Professional

Site Server 3.0

Nick Apostolopoulos, Joey Bernal, Steve Edens, Robert Howard, Stephen Howard, Mike Kendzierski, Steven Livingstone, Craig McQueen, Marco Tabini, Alex Toussaint, Peter Watt

Wrox Press Ltd. ®

Professional
Site Server 3.0

Published by Wrox Press Ltd, Arden House, 1102 Warwick Road, Acocks Green,
Birmingham, B27 9BH, UK
Printed in the United States
ISBN 1-861002-6-96

Trademark Acknowledgements

Wrox has endeavored to provide trademark information about all the companies and products mentioned in this book by the appropriate use of capitals. However, Wrox cannot guarantee the accuracy of this information.

Credits

Authors
Nick Apostolopoulos
Joey Bernal
Steve Edens
Robert Howard
Stephen Howard
Mike Kendzierski
Steven Livingstone
Craig McQueen
Marco Tabini
Alex Toussaint
Peter Watt

Project Manager
Chris Hindley

Design/Layout
Mark Burdett
John McNulty
Frances Olesch

Diagrams
David Boyce

Cover
Chris Morris

Index
Andrew Criddle

Managing Editor
Dominic Shakeshaft

Development Editor
Jeremy Beacock

Editors
Peter Jones
Joanna Mason
Karli Watson

Technical Reviewers
Nick Apostolopoulos
Dinah Berry
Michael Corvese
Ellen Davidson
Charles Fichter
Richard Harrison
Stephen Howard
Tim Huckaby
Marc Kuperstein
Stephen Leonard
Craig McQueen
J. Boyd Nolan
Mark Oswald
Brad Sherrell
Beverley Treadwell
Adwait Ullal
Peter Watt
John Wootton

About the Authors

Nick Apostolopoulos is a software consultant, developer, and trainer in San Diego, California. His company, A13 Digital Media, specializes in the design and development of Internet and Multimedia solutions, with a primary focus on E-Commerce applications using Site Server. He would like to make the following acknowledgements:

To Jeremy Beacock, thank you for giving me this opportunity, in spite of all of the obstacles. To Chris Hindley, Joanna Mason, and Peter Jones, thank you for all of your patience during my struggle to complete this project. I am forever grateful.

Joey Bernal. Anthony (Joey) Bernal is the Director of Information Technology at Impact Performance, a performance improvement company based out of Minnetonka, Minnesota. Joey has worked for or provided consulting services to an array of business and government organizations worldwide including Electronic Data Systems (EDS), Price Waterhouse, the U.S. Dept. of Health, the U.S. Forest Service, Firstar, CNS, and Jostens.

Joey has a B.S. in Computer Science and has several years experience teaching at the University level. He lives in Eden Prairie, Minnesota with his wife Christiane and their 4 children, Daniel, Christopher, Julia, and Oliver.

Steve Edens is a principle consultant and developer for NetSail Internet Commerce, an Internet Service provider for Microsoft Site Server solutions. Prior to being a founding member of NetSail in 1996, Steve was a Manager and Systems Engineer for IBM for thirteen years focusing on Customer Relationship and Satisfaction systems. Steve teaches Electronic Commerce at the New England Institute of Technology and has a wonderful family with three children. In his spare time, if any, he likes to jog and ride his bicycle.

Robert Howard is a Technical Evangelist for Microsoft's Developer Relations Group. He advises organizations on how best to implement Microsoft products. He also writes and reviews code and provides technical support for these organizations.

Stephen Howard is a Consultant/Developer with Breakaway Solutions, Inc. He is responsible for the development of Internet Applications, primarily using Microsoft technologies. Currently, he is working on an institutional investment research site using Microsoft Site Server. Prior to software development, Stephen pursued a career in telecommunications.

Stephen is originally from the UK although he now lives and works in Philadelphia. He would like to thank Jeff Freedman and Gene Wenning for their invaluable assistance.

Mike Kendzierski, Director of Internet Services at USWeb/CKS Cornerstone brings extensive experience deploying and developing complex client-server and Internet e-commerce systems. Mike is a regular speaker at technical conferences such as Microsoft Explorer and ASPDevCon on topics ranging from e-commerce systems to systems design and network architecture for high performance web sites.

Mike is also a published technical author with titles including Windows NT and BackOffice technologies such as Site Server and Internet Information Server. When he's not busy wandering the streets of the Upper East Side in NYC, you can find him at Barnes & Noble sipping coffee and reading magazines for free. Mike welcomes e-mail, and can be reached at mkendzierski@att.net.

Steven Livingstone is based in Glasgow, Scotland and specializes in developing distributed web applications for business, as well as the creation of Electronic Commerce stores using Site Server and XML. He also maintains the `citix.com` and `deltabiz.com` web sites. He enjoys trying to learn other languages, travel and sport, especially watching Celtic (when they win). He would like to make the following acknowledgements:

I would like to thank everyone I know for the patience they have shown while I was writing and my cat Rambo for the important code changes she made whilst constantly walking over the keyboard. I would also like to dedicate my section of the book to my Grandma and my late Grandad, Daniel O'Sullivan, who have always been an inspiration to me. I can be contacted at `ceo@citix.com`.

Craig McQueen. Craig is a Principal Consultant at Sage Information Consultants, Inc. His role at Sage is to guide clients in their adoption of Internet technologies into their existing business. Recently, he led an e-commerce implementation of Site Server at a major consumer electronics company. Previous to consulting, Craig led the development of two retail Internet products: InContext WebAnalyzer and InContent FlashSite.

Craig has a Master of Science degree from the University of Toronto where he specialized in Human-Computer Interaction. He can code for hours at a time as long as he has good music to listen to.

Marco Tabini is an electronic commerce specialist based in Toronto, Canada. He specializes in creating digital nervous system and electronic commerce infrastructures based on Microsoft technologies for customers in North America.

Marco would like to thank the editors and technical reviewers for their contribution to the creation of Professional Site Server. A word of thanks also goes to Josh Axelrod and Ken Knight from the Microsoft Site Server group for their help and support.

Alex Toussaint has been working with e-commerce Web applications for the past five years. He is currently working with Works.com and their new commerce site. Previous projects include sites for Motorola, Ziff Davis, and PCOrder. He also writes technical articles for different web sites including Microsoft MSDN. Most recent article is about credit card processing using MS Site Server 3.0 Commerce Edition found at `http://msdn.microsoft.com/workshop/server/commerce/creditcard.asp`. When not traveling to Brazil or Hawaii he can be seen in Austin, Texas. If you have any questions or comments he can be reached at `netoz@yahoo.com`.

Peter Watt is a Principal Consultant in the Microsoft Solutions Group at Optimation, New Zealand's premier technical consultancy company. After a number of years as an IBM mainframe systems programmer, Peter's recent focus has been on the use of Windows NT in large enterprises. He is a specialist in the use of Internet technologies, with a particular interest in Directory Services and Public Key Infrastructures.

Peter only tinkers with computers in his spare time. His real job involves trying to keep up with his soul mate Wilma and his five children. He also wants it known that he is the proud owner of a new Jeep Wrangler, and that those things really do go anywhere.

You can reach Peter at `peterw@optimation.co.nz`.

Table of Contents

Introduction

The Web is a fast-changing, fast-growing environment, and there are ever-expanding opportunities for businesses to take advantage of. However, producing Web-based solutions in a feasible time-scale is often a challenge. Any Web solution for a business is likely to incorporate a number of different technologies: dealing with data access, mailing, and so on. Applications that draw on all these different technologies can become very complex, but the demands of the Web mean that such applications should also be flexible and scalable. As more and more people become connected to the Internet, and businesses put larger portions of their operations online, your Website may well experience higher volumes of traffic than originally bargained for, and it's essential that your site can keep up with increases in demand.

In this sort of environment, starting from scratch in building a complex, scalable site can be an expensive task. Site Server 3.0 gives you a head start in putting your site together, and building a scalable configuration. Site Server, in essence, is a collection of tools that cover a huge range of functionality: content management, searching and indexing, setting up membership for your site and then personalizing content for those members, and analyzing usage patterns on your site, to name but a few of the options available. With Site Server 3.0 Commerce Edition you also have all the tools to create and maintain an online store.

You may not want to use every tool provided with Site Server, or implement every feature, but if you are trying to develop an integrated, dynamic site then Site Server can save you having to start from square one. This book provides an introduction to installing, configuring, and using Site Server, and will help you get the most out of it for your Web site.

What Does this Book Cover?

This book can be divided into five sections. Overall we'll progress through planning considerations and installation, through the Content Management and Personalization and Membership features of Site Server, to Commerce and Commerce components. At the end of our discussion of the standard Site Server features you'll find the first case study, pulling together all the topics discussed so far. The second case study comes at the end of the book and provides an example of the versatility of Site Server for e-commerce applications.

There is no compulsion to set up any particular feature of Site Server. If you're not interested in using a particular feature on your Web site then you can skip the appropriate section, and move on to the features you want to use. Because Site Server is more a collection of tools than one unified utility, there is not necessarily a linear structure to learning how to use it after installation. However, if you work your way through the sections in this book, you will gain a good overall understanding of the structure of Site Server and the functionality available.

Let's look at each section in a bit more detail.

Section I — Preparation and Installation

This first section of the book sets the scene for Site Server, discusses its foundations and takes us through installation and the means of administering our Site Server Web site. We start by answering the question "What is Site Server?" and look at the various features it provides and what they can do for us. Then we look at how to set up our Site Server platform, and discuss some initial scalability considerations. We look at security, and lay some foundations for the aspects of security we'll come across in later chapters. With all the basic concepts covered, we then set about installing Site Server — quite a complicated process. Finally, to round off this section, we look at the tools we have for administering Site Server.

The chapters in this section are as follows:

- What is Site Server
- Preparing for Site Server
- Security Overview
- Installation
- Site Server Administration Tools

Section II — Managing Content

At this point in the book we're ready to start actually using Site Server. We've seen the tools and components that Site Server consists of, we've looked at overall site design, and we've covered installing Site Server and all the associated software. So, now we can start to make Site Server work for us.

This section covers how to deal with the content of a Website. The tasks involved in first building content, then updating and deleting it, and finally configuring indexes and search mechanisms, can be both complex and time-consuming. Site Server provides a lot of what you need to carry out these tasks, without having to code all this functionality yourself. However, some time is needed to establish exactly what Site Server provides, and how to make the most of it. In addition, you will probably want to customize search and content management procedures to suit your particular site, and maybe automate some of the routine functions.

The chapters in this section are as follows:

> ➤ Content Management
> ➤ Search
> ➤ Knowledge Management

Section III — Personalization and Membership

The Personalization and Membership section introduces both of these named Site Server features, as well as two more: Analysis and Direct Mail. Through Membership you can set up a dedicated data store for your user information (the Membership Directory). This information can then (among other things) be used to personalize a user's session, or be imported into the Analysis component of Site Server to provide information about a user's progress through the site. Through Site Server Analysis you can also analyse the content of your site– for example identify broken links. Finally the Direct Mail component provides an easy way to deliver mail packages and generate mailing lists – and it can also be integrated with other components, such as Analysis, to reach particular groups of users.

The chapters in this section are as follows:

> ➤ Membership
> ➤ Personalization
> ➤ Site Server Analysis
> ➤ Delivering Direct Mail Packages

Case Study — Integrating Site Server

At this point of the book we've covered most of the features that you get with a standard installation of Site Server. This first case study gives an example of how to integrate the components of Site Server that we've seen into a Web site, and also how to integrate other technologies such as XML.

Section IV — Site Server Commerce

This section provides a comprehensive introduction to electronic commerce and what Site Server Commerce Edition offers. We progress through the basic principles of e-commerce to the structure of an online store, and how this maps on to the structure created by Site Server Commerce. We go through the objects provided, and how they fit into the online store, before moving on discuss pipelines (Commerce Server transaction processing mechanisms) in some detail. Finally we look at how to write our own pipeline components.

The chapters in this section are as follows:

> ➤ Electronic Commerce 101
> ➤ Anatomy of an Online Store
> ➤ MSCS Objects within a Store
> ➤ Pipelines – Stages and Components
> ➤ Using Pipelines
> ➤ Extending your Pipelines

Section V — Additional Commerce Components

The fifth and final section in this book provides a brief round-up of three further components provided with Site Server Commerce Edition. The first of these is the Ad Server, which is used to manage advertisements on your site. Next we look at Microsoft Wallet, a client-side component that can be useful for storing payment details. Finally we discuss the Predictor component, predominantly used to provide the capability for historical cross-selling within an online store.

The chapters in this section are thus:

> ➢ Using the Ad Server
>
> ➢ The Microsoft Wallet
>
> ➢ Historical Cross-Selling and the Predictor Component

Case Study — Outlining a Business-to-Business Solution

Finally in this book, this case study walks the reader through the business case made for implementing a Site Server solution for a major company, and then discusses in detail the construction in Visual J++ of the key pipeline component involved.

Who is this Book For?

This book is aimed at developers who need to get to grips with Site Server, and need to solve real-world problems using the functionality that Site Server 3.0 can provide. Site Server combines many different technologies, and while you may not be an expert on all of them, some prior understanding of the key technologies will help you get the most out of this book and Site Server itself.

We've used both SQL Server and Access as the example databases in this book. In addition you will find it useful to be familiar with NT and IIS, as these form the platform for Site Server, and ASP, as this is the example scripting environment we have used for programming with Site Server. In the later stages of the book we also look at using XML, and see some examples of building components in VB, Visual C++ and Visual J++.

Site Server provides a number of graphical user interfaces and wizards, so how much you want to code with Site Server will depend on your requirements. If you want to customize the standard sites provided with Site Server you are going to need to delve into the code at some stage. We've tried to provide information at the GUI level, and also look at some of the code. The first of these enables you to get started quickly and understand what Site Server offers. Looking at what's going on behind the scenes, however, can be the key in adapting Site Server to your specific needs.

Conventions

We have used a number of different styles of text and layout in the book to help differentiate between the different kinds of information. Here are examples of the styles we use and an explanation of what they mean:

Advice, hints, and background information comes indented and italicized, like this.

> **Important information comes in boxes like this.**

Bullets are also indented, and appear with a little box marking each new bullet point, like this:

- **Important Words** are in a bold type font
- Words that appear on the screen in menus like the File or Window are in a similar font to the one that you see on screen
- Keys that you press on the keyboard, like *Ctrl* and *Enter*, are in italics
- Code has several fonts. If it's a word that we're talking about in the text, for example when discussing the For...Next loop, it's in a fixed width font. If it's a block of code that you can type in as a program and run, then it's also in a gray box:

```
Set oCars = CreateObject("WCCCars.Cars")
Set recCars = oCars.GetAll(RegistryRestore("Showroom", "Not Set"))
```

- Sometimes you'll see code in a mixture of styles, like this:

```
If IsMissing(ConnectionString) Then
    varConn = RegistryRestore("Showroom", "Not Set")
Else
    varConn = ConnectionString
End If
```

The code with a white background is code we've already looked at and that we don't wish to examine further.

These formats are designed to make sure that you know what it is you're looking at. We hope they make life easier.

Tell Us What You Think

We've worked hard on this book to make it useful. We've tried to understand what you're willing to exchange your hard-earned money for, and we've tried to make the book live up to your expectations.

Please let us know what you think about this book. Tell us what we did wrong, and what we did right. This isn't just marketing flannel: we really do huddle around the e-mail to find out what you think. If you don't believe it, then send us a note. We'll answer, and we'll take whatever you say on board for future editions. The easiest way is to use e-mail:

`feedback@wrox.com`

You can also find more details about Wrox Press on our Web site. There, you'll find the code from our latest books, sneak previews of forthcoming titles, and information about the authors and editors. You can order Wrox titles directly from the site, or find out where your nearest local bookstore with Wrox titles is located.

Customer Support

If you find a mistake, please have a look at the errata page for this book on our Web site first. If you can't find an answer there, tell us about the problem and we'll do everything we can to answer promptly! Appendix I outlines how can you can submit an errata in much greater detail. Just send us an e-mail:

`support@wrox.com`

or fill in the form on our Web site:

`http://www.wrox.com/Contacts.asp`

What is Site Server?

Microsoft Site Server is a suite of Internet tools, applications, objects, utilities, and services designed to aid developers in the rapid design and deployment of powerful, full-featured web sites. This collection of software and management tools covers virtually every aspect of web site functionality, and provides us with a solid foundation for building many different types of web sites, including intranets and extranets. In this book, we'll be covering the various pieces of Site Server, how they work, and the best ways to implement each component or technology.

Although generally referred to as just Site Server, this product actually comes in two flavors. The first is just plain old Site Server, which contains all of the necessary pieces for building robust information-type web sites, such as corporate intranets. For example, it comes with components for the personalization of content, content management, traffic analysis, knowledge management, access control management, etc. The second version is known as Site Server Commerce Edition. As its name implies, this version is targeted at the growing e-commerce segment of the web, and is fast becoming the most common Site Server implementation. It contains all the functionality of the base product, plus additional tools for building transactional e-commerce web sites, including advertisement display and tracking tools, sophisticated order tracking and processing components.

Site Server's power derives from the way in which it leverages many existing and emerging technologies, and provides an integrated environment for developing robust, highly scalable Internet applications. While it may sound like a stand alone product, Site Server is actually installed on top of Microsoft Internet Information Server and Windows NT, adding components and services to fill in the gaps. Working in conjunction with existing IIS and NT technologies, such as ASP, Site Server creates a broad foundation upon which to build a large variety of web based applications.

With that in mind, here are the things we'll be discussing throughout this chapter:

> **Life Before Site Server.** First, we'll take a look at the evolution of Internet applications, and the early technologies that developers were limited to working with. We'll explore the limitations of these early technologies, and the concessions developers were forced to make because of them.

> **Site Server to the Rescue.** Next, we'll discuss how Site Server solves many of the problems early developers had to contend with. We'll explore the various pieces of Site Server in more detail, and discuss the improvements that each piece provides.

> **Site Server's Many Technologies.** Lastly, we'll look at the various technologies leveraged by Site Server, and we'll discuss what these technologies mean to you, the developer. Developing a web site with Site Server requires understanding of a wide range of technologies, and we'll discuss what it takes to build a solid Site Server implementation.

When we're done, we will hopefully have gained a better understanding of the problems early developers had to deal with when designing complex web sites. We'll also see how Site Server helps to solve many of these problems, and in fact, in many cases, changes the way we design and develop web-based applications all together.

Life Before Site Server

In the early days, which is to say just a few years ago, most web sites were fairly uncomplicated. Much of the content they contained tended to be rather static, and this content was generally updated and maintained by one or two people. Whenever changes to the site needed to be made, the "webmaster" responsible for maintaining the site usually updated the various pages manually using some rudimentary HTML editor, or perhaps even a simple text editor. These sites were primarily informational in nature, and there was very little need for any real security or other complicated means of customization.

However, as the Internet began to grow and become more commercialized, the role of the webmaster began to change and grow much more complex. Increasingly, more and more companies began to launch web sites in support of their primary business. Also, many entirely web based businesses were beginning to emerge as well. As this happened, the demands placed on developers began to increase as the range of features being built into these sites kept increasing. The desire to customize the content being displayed for each user became stronger as web sites kept searching for ways to differentiate themselves from the competition.

Also, as Internet usage increased, many companies began to take advantage of the great emerging opportunities for selling goods over the web, and electronic commerce began to flourish. This lead to a host of new issues, and once again, the technologies available were very limited. Let's take a look at some of those early problems, and the limitations of the early technologies.

CGI and Other Technologies

In the early days of the World Wide Web, most web servers were written for a very specific purpose, to send HTML to the web browser. Sure, there were some rudimentary tools, such as server-side includes (SSIs), which were generally predefined functions that we could embed within the HTML, but these were very limited in their usefulness. The web server would catch these special tags and then replace them with some sort of dynamic content, such as the current date and time. However, for the most part, the processing of these includes was not conditional, meaning that every time that page was viewed, the dynamic content would be displayed.

It soon became evident that something more was needed, and in came the **Common Gateway Interface** (CGI). The primary purpose of CGI programming was to capture data from the user, and perhaps then to display some response based on that data. The problem with the CGI model is that it requires the web server to hand off the incoming data to some external process, since an external program, usually written in a language such as Perl, generally handles the CGI processing. This can also just as easily be done in Visual Basic, for example, or any other CGI compliant language.

Spawning a separate process, however, typically creates an enormous amount of overhead, since each CGI request must be handled by a new instance of that process. Also, it can be rather complex and cumbersome to continually write and maintain separate pieces of code for handling the many different customized pieces of a large and complex web site.

Soon, many additional server-based applications environments began to emerge. These new environments, such as Cold Fusion, iHTML, ASP and others, were unique in that they were capable of supporting various inline-scripting languages. There were a number of benefits to this new model, but the primary gains were speed and ease of use.

First of all, since these new applications processed scripting embedded directly into the HTML file, it now became much easier to develop and maintain complex web-based applications. In addition, these new environments also took advantage of the extensibility of the various web servers running on the Internet, and were written to run within the same process as the web server itself. This meant that this newly embedded scripting was now being processed directly by the web server, instead of as a separate process, which meant a great increase in processing speed.

ASP, or Active Server Pages, is Microsoft's version of this in-process environment. However, unlike many other application environments, such as Cold Fusion, which require the use of a proprietary scripting language, ASP leverages the power of ActiveX scripting. This means that ASP acts as an ActiveX Scripting Host, and can thus process script written in any number of languages, including JavaScript and VBScript, making it extremely flexible.

VBScript is the most common language used when writing ASP pages. In addition, since VBScript is basically a subset of Visual Basic for Applications, it has access to the world of COM (Component Object Model). This means it can interact with the filesystem or even databases through various COM objects, such as ADO (ActiveX Data Objects). Finally, developers had a quick and efficient way to develop complex, robust web-based applications. However, there were still a number of other unsolved problems. For example, there was still no efficient way to maintain information about each web user's current state, as we'll see in a moment in our discussion of user authentication and management.

Of course, there are many solutions and workarounds to address these problems, and none of the issues we've raised here are insurmountable, by any means. However, the idea here is that every change to the system, every new feature addition, even just natural growth issues, can require broad changes to the way our system has been designed and developed. In the rapidly changing world of the Internet, it is imperative that the tools we have at our disposal provide us with the fastest, most efficient means possible for meeting these challenges.

User Authentication and Content Personalization

Probably one of the earliest problems facing web developers was the question of user authentication. This is a very complex problem, and especially so in the past given the tools that were available at the time. Implementing a truly useful security system meant tackling a wide range of thorny topics.

First of all, we need to determine how we are going to store each user's data. For starters, we have to develop some sort of database schema that fits our current needs, and yet is somehow easily extensible. This is of the utmost importance, since we will invariably end up adding to the list of attributes we wish to know about any given user. And once we have designed and tested our data schema, we need to devise some method for accessing this information about our users.

Chances are we are not going to want to do this directly from the ASP pages, since it will require embedding a large amount of SQL into our web pages. Typically, we would probably design one or more middle tier objects, probably in combination with some stored procedures within our database, so that we can quickly and easily authenticate our users. All of this, and we haven't even discussed how to integrate our new authentication model into our actual web site yet!

We must now devise a way to secure the various pages within our web site based on the current user's privileges. This would most likely involve some complex set of include files designed to test each user's privileges. For example, when a user logs into our site, using a HTML based form we provide, we could then check that user's name and password against our database to make sure they are a valid user of our site. Then we would use include files in each page to determine whether or not that user has permission to view that particular page, and then either allow them to view the page or possibly redirect them to some other part of the site.

In order to do this, we must, of course, come up with a method for passing at least the most basic information about each user from page to page within the site. We could actually do this using a "cookie", for example, or perhaps even a session variable (which is less than desirable, since it can drastically slow server performance when there are a large number of concurrent users). The problem with this approach is that when our site usage grows, and we are forced to add additional web servers to take up and balance the load, we begin to lose the user state we have worked so hard for. The minute someone gets bounced to a different server, they would be required to log in all over again, which is clearly unacceptable.

Using IIS and Windows NT, we could overcome this problem with native NT security. However, this is not an ideal solution for a number of reasons. First of all, this would mean that every web site member would now have an actual NT account on our web server. This is perfectly acceptable in an Intranet setting, where all our members probably already have domain accounts we could easily use. However, for say a commercial Internet site, this could pose a significant security risk, especially if your web server lives within your internal domain. Also, the Windows NT Security Accounts Manager (SAM) was not designed to handle an inordinately large amount of users, and thus does not scale well. Again, this is probably just fine for an Intranet, where the number of users will probably be in the thousands. However, when site membership extends into the tens of thousands, you'll be forced to find a new way to authenticate your users.

Also, once the user has been properly authenticated, how do we deal with the customization of content on each individual page that the user is allowed to see? How do we determine what content we are going to display, and what content they will not be allowed to view. This, again, is a rather difficult task, and usually involves some rather intense coding. To make things a bit simpler, we would probably design and build yet another set of middle tier objects to handle this for us. We would basically be building a set of rules processing objects designed specifically for customization purposes. While we might also use this approach even with a Site Server installation, it is far easier since there are a number of tools included for accessing our membership data.

These home grown systems usually served their purpose fairly well. However, they generally were not very extensible, and invariably as the business needs changed, the system would require major reworking or need to be replaced altogether. Also, as the number of users increased, these systems were not generally prepared to handle the load, and there was often little planning or forethought given to such growth. Once again, a better solution was needed, and Site Server provides such a solution.

Site Indexing and Searching

Indexing and Searching may not seem like a big stumbling block in web site development, considering the existence of Index Server, the free content indexing tool available from Microsoft. Index Server is a powerful tool, allowing you to catalog all types of web content. You can then allow your web visitors to search this catalog for the content they are looking for. However, when you take into consideration the issues we talked about above, Index Server begins to fall short of our needs.

Imagine a site that is highly restricted in places. If you are using Windows NT based security, there is no problem, since the Windows NT permissions set on each file or directory will be used, and you will not be allowed to view any content for which you do not have the proper permissions. Unfortunately, if you choose to establish your own security model, as we discussed above, this is no longer true. When you catalog that site, all of the available pages will turn up in a search whether the user has access to them or not.

This is no big deal, you say. When the user tries to access the page by following the link, they will simply be denied access by our page level security system. Well, this works fine for most situations. However, I was recently working on a project for a very large company that had many sales agents out in the field and these agents needed access to various forms and newsletters through the Internet. The problem was that the agents all had various levels of privileges, and many agents were not even allowed to know about the existence of the other types of agents, or for example, the newsletters available to these other agents. It was absolutely crucial to make sure that even when performing a search, they never had access to a single link that would tip them off about the existence of these other groups. Without Site Server, this would have taken forever to pull off. Even with Site Server, it took weeks of planning.

Content Management

Another important aspect of web site management is keeping control of the reams of content you will invariably end up with in your site. Earlier we discussed how for the most part, web sites were generally maintained by one or two "webmasters" who were in charge of managing all of the content on the site. Whenever content needed to be added or updated on the site, it had to pass through their hands so as to ensure that it fitted into the site properly and did not create broken links and the like.

This gets especially tricky when you begin trying to organize content so that it can be easily searched through, as we talked about just moments ago. It's possible to organize the various files that make up any given web site by, say, directory, but how do you handle a situation where content relates to a number of other sections of your web site?

As we'll see in a moment, Site Server allows us to mark, or tag, our content, so that not only can we effectively organize and retrieve it, but we can also use this tagging in conjunction with our search catalog to enforce our security restrictions as well.

Content Publishing

Even once you've got all of your content properly placed and catalogued, etc., how do you safely move all of your changes into production? Once again, this is all too often a manual procedure. Now manually updating content is generally OK, as long as you have a small number of people to contend with. However, as the number of people involved in maintaining your web presence grows, the number of mistakes will invariably multiply. How do you make sure that all of the pages that you recently updated get moved into production? And even more importantly, how do you make sure that the pages you have not yet finished updating *do not* get moved into production prematurely? This can be a major chore.

But let's say you've got that licked. You've got a sure fire little tracking system that you've put into place, and nothing goes live unless it goes through the proper approval process. How do you now get those files from your development environment out onto the actual production servers? If you just have a single web server, and it's attached to your network, then this is a reasonably simple procedure. You just copy the files into the proper directory on your web server, and you're ready to roll.

Things get complicated, however, when you begin adding extra web servers into the equation. Once again, you've got to develop some manual scheme for ensuring that your changes get moved to *all* of your machines properly. Not a major problem, but potentially another manual point of failure nonetheless.

Now let's take this one step further. Your web presence has grown so large that you have now moved the actual production servers offsite to your ISP's facilities so that you can maximize your bandwidth. Or, perhaps for security reasons, your servers are located outside a firewall, and you have no direct access to them for mapping drives or other resources. Now you're forced to FTP the files, or use some other form of transfer, such as Microsoft FrontPage publishing. Again, you still need to make sure that everything makes it out to all of the servers as quickly as possible. The bottom line is that there is just no easy way to ensure that the right files get moved to the correct servers in a timely manner, especially when you do not have direct access to your production machines. Site Server addresses all of these problems, and provides us with a single, simple solution, which we'll look at in a moment.

Site and Traffic Analysis

When it comes to web site analysis, there are plenty of third party tools available that do a great job of analyzing web site traffic and usage. The problem is that they are generally stand-alone products, and they offer no easy way of relating this information back to our list of users, or site members. Trying to integrate some level of site analysis with the usage patterns of your site, and then again trying to tie this information back to the registered user of your site can requires a substantial amount of extra coding. Site Server addresses many of these problems with its various analysis tools.

E-Commerce

Electronic Commerce is quite possibly the fastest growing portion of the Internet today. And as more and more people begin to gain access to and get comfortable with using the Internet, this is sure to increase even more quickly in the future.

Now, developing a basic order taking web site is actually a rather simple prospect, and has been from the very beginning. It's rather simple to develop some product filled pages, and then, through CGI, allow our customers to put products into a virtual "basket" while they shop. Since we're already keeping track of the users as they travel our site through some mechanism or other, we simply need to add some data signifying the products they're choosing to our collection of data. Unfortunately, this is where the simplicity ends.

Products

Our first concern is with product management. We need some way to easily add products to our inventory without having to modify our product display pages every time we update our product offering. This involves designing some sort of data structure for storing our product information, again making sure that it covers all of our present and future needs. This can be a time consuming project, since we may have products with varying attributes. For example, some products may have size and color choices, while others may come in various formats or types.

Once we get our data organized and in place, we now need to build our product navigation and display pages. These pages need to be linked to our data in such a way that they properly display each of our different product types. We also need to design and implement some product management pages, so that we can easily add or delete products from out inventory without having to manipulate the database directly. All of these dynamic pages must be designed from scratch, and this can take a fair amount of time, especially if we have multiple product types, departments, etc.

Pricing

Then there is the issue of pricing. It's pretty simple to just list a price with each product in our database, but what if we want to put certain items on sale. We could, of course, simply adjust each product's pricing manually through our new management tool, but what about the duration of our sale? Using our current method of discounting, each product remains at its discounted price until we remember to change it back to its original price. When we start getting into the hundreds of products, manually making sure that each product goes on and comes off sale at the proper time starts to get a bit confusing.

And what about cross selling, up selling, or other price promotions? Suppose we want to offer a two-for-one or a buy-two-get-one-free promotion. Better still, suppose we want to offer a special where if you buy product A, you get product B at half price. Well, this would require quite a bit of design and programming, as you can well imagine. We would first need some way to track the various promotions available for each product, and then we would have to design some mechanism for enforcing our special pricing rules – a major task, to say the least.

The Purchase Process

And now that we have our pricing structure in place, it's time to verify and process the orders. For this we would need to develop yet another process for collecting our users' personal information, unless we already have it on file. Then we need to total up the order, and account for any sales tax or shipping charges that need to be added to the bill. We may even want to check to see whether the items our user is ordering are even in stock, or whether they are back ordered, in which case there will be a delay in shipping these items. Eventually, through a fair amount of programming and rule checking, we assemble a valid order, complete with a total amount due.

Well, now it's time to collect the money for this purchase from our happy customer, and this usually involves the ever-so-popular credit card. At this point we need to verify that the credit card number that we have received is indeed valid, and if it is, then we need to process the charge. If the card is declined for any reason, we need to make sure that we inform the customer, but more importantly we need to make sure that we do not process the order. Ensuring that this part of the transaction goes smoothly is paramount, since any slip up here can result in either shipping merchandise that hasn't been paid for, or worse yet, charging a customer for an order that never actually gets placed. Assuming, however that the card is valid and the charge is approved, it's time to fulfill the order.

The actual order fulfillment process can be the trickiest part of the whole process, especially when there are multiple vendors involved. Many large e-commerce sites sell products that they don't actually have in their own inventory. In these cases the order must be properly sent to the actual manufacturer of each product, and this can get very complicated. Having some sort or business-to-business processing system helps in this process tremendously.

Finally, once we've completely processed the order, it would be nice if we could add this order to our records. This requires yet another data store, and ideally one that relates directly back to our product and customer database tables. In this way, our customers could then track the status of their orders or even view their ordering history right online. Again, to do this requires customer management pages to be written that can access and display that data in an easily understood fashion for the customer.

As you can see, building a robust e-commerce site from scratch is a daunting task. When you take into account, on top of everything else, the desire to personalize the shopping experience, it could takes weeks or even months to design something like this from the ground up. And especially when electronic commerce is something that is so common on the Internet today, it seems pretty silly to reinvent the wheel each time we develop another electronic storefront.

Site Server to the Rescue

Then along came Site Server, which, as we are about to see, solved many of these problems. The beauty of Site Server, as we've already said, is in its role as the glue that binds many disparate technologies together, and thus provides us with a basis upon which to build our applications. Site Server is actually a collection of a number of different products, or services, which, as a whole, cover just about any functionality we could possibly need when building an Internet-based application. You may not want to use every single tool provided by Site Server, but others will save you a lot of time and energy. Below, we'll cover many of these services in more detail, and explain the advantages of these solutions over previous methods.

Personalization & Membership

Next to Commerce, Personalization and Membership is probably the most widely used feature within Site Server. These days, pretty much any large scale web site worth its salt contains customized content based on either a user's browsing or purchase habits, or perhaps based on a user's attributes or personalized preferences. Site Server Personalization and Membership supplies a robust framework for building a highly scalable personalization system.

Membership

But even before we can personalize content, we need to know who the user is, and whether that user has access to that content in the first place. This is where Membership comes in. The greatest benefit of Site Server Membership is its ability to both authenticate the user, and then, based on that user's privileges, decide what that user is authorized to see, without having to use Windows NT security. This means that we gain all of the advantages of a stand-alone authentication scheme, as we discussed earlier. And the best part is that it accomplishes this through a thorough integration with Internet Information Server.

With Site Server Membership you can choose to use either standard IIS/Windows NT authentication or Membership authentication. The first of these, called Windows NT (Intranet) Authentication in Site Server, is, as the name suggests, most suitable for an Intranet, as all the users you authenticate through your web site will have to have accounts in the Windows NT SAM. Membership authentication on the other hand enables you to store all user credentials in a specialized directory, which we'll discuss next. This makes it easier to cater for large numbers of possibly short-term users, without the administrative burden of managing large numbers of NT user accounts.

The other thing to note about Membership is its support of extra authentication methods, in addition to the ones offered by IIS (which are anonymous access, basic authentication and challenge/response). Site Server Membership authentication supports a number of distinct forms of authentication, some of which were previously unavailable to developers:

> ➤ **Anonymous Access.** Anonymous access under Site Server is identical to that used by Internet Information Server, and is achieved using an anonymous NT user account, which has access to all anonymous content. Any non-authenticated user is viewed by IIS as this account.

> ➤ **Cookie Authentication.** Automatic cookie authentication is pretty much just what it sounds like. Once a user logs into the site for the first time, they are issued a cookie containing a GUID identifier, which is used to authenticate them the next time they visit the site.

> ➤ **HTML Forms-based Authentication.** HTML forms-based authentication looks very similar to the old-style common authentication method of submitting an HTML form. Under Site Server Membership authentication, the information submitted through the form is passed off to Site Server for verification.

> ➤ **Distributed Password Authentication (DPA).** DPA is basically a distributed version of NT LAN Manager (NTLM) Challenge/response authentication, and is highly secure. However, because of this NTLM similarity, DPA is only supported by Microsoft Internet Explorer browsers.

> ➤ **Clear Text/Basic Authentication.** Clear Text authentication works exactly as it sounds – passwords are transmitted in clear text. However it is less secure than DPA authentication, but is very useful if you need to support browsers other than Internet Explorer.

The Membership Directory

Another huge benefit of Site Server Membership is its use of the Membership Directory, which is the directory service used to store all of our Membership information. A directory service is basically an object-oriented data store, which means that the data is stored in logical units, or containers. Because of this, the directory is hierarchical (instead of relational) in structure, and is highly optimized for retrieving data. This works perfectly for our Membership environment, since we are more often that not trying to retrieve information about a member or members. And, as you'll see later, since different containers, such as employees and customers can be spread out across multiple directory stores, it's also highly scalable, with the ability to handle many, many users.

Also, access to this data store is handled transparently through LDAP, the Lightweight Directory Access Protocol. As we'll discuss later on, LDAP is an industry standard protocol, which means that we can actually use any LDAP compliant directory service to authenticate our users or carry out our personalization. While it's definitely preferable to have all of our user data in a single location, we have the possibility of connecting to another data store.

Personalization

Now, once we know who's visiting our site, it's time to make them feel right at home with a little personalized content; and Site Server handles this splendidly. Not only can we control the user's access to content on a page-by-page basis by checking their permissions, but we can now also offer that user a customized experience based on his or her attributes or preferences. To make this possible, Site Server comes with a COM component called the Active User Object, or AUO.

The AUO gives us a way to get access to the Membership Directory directly from within our ASP pages. In fact, the AUO object, when instantiated in an ASP page that is under Membership authentication, knows who the current user is. This means that we only need to instantiate the object, and then we can immediately begin to retrieve various attributes for the current user. This is far easier that if we had simply designed our own membership system.

With this power, we can now customize the content within a page for each specific user. This is most powerful when our objective is to define different levels of access based on, say, the groups a user belongs to. For example, we could use the AUO object to find out if the current user is a manager or not, and then display or suppress each employee's salary information when retrieving employee information.

The idea of personalization takes on an even bigger meaning when we start to discuss electronic commerce. With Site Server Personalization, it's easy to offer discounts to preferred customers, for example. Or perhaps display some particular product special offer only to first time visitors. It's even possible to store important dates for your customers, such as their relatives' birthdays. Then, with the direct mailer, which we'll look at next, you can send them an advanced email reminding them to purchase a gift through your online store. The possibilities are truly endless.

Direct Mailer

The Direct Mailer feature of Site Server works directly with Membership to provide a powerful means of keeping in touch with our site's many users. Just as we would send out bulk mailing to our customers in an effort to keep in touch, or notify them of news and information about our business, we can use the Direct Mailer to send bulk e-mail to our web based clientele. We can even automate the mailings so that they take advantage of certain conditions within our site. For example, we could automatically send out an email message each week to the users that had accessed a specific section or page in our site within the last week.

Also, the mail we send out can be personalized for specific users or user groups based on a number of customizable factors, such as:

> The places within the site that a given user has visited. For example, we could send a special promotional email to those users who have browsed the product information for our newest product. (This information is derived from the usage logs.)

> Personalized information provided by the user. For example, we could send a custom message promoting the release of our new children's toy to each of our users who have indicated they are parents. (This sort of information is stored in the Membership Schema as a user attribute.)

> The frequency with which the users visit our site. In this way, we can target frequent visitors or customers for special thank you messages and promotions.

As you can see, Personalization and Membership makes it extremely easy to design and deploy user friendly web sites that cater to the needs of individual users, without having to spend days or even weeks designing this kind of solution from scratch. Plus, owing to the use of LDAP and the directory service model, this solution is highly scalable and primed for growth as new technologies emerge. Having this functionality alone makes Site Server worth the price of admission.

Search

Site Server includes some great search and indexing technology. With Site Server's search tool, you can build multiple catalogs, each containing its own set of materials, and then you can propagate these catalogs to other servers, allowing users of your web site to search through material available through other sources. In an Intranet environment, this can be extremely useful, since you can offer a web search tool for finding corporate documents, for example, that live on some internal file server. Also, in conjunction with document tagging, which we'll talk about in just a moment, it's possible to customize the various search catalogs so that your site members see specialized content based on their membership attributes and permissions.

Content Management

With Site Server's Content Management functionality, you can define content types for the various pieces of content in your site. Using the Site Server Tag Tool, it's possible to apply tags to the HTML documents that make up your web site. As we said earlier, you can use these content tags to help you manage your content, and to build custom search catalogs based on your membership groups or other member attributes. You then have more control over the content being added to your site, even when it comes from other contributors within the organization. You can create and delete different content types, approve new content for display, or even move and catalog entire content stores. Content Management gives you the ability to stay in control of the volumes of content that will invariably find it's way into your site.

Content Publishing — CRS

Again, once you've got all of your content under control, it's time to publish that content, and this means moving that content out to your live production servers. With Site Server's Content Replication Service (CRS), this is simple and easy. The power of CRS is in its ability to completely customize the way in which you deliver content to your production environment. And whether you're connected to your live machines locally or over the Internet, CRS can even retain the Windows NT Access Control Lists (ACLs) that go along with the files you are moving.

CRS can be setup to move files only when you tell it to, or whenever it detects changes in your content. Either way, you can always be sure that all of your changes are being properly propagated to the proper machine. With CRS, you can even define routes along which content should be published, ensuring that each and every machine that is supposed to receive updated content actually receives it, all with a single mouse click. And to top everything off, CRS replication is lightning fast. When you need a fast and reliable way to publish your content, CRS definitely the way to go.

Analysis

As we discussed earlier, analyzing your site and its usage is an important part of web site management. For this purpose, Site Server includes a number of helpful tools. The first is a web site traffic analyzer and report writer. Using this tool, you can quickly and easily generate reports of various usage statistics of your site. The report writer allows you to choose from various pre-defined reports, or even create reports of your own. You can also schedule these reports, so that you are always assured of having the latest data at your fingertips.

The other part of site analysis is the Content Analyzer, which allows you to examine your site from the developer's point of view. With this tool, you can find and fix broken links, examine various site-specific resources, search the site for specific content, or even visualize your site usage data. You can even generate a map of your site, and design and print out content reports. This is the perfect tool for tracking and maintaining your site's content.

Commerce

The Commerce portion of Site Server is perhaps the easiest piece to use right out of the box. Once all of the necessary software has been installed, building the framework for a robust commerce site is just minutes away. The real work comes when it's time to customize the look and feel of the site, and when you are ready to extend the basic functionality of a standard store. In most cases, however, the store created for you by Site Server will more than adequately fill the needs of the majority of e-commerce solutions, so that once you have applied your look and feel to the store, you'll be ready to go.

First off, you'll run the Site Foundation Wizard, which, as its name implies, establishes the foundation for your new store. This wizard creates the virtual directory your store will live in, and sets up all of the appropriate database connections, etc. Next you'll run the Site Builder Wizard, which will run you through the creation of your actual store. It is at this point that you enter the specifics about the type of products you'll be selling, how you want to handle customer receipts, etc. When you are finished, the wizard then generates all of the pages for your site, including the data schema and even sample data if you wish.

Commerce builds your entire store for you, complete with product navigation pages, a shopping basket system, and even a section where customers can view their current order and order history. Commerce also provides you with a complete set of store management pages, including sections for managing your products and the departments they will belong to, and customer management pages. Also, if you requested this functionality while running the wizard, Commerce even create a set of management pages for all of your price promotion and cross selling needs.

Behind the scenes, Commerce sets up what are known as order and purchase pipelines, which we'll discuss later in the book. In a nutshell, these pipelines are responsible for all of the back end processing involved in completing our customers' transactions, including order verification, payment processing, and even order fulfillment. This ensures that all of our orders are processed properly or not processed at all. And, when all is said and done, the orders are entered into our database so that we, and our customers, can track them.

Of course, this explanation sounds overly simple, and it is. With Site Server Commerce you can create both business-to-consumer and business-to-business stores. No two stores are alike, and there are bound to be places where you'll have to go in and modify the standard functionality; but this is where the fun starts. For example, if you are going to process credit cards through your site, you are going to have to choose a credit card clearing house, and you still need to set up an account with them, etc. However, most major clearing houses can provide you with a component that plugs directly into the commerce pipeline, and will handle the actual credit card approval for you, without having to write a single line of code. That's some pretty powerful stuff.

Active Channels

At first glance, push technology is not necessarily an integral part of a web-based application. However, if actively keeping in touch with your users is something important you, then Active Channels can be very useful. Active Channels allow us to customize content or information based on a user's preferences, and then deliver that content directly to the user in a timely manner. Then, if there are ever any modifications or updates our user needs to be aware of, we "push" this new information to them very quickly, without having to wait for them to return to our site.

This can be a very powerful tool for managing our customer satisfaction and loyalty. For example, if we are offering some sort of product special, or perhaps a special training session of interest to specific users, we can notify them in advance of the general public. And since channels are subscription based, we are never bothering people with information they have no interest in receiving. On the other hand however not all browsers support Active Channels, which means that they are only really reliable in an environment such as an Intranet when you know that all users will have the same browser.

There are two parts to the Active Channel portion of Site Server, Active Channel Server and Active Channel Multicaster.

Active Channel Server

The Active Channel Server allows us to quickly and easily define the content to be delivered through our various channels. The specific configuration information for each channel is stored in a CDF (Channel Definition Format) file. When a user subscribes to one of our channels, their browser downloads our CDF file, and they then begin to receive our customized content. If we make any changes to the channel at a later time, the new information, links, etc, are automatically updated on the user's machine.

Active Channel Multicaster

The Active Channel Multicaster (ACM) is an advanced content delivery server designed to conserve valuable network bandwidth. In order to take advantage of the features it offers each of the browsers subscribing to our channels must be using Multi-Cast Delivery Agent. The Active Channel Multicaster then takes over delivery of our channel content. Instead of delivering the CDF file to the browser, the ACM delivers the actual content. However, it does this through a single transmission to all of the channel's subscribers, and thus saves us from the bandwidth requirements of fulfilling each of those information requests separately.

Site Server's Many Technologies

As we've said throughout, Site Server accomplishes much of it's magic through the use of many varied technologies. When designing and developing web sites that are going to use some implementation of Site Server, it's important to be familiar with as many of these technologies as possible. Of course, no one person can be an expert in each of these areas, but by understanding the basics, it becomes much easier to work as part of a team of Site Server developers.

Understanding the many different technologies in use will make for a better understanding of how all of the pieces of Site Server fit together. We'll briefly discuss some of these technologies below, and we'll touch on how they impact our development, and what changes we're likely to see in the future.

ASP

Just as when using IIS (Internet Information Server) in a stand-alone environment, a Site Server site's foundation is based upon ASP (Active Server Pages). ASP, as we discussed earlier, allows us to add inline scripting to our web pages, which are then processed by the web server, and then delivered as customized HTML pages to the browser. It is from within the ASP that we make most of our calls to either external Site Server objects or objects of our own creation. Most, if not all, of the pages that make up our site will use ASP as their foundation.

LDAP

As we saw earlier, Site Server Personalization and Membership features make extensive use of LDAP (Lightweight Directory Access Protocol). LDAP is an Internet standard for directory services, and while the Membership Directory is generally implemented on top of MS SQL Server, we could theoretically use any LDAP provider for our Membership Directory. In the future, with the release of Windows 2000, the Active Directory will become the directory service of choice, since it will become the central repository for all Windows NT users and other system information.

ADSI

ADSI (Active Directory Services Interface) is a collection of COM interfaces that allow developers to access a wide variety of network resources, including directory services, using a common interface. It acts much like ODBC (Open Database Connectivity), in that it allows developers seamless access to different directory services or other data stores through a "generic" interface. In fact, through ADSI, you can access resources such as an Exchange server, or even other non-Microsoft directory services.

MTS

MTS (Microsoft Transaction Server) is an extension of Microsoft's Component Object Model (COM) that allows for an incredible amount of flexibility and growth in building large scale web site and web applications. It accomplishes this in a number of different ways. First of all, MTS uses processes known as thread pooling and connection pooling, which, for example, minimize the number of actual database connections needed by sharing the connections across multiple object instances. It also utilizes JIT, or Just-In-Time activation, which means that components are loaded into memory only when they are needed to complete a method call, and then they are removed. The bottom line is that MTS allows many users to instantiate numerous COM objects with far less overhead than without MTS.

MTS is an integral part of building a truly scalable Internet application, and any middle tier objects you build for your applications really should be designed with MTS in mind. For example, all of the Commerce objects deployed by the Commerce portion of Site Server reside in MTS, both for possible transactional benefits as well as the definite scalability gains.

There are also other technologies that we could add to this list – for example ADO – that you might use as you develop web applications based on Site Server. In order to get the most out of Site Server your Site Server team would also need to have between them some scripting skills, some knowledge of NT security, and database knowledge – probably SQL Server, as this is the only database supported by all the components of Site Server. We'll be coming across all the technologies we've just mentioned throughout the book.

Summary

In this chapter, we've covered the basics of Site Server. We've seen how difficult it can be to develop complex web sites without any of this technology, and we've seen how Site Server steps in and fills the gaps necessary to more easily and quickly develop complete Internet solutions.

Some of the important things we've learned in this chapter are:

> Site Server attempts to solve many of the problems developers face when building large, complex web sites. As web site complexity has evolved, Site Server has stepped in to help fill the gaps in Internet technology.

> Site Server integrates a number of technologies to provide web developers with solid tools for rapid development of truly robust web sites. These technologies include ASP, LDAP, MTS, ADSI, COM, and many others.

> Site Server is a complex piece of software, and includes many components, including solutions for Personalization and Membership, Content Management and Replication, Commerce, Content Analysis and Reporting, and many more.

> Site Server is a truly powerful piece of software, but the power comes at a price. It takes a wide range of expertise to successfully implement and maintain a Site Server site.

There is so much to Site Server that in this chapter we have only been able to gain a brief idea of what we can do. As we progress through the book, looking at areas of Site Server in detail, we'll show how to exploit Site Server functionality to the full.

In the next chapter we'll explore the issues involved in designing a Site Server site. We'll take a look at various design and scalability considerations, and we'll discuss how to get the most out of Site Server through early and thorough planning.

Preparing for Site Server

As we saw in the previous chapter, Site Server is an extremely powerful tool for building robust Internet and Intranet applications. It solves many of the problems faced by early Internet developers, primarily through the integration of numerous new technologies, and provides us with a great starting point for building complete Internet and intranet solutions. However, all of that power comes with a price: Site Server is probably one of the most difficult server programs to install and configure properly.

There are many things to think about before you begin building your Site Server site, including many design and planning issues that, if addressed early on in the development cycle, will save you a lot of time and frustration later in the process. Because it is such a large, complex product, Site Server also introduces many idiosyncrasies that you'll need to be aware of as you develop your site. Knowing about these potential pitfalls in advance will make for a much easier transition from development to production.

In this chapter, we are going to take a look at the following:

➤ **Site Server Architecture**
We'll look at Site Server's data storage requirements, and see how we can distribute these components across machines according to different requirements. We'll also take a look at partitioning.

➤ **Load Balancing**
In this section we'll discuss various options for balancing traffic across several machines, looking at some of the products available.

➤ **Design considerations**
Here we'll take a look at some of the quirky things that Site Server likes to throw our way, and we'll tackle some of the little tips and tricks that will save you development time, and increase the performance of your finished application.

> ➤ **Going Live.**
> Everything is designed and built, and now it's time to flip the switch, but you're not done yet. It's worth taking a look now at the things you'll need to do to make sure the transition from development to production goes smoothly.

When we're finished, you'll be ready to install Site Server, and you'll be aware of many of the pitfalls and workarounds you'll encounter as you move forward. We'll also have a good foundation in place so that as your site grows, you'll be prepared to address scalability quickly and easily.

Hardware Architecture

In setting up your Site Server site you have a number of options open to you when determining the machine configuration you want to use. This may well be constrained by the machines available to you – even if you are starting out with brand new machines there are unlikely to be unlimited numbers of them available. In addition you will probably want to implement different configurations depending on whether you are setting up development and test environments, or putting together a production environment.

Before we go on to look at machine configurations for development and production environments however, we need first to establish what the components of Site Server are that we need to think about. We can install all these components on one machine, or we can split them out across multiple machines in order to help balance the processing load.

Components of Site Server

In the previous chapter we looked at the different areas of functionality provided by Site Server: Content Management, Search, Personalization and Membership, Commerce and so on. These components each have different storage requirements. When you install Site Server, as well as storing information in the Windows NT Filesystem the installation program generally requires a database. We'll see what we need to do to set up the necessary databases in Chapter 4, *Installation*. However, when thinking about our machine configuration, we need to be aware of Site Server's storage requirements.

There are two main logical parts to a simple Site Server configuration: a web portion and a database portion. The first of these is clear-cut; Site Server is a collection of web tools, and must be installed on to a web server, in fact IIS 4.0 is a pre-requisite of the install. However, why do we need to think about databases right from the beginning?

The following diagram shows, at a logical level, the four main areas for data storage in Site Server.

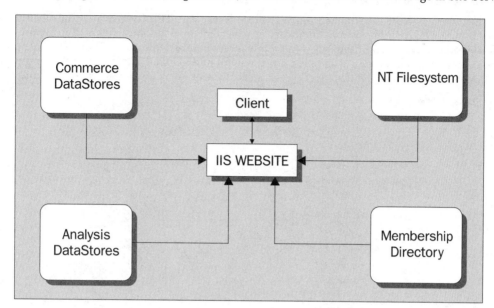

As you can see, in addition to the Windows NT Filesystem, there are up to three other data stores for Site Server, depending on which features of Site Server you want to use. The Commerce and Analysis components both need at least one data store. Also, as we mentioned in the previous chapter, the Personalization and Membership component requires a Membership Directory data store to hold user information. In fact Content Management also uses the Membership Directory, as we'll see in Chapter 6.

We will probably have at least one of these data stores as part of our Site Server architecture. This data store can co-exist with the web server on the same machine. However, we can also distribute Site Server components across machines, depending on the environment we are setting up and the load they will have to handle. There's also one further component we'll be able to separate out if the load gets very heavy: the LDAP service. All requests to the Membership Directory from Site Server go through LDAP, so if necessary we can provide a separate machine to process these LDAP requests. Let's look at some of the options open to us.

A Development Environment

The first thing we need to decide when we are designing our hardware architecture is what our development setup is going to look like. This is not extremely crucial, since we can generally change this configuration down the road, usually adding slightly more complexity, without any real impact to our systems. However, since this is where we are going to develop and update our applications before sending them out to the real world, it pays to have some sense of how this all fits together from the beginning.

Single Development Server

In most cases, a single development server will work just fine. This is especially true when the site in question is primarily informational in nature and mostly contains static content. Since most of the updates and changes can be easily tested on this server before deployment, there is really no need for a more complex setup. Even if there is a large amount of dynamic content on the site, or even a Commerce site, a single development server is usually more than enough to handle all your basic needs.

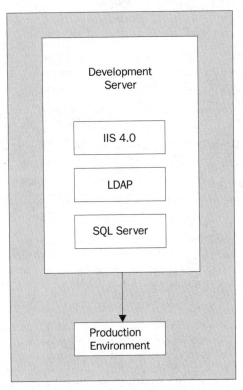

As you can see, we have our web server and our database server on a single machine. We have an IIS 4.0 web server, an LDAP Service and a SQL Server database. This is probably how you will want to set up your test machine when you install Site Server for the first time.

Separate Development and Staging Servers

In more complex sites, however, it may become necessary to use a two-server development system. In this setup, the first server serves primarily as an application development platform, while the second serves as a staging area for new content, and as a test platform for any newly developed pieces of your application. This may seem like overkill. However, when you have a large, complex site where your application is continually being updated and changed, it is extremely nice to have a test platform to work with. This way you can ensure that nothing moves to the live site until it has been thoroughly reviewed by your entire team.

In addition, during multi-tier application development, it can often be necessary to reboot your development server continually throughout the day. This is especially true when you are developing and testing a new COM object, for example, or making other substantial changes to your development environment. If you also have a large staff making regular content changes to the site, it is paramount that they have a stable platform to work on to maintain their productivity. In this scenario, the content developers can continually add new content to the staging server without any interruptions from the application development team.

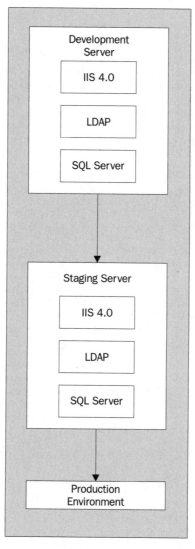

In this configuration we have two machines set up with the same configuration: each machine is both a web server and a database server. Using the second machine as a test environment as shown here, makes sense when we don't have a heavy load on either machine. However, both Site Server and SQL Server are resource-intensive, and in a production environment you will need to cater for much heavier traffic. In this scenario, with two machines, we would probably want to use one machine as a web server and the other as a database server, as we'll go on to discuss.

A Production Environment

Now it's time to discuss the live production environment. Before you begin developing your application, you should have a very clear picture of what your production environment is going to look like. Changes to this piece of the puzzle become extremely difficult as time goes on, and especially after your site is first launched live to the world. Let's take a look at some possible production server configurations, and discuss the various Site Server usage scenarios that could best utilize each.

One Production Server

The simplest configuration is obviously just a single server. This is by far the easiest setup to maintain, since it is most likely a mirror image of your development environment. A single server setup is ideal for web sites that contain a large amount of static content, such as an online catalog or reference site. It is also a viable solution for a smaller commerce or membership site that uses some light personalization, such as an Intranet installation, etc. However, if the needs of your site change, it could be rather difficult to expand this site without a fair amount of pain.

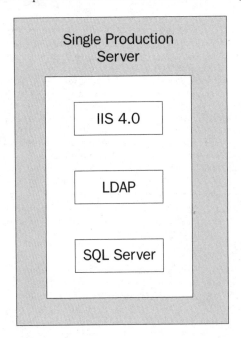

As in the development scenario we looked at earlier, here we have all the components of Site Server on one machine.

Two Production Servers

The next option is to split out your live setup onto two different machines. This is an excellent option for a commerce site that employs no personalization, for example, since the dynamic portion of your site is limited to your online store. In this case, you would run IIS on the primary server, and SQL server on the backend server. This would be perfect for a medium to large commerce site, and could more than handle most of the traffic and growth you may experience.

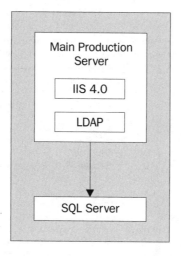

This would also be a great configuration for perhaps a news and information-type site where much of the content is generated dynamically from a SQL Server database. Again, the growth you might experience in this case could easily be handled by either growing the existing servers or adding a machine or two where needed. The only real drawback to this setup is that it would take a little bit of work to add features such as personalization to the web site. However, this could be overcome fairly easily by simply adding another server and expanding the production system from a two server into a three server setup.

Three Production Servers

The three-server production server model is probably the most preferred setup among seasoned Site Server veterans. The reason for this is that it is the most easily scalable setup available, since it is simple to track down any bottlenecks in your application, and then just address that issue directly. For example, if you are having trouble with membership authentication, and the LDAP server is the culprit, you can simply make the necessary modifications, such as the addition of RAM, and be on your way. Additionally, when any one part of the system begins to reach its load limit, you can quickly and easily beef up that part of the system without having to spend hardware resources in places that are just not necessary.

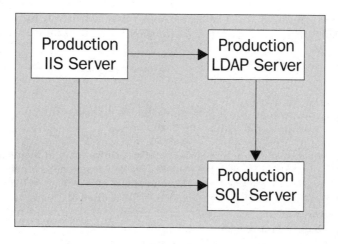

The Big Picture

In the end, if you are building a truly sizable and complex web site, you'll probably want to go with the best of both worlds. Using two separate development servers will provide you with the most flexible environment possible for updating and maintaining your Site Server installation. And in the live environment, the three-server scenario is going to provide you with the most room for scalability and growth.

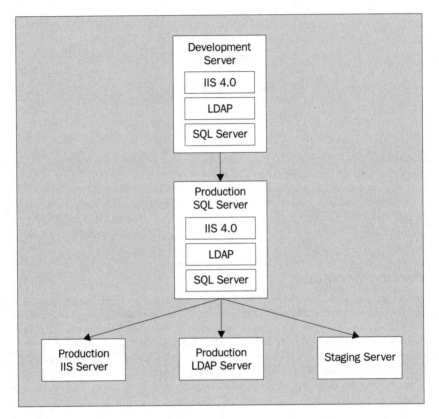

As a complete solution, this setup can't be beaten, and is used extensively by many Site Server developers, especially when running a full scale Commerce site that's fully integrated with Personalization and Membership, etc.

Partioning

There is another way that for one of our data stores, the Membership Directory, we can distribute the load across different machines, and that is with partitioning.

One of the oft-trumpeted strengths of Site Server 3.0 Personalization and Membership is that the Membership Directory is massively scalable – that is, we can design our Membership Directory in advance so that it is ready to store the data of huge numbers of members. We do this by distributing the Directory over a number of SQL Server databases. To begin with, these databases might all live on a single SQL Server machine; but as your system grows, you can migrate individual databases to their own dedicated SQL Server machine.

By using a sufficient number of SQL Servers, and sufficiently many databases, you can allow yourself enough memory to cope with just about any number of members you can throw at it, and room for further expansion.

So how to multiple databases manifest themselves within the Membership Directory? The answer is **partitioning**. We use the logical structure of the Membership Directory to determine what type of data goes into which database.

We'll look in detail at the structure of the Membership Directory further on in the book. For the moment all we need to know is that the structure is arranged hierarchically in terms of container objects, which can then contain other container objects or leaf objects, in a simple tree structure. In fact you most commonly need to partition the container holding all the members of your site.

There are two types of partitions – **namespace partitions** and **value partitions**. Let's look at each of these, and find out how they work.

Namespace Partitions

We use a namespace partition when we want to create a dedicated database to store all the data within a given container. For example, we could put the entire contents of one container on to a separate database:

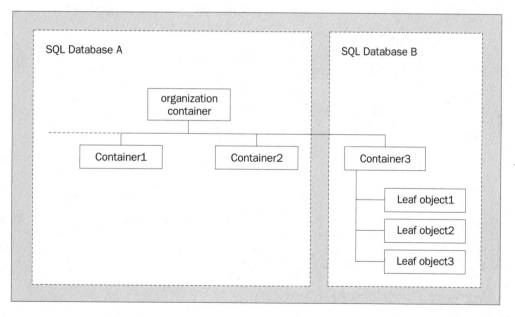

Container3, and all its leafs and sub-containers are contained in SQL Database B, while the remainder of the Membership Directory is contained in SQL database A. Note, however, that the LDAP Service works with the logical structure of the Membership Directory, and therefore sees the *entire* Membership Directory.

Namespace partitions give us the capability to use a different database for each container, if we so choose. For example, if an ISP host uses a single Membership Directory to host many customers, it would be possible to set up a container for each customer, each with its own dedicated database.

Value Partitons

We use a value partition to distribute the contents of a container across two or more physical databases. The distribution is more-or-less even. We can only value-partition a container at the time we create our Membership Server. However, we can create a number of value partitions on a single machine to begin, and – as the size of the container grows – we can migrate each value partition to its own dedicated SQL Server machine.

This way we can allow a large degree of scalability for each container, spreading it over multiple databases and ultimately over multiple machines, provided we plan the partitions in advance.

In the following diagram, the Container3 is value-partitioned into two physical databases. The contents of Container3 are split between the databases.

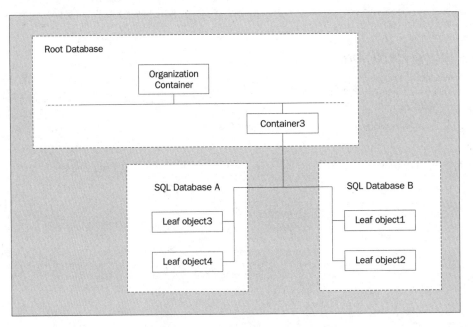

The value partitions of a container are distinguished by the hashing value – as in partitions #1 and #2 in the figure above. The Membership Server decides where a member will be stored, and does its best to distribute members evenly across the two value partitions. Value partitions, like namespace partitions, are transparent to the LDAP Service, which sees the entire Directory.

Planning your Partitions in Advance

As we've mentioned, it's vital that you plan your site requirements in advance. Site Server 3.0 doesn't allow you to re-partition your Membership Directory once you've started using it, so you should plan your partitions in advance. If you don't have the hardware available when you create the site, then it's essential to estimate the amount of traffic you expect you see in 1 or 2 years, and create the partitions when you create the Directory. Once you've prepared your partitions, you can always obtain hardware and migrate databases later on.

> *There's a useful paper on Site Server Capacity and Performance Analysis, which you can find at*
> `http://www.microsoft.com/siteserver/intranet/Update/performance.asp`.

Load Balancing

As your site grows, it may become necessary to add additional servers to your production system in order to handle the load. When this happens, you'll need to explore the various methods at your disposal for balancing the incoming traffic load across these new machines. Let's take a look at a couple of possible options and explore the pros and cons of each.

Round Robin DNS

Round Robin DNS is a software-based load balancing solution that directs incoming web traffic to one of a designated group of web servers, usually in a looping order. Each consecutive client request is routed to the next server in the round robin list, and when the last machine is reached, the loop just starts back at the first server again. This load balancing solution is easy to implement, since it simply requires the addition of a few more web servers, as well as the installation of some round robin DNS software on the already existing DNS servers.

Pros

This solution is very easy to implement, and provides us with a number of advantages. Since the load balancing is accomplished by redirecting the client directly to an actual web server, any subsequent requests that particular client sends are guaranteed to go to the same server. This is very important, since it allows us to continue keeping track of the user's session if we are doing so using session variables, etc.

Cons

The problem with a round robin DNS approach is that it is not truly fail-safe. In other words, if one of the servers in the round robin should fail, the DNS server will not be aware of this, and that machine will continue to receive its share of requests, and a certain percentage of client requests will fall on deaf ears. This situation will continue until either the machine in question is restored to working order or removed from the list of servers in the round robin. Of course, most often our user will successfully reach a functional server on their next attempt to connect to our site, but this situation is still less than ideal.

Another problem with this solution is that it is not a true load balancing solution. Requests are merely doled out in a preset order, so that it is still possible, though rather unlikely, that there will be an uneven load across the various servers. Obviously, though, the more servers we include in the round robin list, the less likely this is to happen.

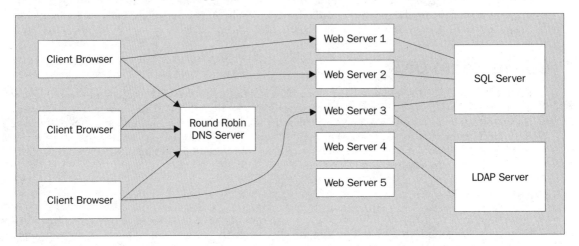

Proxy Arrays

A proxy array, unlike the round robin DNS solution we just discussed, is designed to consolidate the various web servers in our array. In this way, a proxy array presents a single large interface through which the various web clients will connect to our web site. Because of this, each of the machines in our array is aware of the other machines in the array, and hence they can work together to balance the incoming load among themselves. Additionally, they'll be able to detect and compensate for any machine that might go down by redistributing the requests to the remaining servers.

Pros

In addition to the benefits described above, proxy arrays are also particularly effective at reducing the web server load when there is a large amount of static content mixed in with your application. This is accomplished through extensive caching of the static content, so that web client requests for this static content can be fulfilled without even hitting the primary web servers. This can greatly decrease the load on your web application, and free up IIS and Site Server resources, resulting in a dramatic speed gain for all users.

Cons

The main drawback to implementing a proxy array is that since each request is doled out to the server with the lightest load at the moment, there is no guarantee that any given user will hit the same server as they did last time. In fact, it is highly unlikely. This means that it becomes much more difficult to maintain state, since we will can no longer use server variables to do this.

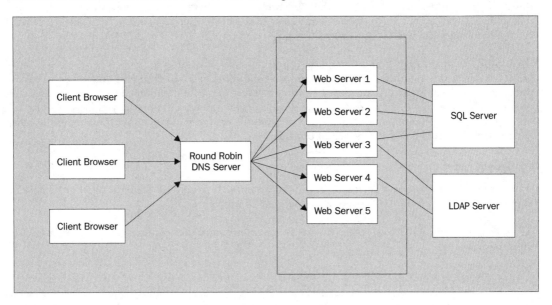

Windows Load Balancing Service

Another option is Microsoft's Windows Load Balancing Service (WLBS). By combining the best of the round robin DNS and proxy array approaches, WLBS offers true fault-tolerant server clustering and load balancing. In fact, it even allows various servers in the same cluster to perform different tasks within the cluster, enabling you to allocate hardware resources where they are most needed.

The WLBS architecture works by clustering all of the servers in your application so that they respond to a single IP address. Because the servers are completely aware of one another, if a single machine fails, the other machines in the cluster are able to compensate and pick up the load. When a down server is restored, it is automatically added back into the cluster and resumes its share of the work. WLBS even allows you to configure the load percentage that each machine should handle, thus enabling you to group machines of various capabilities into the same cluster.

Also, as requests are made, the incoming traffic is routed equally among the various servers in the cluster. This means that, for example, the various graphics necessary to fulfill a web page request would be handled by different servers within the cluster, thus speeding up the overall retrieval of the page.

Even though WLBS is packaged with Windows NT Enterprise Edition, it is currently available for any Windows NT server system, and can be downloaded from the Microsoft web site. For more information go to `http://www.microsoft.com/ntserver`. Of course, WLBS will also be tightly integrated with Windows 2000 when it is released.

Design Considerations For Your Site

Sites built using Site Server are basically Windows Distributed INternet Architecture (DNA) applications. As such, they benefit greatly by taking advantage of the many features that a true multi-tier environment has to offer. However, planning and deploying your application using this distributed multi-tier architecture can be a bit tricky, since there are many new decisions that need to be made that can have a huge impact much later in the development process. We'll see more on this as we go through the book.

In addition to the various planning and design decisions you need to make before you begin building your site, there are a number of other issues you should be aware of. Some of these are tips for increasing your site's performance, while others are just things you will need to be aware of so that you can plan ahead and work around them during development. Either way, you'll want to be sure to understand each of these possible problems and pitfalls so that you can avoid them from the outset. These are what we'll cover in the rest of this chapter.

Session State

If you are going to be using Personalization and Membership, you are going to need to be able to keep track of the current user. There are a number of ways to do this.

One of these is the AUO object that we met in Chapter 1, and that comes with Membership. Other options are:

> **Session Variables.** Using a session variable is a fairly simple way to keep track of the current users CN. However, as you probably already know, session variables can slow down your servers' performance, sometimes dramatically. Also, they can also have an impact on the future scalability of your site, since session variables only live on the server on which they were created. If a user session spans multiple web servers, session variables will no longer work.

> **Cookies.** Cookies are an excellent option, especially since they can be set up so that the users do not ever need to login to the site after their first session. However, this option is not very well suited to sites that require a high level of security, since any user could conceivably walk up to that machine and gain unauthorized access to your site.

> **Server Variables.** You can also usually retrieve the CN of the currently logged on user through the REMOTE_USER server variable, `Request.ServerVariables(REMOTE_USER)`. However, I've found that this option does not work 100% of the time. You will need to test this option on your particular server to see whether or not this variable is storing the proper name.

While none of these options is perfect, it is important to spend ample time determining which option will work best for your needs. This early decision can also have a serious impact on the future growth and expansion of your site, particularly in relation to the load-balancing options we've just discussed.

Consistent Names and Versions

It's extremely important to establish naming conventions as early as possible in the design process. Many of the Site Server features and services you will be using rely heavily on hard coded machine names, which are embedded within numerous configuration files during the setup process. This is especially true with Commerce Server. If you choose to use IP numbers during development, or perhaps you decide to change machine names somewhere down the road, you may end up spending a great deal of time and effort tracking down the many places that need to be updated to get everything running smoothly again.

It's also important to make sure that you are consistent in using identical versions of the many pieces of software that are duplicated across the various machines in your development and production environments. Adding something as simple as a service pack or a new version of Internet Explorer to one machine without performing the same upgrade on all of your machines could result in major problems when you begin to migrate newly developed content from one machine to the next. Also, since your production environment will most likely consist of multiple servers, communications between these machines could also be adversely affected when there are version incompatibilities among these machines. We'll see a common version-related error a little further on.

Domains or Stand-Alone Servers

Along the same lines as having a solid naming convention in place before you begin, is the question of domains. You need to decide in advance how each machine will interact with any existing domains you are running. The reason for this is that many Site Server services and MTS components run in the security context of the currently logged on user. This means that once you have completed your Site Server installation, you should avoid moving that server into or out of a domain at all costs.

Generally, you'll want to install any machine that will live in the 'de-militarized zone' (DMZ) as stand alone servers that are not part of any domain at all. This means that there will be a local administrator login, and that all of these services will run in the context of that user.

Going Live

The most important thing to remember about going live with your new site is to **test extensively in your live environment**. This cannot be stressed enough. Site Server applications are inherently Windows DNA applications, which means that the various servers in your production environment must be able to communicate with one another. Most developers are not prepared for this transition, since generally web applications run solely on the web server, with perhaps some occasional communication with the SQL server for data retrieval.

However, you must remember that, in most cases, the bulk of your development will have been done in a single server environment. Many things that work just fine in this environment could suddenly stop working once you move your application to your production servers. Let's take a look as some of the more common problems you are likely to encounter during this transition.

Failed to Enlist on Calling Object's Transaction

This is probably the most commonly encountered, and most frustrating, problem while moving a Site Server site into the production environment. However, if you don't know why it's happening, it can be downright nasty to try and track down, especially since the error message really isn't all that helpful.

If you do find help, it will tell you that you must make sure that the DTCs (Distributed Transaction Coordinators) on your servers must be running, and that your servers can properly communicate with each other. However, with Site Server, this is rarely the problem. It generally boils down to version incompatibilities between the DTCs running on the web server and the SQL server, and is caused by the SQLItemAdo component in the Commerce purchase pipeline. There are a number of solutions to this problem, but by far the easiest is just to install MTS from the NT Option Pack on each machine, so that they are running the same version. You'll also need to make sure that both services are started, and are set up to start automatically at boot time.

You can find more information on this problem at the following URLs:

> `http://support.microsoft.com/support/kb/articles/q191/1/68.asp`

> `http://support.microsoft.com/support/kb/articles/q201/1/43.asp`

> `http://www.adiscon.com/mts/FAQDetail.asp?ID=42&T=0`

MDAC Versions

In a two-server production environment, you may experience yet another version problem. If your web server and LDAP server are on the first machine, and SQL Server is on the second, SQL Server can interfere with your LDAP server connection, causing membership functionality to fail. If this happens, you will need to upgrade to MDAC version 2.1. You can get version 2.1 from the IE5 installation disk, the SQL Server 7 disk, or a number of other places. However, be aware that if you install MDAC 2.1 on your web server running Site Server, you will encounter problems with ADSI 2.0 (part of the Site Server 3.0 installation). The recommended solution for this is to upgrade to ADSI 2.5 on machines where you are running both MDAC 2.1 and Site Server 3.0, although even this then involves a workaround for some Membership functionality. You can find more information on this problem in the Knowledge Base article at `http://support.microsoft.com/support/kb/articles/Q216/7/09.asp`.

Summary

In this chapter, we've covered many of the design and planning issues you will need to keep in mind as you begin to build your Site Server site. We've looked at installation issues, as well as planning for scalability and growth. We also covered some of the pitfalls to avoid as you get ready to take your site live.

Some of the important things to remember from this chapter include:

> Proper design and planning are crucial to the success of any Site Server site. This is especially true with Site Server, since there are so many interdependent parts. Something as simple as changing a resource name can cause hours or even days of work hunting through the various affected parts of the site.

> Scalability is an important factor to consider when designing a Site Server site. In most Site Server installations, many different components will be spread across multiple machines. It's important to understand the load handling capabilities of each, and to properly plan for future growth.

> Once you've developed your Site Server site, there are still many issues you must tackle as you prepare to move everything into production. Making sure you understand how your production servers are going to talk to the rest of your setup is crucial.

Design and scalability are not isolated issues, which only need to be addressed at the beginning of the installation. As we move through the book we'll see that it is important to bear design considerations in mind to create a maintainable site. We'll also come across other ways of addressing scalability problems before they happen, for example by using the NT Performance Monitor tool.

Next, we'll look at security considerations when implementing Site Server, before finally moving on to installation, by when we should be well-prepared!

3

Security Overview

Somewhere in California, USA. Local time 3:35 AM.

Site Admin: Uh... I think we have a problem...
Manager: What's happening?
Site Admin: All the user accounts have been erased!
Manager: What do you mean? All 100,000 users?
Site Admin: Yes, I'd better check out our back-up data!
Manager: How did this happen? What went wrong?

When thinking about security for a web site you should keep in mind that not all sites have the same security requirements. Each site has different needs; the security needs of a large e-commerce site like Amazon.com may well be different than the security needs of an academic institution. Any security plans have to conform to the needs and purposes of the site. Today the Internet allows for anybody with computer access and a modem to visit sites all over the world just a click away. Now a person can check hundreds of sites for vulnerabilities in just a few hours.

As you prepare to build a web site you will quickly realize that the more you read about security the more prepared you will be to implement an efficient security strategy. This is an ongoing process for which you or someone else on your company must focus their attention. It takes time to build the trust of users on the net and all it takes is perhaps one incident and your whole user base may go away. I cannot begin to emphasize enough how important security is for your web site.

You and your team should spend some time thinking about what you are trying to protect, and who you need to protect it from. Also what is the likelihood of actual threats, security breaches, etc? Prevention is one of the main keys to security. For example, the Computer Emergency Response Team/Coordination Center (CERT/CC) at Carnegie-Mellon University (CMU) estimates that over 80% of the problems that they see have to do with poorly chosen passwords. Simply instructing users on choosing proper passwords could prevent many problems in your site.

Consider running a risk analysis dividing your assets and threats and outlining what is an acceptabl level of security and how your site would be impacted if there were a security break-in on those areas. For each private area on your system such as the user billing address, credit card information or any type of financial data, the basic goals of security are availability, confidentiality, and integrity.

Most e-commerce sites, either business-to-business or business-to-consumer, that handle for example credit card transactions, financial information, user's private information are more likely to require a greater deal of security than plain information sites. You also should consider all aspects of your operation such as network security, hardware security, software security and any other area related to the project.

Finally, this chapter can only be a starting point for thinking about the security of your site. I suggest that you get hold of as many publications and as much documentation as you can get on this topic, such as ASP/MTS/ADSI Web Security ISBN 0130844659, by R.Harrison. There are too many areas related to security to fit in just this chapter.

In this chapter we'll be looking at the "big picture" about security issues. We'll look at the different layers of security you need to consider when implementing a Site Server site, and discuss security in relation to the technologies that make up Site Server. The chapter will discuss the following areas:

> General security concepts

> Securing your hardware architecture with firewalls

> NT security, in particular controlling access to filesystem resources

> Options for securing IIS

> Encryption and LDAP.

We'll start by setting the scene for web site security.

Important Security Concepts

As you identify the most critical areas of your site and what levels of security are needed to protect those areas, you have to make sure that three properties essential for good security are present. These are confidentiality, integrity, and availability. You cannot have good security with only one and without the others. Below is a brief description of each property:

> **Confidentiality** is the concept that information is available only to those who are authorized to access it. Rigorous controls must be implemented to ensure that only those persons who need access to certain information have that access. For example: only the user himself or herself should be able to update his or her shipping and billing information, this also applies to other areas such as credit card information.

> **Integrity** ensures that information cannot be changed in unexpected ways by unauthorized people. The consequences of using inaccurate information can be disastrous. If data is improperly modified it can become very dangerous. Your site should ensure the accuracy of data at all times and keep a log of any major changes that take place. This is a beyond the traditional backup and maintenance in terms of databases. It goes deep into the heart of security where data can be accessed and manipulated by unauthorized personal.

> ➤ **Availability** prevents resources from being improperly deleted or becoming inaccessible. This applies not only to information, but also to networked machines and other aspects of the site infrastructure. Ensuring the physical security of a network or system is one way to cover availability. By limiting physical access to critical machines or data sources, the incidence of inaccessibility will be reduced.

Each area that requires secure access should reflect these three properties. As you are planning the implementation of your site run the C.I.A test on all relevant areas as you build them. You will gradually realize this is not a trivial task. However the sooner you run these types of checks on important areas of your site the easier it will be to ensure security.

Security Architecture: Firewalls

The design of your security architecture has to consider hardware and software components as well as physical considerations such as the location of the site.

> *There is very good information on securing your site in the Site Server documentation, including information on secure network configurations – this is essential reading before setting up a production site.*

In the previous chapter we looked at the various machine configurations for setting up Site Server. In terms of security, we need to consider network access to these machines. If you are implementing a website that has connections through to your internal company network one common security mechanism is a firewall, and this is what we'll look at in this section.

In brief, a firewall is what stands between you and the outside world. A firewall could consists of a variety of items, including computers, routers, and services. Depending on your network, you may have multiple firewalls, multiple internal networks, Virtual Private Networks (VPNs), and extranets.

Some sites will be connected only to other sites within the same organization and will not have the ability to connect to outside networks. A firewall system should be rigorously controlled and password protected. External users accessing it should be constrained by restrictions to only access certain areas.

A firewall can improve the security of your network in three ways.

Packet Filtering

Originally firewalls really were just nothing more than specialized routers. The firewall performed a very basic function, to examine each network packet as it came down the wire to ensure that the address was coming from an authorized client. This is still an integral part of a firewall strategy. It has the benefit that it is very efficient and speedy, since it just looks at the network packet header, making no changes, and simply allows or denies entry.

For example, if it finds an IP address in a header that should be an internal IP address, but it is coming across the public Internet, then that is a danger sign. Basically, no internal IP should be showing up on your network's front door. Someone may be trying to impersonate one of your internal servers. Packet filtering can be either inbound or outbound. An additional benefit of packet filtering is that it generally requires no knowledge or explicit cooperation from the user.

Circuit Proxy

The second approach is through the use of what is called a circuit proxy. The difference between this and the packet filter is that the circuit proxy forces all communicators (client or server) to address their packets to the circuit proxy, not directly to the intended target. So the proxy gets a packet addressed to it, and then changes the address to represent the internal target. As you can imagine, performance is not quite as good as plain packet filtering. The main advantage is that it hides the real IP address, which, to someone trying to gain access to your system, is one of the most important information tidbits. This technique is also known as NAT, network address translation. However, NAT can have implications for Site Server, which we'll talk about below.

Application Proxy

The third approach uses what is known as an application proxy. The application proxy understands the application protocol and data, and intercepts any information intended for that application. A mail server is a good example of this. The mail server receives e-mail messages via a particular protocol from a mail client. Users can check e-mail on the mail server, which works as an intermediary of the information. The application proxy can do such things as authenticate users, instead of simply relying on IP addresses, and even determine if the actual data represents something that could be harmful. This is much more intensive than packet filtering.

Firewalls and Site Server

Below is a simple network diagram to illustrate how a firewall can be part of your site architecture. Note that this is a simple architecture, you may use one or more firewall combinations in your network. You should allow a network engineer to design the layout of your network and help you choose the right hardware.

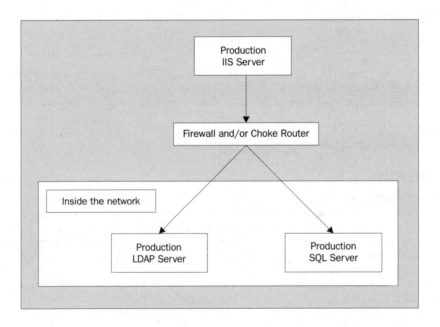

There are several possible configurations for your network. In this example site the database server is behind a firewall and the web server is outside. The separation between your database servers from your web servers can be very useful in order to control access. Only specific machines should be allowed to contact your database server. This also allows you to separate its physical access and personal access from the other servers. In particular, if possible you should keep the machines that handle most of your commerce transactions in a separate environment with very restricted access.

However there are some restrictions when using firewalls with Site Server. For instance if you had the configuration outlined above, with your IIS server and database server in different sides of a firewall, you would encounter some problems if you wanted to use NAT (Network Address Translation) between them.

This is to do with DCOM (Distributed COM). DCOM needs to see the actual IP addresses of the relevant machines, and thus cannot work with NAT. One element of Site Server that uses DCOM is the MMC, so if you were running NAT between your web server and your database server you would not be able to reach the database server through the MMC.

However, other components of Site Server access the database server differently. Within Site Server Commerce, if you were using transactions for parts of your pipeline, you would need the MSDTC (Microsoft Distributed Transaction Coordinator) service running on both the web and database servers, and MSDTC can work through NAT.

> **To work through a firewall, both DCOM and MSDTC require RPC (Remote Procedure Call) to be enabled through the firewall.**

For more information on this see the white paper *Using Distributed COM with Firewalls* by Michael Nelson, available at `http://www.microsoft.com/com/wpaper/dcomfw.asp`.

It's important to note that having a firewall between your web and database servers may not be the best solution for your particular configuration. A further possibility would be to have the web server and database server together behind a firewall, and then have a proxy server outside which would pass requests through the firewall to the web server.

Alternatively you could set up a DMZ (Demilitarized Zone), which essentially provides a buffer between your network and the outside world. We can't go into a detailed discussion of a DMZ here, but for more information see `http://www.whatis.com/dmz.htm`.

Deploying Firewalls

Firewalls and routers can also cause many headaches during your initial deployment. You will need to work closely with the various network administrators who control your company's Internet access and security. This may be something new to you, but it will become increasingly necessary as you develop and grow your multi-tiered application.

Depending on the level of security employed by your organization, you can begin to experience some very strange problems. On a recent project, we began experiencing serious performance problems when connecting to our LDAP servers. After quite a bit of investigation, it turned out that because of the way the DMZ was setup, each connection was making 11 hops before reaching our LDAP server.

Testing Firewalls

Testing your firewall is not very easy. It involves tracking network packets, understanding of different network protocols, and network routing knowledge. Again this is where a network engineer can help with your project. You need to understand several security concepts related to your choice of hardware, have an in-depth understanding of TCP/IP, and be familiar with various methods of attack, such is IP spoofing, denial of service, information theft, and the list goes on. It is critical to test a firewall because even a minor mistake in configuration can lead to holes in your network.

One of the most famous tools for testing networks is SATAN (Security Administrator Tool for Analyzing Networks). For more information on SATAN visit: `http://stos-www.cit.cornell.edu/Mark_html/Satan_html/docs/satan_overview.html`.
It is designed to expose problems in your security, and let you know what they are. However be aware it can also be used by hackers to uncover weaknesses.

You'll also need to make sure that you have the access you need between these servers, since a large part of Internet security involves blocking network traffic over various ports. Let's look at these key ports.

Ports of Interest

You'll need to make sure that the ports for the services you are using are opened up through the firewall, so that your Web server can talk back and forth to your SQL and LDAP server. In some cases, such as SMTP, you need to make sure that your web server is allowed to communicate out on that port so that it can send confirmation e-mails, etc.

Port Number	Use
21	FTP – For file transfers, etc.
25	SMTP – For sending e-mails, etc.
53	SQL Server – name lookup
80	HTTP
135	DCOM session establishment
137/8	File Shares – name lookup; SQL Server – RPC
139	NetBIOS – file share session; SQL Server – session; Windows Challeng/Response authentication
389	Default for LDAP / Membership Directory Manager (MDM)
443	HTTPS / SSL
507	Site Server's Content Replication Service
636	LDAP (SSL)
1433	ODBC / MS SQL. This is the default but can be changed during installation to make life awkward for potential hackers.

Port Number	Use
1002	Membership Server with Windows NT Authentication. This is the port for the default Membership Server created at installation.
8000	Cybercash (credit gateway)
8001	Cybercash (admin)
8002	Cybercash (coin gateway)
8283	IIS Admin

Securing the Software Platform

As we've discussed in the previous two chapters, Site Server is essentially a collection of tools that have dependencies on several other products, principally NT, MTS, SQL Server (or other database) and IIS. In establishing a secure environment for a Site Server site, it is essential to secure the various elements of the Site Server platform. In fact, when we talk about Site Server security, what we are actually discussing is a combination of NT security, IIS security, and additional Site Server-specific features. We'll discuss each of these three layers in turn, and see what is involved for each one and how they integrate. First however we need to take a brief look at users and groups in Site Server.

Users and Groups

There are two main aspects of security to discuss in relation to users: authentication and authorization. Authentication, the process of identifying a user, is the first test a user will face, for instance through logging on and providing a password. Site Server provides a variety of different ways of authenticating users, which all involve access through the web site, so we'll see these when we move on to discuss IIS.

The second part of the process, authorization, involves verifying that the user we've identified does in fact have permission to view a particular file. For example, we might have set up areas of our site to offer some special offer details, which we only want subscribers to see. We could thus authenticate the user, and let them browse the site, and then check to see whether they are authorized to receive the special offer. The authorization component of security is handled through NT.

We need to bear in mind that, although most of the security processes we'll discuss in this chapter are geared towards users accessing our site through the web interface, there should also be security measures in place for users accessing the setup as administrators. This can be just as much to prevent a user accidentally damaging areas of the site, as to avoid deliberate security breaches. As we'll see in Chapter 5 when we discuss administration, we can set up administration rights that are restricted to particular areas of Site Server. This is controlled through Site Server groups that are created at install.

The permissions for what members of a group may access, however, are set at a file system level, with NT access control settings, and this is what we'll look at next.

NT Security

At a basic level, NT permissions control access to files, directories and other file system resources. This is done through a mechanism of Access Control Entries (ACEs), Access Control Lists (ACLs) and security descriptors. Each individual file can have its own permissions. This security information is stored in a security descriptor, which includes the name of the object owner and an ACL. Let's look at these in more detail.

Access Control Entries

An ACE controls or monitors access by a specified trustee to an object. Windows NT/Windows 2000 currently supports six types of ACEs. There are three ACE types supported by all securable objects. In addition, there are three types of object-specific ACEs supported by directory service objects. All types of ACEs contain the following access-control information:

> ➤ A security identifier (SID) that identifies the trustee to which the ACE applies.
>
> ➤ An access mask that specifies the access rights controlled by the ACE.
>
> ➤ A flag that indicates the type of ACE.
>
> ➤ A set of bit flags that determine whether child containers or objects can inherit the ACE from the primary object to which the ACL is attached.

Access Control Lists

An access control list (ACL) is a list of access control entries (ACEs). The security descriptor for a securable object can contain two ACLs: a DACL and a SACL.

A discretionary access-control list (DACL) identifies the trustees that are allowed or denied access to a securable object. When a process tries to access a securable object, the system checks the ACEs in the object's DACL to determine whether to grant access. If the object does not have a DACL, the system grants full access to everyone. If the object's DACL has no ACEs, the system denies all attempts to access the object because the DACL does not allow any access rights. The system checks the ACEs in sequence until it finds one or more ACEs that allow all the requested access rights, or until any of the requested access rights are denied.

A system access-control list (SACL) enables administrators to log attempts to access a secured object. Each ACE specifies the types of access attempts by a specified trustee that cause the system to generate a record in the security event log. An ACE in a SACL can generate audit records when an access attempt fails, when it succeeds, or both. In future releases, a SACL will also be able to raise an alarm when an unauthorized user attempts to gain access to an object. Do not try to work directly with the contents of an ACL. To ensure that ACLs are semantically correct, use the appropriate Win32 functions to create and manipulate ACLs.

Securing the Membership Directory

It's worth noting, while we're on the subject of ACLs, that a good illustration of these is provided by the Membership Directory. By default the Membership Directory allows users unrestricted access, as the root object in the Membership Directory contains the Public group (for Membership Authentication) or the Everyone group (for Windows NT Authentication). The public group is a P&M built-in group to which every Membership Directory user belongs by default. The Everyone group is a Windows NT built-in group to which every user in the Windows NT directory database belongs.

The default access setting on the Membership Directory Manager node for these groups is Full control with Full inheritance. Therefore, by default, every object in the Membership Directory can be accessed by all users. Anonymous access is also enabled by default on the Site Server LDAP Service. This condition in combination with the Public or Everyone ACE on the root node allows access to the Membership Directory without requiring authentication.

This default condition of the Membership Directory is designed to allow you to set up an initial test Membership Directory without worrying about authentication. However, before making your Membership Directory accessible to other users, it is a good idea to remove the Public or Everyone ACE.

To secure a Membership Directory:

➤ Remove the Public group ACE or Everyone group ACE from the Membership Directory Manager object.

➤ If you want no public access to any Membership Directory objects, you can also disable Allow anonymous.

IIS Security

Through IIS you can configure two principal aspects of your site security. The first aspect is authentication, (as we discussed at the beginning of this section). The second aspect concerns the actual transmission of information from your web server to the client, and how this can be secured through Secure Sockets Layer (SSL).

Access To Your Site

We'll be discussing the various authentication methods in detail in Chapter 9, *Membership*. At this stage however, it is useful to understand the different levels of content to which we may want to restrict access, and the different types of user who will be accessing the site. Let's look first at content.

Access to Content

There are different levels of user access you can provide with Site Server 3.0. When choosing one of them you need to consider the type of information to which the user will have access. Below is a summary of content areas:

➤ **Public Content**.
Pages that are visible to all users, such as a Home Page or an About Your Company page. Authentication is not needed on these pages and access control is not enforced on these pages.

➤ **Restricted Content**.
Pages that are only visible after a user provides some information or answers a series of questions. There is no login screen and the users are not required to be registered users at this point. This area can be used to take users through a guided tour or to download special content.

➤ **Private Content**.
Pages that are only visible by registered users. A login screen will appear and require the user to provide some identification before showing information.

> **Secure Content**.
> This area is protected by SSL, and all interactions between the browser and the pages is encrypted. Pages that are only visible to registered and authenticated users. It provides the highest security and is the best choice for safeguarding user's private and financial data, such as credit card numbers. Usually this is also applied to shopping checkout areas, fee-based information access, download of software updates, etc.

Different e-commerce sites may have several public areas and at least one secure content area for account information and financial data. Areas such as check out, user account maintenance, and any report information you may provide should be under secure content areas. Usually secure content areas are provided with secure socket layers (SSL) to greatly improve security. I will go over SSL configuration later.

User Access

When a user comes to your web site you can choose whether to allow them unrestricted anonymous access, or whether to identify them, such as with a password. We have several authentication methods available to us, and there are a number of different types of user. Site Server 3.0 makes a distinction for the following type of users:

> **Anonymous Users**.
> Users that are allowed to visit the site, but are not tracked and therefore cannot receive personalized content. Since they are not tracked and are anonymous, Site Server does not assign them any credentials (such as username or password).

> **Cookie-Identified Users**.
> These users are tracked by Site Server, and their anonymous ids are kept in the "ou=Anonymous" container inside the Membership Directory. A globally unique identifier (GUID) is automatically created and assigned to the user's cookie. This GUID is also kept on LDAP. Cookie-identified users can receive content with personalization and there is a security context created via the Automatic Cookie Authentication mode, however there is no logon. This security context holds the information that establishes what kind of information the user will be able to access. Site Server does not know the identity of a cookie-identified user unless you specify it to collect that information. Under Membership Authentication, cookie-identified users can be put into groups and can therefore be given access to restricted, but not private or secure, content.

> **Registered Users**.
> These users are authenticated and tracked by the Membership Directory or the Windows NT Server directory. They can receive personalized content, become members and part of groups. You can assign different access levels to different groups, therefore creating traditional restricted areas, premium areas, and other areas with different levels of security. The registered user's username and password or client certificate are the credentials by which the user is authenticated at logon time.

Once you have a good idea of the different areas of your site and the types of users that can visit these areas, then you can start thinking about the authentication methods that best fit each area.

Site Server 3.0 comes with two authentication modes, NT Authentication and Membership Authentication. Each mode comes with several authentication options. With Membership Authentication user accounts are stored in the Membership Directory, while under Windows NT Authentication each user must have an NT user account, stored in the Windows NT SAM (Security Accounts manager). This means that under Membership authentication you can support many more users. NT Authentication supports up to eighty thousand users while Membership Authentication can support hundreds of thousands. If you are building a small Intranet site with a small user base, NT Authentication should work fine for you. However, if you are in charge of building a large commerce site, Membership authentication is what you need. We'll discuss this in detail in Chapter 9.

IIS SSL/HTTPS and Site Server.

Client applications can establish a connection to the server over a Secure Sockets Layer (SSL) encrypted channel. The server being connected to identifies itself reliably to the client. Non-SSL connections occur over a clear channel with no encryption. Clear channel transmissions are faster than encrypted transmissions, but are less secure.

SSL protects sensitive data from network interception by packet filtering software. Both Membership Authentication methods and Windows NT Authentication methods can be used over a secure channel. You can use Secure Communications settings on the Site Server LDAP Service and on your web site.

We'll go through the steps for enabling secure communications. However, you may want to come back to this section a little later on, when you've read the Membership chapter and are more familiar with the Membership setup.

Setting up Secure Communications

To use secure communications on your server, you must first enable the SSL port on the server to receive communications. To enable the SSL port, you can use the Key Manager, located in the IIS service manager under the security tab, to install a server certificate and create a key pair.

SSL and a server certificate ensures an encrypted channel connection between client applications and a Membership Server running LDAP, and between client browsers and web servers running WWW, SMTP, and NNTP. The certificate provides a digital identification of the organization that owns the server to the client, and the SSL channel provides data integrity and encryption. Below are the steps to configure SSL and HTTPS on your IIS server:

> In IIS Internet Service Manager, click the Web site or other Application server, or click a directory or file within the server hierarchy.

> On the Action menu, click Properties.

> Click the Directory Security tab, and then under Secure Communications, click Edit.

You should then see the following dialog box:

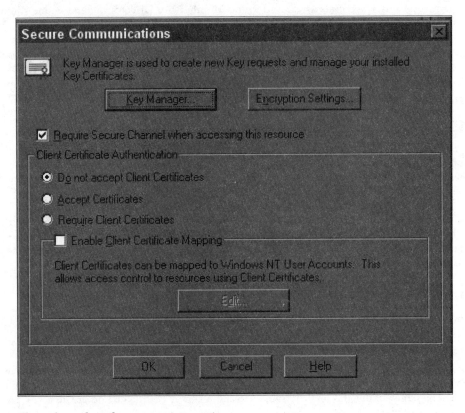

Here you will need to select the appropriate settings:

> ➤ Require secure channel. The clear channel is not available.
> ➤ Do not accept client certificates. Clients cannot be authenticated using certificates. They must provide a valid username and password.
> ➤ Accept client certificates. Certificates can be used for authentication, but they are not required.
> ➤ Require client certificates. The client must have a certificate to be authenticated to use the resource.
> ➤ Enable client certificate mapping. The certificate is mapped to a user account in the Membership Directory or Windows NT Server directory database, depending on the authentication mode being used.

When you are finished selecting options, click OK.

For more information about obtaining and installing a server certificate and about creating and managing server key pairs, see the Security topics in the Internet Information Server (IIS) documentation.

Encryption

One important security measure we haven't yet talked about is encryption. You can use encryption for guarding passwords or a user's financial information such as credit cards, or other critical data. Even if a hacker invades your site and gets to your most sensitive data, if it is encrypted you are still better off than if it was plain text. Encryption is part of Secure Socket Layer, SSL, which as we've discussed is used widely used on the web as a means to secure communication between a browser and the server. One of the most used encryption systems is Public Key encryption.

In a public key encryption system, two different keys are used. When one key encrypts something, the other can decrypt it. The user gives his or her public key to others, and keeps the private key. It is okay for you to give your public key to others without compromising your security; it is very difficult to figure out a private key from a public key.

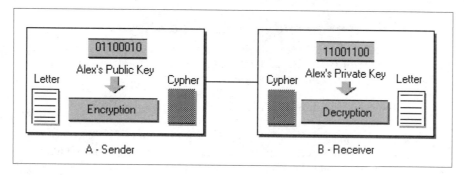

In this scheme, the public key is used to authenticate the originator's use of his or her private key, and hence the identity of the originator is more rigorously proven. The most widely known implementation of a public key encryption system is the RSA system.

We'll come back to encryption in a moment; first we'll look at the Site Server LDAP service.

The LDAP and Authentication Services

The Site Server Authentication service is used by Site Server Membership to authenticate a user from IIS. The Authentication service offers four main services: password validation, security context to support Windows NT security model, the mapping of Membership Directory groups to Windows NT groups, and retrieving user properties from the Membership Directory. You should always have this service running.

The LDAP services provide applications to connect to the Membership Directories on the same machine or on different machines. This service is similar to the W3SVC service – services used by IIS to get web requests – in that clients connect via TCP/IP and it is up to the service to respond to the request.

Both the LDAP service and the Authentication service are required to be on in order to run Membership authentication in your site.

The Authentication Service connects to an LDAP Service, which it will use to access the Membership Directory. When the Authentication Service starts up, it immediately contacts its designated LDAP Service. The LDAP Service itself authenticates the Authentication Service. Once this connection has been established, the Authentication Service can access user information without going through the Membership Directory ACLs. This significantly improves the speed of the Authentication Service's operations. If the Authentication Service resides in a Membership Server that also includes an LDAP Service, the Authentication Service typically uses that LDAP Service. However, it can use an LDAP Service residing in another Membership Server. The other Membership Server can be located on the same computer, or another computer on the same Local Area Network (LAN).

When you create a Membership Server that will use Membership Authentication, an Authentication Service is automatically created and connected to the LDAP Service in that Membership Server, or to another LDAP Service you specify. If at some later time you want to use a different LDAP Service (such as for improved performance) you can do so as long as the new LDAP Service serves the same Membership Directory as the original LDAP Service.

LDAP Password Encryption and the Encryption Keys

The Site Server LDAP Service automatically encrypts all passwords in the Membership Directory before they are written to the underlying Membership Directory database. They are decrypted when the LDAP Service reads them from the database.

Two keys are used to encrypt and decrypt user passwords:

> ➢ Password encryption key (PEkey). Stored in the Membership Directory database and used to encrypt and decrypt user passwords. When a new LDAP Service instance starts, it reads the PEkey from the database so that it can process passwords. PEkey is randomly generated by the first LDAP Service instance to use the store. A user cannot modify PEkey.

> ➢ Key encryption key (KEkey). Stored in the Membership Directory database and used to encrypt and decrypt the PEkey. By default all LDAP Service instances use the same KEkey, making it possible for any LDAP Service instance to retrieve the PEkey. Any LDAP Service instance that can retrieve the PEkey can thereby read and write user passwords.

If the KEkey is changed, the PEkey is re-encrypted. When re-encryption of the PEkey occurs, an LDAP Service instance using the previous KEkey value will not be able to read user passwords. If the KEkey is changed for one LDAP Service instance, it must be changed for all LDAP Service instances that access the same Membership Directory database. The PEkey is never changed; it is only re-encrypted. Changing the PEkey would make all passwords unreadable by LDAP.

Security in General

There are a number of other aspects of security, in addition to the ones we've discussed, which if you bear them in mind, can help to avert the sort of security nightmare that we saw at the beginning of this chapter. In terms of hardware you should consider items such as maintaining a full back up storage for your data, and the physical access to your system. As for software you should look into such things as network monitoring software, the logging capability of your systems, use of encryption of critical data, and configuration management of your system. We'll look at some of these areas in a bit more detail.

System Back-Ups

Always have several full back-ups of your system or incremental back-up if more appropriate. Full back-ups can be system intensive and if you are operating a very popular site this could become a problem in terms of performance. If possible perform your back-ups during off hours time of the times where traffic is minimal. The more back-ups you have the closest you will be able to restore your system to its original state. This literally can save your operation if it is done often. It could potentially damage your business if not done at all.

For example, what would happen if some of your current user data got deleted right at this moment? This could be very difficult to detect and may go unnoticed for days. Would you be able to restore it to its previous condition in a somewhat painless procedure? Full back-ups of your system's sensitive data is a requirement for any e-commerce web site. The bottom line is that only the authorized people should be able to get to your data. No one else should be able to get to it. You must do whatever it takes to assure this by applying as many security layers as possible.

Passwords

Be sure to protect your database with hard-to-guess passwords and always update the password associated with the "sa" account for Microsoft SQL server users. Use a mix of numbers and letters i your password. Create users in the database with very specific access rights that can be used by external users accessing your data.

Site monitoring

Site monitoring can be done either by a system or site administrator, or by special software created for the purpose. Monitoring a web site involves looking at several areas of the site and searching for anything unusual. The most important thing about monitoring an e-commerce site is that it needs to be done on a regular basis if not at all times. Picking one day out of the month to monitor the system is pointless, since a security breach can be isolated to a matter of hours. Fortunately, you can use a combination of tools and strategies to accomplish continuous site monitoring.

> **Logging**
> Most operating systems store numerous bits of information in log files. Examination of these log files on a regular basis is often the first line of defense in detecting unauthorized use of the system. Also make sure your logs can capture the client's IP number and perhaps the referrer web site or link. This is valuable information.

> **Monitoring Software**
> Monitoring tools, such as SiteScope from FreshWater (`http://www.sitescope.com/`) can monitor several aspects of your site and is used by large sites such as Works.com, BarnesAndNobles.com, and Citibank.com. Other tools can easily be constructed by using standard operating system software, or by using several, often unrelated, programs together. Periodically you can create a list of files with checksums. Then these lists can be reconstructed regularly and compared against the master checklist. Differences may indicate that unauthorized modifications have occurred. Network monitoring software is also important. It can be used to look for any spike in traffic or unusual traffic load from a particular location.

If possible, do monitoring at all times. If this is not possible, then be sure to alternate schedules. The task of site monitoring is not as daunting as it may seem.

Configuration Management Procedures

Configuration management is generally applied to the software development process. However, it can also be used in an operational sense. Consider that since many of the system level programs are intended to enforce the security policy, it is important that these be known as correct. That is, one should not allow system level programs (such as the operating system, etc.) to be changed arbitrarily. At very least, the procedures should state who is authorized to make changes to systems, under what circumstances, and how the changes should be documented.

In some environments, configuration management is also desirable as applied to physical configuration of equipment. Maintaining valid and authorized hardware configuration should be given due consideration in your security policy. You want to be able to reproduce good systems and have them ready to become part of your server farm or round robin setup in case a machine is down.

Sometimes, it may be beneficial to have a slightly non-standard configuration in order to thwart the "standard" attacks used by some intruders. The non-standard parts of the configuration might include different password encryption algorithms, different configuration file locations, and rewritten or functionally limited system commands.

Non-standard configurations, however, also have their drawbacks. By changing the "standard" system, these modifications make software maintenance more difficult by requiring extra documentation to be written, software modification after operating system upgrades, and usually, someone with special knowledge of the changes.

Attacks On Your Site

As individuals and businesses increase information sharing and communication via the Internet, vulnerability to attack or intrusion rises. Authorization, access controls, and confidentiality requirements are some examples of the technological components available in security policy. In the world of technological evolution, everyone is a target of electronic crime and needs to be concerned about security.

Keep in mind the following concepts just in case an attack takes place:

> **Containment**
> The purpose of containment is to limit the extent of an attack For example, it is important to limit the spread of a worm type of attack or a virus on a network as quickly as possible. An essential part of containment is decision making, such as determining whether to shut a system down, to disconnect from a network, to monitor system or network activity, to disable functions such as ftp or IIS.

> **Eradication**
> Once the incident has been contained, it is now time to eradicate the cause. Software may be available to help you in this effort. For example, eradication software is available to eliminate most viruses, which infect small systems.

> **Recovery**
> Once the cause of an incident has been eradicated, the recovery phase defines the next stage of action.

> ➤ **Follow-up**
>
> One of the most important stages of responding to incidents is also the most often omitted. This stage is important because it helps those involved in handling the incident to develop a set of "lessons learned" to improve future performance in such situations. This stage also provides information, which justifies an organization's computer security effort to management, and yields information, which may be essential in legal proceedings.

Last but not least, seek professional security auditing at least one month before deploying your e-commerce site. This can be provided by your local ISP or by specialized consulting firms. During a security audit the group you have hired will try to break into your network and your site. They will later provide you with a full report of your weaknesses. This is very useful since it will allow you to run a simulation of what a possible security issue can be. Ideally you want to be able to go back to the results and fix all major issues before the site goes live.

Summary

In this chapter we discussed different security aspects that one must consider when creating a commerce web site. Again I would suggest reading as much as possible about security and how to prepare your commerce sites before going live.

Site Server's default settings provide a balance of security, performance, and administrative convenience. Some settings can be changed in order to increase security. In addition, you strongly influence the effective level of security at your site by your operational approach to security issues. In some cases, you may experience a cost in adding security with a reduction in performance or a reduction in administrative convenience. However, as always, a balance has to be found between the need to protect your site and practical access.

We've now discussed all the foundations you should need in order to be able to install Site Server, so this is what we'll do in the next chapter.

4

Installation

Ready to start using Microsoft Site Server? If you are like me, then you were ready from the moment you held that CD in your hand. Unfortunately, installing Site Server is a fairly complicated process and unlike other Microsoft products with which you simply plug in the CD and go, there are a lot of steps to consider before you are even ready to put the Site Server disk in the CD-ROM drive. The first time I installed Site Server, I dropped the CD into the drive, ran the install program and assumed I was off and running. Nothing was further from the truth. The next day when I booted up my test machine (always use a test machine), nothing worked! It was then that I began to realize how complicated and powerful Site Server really is.

Please don't get me wrong. I am not saying that you will have the same problems that others have had installing and using Site Server 3.0. Check any of the newsgroups surrounding Site Server 3.0 and you will see, amid the cries for help, that many people run the install program and everything works fine. Microsoft Site Server 3.0 is a member of the BackOffice family, however unlike other BackOffice products Site Server needs to integrate with several other Microsoft Server and BackOffice family members in order to function correctly.

That's what this chapter is all about. Starting with an explanation of the system requirements and explaining all the pieces that come together to allow Site Server to function, we will proceed through the installation process and show the step-by-step process to ensure a successful installation. Only then will you have a strong foundation upon which to build your Site Server knowledge. Also keep in mind that patience is the watchword for this chapter and the installation process. Starting from a clean target system, a full Site Server installation can take several hours if not a day or two depending upon your level of experience with Microsoft Windows NT and Microsoft SQL Server. Even after you have done it a couple of times, mistakes can still be made during the installation process. Setting up a full test-bed development environment with SQL Server will take even longer and is prone to even more errors.

In developing Site Server 3.0, Microsoft has definitely raised the bar in terms of web development, hosting and administration. But if you are serious about using Site Server 3.0 as a platform for building powerful web solutions then it is well worth the effort.

System Requirements

Microsoft Site Server represents a new generation of web development technology. However it builds on already existing technology such as Windows NT 4.0 and IIS 4.0. Because of this, hardware and software requirements are similar to what is required for hosting a basic NT web server. However, Site Server is also very resource intensive and for optimum performance the minimum requirements are simply not powerful enough. It is recommended that you exceed the basic requirements if you wish to have any kind of performance out of your Site Server machine.

Hardware Requirements

Although as I mentioned above the actual hardware requirements will vary based on the volume of traffic your web site is expected to receive, here is a list of the minimum requirements as recommended by Microsoft:

> ➤ Intel Pentium 100 MHz or faster processor (Intel Pentium 166 MHz recommended), or a Digital Equipment Corporation (DEC) Alpha processor
>
> ➤ 64 MB of RAM, 96 MB if SQL Server is installed on the same computer (128 MB recommended)
>
> ➤ 128 MB of virtual memory
>
> ➤ 1 GB of available hard disk space (2 GB recommended)
>
> ➤ CD-ROM drive
>
> ➤ Network adapter card
>
> ➤ VGA or Super VGA monitor compatible with Microsoft Windows NT Server 4.0 set to 1024 x 768.

This list from Microsoft gives us a minimum requirement list upon which the software will run. It does provide us with a good starting point, however it does not provide any information as to what it takes to get good performance. Again I stress that a machine that only meets this minimum hardware configuration will slow down to a crawl once Site Server is installed and running. It will be even slower if you install SQL Server on the same machine.

In testing, I have installed Site Server 3.0 and SQL Server together, on several machines that have a similar configuration to the list above with good (albeit slow) results. Nobody's hardware budget is unlimited (especially when it comes to a test environment) and I have several machines that get rebuilt often, depending upon the current project. Having such a machine configured and located right next to my desktop machine, I have sometimes waited for over a minute for the results from a request.

Removing SQL Server to a separate machine can cut the wait time dramatically, sometimes in half, depending upon what type of information you are requesting from the server. This allows the machine to expend more resources toward processing your request and not having to split available resources between processing web requests and SQL Server requests.

So what does it take? Well, my high-end web servers contain dual Xeon 450 processors and about 512 MB of RAM. Each machine also has about 12 GB of usable hard disk space with a RAID 5 configuration. Coupled with this I have my database server, hosting SQL Server 7.0. This machine has a similar configuration except that it has 1 GB of RAM and more hard disk space. I have tested this setup using the Microsoft Web Capacity Analysis Tool (WCAT) and its predefined tests have found that performance does not fall below reasonable limits.

These high-end servers are by no means the best that money can buy. They are the result of budget vs. need. Depending upon what you will expect your site to do, this type of setup can be overkill or just scratching the surface. Technology is improving all the time and as a result costs are coming down on hardware that can provide acceptable performance for just about any web project.

Software Requirements

The software requirements for setting up Site Server are also pretty involved. Make sure that you have the following software on hand before beginning your Site Server installation. Additional software requirements will be discussed within the setup instructions.

- Windows NT Server version 4.0 or later
- Windows NT Service Pack 3 or later (Service Pack 3 is also included on the NT Option Pack CD)
- Internet Explorer 4.01 or higher (included on the NT Option Pack CD)
- Windows NT Option Pack
- FrontPage 98 (Optional) (included on the Site Server CD)
- Microsoft Visual Studio (Optional) (Visual InterDev 6.0 is included on the Site Server CD)
- SQL Server 6.5 or higher (an evaluation copy of SQL Server 6.5 is included on the NT Option Pack CD). We will be installing SQL Server 7.0 in our installation.
- Microsoft SQL Server hot fixes and Service Packs (Download from Microsoft)
- Microsoft Site Server
- Microsoft Site Server Service Pack 2 or later
- Latest FrontPage Server Extensions (Download from Microsoft)
- Latest Site Server hot fixes and updates (also download from Microsoft).

All of the items listed above will be discussed later in the chapter as we go through the installation process. Several of the items mentioned are optional and a decision will need to be made as to whether this is an element that you wish to install.

One piece of software not mentioned on this list is Windows 2000. As of this writing it is not recommended since Site Server is not designed to work within the Windows 2000 environment. Site Server Service Pack 3 is supposed to fix this compatibility problem, however it is not known when this Service Pack will be released.

Choosing a Database Platform

A number of Site Server components require a data store. These should be familiar from the first two chapters:

- Personalization and Membership, and some of the Content features, require a separate database set up as a Membership Directory. You have to create a Membership Directory when you install Site Server.
- Analysis requires a database to hold the statistical data against which to run reports.
- Commerce requires a database for the purchase and product information necessary for an online store.
- Finally you'll also require a database in order to install Ad Server.

In the course of setting up Site Server you will set up between one and four databases, depending on whether you setup all the components of Site Server and Commerce. Currently the choice of which DBMS to use for the standard version of Site Server is limited to two main choices. We can use Microsoft SQL Server or Microsoft Access. Site Server Commerce Edition supports Microsoft SQL Server or Oracle databases, but not Microsoft Access. Before we can proceed much further we need to make a decision about which system to use.

Standard Site Server 3.0 can work with both Microsoft Access and SQL Server. Which one you use is really a matter of what you are going to do with your site, the amount of traffic you expect to receive, and the response time that you would like to have (or are willing to accept) for accesses made to the database.

If you have never used, or aren't quite comfortable with, SQL Server and you are just setting up Site Server 3.0 for the first time to explore its capabilities, you may want to stick with Microsoft Access initially and then move to SQL Server once you are comfortable. Trying to learn Site Server and SQL Server at the same time can be somewhat of a daunting task. If problems arise while you are building your site, it can be difficult to determine exactly where the problem is coming from. Don't be too afraid however, we will talk you through the process of installing and setting up both Site Server and SQL Server in this chapter.

Microsoft Access is a fairly powerful piece of desktop software that can be used to build small to medium size database applications. Even bigger sites that have a lot of data in the backend but don't necessarily receive a lot of traffic perform adequately using Microsoft Access. Many developers (myself included) still use Access day to day as a development environment to design and test the building of new databases, and then upsize or rebuild the database structure in SQL Server when it comes time to go into production. Access is particularly useful with Site Server if you want to start by just installing the standard edition (without Commerce) and learn your way around Content Management, and Personalization and Membership. The install program can automatically create a Microsoft Access Membership Directory for you.

All this may sound as if I am suggesting you use Microsoft Access. Actually, my recommendation is to use SQL Server as your Site Server backend. The initial installation and setup for SQL Server is described in this chapter or a beginning book on SQL Server can be purchased if you need more information. If you want to install Commerce you will need SQL Server or Oracle anyway, so for a complete test installation I would recommend you use SQL Server.

The test-bed installation in this chapter is designed to simulate our production environment as closely as possible, while not making things too complicated. We assume that SQL Server is being used in our production environment to provide us with the high volume transaction processing and scalability that we imagine (hope) we will require, as your site becomes one of the most popular sites on the Internet.

Installation Scenarios

From our previous discussion in chapter 2 you may well have guessed that there are countless installation scenarios for creating a Site Server environment. To cover the install process, in this chapter we are going to use a two-tiered installation. We are going to install Site Server on one machine, and SQL Server on a separate machine. Even in a test and development environment this setup make a lot of sense because of the load that each of these servers individually can put on a machine.

Another factor is that since SQL Server is a large-scale database management system, it makes sense to install and configure it on a separate machine for use within your network environment. If you are using machines with the minimum recommended requirements as described above then this type of environment will be a lot faster then putting everything on one machine. Some of you may already have SQL Server installed and running in your environment. In this case you can create the databases that are required and proceed with the Site Server installation.

Finally, we are going to install SQL Server 7.0, and Microsoft strongly recommend against installing SQL Server 7.0 and Site Server 3.0 on the same machine, unless absolutely necessary. This is because SQL Server 7.0 includes version 2.1 of Microsoft Data Access Components (MDAC) which has compatibility problems with ADSI 2.0 (installed with Site Server 3.0). We mentioned this version problem within Chapter 2; for more information refer to `http://support.microsoft.com/support/kb/articles/q216/7/09.asp`.

I realize that not everyone has the luxury of having two spare machines just sitting around waiting for you to do something with them. If you are limited to only one server, don't worry, we will cover that contingency by detailing where in the installation process to install SQL Server in a single server setup.

Preparing Your Database Server

Before we actually install Site Server 3.0 itself, lets make sure that our database server is setup and ready to go. Installing and setting up SQL Server 7.0 is not a trivial task and requires some basic database knowledge, which is beyond the scope of this book. In our setup we are going to be using Microsoft SQL Server 7.0. This is the latest version of SQL Server.

The Site Server documentation comes with a simple step by step guide to installing and setting up SQL Server 6.5 for use with Site Server 3.0 and Site Server 3.0 Commerce Edition. An evaluation copy of SQL Server 6.5 is included on the Windows NT Option Pack CD since version 7.0 was not available at the time Site Server was released. Since that time SQL Server 7.0 has been released and is fully available. You can request a 120-day evaluation copy of SQL Server 7.0 from the Microsoft SQL Server Web site at `http://www.microsoft.com/sql/`.

Hardware and Software Requirements for SQL Server 7.0

Until recently Site Server 3.0 had some serious compatibility problems with this version of SQL Server. More specifically in many cases it did not work. Site Server 3.0 Service Pack 2 has taken care of most of those problems so we are safe in using this version of SQL Server. For more information about specific problems and what the fixes are go to `http://support.microsoft.com/support/siteserver/servicepacks/sp.asp`.

However, be aware that there are still potential problems with installing SQL Server 7.0and Site Server 3.0 on the same machine. See Chapter 2 for a description of the MDAC and ADSI version problems that result from this.

Depending on which version of SQL Server you have or what setup type you choose to install, SQL Server has the following requirements.

> ➢ Intel or compatible 166 MHz Pentium or Higher Pentium PRO, or Pentium II, or DEC Alpha machine

> ➢ Windows NT 4.0 Workstation or Server, Windows 95/98

> ➢ If you are installing SQL Server 7.0 on Windows NT, you also need to install NT Service Pack 4 and NT mini-service pack 2 (included with SQL Server). When installing Service Packs it is always a good idea to install Service Pack 3 and then Service Pack 4

> ➢ A minimum of 32 MB RAM

> ➢ CD-ROM Drive

> ➢ Between 75 and 200 MB Hard drive space depending on the setup type you choose. This space is just to hold the installed files and not what is necessary for Windows NT and the data that you are going to be storing.

As we discussed in the hardware requirement section for Site Server this is a minimum list for what it takes to install and run SQL Server. Performance is a completely different issue and must be considered as you create your environment. There are several very good books on SQL Server 7.0. These would be a good place to start in determining your actual requirements.

Starting the Installation Process

There are several different setup versions that we can choose from, such as the desktop, standard, or enterprise version. For our installation of SQL Server we are installing the standard version of SQL Server 7.0.

Also worth mentioning in this section is that there are limitations on the version of SQL Server that you can install depending upon the Operating System you are using. For example, if you wish to install the enterprise version of SQL Server 7.0 it must be installed on Windows NT 4.0 Enterprise Server.

> ➢ Start by logging into your SQL Server machine using an account with Administrator privileges.

> ➢ Create SQL Server Service accounts if not already created. This is a domain wide account that SQL services can use to run under. If you are only using a single SQL Server in a small environment then this step may be unnecessary. For any environment where you may have multiple SQL Servers running a single domain account is a good thing. A single account with a name such as SQL_Services_Account will suffice. You can have all SQL services in your domain use this one account.

> ➢ Insert the SQL Server CD into your system and wait for the setup screen to automatically be launched. If autorun is disabled on this machine then choose Run from the Start menu and type `<CDROM Drive>:\autorun`.

> ➢ From the main menu select Install SQL Server 7.0 Components and then Database Server – Enterprise Edition or Database Server – Desktop Edition depending upon which version you need to install.

> ➢ Begin the installation process. Once you get beyond the initial Welcome, Copyright Agreement, and Registration screens, choose a Setup Type from the setup types dialog box.

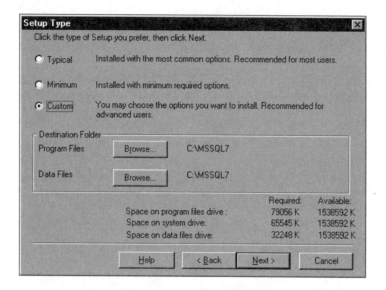

There are three different setup types available in the SQL Setup.

> **Typical Installation:** Automatically installs SQL Server with the default installation options. This installs the most common components that you will use. This option needs about 163 megabytes of hard disk space.

> **Compact Installation:** Loads the minimum file configuration necessary to use SQL Server with all the default options. This option needs about 74 megabytes of hard disk space.

> **Custom Installation:** Custom setup allows you to pick and choose the components that you want to install. Hard disk space needed by this install depends upon the components that you choose to install.

Choose **Custom Install** at this point so that we can examine some of the configuration options that are available and then click **Next**.

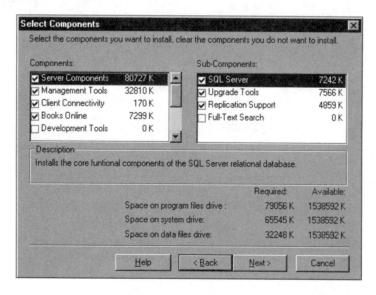

SQL Server provides for a number of standard configuration options to provide the maximum flexibility during an install. On the Character Set / Sort Order / Unicode Collation dialog below are several options that you should understand as you install to program.

> Choosing a Character Set allows SQL Server to determine what combination of characters and numbers that SQL Server can recognize. This will ensure that information sent between the client and SQL Server will be understood and accepted. SQL Server includes 14 different character sets. The default is the ISO or ANSI Character set, which is compatible with Windows NT and 95/98.

> SQL Server also lets you determine a Sort Order, which is used to resolve queries and sort data. The sort orders are available based on the default Character Set that you choose. The default sort order for the ISO Character Set is Dictionary Order, Case-Insensitive.

> Unicode Collation type is used to sort Unicode data which can also be stored in SQL Server.

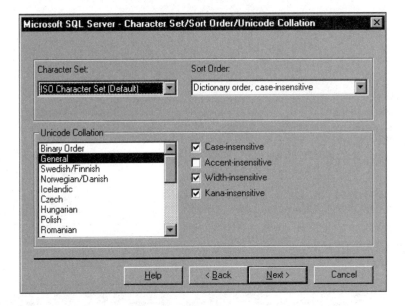

On this screen, ensure that ISO Character Set (Default) is chosen and that Dictionary order, case insensitive is selected.

In order for clients such as Site Server to communicate with SQL Server over the network, they must use a common set of communication protocols or an Inter-Process Communication (IPC) strategy. Communication with SQL Server is supported in the form of Network Libraries. SQL Server uses three main libraries by default and several additional options that can be added.

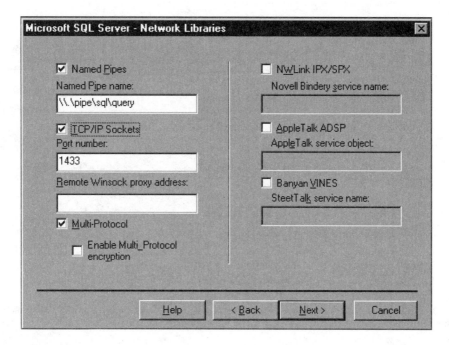

One or all of these libraries can be included in SQL Server to ensure that communication between many different types of clients can occur.

> **Named Pipes:** Named Pipes is a communication system that is traditionally used by Windows NT Server and other Microsoft BackOffice products. Named Pipes communication occurs when the server listens for clients using a hidden share identified as \\sql_server_name\pipe\sql\query.

> **TCP\IP Sockets:** TCP\IP Sockets library uses the traditional TCP\IP protocol as the communication mechanism. By default SQL Server listens on the port number 1433 which is assigned to SQL Server by the Internet Number Authority.

> **Multi-Protocol Network Library:** This library supports a communication mechanism called remote procedure calls (RPC). Essentially RPC is able to support most of communication mechanisms supported by Windows NT, including Named Pipes, TCP/IP Sockets and NWLink. Because of this it is a very flexible library able to support a wide variety of clients.

> **Additional Network Libraries:** Additional libraries include NWLink (IPX/SPX) support for Novell network support, AppleTalk ADSP network library for Apple Macintosh clients, and Banyan VINES (SPP) network library support.

The Named Pipes library must be included in the SQL Server install or the program cannot be installed. For Site Server you will also need to select TCP/IP – we'll see why a little further on. Additional libraries can also be added at this point or added or removed after the program is installed. On the Network Libraries screen, verify that Named Pipes and TCP/IP Sockets are selected. Make sure the Port Number is set to 1433.

At this point SQL Server should have enough information to be installed on your target machine. Click Next to allow the setup program to finish the install process. Setup will start copying files to your machine. When finished the SQL Server setup program will announce to you that it is finished installing all the system files. Next we need to configure SQL Server and create our databases for use with Site Server.

Making Sure SQL Server is Running

Before we can configure SQL Server for use with Site Server we need to make sure SQL Server is running by starting the MSSQLServer Service. Bring up the SQL Service Manager by clicking on Start | Programs | Microsoft SQL Server 7.0 | Service Manager.

This will bring up the SQL Server Service Manager dialog box as shown above. In the Server box the name of your computer holding SQL Server should appear. This is how we identify our server. Click on the Start/Continue button to start the MSSQLServer Service. The stoplight icon next to the server should turn green to indicate that the service is now running. Close the SQL Server Service Manager.

Using the SQL Enterprise Manager

Now that we have SQL Server up and running we can configure our system to work with Site Server 3.0. From within the SQL Server Enterprise Manager we can perform all of the operations that we need to configure SQL Server. Launch the SQL Enterprise Manager by clicking on Start | Programs | Microsoft SQL Server 7.0 | SQL Server Enterprise Manager.

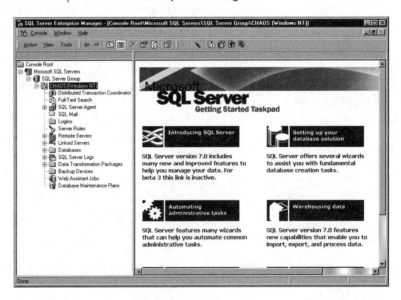

The SQL Enterprise Manager is a Microsoft Management Console (MMC) snap-in. It is used to manage SQL Servers not only on your local machine but also SQL Servers installed on remote machines located across the network. The first thing that we need to do is register your SQL Server with SQL Server Enterprise Manager, and the easiest and quickest way to do this is with the Registration Wizard.

> ➢ Right click on Microsoft SQL Servers in the console tree window of the SQL Enterprise Manager and choose Register SQL Server.

> ➢ This will bring up the Register SQL Server Wizard, and you can follow the steps in the wizard to complete the registration.

When you register a server with the SQL Enterprise manager you are deciding a couple of things. First you are showing SQL Enterprise manager that the server exists and providing its name. Also you are placing a server in a server group and determining the logon name and password for that server. Server groups allow you to group servers of the same type together. This will be more useful to you as your SQL Server implementations grow and managing them becomes more work.

Using TCP/IP for SQL Server

You should configure the SQL Server Client to use TCP/IP as its default network library, rather than Named Pipes, for use with Site Server This is currently Microsoft's recommendation, in order to avoid a common error when using transactions, where the object "fails to enlist". To set up TCP/IP as the default client library click Start | Programs | Microsoft SQL Server 7.0 | Client Network Utility. On the General tab select TCP/IP from the drop-down list for the Default Network Library.

Creating the Site Server Databases

Microsoft has greatly simplified the process of creating databases in SQL 7.0 from the process in SQL 6.5. The use of wizards allows even the greenest of SQL Server administrators to create databases quickly and easily. Below is a table of the databases that you will want to create for use with the standard edition of Site Server 3.0.

Database Name	Database Size	Transaction Log Size
SSMembership	40 MB	10 MB
SSAnalysis	50 MB	10 MB

If you want to use SQL Server for your Membership Directory (the SSMembership database in the table above) you need to set up this database before you install Site Server. However, you can choose to set up the Analysis component of Site Server at a later date, so you don't necessarily need to create the SSAnalysis database at this point.

Note that if you are using SQL Server 6.5 you will need to adjust the size of your TempDB to 25 MB. In SQL Server 7.0, TempDB is set to autogrow as needed.

If you are going to be installing Site Server 3.0 Commerce Edition in addition to Site Server create two additional databases. The following table provides recommended settings.

Database Name	Database Size	Transaction Log Size
SSAdServer	10 MB	5 MB
SSCommerceServer	20 MB	5 MB

Creating the SQL Server 7.0 Databases

Open up the SQL Server Enterprise Manager and click the databases item under your server name. Then in the console Action menu click New Database. This will bring up the Database Properties dialog box:

> Type in the name of your new database next to Name and the initial size in megabytes that you want the database to have under Initial size (MB). Under file properties the default should be set to Automatically grow file. File growth should be set to 10 percent. Maximum file size should be set to the default of Unrestricted file growth.

> Next click on the Transaction Log tab and update the Initial Size (MB) to the Log Device Size that you require for this item.

> When you are finished setting the required properties click OK and SQL Server will create the database that you configured.

> Once your databases have been created you should edit each database by right clicking on each one and selecting Properties. Select the Options tab and enable Select into / Bulk Copy and Truncate Log on Checkpoint. Click OK when you are finished.

Performing the Site Server 3.0 Installation

As I have mentioned before several times, in our test-bed installation we will assume that we are using two different servers: one to hold our Site Server 3.0 installation, and one to hold SQL Server. Although we can install SQL Server 6.5 and Site Server 3.0 on the same computer, and in many cases developers will do this, even in a test environment this is not the best solution. The installation documentation that comes with both Site Server 3.0 and Site Server 3.0 Commerce Edition provides complete step-by-step instructions on setting up a machine that includes both SQL Server 6.5 and Site Server 3.0. However Microsoft also recommend not installing SQL Server 7.0 and Site Server 3.0 on the same machine, because of the MDAC version problem we've mentioned before.

In our test setup we've installed SQL Server 7.0 on a separate machine, so we'll only install the ODBC data sources and the Database Transaction Processor on our Site Server 3.0 machine. We'll see when to install these as we step through the install process. Before we start however, there are a few guidelines to bear in mind.

Site Server Pre-Installation Suggestions

There are number of rules we can follow which will make our Site Server installation simpler.

> Do not install Site Server on any type of Domain Controller. Although officially the documentation states that you can install Site Server 3.0 on either a Primary Domain Controller or a Backup Domain Controller, both of these machines have their hands full with other issues and can this can cause resource problems. Current advice from Microsoft in not to install Site Server on a BDC. BDC's can sometimes encounter synchronization errors when installing IIS and Site Server Components. There is also an issue with the NT user accounts that are created by Site Server 3.0 during installation.

> Don't install other resource intensive products on the same machine as Site Server. This kind of goes hand in hand with the first suggestion. Site Server takes up a lot of resources. Other resource intensive products such as Microsoft Exchange or Microsoft Proxy Server will only serve in slowing all of your services down to a crawl.

> Do not install Site Server on a Clustered NT System (MSCS). We'll talk more about this later in the chapter.

Preparing your System for Site Server

Taking a machine from ground zero to a full Site Server 3.0 or Site Server 3.0 Commerce Edition installation is a lengthy process. Not only is the entire procedure time consuming, it is extremely prone to mistakes or to getting the installation process out of order. Over time as you install Site Server more then once you will become familiar with the procedure and how to make things go more smoothly. For now though, be prepared to take your time and do not try to hurry the process.

Installing Windows NT 4.0 Server

The first step in setting up your computer is to install Windows NT Server version 4.0 and Service Pack 3. Windows NT provides security and networking services that are necessary for running Site Server. Service Pack 3 provides essential updates to Windows NT Server such as enhanced security features. We will be adding Service Pack 4 later in this chapter, but we don't want to install it here, so make sure you follow everything in sequence.

> Use only alphanumeric characters in the computer name. SQL Server supports only a limited character set in server computer names.

> Format the hard drive with the Windows NT File System (NTFS) to allow for greater security and the setting of discretionary Access Control Lists. Although officially you can use the FAT file system with file server it is not recommended.

> Service Pack 3 is contained on the Windows NT 4.0 Option Pack CD.

Increasing Paging

Before we go too much farther we need to increase the paging file size on your system. Windows NT uses the paging file when it runs out of available RAM. As you may have figured by now, Site Server can be pretty resource intensive depending upon what type of application you are running. Increasing the paging file size will ensure that Site Server 3.0 has enough room to handle whatever you throw at it. To increase your paging file size perform the following steps.

> Right-click on the My computer icon, and then click Properties.

> When the System Properties dialog box appears, click the Performance tab and then click Change. The Virtual Memory dialog box will appear.

> In the Initial Size box, type 128. The value in the Maximum Size box must be greater than 128.

> Click Set, and then click OK. Click Close on the System Properties box.

> When prompted, restart your computer.

As an administrator you must ensure that the account that you are using has administrator privileges. It is suggested in the Site Server installation documentation that you add your own Windows NT user account to the Administrators group on the computer on which you will be installing Site Server 3.0.

It is useful to have several accounts available for administering and testing your Site Server applications. The administrator account I use for administering my Site Server installations has domain administration privileges since I am administering several installations at any given time. However it is also helpful to have accounts available with standard user privileges to test the applications that you are building. This is helpful in ensuring that permissions are properly configured.

> If you are installing SQL Server 6.5 on the same computer as Site Server, you should install it now. You should also install Service Pack 4.0 for SQL Server 6.5, and the fix 297 that you'll find on the Site Server CD. (There's a separate fix, 318, for SQL Server 6.5 Enterprise Edition). However you should not install Service Pack 5 until after you've installed Site Server 3.0 Service Pack 2.0.

Installing Internet Explorer 4.01

Before you install Microsoft Internet Information Server 4.0 (IIS) from the Windows NT Option Pack CD, you must install Internet Explorer version 4.01 or later. Site Server 3.0 will detect during the install process whether this browser is installed or not, and if necessary, guide you through the setup process. In most cases it is recommended to choose the standard install option for IE 4.01 when installing. If you wish you may also choose to install IE 4.01 using the full installation option. Site Server 3.0 Commerce Edition when used with electronic mail uses several files that are installed with the standard or full installation.

Installing Windows NT 4.0 Option Pack

The Windows NT 4.0 Option Pack allows you to install several applications that are necessary for installing Site Server 3.0. Among these applications are Internet Information Server (IIS) 4.0, Microsoft Index Server, and Microsoft Management Console (MMC). When you install Site Server 3.0 from its CD; the Site Server program detects automatically whether these applications have been installed. If they are not present, Site Server Setup guides you through the process to install them.

- When you install the Windows NT 4.0 Options Pack follow the online instructions to perform a Custom install.

- In the Select Component dialog box, verify that FrontPage 98 Server Extensions is **not** checked. You should download and install the most current version later in the installation procedure.

- Select Internet Information Server (IIS) and the click Show Sub-components.

- Check Internet NNTP Service. If you want to enable users to search newsgroup messages in Knowledge Manager or Search, you must have Internet NNTP Server installed on your Search Catalog Build server.

- Ensure that SMTP Service is checked. This service is required in order to support sending of electronic mail from your web site.

- Make sure that all Microsoft Index Server components are checked. Site Server requires these components.

- Click Next.

- Make sure you configure MTS for local (not remote) administration.

- For the remaining dialog boxes, accept the default setup options.

- Once all files have been installed, click Finish.

- On the Systems Settings Change dialog box, click Yes to restart your system.

Installing Front Page Server Extensions and Visual Interdev

To help you build and develop your Web site, FrontPage 98 is included with Site Server. FrontPage makes it easy for new users and professional Web developers to create professional quality Internet or Intranet sites. Site Server does not require FrontPage, but if you are going to use it, you must install it before installing Site Server. Microsoft maintains the most current version of the FrontPage Server extensions available for download at
`http://officeupdate.microsoft.com/frontpage/wpp/`.

For developers who want to build dynamic Web applications, Microsoft Visual InterDev can be also be installed at this point.

> **Installing FrontPage or Visual Interdev is not recommended, especially in a production environment.**

For a test bed installation such as this one where you are going to be developing and hosting on a single machine it is permissable, but not recommended, if that is what you need to build your web pages.

Setting up your Database

Ideally we've installed our database software, SQL Server, on a separate machine. If this is the case then we simply need to install the Distributed Transaction Coordinator as described below and set up our DSNs, and this is what we'll look at next.

> **You can install SQL Server 7.0 on the same machine as Site Server,**
> **although remember, this is *not* recommended. For those of you who have to**
> **do this, you would need to install Windows NT 4.0 Service Pack 4.0 and SQL**
> **Server 7.0 now. For more details on this particular configuration refer to**
> **http://support.microsoft.com/support/siteserver/**
> **install-sql70.asp.**

The Distributed Transaction Coordinator

If your SQL Server resides on a remote computer, the MSDTC service (Microsoft Distributed Transaction Coordinator) must also be installed and started on both the local (IIS) computer and the remote (SQL Server) computer.

The Microsoft Distributed Transaction Coordinator (MSDTC) tool is a client-based administration tool that provides distributed transaction support. It only need to be loaded onto clients that run a SQL Server application that require its use, such as Site Server 3.0. The MSDTC tool is provided on the SQL Server 7.0 CD.

You can install the Distributed Transaction Coordinator by running the program is located at E:\x86\other\msdtcsetup.exe where E is the letter of your CD-ROM drive. This will install the MSDTC on your system. Once the Transaction Coordinator is installed, it should be set to start automatically in the services dialog box. Open the Windows NT Services window by clicking on Start | Settings | Control Panel and then double clicking on Services.

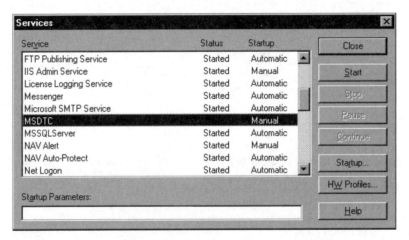

Once you have the MSDTC option highlighted, you can click Startup to open the startup options dialog box for this service. Under startup choose Automatic and then click the OK button.

Create your System DSNs

At this point we will need to create our ODBC system data source names (DSN) for the databases that we created within SQL Server (See *Preparing Your Database Server*). During the installation and setup of Site Server and Site Server Commerce Edition we will be prompted for the System DSN pointing to the databases that we created earlier. Creating a system DSN for Ad, Analysis, Commerce, and P&M Databases is done through the **ODBC Data Source Administrator** dialog box. Below is a table listing the DSNs that will need to be created.

Data Source Name	Database Name
SSMembership	SSMembership
SSAnalysis	SSAnalysis

If you are going to be installing Site Server 3.0 Commerce Edition in addition to Site Server create two additional DSNs. The following table provides some suggested DSN names.

Data Source Name	Database Name
SSAdServer	SSAdServer
SSCommerceServer	SSCommerceServer

Each of the above Data Source names corresponds to a database that you created earlier in this chapter. For a full Site Server 3.0 and Site Server 3.0 Commerce Edition install you must create four different DSNs. Ensure that you are logged on with administrator privileges before you attempt to setup these ODBC data sources.

➤ To open the **ODBC Data Source Administrator**, double click on the **ODBC** icon in the **Control Panel**.

➤ Once the dialog box appears, click on the **System DSN** tab and then click **Add** to open the **Create New Data Source** dialog box.

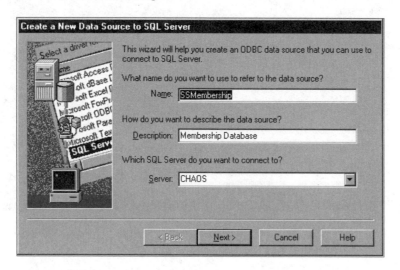

This Create Data Source wizard is designed to help you to complete the setup of your ODBC Data Source. The wizard will take you through a series of dialog boxes in the creation of your new DSN. For the most part you can accept the default values.

> On the Microsoft SQL Server DSN Configuration dialog choose With Windows NT authentication using the network login ID and check Connect to SQL Server to obtain default settings for the additional configuration options. Click Next to continue.

> On the Create a New Data Source to SQL Server dialog box click Change the default database to:. In the drop down box choose the corresponding database that you created earlier in this chapter. Ensure that Use ANSI quoted identifiers and Use ANSI nulls, paddings and warnings are both checked. Click Next to continue.

> In the next dialog ensure that none of the options are checked and accept the default entries. Click Finish to continue. After all the configuration options have been chosen click Done, and finish the setup. Before you close the dialog box, make sure to test your setup when you are finished to ensure the connection is correct.

Now go ahead and create any additional DSNs that you may need based upon the table above before you proceed to the next section.

Installing Site Server 3.0

Ok, it looks like the time is finally here. When you load the Site Server CD into your target computer, the autorun feature of Windows NT will launch the Site Server splash screen onto your system.

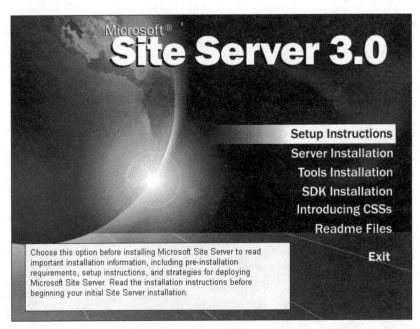

There are several options available to you here, which may or may not be intuitive depending upon your experience. A couple of the options I should point out are:

➢ **Server Installation**: This is the main Site Server installation option that we will be installing later in this chapter.

➢ **Tools Installation**: The tools installation option is available for installing certain tools to administer and use Site Server features. These tools are automatically included as part of the server installation, however this option is available to allow you to include only a minimum subset. The tools installation will allow you to administer Site Server or use features such as Report Writer from a remote location or a client computer. The minimum requirement for this installation is a Windows 95 machine with at least 32 MB of RAM. Do not install these tools on a network drive.

➢ **SDK Installation**: The Site Server Software Development Kit (SDK) is also available for installation seperately from the server installation. This SDK installs samples and documentation for all of the COM objects that are included with Site Server. To run the samples, you must install the SDK on a computer that has Site Server installed.

At this point it is probably a good idea to look through all the available options and view the documentation before you jump right in and start installing Site Server. On the other hand by now you are probably chomping at the bit to finally get Site Server installed. If you do have any patience left take a look through the documentation, otherwise click on Server Installation.

When you install Microsoft Site Server 3.0 from its CD, the Setup program detects whether Microsoft Windows NT Service Pack 3, Microsoft Internet Explorer 4.01 and the Windows NT Options Pack have been installed. If you have followed the directions up to this point then Site Server will continue with its setup. If one or more of these options are missing then Site Server will detect and guide you through the process to install them.

Setup also checks for the file system type (FAT or NTFS). Since there is no security provided for FAT systems it is recommended that you stick with NTFS for both evaluation and production environments.

Choosing an Installation Type

During the setup process Site Server 3.0 Setup will prompt you with three basic setup options:

➢ **Typical.** Enables you to install Site Server features configured for a typical Intranet solution. It installs the Publishing and Analysis features, and the Knowledge Manager customizable application. It does not install the Active Channel Multicaster.

➢ **Complete.** Enables you to install all of Site Server configured for a complete Internet solution, using a Microsoft Access database. As we discussed earlier in this chapter, if you are working with Microsoft Access as your primary DBMS, or are just trying out Site Server to see what it is capable of, then this would be a good option to get you up and running quickly.

➢ **Custom.** Enables you to install all of Site Server, or select only those features you want to install. Select this option if you want to use Site Server with a Microsoft SQL Server database.

Performing a Custom Install

After you select the Custom Install option Site Server will present you with the Select Features dialog box. Here you will select the Site Server options that you would like to install.

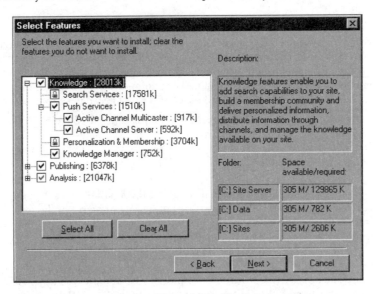

Here is a list of the options and the text that accompanies each item. It may help to point out that several of the features become locked when you choose to install a category. This represents a minimum install for that category or set of features. Additional features may or may not be necessary depending upon your requirements.

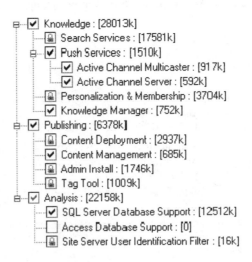

> ➢ **Knowledge.** Knowledge features enable you to add search capabilities to your site, build a membership community and deliver personalized information, distribute information through channels, and manage the knowledge available on your site.

➢ **Search Services.** Search provides site administrators with a tool to gather and index information and create keyword search capabilities on your site.

➢ **Push Service.** Push automates the process of information delivery by providing users with channels that deliver specific content directly to their desktops.

➢ **Active Channel Multicaster.** Active Channel Multicaster enables multicast delivery of Web content. Multicast delivery saves network bandwidth and makes a user's Web browsing more efficient.

➢ **Active Channel Server.** Active Channel Server enables you to create channels, collect content items from a variety of sources, and manage refresh and delivery schedules.

➢ **Personalization & Membership.** Personalization & Membership (P&M) enables any Internet or intranet site to manage memberships, understand customer usage patterns, build community among members, and direct personalized information to individual users.

➢ **Knowledge Manager.** Knowledge Manager provides site visitors with a single application for browsing online corporate information, viewing new or updated information, and sharing their expertise with colleagues.

➢ **Publishing.** Publishing allows the replication of documents, files in multiple formats, and content between Publishing Service systems using reliable and secure technology.

➢ **Content Deployment.** Content Deployment helps you replicate file-based content, such as files, directories, metadata, and access control lists from directory to directory, between local servers, or across the Internet or a corporate intranet.

➢ **Content Management.** Content Management enables content authors to submit, tag, and edit content and enables site administrators to review, manage and publish content on a corporate intranet or the Internet.

➢ **Admin Install.** Admin Install provides administrative control of Content Deployment services using a Microsoft Management console (MMC) snap-in module.

➢ **Tag Tool.** Tag Tool helps you assign specific properties to content, tagging them, prior to the cataloging of the content, ensuring that specific queries will return the tagged content.

➢ **Analysis.** Analysis provides you with a tool to analyze content, site structure, links, and site usage and enables you to convert your analysis data into usable reports.

➢ **SQL Server Database Support.** SQL Server Database Support installs the components necessary to use Microsoft SQL Server as your Analysis database. This option is not available for installation if Access Database support is selected.

➢ **Access Database Support.** Access Database Support installs the components necessary to use Microsoft Access as your Analysis database. This option is not available for installation if SQL Server Database Support is selected.

➢ **Site Server User Identification Filter.** Site Server Identification Filter lets you implement the preferred logging mechanism for an IIS server, the ISAPI filter, this allows the server to generate cookies.

In most cases you may choose the default items in this dialog box, however under Analysis you will want to ensure that SQL Server Database Support is selected. Site Server defaults to Access Database Support if you do not explicitly choose the SQL Server option.

Configuring User Access

Site Server setup will prompt you for the Start menu folder to install Site Server to, and then display the Configure User Access dialog box. Setting the User Access accounts for two of the main Site Server components will allow you to access the components later to configure and maintain them.

The features that will use these accounts are Publishing and Search. Depending upon the type of application that you are creating and deploying these can either be the same account or two separate accounts. The Publishing account will be used by Content Deployment when it replicates content to other computers. Search will also use an account when it creates search catalogs. In a production environment it is recommended that you create and use two separate accounts, one for each Site Server feature.

Site Server Feature	Account	Account Permissions
Publishing	SSPubAdmin	Domain Administrator
Search	SSSearchAdmin	Domain Administrator

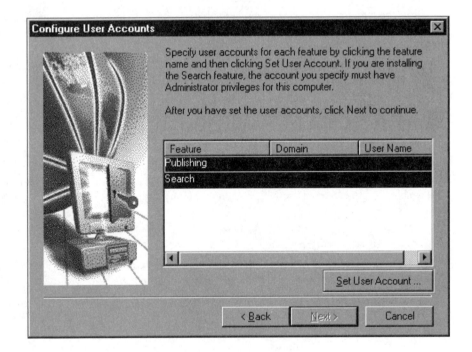

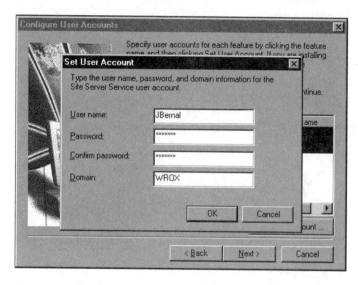

Select the feature that you wish to configure with a user account and then click Set User Account. The Set User Account dialog box will appear allowing you to specify the account information for the feature(s) that you have highlighted.

Completing the Site Server 3.0 Install

Before copying the files and completing the installation process, setup will stop any running services and prompt you to confirm the choices that you made during the setup process.

After confirming this step and making a final confirmation on the files that Site Server will install, the file copy process will proceed. Once the installation process is complete Site Server will display a Setup Complete dialog box to assure you that the setup process if complete. Click the Finish button to complete the installation process.

As I discuss below it is probably a good idea to shut down and restart your computer at this point. Before you install Site Server 3.0 Commerce Edition you will need to reboot your system. It is also a good check to see if any errors have arisen in the installation process. However, you may find you need you need to wait for Index Server.

Index Server Runs Amok

Something else to keep in mind while you are installing Site Server is the Index Server. By design, Index Server comes to life each time the server is restarted, and it begins looking for any content that has been changed or that it has not yet indexed. If it finds any new files that it was previously unaware of, it immediately begins to index these files without regard to anything else happening on the server. This is normally not much of a problem, and you can usually just let Index Server do its thing.

However, when installing Site Server on slower, less powerful machines, such as your development server, for example, Index server can begin to cause some problems. When you install Site Server for the first time, you are prompted to reboot the machine at the end of the installation. When the machine comes back to life, Index server is all of a sudden presented with at least a good 500 files (mostly HTML help content) that it realizes it must now index. On a slow machine, this can bring everything to a crawl.

The key to overcoming this problem is just to wait until Index server has finished its tasks. The best way to monitor this is to simply open the Task Manager and wait until the CPU usage returns to normal. While Index Server is still running, you will see wild spikes that continue for a couple of minutes. Simply resume your installation as soon as Index server has finished and relinquished control of the CPU once again.

Installing Commerce Server 3.0

Microsoft Site Server 3.0 Commerce Edition is a separate installation, required to install the e-Commerce components of Site Server 3.0. If you do not require the Commerce Edition components then skip this section and move to the Final Site Server Installation Considerations section below.

Site Server 3.0 Commerce Edition allows you to install several additional components such as Commerce Server and Ad Server. As we discussed in Chapter 1, Commerce Server is an e-Commerce solution, that allows you to quickly and easily build your own online store.

Ad Server, which is also included with Site Server Commerce Edition, is a tool that allows the management of scheduling and delivery of Web site advertisements. Commerce Server integrates well with the other components of Site Server such as P& M, Searching, Indexing and Usage and Content Analysis.

Performing the Install

Before we go any farther with this process, you should have shut down and rebooted the machine on which you just installed Site Server. A reboot allows all new components and registry entries that have been added with your Site Server installation to take effect.

Installing Site Server 3.0 Commerce Edition is similar to installing Site Server 3.0. Once you get through the splash screens and the licensing agreement Site Server Commerce Edition 3.0 displays the setup types dialog box. Choosing Custom install will bring up the advanced user setup.

The next dialog that is displayed allows you to select the components that you want to install.

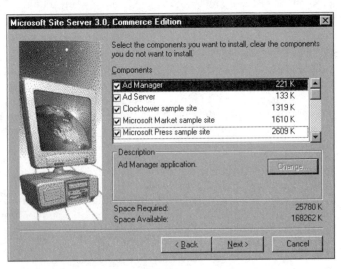

Choose all the components that are available, including the sample sites, in order to get the full set of Commerce tools. I always install the samples for several reasons. First, to ensure that everything was installed correctly and is working properly. Secondly I often refer to the sample sites for sample code or examples of how I should configure or design some part of a web site.

Next you will need to select DSNs for each component of Commerce Edition that you are installing. Earlier in this chapter we created four DSNs which correspond to the four databases that were created in SQL Server. We used two of these DSNs during the installation of Site Server 3.0. We'll use the third and fourth DSNs during the setup of Commerce Edition:

System DSN	Site Server Component
SSAdServer	Ad Server
SSCommerceServer	Clocktower
SSCommerceServer	Vocano Coffee
SSCommerceServer	Microsoft Press
SSCommerceServer	Trey Research
SSCommerceServer	Microsoft Market

You can see from this table that we choose the SSAdServer DSN for the Ad Server component and SSCommerceServer for all of the sample sites that we have chosen to install.

Finally, Site Server Commerce Edition will copy the files to your system and perform several configuration changes.

Finishing the Site Server Installation

By now you probably realize why I gave you all those warnings back at the beginning of this chapter. There is a lot going on in a full Site Server install and a lot of pieces to keep track of. We are almost finished and ready to take Site Server out for a spin.

Installing Additional Software

As with other Microsoft products, Services Packs are the standard way to update Site Server 3.0. Service Packs are used to help keep Site Server and other software current with new technology. Service Packs can also include additional components that may increase or add new functionality to Site Server.

After the Commerce installation has completed you should install Windows NT Service Pack 4.0. However, you shouldn't install Windows NT Service Pack 5.0 until after the next step, installing the service pack for Site Server.

The most current Service Pack release as of this writing for Site Server is Service Pack 2, often seen as SP2, which fixes several issues include those concerning using Site Server with SQL Server 7.0. You should install this after Windows NT SP4.

Additionally you may want to install the following Service Packs and additional software.

> ➤ If you installed Visual Studio at the beginning of the installation you can install Visual Studio 97 Service Pack 3 or Visual Studio 6.0 Service Pack 2.

> ➤ In the next chapter, *Admin*, you will be introduced to the Microsoft Management Console. You should install the latest version of the MMC version 1.1 at this time.

For more information on additional fixes and software to install see
`http://support.microsoft.com/support/siteserver/install_ss3.asp`.

Checking Your Installation

Congratulations! If you have made it this far then you have Site Server up and running. At this point you are probably wondering whether anything went wrong during the installation process. There are several ways that you can determine whether anything went wrong or some component did not get properly installed. Unfortunately since there are so many components that we installed, checking all of them at once is not a simple option.

> ➤ **Using the MMC to verify component installation**
> You can open up the MMC to view the components of Site Server that you've installed. The next chapter explains using the Microsoft Management Console (MMC) to administer site server similar to how you administer IIS and Transaction Server. I won't attempt to discuss this powerful tool in any detail here, however you will probably want to spend some time when it's been discussed in the following chapter to see if all the components you choose to install are actually there.

> ➤ **Checking the Sample Site**
> Another quick way to ensure that everything is installed ok and working correctly is to try out the samples that are installed during the Site Server installation process. In the browser on your Site Server machine type, `http://localhost/siteserver/`. This will display the site server main web page. From here you can view the web administration features of Site Server and look at the sample sites that are also installed.

Where to find additional help?

If you do happen to get an error message, or something does not appear to be quite right there are several sources that you can turn to for help. The Site Server documentation itself should be your initial source for questions about how things should work or steps. Microsoft TechNet (`http://technet.microsoft.com/cdonline/default.asp`) and online support should be your primary source for troubleshooting, updates, or links to hot fixes and new Service Packs.

Microsoft also hosts several newsgroups (e.g. `msnews.microsoft.com`) on Site Server that are filled with information from people who have been working with Site Server since the beginning. Additionally there are several other web sites that are devoted to Site Server and its use. You can find a list of useful resources in Appendix H.

Windows NT Additions

Most BackOffice components when installed on Windows NT add some additional services and performance monitoring tools. In this section we will examine some of those additions and see how we can use them to track our Site Server installation.

Site Server Services

Site Server 3.0 installs several new NT services when it is installed. Not all of these services are required depending on how Site Server is to be used. However, after installation, all these services are set to automatic startup by default. Any service that is started and running in the Services dialog that is not necessary is consuming precious resources. Stopping services and configuring services not to start up automatically is a good way to increase system performance.

Performance Monitor (Perfmon) Objects and Counters

Probably one of the most effective ways of monitoring detailed performance information is through the Windows NT tool called Performance Monitor, or PERFMON. When the Windows NT 4.0 Options pack and Site Server are installed on the system, a number of performance counters are installed on the system as well. Counters provide an inside look at the way a part of the system is performing.

Performance Monitor is a native standard component of Windows NT. It can be used to read the performance counters of any accessible object for the purposes of real-time charting, logging, and report generation, as well as for issuing alerts. You can open Performance Monitor from the Start Menu by clicking on Start | Programs | Administrative Tools | Performance Monitor.

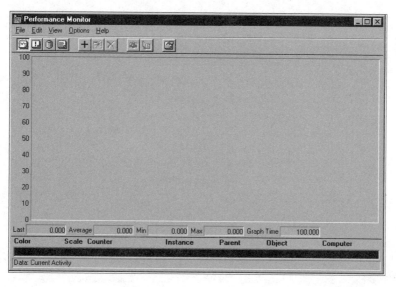

Any computer system, whether a desktop workstation or an Internet Information Server hosting enterprise-level Web sites, should operate at a level sufficient and adequate to support its assigned tasks. Otherwise, the services offered by that computer will fall short of user expectations. Performance monitoring is the act of measuring how a computer system is in carrying out its instructions and activities. Comparing the expected or normal levels of operation to the current real-world levels helps administrators determine how well a computer or service is performing and whether it needs tuning or upgrading.

Performance Monitor is able to monitor the activities hosted on a Windows NT computer because of its framework design, which allows new monitoring components to be added easily. Basically, everything within NT that can be named or accessed by a user or a process is an object. A Windows NT object is comprised of three main components.

> **Type:** A classification designation that defines the class of services and form of attributes that can be associated with an object.

> **Service:** The behaviors possible for an object. Includes methods, services, and functions that can be used to manage, modify, or manipulate the object's attributes.

> **Attributes:** The contents of the object itself (data or services), the identity of the object (including the Security ID and, typically, a NetBIOS name), and the access control list that prescribes the access permissions for the object.

Performance Monitor ties into the services of an object to extract performance information. Performance information is read via specific metrics or counters associated with a particular service. Counters can measure point activity, average activity, or difference activity.

Viewing Site Server Objects and Counters

Site Server installs several objects and counters to help you track and maintain the performance of your system, as you can see from the figure below:

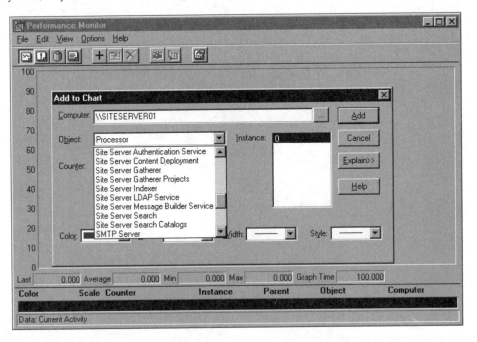

Appendix F is a complete list of the counters that Site Server installs. Take a moment to look through the some of the objects and counters that are available to ensure that you are familiar with the monitoring tools that are available for your use.

Summary

Wow! We have definitely covered a lot of material in this chapter. Hopefully you have taken it all in without feeling like Site Server 3.0 is beyond your ability. If this is your first time being introduced to Site Server then you maybe simply read through the chapter before actually attempting the installation. You probably understand why the beginning paragraphs of this chapter are laced with all those dire warnings. Some of the things that we have discussed in this chapter include:

> Hardware and Software requirements for installing and using Site Server effectively.

> The installation process for Site Server 3.0 and Site Server 3.0 Commerce Edition.

> Simple steps to ensure that your Site Server installation is complete and correct.

> Performance Monitor Counters and Objects that Site Server installs for monitoring your system performance.

In the next chapter you will look at how to administer the Site Server 3.0 site we have created.

Site Server Administration Tools

You are going to build a web site that will be used on the Internet or on your corporate intranet. Most of the content of this web site will be created by you and your colleagues, but much of the software used to run the site was created by Microsoft. You need to be able to configure Microsoft's software to meet your needs. Microsoft has provided some tools to allow you to change the way their software works, the way it is tuned, the way it is secured, and the way it is customized to your requirements.

Life is Complicated

There are four distinct administration contexts that we need to consider, each with different technical and security implications.

Firstly, there is the situation where you are physically logged on to your server. You have a valid security context in the Microsoft Windows domain, and you have full access to all of the available tools and utilities installed on your server.

More often, perhaps, you are seated at your desk and accessing the server over a network. You are still likely to have a Microsoft security context, but some of the tools and utilities will no longer do everything that you want them to do.

The third context is the remote context. You are either dialing into a corporate network, or accessing the server across the Internet or another large network. There may be all sorts of network devices between you and your server that filter out traffic that they are unfamiliar with. This may make it impossible to obtain your normal Microsoft security context or to run the tools that you normally use. In any case, the client machine you are using may not have all of your normal tools installed.

A fourth case is the batch environment. You may have work that needs to be run on the server on a regular basis, or at a scheduled time, without user interaction. This work needs to run in a valid Microsoft security context, and it probably needs to run in such a way that it will not require any input from a screen.

We need to consider each of these cases.

The Microsoft Management Console

When you installed Site Server, it included a management program called the Microsoft Management Console, or MMC. This program was installed on the machine running Site Server, but you can also install it on any other Windows NT 4.0 or Windows 2000 machine on your network, provided you have a Site Server Client Access License for each user. That way, you don't have to be in the same room as your Site Server to be in control. You can change the way this program looks so that it has just the tools that you need for your site. You can also give any sections of the tools to other people, so they can administer just some areas of your site. And if you have written your own software to extend Site Server, you can also add your own management module to the Management Console.

Using a Browser

Site Server is, after all, a web program, and Microsoft has provided Web Administration access to most of the configuration settings that are controlled by MMC. Perhaps you need to manage your server over the Internet, and you don't want to expose the management program to every hacker who happens to have a copy of MMC. Perhaps you need to access your server through a firewall and you are limited in which TCP ports you are able to use. You may want to use the SSL protocol to encrypt your network traffic. Or perhaps you want to access the server from a non-Windows platform, like a Macintosh, a UNIX workstation, or Linux. You will find that the browser interface can do most, but not all, of what MMC can do.

But Wait, There's More!

With the choice of two management tools, why would you also want to be able to issue commands from the command prompt?

Well, firstly, because there are some things that you can't configure using MMC or WebAdmin, but that you can do using a command. But a more important reason to learn about commands is so that you can automate your server.

> You might want to email yourself, or the Help Desk, when there is an unusual condition on the machine, like an error message on the NT Event Log.

> You might want to delete some non-essential files when the server looks like it is about to run out of disk space.

> You might want to be paged when CPU usage exceeds a certain value.

> You might want to change a tuning parameter just before the busiest time of the day, and then set it back later in the day.

> You may need to bulk load a large amount of existing data.

> Perhaps you need to extract data from the Membership Directory and load it into a spreadsheet.

> You will almost certainly want to take regular housekeeping actions, such as backing up your server, deleting obsolete files and de-fragmenting your disks.

You can do all of these things by issuing commands from a DOS .BAT file; and you can do a lot more by running a VB Script, a JavaScript, or a PERL script using the Windows Script Host, and managing the task automatically using the Windows Task Scheduler.

We will discuss the tools that you can use to perform all of these tasks, and more, in this chapter.

The Microsoft Management Console

The Microsoft Management Console (MMC) is a container that hosts management tools, known generically as snap-ins. Instructions on writing tools that will run using MMC are published in the Windows Platform SDK. Microsoft is promoting MMC as a management facility in order to encourage software developers and customers to produce their own tools that run in this environment.

In designing the MMC, Microsoft's goal was to provide a common environment in which software vendors could run their management tools. Microsoft wanted you to be able to:

> Navigate the tools easily and intuitively, by developing tools with a common look and feel, and with a common style of navigation.

> Organize together, in one place, tools from different software vendors and different products.

> Add and remove tools according to your specific requirements.

> Reuse your chosen configuration at other times and on other machines.

There are many proprietary initiatives of this type in the world of network and systems management. The MMC deserves your attention because:

> It satisfies the above four design goals.

> It is open. You can develop and add your own tools to the environment.

> It is available now, and is not merely a proposal.

> It is free. You can install it on as many Windows 95, Windows 98, Windows NT 4.0, and Windows 2000 machines as you like.

> Because it is an internal standard within Microsoft; more and more Microsoft products will provide tools that run in this environment. Most of the administrative tools in Windows 2000 run in this environment. We can be fairly confident that MMC will be around for a while.

> Site Server is one of the first products to take advantage of MMC. In fact, it is the main mechanism used to manage Site Server.

Let's see how we go about installing and using the latest version of the MMC.

Installing MMC 1.1

While MMC Version 1.1 is largely a maintenance release that adds features for snap-in developers, it is well worth the effort to download and install it from the Microsoft web site. It is noticeably more stable than the Version 1.0 that installs with the Windows NT Option Pack. You will also need at least Version 1.1 if you want to run the Commerce Interchange Pipeline Manager (CIPM) snap-in (a recent addition to the Site Server toolkit).

You can download the latest version of the MMC from
`http://www.microsoft.com/MANAGEMENT/MMC/default.htm`.

Starting the MMC

Take a few minutes to get familiar with the MMC. You are going to be seeing a lot of it in the future.

You can start MMC by:

1. Running any file with a `.msc` extension. When you installed MMC it was registered as the default application for files with this extension. You will find that both the NT Option Pack and Site Server have added shortcuts to your Start menu that point to pre-configured MMC consoles.

To run a pre-configured console that includes the NT Option Pack snap-ins, click on Start I Programs I Windows NT 4.0 Option Pack I Microsoft Internet Information Server I Internet Service Manager.

To run a pre-configured console that includes the Site Server snap-ins, click on Start I Programs I Microsoft Site Server I Administration I Site Server Service Admin (MMC).

2. Running mmc from the command line.

If you have a pre-configured console you can include the file name as an argument:

`mmc path\filename.msc`

3. Clicking on Start I Run and entering the mmc command.

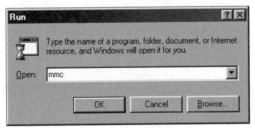

The Multiple Document Interface

MMC is designed as what Microsoft calls a Multiple Document Interface (MDI). That means that the outer shell or parent frame can hold several child windows or views, each being its own self-contained environment. This is perfectly familiar from popular office products, which usually allow you to have multiple documents open at once.

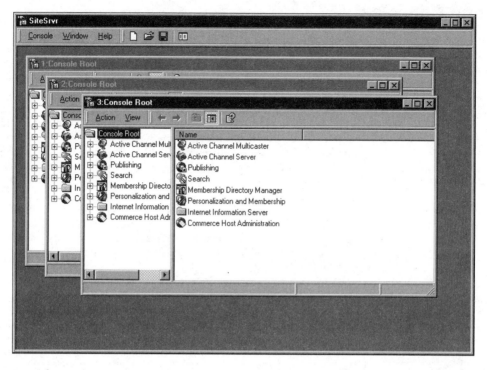

The normal view has two panes, modeled on Windows Explorer. On the left is the **console tree**, which consists of containers and objects. Containers such as the Console Root are holders for other containers and objects. By clicking on the plus sign (+) of a container you can expand that container to view additional containers and objects.

On the right is the **details pane**, which usually shows the contents of the selected item in the console tree. In the adjacent screenshot we can see that a web page is the object that has been selected in the console tree and the contents are displayed in the details pane on the right.

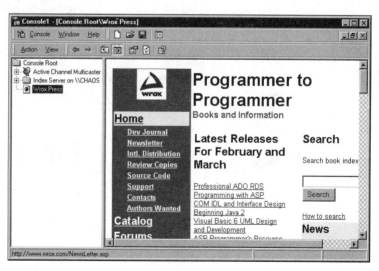

Creating Consoles

The whole aim of MMC is to assist you with customizing management tools to your own requirements, displaying just the tools that you need, in a layout that suits you. You do this by creating **consoles**. A console is a group of settings that is saved in a file with a .msc extension. If you look on your disk you will see that the installation of the NT Option Pack and Site Server created several .msc files with default console settings for you to start with.

Using the Console menu, you can create new consoles. You can add and remove the snap-in tool modules, configure the number and layout of the windows, decide whether both the console tree and the details pane are to be visible, and choose the authoring mode (described below). You save your settings in .msc files, which you can then distribute to other people, simply by copying or emailing the .msc file to them.

It is worth pointing out that having a .msc file is not, in itself, sufficient. The person who wants to use your console must also have the relevant snap-ins installed on their machine, must have appropriate file permissions to run the snap-ins, and must have permissions to actually administer the target system. Additionally they must have a version of MMC installed on their machine the same as, or newer, than the one in which the console was built.

Anyone with MMC installed can also use it to build their own consoles, completely bypassing any consoles that you might have built on their behalf. Do not mistake the ability to build MMC consoles for a security mechanism that will control what other users are able to do. It is simply a method to customize views of the management tools. To control security, you must configure your server correctly.

Creating a New Console

To create a new MMC console, click the New menu option on the Console menu or press *Ctrl+N*. This will bring up a new console window with the console root as the only available item. From here you can begin to add snap-ins and other items to configure a console that is right for your administrative purposes.

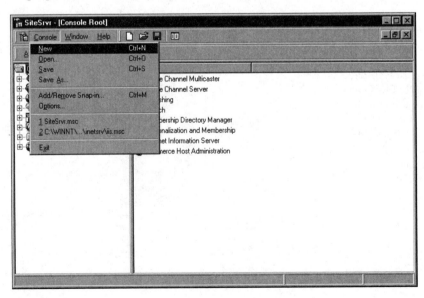

Building Your Console

As we mentioned earlier, the management tools that run in MMC are called snap-ins. You add and remove the snap-in modules by clicking on the Console | Add/Remove Snap-in... menu item (or by pressing *Ctrl+M*). A dialog showing the snap-ins you already have in the console will appear.

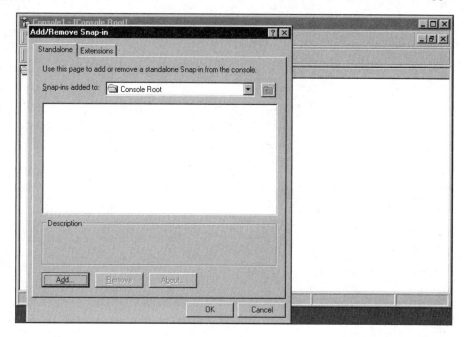

If you click Add... at the bottom left of this dialog box another will appear showing all of the snap-ins available on your machine.

You select Folder to add a folder to your console tree: in this way, you can organize your console into a tree structure. This allows you to close folders when you want to hide items from view.

If you select Link to Web Address you are prompted to enter a URL, and you can enter a reference to any web page. When you click on this item in the console tree, the web page will appear in the details pane. You might use this feature to provide quick access to a test page on your server, or to technical support pages on the Internet.

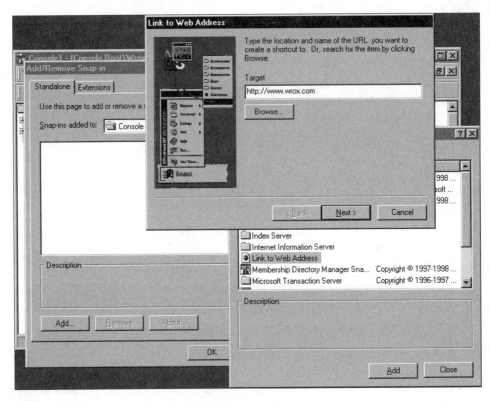

Be aware that you can also use Link to Web Address to display any directory in the details pane, using the Windows Explorer, or to start any script or program.

Do not be afraid to remove snap-ins from the console if you don't need them. You are not actually deleting them from the machine; you are simply removing them from the current console view and can add them back at any time.

Authoring Modes

You can designate whether your console will be opened in **author mode** or **user mode**. You choose the mode of a console by clicking on the Options menu item on the Console menu.

In author mode, the user who opens this console will be able to further customize the console to their requirements, just in the same way that you can. They will be able to add and remove snap-in modules, and configure the number and layout of the windows and whether both the console tree and the details pane are visible.

In user mode, changes to the `.msc` file are controlled. Users pick up the settings that were chosen by the author. You can designate any one of three user modes:

> **User Mode – Full Access**
> Displays the entire console tree, but prevents users from adding or removing snap-ins or changing console properties.

> **User Mode – Delegated Access, Multiple Window**
> Displays only portions of the console tree and prevents users from adding or removing snap-ins, or changing console properties.

> **Use Mode – Delegated Access, Single Window**
> Same as for delegated access for multiple windows, but prevents users from creating new windows.

Again, do not mistake user mode for a security setting. It is simply a way to make it less likely that your console settings will be accidentally changed. A user can always bypass your mode setting. Regardless of your setting, the console is opened in author mode if:

> MMC was already running in author mode when the console was opened

> You right-clicked on the .msc file in Windows Explorer, and chose the Author option

> The console is opened at the command prompt with the /a option

> You have checked Always open console files in Author mode on the User tab under Console | Options

Adding Snap-ins and Other Items to a Console

Let's start with a new console and add in a snap-in.

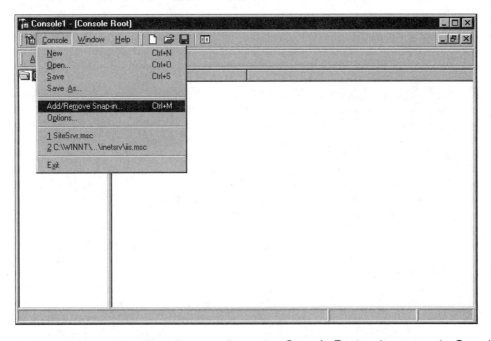

If you look on the screenshot that follows you'll see that Console Root is showing in the Snap-ins added to dropdown box. This means that any items that we add at this point will show up under the Console Root item in our console tree. Click on Add to bring up the Add Standalone Snap-in dialog box.

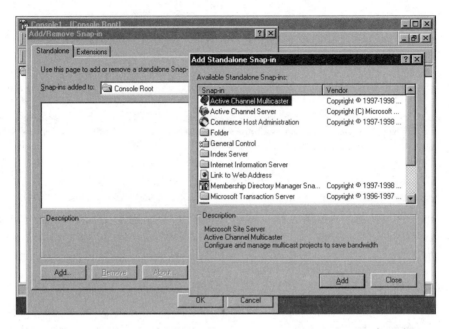

From the **Add Standalone Snap-in** dialog, add whatever snap-ins or other items that you need to configure your new console. By choosing an item from the list and clicking **Add** you can add items to the **Console Root** of your main console tree. Some snap-ins launch a wizard when added. This allows you to provide information about the resource that this item will administer.

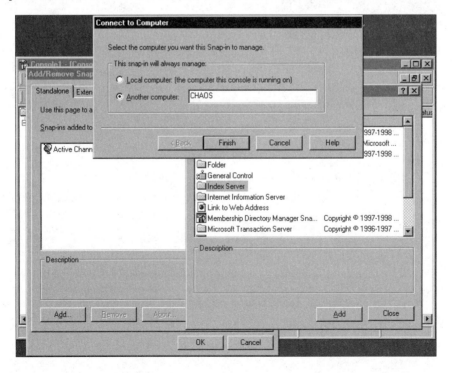

In this case we are adding an Index Server snap-in that will administer the Index Server on the machine on our network named "CHAOS".

Extension Snap-Ins

Snap-ins come in two flavors: **stand-alone** snap-ins and **extension** snap-ins. Stand-alone snap-ins run independently, in the MMC environment. Extension snap-ins add menus, property pages, toolbars, wizards, and Help screens to stand-alone snap-ins, and cannot be run by themselves.

Site Server contains an extension snap-in. If you add the Internet Information Server snap-in from the Standalone tab, a Personalization and Membership snap-in will appear on the Extensions tab. Select the checkbox to add this snap-in to your console.

Saving a Console

Once you have configured your console with the items that you need, you can save your configuration to a file. This allows you to return to this configuration any time that you need to access this set of tools. You can also send your configuration file to other administrators. To save a console, use the Save As menu option on the Console menu, or press *Ctrl+S*.

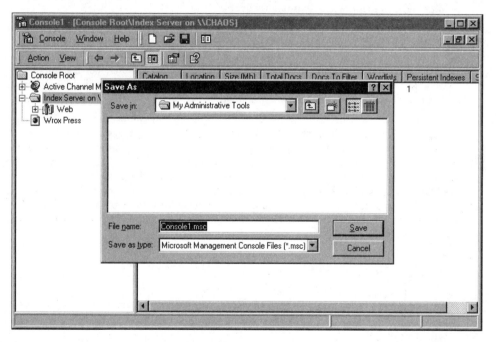

MMC consoles are saved with the file extension `.msc`. By default, a saved console is saved in the My Administrative Tools folder on the system that it was saved on. You will find this folder in your profile. On a Windows NT 4.0 system, for example, it will probably have a name like `C:\Windows\Profiles\username\Start Menu\Program\My Administrative Tools`.

I Lost My Snap-In

Sooner or later you are going to see a message like this:

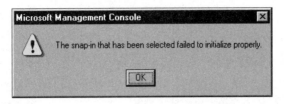

Remember that there are several conditions necessary for you to run a snap-in:

> You need a console, that is, a valid MMC configuration, which will probably be saved in an .msc file. Like any other file, this file can become corrupted, in which case you must delete it, and either restore it from a backup or create a new console. This is a binary file, not an ASCII file, and there is no easy way to fix it.

> Do you have the current version of MMC? If the console that you are trying to run was created in a more recent version, you will probably be unable to run it.

> You need the snap-in installed on your machine. A snap-in is just like any other component: a group of DLLs, EXEs, registry settings, and other files. Unless all of these items are present and correct, the snap-in will not function.
> Was the snap-in installed on this machine? On *this* particular machine? Have some of the files been deleted or moved? If they have been moved there is a good chance that the system cannot find them. Has a directory or file been renamed?

> Never underestimate the ability of file permissions to prevent you from doing what you want to do. That's what they are for, after all. If you don't have permission to either read or execute that snap-in, and every file that it needs, then it isn't going to run. Are you logged on with sufficient permissions? Are you *sure* you are logged on with sufficient permissions? Did someone else log onto this machine as another user when you weren't looking? Has someone "improved" the security on this machine? Did someone change or delete one of the group definitions in this NT domain so that you are no longer running in the same context that you were yesterday?
> To determine what username and domain you are logged into, go to the command line and issue these commands:

```
echo %USERDOMAIN%
echo %USERNAME%
```

> Quite apart from file permissions, some snap-ins will only run correctly in the same security context that they were installed in. Others will only run correctly if you are logged on as an Administrator.
> Try logging on as "Administrator" and see if this solves your problem. If not, ask yourself whether you are also considered an Administrator on the target system. Try adding yourself to the Administrators group there.

If all else fails you will know from bitter experience that the quickest way to get going again is to reinstall the product. Don't be proud: go and find the CD-ROM.

Installing Snap-Ins

Microsoft wants you to freely and easily add snap-ins to MMC so that you can remotely manage their servers. They probably have a web site where you can download the snap-ins and install them on the operating system of your choice, right?

Wrong. For reasons known only in Redmond, the snap-ins are buried deep inside other setup packages. The screenshots that follow show the MMC related files on the NT 4.0 Option Pack and the Site Server installs, respectively:

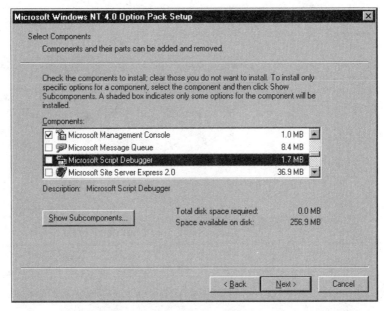

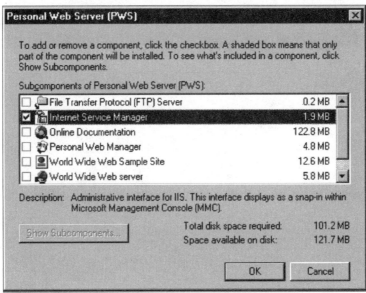

And adding these particular snap-ins is not supported on Windows 95 or Windows 98.

Remember that these snap-ins are already installed on your Site Server machine. Follow this procedure if you need to install them on another Windows NT 4.0 machine:

On NT 4.0 Workstation, do a Custom Install of the Windows NT 4.0 Option Pack. You can select MMC 1.0 from the main menu that is presented.

In the Personal Web Server Custom install the IIS snap-in is described as the **Internet Service Manager**. (There is no need to actually install the whole of Personal Web Server.) Be careful not to uncheck boxes for any existing components already on the machine. You don't want to uninstall software that somebody else is using.

You can install the Site Server snap-ins by choosing Tools Installation from the Site Server CD-ROM.

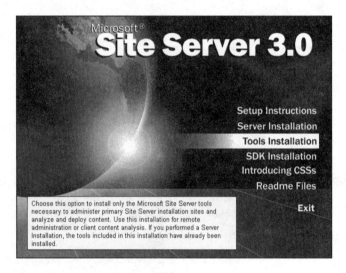

Here, the snap-ins are described as Remote Administration (MMC).

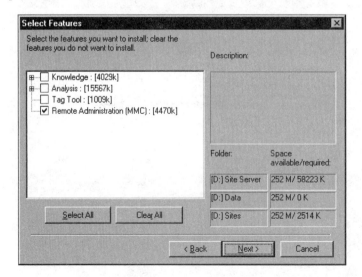

As there is maintenance for at least one snap-in in Site Server Service Pack 2, you need to install this as well. You can download Site Server Service Pack 2 from
`http://www.microsoft.com/SiteServer/site/30/downloads/sp2.htm.`

Writing Your Own Snap-Ins

You may decide that it is worth developing your own management tools and integrating them into the MMC console environment. The COM interfaces to MMC are documented in the Microsoft Platform SDK. At present only C++ is supported.

A good place to get started is
`http://www.microsoft.com/MANAGEMENT/MMC/authorsguide.htm.`

The Site Server Snap-Ins

As you install various programs onto your target system, snap-ins are also installed and made available to help you administer these programs. When you installed the NT Option Pack, it included MMC version 1.0 and the snap-ins for Internet Information Server and Microsoft Transaction Server. When you installed Site Server 3.0, you added snap-ins that you now can use to configure and administer your Site Server environment.

As you can see in this screenshot it is possible to administer Site Server installations on more than one machine via the same console:

Work through this procedure now to configure your own console and to become familiar with each of the snap-ins:

1. Click on Start | Programs | Microsoft Site Server | Administration | Site Server Service Admin (MMC) to bring up a console containing most of the snap-ins.

2. Click on Console | Save As so that you can modify it without losing the Microsoft sample console. You may like to save it in the My Administrative Tools folder so that it appears on your Start menu. The full path name is likely to be something like
   `C:\WINNT\Profiles\Administrator\Start Menu\Programs\My Administrative Tools`.

3. Click on Console | Add/Remove Snap-in.... Click on the Add button to add the Internet Information Server snap-in to your console.

4. Click on the Extensions tab and select the checkbox for the Personalization and Membership extension snap-in.

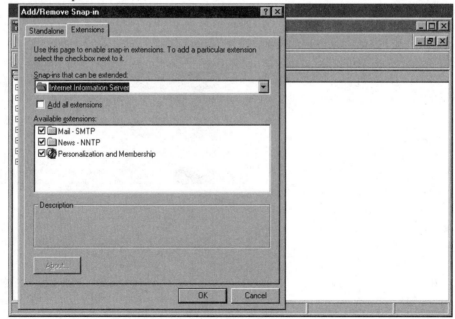

5. Click OK to close the dialog box.

6. Click on the Internet Information Server snap-in. Click Action | Connect to identify your Site Server. Enter the host name or IP address of the machine that you would like to connect to.

7. Explore the Internet Information Server branch by clicking on the plus signs (+). Examine the objects in the tree. Most objects have extensive properties pages that you can display by clicking on the Properties button on the Toolbar, or by clicking Action | Properties, or by right-clicking on the object and selecting Properties.

Many objects have other actions associated with them. You can identify these actions by clicking on the object and examining either the Action menu or the context menu that appears when you right-click.

The IIS snap-in is used to configure, tune, and secure your web site. Nearly all of your work is done using the property pages of various objects. You will need to examine the properties pages and action menus at various levels in the console tree, to get a feel for where everything is found.

8. Click on the Personalization and Membership snap-in. Click Action | Add Host to identify your Site Server.

The Personalization and Membership snap-in is used to create, secure, and configure Membership Servers, Membership Directories, AUO providers, the Site Server Authentication Service, the LDAP Service, and the Message Builder Service.

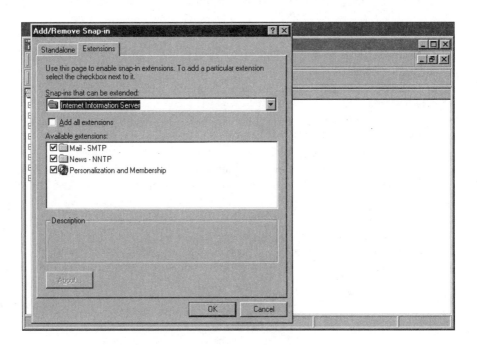

9. Explore the properties pages and action menus for the objects in this branch of the tree.

10. Identify the TCP port that will be used by the LDAP service: you will need this in the next step.

The default port number for LDAP is 389.

11. Click on the Membership Directory Manager snap-in. Bring up the properties page for this snap-in and identify your server. Identify the LDAP port number that you noted in step 9.

Don't worry about the **root node** as the MMC will work this out for itself.

12. When you click on the OK button you will be prompted to logon to the Membership Directory. This is not your Windows domain logon. This is your logon to the directory tree held within the Membership Directory. When you first install Site Server, anonymous access gives you full access to the data. There is also a default administrative account 'administrator' with password 'password'.

The Membership Directory Manager is used to create, modify, and secure objects in the Membership Directory. If you want some administrators to logon to the Membership Directory with less than full Administrator rights, you will need to create accounts for them. You do this by clicking on ou=Members in the console tree, selecting Action | New | User, and completing the wizard that appears.

13. Click on the Publishing snap-in. Click Action | Add Host to identify your Site Server. Explore the properties pages and action menus for the objects in this branch of the tree.

You will be able to show:

➢ **Event Reports**, which contain reporting options that allow the administrator to view what is happening with the publishing process on your server.

➢ **Projects**. which hold information about publishing information: what type of information is contained, the route it needs to take, and what time schedule it should follow in replicating data.

➢ **Routes**, which contain information about where information should go during publishing. You can specify the staging location, any mid-point locations for your information, and where its final destination should be.

14. Click on the Search snap-in. Click Action | Add Host and complete the wizard to identify your Site Server. Explore the properties pages and action menus for the objects in this branch of the tree.

15. If you are going to use this component, click on the Active Channel Server snap-in. Click Action | Add Host to identify your Site Server. Explore the properties pages and action menus for the objects in this branch of the tree.

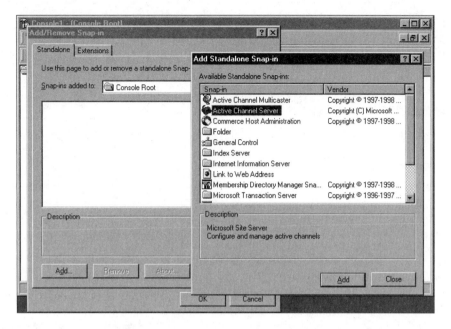

16. If you are going to use this component, click on the Active Channel Multicaster snap-in. Click Action | Add Host to identify your Site Server. Explore the properties pages and action menus for the objects in this branch of the tree.

17. If you are using the Microsoft Site Server Commerce Edition, configure the Commerce Host Administration snap-in now. The Commerce Host Administration snap-in is shipped and installed with Site Server, but it will not function unless Microsoft Site Server Commerce Edition is installed.

You can start the **Site Foundation Wizard** by right clicking on the host name under the Commerce Host Administration snap-in. The wizard is a Web Administration tool that guides you through the process of creating a Commerce Site Foundation.

18. If there are any Site Server components that you are not currently planning to use, remove the snap-in for that component. This will make the console easier to manage.

This will not actually remove the snap-in from your machine, just from this console.

19. Click on Console | Options to choose the authoring mode that will be used when the console is opened in a new instance of MMC. It might be a good idea to save it in User Mode – Full Access. This will help prevent you from accidentally changing your new console file, and it will get rid of irritating "Do you want to save?" messages that pop up each time you exit from MMC in Administration mode.

20. Save your console.

21. Exit from MMC.

22. Test your new console by locating it under My Administrative Tools on your Start menu.

> Since Site Server 3.0 Commerce Edition shipped, Microsoft have released an extra snap-in called the Commerce Interchange Pipeline Manager (CIPM). This snap-in requires MMC Version 1.1. You can read all about it at:
> `http://www.microsoft.com/SiteServer/COMMERCE/30/DOWNLOADS/MSCIPM.HTM`

Understanding the Environment

Let's consider some of the issues involved in getting MMC to work in your environment.

Same User Account

Some snap-ins will only run correctly using the account that was used to install them.

Avoiding MMC crashes

There are fixes in Site Server Service Pack 1 that stop MMC crashing when you create new classes or attributes.

Handling Change in the Environment

You may find that snap-ins remember more about the environment than you expect. For example, if you move between NT domains you may find snap-ins attempting to connect to the old domain. If you change the IP addresses of your servers, or remove servers, your console may continue attempting to connect to the old IP addresses. Go into console authoring mode, remove those snap-ins, and add them to your console again to get fresh configuration details.

Proxy Settings

If you do not have the proxy settings on your client machine set correctly, you may not be able to find the target server even though it is on your local network. You may need to add this machine to the list of machines that do not use the proxy server. If you are using Internet Explorer 5, this setting can be found under the LAN Settings option on the Connections tab of the Internet Properties pages, accessible from both the IE toolbar and from the Control Panel.

Dynamic Ports

Most of the work that you will do with MMC uses Microsoft's remote procedure call (RPC) protocol. These applications use dynamic ports; that is, the TCP ports that they use to communicate with are not allocated until you run the program. RPC connections are established on port 135, but they may continue on any port from 1024 to 65535. This clearly causes issues if you need to run these programs in a complex network or through firewalls.

The paper at `http://www.microsoft.com/com/wpaper/dcomfw.asp` will assist you to configure RPC to reduce the range of ports that it uses.

Use of UDP

By default, Windows NT 4.0 uses UDP rather than TCP to establish RPC connections. It is more difficult to secure UDP connections than TCP connections, and it is likely that UDP will be blocked by your firewall. In this case, you may experience a delay of 30 to 45 seconds when connecting to a server on the other side of a firewall, whilst the UDP connection times out. After failing to make a connection with UDP, Windows NT 4.0 will then try and make a connection using TCP.

For security reasons, your network designer may be prepared to allow TCP traffic through the firewall, but not UDP. In this case, you can make TCP rather than UDP the default protocol on MMC clients and servers by modifying the Registry on both machines. Refer to `http://www.microsoft.com/com/wpaper/dcomfw.asp` for details.

Microsoft Security Context

Most of these programs expect you to have a Microsoft security context in the target domain. Getting a Microsoft domain security context means participating in a NetBIOS over TCP, or NetBT, network. This, in turn, means exchanging packets on ports 135, 137, 138, and 139 on both TCP and UDP protocols. You are unlikely to open up these ports to a public network, like the Internet, because this exposes your whole Microsoft domain to attack. If you don't understand the technical details of this issue, then you should not consider it without specialist assistance.

There is a useful list of port settings used by NT Server in a Microsoft document entitled "Filter Settings for Windows NT Services". This document can be found at `http://www.microsoft.com/MCIS/reskit/docs/rk_FltrSet.doc`.

Web Administration

You have already installed two web sites that you can use to do many, but not all, of the things that MMC can do. IIS installs a web site called the **Internet Service Manager**, and Site Server installs a web site called **Site Server Web Administration**.

Because Web Administration only requires that you have a JavaScript-capable browser installed on your machine, you will choose Web Administration when:

> You do not have MMC installed, or you do not have the appropriate snap-in installed

> You are running on Windows 95 or Windows 98. The MMC snap-ins that we want to use are not supported on these platforms

> You are on a non-Windows platform, a machine that does not support MMC

> There is a firewall or other network device between you and your target server that is preventing you from using MMC

> You want to use SSL to encrypt your network traffic

Let's look at these two web sites in turn.

The Internet Service Manager

When the Internet Service Manager is first installed, it is configured to only allow access from the local IP address (127.0.0.1). You will need to change this restriction if you want to be able to access this site from other computers.

You can do this using MMC, or by logging on at the server in question and running a browser there. You need to edit the IP Address and Domain Name Restrictions, on the Directory Security tab, on the properties pages for this site.

While you are at it, review the port number. This web site is installed with a random port number as a security measure, and if you do not change this, or make a note of it, you will be unlikely to be able to guess the port number and connect to the web site. It is probably a good idea to make this number the same for all of your servers, so that is it easier to remember. This parameter is found on the Web Site tab on the properties pages for this site.

Another way to find the URL of the Internet Services Manager is by examining the shortcut that was placed in the Start menu on the target machine. On the Start menu, point to Programs, and then point to Windows NT 4.0 Option Pack. The site is accessed using Internet Service Manager (HTML).

Note that because the site does not use port 80 (unless you modify it to do so), the port number must be included in the URL. It will probably look something like this: `http://myserver:nnnn` where *nnnn* is the four digit number of the TCP port assigned.

Site Server Web Administration

Site Server Web Administration can be found at `http://myserver/siteserver/admin`.

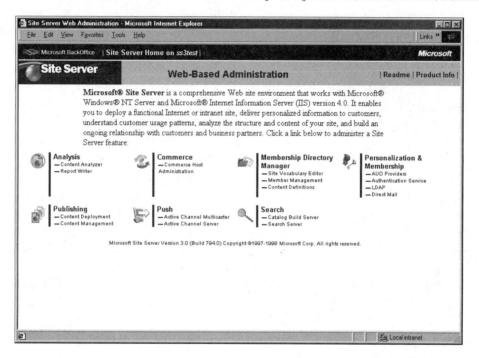

Remote Access

As we have seen, you have the ability to choose the TCP port numbers that the Web Administration applications use. This makes it possible for you to configure your site to allow configuration through firewalls.

You will need to set up your site with an appropriate authentication method, so that you can control who is able to administer your site. Authentication methods are described in detail in Chapter 11 on "Membership".

Using Commands

Now let's take a quick tour of the options available for command line administration.

Building Scripts

There is a power of difference between a command file and a script. The old DOS command file had such primitive logic facilities that it was a feat of ingenuity to get much of anything done. Now, of course, there is a better way. Today's batch execution environment is called the **Windows Script Host.**

You probably installed the Windows Script Host (WSH) when you installed the NT Option pack, but this technology is developing rapidly. The current release of WSH, version 5.0 can be downloaded from `http://www.microsoft.com/msdownload/vbscript/scripting.asp`. This will install:

> ➤ Visual Basic Script Edition (VBScript) Version 5.0
>
> ➤ JScript Version 5.0
>
> ➤ Windows Script Components
>
> ➤ Windows Script Host 1.0
>
> ➤ Windows Script Runtime Version 5.0

You will also see this group of programs referred to as **Windows Script Host**, or **Windows Script**. To further confuse things, Windows 2000 includes WSH 2.0 (available at the time of writing as a separate beta release), which currently requires Windows Script 5.0 as a prerequisite. You will need to visit `http://msdn.microsoft.com/scripting/default.htm` to get the current status and to download up-to-date documentation.

Note that version 5.0 of WSH includes regular expressions, a powerful string parsing facility that has been taken for granted in the UNIX world for years. The regular expression engine is implemented as a COM object that can be called from scripts, ASP pages, or programs.

Briefly, the language choices are:

VBScript	Site Server includes some files with `.vbs` extensions. These are scripts that are written using Visual Basic Script Edition.
Jscript	Windows Script Host also ships with support for Microsoft's implementation of JavaScript (also known as ECMAScript). JavaScript scripts have a `.js` extension.
PerlScript	If you prefer to work with Perl, you can download the PerlScript scripting engine for the Windows Script Host from `http://www.activestate.com`.

Running Scripts

Scripts can execute in either of two contexts: Windows based, or command line based. Because we don't want our scripts to create windows or dialog boxes, we will use command line based scripts.

You can start a script by issuing this command:

```
cscript path\scriptname
```

To make command line based execution the default, rather than Windows based execution, type the following command:

```
cscript //H:Cscript //S
```

You will then be able to run your command without typing "cscript", like this:

```
path\scriptname
```

Running Commands Remotely

You are very unlikely to be sitting at your Site Server machine all of the time. You will probably want to execute commands on this machine, but remotely from another machine. There are various ways that you can achieve this, whilst maintaining control over who is able to execute the commands.

You could write ASP pages that perform the functions that you need, and secure these ASP pages using the standard mechanisms in NT and IIS that allow you to control who is able to execute the ASP page: you can control access to individual pages using NT Explorer, and you can control access to web sites using the Internet Information Server snap-in of MMC.

Another approach is to directly access the command line on the remote computer. You will need to install a utility on both the client and the server, and consider security issues.

This is not a standard facility in Windows NT, but there have been a number of utilities released in the NT Resource Kit that will allow this. In choosing the best utility, you will be concerned firstly with security: you do not want just anyone to be able to access the command line on your machine. Secondly, you will be concerned with the abilities of your chosen tool. Do you need to be able to pipe data between machines? Do you need full-screen DOS commands, like EDIT?

You can download a subset of the NT Resource Kit tools from http://www.microsoft.com/NTServer/nts/downloads/recommended/ntkit/. This package includes tools called **Remote** and **WSRemote**, which provide client and server programs that will give you a remote command line.

Because of their limitations, you would probably only use these tools during development, on a private network. If you have the NT Resource Kit Supplement 3, or a subscription to Microsoft TechNet or MSDN, then you have access to a better utility called **Remote Console** that allows you to:

> - run the console server automatically as an NT service
> - log on to the remote machine with a particular Microsoft security context
> - encrypt your network traffic
> - record activity in the NT Event log
> - resize the console
> - run full screen DOS programs

Do not get this tool confused with **Remote Command**, which is a similar but less feature rich utility.

Running Tasks at a Specific Time

The ability to run a script or command file at a designated time, to process the output of the commands, and to keep a log of what has happened, has always been a standard part of UNIX; perfectly straightforward, really. Why does everything seem harder in the NT world?

Let us review some of the history. There may well be bits and pieces of this history littered around different machines at your site, which helps to explain why some machines behave differently than others.

> ➢ There has always been a simple AT command in NT. This is sometimes referred to as the Win AT Scheduler, or WAS.

> ➢ Successive releases of the NT Resource Kit have included Windows utilities to help you manage your AT commands.

> ➢ Third party software vendors have improved the basic service by releasing software products. A list of some of these can be found at
> http://www.microsoft.com/ntserver/nts/exec/vendors/freeshare/Maintnce.asp#cron

> ➢ The Analysis component of Site Server includes its own task scheduler. This facility is found on the Tools menu in the **Usage Import**, **Report Writer**, and the **Custom Import** programs.

> ➢ Since Version 4.0, Internet Explorer has included the **Microsoft Task Scheduler 1.0**. (Just to add to the confusion, this is also described as the Windows NT Task Scheduler, or WTS). It is probably already installed on your machine, perhaps without your knowledge. You can find it by looking for the Scheduled Tasks icon in My Computer.

> All old tasks now appear in this new Task Scheduler, even if you had previously disabled the Scheduler service. If you now use this new task scheduler to modify a job created with an older scheduler, it changes the format of the schedule entry, and the job cannot be used by the older scheduler.

> Be aware that if you now start the Site Server task scheduler, the job may get rescheduled by this older scheduler *as well.* The duplicate job duly appears in the new Microsoft Task Scheduler window, where it causes consternation – yours.

Our recommendation is that you stick to the most recent interface, Microsoft Task Scheduler 1.0. You can:

> ➢ start, stop, pause, or continue Microsoft Task Scheduler 1.0
> ➢ be alerted when a job fails to run
> ➢ use it to manage jobs on other machines
> ➢ view a log of the jobs that have run

Here is a screenshot of the Task Scheduler in Site Server Analysis:

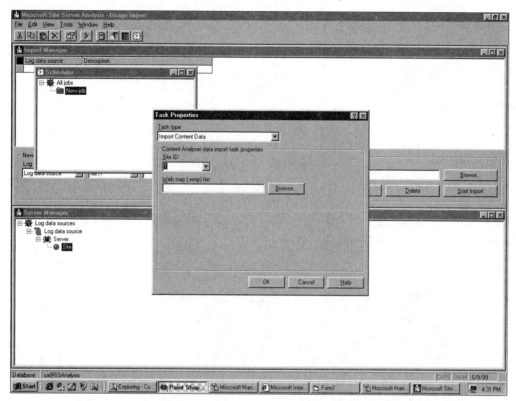

Context

Each job runs in the security context that you choose. If you want the job to run *as if you had logged on and run it,* you would put your username and password in the Run as box. This is not a very good idea though, because you will soon forget that this job is using your username, and next time you change your password, or your permissions, or the groups you are a member of, or your username is deleted, the job will fail. It is best to assign a special username just for scheduled tasks. Make sure that your chosen username has the permissions that it needs to do its work.

Sending E-Mail From a Script

It is often useful to be able to send email from a script. You might, for example, want to email yourself a regular report, or email the Help Desk to alert support staff of unusual events.

You will almost certainly have an SMTP server somewhere on your network. There are many components available that will allow you to send mail to an SMTP server with only a few lines of code. If you install the SMTP server that ships with IIS 4.0, you have already installed the Collaboration Data Objects for Windows NT Server (CDONTS).

However, in the time it takes you to dig out documentation for this component and discover its shortcomings, you could have downloaded **AspEmail** from http://www.aspemail.com/. This component is easy to install on NT Server or NT Workstation, is well documented, feature rich, and free. You can call the component with just a few lines of code from a Windows Script, from an ASP page, or from an application.

Here is an example of a VB Script that uses AspEmail to send an alert of an event.

```
' Alert.vbs

Set Mail = WScript.CreateObject("Persits.MailSender")

Mail.Host = "SMTPhost"
Mail.From = "auto@sitesrvr"
Mail.FromName = "Automatic alert"
Mail.Subject = "An event has occurred"
Mail.Body = "Text of your choice"
Mail.AddAddress "yourname@wrox.com"
Mail.Send

Set Mail = Nothing
```

Recognizing Performance Thresholds

The NT Performance Monitor has the ability to run a command whenever a threshold that you designate is reached. You can configure this tool to run a script that emails you or takes remedial action. You might choose to do this when the CPU usage exceeded 80%, or when disk space on the machine fell below 200 MB.

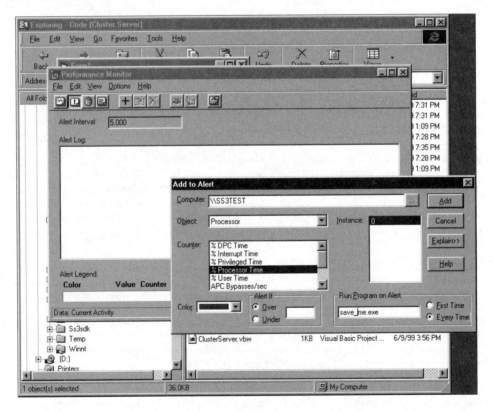

Monitoring the Event Log

You may wish to be aware of certain events being written to the NT Event Log. There is no inbuilt mechanism to monitor the log and send alerts, but there is a utility in the BackOffice Resource Kit that can assist you. If your organization subscribes to the Microsoft TechNet or MSDN services, you will have access to this tool. It is not particularly robust or flexible, but it may be sufficient to meet your needs.

The tool is called `evtscan.exe`. However, it is only able to monitor the Application Log, not the System Log or the Security Log.

If you want `evtscan.exe` to be able to send you an email, you need to install it on a machine with MAPI support. Also, be sure that `C:\Windows\System32\Inetsrv` is in your path, because `evtscan.exe` uses DLLs from this directory. You can change your path by clicking on Start | Settings | Control Panel | System, and modifying the Environment tab.

The Windows Management Instrumentation (WMI) SDK has a facility for monitoring the NT Event Log. To use this, you will need to download and install the **WBEM Core Components** on your server. This download is available at
`http://www.msdn.microsoft.com/developer/sdk/wmisdk/download.asp`.

The following VB Script waits for specific messages to appear on the log, and then takes action:

```
Set theEvent = _
GetObject("winmgmts:{impersonationLevel=impersonate}").ExecNotificationQuery _
    ("select * from __InstanceCreationEvent _
    where TargetInstance isa  'Win32_NTLogEvent'")

While true

    Set myEvent = theEvent.NextEvent

    wscript.echo myEvent.targetInstance.EventIdentifier
    wscript.echo myEvent.targetInstance.RecordNumber

    If InStr(myEvent.TargetInstance.Message,"My message text") Then

        ' Take action
        wscript.echo "Hello, world"

    End If

    If myEvent.TargetInstance.EventIdentifier = 123 Then

        ' Take action
        wscript.echo "Hello, world"

    End If

Wend
```

For more extensive and manageable Event Log monitoring, you will need a third party product. You might like to consider OpalisRobot, which can be found at `http://www.opalis.com/`, or RoboMon NT, at `http://www.heroix.com`.

> WMI makes all sorts of interesting information about your server available to your scripts. You can, for example, find out and control the status of the processes and services on your machine, check device, network, and printer status, and determine security settings.

Useful Commands

Starting and Stopping Services

If you want to stop and start services from the command line, or from a script, you can use the `net` command. Here are some examples:

`net start` Display all the services that have been started

`net start xxxxx` Start the named service

`net stop xxxxx` Stop the named service

You will need to know the service names in order to use this command. The service names are as follows:

IIS (the World Wide Web Publishing Service)	`w3svc`
Site Server Active Channel Multicaster	`acmsvc`
Site Server Authentication Service	`broksvc`
Site Server Content Deployment Service	`crs`
Site Server Gatherer Service	`gthrsvc`
Site Server Message Builder Service	`msgbldsvc`
Site Server List Builder Service	`tmlbsvc`
Site Server LDAP Service	`ldapsvc`
Site Server Search Service	`sssearch`
IIS Administration Service	`iisadmin`

PMAdmin

If you choose, you can configure every aspect of the Personalization and Membership component using the `PMAdmin` command. `PMAdmin` is actually a Visual Basic script, so it is necessary that the Windows Script Host be installed. You will also need to have a path to `Microsoft Site Server\bin\P&M`.

Commands are issued in the format:

`PMAdmin` *verb attribute /switches*

You can get help by typing the command name followed by `/?` or `/help`.

Try a couple of commands now. Go to the command line *on the server* and type:

```
PMAdmin get instance
```

This will give details of the Membership Directories on this machine. While:

```
PMAdmin status ldap
```

Will show the current status of the LDAP service on this machine.

You can find a complete list of the PMAdmin commands in the Site Server documentation. Click on Start | Programs | Microsoft Site Server | Site Server Documentation. Click on the Index tab, and enter "Command-line interface (P&M)".

SSSAdmin

A similar facility is provided for the Search component using the `SSSAdmin` command. You will also need to have a path to `Microsoft Site Server\bin`.

You can find a complete list of the `SSSAdmin` commands in the Site Server documentation. Click on the Index tab, and enter "Command-line (Search)".

Summary

In this chapter we looked at the administration tools that Microsoft has made available for managing a Site Server installation. We reviewed technical and security issues concerning the Microsoft Management Console, the Web Administration interface, and Site Server's command line tools.

When you are *physically logged on* to your server, you will probably prefer to use MMC. This is the most feature rich tool and it can be customized to your requirements. You may also choose to run batch scripts that you have previously prepared. These scripts may use the facilities of the Windows Script Host.

You will also probably use MMC when you are accessing the server over a corporate network. You may use a remote console facility to access the command line. If you are not using your normal machine, you may not have MMC installed and will have to use the browser interface instead.

When you are dialing into a corporate network, or accessing the server across the Internet or another large network, you are most likely to use the browser interface. This is the method most likely to work correctly across corporate firewalls, and does not require special software on your client machine.

To run work on the server on a regular basis, or at a scheduled time, you will probably use the Microsoft Task Scheduler to run Windows Scripts. You may also use various tools to trigger scripts when unusual or interesting events occur.

6

Content Management

There is something wrong with how the content on many web sites is managed. How many times have you seen the following situation? A business user creates a new document that needs to be publicly available. It is e-mailed to a person in Information Technology (IT). The IT person copies the file to a directory on a web server. The web master then creates links from the existing web site to the new document and the information is finally available. The problem is three days have elapsed since the process first started and the content was a time-sensitive press release!

Many manual processes and inefficiencies are described in this scenario. The purpose of Site Server's Content Management feature is to overcome these inefficiencies and automate the process. Site Server puts control of content in the hands of the people creating it.

Consider another problem. You have many files in your organization. The documents exist on both public file servers and individual workstations. You need to find all the files relating to a certain client. How do you do that? Content Management also takes on the responsibility of organizing your files. It tags them with attributes so you can then search based on these attributes to find documents.

Content Management in Site Server means the ability to automate submission and publishing of files to a web site. Content Management makes the files more useful by giving them **context**. At the time of submission, the publisher must provide information about the file such as title, author and keywords. The content can be any type of file including Word documents, HTML files, Excel spreadsheets and even images.In the context of an entire Site Server application, Content Management manages the flow of information from submission to approval to searching, and finally, viewing.

One example would be an entertainment site divided into sections such as videos and music. A user posting a document to the site about a CD would tag it as music, and might also apply other tags such as its title, artist and producer. The documents would then be posted to the music section, and using the meta-information in the tags we could organize our documents intelligently or search for particular artists.

In our discussion of Site Server Content Management in this chapter we will:

> Describe Content Management and its benefits
>
> Demonstrate Content Management by walking through a sample site
>
> Describe the planning phase of a Content Management implementation
>
> Show how to implement Content Management
>
> Highlight maintenance issues of a Content Management application
>
> Finally, describe the process of content deployment.

This aim of this chapter is not to repeat the Microsoft Site Server documentation but rather to emphasize the process of planning and implementing Content Management and highlight some of the issues that you are likely to run into along the way.

Content Management Benefits

Using Content Management benefits both the business user and the application developer by putting control of managing information in the hands of the information producers of the web site. The information producers do not have to pass files to an IT person who then puts them on the web site, they can publish the files themselves. In this way, Content Management introduces self-service to the control of web site content. Content creators can solve their own problems. In addition, the IT department can focus on making the information systems perform well rather than being burdened by the manual task of uploading files.

Some content may need approval before being published to the web site. Content Management also has an approval process built in. The approval process is centralized through a web-based interface so the problem of keeping track of different versions of files is reduced and the risk of the wrong version being put on the web site is minimized.

The consumer of the content (i.e. the user of the web site) also benefits from Content Management through rich search mechanisms. Since attributes are assigned to all published content, it is easy to find content based on attributes.

Finally, Content Management allows the application developer to shine. The developer can leverage the Content Management functionality built into Site Server rather than having to create that functionality from scratch. This means less code has to be designed, written and tested resulting in a web site application being developed faster and with fewer bugs. Since Content Management provides a structure for maintaining content, there is less chance a developer will need to be called in at a later time to make changes. Finally, since Content Management is a feature of Site Server rather than a custom-made solution, the developer can transfer their Content Management knowledge to another Site Server application as needed.

Content Management vs. Document Management

There may be a temptation to use Content Management as a company's overall document management solution. However, Content Management does not have a complete set of document management features. In particular, Content Management does not provide a revision history for a document. It also does not have the ability to check documents in and out. If these features are required, it is better to adopt a more full-featured document management tool. There are document management systems available that have a web-based client such as CyberDocs from PCDOCS Inc. (http://www.pcdocs.com).

Applications of Content Management

Content Management can be used for many different purposes both in large-scale Internet applications and small Intranet applications. Let us consider a few scenarios with which Content Management can be used. The common threads in all these scenarios are:

> Control of publishing content is placed in the hands of those who generate the content

> Content is classified as it is published

> No changes have to be made to the web site to make new content available

In the first scenario, consider a public company that has a web site for marketing and investor relation purposes. The types of content published are press releases, quarterly results, annual reports and product brochures. Different people generate the content: the publicist generates the press releases, accounting creates the quarterly results and annual reports, and marketing creates the product brochures. However, before anything is published to their web sites the company president must approve it. Content Management enables the different groups (e.g. accounting) to submit their content for approval and, if approved, to automatically have it published on the web site.

Content Management does not need to have a big web site to justify its use. Once someone understands Content Management, relatively little effort is required to create a Content Management application. Consider an insurance company that has a small intranet. This company has many types of documents required by the employees such as: policy guides, a monthly newsletter, Word templates for forms and the current rate schedule. For the insurance company to be effective in servicing their customers the employees must have the most recent information and they cannot afford to have multiple versions of the same type of information. Content Management centralizes the publishing and distribution of relevant business content thus making the company work more effectively.

WebSoft Consulting

For the last scenario, consider a software consulting business, WebSoft Consulting, that sells its services to various clients. It has a number of consultants that work on different projects building software solutions. As part of a project, there are many types of required documents including a contract, requirements, and a project plan. As well, a status report must be submitted every week. Internal to WebSoft, a budget spreadsheet is prepared monthly.

Currently, the only control over these documents is a directory structure that documents are manually placed in. Often documents get misplaced and there is no control over consultants being able to view other consultants' documents. The other problem is the client sometimes requests project documents and the consultant needs to pass a copy along. This results in many versions of the same document being distributed.

In the course of this chapter we will be coming back to this scenario, to understand how we can use a Content Management scheme to address WebSoft Consulting's problems.

Overview of the Content Management Process

The Content Management process involves a series of steps that are performed by the content provider, the content administrator, or both, before the document becomes available to the general user.

Content Management uses a specific area of a web site, or content store, to which content providers can post their documents, and these documents can then be administered by content administrators and viewed by other users. Providers upload their content to the store and apply tags to their documents. These tags describe attributes of the document they are uploading, such as the type, the author's name, the date of expiry, an abstract and many other possible properties. Content providers are also able to delete and modify attributes of the content they have uploaded, via their web browser.

Content administrators however have the ability to manage all documents uploaded by content providers. They can edit the attributes of documents and remove or approve these documents.

When the content has been approved, it is normally deployed to a staging server. This server acts as a broker between the development server(s) and the production server. You should not be editing on the staging server, and your content should not be viewed by users on this server either. It should mirror your production environment as closely as possible and gives you the option of preventing deployment of unsuitable content to the live environment.

You can then set up your staging server to deploy the content to your production server(s). This is typically done twice a day and is best done at the quietest periods of server activity. Users coming to your site would use the production server to view content.

The diagram and accompanying commentary outlines the Content Management lifecycle:

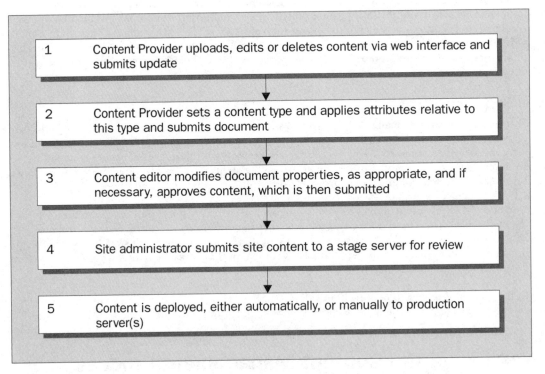

We will look at each of the stages in more detail as we progress through the chapter. However, first let's look at the content management features that we should have on our machine, after installing Site Server (in Chapter 4).

As a minimum Content Management (CM) requires that Publishing, and Personalization and Membership (P&M) have been installed, as much of the information used in Content Management is stored in P&M. The install also includes two sample sites, namely CMsample and FPsample, which you can use as templates to create and then customize your site. The first, CMsample, is designed to be used to upload all types of documents (*.htm, *.doc, *.xls, etc...) directly from the content provider's PC, whereas the FPsample site has been designed primarily for use with FrontPage (it makes use of themes and other FrontPage features). We'll discuss these sites in more detail further on in the chapter. First let's look at the elements of Content Management we can see in the Membership Directory.

Content Management in the Membership Directory

As with the rest of Site Server's features, there are two ways to administer Content Management: through the Microsoft Management Console (MMC) and through WebAdmin. Much of Content Management is most easily administered through WebAdmin, and this is what we'll be using for most of this chapter. However it is also possible to view the structures where relevant information is stored in the Membership Directory with the MMC. The preceding chapter covered the basics of the MMC, so here we'll just establish where Content Management can be found within the **Membership Directory Manager** (MDM) snap-in.

Click on Start | Programs | Microsoft Site Server | Administration | Site Server Service Admin (MMC) and click on Membership Directory Manager. If this is a fresh installation, then the Membership Server will be mapped to the first LDAP port it finds (port 1002), which is the correct port for our default Content Management installation, and the Membership Directory Manager will be displaying the directory for that Membership Server.

> *Note however that if you have been working with P&M, then the Membership Directory that you should bind to may be different.*

If you don't have a fresh installation you can check the port and Membership Server mappings through the following steps:

> ➢ To determine the port to which your content stores have been mapped, select the IIS snap-in, expand the computer on which you installed the content stores and right-click on the web site that you installed the stores to (on a fresh install this will be the Default Web Site). Select All Tasks | Membership Server Mapping and a dialog box will appear telling you the name of the Membership Server that this web site is currently mapped to. Make a note of the name of this instance.

> ➢ Next, expand the Personalization and Membership snap-in and then the name of the server on which you installed your content stores. There will be an instance shown which has the same name as the Membership Server instance you noted from the previous paragraph. Expand this, right-click the LDAP icon that appears, and select Properties. In this LDAP Properties dialog box the TCP Port field shows the port you will need to bind to in order to access the Membership Directory for that Membership Server. Take a note of this port number.

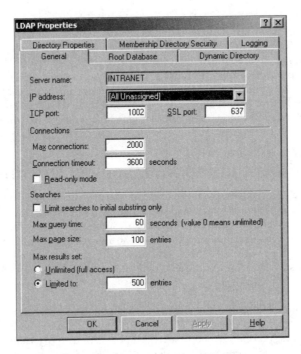

> Now, right-click on the Membership Directory Manager snap-in and select the Properties option. Ensure that the value for Hostname is the name of the computer your LDAP service is using, and that the value for Port is the port number you recorded in the previous step.

You may be asked to log on to the directory, depending on what authentication settings have been configured for your site. For more information on configuring IIS authentication settings please refer to Chapter 9, "Membership".

Containers in the MDM

After performing the above steps, you are presented with the six containers in the root of the Directory Information Tree, as shown below:

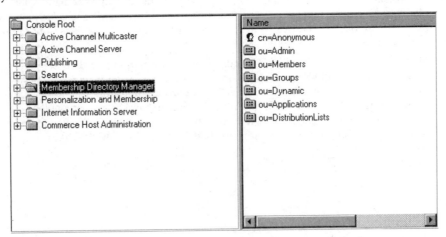

The cn=Anonymous icon you can see is the user account for anonymous logons to the Membership Directory – we'll cover it in detail in the Chapter 9, "*Membership*". A brief overview of each container is given below:

> ➤ **ou=Admin** – Stores administrative and configuration information relating to the Membership Directory
> ➤ **ou=Members** – Stores membership information such as usernames and their attributes
> ➤ **ou=Groups** – Defines the membership groups which members can belong to
> ➤ **ou=Dynamic** – Temporary storage container (similar to the ASP Session and Application objects)
> ➤ **ou=Applications** – Used to store data for a specific applications using the Directory
> ➤ **ou=DistributionLists** – Used by Direct Mail

To see those containers which have an impact on Content Management expand the ou=Admin/ou=Other and three containers will be exposed:

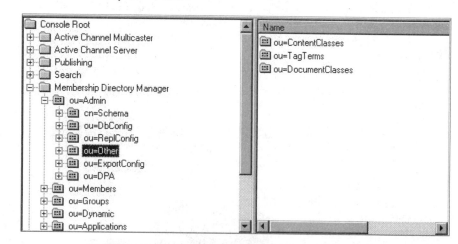

In the right pane, we see three containers which play an important part in working with Content Management, namely ou=ContentClasses, ou=TagTerms and ou=DocumentClasses. This is where information about published content is stored, such as the attributes for tagging content. For instance, the adjacent screenshot shows the content types that have been defined for the CMsample site:

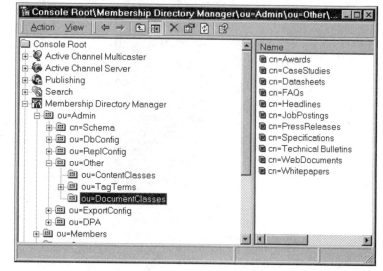

Before we can fully understand how these containers are used however, we need to understand the publishing process. A good first step is to look at a sample site.

Samples Available with Site Server

Let us not go too far without having some fun and trying some of the Content Management functionality. Site Server comes with two sample web sites for Content Management: CMsample and FPsample. CMsample is for people comfortable coding HTML directly or who use scripting such as Active Server Pages. FPsample, as can be inferred from its initials, is for those people more comfortable using Microsoft FrontPage.

These samples are interesting in that they serve a number of purposes. Not only do they demonstrate Site Server Content Management features, but the ASP scripts provide a model that can be used as the starting point for your own Content Management applications. In addition, these samples can be used as the first step in making sure Site Server was correctly installed.

For the time being, we'll content ourselves with a look through the essential processes of the CMsample site. We'll see more of FPsample later.

CMsample

CMsample demonstrates all aspects of Content Management. Your Content Management application will be modeled on CMsample – just branded differently. As you try the features, I will describe what is happening on the web server.

The CMsample site was built using an HTML editor. To access the sample, type in your web browser: http://<your server name>/cmsample. You should see a screen like this:

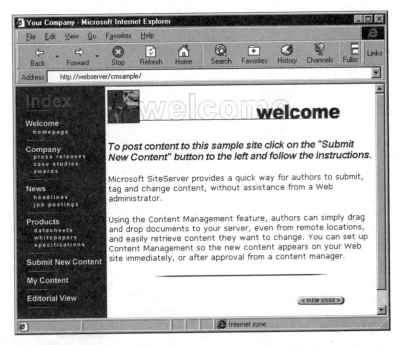

As you can see, navigation of the site is straightforward. Menu choices are along the left and the content is displayed on the right. All of the menu choices call ASP code that use various aspects of Content Management. In the lower right-hand corner note the "<VIEW CODE>" button. This is a great learning feature as you walk through the sample. On most of the pages in the sample web site you will see this button. When selected it will display a color-coded version of the ASP that created the HTML page sent to the browser. Give it try!

For a company like WebSoft Consulting, the menu on the left would list all their document types such as contracts, requirements and project plans.

Viewing Content

Choose one of the options under 'Products' such as 'datasheets' or 'whitepapers'. If you select 'whitepapers' you should see the following:

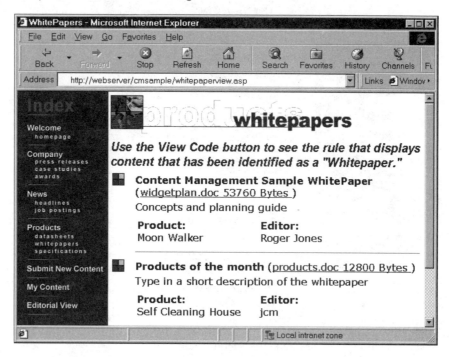

When you make a selection, Content Management fires a query that finds all the documents in the selected category and displays them in a list along with other attributes assigned to the document. In this case, the query found all documents where the category is "whitepaper". Each whitepaper has a title, subject, product and editor. The person who submitted the content has set these attributes. The attributes are returned as ADO `Recordset` fields. You can look at the code in `whitepaperview.asp` (using the <VIEW CODE> button) to see how the HTML formatting is wrapped around the `Recordset` fields.

Select the content filename to display the content. The content will be displayed in the browser if you have a viewer installed for that file type (e.g. Microsoft Word for `.doc` files).

> Note that if your system is behaving in a different way than has been described so far you might want to take a step back and verify that your Site Server installation was successful.

Submitting Content

This section demonstrates how documents are put into the Content Management system. If you are running IE 4.01 you will see the following:

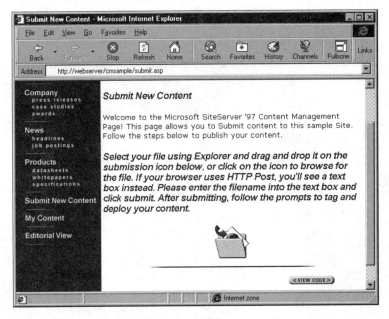

The file `submit.asp` detects the browser type and determines which code to send. In that file you will see a variable named `g_fUseActiveX`. This variable is actually defined in the include file `/SiteServer/Publishing/upload.inc`. If this variable is `true` not only will the client use the ActiveX Upload Control but also VBScript will be sent to the client instead of JavaScript. This is an important consideration if you are going to customize this page.

If the browser does not support ActiveX Controls, Content Management will automatically create a file upload form instead of using the ActiveX Control. In both cases, ActiveX Control or not, after selecting a file, it is transferred to the web server and placed in a directory called 'upload' which is a temporary holding place until the rest of the upload process is complete. Note that with the ActiveX Upload Control you can upload multiple documents. All the files selected will be transferred and then the user is prompted to define the attributes for each file separately. If you want to put many documents into Content Management, all with the same attributes use the Site Server Tag Tool. Note that the Tag Tool is restricted to tagging HTML documents.

If you are following along with the CMsample application, trying uploading a document at this point. The next screen you will see is to select a content type that describes the category that the document belongs in:

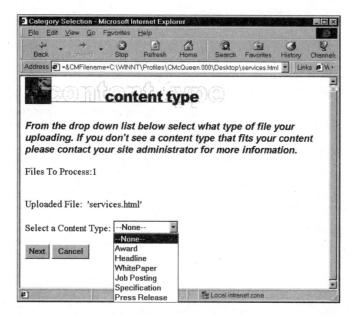

This is the file `type.asp`. It dynamically determines the content types in your Membership Directory and puts them in a drop down box. The code that does this is in `/SiteServer/Publishing/submit.inc`. Let's have a look at it. It is a good example of how to walk through the LDAP hierarchy.

> Since `type.asp` relies on getting information from the LDAP Server if it is not working this page will fail.

When working with LDAP the first step is to get the path to the root of the Membership Directory hierarchy (in order to be able to bind to it later on), as we can see highlighted here.

```
Sub LoadContentList
    Dim    oApp, arrDocTypeList, strRootPath, I, oUser, oDocType, strDN

    On Error Resume Next

    strRootPath = GetLDAPRoot()
    If Len(strRootPath) = 0 Then
        DumpError "Failed to get ADS Root Path"
        Exit Sub
    End If
```

Next, an Active User Object for the user doing the query is instantiated. This object is required to set the security context for ADSI queries.

> *The Active User Object (AUO) is a server-side COM object, which, when instantiated, retrieves the context of the current user using the `OnStartPage` method. We can then use this user object to bind to the Membership Directory and retrieve further information, assuming of course that the current user has the requisite permissions. We'll look at the AUO in detail in Chapter 10, Personalization. You can also find details of the three interfaces it consists of in Appendix E.*

```
Set oUser = Server.CreateObject(UserProgId)
If Err.Number <> 0 Then
        DumpError "Failed to get user object"
        Exit Sub
End If
```

We then bind to the area of the LDAP hierarchy that contains the application and obtain the `DocumentTypes` property with the `GetObjectAsUser()` method. Note that `ApplicationName` is defined in the file `config.inc`, which is in the root directory of your content store.

```
Set oApp = oUser.GetObjectAsUser(strRootPath & "/ou=Applications/appName=" & _
                                 ApplicationName)
If Err.Number <> 0 Then
        DumpError "Failed to get Application object as user"
        Exit Sub
End If

arrDocTypeList = oApp.GetEx("DocumentTypes")
```

Since `DocumentTypes` is a multi-valued property, we iterated through it as a collection to get all the values.

```
For I = 0 To UBound(arrDocTypeList)
        Set oDocType = oUser.GetObjectAsUser(strRootPath & _

"/ou=Admin/ou=Other/ou=DocumentClasses/cn=" & _
                                        arrDocTypeList(I))

        strDN = ""
        strDN = oDocType.GetEx("displayName")(0)
        If strDN = "" Then strDN = arrDocTypeList(I)
        Err.Clear

        ContentList_Callback arrDocTypeList(I), strDN
    Next
End Sub
```

Note the use of a callback subroutine to return each document type. The callback subroutine is in the file `type.asp` and as you can see it is used to populate a combo box. If you want to customize the content type selection user interface (for instance mark a specific option as 'selected'), this is where you would do it.

```
<%
    ' ===============================================================================
    ' Callback procedure for the LoadContentList function

    Sub ContentList_Callback(strName, strDescription)
            Response.Write "<OPTION VALUE=""" & strName & """>" & strDescription &
CrLf
    End Sub
%>
```

Once submitted, there is a test to see if the file already exists in the directory it will be moved to. If so, the user is redirected to a page (`Exists.asp`) that prompts if the file should be overwritten. Otherwise, the user moves on to `GetProps.asp`. You can see this logic in the function `ProcessContentType` in `submit.inc`.

```
If fFileExists = True Then
    Response.Redirect "Exists.asp?" & BuildTypeRedirectURL(g_arrFileList)
Else
    Response.Redirect "GetProps.asp" & BuildTypeRedirectURL(g_arrFileList)
End If
```

In CMsample, `GetProps.asp` will generate the following page if you select 'whitepaper' as the content type.

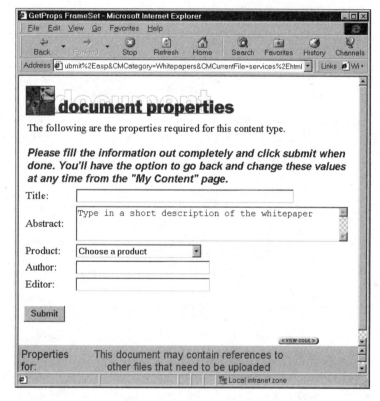

The ASP code `GetProps.asp` looks fairly simple, but it does a lot. It calls a function `GetPropertyPage()` that dynamically forms the file name of the ASP page that will be called. It is obtained from the Content Store attribute 'HTMLForm' for the content type you selected. This page was generated at the time you created that content type.

In this file the subroutine `GenerateLoadFormCode` determines the attributes for the content type you selected. It will also attempt to pre-populate the values of the attributes. Let's look at a section of code in the subroutine `BuildPropertyList` which is called from `GenerateLoadFormCode`.

```
If Not GetOLEProps(strUploadedFile) Then
    If Not GetHTMLProps(Filename) Then
        Response.Write "This file is neither HTML or a Compound Document<BR>"
    End If
End If
```

This is the logic that attempts to get any attributes embedded in the file being uploaded. It 'works' by failure. First it attempts to parse out OLE properties that exist in Microsoft Office documents (e.g. Word, Excel) using GetOLEProps. The parsing of the document is done through the COM object SiteServer.DocProp.1. If this fails it tries to parse the file as HTML using GetHTMLProps. The HTML parsing is done using the COM object TagAuto.TagDocument.1. If this fails it does nothing else. It is curious though that there is a line commented out in the shipping version of Site Server indicating the file is neither HTML nor a Compound Document.

This method can cause serious problems if you are trying to publish files other than Office documents or HTML (e.g. images, Adobe .pdf). Site Server will try to parse any non-Office file as an HTML document even if it is a binary format. If you are lucky, it continues on and you can successfully publish your file. If you are unlucky, the COM object TagAuto.TagDocument.1 gets into a bad loop causing the CPU utilization on the web server machine to skyrocket. I have had cases where some .pdf files caused it to go to 100%. In addition, the client who submitted the document will hang and eventually time out. Not a good situation!

How can you solve the problem so that a non-Office, non-HTML document can be published? Part of the key is in the file LibCM.inc. The file LibCM.inc seems to have better code quality than submit.inc. For instance, LibCM.inc uses constants to define Prog IDs whereas submit.inc does not. Let's look at a section of code in LibCM.inc in the function SaveProperties that is similar to what we've just looked at in submit.inc.

```
    If Not SaveOLEProps(Filepath, Cat, fSaveInternal, PropertyList) Then
        If IsHTMLFile(FilePath) Then
            If Not SaveHTMLProps(Filepath, Cat, fSaveInternal, PropertyList) Then
                DebPrint "Failed to save properties for " & Filepath
                SaveProperties = False
            End If
        Else
            'Open or Create a stub file
            If Not SaveStubProps(Filepath, Cat, fSaveInternal, PropertyList) Then
                DebPrint "Failed to save properties for " & Filepath & " in Stub
file"
                SaveProperties = False
            End If
        End If
    End If
```

It again relies on a function failing for the OLE properties but notice there is a test to see if the file is HTML before it goes ahead to try and parse it. I recommend taking a similar approach and modifying submit.inc to use IsHTMLFile before GetHTMLProps is called. (Of course you are still at risk from someone naming a binary file with the file extension .htm)

Once the attribute values are assigned to the file and submitted, the document is moved out of the Upload directory to either the directory for the Content Type or to the Approval directory if approval is required. If the document is not an HTML document a stub HTML file is created at this point (as can be seen in the code listed above). The stub file is described in detail in the Content Stores section later.

My Content

After you have submitted a new document, choose the "My Content" menu item. This page displays all the content submitted by you. From here you can edit content attributes or delete content from Content Management. When you select EDIT CONTENT, Site Server uses the same parsing logic to obtain document attributes as before when submitting files. However, at this point, a stub file has been created for non-HTML files so you are not at risk of Site Server trying to parse a binary file as HTML. However, if you have changed the submission process to account for non-HTML, non-Office documents you should make sure that the edit content option still works.

If you have just published a file you may not see it in the list. Content does not appear in the Content Management system until Microsoft Index Server has made its rounds to index new files. If this if the case, you will actually see the following icon that indicates the index is not up-to-date. After a couple minutes the index will have incorporated the new information.

Now that we've seen a bit about what Content Management is and how it works, we're now in a position to consider planning for its implementation on a web site.

Planning

Because much of a Content Management implementation is configuration, planning plays an important part in building the solution. Planning the solution prior to implementation results in a better overall system. Planning models the business process of managing content. Planning a Content Management application consists of three areas:

> defining the content used in the application
> defining roles of users
> determining how content is accessed

Content Definition

Content Definition is similar to defining the 'classes' used in an object-oriented application. A submitted file is an instance of content similar to how an object is an instance of a class. Defining content consists of defining Content Types and Content Attributes for each of the types.

Content Stores

When your documents are uploaded using content management, they are published to a **content store**, which is basically an area on a web site that has been configured to work with Site Server Content Management. A content store is physically represented by one or more directories, into which content posted to your site is placed.

Looking back at the MDM, click on the ou=Admin/ou=Other/ou=ContentClasses container, shown in the next screenshot, to reveal the content stores which have been installed on the site. All content stores that are created *for a specific membership instance*, have an entry placed here. If in the web site you create the Content Store is mapped to another Membership Directory, then the content store will be found in the same container location within that directory (i.e. you need to bind to the other instance as described a couple of sections ago).

The default installation we followed earlier has installed two entries, namely cn=FpSample-ContentManagement and cn=CmSample-ContentManagement, of Type 'TripoliSource' (the Type used by Content Management stores). Other content sources, such as Knowledge Manager sources, which are looked in a later chapter, are also stored here. The screenshot illustrates the entries within this container.

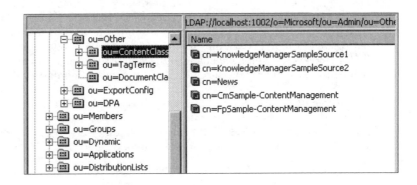

These two sample sites, which are provided with Publishing, namely FPsample and CMsample, are content stores which you can customize for your own site. Later on, we shall be creating an empty content store, as well as a customized content store based on FPsample.

All content that is placed into content stores is tagged as being a specific content type. Let's look at what that means now.

Content Types

Content Types are the categories of content (such as the specifications, project plans, and status reports mentioned in the WebSoft Scenario) used within an organization. The Content Types don't need to be just documents; "Employee Photos" could be a Content Type for pictures of employees in an organization. Similarly, the submitted files don't have to be the same file type within a Content Type. For example, the "Employee Photos" Content Type could contain GIF, JPEG and bitmap files (or even a Word document).

This structure is represented by directories within the content site, each Content Type having a directory of the same name where its documents are stored. So if you have a Content Type called "Headlines", a directory called Headlines will be created within the root of your content store and all "Headlines" documents will be stored there. Each content type is also stored within the Membership Directory Manager under the ou=Admin/ou=Other/ou=DocumentClasses container. You can see this by clicking on the ou=DocumentClasses container in the MDM, as shown in the following screenshot.

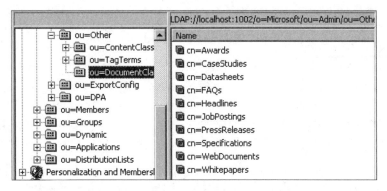

When content is posted to your content store, it is tagged with one of these Content Types using tools provided with Site Server, which we shall see in action later in the chapter. You therefore now have the ability to group all the "PressReleases", for example, which have been posted to your site by content providers. Content Types are useful for gathering documents of the same general type, but we can also apply attributes to further define each document. We shall look at this now.

As you plan for your implementation of Content Management the first step is to decide what Content Types exist within your organization and write them out in a list. Let's make a list for the WebSoft Scenario:

- Contracts
- Budgets
- Requirements
- Project Plans
- Status Reports

With this as a starting point, we need to assign attributes to each of the Content Types.

Content Attributes

Content Attributes describe some aspect of a Content Type such as author, title and keywords. When attributes are assigned to submitted content, they become properties of that content. Content Attributes are used to manage content posted to your site, to define search criteria for finding content and to produce reports using Site Analyst (see Chapter 12, "*Using Site Analyst*").

If possible, each attribute is stored within the file, as meta-tags in HTML documents and in the document properties of Excel and Word documents. Documents for which information cannot be directly written into the file (e.g. .exe files) have a HTML stub file created for them which stores the content attributes as meta-tags and has a redirect to the actual file.

The ou=Admin/ou=Other/ou=TagTerms container defines a hierarchy of logically related items known as the Site Vocabulary which are used to tag documents. So, for example, the "Document" Content Type may have attributes defined in the Site Vocabulary such as "Author", "Creation Date" and "Security Level".

We also have the ability to create our own custom Content Types. We shall look at exactly at how we create these using Site Server later in the chapter, but the following diagram shows the range of attributes types and their syntax types that can be created:

> **String** – An attribute accepts a string value; e.g. `"Author"`

> **Binary** – A property has a TRUE/FALSE value; e.g. `Expired`

> **Integer** – The attribute accepts only Integer values; e.g. `DocumentId`

> **Generalized Time** – The property has a time as its value; e.g. `LastUpdate`

> **Enumerated List** – The attribute accepts one of a number of user-defined values; e.g. `Public | Private`

> **Vocabulary Term** – The property is one of the site vocabulary, which is a hierarchical tree containing possible values which an administrator can define for a site.

> **Distinguished Name** – A distinguished name defined in the membership directory.

In our Content Management process, once you have decided on Content Types, you need to choose the attributes for each Content Type. Let's choose some attributes for WebSoft Consulting (the Content Management scenario introduced earlier in the chapter). Some attributes will be common across all content types and some attributes will only be for specific types of content.

	ATTRIBUTES				
	Author	**Submission Date**	**Title**	**Project Code**	**Account Number**
Contracts	X	X	X		
Budgets	X	X	X	X	X
Requirements	X	X	X	X	
Project Plans	X	X	X	X	
Status Reports	X	X	X	X	

Users and Groups

So far we've categorized and described the type of content to be used on the web site. We have not discussed who will create the content and who will use the published content. Obviously, people that use the Content Management application have different roles and thus fall into different categories or groups. Three groups of users are Content Producers, Content Editors and Content Consumers.

A Content Producer is someone who creates and publishes content to a web site. The Content Producer is the source of the information. A Content Editor controls the publication of content to a web site. Some content may be published directly but others may require an approval step before they are made available to the Content Consumers. A Content Consumer reads the content published on a web site.

The users will fall into at least one of these three groups. The first step is determining who the application's users are. Then each of these users will be assigned permissions according to what their roles and responsibilities are within the Content Management application.

For the WebSoft scenario we will use the following generic users:

> President
> Office Administrator
> Project Manager
> Developer
> Client Manager
> Client Developer

The terms "Client Managers" and "Client Developers" refer to clients of WebSoft. They are not WebSoft employees yet are interested in the documentation produced with respect to their project. Let's look at how each of these users falls into the Content groups.

Content Producers

For WebSoft, the Content Producers are the President, Product Managers and the Office Administrator. The Project Managers create all the documents associated with their projects and are responsible for maintaining them throughout the project. The Office Administrator is responsible for creating budget spreadsheets and filing business related documents such as contracts. The following chart indicates the relationship between who will be creating which types of content. 'Some' indicates the person will only be publishing content for their assigned projects.

	CONTENT TYPE				
	Contracts	Budgets	Requirements	Project Plans	Status Reports
President	All				
Project Manager		Some	Some	Some	Some
Office Admin	All	All			

Content Editors

For WebSoft, the President wants to see Budgets before they are published on the web site so Budgets are identified as requiring approval before being published. This will be the only Content Type requiring approval.

	CONTENT TYPE				
	Contracts	Budgets	Requirements	Project Plans	Status Reports
Approval Required	No	Yes	No	No	No

Content Consumers

The consumers with WebSoft are the Project Managers, Developers, President and Office Administrator. The consumers with the client are Client Manager and Client Developer. The following chart indicates who will be accessing which content.

	CONTENT TYPE				
	Contracts	Budgets	Requirements	Project Plans	Status Reports
President	All	All	All	All	All
Project Manager		Some	Some	Some	Some
Project Developer			Some	Some	
Office Admin	All	All			
Client Manager	Some		Some	Some	Some
Client Developer			Some	Some	

Accessing Content

Once content is "in the system" there have to be methods to access it. To a Site Server developer, accessing content comes down to returning lists of content based on certain criteria. However, to a user, it is usually visually accessible in two ways: as a predefined list or by explicitly executing a search. Another important consideration is deciding if access to certain content should be restricted.

For planning your Content Management application decide which content you will want available as a linear list and which content the user will be able to find using a query.

Lists of Content

Lists of content are usually a pre-configured list. All the content access in CMsample is created this way. The lists are usually constrained by time, such as press releases of the week, or as an ordinal list, such as the top ten projects which have overrun the budget. Often the list is constrained using the Content Type (such as "whitepapers" in CMsample). However, the list can also be created based on the Content Attributes.

For lists of content, you as a Site Server developer decide the search criteria. This makes it easy for the users to navigate the user interface because the only decision they have to make is which link to click on. However, the ease of use results in sacrificing flexibility. To make the application more flexible, creating the search criteria is put in the hands of the user.

For WebSoft consulting, they will have many different lists depending upon the view desired by the user. One list might be a view for the President that lists all documents of Content Type equal to "Contract" published in the last month. Another view might be for a Project Manager that lists many documents of different Content Types belonging to the same project (that is the attribute "Project Code" would be the same for all documents in the list).

Searching for Content

Sometimes a predefined query such as "whitepapers" will not get the content a user wants. For example, a user might want a list of content across all Content Types for a specific product. In this case, the user is able to provide parameters to the query to customize the content search. Creating a parameterized query will be covered in the section on Rulesets.

In the planning phase, you must find out what types of queries the user will want to perform to find documents.

For WebSoft Consulting, a search may be provided to find all documents published by a particular person. Another search may be provided to find all contracts belonging to a particular Account Number.

Controlling Access

Finally, once the users and Content Types have been identified, you must decide which users have access to which content. The easiest way to control access to content is based on Content Types.

Merging the tables already created in the Content Producers and Content Consumers sections would create a permissions table for WebSoft Consulting.

| | CONTENT TYPE | | | | |
	Contracts	Budgets	Requirements	Project Plans	Status Reports
President	RW	R	R	R	R
Project Manager	None	RW*	RW*	RW*	RW*
Developer	None	None	R*	R*	None
Office Admin	RW	RW	None	None	None
Client Manager	R*	None	R*	R*	R*
Client Developer	None	None	R*	R*	None

Where:

> ➢ R – read access
> ➢ W – write access
> ➢ None – no access at all
> ➢ * - only for specific projects

So for example, Developers can read (but cannot create) Requirements content for the projects they are working on. Similarly, the President can read and create all Contract content.

Planning Summary

The planning process outlined here provides a strong base for implementing Content Management. At the end of the planning process, you should have a document with tables similar to the ones described in the previous sections. Planning gets the business issues out the way and allows you to focus on technical issues during implementation.

Implementation

Now that the groundwork is finished it is time to put the plan into action. The implementation steps parallel the planning steps just covered. First we will create the Content Store which contains the Content Types and Content Attributes. Then assigning content permissions to users and groups will be discussed. Finally the content will be made accessible by building some ASP code.

What is a Content Store?

We mentioned the Content Store earlier in the chapter. Content Management revolves around a Content Store. A Content Store is the storage facility for published content and its attributes. It is possible to create and use a Content Store without knowing what is going on behind the scenes. However, to assist debugging and recovering when things go wrong (as they always seem to) it is best to understand how a Content Store works.

We have already seen that the Content Store "class" is stored in a Personalization and Membership (P&M) Membership Directory. Because the Content Store is stored in a Membership Directory, it can be shared with other services such as P&M, Analysis and Microsoft Content Index Server. As well, this means the Content Types and the Content Attributes are stored in the Membership Directory that, in the Microsoft recommended installation, in turn resides in a SQL Server database. The type of database depends on how you configure the Membership Directory (see P&M chapter), but we will stick with SQL Server here.

You can have multiple Content Stores for a web application. Each Content Store has a file system directory associated with it. The web server maps a virtual directory to the file system directory where the Content Store exists. Under the Content Store directory there are subdirectories for each Content Type. Note that the published content is not stored in a database; rather, it is stored as a file in the file system and is served via HTTP just like any other file that is served by your web server.

The Content Attributes values for a content item are stored as HTML <META> tags. <META> tags provide additional information about an HTML document. The information is provided as name-value pairs within the <META> tag such as "Title=My Favorite Document". There is one name-value pair for each <META> tag. When Index Server indexes the directory containing the content it uses the <META> tags as part of the indexing process. With this information stored, a query for a document can be made to Index Server based on any of the <META> tags and thus on the Content Attributes.

But wait – what if you are publishing documents that aren't HTML? If the stored content is not an HTML document, an HTML 'stub' document is created which contains the <META> tags and a link to the content file. The following is an example of a 'stub' document that might be created for a WebSoft Consulting functional requirements document:

```
<!DOCTYPE HTML PUBLIC "-//W3C//DTD HTML 3.2//EN">
<!-- Microsoft Site Server Stub File -->
<HTML><HEAD>
<META NAME="Title" CONTENT="Project X Functional Requirements">
<META NAME="PublicationDate" CONTENT="4/23/99">
<META NAME="Publisher" CONTENT="JCM">
<META NAME="Project" CONTENT="MEGA-X">
<META NAME="Owner" CONTENT="cmcqueen">
<META NAME="SubmitTime" CONTENT="1999/04/26 14:30:25">
<META NAME="ContentType" CONTENT="Requirements">
<META NAME="Approved" CONTENT="Yes">
<META NAME="GENERATOR" CONTENT="Microsoft Site Server">
<META HTTP-EQUIV="Content-Type" CONTENT="text/html; CHARSET=ISO-8859-1">
<META HTTP-EQUIV="Refresh" CONTENT="0; URL=funcReq.doc">
<TITLE>DPS Stub Properties File</TITLE>
</HEAD><BODY>
<A HREF="funcReq.doc">
If your browser doesn't support automatic refresh,
select this link to retrieve the real document
</A></BODY></HTML>
```

Let's look at the various pieces of the stub document. The document is a valid HTML document, with <HTML>, <HEAD> and <BODY> elements. The <META> tags record the attributes of the document that the stub file points to. In this example, the 'Publisher' attribute is 'JCM'.

Also notice the HTTP-EQUIV attributes in the <META> elements. These elements are added to the HTTP response header if the browser supports them. For instance, the "Refresh" HTTP-EQUIV command tells the browser to load a different document. In this case, the stub file redirects to the actual document (e.g. funcReq.doc).

Let's review with the diagram opposite. The Content Store directory is at the top and each of the Content Type directories are below it. The submitted files are contained in the Content Type directories. If the submitted file is not an HTML document then an HTML stub is created (the shaded object in the diagram) that points to the actual content file.

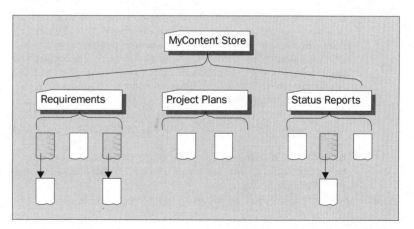

Publishing to the Content Store

When a file is published, it is transferred from the client computer via HTTP to the web server. The web server moves it to an upload directory. When the process is complete it is moved from the upload directory to the subdirectory belonging to the content type unless it is marked for requiring approval. There is an Approve directory that is a temporary stored area for documents as they wait for approval.

Uploading Files

A key piece of Content Management is the ability to upload files to a web server. If this piece doesn't work Content Management is useless. For this reason, let's look at the upload process and the participating technologies.

HTTP Post

"HTTP Post" is a proposed Internet standard for uploading files using HTTP. It is described in the document "Form-based File Upload in HTML" and can be downloaded from `ftp://ds.internic.net/rfc/rfc1867.txt`. The browser has to know how to upload the file and the web server needs to know how to receive a posted file. Microsoft Internet Explorer 3.02 or later, and Netscape Navigator 2.02 or later support HTTP Post. As we noted earlier in the chapter, Site Server tries to improve upon the native browser upload by providing an ActiveX Upload control (which is described below). Site Server detects if the browser supports ActiveX; if it does code is sent to the browser to use it, otherwise the browser uses the native HTTP Post functionality.

Microsoft Posting Acceptor

Site Server uses the Microsoft Posting Acceptor as the method of receiving files. Posting Acceptor exists on the web server and comes with a number of Active Server Pages. See the Site Server documentation or the Internet Information Server documentation for details about the Posting Acceptor.

> If you change the default document of your web site that provides file uploading you may get a dialog box with the message "The Web server you have selected does not indicate support for the service provider you selected." The posting acceptor inserts a `<META>` tag into the default document and if this `<META>` tag does not exist it cannot find the `postinfo.asp` file (which is used to obtain configuration information). The solution is to make sure the default document has the following line:
>
> `<META NAME="postinfo" CONTENT="/scripts/postinfo.asp">`
>
> In addition, if your site's default page performs a re-direct, then make sure you call `Response.Flush` so that section of HTML makes it to the client before redirecting.

File Upload ActiveX Control

The File Upload ActiveX Control is used by Site Server to provide more value to the user above standard HTTP Post. If the user doesn't have it installed, they will be prompted as to whether they wish to download it (depending on their security settings). Consider if your users are willing to download an ActiveX Control. If it is an issue in your organization (as part of its security policies) you may want to force Site Server to use HTTP Post.

The following code is taken from the submission page and shows how the File Upload control is included in the web page.

```
<OBJECT
    CLASSID="clsid:886E7BF0-C867-11CF-B1AE-00AA00A3F2C3"
    ID=UploadIt WIDTH=60 HEIGHT=60 ALIGN=textmiddle COLOR=green
    CODEBASE=http://webserver/SiteServer/Publishing/FlUpl.cab#Version=7,0,783,0>
    <PARAM NAME="AlternateGraphic" VALUE=1></PARAM>
</OBJECT>
```

If you are interested in customizing how the File Upload control behaves (or are just interested in the options available) you can have a look at it on an installed machine using an object browser. The file name is Flupl.ocx, so you can attach Visual Basic to it and look at its methods and properties with the object browser (as displayed in the picture opposite).

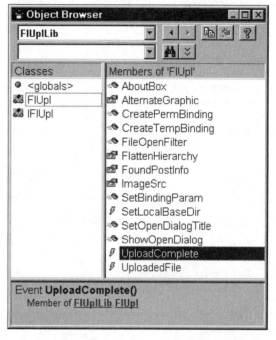

Details of the API for the Upload control are in the "Web Publishing Programmer's Reference" under "The File Upload Control Interface".

Multiple File Upload

There may be situations where you have many documents that you want to upload and they all have the same attributes. In these situations use the Site Server "Tag Tool". Tag tool can only be used for HTML documents but is a convenient way to set the <META> tags. With Tag Tool you can select many documents and assign the same set of attributes to them.

WebSoft Consulting has a number of HTML documents used as functional specifications for a particular project. They could use Tag Tool to assign the same Project Code to all the documents in one operation.

Microsoft Index Server

Microsoft Index Server indexes the contents and properties of files used by Internet Information Server. The Content Attributes stored in the HTML pages' <META> tags are recorded by Index Server. This makes it possible to search for content based on Content Attributes.

Note that Content Management does not use Site Server Search (which is discussed in a later chapter). Site Server Search is for indexing documents from diverse sources by explicitly 'crawling' the documents. Index Server is for indexing documents in a file system. Since all of Content Management is through the file system, Index Server is used. Index Server also receives file system notifications when documents change or are added. It then indexes them after receiving the notification.

As we shall see a little later on, Site Server comes with a script called makeCM.vbs that automatically performs the configuration to create a Content Store. The script configures Index Server to include the new Content Store in the list of directories it indexes. The following code is a section of the script file that adds the Content Store to the index.

```
Set oCI = CreateObject(ContentIndexProgId)
If Err.Number <> 0 Then
        DumpError "Failed to get Content Index cache object"
        Exit Function
End If

oCI.AddScopeToCatalog "ContentManagement", strApplicationDir, 1
If Err.Number <> 0 Then
        DumpError "Failed to set Add Scope " & strApplicationDir & " to Content Index"
        Exit Function
End If
```

After the script has run, you can go into Index Server administrator (ciadmin) and see the Content Store listed as in the following screen shot.

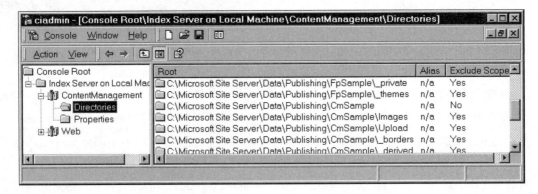

Multiple Approval

There may be cases where you want to have multiple approval stages before a document is published. Just as Content Management is not supposed to be an enterprise document management system it is also not a workflow system. However, with a little bit of customization, you can have a multiple approval process with Site Server. The details are listed in a Microsoft white paper, which can be obtained at
http://www.microsoft.com/siteserver/site/30/whitepapers/MultipleApproval.htm.

WebSoft Consulting might want to implement multiple approvals if they want press releases to be approved by the Director of Marketing and then the President before they are published to their web site.

With some modifications, the instructions for multistage approval can be made to include versioning of submitted documents. You need to add an attribute for the document version number and put previous document versions in other directories for storage. As well, you would need to construct ASP code for retrieving earlier versions of documents.

Creating a Content Store

Creating a Content Store basically involves configuring a number of pieces installed on Site Server including Internet Information Server and a Membership Directory. You could configure all the pieces manually to create a Content Store, however, as we mentioned earlier, Site Server comes with a script called `makeCM.vbs` that does this automatically.

This script can also be extended to automatically create Content Types and Content Attributes. The `makeCM.vbs` file with each of the sample sites has been customized to automatically create the Content Types and Content Attributes specific to those Content Stores. The advantage of extending the script is that you will have a script that automatically configures your entire Content Store to the point where you can immediately upload documents. You will also have a script that makes it easy to create a Content Store with an identical schema on another machine. The disadvantage is that if Content Types or Content Attributes are added via WebAdmin or MMC the script becomes out-of-date.

For our demonstration we are not going to modify the `makeCM.vbs` script. This means the Content Store will be created but we will have to manually add the Content Types and Content Attributes. Let's walk through the steps of configuring a Content Store.

Create a subdirectory on your Site Server machine to contain the Content Store. Microsoft recommends that it be in the path `Microsoft Site Server\Data\Publishing`, however you are free to use any other directory location. The important point to consider is that the web server needs to serve documents out of that directory so it must have the correct permissions. Also if you backup your web site you will want to make sure the directory you specify for the Content Store is in the list of backed up directories.
Copy `makeCM.vbs` from `Microsoft Site Server\Siteserver\Publishing` to the directory you created.

Copy the following files from `Microsoft Site Server\Data\Publishing\CMsample` to the directory you created. We looked at some of these files earlier as we walked through CMsample.

> ➤ `saveprops.asp`
> ➤ `getprops.asp`
> ➤ `type.asp`
> ➤ `common.asp`
> ➤ `submit.asp`
> ➤ `mydocs.prf`
> ➤ `cpview.asp`
> ➤ `approve.asp`
> ➤ `approve.prf`

- ➢ adminlist.asp
- ➢ exists.asp
- ➢ repost.asp
- ➢ defaultviewtemplate.ast
- ➢ files.asp
- ➢ filename.asp
- ➢ deploy.asp

Open the cmd program and at the command prompt change to the directory you created earlier. Type:

```
cscript makeCM.vbs /s:<web server name> /v:<vroot for content store> /a:<storename>
/d:<"full directory path of store">
```

The four parameters in angle brackets are all the required parameters to run the script. See the Site Server documentation for a list of all the required and optional parameters. For WebSoft, the command line would look something like:

```
cscript makeCM.vbs /s:webserver /v:WebSoftContent /a:WebSoftContent
/d:"c:\microsoft site server\siteserver\publishing\WebSoftContent"
```

The following the table describes all the command line arguments available for makeCM.vbs.

Parameter	Description	Optional/Required
/s:<server>	Replace <server> with the name of the Web server on which the vroot will be created. (The LDAP server is derived from this information unless supplied in the /l:<LDAP server> parameter.)	Required
/v:<vroot>	Used to specify a name for the vroot to create and configure for this Content Management site.	Required
/a:<application>	Lets you set a unique name used to store information about this site in the LDAP server.	Required
/w:<virtual web server instance>	The name of your virtual web server.	Optional
/d:<directory>	Full path of the directory containing the Content Management site you are using makeCM.vbs to build.	Required
/l:<ldap server>	Sets the name of the LDAP server to write information about your site to. This can contain the port number (for example, /l:LDAPservername:1002).	Optional

Parameter	Description	Optional/Required
/u:<username>	Name of a user that has the authority to create all Content Management information in the LDAP server.	Required (see note below)
/p:<password>	Sets the password for a given user name.	Required (see note below)
/uninstall	Uninstalls the site. Performs a full uninstall except for the user files and Content Types.	Optional
/RemoveUserFiles	Removes all user files in an install. Must be specified with /uninstall.	Optional
/RemoveDocTypes	Removes all Content Types in the site: both CMsample and FPsample type sites. Must be specified with /uninstall.	Optional

> One very important optional parameter to makeCM.vbs is /l:<ldap server>. If you have already created a Membership Directory for Personalization and Membership you want to make sure that same Membership Directory is used for your Content Store. This is because you can only associate one Membership Directory to a web site. For example, if your P&M Membership Directory is running on port 1003 you would use /l:localhost:1003.
>
> Additionally, if your Membership Server is not using Windows NT Lan Manager (NTLM), you will need to provide a username and password on the command line with /u and /p.

To see if your Content Store was created, go into the Publishing component of WebAdmin (i.e. http://<webserver>/SiteServer/Admin/Publishing/) and select "Content Management". Select the Membership Directory you are using and login. You should then see your Content Store. The table below outlines the main pages and their functions:

Page	Function
Submit.asp	Content providers post their content to the web store via an ActiveX Control (Internet Explorer users) or using HTTP Post (RFC1867)
Approve.asp	Content administrators can approve, edit and deploy files which have been uploaded
Cpview.asp	Content providers can edit and remove previously submitted documents of which they are the owner

Table Continued on Following Page

Page	Function
`DefaultViewTemplate.ast`	The template file from which all pages are created. This can be customized for your site
`Approve.prf`	Contains rules for approving documents and can be customized using the Rule Manager
`Menu.txt`	Stores the navigational structure for your site and can be customized

Creating a Custom Content Store

At this point you will need the files from `WroxStore.zip` which are part of the download files for this book, available from the Wrox Web Site, `http://www.wrox.com`

Now that you know what the basic files are and what they do, let's take a look at what is involved in creating a custom Content Store. Navigate to `C:\Microsoft Site Server\Data\Publishing` and create an empty directory called **WroxStore**.

Now, unzip the `WroxStore.zip` files into the `WroxStore` directory. The following files should be shown in the directory you created.

Name △	Size	Type
images		File Fold
ADMINLIST.ASP	2 KB	Active S
approve.asp	3 KB	Active S
approve.prf	7 KB	RuleSet
background.gif	1 KB	GIF Imaɡ
common.asp	1 KB	Active S
config.inc	1 KB	INC File
cpview.asp	2 KB	Active S
default.asp	3 KB	Active S
DefaultViewTempl...	3 KB	AST File
DEPLOY.ASP	2 KB	Active S
Exists.asp	2 KB	Active S
FileName.asp	2 KB	Active S
FILES.ASP	3 KB	Active S
GetProps.asp	1 KB	Active S
horz.gif	1 KB	GIF Imaɡ
leftnav.gif	5 KB	GIF Imaɡ
makeCM.vbs	63 KB	VBScript
menu.txt	3 KB	Text Doɡ
mydocs.prf	7 KB	RuleSet
repost.asp	1 KB	Active S
SaveProps.asp	2 KB	Active S
submit.asp	4 KB	Active S
Type.asp	3 KB	Active S
welcome.GIF	5 KB	GIF Imaɡ

You will no doubt recognise many of the files used in creating an empty content store that are copied from the CMsample site. However, some of these have to be customized for each store, so let's look at the files that have been customized for our WroxStore Content Management site.

Customizing DefaultViewTemplate.ast

DefaultViewTemplate.ast contains the template for all of the view files that will be generated by the Content Store, so instead of customizing each and every file after creation, we can simply customize this template file to create a consistent look.

> **The first and most important thing to do is to replace all instances of the name "cmsample" with the name of your new store (in our case "WroxStore"), so that all the links created in each view file point to your new store.**

Let's walk through the code. Below is the first section of the file.

```
<!--#include file="common.asp" -->
<html>

<head>
<title>Datasheets</title>
<meta name="GENERATOR" content="Microsoft FrontPage 3.0">

<meta name="Microsoft Theme" content="none, default"><meta name="Microsoft Border"
content="none, default"></head>

<body background="images/background.gif" bgcolor="#000080" topmargin="0"
leftmargin="0">

<table width="100%">
  <tr>
    <td valign="TOP"><table border="0" width="24%">
      <tr>
        <td width="100%">
          <!--#include File="menu.txt" -->
        </td>
      </tr>
    </table>
    </td>
    <td valign="TOP"><table width="100%">
      <tr>
        <td style="margin-left: 10px"><font face="arial"></font>
        <font face="Verdana" size="2">
      </tr>
    <tr><td><% =g_fntStartInstructions %>
    Use the View Code button to see the rule that displays content.
  <% =g_fntEndInstructions %>
  </td></tr>
<tr><td><table>
```

Notice that the first line includes common.asp, which contains information for checking that a valid user is requesting the page and some constants that will be used throughout the files. Running through the code, the next important line is the #include instruction for menu.txt, a file that holds the navigation format for the site, to be included in every page. Note also the use of the constant g_fntStartInstructions which is part of common.asp and simply defines the format of the text in the menu.

Finally, the section of code starting with:

```
<!--METADATA TYPE="DesignerControl" startspan
<OBJECT ID="FormatRuleset1" WIDTH=487 HEIGHT=237 CLASSID="CLSID:F78EAED2-F867-11D0-
9F89-
    0000F8040D4E">
```

... and ending:

```
<!--METADATA TYPE="DesignerControl" endspan-->
```

... is best left as it is. It defines a design-time control (`Membership.FormatRuleSet`) which returns a recordset according to the rules defined in the rules document it uses. The Personalization and Membership Site Server help documents have more detail on working with the `FormatRuleSet` DTC.

It is worth noting that the following line has been removed and should be for all files in your Content Store.

```
<!--#include Virtual="/SiteServer/Publishing/codeview.inc" -->
```

This is only used in development to view the code that makes up the page.

You can add a theme in `DefaultViewTemplate.ast`, and change the page colors and background image to affect all pages. For our purposes, we will look at the `menu.txt` file, which describes the basic menu hierarchy that will be displayed on all pages. This file should point to the following file types, and needs to be updated if changes to the structure of the store are made:

> All of the view pages (this is done automatically using a Rule, as shown below)
> Submission page
> Content Provider View Page
> Approval Page

The code below shows the new code for `menu.txt`:

```
<TABLE width="138" height="359" border="1" VALIGN=TOP BGCOLOR=LIGHTBLUE>
<TR VALIGN=TOP>
<TD>
<CENTER><H2>Wrox Publishing</H2>
<A HREF="approve.asp">Approve Content</a>
<P>
<A HREF="cpview.asp">View My Content</A>
<P>
<A HREF="submit.asp">Submit New Content</A>
<P>
<A HREF="default.asp##_parent">Home</a>
<P>
<HR>
Content
<HR>
<%
    DisplayDefaultViews
```

```
'  ==========================================================================
   Sub DefaultViews_Callback(strURL, strDescription)
      If Len(strDescription) = 0 Then strDescription = strURL
         Response.Write "<BR><A HREF=""" & strURL & """><font color=""white"">" &
   strDescription &
                           "</font>" & CrLf
      End Sub
   %>


</CENTER>
</TD>
</TR>
</TABLE>
```

You should edit the content of the above pages to suit your own site. The new customized Editorial View is shown below:

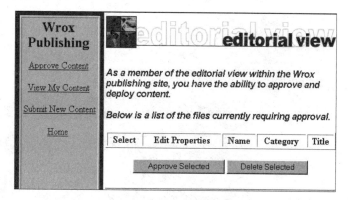

The `default.asp` file included with the WroxStore samples includes the `menu.txt` file by default. In your own Content Management site you may wish to modify the text in the `default.asp` file to suit your own organization's look and feel, but you should not modify any of the ASP (i.e. any code between `<%` and `%>` characters).

We have now configured the files needed for our site and are in a position to actually create the site's Content Store. So, now we shall create WroxStore.

Creating the Store

> **The following instructions assume that you have followed the steps from the beginning of the chapter.**

You now have to create the content store using the following steps:

1. Open a DOS window and at the Command Prompt, change to the directory
`Microsoft Site Server\Data\Publishing\WroxStore`

2. Run the following at the command line:
`cscript makeCM.vbs /s:<servername> /v:WroxStore /a:WroxStore /d:"c:\Microsoft Site Server\Data\Publishing\WroxStore"`
Replacing `<servername>` with the name of your server.

When this command has completed, you should open the Microsoft Management Console and check that the Store application has been created. In our case, we should see the WroxStore application directory as shown in the following screenshot:

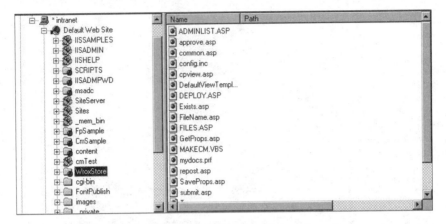

Creating Content Types

If you used the generic makeCM.vbs script you won't have any Content Types yet. Adding Content Types is easiest through WebAdmin. Got to http://<your web server>/ SiteServer/Admin/ Publishing and select "Content Management" from the Menu.

You will then be asked to logon to the appropriate Membership Server with the username and password you specified during installation. Assuming you have got this correct, you will be shown a list of all the content stores within the web site and you should select your storename (WroxStore) and click Properties.

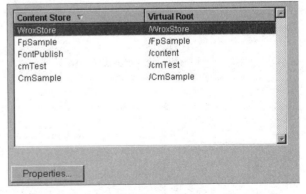

Finally pick "Content Types". From here you can manage the Content Types for your Content Store. As well, from here you can set whether the document requires approval or not. Setting up the Approval mechanism will be discussed later.

Start by selecting the "**Create**" button to create a new Content Type. You should see something similar to the following screen.

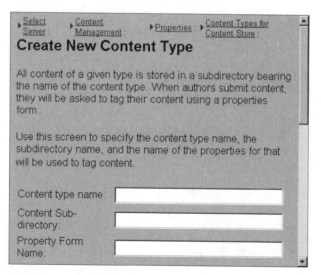

Here you enter the Content Type name. You also enter the name of the sub-directory under the Content Store directory where files for this Content Type will be stored. It can be different from the Content Type name but it is easier to maintain if they are kept the same. The Property Form Name is also specified. This is the ASP that will be generated that contains all the form fields for entering attributes values for submitted content of that type. Again, it can be different but it is easier to keep its name is similar to the Content Type name.

In the Content Type Name textbox, type Books. Pressing *Tab* will automatically fill the Content Sub-Directory and Property Form Name values. Finally, ensure that the Generate Properties Form and Generate View Page checkboxes are both checked and click the Submit button. The page will now refresh and the Content Type Name will be grayed out as read-only. We have now added a new Content Type.

Creating the Property and View Pages

We mentioned above the two check boxes near the end of the "Create New Content Type" form labeled "Generate Properties Form" and "Generate View Page". If checked, some ASP files are automatically generated. Any modifications you make to these files will be overwritten if the files are regenerated. Also, if you place your Content Management project under source control you will need to check out the files before regenerating them otherwise the files will be read-only and the regeneration will fail.

The Content Type configuration that we've just run through has the effect that three files, Books.asp, BooksView.asp and Books.prf, are created. BooksView.asp is added automatically to your menu on every page to allow people to view the content presented there. It appears at the bottom of our WroxStore menu:

The Properties Form is the ASP page used during the submission of content to obtain attributes values for the submitted content. If you add more attributes, you will need to regenerate this page or manually change it. The filename used for the Properties Form page is the one specified in the "Create New Content Type" form (e.g. Books.asp).

The View Page is an ASP file displaying the submitted content in a generic form. Note that it does not display the content itself, rather it displays the attribute values associated with the content. The filename for the View Page is the Properties Form name with 'view' added (e.g. BooksView.asp).

Books.prf is a rule set file for the Content Type. We will deal with rules and rule sets later on in the "Accessing Content" section.

Next, we'll configure the attributes for the new Content Type.

Setting the Content Attributes

Now that we have added a new 'Books' Content Type, we must specify attributes for it. Click on the Add button under the Specify Attributes section.

Standard Attributes

There are a number of Content Attributes already in the Membership Directory that you can use for describing your Content. To add a stock attribute, press the 'Add' button under the text area that lists the Content Type's attributes. A list similar to the following should appear in the web page.

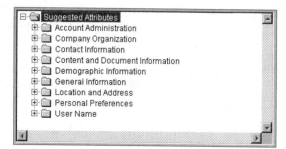

Each category has a number of attributes already in the Membership Directory. Browse through it to get familiar with the available stock attributes. It is easy to use an attribute that already exists and it also maintains naming consistency across the Membership Directory.

Add in the attribute Content Editor that can be found under Content and Document Information as shown here:

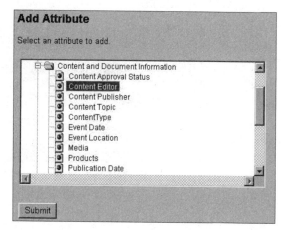

Repeat the above steps for the attribute User Email in under Contact Information. These should both appear in the Attribute box in the Specify Attributes section. Finally, we want to add our own custom attribute.

Custom Attributes

There may be times when an attribute does not exist for your needs. Under Specify Attributes, click the "Create Custom" button beside the "Add" button and you'll be taken to the Create New Attribute entry form. You will see a screen similar to the following.

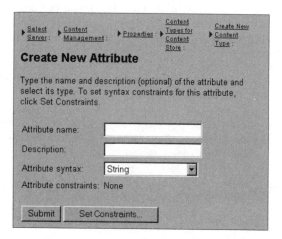

Here you provide the attribute's name and description. You also get to choose a syntax type from the drop down box. If you wish to apply constraints to the attribute's value, such as limiting a string to be between 4 and 10 characters, you can do that through the "Set Constraints" button.

We now wish to add a custom attribute called WebType which will be an enumerated list of different web-based topics from which the user can choose. Enter WebType as the Attribute Name, and for the description enter the text, "Describes the web area into which the book falls." Finally select Enumerated List as the Attribute Syntax and then click on the Set Constraints button.

Next, clicking the Add button will produce a JavaScript prompt asking you to enter a value. Add the following, one at a time:

> ➤   Site Server
> ➤   XML
> ➤   Web Applications

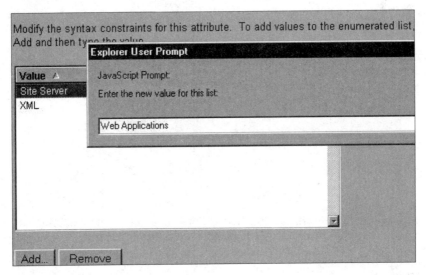

It is worth noting that the enumerated list you have created for this attribute gets added to the Site Vocabulary. You can access this from the Membership Directory Manager and have the ability to modify and add to the attributes from ou=Admin/ou=Other/ou=TagTerms in the Membership Directory.

Finally, click on Edit Properties for the WebType at the top right of the page and then click Submit in the Create New Attribute form.

> It is very important to remember to ensure that the **Generate Properties Form** and **Generate View Page** checkboxes are checked when you make changes, so that these are reflected in your web site.

These attributes can now be used by the content publishers to tag the documents according to the constraints that the content administrator has set.

Setting Content Approval

It may be that you do not want a particular Content Type being published until an authorized editor has approved it. We have the ability to do this within the Content Types administration section for our WroxStore Content Store.

To do this, we should click on the 'Content Types for Content Store' link at the top of the page. We should then be shown the list of Content Types again. Click on the 'Books' Content Type that we created earlier and then click the Approve button. You should see the value in the Approval Required column change to 'Yes' as shown in the next screenshot:

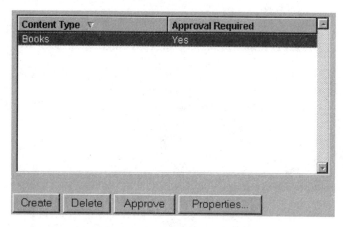

We have now fully set up our Content Management system for users publishing to the WroxStore area. We now have to look at the content uploading and management procedures, which are the other pieces of the jigsaw. There are in fact two ways to control this: via Web Admin, or via the web page directly. I suspect that most people will want to distribute the content management and approval process among multiple authors and so the web page is simplest for this, and is the approach I shall be taking. Working with the Web Admin is a very simple process for the administrator and is documented in the Site Server Publishing help document.

Core WroxStore Content Pages

Now that the Content Store is in place, some ASP files may need to be modified to create the user interfaces you need for your store. The core sample pages that we've borrowed from the CMsample site mirror the Content Management steps: submission, approval and view. The following table summarizes the main files to modify, the users of the file and the purpose of each file.

File	User	Purpose
submit.asp	Content Producer	Used to publish documents to Site Server
cpview.asp	Content Producer	Used to managed published content
approve.asp	Content Editor	Used to control publishing of content
<type>View.asp	Content Consumer	Used to list content of type <type>

Note that links (e.g. images and includes) referred to after you have copied the files from CMsample may be broken. You will either need to copy the referenced files or remove the links. Also, as we mentioned earlier in the chapter, before you deploy these pages on your site don't forget to remove any lines of code that read:

```
<!--#include Virtual="/SiteServer/Publishing/codeview.inc" -->
```

Otherwise, the pages of your site will contain a button that will enable the site's users to see all the code of the page they are viewing.

Adding New Content in WroxStore

Let's now focus on the content by looking at how it gets to the web store and how it is managed. We shall continue with our WroxStore example to illustrate the first of these – uploading the files.

Two files are used for uploading in the sample, namely ss.doc and publish.jpg, although any documents you choose can be uploaded. These documents are in the `Microsoft Site Server\data\publishing\WroxStore` folder that we created for the store earlier.

Uploading Files

Navigate to `http://<yourservername>/WroxStore/default.asp` in preparation for accessing the content upload section for the site. Click on the link to `submit.asp` ("Submit New Content" in our case) and you will be taken to the upload submission web page. Click on the Browse button (or folder icon) and navigate to the `ss.doc` file described above. Click on Open and the path will be inserted into the text box. Click on the Upload button and you'll then be asked to select a Content Type. Select the Books value and click the Next button to continue. The properties you applied to this Content Type should now be shown.

Select Site Server as the WebType and input an e-mail address and editor name of your choice. The frame at the bottom of the page will let you know that the document requires approval before it is made available for viewing.

> If you do not see the properties you expected and defined for this Content Type, it is probably because you did not check the Generate Properties Form box when you modified the Content Type in the web administration form. You must go back into WebAdmin, select the Content Type and check the Generate Properties Form box to force this process, and the new properties will be reflected.

Continuing, you should click on the Submit button and the following page will run through a process of publishing the page. After, you can return to the `default.asp` home page.

Content Administration

Now that we've posted content to the site, how do we go about viewing and editing it for administration purposes?

Viewing Submitted Content

As the owner of the content, you have the ability to view any file you have posted to the web, before or after approval, and to edit its properties or delete it completely. The page that lets you view your files is `cpview.asp`. In our case, click on the **My Content** menu option and the file that you posted to the site will be displayed. Currently, this should only be `ss.doc` as shown in the next screenshot:

The items listed below are pieces of content that you have submitted. You may select a piece of content and delete it, or click the "Edit Properties" graphic to modify previously entered properties. You may also view the file by clicking on its name.

Select	Edit Properties	Name	Category	Title
☐		ss.doc	Books	

Delete Selected

You can edit the document's properties by clicking on the 'scroll and quill' icon in the **Edit Properties** column, and even delete the document by checking the select checkbox and clicking on **Delete Selected**.

> If you do not find a file which you have previously submitted, it is probably because it has either not been indexed yet by Index Server (it can take up to 30 seconds) or the Index Server Content Management Catalog is corrupt. Try forcing index generation from the Index Server snap-in in the MMC.
>
> To force a scan, first launch the Index Server MMC from **Programs | NT Option Pack | Index Server | MMC Administration**. Right-Click on the entry for Content Management and select **Merge** and force a merge. You should then return to your Content Management site through the browser to see if the file has now been added.

Approving Content

We will now look at the view the content administrator gets, so browse to the content store homepage at `http://<yourservername>/WroxStore/default.asp` and click on the **Approve Content** link. As a content administrator, you have almost the exact same view as described in the previous section, however, there are a further three buttons which you can select. These allow for approving selected documents, as well as starting and stopping deployment of content to the web site.

When approving documents for a particular Content Type, each and every document must be individually approved for that Content Type. So, continuing with our example, click on the select checkbox for `ss.doc` and click **Approve Selected**. A page will then tell you that the document is being published and you'll then be taken back to the editor's view for approving more documents.

Viewing Content

Once an administrator has approved the document, it is available for viewing by other users. Documents that have been posted as a particular Content Type can be viewed via a link on the navigation menu, where the link name is an ASP file with the content name and "View" appended to it. Hence, in our case the file will be `BooksView.asp`. Clicking on this file shall show `ss.doc` and some of its properties.

Repeat the above process for the `publish.jpg` file. After completion, the `BooksView.asp` link will display the following:

Use the View Code button to see the rule that displays content.

 ss.doc 19968 Bytes

publish.jpg 899 Bytes

Now let's look in more detail at using the Site Server Tag Tool to prepare documents for the Content Store.

Tagging Files

Before you upload files, it is useful to use the Tag Tool provided with Site Server, as among other reasons, you can apply tag changes to multiple web files or whole folders at the same time. We'll now use the Tag Tool to apply tags to two HTML documents at the same time. When we upload these documents, all of the information will already be filled in.

The Tag Tool is installed when you install Site Server, but it can be installed as a separate application on a content provider's PC. To do this, you should instruct your clients to run the Site Server CD and click on the Tools link when the installation window appears. This will allow the user to install only the client tools, of which the Tag Tool is one.

> **One Site Server license allows you to install the Site Server Tools on as many client PCs as you wish.**

When first run, the user may be asked to log onto a server, and should choose the server relevant to the site. To access the Content Types available for a particular Membership Directory, select the View I Options dialog, type the name of the relevant web server instance and click OK.

We will now add some sample files, `tag.htm` and `tag2.htm`, to the site and use the tag tool to pre-tag these files before uploading. Launch the Tag Tool from Programs I Microsoft Site Server I Tools I Tag Tools and if you are on a remote client, connect to the web server instance where Site Server is installed (as described above).

In the top left pane, navigate to `C:\microsoft siteserver\data\publishing\WroxStore\Temp` and the bottom left-hand pane will list the available web files. Double-click on the `tag.htm` file and it will be displayed in the bottom half of the screen. Click on the Content Type combo box and select cn=Books and the range of available tags will be displayed.

Enter the appropriate values for each of these tags. An example is shown below:

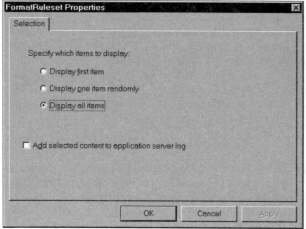

Select **File | Apply Changes to Other Files** and select `tag2.htm` in the right hand pane. Clicking **Next** will alert you as to the changes that will be made and clicking **Finish** will show the **Bulk Tag** dialog box. When this has been completed, all files will have been tagged and are ready for express uploading. You can repeat the application of the tagging of tag.htm for as many files as you see fit. The functionality of this tool becomes more important as the number of tags increases with the range of web documents.

We shall look at tagging in FrontPage in a later section.

Accessing Content

Once the Content Store is created and content is submitted, there has to be a way to access the content. Most likely there will be multiple ways to access the content including a direct link to the content, a user query to find content or a selection that invokes a pre-defined query.

Linking to existing content is a simple matter of creating an anchor to the content within the Content Store. For instance, to access a Books document titled `ops.doc` in the WroxStore Content Store, the anchor might look something like the following:

```
<A HREF="\WroxStore\Books\ops.doc">Obfuscating Project Specifications by Mr. Messy</A>
```

This method does not use Site Server to obtain content – it is just a regular HTML anchor. The disadvantage of this method is that if the content is removed from the Content Store the link will be broken.

The other way to access data is to create a query to return a list of documents that match the query. A query could be formed to return the `ops.doc` document. If the document were removed, the query would return an empty list of documents. The situation is then handled more gracefully than having a 404 error returned to the user. Let's look into the details of creating queries by using the Rule Manager.

Rules and Rule Sets

Rules are covered in the Personalization and Membership section of the Microsoft Site Server documentation. However, rules are very important for being able to query for content. Rules consist of one or more conditions together with actions that would execute if the conditions were met. A rule set is a collection of prioritized rules. The rule set is stored in a rule set file with a `.prf` extension (e.g. `Books.prf`, as we saw when we created the "Books" Content Type). The file is actually just ASP code that generates a list of content based on the rules specified. The ASP code is included into another ASP page (using a Design Time Control described below) that puts the formatting around the content list. In addition there is instruction code within comments that informs the Rule Manager (discussed next) how to create a User Interface to modify the rule set code.

Rule Manager

Rule Manager is the starting point of the rule creation process. It is used to create and modify rule set files (`.prf`). The Rule Manager lets you create queries based on both Content Attributes and user attributes. The Content Attributes allow you to select a type of content. The user attributes let you target the content to what the user would be interested in or limit the content based on their attributes.

Unfortunately, the Rule Manager can only generate static queries. That is, the parameters to the queries are fixed – a user of an application cannot specify them. For instance, if you want the user to specify a keyword to look for in the title of documents, you cannot do that with Rule Manager. You need to modify the rule set file – which we will look at shortly.

The Rule Manager is covered well in the Site Server documentation so we will not cover it in detail here. Instead we will look at using and modifying the `.prf` files it generates.

Modifying Rule Code

At the most basic level, content is obtained by executing a SQL query against Index Server using ADO and the Index Server OLE DB Provider (MSIDXS). Rules and rule sets are a way to abstract the query to a higher level so the developer can focus on creating the query rather than worrying about getting the SQL syntax correct.

Once you start modifying a rule set file don't expect Rule Manager to be able to reload it. Even if Rule Manager is able to load the rule set back in, you may lose the changes you made when it is saved back out. Use Rule Manager only to generate your initial rule set code. If you have to modify the rule set code, don't try to use it in Rule Manager again. Instead, continue to change it with your editor (e.g. Visual InterDev).

Why would you need to manually modify the rule set code? The rule set code is really good at creating static queries. However, if you want to parameterize the query (e.g. letting the user choose a value for an attribute to query on), you will need to modify the code.

Modifying the code is straightforward. You just need to change the SQL SELECT statement to be dynamically formed instead of being static. Consider the SELECT statement in `whitepapers.prf` (from CMsample). The following code is taken from this rule file. This code forms the 'WHERE' clause of the SQL SELECT. It selects all content that is approved and of type 'whitepapers'.

```
If Len(bstrSSPMQuery) > 0 Then bstrSSPMQuery = bstrSSPMQuery & " OR "
bstrSSPMQuery = bstrSSPMQuery & " ( CONTAINS(approved, 'yes*') > 0 "
If Len(bstrSSPMQuery) > 3 Then
    bstrSSPMQuery = bstrSSPMQuery & " AND "
End If
    bstrSSPMQuery = bstrSSPMQuery & " CONTAINS(contentType, 'whitepapers*') > 0  ) "
```

Consider if you want to let the user search for all whitepapers that contain a certain keyword. A way to do this is to pass a keyword to `whitepapersview.asp` as a form variable (e.g. named `txtKeyword`). Then in `whitepapers.prf` you would insert the following code immediately after the previous code just listed.

```
If Request( "txtKeyword" ) <> "" Then
bstrSSPMQuery = bstrSSPMQuery & "AND CONTAINS(DocKeywords, '"" &
    Request.Form( "txtKeyword" ) & "*"') > 0 "
End If
```

Therefore the entire `WHERE` clause would select all approved documents of type whitepapers with the keyword specified in the form variable. You can use the same technique to search on any of the other attributes associated with the Content Type you are querying.

There is another change you should make to the rule file. The generated rule file hard-codes the file path to the content source. In the `SELECT` statement, you will see a function `GetFromClause()` which returns the value of `FromClause`. This constant is stored in the file `config.inc` of your content store. For CMsample this file looks like the following.

```
<%
const DPSVRoot = "/CmSample"
const LDAPServer = "webserver:1002"
const ApplicationName = "CmSample"
const FromClause = " FROM ContentManagement..SCOPE(' ""C:\Microsoft Site
Server\Data\Publishing\CmSample"" ') "
%>
```

If the content source is moved to another location you will have to modify this line. Alternatively, I suggest you use `Server.MapPath` so that you can physically move the content store somewhere else without breaking it. The important point is to keep the virtual directory the same. As example, the `FromClause` of CMsample could be changed to the following.

```
FromClause = ContentManagement..SCOPE(' "" & Server.MapPath( DPSVRoot ) & "" ')
```

The Rule Set Design Time Control

Once the rule set file is created, it has to be embedded in an ASP file. Site Server has a Design Time Control (DTC) to make this easy. After the rule set has fired, the results are stored in an ActiveX Data Object (ADO) recordset. The Content Attributes are fields within each record. You can choose which of these fields you want displayed and how they are formatted in the HTML page.

The following is an example of the DTC in an ASP file.

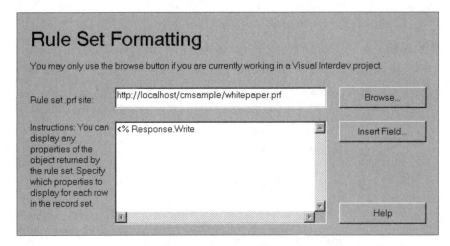

The .prf file is specified as well as formatting code for attribute values. Pressing the "Insert Field" button allows you to add fields to the HTML sent to the browser.

When multiple rows are returned, you can configure which rows are displayed by using the "Properties" dialog of the DTC.

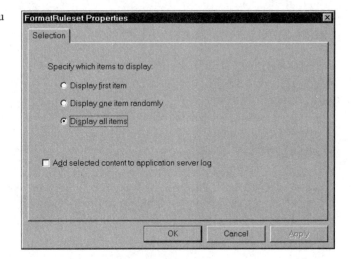

As with any DTC control, at some point you can decide to work with the code generated by the DTC instead of through the DTC user interface. To use the Rule Set DTC to include the .prf without inserting any formatting code, enter the URL for the .prf file in the DTC property page but leave the formatting area blank. When the DTC is closed, the ASP file will contain the generated code to include the .prf file.

Securing the Content

There are two areas of securing content that need to be addressed. The first is limiting search results to only have content available for the user performing the query. This doesn't actually prevent the user from obtaining the content though if the URL is known. The NTFS permissions have to be set on the content files to make sure they are only accessible to those authorized to obtain them.

You will want to secure more than just the content, you will also want to secure the ASP files. Most ASP files used with Content Management have specific functionality associated with them (e.g. `submit.asp` is used for submitting files). Therefore, these files should be restricted to the people allowed to use given functionality.

Programmatic Authorization

Programmatic Authorization is restricting query results based on the identity of the person doing the query. This way the content list does not contain references to content an unauthorized user is not supposed to see. It does not prevent the user from obtaining the document if they know the URL and it is not secured.

For instance, for WebSoft Consulting contracts may not be made available to developers. In this case, when constructing a menu of Content Types to view, there would be logic in the ASP to exclude the hyperlink for contracts if the user is a developer.

To restrict query results, the rule for generating the query contains a condition based on the groups the user performing the query belongs to. Rule Manager allows you to incorporate attributes of the user making the query.

NTFS Authorization

By default, all web site users will have access to all the content on the site. As a first step, set the following permissions using Windows Explorer.

Group	ASP Files			Sub-directories		
	Submit.asp	Approval..asp	Cpview..asp	ContentType	Upload	Approve
Content Producers	Read	No Access	No Access	Write*	Write*	Write*
Content Editors	No Access	Read	Read	Change	No Access	No Access
Content Consumers	No Access	No Access	No Access	Read	No Access	No Access

* Creator/Owner is given Change access so Producers can change their own content.

You may want to assign the Content Type Read access of the Content Consumers to a finer degree. For instance, there may be a group of Content Consumers who only have access for a particular Content Type.

Taking the planning we did for WebSoft and applying file and sub-directory access control, we come up with the following two tables.

	ASP Files		
	Submit.asp	Approval.asp	Cpview.asp
President	Read	Read	Read
Project Manager	Read	No Access	Read
Developer	No Access	No Access	No Access
Office Admin	Read	No Access	Read
Client Manager	No Access	No Access	No Access
Client Developer	No Access	No Access	No Access

	Sub-directories						
	Contracts	Budgets	Requirements	Project Plans	Status Reports	Upload	Approve
President	RW	R	R	R	R	W	W
Project Manager	None	RW	RW	RW	RW	W	W
Developer	None	None	R	R	None	None	None
Office Admin	RW	RW	None	None	None	W	W
Client Manager	R	None	R	R	R	None	None
Client Developer	None	None	R	R	None	None	None

Creating a FrontPage Publishing Site

FrontPage is a web authoring and design tool from Microsoft that enables the creation and uploading of web content using a simple and intuitive user interface. It is a client-based tool and connects directly to the web server rather than via the web browser, and so allows you to directly upload and tag content for a content store, without necessarily using the browser-based submit and tagging features.

Setting Up the FrontPage Web

The FPsample site contains all of the Active Server Pages you need to enable your Content Providers and Content Editors to submit, tag and approve content, as well as View pages for a variety of Content Types. The FPsample site is best customized with FrontPage.

If we have a FrontPage local directory structure which was created from another FrontPage web and we want to create a FrontPage Content Management site then we have to restore it from this "disk-based web" to a full FrontPage web.

> A "disk-based FrontPage web" is simply a local directory structure that was a FrontPage web. This allows us to pass FrontPage webs around in, for example, a .zip file and it can be unzipped by the client and restored on the web server to a full FrontPage web site using the methods below.

Restoring the FPsample Web

We are going to illustrate how to convert an existing directory structure, or disk-based web to a FrontPage web site, but as there is a slight difference in how FrontPage 98 does this compared to FrontPage 2000, both methods shall be shown.

FrontPage 98

We must first restore the current disk-based web for the FPsample web. To do this launch FrontPage 98 and open a FrontPage web, except we click on More Webs and when presented with the following dialog, we should insert `C:\Microsoft SiteServer\Data\Publishing\FPsample` as the web location and press OK twice.

Now that we have the disk-based web restored, we must convert this to a web-based URL. We should select the File menu and, after selecting Publish FrontPage Web, the publish dialog box should be displayed. After clicking More Webs we will be presented with the Publish FrontPage Web dialog box asking for the location to publish our web.

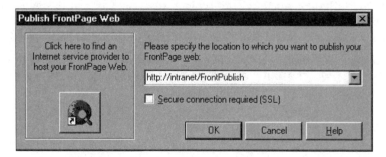

Insert `http://<yourservername>/FrontPublish` as the location where `<yourservername>` should be replaced by the name of your server. Pressing **OK** to publish your web will create a virtual root pointing to a directory under your default web site and FrontPage will place your content there. Now check that this has been created by opening the web in FrontPage.

FrontPage 2000

For FrontPage 2000 the process is a little different. Launch FrontPage 2000 and open a FrontPage web, click **File | Open** and navigate to `C:\Microsoft Site Server\Data\Publishing\ FPsample`. The FPsample directory will have a blue icon on it. Double-click on it and then click the **Open** button.

Now that we have the disk-based web restored, we must convert this to a web-based URL. We should select the **File** menu and after selecting **Publish Web**, the publish dialog box should be displayed.

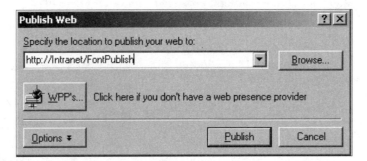

Insert http://*<yourservername>*/FrontPublish as the location where *<yourservername>* should be replaced by the name of your server. Click **Publish** to publish your web; the wizard will create a virtual root pointing to a directory under your default web site and will place your content there. Now check that this has been created by opening the web in FrontPage.

Creating the Content Store

We must now run a script that will build our content store and create the necessary upload, tag, approve and publish Content Management pages properly.

> There is a possibility that when the site is copied over, that it still uses the FPsample virtual directory as its base. This will cause problems later. To check this, open the file `DefaultViewTemplate.ast` and search for the text 'fpsample'.
>
> If you find this, then you'll have to replace all occurrences of this with the name of your store (FrontPublish) in this file, the `default.asp` file and each of the view pages for each Content Type. It will then point to the correct area.
>
> This assumes that you do not remove the content pages and their view pages which come with the sample (if you are going to insert your own).

Follow the following steps to correctly set up the FrontPage Content Store:

3. Change to the directory where the FrontPage web has just been installed
(C:\InetPub\wwwroot\FrontPublish)

4. Type the following command :
cscript makeCM.vbs /s:<Servername> /v:content /a:FrontPublish
/d:"c:\Inetpub\wwwroot\FrontPublish"

```
C:\WINNT\System32\cmd.exe                                          _ □ ✕
03/24/99   09:14p      <DIR>         _derived
03/24/99   09:13p      <DIR>         _fpclass
03/24/99   09:14p      <DIR>         _overlay
03/24/99   09:14p      <DIR>         _private
03/24/99   09:14p      <DIR>         _themes
              68 File(s)         261,644 bytes
                             1,405,863,424 bytes free

C:\InetPub\wwwroot\FontPublish>dir *.vbs
 Volume in drive C has no label.
 Volume Serial Number is 587A-2B61

 Directory of C:\InetPub\wwwroot\FontPublish

02/26/98   12:29p                61,437 makeCM.vbs
              1 File(s)           61,437 bytes
                             1,405,863,424 bytes free

C:\InetPub\wwwroot\FontPublish>cscript makecm.vbs /s:Intranet /v:content /a:Font
Publish /d:"c:\inetpub\wwwroot\FontPublish"
Microsoft (R) Windows Scripting Host Version 5.0 for Windows
Copyright (C) Microsoft Corporation 1996-1997. All rights reserved.

C:\InetPub\wwwroot\FontPublish>_
```

We can now view the new Content Management site we have just created by browsing to
http://<yourservername>/FrontPublish. In our case the following is one of the pages that
will be displayed by default.

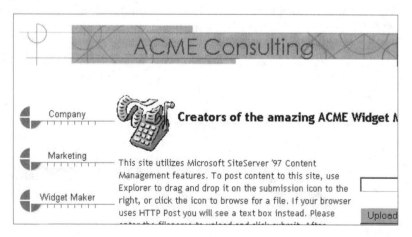

However, I expect the majority of you will want a different look to your site and will probably not be
called ACME Consulting, so let's customize our site.

Customizing the Site

Using FrontPage for our development gives us the advantage of using **Themes** to maintain the same look and feel throughout the entire site. Note that to alter the Theme throughout the site, you simply open the `default.asp` page in the FrontPage editor and select Format I Theme and choose your desired Theme.

To complete the design customization, the files `CompanyView.asp`, `Marketing.htm`, `DataSheetView.asp`, `FaqsView.asp`, `Products.htm`, `SpecificationsView.asp`, `WhitePapers.asp`, `Cpview.asp`, `Approve.asp` and their respective properties pages should be edited and replaced by your company-specific information.

The current `default.asp` page contains links on the left allowing users to view the content for the various Content Types which have been created for the FrontPublish site, as well as a link for viewing content you have previously submitted, a link for content administrators to approve posted content, and a link to create a channel for your company.

The method for adding Content Types and attributes is the same as described previously for the WroxStore sample, so we'll look at how we can allow users to upload to a store via FrontPage.

The scenario of the example we shall now work with, is that of a site where 'press release' documents are created directly on the web site and are available to users immediately without approval. To get this to work, we must modify attributes directly in the Membership Directory Manager, as well as modifying the rule for the press release (`pressreleases.prf`).

Modifying Attributes with the Membership Directory Manager

When you upload a document via FrontPage, an owner tag is not added to it automatically, so a content provider would be unable to view content he has posted to the server. The following steps show you how to use the Membership Directory Manager MMC snap-in to add Owner as an attribute which will be available to the Tag Tool and so can be specified by the author at design time.

Run the Site Server MMC from Start I Programs I Microsoft Site Server I Administration I Site Server Service Admin (MMC). Click on the Membership Directory Manager snap-in and navigate to the ou=Other /ou=Admin /ou=DocumentClasses container. You should see the following:

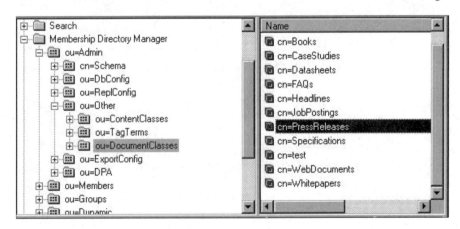

Right click on cn=PressReleases, select Properties and click on the may-contain attribute. Click on Add Value and type Owner into the text box with focus as shown opposite:

Click on OK and the Owner attribute will now be explicitly available to the FrontPage tag tool.

Modifying Content Management Rules

As we are allowing users to directly upload their files to directories via FrontPage, we must remove the rule that checks for approval information. Fire up the Rule Manager from Start I Programs I Microsoft Site Server I Tools. When the application is loaded, if you are on a client machine, select View I Options, enter the web server instance and click OK. Otherwise, choose File I Open and navigate to InetPub\wwwroot\FrontPublish and open pressreleases.prf. When this has finished, click on the "and where approved contains yes". Once this is selected, right-click and select Clear, as shown below:

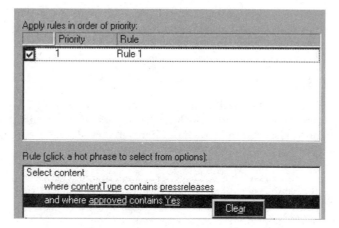

Click on Save and exit the application. Now, for the "PressReleases" Content Type – no approval tag will be needed and documents will be immediately available.

Publishing a FrontPage File

In this example, we shall use FrontPage to create a file called `fp.htm` within the `PressRelease` directory in the FrontPage web. Create this document with "This file was published using FrontPage" as the document text.

If we wish the file to be available, then the content provider must provide all of the attributes of the documents via the FrontPage Tag Tool utility, which will be available if you install the client Tag Tool provided with Site Server, as described a few pages ago. To tag the document from FrontPage, you should select Tools | Tag this Page and the content provider will be presented with a list of Content Types.

Ensure you select "Press Release" from the drop down box and enter your full domain and username as the owner. Input the other types of information as desired and click OK and save the file.

You can now navigate to the homepage of FrontPublish and view the press releases content. You will see that your document has been added. You can also navigate to `cpView.asp` to remove or modify the file attributes if you want to update the file.

We have been working with a setup where content providers have direct access to the content and their modifications (and mistakes) are effective immediately. If there is a lot of work going on, access to the server could be slow for users, so it makes sense to have a production server to store content which users have access to, and keep the development server separate.

Let's now move on and have a look at some of the maintenance issues involved in Content Management.

Maintenance

There are some other issues surrounding Content Management that come up in the course of developing and deploying a Content Management application. Three that we are going to look at are: Source Control, Recovering a Content Store and Moving a Content Store.

Source Control

Source Control is managing files used during the development process by keeping track of different versions. As well, source control identifies which developers made the changes and when they checked them in. For Visual InterDev projects, Microsoft Visual Source Safe is typically used for source control.

Getting source control to work with Site Server is a challenge in itself. If you have not attempted it yet be sure to read the Site Server documentation that refers to using Visual InterDev, Visual Source Safe and Front Page Extensions. If you have source control working successfully, you must decide which portion of your Content Management application to put under source control.

What to Put Under Source Control

Obviously, any ASP or HTML pages that you create from scratch should be placed under source control.

Also, any of the files copied from CMsample to your Content Store that were changed should be placed under source control. Specifically, the following files.

- ➢ `submit.asp`
- ➢ `cpview.asp`
- ➢ `approval.asp`

Any `.prf` files generated by the Rule Manager should be placed under source control. Remember that if you go back into Rule Manager to change them, they will first need to be checked out using Visual InterDev or Source Safe.

The Content Type Property and Content Type View pages may be put under source control. If you are changing those pages from what is automatically generated you will want to place them under source control. This will reduce the risk of accidentally overwriting them when changing attributes for a Content Type. However, if you do modify the attributes for a Content Type, you will have to manually update the Property and View pages. If you are not modifying the Property and View pages you do not need to place them under source control. Additionally, you can take advantage of the automatic generation process when the attributes change for a Content Type.

What Not to Put Under Source Control

The content files or the stubs for the content files should not be placed under source control. This might seem counter-intuitive since the content is a valuable part of the web site. However, if content is under source control this means that the users would have to use Source Safe to check out content before it can be changed. Since attribute values are stored in a stub file this means attributes cannot be changed unless the stub file is checked out as well. Additionally, when content is published, someone would have to manually add the content to source control using Source Safe.

The goal of Content Management is to place control of the content in the hands of the Content Producers. Mostly likely the Content Producers will not be happy if they have to use an additional tool that is not related to the job they are trying to accomplish – getting content published to the web site.

Remember that Content Management is not a substitution for Document Management. It does not provide revisions control or file locking. Content Management's strength is an easy way to make information available via a web site.

Recovering a Content Store

It is bound to happen. You have to re-install a portion of your machine. It might be Site Server, SQL Server or even NT itself. How do you recover and recreate your Content Store without having to submit all your documents again? Well, you won't find the answer in the documentation. Here is what I found works.

There are two pieces you need to recover a content store – the Membership Directory database and the file system hierarchy under the Content Store sub-directory. Hopefully you have these backed up.

If you have to reinstall Site Server you will lose your Membership Directory configuration, which has a lot of the information about the Content Store. However, that information ultimately resides in your database. So the trick is to create a new Content Store (and thus Membership Directory) and map your restored database to that Membership Directory.

If you have lost the Content Store directory structure you will have to replace it from backup. This Content Store directory structure is the one depicted in a diagram in the "What is a Content Store" section. Make sure the directories are placed in the same location as they were before.

Moving a Content Store

A web-based architecture often has many different web servers. For example, there may be a development server, a staging server for Quality Assurance and finally one or many production servers. So you will want to propagate the Content Store from one machine to another. There may be another reason that you want to change the machine that a given Content Store is located on. Unfortunately, this is not a one step process and is not documented in the Microsoft Site Server documentation. I have found though that the following steps work for moving a Content Store:

> ➤ Move The Membership Server Database
> ➤ Configure a Content Deployment project
> ➤ Move the Index

Use your favorite method of moving a database. A backup and restore is probably what you are used to. I recommend you keep the name of the Membership Server database the same. That way any queries will not have to change.

> **Make sure that you have the same version of Site Server, including service packs, on both machines otherwise the database schema for the Membership Directories may be different.**

The Membership Directory has the name of the Membership Server it is associated with encoded in the database. If you've moved the Membership Directory into another database on a different machine, this can be really deceiving because from the outside, LDAP queries will say they using the new server while in fact it is performing the queries using the original one. Assuming the other server is still on the network, with this configuration Site Server does not even fail - it performs the queries against the Membership Server instance the Membership Directory was originally associated with on the original machine. Check the field `vc_ServerName` in the table `DsConfiguration` and the field `vs_Datasource` in the table `DsoGrid` to ensure they have the correct server name.

Once the database has been migrated, create a new Membership Server instance. Follow the same steps as for creating a new Membership Server except you select "**Connect to an existing Membership Directory**" as shown in the screenshot.

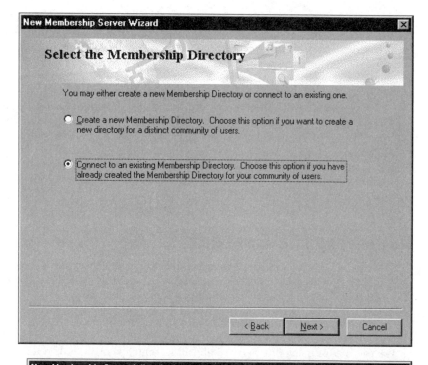

After selecting '**Next**' you are asked for the existing database. Note that after filling out the database information Site Server checks to make sure the database connection is valid before continuing on to the next dialog. However, it does not check that the database specified is the same as the machine name in the database. This is why it is important to check those fields in the database. This screenshot shows an example of connecting to an existing SQL database.

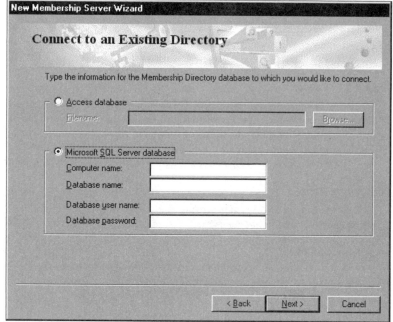

The next step is to move the actual documents from one server to the other. The easiest way to do this is to configure a Site Server deployment project (we'll look at this in a moment). Move the directory and sub-directories specified for the Content Store on the original server. Once the project is deployed, verify the permissions on the directory of the end-point server. It is important that content authors have write permissions on the 'Upload' directory.

> As mentioned earlier in the chapter, if your Content Store is moved to a different physical directory, you will need to modify the file config.inc.

At this point it is possible to publish documents to the replicated server. However, existing documents will not appear in a search because they have not been indexed. To move the index, copy the directory Catalog.wci for the source Content Store to the index directory for the destination Content Store.

Deploying the Content

In a typical web content lifecycle, users develop their content on a development server and when ready, their content is published to a staging server from where it will be automatically published to a production server and will be available to users for browsing.

Currently, we have published all of our FrontPage content to a development server, so in order for users to be able to access this content, we should define a process where the content is propagated. We can do this using Site Server Publishing, which we will look at now.

Configuring the Servers

Prior to actually deploying your content, you must configure all servers by firstly installing the Site Server Publishing Service on each and also configuring access for Publishing operators.

Installing Publishing

Publishing is installed as part of the default installation for Site Server, but it can also be installed independently on another machine. You install this by clicking Setup.exe on the Site Server CD and selecting only the Publishing option from the Custom configuration. You can check that the Publishing has been installed if you look in Start | Setting | Control Panel and select Services. You should find the Site Server Content Deployment service has been started.

Configuring Access

When Site Server Deployment publishes across multiple servers, it uses a specified username and password to log onto each server. For this reason it is essential that it logs on as a user who has publishing privileges and is in the Site Server Publishing Operators group.

Create an account on all participating machines with the username "pub" and password "pub" and add this user to the Site Server Publishing Operators group on all computers using the NT User Manager for Domains.

Creating Deployment Projects

We are going to create a relatively simple, but effective deployment solution that will involve the current development server, a staging server and a production server.

Staging Server Content

The staging server will be operating on the same server as the development web, but will not be accessible to users via a browser or FrontPage. Content is stored in the staging area in preparation for production deployment and mirrors exactly the content that will appear there, so we should remove any extra unnecessary directories created by FrontPage.

Click on Start | Programs | Microsoft Site Server | Administration | Site Server Service Admin (MMC) and select the Publishing snap-in. Click on the Projects entry and select New | Project with a Wizard. When the wizard appears, click Next. Enter "FrontPublishToStage" in the Specify a Project Name textbox and click Next. In the Project Type dialog, keep the default Deploy content from a local directory as shown in this screenshot:

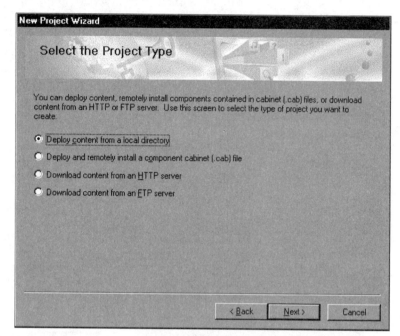

Click Next and enter the path of the FrontPublish Directory (e.g. C:\Microsoft Site Server\Data\Publishing\FrontPublish) and click next. On the Specify the Project Definitions box, click Add and a dialog box will appear. Click the Directory radio button to specify that we first want to deploy our content locally. Enter the path to a directory called C:\InetPub\Stage (where we'll stage our content) directory in the edit box as in the opposite screenshot, and click OK.

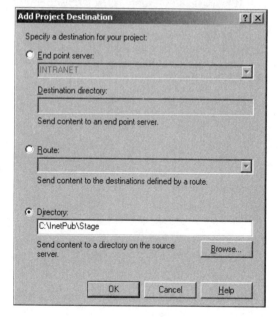

Click Next twice and in the Create Project Schedule screen, check the box to Deploy the Content Automatically when it changes and click Next. Finally click Finish and your project will be created and appear in the Projects list for your server under the Publishing snap-in of the MMC.

We are not quite ready to deploy our content though – we will encounter authentication errors if we do. We should now specify the username and password of the operator we created earlier as the user that Publishing should log on as. To specify that we want to use this user, select the Properties on the FrontPublishToStage project and when the dialog box comes up, click the Security tab. In the Authentication section, enter the details for the Pub Account and click OK twice.

Now right-click on the FrontPublishToStage Project and select Start. Then click Start Replication, and your FrontPublish Project will start running and content will start to be deployed. After a few minutes, you can look at the new stage directory and you'll see that it now consists of the FrontPage files from FrontPublish.

> **You can also apply a filter to the project by selecting the project name and then Properties | Filter. This can be useful for preventing the deployment of all the FrontPage directories that are created on the development web server.**

Production Server Content

We can now create a production project where content will be deployed on a daily basis. To create this project, follow all of the steps above (enter FrontPublishProd as the name), but when asked to specify the project source, enter the path to the Stage directory we created earlier (C:\InetPub\Stage). In the Specify Project Destinations dialog enter the production server, which you have installed Site Server Publishing on, as the End Point Server and enter a valid directory residing on that server (e.g. C:\InetPub\wwwroot\FrontPublish).

When asked to Create a Project Schedule, click the Add button and, as we want to schedule a daily replication, click the Weekly radio button and check all of the days available (i.e. Mon – Sun), as shown in this screenshot:

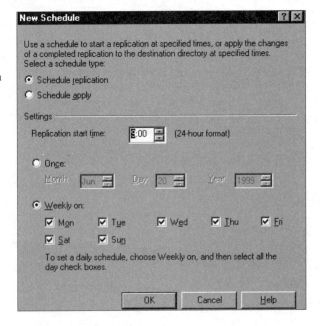

Once again, enter the user account we specified earlier as the authentication account and start the replication as before. The content should then be available to users browsing the live web site.

Summary

Researching and classifying the information and the people involved are the first steps to designing a Content Management application. Content Management puts a process in place for publishing and controlling content: the Information Systems department benefits by being relieved of the manual task of uploading documents on a web server; the Business Users are happy because they are given control of their own content; the web site users are happy because they can quickly search for information within the organization.

In this chapter we have covered the following areas:

> Planning Content Management before it is implemented
> Creating a Content Store and attaching it to an existing Membership Directory
> Creating Content Types and Content Attributes
> Dealing with issues during deployment and maintenance

Once in place, Content Management will make your organization more efficient, put control over content in the hands of its producers, and make information timely and easy to find.

7

Search

The focus of today's employee should be on solving business problems and not manual processes. Many companies have taken the first step towards this goal by storing the company's information in digital form. However, there is still a lot of valuable time spent looking for the digital documents. The phrase has changed from "where did I leave that piece of paper?" to "where did I put that file?"

One solution is to put a process in place so that content is categorized before it is made available. Chapter 7 – Content Management, demonstrated this solution. However, with Content Management you must go through the submission process for the files. What if you already have thousands of files spread over a number of servers that you want to provide easier access to immediately? Simple! You use Site Server Search.

Information is available in many forms and from many sources. For instance, when you as a developer run into a problem, there are a number of resources to check for answers like the Microsoft Knowledge Base, many newsgroups, and information posted to Microsoft Exchange Public Folders on your Intranet. It is tedious to search through all these sources individually. Site Server Search allows you to execute one query against all these information sources at once.

In this chapter you will see:

> An overview of Search functionality and its benefits
> Planning to use Search
> Sample Search catalogs and Search pages available with the Site Server package
> Implementation of Search

Let's fit Search into the context of Site Server as a whole, see the benefits it offers you and the situations in which you would use it.

Overview

Search is used to gather information from diverse sources and index it into a catalog. The sources of information can be web sites, file systems, newsgroups, Microsoft Exchange public folders and ODBC databases. Additionally, Search can be configured to regulate the amount of information obtained from these sources.

Once data is indexed, queries can be performed against the catalog to find information. Any documents that match the query are listed on a results page. The results page has a description of the matches with hyperlinks to the documents concerned.

Search's Relationship to Index Server

You might be thinking, "But how is this different from Microsoft Index Server?" Well, Search uses the same indexing engine as Index Server. This means that once data is obtained, it is processed in the same way. The difference with Search is how and from where the data is obtained. The main purpose of Index Server is to index documents on a file system whereas Search is designed to index content from many diverse sources. Additionally, Search gives you more fine-grained control over what is indexed and what is not.

Index Server generates its index automatically. It tracks file changes in directories that have been selected for indexing. When a file has been added to a directory selected for indexing Index Server adds that file to its index. To set this up, in the property page for a web site in the MMC for IIS, you tick the check box under "Content Control" to indicate that Index Server should index a directory.

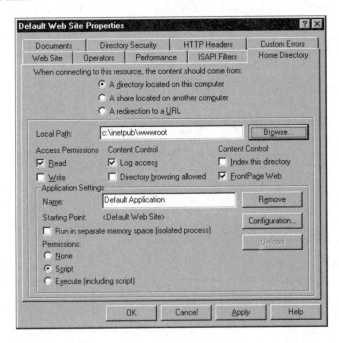

Index Server can index the web site documents because Index Server is on the same machine as the web server and therefore has access to the web documents through the file system. Index Server cannot index documents on a web server that does not expose its documents through the file system.

Search can index documents from other web servers because it can use HTTP to obtain documents. However, HTTP does not have any file notification built in so Search has to periodically re-index documents according to some schedule or explicit command in case they have changed, instead of just re-indexing certain folders or documents whenever notification of a change is given (file change notifications and IIS `vroot` changes) as is the case with Index Server. (However, as we will see later, there is a workaround to make Search index in response to notifications of changes.)

> *Index Server obtains the documents it indexes through the file system. However, there is a link into Internet Information Server. The link enables the physical file path to be mapped to a virtual directory. Therefore, when a list of search results is obtained, the URL of the file (if it is under wwwroot) can be obtained from the file path. However, because of this link, if any of the virtual directories in IIS that map to file directories that are indexed change (a `vroot` change), a 're-indexing' has to take place.*

Another important distinction is that Index Server indexes documents from a server's point of view whereas Search indexes document from a client's point of view. For example, Index Server will index the actual Active Server Page code of an ASP file whereas Search makes a request for that ASP file, the ASP file gets processed and Search indexes the HTML returned by the web server.

With Search an index must be explicitly defined using a catalog definition. The catalog definition says exactly where the source of the content is and how the indexing should be done. You also have the option of including and excluding specific types of content and you can create a schema for each catalog to control which properties of documents are catalogued.

Both Index Server and Search can use the Windows NT Performance Monitor. Search can also use the Analysis tool of Site Server to provide reports on site visitor query patterns.

Lastly, Index Server offers search term highlighting, whereas Search does not. Search term highlighting means that when Index Server returns a document satisfying a query, the words used for the query will be shown in a different color.

Benefits

The focus of Search is to make information easily accessible. The result is people work more effectively, it takes less time to find documents and people's productivity is enhanced.

Search does its best to categorize information as much as it can. For example, for a Microsoft Office document, Search will record information such as the author and title. The result is you can perform a context sensitive search (e.g. selecting all documents where the author is Craig instead of selecting all documents where the word Craig occurs) resulting in a much better result list. Search also automatically detects the language of the documents it catalogs. This means the site visitor can specify the language of the documents they want to search for.

Search provides a single access point to information stored in diverse locations. Instead of using many different applications to find a document, Search provides a web-based interface to query for documents. Once the document is found then the relevant application can be launched to view it.

In addition, although Search can be administered from the Microsoft Management Console (MMC) used in Windows NT, it can also be managed remotely using the Site Server WebAdmin interface. For most of the samples in this chapter we will be using the MMC. However, to administer search from WebAdmin, go to `http://yourwebserver/siteserver/Admin/Knowledge/Search/`.

You might also be wondering if Search can be used to create a search web site like Altavista (http://www.altavista.com) or Yahoo (http://www.yahoo.com). It can, but certainly not at the same scale. However, Search employs similar technology, acting as a web crawler so you can point it to many web sites and it will automatically walk through the links, indexing the content as it goes.

Now let's look at some key concepts.

Concepts

There are four parts to Search – defining the data to index, gathering data for indexing, moving the generated index to a Search Server and executing queries against the index. Search does not have one massive index containing all the information; rather it organizes indexed data into catalogs. Lets look at how the key concepts fit into place.

> **Catalog** – an index created by Search according to criteria (a Catalog Definition) defined by the developer

> **Catalog Definition** – the instructions and parameters for creating a catalog

> **Query** – a description of information passed to a Search Server used to try and find matches in a catalog

> **Propagation** – moving a –catalog to one or many Search Servers

Note, the words 'catalog' and 'index' essentially mean the same thing when dealing with Site Server Search.

The catalog is created using the **Catalog Build Server**. Once created the catalog is passed to the **Search Server**. The Search Server is responsible for receiving queries, executing them against an index and serving the results back to the client.

Catalog Build Server

The Catalog Build Server takes a catalog definition and executes it, resulting in a catalog. Creating a catalog can be a *very* resource intensive operation therefore it is important to have an understanding of how much data is being indexed and how often it is being indexed. A Catalog Build Server then deploys the catalog to a Search Server. The Catalog Build Server runs as the Site Server Gatherer service.

Search Server

The Search Server gets all the credit. It takes the hard work of the Catalog Build Server and satisfies requests of the user. The user passes a query to the Search Server, which looks up the query in the catalog and returns the results. The Search Server runs as the Site Server Search service.

Now let's take a quick look at some of the issues to bear in mind when implementing Search.

Planning and Configuration

Planning and configuration go together. Having decided what you want to be able to do, you should then be able to work out in rough measure the resource demands that will be placed on the system. With this information you can decide on how the system can be configured. Depending on just what configuration options are available you may have to then go back and revise your planned implementation somewhat.

Planning

Search can potentially impose a large network and CPU load on a system, as it may need to obtain files and data from many other machines, which means they are pulled over the network. Once the data is obtained it is indexed, which is a resource intensive task. This is why it is important to have an idea of the type of data being indexed, and where it is coming from.

Planning your Search application will help with configuration since you will have a good idea of the load placed on the servers. Planning will also make the application more useful to the end user since you will understand the person's workflow before building the application.

Planning consists of determining your users needs, and in light of these requirements defining the data to index, grouping the data into catalogs and determining accessibility to the content. The more data there is in a catalog, the more the performance drops; however, you also don't want a user to have to search across many catalogs to get the information they are after. Search supports 5 million documents per catalog and up to 32 catalogs per Search Server.

Let's work with a hypothetical scenario to help us work through the implementation of Search.

WebSoft Consulting

WebSoft Consulting has a file server at their main office where they store all their documents. Examples of files are functional requirements documents, budget spreadsheets, and project plans. They have tried their best to maintain some order by creating a directory structure that people are supposed to adhere to, but it is still difficult to find documents. Not only that but they have just opened two other offices and have clients' documents stored on the other servers as well. By implementing Search they should be able to index all the directories and provide easier access to documents.

The company also wants to provide the sales and marketing employees with up-to-date intelligence on their competitors. To get this information, Search needs to be configured to crawl the competitors' web sites and store this information in a catalog.

WebSoft also has a number of domain experts within the company. Other consultants use these experts as resources. Unfortunately WebSoft has only one Site Server expert and she is getting tired of everyone asking her Site Server questions. She is going to solve her problem by setting up a repository of Site Server information using Search.

In order to get to grips with implementing Search in this scenario we first need to understand the concept of a host.

Working with Hosts

A **host** is defined as a computer on the network that is available to do some work. In the case of Site Server Search this means any Window NT Server machine on the network on which Search is installed. So you can have many Search hosts on your network if necessary. The work you do in the planning stage should help guide your choice of how many hosts you need and how they should be configured.

In the case of WebSoft we have one main and two subsidiary file servers, and in addition they need to obtain data from a number of web sites. Since the file servers contain operational data for the company (data that is used in the course of the business' everyday activities) it makes sense for the indexes for the file servers to be updated every fifteen minutes or so, if not more often.

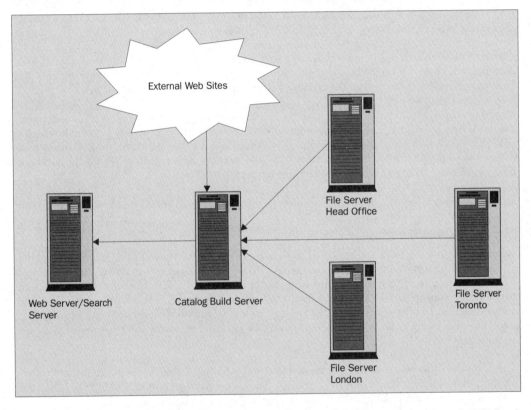

As mentioned earlier, the two resources strained by Search are network bandwidth and CPU load on each host. The network bandwidth is used because the Catalog Build Server needs to obtain the data from the source machine to index it. The source machine could be a file server, web server, exchange server, database server or news server. Note that the indexing process itself is much more greedy in terms of the demands it places on the system resources available than the process of serving up a document across the network to a client that requests it.

Thus, if the Catalog Build Server were to operate at maximum intensity on the same machine as the file system itself, the activities of the company would almost grind to a halt every time anything was indexed. So it makes sense for WebSoft to implement a dedicated server for the Catalog Build Server. You might think that if they were really short of money they could get around this problem by scheduling the index building activity to occur at times when the file system was not in use (e.g. between 3 and 4 a.m. in the morning). But let's imagine, as we have in the diagram shown earlier, that WebSoft is an international company with offices in different times zones so there really isn't any gap in the company's activities. Then it really does make sense for the company to put a dedicated Catalog Build Server on the network.

If there is a truly vast amount of data that needs indexing and constantly updating then, of course, one dedicated Catalog Build Server might not be enough. You may want to separate hosts depending on the content that they will be indexing. For instance, if you have five catalogs with only one on a high frequency indexing schedule you might place the four low-frequency catalogs on one host and the high-frequency catalog on its own host. With Search each host can be configured differently with respect to system resource use, the administrative and content access accounts it uses, and the location for storing catalog files.

To reduce the traffic created during the data gathering, place the Catalog Build Server in close physical proximity to the server with the data to be indexed. Ideally, the machines should be on the same network sub-net so the traffic does not have to go beyond the borders of the physical network. In the case of the web crawling that the WebSoft Catalog Build Server will have to do in order to index the data gathered over the Net, it might also make sense to implement a dedicated connection to the Internet so as not to slow any other Net access needs the company has.

Microsoft has performed an extensive capacity and performance study on Site Server Search. It is documented in the whitepaper available from `http://www.microsoft.com/siteserver/site/30/gen/per_search.htm`. This paper suggests calculations for capacity planning, gives results of tests based upon the calculations and lists some of the performance counters that should be monitored. The following assertions about scaling and performance for the Search Server part of Site Server Search are taken from this whitepaper:

> ➢ Scaling is reasonable from 1- to 2-processors, with a fifty-percent gain in query rate. From 2-processors to 4-processors scaling is insignificant, with only a fourteen-percent gain. Query rate may drop in 4-processors if the system is pushed beyond optimal performance, as a result of context switching.

> ➢ CPU is the primary bottleneck in 1- and 2-processor systems for small to moderate values of `MaxRecords`.

> ➢ Peak query rate falls when performing searches with hit count on and `MaxRecords=1`, when the property store size is significantly larger than system RAM size. However, as `MaxRecords` is increased, this loss in performance becomes increasingly less significant.

> ➢ Hit count makes a significant difference in query rate. With hit count off, 4- and 2-processor systems with `MaxRecords=1`, query rate peaked at approximately 60 queries/sec, versus 16 with hit count on.

> ➢ Size of the result set returned (as defined by `MaxRecords` in the search .asp) significantly impacts the query rate.

> ➤ Searching against catalogs in which security is applied to each document generally causes a reduction in the query rate by as much as fifty-five percent relative to corresponding anonymous query rates, when `MaxRecords` is small and the hit count is off. Under the same conditions, but with hit count on, a reduction in the query rate is also observed when searching against Exchange catalogs. In all other scenarios studied, the effects of security on query rate were minimal .

Query rate is the number of queries per second that the Search Server can cope with simultaneously. Context switching is when a multitasking operating system stops running one process and starts running another. `MaxRecords` is an ASP control variable limiting the number of records returned by each query.

Setting File Locations

The size of the index can get large if you are indexing a lot of information. For this reason, or perhaps for reasons of security, you may want to change the initial location that the Catalog Build Server files are stored at.

To change the locations of files from WebAdmin, start at
`http://yourWebServer/siteserver/Admin/Knowledge/Search/`
and click on **Server Properties** in the menu frame. On the **Server Properties for Host** page, click **General Properties**.

Temporary Catalog Build Files

When a Catalog Build Server creates catalogs, it creates temporary files. By default, these files are stored in the system's `temp` directory.

Catalog Definition Files

By default, files for catalog definitions are stored in the following directory on the Catalog Build Server:
drive:`\Microsoft Site Server\Data\Search\Projects\`*catalog_name*`\Build`.

Completed Catalogs

By default, files for completed catalogs are stored in the following directory on the Search Server:
drive:`\Microsoft Site Server\Data\Search\Projects\`*catalog_name*`\Search`.

Each Search Server machine has its own configuration. Therefore, if the Search Server is on a different machine than the Catalog Build Server, the deployed catalog will be placed in the directory configured for that Search Server – not the directory configured on the Catalog Build Server machine. To configure Search Server for a particular machine you need to go to WebAdmin for that machine.

Now let's look at the security accounts needed to be able to administer intranet, Internet and extranet Search as these are essential for the successful completion of catalog building activity on a modern corporate networked system.

Search Accounts

Accounts are required for administering both the Catalog Build Server and the Search Server. Alternatively, you can use the same account for both. When you install Site Server, you specify a default account with a user name, password, and domain. This account is used for both the administrative access and content access accounts. This account can access servers that allow anonymous access. However, you cannot propagate catalogs to other hosts using this account unless this account has administrative privileges on the hosts being propagated to.

When you configure the account, it must have the following properties:

> ➢ Domain account
> ➢ Membership of local administrators group or optionally one of the following on the Catalog Build or Search Server: SiteServer Administrator, SiteServer Knowledge Administrators or SiteServer Administrators
> ➢ Password never expires
> ➢ Read access to all information sources to be crawled (per-site accounts can be set for crawling secured content as was discussed earlier in the section discussing Site Rules for Creating a Catalog)

Preparing the Content

The standard phrase "Garbage in – Garbage out" also applies to Search. Your query abilities will only be as good as the content being indexed. However there are a few steps you can take to ensure your documents are indexed correctly and effectively.

The IFilter Interface

For example, imagine that WebSoft has a number of sales brochures they would like indexed with Search. These brochures are stored as Portable Document Format (.pdf) files. Site Server Search is limited to a specific set of document formats it can index with the standard installation and .pdf is not one of those document formats. Let's see how we can extend the document types Search can index.

Content is stored in many different formats like plain text, HTML and Word documents. Information that is semantically the same is stored in different ways within these documents. For instance, a HTML document has a <TITLE> element whereas a Microsoft Office document keeps the title in the document properties.

To accommodate these differences in document types, Search uses an IFilter COM interface to query for properties. IFilter is a specification for how to write filters and return file properties. The IFilter interface used is based on the file's extension. If the IFilter for a file type is not included with Site Server, it may be available from a third-party provider. For instance, a common IFilter not packaged with Site Server is for Adobe .pdf files. Adobe does have one available that you can download and install. Search the Adobe web site (http://www.adobe.com) for IFilter to get more information about it.

As part of planning and configuration you should find out if there are documents you want indexed that are neither HTML nor Microsoft Office document types. If so, find out if an IFilter component is available for that document type and install it.

Making Content "Search Friendly"

As mentioned earlier, Search uses the IFilter interface to obtain context information about a document. However, for that to be effective, the document must have those fields stored in the document. For HTML documents, using <TITLE> and <ALT> tags can improve search ability as well as putting information in <META> tags. Using Site Server Content Management to submit documents or the Site Server Tag Tool (see later) will automatically put values in the <META> tags.

To improve the information obtained in Microsoft Office Documents, it is important to fill out the document properties. The following screen shot shows an example of how WebSoft should fill out a few of the fields used in a Word document.

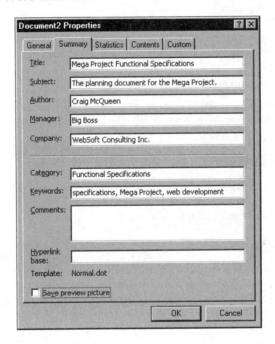

Tag Tool

To give an HTML document more context, it is important to include <META> tags within the document. That way, users can target their searches more to the information they are looking for. Tag Tool provides a way to add <META> tags to documents rather than changing the HTML manually.

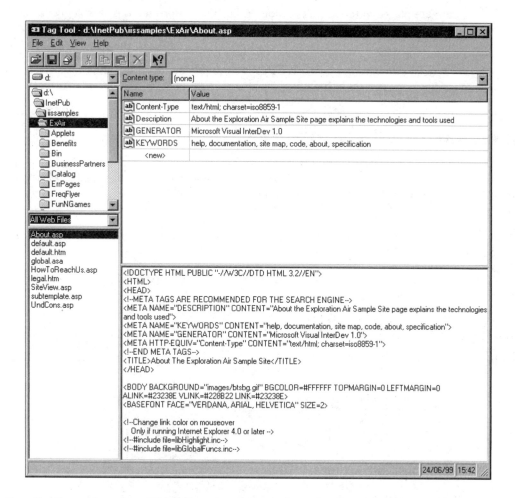

Say, that for each project, WebSoft maintains a number of web pages including a team member contact list, project status and documentation. Tag Tool can apply <META> tags either a document at a time or the same <META> tags to many documents. For example, the following <META> tags can be applied to all HTML documents related to a project:

```
<META name="Project" content="Mega Project">
<META name="Practice Area" content="Web Development">
<META name="Program Manager" content="Benny Hill">
```

Once the common tags are added to the documents, specific tags can be added to the individual documents. For instance, the web page that lists the team members, their responsibilities and contact information might have the following tags:

```
<META name="Content Type" content="Team List">
<META name="Author" content="Joe Maintainer">
```

195

The <META> tags are placed in the header section of the HTML document. A search query can then be formed that explicitly has 'Project=Mega Project' rather than just having the words 'Mega Project' in the text.

Now let's take a look at the samples for Search that are provided in the Site Server package, so we can run through the basic process of building a catalog.

Samples with Site Server

There is sample content available with Site Server for building sample catalogs, and sample search pages for creating queries against the sample data. The sample content can be found in Microsoft Site Server\Sites\samples\knowledge\search in folders called contentX. The sample search pages (all called search.asp) are in other sub-folders in the same directory.

Running through the process of enabling and using the sample material will help us to see what needs to be done in the case of the WebSoft scenario.

The Site Server sample content is a set of HTML pages. In order to try the samples, the HTML files first have to be catalogued.

Building a Sample Catalog

Start by opening MMC for Site Server. In the Search area you should see something similar to the following screenshot.

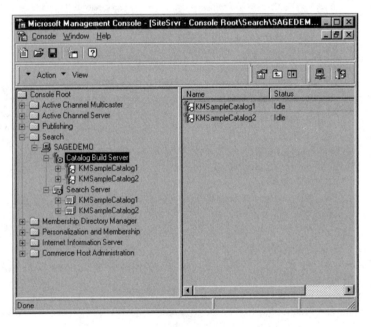

The KMSampleCatalogs are Site Server demo catalogs. They have already been defined for you but have not been built. In a production system you will want to delete these catalogs so their content doesn't get included in your search. As you can see, there is one section under Search for the Catalog Build Server and one for the Search Server. When catalogs are defined they are placed and controlled under the Catalog Build Server. Once catalogs have been propagated, a listing appears under the Search Server.

A Catalog Build can either be scheduled or run manually. Let's try a manual build. Right-click on KMSampleCatalog1 under Catalog Build Server to bring up the content menu and select "Build". The Catalog Build Server will take the sample catalog definition, crawl the sample web pages and create a catalog.

Once a catalog is built is it automatically propagated. However, you can also propagate a catalog as it is being built. You might want to do this if a build takes several hours to complete. You can also manually propagate a catalog either from MMC or WebAdmin.

If you cannot propagate the catalog there are a few things you can check. It may mean that the Catalog Build Server cannot access the Search host. Be sure you typed the host name correctly and that the host is accessible by the Catalog Build Server. If you are propagating to a host separate from the one with the Catalog Build Server on be sure the administrator access account is correct and has administrator privileges on the host being propagated to. Also be sure the host you are propagating to has sufficient disk space.

You can monitor the status of a catalog build through the MMC. In the scope pane of the MMC click Catalog Build Server to see a brief status of the catalog. The status is displayed in the Status column of the results pane of the Microsoft Management Console. For more detail select your catalog and on the "Action" menu click "Properties". By clicking the "Status" tab you will see the Status Property page showing the current activity. We will see an example of the status later in the chapter.

Sample Search Pages

Once a catalog is built and propagated, it is ready to be used by site visitors searching for information. Site Server has sample search pages that demonstrate various ways of querying a catalog. Note that some of them are hard-coded to use the catalogs named "catalog1" and "catalog2", which are the Site Server sample catalogs. It can be a handy way to try out a catalog before you put a lot of effort in creating a customized search page.

You can browse the different search pages available from the "Site Server Search Samples page" (try saying that phrase fast!), located at
`http://yourWebServer/SiteServer/samples/knowledge/search/`

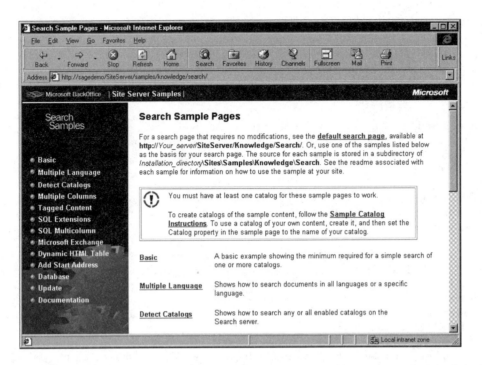

Note the text box with the exclamation mark on this page. You need sample catalogs built before you can use the sample search pages. This text box points to step-by-step instructions for building the sample catalogs. If you want to try searching your own catalogs rather than the sample catalogs I suggest using the Search Samples "Basic" or "Detect Catalogs", as they will work with any catalog.

The samples are well documented with each having a readme page and each having easily accessible color-coded, commented source, so I encourage you to go through them. The sample search pages available demonstrate the variety of ways queries can be formed. Most of the sample pages have a "View Source Code" link that will display a color-coded version of the ASP. There is also a "Readme" link to a page discussing the features of the page, required setup and how to incorporate the sample into your site.

Let's take a quick look at the code for the 'Basic' search page.

First, a Query COM object is created.

```
' Create the Query Object, and set properties for the search.
set Q = Server.CreateObject("MSSearch.Query")
```

The HTTP QueryString used for the search is set.

```
Q.SetQueryFromURL(Request.QueryString)
```

The name of the catalog to search is set. In this case, the name of the catalog is passed as a form variable.

```
Q.Catalog = Request("ct")
```

The columns to return from the search are set.

```
Q.Columns = "DocTitle, DocAddress, FileName"
```

The query is executed and the results are return as an ADO `Recordset`.

```
' Execute the query and create the recordset holding the search results.
on error resume next
set RS = Q.CreateRecordSet("sequential")
Response.write "<p>"
```

After the query is executed, the error object is checked. If the query was successful, you then iterate through the results just like a regular ADO `Recordset`.

```
' If the query can't be executed, print out the error description.
if err then
  Response.write err.description & "<p>"
elseif RS.BOF and RS.EOF then
  if Q.QueryIncomplete=true then
    L_TooComplex_Error = "Your query was too complex. Try a simpler _
                query."
    Response.write L_TooComplex_Error & "<p>"
  else
    L_NoMatch_Error = "No documents matching your query were found."
    Response.write L_NoMatch_Error & "<p>"
  end if
else
  ' Set up table for displaying results.
    Response.write "<table cellpadding=3>"
    ' Set up loop to iterate through results.
      Do while not RS.EOF
        ' If a blank title is found, use the filename or address
        ' instead.
        if RS("DocTitle") <> "" then
          DisplayTitle = RS("DocTitle")
        elseif RS("FileName") <> "" then
          L_NoTitle_text="No title"
          DisplayTitle = L_NoTitle_text & ": " & RS("FileName")
        else
          L_NoTitle="No title"
          DisplayTitle = L_NoTitle_text & ": " & RS("DocAddress")
        end if
        ' Display one table row for each result.
%>
        <tr><td><font size=2>
         <a href="<% = RS("DocAddress") %>"> _
                <% = DisplayTitle %> </a>
        </font></td></tr>
<%
        ' Increment the results.
        RS.MoveNext
      Loop
    Response.write "</table>"

end if ' End of check for successful recordset creation.
%>
```

Default Search Page

Site Server also has a default search page. The default search page can be used to search any catalog in your Site Server system. It can be found at
`http://yourWebServer/siteserver/knowledge/search`. You can search all catalogs or just an individual catalog. The results are displayed in the right hand frame. The following screenshot shows the results of a search in the KMSampleCatalog1 for the word "product".

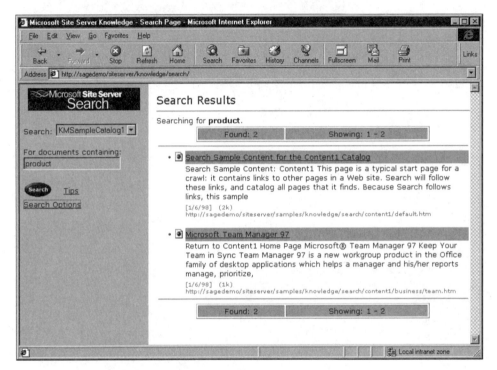

Creating a Catalog

It is time to solve WebSoft's Site Server expert's problem. Recall that many of the consultants came to her when they had Site Server questions. She wants to make an information repository for Site Server that the consultants can query instead. Let's create a catalog for Site Server information. We will use the Microsoft Site Server web site, `http://www.siteserver.com` and the local documentation installed with Site Server. The resulting catalog will have indexed information from two web sites and the local file system.

Creating a Catalog Definition

In the MMC under 'Search', right-click on the Catalog Build Server and select "New Catalog Definition" from the menu:

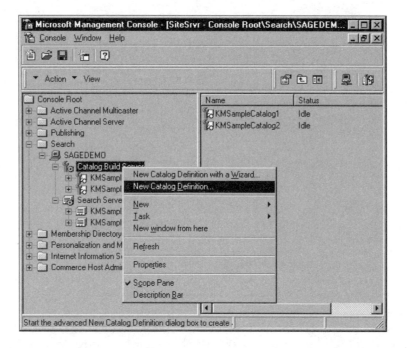

Give the catalog a name – in this case we are going to use "SiteServerInfo". Be sure to give the catalog an appropriate name because the name will be used for any programmatic access to the catalog.

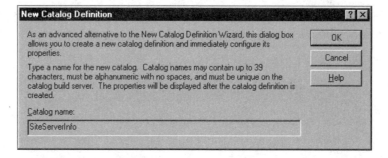

Crawling a Web Site

Next, the type of catalog needs to be indicated. Crawl indicates the Catalog Builder will periodically visit the documents defined within the scope of the crawl to update the index. For this demonstration, all the types will be "Crawl". Click "Add" to add a crawl type.

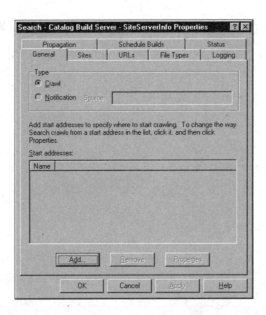

A "Notification" type catalog is built by accepting information from a notification source. The notification source informs Search when content has changed indicating that the information should be catalogued again. The notification source is a software component that implements the IGatherNotify COM interface. The Site Server SDK (available from http://www.microsoft.com/siteserver) has details of the IGatherNotify interface and a sample that uses it called DirMon. DirMon demonstrates how you can use the IGatherNotify interface to manage a notification-based catalog, and how to monitor a directory for file changes.

Make sure "Web link crawl" is selected and press "Next".

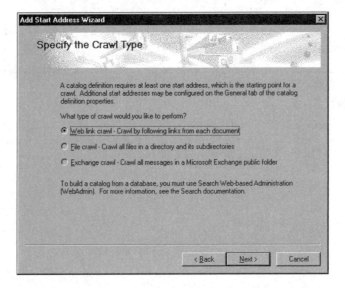

Enter the start address `http://www.siteserver.com`. We don't want the crawler to leave the web site and start crawling other web sites, so make sure that the "Site hops" box is selected and set to 0. Setting the "Page hops" means defining the depth that the crawler will travel. For instance, if it is set to 1, that means it will index each page linked to the Start address but will not visit the pages linked from there on.

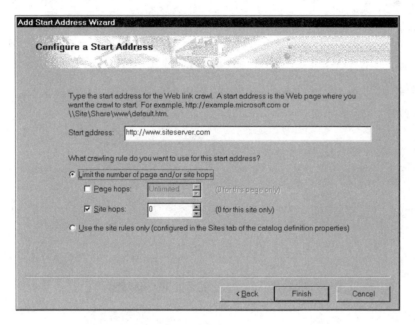

If you want finer grained control over how the crawl is performed you can use "site rules", which we'll cover next.

Crawling a Portion of a Web Site

The next set of documents we are going to add to the catalog is at `http://www.microsoft.com/siteserver`. There is an important distinction to make between a web site and a path. In the URL we just configured "`www.microsoft.com`" is considered a site and "`/siteserver`" is considered a path. Unless it is constrained, if there is a page within `http://www.microsoft.com/siteserver` that links to another portion of the Microsoft web site, say for example `http://www.microsoft.com/iis`, the crawler would continue to follow those links. We definitely don't want to index all of the Microsoft web site so we will configure this crawl using site rules.

As before, add a new start address to the catalog. This time however, specify the Start address as `http://www.microsoft.com/siteserver` and select "Use the site rules only".

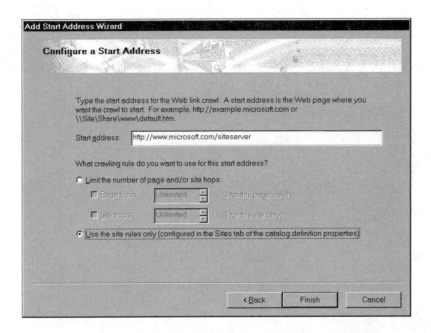

After clicking finish, bring up the properties for the catalog and select the "Sites" tab.

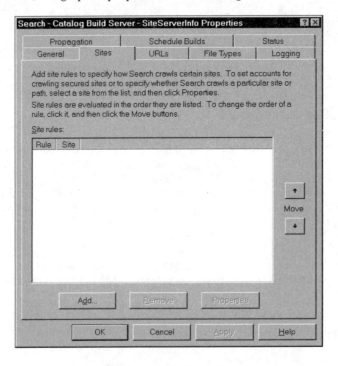

This property page is used to control which portions of a web site are crawled. As well, if portions of a web site are password protected, you can configure a username and password that will be automatically provided when that portion of the web site is entered.

What we need to do is tell the crawler to stay within the \siteserver path but stay out of the rest of the www.microsoft.com web site. Click on the "Add" button to add a site rule and fill out the dialog as in the following screenshot.

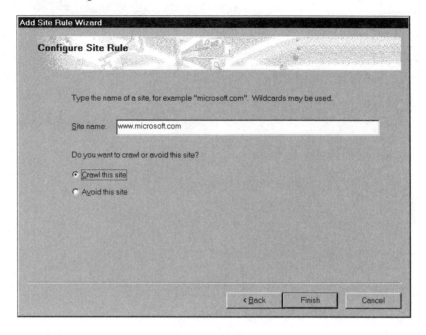

After clicking "Finish", bring up the properties for the site rule just added and add a path rule. Configure the dialog as in the following dialog.

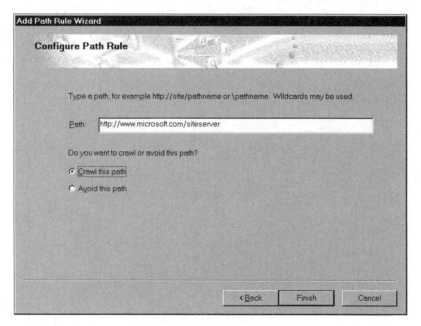

One more path rule needs to be added to tell the crawler to avoid the rest of the Microsoft web site. So add another rule and configure it as in the following screenshot.

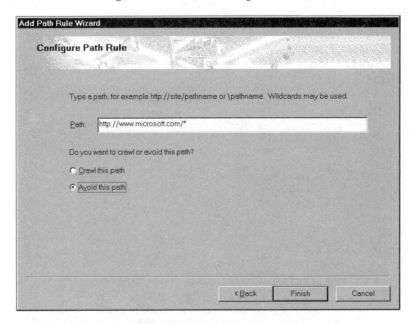

The resulting configuration should look like the following.

The important thing to note is the order of the path rules. Since the Crawl `/siteserver`
path rule is before the Avoid path rule, the Crawl path rule takes precedence – so
`/siteserver` will be crawled.

Crawling a File System

Another rich area of
information is the file system.
Let's add the Site Server help
documents to the catalog.
Choose "Add" again but this
time select "File Crawl" and
press "Next".

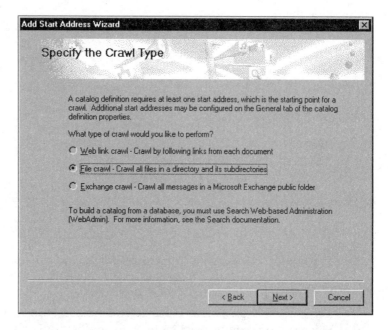

For the "Start address"
specify the location of your
Site Server help documents.
Note the file path can be a
local path
(`c:\Microsoft Site
Server\SiteServer
\Docs`) or a network path to
another machine
(`\\webserver\Share\Do
cs`). You can also limit the
depth of subdirectories to
index at this point at well.

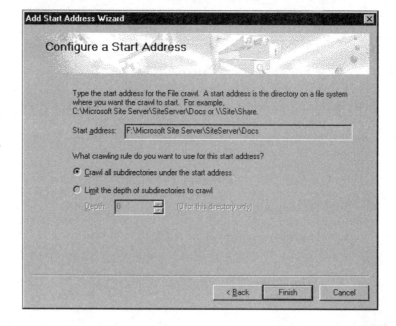

207

Your final catalog should look something like the following catalog. The next step is to build the catalog according to the definition you just gave. Click "OK" to close the window.

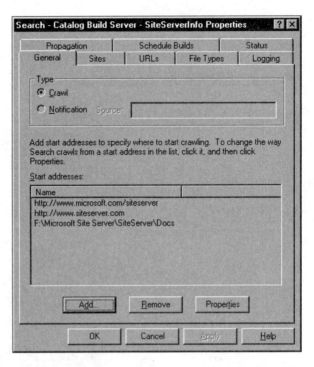

Note the "File Types" tab in the Property Sheet. That property page allows you to specify which files to crawl and which to avoid. For instance, if you wanted to exclude .css stylesheets, you would specify it there.

> You need to carefully consider how you define your catalog. You want to make sure the crawler obtains all the documents you want indexed yet does not have such a large scope that it never finishes crawling.

Crawling Forms-based Authenticated Sites

WebSoft could run into trouble when creating their search catalogs. Since Site Server is part of their Information Technology strategy they may be using HTML-forms-based authentication to protect some areas of their Intranet. Forms-based authentication causes problems for Search. Search cannot automatically type a username and password into an HTML form. This means they would not be able to crawl web sites that use forms-based authentication.

However, if you are using Site Server with forms-based authentication you do have an option. You can take the same approach as mentioned in the Site Server documentation for using Visual InterDev with a web site protected with forms-based authentication (search the Site Server help for "FrontPage Extensions" and "Authentication" to get more details for Visual InterDev). Let's adapt this technique for crawling forms-based authenticated sites.

Set up a new virtual directory that points to the same files that are protected with forms-based authentication. For this new virtual directory set the authentication to 'Basic/Clear Text' rather than forms-based authentication. Configure Search to index this new virtual directory. Since it uses Basic/Clear Text authentication, you can configure Search to provide a username and password when indexing the virtual directory. As an added security measure, use the MMC to deny all computers access to the new virtual directory except the IP address of the machine doing the catalog build.

There is one more step you need to take. Returned search hits will have the address of the virtual directory that denies access to everyone except the Catalog Build Server. For the URLs in your search results page you will have to programmatically swap the search virtual directory name with the proper one.

You might think, "Well, if the files are on their intranet, how come they just can't use a file system crawl to index the documents?" Remember that if you use a file system crawl the content of the file will be indexed, *not* the content generated from the file. Specifically, if the file is an ASP, the ASP code will be indexed. However, if you use a web-based crawl the content generated from the ASP (i.e. the HTML) will be indexed.

Crawling Databases

So far WebSoft has included information from web sites and file systems into their catalogs. Someone from the WebSoft Sales department pointed out that they have a "Sales Tips" database on a legacy system. It contains all kinds of sales tips and information that has been acquired over the years. The Sales Manager would really like to make this information available to the sales team and consultants via a web-based application. Specifically, he would like the team to be able to search for tips in the database. It turns out that Site Server Search can solve this problem too.

You can build a Search catalog from a database provided you have an ODBC driver for the database. Microsoft has a whitepaper on the subject that can be obtained from http://www.microsoft.com/siteserver/site/30/whitepapers/SearchDatabase.htm. It describes the process of full text indexing Microsoft SQL Server and Access databases using ODBC and Active Server Pages. It describes in detail how the process works and walks through a sample.

It might sound strange to "crawl" a database. With Site Server Search you are not really crawling the database but instead you are creating HTML pages from queries to the database and are crawling the resulting pages. When you configure a catalog definition based on a database Site Server generates some ASP files. These ASP files perform ADO queries to obtain the data from the database and render the results as HTML. The HTML generated from the ASP files is actually what is indexed.

The documentation says the process is tested with SQL Server and Microsoft Access only. However, any database accessible through ODBC should work. I have successfully created a catalog using an ODBC connection to an IBM AS/400 database.

If WebSoft was starting the "Sales Tips" database from scratch and was using SQL Server 7 they would probably take a different approach. Since SQL Server 7 has full text indexing built in, it is more efficient to rely on the database index than to create HTML from the database and index the HTML.

Crawling Dynamically Generated Content

As mentioned before, dynamically generated content should be treated differently from static content. Again, static content, like an HTML file, is in most respects the same on the file system as it is when delivered to the client. This means it can be indexed either through a web crawl or a file system crawl. Dynamically generated content however, is different on the file system compared to what the client receives. Specifically, an ASP file is not the same as the HTML it generates and sends to the web browser. Most of the time it is the HTML that should be indexed not the ASP.

WebSoft has a situation where the same ASP page generates many different documents depending on the parameters passed to the ASP via the query string. They have two options to index content dynamically generated in this way. One way is to specify the entire URL including the query string as a start address. Another way is to create an HTML page that has a list of anchors in it. Each anchor would have the URL of the dynamically generated web pages. Just the 'container' HTML page would be added as a start address and each anchor in it would be followed by the Search crawler – thus causing all the dynamically generated content to be indexed. This method is the way database indexing works with Site Server.

Building the Catalog

Once the catalog is defined, it needs to be built. Building means taking the definition of where information is located, obtaining the information and indexing it. In the case of a web crawl, the Catalog Build Server will obtain all the links within a web page, decide if they need to be followed and if so put them in a queue for processing. In the case of a file system, the file hierarchy is crawled according to how you configured the crawl.

Note that if you configure a file crawl for a directory of HTML files you may obtain different results than if you configure a web crawl for the same files. This is because the Catalog Build Server processes the information in two different ways. One example of the difference is that 'orphaned' files (HTML files that no other pages link to) will get indexed with a file crawl if they are in the directory being crawled but would not be indexed using a web crawl.

To build the Site Server Information catalog defined in the previous section, select the catalog from the MMC under Search, right-click to bring up the context menu and choose "Start build".

Within the property page of the catalog you can watch the progress of the build by clicking on the "Status" tab. Here you can see all the documents that are currently being indexed.

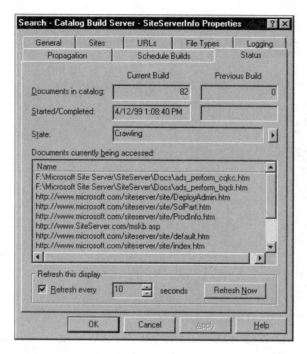

If you stop a build during processing you may get a warning saying that it may take some time. The reason is the Catalog Build Server has to wait for all outstanding requests to complete before it can stop.

In this case we manually performed the build. However, you may want to schedule the build (as we discussed earlier when considering WebSoft's options).

To set a schedule, click on the "Schedule Builds" tab in the property page for the Catalog Build Server. From here you can schedule "Full builds" and "Incremental builds". A full build will index all documents. An incremental build will only index those documents that have changed since the last build. An incremental build will take less time and resources than a full build. If "last modified" dates are not available with your information source, you will have to do a full build.

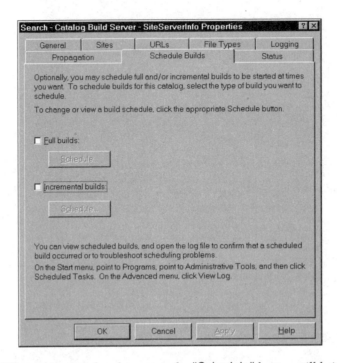

Selecting either full or incremental and pressing the "Schedule" button will bring up property pages to set the schedule and configure the account the task will run as.

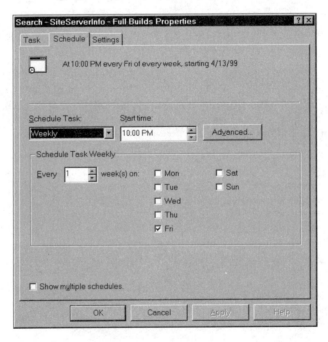

Making Searches "Server Friendly"

The Internet has made information free. Building a catalog based on other people's web sites is leveraging all that free information. The result is a comprehensive index from diverse information sources. WebSoft's Site Server catalog is leveraging the information prepared by the good folks at Microsoft and SiteServer.com (http://www.siteserver.com).

However, it is also important to respect other people's web sites when crawling them so you don't overload their server. If an automated crawler floods a web site with requests, less server time is available to serve requests by individuals visiting that site.

What motivation should you have to be "server friendly"? If web masters see that you are flooding their web server they might decide to block requests coming from your IP address. In this case, their information will no longer be available to you. WebSoft certainly doesn't want to get blacklisted by Microsoft.

The other advantage to being server friendly is that it can also reduce the amount of work your Catalog Build Server has to do. For instance, as you will see in the next section, sites that use the Robot Exclusion Protocol can instruct your Catalog Build Server to avoid areas of the web site that have information of little value.

Robot Exclusion Protocol

The Robot Exclusion Protocol is a method for administrators of a web site to give instructions to web robots as to which areas of the web site can be indexed and which should be avoided. It is currently an Internet Draft meaning it is not an official standard yet. However, there are no competing schemes in the market so chances are people implementing the Robot Exclusion Protocol have do so consistently. The best starting place to learn about it is at the web site http://info.webcrawler.com/mak/projects/robots/robots.html.

The Catalog Build Server will look for the robots.txt file before it starts crawling the web site. It then obeys the rules contained within the file. As well, it will obey any <META> tags in the documents that exclude robots. For example, <META NAME="Robots" CONTENTS= "NOINDEX, NOFOLLOW">.

To see what Microsoft uses for robot exclusion, enter the following URL into your browser: http://www.microsoft.com/robots.txt

You browser should show something similar to the following:

```
# robots.txt for http://www.microsoft.com/
# do not delete this file, contact MSCOMHLP for edits!!!!
#

User-agent: *
Disallow: /isapi/# keep robots out of the executable tree
Disallow: /scripts/
```

This robots.txt file says "allow all user-agents, do not index the /isapi/ directory and do not index the /scripts/ directory". Those directories are excluded because there is a performance hit accessing dynamically generated pages and Microsoft doesn't want robots loading their server.

Obviously, if you are implementing a web site, there will be parts of your site that you will want to prevent other search crawlers from indexing and you will want to write a robots.txt file of your own.

Hit Frequency

When an HTML document is parsed during a crawl, all the links contained in it are put into a queue for the crawler to follow. Requests for all these documents can be submitted almost simultaneously. When each of these documents is returned, they are parsed and all links contained within them are put into a request queue. As you can see, there could be an exponential growth of HTTP requests sent out to the web server. For example, if you assume that an average page has 10 links on it, after the initial page is parsed there will be 10 HTTP requests queued up. Once all those documents are obtained and parsed then would then be 100 HTTP requests queued up, and the web site walk has only gone 2 levels deep.

There are two ways you can control the requests sent to a web server being crawled: you can limit the number of simultaneous requests and you can specify a delay between document requests. Limiting the number of simultaneous requests means that once the limit is reached, all other requests are blocked and queued up until one of the outstanding requests finishes. Specifying a delay means that Search will wait the given amount of time before the next HTTP request is sent to the server.

The number of simultaneous requests and the delay can be set from "Server Properties" in WebAdmin or in "Catalog Build Server Properties" in the MMC.

Identifying the Crawler

An optional HTTP header field used by Search is the "From" field. It specifies the email address of the person making the HTTP request. The web server can log it, giving web administrators the ability to contact the person at this email address if they decide that the requests are causing problems. Search requires that an e-mail address be specified to crawl web sites, but it is not required for crawling file systems. The e-mail address is set in the "Properties" dialog for the Catalog Build Server in the "Settings" under the "General" tab.

Propagating the Catalog

Once the catalog is built it needs to be propagated to the Search Server. The Search Server may be on the same machine as the Catalog Build Server, or it may be on another machine. It is possible to propagate the catalog to many machines on a network, and as long as each machine has Search Server it can make use of the catalog.

When propagating to a machine different than the Catalog Build Server you have to be careful with catalogs built from a file crawl. The catalog records the file location when it performs the crawl. When a query hit is returned for that file, so is the file location. For instance, in the WebSoft Site Server catalog, a hit on the Site Server Search help page would return F:\Microsoft Site Server\SiteServer\docs\top_sss.htm. If the help documents don't exist on that Search Server the user will not be able to get that document.

Because of this problem, it is better to use the network path to shared files rather than the physical path even if the files exist on the Catalog Build Server. This way if there is a hit on a document, the network path will be returned and users will be able to get the file if they have sufficient NT permissions. If the files aren't shared there is probably a security reason and therefore they should not be included in a file crawl.

To configure where the catalog is propagated, click on the "Propagation" tab in the property sheet. Add hosts by clicking "Add" and making sure the checkbox is checked.

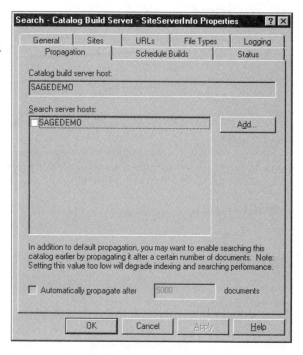

You can force propagation by selecting the appropriate menu item in the MMC as demonstrated in the following screen shot.

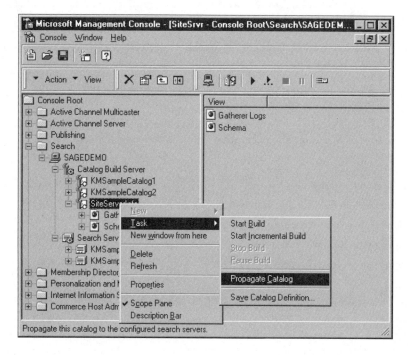

Testing the Catalog

Once you have defined, built and propagated the catalog, you will want to test it to make sure that it indexed the information you are interested in, and that you are able to access the documents you want to search for in the correct way. The easiest way is to go back to the default search page at: `http://yourWebServer//siteserver/knowledge/search` and try some queries. Alternatively, the MMC brings up a search page in the right-hand pane when you select a catalog.

Windows NT Access Control Lists (ACLs) permissions for each file indexed are recorded when Search performs a file or Microsoft Exchange crawl. Users who do not have the correct permissions to access a file will not see that file in the results page for a search query – returned query results will have all documents for which a user does not have proper permissions filtered out. Therefore, two people may get different query results if they have different file access permissions.

Indexed content from crawls performed over HTTP will be visible in the search results for all users.

Search and Usage Analyzer

Search can be integrated with other tools in the Site Server package to help optimize the searching process. For example, once Search is deployed within their organization, WebSoft would like to monitor which types of information their consultants are searching for, so they know what the most valuable type of information is for that group. Additionally, WebSoft is interested in finding out what topics people cannot find information for. Among other things, this analysis could be used to drive optimizing which information is indexed and the way the catalogs are organized. Fortunately, another feature of Site Server, Usage Analyzer, can integrate with Search to produce these reports. We will only mention a few features of integrating the Usage Analyzer with Search here, as we will cover the Site Server Analysis Tools in detail in Chapter 11 on 'Site Server Analysis'.

Basically, Usage Analyzer is used to create reports about web site usage. It is possible to save information to the IIS 4.0 log file about search queries requested and the results returned. Usage Analyzer can generate reports based on this information. There are two standard Analysis reports that use Search information: "Search Top Query" and "Search Trends".

Search Top Query

This report provides information about common queries and common problems. It contains the following information:

> Top 20 search queries

> Top queries based on catalog searched

> Which catalogs are used most frequently

> Queries that returned > 200 results

> Queries that returned no results

Search Trends

This report provides information about queries over time. It contains the following information:

> Search use by week
>
> Search use by day
>
> Search frequency
>
> Number of unique searches by day

Either of the packaged reports can be customized. Additionally, new reports can be created using Report Writer (another tool in the Site Server Analysis package). The information gathered from these reports provides valuable insights into future site design. For instance, the WebSoft web master may decide to create predefined queries according to the most common search queries.

Search and Knowledge Manager

Hopefully you now have an understanding of how to gather and index various types of information. The next step is to create an "information portal" as a sophisticated front-end for searching and viewing the information. Site Server's Knowledge Manager can do this for you. We will look at this Site Server feature in the next chapter.

Search SDK

There is also a section for Search in the Site Server SDK 1.1 that is downloadable from `http://www.microsoft.com/siteserver/site/default.htm`. The SDK describes two COM classes, SearchAdmin and CGatherNotify, that provide programmatic access to a set of collections, properties, and methods to administer a Search system. These COM classes provide a way to embed search functionality into your existing web applications.

SearchAdmin is used to manage catalog definitions, build catalogs from the catalog definitions, and propagate the resulting searchable catalogs to the Search servers in the system. With SearchAdmin you could build your own webcrawler without having to worry about the details of making HTTP requests and parsing HTML.

CGatherNotify is used to notify Search that content has changed and should be re-indexed. Being able to drive indexing from notifications instead of schedules is more efficient because only changed information is re-indexed. An example of when you might implement CGatherNotify is integration with your deployment mechanism so content is re-indexed after it is deployed. As mentioned earlier in the chapter, the SDK contains a sample that uses CGatherNotify to indicate when files change in a directory.

Summary

This chapter introduced the concepts of Site Server Search. The purpose of Search is to gather information from many diverse sources and integrate it into a catalog. This chapter demonstrated how to get information from web sites and file systems. Limiting the scope of the crawl of a web site was also shown. Specific aspects of Search covered were:

➢ Creating a catalog definition

➢ Building a catalog

➢ Propagating a catalog

➢ Using search pages

➢ Tips for improving catalogs

Catalogs built by Search are key components used in the next chapter, which is about the Knowledge Manager.

8

Knowledge Manager

Much of the book so far has discussed services provided by Site Server. Knowledge Manager is different because it's a web-based application within Site Server rather than a service. It can be used within your organization "out-of-the-box". It requires configuration, but no Active Server Page programming – unless of course you want to customize it.

The Knowledge Manager utilizes the following features of Site Server:

- ➢ Personalization & Membership
- ➢ Content Management
- ➢ Search
- ➢ Direct Mail

Two of these features we've already seen: Content Management and Search. The other two, Personalization and Membership and Direct Mail, were introduced in chapter 1 but we haven't yet covered them in depth. We won't go into them in detail in this chapter – however if you'd like more information you probably want to refer to the relevant chapters. This chapter discusses the following:

- ➢ Knowing when it is appropriate to use the Knowledge Manager
- ➢ Understanding of the concepts behind Knowledge Manager
- ➢ Creating and configuring various sources of information to use with Knowledge Manager
- ➢ Creating a Content Source from a Catalog
- ➢ Providing easy access to information for users

In the Search and Content Management chapters you were introduced to WebSoft Consulting. WebSoft has a number of domain experts within the company that other consultants use as resources. In the Search chapter we created a Site Server information repository so that the WebSoft Site Server expert doesn't have to spend as much time answering people's queries. We will continue to try to ease the workload on the WebSoft experts using Knowledge Manager.

Overview

Let's start with a quick review of some of the Site Server concepts used by Knowledge Manager.

In Chapter 9, *Membership*, we'll learn about the concept of a Membership Directory, how to define users and groups within Site Server, and how to assign attributes to them.

In Chapter 6, *Content Management*, you learned how to give context to documents by assigning attributes to them as they were published. The concept of Content Sources was introduced. You saw how files in a Content Source can belong to different Content types and have attributes assigned to them.

Chapter 7, *Search*, discusses how to create a catalog by gathering and indexing information from many diverse sources. It also demonstrated how to execute a query to find information stored in a catalog.

Once you have implemented these features you have a rich source of information. The data is indexed and stored with context associated with it. If you have implemented Personalization and Membership, user's preferences and interests are known. However, by itself, the information is not very interesting. What is required is an application to bring it all together. The answer, as you can probably guess, is Knowledge Manager.

Knowledge Manager does not bring any new base features to Site Server itself, rather it uses the rich information created by the existing services making it useful to a user. Content Management and Search categorize and index information; Personalization & Membership identifies a user's preferences; Knowledge Manager matches these up, targeting information that is appropriate to a user.

Many Search sites have re-branded themselves as information **portals**. Instead of being general search web sites they are moving towards categorized, personalized information. As well as this, some of the information is 'pushed' to the web site user as brief clips of information on the logon page – targeted to the user's interest. A example of a portal site is `http://home.microsoft.com`.

Knowledge Manager is similar to an information portal and offers similar benefits. The difference is that Knowledge Manager is much more targeted – your organization decides what information is available through the portal and how it is categorized. With Knowledge Manager, users can quickly obtain the information they need both actively and passively. They can hunt for information using the search features of Knowledge Manager, and they can periodically scan the published information specific to their interests. Alternatively, users can have information e-mailed to them instead of going to the portal.

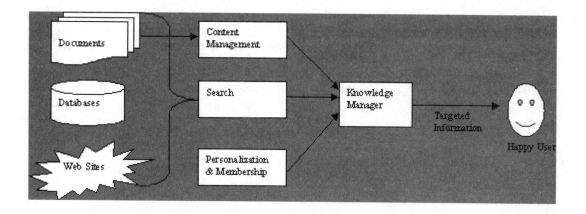

Concepts

Knowledge Manager uses some concepts that if understood first, make learning the application much easier. The information used by Knowledge Manager is available through **briefs**. Using the Portal analogy, a Brief is similar to the first page of a portal. A brief is a collection of categorized information with summaries available for each piece of information. Each user has a **private brief** and access to **shared briefs**. A private brief is information collected and organized by a user for their personal use. A shared brief is information collected and organized by someone and then made available to others.

Shared briefs are generally setup by **experts**. In Site Server terms, an expert is just a Knowledge Manager user who has been given permission to publish shared briefs. An expert is responsible for collecting information for a particular topic, creating a shared brief for that topic and maintaining that shared brief once it is published. For instance, WebSoft Consulting has a Site Server expert who would be responsible for collecting and publishing information about Site Server.

A brief is composed of organizational units based on different topics, called **sections**. The pieces of information within a section are usually related to each other in some way. There are two types of sections: saved searches and links list. A **saved search** is a record of the parameters for a query, assigning these a title and description for easy recall later. A **links list** is a list of URLs with descriptions.

Information used with Knowledge Manager is stored in **content sources**. A content source is an object stored in a Site Server Membership Directory that defines content and its location. Note that it doesn't contain the content itself. Content sources are discussed further in Chapter 6 – Content Management. The Membership Directory is discussed further in Chapters 9 and 10 – on Personalization and Membership.

Information within a content source can be tagged using a **site vocabulary**. A site vocabulary is a hierarchically arranged set of possible values for user and content attributes. The site vocabulary is stored in a P&M Membership Directory and is used to ensure that information is described in a consistent way.

In addition to searching properties of content, Knowledge Manager also searches the content itself. For this to be possible, a **catalog** needs to be created. A catalog is an index and property store that can be searched.

Once gathered, one of the ways to distribute information to people is through a **channel**. A channel is a definition for a set of information to be automatically delivered to users. Channels are part of Site Server Push, specifically Active Channel Server. Information defined in a channel is updated on a user's computer according to a defined schedule or set of rules.

With those concepts explained, let's see how they are used in practice by taking a tour of Knowledge Manager.

Tour

Knowledge Manager is a complete application. However, to be useful it requires sources of information. Let's take a tour of Knowledge Manager using the sample data provided with Site Server.

> **Make sure that you have built and propagated the sample catalogs discussed in the Search chapter before you use this Knowledge Manager sample.**

Authorization

The Knowledge Manager application is started from the URL:
`http://yourWebServer/SiteServer/Knowledge`.

Knowledge Manager uses whatever authorization has been set up with Personalization and Membership. For example, if the web site is protected with Basic Authentication, the user will be prompted for a user name and password before using Knowledge Manager. Since the user is authenticated, Site Server knows various attributes about the user from the Membership Directory. If the Membership Directory has a first name, last name and e-mail address for the user, the user will be immediately put into Knowledge Manager. If any of those fields are missing in the Membership Directory, the user is required to provide that information before continuing. Once entered, Knowledge Manager updates the Membership Directory with this new information.

If anonymous access is allowed, users are recorded as Anonymous users, and they will be required to provide contact information. Site Server returns a cookie to their browser so it knows that they have already registered with Knowledge Manager.

If you are prompted for the contact information, fill in this information similar to the following screen shot.

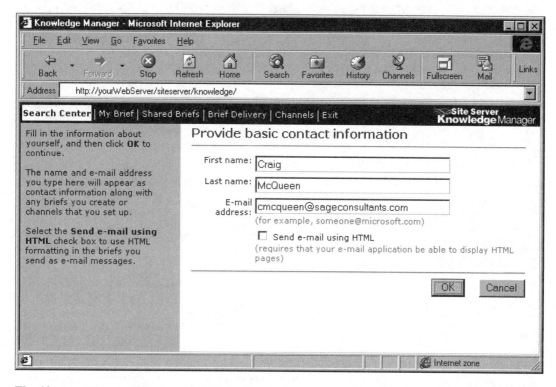

The file `EditUserRight.asp` (which is the page you just saw) contains all the logic for the contact information. You may want to modify the page if you have other attributes you want to ensure are recorded for a user. For instance, WebSoft might want to make sure they had an employee ID for each person that uses Knowledge Manager.

The name and e-mail address in the contact information is associated with any briefs or channels you set up. We will see later in the chapter how you can choose to have briefs delivered by e-mail. If your e-mail client supports the display of HTML, check the box titled Send e-mail using HTML to receive a richer view than with plain text. A brief e-mailed as HTML will look almost the same as it would using the web-browser. A brief sent as text will have all the content but will lack the formatting.

You can change the contact information anytime by selecting Change Personal Settings. Note that if you do change the personal settings it will update the Site Server Membership Directory and be reflected in any other applications that use that membership directory.

After you press the OK button, you will see a web page similar to the following.

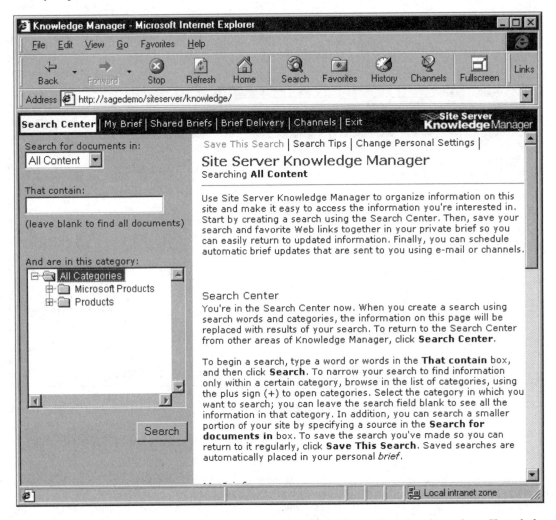

This page is the main user interface of Knowledge Manager. You will notice throughout Knowledge Manager a lot of text displayed describing the application. The options along the top menu are:

> Search Center
> My Brief
> Shared Briefs
> Brief Delivery
> Channels
> Exit

Let's look at each of these choices (except Exit, which we will look at in a later section of the chapter).

Search Center

The user interface for Search Center is in the left-hand pane. The Search Center is similar to the Search page at `http://yourWebServer/siteserver/knowledge/search/`. We looked at this page in Chapter 7 – Search. You'll notice that both Search interfaces allow you to search documents within a catalog (or in all catalogs).

A difference between the user interfaces is that the Knowledge Manager Search Center allows you to specify a category where Search does not. A category is a value in the Site Server Site Vocabulary. Categories are used in this case as an attribute of a document. For an HTML document, a category is specified using the meta tag `topic`. For example, the following meta tag would identify an HTML document as a development specification for `ProjectX`.

```
<meta name="topic" content="\Development\Specification\ProjectX">
```

In order to use categories, Knowledge Manager queries content sources rather than a catalog. Knowledge Manager 'wraps' catalogs with additional metadata to create a content source. We will see later in the chapter how to make a content source from a catalog.

Recall that in the Search chapter that we created a Site Server Search Catalog containing information about Site Server from various sources. WebSoft consultants could query the catalog to find answers to their Site Server questions. One problem is that they had to re-enter a query every time they wanted to run it. For instance, if someone's search was "Membership.UserObject NEAR Active User Object", they would have to re-type it every time they performed the search. Knowledge Manager lets you save a search. This way, once you refine a search to the results you want, it can be recorded for future use and even shared with others. Let's start by seeing how we perform a search within Knowledge Manager.

Performing a Search

Queries can be performed against a category of information rather than globally. For instance, the following example shows a search for all Microsoft **Business Products** that contain the word 'Web'. This means all the found documents would have the following meta tag:

```
<meta name="topic" content="\Microsoft Products\Business Products">
```

Since the drop-down box is selected for **All Content**, all catalogs will be searched. The search results are displayed on the right hand side. A smaller, more specific list of hits is returned compared with a global search. Try a global search by selecting **All Categories** instead of **Business Products**. You should get a greater number of hits. Be sure to try both to see the difference.

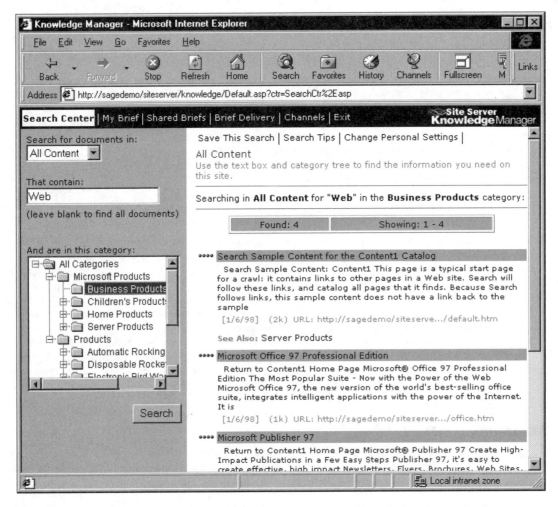

The category, such as Business Products, is mapped to the Site Vocabulary hierarchy for your content store. Each document in the sample content has a tag that matches the Site Vocabulary.

Another way to constrain the search is selecting only one content source in the drop down box rather than using the default of All Content.

Saving a Search

After receiving the query results, in the top left corner of the page you will notice a link to Save this Search. This feature lets you record a search for quick reference later. It is a key way of organizing important information with Knowledge Manager. The search is stored in a Microsoft Access database – we will look at the Knowledge Manager database later in the chapter. Click on it, fill out the dialog that comes up (looking something like the following screen shot) and press the OK button.

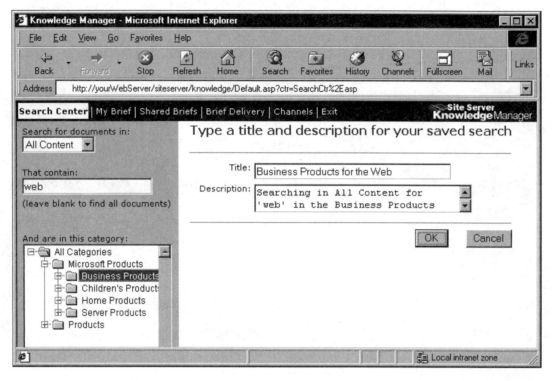

Note the description is already filled out for you, although you can change it if you wish. We will see how to access stored searches in the next section.

For WebSoft Consultants, the ability to save searches means that they have easy access to customized lists of resources they use on a regular basis. In fact, they are beginning to wish that Microsoft's MSDN library would allow them to save searches!

My Brief

My Brief is your private or personal brief in Knowledge Manager. As discussed earlier in the chapter, briefs are comprised of sections. A section can be a saved search or a list of Web links. Use this page to add or change a brief's title and description and add or remove sections.

Sections for Saved Queries

When you first click on My Brief it will look something like the following screen shot. This page contains searches you have saved and your favorite web links.

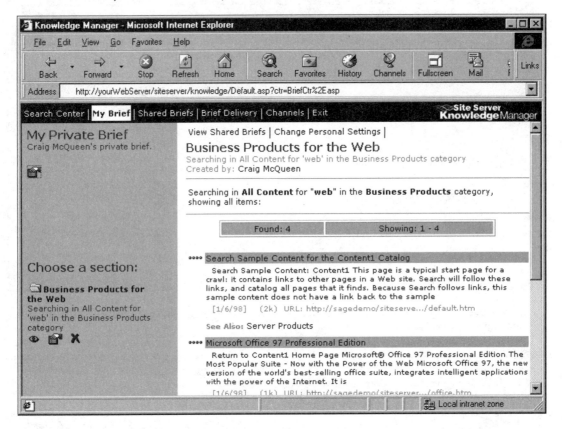

Since we have already saved a search, it is listed here. Note also that the query is automatically run when you go to My Brief and the results are displayed in the right-hand page.

You will notice three icons with the section, these are for viewing, editing and deleting the section. Viewing will execute the query associated with the section. Delete will remove the section from My Brief. Edit allows you to change some of the properties for the brief – the title and description of the section can be changed but the actual query parameters cannot.

The page allowing you to do this looks remarkably similar to the page we used to enter the details of our saved search earlier, so I won't show it here.

Link Sections

The other type of section you can add to My Brief is a link to a URL. Note that a link can be any valid URL, including links to web pages, newsgroups, ftp sites and e-mail addresses. The links are divided into sections. Each section should have a particular subject. Let's build a section composed of links to helpful pages for ASP developers at WebSoft Consulting.

Click on the icon under My Private Brief. You will see the following screen:

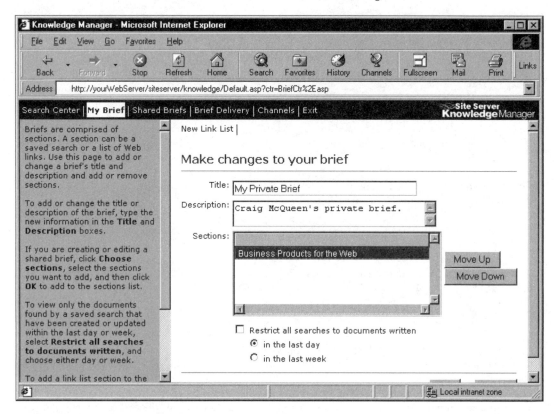

From this page you can change the title and description for your private brief. As well as this, you can filter your search based on whether the document is new within the last day or last week. If you decide you want to run the query with some other time interval than the last day or the last week the file you will be interested in is QueryUtils.inc. In there you will find a function called RunQuery with a parameter called in_iSince. If the value is −1 the documents returned would be for the last day, otherwise if the parameter is greater than zero the query is performed for the last in_iSince weeks.

The right-hand frame for editing briefs is named EditBriefsRight.asp. In there is a variable m_iBriefFreq, which contains the time restriction for which documents are returned. With the current ASP the value can only be −1 (last day), 0 (no restriction), or 1 (last week).

Have a look at the `GetFreq()` function taken from `EditBriefsRight.asp`:

```
function GetFreq()
{
    var iReturn = "";
    if (document.frmEditBrief2.chkRestrict.checked)
    {
        if (document.frmEditBrief2.rdoRestrict[1].checked)
        {
            iReturn = <%= FREQ_WEEKLY %>;
        }
        else
        {
            iReturn = <%= FREQ_DAILY %>;
        }
    }
    else
    {
        iReturn = <%= FREQ_ALL %>;
    }
    return iReturn;
}
```

The function `GetFreq()` is a client side function that obtains the value from the HTML form. It is then assigned and submitted to the web server as a form variable:

```
document.frmEditBrief.<%= PARAM_EDIT_FREQ %>.value = GetFreq();
document.frmEditBrief.submit();
```

Once at the server that form variable is assigned to the variable `m_iBriefFreq` with the line (in the file `EditBriefsRight.asp`):

```
m_iBriefFreq = Request(PARAM_EDIT_FREQ)
```

There is no reason you couldn't change the page so the user could specify the number of weeks. You would change `GetFreq` to return the number of weeks. Without any other changes eventually this value would be assigned to `m_iBriefFreq` and be passed to `RunQuery`.

You can also change the order of sections. The important point about the order of sections is that the section listed first is the one automatically run when you go to **My Brief**.

For now, click on **New Link List** near the top of the page. Fill out the page that comes up like the following screen shot and press **Add**. The link being added here is to the Wrox ASP developer web site http://www.asptoday.com.

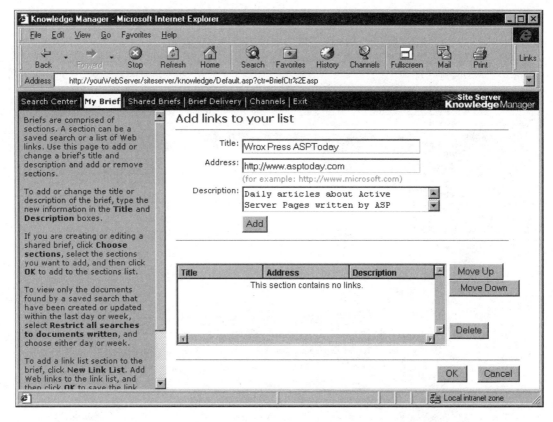

Lets consider some developer links that some of the WebSoft developers might be interested in, such as:

> MSDN web site
> Microsoft Active Server Page newsgroup
> Microsoft support e-mail

The result will look something like the following screen shot:

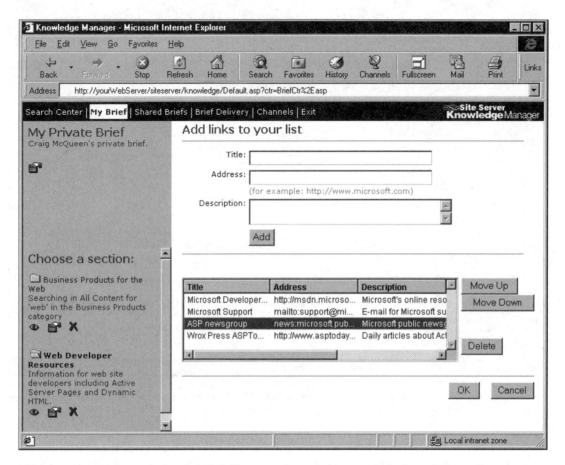

When you have all your links click OK. You can always add more links later. Fill out the next form something like the following:

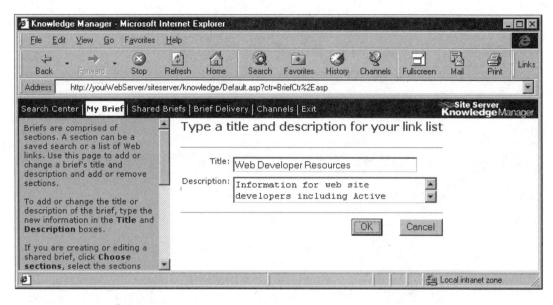

After pressing the OK button your screen should look like the following.

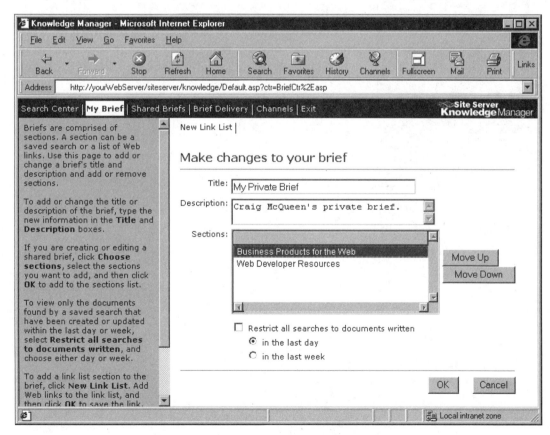

We are now ready to see the results of our work. Go to the main My Brief page and click on the view icon for the new section. You should see a web page with your links. The configuration just described looks like the following. You can click on the title of a link to go to the URL.

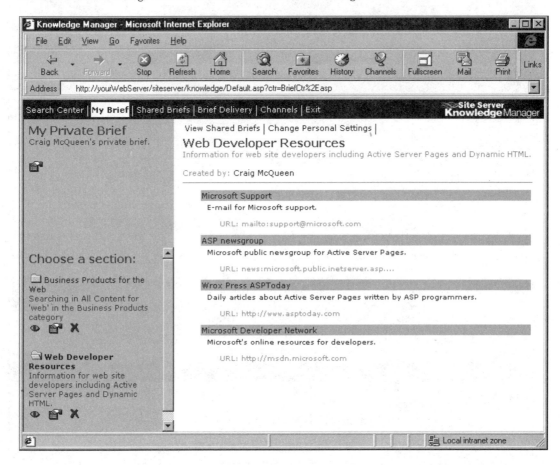

Note that in the left-hand page the folder is open and the title of the section you are currently viewing is highlighted.

Sample Shared Briefs

There are two sample shared briefs available with Site Server. Click on the Shared Briefs tab and then Sample Briefs. You should see the following:

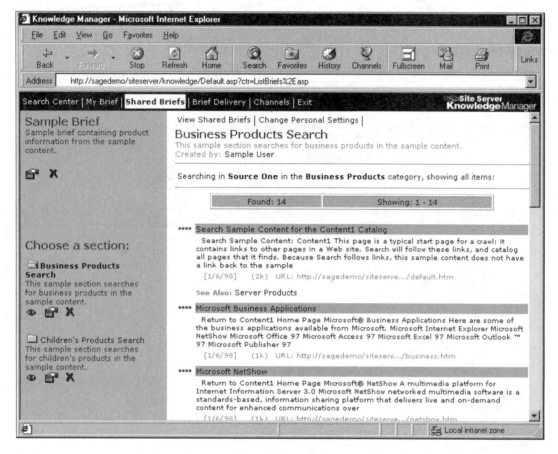

Both are sample sections created by searching and then saving the search query. The results of the first section are automatically displayed when you enter Shared Briefs.

As you can see, the shared briefs are very similar to My Brief. The difference is that the shared briefs are available to many people.

Knowledge Manager itself does not have any mechanism to control access to shared briefs. Access is dependent upon the catalog built with Search. By retrieving a shared brief, you are running a query against Search Server. This means that a shared brief obeys the same rules as queries run against Search Server. Specifically, if the catalog the content source is based on was generated with files that have NTFS permissions, the result set will reflect the privileges assigned to the user who ran the query. Users will only see documents that they have permissions to see.

Later in the chapter you will see how to create Shared Briefs.

Brief Delivery Methods

Knowledge Manager is about making a user more efficient by providing a mechanism of collecting and delivering targeted information. So far we have collected and organized the information. However, the user still has to visit the Knowledge Manager page to get the information. Let's look at two other methods of getting the information to the user.

Briefs by E-Mail

Instead of having to go to Knowledge Manager to get your briefs, you can have them sent by e-mail. Click on the Brief Delivery tab and you should see the following.

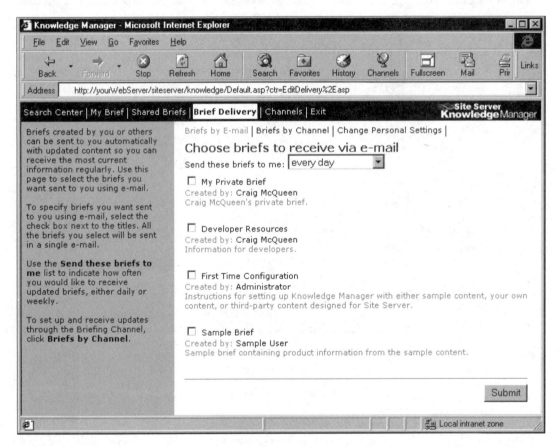

From here you can select which briefs you want delivered to you by e-mail. If you have Send e-mail using HTML checked in your Personal Settings, you will receive an HTML document containing the brief – similar to what you would see in the web page anyway. If you don't have this checked then the e-mail will be sent as plain text. You would only want to send it as plain text if your mail client doesn't support HTML. Note the drop down box with which you can choose when the brief is sent.

WebSoft Consulting has Knowledge Manager set up on their Intranet. As a result, it can't be accessed from outside of the organization. Many off-site WebSoft consultants have their briefs delivered by e-mail as just demonstrated so they can receive information in a timely fashion.

Briefs by Channel

Alternatively, you can have the brief delivered to you as an HTML page by a channel. Before you can do this you have to configure Site Server with a channel to deliver briefs. To do so, go to the web page `http://yourWebServer/Siteserver/Knowledge/CreateBriefingChannel.asp`. You will see a form similar to the following. After pressing the Submit button a channel will be created for delivering the briefs.

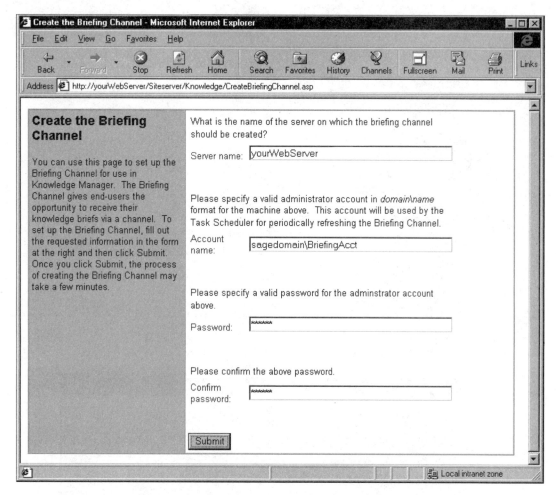

If you click on Briefs by Channel you will see the following page.

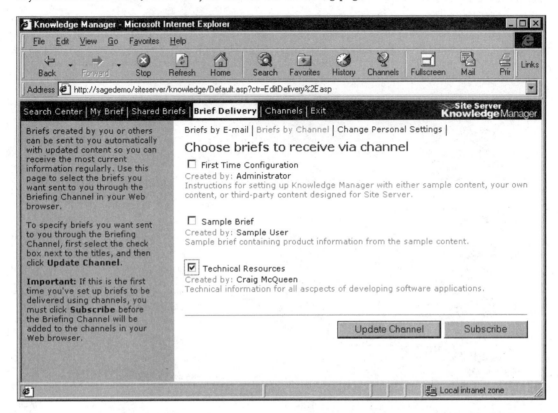

Before briefs can be delivered to you, you must first subscribe to the briefing channel. Click on the Subscribe button. You will get the standard dialog box for subscribing to a channel:

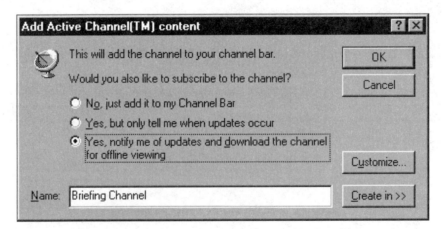

You can't have your private brief delivered by a channel so only the shared briefs are listed. Selecting a shared brief will include it in the channels delivered by the Briefing Channel.

Channels

By clicking on the Channels tab in the top menu, you will see channels set up by the Active Channel Server. You can subscribe to any of the channels from this page.

Implementation Details

Now that we have taken a tour of the Knowledge Manager features, let's look at some of the specific tasks required for implementing Knowledge Manager in your organization.

Creating Experts

As we have seen, WebSoft has domain experts within their organization. Example areas of expertise are: ADO, Site Server and NT security. Often, being a technical expert just means knowing where to go to get an answer. By using Knowledge Manager, WebSoft hopes to record the information sources the experts use and make it available to the entire organization.

Becoming an Expert within Knowledge Manager is easy – you just have to belong to a group with the correct permissions. Too bad it's not that easy to become an expert in real life! Site Server tracks which groups are experts by looking at the access control list (ACL) for the file experts.txt, located in the directory Installation_Directory\SiteServer\Knowledge\.

There is a function called CheckExperts in the file GeneralUtils.inc. You can use it to test whether the logged in user is an expert. It looks like the following:

```
Function CheckExpert()
    Dim oChecker, bExpert

    Set oChecker = Server.CreateObject("IISSample.PermissionChecker")
    bExpert = oChecker.HasAccess("Experts.txt")
    Set oChecker = Nothing
    CheckExpert = bExpert
End Function
```

Also, if you want to change the way Knowledge Manager determines if the logged in user is an expert, this is the function that you would change.

Site Server does not create a default group for Knowledge Manager experts. However, users in the Administrators, SiteServer Administrators, or SiteServer Knowledge Administrators groups on your server are automatically considered experts by Site Server. People in these groups can create, edit, and delete shared briefs. They can also administer Search, Push, and Personalization & Membership (P&M).

Since Knowledge Manager experts shouldn't need to administer Search, Push and P&M, you should create a separate group for Knowledge Manager experts. Use NT Server's User Manager for Domains to create a new group, such as Knowledge Manager Experts. Make sure your 'expert users' belong to that group. Finally, give the Knowledge Manager Experts group full control on the experts.txt file.

The only additional functionality a user will get by being an expert is the ability to create and delete shared briefs.

Creating Shared Briefs

Creating a shared brief is very similar to creating a private brief, you just do it from a different location. WebSoft Experts would start from here to create a shared brief to make available to the rest of the organization.

Start by selecting **Shared Briefs** from the top-level menu and then **Create a New Brief** from the menu in the Shared Briefs area. This menu selection will only be available for experts. You can see the logic in the file `ListBriefRight.asp`:

```
<% If (m_bUserExpert) Then %>
    <% CreateTextbarButton CreateCancelableURL( FILE_EDITBRIEFS ), "_parent", _
    L_strCreateNewBrief, True %>
<% End If %>
```

The variable `m_bUserExpert` is set in the file by calling the function `CheckExpert`, which we looked at in the last section.

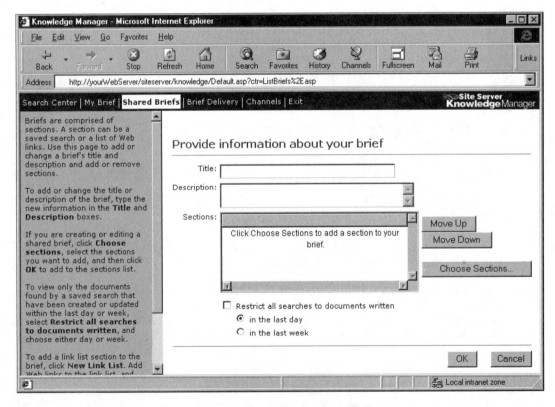

From this page you can configure a shared brief. The **Title** and **Description** is for the entire shared brief. You then add the sections you want to appear in the shared briefs. Note that these sections have to be previously created. You can also specify the order the sections will appear. Remember, the first section will be automatically run and displayed when the user first goes to the shared brief. Let's add the section **Web Developer Resources** that we created earlier.

After pressing the Choose Sections button you will get a list of your Saved Searches and a list of your Link Lists. Check the ones you want to make available to other people and then press OK.

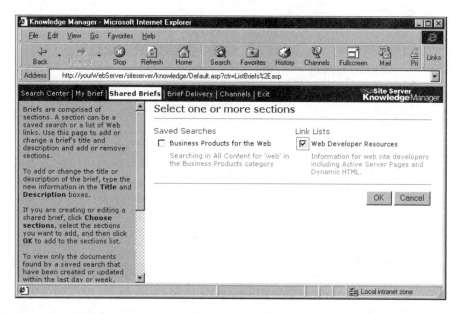

If you haven't done it yet, you now have the option of giving the shared brief a title and description:

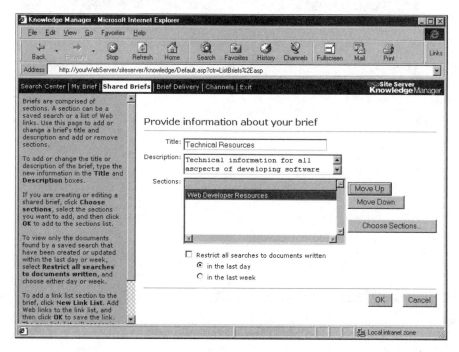

After pressing OK, you will see what your shared brief looks like:

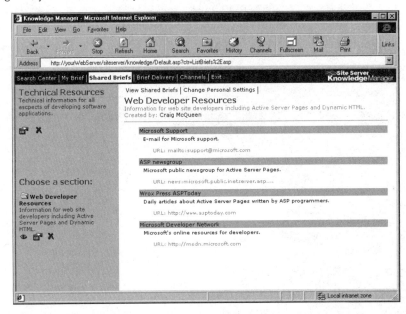

The next time a user looks at the Shared Briefs tab, your newly created brief will be listed. Now all of the WebSoft developers can go to one area to find information about ASP development:

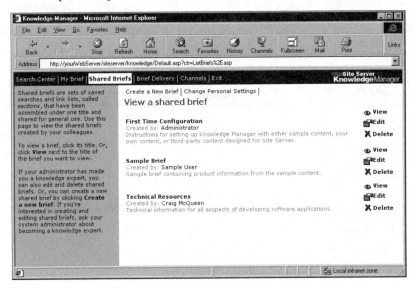

Creating a Content Source from a Catalog

In Chapter 7 – *Search* we looked at how to build catalogs. Knowledge Manager needs to have the catalogs converted to content sources. For this exercise you need to have built and propagated the sample catalogs as demonstrated in Chapter 7. If you created the WebSoft catalog for the Site Server information in the Search chapter you can also use it for this exercise. Let's create a content source using one of the sample catalogs.

From the Site Server web administration tool, click the Membership Directory Manager link and select the membership server for adding your content store. Once you log in, select Content from the menu on the right-hand side and then Content Sources from the left-hand pane. You will see a list of your content sources:

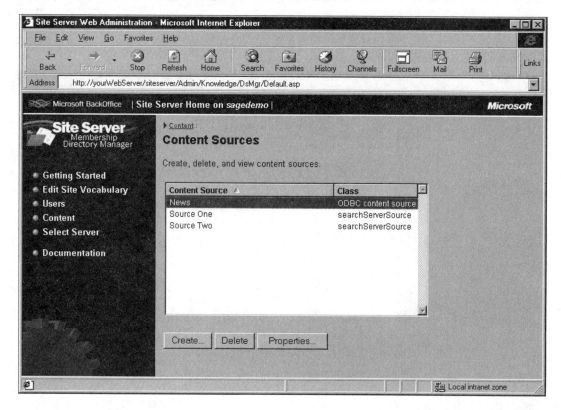

Select **Create** to add a new content source. For this exercise, we will be creating a content source from a sample catalog that is included with Site Server.

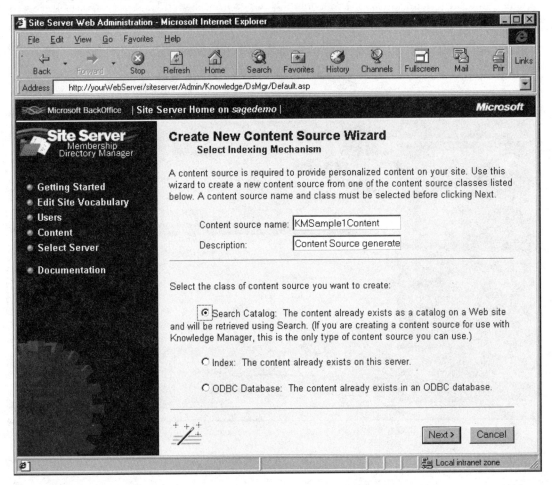

Give the content source a name and description. The class of content store you want is Search Catalog which is set as the default. As indicated on the page, this class is for content already existing as a catalog on a web site. After pressing **Next** you select the search catalog to use for the content source. In this case, the two Site Server sample catalogs are listed. They should look familiar if you have read Chapter 7 – Search.

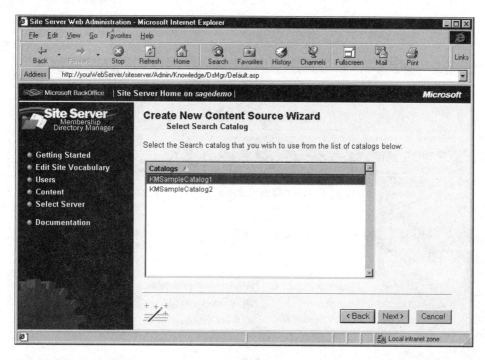

Next, select the content types to include in this content source:

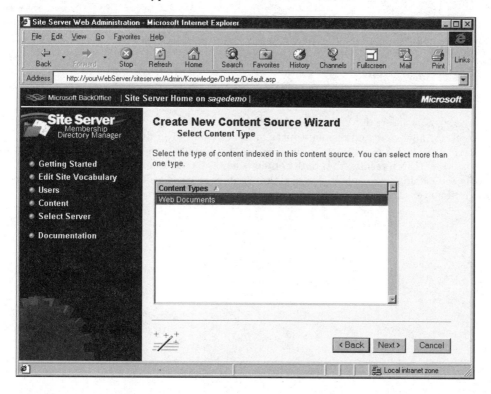

Finally, you get a summary of your content source configuration. If you want it created press Finish otherwise to abort press Cancel.

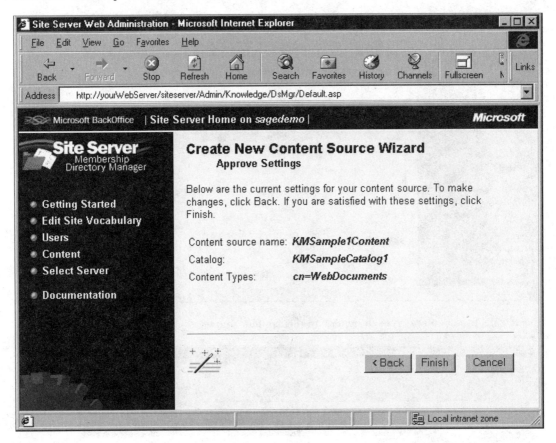

The content source now shows up. When you go to Search Center in Knowledge Manager, you will be able to search the newly created content source in the category drop-down box. Note that the content source just created is based on the same catalog as the content source sample Source One so you will get the same search results from both content sources. As mentioned early in the chapter, the difference between catalog and content source is that content source has additional information used by Knowledge Manager. This additional information is used to tie into the Site Vocabulary.

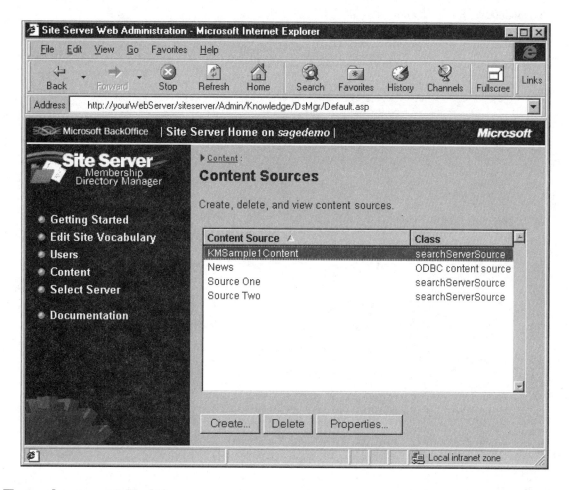

Entering and Exiting

To use the application, users simply have to enter the URL for Knowledge Manager. which is typically `http://yourWebServer/siteserver/knowledge`. However, your organization most likely has an Intranet web site set up already. In this case, you can make a link from your Intranet web site to the Knowledge Manager.

For some reason the default link for Exiting Knowledge Manager (from the menu option in the top menu bar) is to go to the Microsoft Site Server home page. This is probably not very useful for your users. You probably want to change the exit page to something like your Intranet home page.

To change the Exit page, open the file
`Installation_Directory\SiteServer\Knowledge\config.inc.` Make the change in the
line indicated in the following code:

```
' =============================================================================
' FILE: CONFIG.INC'' DESCRIPTION:
'      These constants are set by the administrator, and used for the
'      Knowledge Manager Search Center and Briefing Center. This file
'      also includes descriptions of constants that must be changed
'      in the Channel Center configuration file, BriefingAgent.vbs.'
' Copyright (c)1997, 1998 Microsoft Corporation.' All rights reserved.
' =============================================================================

' DSN for the database where briefs and sections are stored.
  Const ADMIN_DSN = "Knowledge"

' Search column to use for category searches. This should match the tag
' name used to tag your content.
Const ADMIN_SEARCHCOLUMN = "Topic"

' Text for the Exit button. The text you enter here will appear as the last
' link in the top toolbar
Const ADMIN_HOMETEXT = "Exit"

' Link for the Exit button. This should point to the home page of your intranet.
  Const ADMIN_HOMEURL = "http://www.microsoft.com/siteserver"

' E-mail address of the site administrator. This address is included in all
' Knowledge Manager error messages.
Const ADMIN_EMAIL = "admin@localhost"

' Number of search results to show per saved search section when the
' information is displayed on a Web page.
Const ADMIN_PAGEHITS = 25

' Number of search results to show per saved search section when the
' information is displayed in an e-mail message.
Const ADMIN_EMAILHITS = 25%>
```

You can see many of the other configuration options in this file, which are self-explanatory.

Maintenance

Much of the maintenance of Knowledge Manager relies on its information sources being maintained
correctly. However, there are some specific tasks associated with maintaining Knowledge Manager.
In the event of your system crashing, maintenance ensures Knowledge Manager can be returned to its
previous state.

Knowledge Manager Files

If you customize any of the Knowledge Manager files you will want to back them up. All the
Knowledge Manager files are stored under the directory
`Installation_Directory\SiteServer\Knowledge.` Specific files that are important to
backup are: `config.inc`, which contains the administration settings, and `Experts.txt`, whose
access control list (ACL) is used to determine whether a user is a Knowledge Manager expert.

Database Backup

Information specific to Knowledge Manager is stored in a Microsoft Access 97 database named `Knowledge.mdb`. You don't have the option of storing the data in SQL Server. There are four tables in the database, named: `Briefs`, `Filters`, `Details` and `URLs`. The `Brief` table contains information such as the authors and creation dates of briefs, along with whether briefs are shared. The `Filters` table contains information about the sections that have been created. The `Details` table links the `Briefs` and `Filters` table. Finally, the `URLs` table contains information about the link list sections that have been created. Note that the content itself is not stored in the database. The content (such as HTML files) is stored in the file system. User attributes (such as e-mail address) are stored in the Membership Directory.

By default the database is stored in the `Installation_Directory\Data\Knowledge` directory. If you need to restore the database to system default, use the empty database provided in the directory `Installation_Directory\SiteServer\Knowledge\Database`.

To backup the Knowledge Manager database, just copy `Knowledge.mdb` to another location. Note that Access databases should not be backed up while they are in use. Either schedule backup for a time when there are no users on the system or temporarily disable the Knowledge Manager web pages.

Deleting Users from the Database

Occasionally you may need to remove users from Knowledge Manager. To do this you need to modify the Knowledge Manager database directly:

> Use Microsoft Access to open the `Knowledge.mdb` database

> Each user has a globally unique identifier (GUID) for unique identification. Go to the `Briefs` table in the database to find the user and the associated GUID

> In the `Briefs` table, remove anything associated with the user's GUID

> In the `Filters` table, remove anything associated with the user's GUID.

Note that it is wise to backup the database before deleting any users.

Tips

There are also some tips to accomplish tasks that you may run into when implementing Knowledge Manager.

Removing the Sample Content Sources and Catalogs

In a production system you will want to remove the sample content sources and catalogs so they are not included in search results. To remove them, follow these steps:

> ➤ From within the web administration tool click Membership Directory Manager
> ➤ Select Intranet (Windows NT Authentication) Membership Server and log in
> ➤ Select Content and then Content Sources
> ➤ Select Source One and then click Delete
> ➤ Select Source Two and then click Delete.

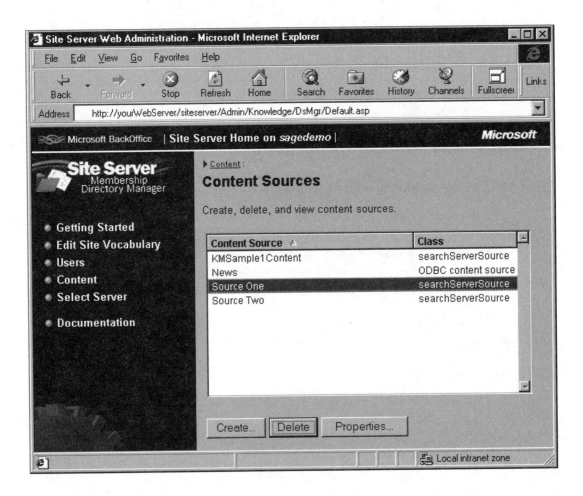

Hiding a Content Source

An alternative to removing a content source is to designate it as non-browsable. For example, you might make time-sensitive information non-browsable if you want to prepare content for Knowledge Manager and make it active on a given day. WebSoft received some early documentation for Windows 2000, which they will keep non-browsable until the day Windows 2000 launched. Browsable is a property of content sources within the membership directory.

To hide a content source, start the MMC for Site Server and expand the Membership Directory Manager for the membership directory containing your content source. Expand the ou=Admin node and then the ou=Other node. Select ou=ContentClasses to see your content sources. You should see something like the following.

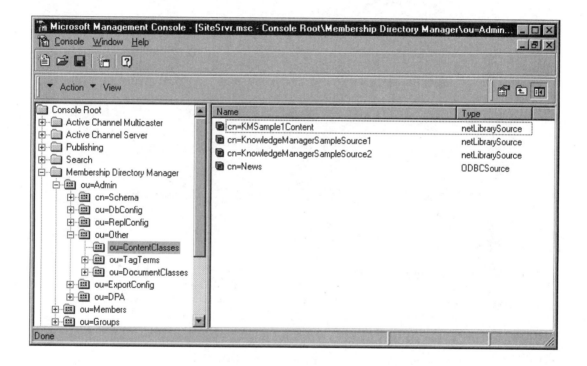

Select the content source you wish to hide and then select Properties from the Action Menu. Change the Browsable property from 1 to 0.

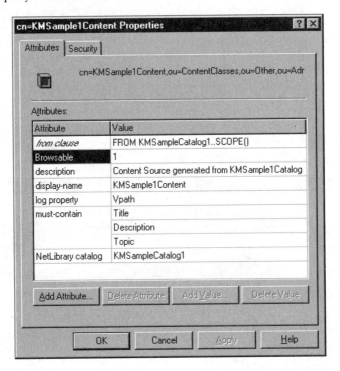

Summary

Knowledge Manager is an application within Site Server that leverages the Search, Personalization & Membership and Content Management features. Many of Site Server's features gather and categorize information, Knowledge Manager takes this work and presents it in an effective user interface.

Knowledge Manager is like an information portal for your organization's Intranet. In this chapter we learned:

> Concepts used by Knowledge Manager
> Creation of private and public briefs
> Different ways to deliver briefs
> Making users Knowledge Manager experts
> Making search catalogs available to Knowledge Manager
> Maintaining Knowledge Manager

With Knowledge Manager in your organization people will spend less time searching for information and more time using information.

Membership

"When I
get a little
money
I buy
books;
and if any
is left
I buy food
and
clothes."

-Erasmus

Site Server Personalization and M   will use to personalize a user's
experience or secure content whi   technology is called
Personalization and Membership   rsonalization, and because of
this it makes more sense to me to   order. In this first chapter
we'll cover Site Server Membersh   cover Site Server
Personalization.

Why the ordering switch? Simpl   ience for a user coming to
your web site, you must first kno   apter, Personalization, I'll use
the analogy of a restaurant waite   personalized service.
However, before the waiter can   rant must first determine who
the customer is – the customer   e and I had a reservation for
6:00'.

The same is true for a web site.   t for your user, you must first
recognize who the user is. The   what enables us to do this. In
fact, my personal opinion is tha   t of the technologies to
implement simply because it in   software design.

Site Server is a collection of to   oft's powerful Internet
Information Server 4.0 web se   n mind when developing with
Site Server. Site Server is not a   s you need to build your own
solution. For example, IIS 4.0   ip in the anonymous account:
IUSER_[server name]. Site Se   adds to the Windows NT
security system, by providing

> ➢ Recognize the user
> ➢ Provide secure access

Let's take a brief look at what we'll be covering in this chapter:

- **Introduction to Directories and LDAP** – Since the Site Server Personalization and Membership technologies rely upon the use of an LDAP directory to store information, we need some background on what directories and LDAP are.
- **Overview of the MMC Snap-ins** – Here we'll examine – at a high level – the two MMC snap-ins added after the installation of Site Server Personalization and Membership.
- **Membership and Windows NT Modes** – In this section we'll discuss Membership and Windows NT Modes. These are the two different types of authentication you can choose to use when a user comes to your site.
- **Creating a New Membership Server** – After we learn the difference between the two authentication types that Site Server P&M supports, we'll examine the necessary steps to create a new Membership Server. A Membership Server is what we then map to an IIS 4.0 web site to utilize the features of Site Server P&M.
- **Membership and Personalization with IIS 4.0** – To use this technology with a web site, we also need to tell the IIS 4.0 web site – the only web server this technology works with – some specific information. This information is available through a Membership Server, which is associated with the IIS 4.0 web site where it is to be used.
- **IIS Authentication Configuration** – Finally, after mapping the Membership Server to an IIS 4.0 web site, we can configure the various authentication options for IIS to use to recognize members.
- *Authorization and Security* – After examining authentication, we'll look at another aspect of security: Authorization.

It's important that, before we begin any discussion of Site Server Personalization and Membership, you understand one of the more esoteric areas of this product, namely the Membership Directory and LDAP.

Introduction to Directories and LDAP

Site Server Membership introduces a concept new to some developers – that of an LDAP directory used to store information. So, before I dive into the details of how Membership works, I'll give a little background on directories and LDAP, and explain some of the common syntax I'll be using in this chapter and the next.

What is a Directory

A directory is a storage structure used to store information organized much like a phone book. It is said to be a 'namespace' in that if we have the name (think key) of the object we want, we can easily look it up.

For example, I have a friend with the last name White that lives in Denver, CO. I can open up a Denver, CO phone book and find White listed under W. The directory used by Site Server is called the Membership Directory. It too is similar to a phone book, but instead it has a digital representation that we can use for various applications. Digital directories, like their analog counterparts, are great for managing information that does not change frequently and is organized in a namespace.

Information in the directory is stored in a hierarchical manner, and has it's own syntax used to describe information in the directory. This syntax can be confusing, and is worth examining before we move on to more interesting topics:

Directory Syntax

Later, we'll use a tool via the Microsoft Management Console to view the Membership Directory. What we'll see is a tree-like structure with a format similar to using Windows NT explorer to navigate the file system. The structure you will see is known as the Directory Information Tree (DIT).

Directory Information Tree

The DIT is term used to describe the structure of a directory; the structure being not the objects within the directory, but the containers of these objects. Going back to our file system analogy, containers are similar to directories. A new Membership Directory contains one root container, and 6 sub-containers. Each sub-container may or may not contain further containers. Here is what this base DIT looks like through the MMC tool we'll use later (the Membership Directory Manager Snap-in):

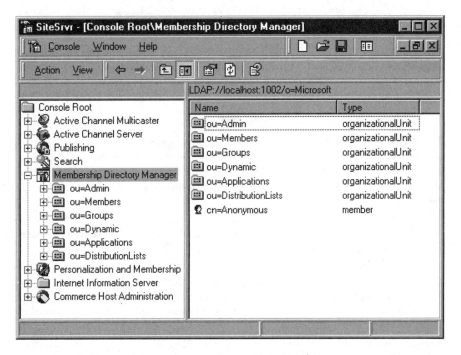

Note that this screenshot is of Version 1.1 of Microsoft MMC (the most up to date version at the time of writing). If you have a different version things might look a bit different.

A directory is great for storing highly structured information that is read more often than written. Site Server Personalization and Membership makes use of this directory for storing information about members, but the concept of a directory is also the foundation for the Windows 2000 **Active Directory** – a directory to be utilized by Windows 2000 for globally important information, such as users, groups, etc.

Unlike a conventional phone book that is dropped off at your front door every 6 months, the directory is a resource available to many users. Because of this, a protocol is necessary so that all users can share this common directory and look up information. This common protocol is the **Lightweight Directory Access Protocol** (LDAP).

LDAP

Think of Lightweight Directory Access Protocol (LDAP) as the phone operator you speak to when you dial 0 on your phone. Much like an operator, LDAP handles requests for information from the directory. Since the directory is digital and globally available (not to mention can be large) you don't necessarily want to hand out the directory to each user.

Going back to our earlier example, if I wanted to look up a friend in Denver, CO with the last name White, and I had to use an operator, I would tell the operator my friend's information and the operator would look up my request and return the appropriate information.

Similarly, LDAP provides the interface for the directory, in our case the Membership Directory. If we want to bind to a member, we would need to request the bind through LDAP. LDAP is run as a service on an LDAP server, and a protocol that is used for communication. Just as HTTP is a protocol used to communicate with HTTP servers.

In the following chapter we'll examine how to perform these binds using Microsoft's **Active Directory Service Interfaces** (ADSI), the API for working with directories and LDAP.

So what *are* the most attractive benefits to be gained by employing a directory service and LDAP? Well, we can summarize them as follows:

> **LDAP is an open, standards based, cross-platform protocol.** Hence, any client or service that supports LDAP can use this technology to share information across network, operating system, and application boundaries. Cross-platform interoperability means that two distinct operating systems – such as Windows NT and UNIX – can both use the same LDAP directory to share information.

> **The schema is exposed.** The schema of a directory is the definition of the various objects and property types the directory supports. The schema of a directory is exposed and accessible, meaning that any application can query the schema to learn what a particular object looks like and what its relationship is to other objects.

> **The directory service is simply a database that is optimized for reads.** The design of the directory is around providing storage for common information that does not change regularly. Since a large number of the requests for the directory are for data, a higher importance is placed on reading information.

> **Directory services and LDAP are designed for distribution.** Both the directory and the LDAP Service are network services that can reside on different network segments and separate machines. The only requirement is that the machines can find each other and clients can find the LDAP Service. What this really means is that directories are extremely scalable.

> **Directory services are designed with a highly organized structure.** The directory is designed around an object-oriented architecture that uses instances of objects and containers to organize information in a logical manner. You can compare it to the way that a phone book organizes data – objects are stored in containers, in the same way that the name *Fell* is stored under the letter *F* in a phone book. The structure of the directory and of LDAP lends itself to simplified maintenance, scalability, and distribution.

> **Open security standards such as SSL.** Security standards such as Secure Sockets Layer (SSL) can be used as long as the client knows how to use them. Using SSL enables us to provide a secure mechanism for exchanging information with the directory.

> ➤ **Many organizations are moving to directory services to organize and expose their data.** As the Internet grows and evolves, many organizations and software developers are using LDAP Services and directories to share information more easily.

Now that you have a cursory understanding of what a directory is, and that LDAP is used to communicate with the directory, let's look at the Microsoft Management Console; the tool used to manage Site Server Membership.

Overview of the MMC Snap-ins

After Site Server 3.0 is installed, there are several MMC snap-ins installed. The two relevant to our discussion of Personalization and Membership are the Personalization and Membership and the Membership Directory Manager snap-ins.

We won't be able to delve into the full details of both of these snap-ins, but we will cover the highlights of both.

Personalization and Membership

The Personalization and Membership snap-in is used to view and manage Membership Server instances. Each instance of the Membership Server is a virtual representation of the aggregated services that Membership Server provides.

So what does that mean? Several things. The Membership Server instance itself is not something that can be started and stopped. However, the services running within an individual Membership Server can be stopped. For example, the LDAP server runs within the context of the Membership Server. If you wish to stop/start a particular LDAP server, you don't stop the Membership Server, but you do expand the appropriate Membership Server to stop the corresponding LDAP server.

In addition to the LDAP server exposed in the Membership Server, there are also settings for Direct Mail. Direct Mail is an application provided with Site Server that can read in a list of users out of the Membership Directory and, based on their attributes or usage patterns, send appropriate e-mails tailored to each user.

These custom tailored emails are built from Active Server Pages that are executed to generate the custom message in the context of the user that the mail will be sent to. This way, logic can be built into the Active Server Pages to display certain content to specific users based on their attributes.

The screenshot below shows the Personalization and Membership snap-in expanded. Additionally, the Intranet (Windows NT Authentication) Membership Server – the default Membership Server installed – is also displayed and expanded. Note, this instance of the Personalization and Membership snap-in is only showing 1 Membership Server. The Personalization and Membership snap-in can manage multiple Membership Servers... even on separate machines!

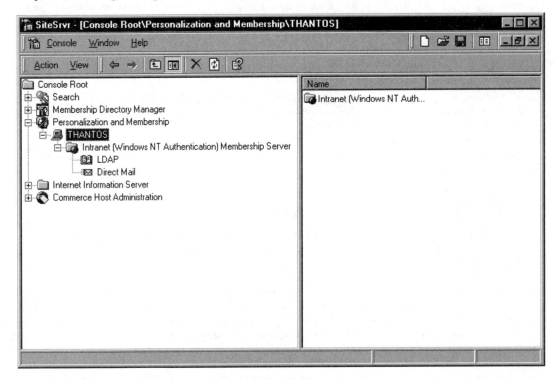

In the screenshot you can clearly see the LDAP server instance used for this Membership Server. The LDAP Server provides services for accessing the Membership Directory while Direct Mail provides services for interacting with a SMTP server for sending personalized email.

We've introduced another point of confusion here. How do these pieces – Membership Server, LDAP Server, Membership Directory, etc. – all fit together? Examine the diagram overleaf:

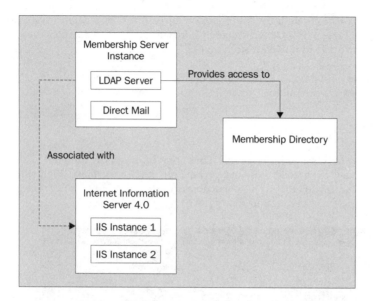

The Membership Server instance is associated with an instance of an IIS 4.0 web site, for example the default port 80 web root. Once this mapping is complete, IIS 'knows how to use' the features of Site Server (we'll look at this later in the chapter). Since IIS now has access to the features, it also has access to the associated LDAP server, which it can use to communicate with the Membership Directory.

> **A Membership Server is the virtual representation of the services provided by the aggregation of the LDAP Service and/or Direct Mail.**

In addition to managing the various services and properties of the Membership Server instances, the Personalization and Membership snap-in is also used to create new Membership Server instances. We use Membership Server instances to associate different Site Server capabilities with different web sites. For example, if you ran an ISP and hosted two sites: Competitor A and Competitor B, you wouldn't want them to share the same Membership Directory and Membership Server settings. Instead, you would create two separate Membership Server instances each with its own Membership Directory to provide distinct services for both of these organizations.

Once you've created a new Membership Directory – which we'll do later – you will use the Membership Directory Manager snap-in to manage it.

Membership Directory Manager

The Membership Directory Manager is a tool used to view a Membership Directory. Additionally, we can use the Membership Directory Manager to modify, add, or delete entries in the directory. Most of this functionality is provided through wizards.

Navigating the Membership Directory

Navigating within the Membership Directory is much like navigating a file system with the Windows NT Explorer. The left-hand window represents the containers and presents a broad overview, while the right-hand window presents the details of each container.

When the Membership Directory is first created, the Membership Directory is populated with a pre-determined Directory Information Tree. Within this Directory Information Tree, a default set of containers, objects, and attributes are added during installation.

Understanding the purpose of these containers is important, because some containers, like the ou=Members container or the ou=Admin container, contain important entries – such as members and the schema.

Containers

When the Membership Directory is first created, the default Directory Information Tree (DIT) contains six containers under the root. Several of these are parents for other containers, each with a specific purpose. The containers created include (in no particular order): ou=Admin, ou=Members, ou=Groups, ou=Dynamic, ou=Applications and ou=DistributionLists:

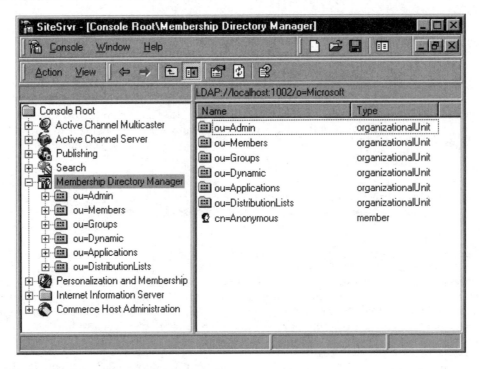

Let's start by examining the ou=Admin container.

The Admin Container (ou=Admin)

The ou=Admin container represents the administrative settings and configurations for the Membership Directory. In it we'll find cn=Schema, ou=DbConfig, ou=ReplConfig, ou=Other, ou=ExportConfig, and finally ou=DPA.

Let's examine the more important of these in more detail, starting with cn=Schema.

The schema container is a special container used to hold the cn=attributeSchema and cn=classSchema entries, which define the Membership Directory. Also, the schema container is the only common-name (cn=) container in the Membership Directory. This is where the schema that represents the relationships between objects is exposed in the Membership Directory.

The schema provides the ability for any application to connect to the Membership Directory and view the available schema – the design of the directory. We'll learn how we can use the entries in the cn=Schema in the next chapter, where we'll programmatically discover what attributes a member has.

Members Container (ou=Members)

The ou=Members container is the default container used to store all members of a Personalization and Membership site.

The ou=AnonymousUsers container underneath the ou=Members container is a special container that Membership uses for all users who authenticate using Automatic Cookie Authentication that the site does not recognize. We'll talk about the authentication methods, such as Automatic Cookie Authentication, later in this chapter.

Groups Container (ou=Groups)

The ou=Groups container is used to hold groups that site members can belong to. A directory using Membership Authentication also uses groups to authorize access to content protected by Windows NT security.

Windows NT groups are creating in the Membership Directory automatically, as part of the default DIT. Members can belong to these groups – we'll cover how to create groups and add members later in this chapter.

Dynamic Container (ou=Dynamic)

The ou=Dynamic container holds entries in memory on the LDAP server. The dynamic container is different from all the other containers, in that objects created in this container have a specified time to live. Since the dynamic container is in memory, access to this data is very fast. We'll learn how to use the dynamic container in the following chapter when we discuss optimizations.

Application Container (ou=Applications)

The ou=Applications container is used for defining attributes specific to an application. If you design an application that uses the Membership Directory to store application specific data, the data should be stored in the ou=Applications container. Entries in this container are of class type application and simply store attributes about the application.

After the creation of a Membership Directory, you should have one application installed and configured – MS-NetMeeting. This application is a dynamic container used by Microsoft NetMeeting clients.

Distribution List Container (ou=DistributionLists)

Finally, the last of the six root containers in the Membership Directory DIT, the ou=DistributionLists container is used to contain distributionList entries used by Direct Mail.

These `distributionList` entries define users to receive a Direct Mailing. If we examine one of the default entries `cn=KmBriefList` inside the `ou=DistributionLists` container, we'll notice that it allows us to enter members:

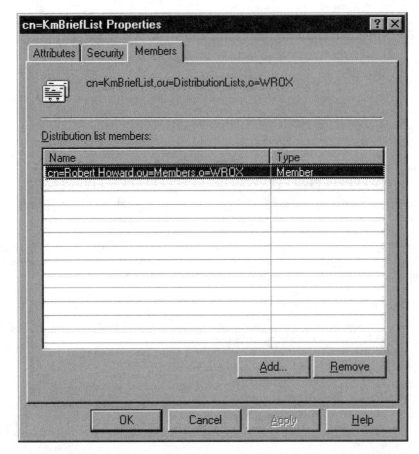

The Direct Mail tool uses a `distributionList` entry, specified when we use the tool, to read out the member distinguished name entry and generate a personalized page using each individual member's attributes.

Before we can move on to look at how to create a new Membership Server instance we need to look at something else: authentication modes.

Membership and Windows NT Modes

In the opening sentences of this chapter I stated that Site Server Membership is one of the more difficult pieces of Site Server to implement. One of the reasons for this is the confusion between the two authentication modes that Site Server Membership supports: Membership Authentication and Windows NT Security.

The differences between these two modes affect the security and authentication methods used by your web site. Before we continue and dive into the discussion of these two types, let me first make a recommendation. Select Site Server Membership Authentication mode if you intend to run your site on the Internet and use Site Server Windows NT Authentication mode if you intend to run your site on the Intranet. The importance of this will become clear shortly.

Let's begin our discussion of the two authentication modes with Windows NT Authentication.

Windows NT (Intranet) Authentication

When Site Server is used on an Intranet and Windows NT users are already mapped to the file system resources, integrating with Site Server is straightforward. Instead of authenticating users from the Membership Directory, either NT LAN Manager (NTLM) or an anonymous account can be used.

Site Server personalization services are still available, since Windows NT users are associated with members in the Membership Directory. However, the Membership Directory is not used for authentication.

Using Windows NT (Intranet) Authentication with Site Server is a great solution for sites that already have Windows NT Authentication mechanisms in place, but still want to use Site Server 3.0's Membership Directory for their data storage.

However, organizations that are planning for a large amount of web traffic should take a close look at Site Server Membership Authentication to 'abstract' the web members from the Windows NT account database.

Membership Authentication

The first form of authentication we'll discuss is Membership Authentication. Membership Authentication uses the **Security Support Provider Interface** (SSPI) of Windows NT Internet Information Server 4.0 to validate who the user is. The SSPI is a security interface that allows for Security Support Providers (implementing various authentication methods such as clear text/base, HTML forms, NT Challenge Response) to be used to securely authenticate a user. You don't need to worry about writing SSPs, or even how to use the SSPI, because Site Server provides everything you need. In fact, Site Server Membership Authentication provides some new SSPs that we'll be discussing in more detail later: Cookie Authentication, HTML Forms Authentication, and Distributed Password Authentication. All you need to know about all this is that it's there, it's written, and you can take advantage of it.

The next important part about Membership Authentication is that these SSPs don't authenticate against the Windows NT **Security Accounts Manager** (SAM) database – the SAM is the local or domain directory that maintains the list of users and groups, along with their Security IDs. Whenever you log on (*Ctrl-Alt-Del*) to Windows NT, you are authenticated against the SAM, shown below:

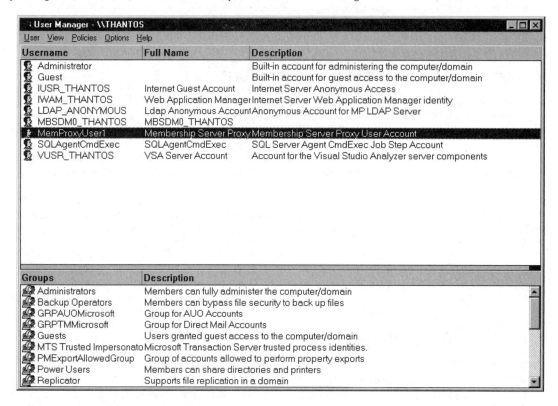

Using Site Server Membership on your web site, your users will authenticate against another separate directory: the Site Server Membership Directory.

But how do I access content on my file system secured by Windows NT security? Glad you asked! Site Server Authentication does a little sleight of hand behind the scenes: it uses a proxy user SID along with proxy groups – that map to groups in the Membership Directory – to give you secure Windows NT authorized access to content.

In fact, if you refer to the screen shot of the tool used to manage the SAM above, you will notice a particular user highlighted: MemProxyUser1. MemProxyUser users are the proxy users used by a Site Server mapped web site to impersonate users; one for each new Membership Server you create (hence the suffix '1' in the screenshot, if more Membership Servers are created they will be numbered accordingly).

Why is this important? Again, another great question! It's important because now we:

> Don't rely on the SAM to store all of our web users; remember, we might have millions!

> Don't need to lay awake at night thinking that all of your web users each have a Windows NT account. Well, actually they do, but it's abstracted in such a way that they can't log on your system through the NT log on dialog.

I've said that Site Server Membership Authentication implements some Security Support Providers to authenticate users. For now, it's enough to say that each of these authentication types is configured either through the MMC IIS 4.0 snap-in, or programmatically.

Here's what you need to know about Site Server Membership Authentication:

> **Usernames and passwords are stored separately from the Windows NT SAM** – The MemProxyUser exists in the SAM, but the usernames and passwords used to authenticate are stored in a separate data store known as the Membership Directory; which we looked at earlier.

> **Membership Authentication is more scalable than Windows NT Authentication** – Windows NT Authentication stores all users in the Windows NT SAM. Once the SAM contains upwards of 85,000 items, the performance starts degrading. The Membership Directory can contain millions of users.

> **Membership Authentication is more flexible than Windows NT Authentication** – Membership authentication methods, such as cookie authentication, do not exist for Windows NT Authentication.

> **Programmability** – Although tools such as the Windows NT User Manager exist for managing users in Windows NT, you could argue that the programming model is simpler with Membership.

Site Server Membership Authentication provides the flexibility that developers who are writing solutions for large web sites need.

Now that you're clear on the two different authentication types, let's go on to create a new Membership Server instance using the Personalization and Membership snap-in.

Creating a New Membership Server

There are three ways by which you can create a new Membership Server: using the New Membership Server Wizard from the Personalization and Membership snap-in; using the PMAdmin tool from the command line; or programmatically using the appropriate COM objects. I've chosen only to show how to create a new Membership Server through the MMC, since the process itself is more important than showing you the code. Once you understand the process, stitching together the code is a snap. For reference to the relevant objects, see Appendix B.

The PMAdmin tool is a Visual Basic Script utility. It provides a method that uses the necessary COM objects to create new Membership Server instances from the command line. You can find full details in the documentation.

Finding the New Membership Server Wizard

The New Membership Server Wizard is available by right-clicking on the host name which represents the computer on which you want to create the new Membership Server, and selecting New | Membership Server Instance:

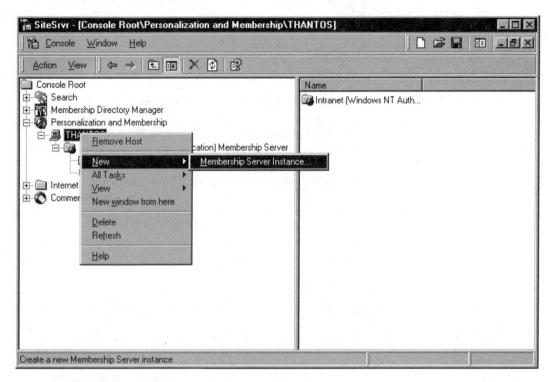

The New Membership Server Wizard is the simplest way to create a new Membership Server. Each dialog box represents a different configuration option. Let's examine how we create a new Membership Server that uses SQL 7.0 for its data store (in the next chapter we'll learn how to access associated data from other data stores), and Membership Authentication as its Membership mechanism.

Membership Authentication and SQL Server 7.0

The New Membership Server wizard has a total of 15 screens. The screens we cover – those relative to Membership Authentication mode and SQL 7.0 – don't represent all of the options available, but do represent the majority that you will encounter.

> *The New Membership Server wizard is also used to create new Windows NT Authentication Membership Directories, create new Membership Directories using an existing LDAP, and can also create Membership Directories using Access as the data store.*

The table below outlines the screens that we will be reviewing in our creation of a new Membership Server.

Screen	Description
Screen 1	Splash Screen
Screen 2	Select Configuration Mode – Custom Configuration
Screen 3	Select Configuration Options – AUO, LDAP and/or Message Builder
Screen 4	Select the Membership Directory – Create a new Membership Directory
Screen 5	Select Authentication Mode
Screen 6	Name the Membership Directory and Create Account
Screen 7	Select the Database Type – Microsoft SQL Server
Screen 8	Type SQL Database Information
Screen 9	Create Local LDAP Service
Screen 10	Message Builder Configuration (If Message Builder service selected in screen 3)
Screen 11	Complete the Configuration

Wizard Screens

Each screen in the wizard represents a different configuration option for the behavior of the Membership Server, and the services it will represent.

In order to create a new SQL Server Membership Directory, we need to have already created and configured an empty SQL Server database. However, the wizard can also automatically create an Access Membership Directory, useful if you want to set up an initial test environment.

Screen 1: Splash Screen

The splash screen lists the functions of the wizard:

The New Membership Server Wizard has the ability to create a new Membership Server with a new Membership Directory, or can create a new Membership Server to use an existing Membership Directory.

Screen 2: Selecting the Configuration Mode

Screen 2 of the wizard presents us with the option of how we want to configure this Membership Server instance:

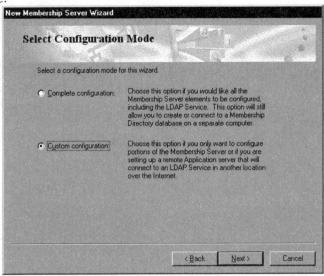

We are presented with a choice: we can select the complete configuration or the custom configuration option. Each of these choices is described on screen. For the purpose of the book, we will select the custom configuration – this will allow us to examine the other available settings.

Screen 3: Select Configuration Options

After selecting the custom configuration option from screen 2 of the wizard, screen 3 presents you with three configuration options:

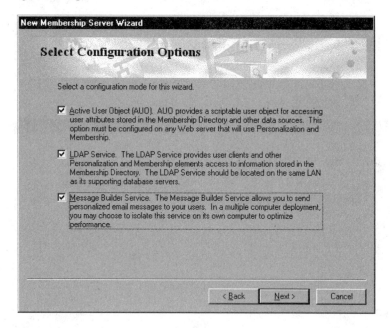

Active User Object (AUO)

The **Active User Object** is a wrapper for a lower level set of interfaces, the Active Directory Service Interfaces, used to navigate and manage a directory – in our case the Membership Directory. ADSI is a set of objects you use to work with a directory and we'll examine the AUO and ADSI in detail in the following Personalization chapter. For now, think of the AUO as the programmatic representation of a user which you can use inside Site Server and Active Server Pages, to manipulate or request member properties mainly for personalization purposes.

If you don't intend to use Site Server Personalization, and all you care about is using the membership (or authentication) features of the Personalization and Membership system, then you won't need the AUO.

However, if you do want to customize your pages based on your attributes, or dynamically interact with the Directory Service, then you definitely want to select the AUO.

LDAP Service

You should select the LDAP service checkbox if you need to either create a new Membership Directory, or connect to an existing directory. Remember, the LDAP service provides the ability for applications to communicate with the Membership Directory through the LDAP protocol. For example, the AUO uses LDAP to communicate with the Membership Directory.

273

Message Builder Service

Selecting the Message Builder Service determines whether or not e-mail can be sent via the Direct Mail server. Although not covered in this chapter, Direct Mail is another Site Server tool that can be used to send mail to registered users of your site.

Screen 4: Select the Membership Directory

If you select the LDAP service option, along with either (or both) of the other services, you will be presented with a screen that allows you to either create a *new* Membership Directory, or connect to an *existing* Membership Directory.

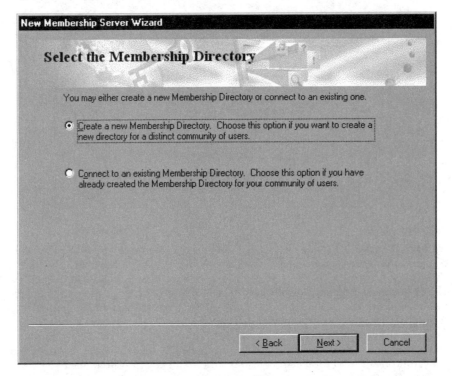

By opting to create a new Membership Directory, the wizard will apply the Membership Directory Directory Information Tree structure to the database you specify later in the wizard. This database will provide the services of the Membership Directory.

By connecting to an existing Membership Directory, the wizard simply allows for the creation of a new LDAP Service or Active User Object to use against the Membership Directory selected later in the wizard.

Screen 5: Select Authentication Mode

If (in screen 4) you selected to create a new Membership Directory, you'll be prompted to select an authentication mode.

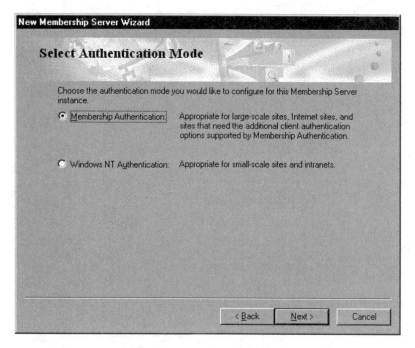

Remember our previous discussion of the two authentication types: Membership Authentication stores member credentials in the Membership Directory, Windows NT Authentication stores member credentials in the Windows NT SAM. However, both still use the Membership Directory for personalization.

Screen 6: Name the Membership Directory and Create an Account

The Membership Directory Name is used as the realm for authentication. The realm is displayed in the Clear Text/Basic and Distributed Password Authentication and is a simple way of letting the user know what they are providing credentials for.

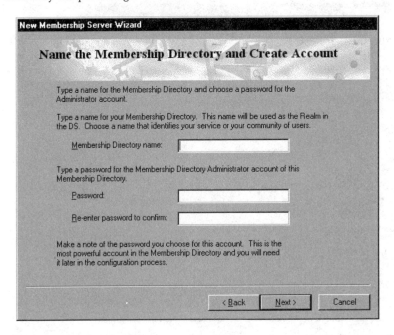

The password for the Membership Directory Administrator account is the password for the first account created in the Membership Directory. The Administrator account should be used for Administration purposes only, when first connecting to the Membership Directory through the Membership Directory Manager snap-in and when creating other users. The Administrator account will be given the SUPERBROKER privilege in the Membership Directory.

The SUPERBROKER privilege identifies a member in the directory as having full and unrestricted access to all information stored in the directory. Similar to the file system, the Membership Directory uses security to control what users have access to. The SUPERBROKER privilege simply tells the Membership Directory to ignore security checking, since this is the super-user. In other words, be extremely careful about who you assign this privilege to (it has to be explicitly granted).

Screen 7: Select the Database Type

Since the Membership Directory itself is nothing but a database schema with data, you must specify a database where this schema, and its data, will exist.

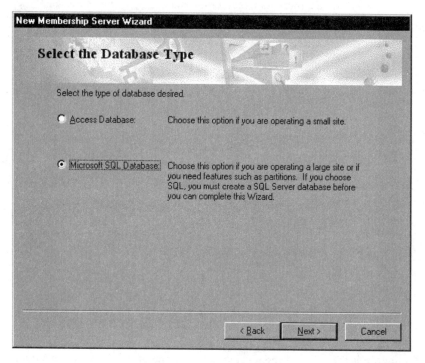

Site Server Service Pack 2 allows for Personalization and Membership to use SQL Server 7.0 as the data store for the Membership Directory. Unfortunately, the Membership Directory does not support non Microsoft databases such as Oracle or Sybase.

Screen 8: Type SQL Database Information

Next, you need to tell Site Server where the database that you created exists. You do this by specifying the server, the database name, and then the username and password (use an account such as sa) for Site Server to use when creating the Membership Directory tables in the database.

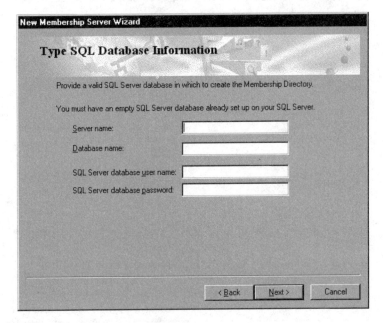

The Server name is the name of the machine that has the new SQL Server database that is to be used for the Membership Directory. The Database name corresponds to the name of the database that we created to store the Membership Directory, and the SQL user name and password should be equivalent to the sa permission level.

Note: If you use SQL Server 6.5 for your database, ensure that TCP/IP is one of the network protocols that is selected. By default it is named pipes only.

Screen 9: Create Local LDAP Service

When a new LDAP service is created on a machine, a port number and IP address must be assigned to it. Site Server will pick a port for you, starting with the first LDAP server on the machine, at port 1002. However, 1002 will be used by the default Windows NT Authentication Membership Server – if you can, I would suggest that you use the default LDAP port number, 389, if at all possible. 389 is simply the common port for LDAP, much as 80 is for HTTP.

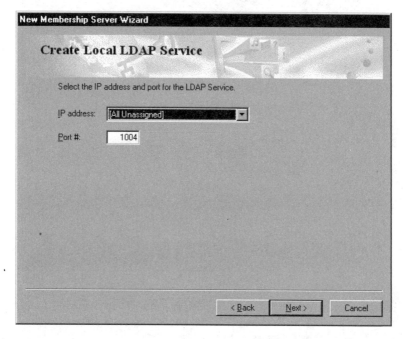

If you are using Microsoft DHCP on your network to dynamically assign IP addresses, leave the IP Address selection drop-down set to [All Unassigned] – this way, the machine can support Domain Name Service resolution and will only be dependent upon the port number. However, if a static IP is assigned to the machine, assign that IP address to the LDAP service as well.

Screen 10: Message Builder Configuration

In order to use the Direct Mail feature of Site Server Personalization and Membership, a SMTP mail server has to be provided. The **Simple Mail Transport Protocol** (SMTP) server installed with IIS 4.0 suits this role quite well; it can reside on any machine with IIS, and is installed from the Windows NT 4.0 Option Pack.

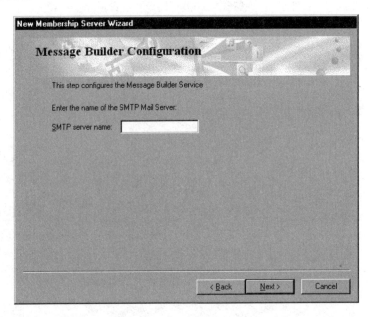

The SMTP Server, provided with IIS 4.0, is only a relay server, and requires another server (such as Exchange 5.5 or the POP3 Server provided with MCIS) to send email to the Internet.

To configure Site Server to use a SMTP server, simply enter the name of the server that SMTP services are running on.

Screen 11: Complete the Configuration

Once all of the parameters have been fulfilled, the wizard presents the most important screen of all. The Complete the Configuration screen provides the user with some of the most critical information that should immediately put to memory (or better still, written down!).

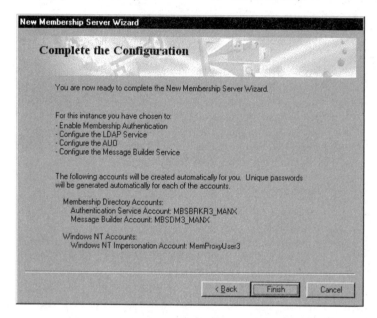

The screen gives a brief overview of the Membership Server features installed by the wizard as well as the accounts that are used for system and authentication purposes. The Membership Directory accounts correspond to accounts in the Membership Directory that fulfill certain 'system' roles:

> **Membership Directory Accounts** are accounts that exist in the Membership Directory:

Account	Description
Authentication Service Account	The Authentication Service Account is only necessary for a Membership Directory configured for Membership Authentication mode. The account is used by the LDAP service to connect to the Membership Directory and retrieve user information to be compared against information that is presented when a client is challenged.
Message Builder Account	The message builder account is another special account that is added when Message Builder services are installed for the Membership Server. The account is used to access the Membership Directory and impersonate users, or to perform necessary actions to generate content for personalized mailings.

> ➤ **Windows NT Accounts** are accounts created for impersonating the Membership User when accessing Windows NT resources through the Personalization and Membership system. A single account of this type is created for Membership Directories that use Membership Authentication – they are not necessary for Membership Directories that use Windows NT authentication since the Windows NT users already exist.

Account	Description
Windows NT Impersonation Account	The Windows NT impersonation account, MemProxyUser, is a special account used by the Personalization and Membership system to impersonate the user currently accessing the Internet Information Server web mapped to a Membership Server in Membership authentication mode. Each Membership Server instance creates a new MemProxyUser account. The number you see in the above screen shot simply means that this MemProxyUser corresponds to the Member Server with the instance ID of 3.
	Whenever a request is made for a file system resource, a Security Access Token (used to grant access to resources to security principals) is created using the Security ID (unique identifier) of the MemProxyUser, as well as the Security IDs of the corresponding membership groups they belong to (that correspond to Windows NT groups).

> Never assign any resource permissions directly to **MemProxyUser**, because every membership user will then have access to that resource. Instead, assign members to groups in the Membership Directory, and use groups to allow or deny access to resources. We'll read more about this later in the chapter.

Now that you've created a new Membership Directory, we'll use the Membership Directory Manager to view our new directory.

Connecting to a Membership Directory

The Membership Directory Manager uses LDAP to connect to the LDAP Server providing the Membership Directory. Therefore, using the Membership Directory Manager, we can connect to any Membership Directory whose LDAP Server is accessible from our computer.

To specify which LDAP Server to connect to, we need to modify the properties of the Membership Directory Manager snap-in.

Setting the Properties

The Membership Directory Manager properties tell the Membership Directory Manager which LDAP Service to connect to. To find the Membership Directory Manager properties, right-click on the Membership Directory Manager snap-in and select Properties. This should give you the following dialog box:

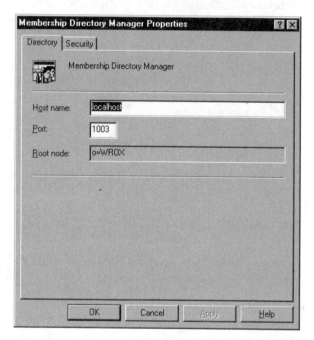

If, at any time, a dialog box prompts for logon while configuring the snap-in, just press OK. This dialog box is prompting us to login to the Membership Directory. Assuming the Membership Directory has not been secured, we can login anonymously. We'll cover this dialog box in more detail a little bit later in the chapter.

From the Membership Directory Manager Properties dialog, enter the name of the server and port number of the LDAP Service configured for the Membership Directory you wish to view. The server and port number are the ones we previously used in creating the new Membership Server.

> *If the Membership Directory is on the local machine, then you can use localhost as the server name.*

The port number corresponds to the TCP port of the LDAP Service instance to be connected to. To determine the port number from the Personalization and Membership snap-in, right-click on the Membership Directory LDAP instance, for the appropriate Membership Server, select Properties, and look under the General tab for the TCP port value:

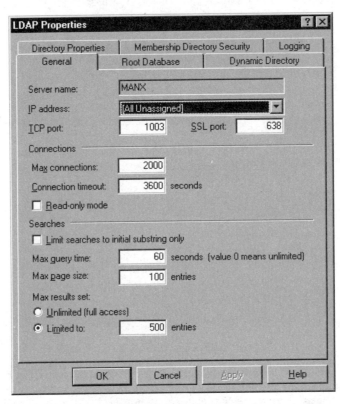

After entering the appropriate TCP port number and server name for the LDAP Service, press OK on the dialog. A dialog box should appear prompting for authentication:

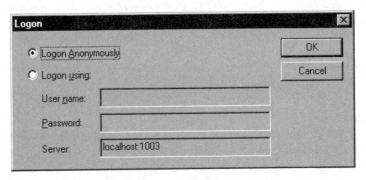

Note: We'll only be prompted for authentication if the Membership Directory being connected to uses Membership Authentication. A Membership Directory using Windows NT (Intranet) Authentication uses the context of the user running the Membership Directory Manager to connect.

If we were to configure the Membership Directory Manager to connect to a Membership Directory that used Windows NT (Intranet) Authentication, and we were connected to the Windows NT machine as the Administrator, we would be logged in as the Administrator in the Membership Directory Manager as well.

Authentication

Two choices are presented for logging into the Membership Directory: Logon Anonymously, or Logon Using.

Logon Anonymously — Membership Authentication

Logging on anonymously (for a Membership Directory which uses Membership Authentication) uses the cn=anonymous member account in the root container of the directory:

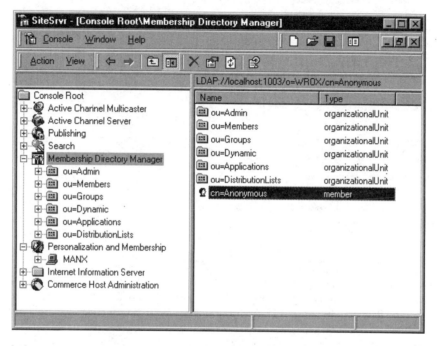

This user belongs to no groups, and only has the permissions of the public group, which all members belong to. The public group is similar to the **everyone** group in Windows NT, except that it applies only to the Membership Directory.

By default, when a new Membership Directory is created for Membership Authentication mode the public group has full permissions throughout the entire directory. Since all members have full permissions, the cn=anonymous user will have full access to anything in the Membership Directory; including adding members to Windows NT groups.

Logon Anonymously — Windows NT (Intranet) Authentication

When an anonymous logon is performed on a Membership Directory that uses Windows NT (Intranet) Authentication the context of the logon is performed through the LDAP_ANONYMOUS account (an account the is automatically created by Personalization and Membership) in the Windows NT Security Accounts Manger database:

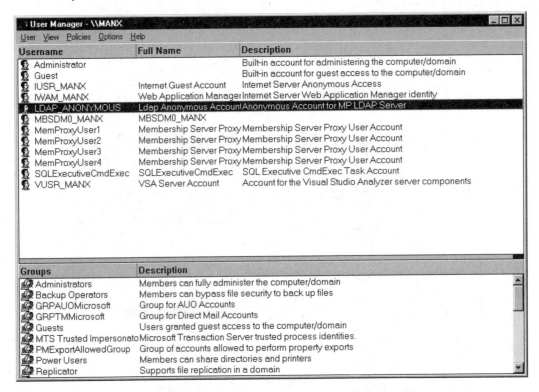

When a new Membership Directory in Windows NT (Intranet) Authentication mode is created the everyone group has full permissions throughout the entire directory. This gives the LDAP_ANONYMOUS user full access to anything in the Membership Directory, including adding users to Windows NT groups.

You may be a bit confused since earlier we read that a Membership Directory using Windows NT (Intranet) Authentication doesn't prompt for a logon. This is still true, but later, when we learn how to connect programmatically to a Membership Directory without providing credentials, we'll be binding as the LDAP_ANONYMOUS user.

Logon using — Membership Authentication

When we connect to a Membership Directory that authenticates through Membership Authentication we can connect to the directory as a particular member in the Membership Directory.

When we use a particular member (such as Administrator), the security privileges of that member are applied to the Membership Directory Manager. We can view or modify any objects or entries for which we have permissions; any objects and entries for which we don't have permissions are not visible.

Once the Membership Directory is secured, the Administrator account should only be used for administration purposes.

Logon using — Windows NT (Intranet) Authentication

We don't need to create members for Membership Directories that use Windows NT (Intranet) Authentication. If the user already exists in the Windows NT SAM, they are added automatically to the Membership Directory. Additionally, if the user is a domain user, a new container is auto-magically created under the ou=Members container with the name of the domain.

> 'Users' refers to users in a Membership Directory that uses Windows NT (Intranet) Authentication, and 'members' refer to members in a Membership Directory that uses Membership Authentication. We differentiate because users also exist in the Windows NT SAM.

Now that we've created a new Membership Server, and used the Membership Directory Manager (MMC snap-in) to view the Membership Directory, let's apply Membership to IIS 4.0.

Membership and Personalization with IIS 4.0

Before we can use Site Server Personalization and Membership with Internet Information Server 4.0, we need to map the Membership Server to an Internet Information Server 4.0 web site. Mapping is the process of associating a Membership Server with an IIS 4.0 web site. This association does several different things – like adding a new virtual directory (_mem_bin), and, if the Membership Server is in Membership Authentication mode, installing several Security Support Provider Interfaces and an ISAPI filter (AuthFilter).

This mapping process is actually easier than it sounds. In fact, it's only a two step process from the MMC. After mapping the Membership Server, we can configure different authentication methods for each item in the IIS 4.0 web. However, depending on the Membership Server mode (Membership or Windows NT Authentication), the authentication methods will be different.

> Personalization and Membership will not work with Internet Information Server versions earlier than 4.0. Moreover, an IIS web instance can only have one Membership Server mapping (but remember, IIS can support multiple web instances).

Mapping a Membership Server

The process of performing the mapping is simple. First we select the IIS 4.0 web site that needs to be mapped. Second, we select the Membership Server to map to, and Site Server takes care of the rest.

If you are experimenting with this you may find it useful to create a new web site to play around with. To do this, simply right click on your host under the IIS snap-in and select New | Web Site*. The dialogs that follow are fairly self-explanatory.*

Let's take a look at the process of mapping a Membership Server to an IIS 4.0 web site just a little more closely.

Steps for Mapping a Membership Server

First, open the Microsoft Management Console installed with Site Server 3.0 to manage both the Internet Information Server 4.0 and Membership Servers that need to be mapped – found under the program group: Microsoft Site Server | Administration | Site Server Service Admin (MMC).

Next, expand the Microsoft Management Console snap-in for Internet Information Server. Now right-click on the Internet Information Server 4.0 web site that is to be mapped, and select Task | Membership Server Mapping:

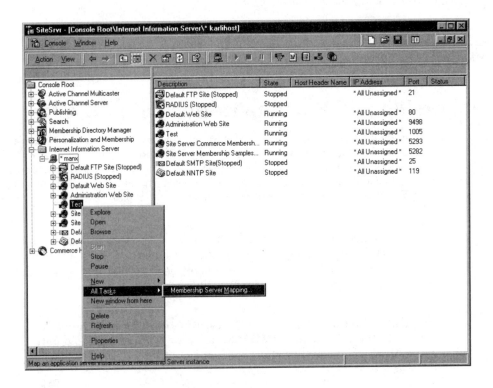

This selection brings up a dialog box that lists all the available Membership Servers on the local machine:

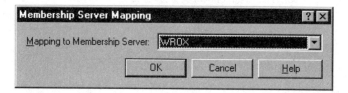

Use this dialog to select the Membership Server that represents the Membership Directory that is to be used with the IIS 4.0 web site you are mapping to. The available Membership Servers listed in the Membership Server Mapping dialog box represent the Membership Servers in the Personalization and Membership snap-in.

We can only map Membership Servers that are on the same machine that IIS is on. However, either the Membership Server's LDAP service or the Membership Directory that the LDAP service points to can be on different machines.

When you've made the selection, press OK; you'll have to wait for a few seconds while the Membership Server mapping completes. Then, you can configure the Membership Authentication methods for the Internet Information Server 4.0 web site.

IIS Authentication Configuration

Configuring authentication for an IIS web site is simply a matter of selecting the authentication method to use for the resource. It's a straightforward task to set the authentication types through the Microsoft Management Console, and that's what we'll cover here.

As mentioned, there are two options for authentication: Windows NT Authentication and Membership Authentication. Depending on the type of authentication used by the Membership Server you mapped to your web site you will get different options for the properties of that web site (or its component resources). The following sections address the two possibilities.

IIS Authentication Properties under Windows NT Authentication

If you chose Windows NT Authentication when creating a new Membership Server, then you've effectively told the Membership Directory that it must authenticate users based on the accounts in the Windows NT Security Accounts Manager (SAM). As I've already said, a Windows NT authentication with Site Server is a great solution for sites that already have Windows NT authentication mechanisms in place but want to utilize Site Server 3.0 personalization.

Where does the Membership system get its user information? Well, it takes copies of the appropriate Windows NT account entries from the SAM and stores these copies in the Membership Directory. Note that all authentication is performed against the Windows NT SAM database – regardless of whether the account exists in the Membership Directory.

As we've already seen, Windows NT authentication and Membership authentication both use Windows NT accounts to authorize access to system resources. Membership authentication adds a layer of abstraction, by storing credentials in the Membership Directory and using a Windows NT impersonation account for authorization. It's important to understand that all system-level security is done with the Windows NT 4.0 security subsystem.

Using the Authentication Methods Dialog Box

In this section we'll go through the configuration for Windows NT authentication. The dialog for this is easy to find. Within the Internet Information Server snap-in representation of the MMC, simply choose a web site object (associated with the appropriate type of Membership Server), and right-click. Select Properties, and then choose the Directory Security tab:

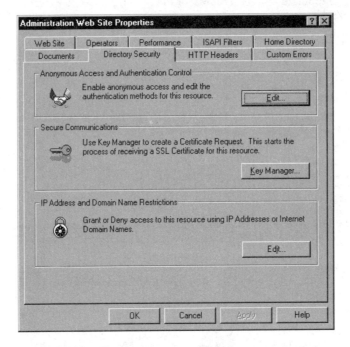

The screenshot above shows the authentication properties for a whole web site. It is possible to set properties for individual resources, in which case there will be a 'File Security' tab showing the same information and options as above.

Finally, select the <u>E</u>dit button of the Anonymous Access and Authentication Control frame. We are presented with the Authentication Methods dialog box:

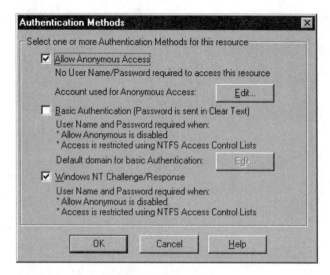

The dialog presents us with three options: <u>A</u>llow Anonymous Access, <u>B</u>asic Authentication and <u>W</u>indows NT Challenge/Response. Let's take a look at these different options and see how they interact with the Membership Directory.

Allowing Anonymous Access

With the <u>A</u>llow Anonymous Access option selected, the Security Support Provider Interface uses Windows NT's special anonymous user account, IUSR_[*server_name*], for any user that the system does not recognize.

> *The Security Support Provider Interface is what provides IIS 4.0 with the ability to use credentials given by a member and create a Windows NT user thread context. If properly authenticated, the thread serving the request will switch to the user whose credentials were passed by the Security Support Provider.*

In fact, when a new web site is created with IIS's New Web Site Wizard, the Allow Anonymous Access option is selected by default, as you can see from the screenshot below:

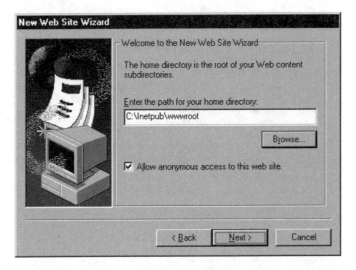

Why would we use this option? For example, on a large public web site it's often the case that only *some* of the available information needs to be authenticated and/or personalized. This is the case if most of the stored information is general product information, or other information that is intended to be accessible by *any* user. By using Site Server to provide Personalization and Membership services to the site, the administrator can mark these 'general information' pages with Allow Anonymous Access. Thus, any user attempting to access this information can do so without providing user credentials.

So, what actually happens when this access method is selected? Whenever a client requests access to a resource, IIS and Windows NT check the user's permissions to determine whether or not access should be granted. Anonymous access will be granted *only* if the requested resource has the IUSR_[*server_name*] account (or has either the Guest group or the Everyone group), with Read/Execute ACEs for both the directory and file.

> *You can view the permissions and user information of the IUSR_[server_name] account, by using the local machine's Windows NT User Manager. To start the User Manager tool, use the command* usrmgr \\[machine_name] *in the* Start | Run *dialog box.*

Since IUSR_[*server_name*] is the *anonymous user* account, there's no way of associating it with any particular user. Because of this, Site Sever is unable to store member information in the Membership Directory, and so Site Server itself doesn't handle the IUSR_[*server_name*] account.

> *In fact, it's not possible to store member information for IUSR_[server_name] under the Membership authentication configuration either. However, Membership Authentication does provide a way to handle anonymous users separately to the IUSR_[server_name] account – we'll cover this in the* Membership Authentication *section, overleaf.*

IUSR_[*server_name*] is the default anonymous user account. You can change the Account used for Anonymous Access by hitting the first Edit... button, which you can see on the Authentication Methods dialog box above:

In the resulting dialog, you can enter your chosen anonymous user account and password (after it has been created in the Windows NT SAM). Once we've selected the appropriate user, if the Enable Automatic Password Synchronization box is checked, this facility synchronizes the password with the Windows NT SAM automatically.

Using Basic Authentication (Password is sent in Clear Text)

If the Basic Authentication checkbox is checked, then the user will be authenticated against a Windows NT SAM database each time he requests a resource. When the user requests a resource, he is challenged by the following authentication dialog:

The user must supply his username and password. If the user's credentials match those in the SAM user database, then access is granted – and the corresponding account in the Membership Directory is made available as the current 'member', along with all the attributes and values. If access is denied, then the user is redirected to the IIS 4.0 page that is displayed for 401.1 server access-denied errors.

By default, the domain members are the users from the Windows NT Server SAM providing the web service (for example, Manx in the dialog above). However, the administrator has the ability to specify the domain from which users are authenticated. This is done by selecting the second Edit... button from the Authentication Methods dialog box, which results in the following dialog:

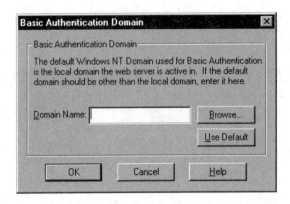

The Clear Text/Basic Authentication method is supported by a number of applications, including Netscape, and most clients should be able to use it. Indeed, HTTP clients such as Netscape can *only* access the Site Server site through the Basic Authentication and Anonymous Authentication methods (there's more on this at the end of this section). However, the Basic Authentication method passes the user's authentication credentials back to the server as clear text, in base 64 UUEncoded format. The existence of network sniffing tools, which can easily detect and decode information that is transported in base 64 UUEncoded format, means that this is an important security concern.

Indeed, if you take another look at the default checks in the Authentication Methods dialog box above, you'll see that, by default, the Basic Authentication box is *not* checked. If you check the box, then IIS displays the following warning:

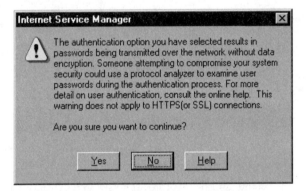

The solution to this is to implement Secure Sockets Layer (SSL). This is a 40-bit or 128-bit encryption protocol, which can be used to encode authentication information as it's sent. With SSL implemented, a higher level of security can be achieved.

We discussed SSL in Chapter 3, earlier in the book. If you want to know more about using SSL with IIS 4.0, then you should refer to the IIS 4.0 Resource Kit.

If a user account is authenticated using Clear Text/Basic Authentication, the account is written to the Membership Directory automatically. A user can log into any domain, simply by specifying the domain as part of the username when sending the logon credentials (that is, by specifying the domain and username, separated by a backslash, in the form domain\username). When the user account is authenticated, and if the credentials are not from the root domain, the domain for the user is created as a container under the Base Distinguised Name (BaseDN) container.

The base distinguished name (BaseDN) represents the container from which members will be authenticated. By default the BaseDN is the ou=Members *container, but can be changed through the* PMAdmin.vbs *tool. When a member passes credentials for authentication a path is built to that member using the BaseDN.*

Let's consider a brief example. Suppose we have a user who is a member of a domain that has access to resources on the network. Suppose that the user accesses the domain by authenticating himself with Clear Text/Basic Authentication, and that the user is visiting the site for the first time. Since our site is mapped to a Membership Server that uses Windows NT Authentication, a new member instance will be created for the member in the Membership Directory. Moreover, if the domain is *not* the base domain for the site, then a new container will be created under the BaseDN container of the directory, with the name of the domain. With all this set up, the P&M system is now in a position to store personalized data about this member.

Clear Text/Basic Authentication provides us with some of the functionality that we need to secure a site. Used in conjunction with Secure Sockets Layer encryption, the Basic Authentication method can provide us with a viable solution that works for all browsers.

However, for users accessing the site via a browser that supports NTLM, we can make use of the **Windows NT Challenge/Response** (also known as **Windows NTLM**) method to handle authentication. It's the third option in the Authentication Methods dialog box, and we'll look at it next.

Using Windows NT Challenge/Response (NTLM)

The beauty of this method is that – unlike Clear Text/Basic Authentication – there's no need to send user credentials across the network. Instead, Windows NT (or whatever clients are accessing the resources) sends a series of challenges and responses back and forth between itself and Internet Explorer.

First, the server challenges the client. To do this, the server applies a series of numerical algorithms (called **hashes**) to the username and password, and sends the encrypted result to the client. The client then creates a response. The response is constructed as a hash of the user's password, plus the random challenge that was originally sent by the server – these two items are packaged up and sent back to the server. The server examines the response, checking that the user's credentials match – if so, the user is authenticated and the Security Support Provider Interface maps the thread to the user's security ID in the SAM. As long as the session is active, any further requests are made with the authenticated thread. The real beauty of NTLM is that the user's password is never sent across the wire, only the hashes.

If an account is authenticated in this way, Site Server handles it in just the same way as if it had been validated through Clear Text/Basic Authentication. Thus, the user account is written to the Membership Directory automatically, and the domain for the user is created as a container under the BaseDN (if the credentials are not from the root domain).

Using Combinations of Authentication Methods

Of course, it's possible to select both Allow Anonymous Access and Basic Authentication simultaneously. In this case, when a user attempts to access content without the appropriate group or user Access Control Entry for the IUSR_*[server_name]* account, then he sees only a Basic Authentication dialog box.

By marking resources as supporting Allow Anonymous Access with either Basic Authentication or Challenge/Response, we can manage the resource's security from the normal Windows NT security mechanisms.

A Note on Netscape and Trusted Domain Authentication

We've already mentioned that HTTP clients such as Netscape Navigator can only access Site Server through Anonymous Authentication or Clear Text/Basic Authentication. When a user tries to access a particular domain through a browser that *doesn't* support Challenge/Response authentication, and IIS is on a *separate* trusted domain, then the client will be denied access to the resource:

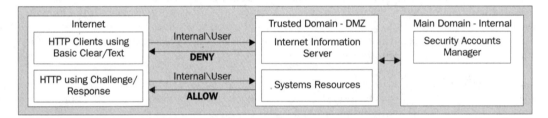

The only exception is when domain users that need to access the site are added to the users group (or another appropriate group) on the trusted domain.

IIS Authentication Properties under Membership Authentication

Having covered the IIS authentication configuration options for a Membership Server under Windows NT authentication, let's move on to consider the configuration options for a Membership Server under Membership authentication. If you chose the Membership Authentication option when creating a new Membership Server then you've told the Membership Server that it should use the user credentials that are stored in the Membership Directory.

Later, once a member has been authenticated, a security context is created with a Windows NT impersonation account (the default impersonation account is called MemProxyUser) – and the member gains access to the system via an instance of the impersonation account. The system creates an in-memory copy of the impersonation account, and assigns a unique Security ID (SID). Thus, many members can be signed on simultaneously, and these members will have different SIDs that don't conflict.

The configuration steps for Membership Authentication are a little different to those that we've seen for Windows NT Authentication.

Configuring Membership Authentication

In order to configure IIS authentication properties under Membership Authentication, fire up the MMC and right-click on the appropriate web site object in the Internet Information Server snap-in. Then select Properties, and choose the Membership Authentication tab – this presents you with the supported Membership authentication methods:

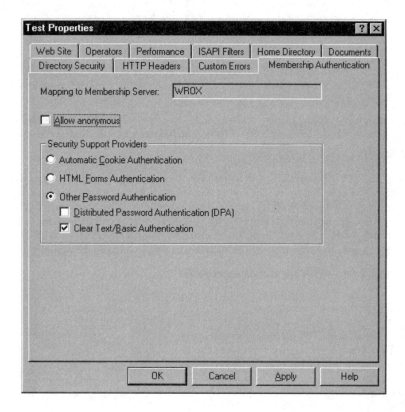

Again, this information is available for component resources of the web site, although the tabs might be different.

The dialog box shows the name of the Membership Server that the IIS 4.0 web site is mapped to, and also displays the possible authentication options. Remember, we can only map one Membership Server to any IIS 4.0 web site. However, we can support multiple sites on one machine, so each site can use a different Membership Server.

So what do all these methods do? Let's start with the Anonymous Authentication type.

Allowing Anonymous Authentication

If the Allow Anonymous checkbox is checked, then the IIS 4.0 web will allow unrecognized users to access the site as the IUSR_[*server_name*] account.

> *Note that the Allow Anonymous checkbox in this dialog is not related to the anonymous membership accounts created in the* ou=AnonymousUsers *container in the Membership Directory. This is a common cause of confusion – I know a number of developers who have made the mistake of associating Allow Anonymous with Automatic Cookie Authentication. We'll come onto the latter in a moment.*

> *The Allow Anonymous checkbox represents IIS's IUSR_[server_name] anonymous access method. Like Windows NT (Intranet) Authentication, it is not used by the Membership system.*

What's the purpose of the Allow Anonymous checkbox? If part of a Membership-enabled web needs to allow access to all users, and doesn't need to be concerned with personalization, we can use Allow Anonymous to remove the necessity of providing authentication.

Let's expand on this a little. Obviously, there are some sites that *do* need to authenticate every member that visits the site. However, there are also many sites for which this isn't necessary – there's no reason why these sites should suffer the overhead associated with Membership authentication (stemming from cookie creation, or Membership Directory new member instance creation, for example) when their resources don't need these services. We can mark resources like this as Allow Anonymous – as long as the resource's allows the appropriate security principals.

If Allow Anonymous Fails — Having the Correct ACEs

Access to a resource will be denied if the requested resource's Discretionary ACL does not have the appropriate ACE for the Windows NT anonymous user (just as if we were using the Windows NT Authentication method). In this case the authentication process will default to a Membership Security Support Provider that has to be used in conjunction with Allow Anonymous. A possible order of events is demonstrated in the figure to the right:

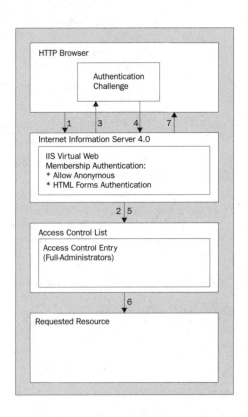

> **Resource is requested anonymously (1)** – An HTTP browser attempts to access a resource on an IIS 4.0 web site (the IIS4.0 web site is using the Membership authentication method, but supports Allow Anonymous). The client attempts to access the resource via IIS's IUSR_*[server_name]* anonymous account.

> **Access is requested via the anonymous account (2)** – The Windows NT security system attempts to access the resource as the anonymous account. If the proper ACEs are not available for the security principal performing the request (IUSR_*[server_name]*), access is denied.

> **Membership authentication (3)** – If access to the resource is denied, the Membership system attempts to authenticate the user with the Security Support Provider selected.

> **Membership credentials (4)** – Based on the information provided by Membership authentication, access is either granted or denied. If access is granted, the member accesses the resource as the impersonation account (MemProxyUser) and receives the Windows NT group Security IDs that match the corresponding groups in the Membership Directory.

> **Access is requested via the impersonation account (5)** – If the impersonation account has the necessary Security IDs that match the access type supported in the ACE, then access is allowed. Otherwise, access is denied.

> **The resource is exposed (6)** – The resource is now available to the requesting account

> **Displayed to the browser (7)** – Finally, the resource is processed by IIS and served to the HTTP browser.

Forcing Anonymous Authentication

There is a little secret that we can use to force anonymous authentication. By selecting Allow Anonymous and Other Password Authentication, but not selecting an Other Password Authentication method such as Clear Text/Basic Authentication, we force anonymous authentication. In some cases, such as using ASP to generate content that we don't want to be directed through the ISAPI, this is extremely valuable.

Now that we've covered Allow Anonymous – which is identical to the Allow Anonymous Access option for Windows NT Authentication – let's talk about the new authentication methods provided by Site Server, the Security Support Providers.

Security Support Providers

There are four Security Support Provider authentication methods provided by Site Server Membership:

> Automatic Cookie Authentication

> HTML Forms Authentication

> Distributed Password Authentication

> Clear Text/Basic Authentication

> **We can use a combination of different authentication types on resources, depending upon the amount of security that the resource demands.**

The SSPs work with IIS 4.0's Security Support Provider Interface (SSPI) and the Membership authentication type to map Membership Directory accounts to a Windows NT impersonation account (by default, this is the MemProxyUser account). Let's walk through these SSPs now.

Automatic Cookie Authentication

Cookie authentication provides us with a quiet and discreet authentication method for both anonymous users and registered members. Cookie authentication uses two cookies – SITESERVER and MEMUSER – to store information on the user's computer. If the user doesn't accept cookies then they will not be able to access the site. As long as the user is prepared to accept cookies, we can authenticate and track the member throughout the site.

When Automatic Cookie Authentication is selected, the ISAPI filter (which was installed by the mapping of the Membership Server) parses the headers of the client and looks for the SITESERVER and MEMUSER cookies. There are three possibilities. If the cookies exist then the information found therein is used to authenticate and bind to a member. If the cookies are invalid then the member is redirected to an ASP page in the _mem_bin virtual directory; we'll come back to this shortly. If the cookies don't exist then the ISAPI filter creates and binds to a *new* member in the Membership Directory, in the ou=AnonymousUsers container. Once bound to this user, two new cookies are written to the browser. These two new cookies SITESERVER and MEMUSER will be used in future sessions to identify the member uniquely.

> If a user is to be authenticated via **Automatic Cookie Authentication** then he must have agreed to accept cookies. All authentication methods except for **Allow Anonymous** (which can't be personalized), **Basic/Clear Text** and **Distributed Password Authentication (DPA)** rely upon cookies to maintain member state.

In addition to tracking members, Automatic Cookie Authentication accommodates each new member by sending cookies to the new member and automatically creating a new account in the Membership directory, under ou=AnonymousUsers, ou=Members, o=[*organization name*]. This anonymous account can be used to personalize information about the visitor, and later to provide the functionality for migrating the anonymous member (and all its member information) to a new account in the ou=Members container (or some other container).

Let's have a look at the two cookies that Automatic Cookie Authentication uses. The SITESERVER cookie represents the GUID (or Globally Unique Identifier), and corresponds to the value of the member GUID attribute. When the user is asked whether he is prepared to receive a cookie, he sees the following dialog:

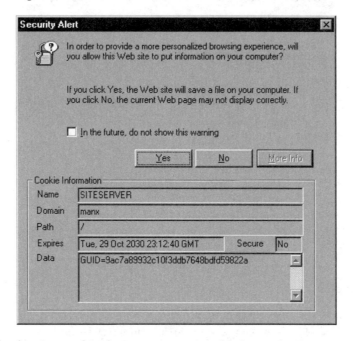

In this case, the data is stored in the SITESERVER cookie is:

```
GUID=9ac7a89932c10f3ddb7648bdfd59822a
```

The MEMUSER cookie represents the **distinguished name** (DN) of the member represented – this value should be the same as the name of the member in the Membership Directory:

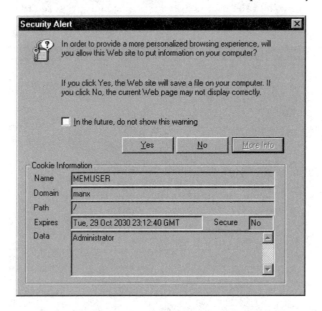

In this case, the accepted cookie will contain the data string Administrator.

The values contained in the SITESERVER and MEMUSER cookies are used to look up the corresponding member information in the Membership Directory – and to use that member (and its corresponding Windows NT group Security IDs) to access resources on the Windows NT Server. In the HTTP header HTTP_COOKIE value, these cookie values appear together as

```
SITESERVER=GUID=9ac7a89932c10f3ddb7648bdfd59822a; MEMUSER=Administrator;
ASPSESSIONIDGQQQQQBB
```

Notice the normal GUID decorations (curly braces and dashes) are not stored in the cookie GUID value.

> **A brief note about security: Automatic Cookie Authentication is a useful form of authentication. However, it's not the most *secure* form of authentication. Cookies can easily be copied, e-mailed, and used in any other similar browser type. Automatic Cookie Authentication works best for displaying non-secure personalized content to the user.**

So, suppose we want to write some simple personalization into a web page (such as greeting the member). Suppose also that the contents of our web page are not highly confidential. In this case, Automatic Cookie Authentication would be quite suitable. However, if the page contained more sensitive information – such as financial data – then we would want to use a more interactive authentication method.

Automatic Cookie Authentication with Allow Anonymous

We can use Automatic Cookie Authentication and Allow Anonymous simultaneously. In this case, IIS first determines whether the user has access to a resource, by attempting to use IIS's anonymous account, the IUSR_*[server_name]*, to access a resource (you'll recall this from the diagram in the *Allowing Anonymous Authentication* section of this chapter). If access is granted, then the user accesses the resource through the IUSR_*[server_name]* account.

If access is denied, the Membership system will attempt to authenticate the user by requesting the Site Server 3.0 cookies. If the SITESERVER cookie exists, but the MEMUSER cookie is blank, it is assumed that the member will be found in the ou=AnonymousUsers container. Alternatively, if the MEMUSER cookie *does* exist then the information is used to bind to a member whose GUID attribute value matches the SITESERVER cookie, and whose member RDN matches the value of the MEMUSER cookie.

If the system is able to bind to the appropriate member then the Security Support Provider Interface will handle the impersonation process and mapping of the member to the Windows NT impersonation account (you'll recall that the default impersonation account is called MemProxyUser).

HTML Forms Authentication

To provide a more secure (but equally simple) form of authentication, we can use HTML Forms Authentication. This method of authentication uses HTTP's POST method to send the user's credentials to an ASP page, which handles the submission – the credentials are sent via the headers of the page. Then, the ASP page makes use of a special COM object – the VerifUsr object – to verify the user's credentials.

Moreover, it's possible to combine HTML Forms authentication with Secure Sockets Layer (SSL), so that data is encrypted as it is sent across the wire.

HTML Forms Authentication also makes use of the ISAPI Membership Authentication filter – you'll recall that this filter is installed when a Membership Server, using Membership authentication, is mapped to an IIS 4.0 web site. When a user makes a call to a page that uses HTML Forms Authentication, ISAPI traps that call and redirects it to a special ASP page called FormsLogin.asp:

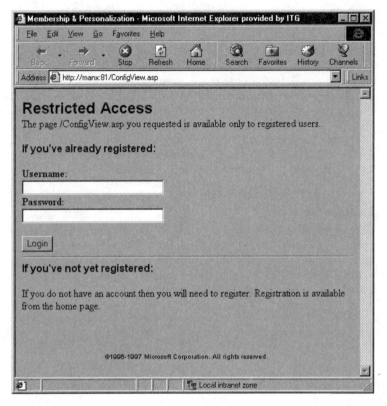

The FormsLogin.asp page is provided in the _mem_bin web application. We can modify this page; or supply our own version of the FormsLogin.asp page – it should either be placed in the same directory as the requested resource, or in the resource's parent directory. The authentication filter will look for the FormsLogin.asp page – first in the same directory, then in each successive parent directory, and finally in the _mem_bin virtual directory web application.

> *HTML Forms Authentication sets a 120-character limit on the number of characters in the password. It's possible to enter up to 256 characters – but only the first 120 characters are significant.*

In order to gain access to the resource, the user must complete the FormsLogin.asp HTML form and hit the submit button. This submits the contents of form to an ASP page called VerifPwd.asp. This page creates an instance of the Membership.VerifUsr.1 COM object, which accepts the username, password, and HTTP path of the URL resource that has been requested. (In fact, this URL is used only for redirecting back to the original page – it doesn't have any bearing on the security context).

If you wish, you can replace the code in the existing `VerifPwd.asp` with the following code, which is a little clearer and more efficient:

```
<%
Option Explicit
On Error resume next

' ***********************************
' Use the Membership.VerifUsr object to
' verify the Member's credentials
' ***********************************

Dim objVerif
Dim strURL
Dim strUserName
Dim strPassword

' Grab passed form items
' ***********************************
strUrl = Request.Form("URL")
strUsername = Request("Username")
strPassword = Request("Password")

' Create the VerifUsr object
' ***********************************
Set objVerif = Server.CreateObject("Membership.verifusr.1")
If Err.Number <> 0 Then
  Response.Write "Authentication failed. Please try logging in again.<br>"
  Response.Write "The URL " & strUrl & " cannot be accessed.<br>"
  Response.Write "Use the back button on your browser to try again."
  Response.End
End If

' Call the VerifyCredentails method
' to validate the account
' ***********************************
strUrl = objVerif.VerifyCredentials(strUsername, strPassword, strUrl)

' Handle errors or redirect
' ***********************************
If (Err.Number <> 0) Or (strURL = "") Then
  Response.Write "Authentication failed. Please try logging in again.<br>"
  Response.Write "The URL " & strUrl & " cannot be accessed.<br>"
  Response.Write "Use the back button on your browser to try again."
Else
  Response.Redirect strUrl
End if
%>
```

Compare this with the following code, which is the version of `VerifPwd.asp` provided with `_mem_bin`:

```
<%
  On Error resume next
  set x = Server.CreateObject("Membership.verifusr.1")
  strUrl = Request.Form("URL")
  strUsername = Request("Username")
  strPassword = Request("Password")
    REM VerifyCredentials verifies that the username/password
    REM specified is correct. If the credentials are valid,
    REM VerifyCredentials issues the FormsAuth cookie to the user.
    REM VerifyCredentials returns the URL to which a redirect
    REM must be sent.
  y = x.VerifyCredentials(strUsername, strPassword, strUrl)
  if y = "" Then
    Response.Write "Authentication failed. Please try logging in again.<br>"
    Response.Write "The URL " & strUrl & " cannot be accessed.<br>"
    Response.Write "Use the back button on your browser to try again."
  Else
    Response.Redirect y
  End if
%>
```

As you can see from the code above, HTML Forms authentication makes use of
`VerifyCredentials`, which is a method of the `Membership.VerifUsr.1` COM object. The
`VerifyCredentials` method has three arguments: `strUsername`, `strPassword` and `strURL`
(corresponding to the user, their password, and the URL that they are trying to access).
`VerifyCredentials` performs the calls to the Security Support Provider Interface, to map the
running thread to the appropriate impersonation account, and adds the appropriate Windows NT
Security IDs that correspond to the Membership group mappings.

> **Any ASP page called `FormsLogin.asp` can be used; the only condition is
> that it must call `/_mem_bin/verifpwd.asp` (or some other ASP page that
> provides identical functionality by using the `Membership.VerifUsr.1`
> COM object).**

HTML Forms Authentication uses just a single cookie, called FORMSAUTH. The FORMSAUTH cookie controls the length of the HTML Forms authentication session. The session length determines whether or not the current session is valid. This value is set under the properties of the Membership Server through the Personalization and Membership snap-in, and defaults to 10 minutes. The member must accept the FORMSAUTH cookie, otherwise they will not be authenticated:

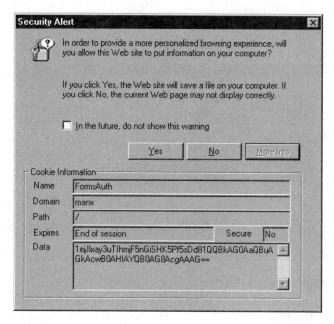

The cookie will always be set to expire after the time period specified in the Membership Server, and is reset on every subsequent visit to the site.

The main advantage of HTML Forms Authentication over Automatic Cookie Authentication is that HTML Forms Authentication forces the member to authenticate before gaining access to content. (Automatic Cookie Authentication authenticates based on the cookie alone, so no password is required.) This eliminates the chance that security will be compromised through Members sharing cookies, since we require an authentication regardless of the cookie credentials.

Furthermore, unlike other methods of authentication, HTML Forms Authentication can take advantage of the look and feel of the web site. It's possible to handle the logon process through a set of ASP pages with which the user is familiar – instead of relying on login dialog boxes as used in Distributed Password Authentication or Clear Text/Basic Authentication.

Finally, it's possible to provide other login credentials that we can check after calling the VerifyCredentials method – for example, it may be convenient to include an attribute to store the user's lastVisit.

There are two other authentication methods, which provide a more elegant 'under the covers' solution than we've seen so far. These two authentication methods are provided within the Membership Authentication tab, under the Other Password Authentication option. Both are, to a large extent, similar to the corresponding settings under Windows NT (Intranet) authentication – therefore we'll mention them only briefly here.

Distributed Password Authentication (DPA)

Distributed Password Authentication (DPA) works for Membership authentication in much the same way as Challenge/Response works for Windows NT authentication. You can probably guess the main difference: for DPA, users are authenticated against the Membership Directory (rather than the Windows NT Security Accounts Manager database). It's only possible for Windows Internet Explorer clients to use DPA, and usernames and passwords are hashed with a challenge sent by the server.

Here's what the user sees when he attempts to gain access through DPA:

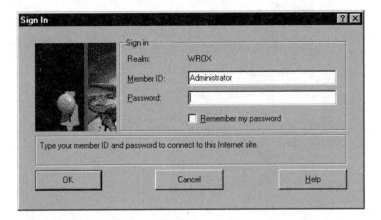

Clear Text/Basic Authentication

When we select **Basic Authentication**, we authenticate any user that requests a resource against the credentials stored in the Membership Directory. We can also specify extra information along with the username, a bit like the way we could specify a domain name for Basic Authentication under Windows NT (Intranet) authentication. However, with Basic Authentication under Membership authentication the information represents a sub-container.

This 'extra information' specifies the container below the base distinguished name (BaseDN) container from which authentication occurs. If no sub-container is specified, then the authentication will assume that all accounts live in the BaseDN of the Membership Directory. For example, suppose that the BaseDN value of our Membership Directory is ou=Members, and that the user information passed from the authentication dialog box is Premium\Robert. Then members will be authenticated from the ou=Members\ou=Premium container.

The Clear Text/Basic Authentication method is supported by a number of applications, including Netscape, and most clients should be able to use it. (As we mentioned earlier, this is also true for Clear Text/Basic Authentication under the Windows NT (Intranet) authentication method.)

A Few Final Remarks

DPA and Clear Text/Basic Authentication can be selected simultaneously. In this case, the server will first attempt to issue a DPA authentication challenge. If (and only if) the client cannot interpret the challenge, the server will offer the Clear Text/Basic Authentication request.

If Allow Anonymous and Clear Text/Basic Authentication have been selected simultaneously, then the user will see a Basic Authentication dialog box *only* if the anonymous user account access has been denied to the resource.

As we've mentioned before, Clear Text/Basic Authentication provides us with some of the functionality that we need to secure a site. If we use it in conjunction with Secure Sockets Layer encryption, we can provide a viable solution that works for all browsers. However, by restricting ourselves to Internet Explorer browsers, we can use Site Server Distributed Password Authentication to handle more secure Membership Authentication. DPA works similarly to Windows NT Challenge/Response, and the username and password is never sent across the wire.

Summary

We've had to cover a lot of ground in this chapter, but we've made it to the end! You should now have enough data to effectively implement Site Server Membership – in either Windows NT or Membership Authentication mode – on your own web site.

In the opening paragraphs of the chapter I stated that "although the technology is called Personalization and Membership, I prefer to call it Membership and Personalization." As you can see, we must recognize (authenticate) a user before providing personalization for then. This is what we will look at in the next chapter.

10

Personalization

How much more would you enjoy going to your favorite restaurant if the moment you walked in you were greeted by name, shown to your favorite table, and then poured a glass of your favorite Cabernet wine? The food wouldn't necessarily be any better, but chances are you'd be back.

Why will you be back? More than likely you've developed a relationship with the restaurant, and vice-versa. In other words, the restaurant so treasures your business that it wants to provide the best possible service for you, the customer. One way it chooses to do so is by distinguishing it's customers by name, and pouring them a glass of their favorite drink upon arrival.

The web is no different; you have customers, and if you treat them well, they will return – actually statistics show that 60% of all users that personalize do return.

> *If you would like more evidence to support this, I suggest you purchase the IDC (http://www.idc.com) Personalization document that gives credibility to the importance of personalization on a web site.*

Just as the previous chapter showed you the role of Site Server Membership, this chapter will show you how to implement Site Server Personalization. Here's a look at what we'll be covering in this chapter:

- ➤ **Why You Should Personalize** – What are the motivations behind personalization? We'll address this question, as well as the two methods to acquire information for personalization.

- ➤ **Technical Implementation** – Here we'll examine what you need to know to implement Site Server Personalization. We'll start by examining Active Directory Service Interfaces – the API set for working with a directory – and conclude by examining the Active User Object – the object used to represent a user.

> ➢ **Using ADSI and AUO** – After examining ADSI and AUO, we'll look at some common examples where we would use both these technologies. We'll use ADSI to create a new member and a new group, and we'll use the AUO to do some simple personalization.

> ➢ **Performance and Directory Strategy** – Here we'll look at some performance and design strategy tips to help you build a successful Membership Directory. We'll examine dynamic data, object relationships, and how to get to related data in a database.

Let's start by looking at why you should personalize.

Why Should You Personalize?

If you have any doubts about the need for personalization, ask yourself the following two questions:

> ➢ How long does a user stay on my web site?

> ➢ How much link navigation does the site require for the user to find their desired information?

Fundamentally, this begs the question:

> ➢ How long does it take for a user to find the information they are looking for?

Identify Goals

If you can give quantitative answers to the above questions – such as 10 minutes and 6 clicks – you can make determinations about the content of your site; perhaps even some insights as to how far away the 'important' information is from the user. The relevance of the information is key to building a successful web site. It is, of course, why people come to your site in the first place.

Now that we've identified the two key questions we should ask, we could also define two goals for our site:

> ➢ **Users will stay longer** – The availability and location of information is so readily available that users will want to stay longer and return frequently.

> ➢ **Users have to navigate less to find the information they want** – Users should be able to find the desired information in the least amount of navigation (clicks) as possible.

The bottom line being: personalization avoids information overload by enabling a user to quickly locate the information they require.

Solution: Personalization

One possible answer – and my personal favorite – is of course personalization: identifying user's behaviors and interests through explicit and implicit behavior profiling as users move around your site. Of course, there are various ways to do this: manually examining the log files and making modifications to the anchor orders on the web pages, customer surveys, or writing your own member tracking solution. However, Site Server Personalization and Membership is a very powerful and flexible tool, allowing you to focus on solving the business problem rather than the infrastructure problem (as would be the case with writing your own P&M solution).

It is, however, important to recognize that Site Server Personalization and Membership is just a set of tools that make the task of building a solution easier. Just think of Site Server as a package that solves your simple business rules and infrastructure problems. You still have to write the code to tie all the pieces together. Throughout this chapter we'll look at how you put these different puzzle pieces together to build a Personalization and Membership solution using Site Server.

Now that we have identified the problem and a solution, let's examine how we collect the information used for personalization. We'll start with explicit profiling.

Explicit Profiling

Do you run a commerce site? Do you provide for the capability for users to sign up for newsletters, or provide forms that users can use to provide feedback or purchase products? For example, examine the following screen shot from `barnesandnoble.com`:

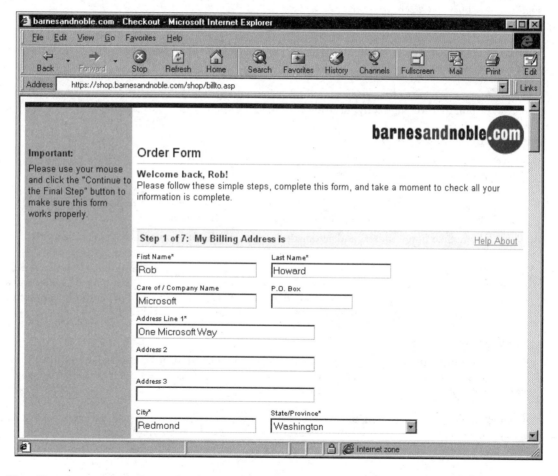

Here I've chosen to purchase a book from Barnes and Noble's web site. However, before I can complete the transaction, I must provide some information about myself, such as my billing address.

Are you already doing something similar to this? If so, congratulations! You're already explicitly profiling your users – collecting data by asking for it!

Explicit information is *information that you ask for*, or that is required before the user can perform a specific task on your web site. Of course, the best example of this is a commerce site!

This manner of behavior profiling is probably one of the easiest ways to implement personalization, and provides the most immediate benefits for a commerce site. The next section gives an example of this.

Explicit Profiling Example

My wife and I are true net citizens, we shop online for everything from groceries to clothes to airline tickets – interestingly enough my wife is usually one of the best resources I use for critiquing web sites. She doesn't have a propeller-head view of the technology, and is only concerned with getting her online 'business' accomplished.

Visiting a new site for the first time and purchasing a product easily and hassle free usually lends itself to repeat business. However, there is nothing more frustrating for either of us than to have to re-type all of our information again and again.

Frequently we purchase airline tickets online. When purchasing these tickets, we constantly have to tell the system that we will be flying from Seattle, and re-enter our Seattle address.

Immediate Benefits

If I were running this web site (or were advising them on how to better their site as I do as a Microsoft Evangelist), I would do two things immediately:

> Ask the user if the departing city is their home city, and if it is then automatically use that value for later visits; perhaps as a pre-selected value in an HTML drop down list.

> Store their home address and automatically populate the form automatically on future visits.

We've introduced another concept here, that of privacy. It's my personal opinion that you should always give the user the *option* to remember their data, and let them have access to the data you store about them. Your users will be happier and will be more willing to share information knowing that they have some control, and the data you collect will be much more accurate.

Just Ask for the Information!

Explicitly profiling the users is easy if your web site is a commerce site and you require data from your users so that they can navigate. However, what if your site isn't a commerce site and you still want to personalize? Easy, just ask for the information!

As an example of this, let's look at `home.microsoft.com`. This is a non-commerce site that makes heavy use of personalization (the site asks how the user would like to view content).

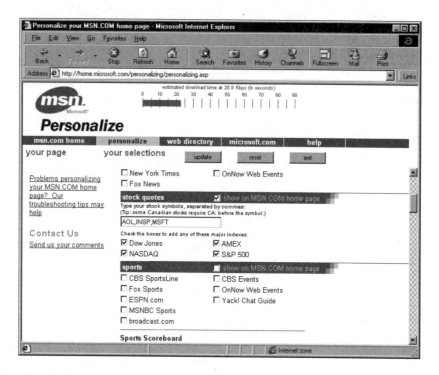

After asking for this information, `home.microsoft.com` uses this explicit information to change the behavior or display of the site – such as displaying favorite stock quotes, local weather and news, and favorite links.

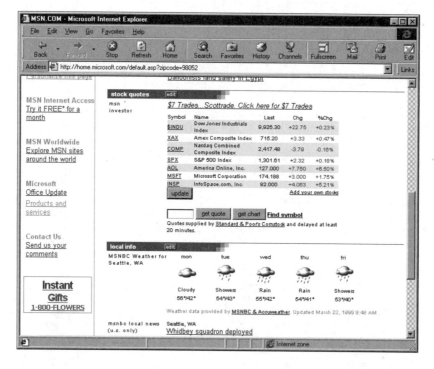

By asking the user for explicit feedback, information that they would either already provide, or want to provide to enhance their own experience, you can easily implement personalization; we'll examine how this is done through code momentarily.

Now that we're clear on what explicit personalization is, let's look at what implicit personalization is, and how we use it.

Implicit Profiling

If explicit profiling is asking the user for information, then implicit profiling is profiling the user based on actions they take while on the site – users are still providing information, but now this information comes from other sources, such as the web logs, purchasing patterns, or other user behaviors.

> Notice the constant use of the word behavior. **Personalization is about identifying user behaviors, and capitalizing on these behaviors to enhance the users' experience.**

Now, you could say that we implicitly profile a user when we ask for their address or billing information as part of a commerce site – from our above explicit profiling example – but we still ask for this information. You should consider any information that is not explicitly asked for as implicit profiling.

One way we can implicitly profile behaviors is through one of the Site Server integrated tools, **Analysis**. We stated earlier that Site Server 3.0 is a collection of tools and utilities used to aid the developer in building a complete web site. Analysis is one such tool.

Analysis

Site Server Analysis is a tool used examine log files written by IIS – actually by any web server, but in this context it is relevant only to Internet Information Server 4.0, since that is the only web server that supports Site Server 3.0 Personalization and Membership.

When a user visits an IIS 4.0 web site with logging and Site Server Membership enabled – as examined in the previous chapter – log files are generated by the requests the user makes from the web server. These logs provide a good resource to determine the path of a user through the site. And with Site Server Membership, the member visiting the site has his or her username stamped in the log.

The following script, AuthUser.asp, is a relatively simple Active Server Page that dumps the server variables. If you were to save the following script sample as AuthUser.asp in a Site Server Personalization and Membership enabled web (see previous chapter) and were to request it, you would see the AUTH_USER server variable return value equal to the cn of the requesting user.

```
<%
Option Explicit

Dim varItem
```

```
Response.Write "<FONT FACE=ARIAL>"
Response.Write "<HTML><TABLE BORDER=1>"
Response.Write "<TR><TD><B>Key</B></TD>"
Response.Write "<TD><B>Value</B></TD></TR>"

' Write out Server variables
' *********************************
For Each varItem in Request.ServerVariables()
  Response.Write "<TR><TD>" & varItem & "</TD>"
  Response.Write "<TD>" & Request.ServerVariables(varItem) & "</TD></TR>"
Next

Response.Write "</TABLE></HTML>"
%>
```

After using one of the authentication mechanisms, we would see the following value for AUTH_USER.

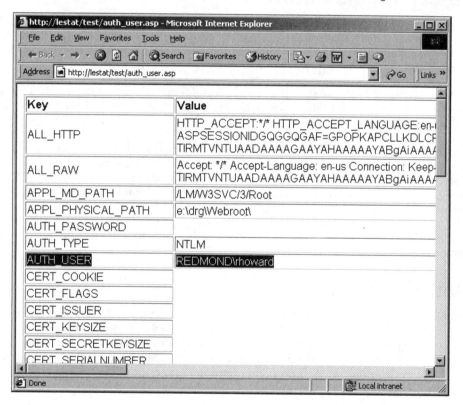

For example, if we authenticated as Scully, we would see an AUTH_USER value of Scully. This AUTH_USER value is written to the log files, as part of the 'stamp' as we navigate through the site.

Using Site Server Analysis, we can then examine all of the log file information, cross-reference it with Members in the Membership Directory, and build a behavior pattern. Later, based on this behavior pattern, we can modify our sites' content – or personalization attributes about our members – to reflect this knowledge.

Trends

There is something you should consider if you plan to implement implicit profiling in your site: trends and data. A high performance web site needs to be efficient in its use of information, and this definitely holds true for the data used in implicit profiling. If you are trying to establish trends in your data, for example top traffic locations for a specific user set, don't examine all the data. Instead, select a sample of the data. This is especially true if you're implementing a 'trends' based implicit profiling commerce solution. You don't need to know all the data about all the users, just the trends for the majority of the users.

Now that we've looked at how you can explicitly or implicitly profile members of your site, let's get to the good stuff... how it's done!

Technical Implementation

In the previous chapter, we discussed Membership. Of the two pieces of the technology, Membership is by far the more complex to configure. Personalization, on the other hand, is quite simple and straightforward from the technical implementation perspective... that is, once you have the data to personalize with!

Once we've identified (authenticated) the user through Membership, we use a special object that can receive the context of the authenticated user. Before we go on to discuss the object, let's examine what is meant by context.

The context of the user is the instance of a user performing a specific action upon our IIS web through the Internet. The context includes any temporary memory set aside for the user – for example, while the Active Server Page is executing, the user has variables that are identified with their context. In addition to memory, the context also includes security permissions that are assigned to the user when the execution of code is performed. By default the security context is anonymous (IUSR_[*server name*]), but remember that with Membership this security context is extended beyond the traditional boundaries of Windows NT in Membership Authentication, as discussed in the previous chapter.

The Active User Object

The object we use for personalizing the user's experience is the **Active User Object** (AUO). The AUO is a COM component that is capable of retrieving the current user's context once instantiated. In fact, the AUO is designed specifically for Active Server Pages. Active Server Pages attempt to call the entry point OnStartPage() on any object instance created. Since the AUO implements the OnStartPage() method, the AUO is able to retrieve the context of the current execution of the Active Server Page document.

So how is the context passed? Well, ASP supports an ObjectContext object that may be passed around to share the current ASP context. This ObjectContext is exactly what is passed to the implementation of OnStartPage() in the AUO. The AUO can then use the passed ObjectContext to retrieve information about the user the ASP is executing for; thus binding to the appropriate member in the Membership Directory and providing access to properties.

Let's look at another code sample, SimpleAUO.asp, which shows just how easy personalization using the AUO is. The following code sample creates an instance of the AUO and then uses that instance, calling the Get() method to retrieve a member attribute. In this case we'll be retrieving the common name (cn) value of the current member executing this ASP:

```
<%
Option Explicit
On Error Resume Next

Dim objAUO

Set objAUO = Server.CreateObject("Membership.UserObjects.1")
If Err.Number <> 0 Then
  Response.Write "Unable to create the AUO."
  Response.End
End If

Response.Write "Hello " & objAUO.Get("cn") & "!"

Set objAUO = Nothing
%>
```

If you applied Clear Text/Basic Authentication – or for that matter any form of authentication that allows you to identify the user – and authenticated with a valid user (in this case I used rhoward) you should see:

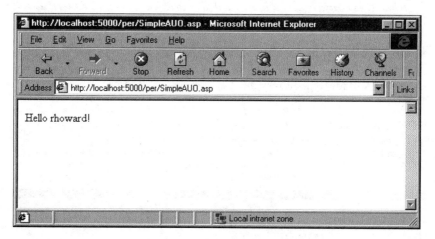

The AUO is designed for use with Active Server Pages. Outside of this programming paradigm, the effectiveness of the AUO diminishes because more work is required than is necessary to get to member data. Although you could use the AUO for other purposes, for example in a Visual Basic application to administer the Membership Directory, or a C++ COM object used to write Access Control Entries in the directory, you shouldn't. Using the AUO in ASP requires no method calls to initialize or bind to the correct Membership Directory. Outside of the scope of ASP, you would have to initialize and bind to the correct data structures yourself. In such an environment you should use the Microsoft API for working with directories and namespaces: **Active Directory Service Interfaces** (ADSI). More details about this distinction are given later in this chapter.

> *Specifically, if you needed to use the AUO outside of the scope of Active Server Pages, you would need to call the Init() method and several others yourself. For more on AUO methods and properties see Appendix E, and for more on the AUO see Site Server 3.0 Personalization and Membership by Robert Howard (Wrox, ISBN 1861001940).*

The AUO itself uses ADSI, exposing interfaces allowing you to work with directories. Because of this, let's start our dissection of the Active User Object by examining ADSI.

Active Directory Service Interfaces

If you develop with Microsoft Windows, ADSI is one of the better technologies to learn. Not only can you use ADSI to manage the Site Server Membership Directory, but the same skills can be applied to the Internet Information Server 4.0 metabase (the structure that IIS stores all site specific data in), the current Windows user directory (Security Accounts Manager or SAM), and, more importantly, Windows 2000 Active Directory (the directory that Windows 2000 uses both to replace the functionality of the SAM and to store other globally important data).

Learning ADSI is also important because the Active User Object exposes two ADSI interfaces: IADs and IADsContainer. Working with the AUO, you'll become intimately familiar with these two interfaces, whether you like it or not!

The way I learned ADSI – other than day-in and day-out use! – is by examining the interfaces, methods, and properties through OLE/COM Object Viewer.

> *OLE/COM Object Viewer (installed with Microsoft Visual Studio) is one of the many tools available to the developer provided in addition to the already complete development package of Visual Studio. If you've never used this tool, and plan to do any serious object level development and implementation, I suggest you investigate it!*

OLE/COM Object Viewer

The OLE/COM Object Viewer allows you to examine the ADSI type library. After installing Site Server, you should find this type library in <system drive>\winnt\system32\, named activeds.tlb.

To use OLE/COM Object Viewer to view the activeds.tlb type library select File | View TypeLib... and navigate to the appropriate location. After opening activeds.tlb you can see all the ADSI interfaces and their methods. For example, here is the information we can see for IADs:

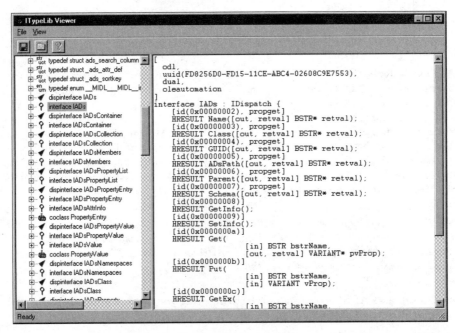

Unfortunately (or maybe not, depending upon your perspective!), you won't be learning all of these interfaces and methods to work with the Membership Directory. There are quite a few interfaces, 46 by my count, but the Membership Directory supports only 5 of these – the others are for use with Windows 2000 Active Directory and other ADSI directories. There are only 3 interfaces that are 'truly' relevant to our work in the Membership Directory, so these are the ones that we'll concentrate on here.

For a complete list of the interfaces supported by the Membership Directory, and their methods and properties, refer to Appendix D.

The 3 Active Directory Service Interfaces you should learn are:

➢ IADs – Used for working with objects in the directory

➢ IADsContainer – Used for working with containers in the directory

➢ IADsOpenDSObject – Used for binding to the directory

In the following diagram you can see how IADs is used for objects and IADsContainer is used for containers:

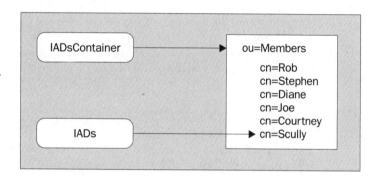

The IADsContainer interface is used for working with the ou (organizational unit) structure of a directory, while IADs is used to work with class instances, our user, Scully, for example.

For now, let's look at some of the more important methods provided by each of these interfaces. We'll start with IADsOpenDSObject:

IADsOpenDSObject

The IADsOpenDSObject interface only has one method, making it one of the easier interfaces to learn. This single method, OpenDSObject(), returns a pointer to an object – specified by the first parameter – in a directory. However, we can use this to bind to a directory as a *specific user*. Remember how in the previous chapter we had to enter a username and password when accessing the Membership Directory through the Membership Directory Manager? This uses the same concept, only now we'll do it through code.

Here's the method definition from OLE/COM Object Viewer definition of the IADsOpenDSObject's dispatch interface definition:

```
IDispatch* OpenDSObject([in] BSTR lpszDNName,
                        [in] BSTR lpszUserName,
                        [in] BSTR lpszPassword,
                        [in] long lnReserved);
```

Let's examine each of these parameters in more detail.

> lpszDNName – defines the distinguished name – or unique path – of the object to bind to. If we wanted to bind to a Membership Directory on a machine named LDAPServer on port 389, we would specify:

```
"LDAP://LDAPServer:389"
```

Port 389 is the default LDAP port much in the same way that port 80 is the default WWW port. We don't need to specify port 389 for LDAP; I have only done so here for the sake of clarity.

> lpszUserName – specifies the user to perform the bind as. However, rather than merely passing the name of the user, we must specify the location of the user in the Membership Directory. For example, if our Membership Directory's root name was MemDir, and we wished to bind as Administrator, we would pass the following value:

```
"cn=Administrator, ou=Members, o=MemDir"
```

> lpszPassword – once we've identified the distinguished name of the member we wish to authenticate with, we pass the password value of our member through the third parameter, for example:

```
"password"
```

> lnReserved – the last parameter determines the type of bind to perform, and can be any of the following constants (whose definitions are found in the IADs.h header file):

```
#define ADS_SECURE_AUTHENTICATION  (0x1)
#define ADS_USE_ENCRYPTION         (0x2)
#define ADS_READONLY_SERVER        (0x4)
#define ADS_PROMPT_CREDENTIALS     (0x8)
```

> **Site Server 3.0 installs ADSI version 2.0, in which the lnReserved parameter of the OpenDSObject() method is reserved for future use. ADSI version 2.5, which may be installed after applying Site Server Service Pack 2, recognizes these parameter values.**

Example Use

The following code sample demonstrates how you could use the IADsOpenDSObject interface along with the OpenDSObject() method to bind to the Membership Directory as a specific user. Why would you do this? For the same reason that you use different users to bind to a database. Different users are allowed to perform different tasks; sometimes you don't want a user to be able to perform a specific task without explicitly giving them the permissions to do so. In this example, the correct permissions are needed to bind to a specific resource in the directory. Once this resource is obtained, actions, such as creating new members or adding members to groups, may be performed.

For example, if this was an internal management page for our Membership Directory, we could programmatically bind as `Administrator` to perform some action, even if the current user (the user that the AUO would be activated as) executed the ASP:

```
<%
Option Explicit

On Error Resume Next

Dim objIADs
Dim objOpenDSObject

' Bind securely
' *****************************************
Const STR_LDAP_PATH = "LDAP://localhost:1003/o=Memdir/ou=Dynamic"
Const STR_SECURE_BIND_USER = "cn=Administrator, ou=Members, o=MemDir"
Const STR_SECURE_BIND_PWD = "password"

' Bind to LDAP
' *****************************************
Set objOpenDSObject = GetObject("LDAP:")

' Bind to the appropriate container (in this example the dynamic container)
' **************************************************************
Set objIADs = objOpenDSObject.OpenDSObject(STR_LDAP_PATH, _
                                           STR_SECURE_BIND_USER, _
                                           STR_SECURE_BIND_PWD, _
                                           1)

' If no errors occured, we bound successfully
' *****************************************
If Err.Number = 70 Then ' 70 is Permission Denied
  Response.Write "Permission denied, please bind with another user."
Else If Err.Number = 0 Then
  Response.Write "Bound succesfully!"
Else
  Response.Write "General error, check the code ;)"
End If
%>
```

The above code sample uses the user `Administrator` with the password of `password` to bind to the `ou=Dynamic` container of the Membership Directory. The `ou=Dynamic` container is a special container of the Membership Directory that we'll look at later.

One of the interesting things that you might have noticed is the following call:

```
' Bind to LDAP
' *****************************************
Set objOpenDSObject = GetObject("LDAP:")
```

The `GetObject()` call is intrinsic to VB/VBScript and is similar to the `CreateObject()` call, but instead it binds to an already running service or object. `LDAP:` is what is known as a COM moniker. Think of a moniker as a common name for a binary object or service. The `LDAP:` moniker actually calls a COM object and returns a reference to an object that you can use to converse with a directory.

After getting a reference to the LDAP moniker, we'll use the `OpenDSObject()` method with the value of the constants defined earlier. So, you might ask, how can you call through to `OpenDSObject()` via the reference returned by `GetObject("LDAP:")`? Well, The object returned exposes the `IADsOpenDSObject` interface, and via the magic of dispatch interfaces is able to translate our call to the appropriate method. If the bind is successfully completed, a pointer is returned to another ADSI interface: `IADs`.

Although this is a fairly simple sample of how to use the `IADsOpenDsObject`, we'll be building on this sample code throughout the remainder of the chapter.

Since our `OpenDSObject()` call returned an `IADs` reference, let's examine that interface next.

IADs

If you choose to learn one ADSI interface, this is the one. The `IADs` interface provides all the methods necessary to retrieve and update attribute values in a directory, or from the ADSI cache. ADSI implements caching for attributes returned from the data source. One of the methods we'll examine in a moment is the `Get()` method. The `Get()` method is actually very unique, since behind the scenes it first checks to see if an attribute value is in the ADSI cache. If it's not, the first programmatic call of this method for any attribute will result in the entire local ADSI cache being updated; thus making subsequent requests less expensive.

> *Once again, to clarify, an attribute is the loving term we give to properties of an object in a directory. An object is described by attributes, `telephoneNumber` for example. When you see attribute, think property (or vice-versa).*

The three most important methods of `IADs` that we'll discuss are: `Put()`, `SetInfo()`, and `Get()`. Let's examine each of these in more detail.

The Get() Method

We use the `Get()` method to retrieve the value of an attribute from the ADSI cache. Behind the scenes this value is either retrieved directly from the directory along with all other attribute values (for the first call) or from the ADSI cache for every subsequent call.

> *All though we're not discussing them in this book, there are other methods used to work with attributes and attribute values, namely `GetInfo()` and `GetInfoEx()`.*

You use the `Get()` method explicitly, like this:

```
strName = objAUO.Get("givenName")
```

or implicitly, like this:

```
strName = objAUO.givenName
```

Before we look at a code sample, let's explain the single parameter required by `Get()`.

> ➢ `bstrName` – the `Get()` method let's us retrieve the value that an attribute contains, but to retrieve the value, we have to specify the attribute. `bstrName` represents the name of the attribute whose value we wish to retrieve.

Example Use

By way of an example, let's imagine we have a Membership Directory on machine A and a client on machine B. We can bind to the Membership Directory on machine A from machine B and view a cache in action. If we used the following code, and have debugging turned on via the properties of the IIS 4.0 web site, we could actually disconnect the physical network connection between the two machines when we encounter the stop directive (with debugging turned on the ASP command `stop` tells the compiler it has encountered a break-point and to open the debugger). After disconnecting we can continue our code and still view attribute values – taken from the cache, which will then contain all available attribute values in local memory.

```
<HTML>
<BODY BGCOLOR=WHITE>
<FONT FACE=ARIAL SIZE=3>
<B>
Active Directory Caching
</B>
<HR SIZE=1>
</FONT>
<FONT FACE=ARIAL SIZE=2>
<%
On Error Resume Next

Dim objAUO

' Create AUO
' **************************
Set objAUO = Server.CreateObject("Membership.UserObjects.1")
If Err.Number <> 0 Then
  Response.Write "Error creating AUO"
  Response.End
End If

Response.Write "The cn of the user is: " & objAUO.Get("cn")
Response.Flush

' Disconnect network here
' **************************
stop

Response.Write "Your password is: " & objAUO.Get("userPassword")
%>
</FONT>
</BODY>
</HTML>
```

`Get()` is the method you will use for almost all your personalization needs. You will simply get the attribute value, such as `favoriteLinks` (an example of a custom attribute), or `givenName` (an example of a provided attribute). Either way your local variable on the left hand side of the assignment receives the value of the attribute. The local variable is then available for your own programmatic use.

Now that you know how to get values out of the cache and from the directory, let's see how we put them back in.

The Put() Method

The `Put()` method is used to add values to the attributes of a class instance. For example, if you wanted to add the value of `Jon` for the `givenName` attribute, you would use:

```
[object].Put("givenName", "Jon")
```

If the object you are doing the putting with was a Member and exposed the `givenName` attribute, this would be a valid action.

However, the `Put()` method *only* updates the ADSI cache – in local memory – for the current object. For the values to be written back the Membership Directory, we have to call the `SetInfo()` method; another method of `IADs` that writes the cache to the physical directory, we'll examine it a bit later.

If we were to call a series of `Put()`s on an object, but never call `SetInfo()`, the memory would be flushed and our updates lost as soon as you lose the reference to the object. But you only need to call `SetInfo()` once after you've completed your series of `Put()`s.

Note that we can use the `Put()` method explicitly, like this:

```
objAUO.Put "givenName", "StephenS"
```

or implicitly, like this:

```
objAUO.givenName "StephenS"
```

For the sake of clarity and ease of use, I suggest you use the explicit method. Also, for attributes that have the same name as property values of the `IADs` object such as `GUID`, you'll run into problems.

Now, let's examine the parameters of the `Put()` method, `bstrName` and `vProp`.

- ➤ `bstrName` – represents the name of the attribute to be updated. For example, if we wanted to update the `givenName` of a member, we would pass `givenName` as the `bstrName` parameter value.

- ➤ `vProp` – after specifying the attribute to update, we pass the value for the attribute through the `vProp` parameter.

Example Use

Let's look at an example that uses the AUO and ASP to `Put()` some attribute values for a member. However, let's see a little background first.

`Put()`ing itself is not an expensive operation, but `SetInfo()` is. Of course, there is little point in updating only the ADSI cache without calling `SetInfo()`, but you should try and be discreet about where and when you add values to the Membership Directory. We'll talk more about this in the strategies section towards the end of this chapter.

```
<HTML>
<BODY BGCOLOR=WHITE>
<FONT FACE=ARIAL SIZE=3>
<B>
IADs - Put
</B>
<HR SIZE=1>
</FONT>
<FONT FACE=ARIAL SIZE=2>
<%
On Error Resume Next

Dim objAUO

' Create the Active User Object
' *******************************************************
Set objAUO = Server.CreateObject("Membership.UserObjects.1")
If Err.Number <> 0 Then
  Response.Write "Unable to create the AUO."
  Response.End
End If

' Use the Put Method
' *******************************************************
Response.Write "<P> The Put method adds values "
Response.Write "for mustContain or "
Response.Write "mayContain attributes "
Response.Write "for members.</P>"

objAUO.Put "givenName", "Brian" ' First Name
objAUO.Put "sn", "White"        ' Last Name
```

The ADSI cache now has values for the `givenName` and `sn` attributes of our member. We can ask for the values straight away, even though they don't yet exist in the physical directory.

```
' Read from the ADSI cache
' *******************************************************
Response.Write "First Name: " & objAUO.Get("givenName") & "<BR>"
Response.Write "Last Name: " & objAUO.Get("sn")
%>
</FONT>
</BODY>
</HTML>
```

The attribute values from the `Put()` sample code are never written to the directory – we'd have to call the `SetInfo()` method for that. The attribute values reside only in the ADSI cache, not in the Membership Directory.

The code:

```
' Read from the ADSI cache
' *******************************************************
Response.Write "First Name: " & objAUO.Get("givenName") & "<BR>"
Response.Write "Last Name: " & objAUO.Get("sn")
```

Does display values, but remember, these values are being read from memory. If you were to write an ASP that called for these same values from the same AUO instance on a separate ASP, you would not see the same results; not until we called `SetInfo()` from our initial ASP.

The SetInfo() Method

We use the `SetInfo()` method to update the directory with only the items we change in the ADSI cache. There are two points we should remember about a `SetInfo()` call:

> Not all attributes are updated. The *only* attributes updated by `SetInfo()` are those for which `Put()` or `PutEx()` (`PutEx()` is an extended version of `Put()`, not discussed in this book) is called. This means that if an attribute has changed and `SetInfo()` is not called, the value won't be changed in the Membership Directory.

> Only one trip is made to the directory to update the information. This saves network traffic (if the Membership Directory is on another machine), because there's no need to use the network for every single `Put()` or `PutEx()` performed.

The `SetInfo()` method has to be one of the more frustrating calls for any developer working with the AUO or with raw ADSI objects. Personally, I've spent a good deal of time debugging applications that worked just fine until the `SetInfo()` method was called. It's one of the unfortunate things about working with the ADSI cache – it can have some pitfalls when we're adding information. We don't know if we've populated all the required values, or if the values are valid, until `SetInfo()` is called.

For example, you can add any number of attribute values to the ADSI cache with `Put()`, even if the attribute doesn't exist for the particular object class you may be working with. In other words, you're responsible for the semantics of the objects you work with – if you add a value for an attribute that doesn't exist for the class, `SetInfo()` will fail.

Going back to our previous example for `Put()`, we could modify the code to call `SetInfo()`:

```
<HTML>
<BODY BGCOLOR=WHITE>
<FONT FACE=ARIAL SIZE=3>
<B>
IADs — Put and SetInfo()
</B>
<HR SIZE=1>
</FONT>
<FONT FACE=ARIAL SIZE=2>
<%
On Error Resume Next

Dim objAUO

' Create the Active User Object
' *******************************************************
Set objAUO = Server.CreateObject("Membership.UserObjects.1")
If Err.Number <> 0 Then
  Response.Write "Unable to create the AUO."
  Response.End
End If


' Use the Put Method
' *******************************************************
Response.Write "<P> The Put method adds values "
Response.Write "for mustContain or "
Response.Write "mayContain attributes "
Response.Write "for members.</P>"

objAUO.Put "givenName", "Bill" ' First Name
objAUO.Put "sn", "Gates"        ' Last Name
```

```
' SetInfo() on the data to write to MD
' **********************************************************
objAUO.SetInfo
%>
</FONT>
</BODY>
</HTML>
```

Afterwards, if you examined the member in the Membership Directory Manager (our member object is billg), you would see values for the givenName and sn attributes for the member:

Now that you're familiar with the three most important methods of IADs, let's examine the final interface: IADsContainer.

IADsContainer

This interface is used to bind to containers (such as the ou=Members container), and to create, delete, move and get objects in those containers. However, for this chapter we will only be examining two methods: Create() and MoveHere().

These two methods provide the most important functionality of IADsContainer, the ability to create and move new object instances. For example, you might use the Create() method to create a new Member object in ou=AnonymousUsers. After creating the new member, you may decide that the member should no longer be anonymous, but should become a regular member of the site. You would then use the MoveHere() method to move the member from the ou=AnonymousUsers container to the ou=Members container.

Let's begin by examining the Create() method.

The Create() Method

The `Create()` method creates new instances of classes in the directory. This includes new attributes and new classes in the schema, not just class instances – even the schema of the directory is made up of instances of classes.

It has two parameters, `ClassName` and `RelativeName`.

> ➢ `ClassName` – the schema name of the class of object to create
>
> ➢ `RelativeName` - the name of the object as it will be known in the directory

Example Use

If we wanted to write a script to create a new container under the members container we would bind to the `ou=Members` container and use the `Create()` method on this `IADsContainer` object to create a new `organizationalUnit` (ou) object. Passing the `ClassName` of `organizationalUnit` and the `RelativeName` value of the new container, would create the appropriate container for us.

Let's review a code sample that uses the `Create()` method to create a new container called `ou=Premium` under the `ou=Members` container.

```
<HTML>
<BODY BGCOLOR=WHITE>
<FONT FACE=ARIAL SIZE=3>
<B>
IADsContainer - Create
</B>
<HR SIZE=1>
</FONT>
<FONT FACE=ARIAL SIZE=2>
<%
On Error Resume Next

Dim objAUO

' Create the Active User Object
' *********************************************************
Set objAUO = Server.CreateObject("Membership.UserObjects.1")
If Err.Number <> 0 Then
  Response.Write "Unable to create the AUO."
  Response.End
End If

Set objLDAPRoot = objAUO

' Loop to get ldap root
' *********************************************************
Do While Not objLDAPRoot.class = "organization"
  Set objLDAPRoot = GetObject(objLDAPRoot.parent)
Loop

' Use the IADsContainer GetObject method to bind to the members container
' *********************************************************
Set objIADsContainer = objLDAPRoot.GetObject("organizationalUnit", "ou=Members")

' Use the IADsContainer Create method to create a new container called Premium
' *********************************************************
```

```
  Set objIADsContainer = objIADsContainer.Create("organizationalUnit", "ou=Premium")

  ' Call SetInfo to store the new container in the Membership Directory
  ' *********************************************************
  objIADsContainer.SetInfo

  If Err.Number <> 0 Then
    Response.Write "Error: New container not created!"
  Else
    Response.Write "New container created!"
  End If
%>
</FONT>
</BODY>
</HTML>
```

We can see the new container that's been created in the Membership Directory:

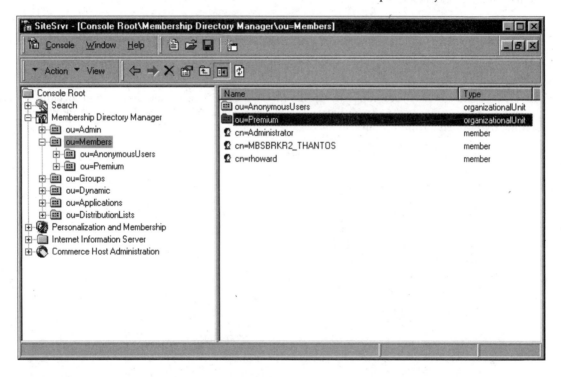

Now that you know how to create a new object, let's learn how to move it.

The MoveHere() Method

You use the MoveHere() method to move class instances from one location (container) to another. The primary use of the MoveHere() method is member management. As we stated earlier, you might want to promote an anonymous user to a fully registered user. To do so you would use the MoveHere() method. Specifically, the member object would be moved from the ou=AnonymousUsers container into the ou=Members container.

Let's start by examining the parameters of this method, SourceName and NewName.

> SourceName – represents the Active Directory path (for example, LDAP://localhost/o=Wrox/ou=Members/ou=AnonymousUsers) from where the object to be moved exists. We could also use the ADsPath parameters from the IADs interface to retrieve this value.

> NewName – represents the new name of the object – such as cn=UsedToBeAnonymous. This parameter can be omitted if no name change is required.

Example Use

The MoveHere() method allows us to move a member that was anonymous to another container, such as the ou=Members container, while retaining all of the member's properties. This is especially important since we can migrate this member without losing all the member information that is being stored about the member.

> **The MoveHere() method allows us to move a user to another container without losing the member information.**

You can use this behavior to implicitly profile members, and later, when they wish to become official members, move them to the appropriate ou=members container while still retaining all of their implicitly profiled attribute values.

```
<HTML>
<BODY BGCOLOR=WHITE>
<FONT FACE=ARIAL SIZE=3>
<B>
IADsContainer - MoveHere
</B>
<HR SIZE=1>
</FONT>
<FONT FACE=ARIAL SIZE=2>
<%
' *********************************************************
' FUNCTION: MoveMember
'
' PURPOSE: Move member from one container to another.
'
' RETURNS: object - object exists / object nothing
'
' PARAMETERS:
'    strADsPathToMember - Path to the member to move
'
'    strADsPathToContainer - Path to move member to
'
'    strNewMemberCn - New common name for member if necessary
'
Public Function MoveMember(strADsPathToMember, _
                           strADsPathToContainer, _
                           strNewMemberCn)

  On Error Resume Next

  Dim objIADsContainer
  Dim objIADsMember
```

```
    ' Assume failure
    ' ************************
    Set MoveMember = Nothing

    ' Bind to the strADsPathToContainer
    ' ************************
    Set objIADsContainer = GetObject(strADsPathToContainer)
    If Err.Number <> 0 Then
      Err.Clear
      Exit Function
    End If

    ' Bind to the strADsPathToMember
    ' ************************
    Set objIADsMember = GetObject(strADsPathToMember)
    If Err.Number <> 0 Then
      Err.Clear
      Exit Function
    End If

    ' Are we passing a new cn?
    ' ************************
    If Len(strNewMemberCn) > 0 Then
      strNewMemberCn = "cn=" & strNewMemberCN
    Else

      ' Get Member Name (RDN)
      ' ************************
      strNewMemberCn = objIADsMember.Name
    End If

    ' Move the AUO user to the
    ' appropriate container
    ' ************************
    objIADsContainer.MoveHere objIADsMember.ADsPath, strNewMemberCn
    If Err.Number <> 0 Then
      Err.Clear
      Exit Function
    End If

    ' SetInfo
    ' ************************
    objIADsContainer.SetInfo
    If Err.Number <> 0 Then
      Err.Clear
      Exit Function
    Else
      Set MoveMember = objIADsContainer.GetObject("member",strNewMemberCn)
    End If
End Function


' ********************************
' Example Use
' ********************************
Dim objAUO
Dim objNewAUO

' Create the Active User Object
' *******************************************************
```

```
Set objAUO = Server.CreateObject("Membership.UserObjects.1")
If Err.Number <> 0 Then
  Response.Write "Unable to create the AUO."
  Response.End
End If

Set objLDAPRoot = objAUO

' Loop to get ldap root
' **********************************************
Do While Not objLDAPRoot.class = "organization"
  Set objLDAPRoot = GetObject(objLDAPRoot.parent)
Loop

' Use the IADs GetObject to bind to the members container
' ********************************************************
Set objIADsContainer = objLDAPRoot.GetObject("organizationalUnit", "ou=Members")

' Use the MoveMember function to migrate the member
' ********************************************************
Set objNewAUO = MoveMember(objAUO.ADsPath, objIADsContainer.ADsPath, "Rob")

If objNewAUO Is Nothing Then
  Response.Write "Failed to move Member"
Else
  Response.Write "Member moved successfully"
End If
%>
</FONT>
</BODY>
</HTML>
```

We've stated that the AUO exposes both the `IADs` and `IADsContainer` to work with objects in the Membership Directory. But, as I said earlier, the AUO should only be used from Active Server Pages. For other uses, you should use straight ADSI rather than the exposed interfaces available through the AUO. Let's examine why that is.

Suggested Use of the AUO

This might seem a bit confusing. I've told you not to use the Active User Object in applications other than ASP. But, if the AUO exposes ADSI interfaces... why not? The answer lies within the purpose and design of the object.

The first ADSI interface we examined, `IADsOpenDSObject`, performed a critical function for us: it allowed us to bind to the Membership Directory. The Active User Object provides this functionality when instantiated in an ASP using Site Server Membership. Once instantiated, the AUO binds to the member in the Membership Directory that authenticated to our web site, exposing the member programmatically to the ASP. Hence the name, **Active User Object**.

It is this reason, and the manner in which the AUO is bound, that we should not use the object from other applications. Let's examine this in more detail.

AUO Architecture

Whenever an Active Server Page is executed, the method `OnStartPage()` is called on every object that is created:

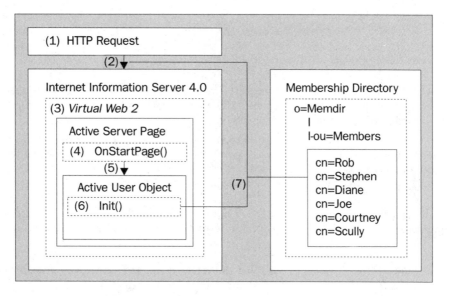

There's a lot happening in this diagram, but the bottom line is that a user requests an ASP, and an instance of the AUO is created. Let's look at each of the steps.

An HTTP Request is made to an IIS 4.0 web server (**1**). This request can be for any resource that exists on the server, but must be made through HTTP so that the web server can trap and authenticate the request with Membership. This authentication (**2**) then queries the Membership Directory to see if the user attempting to authenticate is in fact a member of the site.

> *In our case we'll assume Clear Text/Basic Authentication as the authentication technique, and that the member to be authenticated does in fact exist and his member name is* `cn=Stephen`.

After successfully authenticating the member, the ASP is served (**3**) from a virtual web server #2 (the fact that IIS has virtual web servers will become important soon).

The Active Server Page then begins to execute (**4**), being either called from memory, or parsed by `asp.dll`. Nevertheless, if a `Server.CreateObject()` method is called to create an instance of an object with in the ASP, the `OnStartPage()` method is also called on the object (**5**).

`OnStartPage()` is useful for performing any initialization with an object called from an ASP. In the case of the AUO, it is extremely useful. The AUO supports the `OnStartPage()` method, and in turn calls its own `Init()` method (**6**).

AUO Initialization

The Init() method, exposed by the IUserObjects interface of the AUO, accepts two parameters. Examine the method definition from OLE/COM Object Viewer:

```
void Init(BSTR bszHost,
          BSTR bszUserName);
```

Let's examine these parameters in more detail:

> ➤ bszHost – This parameter represents the id number of the IIS 4.0 virtual server that the object is called from. This value is used by the AUO to look up which Membership Directory is mapped to this web, and then to bind to that directory.

> ➤ bszUserName – The value of the IIS server variable AUTH_USER is passed by this parameter and is used to bind to the appropriate member in the Membership Directory. This binding is performed by a broker – a dedicated user used to perform specific tasks in the directory – and since the user is already authenticated, the password is not necessary.

After the initialization is complete the AUO is bound to the member that authenticated (7). The developer has done no work to get this done! It is all performed by merely instantiating the object.

> Note that although you can also use the AUO from ASPs not participating in membership, you will have to call the Init() method yourself. I recommend that in these cases you also choose to use ADSI for performance and code clarity.

Why the AUO Should Only Be Used In ASP

So, why shouldn't the AUO be used from VB or other non-ASP based applications?

The calls performed by the AUO are redundant to the provided services of ADSI outside of ASP. Using the AUO in ASP simplifies personalization since the process of binding is integrated with the membership features.

However, outside the scope of an ASP page, calling Init() (depending on the Membership Server mapping), and then performing the call directly, short-circuits security and adds more unnecessary overhead to development.

Rather, it makes more sense to bind to the Membership Directory as the particular member using the IADsOpenDSObject interface, binding either directly to the object or to the desired member. This makes the code more flexible since there are no dependencies upon the Membership Server mapping settings that affect the Init() call. Additionally, security is not compromised since the caller has to provide credentials to perform the bind; simply using the Init() method uses a directory broker, without checking security with the binder, and returns a pointer to the member.

OK, you've got all the background you need to start using personalization. As you can see, actually personalizing content is quite simple. You simply request an attribute and write conditional code that directs your application to behave in various manners; piece of cake! Rather than showing you simplistic personalization examples, let's look at some of the more esoteric areas of this product, namely programmatic management of your application and the directory.

Using ADSI and AUO

Now that you're familiar with the object model of the AUO and ADSI, let's look at some code samples that show some common uses of both. We'll start by using ADSI to perform some common tasks, such as creating new member objects and adding members to groups. Next, we'll use the AUO to demonstrate how easy it is to accomplish personalization tasks.

ADSI

One of the most frequent occurring tasks in the Membership Directory is creating new members programmatically. Before we examine the code to do this, let's first set the stage for why the code is written the way it is.

mustContain and mayContain Attributes

Every object in the Membership Directory has a set of attributes (properties) that define the object. For example, a member object is defined by several attributes (not all shown):

Attribute	Description
cn (common name)	Member's username
UserPassword	The password of the member
GUID	Unique identifier for a member object
telephoneNumber	Phone number of the member

What is important to note about these attributes is that, for the instantiation of a new object, some are required and some are not. Any object that is created in the Membership Directory must define these required attributes, known as mustContain or MandatoryProperties, but may also define the non-required attributes, known as mayContain or OptionalProperties. Let's examine these in more detail, since the knowledge of 'creating' a member can then be applied to any object.

mustContain Attributes

As stated above, each object in the Membership Directory contains a set of required attributes. These attributes are defined in the object definition as mustContain attribute of the object. Going back to our member object example, we would need to define values for the cn and the GUID of a new member before calling SetInfo() to create the member in the Membership Directory.

mayContain Attributes

mayContain attributes do not need to be defined to create an object. For example, the userPassword attribute of the member object is defined as a mayContain attribute of the member object. If we wanted to create a new member, we would not need to define a value for this attribute before calling SetInfo() on the new object.

It's very important that you distinguish between these two attribute types when working with the Membership Directory, otherwise it will be completely confusing why, or how, the code you're using works.

Now that you understand the mustContain and mayContain purposes, let's discuss where, and how, we define these types. There are two ways we can view the mustContain and mayContain attributes of an object. Either way, we must examine the object definition in the cn=Schema.

Viewing mustContain and mayContain Attributes through the MMC

We can use the Membership Directory Manager that we examined in the previous chapter to view the mustContain attributes of the member object. To do so, open the **Site Server Service Admin** **(MMC)**. Next, expand ou=Admin and select the cn=Schema in the appropriate Membership Directory:

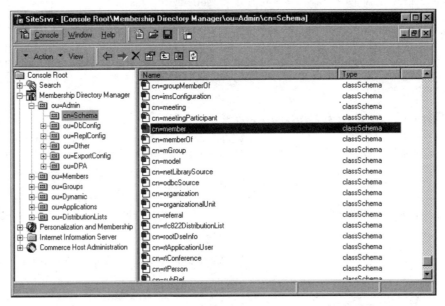

Remember, to bind to a different directory right-click on the Membership Directory Administrator snap-in and modify the properties of the snap-in to point to the appropriate directory.

After selecting the cn=Admin container, select the cn=member object in the right-hand pane of the MMC, right-click, and select properties. Finally, select the last available tab of the now open member object, **Class Attributes**:

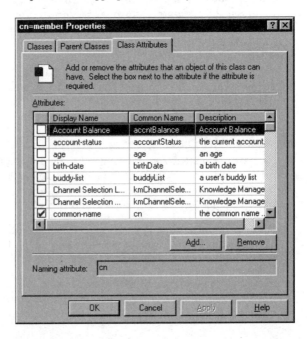

This brings up the definition of the object, displaying all of the attributes that the object supports. You'll immediately notice that two of the attributes, cn and GUID, have a green check placed next to them. This check is used to identify mustContain attributes. Conversely, the attributes that do not have a green check, such as age, userPassword, and telephoneNumber, are mayContain attributes of the object.

Now that we've examined how we use the MMC to view mustContain and mayContain attributes, let's look at some methods that deal with both these categories of attribute.

Adding Attributes to Classes

We've stepped through mustContain and mayContain attributes, but how do we add attributes to existing classes programmatically? The mustContain and mayContain attributes of a class are already populated since the class already exists.

To add attributes to an existing class, first we need to read out the existing attributes and compare them to the attributes we want to add. If there is a match, we don't need to add the attribute. However, if the attribute doesn't exist we need to add it to the array representing either the mustContain or mayContain attributes and save it back to the class.

AddAttributesToClass() Method

The AddAttributesToClass() method takes an array of attributes to be added to a class, the name of the class to modify, and whether or not the attributes are to be added to the mayContain or mustContain attributes of the class.

Its parameters are:

> arrAttributesToAdd – a one dimensional array of attributes to be added to the class. For example, if we wanted to add a new attribute to the member class, such as an existing attribute, 'education', we would pass an array with this one value.

> strClassName – used to pass the class name of the class to add the new attributes to. Using our member class and 'education' attribute example, we would want to pass the string 'member' to tell the method that we want to make modifications to the 'member' class.

> nMayContain – used to tell the AddAttributesToClass() method whether the attributes need to be added to the mayContain or the mustContain attribute of the class to modify. To do this, we'll use constants to represent whether the attributes are mayContain:

```
Const ADDATTRIBUTESTOCLASS_MAYCONTAIN_TRUE = 1
Const ADDATTRIBUTESTOCLASS_MAYCONTAIN_FALSE = 0
```

In the code sample we'll use the ADDATTRIBUTESTOCLASS_MAYCONTAIN_TRUE constant since the attribute 'education' isn't a required attribute for a new member. If we were to use ADDATTRIBUTESTOCLASS_MAYCONTAIN_FALSE constant the method would set the attribute 'education' as a mustContain attribute for the member class. This would mean that any new member that was created would have to declare values for cn, GUID, and now education.

Example Use

The `AddAtrributesToClass()` method depends upon a global object that is a reference to the `cn=Schema` container, `g_objSchema`:

```
<HTML>
<BODY BGCOLOR=WHITE>
<FONT FACE=ARIAL SIZE=3>
<B>
Function AddAttributesToClass(arrAttributesToAdd, strClassName, nMayContain)
</B>
<HR SIZE=1>
</FONT>
<FONT FACE=ARIAL SIZE=2>
<%
Const ADDATTRIBUTESTOCLASS_MAYCONTAIN_TRUE = 1
Const ADDATTRIBUTESTOCLASS_MAYCONTAIN_FALSE = 0

' **************************************************
' FUNCTION: AddAttributesToClass
'
' PURPOSE: Adds attributes to the specified class
'
' RETURNS: True - Success / False - Failure
'
' PARAMETERS:
'    arrAttributesToAdd - Array of attributes to
'                         be added to the class.
'
'    strClassName - The name of the class in the
'                   schema to add the attributes to.
'
'    nMayContain - boolean whether or not the attributes
'                  to be added are may contain. If this
'                  is True they are, if it is False
'                  they are mustContain.
'
Function AddAttributesToClass(arrAttributesToAdd, strClassName, nMayContain)
  On Error Resume Next

  Dim objClass
  Dim arrContain
  Dim nExistingItems
  Dim arrAddAttributes
  Dim nArrayLoop
  Dim nArrayLoop2
  Dim blnMatch

  ' Assume failure
  ' *******************************************
  AddAttributesToClass = False
```

First, we'll use the `g_objSchema`, which is a supplied global object already bound to the `cn=Schema` of the directory, to get the `classSchema` object we wish to modify; this could easily be the member object.

```
' Attempt to bind to the classSchema type
' fail if classSchema type doesn't exist
' *********************************************
Set objClass = g_objSchema.GetObject("classSchema", "cn=" & strClassName)
If Err.number <> 0 Then
  Err.Clear
  Exit Function
End If


' Populate arrays for must and may contain attributes
' based on nMayContain parameter
' *********************************************
If nMayContain = ADDATTRIBUTESTOCLASS_MAYCONTAIN_TRUE Then
  ' modify may contain attributes
  ' *********************************************
  arrContain = objClass.Get("mayContain")
Else
  ' modify must contain attributes
  ' *********************************************
  arrContain = objClass.Get("mustContain")
End If
```

After this segment of our code is called, we now have an array of either the `mustContain` or `mayContain` attributes that we need to modify.

```
' Get the number of existing items
' *********************************************
nExistingItems = UBound(arrContain) - LBound(arrContain)
```

We'll save some time here and use a local variable for the array count of items.

```
' Populate the arrAddAttributes array with all
' of the items in arrContain
' *********************************************
ReDim arrAddAttributes(nExistingItems)
For nArrayLoop = LBound(arrContain) to UBound(arrContain)
  arrAddAttributes(nArrayLoop) = arrContain(nArrayLoop)
Next
```

Next, we'll walk our array with the items to be added, adding the items from either the `mustContain` or `mayContain` array that we want to modify.

```
' Compare new properties in existing. If there is not a match then
' add them to arrAddAttributes
' *********************************************
For nArrayLoop = LBound(arrAttributesToAdd) to UBound(arrAttributesToAdd)
  blnMatch = False

  ' Loop through and compare
  ' *********************************************
  For nArrayLoop2 = LBound(arrContain) to UBound(arrContain)
    If LCase(arrAttributesToAdd(nArrayLoop)) _
       = LCase(arrContain(nArrayLoop2)) Then
      blnMatch = True
      Exit For
    End If
  Next
```

341

```
      If Not blnMatch Then
         nExistingItems = nExistingItems + 1
         ReDim Preserve arrAddAttributes(nExistingItems)
         arrAddAttributes(nExistingItems) = arrAttributesToAdd(nArrayLoop)
      End If
   Next

   ' Set either must or may contain array to
   ' our new array with our desired values
   ' ******************************************
   If nMayContain = ADDATTRIBUTESTOCLASS_MAYCONTAIN_TRUE Then
      ' Put may contain attributes
      ' *******************************************
      objClass.Put "mayContain",(arrAddAttributes)
   Else
      ' Put must contain attributes
      ' *******************************************
      objClass.Put "mustContain",(arrAddAttributes)
   End If
```

After updating the ADSI cache with the appropriate `Put()`, we check for errors and call `SetInfo()`.

```
   ' Error putting new array
   ' *******************************************
   If Err.number <> 0 Then
      Err.Clear
      Exit Function
   End If

   ' Save changes
   ' *******************************************
   objClass.setInfo
   If Err.number <> 0 Then
      Err.Clear
      Exit Function
   Else
      AddAttributesToClass = True
   End If
End Function


' **************************************************
' Example use of function
On Error Resume Next

Dim g_objSchema
Dim blnAddedAttributesToClass

' Create local arrays for the must
' contain and the may contain
' attributes of this class
' *******************************
Dim l_arrMayContain(0)

' Populate may contain array
' **************************
l_arrMayContain(0) = "education"
```

```
' Bind to the schema
' *******************************
stop
Set g_objSchema = GetObject("LDAP://localhost:1003/o=Wrox/ou=Admin/cn=Schema")
If Err.Number <> 0 Then
  Response.Write "Unable to bind to schema."
  Response.End
End If

' Add attributes to class
' *******************************
blnAddedAttributesToClass = AddAttributesToClass(l_arrMayContain, "member",
ADDATTRIBUTESTOCLASS_MAYCONTAIN_TRUE)

If blnAddedAttributesToClass = True Then
  Response.Write "Added attributes to class."
Else
  Response.Write "Failed to add attributes to class."
End If
%>
</FONT>
</BODY>
</HTML>
```

You now have a handy little method that you can use in an install script to move a directory from staging to production. Just write a script to do all your member modifications, rather than using the MMC.

Now that you know what the `mustContain` and `mayContain` attributes are, and where they are defined, let's write some code to create a new member.

Creating New Members

When it comes to creating new members, programmatically is the only way to go. As easy as the Microsoft Management Console Membership Directory Manager snap-in and wizards are to use, nothing beats writing a script to create all those new users automatically – especially when we have a set of pre-existing members to add.

Additionally, there are other reasons to use code to create new members. What if membership for the site is gained simply by asking for it? Well, we can write an Active Server Page that can auto-register and create new members after the user successfully completes a membership registration form. This is much easier than having every individual user e-mail the site administrator and apply for his or her own separate membership account. Not only does it take precious time away from the site administrator, but users have to wait before they can get the information they want – and that's not good!

CreateMember() Method

The `CreateMember()` method requires the LDAP path to the container from the Membership Directory root, where the new member needs to be created. Additionally, the new member name and password is required.

The method returns a member object back to the caller, and this object should be tested with `IsNothing` to determine whether or not the method call succeeded.

Somewhat like the previous examples, the `CreateMember()` method is dependent upon a global object. However, unlike binding to the `cn=Schema`, we need a bound global object to the Membership Directory root – `g_objLDAPRoot`. This object's `ADsPath` value should be `LDAP://[server name][:port number]/o=[organization name]`. An example of this is provided in the code sample.

Let's look at the parameters of this method:

> `strPathToContainerFromRoot` – used by the method to determine what container the new member should be created under. For example, to create a new member in a sub-container of `ou=Members` called `ou=NewMembers` we would pass a `strPathToContainerFromRoot` value of `'ou=NewMembers, ou=Members'`. This path information would then be used in conjunction with a global `g_objLDAPRoot` to bind to.

> `strMemberName` – represents the new member to be created in `strPathToContainerFromRoot`. If we wanted to create a new member `Jon`, we would pass this value for this parameter, and, if successful, `Jon` will be created in the container described by `strPathToContainerFromRoot`.

> `strMemberPassword` – similar to `strMemberName`, `strMemberPassword` is used for the new member to be created. While `strMemberName` represents the `cn` value of the new member object, `strMemberPassword` represents the `userPassword` value.

Now that we've reviewed the parameters, let's take a look at the code.

```
<HTML>
<BODY BGCOLOR=WHITE>
<FONT FACE=ARIAL SIZE=3>
<B>
Function CreateMember(strPathToContainerFromRoot, strMemberName,
                      strMemberPassword)
</B>
<HR SIZE=1>
</FONT>
<FONT FACE=ARIAL SIZE=2>
<%
' **************************************************
' FUNCTION: CreateMember()
'
' PURPOSE: Creates new membership members
'
' RETURNS: Object representing new member (IADs)
'
' PARAMETERS:
'     strPathToContainer - Path to container to
'                          create new member in, such as:
'                          ou=Members, ou=NewMembers
'
'     strMemberName - The username (cn) of the new
'                     member
'
'     strMemberPassword - The password (userPassword)
'                         of the new member
'
```

```
' REQUIRES:
'     g_objLDAPRoot - Root of the Membership Directory:
'                     such as g_objLDAPRoot = GetObject(LDAP://server:port)
'
Public Function CreateMember(strPathToContainerFromRoot, strMemberName,
                              strMemberPassword)
  On Error Resume Next
  Dim objGUIDGen
  Dim strGUID
  Dim objMemberContainer
  Dim objNewUser

  ' Assume Failure
  ' ***************************
  Set CreateMember = Nothing
```

First we need to bind to the appropriate container using some of the passed in references.

```
  ' Connect to the container to
  ' create new objects in
  ' ***************************
  Set objMemberContainer  = GetObject(g_objLDAPRoot.ADsPath & "/" _
                                      & strPathToContainerFromRoot)
  If Err.Number <> 0 Then
    Err.Clear
    Exit Function
  End If
```

Next, we'll use the `Membership.GUIDGen` object to generate `GUID`s for our member. The `GUIDGen` object is a useful object with only one important method: `GenerateGUID()`. You can use this to create `GUID`s in your ASP code.

```
  ' Create the Membership GUID Generator
  ' ***************************
  Set objGUIDGen = Server.CreateObject("Membership.GUIDGen.1")
  If Err.Number <> 0 Then
    Err.Clear
    Exit Function
  End If
```

After we have a reference to the `GUIDGen` object, we'll use it to create a new `GUID`. Remember, a `GUID` is a `mustContain` attribute of a new member object as defined by the Membership Directory schema.

```
  ' Create the Membership GUID Generator
  ' ***************************
  strGUID = objGUIDGen.GenerateGuid

  ' Create the new user
  ' ***************************
  Set objNewUser = objMemberContainer.Create("member", "cn=" & strMemberName)
  If Err.Number <> 0 Then
    Err.Clear
    Exit Function
  End If
```

```
   ' Set some user attributes
   ' ****************************
   objNewUser.put "GUID", CStr(strGUID)                      ' must contain
   objNewUser.put "userPassword", CStr(strMemberPassword)    ' may contain

   ' Call SetInfo
   ' ****************************
   objNewUser.SetInfo
   If Err.Number <> 0 Then
     Err.Clear
     Exit Function
   End If
```

After we called `SetInfo()` to write the ADSI cache, we return a reference to the new member object to the calling code.

```
   ' Pass back the new user
   ' ****************************
   Set CreateMember = objNewUser
End Function


' ****************************
' Example use of function
On Error Resume Next

Dim g_objLDAPRoot
Dim objNewMember

' Bind to root of directory
' ****************************
Set g_objLDAPRoot = GetObject("LDAP://localhost:1003")
If Err.Number <> 0 Then
  Response.Write "Unable to bind to directory"
  Response.End
End If

' Create new member
' ****************************
Set objNewMember = CreateMember("ou=Members", "Robert", "password")

' test for new member existance
' ****************************
If objNewMember Is Nothing Then
  Response.Write "New Member not created."
Else
  Response.Write "New Member created : " & objNewMember.cn
End If
%>
</FONT>
</BODY>
</HTML>
```

This code will create new member objects in the Membership Directory with the default installation of Site Server 3.0.

As I said in the beginning of the chapter, personalization is quite simple once you've created a member, and explicitly or implicitly defined some attribute values. Let's look at a simple example of just how easy personalization is.

Greeting the Member by Name

Greeting the member is one of the simplest tasks that can be done with the Active User Object. It's simply a matter of asking the AUO for one of the attributes stored for the member. In the previous chapter we reviewed the New Member Wizard used for creating new members, from this wizard we could easily add member properties, such as the `givenName` value to store the first name of the member. Then, in the previous section, we just learned how to create new members programmatically. Either way, we can view the member attributes and values from the Membership Directory Manager by double-clicking on the member in the `ou=Members` container:

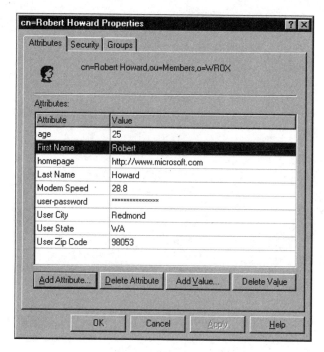

From this screen shot, we can see what member attributes have been set, as well as their values. So how would we read the first name attribute value from the Membership Directory and display it in HTML?

Implementation

We can very easily implement code to display the first name attribute by using the AUO `Get()` method. For example, the following code (`Simple.asp`) shows an ASP that displays the member's `cn`:

```
<HTML>
<BODY>
<%
Option Explicit
On Error Resume Next
```

```
' *********************************************
' Simple ASP to display the current member's
' common name (cn) attribute
' *********************************************

Dim objAUO
Dim strMemberName
```

First we'll create an instance of the AUO. As soon as this instance is created, and assuming some form of Site Server Authentication is enabled, we have the user's identity.

```
' Create the Active User Object
' *********************************************
Set objAUO = Server.CreateObject("Membership.UserObjects.1")
If Err.Number <> 0 Then
  Response.Write "Unable to create AUO. Make sure the "
  Response.Write "web is mapped to a Membership Server, "
  Response.Write "and that authentication is enabled."
  Response.End
End If
```

Next, we'll ask for and display the common name (the same attribute value that the user used to log on to the site with).

```
' Assign the member's common name value to the
' variable strMemberName. This is faster than
' requesting objAUO.cn each time.
' *********************************************
strMemberName = objAUO.Get("cn")

' Display the member's cn
' *********************************************
Response.Write strMemberName
%>
</BODY>
</HTML>
```

After we've run this code – my particular configuration was with Clear Text/Basic Authentication – you should see something similar to:

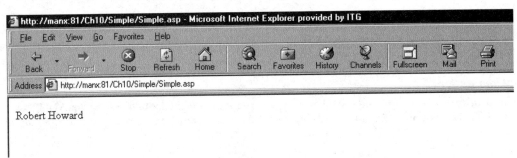

Now that we have the `strMemberName` value, how difficult could it be to integrate this in a more 'personalized' fashion?

Planning the Code

The flow for our example is simple, we create the Active User Object, request and assign the common name attribute to a variable, and display the contents of the variable in the resulting HTML.

The differences between our previous example and a personalized display is integrating the above code into the context of another ASP, such as the `default.asp` provided by IIS 4.0:

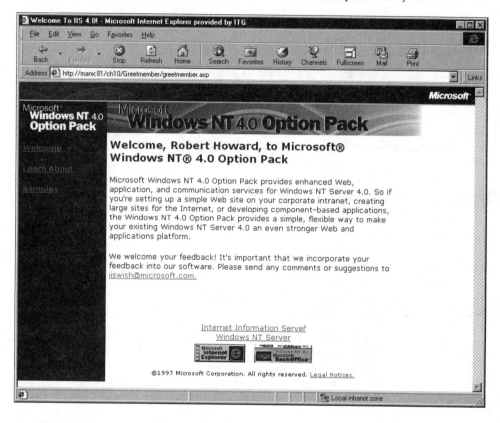

You may be wondering what needed to be done for this page to display the greeting. The `Simple.asp` logic was cut and pasted into `default.asp`, and a single line of code was modified to display `strMemberName` in the welcome:

```
Welcome, <%=strMemberName%>, to Microsoft® Windows NT® 4.0 Option Pack
```

Just to make sure we always displayed something for the welcome message, I also made a minor modification to the `Simple.asp` code to determine if we even had a member name – in case we wanted to also support anonymous:

```
' Determine if we have a valid member name
' ************************************************
If Len(strMemberName) = 0 Then
  strMemberName = "valued customer"
End If
```

We've seen a very simple demonstration of how easy it is to personalize a page. Once a Membership Server is mapped to an IIS 4.0 web site, and we've configured an authentication type, we only need to add a few lines of custom code to display personalized content.

It's pretty easy to display attributes back to the browser through HTML, but what about using HTML as a mechanism for updating information in the Membership Directory? For example, we could use the AUO and a personalized HTML form to allow the user to manipulate their member data.

Performance and Directory Strategy

We've gone over quite a few details in this chapter so far, and you should be ready to implement Site Server Personalization and Membership. However, let me leave you with a word of caution and some information. With Site Server Personalization and Membership, Microsoft has given you an enormous amount of flexibility for implementing a much heralded web technology. However, with this flexibility comes the responsibility for you to properly design your architecture and application. Below you will find some suggestions as to how to design your architecture and your application for optimal performance.

Abstraction of the AUO

A common misconception about Active Server Pages is that including files (files that are included into a document using the syntax below) affects performance:

```
<!--#Include Virtual="include/auo/libAUOInit.inc"-->
```

There is no tangible performance hit associated with using an include file, and the benefits are enormous.

Let's put this in the appropriate context. The number of lines in your ASP code, the code the ASP parser must parse, does affect performance. Include files can only lead to performance degradation when they include excessive code that is part of a library unrelated to the actual calls needed for the document. In other words, you can use include files, but don't bloat your code – better yet, use a COM object!

There are two benefits that you receive by using include files and the AUO. Firstly, your application can abstract the attributes values into a set of local variables. This means that rather than calling directly onto the object you call local variables with in your application:

```
<!--#Include Virtual="include/auo/libAUOInit.inc"-->
```

Default.asp includes libAUOInit.inc, which defines the value for the G_ACCNT_DIS_BRIEF personalization variable. Rather than calling into the AUO again, we can use the abstracted variable reference.

```
DisplayUserAccounts(G_ACCNT_DIS_BRIEF)
```

Secondly, migrations to newer Microsoft personalization solutions, or changes in your implementation, are simple. Think of using include files and local variables as a similar representation of interfaces in COM. The local variables don't change, but the implementation of how those local variable values are derived can be changed easily in one location.

For example, if the implementation for how we derived a value for G_ACCNT_DIS_BRIEF changed, what would be easier to do:

> ➤ Touch 10 files and make 5 modifications to each file? – We would do this if we used a new implementation of AUO on each ASP.

> ➤ Touch 1 file and make 1 modification? – We modify the include file that all other ASPs use for personalization.

I've shown you a good design that you can implement, now let's look at some architectural decisions.

Dynamic Data for Performance

Because the Membership Directory resides in a database on a physical hard drive, the speed at which data can either be read or written is defined purely by the speed of the drive, the way data is stored on the drive (how many partitions are used for the Membership Directory) and the number of attributes an object has. Depending upon the number of service requests per second by the users, correlating to the number of pages served per second, this can cripple a large site.

To bypass this potential bottleneck, Site Server Personalization and Membership allows for memory to be used to store data for a specified duration of time. Data of this type is said to be dynamic.

Dynamic data can be read and written up to three times faster than similar data in the physical data store.

The following code sample shows how to create a member object in the dynamic container. What does this mean? Well, if you configure Site Server to authenticate from the ou=Dynamic container, rather than the ou=Members container, you get a performance boost, since the members are authenticated from memory.

This is good for a site that expects high authentication load – or many requests for a particular object. For example, if you are hosting an auction that goes live at 5:00 PM, and in order to bid users must first log in, you will experience a high volume of authentication for a period of 5-10 minutes. To handle this volume your site needs to be responsive, and what better way than using memory!

Let's look at the code:

```
<HTML>
<FONT SIZE=6 FACE=ARIAL>
Dynamic Example:
<BR>
<%
' Sample to create a dynamic member
' **********************************************
On Error Resume Next

Dim objIADsContainer
Dim objOpenDSObject
Dim objDynamicMember
Dim objGuidGen
Dim objIADs

' Assign Member name
```

```
' ****************************************
Const STR_MEMBER = "Rob"
Const STR_LDAP_PATH = "LDAP://localhost:1003/o=Memdir/ou=Dynamic"
Const STR_SECURE_BIND_USER = "cn=Administrator, ou=Members, o=MemDir"
Const STR_SECURE_BIND_PWD = "password"

' Bind to LDAP
' ****************************************
Set objOpenDSObject = GetObject("LDAP:")

' Bind to the appropriate ou=dynamic
' ****************************************
Set objIADsContainer = objOpenDSObject.OpenDSObject(STR_LDAP_PATH, _
                                                    STR_SECURE_BIND_USER, _
                                                    STR_SECURE_BIND_PWD, _
                                                    1)
```

The code starts by binding to the `ou=Dynamic` container in the Membership Directory. Afterwards, we have a pointer to the container where we can create dynamic objects.

```
' Bind to the appropriate ou=dynamic
' ****************************************
Set objIADsContainer = GetObject("LDAP://localhost:1003/o=Memdir/ou=Dynamic")

' Create a new member -- note this member
' will only exist for the duration of the TTL (default 5 minutes)
' ****************************************
Set objDynamicMember = objIADsContainer.Create("member", "cn=" & strMember)
```

Using the `Create()` method of `objIADsContainer`, we create a new member object. Since this member is created in the dynamic container, it too will be dynamic, meaning that the object will exist only for the lifetime of the object. Afterwards, the object will be removed from memory. I'll say more about this lifetime in a bit.

```
' Create the guid for the new member
' ****************************************
Set objGuidGen = Server.CreateObject("Membership.GuidGen.1")

' Add the required must-have attributes (GUID)
' ****************************************
objDynamicMember.Put "Guid", CStr(objGuidGen.GenerateGuid)

' Now make it a dynamic object.
' ****************************************
objDynamicMember.Put "objectClass", (ARRAY("member", "DynamicObject"))
objDynamicMember.SetInfo

' Set the TTL value in seconds.  600=10 minutes
' ****************************************
objDynamicMember.Put "entryTTL", (600)
```

A dynamic object requires an `entryTTL` – Time-to-live – as a `mustContain` attribute. The `entryTTL` is a counter that counts backwards in seconds. Once 0 is reached, and if the `entryTTL` has not been updated, the object expires and is removed from memory; it cleans up after itself.

This is extremely convenient for ASP developers working with the Membership Directory. When working with dynamic objects, you don't need to write code to manage expiration of the object; Site Server does it for you!

```
' Update MD with ADSI Cache
' *************************************
objDynamicMember.SetInfo

If Err.Number <> 0 Then
  Response.Write "Error creating dynamic member - <B>" & strMember & "</B>"
  Err.Clear ' Clear the error
  Response.Write "<P>"
  Response.Write "Checking to see if already exists...<BR>"
  Set objDynamicMember = _
              GetObject("LDAP://localhost:1003/o=Memdir/ou=dynamic/cn=" &
                  strMember)
  If Err.Number = 0 Then
    Response.Write "Member <B>" & strMember & "</B> already exists in ou=dynamic."
  Else
    Response.Write "Nope... too many bugs"
  End If
Else
  Response.Write "Member - <B>" & strMember & "</B> created!"
End If
%>

<HR>
Display all values in ou=Dynamic
<BR>
<%
Dim objIADs

' Bind to ou=Dynamic
' *****************************
Set objIADsContainer = GetObject("LDAP://localhost:1003/o=Memdir/ou=dynamic")

' Enum IADs
' *****************************
For Each objIADs in objIADsContainer
  Response.Write "-- Common Name (cn): " & objIADs.Get("cn") & "<BR>"
  Response.Write "-- ADsPath : "  & objIADs.ADsPath & "<BR>"
Next
%>
```

So how do you know if the information is truly being 'pulled' from dynamic memory rather than from the SQL Membership database? The easiest way is to use the SQL 7.0 SQL Server Profiler (SQL Trace in SQL Server 6.5) to examine the request that came across the server.

Any request that goes to the physical Membership Directory must first go through our LDAP server, which translates non-dynamic calls to SQL syntax – viewable with the SQL profiler.

To see this in action run the following code, which again binds to the dynamic container. Look for any SQL calls through your tracer; you shouldn't see any:

```
<HR>
Display all values in ou=Dynamic
<BR>
<%
' Bind to ou=Dynamic
' ******************************
Set objIADsContainer = _
                GetObject("LDAP://localhost:1003/o=Memdir/ou=dynamic/cn=Rob")

Response.Write objIADsContainer.ADsPath
%>
```

The dynamic directory adds some complexity to your application development, but the complexity is a direct trade off for performance. Finally, let's look at one of the most important architecture decisions, building out the data store.

Data Storage and OLAP

Usually, most developers I talk with about the Membership Directory have more than one purpose for the directory than as a personalization data store. For example, once the marketing people in your organization find out about your great implementation of Site Server Personalization and Membership, the first thing they'll want to do is mine the data; which has proven to be quite difficult with a directory. I'd like to share some of the design strategies that should help to make your directory more efficient and perform better.

The first strategy is to reduce the number of individual attributes that your member object has.

Reducing Member Attributes

One of the easiest ways to reduce member attributes is to use bit fields to represent attribute values. Rather than use individual attributes for each aspect of personalization, use a bit field so that one attribute can represent multiple values.

For example, if you have numerous options that you wish to show to your user, such as weather, stocks, local news, national news, etc. you could use an attribute called `DisplayType` with a binary attribute definition. Now you can represent all four of these display types:

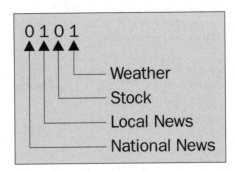

This decreases the footprint of the data, and the number of local variables you need to use to represent the data.

Working with Databases

It's unrealistic to think that everything should go into the Membership Directory. Some data still belongs – not to mention makes more sense – in a database. Data that needs to be searched or used for OLAP is a good example. Although you can search the Membership Directory, it is by no means a fast operation. This is no fault of the directory, but rather the design of a directory. The bottom line is: treat a directory like a directory, and you will be exceedingly pleased with its performance. Use it as an OLAP data store, and you will be disappointed.

For example, if our site sold goods online, we would not want to keep a record of all the purchases made by members in the Membership Directory. It would simply be too inefficient for searches and data analysis later on. Instead, it makes more sense to store member specific information in the Membership Directory, and rely upon a Relational Database Management System to manage customer purchase history.

Here's another example: think of a directory as a digital phone book, think of LDAP as an operator that can look up information for you in the phone book. If you wanted to look up a person or business, and had that person's business or name, the operator would be able to find that information very quickly since the phone book is a namespace organized by names of individuals and businesses (or groups or containers of individuals/businesses as represented by the yellow pages). However, if you asked the operator for all individuals or businesses with a particular zip code, it would mean that the operator would have to flip through every page of the phone book – highly inefficient.

With that said, here are some suggestions for integrating the two:

> Any data that you want to data mine, put into a database.

> Use the GUID of the member object as a foreign key into your database table. A good example of this is using the Site Server Commerce Shopper ID to correlate a Membership Directory to a particular shopping basket.

> Store the member's common name in the database as a foreign key into the Membership Directory. Since the directory is designed for lookups on the cn, having the cn available in the database will make any necessary lookups very quick and efficient.

Don't Use Secondary Providers

The AUO has the capability to be our one-stop shopping source for information about members. The AUO provides the capability to bind to the member in the Membership Directory when instantiated in an ASP, and it also provides what are known as secondary providers, the primary provider being the Membership Directory.

There is a provider for working with databases: SimpleDBMS, but it is limited to working with only one record at a time – not extremely useful for most applications.

Working with secondary providers is extremely difficult and confusing. Just examine the 15 Seconds (http://www.15Seconds.com), Site Server Discussion List!

Secondary Provider Alternatives

Rather than using secondary providers, I suggest you take a more pragmatic approach and do either of the following:

> - Use the cn of the member as a key in your database
> - Store a key in the member profile to the data

Of course, you could always do both!

If you're using the a member profile to look up data, this means that you will need to do a little more work to get to the data than you did with the secondary provider. However, you will also get an increased amount of flexibility as to how you manage the data, and the relationships thereof. You should still keep this nicely abstracted in an include file or COM component.

Conclusion

Personalization is quickly becoming a *de facto* standard on the Internet. Large sites are setting the standards of how sites can personalize experiences for their frequent users. Site Server 3.0 Personalization and Membership is an excellent solution to the problems faced by developers that want to personalize.

All of the necessary tools and technologies are already built, and with the integration of Site Server 3.0 and Internet Information Server 4.0, a powerful personalized web application can be built very rapidly.

We covered some of the basics of personalization in this chapter, here are the highlights of what we covered:

> - There are two ways to collect information about users of the site: explicit and implicit profiling. Explicit profiling asks for information, implicit collects it based on normal user usage of the site.
> - The Active User Object is a specialized COM object that can automatically bind to a member upon activation from a P&M enabled IIS 4.0 Web.
> - Active Directory Service Interfaces (ADSI) is the primary API for working with the Membership Directory; this same API will be used for Windows 2000 Active Directory.
> - Finally, we touched on some strategies that you can apply to your work in the Membership Directory to get optimal performance.

11
Site Server Analysis

Several years ago, an eternity in Internet time, I received an unpleasant phone call from a new client. After some brief agreement that my company had met the specifications for building a new Web site, the client quickly shared some additional disappointment. The client voiced concern that she had spent a great deal of money having my company build her a Web site, but she was uncertain about the results of her investment. Yes, we had worked very hard on the client's site design and the client was not unhappy about the look or performance of the site. However, there was still nagging doubt about the success of the project, because the client's final estimation of our value, as web artists, depended on the number of prospects that we brought to the client's business. That call provided one of my first lessons in electronic commerce. Successful Web commerce projects go beyond fancy artistry, and site value is determined by the quality of building customer-audience communities.

I wish the lesson had ended there, but when we performed a laborious hand-crafted analysis of the site's web traffic, *because this incident predated SiteServer*, we discovered that thousands of visitors had visited the client's Web site. In fact, the clients' site had the most visits when compared with a few other sites that we had implemented on the server we analyzed. Imagine the client's surprise when we showed her the visitation statistics. Ultimately, we helped the client get better responses from web visitors by including such site features as a guest book, discount promotion coupons, e-mail links, etc. Finally, the client began to feel that she was developing an electronic Web-based customer community. However, the primary lesson showed us the importance of site analysis and communicating visitor usage in the overall planning for a Web site production. Needless to say we established new processes and procedures for conducting site analysis, and that is the topic of this chapter.

Today, the Internet has very wide acceptance as a mechanism for conducting electronic commerce, and yet the activities involved in performing site analysis are still frequently afterthoughts in the race to build new sites that are presumed to be attractive to some imagined visitor audience. Many clients have never seen any reports or statistics on visitor usage, and don't know where their site Web logs are archived. Many Internet Service providers still provide usage statistics that aren't meaningful, because they are overly complex and present information from a technical rather then a business perspective.

Having said that, as Web commerce moves beyond novelty, more non-technology business managers are asking for quantitative evidence, The Proof, that the Internet is a viable mechanism for conducting electronic business. A new career path is rapidly becoming available for those individuals who can understand the idiosyncrasies of Web site visitation and content analysis. In one of the companies ranked as an Internet top ten search engine, a new job has been defined: a *site datamining expert*, and the new career role is filled by an individual that can understand organizational, marketing and statistical concepts beyond the scope of Internet technology issues. In another case, a large multinational company has begun applying artificial intelligence neural networking techniques to deduce patterns of visitor behavior beyond the statistical reports provided by most site analysis tools.

For those of us who can't afford to hire a datamining expert, Microsoft Site Server provides excellent tools to assist us in performing site analysis. A market for Web site analysis tools has developed where there are now dozens of products that deliver varying degrees of site analysis features and quality, at prices ranging from $100 to $20,000. The analysis features of Site Server compare very favorably with products costing much more. Perhaps as the ultimate advantage, Site Server is integrated into Microsoft BackOffice and offers Microsoft SQL Server as a data storage manager. The ability to have a robust and industry standard data manager as a foundation for gathering analysis data extends the availability of information, allowing it to be better organized and integrated into a wide variety of statistical and presentation products. This chapter will give you all the knowledge you need to perform site analysis like the pros.

As an introduction to Analysis, it has two dimensions: **visitor usage analysis**, and **content analysis**. You may think of these dimensions as offering two activities of analysis on your site, an outward and inward concept. Usage analysis deals with an outward concept of analysis. In performing usage analysis, we examine the information that concerns visitors. There is also an inward form of analysis called content analysis. In examining content we try to determine useful information from it. Content refers to the pictures, text, pages, and links that comprise the site.

In presenting the Analysis feature of Site Server, there are five programs that can be invoked from the Start button. Four of the programs deal with visitor usage analysis, the interpretation and creation of information that relates to end user site visitation. A fifth program, the Content Analyzer, is the principle subject of this chapter, and deals with the analysis of information that can be gained from studying the resources that comprise a site.

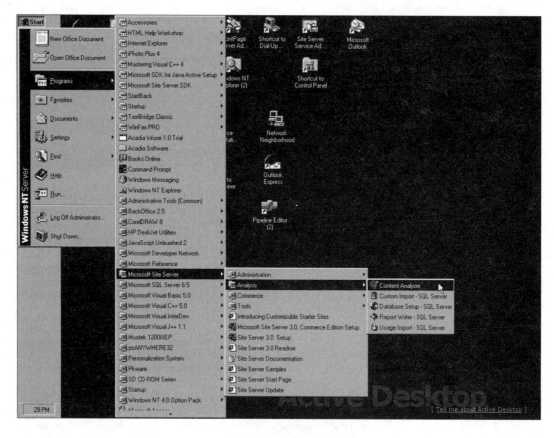

If you have SQL Server 7 installed you may get slightly different options here.

Based on the idea that you will build your content before you need to track usage, we will begin our presentation by looking at the Site Server Content Analyzer.

The Site Server Content Analyzer

The Content Analyzer can help you manage even the simplest Web site projects. You will value it more as your site expands. For those of you who have had experience with building and managing Web sites using Microsoft FrontPage, you have had a chance to appreciate some of the benefits of content management. However, the Content Analyzer, while conceptually similar to FrontPage, offers superior features in an entirely different product, meaning that the program code is different. Not only is the program code and the use of the features in the Content Analyzer different, but Content Analyzer extends beyond FrontPage to include features such as the ability to tag content via **META tags**. You can integrate content analysis into other Site Server programs such as Site Server Membership. As an example, you have the ability to identify and manage a team site project with multiple site authors. These features allow you to further classify and identify your Web site pages and easily perform analysis of questions such as which authors or subject genres receive the greatest visitation.

As a general overview, you can achieve the following with the Content Analyzer:

> Create a inventory of resources used on your site, a 'project', for your site.

> Extend the classification of resources on your site by adding meta data, META tags, on site resources.

> Generate useful management reports.

> Find and fix broken resource links within your site.

> Review sites that link to your site, called referrals.

> Animate and evaluate content usage by integrating content data with visitation data produced in the Usage Analyzer.

Before we jump into the features of the Content Analyzer we should talk about installation considerations. The Content Analyzer is one feature of Site Server that you may want to consider installing on a machine other than your Site Server Web server. The Content Analyzer program is considered to be a member of a set of programs called **Site Server Tools**. The other programs in the Site Server Tools family include the Direct Mailer, the Tag Tool, etc. The theme for the tools programs is that they are not classified as server applications. The suggestion to install the program in a different location to your production Web server is based on the idea that you can take best advantage of the Content Analyzer when the product is installed in concert with web tools that are called **Helper Applications**.

Helper Applications are all the myriad little programs that you use to develop site pages and resources. Examples of a Helper Applications might include graphics programs, or perhaps a MIDI music editor. Potential Helper Applications may be products that are produced by companies other than Microsoft. The most common application for editing HTML is Microsoft Notepad. We will discuss this in more depth later, but the key point here is that the Content Analyzer offers an integrated development environment for Web site design. This integrated development environment is vaguely similar to that offered by Visual Studio, but rather then offering a full workshop for application development, it is more of a workbench for you to make last minute site repairs, which will be inevitable, as an active site changes content on a regular basis.

Many Web design tools are not appropriate for installation on NT production Web servers. For example, some Web tools don't run well on Microsoft NT due to inconsistencies in the graphics drivers. So, there is a need for web design workstations that run both NT and Windows 98 versions of products. These Windows 98 based workstations may be install candidates for the Content Analyzer.

Should you decide to install Content Analyzer on a different machine to your Site Server Web server, then be sure to examine the Readme *file that describes installation procedures. As a general statement, implementing Site Server on separate machines is not for the timid, but it is important to understand that the Content Analyzer is a very different program to the other program members of the Site Server Analysis family. The Usage Analyzer programs need to be installed on a machine that has access to SQL Server. This is not a requirement for the Content Analyzer. The Content Analyzer will install on Windows 9x, and its software licensing allows it to be installed on multiple client machines.*

Starting the Analyzer

The Content Analyzer has three interfaces, possibly four if you include the COM objects. The three primary interfaces are the **Command Line**, **WebAdmin**, and **Windows**. All three interfaces provide access to the Content Analyzer's features and options, although, not all the interfaces offer access the full set of program capabilities.

> *While Site Server provides a solid set of tools, the way you organize and use the tools is pretty much up to you. There are issues in how you allocate responsibility to a variety of individuals with site management responsibility. Furthermore, you will probably want to automate Web operations so that data collection and analysis is automatic from week to week and month to month. Unlike software engineering or Web artistry, there is very little creativity involved in site analysis. The mechanics of site analysis, once established, need to be a routine and automatic part of your site operations.*

We will summarize the command line and WebAdmin browser based interfaces and then spend the remainder of the chapter dealing with the Windows interface. The command line interface lends itself to ISP hosting operations because it can be programmed via scripts. On the other hand, WebAdmin is useful for accessing program features from remote devices. Therefore, they both offer access to a basic set of Content Analyzer features but may be used by different team members in varying circumstances.

> *As a fourth possible interface, Site Server, like many Microsoft products is built using Microsoft COM technology. While it may be possible to integrate these COM objects into your programs, the ability to write scripts to the Command Line interface has proven more than adequate for our operations in a large commercial ISP.*

The Command Line interface

Command line operation may at first seem like a nostalgic throw back to the days of DOS, but it serves a real purpose in providing cross platform feature access, as well as allowing program feature scheduling via Microsoft NT Scheduler. One can obtain a listing of the command line commands by typing `cacmd` from the NT command line interface, as is demonstrated below. Not all Content Analyzer features are available via the command line, but there is a nice basic selection of functions.

```
Command Prompt                                                                          _ □ X

CACMD input options

Opens an existing or creates a new Content Analyzer project. Remaps a project,
finds orphans, creates reports, saves a project file, sets explore limits,
and sets explore options.

Input is exactly one of the following:
    -I=path    Project file to open.
    -N=URL     Start page URL for new project.
    -F=path    Start page path and filename for new project from file. (-R
               option required)

New project from file required option:
    -R=URL     Domain and site root

New project from file options:
    -W[0|1]    If no default file, map all files in directory. (Default=1=true)
    -B=path    Cgi-bin directory

Options are one or more of the following. If more than one, they are executed
in the following order:
    -U=n       Remap the project. (Value for n required. See below for
               definition of n.)
    -V=n       Verify the links in the project. (Value for n required. See below
               for definition of n.)
    -H         Set routes by URL hierarchy.
    -O=path    Find orphans. (-L and -G options required.)
    -G=path+prefix   Generate HTML reports.
    -S=path    Save updated project file. (Required if -N -F -H or -U are used.)

Remap options:
    -U=1       Re-explore previously explored pages only.
    -U=2       Re-explore rest of site.
    -U=3       Re-explore previously explored pages and rest of site.
    -K[0|1]    Create backup project file before remapping. (Default=1=true)

Verify options:
    -U=1       Verify only offsite broken links.
    -U=2       Verify only onsite broken links.
    -U=3       Verify all broken links.
    -U=5       Verify all offsite links.
    -U=6       Verify all onsite links.
    -U=7       Verify all links.

Find orphans option:
    -L=URL     URL prefix for files in directory used with -O.

Explore options:
    -D=n       Level limit. (Default = no limit)
    -P=n       Page limit. (Default = no limit)
    -C[0|1]    Ignore case of URLs. (New project only. Default=1=true)
    -T[0|1]    Honor robot protocol. (Default=1=true)
    -A[0|1]    Explore URLs with arguments. (Default=0=false)
    -X[0|1]    Verify offsite links while exploring. (Default=0=false)
```

By using the NT AT command we could schedule the Content Analyzer as follows:

```
AT 23:00 /every:Monday cacmd -I=M:\WebAnalysis\MySite.wmp -U=1 -V=7
    -G=M:\InetPub\wwwroot\Reports\Mysite\Mysite_ -S=M:\WebAnalysis\MySite.wmp
```

We are getting ahead of our reading in presenting this example with arcane looking parameters. However, this example shows the power of the Command Line interface. In this example, the Content Analyzer performs analysis and writes a report every Monday evening at 11:00 PM. The parameter value of -U=1 tells the program to perform what we will soon present as a re-map of the site and to explore only the previous scope of explorations. (Remapping is the process of performing link analysis on site resources.) The parameter value of -V=7 specifies that the Content Analyzer should verify all links.

The other parameters specify where the program is to find and save resources (such as a new site project file), and where to deposit prepared reports. In this situation we have specified that reports should be deposited in a sub directory under the root of the IIS 4.0 Web server.

In setting up this application we have already set up the directory structure and created a secure Web site, `Mysite`, using NT ACLs. The clients for this site can inspect a report on their site contents on Tuesday morning as they arrive for work. In the last portion of the `-G` reporting parameter we have included the string `'Mysite_'` because this value will be appended as a prefix to all site report HTML pages. We will discuss the reporting capabilities of the Content Analyzer later, for now I'll just say that the program can create elaborate reports. In this example, where we run a commercial ISP hosting operation, the ability to create Content Analysis reports for clients is valued as a unique competitive advantage.

While we have demonstrated an NT Command scheduling example here, there is also a Windows based program called the NT Task Scheduler (available in Microsoft Windows98 as well as in Microsoft Explorer, Version 4.0 or higher). If you host large volumes of Web sites you might find that keeping site operations schedules in a `.bat` file is ultimately more convenient then navigating the Task Scheduler's Windows dialogs.

The WebAdmin Interface

The Web Administration interface (WebAdmin) is a browser HTML based interface that allows you to access some of the primary features of the Content Analyzer. The WebAdmin interface is an optional install feature of Site Server. Perhaps the decision to make the feature an option is viewed as some sort of security risk, so you may not have implemented the feature during your initial setup. The option can be installed at any later time.

The primary benefit of the WebAdmin interface is cross platform remote access to the Content Analyzer features. By using the WebAdmin interface you can grant individuals the rights to manage selected portions of Site Server from remote locations. In addition, WebAdmin can be used through firewalls and can be encrypted with **Secure Sockets Layer** (SSL). Since WebAdmin is a HTML interface, the features offered lend themselves to automation via Active Server Pages programming. The WebAdmin interface provides services beyond Site Server Analysis, and includes interfaces to: Publish, Search, Membership and Personalization. The WebAdmin interface is available via the NT Start menu in the **Microsoft Site Server** program group, or via the URL:

```
http://www.yourdomain.com/SiteServer/admin.
```

The Windows Interface

The Windows, or Win32, interface offers the most comprehensive ability to use the Content Analyzer product. Upon starting the Content Analyzer you are presented with a modal welcome screen. This screen offers a quick start to four program features:

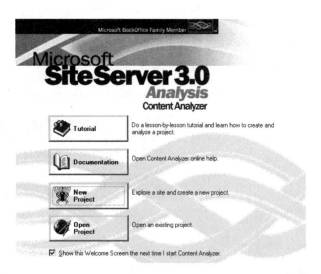

Both the Tutorial and the Documentation buttons will lead you to the Site Server help documentation, which has a pretty good level of detail. After you have used the Content Analyzer for some time, you may appreciate the check box at the bottom of the screen that allows you to disable the welcome screen. If you choose that option, then working with projects is available via the file menu. However, as you first open the Content Analyzer the welcome screen provides you with a quick start. You will want to create a new **Project**.

Creating Projects

The concept behind a Project is to create a repository of data that controls site analysis.

> *While the Content Analyzer may refer to the project as a database, it is not one in the sense that the project resource meta data is being stored in SQL Server. Meta data is data that describes a resource, like a META tag defined the content of a page. Meta data for an image might include the size, width, height, format, etc.*

The Project data encompasses:

> ➢ The definition and scope of a site
> ➢ A map that graphically depicts a site
> ➢ Controls for site exploration

Files versus URLs

Your first choice in creating a project is to provide location information to begin the analysis process. You will need to specify either a URL or a Filename so that the Content Analyzer can build your project. It is easier to supply a URL for your site but the option of specifying a filename is provided in case your site is somehow TCP/IP challenged.

If you choose to specify a filename, you list the root page file name, such as `default.htm` or `index.htm`. You will also need to specify the Web site domain and root directory as well as any CGI-bin directories that are not immediately in the root of your site. After going through the exercise of supplying all this dialog information, you may decide that supplying a URL is an easier method of project building.

Microsoft provides a sample site that you can use to learn and test Content Analysis. The sample site is located in the `Microsoft Site Server\Sites\Tutorial\Exair` directory. It's somewhat amusing to consider that the supplied samples have broken links and other quality problems, so that you don't have to introduce problems into your own site, as if you didn't have any.

Creation Options

Regardless of whether you create your project with a URL or File, there are several options to consider before you proceed toward the final project build. I'll briefly summarize the considerations now, and expand further as we discuss special situations in project creation.

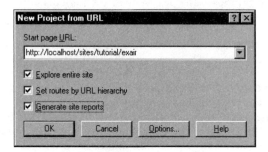

> ➤ **Explore Entire Site** – Un-checking this check box triggers an additional dialog box that allows you to begin controlling the scope of the Content Analyzer's *robot* or *spider*. A spider is a text parsing program that will seek out instances of URLs in HTML and then follow those URLs, thereby traveling the Internet in a process called *crawling*.

> ➤ **Set Routes** – This option begins the configuration of how your project will be organized. We'll discuss this further, but basically a **route** is defined to be the path that is implemented by a link. If this sounds confusing, it might make more sense to understand that a link provides you an address of a resource on the Internet. But that's not the same thing as telling you how to proceed toward reaching a specific resource asset. So, as you examine the graphical panels and windows of the Conent Analyzer, you will discover that there are many different paths that may allow you to get to any one particular resource within your site.

> ➤ **Generate Reports** – You can enable this option if you want to have a site report created in parallel with the project. As the Content Analyser performs an exploration of your site and re-maps your site resources, it will also prepare the reports of analysis on your site and take you directly to a convenient browser based report.

The Options button on the creation dialog box opens a tabbed modal dialog box that offers about a dozen additional options to control project creation. We will discuss these options more, but first we need to cover some basic concepts that concern understanding routes and links.

Understanding Routes and Links

To understand the basic nature of the Web, one needs to appreciate the concepts involving **resources**, **routes**, and **links**. Resources are objects or things that are identified through links. A Resource might be an image, an audio file, a document, or something yet to be invented, perhaps Internet aromas (who knows the future...). The lesson here is that a Web site is composed of resources. Each page or document in your site is a resource, and it may have many other resources within it's content, mostly images and links to other pages. The identifying feature of a resource is the fact that it can be referenced by a link. If you examine the HTML on almost any Web page you can see examples where a link is denoted by specifying an HTML command:

```
<A href="http:www.mysite.com/index.htm">Link to MySite</A>
```

In a simple Web site the images and pages may be in the same file directory. Typically, the images are stored in a directory most aptly named `images`. However, in one music store Web site project the author and his company recently created, the music descriptions and prices for products came from a Site Server Commerce Server database, but the sample music, album art, and artist biographies all came from different servers. These servers were owned by different companies and located across the Internet. Therefore, while the consumer sees one page in the browser, in that situation the resources that composed the page came from perhaps four different locations on the Internet.

The problem for Content Analyzer is to collect data on links and then to present the data in such a way as to provide meaningful value. The answer to the problem is to introduce the concept of the route. As previously mentioned, the route defines the implementation path between two resources. In the features of Site Server that deal with content deployment, the concept of the route is useful for managing issues that deal with deploying content on staging servers and replicating content. For the purposes of the Content Analyzer, the route simply provides you with a handy mechanism for presenting linkage information. Routes let you not only see how your site is organized, but also how visitors navigate the site. As an analogy, think of a link as being similar to the street address of your home or business. A route consists of the directions for arriving at your address. Are there multiple ways to get to your house? Of course. Are there multiple routes to get to the resources on your site? You bet.

When the Content Analyzer builds a project, a spider crawls your site and gathers link data that is used to build a **map**. The map organizes your resources and links and presents a graphical depiction of your site.

Content Analyzer organizes maps by recognizing the idea of **main** and **alternate** routes. For example, the image logo of your company may be referenced many times from many points within your company Web site. The Content Analyzer would designate one route the main and the other routes, subsequent occurrences of resources in the map, as alternate routes. How does the Content Analyser select the Main and Alternate routes?

Content Analyzer offers three methods to organize route selection, that is to say, the organization of main and alternate routes. The three methods are: **URL hierarchy**, **breadth-first**, or **usage data**. The simplest organization to understand is usage data. Content Analyzer can show you the organization of your resources, based upon the number of times that a resource has been used in visitation. While usage data may be simple to understand it is more difficult to implement, because Content Analyzer must import usage data to complete the routing process. Therefore, the other two methods, URL hierarchy and breadth-first route organization, are more common. An example will help clarify the concepts. In the simple schema presented below, there are three links within the site example:

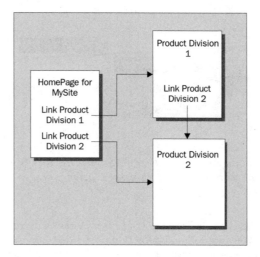

Content Analyzer always crawls through a site by using the breadth-first method. What this means is that the spider explores a site by beginning at the root/home page you define and working through the site in levels. As we discuss the idea of levels, we think about your site as a hierarchy of pages, although, in actuality, it is more like a network, or a web (no pun intended). Your home page is typically at the first level. The major sections of your site are at the second level, etc. In a breadth-first route organization the main route to Product Division 2 would be from the Home Page for MySite page. The next figure shows breadth-first routing. It has been taken from the Content Analyzer **Hyperbolic** window that we will introduce in a moment. The black boxes indicate onsite resources in the main routes for a site. The box in the top right (green on the screen) denotes a resource on an alternate route.

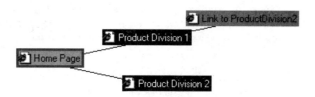

The URL hierarchy routing method is the default organization for the Content Analyzer. URL hierarchy provides a method that recognizes routes based upon the relative positions of the site resources in the directory structure of the site. Suppose you created directories to house the HTML pages for your site. Your home page would probably be in the top-level directory. Perhaps the next sub directory down might include a Product Division 1 directory. Now, let's also assume that the Product Division 2 directory was a sub directory of Product Division 1. In this example, Product Division 2 might be the 'button' division that is part of the 'coat' division. Both buttons and coats are considered products, but they are not of equal stature, at least in the vision of the folks that created the directory structure. In this situation a routing organization of URL hierarchy would show that the main route to Product Division 2 was not from the home page, but is now routed from the Product Division 1 page as shown in the next figure. In the URL hierarchy organization the HTML page for Product Division 1 is superior in the URL (read disk) hierarchy.

It may be worth mentioning that the Content Analyzer always explores sites by using the breadth-first routing method. If URL hierarchy is required, then a conversion is done to that organization.

If that preceding introduction causes confusion, the concept may make more sense if you use the Content Analyzer to create and view a graphical depiction of the map of your site. The idea here is that most Webmasters have a pretty good grasp of the logic behind the organization of their sites so the concept in action will seem clearer.

You have control over how the main and alternate routes are chosen and displayed. You can also reorganize your routes by a process called remapping, and change your routing using any one of the three approaches we have discussed. The Content Analyzer uses color to display resources and routes (black for resources, green for resources on alternate routes). You can also control the level of detail desired in displaying main and alternate routes.

At this point you may be wondering about the value of all these routing concepts. The differences in routing organization have nothing to do with site performance, at least not directly. Your site's web pages will not feed faster if you display your routing in URL hierarchy as opposed to breadth-first. For the most part, the routing organization is provided to help you comprehend your resource links. However, the information you receive from viewing your pages in the different routing formats can help you make decisions on site organization that will indirectly impact your site's performance.

Admittedly, not everyone is trying to tweak a few milliseconds out of a Web site that is feeding pages to millions of visitors. However, for those of you that have even moderate site visitation it may make sense to make sure that resources are located in near proximity to pages that receive heavy usage. Solutions to improving performance may involve moving resources between servers or perhaps caching whole pages.

In short, don't put your main company logo on a server that only has a narrow band modem link to your main site. While that example may sound like common sense, I know of examples where clients have spread various pages used within the frames of a single page across many different servers.

Special Situations

There are several situations that deserve special attention as we present options in project creation.

> **Password protected sites** – Many sites, or portions of sites, are password protected. The Content Analyzer provides special processing for these sites, but some additional configuration is required prior to creating a site. As part of the Tools menu there is a Program Options dialog box with a Passwords tab. You will need to supply a **Userid** and **Password** for each domain that will be considered within the scope of the Content Analyzer's spider exploration. These passwords become properties of the current user for the Content Analyzer tool, this data is not stored as part of the Content Analyzer site WMP file.

The .wmp *name is the file extension for a project file of site data.*

> **Proxy servers** – The Content Analyzer will work with proxy servers, and there are several configuration options. Content Analyzer will automatically use any proxy settings that you have set up for your Microsoft Internet Explorer. Otherwise you can tailor the settings using the Project menu item and a dialog window with Connection and Authentication tabs.

> **Creation options** – As we create a project there is an Options button that opens a dialog window with several tabs offering a variety of options. What follows are some of the key parameters that can be tailored:

Option	Description
Limiting creation	You can limit exploration by an absolute number of pages, by a relative level index, or by both. Content Analyzer will always explore at least one level so the best way to set the property is to choose a level number higher then two. Limiting levels is useful in Web sites where there are great volumes of reference pages at the lower site levels.
Extending URLs and Domains	You have encountered a situation where the scope of your Web management extends beyond a single domain. You can set a check box that allows the Content Analyzer to search on routes beyond your immediate domain. However, you must be careful – if you have a link on your site to a site such as Microsoft you will find that your spider has crawled quite a way beyond your site, and will search the Internet until the Content Analyzer exhausts your machine's physical resources.
	A more common situation is found where your company may own not just a primary company domain like, www.MyCompany.com, but perhaps other domains too, such as www.MyCompanyService.com or www.MyCompanyTech.com. In these situations you can specify the additional domains by name and you can provide a partial domain name such as www.mycompany. You can also set restrictions on domains that are not to be searched.
	A flowchart describing the spider search process is presented in the figure after this table.

Table Continued on Following Page

Option	Description
Site Copy	One of my favorite features is to be able to copy a site. You can specify a local directory to deposit site resources and the Content Analyzer will perform a copy operation while crawling through an exploration. The copy site feature only works in situations where a site was originally specified by URL, not by a File, and CGI scripts don't get copies, so the feature is far from perfect – although it can be very handy. In discussing CGI you may be wondering about ASP. We'll cover that topic later in this chapter.
Honoring Robot protocols	Anyone who has used an Internet search engine has seen that there is quite a bit of information indexed by Internet spiders. To assist in improving searches and protect information many sites have enabled *robot protocols* that limit the searching capability of spiders such as the one used in the Content Analyzer. While this is generally accepted to be a worthy Internet social practice, you may not want to honor robot protocols when performing exploration of your own site. Therefore you have a checkbox that will disable the function. It is normally checked by default. This option is only available if exploring sites by URL.
Testing User Agents	Web sites can be set up to provide varying responses to different browser types. You can control your spider's exploration by setting a user agent parameter that makes the spider appear to web sites as a representative of one browser type or another. The default type is Microsoft Internet Explorer 4.0.

The following diagram shows a flow chart of spider operation:

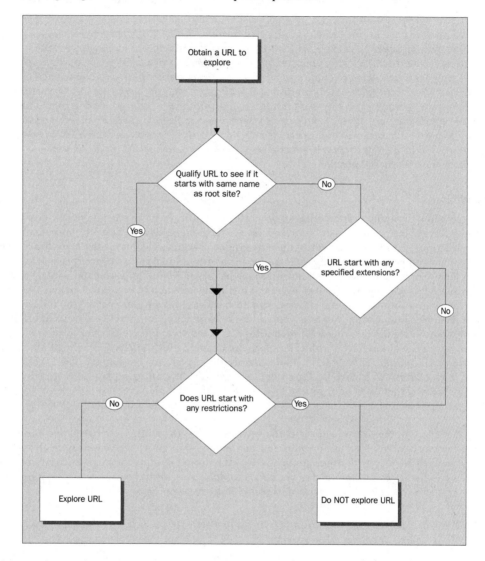

Viewing a Project

We have already had a somewhat lengthy discussion of creating a project, but after you master the concepts and tailor your project creation defaults, the process of creation will take only seconds if you limit your exploration to the domain of your local site. Exhaustive exploration of the Internet is another story, but in any case, the Content Analyzer will eventually present you with a **workspace**.

Understanding the Workspace

The Content Analyzer workspace is comprised of three windows, Site, Analysis, and Properties.

> *As I remember from my first experience with this program, it is at this point that you may experience some confusion, because the Content Analyzer is likely to open quite a few windows with new and interesting toolbar icons. All the Content Analyzer windows employ multiple panes that make the windows more complicated looking, and if you checked the report creation option during project creation, your browser window will also open with the workspace. All together it's quite a show of windows activity and provides good justification for asking your boss about that extra large display monitor that you desire. Before you get too far into analysis you will probably open your help window as well as one of the helper applications, such as an HTML editor so you can justify quite a bit of screen real estate. The recommended screen resolution for Content Analyzer is 1024 by 768 pixels.*

The Site Window

The site window provides a global view of your **site domain**. In more specific terms, you can view an **outline** and graphical map of your site resources, as in the next figure. You will immediately take notice of the graphical map area within the site window because it contains the Hyperbolic pane. The hyperbolic pane bears a superficial resemblance to the hyperlinks pane in FrontPage. However, the Content Analyzer pane is actually an invention of the Xerox Palo Alto Research Center, or PARC. The Xerox PARC is generally reputed to be the birthplace of such innovations such as the windowing GUI interface used in many operating systems and hardware inventions such as the mouse. The Content Analyzer help dialog that tells you about the product contains references to the Xerox companies that provide the hyperbolic technology. It is worth a quick visit over to their sites because you can learn more about how graphical hyperbolic browsing technology is shaping the way we interface to the Internet. This same technology is used in several of the popular tools that assist in site analysis, WebTrends and HotMetal Pro to name a few. It's difficult to explain in words, but the hyperbolic pane responds to your mouse movements. For example, a mouse movement to the right might open up new branches of a tree that exist on the right side of a depicted Web site.

We shouldn't ignore the features of the Outline window, but the ability to expand and contract an outline interface is pretty well understood and implemented in many Windows applications. Perhaps one important difference with other applications is the option of customizing the variety of resource items that are displayed in the outline. There is a toolbar control that produces a dialog box and allows you to check the items you wish to display; images, pages, gateways, etc.

> *A gateway is a program that handles a querystring and provides a gate to a dynamic reaction of a Web site. Forms are processed by gateaays.*

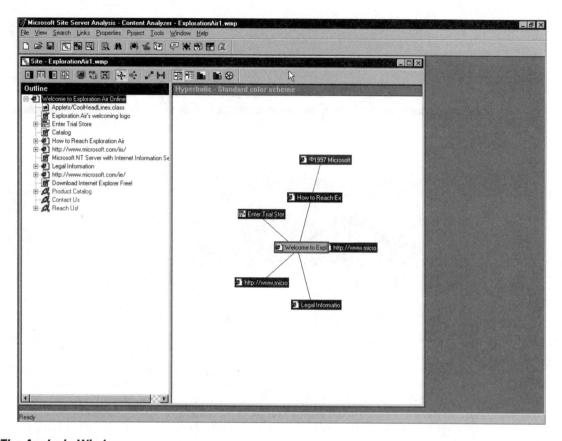

The Analysis Window

The analysis window provides you the mechanism to review the research you conduct on your site. The Content Analyzer provides a lot of information in its basic reports. In the site analysis process you might choose to conduct additional research into various questions about your site. I call this activity Content Mining, similar to the current trends toward data mining. You might want to review the pages with broken links in detail, or you might want to find images that are candidates for improved page loading. We'll talk more about Content Mining in a moment, the idea here is to present the concept of the Analysis window and it's frames. In the next screenshot I've shown an analysis window with the results of searching for all of the images on the Microsoft demonstration site, Exair. The analysis window is divided into two panes. One pane, the **results** pane, provides a tabular view of your search results. The other window, known as the **browser** shows you a specific resource. While the focus of the analysis window is to allow you to compare the properties of a collection of resources, pages, images, gateways, etc., the properties window provides you with a viewing tool to study one specific resource.

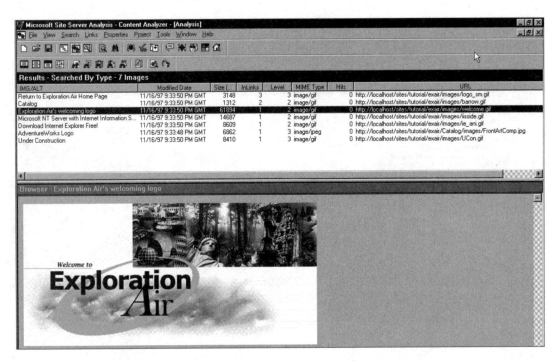

There are many situations where you can click on a resource and have it displayed with your default workstation browser, such as the Microsoft Internet Explorer. However, the browser within the analysis window is an embedded browser, specifically integrated into the Content Analyzer. In the Content Analyzer's embedded browser you can tailor the browser's behavior. For example, you can request that the browser show you the HTML source for each resource, rather then displaying the rendered HTML.

The Properties Window

The properties window provides you two panes as shown in the next figure. The resource pane provides details on the 'properties' of a single resource. The links pane provides details on the links that relate to the resource being displayed in the resource pane.

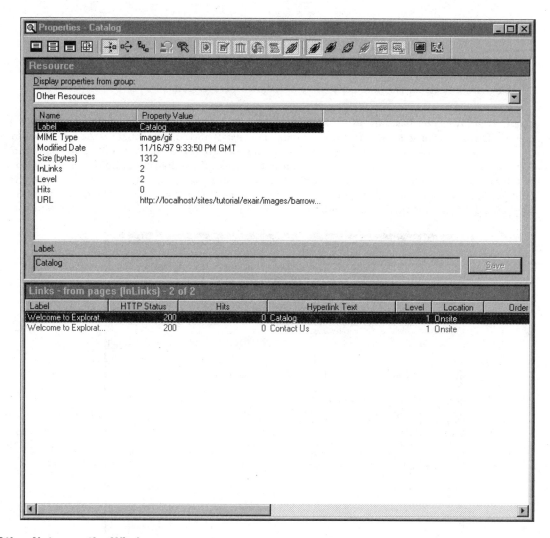

Other Notes on the Windows

All the panes in the workspace windows work in a similar manner, so that if you select a resource in one pane, then the other pane adjusts automatically to focus on the resource that has the window's focus. For example, if you select an image resource in the site window's outline pane, then the hyperbolic graphic images will change, and also the values in the property window panes. If you select a resource in the resource window then the links pane will display the links for that resource.

The Content Analyzer has a variety of window pane controls that can be located on the toolbar. These controls allow you to select whether one or two panes are to be visible when you are working with a specific window. For example, you can arrange for the site window to show only the outline pane, only the hyperbolic pane, or both. There is also an option to allow you to determine if you want the panes to have a **top** and **bottom** horizontal layout or a **right** and **left** vertical arrangement as they are displayed within the window. Finally, the way you lay out and customize the panes is saved from one work session to the next, as is the practice in many Microsoft products.

At this point you may be thinking that the windows of the Content Analyzer are all very nice, but your Webmaster responsibilities might lean more toward server hosting and network control, as opposed to Web site content development. The dilemma for those of you in this situation is how to distribute the Analysis information produced by the Content Analyzer. One solution I've already suggested is to use the NT scheduler to setup automatic report generation.

The Content Analyzer has the ability to e-mail the results of your analysis to single or multiple e-mail clients. The prerequisite for this feature is the need to install a MAPI compliant e-mail application on the machine that is running the Content Analyzer (another good reason for installing the Content Analyzer off your production web servers). Outlook express, the e-mail program that installs as part of the Microsoft Internet Explorer package is a good MAPI e-mail program. Once you are properly configured for e-mail you can use the relevant option under the Tools menu of the results pane to send a URL listing to either a single author (as shown in the figure below), or to a distribution list.

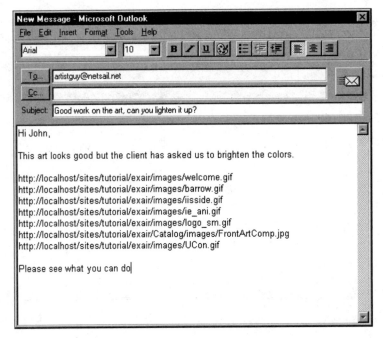

Finally, there may be situations where you want to work externally to the Content Analyzer with some or all the data that is found in the Content Analyzer windows. You have the option to export the data that can be found in the site outline, the analysis results, or the properties link panes. These panes are table like in their data presentation, and the contents of the panes can be exported in either HTML or delimited text format. In our company the benefit of this feature is being able to quickly export data into a spreadsheet format and e-mail information to web clients. The controls for performing the export are located on the File menu item.

Resource Properties

Resources have properties. For example, an image might have the properties of width, height, alternate text, etc. The Content Analyzer has about 100 system-defined resource properties that you can read. A reference guide to these system properties is provided in the Content Analyzer help materials. In addition, there are about a dozen user-defined properties that you can read or write. If all that isn't enough you can create your own new properties. User-defined properties are attached to HTML pages by the use of META tags. The definition of the META tag is part of HTML syntax so I won't describe the mechanics of it here. You can use the Site Server Tag tool to insert META tags onto your web pages. Many HTML editors such as FrontPage will also help you perform the necessary editing.

> *A short editorial comment about* META *tags: spend some time understanding the tags and updating your web pages.* META *tags are still a big factor in the methods that search engines use to characterize the information on the Internet. You will be helping your own promotion and providing less Internet page clutter if you take the time to correctly label your pages.*

The help for the Content Analyzer has a Property Reference Guide to define all the system properties and the default user-defined properties.

> *If you take the opportunity to review the property reference you will notice that some of the property names are capitalized. Those properties concern HTML tags or attributes.*

The rather large volume of properties poses some issues in managing the data, but Content Analyzer has developed the concept of **property groups** to assist in property management. The next screenshot shows the dialog window for grouping some of the properties that might be used to characterize an image resource. You can access this dialog from the Properties menu item, and then by selecting the Properties Groups menu item. The list box on the right is listing the properties that will be part of the group called Images. Notice the buttons to move the selected property URL up or down in the list. As you set the ranking of properties in this dialog window, you are setting the order that the properties will be displayed in the columns of the analysis results pane or the properties resource page.

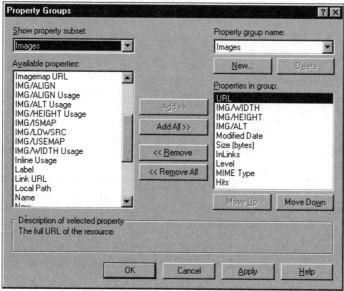

The ability to have dozens of system properties is very useful in performing the complex searches that help to perform the Content Mining that analyzes resource usage. Perhaps the greatest analysis benefit can be found in using the user-defined tags. These tags give you greater control over performing analysis on properties that are unique to your organization or industry.

Tag Name	Description
Author E-mail	The e-mail address for a resource author
Content Author	The name of the person who is responsible for a resource
Content Topic	The topic that is associated with a page
Content Type	The type of content that is associated with a page
Expiration Date	The expiration date that you assign to a resource
Resource Note	A note that you can place on a page
Resource Name	A name that you can associate with a resource or the title property for a page
Source Path	The path to a resource on a local machine
Description	A description that is attached to a resource
Generator	A description of the software that generated a resource

In the process of crawling through the mapping of your web, any META tags that are found on your pages will automatically become user-defined properties. The following is a template of some standard META tags that can be copied into any HTML page and then tailored as required.

```
<META NAME=       "Title" CONTENT="your title">
<META NAME=       "Subject" CONTENT="your subject">
<META NAME=       "description" CONTENT="description here">
<META HTTP-EQUIV= "Keywords" CONTENT="HTML, Reference">
<META NAME=       "Last-Modified" CONTENT="01/01/99">

<META HTTP-EQUIV= "Expires" CONTENT="Tue, 04 Dec 1996 21:29:02 GMT">
<META HTTP-EQUIV= "Reply-to" CONTENT="yourname@yourmail.net">
<META HTTP-EQUIV= "REFRESH" CONTENT="5; URL=http://www.sample.com/next.htm">

<META NAME=       "CONTENTAUTHOR" CONTENT="yourname">
<META NAME=       "TOPIC" CONTENT="Any Topic">
<META NAME=       "CONTENTTYPE" CONTENT="Reference Info">
```

The Content Analyzer will allow you to change user-defined properties from within the resource pane of the properties window. However, you can only change properties that are *not* already defined by META tags. In addition, any changes you make to a property value from within the Content Analyzer will *not* update the HTML. Therefore, the update feature may be valuable to encapsulate some site information you don't want released to the site audience. However, you will probably gain the greatest benefit to your site management efforts if you use the user-defined properties by incorporating META tags in your HTML.

Setting up Helper Applications

At this point you have done almost everything necessary to begin some serious Web site content analysis. The Content Analyzer offers a great deal of flexibility in allowing you to customize both the variety of information on a site, as well as the manner in which that information is displayed. You select the types of information displayed, the routes, the images, the links, etc. You can also select the colors and labels that are used to display resources. We will talk about this in more detail toward the end of the chapter. The Content Analyzer customization is non-mission critical in your quest to start site analysis. However, one additional pre-analysis activity you do want to consider is the configuration and setup of what The Content Analyzer calls h**elper applications.**

Helper applications are independent, non-Content Analyzer `.exe` or **out of process** programs that you configure to be integrated into the Content Analyzer integrated development environment, the **workspace**. As previously discussed, there is no shortage of Web oriented site tools, which can be as rich as Microsoft FrontPage or as common as the Windows Notepad. As you analyze your sites, you will probably want to have handy access to your favorite HTML editor, as well as your image editor, and perhaps an animation editor and audio editor. Therein lies the value of integrated helper applications.

Configuring a helper application is fairly straightforward. You can access the Helpers tab dialog window, similar to the one shown in the next screenshot, from the Tools menu item and the Program Options menu sub-selection.

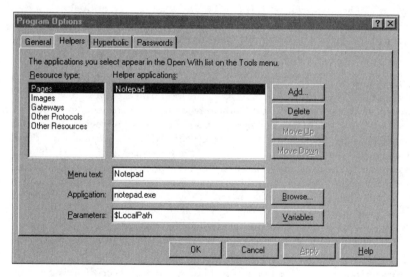

The first potentially confusing part of the configuration activity is to understand that helper applications are usually single purpose in their nature. There are a few "We do everything", Swiss army knife type applications, but generally the idea is that Web page editors are not in the same genre as image editors or audio editors.

Therefore, we need to have some way to link the helper application tool with the type of resource that it can best be used on. Later on we'll see how you click on a resource and the helper application is initialized.

In order to achieve this link, you choose a Resource Type from the list box presented on the left side of the dialog.

The next step is to identify the application you want to add or modify as a helper application. By using the list box on the right hand side you can select current applications, or you can press the Add button to create new applications.

Pressing the Add button is straightforward. You are presented with a small window that allows you to key in the path to your application or browse using your file explorer.

In most cases, you will find your application `.exe` program and the three text boxes at the bottom of the dialog window are filled in automatically. However, there's plenty of room for exceptions. The menu text box allows you to create a friendly name for your helper application. For example, the FrontPage editor program is very popular but as you install it, the default setting in Menu text is the single word fpeditor. You might want to change the default editor naming to something like FrontPage Editor.

The Application text box will be filled in with the execution path to your application. The Browse button on the right seems redundant when you are adding applications, but you will soon appreciate it's value if you need to return to modify an existing helper application.

Finally, there is another potentially confusing final challenge to configuring your application. Most applications can be called with **arguments**. If you open Notepad without any arguments you wind up looking at a blank editor window. In order to provide more automation you might want to call the Notepad using a command that looks similar to: `c:\notepad.exe -f c:\milefile.htm`. The Content Analyzer can help you with this task. The Variables button at the bottom right of the Helper tab lets you configure the method for adding arguments to your program calls. If you spend time modifying dozens if not hundreds of objects daily, then understanding this button is a big help. It can have the following values:

> Local Path – The value of the *local path* is the Content Analyzer default. Unfortunately, this is probably not the best choice in some cases. The local path is populated when you create a project from a file or from a copy of a site. Neither one of these options seem to be the situation for normal commercial ISP/ hosting operations, and I could debate their value in intranet operations. In our ISP hosting operation, we usually analyze the site directly from the production Web server, a machine that is hundreds of miles distant on the Internet. After all, this is the source of the information that the audience really sees. However, we revise the content from a copy of the site that is maintained on a separate development server situated on our Local Area Network. All this may sound confusing because the Content Analyzer allows you to start a project with a site copy. That is a great feature if you are adopting a site that was created by a different web design firm. However, this feature is not as valuable in situations where sites were created from nothing and the development site exists prior to Content Analyzer site project creation,

> URL – The value of the URL seems like a good idea until you realize that, in many cases, you are editing a temporary copy of a resource and not the original object. This is the same situation you see when you exercise the View Source feature from within the Microsoft Internet Explorer. Occasionally, I absent-mindedly start to change the HTML from within Notepad and when I start to save I am then reminded that the original location for the source was a server several hundred miles away, not on my local workstation.

> Source Path – The value of the source path is derived from the `<META NAME= "SOURCE PATH">` tag that you can place in the header of your HTML page. There is value in this feature, but the possible drawbacks include the time taken to maintain the source path META tag (although this is minimal in my estimation), as well as the possible security breach in publicizing details of your internal Web design operations, something that should be encapsulated from the public.

> ➤ **Local Path URL / Full URL** – The final option for specifying the **Variable** button is to select a hybrid of both the **Local Path** and the **URL** options previously discussed. In this option the Content Analyzer will inspect the contents of the local path property and, if present, will convert it to a URL. Otherwise the value of the URL becomes the target of the data substituted on the command line. This approach, while offering some flexibility, suffers from the issues discussed for both **Local Path** and **URL**.

The final task to understanding helper applications is to comprehend their selection as you work the Content Analyzer. As shown in the figure below, a *right* mouse selection on a resource in the Site window's hyperbolic pane offers the **Open With** menu item. By further expanding the menu, you can see that we have two choices for opening an HTML page. The Notepad was listed as a Content Analyzer default, but I added the FrontPage editor during the course of working with the **Helper** tab of the **Program Options** dialog window.

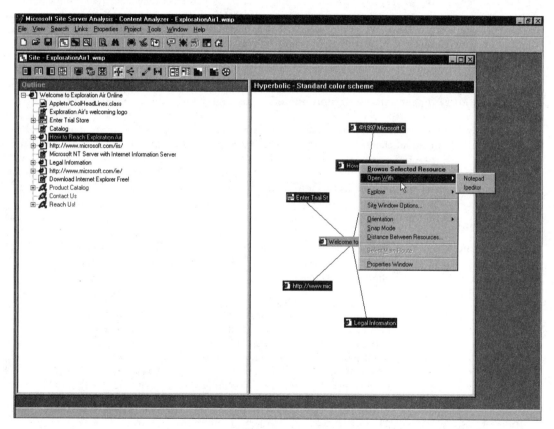

In this example, I could have improved the helper application feature by providing a friendly name for the FrontPage editor program fpeditor. *I could also have moved the Front Page editor to the top of the list, in front of Notepad. All these options are part of the Helper tab in the Program Options window.*

Content Mining

In spite of having spent many pages discussing the customization of Content Analyzer and the creation of projects, the real work of the product, the analysis of Web sites and then content, begins with the topic I call **Content Mining**.

Understanding Web site organization and content

First off, we must differentiate usage analysis from content analysis. Most of the analysis features of Site Server deal with usage analysis, like tracking visitor usage. In contrast, content analysis has more of an inward focus, perhaps much like auditing a company. The idea of content analysis is growing in importance as the size and complexity of Web projects expand. So, what's the difference between content analysis and Content Mining?

The reason for coining a term like Content Mining is derived from the idea that the Content Analyzer only presents you with quantitative, non-subjective information about your site. Perhaps it's an esoteric debate, but the final task of Content Analysis depends on performing some content mining, that is to say, researching data and turning it into information before making subjective judgments on how the information is presented to the audience. The Content Analyzer knows nothing about good taste or fashion, but I would suggest that the final value of Content Analysis is to offer information that can allow you to improve a site's value to its audience. As an example, we have a client who feels strongly that his European Jazz music store should be rendered with a black background.

When performing Content Mining you first need to have some idea on where to prospect. The key point here is to understand the nature of your Web sites and perhaps have a guiding policy toward their growth. Perhaps a guiding phrase is: a mission, a means, a goal... so to speak. To put this in another perspective, what is the community that your site is serving? The following are just a couple of examples; of course the permutations on the basic themes are endless:

Web organization	Description
Brochure Sites	Presents static information billboard style. The cyber calling card never changes once created. Requires very little content analysis after the first instance.
Promotion Sites	Similar to a brochure site, but eventually someone realizes that changing the site content is a good idea. Promotions include news or perhaps coupons to attract customers. Promotion sites are like Brochure sites but are starting to advance toward higher forms of intelligence. Since promotions change frequently, the mining emphasis should be to grammar and spell check pages and look for inappropriate image sizes (we had one instance where a Web artist accidentally put a 1 meg image on a site!), broken links, etc.
Reference Sites	These sites can contain lots of textual, image, or audio information, and are characterized by non-database volumes of pages. The 'encyclopedia site' can be hundreds of megs large and very difficult to maintain due to thousands of links. They may also involve many authors. Reference sites are frequent targets for usage analysis.

Web organization	Description
Author Sites	Where a potentially large team of various authors provides content information. Authors may represent different departments of a company or vendors within an online flea market. HTML skills in multi-author projects can vary a great deal, so performance issues and site consistency are paramount issues.
News Sites	Often have rapid changes to content, possibly by the hour, certainly by the day. Grammar, Spelling, Broken Links, and Missing Resources are all issues.
Portal Web Alliances	Web sites that contain many links to other web sites. The primary problem here is broken links and exploring a variety of domains. Examples here might encompass situations where a holding corporation has a variety of companies in one big corporate family. It is very difficult to explore Web site alliances.
Dynamic database Sites	Sites that may only have a few ASP pages and yet can be gigantic in the dynamic nature of the information they can produce. Difficulties with handling ASP sites are discussed later.

Where Do I Begin?

Depending on the unique needs of your site, you may want to proceed in various directions with your content mining. However, there are probably a few guides to making content mining more of an empirical method as opposed to a black art.

Firstly, you should remember that the Content Analyzer can produce a comprehensive set of reports on demand. In our Web design operations, we have automated the process so that each Web client has a private Web where we run routine content analysis reports and deposit them automatically into the client's private site management Web. Once again, the reports have nothing to do with indicating the value of a site in meeting the needs of its audience. Moreover, the reports are more like a bill of goods in performing an inventory of links and resources; therein lies the idea behind content mining, more so than content analysis.

However, the reports are a good start.

Project searches

The Content Analyzer offers three mechanisms for performing searches:

> Quick searches

> Simple searches

> Advanced searches

All search mechanisms are available via a Search menu choice from the Content Analyzer main window. The analysis window also has toolbar icons to allow various searches.

Quick Search

Quick searches provide a mechanism for performing... well... quick searches. There are ten searches that are created by default, you can add your own unique searches that they can be readily referenced.

Search name	Description
Pages with Broken Links	Identifies pages where there are broken links. Tips for resolving broken links are provided later in this chapter. The broken links section of the Links Pane for a page provides more resources. Solutions include correcting spellings, link verification, etc.
Not Found Resources (404)	Identifies resources that are missing from the target server and thereby creating broken links. The solution is to verify the broken links and replace the resources.
Load Size Over 32K	The load size is the size of the HTML page text plus embedded resources such as frames and images. Possible improvements here include decreasing the quality of JPEG compression, converting JPEGS to GIFS, or using ASP page buffering to display progressive content on pages.
Images with no Height or Width	Locates the images where the HTML IMG tag parameters for HEIGHT and WIDTH are not used. Including values for these parameters will made a page appear to load faster because image frames can be established, otherwise the entire page must be rendered in the browser before display begins.
Resources with Server Errors	This class of error is more unusual than the typical missing resource. Errors in this class are caused by HTTP status codes in the 500 range. Possible issues include internal server errors, bad gateways, or services that are unavailable or not implemented. You will also see these codes when the request query stream on a form has an embedded space.
Unverified Resources	A resource may be unverified because it is really missing, or it might have been unverified due to the happenstance of the Internet traffic during exploration. A good tip is to conduct exploration in the middle of the night, which is becoming more difficult in the global economy. A solution is to Verify Links using the Tools menu item, and the Results Pane sub-selection item.
Resources with External Referrers	Provides a list of the external Web sites that have links into your site. This isn't really a problem, unless you are trying to sell your business plan as being a great Mecca of visitor congregation. But seriously, this is a great feature but it depends upon importing usage data for your site. In order to use this feature you would need to import data through the Site Server Usage Analyst.

Search name	Description
Pages with Forms	Knowing which pages have forms is useful because of the need to write some CGI or other ASP program to handle the form response. In our Web design business, we will sometimes create Web sites in NetObjects Fusion, but handle all the site form pages by building a sub site that is crafted in Microsoft FrontPage. FrontPage has a great feature for building forms with a WebBOT. You can think of a WebBOT as filling the same function as a CGI script. After a site is opened and promoted, forms are eventually handled with ASP pages.
Unavailable Resources	This search is more ambiguous then searches previously defined, and it is not one of my favorites. The search will produce results that mirror the resources not found 404 error, but will also include situations where resources are password protected (401), or the server was down (152). In situations where the server is down, this means that a hostname was resolved by a DNS server, but the Content Analyzer could not connect to the Web server.
Offsite Resources	The identification of offsite resources may not identify a problem, but is useful for understanding the amount of content inventory beyond the scope of the Content Analyzer's spider exploration.

The Content Analyzer help information has additional tips on diagnosing and repairing site problems by explaining the various Content Analyzer window panes and how they can be applied to fixing various issues.

As you perform the various searches offered by the Content Analyzer you can easily create a quick search by selecting the Save Last as Quick Search... item on the Search menu item in the Content Analyzer main window. As shown in the screenshot below, the Content Analyzer will not only save the search query but will also save the configuration settings of the results, resource, and links panes.

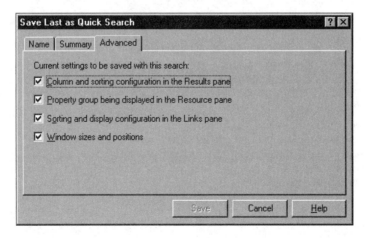

Simple Searches

The Content Analyzer <u>S</u>earch menu item provides four commonly used simple searches. These searches are useful for quickly reviewing the inventory of a site. The searches are described as follows:

Simple Search	Description
Text	This search is probably not what you would assume. A search is performed for a text string, but not in the basic HTML text on a page. Instead, the Content Analyzer searches for a text string that is located in the resource properties you have defined for a site. This includes META tags, titles, headings, hyperlinks, and ALT strings.
Date	This search will be performed upon properties where you have specified dates. There are two default dates given, **Modified Date** and **Expiration Date**. The importance of the Expiration Date is increasing daily. The reason for this is the increasing use of Web page caching. Many Internet servers and routers are now caching Web material to improve performance. The review for the freshness of material is often based on the expiration data of a resource. For example, I frequently update site resources that are located on servers in the Southern US, and I live in New England. In cases of pages without expiration, it sometimes takes up to a hour for site changes to move through the Internet caching system between the providers in the US South and North.
URL	A URL search is similar to a text search, but is confined only to properties that are used to contain URL address information.
Type	There are six types of resource searches that can be performed:
	➢ All Resources – All types of resources
	➢ Pages – HTML Pages
	➢ Images – Images
	➢ Gateways – Programs that process Forms
	➢ Other Protocols – Non-HTTP protocols like FTP or MAIL
	➢ Other Resources – Any other resources not mentioned, e.g. audio

Advanced Searches

Of course, there will be situations where you needs exceed the capabilities of any quick or simple search. In these situations you can use the advanced search capabilities of the Content Analyzer to build just about any query imaginable. The screenshot below shows an example of an advanced search to find large images. The example assumes that a large image has attributes that have been defined for its width and height.

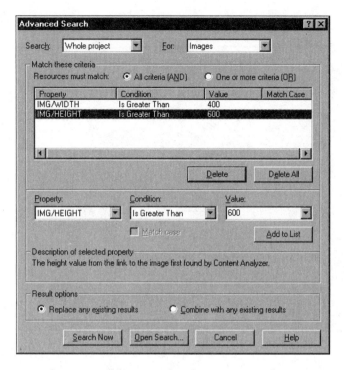

As you perform searches you will begin to develop questions about your site. For example, in reviewing the Microsoft demo site Exploration Air I questioned the number of in-links to the homepage. In any event, you need to know that the Content Analyzer offers you a chance to perform additional explorations after the initial exploration that created your project. The Project menu item from the main Content Analyzer window will let you explore a Site, a Branch, or a Page. The need for additional exploration makes more sense if you have placed limits on your initial project creation exploration.

Remapping Sites

Before we proceed to further discussions on fixing or improving your site, we need to present the concept of project **remapping**. As you make changes to your site, the Content Analyzer project you created becomes stale. There is no real time revision process for your site. Therefore, you will need to perform periodic remapping to refresh the data within your project.

The screenshot below shows the options for remapping a project. For the most part, the options presented have already been discussed, because they can be activated during project creation. One useful option to mention concerns the check box for Show new and changed resources in Results pane. By enabling this option you can view an additional column in the results pane of the analysis window. The column will show True or False for each resource to indicate if the item has been affected by recent mapping operations. A final consideration is to use the Schedule feature and perform a remapping of your site during slow traffic periods of Internet activity. This suggestion presumes that your site will need access to the Internet to verify the links to resources, we'll discuss this issue in more detail as we discuss **link verification**.

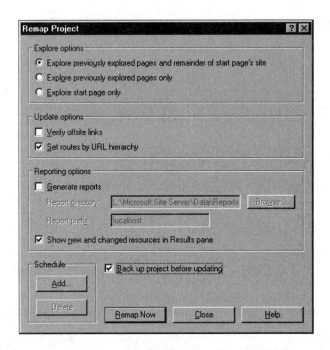

Verifying Links

We have described many ways in which the Content Analyzer can be useful for performing site analysis. Perhaps the most important focus of the application is on managing **links**. Common HTML commands that specify links are <A>, with it's HREF attribute, or < IMG>, with it's SRC attribute. However, there are about 25 different HTML commands and 31 different attributes that can specify links, so a tutorial on link syntax is beyond our mission here. In any event, the analysis and verification of links refers to static HTML links, not the links that are dynamically generated by technologies such as ASP.

Examining links is performed in the Content Analyzer by using both the site hyperbolic map and the property window links pane. For example, broken links are easily identified in the hyperbolic standard color scheme because they are represented as *red* lines.

Information available in Link Types

Usually, you will select a resource in the site window and then select a link type to show in the links pane of the property window. There are three basic types of links presented in the link pane.

> **Links (to Resources)** – In this link type, a table of links is shown for links pointing outward. For example, in the case of a resource that is a page, there will be links for resources that are contained both on the current page and off the page. If the resource in question is an image you will not see any links because you can't link from an image to somewhere else. You link to an image, not out of an image.

A lot of you may be thinking of all the times you have clicked on an image to go to another page. However, in HTML, a click, and therefore a link, is an event and property of the HREF attribute of the <A> HTML command. Images are frequently used as a parameter within the <A> command. Only pages can contain links to other resources.

> **InLinks (from Pages)** – For a specific resource, the InLinks type shows the links that are pointing inward to a specific resource. Similar to the previous example, the degree that you find link data is dependent upon the type of resource that has the focus of the property window. In this situation, an image resource may have lots of incoming links, perhaps the image is a company logo. It may be used on many pages. A home page will probably have many incoming and outgoing links.

When examining the home page in the Microsoft demo site, Exploration Air, there is only one incoming link to the home page. What gives? Why not more? Perhaps it was an intentional trick to provide a tutorial. There is, in fact, only one situation where a link is made to the page named Default.asp. However, there are other situations where a link is made to the home site (not the home page), for example: http://www.exair.com/. In these cases there is an implicit reference to default to the page named Default.asp. That linkage is made in the IIS Web server. The Content Analyizer will not pick up these implicit assumptions.

> **Links on Route to Resource** – In this link type the links on the start page and all intermediate pages are displayed, showing you a route to the resource of your focus.

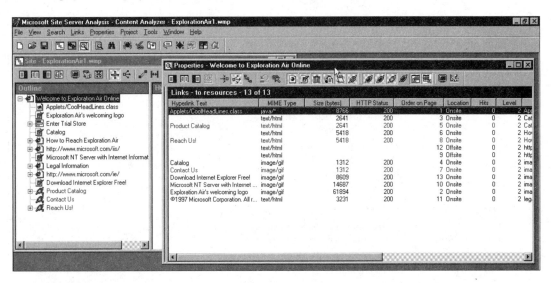

The link pane employs a Microsoft table control. What this means in practical terms is that you can sort on the column information by clicking on the column headers. You can also expand or reduce the size of the columns by manipulating the column headers. You can't drag and drop the order of the columns, but you can customize the data that is shown within a column and the column order of that data. The links customization is available via a menu item called Links, found on the Content Analyzer main menu.

The following is a review of the data content in each column for each link type pane within the Property window.

Property	Description	To Resources	InLinks	On Route
Hyperlink Text	The text associated with a hyperlink, and, in the case of images, the ALT string on the main route. Can be the string you put in a value list, like a select box.	√	√	√
MIME Type	Multipurpose Internet Mail Extensions. This defines a file type for an Internet resource. The MIME type provides a way to link a type of file with a method of handling it. HTML pages get handled differently to spreadsheets. The type is server dependent and can depend on whether you created your project from a URL or a file.	√		
Size (bytes)	The size in bytes of a resource, as returned by the server. The sizes can be quite surprisingly large, a couple of kilobytes for even simple links. This is because the server is measuring the total size of the stub for the link, not just the character text in the link string.	√		
HTTP Status	The HTTP status codes are somewhat industry specific, but some of them apply only to the Content Analyzer.	√	√	
Order on Page	The order for a link as it is found on a specific web page.	√	√	
Location	Can be Onsite, Offsite, or Onpage.	√	√	√

Property	Description	To Resources	InLinks	On Route
Hits	The number of times a resource has been accessed by a site visitor, usage data is required.	√	√	√
Level	A numerical index of level in relation to the start page. Will depend upon how mapping is conducted for a site and how routes are selected.	√	√	√
Link URL	The link URL is for the main route for resources. It can be relative or absolute. In the latter case, you need to figure out the resource's proximity to the root of the site.	√	√	√
URL	The full URL for a resource.	√		
Label	The label depends on how you have selected labeling with the Content Analyzer, meaning that it could be HTML text, or perhaps a URL.		√	
From URL	The URL of a From page for a link.		√	
From Label	The label that is applied to the From page for a link.			√

The help information for the Content Analyzer contains a Content Analyzer Property Reference that contains details on all system defined properties.

Finding and fixing Broken Links

Links can be broken for two basic reasons: there might a mistake in the HTML tag that specifies the link, or the resource that is the target of the link may be unavailable. Having personally created about a zillion broken links, *accidentally*, I can tell you from experience that popular mistakes include specifying relative links correctly and remembering whether pages end in HTM or HTML. While resources can be unavailable for a variety of valid reasons, one situation involves the problem of a resource not being available because of Internet traffic problems during the site mapping exploration process. I once read that resource availability problems could be as high as 36% during peak Internet usage periods, but this estimate was about a year old so it is ancient history by Internet standards. Nevertheless, the lesson here is still valid. It is best to perform site exploration and mapping during quiet traffic periods. We frequently schedule site mappings during the hours of 3:00 AM and 7:00 AM Eastern Standard US time.

Steps to check link corrections

The following is a basic process for resolving broken links.

> ➢ Perform the Pages with Broken Links Quick Search.
>
> ➢ In the Analysis window Results pane look at the URL to validate the URL text.
>
> ➢ Focus attention on the relative linking syntax, if used, and review the file extensions for accuracy.
>
> ➢ If you find a problem with the link syntax, use your favorite helper application to revise the source page with the broken link.
>
> ➢ Save your corrected source in the correct location.
>
> ➢ Remap your project.
>
> ➢ Check for broken links again (and proceed back to the first step if necessary).
>
> ➢ Test your changes in your target browser.

Handling dynamically created pages (ASP)

A frequent question concerns the ability to perform site analysis in situations where the content of a site is dynamically created with popular technologies such as Active Server Pages or ASP. The goal of an ASP page is to dynamically handle and generate the HTML content of a site.

There should be no doubt that dynamically created pages pose a challenge for site analysis. However, the Content Analyzer does have a feature that lets you provide responses to forms and then trace how your site will handle the form information, regardless of whether the form is handled by CGI scripts or ASP. The next screenshot shows an example of creating a response for the Microsoft demonstration site, Exploration Air. The Project menu item on the Content Analyzer main window offers a sub item entitled Add Form Response. In order to enable this menu option, you need to have selected a form from the site window.

In this example, you complete the operation by providing the data required in the form fields and pressing the submit button (labeled Enter Store in this example). After closing the Add Form Response window, you can remap your site and discover that several new pages and their resources are now candidates for analysis within your project.

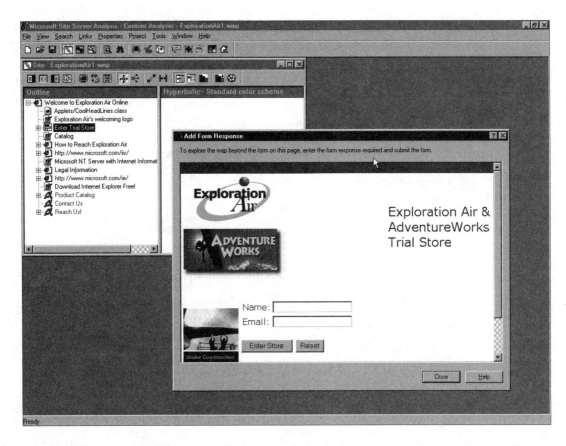

Generating Reports

We will not spend much time on report generation, but the Content Analyzer can produce an impressive Web site of reports at the press of a button. The reports in total present the site author with a bill of materials for all resources within the site, as well as helpful analysis information on broken links and other critical error data, as shown in the screenshot overleaf:

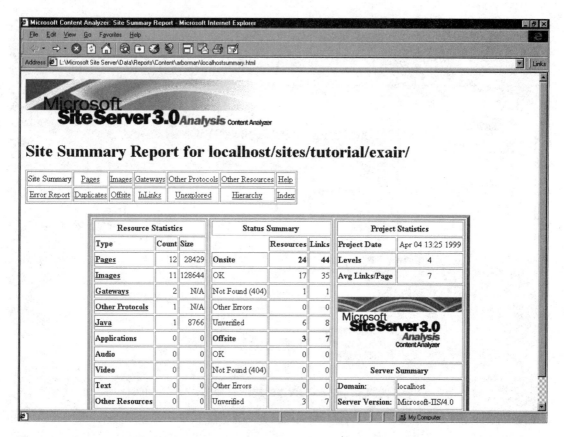

Report generation is offered during project creation, and can be performed anytime as an option from the Tools menu in the Content Analyzer main window. As I mentioned at the beginning of the chapter, my company automates this process and produces weekly reports for a number of sites, where each site author receives a private Web site that aids in site management. The pages of this Web site include both site reports and usage analysis, discussed later. If you choose to develop a report automation process, one tip is to include an additional site page that provides additional help to authors. A Frequently Asked Questions page, or FAQ page is useful.

General Reporting

The following is a brief summary of the Content Analyzer reports:

Report Title	Description
Site Summary	Provides key statistics and a summary of identifying site information. Contains links to all other reports.
Pages	Provides an inventory of pages and shows data on the load size and links contained within them.
Images	Provides an inventory of images and their load sizes.

Report Title	Description
Gateways	Provides an inventory of gateways (forms), showing their methods, Get or Post.
Other Protocols	An inventory of protocols, both onsite and offsite, protocols include FTP, Mail, News, Gopher, etc.
Other Resources	An inventory of other resources such as Java, audio, video, applications.
Help	A basic report description.
Error Report	Unreachable resources.
Duplicates	Duplicate resources.
OffSite	An inventory of offsite resources.
InLinks	An InLink inventory. The concept of the InLink in this venue is to map the links that are coming into a resource, but only from within your site.
Unexplored	Unexplored resources are created when you put limits on site exploration.
Hierarchy	The Hierarchy Report attempts to convey a basic hierarchical structure for your site in outline form.
Index	The index is alphabetical and provides an easy way to navigate the report site.

Reporting on Orphan Resources

One special report worth mentioning concerns the idea of **orphaned resources**. An orphan is a resource that does not appear to have any InLinks. The orphan report is not created as part of the General Reporting process. This feature is activated from the Content Analyzer Tools menu item and a sub-item entitled Find Orphans.

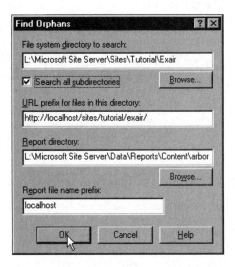

You should be careful before you delete any resources listed in the orphan report, especially if you placed limits on your project exploration and mapping. The orphans may be referenced by some mechanism that is beyond your site.

SiteServer Usage Analyst

There are five programs that comprise the Site Server Analysis family. Four of the programs deal with visitor Usage Analysis, the fifth program, the Content Analyzer, has already been presented.

As a bit of history, the Microsoft Usage Analyzer was conceived by a company called Interse, and purchased by Microsoft in early 1997. The current Usage Analyzer, while having some improvements, still retains much of the flavor of the original Interse product called Market Focus Version 3.0.

It's easy to see why Microsoft admired the product. Firstly, it's one of the few products that has the option of storing its data in a SQL Server database. Perhaps more importantly, Interse was somewhat brilliant in not feeling the need to invent their own proprietary code to provide users with reports and spreadsheets. The product has output all its information as Microsoft Office files from its inception.

There are quite a few products on the market today that can show you Web log usage data that is presented in graphical charts and nicely formatted reports, but the Usage Analyzer still has the advantage in being tightly integrated with SQL Server and Microsoft Backoffice. There's also a tremendous variance in the prices for Web log analysis tools. It pays to shop around, but Site Server offers good value relative to its competitors.

The three key programs that comprise the Usage Analyst are: Usage Import, Custom Import, and the Report Writer. There's a fourth program for Database Setup, this program is used infrequently to provide a wizard database setup to the SQL Server challenged (only available for SQL Server 6.5). Before I get too far in, I should mention that the Usage Analyzer can be implemented using Microsoft Access. For the purposes of this chapter I will point out a few differences between the SQL Server and Access implementations, but I would assume that most organizations that can afford Site Server are probably using SQL Server.

Without having to admit to too much stupidity, I found the Usage Analyzer difficult to understand on my first experience. The program has none of the instant familiarity that you might have when you look at a new word processor, a graphics program, or something you have generally seen before. If you have a job like mine, you're probably rushed to perform many tasks, and log analysis is but one mission in a long day. So, perhaps you might be tempted to rush. The advice is: *don't do it!* You will need to be very specific when you set up the Usage Analyzer to handle your web traffic, else you run the risk of serious time wastage. If you don't set up your infrastructure properly, then you might spend hours importing data that doesn't give you the reports you desired. Fortunately for you, I've already been there and done that, so I'll spare you some grief as you read this chapter. Additionally, Microsoft offers a tutorial that will walk you through the data import and report generation process in a step by step basis.

Installation Considerations

If you plan on installing the Usage Analyzer while you study this chapter, the first thing you should do is find the readme installation file that is kept in the Site Server docs directory. There are a couple of issues to consider for installation. Firstly, there is some minor wisdom to installing the Usage Analyzer on a machine that is not your production Web server. The product does not require any IIS functionality other then having IIS create Web logs, which, after all, can be transported anywhere you can send a file. IIS is not even a prerequisite for the Usage Analyst. It can work with a wide variety of logs produced by various Web servers. Perhaps more importantly, the Usage Analyzer can create reports in HTML, Microsoft Word 97 or Microsoft Excel 97. You may not want to install these products on a production web server due to potential conflicts in DLLs etc.

The Usage Analyst has both a Win32 and Command-Line interface. Unfortunately, the Command-Line interface is only available via Windows NT. To be more specific, the Command-Line interface is *not* available on Windows 9x platforms, so you'll be limited in automating the Usage Analysis process on such machines. Finally, if you plan to import data from Site Server Personalization and Membership (P&M) in order to use P&M's Direct Mail feature, you must install Analysis on the same computer as the Direct Mail List Builder Service. For all these reasons, the ideal platform for a Usage Analysis install may be an NT BackOffice server that is not your primary production Web server.

> *We installed the Usage Analysis programs on a NT Domain Controller and found that setup to work well. While the Domain Controller is pretty busy during the day, there is less activity in the evenings when the batch oriented work of the Usage Analysis programs run. However, there are issues in software licensing. The Usage Analyzer is a key product component of the Site Server family. It is not considered a Site Server tool, such as the Content Analyzer. Therefore, you will need to pay additional licensing fees if you install the product components that are considered non-tools across platforms. But, if money is no object and you have another machine with SQL Server installed, then I suggest getting the Usage Analyzer off your production web server.*

The Site Server Analysis help files have specific suggestions for tuning your SQL Server to optimize it for performance on a dedicated machine for Analysis. There are specific settings suggested for allocating memory, locks, sort pages, and a procedure cache. There is also an interesting warning that suggests not running any combination of the Usage Import, Custom Import, or Report Writer at the same time, due to a risk of database corruption. So, perhaps a dedicated server might help establish an extra measure of application control.

As a final technical glitch, if you go with the plan of installing the Usage Analyzer on a separate machine from your Web server, then you will need to manually install an ISAPI filter called `mss_log.dll`. This filter allows the server to generate cookies so that P&M can identify users. You can find details of this procedure in the readme file.

Understanding Web Logs and Log Data

It's worth spending a minute talking about log formats, but for those of you who are still rushing through this chapter in spite of my advice, you should set your Web server to the Microsoft IIS W3C Extended Log File Format. As I mentioned earlier, there is an ISAPI filter that must be installed during the Site Server installation process. This installation is automatic, and if you are running the Usage Analyst from your Site Server installation primary server then you are set. Having specified those two requirements you're ready to collect all the data for analysis.

For those of you reading at a more leisurely pace, the basic idea behind Log Analysis is to turn the data collected by most Web servers into useful information. There are three types of information that Web servers routinely collect:

> ➤ **Referrer data** – concerns data on the server where a browser request originated. A common example of a referrer server might be America Online, but there are plenty of Internet users that are browsing from their company servers. This data can also be captured and is quite valuable.

> ➤ **User agent data** – is data that concerns the browser environment of the user. It might be important for a web author to understand the versions and types of browsers that form the technical audience for a site.

> ➤ **Cookies** – are information that is stored on user computers, serving a variety of purposes. One valuable purpose is site visitor tracking.

One of the advantages of the Site Server log analysis is the fact that you can combine Site Server data from Personalization, Commerce, AdServer or Search with the data that is collected in your log.

You will notice that the Usage Analyzer supports fifteen different formats in addition to the Microsoft Extended format previously suggested. Obviously, this degree of flexibility is handy for mixed server environments. If you have servers that are running something less then IIS 4.0 then the previous Microsoft IIS Standard Log File Format is different from the new Extended Log File Format. This means that the importing process is slightly different if you are bringing in data from a server that you just recently upgraded to SiteServer 3.0.

I won't have time to present all the differences between sixteen different log file formats. However, before we start performing Usage Analysis we need to perform a little more work on configuring your Web Server.

The next screenshot shows a log configuration example. Log configuration is part of the **Web Site** tab for your default site, and you can reach this dialog window by using the Internet Information Server manager. Other then enabling logging and configuring your log for the **W3C Extended Log File Format**, you should probably change the defaults that can be located by pressing the **Properties** button next to the **Active Log Format** labeled text box. In short, the Microsoft default will create a web log daily and deposit it in your Windows NT directory. You should change the log generation to a monthly cycle and move the log archive to a disk that is not the operating system root disk for your Web server. A frequently asked question concerns the use of ODBC to allow logging straight into a database. Basically, I don't recommend it. The basic assumption here is that your Web server is going to be pretty busy serving up that electronic commerce world of the future. There isn't a big performance hit in using the ODBC logging, but there doesn't seem to be a big advantage either. Perhaps the feature will become more important when the "Real Time, not Batch" Usage Analyzer is announced, if ever.

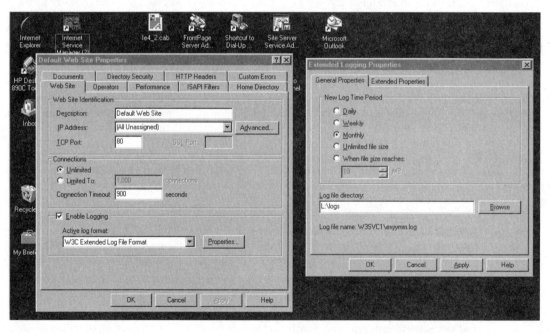

From the window on the right hand side of the screenshot above, you can select a tab called Extended Properties. You will then be presented with a window similar to the one below. The suggested properties to capture are: Date, Time, Client IP Address, User Name, URI Stem, URI Query, HTTP Status, Bytes Sent, User Agent, Cookie, and Referrer.

I'm sure some of you are wondering about some of the data elements that are being collected by your log. Let's take a moment to review some basic terminology.

Data Element Definitions

> **Log File** – A log file is a data file that records the actions of a user who is visiting a Web site.

> **Log Data Source** – A Log Data Source represents a physical machine that generates log data files in a specific format.

> **Server** – A Server provides information in a specific protocol, WWW, FTP Gopher, etc. It is usually associated with an IP address and a domain name. There can be multiple virtual servers for a single Log Data Source.

> **Site** – A site is identified by a domain name and file/URL prefix. The site defines a collection of files or pages. There can be multiple sites for a single Server.

> **Referrer** – A Referrer is the URL of a server that originated a visit to your site.

> **Category** – A category is a value in a site vocabulary.

> **Dimension** – A dimension is a range of values upon which results are grouped in a table or graph.

> **Dimension Hierarchy** – The relationships between dimensions form a hierarchy in the Usage database.

The concept of a Category is further defined into several different types:

- ➤ **Hit** – Most people think of a hit as a request for a resource. When a visitor requests a page, there may be many hits that are counted for that page, depending on the resources contained on the page. A resource may be a page, image, a protocol, (like FTP), a gateway (like a form), or perhaps a video or audio file. A hit is also a line in a log file.

- ➤ **Request** – A Request provides a concept to accumulate hits into something more meaningful to an audience. For example, if a page has many images, they all might be considered hits, but they all might be accumulated to count for one Request.

- ➤ **Visit** – Hits and Requests are further accumulated into Visits. A Visit is defined by the session where a visitor first links into a site and is ended when a period of time has passed without any further requests to the site, usually 30 minutes.

- ➤ **User** – The user is a concept to identify an individual, which is no easy feat in Internet technology. The Usage Import program may look for cookies to identify a user. Other methods may involve a registered user name. If none of these methods exist, the final method will be to look for a host name.

- ➤ **Organization** – An organization denotes a domain name. For example, America Online, AOL, is an organization frequently seen in web logs as there are millions of users at AOL. However, there are plenty of instances where you may find rich data in organization names where individual companies have their own ISP facilities. I've seen many instances where both prospects and competitors could be identified roaming around a company's Web site and being recorded in the site's logs.

Database Setup

Usage Analysis can be performed with either Microsoft Access or SQL Server. The database implementation decision is made during Site Server installation. If you choose to use the Microsoft Access database then the setup of Site Server is automatic. The SQL Server setup requires a little more effort. Microsoft has provided a database setup wizard to make the task easier for those that are not familiar with SQL Server. However, even for the SQL Server Pro the wizard is valuable because it does a quick and painless job of not only creating the necessary database but also loading meta data such as country and postal codes.

The Database Setup Wizard

It only takes a few minutes to run the database setup wizard, and the following screen shots may simplify a view of the process, but not by much. If you choose the typical setup you will need to know your login for SQL Server and make a choice on database disk locations, and that's about it.

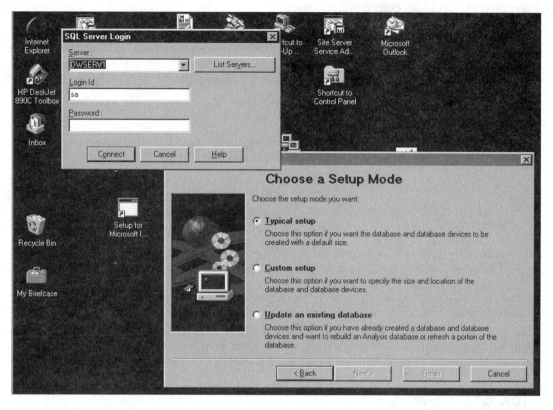

The resulting work of the wizard is the creation and loading of more then seventy-five tables, seven views, and almost a dozen stored procedures.

While taking the 'typical' route for product installation is best for many products, it will almost never suffice for the Site Server database wizard. The issue here is the fact that each user's Web site logs will vary tremendously in size. Therefore, the Custom option of the database wizard is the best choice in most instances. By selecting this option, you will be prompted with a series of questions to help you determine the size of your logs and how they will impact your need for analysis data.

There's always a group of folks that wants to shun the wizards and go it alone. Yes, we know you're out there, that hearty do it yourself group of folks that always has some unique requirement that circumvents use of a wizard. If you fit in this group, you're in for a tough time. Site Server does not provide SQL scripts for you to create or load your tables. Perhaps one solution is to run the wizard to create a test database and then create your own scripts that you can further modify.

After you have performed setup via the database wizard or your own procedures, you are ready to perform the core tasks involved in Usage Analysis.

Starting the Usage Analyzer

You can start Usage Analysis either from a Windows interface or from the Command Line. While we spend most of this chapter presenting the concepts of using Usage Analysis via Windows, you may ultimately find more value in the Command Line interface. The reason for this is that you will want to set up procedures so that Usage Analysis is performed automatically, perhaps on the first Monday of every month.

The Command Line Interface

Type in `uimport.exe -help` at your NT command prompt and you will receive a pop-up window with the following help for Usage Analysis command line operation.

```
UImport.Exe [-?]
UImport.Exe [-silence] db=<Database> source=<LDS1>:<LogFileName1>
[source=<LDS1>:<LogFileName2>] [source=<LDS2>:<LogFileName3>]...
[messagelog=<filename>]
```

IIS 4 introduces the Windows Scripting Host, a language neutral scripting engine that will be a core part of Windows 2000. The Windows Scripting Host will make future automation of Usage Analyzer even easier.

The Windows Interface

After you perform database setup you will begin the visitor analysis process by starting the Usage Anlyzer import program. From the Windows Start menu make your way to Site Server Analysis and start the Usage Import program.

Quick Start Steps

The first time you start the Usage Import program you will receive the following message box:

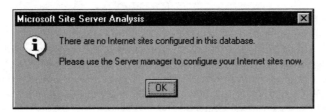

By way of this introduction you will come to understand that the Usage Import program has three panes from which you will operate the programs features: the **Server Manager**, the **Import Manager**, and The **Import History Manager**.

Let's take a quick look at the process involved in performing Log Import.

You've already told your Web Server to collect logs via Extended Logging. You've also set up your database. The following are the steps to produce information via your logs.

In the Server Manager you will identify the major entities involved in the production of information:

> **Add a data source** – First you will create a pointer to the log files that your web server has been creating.

> **Add a server** – Then you will create one or more servers. In a commercial ISP operation, each hosted site is considered a multihomed server, because the IP addresses are unique. In an Intranet you have more virtual sites, within the one IP address of an Intranet server.

> **Add a site** – You will add a site denoting virtual directories. Once again, in a commercial hosting operation, the server and the site are pretty synonymous, albeit this is a conceptual simplification.

> **Rename Servers and Sites** – You will want to perform a renaming of the objects that are created by the Usage Analyzer. The program provides default names like Server 1 or Site 2.

Next, the Import Manager is used to perform the actual input of information into the Usage Analyzer.

> **Import Log Files** – Finally, you will import your log files. In this activity, the data from your Web logs is inserted into Microsoft Access or SQL Server.

The Usage Import program has a few tools that can be used to enhance Log data:

> **Augment data** – There are four additional activities that can help you improve the information you produce from Web log data:

> **Resolving IP addresses** – Perform a reverse DNS lookup to get a domain name for your IP addresses.

> **Performing Whois queries** – Further define IP addresses by finding geographic data on IP addresses.

> **Performing HTML title lookups** – Associate Web page titles with site pages.

> **Importing Custom Data** – The Custom Import program will import personalization, advertisement, and author data.

> **Run Reports** – The Report Writer will process data into Microsoft Office documents.

Finally, the Import History Manager is useful for maintaining log data and operational histories.

Configuring Usage Import

We begin the process by defining the entities that will be involved in the analysis process. The Usage Analyzer Server Manager is the first pane you will use. You will use the Server Manger to define Log Data Sources, Servers and Sites.

Whether you are managing an Intranet or a Commercial hosting operation, you will initially spend a lot of time with the Server Manager, and then return periodically to update changes in new Web sites. If you don't get the initial configuration of your operation correct, then your log import may run for hours and load a lot of incorrect and useless data into your database. At that point you will be introduced to the Import History Manager, which can help you correct the situation. However, the advice here is to get the configuration right from the start.

405

The following screen shot will provide an overview for a configuration scenario. In this situation, two log data sources have been configured. The log data sources relate to physical Web servers. The Web servers are not multihomed, and each one has only one IP address, meaning one server. Also, there is only one web site defined per server. All the names have been provided by defaults in the Usage Import Server Manager.

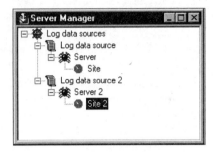

Now, let's see how this is done.

Log Data Sources

First off, we'll need a pointer to a log data source. The log data source represents the logging of one Web Server. Conceptually, you should associate one log data source to each Web server in your installation. To initiate the process, you can select the Edit menu from the Server Manager panel and then select the New Log Data Source menu item. A second, perhaps easier, approach is to double click on the log data sources icon on the initial Server Manager panel.

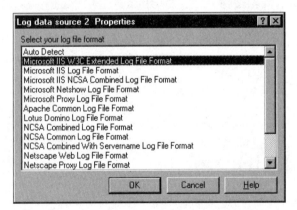

You will be presented with a dialog box allowing you to configure your log source to the many different formats offered by Site Server. If you select Auto Detect then the Usage Analyzer will perform the diagnosis of a log's format. What could be easier?

Since I might assume that most readers will be using IIS 4.0 as a Web server, then most of the readers will probably configure their logs for the Microsoft IIS W3C Extended Log File Format, as recommended. One note of caution is to point out that the new Microsoft IIS W3C format is different from the formats that were previously offered on IIS 3.0. You will find this out when you try to perform your first import of old log data. However, don't worry; a quick return to the properties of the Log Data Source will allow you to easily reconfigure your log format selection, which of course is not to be confused with reformatting the actual log.

Server Definition

When you click OK on defining a Log Data Source, you will immediately be presented with the opportunity to configure a Server, as shown below. You can define a Server at any time, by using the View menu of the Usage Import program, to select the Server Manager pane. Once you have the Server Manager on screen, you can select the New Server item from the Edit menu. However, the ability to select a new Server ID is dependent upon having your mouse positioned on an existing Log Data Source or an existing Server. Conceptually, you should equate the Server Manager concept of a Server with an IP address. In situations such as a Commercial ISP Hosting Operation you will have lots of Servers for a single Log Data Source, because the Web Server is multihomed and each hosted site typically is provided a unique IP address. In Intranet situations, you will more likely have a single IP address for a physical machine, but perhaps may virtual directories, or Sites, within that one IP address. If you are using a Proxy Server then we have a different situation, which we will discuss shortly.

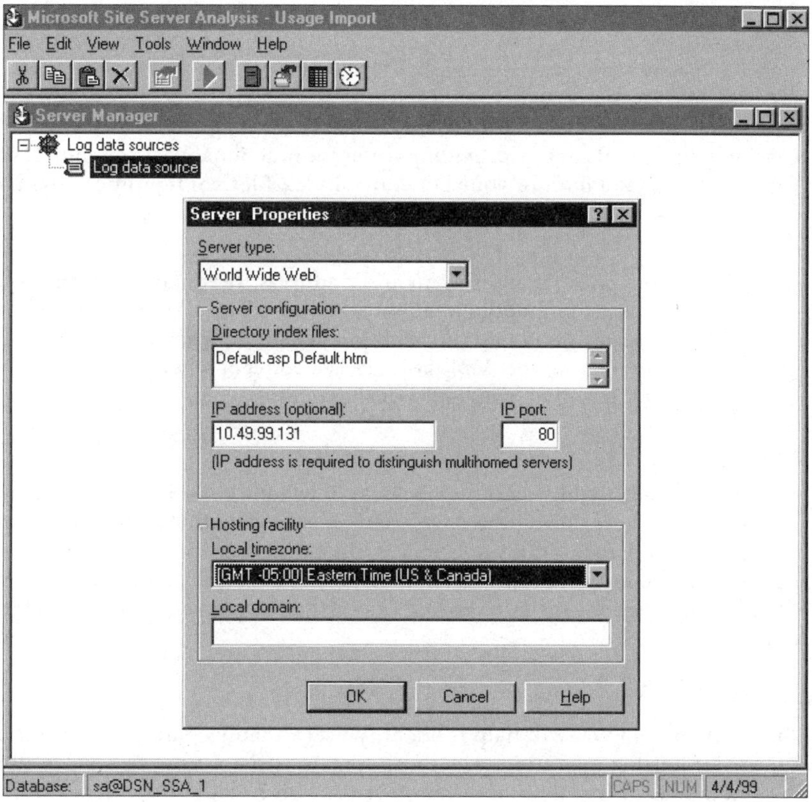

Server Type

When you are presented with the Server configuration dialog window, you will need to specify a few key details. If you selected AutoDetect during your Log Data Source configuration, then a Server type of World Wide Web will probably be the default.

Directory Index files

The entry for Directory Index files is required to target the site page that is returned to the user when they key in your domain name from somewhere out on the Internet. In other words, if a browser requests http://www.yourcompany.com, then what page would they see as your homepage? Historically, Web servers were somewhat limited in specifying the file name for the home page. You would see restrictions that dictated that you name your homepage something like index.html, default.html, or homepage.html. In IIS 4.0 you have more flexibility and can pretty much define a unique homepage name for any site. As you may notice, in our example we allow both default.htm and default.asp.

The Usage Analyzer will count all derivations your directory index files as being one entry point for your site. In this example, a user could enter your web from three different URLs but they would be counted as one page:

```
http://www.yourcompany.com
http://www.yourcompany.com/default.htm
http://www.yourcompany.com/default.asp
```

In instances where your ASP page is providing different functionality from your HTM page, you would be wise not to include both in your Directory Index files configuration text area.

IP Address

Next, you are offered the option of entering in an IP address. If you are a commercial ISP hosting operation then there isn't anything optional about this entry. The IP address is the mechanism that the Usage Analyzer will use to divide up the Web log entries between the various multihomed sites you may find on a commercial server. Multihoming is a concept where several different IP addresses are assigned to one server, usually a single physical machine.

Local Time Zone

The Usage Analyzer needs to understand your local time zone in order to produce reports that will show you visitation variances during the day. There may be situations where a physical server is in one time zone but the audience for a site is located in a different zone. We had one situation where a site that had an audience in Colorado was actually hosted in North Carolina, two time zones distant. Therefore, the visitor usage for the site showed that visitation peaked much later during the day, and into the evening hours.

Local Domain

In setting the local domain you will help to identify usage that is coming from your own organization or from within your hosting operation. The local domain name is used to resolve situations where a host name is ambiguous during the importing process. This is caused by users that might approach your site from a local area network, as opposed to the Internet. Obviously, this would be of great value in determining usage in an Intranet for a large company campus (a LAN environment). In order to configure this entry you would type your domain, such as mycompany.com.

Site Definition

You will automatically be offered the opportunity to configure a site as you complete the configuration of a server. You can create a site at any time by activating the **Server Manager** pane of the Usage Import program from the **View** menu. You can then use the **Edit** menu to select the creation of a **New Site**. However, you must position your mouse on an existing site or server within the Server Manger pane to enable the **New Site** menu sub-selection. Conceptually, I think of the Usage Analyzer concept of a site as being synonymous with the IIS concept of a virtual directory, although I suspect there are some technical differences not worth discussing.

In an example of a company Web site with one server, there are different virtual directories defined under IIS 4.0, and they look as follows:

```
http://www.mycompany.com/
http://www.mycompany.com/support/
http://www.mycompany.com/products/
http://www.mycompany.com/partners/
```

In this example, the different sites are the root at /, but there are also sites at /support/, /products/, and /partners/.

You would therefore create four sites. Each site would have www.mycompany.com as the Home page URL. In the URL path extension you would enter /, /support/, /products/, etc.

In the following example we have entered the URL for the Microsoft example site **Exair**, which is a good site to explore the example features of the Usage and Content Analyzers. It is found in the directory:

```
Microsoft Site Server\Sites\Tutorial\Exair
```

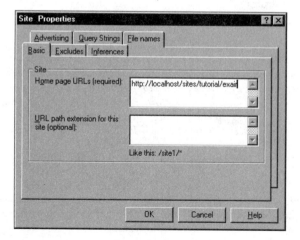

There are several additional options that are selected via the tabs on the **Site Properties** dialog window. However, at this point you've completed the major activities involved in defining a Web operation for analysis. Before we proceed with these details, let's recap an example that shows how a Web operation might be configured using the Usage Import program.

In the following example we have defined two log data sources that represent two production Web servers, WebHost1 and WebHost2. On the physical WebHost1 web server machine we have three virtual servers identified through their IP addresses, which I have named: AcmeCompany_126, Entrepreneur_135, and WidgetsR_US_124. We will discuss the naming of sites later in this chapter, but I think it's a good tip to append the last part of the quad IP address to the name of the virtual server.

Finally we have identified several Sites within the virtual servers. In the case of the AcmeCompany site there is only one Site. However, the WidgetR_US company has several virtual directories that are defined as Sites. Perhaps they have defined a site where users keep FrontPage type forms, WidgetsForms. They have also placed their cyberstore in a separate site. All three of their sites are virtual directories and might have separate global.asa files in operation.

Within this section we will summarize the activities involved in:

- Excluding data
- Dealing with advertising
- Customizing inferences
- Managing query strings
- Controlling file names

The Usage Analyzer will produce a lot of valuable information with minor configuration customization. However, there are many Web site situations where you can dramatically improve the value of the information by performing some configuration fine tuning. Most of these fine tuning operations are quickly entered from the Site Properties window, but understanding all the dozens of configuration options will require many hours of study plus trial and error testing to review the results obtained during log importation. It is best to start with a smaller log and work toward larger log imports.

Excluding data

There are four types of data that might be excluded from Usage Analysis: **Hosts**, **Files**, **Directories**, and **Crawlers**. Excluding data will improve the accuracy of your reporting and also reduces the time for conducting a log import (which is a significant task).

> **Hosts** – Situations that may require host exclusion include skipping the requests that are made by your Web site development personnel. Another situation may be to exclude requests from business partners in order to more correctly understand visits by customers. In any event, you can exclude hosts from the Excludes tab of the Site Properties dialog window. You can use both IP addresses and node names to perform exclusions. You can also use the asterisk as a wild card character. So, for example, "10.49.99.*" would eliminate all requests from workstations on my intranet by using an IP address. In using a node name you could specify "*.mycompany.com" and eliminate all the hosts that are resident on mycompany.com. *Remember to include your exclusions in quotation marks.*

> **Files** – You can exclude files on the same dialog window where you exclude hosts. As you may remember from previous discussions, when a visitor requests a page the there are hits registered for every graphic that is included on that page. Therefore, the number of hits your site receives tends to be much larger then the number of actual pages requested. Most Web site analysis programs make adjustment for this fact and Usage Analyzer is no different. By default, Usage Analyzer will adjust your hit and bandwidth calculations for file types of: "*.gif", "*.jpeg", "*. Jpg", and "*.cdf". You may want to add additional file types, perhaps "*.wav", or "*.mp3". In a more unusual situation, you may want to exclude references to pages that represent navigation in order to focus only on the pages that deliver true content. Use quotation marks and wildcard characters, such as the asterisk, to list your file for exclusion. Also, remember to place a space between entries.

> **Directories** – Eliminating directories is a twist on the manner that you entered your Sites. In a typical site configuration you will have a root directory and then various sub directories. When configuring a Site, you would specify the root as "/" or perhaps list virtual directories as "/mysubsite/". The point here is that if you do not specify a root, but only specify sub directories, then you can effectively eliminate directories that are to be included in analysis by not listing them as part of the Site. The Basic tab of the Site Properties dialog window is where you configure a site's directories.

> **Crawlers** – Eliminating Crawlers seems like a good idea, but the option is not the default. You will probably want to enable the option. As you may remember, a Crawler is a request that is made by a program that is cataloging the Web for a search engine. In most situations these requests do not represent data that reflects the audience for your site and you should eliminate the Crawler activity from your analysis. Excluding Crawlers is not performed on a Site basis. You will select this option for all Analysis, and so it is an option of the Usage Import program. You will need to select Tools | Options to find a tab item for Crawler List. Many of the popular crawlers have already been listed, all you need to do is activate a check box to enable the program exclusion feature.

Dealing with Advertising

Few topics generate as much heated debate as asking a bunch of Internet geeks how they feel about advertising. Whether you are pro or con on the subject it is factual to say that advertising is one of the primary money making activities fostering the growth of the Internet. There are even situations in which individual companies are selling banner advertisements on their intranets. So, the point here is that advertising is becoming more pervasive, and advertisers and their clients want to understand the response rates for their ads.

From the Site Server perspective, there are two types of data to help understand advertising responses: log file advertising data and AdServer data. The Usage Analyzer is focused on performing analysis on log file advertising data. As you'll see later, there are a variety of reports available for you to understand advertising, but you'll need to perform a simple configuration as part of your Site configuration in Usage Import.

From the Properties dialog window on your Site you'll need to specify two directories that relate to your advertising banner ads. The first directory or file system path specifies the location of your advertisements. You would provide an entry similar to /images/advertisements/*. *Notice that quotation marks are not used here.* The second file system path points to the CGI bin directory where typically you find a CGI program that performs redirection of requests for banner advertisements. Perhaps your entry will look like: /cgi-bin/ad_redirect*. As another alternative, you might have an ASP page that performs this same redirection function, in this situation you will provide the URL for that page.

> *By this point, some of you may have noticed that the Usage Analyzer is terribly inconsistent in the way that it requires you to provide data. Sometimes you need to delimit data with quotation marks and other times you don't. In other situations the operation of the program will vary depending on how you supply wildcard characters such as the asterisk. Usually the quotation marks are important to delimit data in situations where multiple arguments will be supplied within one text area.*

Customizing Inferences

It's pretty clear that tracking Site usage wasn't in the minds of the designers of the Web (as if one could really attribute the evolution of the Web to a few individuals). By way of that introduction, you need to understand that the goal of any Site Analysis software is pretty elusive when it comes to creating a picture of site visitation that represents reality. There are a number of issues:

> ➤ Many objects on one page count as hits
>
> ➤ Web caching hides true usage
>
> ➤ Visitors can't be identified

The Usage Analyzer will attempt to compensate for the issues of Web visitation just listed. While the program uses a fair measure of common sense and industry best practices, you will still need to make configuration adjustments to meet the unique needs of your operations. We have already addressed the issue of excluding hit references to objects like images or sound files. The Usage Analyzer allows you to make several adjustments via the Inferences tab of a Site's Properties dialog window.

> ➤ **Missing Referrers** – is a mechanism to try and adjust the referrals for your site. First we need to assume that you are collecting referral information, but given that you are, then your referral data is likely to be skewed because of Web caching. As you may know, there are at least two types of caching currently in vogue. In the first situation, users have traditionally been able to cache web pages at their browsers in order to improve their browsing performance. In the second situation (which is a more recent development), many ISPs have increased their ability to cache entire Web sites into routers or proxy servers. One of the latest entrepreneurial ventures on the Internet are companies that provide the service of distributing your Site contents to servers that are distributed globally, and are therefore closer to the end user audience. Activating the Missing Referrers option in the Usage Analyzer is more likely to help with the first situation of End User browser caching, because, in the latter case, your Web site may never receive any indication that one of your audience has visited your site on a proxy server. If you enable the option of providing Missing Referrers then the Usage Analyzer will invoke some rules that make some adjustments in trying to detect situations where a page might be cached at the user's browser.

> **Visit End Time** – The second option of the Inferences tab allows you to specify a visit end time. The purpose of this parameter is to get a grip on the concept of what constitutes a visit. Why is this difficult? Well, unlike the more traditional design of computer applications where state data is maintained over a user's session on an application, this was obviously not part of the original vision for the Web. Over the last couple of years, various methods have been devised to create some sense of a session. The most popular method are to establish host session tracking or use cookies. By default, the Usage Analyst will try to use cookies to track visitation. In the event that this isn't a workable option, the idea of having a somewhat arbitrary cutoff time establishes the concept of a visit. Therein lies the story behind setting a Visit End time that matches your notions of how long visitors spend on your site.

> **Multiple Users with the same name** – Finally, we mention the option of ignoring user names when identifying users. This option applies to situations where you are not using cookies to identify users. If you have a site, say an intranet or extranet, where users log on via a user ID, you may have many users logging in on one login user ID, say Guest. By toggling the Multiple Users option, which is the default, you will be ignoring the logon username as a method of identifying users.

Managing query strings

Increasingly, the visit requests for a site are being generated dynamically via ASP or Java server apps. In these situations the user's request may not specify a unique site page URL but instead will have a page URL with additional querystring arguments added after a question mark separator. In this example, an ASP page will return some product information based upon the arguments to two parameters, a product type, and a color.

```
http://getProduct.asp?product=widget&color=blue
```

The analysis of query strings can become a career path unto itself. However, there are situations where analysis of query strings is quite appropriate and important. There are many situations where the majority of content on a Web site may be static brochure-type information but also contain (for example) a simple dynamically created product catalog with a low number of products. These situations make ideal candidates for performing query string site analysis using the Usage Analyzer. The key advantage in using the Usage Analyzer to import query strings lies in the idea that the parameters in the strings can become dimensions in the Analysis database. As previously introduced, a **dimension** is a range of values which are used in a table or a graph. Dimensions provide a great foundation for having the Report Writer create a great variety of reports.

> *As you look at the log analysis of query strings it will become apparent that the role of the Web analysis program for this purpose is limited. Quite frankly, in a heavily dynamic site there are simply too many different parameters and possible arguments to provide for efficient log analysis. A better alternative is to build alternate tracking mechanisms at the same time that the dynamic database driven application is being created.*

In the Microsoft example site, Exair, we show the entry that is made to identify the ASP page catalog.asp. This is the page that drives the site's product catalog.

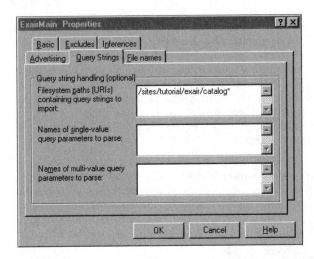

In the Microsoft sample site example provided above we are telling the Usage Analyzer to import the query string provided in the first text area. The program will not import any query strings by default.

In the second and third text areas of the dialog window, we need to provide additional specification on how to parse the parameters that exist within the query string. All you need to do is provide the name of the parameters (in quotes, with spaces between your parameters). Differentiating between single valued and multi-valued parameters will help the Usage Analyzer perform the import more efficiently. In our above example, using the `getProduct.asp` page, you would have two dimensions, `product`, and `color`.

Controlling filenames

A final option on the Site Properties dialog window provides you with a check box to enable the truncation of top level directory names. This feature is mostly of interest to ISPs who file each client's web data in directories that are labeled by client name.

Fine Tuning your configuration

As you enter your log data sources, servers, and sites you will notice that the Usage Analyzer does not provide any dialog windows to offer you an opportunity to provide naming for your resources:

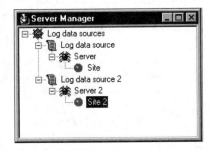

The solution for resource naming is to let your mouse cursor rest on any one resource for a second or so. You will notice that the selection of a resource is then boxed and you are allowed to change the label of the resource. Obviously, you will probably want to choose your own label that matches the name of the resource. However, in the author's operations we also add an IP address at the end of the server names. In this manner we can easily relate each virtual server back to its IP address configuration.

Specifying your default log directory

You are almost ready to start importing your log files. However, before you start the real work of the Usage Analyst you can make your life a little easier by customizing the default directory where the Usage Analyst can find you log files. From your Tools menu you can click on Options and then click on the Default Directories tab. You will want to enter or browse so that you eventually wind up pointing to the directory where you specified that IIS, or your log source Web server deposit log data.

Importing Logs

Finally, you are ready to import your log data. Log importing and data analysis are the activities where you will spend most of your time after you have successfully configured the Usage Analyst.

Steps in the import process

If you have not already done so, then start Usage Import and use the View menu to bring up the Import Manager window. You'll need to select your Log Data Source from the panel at the bottom of the window. If you're using a single Web server with the Usage Analysis then you are given your target server as default.

Browse your way to the directory where your log files are kept and make some log selections. Traditional Windows tricks such as selecting a group of logs with the *shift* key, or individual logs with the *control* key works great in this window. You will need to click Open to close the log selection process. You will also need to click the Add to List button to create an inventory of logs that will be imported.

Then you push the Start Import button and wait.

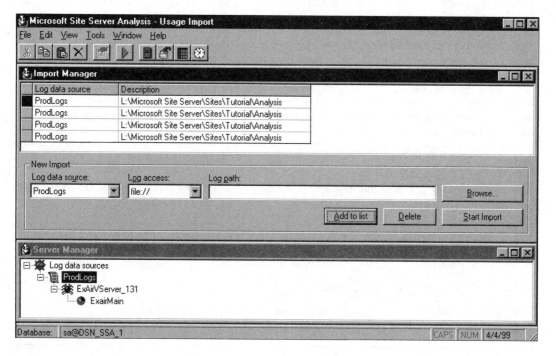

Interpreting Import Statistics

Depending on the size of your log files you may wait a considerable time while the Usage Analyst parses through the data and performs the insertions to place data in SQL Server.

The import statistics window, which appears after an import, provides you with information on the import. In the following example we have tried to import the data that is provided as part of the Microsoft Exair site. The Usage Import Statistics report provided here indicates an unpleasant situation I hope you avoid. Look over the statistics and see if you can find a problem. As a hint, it isn't the statistic that says 57 hits were client errors, but that's close.

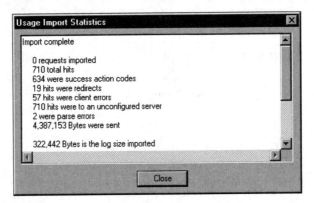

Yes, the problem is that 710 hits were to an unconfigured server. This means that the Usage Analysis essentially ignored all my data on import. This is caused because I didn't enter the Site definition URL of the Exair site as it was listed within the URLs of the Web logs. The details of the error are not important here. It's a pretty good idea to copy the text within the Usage Import Statistics window and save it in a file. You may need to refer back to your import statistics as you review the reports of your analysis later. In my experience there are frequently questions about the content you will see on the reports that will make you wonder how your import impacted your reports.

It's a good thing we didn't try to import several months worth of data. Usage Analyst will churn through all your imported log records, even if you don't have your Site URLs defined correctly. Importing logs can take more then a few moments. Another lesson here it to try to import a small amount of your own data and then look at your statistics and reports. If necessary, you can go back and read the configuration section of this book and spend some time on the help screens of the Usage Analyst.

The following table provides information on the messages you may receive in the import statistics window after an import:

Message	Description
Ad clicks imported	Number of hits to ad clicks.
Ad requests imported	Number of hits to ad requests.
Bytes received	Number of bytes the client sent to the server.
Bytes sent	Number of bytes the server sent to the client.

Message	Description
Hits couldn't be parsed	Number of entries in the log file that did not match the expected format and so could not be imported.
Hits were client errors	Number of hits that had a 400 response code and were not imported.
Hits were from excluded hosts	The number of hits to hosts you have excluded.
Hits were from excluded spiders	The number of hits to crawlers you have excluded.
Hits were redirects	Number of hits that had a 300 response code and were not imported.
Hits were server errors	Number of hits that had a 500 response code and were not imported.
Hits were to an unconfigured server	If the Server ID or name in the log file does not match those configured in the Server Manager, hits to that server are discarded.
Hits were to an unconfigured site	If the Site ID or name in the log file does not match those configured in the Server Manager, hits to that site are discarded.
Hits were to excluded inline images	The number of hits to file types you have excluded.
Missing referrers requests were inserted	Number of missing referrers that were inserted.
Number of open visits	Number of open visits.
Requests imported	Number of successfully imported requests.
Total hits	Number of lines in the log file.

Import Housekeeping

I found the **Import History Manager** more important then I at first though. It seems like I always have someone asking 'what if' type questions that require research with Usage Analyst. Without the Import History Manager it would be very difficult to remember and manage which logs had been imported. The Import History Manager is the tool set for deleting data out of your logs.

As you first bring up the Import History Manager you will see a variety of columns of information. You can control the columns that appear in the History Manager by using the View menu of the Usage Analyst. The columns available are:

Column	Description
Action	Lists the action (either Import, Delete, or Abort). Delete shows if you deleted a request. (If you delete an entire import, the import disappears from the Import History Manager.) Abort appears if you stop an import, if the log file overlaps option is set
Ad Clicks	Lists the number of ad clicks imported (for the entire import).
Ad Requests	Lists the number of ad requests imported (for the entire import).
Description	Depending on the action, lists the name of the first imported log file or the filter used to delete requests.
Duration	Lists the length of time the action took.
Import Size	Lists the total size of the imported log files (for the entire import).
Log Data Source	Lists the first log data source for which log files have been imported.
Requests	Depending on the action, lists the number of requests imported or the number of requests deleted.
Start Time	Lists the time that the action started.
Who	Lists who performed the action.

If you import multiple log files at one time, the import is recorded as one line in the Import History Manager. You can view which log files were imported together by double-clicking on the line, which causes an Import Detail window to appear.

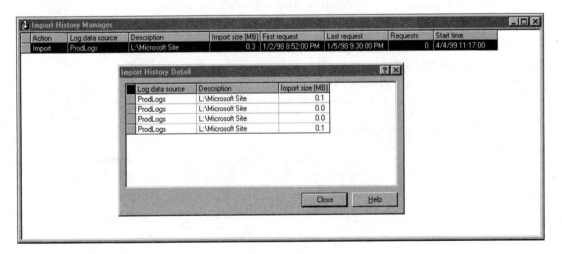

Deleting an Import

If you made an import mistake, as I demonstrated above, then you will want to delete your imports and try again. Occasionally you will want to delete some of your Imports to conserve space. If your interest in deleting Imports tends toward conserving space then I suggest you try to delete Requests, I will show you how in a moment. However, assuming that you have decided to go for the deletion of an Import, meaning a set of one or more log files imported into the database, then perform the following:

> ➤ Select your Import using the gray data button on the right of your Import History Manager.

> ➤ Click on the Edit menu item and select Delete Import. As shown in the next screenshot, you'll then get a final chance to back out, what I call a sanity check.

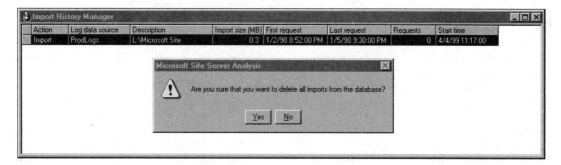

Then the Import will be extracted from the SQL Data and deleted. Once you do this, there is no recovery, no getting the data back. However, you can always re-import the data.

Deleting Requests

Deleting Requests gives you the option to filter the data you would like to delete. You will need to configure a filter by creating some sort of Boolean expression. A Boolean expression involves selecting a variable name, choosing an operator such as > = or <, and then selecting a value. The following example shows deleting requests with dates less then January 3, 1998. Note that the list box where Date is selected is labeled Dimension.

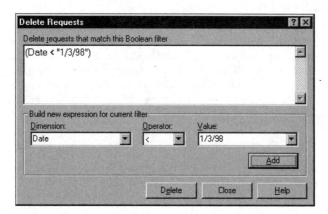

One point worth mentioning concerns the idea that deleting Imports and Requests differs in a very fundamental way. On the one hand you will be deleting a set of data that represents an Import of log files from a specific Log Data Source. However, when you delete Requests, you are deleting data across a variety of Imports that are represented within your data. Don't think that you are deleting Requests from a specific Import – this is not the case. In the example we could be deleting a lot of data when we remove all the log records that predate 1998.

Scheduling Imports

Earlier in this chapter we discussed that there is both a Win32 and a command line interface to the Usage Analyst. I like the command line interface because operations can be easily scheduled and scripted within the NT environment. However, the Usage Analyst has it's own scheduler that can save you the time of writing your own scripts.

Enriching the Data in Your Database

Once you have imported some data you can go ahead and run reports. The reports layout well in Microsoft Word and the graphics are terrific. However, you will probably notice that the information in the reports is not quite as great as it could be. Perhaps you will notice that a lot of your report labels look like IP addresses. Hmmm... getting a lot of visitors from 206.198.16... wonder where that is?

IP Resolution, Whois queries, and HTML title lookups are all ways by which you can enrich your data and make reports more informative. You can run these utilities anytime after you import your data, and you can request that they are automatically run after you perform an import, which is a good idea if you perform automatic import operations overnight. IP Resolution converts the IP addresses in your log files to domain names in the database. Whois queries build upon IP Resolution by finding out more about the domain names you resolved. You can obtain geographical data such as city, state or province, and zip code. Finally, HTML title lookup will convert references to the Web pages in your logs and resolve them to their HTML titles if they have one. All of these tasks will help to enrich your reports. I would suggest to you that these are "Must Do" items that you should pursue as part of your Usage Analyst operations routine.

You can run all three of these utilities from the Tools menu of the Usage Analyst Usage Import Program. The first task you will want to perform is IP Resolution. This is a prerequisite to performing Whois queries, which I will explain in a moment.

IP Resolution

IP resolution works on the principle of Reverse Domain Name Services. Those of you who have had some experience with a Domain Name Server will recognize the concept. In performing Reverse DNS, you can trace an IP address backwards to find its source. For example, the author's primary Web site is located at 206.198.16.29. In performing reverse DNS the search would be reversed and 29.16.198.206 would become NetSail Internet Commerce, the author's business.

IP Address Resolution results will not discover 100% of the IP addresses in your web log. In fact, the results vary. In my ISP operation the resolution typically finds domain names for 75% of the queries. However, I've seen some individual web sites will experience resolution as low as 40%. For a lot of reasons, it depends on the audience for your site. You may perform the utility and find out that all your visitors come from America Online. Of course, this may not be as useful as obtaining a list of specific companies that are visiting your site. The author's company hosts a chemical supply house and IP address resolution on the audience for this site always seems to produce great results in listing lots of individual companies who have their own domain names and IP networks on the Internet. Some Web servers, but not IIS, will perform IP Resolution for you. Having the server perform this service can save time, but it also slows down the server. It's a mixed blessing, and it's your call on which option you choose. In the author's operation we perform IP Resolution with the Usage Analyst and it runs at night. The results are great.

Be sure to examine the IP Resolution configuration options that are provided with Usage Analyst. There are three options, which you can access them via the Usage Analyst's **Tools** menu, clicking on **Options**. There is a tab devoted to IP Resolution. So, if the first time you run IP Resolution you don't find that you achieved the resolution goals you expected, then inspect the IP Resolution Options.

Cache IP resolution

As you gain experience with Usage Analyst you will want to set the Cache IP resolution low, perhaps even to zero. The Usage Analyst will remember how it performed prior resolutions. This is a great feature, but only if the UA performed your resolutions correctly.

Timeout

The Timeout feature is another one to watch out for. It has a default of one minute. However, depending on when you perform your resolutions, this can be a problem. If you try to perform resolution activity in the middle of the afternoon, then maybe you need a higher number. Of course, the higher you set the timeout, the slower your IP Resolution will run.

Resolution Batch Size

The IP Resolution code is multithreaded, and you can batch up a number of resolutions and improve the efficiency of your DNS server. (you need to point to a DNS server to use this utility.) I generally don't set this number too high, 300 is the default. The only advantage in setting the number lower is that you will receive progress indicators of the utility's run. If you perform a run in the middle of the night, then it won't make much difference.

Remember, Not all DNS servers are always set up correctly to perform Reverse DNS lookups. Be sure to check with the WebMaster who maintains your DNS server to see how the configuration of the DNS server could affect your IP Address Resolution.

As a final reminder, try scheduling your Imports and automatic running of IP Resolution at night, approximately 2 AM to 6 AM US Eastern Standard time. The Internet has less activity then and the chances of your resolution proceeding smoothly are increased.

Whois Queries

A lot of the clients of the author's consultancy really like the Usage Analyst reports that detail the geography of visitors. We are getting ahead of ourselves, but the Usage Analyst will provide you reports and charts that break down your visitor usage by specific countries. The ability to have this feature of the Usage Analyst depends on performing something called a Whois Query. In performing a Whois Query, the domain names you identified during IP resolution will be translated to determine organization names, zip codes, cities, states, and of course, the country of the visitor, or perhaps more the point, the country of the visitor's IP address. Obviously, a lot of you are probably wondering how all this works. While the details are beyond my expertise, the key fact is that the Usage Analyst has a great deal of what I would call meta data.

Meta data is basically a concept for data that describes data. In this case, part of your Usage Analyst installation process is to install a lot of data that is used to further define the data you import. The Usage Analyst has knowledge of hundreds of countries and thousands of cities. You can review this data by using the features of the Usage Analyst Custom Import program.

> *You can review your meta data by using the Custom Import program, which we will discuss later. However, one interesting exercise you can perform is to examine your Usage Analyst meta data as it sits in the SQL Server tables. For those of you who are not used to creating SQL Server queries, you can use a product like Microsoft Access to link to the Usage Analyst tables. In using Access, you use the File menu and then select Get External Data. Finally, you use the ODBC data source you already set up to link to your Usage Analyst tables. If you look at the* `tblReferenceCountry` *table you will find that 246 countries have been loaded by the Usage Analyst. In the* `tblReferenceCity` *table there are rows for 7,359 cities.*

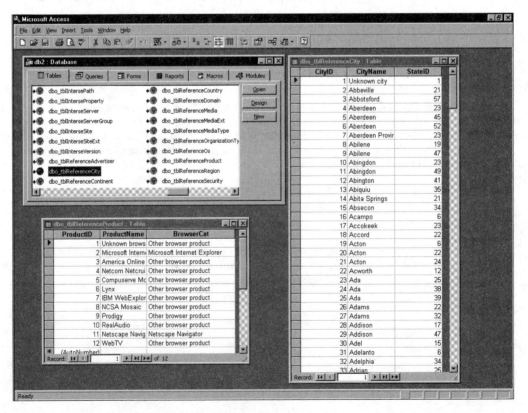

Unlike performing IP Resolution, the activity involved in performing the Whois Queries will not consume as much time, and little if any Internet bandwidth. It takes a couple of moments, but not as long as it takes to perform a Reverse Domain Name search on every IP address.

HTML Title Lookups

Finally, we have the third of what I consider 'Must Do' activities to enrich your data. As soon as you run your first set of reports you will notice that the pages that are referenced in your sites will be referred to by file name. This isn't too much of an issue, but if you perform the HTML Title Lookup feature, you will have much more descriptive reports, given the assumption that Webmasters are a little more elaborate and creative on their page titles. The HTML Title Lookup feature couldn't be more descriptive of its purpose. The feature will look at all the pages that are referenced in your import and then perform a lookup on the title of each page. The titles we are talking about are the ones that can be included in the META section of each page:

```
<TITLE>This is a title</TITLE>
```

Once again, similar to the Whois Queries, this activity takes a couple of minutes but not anywhere near the length of time that was consumed by performing IP Address Resolution. The Usage Analyst will take the time to go find every page included in an Import ant then parse the page to find the title HTML.

A message to Web page designers: you should be sure to include titles on all your pages, including the ones that are part of framed pages. The title of a framed page, meaning a button bar or a footnote bar, doesn't seem that important, as the title is rarely seen within the browser. However, the page can be referenced as an entity unto itself within the Usage Analyst, and it is much more informative to have titles on these resources. If this isn't clear, then the issue might be: How many people click on the framed button bar on the home page, as opposed to the framed footer bar? Maybe this isn't too important a controversy, but you can never tell the questions that a client might ask.

One more item to mention is the fact that the HTML Title Lookup offers a filter that you can use to customize the process to your needs. Usually I just use the filter Title="*", which will make sure that the Usage Analyst will request all HTML files and make all Title translations.

If you are reading this chapter in a linear fashion then at this point in our progress you could close down the Import Usage program and start the Usage Analyst Report Writer. We have now captured a lot of data and you can run some pretty nice reports. If you are inclined to do this, then try to run the Executive Summary from the Report Writer. It is a beautiful HTML or Microsoft Word report full of interesting charts and statistics. However, if you are prone to wanting the full tutorial prior to diving in then let's keep going. The Custom Import program will allow you to continue to polish up a great analysis package started by the Usage Import program.

Importing Custom Data

The Custom Import program provides you with a way to augment your log usage data with a variety of data from other sources. Your log data is valuable but it is not the "be all and end all" data you need to perform the task of Site Analysis. The more you get used to using all the features of Site Server, the more you can make use of a wide variety of data that can be integrated together with your log usage data.

Other sources of data include:

> ➤ Content data from the Content Analyzer
> ➤ User data from Personalization and Membership
> ➤ Advertising data from Advertising Server

And let's not stop with Site Server. The Custom Import program allows you to import data from virtually any source. The next figure illustrates all this:

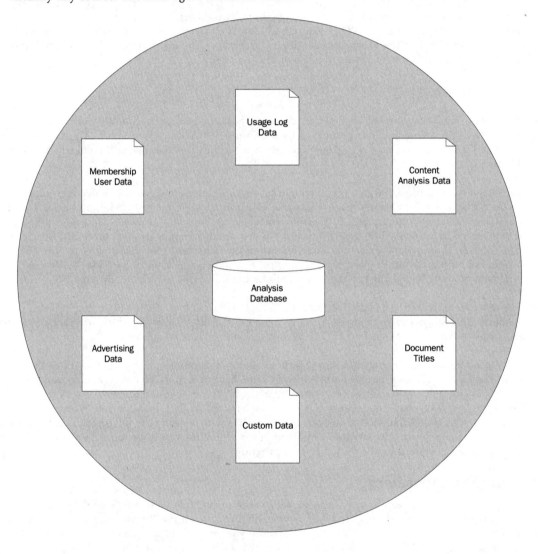

Starting the custom import application

As with the Import Usage program there are two interfaces available to give you access to Custom Import. Each interface offers its own advantages. The command line interface lends itself toward assisting you to automate your operations, although I might mention that the Custom Import program has it's own scheduler as well.

The command line is useful in cross platform (read non-Windows) environments. It is run from the MS DOS window. If you find your way to the `bin` directory of your Site Server installation directory then you can run the program. type the following to receive your initial instructions:

```
C:\Microsoft Site Server\Bin\Cmport.exe -help
```

A small window will pop up to provide you a tutorial on the Command line features of the program, as shown below. That's about it for discussing the command line, we'll spend the remainder of our time on the Win32 interface to Custom Import.

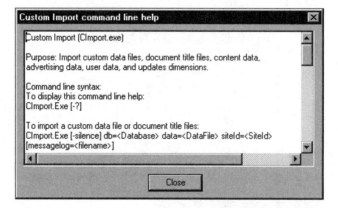

The Windows, or Win32, interface provides access to all the Custom Import features and options. As you bring up the application from the Site Server Analysis start menu item you will receive a modal welcome window (shown below) that gives you a sense that the program is divided into four basic activities. Naturally you can get to these features via the menus and tool bars of the main program window, so you will want to take note of the option of turning off this program feature (via the bottom-left check box).

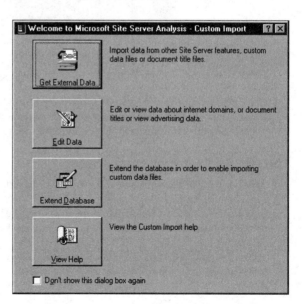

I'm going to spend some time talking about the tasks involved with the Custom Import of data. Then I'll touch lightly on the features of the program that allow you to edit data.

Dimensions and Categories

Up to this point we have managed to discuss importing data into the Usage Analyst without spending too much time presenting a concept of how that data is organized. However, as we consider importing custom data, a prerequisite to this activity involves at least a rudimentary idea of Usage Analyst data organization concepts.

The Usage Analyst is composed of dimensions and categories. You can think of a category as a database table and a dimension as a column in that table. Although Usage Analyst has dozens of tables, there are four main categories: **Organizations**, **Requests**, **Users**, and **Visits**. In each of these categories there is a further delineation of data into dimensions and subcategories. You can view the structure and hierarchy of the data organization by accessing the Custom Import Manager from the View menu item of the main program.

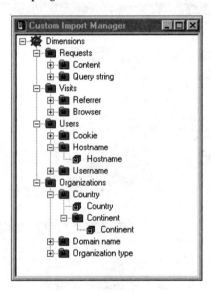

The Edit Menu of the Custom Import program will let you add additional Dimensions and Categories to your data. The Tools menu also has a utility to let you perform database maintenance and review consistency checks via the SQL Server DBCC CheckDB command.

Importing Member User Data

Importing Member or User data allows you to extend the richness of your user data, and therefore to produce more interesting reports that contain rich demographic information. To do this you would need to be using Site Server Personalization and Membership (P&M). You should also be using the new IIS 4.0 log format called Extended Logging.

P&M is configured to export values to either existing dimensions or ones you create in the Analysis database. The particulars for achieving this import depend on how you have your data set up within Membership.

By using the File menu you only need to click on Get External Data and you are presented with a multipurpose import window. What I mean by multipurpose is that the controls that are present on the right side of the window change depending on whether you want to import User data, Content data, etc. In the situation of importing User data, you are asked to login to the application server that is mapped to your Membership Server:

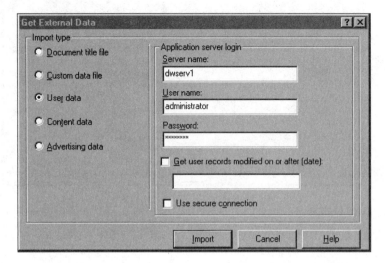

Depending on the size of your user community, the import process can take minutes, or considerably longer.

Importing Content Data

Content data is concerned with the information to be gained from the resources that are part of your site. Actually, you really don't want to import things such as your images into your Analysis Database, but if you've defined meta data on your web pages then this data is valuable for analysis. For those of you who are new to the Web, and I hope that isn't too many, the meta data is a section that is supposed to be at the top of every Web page, of at least the politically correct and socially graceful Web pages anyway. The joke here is that the meta data is optional, but it's increasing in importance for a lot of reasons that go beyond usage analysis. This topic is talked about in more detail in the Content Analyst support materials, so we won't go into details. However, page meta data allows you to identify the type of information kept on a page, as well as the Author and the Topic of the content. All of this can easily be imported using the Custom Import program.

You will need to have used the Site Server Content Analyst prior to importing Content Data. The Content Analyst creates a project file with a .wmp extension. It is this file that you will import using the features of the Custom Import program. Here we are showing the import of the Microsoft demonstration site, Exair:

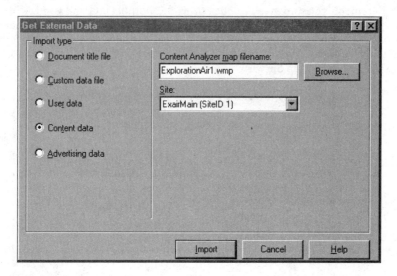

Editing Custom Data

There are several features of the Custom Import program that will assist you in various tailoring activities that will enrich the references in your reports. The three features are:

> ➤ The ability to enhance Internet Domain names
> ➤ Providing additional Document Titles
> ➤ Enriching Advertising data.

Internet Domains

When running a Whois Query there is some risk that you may not be able to resolve all your domain names to geographic information. The Internet Domains feature will allow you to manually enter organizational information such as organization names or zip codes for domains. You will want to perform this activity after you attempt a Whois Query.

Document Titles

You can augment the document titles that you resolved when you ran your HTML Title lookup in Usage Import. You can selectively edit individual titles, or import an entire document title file that will batch load titles for your documents. In future HTML Title lookups you will want to use a filter of Title="" so that the changes you make here in Document Titles will not be overwritten.

Advertising Data

If you have enabled Advertising Data when you performed Usage Import, then your ad clicks are stored in a separate portion of the database, that is to say, different dimensions. However, references to your ad clicks are stored as file names, which may not be as descriptive as you'd like when it comes time to produce reports. Therefore, the Custom Import program provides you with a feature for adding your own data to replace file name references, in the same sense that you did during HTML Title lookups. In this advertising situation you can associate campaigns, advertisers, or advertisements with file names.

Running the Standard Reports

We've covered a lot of ground, but, unless you took a shortcut, we still haven't produced any analysis. We have not run a report. The Report Writer allows you to generate a great variety of pre-designed reports and you can create your own. I would image that most users will find the pre-designed reports adequate, because there are dozens of report options. And the reports look great. You can opt for either HTML, Microsoft Word, or Excel formats, and the content of the reports is full of useful graphics (like charts), and definitions that non-technical business type Web users will find useful. If you are unfamiliar with Usage Analyst reports, then you are in for a treat. I love it when my clients are astonished to understand their visitation stats. What are the top ten companies visiting their site? What countries are represented by the visitors? How much bandwidth are they using on that shared T1 pipe? All of these questions are easily answered by the Report Writer. The following is a sample of a Microsoft Word report that shows you the general layout and quality of the graphics included in the report:

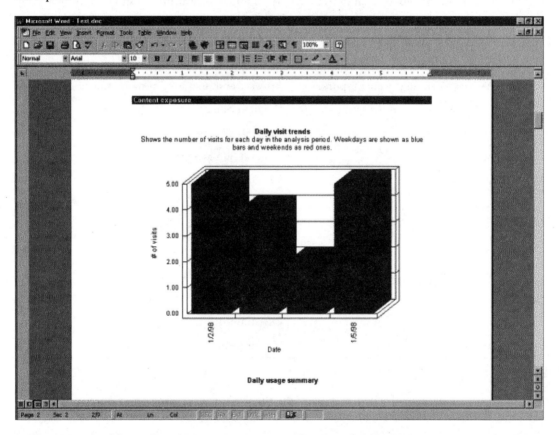

Before we get any further, a word of caution is in order. You should make sure you close Usage Import before starting Report Writer. The Report Writer has three interfaces, as we have discussed for some of the other Usage Analyst programs. The three interfaces: WebAdmin, Command Line, and Windows (Win32) all allow access to some of the features of the program. Only the Win32 interface provides full access to all features.

Report Types

I've divided the types of report into:

> ➢ Detail and Summary reports
> ➢ Site Server reports
> ➢ Intranet reports
> ➢ Advertisement reports

Detail and Summary Reports

The following table provides information on the standard report definitions available in the Detail and Summary folders of the Report Writer catalog. While the report definitions in each folder answer similar questions, the report definitions in the Detail folder answer the questions in more detail:

Report	Purpose
Bandwidth report	Bandwidth and net usage stats.
Browser and operating system report	Browser and operating system information.
Comprehensive site analysis report	Detailed Site analysis.
Content report	Analysis of content resources.
Executive summary	General Site activity.
Geography report	Visitation by geography.
Hits report	Server hit analysis.
Organization report	Organizational analysis.
Path report	Path analysis.
Referrer report	Referring organizations.
Request report	Most popular and least requested documents.
User report	User time spent on site.
Visit report	Visitor trends.

Site Server Reports

The following table provides information on the standard reports available to you if you have imported data from other Site Server features:

Report	Purpose
Advertising summary	Ad click rate statistics.
Commerce Server Top product	Products being browsed.
Content	Content analysis data of Types, Topics and Authors.

Report	Purpose
Content and rule	P&M rules execution stats.
Microsoft NetShow report	Understand the performance and usage of your NetShow media server.
Search data, Search trends	Search usage over time.
Search top query	Identify the keywords users are submitting for searches.
Tags (Ad Server data)	The number of times a tag was passed as a part of a taglist to the Ad Server `GetAd` call.
Top user	Users' most common attributes.
User list	List users in the P&M database that have been imported.
Users by content attribute	Correlation of user attributes to content attributes.

Intranet Reports

The following table provides information on the intranet reports:

Report	Pupose
Intranet content	Intranet content usage.
Intranet traffic by department	Visitation by department.
Proxy report	Site visitation via Proxy Server.

Advertising Reports

The following reports are available if you have enabled log file advertising data:

Report	Purpose
ABVS-compliant report	ABVS information.
Advertisement detail report	Advertisement traffic information.
Advertising detail report	Advertising performance.
Advertising overview report	Advertising Overview.
Advertising placement report	Advertisement placement effectiveness.
BPA-compliant report	BPA information.

Analyzing Usage Data

Previously we discussed the Content Analyzer focusing on analyzing resources as opposed to visitors. However, that isn't exactly true. The Content Analyzer and the Usage Analyzer work together. The Content Analyzer lets you review the usage on any one resource and it has a great feature that lets you animate usage data.

Importing Usage Data

You begin the usage analysis process by selecting the Import Usage Data... menu item from the Tools menu in the Content Analyzer main window. You will be presented with a dialog window similar to that shown in the screenshot below:

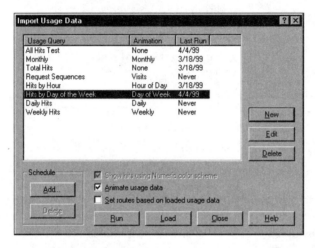

The Content Analyzer comes with many pre-built queries that let help you import usage data. Like almost everything in the Content Analyzer, you can create your own and build a custom library of import queries. The predefined queries are:

- Total Hits
- Hits by Hour
- Hits by Day of the Week
- Daily Hits
- Weekly Hits
- Monthly Hits
- Request Sequences

If you have already read the material on Usage Analysis and performed the sample exercises in importing data, then you can press the Run button and perform an import on the data that pertains to the Microsoft demo site, Exploration Air. Here we have selected the query to review hits by the day of the week. This query lends itself toward usage animation. Only the queries involving time can be animated. After you press the run button, you will be presented with a database login window similar to the one in the figure below:

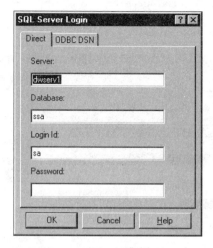

The window and tabs presented in this window are pretty standard for database logins. You should also notice there is a tab that lets you specify an ODBC connection object. After you log in to your Usage database, a couple of moments may pass while the data query and analysis proceeds. A window will inform you of progress:

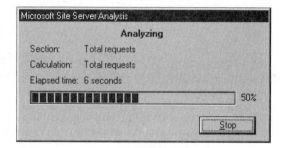

Soon you will be presented with a 'query finished' message that asks you if you want to load your data. At this point you should respond with a **Yes**. You may receive the following message:

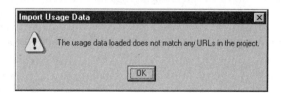

In this situation the URL that you used to import your data in the Usage Import program does not match the URL that you used to create your Content Analyzer project. In the Microsoft examples they suggest using the name `LocalHost` to denote your Web Server, other options might include the IP address of the machine, or the machine node name, which in my case is `dwserv1`. If you mix any of these valid addressing schemes, then your usage animation will fail to load data.

For those of you who have experienced success to this point you should have a screen that looks similar to the one shown below. In this example you are presented with a color legend at the bottom right and an animation control panel at the upper right.

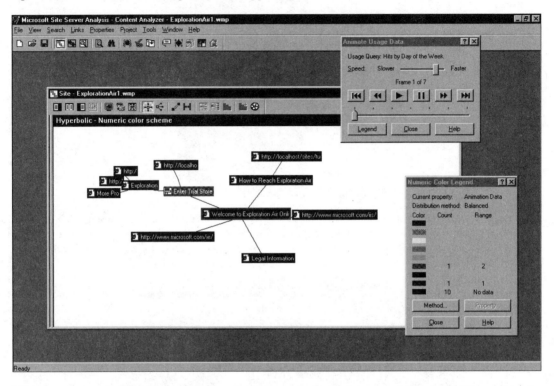

When you press the play button on the animation control panel (upper right), you will see the colors in your hyperbolic pane change for each resource as the day of the week changes.

While the hits by day of the week provides a simple example, the hits by hour can produce a fantastic report on site usage for some sites. One of my wish list items for the Content Analyzer is some way to easily export the Usage Animation into some sort of multimedia animation like an AVI or MPEG.

One of the great uses for Content Analyzer animation is the monitoring of banner ad usage. There is a great deal of interest in understanding which banner advertisements are popular and at what times of the day.

Summary

In summary I believe we could spend more time talking about the multitude of features that will let you customize the Content Analyzer to your unique needs. We could also discuss more tips for setting up scheduling and automation processes. However, for the most part I think I've covered all the features in a pretty deep level of detail, and you can feel comfortable that there aren't any features left untouched.

The future of the Content Analyzer is probably very different to the version we see today. There are new developments in programming environments like ASP and XML that will continue to put a great emphasis on site analysis, but will also demand new features beyond those offered in Content Analysis. In a sense, the Content Analyzer is one of the first products for establishing a formal software engineering quality test plan for Web sites.

We've also looked at the Usage Analysis facilities offered by Usage Import, Custom Import and the Report Writer. Through these you can assemble a pretty good tool kit to perform a wide variety of statistical reports of great interest to the business users of your company or organization. For most companies, the additional time spent in mastering Site Server Analysis can easily be repaid in the new marketing and network analysis information produced from data that is probably untapped but sitting within your organization today.

12

Delivering Direct Mail Packages

Have you ever tried to send email from a web page? Microsoft has made this relatively easy using **CDONTS** (Collaboration Data Objects for NT Server) objects; or there are multitudes of third party components that are equally easy to use. Now, have you ever tried sending email from a web page to 10000 users? CDONTS objects don't fair too well under these conditions. With the built-in CDONTS object you can either build a cc: list with 10000 users (not a great idea as you'd be exposing all the email addresses), or do something similar to this:

1. Create the mail object.
2. Create the mail body and subject, possibly customized for each user.
3. Send the email individually to each user.
4. Loop for each email address.

This doesn't work out too well either. First of all, it is very processor intensive on the same machine that IIS is trying to serve up pages to site visitors. We can always separate the processing load onto different machines, however, if you are like me, this is not always within scope of the project. Secondly, it is prone to errors.

Site Server 3.0 can help make this mail delivery process more efficient with its **Direct Mail** component, which is essentially a bulk mailing service.

Direct Mail streamlines the delivery process by allowing you to develop a **mail package** that includes a list of recipients based on information contained within the Membership Directory. When the mailing is ready to be sent, Direct Mail loops on your behalf for each recipient within the list. There is not a significant difference in performance whether you perform the looping as described in steps 1 through above, or whether Direct Mail loops for you, although the overhead of using ASP script to perform the looping is slightly heavier than letting Direct Mail do this for you. However, one important difference is the fact that Direct Mail can send the mail essentially as a background process, calling on the ASP processing as necessary. This is not the case if you perform the loop yourself, as the ASP page is tied up until processing has completed.

Direct Mail is considered to be a sub-component of Personalization & Membership (P&M); however, as we will see throughout this chapter, its interaction is not just restricted to P&M. In fact, a great feature of Direct Mail is its ability to interact with the Analysis component of Site Server. We are able to generate a list of recipients that is constrained by our specific criteria. For instance, we can just target users who clicked on a given Banner Ad, or users who bought something within the last month.

How Direct Mail Fits Within Microsoft's Web Architecture

We can see how Direct Mail fits within Microsoft's Web Architecture from a processing perspective by examining the diagram below. It was a little confusing to us at first how Direct Mail's process flow actually occurred. This was a result of the online documentation focus of describing how its various pieces can be distributed across different hardware elements. If you're like us, you probably learn things much faster from a procedural point of view.

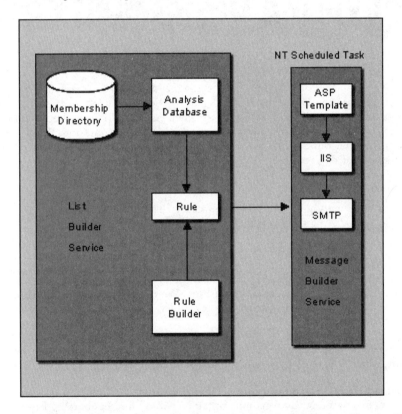

From our vantage point, the driving event for kicking off Direct Mail is initiated by the NT Scheduler service. The scheduler is in charge of executing, i.e. sending the mail package at the appropriate time. It encompasses the List Builder Service and the Message Builder Service that Direct Mail uses to construct and send the packages.

Once activated by the NT Scheduler, the List Builder Service is executed. This service draws upon three major elements of Site Server: the analysis database generated from the Analysis component; the rule set generated by Direct Mail's Rule Builder; and the Membership Server found within the Personalization and Membership component. The analysis database is used in conjunction with the Rule Builder to establish a Rule-Set, which ultimately generates the mailing list from the Membership Directory. Alternatively, a distribution list can be used. Either way, the result of List Builder Service is the generation of the mailing list, which is then used as the input into the Message Builder Service.

The Message Builder Service uses an **ASP message template,** which is used as the e-mail message body. This is a great feature of Direct Mail; we are able to customize our e-mail message by writing the content with standard ASP or HTML pages. Once the message body is assembled, the e-mail is built to the SMTP standard and forwarded to the SMTP server for delivery. As you will see later, the configuration of these services is controlled via a GUI.

About the only limitation we have identified is the inability to dynamically configure the subject of the e-mail. We are almost certain that this will be improved in later versions of Direct Mail. However, even with this minor limitation, Direct Mail provides powerful features and will help reduce your "time to market" for your mail campaign!

Case Study Introduction

To best investigate the inner workings of Direct Mail, we will use a fictitious case study to illustrate the concepts that will be discussed throughout this chapter.

Let's take a look at **Retail Store**, a physical clothing apparel store that also has an online presence. Retail Store's current online presence is nothing more than a static catalogue showcasing a number of their products. The site owner at Retail Store (our client) has the following requirements:

> ➢ Retail Store wants the ability to send a bulk electronic mailing to alert users of upcoming specials.

> ➢ The store management wants this to be a well-targeted mailing so as not to inundate users with irrelevant mail. This is in the hope that the follow-up sales percentage will be higher using a targeted mailing than it would be with a general mailing.

> ➢ Retail Store would also like to personalize the content of the e-mail to provide the user with a more welcoming appearance and targeted content, thereby increasing the likelihood that the user will visit their store.

> ➢ There is an existing group of **premium** customers that the store would like to specifically target; these customers are essentially frequent customers and are rewarded with special sales events.

> ➢ The store would like to send the electronic mailing automatically once per week.

> ➢ The store management mentions one final thing to you as you are preparing to design a solution for them – they would like the site operational in four weeks!

Great! You have four weeks to create the beginnings of an online store. Luckily, they do not have an initial requirement to interactively sell their apparel over the Internet. However, you're thinking ahead and from experience you realize that this is a logical next step in the evolution of this web service. You then realize that Site Server will be able to solve Retail Store's current requirements and also position them to be able extend this into a full-blown online store.

Admittedly, we put a bias in our fictitious case study that made Site Server a perfect solution. Still, the requirements are not exactly out of the ordinary. As more and more businesses move their operations to the Internet, there is an increasing need for help with the migration process. The requirements we mentioned above are very typical of an online business-to-consumer site.

How are we going to use Site Server to build a new site for Retail Store? Well, the following general tasks should help us to setup Retail Store's mailing campaign:

1. Create a new Membership Server instance for the Retail Store.

2. Setup an IIS web site that is mapped to our Membership Server.

3. Configure the Site Server Direct Mail component within our Membership Server.

4. Create a distribution list of mail recipients.

5. Build a mail content template (this will become the message body).

6. Schedule our mail package for delivery.

These steps will allow us to demonstrate Direct Mail clearly here; obviously you may want to adapt some of these tasks to your particular setup, such as using an existing Membership Server instance if you have one.

We will look first at the necessary configuration information for tasks **1** and **2**. This will provide us with a consistent naming convention as we continue through the rest of the chapter. No doubt you will have your own configuration information such as server names. However, by introducing the settings here, you will be able to change them to your own values as necessary.

Setting up the Membership Server and Website

These are the settings we used for creating a new Membership Server instance and mapping an IIS web site to it. We won't go through the details of creating the instance or the web site, as you should already be familiar with the Membership wizard and the IIS snap-in from the earlier chapters in this section. You'll need to run the wizard to create a new Membership Server instance, and fill in the information below as required.

IIS Application Server

The name of the IIS Server is conveniently going to be RetailStore. I can almost guarantee that you have an IIS Server setup and it has a different name. That's ok – just remember that everywhere you see a reference to the RetailStore, put your server name in its place.

IIS Port

We have the RetailStore IIS application set up on port number 8080, but again, you can choose your own port number providing that you make the change consistent in the code examples.

Membership Server Name

We like to use consistent naming across the different components of a project, hence we set the Root Distinguished Name of the Membership Directory to o=RetailStore to match the IIS application name.

> Select either **Complete Configuration** *or* **Custom Configuration** *and* check the **Message Builder Service** option. This is how we include the **Direct Mail** component.

If you are working with an existing Membership Server instance that does not include Direct Mail, you can work around this. Simply create a new Membership Server instance and Connect to an existing Membership Directory when presented with the Select the Membership Directory option in the New Membership Server Wizard. You will then be permitted to enter the connection information for your existing Membership Directory.

You should now have completed tasks 1 and 2, and have the necessary foundation for the examples we'll be discussing in the rest of this chapter. Tasks 3 through 6 are covered throughout the rest of this chapter.

Configuring Direct Mail

As we have already discovered, Direct Mail can be one of Site Server's most powerful features. It is also one of the most frustrating because there is no officially supported object model for this component. The problems that this introduces will become more apparent as we extend our Retail Store example. In particular, we will give the site owner the ability to setup additional mailing campaigns. If you are already familiar with the Direct Mail component of Site Server, then you are probably all too aware of the shortcomings of trying to provide the site owner with the ability to manage his or her own mailing campaigns.

A close look at how Direct Mail is configured should provide a quick illustration of why we encounter problems trying to customize mailing campaigns.

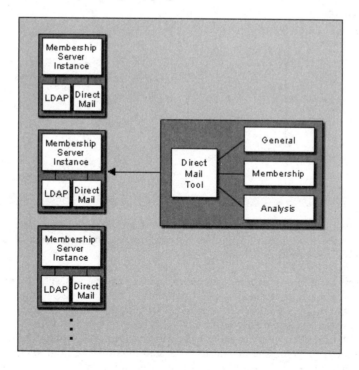

There are two distinct stages involved in Direct Mail configuration as shown in the diagram above. The left side of the diagram shows each of the Membership Server instances set up on a host and the right side shows the **Direct Mailer** tool on that same host. The diagram represents the relationship between the configurable elements and is much akin to the view that we see in the Site Server Service Admin MMC (shown in the next screenshot). It is not intended to be a physical representation of the elements. We will discuss the Direct Mailer tool in more detail as this chapter progresses; however, it is worth mentioning at this point that this tool can only be configured to point at one Membership Server instance at a time.

The Site Server Membership Directory and Membership Server architecture was designed such that each of the Membership Server instances are connected to an LDAP Membership Directory and a Direct Mail service. Each Membership Server instance has settings for its respective LDAP and Direct Mail services, as shown in the screenshot below:

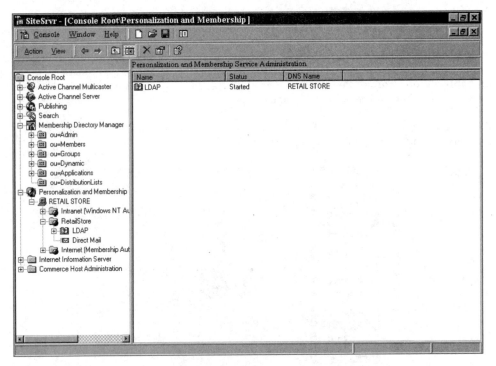

However, unlike the LDAP Membership Directory, Microsoft intended that the Direct Mail component should only be accessed through a GUI and not through a programmatic interface. This approach has resulted in certain drawbacks.

Where are problems encountered when customizing mailing campaigns? The Direct Mailer GUI tool is only accessible on a server that the site owner (whom you have developed the site for) will typically not access. To combat this, we could make a special case and provide some sort of server access for the site owner. However, the site owner will usually not have either the technical expertise or the desire to use this GUI. So then, what is going to happen each time that they want a new mailing campaign? Each time, you as the site developer will need to configure the tool and mailings. A programmatic interface into the Direct Mail component would allow you to provide the site owner with the capability to create a mailing campaign. In addition, it would provide the added safety of isolating the site owner from the rest of the Site Server configuration.

In the next section, we will investigate the two distinct stages of Direct Mail configuration – configuring the Membership Server instance and configuring the Direct Mailer.

Configuring the Membership Server Instance

You should have set up a Membership Server instance that incorporates the Message Builder Service as described earlier in this chapter. We're going to look at the Direct Mail configuration settings for the Membership Server instance we created.

The first thing we need to do is open the Direct Mail configuration dialogue box. To do this, open the Site Server Service Admin MMC and click the plus sign to drill down to the Personalization and Membership and Machine Name nodes. You should see the Retail Store Membership Server. Click the plus sign next to this and you will then see the LDAP and the Direct Mail nodes. Right-click on the Direct Mail node and select Properties. You will now see the Direct Mail configuration dialogue, similar to the one shown below:

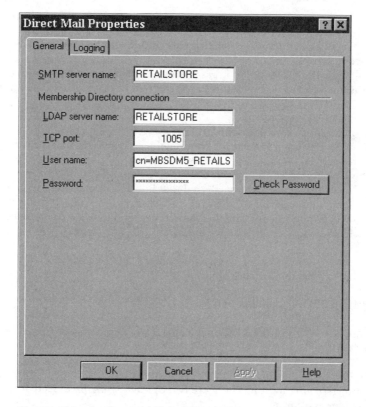

There are two settings within the General Tab and an additional Logging Tab. You will notice that the settings are already completed within the General Tab. These settings relate to the **SMTP server** that will be used to send the mailings and the **Message Builder account** that will be used to connect to the Membership Directory.

SMTP Server

The first step is to choose the SMTP server that will be used to send the Direct Mail packages. This can either be set up on the local host or on a remote host. From a performance standpoint, it is best to have a dedicated SMTP mail server. If this is not possible, there are other techniques that help to reduce the load that Direct Mail imposes on an IIS server. We will cover these advanced techniques later in this chapter.

For help on setting up your SMTP server you can use the Windows NT Option Pack documentation at:

```
http://localhost/iisHelp/iis/misc/default.asp
```

Click on Microsoft Internet Information Server and then Microsoft SMTP service.

Message Builder Account

The Message Builder account has the appropriate privileges to create and send the elements of a mailing campaign. By default, this account belongs to the Site Server Direct Mail Administrator group. The Site Server documentation states that this account can belong to the Site Server Direct Mail Operators group as well. An account belonging to just the Operators group only has the privilege of managing mail packages that it has created. If the account belongs to the Administrators group then there is the additional privilege of having access to mailing packages created by other users.

Our next step is to determine which account we are going to use to manage the interaction between Direct Mail and our Membership Directory. Fortunately, a default account already exists. This is the Message Builder account that was set up when our Membership Server instance was created. It is pre-populated into the Direct Mail configuration dialogue box along with the corresponding password. If you click Check Password, you should be alerted that it is a valid password (assuming that you have not altered any of the account settings). The account name is of the form MBSDM#_machineName and you will find this account in your Membership Directory under the ou=Members container. The # represents the Membership Server instance and machineName is, well you guessed it, the name of your server.

In our case, the Message Builder account is:

cn=MBSDM5_RETAILSTORE,ou=Members,o=RetailStore

As you can see, this account is in **Distinguished Name** (DN) form and will probably have a different value on your server.

Unfortunately, the password for this account is not immediately obvious and we will need access to it as we continue through configuration. There are two options available to us that will provide access to the Message Builder account password.

Changing the Password

We can change the Message Builder account password in our Membership Directory by navigating to the ou=Members container and then editing the userPassword attribute for the appropriate Message Builder account. After doing this, we need to change the password that we entered in the Direct Mail configuration dialogue and then click Check Password again to make certain that the password is valid.

> It is possible to have more than one Message Builder account in the Membership Directory. This typically happens when more than one Membership Server is connected to a given Membership Directory. If this is the case, make certain that the password for the appropriate Message Builder account is used. This account is determined by the default MBSDM#_machineName account that is pre-populated in the Direct Mail configuration dialogue.

Determining the Password

Passively determining the password of the default Message Builder account is the preferred solution since this does not require any of the interdependent account settings to be changed.

The easiest way to passively determine the Message Builder account password is to bind to each user in the Membership Directory with an account that has administrative privileges, and then read the userPassword attribute of any Message Builder accounts. For example:

```
Const ADS_SECURE_AUTHENTICATION = 1

Dim sDNName, sAdministrator, sPassword
Dim oADsRoot
Dim oUser, oUsers
Dim sCN, sPWD

sDNName = "LDAP://localhost:1005/o=RetailStore/ou=Members"
sAdministrator = "cn=Administrator, ou=Members, o=RetailStore"
sPassword = "password"

Set oADsRoot = GetObject("LDAP:")
Set oUsers = oADsRoot.OpenDSObject(sDNName, _
                                   sAdministrator, _
                                   sPassword, _
                                   ADS_SECURE_AUTHENTICATION)

For Each oUser In oUsers
   sCN = oUser.cn
   If InStr(sCN, "MBSDM") Then
      sPWD = oUser.Get("userPassword")
      Response.Write "cn = <b>" & sCN & "</b><br>"
      Response.Write "password = <b>" & sPWD & "</b><br><br>"
   End If
Next
```

Assuming that we have an administrative user where cn=Administrator and password=password, we are able to securely bind to the ou=Members container using the OpenDSObject method:

```
Set oUsers = oADsRoot.OpenDSObject(sDNName, _
                                   sAdministrator, _
                                   sPassword, _
                                   ADS_SECURE_AUTHENTICATION)
```

Strictly speaking, we are not just enumerating every user in the ou=Members container. Our call that binds to the Members container will also bind to any containers or objects that are in the Members container. Therefore, when we are checking to see whether the object's common name contains the MBSDM prefix, we are also making this comparison to the common name of other containers and objects:

```
sCN = oUser.cn
If InStr(sCN, "MBSDM") Then
```

This should not cause any problems, as it is unlikely that additional containers or objects will exist that have a similar naming scheme. If this does cause problems, simply modify your code to be aware of your Members container structure and ignore these extra objects and containers.

If we run MBSDMpwd.asp, we will be returned the password for each account that has the MBSDM prefix. As previously mentioned, it is possible to have more than one Message Builder account in our Membership Directory, so care should be taken to select the appropriate account and password. In practice, any of the Message Builder accounts can be used since they all have the appropriate privileges.

After determining the appropriate password, enter it in the Direct Mail configuration dialogue box and then click Check Password to make certain it is valid.

LDAP Server and Port

To complete the configuration of the Membership Server instance, we need to check the name of the LDAP server that our Membership Server uses. We can access this information by right-clicking on the LDAP node under our Membership Server (as we saw in the screenshot a couple of pages ago) and selecting Properties. Under the General tab, you can read the values for the Server Name and TCP Port. Note that these values are actually pre-populated in the Direct Mail configuration dialogue, just for our convenience.

Configuring the Direct Mailer Tool

In the previous section, we discussed the significance of the Message Builder account and consequently took the time to retrieve its password. All of our hard work will be rewarded now as we continue through the second stage of configuration.

We start by opening the Direct Mailer tool, located in the Tools folder, by selecting this path from the Start menu:

Start | Programs | Microsoft Site Server | Tools | Direct Mailer

Once the Direct Mailer tool is open, you may immediately be prompted with the Direct Mail Settings dialog box. If it doesn't appear, launch it manually by clicking on Tools and then Settings in the Direct Mailer. The Direct Mail Settings box has three tabs; we'll look at each of these in turn.

The Direct Mail Tab

The first thing we need to do is enter the Direct Mail servers on the Direct Mail tab, shown below. When you click on the Direct Mail tab you will notice that there are two sections which each require an application server, username and password combination:

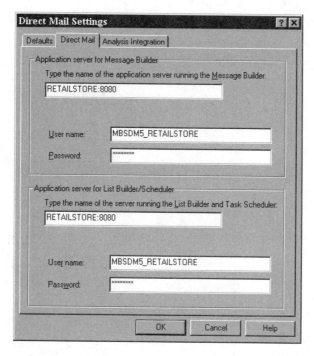

The upper section asks for the application server that is running the Message Builder service. This is essentially the IIS application that we are using.

In our Retail Store example, the application server is:

RETAIL_STORE_WEB_SERVER:PORT

In particular, since the Retail Store example set up IIS on server RETAILSTORE, and created the Retail Store web on port 8080, I enter:

RETAILSTORE:8080

as my application server.

We already know the Message Builder account details from the section *Configuring the Membership Server Instance*, so we can enter this in the username and password.

The lower section of the Direct Mail settings requires the same information as the top section, but this time as applicable to the List Builder service.

Why do we need to enter the information for each service individually? Having it set up this way implies that we can use different accounts and even different servers to handle each of these services. The Message Builder service is responsible for creating the mail packages and the List Builder service is responsible for managing the package schedules. In most cases you will use the same application server and the same Message Builder account for both services.

The only time you will use different Message Builder and List Builder settings is if, for instance, you want a user to be able to edit the mail package schedule, but not edit the actual package contents itself. This can be achieved by giving the user access to the List Builder account only.

For our Retail Store, use the same Message Builder account that you used in the Message Builder Direct Mail settings.

At this point we have our application server set up and mapped to our Membership Server instance, which in turn is connected to our Membership Directory. The diagram opposite helps to make this interaction a little easier to understand:

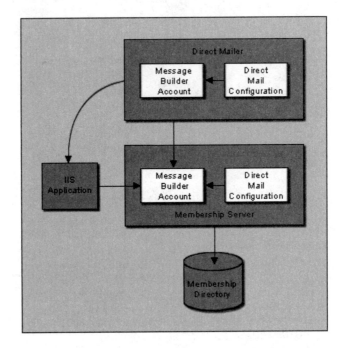

The Message Builder account information is required to configure both the Membership Server instance and the Direct Mailer. We have provided this information already for both of these. The Direct Mailer also requires the connection information to our application server. As we have discovered, this is nothing more than the existing web application and port number that is already mapped to our Membership Server. We can now see how Direct Mail fits in to the whole picture and with these last few pieces of connection information completed, we are nearly ready to create our first mailing package.

Additional Configuration

If you can't wait to send out your first mail package then you can skip ahead to *Using Direct Mail* now – we have all of the necessary basic configuration information. However, I would recommend that you read through the remainder of this configuration section first, or at the very least, return to it at a later date. If you are planning to use Direct Mail with Site Server Analysis, you should definitely plan to read this section.

Before we create any mail packages, let's take a look at some additional settings that we can use to help customize and monitor our mailings.

> *For those of you who are familiar with Direct Mail, note that the customization that we are about to discuss is nothing more than setting the sender email address. We will defer talking about customization of the mail content until the upcoming section on Using Direct Mail.*

The Defaults Tab

Clicking the Defaults tab will reveal the following additional settings:

> **Sender Name**
> This is the From address that appears in each of the email messages sent out to the recipients on the mailing list. The From address is encapsulated in the mail package when it is initially created, however this may cause us problems if we need to change the address at some future date. The Direct Mail settings GUI does not provide us with the ability to edit the From address once the package has been created; this is the price we pay with this one-shot package creation tool. Note that there is no check to see if the address we enter is a valid email address.

> **Status Recipient**
> We have several options open to us for monitoring the status of our mail packages. One of the simplest yet most effective methods is to provide an email address where a status receipt can be sent. A typical successful receipt would look similar to this:

```
Mailing "Weekly Circular" completed. 2 out of 2 messages have been
successfully processed (2 have been successfully sent). If the total
processed does not match the total sent, please see the direct mail
logs for details. Time started: 7/1/99 9:56:40 AM.
```

> Weekly Circular is the name of the mailing as entered in the Create Direct Mailing wizard. Don't worry if this does not mean anything to you right now, we will be covering this shortly.

> Again, the recipient address is encapsulated in the direct mail package and cannot be accessed through the Direct Mail settings GUI (just as with the Sender's Email Address).

> **Message Type**
> The message type can be one of three selections: plain text with uuencode attachments; plain text with MIME attachments or HTML/MHTML. MHTML is the Mail HTML format that allows a message to be sent and displayed as an HTML page, and is supported by most popular mail clients. You will probably find yourself using this message type most frequently since it works closely with the mail content templates. These templates allow you to personalize the mail content that each recipient receives. For a description of the message types, check out Selecting the Message Type in the online Site Server documentation by searching for MHTML MIME.

> For our Retail Store, we will set the message type to HTML/MHTML since we will be using a content template that has HTML and server-side script embedded in it.

> **One of the most common problems encountered when trying to send a direct mail package is the appearance of HTML tags in the message body. This can readily be fixed by simply changing the message type to HTML/MHTML.**

The Analysis Integration Tab

Finally, the Analysis Integration tab is for integrating Direct Mail with the Analysis feature of Site Server.

There are basically two methods that can be used to define the recipients of our mailing campaign. The first makes use of a distribution list that contains the email addresses of all recipients. This distribution list is stored in the Membership Server and can be thought of as a special type of group. The other method, Analysis integration, dynamically generates a list of recipients based on rules that we define.

Using Analysis with Direct Mail itself is fairly straightforward; the difficult part is setting up the analysis database and performing a **Custom Import** of user data. For information on how to do this you'll need to refer to the previous chapter, *Analysis*.

> *You can also find more information on this in the Site Server documentation by clicking* Help *at the bottom of the* Analysis *tab. I also recommend two Site Server online documents: "Exporting User Attributes to Analysis" and "Importing User Data (CI)".*

Assuming that we have our analysis database set up, all we need to do is enter the connection information for it. The analysis database is required so that **rule conditions** can be established. When a rule condition is met, the corresponding email address is added to the list of mail recipients.

There are two alternatives when selecting a database – an Access database or SQL Server database. You should choose the appropriate option that corresponds to your analysis database. You will most likely be using SQL Server if you have a Membership Directory with a large number of users.

That's all there is to configuring Direct Mail. The fact that we had to configure the Membership Server instance and the Direct Mailer tool separately definitely made this process more complicated than it should have been. You should take comfort in knowing that you are now well positioned to be able jump into the remaining material in this chapter, and move on to tasks such as actually running an analysis query. We still have to determine who the members of our mailing list will be, and this is what we'll look at next.

Using Direct Mail

Sending out Direct Mail packages is a relatively straightforward process providing that we have gone through the configuration steps in the previous section. Based on our discussion at the beginning of this chapter, we know the fundamental building blocks that are required to create a Direct Mail package.

As a quick overview, here are the pieces that we will be putting together:

> ➢ Create a Direct Mail package with the Direct Mailer tool.
> ➢ Add a mail content template to this mail package. The content template will contain personalized information for each of the mail recipients.
> ➢ Select our mail recipients from a Distribution List and also from an Analysis query.
> ➢ Add our Direct Mail package as a scheduled task to be run on a predetermined schedule.

These steps capture most of the options that we have for sending out a Direct Mail package. We should be able to achieve our goals of our Retail Store bulk mailing campaign if we are able to successfully complete all of the steps mentioned here.

The mail content template will contain a personalized message for each of our users. We need to watch out for the authentication method that we choose in order to ensure that the message is personalized for each and every user. We'll talk more about this in a moment.

Our Premium group of users can now be defined in a distribution list, which can then be set as the target of our mail package. Alternatively, we can satisfy our need to dynamically generate a list of site users who meet our criterion of having visited a given URL.

And lastly, we can set our mail package to run as a **Windows NT Task**. Don't worry if you haven't used Windows NT tasks before, the Direct Mailer provides us with an easy interface that takes us straight to the tasks that we create. The task scheduler will satisfy one of our goals: Send the messages out once a week automatically without our intervention.

Creating Mail Packages

If it is not already open then start the Direct Mailer program by clicking on:

Start | Programs | Microsoft Site Server | Tools | Direct Mailer

You may be prompted with a login box at this point. If this is the case then enter the username and password of a Site Server account that is a member of the Site Server Direct Mail Administrators group. These steps are covered in the Configuring Direct Mail section of this chapter.

When the Direct Mailer opens up, click on Schedule and Create Direct Mailing (this can also be accessed from the first *envelope* icon on the toolbar). We will be presented with the **Create New Direct Mailing Wizard**.

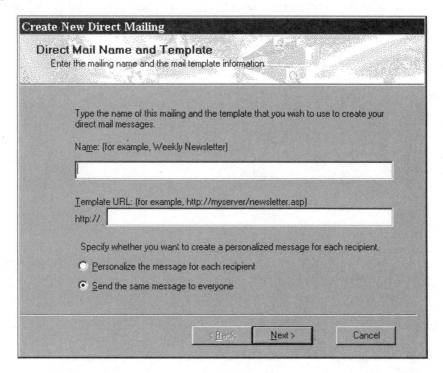

Mailing Name and Template URL

The first step of the wizard asks for the name and message template URL.

Name

The name is the task name that appears in the Direct Mailer main window once we have finished creating our package. This name should be descriptive, and please note that it doesn't appear anywhere in the mail that the recipients receive.

Set the name to Weekly Circular for the Retail Store weekly mail update.

Template URL

The mail content template is next; here we have an opportunity to include a personalized message for each recipient. If we are going to take advantage of the technology that we have at our disposal, the content template should be an ASP page with dynamic content. To really use this technology to its full potential, we should also be personalizing the content by including information that we have collected about our users in the Membership Directory. It is easy to achieve all of this simply because of the tight integration between the Membership Directory, Personalization & Membership and Direct Mail.

> **A word of caution: there is a performance penalty to pay by personalizing for each mail recipient. However, with careful planning, we can minimize this penalty.**

The template file defines the contents and layout of the email that will be sent to each of the mailing list recipients. The template can either be a plain text file with uuencoded attachments, a plain text file with MIME attachments or an HTML/ASP file.

The content template that we are going to use for our Retail Store is shown below in `WeeklyCircular.asp`.

```
<%
Set oAUOUser = Server.CreateObject("Membership.UserObjects")

' Catch Errors
If Err.Number <> 0 Then
  Response.Write Err.Description
  Response.End
End If
%>

<HTML>

<HEAD>
<TITLE>WeeklyCircular.asp</TITLE>
</HEAD>

<BODY>
```

```
<P>
<B>Retail Store</B>

<BR>*************<BR><BR>
Dear
<% Response.Write oAUOUser.givenName & " " & oAUOUser.sn %>

<P>
Welcome to the Weekly Update from the
<A href="http://www.ExampleRetailStore.com">Retail Store</A>

<P>
This week's specials:
<BR>* 10% reductions storewide!

<% IF oAUOUser.shoeShopper = 1 THEN %>
    <BR>* All shoes up to 40% off
<% END IF %>

<BR>* New winter jackets in
<BR>* Free delivery on all items
<BR>* Check out our latest online SPECIALS

<P>
**************************************************

<P>
To unsubscribe from this mail please send a message to:
<BR>
<A href="mailto:support@ExampleRetailStore.com">support@ExampleRetailStore.com</A>

</BODY>
</HTML>
```

The first thing we do is instantiate the **Active User Object** (AUO). This is the key to providing customized content for each recipient. Next we use the AUO to find out the recipient's first and last names. The rest of the content is just plain old HTML except for the conditional logic surrounding the shoe specials. We are making the assumption that the recipients' mail clients can accept this MHTML format (Mail HTML).

There is nothing complicated about WeeklyCircular.asp. As you can see, we are simply using the AUO object to read user attributes and include conditional content based on these attributes. We are able to determine whether each individual user has purchased shoes from us in the past and if he or she has, then we tell him or her about a special shoe sale. Notice how each recipient is personally greeted at the beginning of the mail.

Now, all we need to do is put WeeklyCircular.asp up on our web server and then type the appropriate URL in the **Template URL** field of the Create New Template Wizard. It is a good rule of thumb to create a separate Template directory, for example:

```
http://RETAILSTORE:8080/Templates/WeeklyCircular.asp
```

A Personalized Message

Next, we choose whether to send a personalized message to each recipient or the same message to everyone. For the Retail Store, we have created a personalized message for each recipient that greets him or her by name and also checks an individual attribute. We should therefore choose the Personalize the message for each recipient option in our Retail Store example so that each user receives the appropriate personalized message.

> Selecting **Send the same message to everyone** would result in
> personalization for the first recipient only and then this message would be
> sent to each additional recipient in the mailing list.

Click the Next button to move to the Select Users step of the wizard.

Select Users (mail recipients)

We are presented with two options for the source of our recipients. Both of these options have already been mentioned, so hopefully you are familiar with the significant difference between them. As a reminder, by choosing a distribution list, we are getting a list of users that has been defined in a mailing list. The Site Server Analysis option allows the mailing list to be calculated at the time that the mailing package is sent out based on a set of rules that we invent.

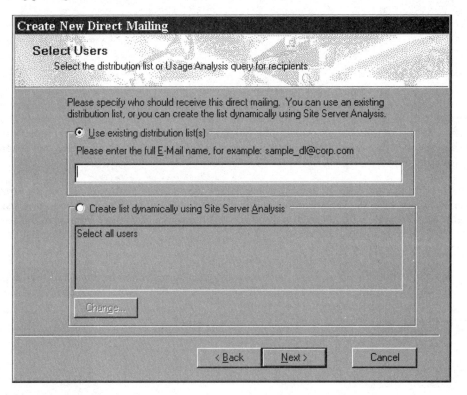

Creating a Distribution List

The two types of distribution list are the inherent Site Server distributionList and the rfc822DistributionList. They are both stored within the ou=DistributionLists container in the Membership Server.

> The advantage of the **rfc822DistributionList** is the ability to add any email addresses to the list, without the dependency of them existing in the Membership Directory.

We are going to create an inherent Site Server distribution list to define a set of Premium Retail Store customers. This is actually very similar to creating a group and then adding members to it.

First, we navigate to the ou=DistributionLists container in our Membership Directory and right-click on it. Click on New and then Object and this will launch the **New Object Wizard**. Click Next to bypass the splash screen. Next, we select the Class of Object that we are creating, and choose distributionList (if you scroll down this list you will notice the rfc822DistributionList). We are going to call this list Premium so type Premium in the Name field. Click Next, and we are then presented with an Add Attribute screen, with an Email Address attribute already added for us. Here we add an arbitrary email address that is used as an alias for our distribution list. Type in:

```
List@ExampleRetailStore.com
```

Click Finish to complete the creation of the distribution list. We should now see the Premium distribution list object in the ou=DistributionLists container.

Before we can use this distribution list as the source of our recipients, we must add some members to it. All we have done at this point is created an empty list, essentially a placeholder for the list members.

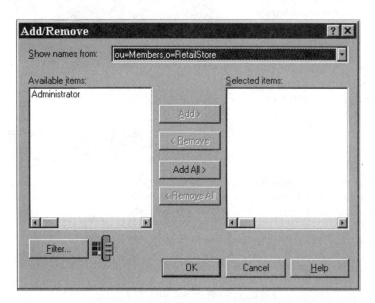

To add members, right-click the Premium distribution list and select Properties. Then click the Members tab and then Add. We can choose to add any existing users in our Membership Directory, although we may need to navigate to the appropriate container.

After you have added your members to the Premium distribution list, click OK and then click OK again to clear the Properties dialog.

Now we can return to the Create New Direct Mailing wizard and enter List@ExampleRetailStore.com as the full E-mail name.

Running an Analysis Query

Although we are using a distribution list to determine our recipients in the Retail Store example, we will briefly cover the process to get the recipients using an Analysis query. In order to run an Analysis query, you must first create an Analysis database and import your user data into it, as discussed in the previous chapter.

Once the Analysis database is in place we can proceed by selecting the Create list dynamically using Site Server Analysis radio option in the Select Users step of the Create New Direct Mailing wizard. Next click the Change button to set up the analysis query rules that will be used to determine the recipient list (that is unless you want to send the mail to each of the users in the Analysis database). Now we choose the appropriate rule conditions that will suitably define the query that will build our recipient list. There is an existing list of rule conditions that can be used in the top half of this wizard (shown opposite). As you can also see, adding a rule moves it to the bottom half of the display where the underlined **hot phrases** can be given values.

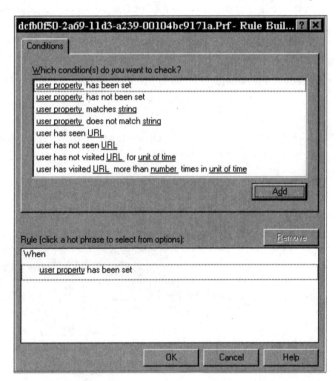

Let's assume that we have a registration process for our Retail Store and we use a Registered attribute that we can import into our Analysis database. Then we can set up a rule condition that only sends the mail to users who have a Registered attribute set.

This would be accomplished by choosing the following rule fragment:

<u>user property</u> has been <u>set</u>

and clicking on <u>user property</u> to select the Registered attribute.

What we have just done is create a rule, which consists of a condition and an action. In our case the condition is that the given user property has been set and the action is to include the content that the Template URL points to. Direct Mail gives us a clean interface into part of the Analysis component. If you are familiar with Analysis then you will notice that we really only have access to a small subset of what Analysis can actually achieve in terms of rules.

Scheduling the Mailing

There are three fields in the last step of the Create New Direct Mailing Wizard. The first two are simply the Sender name and Subject line which are the values that appear in the email From line and Subject line respectively. If you remember back in configuration, we already entered a name that will appear as the sender of the email. The value that you enter here will override the previous value entered in configuration. There is no real advantage in being able to enter this value in either place, in fact it is probably a point of confusion for many people.

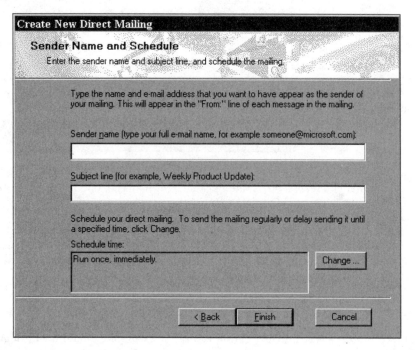

The third section is the piece that lets us schedule mailings. We can click Finish and our mailing will be sent immediately, or the selections can be adjusted to send the mailing at different times. You can experiment with this on your own. For now we are going to go one step further and add our mail package as a scheduled task.

Click on Change... to bring up the Schedule Mailing dialogue. There is no initial task scheduled so we need to click on New which defaults the task to run on a daily basis. You will probably find that the scheduler is a very intuitive tool and should be able to create a schedule that meets your needs.

For the Retail Store, set Schedule Task to Weekly and then change the Start time to 3:00 AM. This will send the mail package out every Sunday morning at 3:00 AM. This is just what we were looking for when we started looking at the Retail Store Example.

Note that you can click on New again. This allows you to combine more than one schedule for this mailing.

Click OK and you will be asked for an account to run this task under. Enter any valid NT account and click OK. Now click Finish and you will be returned to the Direct Mailer main window. We can't see our task in this window, but don't worry. Click Schedule and then Edit Schedule... and our task will be displayed along with the schedule it is set to run on.

Delivering the Package

We don't have to wait until the scheduled run time to see if our mail package was successfully created. Just click on the task name in the task window, as shown here, (this was the name entered in the first step of this wizard) and then click File and Run. Refreshing the screen will keep us updated on the task's progress.

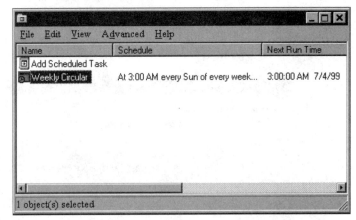

We have just created and sent our first mailing package. Imagine having to do this each time that one of your clients wanted to create a new mailing campaign! As usual, once we have more than one package to send, we will want to automate some of this process.

The following *Scripting Against Direct Mail* section will repeat this procedure by using code. This also addresses our problem of how to give the site owner the ability to create mail packages. With a little effort, we can create a mail package creation utility with a user interface that gives the site owner the ability to create and schedule mail packages to their heart's content.

Troubleshooting

Although the Template URL and Distribution List settings cannot be modified through the GUI once the mail package has been created, they are accessible through a little known script called DMSP.asp which is located in the _mem_bin directory of Site Server. This is usually a virtual directory mapped to:

```
Local Drive:\Microsoft Site Server\Bin\P&M\html
```

unless you have modified its default location.

We will be alerted if we encounter errors while sending our mail package and the mail package will persist in the Direct Mail main window with an Error Status. We can launch the DMSP.asp script by first clicking on the pertinent task name in the Direct Mailer and then clicking Tools and Edit Task Error Information. Alternatively, we can click the Edit Task Error Information icon on the menu bar.

We will be prompted for a username and password to gain access to the Membership Server that this Direct Mail package is associated with. Give the username and password for an account that is in the Membership Server and belongs to the SiteServer DirectMail Administrators group.

Now `DMSP.asp` is opened up in a browser window with the Template URL and Distribution List properties of the invalid mail package available for editing.

Scripting Against Direct Mail

It is possible to perform all of the interactive steps described in this chapter so far through the use of objects in scripts. This allows the automation of many of these tasks.

Why would we want to do this when we could just continue to use the Direct Mailer tool? Well, how are we going to keep up with the high demands of the site owner as he keeps dreaming up bigger and better mailing campaigns? Through scripting, we can write routines that will do exactly what we have been doing so far, i.e. specifying the mail recipients, the content of the message and the schedule. Scripting has the added benefit of providing the site owner with an HTML-based interface. The advantage of this is that the site owner just needs a browser to manage his/her campaigns and not direct access to the server.

The Mail Template

We will use the same mail content that we used in the *Using Direct Mail* section, the `WeeklyCircular.asp` file. Remember that this template was set up to greet each of the mail recipients personally and also to check an additional shoeShopper attribute to see if the user qualified to be shown a special shoe sale notice.

Coding Direct Mail through Objects

Direct Mail was a late feature that was added as a Site Server component. Because of this, all documentation to date concerning Direct Mail discusses only the interactive method for submitting a Direct Mail task. Although it is not documented in the SDK, or anywhere else for that matter, it is possible to replace these interactive portions of the Mailer Tool and the Task Scheduler with ASP code by using several objects. This capability is critical to allowing a "hands-off" mode of operation for direct mailings.

> The description and examples that we provide below have been reverse engineered through inference and experimentation. The discussion that follows is not an attempt to provide complete documentation for these objects. It is merely intended to illustrate the methods by which Direct Mail can be coordinated using these objects. We have successfully tested this approach in our development facility. However, you might need to experiment a little bit to come up with a solution that fits your particular needs.

The Objects

The TaskPackage Object

The TaskPackage object is the primary object for the Direct Mail effort. This object can be created with a call to CreateObject.

```
set package = CreateObject("Membership.TaskPackage.1")
```

The MailTemplate Object

The TaskPackage object includes a MailTemplate object. This object allows us to set the template that will be used to send the mailing, and can also be created with a call to CreateObject.

```
set mailTemplate = CreateObject("Membership.MailTemplate.1")
```

The MailingList Object

The TaskPackage object also includes a MailingList object. We use this object to select the mailing list that will be used to send the mailing. Again, it can be created with a call to CreateObject.

```
set mailingList = CreateObject("Membership.MailingList.1")
```

The SchedulingAgent Object

The SchedulingAgent object is used to add this Mail Package to the NT Task Scheduler. It can be created with a call to CreateObject.

```
Set objScheduler = Server.CreateObject("Scheduler.SchedulingAgent.1")
```

The Task Object

The Task object is used by the SchedulingAgent object, and can be created with a call to the Add method of the Tasks container object within the SchedulingAgent object.

```
Set objTask = objScheduler.Tasks.Add(strJobName)
```

The Code

Example: Creating a Mail Package

First, we'll create the Task Package object with a call to CreateObject. Next we'll get the GUID and parse it into a standardized format for use as the storage file name of the Task Package.

> This example shows a hard-coded path to the Queue directory. Your actual path could vary depending on the options chosen at Site Server installation.

Finally, we'll give the package a name.

```
<HTML>
<HEAD>
<TITLE>Retail Store - Direct Mail Package Creation</TITLE>
</HEAD>
<BODY>

<%
  set pkg = CreateObject("Membership.TaskPackage.1")

  Set objGuid = Server.CreateObject("Membership.GuidGen.1")
  guid = objGuid.GenerateGuid
  Set objGuid = Nothing

  guid1 = Left(guid, 8)
  guid2 = Mid(guid, 9, 4)
  guid3 = Mid(guid, 13, 4)
  guid4 = Mid(guid, 17, 4)
  guid5 = Mid(guid, 21)
  guid = guid1 & "-" & guid2 & "-" & guid3 & "-" & guid4 & "-" & guid5

  Session("guid") = guid
  pkgID = guid

  pkgFileName = "D:\Microsoft Site Server\data\knowledge\membership\" & _
               "ListBuilderQueue\Schedule\" & guid & ".New"


  pkg.Create pkgFileName, pkgID

  pkg.Name = "WeeklyCircular"
```

Now, we can create the `Mail Template` object with a call to `CreateObject`, associate the template file with this object, and associate this `Mail Template` object with the `Mail Package` object.

The `MailTemplate` object's `Type` attribute can have one of the following values:

> ➤ 0 – Plain text / unencoded attachments
> ➤ 1 – Plain text / MIME attachments
> ➤ 2 – HTML / MHTML

```
' *************************************************************************

set mailTemplate = CreateObject("Membership.MailTemplate.1")

mailTemplate.Load()
mailTemplate.URL = "http://RETAILSTORE:8080/Templates/WeeklyCircular.asp"
mailTemplate.Type = 2
mailTemplate.Save()

pkg.MailTemplate = mailTemplate
```

Create the `Mailing List` object with a call to `CreateObject`, associate the distribution list with this object, and associate this `Mailing List` object with the `Mail Package` object.

The `mailingList` object `Type` attribute can have one of the following values:

> ➢ 1 – Distribution List
> ➢ 2 – Usage Analysis Query

```
' ************************************************************************

set mailingList = CreateObject("Membership.MailingList.1")

distribList = "List@ExampleRetailStore.com"

mailingList.AddEx (distribList)
mailingList.Type = 1

pkg.MailingList = mailingList
```

Finish up by filling in some information fields in the `Mail Package` object and saving the changes.

The attributes we can set for extra package information are:

> ➢ `pkg.Owner` – the message builder account
> ➢ `pkg.Pwd` – the password for the message builder user
> ➢ `pkg.Sender` – the identifier that will appear in the 'From:' line in each of the emails that are sent
> ➢ `pkg.SubjectLine` – the text that will appear in the 'Subject:' line in each of the emails that are sent.
> ➢ `pkg.Status` – no information is available on the exact meaning of this attribute, although its value is usually 1.

```
' ************************************************************************

pkg.Owner = "MBSDM5_RETAILSTORE"
pkg.Pwd = "password"
pkg.Sender = "specials@ExampleRetailStore.com"
pkg.SubjectLine = "Weekly Specials at Retail Store!!"

pkg.Status = 1

' ************************************************************************

pkg.Save()

' ************************************************************************

%>


</BODY>
</HTML>
```

We now have a Mail Package saved on disk in the queue directory.

Next, we'll create a scheduled task to execute this mail package.

Example: Creating a Scheduled Task

First, we'll create the `SchedulingAgent` object with a call to `CreateObject`. Then we'll make sure that the task doesn't already exist. Finally, we'll add the task.

```
<HTML>
<HEAD>

<TITLE>Retail Store - Direct Mail Task Creation</TITLE>
</HEAD>
<BODY>

<%

  strJobName = "Direct Print Test"
  pkgFileName = Session("guid") & ".New"

  Set objScheduler = Server.CreateObject("Scheduler.SchedulingAgent.1")

  If (Err.Number <> 0) Then
    Response.Write "ERROR " & Err.Number & ": " & Err.Description & "<br>"
  End If

  'Check to see if task exists
  For Each objTask in objScheduler.Tasks
    If (objTask.JobName = strJobName) Then
      Response.Write "ERROR: Task " & strJobName & " already exists!<br>"
      Response.End
    End If
  Next

  Set objTask = objScheduler.Tasks.Add(strJobName)

  If (Err.Number <> 0) Then
    Response.Write "ERROR " & Err.Number & ": " & Err.Description & "<br>"
    Err.Clear
  End If
```

Now we'll fill in some information fields in the `Task` object.

The attributes we can set are:

> ➤ `objTask.Parameters` – the mail package queue file name
> ➤ `objTask.ApplicationName` – always "TMLstBld.exe". This is the executable that actually does the work.

- ➤ `objTask.WorkingDirectory` – The directory in which "TMLstBld.exe" resides. (Your actual path could vary depending on the options chosen at Site Server installation).
- ➤ `objTask.SetAccountInformation` – "DOMAIN\User", "password": the account information for the user that this task will run as.

> A word of caution here – the username and password combination that you provide should not be exposed directly in the ASP script. You should use either the registry or a COM object to hide this sensitive information. You can find a good example of this if you refer to `RegistryLookup()` function or the `Security.SecureInfo()` VB Class in Site Server 3.0 Personalization and Membership by Rob Howard (Wrox Press, ISBN 1-861001-94-0).

```
objTask.Parameters = pkgFileName
objTask.ApplicationName = "TMLstBld.exe"
objTask.WorkingDirectory = "D:\Microsoft Site Server\bin\P&M"
objTask.SetAccountInformation "RETAILSTORE\Administrator", "password"

' Set Flag to delete task when finished
objTask.Flags = objTask.Flags Or 2
```

Finish up by scheduling this task to be run once and actually request it to run immediately.

```
' Add Trigger
Set objTrigger = objTask.Triggers.Add()
objTrigger.BeginTime = CDate(Request("beginTime"))
objTrigger.Flags = 0
objTrigger.Duration = 0

' Add a Run Once type trigger
objTrigger.TriggerType = 1 'Run Once
Set objTrigger = Nothing

' Run the task Now
objTask.Run

' ***********************************************************************

%>

</BODY>
</HTML>
```

Summary

Direct Mail has given us the ability to create bulk mailings to send out to our web site users. The main elements of a mail package are defining its recipient list, personalizing the message content and then scheduling the delivery of the mail package.

The recipient list can be generated statically from a distribution list or dynamically using the Analysis component of Site Server.

We have taken numerous configuration steps and performed scripting tasks that will make the Direct Mail system easier to maintain and extend. It is worth noting that the most important aspect of Direct Mail from a customer standpoint is the actual message content. We were able to leverage our existing knowledge of ASP to personalize the content sent to each recipient. Admittedly, we did not exactly use rocket science for our ASP page content, however, with a little imagination and effort we should be able to generate some very compelling, data-driven mail campaigns.

One of the most useful discoveries we have made is how to programmatically create and manipulate the elements of a Direct Mail package. The lack of a documented object model has traditionally made this component difficult to script against; however, our investigations have enabled us to work around this limitation.

The popularity of Direct Mail certainly exceeded Microsoft's expectations. This is part of the reason why there is a lack of support and documentation for this component. Fortunately, we can expect a lot more from the Direct Mail component in the next release of Site Server.

Case Study — Integrating Site Server

13

Site Server is one of the most comprehensive suites of products in the Internet market. We have seen, for example, how useful the Content Management product can be to control information on your site, and how search can be used to find documents in numerous disparate data sources. Of course, these individual components are only one part of the suite – the real benefit and power of Site Server is achieved by integrating the various tools.

This case study is designed to illustrate this. Obviously, Site Server is a very powerful product; this case study will show you how to integrate many of its features in a way that can be built upon. We shall be using the WebAdmin and Microsoft Management Console administration tools so that you can become familiar with both of them. Both provide almost identical functionality.

Global Consulting Company

The study outlines a global company, **Citix Consultants Inc.**, which operates across multiple countries, language barriers and currencies, specializing in software development for business systems. This company must be able to share information seamlessly in multiple languages and in their own currency. We are going to concentrate on languages during this chapter as we are illustrating personalizing user content rather than the business process which would underlie a live global application (a typical system may also have to consider different calendar year, date, and currency formats). CCI must also be able to search documents in multiple languages and be informed when documents important to them have been added. This study focuses on the operations between the company's offices in Glasgow (Scotland), Rome (Italy), and the US.

The company is not organized by location, but rather by business units across the globe, allowing members of each unit to be available at all times for users around the world. The four main "business units" are:

- Management Science
- Risk Management
- Software Development
- Performance Analysis

The company hierarchy is quite straightforward, with Directors, Employees and Temps comprising the workforce. In alignment with the companies aim to be available across the globe, members of these levels live on different sites and are native to their country.

This final point provides a challenge for sharing content. Workers must have access to the same content without delay and the content needs to be available in their own language. An additional criterion is that the directors want the information broken into levels of viewing. They are not overly concerned with security, but would prefer that the more important information be hidden from view. However, modifying content within the site must only be done by either an administrator or the content editor. Content is written by various authors, translated into other languages in the company's language administration department (consisting of temporary workers), and published to the web site. It was stressed that they do not want 20 copies of the same document to cater for each and every language and security level – they want one document to do it all.

However, the company is not a small one and each department also has its content divided into four main types for better management. These types (or 'areas') are:

- **Overview** – general information for the department.
- **Research** – research information on the business area.
- **CompetitorWatch** – what the competitors in this departmental area are doing.
- **Technical** – detailed technical information on the department.

The company maintains complete knowledge systems where users from all departments should have ready access to information throughout the company. It is therefore important that the system allow the workers to find information based on their department and/or document type.

They see information as the key to success in their operations and this solution must provide a flexible, but efficient knowledge management system.

Configuring the Corporate Web Site

This section details the setting up of our corporate web site. We will create a membership directory and assign it to the Default Web Site where we will be placing our data.

Before we begin

Before we start the case study, let's ensure that we have all the necessary components to allow us to successfully complete the exercise. If you are unsure of how to install any of these components, refer back to the chapter on Content Management.

To install all the components necessary for the case study, check the Knowledge and Publishing features. You may uncheck the Push Services option, as this is not used in the study. Finally, select the Access Database Support option from the Analysis feature, that's all we need for now although it is recommended that a production system uses SQL Server. The options you have chosen will install P&M, Knowledge Manager, Content Deployment, Content Management, Admin Install and the Tag Tool.

Note that later in the chapter Microsoft Internet Explorer 5 will be needed, so this needs to be installed as well. You can download the browser from `http://www.microsoft.com/ie`.

We are going to map our membership directory to the Default Web Site – if you want to use another web site, then you should look at the Site Server documentation on installing Content Management on a different virtual server.

Creating the Membership Directory

The first step is to set up a membership directory and a user with administrative privileges who can perform our high-level Content Management configuration duties via the Web Administration tool.

For more information on the Personalization processes described here, refer to Chapter 10.

Expand the Personalization and Membership snap-in, right-click on the server and select New | Membership Server Instance to fire up the wizard. Choose Custom Configuration and check the Active User Object and LDAP Service checkboxes. On the next page, ensure Create New Membership Directory is selected; click Next and then choose Membership Authentication. Set the membership directory name and the password of the administrator account to mem, as shown in the figure below. Remember this password; you will need it later. Select Next and stick with the default Access database in the next screen. Click Next and accept the default path of your new Access database. On the following screen, accept the IP Address as All Unassigned and note the Port Number that is being used – this will be very important in our Content Management configuration. Finally, click Next again, read the summary information, ensure that you haven't made any errors, select Finish and go make some coffee. After a few minutes, your new LDAP instance will be created.

Now that we've created our membership instance, I find it useful to create a new user who has administrative privileges for working within the directory manager (although you can use the Administrator account). Before adding a user you should always check the properties of the Membership Directory Manager snap-in to make sure that it is pointing to the right directory. If it isn't, change the hostname points to the server you created the LDAP instance on (localhost in this case) and change the value of Port to the one you recorded earlier. The settings should look similar to those in the screenshot below. When requested, enter Administrator as the username and the mem for the password. This gives us full administrative privileges for the directory.

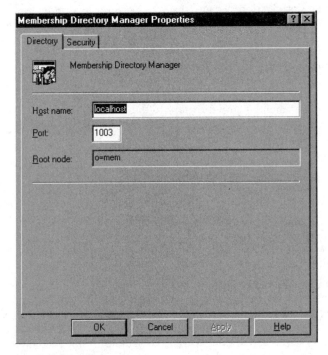

When the directory tree appears, right-click on ou=Members and select New | User. This launches the New User Wizard. Click Next and enter WebAdmin as the name of the user. Click Next again and then click Finish. The user WebAdmin should now be added to the root of the ou=Members container. We must now give this username a password and assign it to the appropriate administration group.

Double click on cn=WebAdmin, click Add Attribute, select user-password from the attributes list and click OK. Clear the asterisks out of the Value field and enter WebAdmin. In order to perform complete administrative tasks, we also need to add the attribute DS-Privileges and set its value to SUPERBROKER. This account bypasses all ACL (Access Control List) checking and has full privileges for creating and modifying all user accounts and privileges in you directory.

Now, click on the Groups tab and then the Add button. Ensure that the Show names from drop down list contains the value ou=Groups, o=mem and double-click on AdminGroup in the Available Items list to add it to the Selected Items list.

Click OK twice to complete this initial section of configuration. Now we have set up the administration side of the directory, let's populate the directory with our user information.

Populating the Directory

We will populate the directory with the three access levels we discussed earlier, along with their respective users. This will allow us to control the customization and content of our site.

Corporate Groups and Group Attributes

Our corporate site is going to consist of three levels of access: Full Access (level 2), Limited Access (level 1) and Restricted Access (level 0), which will be mapped to company responsibilities as shown below:

Access Type	Security Level	Company Responsibility
Full Access	[level 2]	Directors
Limited Access	[level 1]	Employees
Restricted Access	[level 0]	Temps

Let's create the first of these – the Directors group. Navigate to the ou=Groups container of the MDM, and in the right-pane right click and select New | Group to start the New Group Wizard. Click Next and enter Directors as the name of our group. Finally, click Next twice then Finish to complete the addition of the group. Repeat this process to create the Employees and Temps groups.

Now we need to add a security level attribute to each of the groups, as shown above. Go to ou=Admin/cn=Schema and add a new attribute by right clicking on cn=Schema in the left pane and selecting New | Attribute to launch the New Attribute Wizard. Click Next and enter SecurityLevel for Name and Security Level for the Display Name. Click Next and select Integer as the attribute syntax. Complete this process by clicking Next and then Finish.

> *The difference between the Display Name and the Name is that the former is used with the Description to provide user friendly information on the attribute which is being added, whereas the latter is the internally stored name of the attribute. For example, we may have a Display Name of "Private Key ID", a Name of "pkid" and a Description reading "The users Private Key Identification".*

To make it possible for groups to have this new attribute, you need to update the schema of the `mGroup` class, so double-click on `cn=mGroup` and select the **Class Attributes** tab. Clicking on **Add** brings up the attributes list, select the **Security Level** attribute as shown in the screenshot below:

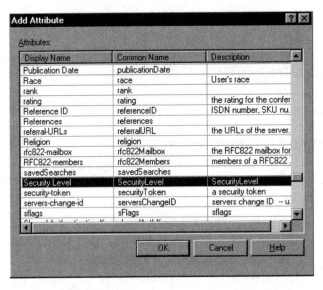

Click **OK** and this attribute can be used in all of our groups. The next screenshot shows the new list of attributes for `cn=mGroup`:

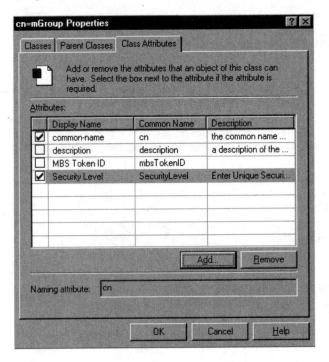

Flag the checkbox on the left of the new attribute to ensure that it is a mandatory part of any group we add to our directory in the `cn=Groups` container. Click **OK** to add the attribute. Next, under `ou=Groups`, double click on the `cn=Directors` entry and then click the **Add Attribute** button to add the **Security Level** attribute. Give this attribute a value of **2** (as shown in the screenshot below) and click **OK** to complete the configuration of the group.

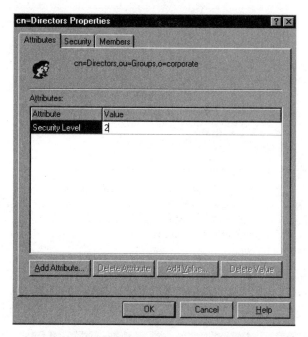

Repeat this for the **Employees** group (Security Level = 1) and **Temps** group (Security Level = 0). You should notice that the **Security Level** attribute is always present – this is because we specified it as being required when we added it to the class attributes of `cn=mGroup`.

Once this has been completed, we need to add some members to our groups.

Adding the members and member attributes

Our members are illustrated below along with their relationships to the groups we have just defined.

Group	Members
Directors	Stefano
	Donna
Employees	Eileen
	Jim
	Catrina
Temps	Anna
	Graham

Each of these members must have two attributes, namely their Countries' Name and the Language they wish to have their articles in. These are as follows:

Member	Group	country-name	language	user-password
Stefano	Directors	italia	italiano	Stefano
Donna	Directors	uk	english	Donna
Eileen	Employees	us	english	Eileen
Jim	Employees	uk	english	Jim
Catrina	Employees	italia	italiano	Catrina
Anna	Temps	italia	italiano	Anna
Graham	Temps	us	english	Graham

Both `country-name` and `language` are already optional attributes for members in the directory, so we can just move on to adding the members. The first will be illustrated, and as an exercise you should insert the other 6 members and their attributes as outlined in the above table. Note that you must also add a `user-password` attribute for each user so they can log in. For simplicity, we are just going to make these the same values as the usernames.

So let's enter Stefano as a new member. Navigating to ou=Members, right-click in the right pane and select New | User and, upon clicking Next, enter the Name as Stefano. Click Next and the Add Attribute button, select the `country-name` attribute, click OK and enter italia as its value. Repeat this for language, but enter italiano as the value, as show in the figure below:

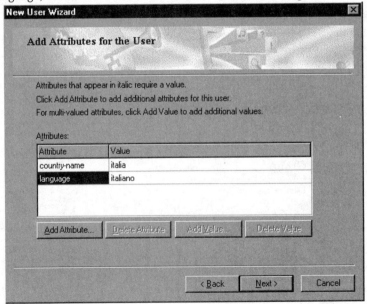

The final attribute you need to add is `user-password`. Add this and give it the value **Stefano**. Click **Next** to take you to the **Add the User to Groups** screen and select **Add** to list the available groups. Double-click on **Directors** and then click **OK** and **Finish** to complete the addition of your user to the membership directory. Repeat this for the other users, following the attributes exactly as laid out in the table above.

When complete, you should have a list of all these users in the `ou=Members` container and you are ready to map the instance to the web site.

Securing the Corporate Web Site

We have completed the configuration of our Membership Directory administration, so we must now assign this instance to our web site. In the Site Server Administration tool, select the Internet Information Server snap-in, right-click on the **Default Web Site** and select **All Tasks | Membership Server Mapping**. Select **mem** from the list of instances. After clicking OK, a few seconds will pass while the site is set up with membership authentication.

> **If this task does not appear on your menu, check the console Snap-in configuration. A Personalization and Membership snap-in will appear on the Extensions tab. Select the checkbox to add this snap-in to your console.**

You have now successfully completed the Personalization and Membership section of the study – well done!

Creating the Site Vocabulary

The **site vocabulary** is one area that wasn't covered in detail in the Content Management section. The site vocabulary can form the basis of your site for both content and navigation. It can store categories of information that can be browsed or searched on by visitors to the web site. It's useful to have the site vocabulary terms match values that may be used in the content types of Content Management. This allows us to define a content type department and select from the departments listed in the site vocabulary.

In our case, the site vocabulary is to be designed around the following structure:

```
Documents
    Units
        Management Science
        Risk Management
        Software Development
        Performance Analysis
    Areas
        Overview
        Research
        CompetitorWatch
        Technical
```

Let's create the site vocabulary now.

We are able to use the default site vocabulary defined when we install site server, but in our case, it does not contain the terms we need, so we have to create our own vocabulary terms. Documents are at the root of our vocabulary, so we need to create this root from the membership directory manager (you are unable to add to the root of the site vocabulary using the web administration tool).

Navigate to `ou=Admin/ou=Other/ou=TagTerms/ModelName=Default`. **Right-Click** on `ModelName=Default` and select **New | Object** to launch the **New Object Wizard**. Click **Next** twice and, when asked to type the **Name** of the object, enter `Documents` and click **Next**. Upon clicking **Finish**, the wizard closes and your object will have been added – note that if the object is not added to the list then you should click the **Refresh** button. What you should see is shown in the screenshot below:

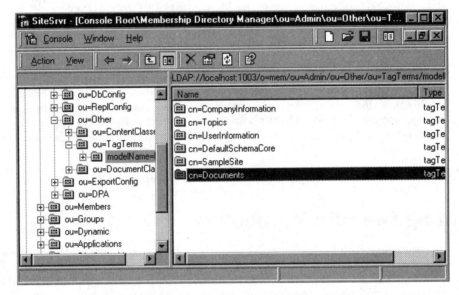

We have now finished working with the MMC, which allowed us to add the `Documents` section to the root of the site vocabulary. Now we'll change to the Web Administration tool to complete the site vocabulary configuration, as the user interface of the web administration tool is easier to use than the raw membership directory. Close down the MMC and fire up the Web Administration utility, entering the username/password of **WebAdmin/WebAdmin**, which you created earlier. When the Admin page appears click on the **Membership Directory Manager** link. When asked to log on to your membership directory instance, ensure you select **mem**, enter **WebAdmin/WebAdmin** as the username/password combination, and click on **Submit**.

Once you have been authenticated, select **Edit Site Vocabulary** from the list of links on the left frame and you should see a list box with `Documents` (and possibly others listed) as illustrated in the screenshot below:

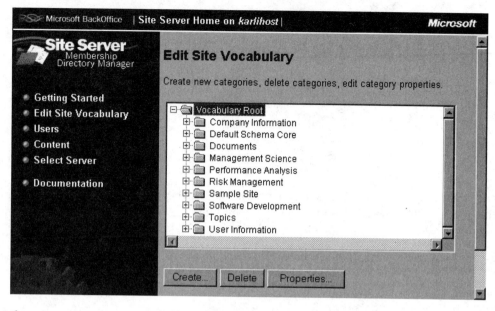

Select the `Documents` term and click the **Create** button at the bottom – the categories we now create are the site vocabulary terms for our corporate documents.

We are required to create two levels under `Documents` – namely `Units` and `Areas`. In the **Category Name** field type `Units`, and enter "**Holds the business Units**" as the description. Leave the Query string blank for the moment and click submit. Repeat the above for `Areas`, this time adding the description "**Describes the document type**". You should now be seeing something like the screenshot below.

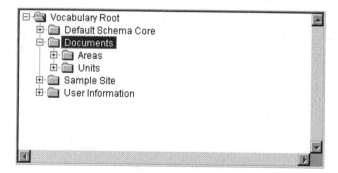

Now, to complete the configuration of the Site Vocabulary, click on `Units` and insert the sub-categories `Management Science`, `Performance Analysis`, `Risk Management`, and `Software Development`. To complete the building of the vocabulary, select `Areas` and add the four sub-categories `CompetitorWatch`, `Overview`, `Research`, and `Technical`.

The next screenshot illustrates what your site vocabulary should resemble.

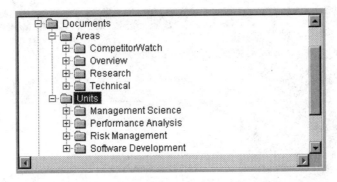

The initial design of the site vocabulary has been completed. We will look at it again during the set up of our Content Management store in the next section.

Creating the Content Management Store

In this section we will create our content management store, adding content types and attributes where appropriate.

Creating the InfoPost Content Store

We now need to create a content store called InfoPost, so we should create a directory called InfoPost in the Microsoft Site Server\Data\Publishing directory. In accordance with the Content Management chapter, we must copy the files shown in the figure below from the CmSample directory (Microsoft Site Server\Data\Publishing\CMSample) to the InfoPost directory we have just created. You also have to copy the file makeCM.vbs from the directory Microsoft Site Server\SiteServer\Publishing to the InfoPost directory. Finally, copy all of the files in the CM.zip archive (which is found in the sample files downloaded from the Wrox web site) to this directory (see the Content Management chapter to get more detail on what files are needed and why). Note we have added the file AllDocs.asp, which is included in the sample, but was not needed in the Content Management chapter. The reason for this is outlined later in this chapter.

The first document, `AllDocs.asp` is of use later when we implement a search tool for the site. It basically has links to all of the files you create for users to view, so the Site Server Search crawler can index these files.

Customising our site pages

Browse the sample files provided in the `CM.zip` download and open the file `DefaultViewTemplate.ast` in a text editor (if you have not met this file before, it is described in detail in the Content Management chapter). Notice that it has been edited, replacing all occurrences of `cmSample` with `InfoPost` to customize it for using within the case study.

We also needed to edit `menu.txt` to create a navigational menu that is appropriate to our site. Note the `DisplayDefaultViews` section, which will write out links to each of the content types we have previously created, followed by links to the approval site, file views, and submit pages. The menu.txt file is shown below with the changes highlighted.

```
<TABLE WIDTH="138" HEIGHT="359" BORDER=0 VALIGN=TOP BGCOLOR="SILVER">
<TR VALIGN=TOP>
<TD>
<CENTER>
<H2>InfoPost</H2>
<%

    DisplayDefaultViews


    ' =======================================================================
    Sub DefaultViews_Callback(strURL, strDescription)
    If Len(strDescription) = 0 Then strDescription = strURL

    Response.Write "<BR><A HREF=""" & strURL & """><font color=""white"">" & _
        strDescription & "</font>" & CrLf
    End Sub
%>
```

```
<P>
Admin
<BR>
<A HREF="approve.asp"><IMG SRC="approve.gif" BORDER=0 WIDTH=45
HEIGHT=35><BR>Approve</A>
<P>
<A HREF="cpview.asp"><IMG SRC="view.gif" BORDER=0 WIDTH=45 HEIGHT=35><BR>View</A>
<P>
<A HREF="submit.asp"><IMG SRC="post.gif" BORDER=0 WIDTH=45
HEIGHT=35><BR>Submit</A>
<P>
<A HREF="default.asp##_parent">Home</A>
<P>

</CENTER>
</TD>
</TR>
</TABLE>
```

Finally, the `default.asp` file (also available from the `CM.zip` download) was customized for our site, at the point where it says, "CUSTOMISE". We must also remove the "View this code" link from the file. A test is done to determine the browser type and the included file, `Upload.inc`, determines what upload control should be used on the client to allow the content providers to post their content to the site (this is detailed in the Content Management chapter). The new `default.asp` file is shown below, divided by commentary indicating the changes that had to be made:

```
<!--#include file="common.asp" -->
<!--#include Virtual="/SiteServer/Publishing/upload.inc" -->
<!DOCTYPE HTML PUBLIC "-//W3C//DTD HTML 3.2//EN">
<html>

<head>
<title>Citix Consultants</title>
</head>

<body background="images/background.gif" bgcolor="#ffe4e1" topmargin="0"
leftmargin="0">

<table width="100%">
   <tr>
      <td valign="top"><table border="0" width="24%">
         <tr>
```

The first notable insert is the navigation menu, which provides links to each of the view pages created for content types, as well as to the administrative areas (submit, content view and approval).

```
            <td width="100%"><!-- #include file="menu.txt" --></td>
         </tr>
      </table>
      </td>
      <td valign="top"><FONT color=dimgray></FONT><FONT></FONT><table
width="100%">
         <tr>
            <td style="MARGIN-LEFT: 10px"><p><FONT color=white face="">
               <!--CUSTOMISE-->
               <!--This just checks that the user entering has a recent browser-->
               <% If IsBrowserOk() Then %>
```

The name of the company is then indicated, along with instructions for content providers:

```
                              <FONT color=dimgray size=6>InfoPost @ Citix.com</FONT>
                              <P>
                              To browse the site, simply select one of the navigation
                              links to the left of the site.
                              <BR>
                              If you wish to view your content on this site or upload new
                              content, then click on the
                              "View my Content" or "Submit New content" links respectively.
                              <P>
                              <B>Only administrators have the ability to administer
                              documents on the site.</B>
                         <% Else %>
                              <FONT color=dimgray size=6>InfoPost @ Citix.com</FONT>
                              <h2>Sorry, but you must upgrade to a newer version of your
                              browser.</h2>
                              <A href="http://www.microsoft.com/ie"><i>Upgrade Now</i></A>
                         <% End IF %>
                              </FONT>
                      </td>
                  </tr>

              </table>
              </td>
          </tr>
      </table>
      </body>
      </html>

      <%
      '  ===========================================================================
```

Finally, a function is supplied to determine the type and version of the browser being used, allowing us to specify the method the content provider uses to upload content (for example, Netscape browsers don't support ActiveX and hence would use the POST method). The Content Management chapter outlines this in more detail.

```
Function IsBrowserOk()
    Dim oBC, strOS

    On Error Resume Next

    IsBrowserOk = False

    Set oBC = Server.CreateObject("MSWC.BrowserType")
    If Err Then
        DumpError "Failed to get BrowserType object"
        Exit Function
    End If

    DebPrint "Browser = " & oBC.browser
    DebPrint "Version = " & oBC.version

    strOS = Request.ServerVariables("HTTP_UA_OS")
    If strOS <> "MacOS" Then
        If Not oBC.Frames Or Not oBC.Tables Or Not oBC.Cookies Then Exit Function
```

Continued on Following Page

```
        'Upload control needs IE 3.02
        If oBC.ActiveXControls And oBC.VBScript Then
            Dim iMinor, iMajor, fVerBad
            iMajor = oBC.MajorVer
            iMinor = oBC.MinorVer
            fVerBad = False
            If iMajor > 3 Then
                fVerBad = False
            ElseIf iMajor = 3 Then
                If iMinor >= 2 Then fVerBad = False
            End If

            If oBC.Browser = "IE" And fVerBad Then Exit Function
        End If
    End IF

    IsBrowserOk = True
End Function
%>
```

The final file to consider is `AllDocs.asp`. This file uses a rule set to generate a recordset of the files within the Content Management site, and creates URL's of these so that Site Server Search can crawl these files. We are going to look at this file in more detail later in the chapter.

Now that we have the customized files, let's configure and run the script to create our new CM site.

Working with makeCm.vbs

We need to create our content store, using the `makeCm.vbs` script detailed in the Content Management chapter. It is possible to customize this file to create the complete Content Management site, with all of the content types and attributes. We would otherwise need to use either the web administration tool or the Membership MMC to accomplish this.

However, fully customizing this file is outside the scope of this study, and can be quite involved. In our study, the `makeCM.vbs` file provided in the downloaded file has no content customization. If you happened to be using a customized version then remove all site customizations – we are going to configure site customization ourselves through the web administration utility. Look in the `makeCM.vbs` file and find the second occurrence of the following text:

```
' ===================================================================
' Start of configurable part
' ===================================================================
```

Notice that all the customization has been removed up until the next occurrence of the text:

```
' ===================================================================
' End of configurable part
' ===================================================================
```

The command line to run this script is different from the previous one, as we are creating in a Membership Directory. I hope you remember the LDAP Port number to which your web site is mapped (my sample number is 1003). With this number in hand, change to the `InfoPost` directory and run the following command line, substituting 1003 for the number of your LDAP Port and ensuring that the path to you store is correct:

> **CScript makeCM.vbs /s:localhost /l:localhost:1003 /v:InfoPost /a:InfoPost /d:"c:\Microsoft Site Server\Data\Publishing\InfoPost" /u:WebAdmin /p:WebAdmin**

The /l defines the LDAP instance used by your website (otherwise the default is used) and the /u and /p parameters specify the admin member you created earlier. Using the Internet Information snap-in of the MMC, check that the `InfoPost` application has been created (as shown in the screenshot below):

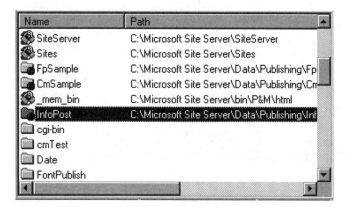

We can now view the Content default page (`http://servername/InfoPost/default.asp`) by browsing to `http://servername/InfoPost` and entering the membership **WebAdmin** username and password. The `InfoPost` start page is illustrated below:

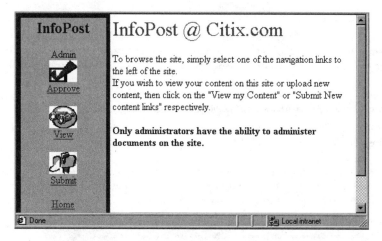

Now that we've created the framework of our site, we need to create the detail – namely, the content types and attributes, but first we need to refine the site vocabulary for this Content Source.

Creating Content Types and Attributes

In accordance with our site design, there are four content types that we must create, namely `Overview`, `Research`, `CompetitorWatch` and `Technical`. The documents to be uploaded with these content types have the attributes `Department`, `Author`, `Title`, `ReviewDate`, `SecurityLevel` and `Abstract`. Let's run through the creation of the Content Type `CompetitorWatch` as well as the attributes to apply to this content type when documents are submitted. As an exercise, you should complete the same procedure for the other Content types – the same attributes should be applied to all documents (although under many circumstances, you may wish to have different attributes for varying content types).

You should now use the web administration utility and select **Content Management** under the **Publishing** section and at `http://yourserver/SiteServer/Admin/Publishing/default.asp`, log onto the "mem" Membership Directory. If all of the above steps have been completed successfully, then you should see `InfoPost` listed in the Content Stores as shown below:

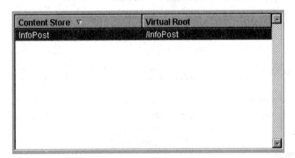

Select `InfoPost`, click on **Properties** and select the **Content Types** link, which will take you to an empty content type list. We now want to create our content types, but before we do this there is a problem that will make this currently unsuccessful. Let's take an aside to see what this is and how to solve it.

Creating Content Types for a Store under Membership Authentication

When a content store has been created using membership authentication, a problem occurs when we come to adding content types. To see this in action, try the following:

Click on **Create** and we should now be viewing the **Create New Content Type** screen. Go ahead and type **Test** as the **Content type name**. Next, press *Tab*, which auto-fill's in the other boxes, and then **Submit**. You'll probably get the following error message:

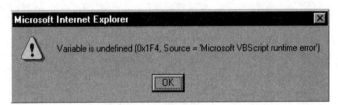

Strangely enough the content type is actually added to the list of Types for the Store, but this hides the fact that a problem prevents your content from being indexed. We get a hint of where the problem lies if we view the DEBUG information generated within the web administration tool. OK the error message and view the source of the HTML page that is displayed (right click on the page and select View Source from there, else you will be looking at the source for the frame instead). A snippet is shown below:

```
...

<!-- Debug=Generating property page -->
<!-- Debug=GenerateHTML  InfoPost::test.asp:: -->
<!-- Debug=Root = /InfoPost -->
<!-- Debug=Filename = C:\Microsoft Site Server\Data\Publishing\InfoPost\test.asp -
->
<!-- Debug=GenerateHTML Succeeded -->
<!-- Debug=test::::test::test.asp -->
<!-- Debug=SetConfig: Dir = C:\Microsoft Site Server\Data\Publishing\InfoPost -->
<!-- Debug=Failed to BeginTransaction on Content Index cache object -- Error
Number=46 (70)  String=Permission denied -->
<!-- Debug=Failed to CreateContentType -- Error Number=1F4 (500)  String=Variable
is undefined -->

<SCRIPT LANGUAGE=JavaScript>
alert("Variable is undefined (0x1F4, Source = 'Microsoft VBScript runtime
error')")
</SCRIPT>
<!-- Debug=Generating view page -->
<!-- Debug=VRoot = InfoPost -->
<!-- Debug=New Attribute =   -->
<!-- Debug=Attributes =   -->

...
```

Notice the lines:

```
<!-- Debug=Failed to BeginTransaction on Content Index cache object -- Error
Number=46 (70)  String=Permission denied -->
<!-- Debug=Failed to CreateContentType -- Error Number=1F4 (500)  String=Variable
is undefined -->
```

These are the keys to the problem. It is caused by the fact that the user in the membership directory does not have enough privileges to update the Search server catalog that was created for our content store. To solve this, we must return to the membership directory we set-up earlier and upgrade the privileges we assigned to our WebAdmin administrator.

Before we do this, let's have a quick look at another problem that may arise. It's possible that you'll get the error below:

```
<!-- Debug=SetConfig: Dir = D:\Microsoft Site Server\Data\Publishing\InfoPost -->
<!-- Debug=Failed to BeginTransaction on Content Index cache object -- Error
Number=80004005 (-2147467259)  String= -->
<!-- Debug=Failed to CreateContentType -- Error Number=1F4 (500) String=Variable
is undefined -->
```

This error arises because the Content Index service is stopped and Site Server is unable to update the Property Set for the Content Management catalog. This property set stores all of the content types and attributes which can be applied to documents, and can be seen by selecting Start | Programs | Windows NT 4.0 Option Pack | Microsoft Index Server | Index Server Manager and selecting Content Management and then Properties. The name of content types and attributes are stored under the Property heading.

We can rectify this error by starting the Content Index Service from Start | Settings | Control Panel and clicking the Services icon. Select the Content Index service and click the Start button.

Now, let's upgrade the privileges of our WebAdmin user. Fire up the Membership Directory Manager, choose our Membership Instance (mem, accessed by changing the properties of the MDM snap-in as detailed earlier) and navigate to o=mem/ou=Groups/ou=NTGroups. Double-click on the cn=Administrators group and view the Members tab. Click on the Add button, select our WebAdmin user from the Available items list, and add it to the Selected items list:

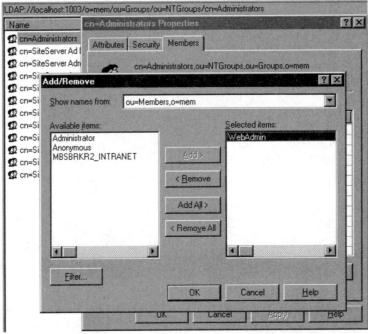

You have now added WebAdmin to an NT Administrators group. This account can now successfully add content types to your Content Source. You can prove that this has been successful if you once again look at the DEBUG information written out within the content type page for our test content type, Test:

```
...
<!-- Debug=Generating property page -->
<!-- Debug=GenerateHTML  InfoPost::test.asp:: -->
<!-- Debug=Root = /InfoPost -->
<!-- Debug=Filename = C:\Microsoft Site Server\Data\Publishing\InfoPost\test.asp -
->
```

```
<!-- Debug=GenerateHTML Succeeded -->
<!-- Debug=test::::test::test.asp -->
<!-- Debug=SetConfig: Dir = C:\Microsoft Site Server\Data\Publishing\InfoPost -->
<!-- Debug=Arr(0) = DocAuthor -->
<!-- Debug=Arr(1) = DocLastSavedTm -->
<!-- Debug=Arr(2) = DocLastPrinted -->
<!-- Debug=Arr(3) = DocLastAuthor -->
<!-- Debug=Arr(4) = DocKeywords -->
<!-- Debug=Arr(5) = DocEditTime -->
<!-- Debug=Arr(6) = DocCreatedTm -->
<!-- Debug=Arr(7) = DocRevNumber -->
<!-- Debug=Arr(8) = DocCharCount -->
<!-- Debug=Arr(9) = DocSubject -->
<!-- Debug=Arr(10) = DocAppName -->
<!-- Debug=Arr(11) = create -->
<!-- Debug=Arr(12) = Characterization -->
<!-- Debug=Arr(13) = attrib -->
<!-- Debug=Arr(14) = allocsize -->
<!-- Debug=Arr(15) = access -->
<!-- Debug=Arr(16) = DocComments -->
<!-- Debug=Arr(17) = shortfilename -->
<!-- Debug=Arr(18) = Owner -->
<!-- Debug=Arr(19) = write -->
<!-- Debug=Arr(20) = workid -->
<!-- Debug=Arr(21) = Vpath -->
<!-- Debug=Arr(22) = USN -->
<!-- Debug=Arr(23) = DocPageCount -->
<!-- Debug=Arr(24) = ContentType -->
<!-- Debug=Arr(25) = SubmitTime -->
<!-- Debug=Arr(26) = size -->
<!-- Debug=Arr(27) = rank -->
<!-- Debug=Arr(28) = path -->
<!-- Debug=Arr(29) = HitCount -->
<!-- Debug=Arr(30) = filename -->
<!-- Debug=Arr(31) = fileindex -->
<!-- Debug=Arr(32) = DocWordCount -->
<!-- Debug=Arr(33) = DocTemplate -->
<!-- Debug=Arr(34) = Approved -->
<!-- Debug=AddContentTypeToContentSource Ok -->
<!-- Debug=AddContentTypeToApp Ok -->
<!-- Debug=CreateContentType Ok -->
<!-- Debug=Generating view page -->
<!-- Debug=VRoot = InfoPost -->
<!-- Debug=New Attribute =   -->
<!-- Debug=Attributes =   -->

...
```

We have proved we can now add content types, so let's continue where we left off.

> Remember to delete the **Test** content type before proceeding, if you added it in the above test.

Successfully Creating Content Types and Attributes

It is important to categorize your content types with your site vocabulary. This gives your users a logical hierarchy to browse through as they select a topic from the vocabulary. If you remember our site vocabulary from earlier:

```
Documents
    Units
        Management Science
        Risk Management
        Software Development
        Performance Analysis
    Areas
        Overview
        Research
        CompetitorWatch
        Technical
```

In our case, it seems reasonable to categorize content types according to both Units and Areas. This would simplify user navigation, allowing a user to find all documents in either of these types (for example, the user could ask for all documents within the Software Development unit, or all Overview documents). Citix Consultants Inc. operates on a knowledge wide basis rather than a business unit basis, allowing all users access to information by type. However, users from certain business units should still be able to focus on documents specific to their own business unit without wasting precious time.

Also important to the organization is control of documentation, so a title and version number must be present with every document, as well as the name of the author who created the document and when it was created. An e-mail address should also be supplied to contact an author if necessary.

Let's stay with a relatively simple structure, maintaining the attributes for each content type, but allowing for specialized attributes (for example, CompetitorWatch documents may contain an attribute containing the name of the company the information pertains to). Shown below is the description of the content type Overview:

Attribute	Type
UnitName	Site Vocabulary Selection
Title	String
Content Editor	String
Publication Date	String
VersionNo	Integer
AuthorEmail	String

You should currently have the web administration tool open, after earlier selecting the InfoPost store from the list of Content Management stores. After selecting Content Types, an empty list is displayed – we should now populate these lists with the above terms.

Click **Create** and in the **Create New Content Type** screen, enter `Overview` as the **Content type name** and press *Tab*, which fills in the boxes showing the **Content Sub-directory** and **Property Form Name**. Now we need to create our `UnitName` attribute. As this is a site vocabulary term we have created, we need to create a custom attribute, so click on the **Create Custom** button. Enter `UnitName` as the **Attribute name**, enter "Describes the business Unit" as the **Description** and select **Vocabulary Term** as the **Attribute Syntax**. We now need to set the constraints on the vocabulary term, so click on the **Set Constraints** button and a tree view of the site vocabulary will be shown. Expand **Documents**, click on **Units** and press the submit button. You should now see something like:

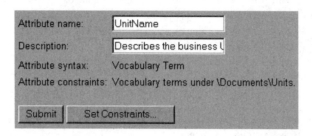

Click **Submit** and, on the properties page, ensure that both **Generate** checkboxes are checked. Now click **Submit** again. When the page refreshes, you shall see an attribute named `UnitNameDisplay` which is used to show the user options – do not remove it.

Now we can create the `Title` attribute, which is already defined in the default site vocabulary provided with Site Server Content Management, by clicking the **Add** button, expanding **Content and Document Information**, and then selecting the **Title** entry and clicking the submit button. Repeat this process for **Content Editor** and **Publication Date** from the same list. We have to create the final two attributes ourselves, so go ahead and **Create** two custom attributes – one called `VersionNo` which is of type `Integer` and another called `AuthorEmail` of type `String`.

You should now be in the position illustrated below:

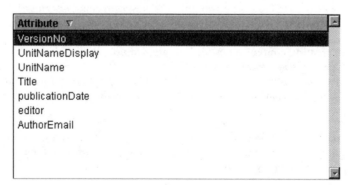

We now need to create the other content types and add each of these attributes. The easiest way I've found to do this is to create a new group in the default attributes list and add the necessary attributes there. To do this, open up the file:

```
<Site Server Root>\SiteServer\Admin\knowledge\dsmgr\users\defaultattributes.asp
```

489

This file contains all of the attributes that you are able to add when you create a content type. Scroll down to the bottom and add the following code just before the `End Sub`:

```
AddNode "Corporate"
    AddChild "VersionNo","VersionNo"
    AddChild "AuthorEmail","AuthorEmail"
    AddChild "UnitName","UnitName"
```

This node is placed in the site vocabulary under the term "Corporate" that we are using to describe content types which are part of our own organization, but which were *not* part of the default vocabulary provided by Site Server. This section (Corporate) contains the three attributes we added earlier, namely `VersionNo`, `AuthorEmail` and `UnitName`.

You can test this change by simply adding a new attribute to a content type of the `InfoPost` store, in the same way we did earlier. You should see the attributes we just added under our new Corporate category.

> *It is important to note that this file is not dynamically generated as you add your own attributes. Any additions need to be made manually, as above.*

You should now add the content types `Research`, `CompetitorWatch` and `Technical` as defined previously, adding the same attributes as we did for the `Overview` content type. Of course, you won't have to create custom attributes this time, as we've just added the ones we need to the default attribute list. Go ahead and do this now, and complete the design of our Content Management store.

> **If you add a content type or its relevant attributes, and find that attributes you have added have disappeared, refresh the page to re-populate the list.**

You may be wondering why we don't repeat this process for the `Units` entries outlined in the site vocabulary (`Management Science` and so on). The key is in remembering that the site vocabulary is a logical pointer to documents, and does not directly correspond to each content type.

When we consider creating content types for our site, we note that each document falls under one of the four content types: `Overview`, `Research`, `CompetitorWatch` and `Technical`. What the site vocabulary structure above allows us to do is to logically organize our documents according to both the content types describing particular documents as well as their `Unit`, which is stored as an attribute of the document.

So, a particular document may be a research document that would obviously be of content type `Research`. Within that content type is an attribute called `UnitName`, which corresponds to one of the entries in the `Units` category in the vocabulary.

When searching for a document we can look for documents of a specified content type, a particular attribute value, or both of these.

Working with the Company Content

Now that we have set up the content store and membership directory, we are in a position to allow content to be stored and shared on our site. The company directors have stated that they want the most efficient method for dealing with the various security levels and languages based throughout the global company. They also know they are dealing with non-programmers, which is also an important factor. These content creators don't want to write multiple documents for the various languages and security levels, they want to be able to write one document which marks sections only available to certain parties and other parts which translate the document into the users language as defined in their membership account. Here's a diagram that illustrates the scenario:

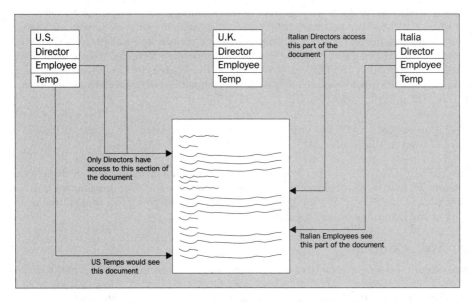

Notice that different levels of users have access to different areas of the document depending on both their locale and security level. Also, notice that the US and UK Directors have the same language and security level, and so have access to the same area of the document.

Developing Content

Now that we have decided we want to maintain only one copy of a version of a document, we have to decide on the best way of doing this. Of course, we could use ASP and P&M to determine what parts of the document the user can see, but this does not account for the requirement that all users must be able to create the documents and submit them for viewing. Alternatively, we could use an HTML editor or Word documents, but how do we then determine what users can see without creating multiple versions of documents and some template to differentiate between them?

Before we begin

This case study focuses on integrating content based on the XML standard, using Site Server features such as Personalization and Membership and Content Management to provide a powerful knowledge management web site.

eXtensible Markup Language (XML) is a meta-markup language that provides a format for describing structured data. This allows us to declare precise declarations of content, perform powerful content searches, and retrieve meaningful search results across multiple platforms. There are three key points in understanding the usefulness of XML compared to HTML:

> XML is **extensible**, allowing us to define as many tags as we need for our document. This differs from HTML, which had a limited subset of tags.

> Data marked up with XML is structured. This allows us to have a tree of tags, for example we could have a `Pages` tag within a root `Book` tag. This makes sense, as we couldn't have it in reverse. We can also implement rules to describe a valid structure of XML data depending on the document being written.

> Using XML we can separate the content from its presentation. HTML would use both content tags (such as `<TITLE>`) and presentation tags (like `<B>`) within the same document, making it difficult to present different views of the same content. **eXtensible Style Language** (XSL) is one technology currently being proposed as a standard for presenting XML documents. Both XML and XSL are supported by IE5 (XML is also supported to a lesser extent in IE4, although direct viewing of XML files is not supported in IE4). It is recommended that you carry out this case study using IE5 (`http://www.microsoft.com/ie`).

For more information on XML and XSL, visit `http://www.microsoft.com/xml` or look at one of the many Wrox books dealing with XML.

We will look at XML in a different perspective because Content Management gives us direct access to XML documents. Of course, to integrate this with Personalization and Membership we must have some way of integrating Site Server. We are going to look at a way of doing this that allows us to bring the worlds of XML and Site Server together.

Working with XML Content

Using XML, we can allow a single version of a document to be marked up so we can easily determine which parts of the content specific users should be allowed to view. So, how – from a content developer's point of view – would content be created so that it would fit all of the criteria stated?

Creating Content

Let's create an example XML template, which we'll call `Template.xml`, for our content providers to use when developing their content (this file is found, along with the other XML files used in this chapter, in `xml.zip`):

```
<?xml version="1.0"?>
<?xml-stylesheet type="text/xsl" href="style.xsl"?>
<document>
    <title>Title of the paper</title>
    <author>Author Name</author>
    <languages_supported>
        <language>italiano</language>
        <language>english</language>
    </languages_supported>
    <abstract>
        <english>English Abstract</english>
        <italiano>Astratto Italiano</italiano>
    </abstract>
    <body>
```

```
        <para security_level="2">
          <english>Info available to US &amp; UK Directors</english>
          <italiano>Per i direttori italiani</italiano>
        </para>
        <para security_level="1">
          <english>Info available to US &amp; UK Employees</english>
          <italiano>Per i dipendenti italiani</italiano>
        </para>
        <para security_level="0">
          <english>Info available to US &amp; UK Temps</english>
          <italiano>Per i impiegati italiani</italiano>
        </para>
      </body>
   </document>
```

Notice that this is just a straight XML document and hence can be opened directly in IE5. In the second line we define a stylesheet used to present the information in an acceptable form, customized for the user. We'll come back to this later, as this will be an important part of the process.

The document defines a title and author as is typical in any content. Specific to this document is a `languages_supported` section, allowing us to specify what languages this document is available in. This would be useful is we wanted to know if a document was available in our language before viewing its content. We also describe a simple document abstract in each of the available languages. We then reach the most interesting part of the template – where we have the ability to tell who can see what parts of our document and in their appropriate language. Each paragraph has an associated Security Level (remember creating this in the membership directory?), allowing the user to limit access to the content to a specified level of user. Each paragraph also has the content available in English and Italian, although this could easily scale and provide different paragraphs in varying numbers and types of languages.

This is all very well, but would you expect a user to start editing your XML source? I didn't think so. This is where we can give them a bit of help with Microsoft's XML Notepad (downloadable from `msdn.microsoft.com/xml/notepad`). XML Notepad gives a graphical interface to the XML source we just created and allows content providers to simply and easily input their information, whilst maintaining the markup and validity of the XML template.

The aim of this case study is not to discuss the pros and cons of the XML editors currently available on the market, rather it aims to show the advantages that can be gained by using XML to markup content within your company. Other commercial editors, more powerful than XML Notepad, are available (check out `http://www.xml.com/xml/pub/pt/Authoring`), and you may find one of these editors more useful. It should be noted that current XML editors are fundamentally different from the Microsoft Word editor users may currently be using. The advent of Office 2000 and its use of XML may have you think that this is the solution to your XML editor problem. However, Word 2000 does not save as pure XML, but rather as a combination of XML, CSS and HTML.

The following figure shows a document created using our XML template. This file is called `CompGlas.xml` in your download package (`xml.zip`):

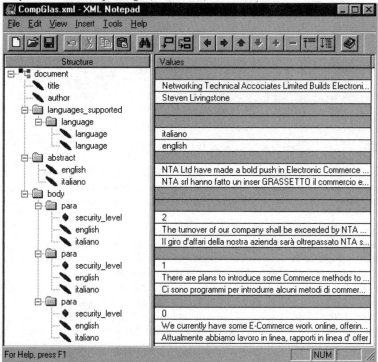

Uploading the Content

Now that the content has been created, we need to deploy it to our web site. You should now go to the `InfoPost` site, click the `Submit` link and upload the file `CompGlas.xml`. Select the content type `CompetitorWatch` and click **Next**. Enter the details as shown in the figure below (the **Title** should be the same as that in the XML document):

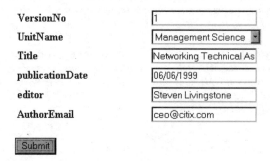

Click **Submit** and the document will be published. It will now be accessible via the link relevant to its content type.

> Note that it takes around 30 seconds before you document is published, while Site Server Search catalogs it.

Repeat this for each of the XML files supplied in `xml.zip`. You are free to enter all the information; the following is the mapping between the `UnitName` and the filename:

File	Content Type	UnitName
ResRiskEcom.xml	Research	Risk Management
OverTurnOver.xml	Overview	Management Science
TechPerfSS.xml	Technical	Performance Analysis
TechManSoft.xml	Technical	Software Development

We have now posted all our XML content to the server and users throughout the company are in a position to start accessing it. This is what the next topic discusses.

Viewing Content

In the normal Content Management solution, various types of files are uploaded and users have direct access to the documents by simply clicking on the link to them within the respective view for that content type. So what's different here? Well, the challenge is that we have allowed all of our information, including security and language, to be put in one document, which we have marked up with XML. Although we can apply a stylesheet to the file, we have no way of determining what language the stylesheet should display, or more importantly what security level to apply – this information is all dependent on user attributes stored in the Membership Directory and accessible via ASP using the Active User Object.

So, how do we get round this? What follows is one way.

Active StyleSheets

> The XML Parser with IE5 is needed to work with the XML documents.

Configuration

The following diagram describes how our site will incorporate information from the Membership database with the XML content developed by providers:

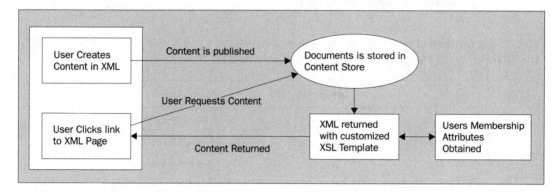

The main crux of this is that we actually set up our XSL stylesheet to be run as an ASP script (it is in fact parsed by the ASP COM object on the server), allowing us to use ASP inside our XSL stylesheets. Therefore, we can dynamically create our stylesheet depending on the user attributes in the Membership Directory. Before this can be illustrated, we must configure Internet Information Server to support such a process.

Right-click on the **Default Web Site** at the root of our web in the Internet Information Service snap-in of the MMC and select **Properties**. Select the **Home Directory** tab, click the **Configuration** button, and, under **Application Mappings**, click **Add**. In the executable box type `C:\WINNT\system32\inetsrv\Asp.dll` (or browse to where your copy of `asp.dll` lives), enter **.xsl** in the **Extension** box and click **OK** three times. The mapping has now been done.

StyleSheet Template

Now that we have set up IIS so that we can integrate ASP with out XSL stylesheet, we must define a template which can then be applied to our XML files. This stylesheet should be placed in the `InfoPost` directory, rather than in every subdirectory – allowing us to update only this copy and have it applied across all documents. Here is the XSL template we shall apply (`style.xsl`):

```
<% Set objMem  = Server.CreateObject("MemberShip.UserObjects")
   strLanguage = objMem.Get("language")
   arr         = objMem.Groups
   Set objCont = GetObject("LDAP://localhost:1003/" & arr)
   intSecurity = CInt(objCont.Get("SecurityLevel"))

   Set objCont = Nothing
   Set objMem  = Nothing
%>
<?xml version="1.0"?>
<xsl:stylesheet

   xmlns:xsl="http://www.w3.org/TR/WD-xsl"
   xmlns="http://www.w3.org/TR/REC-html40"
   result-ns="">
```

```
    <xsl:template match="/">
    <HTML>
        <BODY STYLE="font-family:Arial, helvetica, sans-serif; font-size:10pt;
        background-color:#EEEEEE">
            <DIV>
                <xsl:apply-templates select="document" />
            </DIV>
        </BODY>
    </HTML>
    </xsl:template>

    <xsl:template match="document">
        <xsl:apply-templates/>
    </xsl:template>

    <xsl:template match="title">
        <DIV STYLE="background-color:darkblue; color:white; padding:4px">
        <SPAN STYLE="font-weight:bold; color:lightblue">
            <xsl:value-of /> by <i><xsl:value-of select="../author" />.</i>
        </SPAN>
        </DIV>
    </xsl:template>

    <xsl:template match="abstract">
        <P/>
        <DIV STYLE="background-color:lightblue; color:white; padding:4px">
            <FONT STYLE="font-size=20pt;color=darkblue;">Abstract</FONT><BR/>
            <SPAN STYLE="font-weight:bold; color:black">
                <xsl:value-of select="<%=strLanguage%>" />
            </SPAN>
        </DIV>
    </xsl:template>

    <xsl:template match="languages_supported">
        <DIV ALIGN="right" STYLE="background-color:lightblue">
            <SPAN>
                <xsl:for-each select="language">
                    <B><xsl:value-of /></B><BR/>
                </xsl:for-each>
            </SPAN>
        </DIV>
    </xsl:template>

    <xsl:template match="body">
        <HR/>
        <DIV STYLE="background-color:lightblue; color:black; padding:4px">
            <FONT STYLE="font-size=20pt;color=darkblue;">Information</FONT><BR/>
            <xsl:for-each select="para[@security_level&lt;<%=intSecurity+1%>]">
                <P><xsl:value-of select="<%=strLanguage%>" /></P>
            </xsl:for-each>
        </DIV>
    </xsl:template>

</xsl:stylesheet>
```

> **If you log in as different users to test the different views presented and you
> cannot find the document that has been uploaded, then you should ensure
> that Search Server is correctly indexing your content.**

Notice how we first access the membership directory and get the language attribute for the user and the security level of the group the user is in (note that if your LDAP port is other than 1003, you will have to manually edit `style.xsl`):

```
<% Set objMem    = Server.CreateObject("MemberShip.UserObjects")
   strLanguage  = objMem.Get("language")
   arr          = objMem.Groups
   Set objCont  = GetObject("LDAP://localhost:1003/" & arr)
   intSecurity  = CInt(objCont.Get("SecurityLevel"))

   Set objCont  = Nothing
   Set objMem   = Nothing
%>
```

We then declare the document an XML 1.0 compliant stylesheet and declare the XSL and HTML namespaces:

```
<?xml version="1.0"?>
<xsl:stylesheet

   xmlns:xsl="http://www.w3.org/TR/WD-xsl"
   xmlns="http://www.w3.org/TR/REC-html40"
   result-ns="">
```

We then find the root of the XML document and kick off the stylesheet starting at the document root:

```
<xsl:template match="/">
<HTML>
    <BODY STYLE="font-family:Arial, helvetica, sans-serif; font-size:10pt;
    background-color:#EEEEEE">
        <DIV>
            <xsl:apply-templates select="document" />
        </DIV>
    </BODY>
</HTML>
</xsl:template>

<xsl:template match="document">
    <xsl:apply-templates/>
</xsl:template>
```

When we find a match of the title of the document, we write this out styled by a DIV and SPAN tag, along with the name of the document author:

```
<xsl:template match="title">
    <DIV STYLE="background-color:darkblue; color:white; padding:4px">
        <SPAN STYLE="font-weight:bold; color:lightblue">
            <xsl:value-of /> by <i><xsl:value-of select="../author" />.</i>
        </SPAN>
    </DIV>
</xsl:template>
```

When we find the abstract of the document, we use the language value we got earlier and select text based on this value:

```
<xsl:template match="abstract">
   <P/>
   <DIV STYLE="background-color:lightblue; color:white; padding:4px">
      <FONT STYLE="font-size=20pt;color=darkblue;">Abstract</FONT><BR/>
      <SPAN STYLE="font-weight:bold; color:black">
         <xsl:value-of select="<%=strLanguage%>" />
      </SPAN>
   </DIV>
</xsl:template>
```

We can also inform the user of the languages that this document is available in using the languages_supported tags:

```
<xsl:template match="languages_supported">
   <DIV ALIGN="right" STYLE="background-color:lightblue">
      <SPAN>
         <xsl:for-each select="language">
            <B><xsl:value-of /></B><BR/>
         </xsl:for-each>
      </SPAN>
   </DIV>
</xsl:template>
```

Perhaps the most important part of the stylesheet comes when we iterate through each paragraph and match on the SecurityLevel attribute. If the users security level is greater than the paragraph security level then the document is displayed, otherwise it is ignored.

```
<xsl:template match="body">
   <HR/>
   <DIV STYLE="background-color:lightblue; color:black; padding:4px">
      <FONT STYLE="font-size=20pt;color=darkblue;">Information</FONT><BR/>
      <xsl:for-each select="para[@security_level&lt;<%=intSecurity+1%>]">
         <P><xsl:value-of select="<%=strLanguage%>" /></P>
      </xsl:for-each>
   </DIV>
</xsl:template>
```

Now, when we log into the application, papers are customized according to our identity. The next screenshot shows the user **Stefano** logged in and viewing the document `CompGlas.xml`:

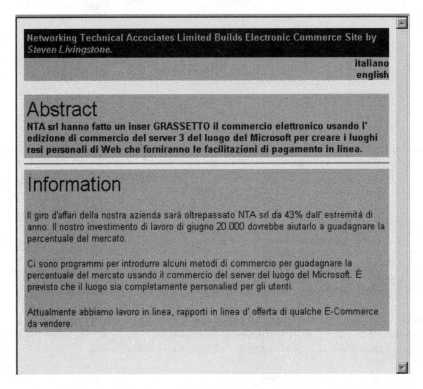

Go ahead and play around with the various uploaded documents and membership accounts to see the changes in content.

If security is of paramount importance to you (which it is not for Citix as explained in the requirements), then this method would not be suitable, as it applies the stylesheet to the XML document when it has already arrived at the client. This would allow the user to retrieve the full XML document from cache. You can see this for yourself: right-click on the text being viewed and select **View Source**.

You can avoid this by parsing the XML document on the server, but this would require an intermediate ASP page. The user would click on a link that would pass the name of the document to be retrieved in the querystring of an ASP page. The ASP page would then parse the document server-side and return the resulting XML to the client.

You may also insert the ASP scripts directly into the XML document and so parse the XML document directly. This technique is open to debate, however, as this would not leave the XML document well formed. You need to compare the advantages and disadvantages of this technique for your own situation.

Configuring this, however, is outside the scope of this study.

Now, let's look at how we integrate all this together with Knowledge Manager.

Creating a Knowledge Base

Knowledge Manager is a suite of facilities provided with Site Server to allow you to manage the information available to your users. You can allow users to browse and search your content in a structured manner according to the site vocabulary you have built up, as well as integrate with personalisation and membership to send e-mails of site information and updates to users on a prepared schedule. This study focuses on the search capabilities that are generally central to a site's information store.

Site Server Search is in fact a powerful tool that allows you to search regular text files, ODBC data sources, Exchange mailboxes, and newsgroups, as well as other sources.

Creating the search Catalog

The whole of Knowledge Manager, and in fact Content Management, uses content catalogs created by Site Server Search. However, the catalogs used to store information about your Content Management site are not compatible with Knowledge Manager. To enable our web content to be browsed from Knowledge Manager, we must create a new Content Source using Site Server Search, which contains additional information important to Knowledge Manager, as we will see later in the chapter.

Before we create this content catalog, let's look at `AllDocs.asp`, which is central to creating a Knowledge Manager site for content managed sites.

Where the Crawl Starts

When we create a search catalog, we must specify the location of files that we want to be indexed. Content Management provides us with a very simple method of locating all the files that have been uploaded to a site and should be indexed – through a file in the root of the site called `AllDocs.asp`.

Our `AllDocs.asp` file is shown below:

```
<!--#include file="common.asp" -->
<!--#include Virtual="/SiteServer/Publishing/upload.inc" -->
<!DOCTYPE HTML PUBLIC "-//W3C//DTD HTML 3.2//EN">
<html>

<head>
<title></title>
</head>
<body>
<!--
    A Simple List of all the documents on the site so that Crawler software, i.e.
    Site Server Search, can find all the documents, without needing to navigate
    personalized pages etc
-->
```

```
<!--#include Virtual="/SiteServer/Publishing/alldocs.prf" -->
<%
    Do While Not MemRecordSet.EOF
        Response.Write "<A HREF=""" & GetDocUrl(MemRecordSet("path"), _
                        MemRecordSet("ContentType")) & """>" & _
                        getfilename(MemRecordSet("FileName")) & "</A><BR>"

        MemRecordSet.MoveNext
    Loop
%>
</body>
</html>
```

If you glance just over half way down the code, you can see the rule `alldocs.prf`, which simply returns a recordset of all the content files within the `InfoPost` site.

> **Rule Files (extension .prf) and rule sets are a way of streamlining the SQL queries and ActiveX Data Objects (ADO) that can always be used to select and display content to users. Instead of putting together a complicated set of queries to personalize content for user segments, you can use a rule set. We can then retrieve a recordset of files from content sources valid for a particular user.**

The following section writes out the names and a link to each of these files, which allows a search crawl to follow these links.

Configuring the search

Let's now create the catalog of our site. Fire up the MMC and select the Search snap-in. If you now select the **Catalog Build Server** a list of the current catalogs is displayed. Right-click on **Catalog Build Server**, select **New Catalog Definition with a Wizard**, and enter **Corporate** as the name of the catalog. Leave the default **Web Link Crawl** as the search type. Click **Next** and, when asked for details on starting the search, enter the path to `AllDocs.asp` as the **Start address**. This file takes us directly to each document within our site, so we should select **Page hops** and enter **1** as the maximum number of pages to visit for each link in **AllDocs.asp**. This is shown in the screenshot below:

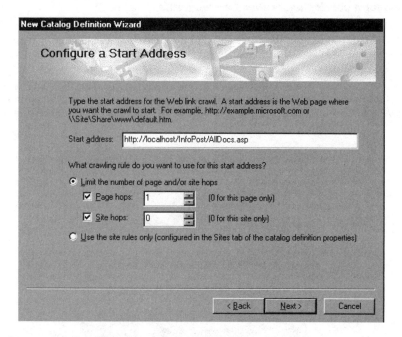

Click **Next** twice and then **Finish** and you will be returned to the list of catalogs you saw earlier, with the new **Corporate** catalog added. You have now configured the basic features of the search catalog for `InfoPost`, but we are not quite ready to build our catalog. If you right-click on the **Corporate** catalog and select **Build**, your PC may whir for a few seconds and you might think that you have now created you catalog, but take a quick look in the **Gatherer Logs** (or the Event viewer). An error will be displayed telling you that access was denied to the `AllDocs.asp` file. This can seem a bit confusing at first, but let's look at what's happening.

Configuring Access for a catalog under Membership authentication

When the Gatherer service of Site Server Search starts, it crawls through the web site as a normal web user would and so needs to log onto the site as a valid membership user. Right-click on the **Corporate** catalog and select **Properties**, which will display the **General** tab with the start address you specified earlier. Click on the **Sites** tab and click on the **Add** button. Enter **Localhost** as the **Site Name** and click **Finish** to add the new rule to the sites list. Now click on this new rule, select **Properties** and then the **Account** tab. Select **Use the account below** and enter a valid user in the membership directory – **WebAdmin** in our case. Ensure that **Basic (clear text)** has been selected, as shown in the screenshot, and click the **OK** button.

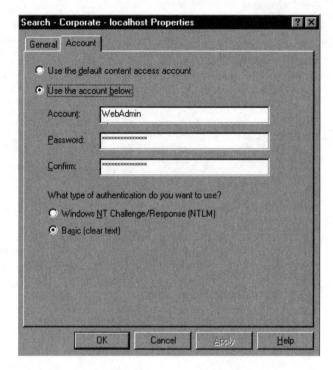

We are almost ready to build our search catalog, but there is one final part we must configure.

Adding the file types

When a file is uploaded to the Content Management site and the information it is tagged with cannot be directly embedded in the document (such as a `.exe` file, or an file format unknown to Site Server Content Management such as `.xml` files), a stub file is created which stores the content types and acts as a proxy/redirect to the real file. The stub file (a text file of extension `.stub`) for the XML file `CompGlas.xml` we uploaded earlier is shown below. The file is in the same directory as `CompGlas.xml`, but is called `CompGlas.xml.stub`:

```
<!DOCTYPE HTML PUBLIC "-//W3C//DTD HTML 3.2//EN">
<!-- Microsoft Site Server Stub File -->
<HTML><HEAD>
<meta name="VersionNo" content="1">
<meta name="UnitName" content="\Documents\Units\Risk Management">
<meta name="UnitNameDisplay" content="Risk Management">
<meta name="Title" content="RAROE in Electronic Commerce">
<meta name="publicationDate" content="01/02/1999">
<meta name="editor" content="Steven Livingstone">
<meta name="AuthorEmail" content="ceo@citix.com">
<meta name="Owner" content="Stefano">
<meta name="SubmitTime" content="1999/06/08 01:55:47">
<meta name="ContentType" content="Technical">
<meta name="Approved" content="Yes">
<META NAME="GENERATOR" Content="Microsoft Site Server">
<META HTTP-EQUIV="Content-Type" Content="text/html; Charset=iso-8859-1">
<META HTTP-EQUIV="Refresh" CONTENT="0; url=CompGlas.xml">
<TITLE>DPS Stub Properties File</TITLE>
</HEAD><BODY>
<A HREF="CompGlas.xml">
If your browser doesn't support automatic refresh, select this link to retrieve
the real
document
</A></BODY></HTML>
```

This file shows each of the content attributes and respective values as well as the redirect to the real XML file.

So why is this of interest? Well, when search chooses documents to index, it only selects those document types that have been explicitly defined. Fire up the MMC and view the `Properties` of the `Corporate` catalog. Choose the **File Types** tab and you should see a list of the document types which are currently indexed – notice that the stub file type is absent. Click on **Add**, insert `stub` as the file type and click **OK** twice to return to the catalog list. Search can now use this stub file to search for meta properties of the XML document – the information cannot be directly embedded into the XML document (as this would likely make the file invalid). Site Server Search does not currently provide a mechanism for direct searching of XML documents.

You are now in a position to create the Corporate catalog, so select the catalog and choose **All Tasks | Start Build**. After a few seconds your catalog is built. Have a look at the gatherer log to confirm that you received no permission denied errors this time.

Although the search catalog has now been created, we must now wrap this in a content source that is supported by Knowledge Manager, which is what we are going to do now.

Creating a KM Content Source

Launch the Site Server web administration tool and select the Membership Directory Manager link. Log in to the mem server and choose the Content link from the left pane (taking you to `http://yourserver/siteserver/Admin/Knowledge/DsMgr/Default.asp`). Choose Content Sources, click the Create button and enter Corporate as the Content source name. Ensure that the Search Catalog option is checked, as this is the only type that can work with Knowledge Manager, and click the Next button. A list of the available catalogs is now displayed, as shown in the following screenshot, from which you should choose Corporate and click the Next button.

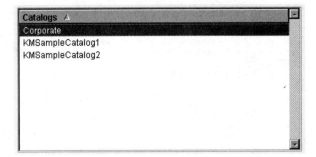

Select all of the available content types from the list and click the Next button, which displays summary details of the new content source. Click Finish to complete, and the new content source is added to the list (as shown below). Notice that the Class is `searchServerSource`, which is supported by KM.

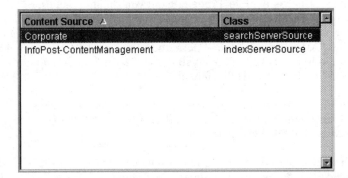

Our new catalog can now be used with Knowledge Manager. You can see this if you go to Programs > Microsoft Site Server | Tools | Knowledge Manager on the Start menu and select from the drop down box entitled "Search for documents in:" in the top left frame (you may be asked to enter a valid username and password). You should select the Corporate option and then the screen should refresh showing a tree listing of the site vocabulary in the category list in the left frame, as shown in the next screenshot:

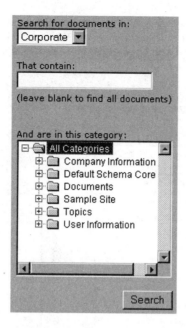

Notice that this shows the whole default site vocabulary, but we only want users to browse the vocabulary where we have designed ourselves. To do this, we must anchor our content source, which is what we need to look at now.

Anchoring the Vocabulary for our Content Source

Now that we have added our content section, we need to set up the section as the default starting point or root for our site vocabulary. Fire up the MDM and instead of logging on anonymously, log on as **Administrator** using the membership directory password (if you followed the earlier instructions, this is **mem**). Once authenticated, navigate to `ou=Admin/ou=Other/ou=ContentClasses` and you shall see our content source, `cn=Corporate`, in the right pane, as shown below:

The site vocabulary installed by site server is our default vocabulary, but we're defining our own site vocabulary, so we want to limit browsing from all terms under the `Documents` category. To do this, we must apply an Anchor to our content source, which sets the root of our site vocabulary to be the `Documents` category.

> **The Content Source Anchor is used as a node in the Site Vocabulary whose child categories appear in the Knowledge Manager's content browser, as terms that can be browsed when the content source is selected.**

Note that you can delete the default vocabulary terms if you wish – we won't be using these.

Right-Click on the entry cn=Corporate and click **Properties**. When the attribute list appears, click on Add Attribute and, from the list that appears, select **Anchor** and click **OK**. In the **Value** box of the Anchor attribute, click the **Select** button and choose the Documents Category as shown below:

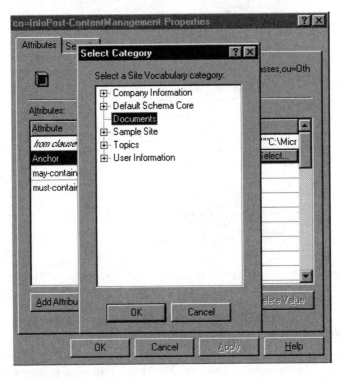

Click **OK** twice to confirm the anchor. Now, when it comes to adding terms from the site vocabulary, we'll only be able to choose from values starting from the Documents root.

At the moment, however, browsing through the category list in Knowledge Manager has no effect. We can however attach searches to this category list, so, for example, a user browsing to Research could get all of the Research documents. Let's look at how we do this.

Integrating Knowledge Manager

With Knowledge Manger, we can allow users to browse the site vocabulary and have documents relevant to that category returned to them. Before this can work, however, we must first associate a query with each category so that the correct documents are pulled back. To do this, we must revisit our site vocabulary and set up associated queries with each major category. Fire up the web administration tool, select **Membership Directory Manager**, log in, and choose the **Edit Site Vocabulary** link from the left pane. Now click the Plus (+) sign next to the Documents category and then the one for Areas, which should expand the view to the four sub-categories you entered here earlier. Select the Technical category and click on the **Properties** button.

Now, the **Query string** textbox should be empty. Text entered in here is equivalent to a user typing it in themselves, but since we want a user to click on the Technical category and retrieve documents which have been tagged as Technical, we need to do more than just type a simple text query. All the information is stored as meta-data; so we need some way of querying our meta-name ContentType, which would store the fact a document fell under a particular Area and query if this Area was Technical. The syntax to query meta data is:

@meta_ContentType ContentValue

So, in the **Query String** textbox, enter:

@meta_ContentType Technical

> Click the **Submit** button and you will be returned to the site vocabulary list. So, has this worked? Well, you can test it out by going into Knowledge Manger, selecting the Corporate catalog as your search scope and navigating to **Areas | Technical** in the **Category** list. Click on the **Search** button and you shall be returned a list of documents that have been tagged as ContentType Technical, similar to that shown below:

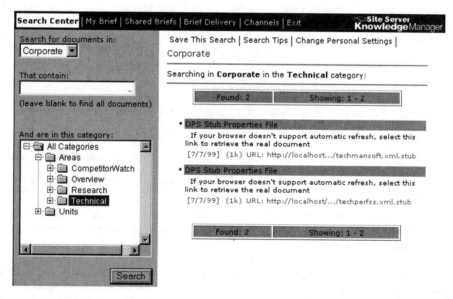

You can see that users can even add further search criteria in the textbox on the left pane. For example, the above search could be easily extended in the Corporate environment to search for all Technical documents which had been placed on the site in the last week and contained the text SiteServer.

Now, complete our tagging of `Areas` by applying the rest of the search query strings to the relevant content types. The full list of these is shown below:

Area	Query String
Technical	@meta_ContentType Technical
CompetitorWatch	@meta_ContentType CompetitorWatch
Overview	@meta_ContentType Overview
Research	@meta_ContentType Research

We now need to complete our tagging of the site vocabulary by applying query strings to our `Units`. Navigate to Documents | Units, click on Management Science and select Properties. Type the following into the Query String:

@meta_UnitName \Documents\Units\Management Science

The path name you have entered is the site vocabulary term we use for specifying the `Unit` of a document.

Click Submit and check that this has worked in Knowledge Manager. Select the Units | Management Science category, click Submit and a list of tagged documents is shown. Once again, repeat these steps for the following other Content Types, entering the pathname to the `Unit` as defined in the site vocabulary:

Unit	Query String
Management Science	@meta_UnitName \Documents\Units\Management Science
Performance Analysis	@meta_UnitName \Documents\Units\Performance Analysis
Risk Management	@meta_UnitName \Documents\Units\Risk Management
Software Development	@meta_UnitName \Documents\Units\Software Development

Now that this task has been completed, users can have intelligent access to your content. New categories can be added transparently so that Italian users could be returned only documents available in their language or locale.

We now have a complete company Knowledge Management system for Citix, for multiple departments and languages. We have completed our study of a knowledge management system, but Site Server and other Microsoft tools allow us to make such a system even more powerful.

Further Possibilities

Although we've looked at the searching capabilities of Knowledge Manager in detail, it offers a lot more which can all be combined to provide a very powerful Knowledge center. The Search center allows us to save searches we have made to a personal (private) or shared (public) brief. We can then customise these briefs and have the results sent to users according to a schedule, allowing them to know when documents they are interested in are added.

For example, you could imagine a brief that composed a search for the Documents\Units\Risk Management vocabulary selection that was delivered to a user on a daily basis. Employees of the Risk Management department around the world could then be automatically notified of ongoing work.

Indeed, all areas of Site Server can be integrated to provide a very powerful content management and information center.

14

Electronic Commerce 101

Looking back at the recent past, it's interesting to take note of how many technological innovations have originated in a garage, usually the result of the efforts of a few teenagers (and two seems to be the magic number) who got together and created the next big thing.

Sure enough, people tend to forget that not many of these kids are exactly penniless when they start their soon-to-be technological empires (after all, should we ignore the fact that Bill Gates' father was—and still is—one of Seattle's most influential lawyers?). Their true advantage, however, is that they are pioneers in uncharted territory, and therefore no competition prevents them from claiming a new market as theirs, growing rapidly as the demand for the new technology greatly surpasses the available supply.

The history of electronic commerce, which for the moment we shall consider the ability to sell goods over the Internet, wasn't much different. Once a "critical mass" of people gained access to the World Wide Web, a group of people figured out that it would have been extremely easy to create a "virtual catalog" of items—books in this case—that could be sold directly through a web server. The advantages were clear: there was no physical location to maintain (and therefore the prices could be conveniently kept low), and people had no problem in trading the accessibility, convenience and wide variety of books offered with the need to wait a few days for delivery.

The lack of a physical point of sale also means that not all the inventory has to be kept in stock—in fact only a small portion of it is readily available, while other titles must be ordered from the various suppliers, and sometimes will never become available again. People don't seem to mind, though, perhaps because those books are often out of print and the expectation level is low from the very beginning. You've got to admit, however, that being able to bolster a catalog whose title count can only be expressed using *a lot* of digits does miracles for marketing purposes.

Sooner or later, though, the rest of the world catches up with these innovators, and the pursuit of market share becomes suddenly more difficult. This is particularly true when traditional retailers, whose names are well known to the general public and who are considered reliable and trustworthy, enter the scene and start competing aggressively against the original market leaders. They usually have more resources and can draw upon a more seasoned pool of marketing and retail experts, and can easily become a threat to the aforementioned whiz kids.

The only real way of competing effectively at that point becomes understanding the true possibilities of the technology itself and taking full advantage of them to create more and more advanced features aimed at making the customer's experience more and more enjoyable. It's a known fact that Internet shoppers look as much for convenience as they do for a good deal; therefore, being able to make the purchase process truly customer-friendly becomes extremely important.

You can compare this concept to buying a coffee at Starbucks or in a less trendy coffee shop. Internet users are mostly the Starbucks types—not as much interested in the price of the beverage as they are in the quality of the environment in which they will be drinking. In the end, both stores sell the same product (we won't argue about the quality of the coffee here) but Starbucks makes more money, because it understands its customers better. As Tom Hanks' character in *You've Got Mail* puts it, "The whole purpose of places like Starbucks is for people with no decision-making ability whatsoever to make six decisions just to buy one cup of coffee."

There's more to consider, though. I'm sure that you have noticed how many Starbucks locations look alike: same furniture, same design and same machinery. At first glance, the obvious reason for this is that Starbucks can save money by buying all this equipment in bulk and then placing it in its stores. The truth, however, goes a little beyond that: by creating a consistent look-and-feel for its point-of-sales, Starbucks lets its store operators focus on more important aspects of their business, such as planning, special offers, advertisements, and so on.

What Does This Chapter Talk About?

The goal of the electronic commerce products in Site Server is not all that dissimilar from that of the equipment in a Starbucks store: to provide store developers with a "foundation" of solid, lower-level functionality on which they can build the truly unique identity of their sites. In the course of the following few chapters, we will analyze in technical detail how the electronic commerce functionality of Site Server can be programmed and extended by using common development tools, such as ASP, Visual Basic and Visual C++.

Developers, however, are not coding machines (contrary to what some business people seem to believe), and do gain in professional value from a more complete understanding of the business case on which a technology has been built. Therefore, the goal of this chapter is to provide a general overview of the concepts behind electronic commerce. As such, it will not be not be extremely technical in nature, but will focus on what electronic commerce is and how it works. At the end of this chapter you should understand enough about electronic commerce to be able to conceptually picture the architecture of your own point of sales.

To better identify the key topics that we will be discussing, I have divided the chapter in five parts:

> **The nature of electronic commerce**
>
> This section tackles the basic nature of electronic commerce. A lot of useful terms are explained here, like *store*, *shopper*, and *products*. We'll also discuss briefly the difference between business-to-consumer and business-to-business electronic commerce.

> **A crash course in Internet selling**
>
> Once your mind is fixed on what electronic commerce really means, we'll see how products are sold on the Internet and what the basic concepts for doing so are. We will discover that, although some new ideas had to be created to accommodate the uniqueness of the Internet as a communication and transport medium, there are a surprisingly high number of notions that closely mimic the traditional retail environment.

> **Content personalization**
>
> Earlier in the book, you probably had chance to take a look at the Personalization and Membership functionality of Site Server. If you haven't done so yet this would be a great time to go back to it and study it in detail. As we shall see in this section, being able to tailor a site's content to the preferences of an individual user is part of the feature set that is rapidly defining the difference between winners and losers in the contest for most successful online store.

> **Applications**
>
> If electronic commerce is not only selling books online, then what is it? In this section, we'll examine several—but by all means not *all*—of its possible applications, and we will find out that there is more to see than meets the eye. We will also discover that sometimes an online store doesn't have to *look* like one—we'll call these sites in disguise "electronic commerce applications".

> **Microsoft Site Server, Commerce Edition**
>
> The last part of the chapter will introduce you to Microsoft's electronic commerce platform, which is part of the Commerce Edition version of Site Server 3.0 and is also known as Microsoft Commerce Server (MSCS). We will match all the concepts discussed earlier in the chapter to the functionality offered by MSCS; we will also examine its basic architectural elements in some detail.

The Nature of Electronic Commerce

As we mentioned above, this section will take care of defining some important terms that we will be using consistently throughout the entire MSCS part of this book. These terms are also used widely in the electronic commerce industry (now that there *is* one), so it's a good idea to get to know their correct meaning.

The Electronic Commerce Metaphor

Despite the fact that electronic commerce is a relatively new, if popular, topic, we have learnt to accept several terms that we use to identify concepts that are tied to it. As it often happens, however, these terms have not been created from scratch but rather adapted from other scenarios to which people are more accustomed.

Even though this is a fairly common way of making things easier to understand, it tends to cause a little confusion when the real-life terms are too closely related to their electronic counterparts; as it is the case with the topic of this chapter, starting from the term "electronic commerce" itself—and continuing down to many of the other terms that are commonly used in the field. Therefore, we are going to take a look at what we will call the *electronic commerce metaphor*.

It Is Commerce, But It Doesn't Sell

If you take a look at the description of the word "commerce" in a dictionary, it will read something like this:

com·merce, n. *('kä-(")m&rs): the exchange or buying and selling of commodities on a large scale involving transportation from place to place*

This is the common definition of commerce that everybody is familiar with: the action of purchasing or selling goods in exchange for money or other goods. The interesting part, however, comes when we keep on reading the alternative definitions that the dictionary has to offer:

> **2:** *social intercourse: interchange of ideas, opinions, or sentiments*

Now, this offers a somehow different point of view on the whole concept. It doesn't necessarily have anything to do with buying or selling, or even with physical goods (we'll come back to this last concept later on in the chapter). All that commerce really means is the exchange of things between two people or companies.

This is the definition that best fits the concept of electronic commerce, because an online store doesn't really buy or sell any physical goods, but acts as a proxy between a seller as a buyer, and therefore only deals in *information*. The buyer transfers his or her personal information—like shipping and billing information, or credit card data, for example—to the owners of the store, who in turn provide information regarding the merchandise that is sold, its availability and so on. The store itself doesn't directly deliver anything to the user, and its core functionality doesn't really bother with the line-of-business functionality that is required to turn the user's request into the action of actually shipping the goods. The following diagram shows all the entities that play a fundamental role in an online store.

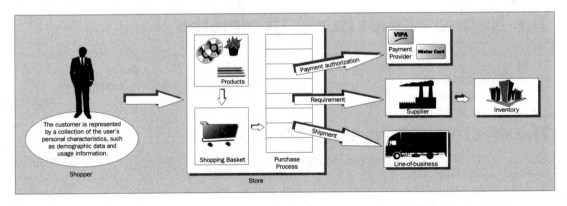

Naturally, you will find examples in which the line between electronic commerce and line-of-business application blurs significantly. This mostly happens in small to medium-sized online stores, whose owners don't have the need for or can't afford a separate line-of-business system. In those cases, the store takes also care of fulfilling orders (i.e. creating receipts, printing labels, and so on). Still, based on the definition that we just saw it becomes easy enough to determine what belongs to online commerce and what doesn't.

Just Because It's A Store, It Doesn't Have To Look Like One

Let's now move on to the concept of a *store*. In real life, we are used to walking into a store, browsing through its aisles and picking up products from it. Naturally, we don't really walk into an online store, neither do we really walk through its aisles and pick up any products. As we shall see later on, this last concept in particular raises some interesting issues when dealing with how products are assigned to customers who haven't paid for them yet.

Some people do think of an online store as something similar to the online version of a mail-order catalog, noting that there are some strikingly similarities between the two. Like the fact that they both are, fundamentally, lists of products that can be used to tell the catalog owners that the customer would like to buy something and receive it through the mail.

There are, however, a number of striking differences between an online store and a mail-order catalog. For one thing, the online store is an *interactive* tool, allowing the user to restrict the range of products that are presented to him or her to only those he or she is interested in. Moreover, the online store can be an *adaptive* instrument that changes to provide the content that best fits the preferences and habits of a specific user. Finally, an online store is a self-sufficient tool: you can't really place an order using a mail-order catalog—there has to be somebody who takes your order, either through the mail or over the telephone, and stores it into the company's line-of-business system, whatever that might be.

The result of all this is, obviously, that the online store offers many more opportunities than the printed catalog, both for the user—who enjoys the added functionality—and the owner, who needs much less manpower and can rely on a completely computer-based system to handle his or her business.

Inside the Store

In real life, you *do* know when you're walking into a store. The store owner has a concerted interest in making it very clear that he or she *sells* something, and does not really hide the fact that somebody is expected to come in and buy something or at least inquire about a product.

Because of the definition of electronic commerce that we gave before, an online store doesn't necessarily have to publicize the fact that it sells something. Let's, for example, consider the case in which the user is buying an electronic license to use a piece of software. We will see how this works in detail only later on in the chapter, but for the moment it shouldn't be difficult to imagine that this kind of store wouldn't work well with the traditional store metaphor. Most likely, the users would enter the site as part of some kind of registration process, and expect to just choose a licensing option, maybe enter some information about themselves, and pay for the license. Keep in mind that the payment doesn't necessarily have to take place. The important part, as we saw earlier, is the *exchange of information*.

The Shopper

From the owner's point of view, the shopper is arguably the most important part of the whole electronic commerce concept. However, it is also the part that carries the most unknowns, because shoppers are traditionally anonymous as they visit a store, whether physical or virtual.

As we identified before, however, the online store has a tremendous advantage over the traditional one in the fact that it can *adapt* to the needs and habits of the individual user. Imagine this as the equivalent of having to identify each shopper who enters a grocery store and completely rearrange all the items on display so that only the products that he or she is interested in are displayed and in the particular order that fit his or her preference, a clearly practically unrealizable proposition.

In an online store, though, there is no physical display. All the information, as we shall see in the next few chapters, is stored in a database, whose only goal is to provide data arranged in a given format. Creating customized versions of the store, therefore, becomes a relatively easy process. Moreover, while our customers will, most likely, browse through the store in an anonymous fashion, certain Internet technologies–such as cookies–allow us to uniquely identify their browsers and collect information about the way they behave during their visit to the site. This information can then be processed and used to generate an adaptive version of the store that rapidly changes to make the information that the user is probably interested in more readily available; which in turn makes the store visit more enjoyable and productive for the customer.

What is a shopper, then? Well, since there is no physical contact between customers and the store, we will have to settle for a collection of *attributes* that we can use to do many things, such as:

> ➤ Delivering personalized content
> ➤ Group orders by customer to improve customer support
> ➤ Create reports which will help us understand our audience better
> ➤ Send targeted information to users who are interested in specific information

The Shopping Cart

We are probably used to grabbing a shopping cart as soon as we enter a large grocery store. For visits to a smaller store, we might use a basket; even a visit to the small bakery store around the corner requires us to collect the items we want to buy in our arms.

Since the same need does apply to an online store, the concept of a shopping cart has been transferred to electronic commerce as the repository of items that the customer intends to purchase from the store. As has happened for the other concepts, however, some differences do arise.

First of all, let me reiterate something: there is *nothing* to buy in an online store. Users don't really go around and pick up any product–they are merely asking somebody to pick the products up and send them to them. Therefore, while items in a real shopping cart must be put back into their own aisle (at least in theory), an online basket's contents can be changed at any time.

Additionally, in a real store whatever goes into a user's shopping cart cannot be picked up and purchased by another customer (other than a really rude one). The online shopping experience does not know this concept at all. Until the moment the shopper sends a purchase request to the store, he is merely expressing a *preference* for a certain product rather than another. In other words, the quantity of products available, or *inventory*, does not change until the store sends a request for shipment to the line-of-business system. Naturally, this also means that an online store can be fine-tuned to predict the inventory requirements (which are usually considered a liability) and reduce them to the minimum amount needed to quickly satisfy the customers' needs.

Finally, when a shopper leaves the store, he or she will also leave an empty cart behind. Since the basket's contents do not really correspond to any physical allocation of the goods sold, it's very easy to save them in the store's database and make them available when the user returns. This is also very convenient for the shoppers, since they don't have to remember everything they wanted to buy if they have to leave the store in the middle of their visit and want to return to the shopping later.

Products

Because of the distinction between the online store and the line-of-business system that we made earlier in the chapter, there are some special considerations that must be made about products. First of all, the products in the store are simply *information*. As a result, they can be just about anything: books, compact disks, documents, stock quotes, software licenses. They are all the same things to an online store—the real distinction comes at the line-of-business level.

This distinction also means that there are different levels of information about a product that can be transmitted by the store to the customer. A description, for example, is an important part of the product presentation, but is not really crucial to the actual process: you can buy a car even if you don't know that it's black and has four-wheel drive. The availability of the product, however, *is* of extreme relevance in the purchase process—you can't buy a car if the store doesn't have one to sell to you.

Sadly, the really important information about product availability is most difficult to obtain, because it is stored in the line-of-business system, which, in most cases, is often completely separated from the online store. Traditionally, these systems—at least in large organizations—are based on technology that can only be integrated with the store by spending a considerable amount of time and money, something that the store owner is not always keen on doing. A typical example is trying to interface your Windows NT machine, running Site Server, with an IBM AS/400 system that runs your supplier's warehouse.

Naturally, there are companies whose only business is to perform integration tasks between Site Server and other systems, but the costs are high and most likely require some work to be done at your supplier's site. As a result, smaller companies have sometimes to resort to complex e-mail systems that do not provide real-time information and can sometimes lead to the scenario where the store thinks that a product is available while it is not anymore.

Departments

We can compare the concept of a department to that of an aisle in a supermarket. Products in our store are grouped logically into well-defined categories that can be used by the customers to narrow their research for items for purchase.

However, it is worth noting that since an online store does not deal with physical products, but only with information about them, an item can actually sit in more than one department—usually because it doesn't really fit well just in one. This is not always possible in a real-life store because having to show the same product in two different aisles can become expensive in terms of having to stock too much inventory.

Departments are a very important means for discovering what your users are really interested in. I'm sure that you are all familiar with the thirty or so years of research that supermarket owners have put into trying to understand their customers better by recording and analyzing their behavior while browsing through the store. Unfortunately, they weren't really able to understand much from those recordings, mainly because it was very difficult to automate the analysis process.

In an online store, though, the process is *already* automated. In fact, the whole store is! Therefore, analyzing the behavior of your users is a much easier—as we will see later on—and more profitable task. Knowing what your customers are interested in gives you an advantage in offering a more advanced shopping experience that can lead to higher sales.

The Purchase Process

Buying something from a store is an easy process for everybody. The customer just goes in, picks something, carries it to the cashier, pays for it and takes it out. Thereby ends the relationship between buyer and seller, unless the product is defective or the seller is particularly annoying.

Not so in an online store. Remember, customers aren't really buying anything, but they are rather asking you, the storeowner, to ship something to them, so the relationship doesn't end at the moment in which the customer essentially says "I want to buy this, here's the money". As a result, you will have to initiate a *purchase process* that will begin with the purchase order and terminate only when the user has received the product (again, unless the product is defective or your online store allows returns).

The purchase process, as you can imagine, takes care of a number of important steps. First of all, its responsibility is to calculate all the taxes, handling and shipping fees that are to be applied to the order. Next, it will have to communicate with your line-of-business system and make sure that the order is sent on to shipping. During this process, being able to inform the users as to the status of their orders is extremely important to keep customer confidence up and client support-related costs down. (Don't you hate it when the customer keeps on calling in to know when his or her products will be arriving? Well, chances are that your online store won't mind, and will let the user check the order any time of the day.)

Another important task for the purchase process is making sure that the payment for the order will effectively be received and is not fraudulent. Now, this is normally a difficult task for a physical-location store, which however has the advantage of (a) eye contact with the customer and (b) being actually able to see the payment method and to verify the customer's identity (for example by looking at the signature on a credit card). For an online store, absolute certainty is only a dream from which to awake when the first charge refusals start to come in from the credit card company.

There are certain methods that can be employed to protect the store's owners, such as asking the users to fax in a copy of their credit card, or using the Address Verification System (available in the United States only) to make sure that the address to which the product is sent is the same as the one where the credit card is registered and verifying that that particular credit card doesn't have a history of fraudulent purchases. However, you will have to accept a certain (hopefully small) amount of fraud as one of the facts of life and keep it in mind when calculating your earning projections and safe risk acceptance.

Types of Electronic Commerce

Even though, fundamentally, all electronic commerce stores follow the same basic rules, such as dealing in an exchange of information rather than a direct exchange of goods, the nature of their audience dictates largely what kind of information they will be exchanging, and how.

Business-to-Consumer Electronic Commerce

If you are selling products to the public-at-large, or even only to people who have registered to become members of your site but are still private citizens (or treated as such), your store deals in business-to-consumer commerce. In this case, the information you collect is probably simple ship-to and bill-to addresses and payment data. You have no ongoing generic business relationship with them, and you simply request all the information every time.

The preferred method of payment for this kind of online store is the credit card or an equivalent payment system such as CyberCash. Generally speaking, the online store maintains one set of pricing for all its customers and receives the money directly as a result—and in most cases as a pre-requisite—of the purchase.

Business-to-Business Electronic Commerce

If your audience is mainly made of businesses with which you have an established relationship, the way you do business with your customers differs significantly from doing business with the public-at-large.

First of all, you will most likely maintain a different set of pricing rules for each of your customers. This is because "good clients", or high volume buyers, receive better discounts than others, or because you have a special agreement with another company (for example to exchange some of the goods with a one-time payment every year). Clearly, what we are talking of here is a very complex store to maintain, because the price of each product for sale has to be updated keeping in mind every single customer, and therefore each customer has to be authenticated before he or she enters the store.

In addition, the payment for purchases is normally not done when the orders are entered or delivered but deferred in accordance with the particular agreements in force between the seller and the buyer. Typically, this means that the seller grants the buyer a certain amount of credit for a certain period of time, based on factors like the buyer's credit history. As a result, business-to-business commerce is based essentially on an *exchange of documents*. This means, for example, that when a purchase takes place, your customers will send you a *purchase order*, and you will reply with an *invoice*. No money changes hands at that time.

Business-to-business commerce works the other way too—owners of online stores usually deal with their suppliers by exchanging purchase orders and invoices, and deferring the payment to certain dates. Therefore, the importance of this type of electronic commerce becomes twofold, in that it benefits both the owner of a store and, potentially, its customers, and also its applications will be wider than those of business-to-consumer commerce in the future, to the point that some analysts predict that in a few years as much as 95% of Internet-based trade will be between two businesses.

Generally speaking, business-to-business is said to operate across "Extranets", that is, by creating a private or privileged communication channel between two or more parties in which the data flows across the Internet's public system. Private communications are usually created through Secure Sockets Layer (SSL) connections and secured logins, but can be handled through other means as well, such as Private Networking applications, and so on.

A Crash Course in Internet Selling

In the following few pages, we will explore the world of online commerce, and the techniques that make selling online an effective business proposition. The concepts that we'll examine, unless otherwise noted, apply to both business-to-business and to business-to-consumer stores.

The basic anatomy of an online store, stripped of all the functionality that is not strictly necessary to its working properly, is shown in the figure that follows. As you can see, the idea here is very simple, and the goal is to take the user to the purchase process as easily and quickly as possible. In other words, "all the roads lead to the shopping cart".

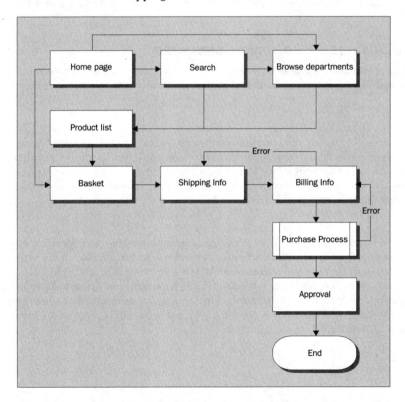

Cross-Selling and Upselling

When we enter a real-life store, we are used to dealing with human beings. In smaller shops, or in those stores that require human contact to the extreme degree, a salesperson will come to bid us welcome as soon as we enter the store's premises and guide us through the purchase process, from selecting the products that are right for us, to suggesting items that could well complement our choices, and to printing out an invoice and–gladly–swiping the money away from our well-worn credit cards.

Naturally, an online store does not have any of this–it is actually the major benefit of electronic commerce to be able to run without any human intervention on the owner's side. Therefore, the visitor must be able to browse around the store and find what he or she is looking for without any outside human help. Customers tire easily–an inevitable drawback of capitalistic competition–and therefore the store must give them what they want very efficiently.

In addition, the store must be able to suggest and recommend products based on what the user is about to purchase and what his or her preferences are. This is the electronic equivalent of a salesperson throwing the casual "you know, that pair of shoes would really look good with this shirt" or "you really can't buy that and not buy the batteries!" Chances are, your store will actually be less annoying than a salesperson, and your customers will like buying from your online store much more than going to the one around the corner. This will only happen if the logic that provides this functionality is well tuned, however, because suggesting a blue shirt with a brown pair of pants is an all-too-effective way to remind your customers that the next online store is only a few keystrokes away.

Complementary Cross-Selling

An interesting and easy way of luring your customers into buying something from your online store is to present them with a list of products that is complementary to – and possibly costs more than – some product that the user is currently examining.

For example, don't you hate it when you go to a store, buy something and then go home just to find out that you forgot an important component, like that special cable or–even worse–the battery? Well, I do, and I usually tend to think that the salesman I was dealing with did a poor job (especially considering that he would have made more money had I bought *all* the stuff I needed). If I bought the product at a supermarket, I can't help wonder why their computer systems–more and more advanced–failed to advise the cashier that I didn't have all I needed, or that perhaps I could have used something else.

Whether you share my opinion or not, you'll agree with me that all these people are missing a great opportunity to make more money. Whether it's because the salesperson forgot to mention something or because the owners of a supermarket are justly concerned with the fact that if everybody were allowed to remember something while at the cashier it would take an average of three weeks to buy the next round of groceries, it's obvious that an online store shouldn't have any problems. First, there's no salesperson, second, many users can check out at the same time, and any of them stopping to think whether they need some more items doesn't prevent anybody from buying the same items.

An online store can (and should) take full advantage of its interactivity by providing the customer with a list of items that show affinity with the products that he or she has in his or her basket, thus providing at the same time a benefit for the user and an advantage for its owner.

Complementary cross-selling is the most basic form of cross-selling, and it can be usually performed by organizing the products in your store wisely. Once that's done, all you need to do is just display a few selected items from the same department the main product on display belongs to and, *voila*, the trick is done.

Historical Cross-Selling

Another very interesting—and more complex—type of cross-selling consists of recommending complementary products based on what other users have bought in the past. You have probably seen this technique applied to several online stores, typically under the form "customers who bought this product also bought".

The trick here is in knowing what previous users have purchased in the past and being able to analyze that historical data effectively. The analysis, in particular, might sound like an easy thing to do, but it really isn't. To make this clearer, let's consider an example.

Your store, which sells shoes, receives one purchase:

1	pair of blue shoes
1	pair of white shoes
2	pairs of red shoes

At this point, if somebody else wants to buy a pair of blue shoes, it's easy to figure out—based on the historical data collected—that he or she may also be interested in one pair of white shoes and two of red shoes.

As soon as you receive another purchase, however, things get immediately more complex:

1	pair of white shoes
1	pair of green shoes
1	pair of brown shoes

Keeping in mind both purchases, it's not easy to be sure what a person who buys a pair of white shoes will be interested in. This is because we don't really know *how much* the other people were interested in the other products, and how much each one of them represented a reasonable average.

You can compare this situation in trying to figure out the trend of a curve based on a limited number of points. For example, lets consider a Cartesian plane on which we have plotted the two points A (1;0) and B (2;1), which could, for example, represent the two purchases that we mentioned above. The third customer, the one interested in the white shoes to which we have to propose some cross-selling items, will be somewhere on one of the possible curves that pass through the two points.

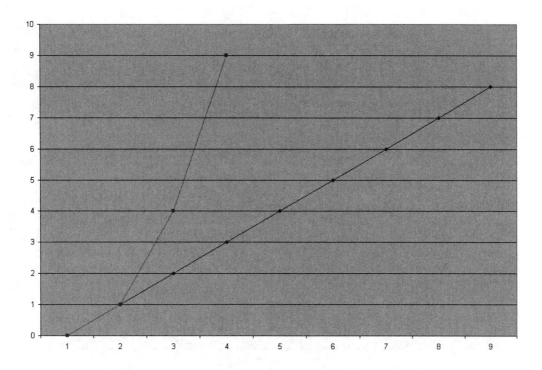

The real problem is that there are an *infinite* number of curves the meet this requirement! (Do keep in mind that we are talking about curves and not straight lines). Therefore, even though we can only approximate the correct curve, with a high number of given points it can become easier to get closer and closer to a realistically correct match. Unfortunately, we also have to keep in mind a basic fact: that we are dealing with human beings, who are generally not very predictable. This means that, every once in a while, we will get some "spurious" data—for example, somebody who purchases something by mistake or who is buying something for himself and some other product as a gift to a friend—that is not representative of the average cross-selling profile.

Plotting this data on the Cartesian plane results in points that are far from the rest of the points collected and therefore they risk altering the trend of the curve outside the path of reality. In the next diagram, for example, the point plotted where x = 6 is obviously spurious because it "sticks out" of the trend generated by the rest of the points.

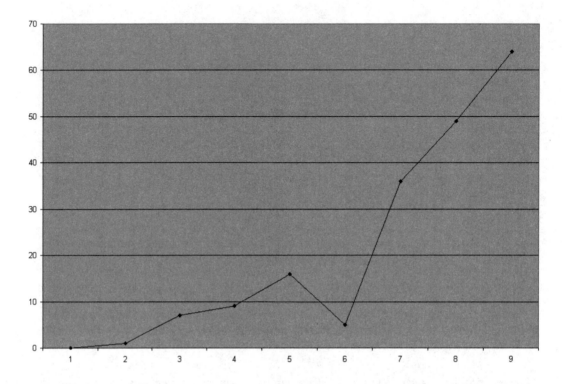

While it's easy (at least in this case) to tell actual data from spurious elements, from a mathematical point of view it's much more complex. To make things worse, in real-life scenarios we don't deal with two-dimensional problems but rather with n-dimensional ones, because the amount of parameters that regulate the cross-selling action are many.

Upselling

If your potential customer is looking at a pair of shoes, your store might nonchalantly suggest that he or she also take a look at other shoes of the same or a similar kind. This way of making business not only tends to attract your customers toward making a more expensive purchase (a more than welcome event, in any case), but also raises the possibility that a customer will make a purchase from your store because he or she is presented with a wider variety of products to choose from than they might have been aware existed.

Keep in mind that "wider variety of products" refers to being able to display more items of the same category—somebody looking at shoes will not necessarily be looking for shirts! However, it is possible that the shoes he or she is looking at are not exactly what he or she was really after; by looking at other pairs, however, the customer might see something more to their liking and buy that instead of going to another online store.

The benefit of implementing *upselling* functionality, of luring the customer toward upgrading the quality and price of his or her purchase, is obvious.

Content Personalization

There's a small tailor's store I usually go to when I need to buy some new clothes. Now, before you dismiss the last sentence as an obvious sign of my snobbery, I must warn that the reason why I don't buy the clothes I wear at a department store is that, for some reason, the people who run them seem to believe that the entire population worldwide wears small- or medium-sized clothes. Unfortunately, not falling into that category, I have to spend more money in a tailor's—something I would gladly do without.

Going back to the aforementioned tailor, he is an Italian fellow (what else), and really not the most economical. But, he makes good clothes and he knows me. This means that, when I go there, all I have to do is pick the kind of cloth and my pants will be ready in a couple of weeks. No taking measurements, and usually I don't even have to try the new clothes on, because the tailor knows me so well that they are perfect from the start. So, I'm glad to spend the few dollars more because going there saves me time, gets me good quality merchandise and provides me with a less humiliating experience than the "try this on and see if it fits" at the department store that always ends up in my wife giving up and telling me I just *have* to pay the tailor a visit.

This Time, It's Personal

The point that I was trying to make is that people *do* care about receiving a personalized treatment. As much as they are hunting for the best bargain, having to look through tons of products to find the right one is not a task most of us look to eagerly. Some are even ready to pay the extra buck in order to avoid it.

On the Internet, the need to provide a custom-tailored shopping experience is even greater, because the next online store is just a mouse click away. While in a real-life store going somewhere else costs a lot of time and effort, all that's needed to visit another online store is to type a different URL in your browser's window. At the same time, while customizing a real-life store is practically impossible, it can be done in a relatively easy way using powerful tools such as Site Server.

Tell Me Who You Are, I'll Tell You What To Buy

The first step toward creating a store able to adapt to the preferences and behavior of the user consists in *knowing* your users. This will indeed allow you to serve the correct content and point the user to the right areas. There are two basic ways of collecting user information: **explicit personalization** and **implicit personalization**.

Explicit personalization consists in collecting information by asking the user a series of question. The term "explicit" comes from the fact that the user must voluntarily answer a set of questions in order to activate the personalization feature. This means that the user will know that the store will be modified to fit his or her profile.

Unfortunately, there are several drawbacks to this method. First of all, many potential customers don't like to give out personal information of any kind. If you think about it, that's really understandable, considering the vast amount of spamming most Internet users have been subjected to. Thus, your personalization feature would run the risk of not being used, wasting the costly time and resources you had to invest to implement it.

What's even more problematic is the fact that your store is actually personalizing its content based on a "snapshot" of the user's preferences taken at a very specific moment in time. What happens if the user's own predilection for certain items changes over time? The risk, in this case, is that your personalization system will not dynamically follow the evolution of your customers, on whom you certainly can't count for keeping their own profiles up-to-date (after all, from their point of view, they are doing you a favor, and not the opposite).

A better way of personalizing a store's content is by analyzing what the user does while he or she is visiting the site and extrapolating a profile from that data. The result is of greater quality than before, because both big problems of explicit personalization have been solved: there's no more need to ask the user any questions, and the profile information is always up-to-date.

However, even implicit personalization—which, as you might have imagined, is this technique's name—has its own drawbacks. First of all, it cannot be used since the very beginning, because very little will be known about the user at that time, and therefore the personalization will be very imprecise (so imprecise, in fact, that you will run the risk of annoying your customers because it will be too obvious that you are suggesting content based on their immediate actions). In addition, collecting information about a user's behavior without letting the user know may lead your customers—and the ever-annoyed media—to think that you are assuming a "Big Brother" attitude towards your audience.

These suspicions, of course, would be legitimate if you were collecting the data to sell it to some third party who could use and abuse it. In most cases, however, you are just trying to offer a better service to your customers and have the best of intentions. The fact is, a lot of people won't disallow you from doing that, but you will have to ask them and accept the fact that they might not like the idea.

Since you will have to ask something, then, why not also offer the possibility of a quick registration that could give you enough data to use explicit personalization until you have collected information sufficient to provide accurate personalization features based on the user's behavior? A combination of the two data-collection techniques will generally offer the best results on all fronts.

Recognizing Your Customers

During my early visits to the Italian tailor that I just introduced earlier, I was worried sick every time that he would not remember who I was and would either (a) force me into the measurement torture or (b) produce a pair of "armpit underwear", as we call it in Italy.

Remembering who your users are is not necessarily an easy task, but it certainly is an important one. As you have seen in the section of this book dedicated to the Personalization and Membership part of Site Server, there a few different methods, each one with its own drawback. In particular, depending on the information that you decide to store in a user's profile, you will probably want to avoid using the less secure ones. For example, you should not use cookie authentication if you're storing credit card numbers!

Serving Content

Once you are able to establish a user's profile and recognize your customers, the store can start serving personalized content. The matter at hand, now, becomes deciding *what* content should be personalized. The answer is simple: *as much as possible*. The store's success will largely depend on how well it will be able to adapt to the user's preferences.

A good idea is to tie cross- and up-selling functionality with the personalization system so that the products featured are not only based on the shopping cart's content, but also on what the user likes. It is also possible to arrange the layout of the site so that it better reflects the user's profile. For example, if the personalization system detects a pattern in the fact that the user seems to particularly like a section of the store, the latter should be prominently featured at the beginning of the pages. However, this approach is also quite complex to implement for two reasons. First of all, you will have to create a site design that is flexible enough to allow for such changes; second, you will have to fine-tune your personalization system so that the information displayed will be consistent enough not to confuse your customers (can you imagine having links in different places at every new visit?)

How Does Site Server Help Me?

The only personalization system that is available with Site Server is the Personalization and Membership server that has been discussed earlier in this book. To avoid repetition, I will not suggest whether you should use it or not *in general*, but I'll rather stick to whether you should or should not use it *for electronic commerce*, since that's what I'm talking about here.

Even though P&M is indeed a powerful system, I would think very carefully about whether you should use it in your store or not. For one thing, working with implicit personalization is very difficult—as in fact it is not really something that the creators probably thought about.

The membership part, however, does add a lot of value, but you will still have to implement an engine to deliver personalized content. In addition, there's a pretty good chance that the next version of Site Server, whenever it might come out, will be based on Windows 2000, which features the Active Directory, which is LDAP compliant just like the Membership Directory. Migrating from the MD to the AD will certainly entail at least some work—even more so if you consider that Microsoft's recent acquisition of FireFly, a company that has been working in the field of content personalization, will probably have some impact on the functionality offered by P&M as well.

Applications

There is an example that I always make when I try to explain why electronic commerce is a vast field that nobody has yet explored thoroughly. It has to do with the transition from radio to television that took place some fifty years ago. At the beginning, TV shows were simply the equivalent of radio shows, the only difference being that the audience could actually *see* the person who was speaking to them. Now, that was undoubtedly a very powerful experience for the time, but it wasn't television. It took several years before people were able to discover what could really be done with the new medium: shows, movies, games, newscasts, and so on.

History repeats itself, once again, with electronic commerce. Somebody came up with the idea of selling books online, and they made millions. But that's not all there is to electronic commerce—they have just placed an existing concept on a new medium that broadens its reach to millions of people all over the world.

So much more, however, can be done with the Internet—a medium whose true potential we are just beginning to understand now—that it's hard to believe that electronic commerce stops just there. As a matter of fact, it doesn't! The figure below illustrates a few of the disguises under which an online store can appear.

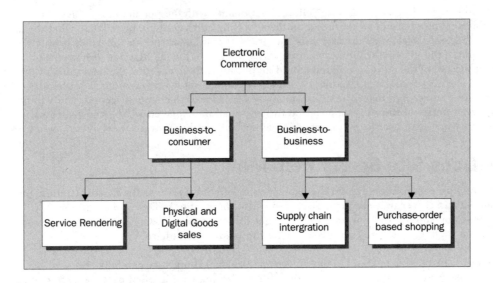

Digital Delivery of Goods

Until now, we have talked about stores that physically delivered the products to the customer's doorstep. We'll call that *physical delivery of goods*, and we're already pretty familiar with the way it works: somebody visits the site and asks for a product to be shipped out to him or her in exchange for a sum of money (or, in the case of business-to-business applications, in exchange for the *promise* to pay a sum of money). As we have just seen, in these cases the store itself is simply the middleperson between the customer and the line-of-business system that runs in the backend.

Let's now consider the scenario in which the product that the store sells is not physical. This concept can be applied to just about any pay-per-something site on the Internet. It doesn't matter what the site is requesting payment for, stock quotes, news, or software, there always is an exchange of information that can be considered the delivery of *digital goods*.

While most of the concepts that we have examined earlier still apply to this kind of store, there are a few significant differences. First off, the line that divides the online store from the line-of-business system becomes very blurred. There is no need for interfacing with a warehouse and having to keep control over what happens to the package that has to be delivered to the user. The goods are paid for and delivered immediately *by* the store through the Internet. Furthermore, in this particular case it's reasonable to believe that the line-of-business functionality be provided by the same system that operates the store. As a result, certain information that can usually only be updated through complex replication procedures, because the line-of-business system and the store are implemented on different platforms, is readily available.

Being able to recognize users with the minimum error possible is paramount in these cases, since the goods you will be delivering have a value as an intellectual property, rather than as a physical entity, delivering them to the wrong user can mean a total loss that you will never be able to recover. Think of two different people sharing the same account on your news service, for example: if you are not able to prevent one of them—the one who *didn't* pay for the service, possibly—from accessing the information, you will have realized a loss of gains that, on a larger scale, can significantly affect your bottom line.

At the same time, you will have to compensate for the limitations of the Internet that risk interfering with your business. For example, if you are selling software online and allow for direct download, you'll have to cope with two problems:

> Sending large amounts of data over the network can be a very slow operation, depending on the kind of connectivity that your customers enjoy. Uploading a game that takes three CDs, for example, is unthinkable with today's connectivity (with most users are still running at baud rates lower than 56.6 kbps).

> Uploading data over the Internet can be problematic also from a continuity point of view. In fact, connections can be unexpectedly dropped (i.e. because the user's phone line quality deteriorates, and so on) before the transmission is completed, leaving the customer with having paid for something that he or she won't be able to use. At the same time, how are you going to be sure that the user has really paid for it and not completed the download?

Luckily, some solutions to this problem are just around the corner. High-speed connections, such as Digital Subscriber Lines (DSL) and TV cable modems are rapidly reaching more and more people, although only in North America, where most of the market for electronic commerce still is, though. Additionally, some companies are already experimenting with safer ways of transmitting large amounts of data over the Internet, taking care of data security and recovering from connection drops. Microsoft, for example, has recently begun offering most of the popular Developer Network (MSDN) library online, while still maintaining the regular CD shipments for those users who can't afford to download several gigabytes of data with their connections.

It is worth noting that all the concepts that apply to physical-goods stores are still valid for this kind of application. You will find products, probably organized in departments or categories, and you will still be able to use techniques like cross-selling and up-selling successfully.

Service Rendering

There are some cases in which an online store can be so well concealed that you won't actually realize that you are buying something because nothing is being sent to you in any form. This is the case, for example, with companies that offer you *services* rather than goods.

In this case the line-of-business system disappears almost entirely, fundamentally because there are no products that have to be tracked to a warehouse or delivered to the user in any way. Most of the time, however, there will still be a need for some kind of tracking system, so that the user can know what is happening to their service without having to ask your always-too-busy support staff.

A typical scenario for this kind of electronic commerce application is the one where an ISP provides Internet access to a number of customers. As you can imagine, there really isn't anything to buy and deliver to the user, beside a good connection to the Net. Still, you'll have to provide feedback to the user as to what the status of his or her account is without him or her having to call you by phone.

Several of the electronic commerce concepts that we saw earlier have to be bent a little to fit this model, but they don't need to change radically or disappear altogether. In fact, you'll find that the basic concepts, like shoppers, shopping cart, products and departments will fit any possible application of electronic commerce that can come to mind.

In this case, you will have to consider the services you offer as your products. This might seem a bit of a stretch, because there's nothing that's actually being delivered to the user, to the point that you are not going to need a line-of-business system anymore, but, if you think of it, that's exactly what you're selling. Even the concept of departments doesn't need to be thrown away—after all, you will offer different types of services (i.e. business and household connections) and you will need to categorize your products accordingly.

The only idea that seems to be completely out of place is the shopping cart. After all, your customers don't need to pretend they are in an online store—most likely, they won't even *know* they are in one—and it seems hard to believe that more than one product will be bought at any given time. However, keep in mind that we are trying our best to adapt a generic system—our definition of electronic commerce (and its Site Server implementation, as we shall see later on)—to different models. Therefore, it doesn't hurt to think of the shopping cart as the repository where the services chosen by your customer will be stored for retrieval by the purchase process.

Speaking of the purchase process, the latter is probably significantly simpler than the one that has to be used for a physical merchandise store. For one thing, you don't have to worry about shipping costs (unless some are connected with the service you provide, although in that case you'd probably fall back to a physical goods delivery store), which can be a very difficult issue to deal with. By the same token, the availability of the products won't be a source of concern, since you are not really selling anything.

Software Licensing

The third business-to-consumer application of electronic commerce that we are going to examine concerns the sale of licenses for use of a software program. In the typical scenario, a customer will usually receive the software free of charge (i.e. through an Internet download), but will have to pay for its usage.

Even though, at first sight, this kind of model might look similar to the service rendering, many of its aspects present unique challenges. For one thing, you will have to come up with a viable system to license your software. "Viable", in this case, means reliable, secure and safe for the vendor. In fact, you don't want to sell something to the user that he or she can't use for some reason, and at the same time you don't want anybody else than the licensed customer to use the license that you distribute.

Another interesting point to keep in mind is that, in this case, the store will have to somehow send a license to the software to activate it for the prescribed number of uses or period of time. So, software licensing forces you to deliver a product that is different for each user—since each license that you hand out will be custom-tailored to the user machine and usage parameters.

Again, all the concepts that we have examined work well in this scenario, too, especially if you keep an open mind as we just did for digital goods. In the case of software licensing, the licenses will be your products, and they can well be categorized in departments. Once more, you will have to stretch the concept of the shopping cart to make it work here, but I'm sure you're getting used to it anyway.

Let's now make an example of how software licensing works. Several companies, these days, are bringing the convenience of the Internet to the backup software scene. The advantages in backing up data through the Net are threefold. First of all, the service providers make sure that you never run out of space (a much dreaded problem for everybody who ever lost data and turned faithfully to the mystical tape only to find out that it had ran out of space three days before). Second, you will most likely be able to schedule the entire backup system so that it runs completely unattended. Third, your data will be automatically backed up out-of-site, so that any accidents that might happen will not affect your data. (Isn't it so reassuring to know that, in the event of a fire, you will burn to death but your data will be somewhere else? I remember once being in a backup lab—one of those buildings allegedly capable of withstanding the Wrath of God itself—and seeing a sign that read "In case of fire, retrieve daily backup tapes and *then* leave the building").

Thus, as you can see, these programs take care of the three main problems of backups: availability, consistency and durability (it's very unfortunate that a similar service doesn't exist for cars). The issue, of course, is that customers have to pay for the service they're getting, and they will usually do this by purchasing licenses to use the backup program.

As you may have noticed, the online store is but one piece of the puzzle in this scenario. You will need a good licensing system (and there are *very* few) that has been designed to work across the Internet and that can be integrated with the application without too much trouble. At the same time, you will have to make absolutely sure that nobody is using your product without having paid the appropriate fee. In the case of data backup, this is a relatively easy task, since the backup software itself is pretty useless if it can't access the backup server, and you can always deny access to a server if a user account is not in good shape, or if the user is not registered at all. In other cases in which the software operates in standalone mode (like computer games, for example), not only will you not be able to prevent users from fraudulently using your product if the licensing system is not secure and safe: your technology will not enable you to recognize that this is happening at all.

Business-to-Business Scenarios

The models that we have looked at so far work well in a business-to-consumer environment, in which your audience is the general public. Things are a little different, as we mentioned before, when it comes to business-to-business electronic commerce.

Corporate Procurement

This is the equivalent of a typical online store, only for businesses. Through it, it is possible to purchase any item of any kind. However, there are three important aspects to keep in mind:

> A customer is not spending his or her own money. Therefore, it might be necessary to either limit the maximum amount that any given user can spend, or require approval from the user's supervisor before accepting a purchase above a certain limit.

> The customer is not going to be paying for the merchandise directly. This means that (a) the store must be *absolutely* sure about the user's identity, and (b) it must be tightly integrated with the line-of-business system in order to emit invoices properly to the customer's organization. Also, most companies only grant so much credit to any given business partner before they require a payment to be made in order to continue placing orders—and the store must be sure to keep this fact into account.

> Finally, each organization is given its own pricing model, which can be different from other organizations shopping at the same store. Although producing different prices for different users sounds like a simple enough proposition, managing the products' prices can become a tricky task.

If you think of it, what all three requirements really mean is that there is a strong need for a good personalization system that runs side-by-side with the store and provides it with useful information, such as spending limits and other user data. The Personalization part of Site Server fits in really nicely here, in particular because you will not have to worry too much about the problems that arise when you need to scale the Membership Directory—a little bit of planning ahead will give you exactly what you need.

Supplier-Chain Integration

Another application of business-to-business electronic commerce is the integration of the store with certain (or all) aspects of a line-of-business system. You will have to deal with this kind of situation if you open a business-to-consumer online store but are not directly fulfilling your orders. In that case, you will most probably delegate the task of sending the merchandise to your customers to one or more third parties, or *suppliers*, who, in turn, will be using their own fulfillment system to send out the products.

From a technical point of view, there is no real difference between this model and the corporate procurement one. In the end, your supplier will be dealing only with you, and you will fundamentally adhere to the basic rules of business-to-business commerce: you'll pay through a purchase order/invoice/deferred settlement system; you will need to authenticate yourself in order to transfer a purchase; and so on.

From a logical standpoint, however, the problem is very different. First of all, you will not be the ultimate recipient of the merchandise that you buy. The store will therefore need to implement a feedback system so that your customers will be able to track the status of their orders, and you will be able to know that whatever has been purchased by them, through you, has actually been delivered to their doors.

Finally, looking at the practical side of things, there's a fairly good chance that your online store will be implemented on a platform that is completely different from the one used by your supplier. This is a simple consequence of the fact that, traditionally, wholesalers have been managing their warehouses with minicomputers, like the ones from the IBM AS/400 series, whereas most startup online stores tend to enjoy the affordable price of PC-based systems like Windows NT and Site Server. Now, the main problem here is in the fact that NT and, say, an AS/400 don't really talk well to each other. In fact, they don't at all! What you need, therefore, is a middle tier that takes care of all the transfer of information between the two systems.

Luckily, as we shall see in a moment, Microsoft offers all the functionality that you need to interface the two systems through the SNA Server product (or alternatively one could use IBM's Client Access), while Site Server itself features a business-to-business functionality that is flexible enough to support the exchange of data between any two systems.

Microsoft Site Server, Commerce Edition

It's now finally time to move on and find out what Site Server has to offer in terms of electronic commerce. First of all, it is worth noting that there are two versions of the product: one of them carries the longer name of *Commerce Edition*, and, as you can imagine, it's the one that actually provides the functionality that we will be talking about in the next few chapters.

A Brief History of Microsoft's Commerce Technology

Looking back at the last few years of software development, it's surprising to notice that, even though Microsoft didn't have any Internet technology at all as late as the end of 1996, Site Server is now in its third version. This is certainly due at least in part to the great effort that the company is putting into gaining market leadership in the field, but also owing to the fact that the technology currently in Site Server was acquired in 1996 through a merger with eShop, a small California-based company focusing on electronic commerce. To be fair, Microsoft had already initiated an internal development effort aimed at creating a commerce platform, but they probably figured out that merging with an existing company and acquiring its technology would have given them a boost in their race against major rivals, such as IBM or Oracle, which were already shipping similarly targeted products.

The funny thing is that eShop's technology wasn't Internet-based at all, but worked on a completely separate network, similar to other service providers at the time, like the Microsoft Network or America Online. Potential customers received proprietary client software on a floppy disk through the mail and could connect to the proprietary network through a normal phone line. eShop signed up a few vendors, who eventually ended up implementing Microsoft solutions in their Internet stores later on.

Why did Microsoft choose eShop, then? Well, they are probably the only ones who really know the answer to that question, but the technology must have fitted really well in the corporation's plans, because by the end of 1996 the first version of their Internet commerce software, called *Microsoft Merchant Server 1.0*, was available for purchase.

Merchant Server was a much simpler product than Site Server is today, as it really only included basic electronic commerce functionality (therefore this book would have been a lot shorter back then!). However, it was already entirely based on Microsoft technology, from NT to Internet Information Server to SQL Server, and was designed to be easily expandable–a fundamental characteristic that it preserves to this day. COM was not an extremely well established concept in Merchant Server, therefore much of the customization had to be done by writing C++ components based on a proprietary interface. The software was also designed to provide an easy interface to the underlying database, which in some way limited what could be done with it because the table structure was "hidden" from the web application. Certain aspects of this approach still remain in the current product, as we'll see in the next chapters.

A license to use Merchant Server cost $15,000. You can count the zeros, if you like to, but I can spell it out for you in letters: fifteen thousand dollars. Well, if you think that's a tad too high a price, you can find comfort in the fact that you're not alone–this kind of pricing is in clear contrast with Microsoft's basic philosophy of delivering high quality products at low prices by targeting a wide audience. As a matter of fact, when Merchant Server's successor, called Microsoft Site Server 2.0 came out in 1997, it only cost $5,000 and provided functionality that went beyond electronic commerce in fields like personalization and membership, content publishing, and so on.

Site Server 2.0 came in two flavor: the Standard Edition and the Enterprise Edition, which also contained Microsoft Commerce Server, the new name for the functionality previously provided by Merchant Server. The new software was finally entirely based on COM and all of Microsoft's technologies, such as ASP. However, because of certain limitations in the way Visual Basic worked, Visual C++ was realistically the only tool that could be used to develop the plug-ins for expanding the order processing system.

Site Server 2.0 also introduced the *Microsoft Wallet*, a browser plug-in that allows the user to securely store personal information on his or her computer and then authorize its transfer to a Site Server-based online store by typing in a password. The intent was, obviously, to facilitate the purchase process by making it possible for the user to transmit all his or her personal information–shipping and billing addresses and credit card numbers–without having to retype it every time. Commerce Server came with two versions of the Wallet, one for Internet Explorer and the other one for Netscape Navigator, and was once again based on a model that could be expanded through COM to implement different authentication methods and new types of credit card. We'll talk more in detail about the Wallet in later chapters.

In 1998, Site Server 3.0 was released. Once again, it was split in two different products. The standard version was presented mainly as an intranet tool, and provided Membership, Personalization, Publishing and Analysis functionality. The other one, called *Commerce Edition* also included the successor to Commerce Server and the Ad Server, a new piece of software that made it possible to deliver advertisements online (and which will be the topic of Chapter 20). Site Server 3.0 is even more integrated with the latest Microsoft technology. For one thing, it is entirely based on ASP and COM/DCOM; in addition, it makes a heavy use of Microsoft Transaction Server, which is very appropriate considering the fact that an online store is *entirely* based on transactions. Thanks to a modification to the threading model in Visual Basic 5 Service Pack 1, later on maintained in Visual Basic 6, it is now possible to write the expansion plug-ins in that language too, albeit not without a certain performance impact.

Site Server 3.0 also includes business-to-business functionality, a major advancement from the previous versions. The business-to-business system is still in its infancy, but provides an incredibly wide array of applications that can be used to integrate with just about any other line-of-business or corporate procurement software–even though it has been optimized to work with another Site Server site at the other end. The licensing system has been changed again–even though prices tend to be close to the ones that were paid for version 2.0.

The Commerce Server Design Philosophy

As you might have guessed by the fact that I have mentioned it about once in every line of text over the last two pages, Commerce Server (MSCS from now on) has been primarily written as a platform. This means that its goal is to provide solid and reliable *building blocks* that can be used by a developer to create an online store. Thus, the functionality provided by MSCS is very horizontal, and can be adapted to just about any scenario. The downside of this is that it's a little difficult to grasp the technology as a whole, because of its breadth. Luckily, the software is sufficiently automated in the creation and management of online stores, so it's not that difficult to get started.

The Store

At the core of the MSCS implementation is the server, which is fundamentally a standalone IIS application. Any given site can contain an arbitrary number of stores, each in its own virtual folder. A store cannot reside in the root folder of a site–unless you make modifications to the ASP code that is generated by MSCS.

Each store is composed of a set of steps whose goal is to drive the user toward loading items in his or her shopping cart. We'll look at these steps in the following chapters.

The Purchase Process

Once the user expresses a desire to buy the products in his or her basket, the control of the application is handed over to the purchase process, which is fundamentally different depending on whether the store provides business-to-consumer or business-to-business functionality.

In the first case, a group of ASP pages guide the user through the process of entering all the information that is needed to complete the order. In most cases, this will include shipping and billing addresses, as well as a credit card number. The order is then processed by the *Order Processing Pipeline*, a series of processes, organized in a transaction, whose goal is to make sure that all the information collected for the order is correct and that the order can be successfully accepted by the store.

The pipeline technology is a very important piece of MSCS—to the point that we will dedicate a couple of chapters to it later—as it provides an organized approach to order processing. Internally, it is divided into a set of *stages*, each one of which is dedicated to addressing a particular aspect of the process (e.g. verifying that the shipping information is correct; making sure that the credit card can be charged; and so on). Each process, in turn, executes a customizable set of *components*, each specialized in taking care of a particular issue. Pipeline components are essentially ad-hoc COM objects, which means that pipelines can be easily expanded using either Visual Basic or Visual C++.

If your store is a business-to-business application, the purchase process will be radically different. In fact, there will be no need to specify either billing or shipping information, but other steps will have to be taken. These steps are handled by the Commerce Interchange Pipeline (CIP), whose essential task is to manage the exchange of documents with other partners.

The CIP is based on the same fundamental technology that powers the Order Processing Pipeline, but its chores include tasks like sending purchase orders, requesting supervisor authorization for completing orders above a user's purchase limit, and so on.

The Store Manager

An online store developed using MSCS doesn't just provide the interface to the client and the functionality required to process an order, but also features a complete Web-based management system that can be securely accessed using a browser.

The implications of this concept are interesting. For one thing, the store's management team is able to handle all the aspects of the store from anywhere—there's no need for costly terminal equipment and dedicated management applications. Additionally, because the management interface is based on exactly the same technologies used to run the front-end, implementing new functionality—or expanding the existing one—is a relatively easy task.

More Business-to-Business Functionality

Since the CIP's main task is to handle the transfer of documents, one of its obvious uses is in the handling of supply-chain integration. As a matter of fact, the pipeline has been designed to provide a broad range of functionality that enables it to support technologies as diverse as simple e-mail or HTTP communication and the more advanced Electronic Data Interchange (EDI), supported by many of the larger suppliers in several industries.

The CIP can also be used as an integration tool on its own, without needing any translation to another protocol in the middle. In fact, two Site Server applications can talk to each other directly through the pipeline, and can therefore provide a complete supply-chain system that communicates on one end with the online store and on the other with the line-of-business system, whatever that might be.

Summary

The one important concept that you should have acquired from this chapter is that we are only beginning to understand the many implications of electronic commerce. Its applications span a multitude of possibilities, the most important of which we have discussed early in the chapter.

We also had the time to stop and examine the relevant concepts of electronic commerce, which we have discovered to have been, as so often happens, borrowed and adapted from other areas of activity. Finally, we examined Microsoft's electronic commerce platform, Microsoft Site Server, Commerce Edition, and saw the design principles on which it is based.

15

Anatomy of An Online Store

Every time we enter into a real-life store, we immediately recognize certain familiar elements, such as the aisles (or whatever is used to show the products), the cashier, the store's personnel, and so on. The ability to identify these constituents of the store is so automatic for us that we don't even pay attention to it anymore. For example, I have a shirt that looks exactly like the one that the employees of a popular furniture store chain wear while at work. Incidentally, that shirt is also one of my favorites; so there's a good chance that, whenever I go there to see for, say, a new desk, I'll be wearing that shirt, too.

Now, my shirt looks *similar* to the one worn by the employees, but it is not by any means the same: mine has no logo—of course—and the pattern is slightly different. Nonetheless, every time I go there with my favorite shirt I am continually harassed by customers asking me how much that beautiful sofa costs. People don't stop to consider that, although the shirt I wear looks similar to the one the employees have on, it is by no means identical. They simply direct their attention to what looks familiar and go for it.

In an online store, as we have seen in the previous chapter, the problem is not so much in showing the elements, but in doing so the proper way. After all, we were able to adapt just about any model that we could think of to the basic concepts of store, shopper, shopping cart, and so on. This means that they must be there, even if we don't see them or if they are presented to us under a disguise.

In this chapter, we will examine the fundamental structure of an online store, both for business-to-consumer and business-to-business applications. We will also pay a visit to the sample stores that are shipped together with SSCE and look at the kind of functionality that they offer.Finally, we will take a look at the store creation tools that are part of MSCS, how they work and what the basic architecture of a newly born site is.

> In order to be able to see the sample stores on your server, you will have to make sure that they have been installed during the setup of Site Server. If they haven't, simply launch setup again and install them.

Here's a preview of this chapter's content:

> **Architecture of a business-to-consumer site**
> This section will describe how a business-to-consumer site works from an architectural point of view. We will also follow the site's structure with online examples that are taken from the basic Site Server-created store. To demonstrate more realistic implementations, we will then take a look at the sample stores that are provided by MSCS.

> **Architecture of a business-to-business site**
> Similarly to the previous one, this section will focus on the structure of a business-to-business site. We will examine a typical store and point out how it differs from a business-to-consumer site. Once again, we will take a look at Microsoft Market, the only business-to-business sample store that is offered by MSCS.

> **Store creation tools**
> Finally, the last part of the chapter will be dedicated to learning how the two wizards that are provided by MSCS can facilitate the creation of a new store. We will also take a look at the basic structure of a newly created store.

Architecture of a Business-to-Consumer Store

A plain online store—one that only provides the functionality that is strictly needed to make a purchase—can be divided into three different areas. The **store browsing** part corresponds to walking around in the aisles of a store with your shopping cart and choosing the products you want to buy.

For customers who are really interested in something but can't find it by just browsing through the available products (something that happens all-too-often in real life and can only get worse in an online store with thousands of products), the **search** functionality makes it possible to find just about anything without going crazy. This corresponds to asking a store clerk where a product is located in a normal store, with the difference that (a) a good online search system will know of *all* products (try that with a clerk) and will (b) actually show the customer all the products that match his or her description in the same place, rather than directing him or her to the various aisles.

Finally, all sections converge into the **shopping cart**, sometimes called the *shopping basket*, which contains all the products that the user wants to buy. From the basket, they can proceed to the **order processing** section of the site, which guides them through all the steps necessary to complete their purchases, computes all the costs and performs all the operations needed to pass the order on to the line-of-business system.

The Home Page

The entry point of an online store is, usually, the home page. The reason why I'm using the term *usually* is that this might not always be the case: for example, if you're entering the store following the URL provided by an online ad for a special offer, you may be taken to an introductory page first.

As you can see from the following screenshot, the home page generally contains some information about the nature of the store (although more information is usually provided in a separate section, which is not strictly needed to purchase something) and, often, provides direct links to products that are on special offer. Everything that you see in an online store should be done with the goal of increasing the possibility that a customer makes a purchase; as such, the home page often contains direct links to products that are on sale, information about special offers, and so on.

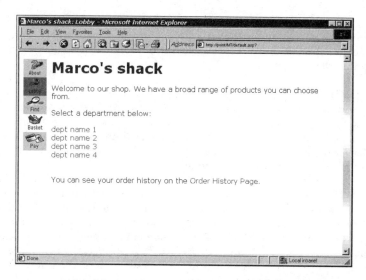

For consistency, every store should contain certain recurring elements that appear as part of every page—no exclusions allowed—and occupy always the same spot. These elements have two main aims: first, they represent the fingerprint of the store and make it easier for the users to remember where they are; second, these elements provide navigational elements that are useful throughout the entire shopping experience. In the previous screenshot, they are on the left side and provide links to the main sections of the site: the site information section, the home page (called "Lobby" here in respect of the store's metaphor), the search section, the shopping cart, and the purchase process ("Pay").

In our case, the body of the home page contains links to various departments (our aisles), and, although this is not always the case, on many sites departments are often part of the navigational elements common to every page. Here, each department link is our main door into the store browsing section.

The Department Page

The screenshot that follows shows what you see when you click on a department. As you can see, the first step into store browsing is usually a list of products that belong to a given department. Each list entry provides a link to a page that offers more information about a specific product, as we will see in a moment. In addition, a brief description of the department itself (usually together with a brief portrait of the products it contains) is given as well.

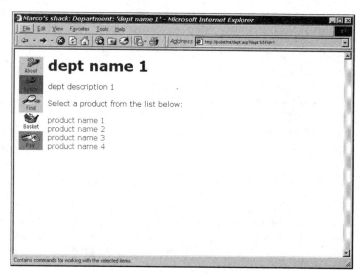

Again, a more evolved store than ours might want to maximize the potential of this page, which will probably register most of the impressions after the home page, and display more focused information, like the department's specials or best sellers. The list of products, in that case, will be displayed as a secondary step into the navigation.

This approach to shopping, which is the most common in a real-life store, has a significant handicap in the online world. As you can see from the picture, the entry for each product is pretty anonymous—you can only see the product's name. No picture, not even a price. Once again, more evolved stores *do* offer additional data, like a price and, sometimes, a small picture. The problem is that the store can't really offer more than that because the download times for the page would dilate significantly, since several different products are displayed in it.

In addition, an online store often offers a variety of products that a normal store, for stocking reasons, cannot provide. As a result, a department might be made of hundreds, or even thousands, of individual products. Showing all these products in a single list is impractical—that would mean a lot of bandwidth usage both on the store's and the user's end—and having to browse through many pages of dull product entries is a time-consuming experience. This is especially true if the user doesn't know where the product he or she is looking for is in the list—sometimes, albeit not always, products are sorted in alphabetical order, and the only navigation possibility offered is a link to the next page and a link to the previous one. Now, if the department contains ten thousand products and the one the user is looking for begins with the letter Z, an arbitrary number of pages further on, then you can be certain that the user will go somewhere else. Other sorting options, such as by price and by availability, can be chosen as well, and in some cases they will offer a better approach to listing the products in your store. In general, however, you should also provide some sort of search functionality to help the user.

The Product

Clicking on a product entry in the listing provided by the department page will cause more information about that specific product to be displayed. As you can see from the next screenshot, this page provides much more detail about the product than the previous one: there is plenty of space for a good picture, a detailed description and pricing information. If the product is on sale, or part of a special promotion, this would be the right place to let the user know about that too.

Looking at this page, you can probably imagine how inconvenient it can be for the user to access information about many products in this way. Therefore, when designing an online store, much care should be taken in making the navigation system as flexible and powerful as possible, to guide the users to the correct products without annoying them.

This is also the very first page where we see an **Add to basket** link. As I'm sure you have already figured out, clicking on this link causes the product to be added to the user's basket (whose page we'll see later on). Usually, the product is added with a quantity of one item, but this may vary according to what the store sells (if you're into groceries, for example, and sell something by the gram, then maybe you'll want to add a minimum quantity of 500g).

In a more realistic store, the **Add to Basket** link will be all over the place—main page, department page, special offers page, and so on—because the store designer will have wanted to facilitate the act of adding products to the basket to the maximum extent possible. Maybe it's not so evident by looking at the generic store that we see here, but let's assume that you had found a product you really like in the listing. If you know the product well, then it's annoying to have to view one additional page to be able to add it to the basket!

The product page concludes the navigation section of the site. As you can see, even in this simple store of ours, the navigation is very streamlined, and the user doesn't need more than three clicks to add something to the basket. This is a very important particularly because, once again, you want to keep the store as straightforward as possible for your users.

The Search Functionality

In the previous paragraphs, we have mentioned how department browsing is really not the preferred method for finding a product in an online store. As a matter of fact, statistics show us that most people who buy online have a good idea of what they want even before they enter the store.

As a result, when a user enters an online store, most often he or she will want to find something using some focused search tool, rather than having to guess where that product might be in the store. The search functionality offered by the store, then, arguably becomes its single most important aspect (besides actually having what the user is looking for and being up and running).

If we click on the Find link provided by the site navigation of our store, we'll end up in a page similar to the one shown in the next screenshot. As you can see, our search functionality is *extremely* simple—all the user has to do is type in some text and click on Find. The search results (in the screenshot overleaf) are somewhat similar to a department listing page, and the links to the individual products point, once again, to the product page that we just saw a moment ago.

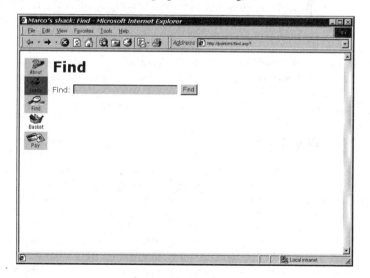

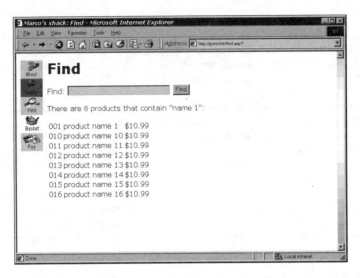

Many online stores offer the basic functionality that our store provides as part of the navigation elements that are common to all pages. This means that, from any page in the store, the user can just type in what he or she is looking for and click on a Find button to launch a "quick search" against the site's product database. Obviously, tools like natural language search–that allow the user to type in questions in plain English (or any other language that the store supports) and find what he or she is looking for–are extremely useful in this context, even though most stores only provide simple keyword search on the database's contents.

Characteristic of more and more online stores is an **Advanced Search**, which makes it possible for the user to specify targeting parameters with greater detail than the quick search. For example, in a music store, the advanced search functionality might allow the user to specify price range, title keywords, producers/publishers, format (CD or tape), and so on. The result is a much more focused search, usually producing results that better reflect what the user was looking for.

From a technical point of view, it's important to understand that there really isn't any huge difference between performing a search and browsing the catalogue. In most instances (excluding the natural language search that we mentioned above), both actions will result in a query being executed against the database and the same result set being shown to the user.

The Basket

Whenever the user decides that he or she wants to buy something, the product ends up in his or her basket. As we saw in the previous chapter, the basket is more similar to a shopping list than to a shopping basket, in that the products it includes are not really "taken off the shelves" until the order is processed.

The next screenshot shows the basket page of our bare-bones online store. Notice how certain information is displayed about each product: the name, the per-item list price, the actual cost (after applying discounts), the quantity and the total price that the user will be paying (excluding taxes, shipping and handling). To be honest, our store has nothing to add in this case, because the information that is displayed is exactly what's needed–there would be no point in including a picture of the product or its description here, since the user has already expressed the intention of buying it.

Naturally, this model doesn't necessarily apply to any store. A site whose products are very visual, like a clothing store, for example, might need to include a picture or a better description so that the user knows exactly what he or she is going to buy. This is particularly true in those cases in which a single product can be purchased in many variants (i.e. a shirt can have different colors and sizes).

It's important that certain tools be provided to the user as part of the basket page. First of all, the user must be able to change the quantity of a product that he or she is buying (hopefully to increment it), and be able to proceed quickly to the order processing phase. In our case, the quantity of an item is stored in an edit box, which means that the user can change it at any time. If we had more than one item in the basket, naturally the user would be able to change the quantity of as many items as needed and then click on the Update Basket button to commit the changes. Moving on to the order processing stage is equally simple—all the user has to do is click on the Purchase button.

As you have probably already guessed, setting an item's quantity to zero and clicking on Update Basket causes that item to disappear from the basket. If you have several items in your basket, however, this deletion method can be awkward—the fact that you don't want your users to delete items is understandable, but this might be a little too obvious—and therefore the store provides an Empty Basket button that does the job of clearing up the basket's contents.

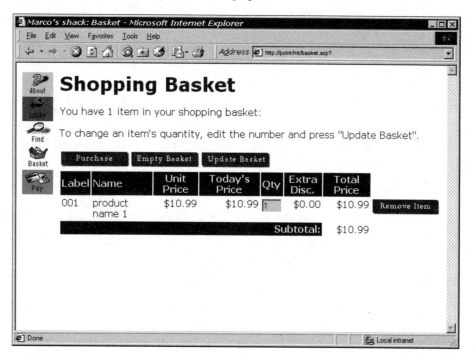

The Purchase Process

A decision has been made by the user: I want to buy! Now what? Well, there are a few things that you must still ask the user before you can be sure that (a) you'll be able to send him or her the merchandise (whatever that is) and (b) he or she will be able to pay for it. The procedure of asking for the necessary information and evaluating it is called the **purchase process**, or sometimes the *check-out* process.

Shipping

The first thing you will want to know is who the recipient of the merchandise is. In a physical goods delivery store, this is an important step because the ship-to location will most likely influence the total cost of the order, and in certain cases (e.g. if you're selling regulated encryption software) will determine whether you can ship the merchandise at all.

The next screenshot shows our shipping page. As you can see, there is a strange-looking box in the middle of the page, instead of the more familiar form fields that one would expect. That's the **Microsoft Wallet**, whose task is safely storing the user's data on his or her computer and then releasing it, upon authorization from the user, of course, whenever a site needs it. Its goal is to improve the shopping experience by facilitating the exchange of data between the user and the site.

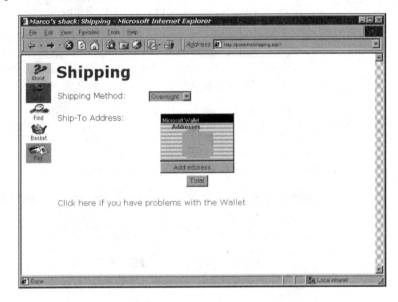

The Wallet also provides storage for the user's credit card information (remember, all the data is stored in encrypted format on the user's local machine and released only if the user decides to by typing in a password that is *not* sent to the site), and features a COM-based interface that can be extended to include private-label cards, debit-cards, and so on.

For more information on the Wallet you can refer to Appendix B; for the moment, take note of the fact that it exists and that it is obviously a browser plug-in. This means that (a) not all the browsers will be able to support it and that (b) in most cases the users will have to download it from either your site or Microsoft's. Since you want the store to be accessible to as wide an audience as possible, you will also provide the appropriate means for your users to avoid using it. In our case, this is done by clicking on the Click here if you have problems with the Wallet link, which brings the user to an alternate shipping page that uses standard HTML forms (see the next screenshot). The same page is also shown if the browser does not support the Wallet at all.

The data that is asked for during the shipping phase is pretty straightforward. With a little hands-on experience, however, you will find that the Wallet asks for more information than the HTML forms. In particular, the latter doesn't require the user to type in an e-mail address. Now this is understandable, because the recipient, who is not necessarily the person who is placing the order, might even not have Internet access at all. However, e-mail is arguably the cheapest and best way to get in touch with a person, therefore it's a good idea for an online store to be asking for it, too.

Clicking on the Total button will cause the system to verify the information that the user has typed in and, if it doesn't find any problems with it, it stores it in its internal database.

Billing

The next page in line is there to ask the user about how he or she intends to pay for the purchase. The screenshot shows us the billing screen from our store. As you can see, a complete order detail is presented to the user again; there are two reasons why this happens.

First of all, the store is now able to calculate the *final* cost of the order, including shipping, handling and tax fees. This wasn't possible before, as we didn't know where we were going to ship the merchandise and, therefore, were unable to calculate all the fees correctly. Second, the user is now going to officially approve and authorize the purchase, therefore it is important that he or she be able to see what the costs are going to be, particularly from a legal standpoint.

Once again, there is a box on the page, and this time it's got a huge Visa logo on it. As you probably have already figured out, this is just another manifestation of the Wallet, which this time can be used to send over pre-stored payment information. As was the case for the shipping page, here we have a link that allows us to use a standard HTML form rather than the Wallet. As you can see from the next screenshot, the page asks for the usual credit card information. If you go back and forth from the shipping to the billing page, you will notice that any text that you store in the credit card information box is not retained by the store and doesn't appear when you go back to the billing page. This behavior is by design, because it is possible that the same computer be used by two different people and keeping this kind of data might prove to be disastrous. We'll talk more about tracking users later on in the chapter.

Using the Wallet

For the moment we'll focus on the Wallet's interface with the user. As you can see, the Wallet initially contains no data. This means, of course, that it's not possible to use it for completing a purchase unless some information is stored in it.

To do so, the user clicks on **Add Address...** (or **Add card...** from the billing page), causing the Wallet to display a dialogue box similar to the one shown in the next screenshot. Once all the data has been filled out, the user can click on **OK** to save it in the Wallet's internal storage system.

It's worth noting again that any data entered in the Wallet is stored on the local computer in encrypted format. The user is also asked for a password whenever this information needs to be released, and the password is never sent over to the requesting site. This offers a good degree of security for your personal information.

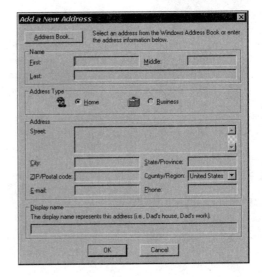

Installing the Wallet

Let's talk for a moment about how the Wallet is installed—this is particularly important if you consider that most of your users might well not have it installed when they first visit the site.

First of all, Microsoft provides two versions of the Wallet, one for Internet Explorer and the other for Netscape Navigator. In both cases, however, the amount of data to download is pretty high, resulting in a wait time of several minutes on a typical modem connection.

As a result, those users who don't already have the Wallet (it comes as an option even in IE4 and IE5) will not really want to wait for their browsers to download it and install it on their computer. The problem here is that IE, contrary to Netscape, will automatically start downloading the plug-in without any manual intervention, and this might be confusing for your users, who will not easily realize what's going on.

In consideration of all these issues, I recommend that you include the Wallet as a second-choice option for your customers, and offer the HTML forms as default, essentially inverting the scenario that we just went through. This way, you will be sure that *all* your users are able to complete a purchase without any problem, while those who want to take advantage of the Wallet's advanced features will be able to do so by clicking on the appropriate link.

The Confirmation Page

When the user clicks on the Purchase button from the billing page, the store proceeds with the final processing of the purchase. This includes making sure that all the information entered is correct and compatible with the operating parameters of the store, that the merchandise requested is available for delivery, and that the payment information is correct from all points of view. Larger online stores also pass the payment data through a credit card processor to make sure that the data provided by the user is correct, but this involves the purchase of (often) expensive verification software that not all site owners can afford. As a result, most small to medium stores still process credit cards manually, and the user's order is accepted without really verifying that he or she has the buying power needed to complete it.

In any case, once the purchase is approved, the user is redirected to a confirmation page, similar to the one in the next screenshot. The goal of this page is to tell the user that his or her purchase went through successfully, and to provide a **reference number** (or Order ID) that can be used to reference the order in the future. This number becomes particularly useful whenever a communication of any kind must take place between the store and the customer concerning the purchase; in that case, understanding what the conversation refers to will be much easier.

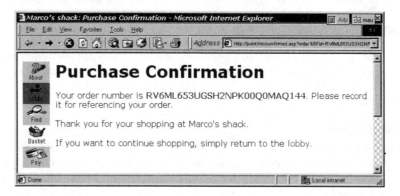

Unfortunately, as you can see, the order IDs that MSCS provides are way too long for any practical use. As a matter of fact, asking a customer to remember—or even write down—such a long sequence of letters and numbers means almost certainly that you will be in trouble sooner or later, when your users start calling in for questions or complaints and your attempts to find their orders only add to their frustration. The reason why MSCS uses such a long number is that it generates a GUID (Globally Unique IDentifier)—a 128-bit number that is likely to be unique among all the machines in the world—and uses that to uniquely identify each order.

This ensures that, no matter what database system is used in the backend, each order will be assigned a unique number. The same, however, can be achieved, if you're using a SQL Server, by implementing a self-incrementing primary key integer field that starts from any number (usually 100, so that your customers don't think your store is *that* new to the scene) and automatically updates itself every time a new order is added to the appropriate table. This way, the order IDs will have a shorter length (it will take a lot of purchases before you'll even reach six digits!) and it will be easier both for you and your customers to track them.

Security and Cookies

An important aspect of an online store is its security, which we can divide into three equally important aspects (their importance is the same in that if any of them fails you will end up with a lot of upset customers):

> **Data transmission**
> This type of security has to do with how much, how often and through what channels sensitive data is exchanged between the user's browser and the server.

> **Data retention**
> When the user sends data to the store, the latter will have to save it somewhere and may make it available to the user to expedite future purchases. It is imperative that the store ensures that that data is not sent to the wrong user by mistake!

> **Data storage**
> Finally, the site will have to store the user's information somewhere—usually a database—and it's important to ensure that that place is *not* accessible to unauthorized people.

What Data Anyway?

Let's spend a minute discussing about what this "data" is; fully understanding the nature of the data you have to handle is important because secure transmissions and storage are costly. In fact, sending data through a secure connection, such as SSL, is slower and takes more bandwidth than transmissions in the clear, and securing a database from physical and logical access can be expensive.

What you should be securing is all the data that can give away the user's identity and payment information. This includes billing and shipping addresses, and credit card data, but not, for example, the basket's contents. MSCS doesn't do a great job from this point of view, since most of the ship-to and bill-to data is preserved, and this is done on the basis that either the store owner has a reasonably good method for recognizing customers (i.e. through a login), or that the customer is aware that some of his or her data might be visible to other users.

Data Transmission

This is probably the easiest security problem that you will have to solve, since Site Server already provides support for SSL-encrypted transmissions. In particular, the basket, shipping, billing and confirmation pages are protected, while the others, which are not deemed to contain any confidential data, are sent over to the user in clear text.

As I mentioned in the previous section, there really isn't any need to force an HTTPS connection to the basket; the data that it contains really has no confidential value, as nobody can steal anything by knowing it, and it would be very difficult to recognize who a user is by looking at it.

If you look closely at the pictures in this chapter, you will notice that none of them uses an SSL-encrypted connection. Although this may seem to contradict the previous paragraph, you should keep in mind that the store was running in a test environment, in which using HTTPS will just bring additional headaches (not to mention the need of an additional digital certificate). MSCS provides several functions that allow the creation of links that can be made secure by changing a setting in the store configuration, thus allowing the developer to use clear-text communications during the development phase, and then switching easily to SSL once the site goes live.

Data Retention

This is a much more difficult problem to address, and it has to do with the way that MSCS recognizes users. In spite of the fact that they ship together, the various components of Site Server 3 do not integrate *that* easily. Thus, by default, MSCS doesn't use the functionality provided by Personalization and Membership to recognize users, but rather its own internal engine. (Of course, this can also be thought as a good thing, since you don't need P&M to run an online store).

As a result, users are tracked in one of two ways. In the first scenario, cookies are used to determine who a user is. Please keep in mind that, as we shall see later on in the chapter, MSCS turns off IIS support for Session objects by default, and forces the use of its own internal tracking system (which is still based on cookies) instead. The reason why this takes place is that sessions are unique to each web server, whereas MSCS's system works by storing all the information in the database, which can be shared across several web servers. As a result, sessions don't work well in a server farm, in which a user can be redirected to any server at any moment, while MSCS works well across any number of servers and is fully scaleable.

There are two main problems with cookies. The first one is that some browsers don't support them, and a lot of users turn them off even if their browser does. The second is that they do not guarantee recognition of a user, but only of a browser. Thus, if more than one person uses the browser, as is often the case in offices or Internet cafés, there is a risk that whatever data is persisted for one user may be visible to the next.

Alternatively, MSCS tracks users by means of a token, called Shopper ID, that is passed on as an HTML parameter in the URL query string. The use of this parameter guarantees that the shopper is recognized throughout the session even though he or she doesn't allow cookies to be employed. However, there is no way to persist the data across sessions, and, since all the information is stored in a database, the store will end up with a lot of wasted storage space. In addition, because users will not be recognized across more than one session, they will have to re-enter all their information every time they need to make a purchase, something that can make shopping at your site less than convenient.

If you are going to need your customers to log in, they should be required to do so only when strictly necessary, such as when accessing their personal information and/or making a purchase. In this case, integrating your store with Personalization & Membership is really a good idea, since you can maintain all the user data, including basket information, in a single place.

Data Storage

All this brings us to the store's database. Many people think that putting a firewall in front of the database server, or even only connecting it to a private network whose only point of access is the web server, is a sufficient measure to keep the data secure.

There are two holes in this way of reasoning. First, many hacking attempts are done from within an organization. There is no simpler way to steal data than entering the server room, logging onto the database server and dumping the tables that hold the user's information onto a floppy disk. Easy and, because most of the time auditing will be off (and even worse, somebody else will have already logged onto the machine, forgetting to lock it when they left), clean.

Second, even if the server is on a network that is not accessible from the outside world, don't forget that the web server must have access to it and, on reflection, anybody who has access to the web server also has access to the database. In fact, users normally have access to it, albeit only to that part of the data that concerns them. If somebody were to somehow hack into the web server and change the ASP scripts so that they return information about any user, that somebody would have successfully hacked into your database server as well, no matter how well protected it is.

Thus, protecting the data storage means making sure that the web server is bulletproof as well. You can do this with a firewall, even though it can turn into a single point of failure. In fact, if you are running a server farm, in which multiple computers provide service redundancy, if the firewall alone goes down, your customers won't be able to view any of the web servers anyway.

There is another way of protecting your data storage. It probably isn't as functional or even as secure as using a firewall, but it's definitely cheaper (firewalls run at about $15,000 apiece). All you need to do is take advantage of NT's built-in security features. They can be accessed through the Control Panel/Network interface (or, alternately, by right clicking on the My Neighborhood icon on the desktop and selecting Properties). The next screenshot shows the Protocols pane of the resulting dialogue box, from which you can access the TCP/IP properties by double-clicking the TCP/IP protocol.

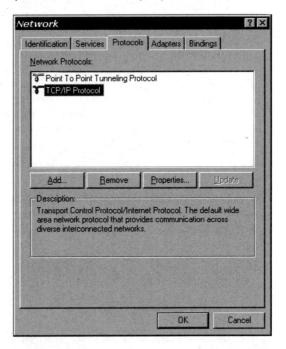

Once you are into the TCP/IP protocol properties, just select Enable Security, then click on Advanced and add the TCP/IP ports that you want to allow access on. In most cases, you will only need port 80 (HTTP) and 443 (HTTPS), while everything else should not be allowed—including the NetBEUI ports that are a hacker's heaven. This configuration will make accessing data on the server through normal NetBIOS sharing impossible, even for authorized persons, but will help in protecting your site from outside attacks. In this case, you can use a staging server for making changes to your site, and then replicate the changes by temporarily restoring access to the server.

The Store Manager

In the previous chapter, we mentioned how it should be possible to manage an online store through a web browser. This is a good idea, if you consider that you will have to create all the logic needed to run the entire site anyway, and you will most likely be able to recycle a good part of it if you decide to create a management interface for the store.

The creators of MSCS must have believed that this was a good idea too, since a store created with the software provides an interface that makes it possible to handle all the management functions entirely online. Access to the interface should only be granted to authorized users–usually people whose task is managing the store–and nobody else. If your store manager isn't protected, it doesn't matter how far you will have gone to secure your data, because just about anybody will have access to it anyway!

We can divide the Store Manager interface into four different areas:

> **Merchandising**
> Functions that are provided within this section can be used to access and modify the product database. This includes changing actual product data *and* the way products are organized in departments.

> **Transactions**
> From this section, it is possible to examine and work with the orders as they are received by the store. This includes viewing orders, authorizing their shipment, and so on.

> **Marketing**
> Being able to offer cross-selling, up-selling and special deals is a very important aspect of doing business online. This kind of functionality is usually grouped in the Marketing section of the Store Manager.

> **System**
> Finally, let's not forget that the web site is, essentially, a software product. As such, there are certain tasks that it must be possible to perform, like opening and closing the store, or configuring the purchase process. We'll consider all these operations as part of the System section.

The Home Page

As for the storefront the main point of entry for the Site Manager is its home page, shown in the adjacent screenshot. As you can see, Marketing and Merchandising functions are grouped together– mainly because there isn't much marketing functionality in general, since the only supported function is creating and managing promotions.

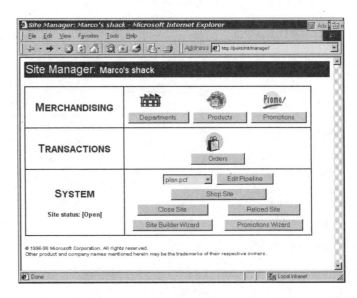

Now, there is one main problem with this page, and it's that everybody has access to everything. As a matter of fact, once you've made your way through the Manager, you will be able to access all the functionality, regardless of whether you are the CEO or the guy who works in the warehouse. This can be a risky proposition, if you consider that some store owners will not want just about anybody in their organization to have access to certain data—and having access to information you're not supposed to see means that sooner or later somebody will make a mistake where he or she wasn't even supposed to look into.

You will notice how the layout of the main page—whose spirit is more or less maintained throughout the management site—is extremely slim: the pictures are few and very small, and there is little explanatory text. Although this might have been said of the storefront as well, in this case it is so by design. In fact, you will want the Manager to be as efficient as possible, rather than "good-looking", because its use is limited to a restricted number of busy people who belong to your organization. This doesn't mean, however, that the management portion of a site should not be designed to be user-friendly and easy to use—just that the appearance will not be as important as the functionality it offers.

Merchandising Functions

As you can see from the previous screenshot our store provides two merchandising functions: access to the product database and access to the department database.

The Department Database

Clicking on the Departments button will take us to a page similar to the one shown in the next screenshot. The layout of this page is slightly different from the home page: a header and a footer containing the same information are provided as part of the page. The reason why they provide the same information is that you might be forced by the length of the page itself to hide either one outside your browser's viewable window, and therefore you'll be able to use the other to jump from one section of the site to the other.

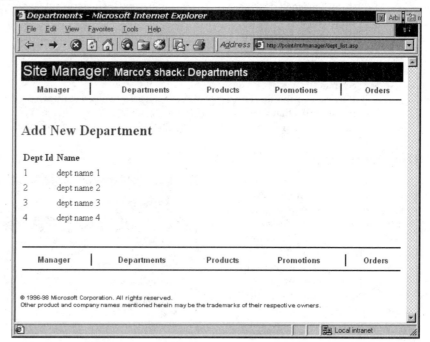

The rest of the page shows an interface that we'll find replicated across the entire site (as a matter of fact, many pages are shared by different functions within the Manager). The first link allows us to add a new department; by clicking on it, we'll be taken to the page shown in the following screenshot, which asks us a for a department ID (unique to the store and used to identify the department in the database), a name and a description. The name and description will be used in the storefront pages.

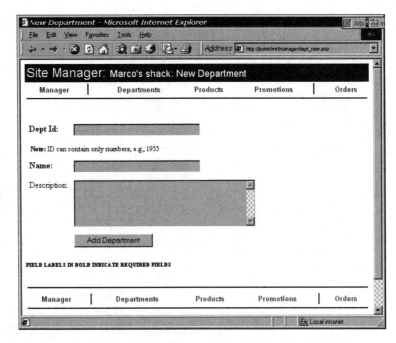

Editing departments is equally easy—all we need to do is click on a name and edit the data. You will notice that we are not allowed to change the department ID in the editing page; this is because that number is used as the primary key in the department table and therefore cannot be changed, otherwise the system won't be able to recognize the correct record for that department.

The Product Database

The product interface shown in the next two screenshots works in a similar way; the only significant difference is in the fact that there are many more fields to fill out here. You will also notice that, because there are more than ten products, the main list has been divided into pages. This is a very useful function, because some of these lists can get very long and, therefore, very difficult to manage. However, you will most likely want to add more functionality yourself, like the ability to reduce the number of items in the list by modifying the database query that generates it.

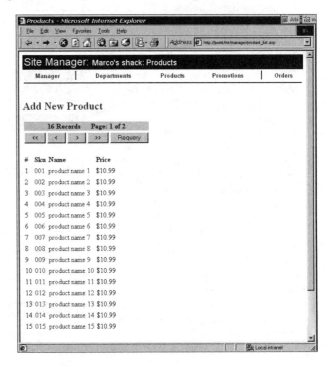

The fields used to create or edit a product (see next screenshot) are all very straightforward, but a few words should be spent talking about the Sale fields (the last three fields) and the department list. As you can imagine, the sale fields are used to determine whether a product is on sale. It is possible to specify a start and an end date for the sale, and a sale price. The system will automatically apply the sale price to all purchases within the specified amount of time. The department list, on the other hand, makes it possible to associate a product with one or more departments–pressing *Control* while clicking on any department will alternately add or remove it from the list of linked departments.

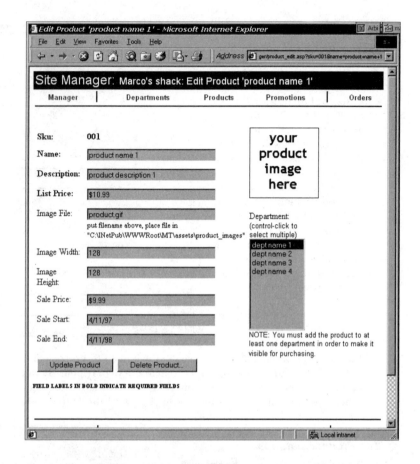

Transactions

The transactions section of our Store Manager only contains one button, which brings us to the list of orders, sorted according to certain parameters. If you choose to view orders divided by month, year or product, you will be shown a non-editable list of orders similar to the one in the following screenshot. Otherwise, you'll see something similar to the screenshot after that: a list of the orders available in the store. If you thought that the string used to identify orders was extremely long, take a look at the Shopper ID! As you can imagine, having it there, as it is, is not a great help–if anything, it makes reading the list more difficult.

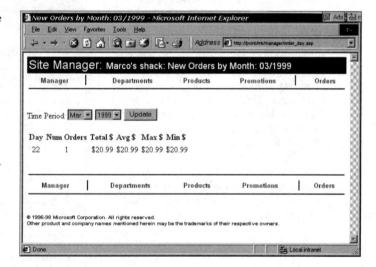

Clicking on an order ID brings up a page with more detailed information on the order. Shipping and billing information are provided, as well as a complete breakdown of the items that were purchased. You will probably find the fact that no credit card information is displayed annoying, but I can assure you that it's there and can be retrieved easily, as we shall see in the next chapter.

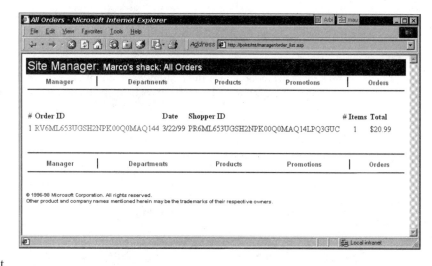

However, what's really missing here is a link to a line-of-business system. Naturally, there is a reason for this: it's impossible to write a generic sample that will be able to interface successfully with all the possible line-of-business systems. Therefore, the MSCS team thought that they would provide an interface suitable for a store that doesn't have a real system designed to handle and dispatch orders, and leave the implementation of such system to the site developer. As a matter of fact, MSCS does provide all the necessary functionality to do so relatively easily, as we will see later on.

Marketing

The only marketing function provided by the store is grouped together with the Merchandising functionality. As you can see from the next screenshot, there are two categories of marketing promotions that we can set up: price promotions and cross-selling promotions.

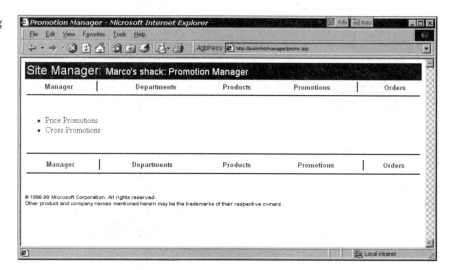

A Marketer's Dream: Price Promotions

If you've had a chance to work with marketing people in the course of your career, you will know how difficult it can be to translate their ideas into something technically viable. Their concept of "special offers" can take on the most convoluted forms, and they will always expect you to promptly generate the code that will make these "promotional Frankenstein's monsters" come alive.

MSCS provides a set of standard price promotions that can save your life. As a matter of fact, out-of-the-box it is possible to generate three different types of promotions:

> **buy x and get y at z% off**
> This kind of promotion gives the customer a discount on one item if another one is also purchased. The discount is expressed in percentage points.

> **buy x and get y at $z off**
> This promotion is exactly the same as the previous one, except that the discount is expressed as a dollar amount.

> **buy 2x for the price of 1**
> The third possible type of promotion is a variation of the first one. If the customer buys two (or a multiple of two) items of the same product, he or she will receive the second one(s) for free. As you have probably already envisaged, this is the same as offering a 100% discount on a product if the same product is present twice in the basket.

With a little effort, it's possible to imagine how all the three built-in promotions are really all variations of the same operation. In fact, if, after adding a promotion, we click on the Advanced Attributes link, we will always be presented with the same page, visible in the following screenshot. This screen makes it possible to modify the parameters of the offer with a higher degree of freedom than by using the pre-canned entry screens that we just saw.

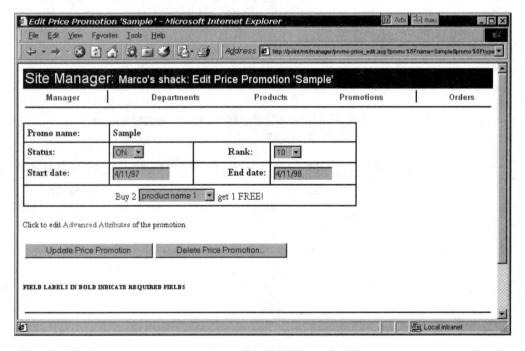

An important element of a promotion is its **rank**, which expresses its importance or—in other words—the order in which it will be applied to the orders. The need for the rank derives from the fact that two or more promotions might be in conflict with each other and, because only one promotion can be safely applied to any given product (with the goal of preventing paradoxical scenarios from happening), the promotion engine must be able to decide which one is applied in every specific case. The lower the ranking number, the higher the priority that a promotion has; i.e. a promotion with rank 10 will take precedence over another one with rank 20, and so on.

Cross-Selling Promotions

As we mentioned above, cross-selling is an important part of a site's interface with the user. MSCS supports cross-selling promotions through the management interface shown in the next screenshot. As you can see, the system is very simple, and it practically allows the store manager to associate products with others as part of the promotion. Once we have added a new promotion, it appears on the web site in the product information page as a complementary product suggestion.

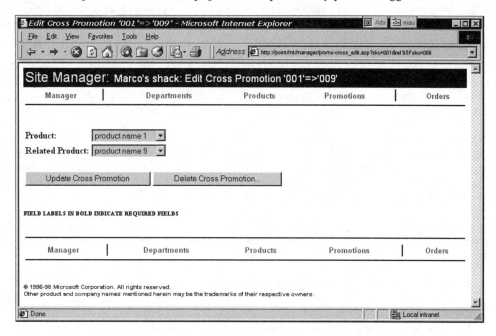

While this cross-selling system allows us to handle both cross-selling and up-selling (we'd just have to add promotions between a product and its accessories, for example), it readily becomes awkward if you have a large database of products, and it is unable to handle historical cross-selling (although MSCS provides this kind of functionality through the Predictor component that we'll see in the next chapter).

System

The system functions that are provided by our sample store are very basic (as is the store itself). The first part allows us to edit the pipeline files, which, as we'll see in the coming chapter on Pipelines, are used to configure the Order Processing Pipeline and manage the handling of orders.

Next, we can jump to the storefront (using the **Shop Site** button), close the site and force IIS to reload the store's Global.asa file, which resets the entire ASP application. We'll talk about the last two buttons, **Site Builder Wizard** and **Promotions Wizard** later on in this chapter.

Let's talk for a moment about the closing and opening operations. The concept that they control is quite simple, as you have probably already figured out: when major updates, or redesign changes, are required, the store can be temporarily "closed" so that users cannot browse through it or make purchases. A closed store will usually display only an informational page, or be restricted to the non-commerce related functionality. In any case, displaying this kind of interface is much better than taking the site down!

How does MSCS handle a "closed" store? As we'll see in the next chapter, the user is simply redirected to an entirely different set of ASP pages when the Close Store button is clicked on.

Sample Stores Provided With MSCS

The basic store that we have been looking at so far wasn't much help in demonstrating the true power of MSCS's functionality. As we shall see later on, however, there is a good reason for that—the fact that this store is the *blueprint* that MSCS provides for developers who want to build their own sites, and therefore has to be extremely simple in its structure.

Together with MSCS, however, come a few "sample" stores that are intended to represent closer representations of online stores created using Site Server. Keep in mind that these are not *real* online stores, and therefore still miss a lot of elements that a real site should have, such as order processing and line-of-business functionality.

All the business-to-consumer sample stores require a credit card to successfully complete a purchase; even though no credit card processing actually takes place, you will need a valid credit card number. MSCS provides a few test numbers that you can use (it's always better not to use your own, because the store might be accessible to other people with whom you wouldn't necessarily want to share *that* kind of information), but I find it fun (and useful) to calculate some.

The algorithm used to compute a credit card number is called the *Mod10* or *Luhn Check Digit Algorithm*. It uses the last digit of the credit card number as a checksum to verify that the number is indeed valid. It works like this:

> ➢ Double the value of alternate digits of the primary account number beginning with the second digit from the right and working toward the left (the first number on the right is the check digit).
> ➢ Sum the resulting digits to the remaining digits (including the check digit).
> ➢ If the resulting sum modulo 10 results in a value of 0, the credit card number is valid.

Obviously, the algorithm can be easily reversed to *calculate* a credit card number. Let's take a VISA card, for example, which always starts with the digit 4 and has either thirteen or sixteen digits in total. The second, third and fourth digits from the left identify the issuing institution—we'll use 000, which shouldn't correspond to any existing bank. The remaining eight or eleven digits (excluding the check digit) are the account number (you can use any number you want). In our case, we'll choose a sixteen-digit card:

$$4000 \quad 1234 \quad 5678 \quad 901x$$

Applying the reverse Luhn algorithm to this sequence of number we find the following:

x
$1 * 2 = 2$
0
$9 * 2 = 18 \rightarrow 1 + 8 = 9$

8
$7 * 2 = 14 \rightarrow 1 + 4 = 5$
6
$5 * 2 = 10 \rightarrow 1 + 0 = 1$

4
3 * 2 = 6
2
1 * 2 = 2

0
0 * 2 = 0
0
4 * 2 = 8

We'll then sum all the resulting values:

$$x + 2 + 0 + 9 + 8 + 5 + 6 + 1 + 4 + 6 + 2 + 2 + 0 + 0 + 0 + 8 = 53 + x$$

Now, the one digit that added to 53 would make the total perfectly divisible by ten (and therefore the result of the modulo 10 operation zero) is 7. With that digit appended at the end, the credit card number is complete:

4000 1234 5678 9017

Try it by yourselves, and you'll find out that MSCS will accept it, even though it won't accept the same number ending in 6 or 8.

A word of caution: the numbers that we have just generated *do not* correspond to real credit card numbers; therefore, although MSCS's sample stores will accept them because they are not linked with the credit card processing circuit, they will not be accepted by any real store. Credit card fraud is a serious crime, and using a fake number will, in the best of causes, be source of a lot of embarrassment!

The Simplest Sample: Clocktower

Let's now move on to examining the sample stores that are provided with MSCS. We'll proceed in order of complexity, with the simplest store first and more complex ones to follow. The first site on the list will have to be *Clocktower*, a fictitious online store that sells clocks.

Clocktower shows the most basic functionality provided by MSCS, and is in fact very close to the "unbranded" store that we have used for visuals so far. You can access the store through the following URL:

http://*your_host*/clocktower

where *your_host* is the name or IP address of your computer (depending on how you set up your installation of IIS).

You will only be able to see the Clocktower store if you have correctly installed MSCS and Site Server. The samples are installed as part of the setup process for Disk 2 of Site Server, Commerce Edition.

Clocktower's Home Page

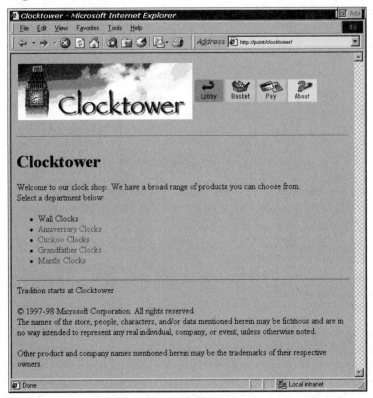

As you can see from the screenshot, the home page for Clocktower can be divided into three different areas, each one designed to fit a specific purpose:

> **The header**
> This section's task is to provide links to the main sections of the site. Because Clocktower is a very basic site, the sections presented are exactly the same as those that are part of the standard store we looked at earlier. As a matter of fact, the header serves the same purpose as the navigation bar that was on the left side of that store's pages. You might find it strange that the home page contains a link to itself (Lobby), but you should keep in mind that those links are supposed to be consistent throughout the site.

> **The body**
> The actual content of the home page is shown in this section. Clocktower's designer has decided to include in it a brief description of what the site offers and a list of the available departments. Comparing this home page with the one that we saw for the unbranded store, you'll probably notice a certain amount of similarities. Actually, to be honest, the format of the two pages is exactly the same (including the generic description text)!

> **The footer**
> Finally, the last portion of the screen is dedicated to the usual legal disclaimers and notices. The idea here is to bring a sense of closure to the page; other online stores sometimes take advantage of this space to provide useful links, such as one to the Customer Support section of the store, or to provide text versions of the images shown in the rest of the page for text-only browsers.

As we already mentioned, Clocktower is fundamentally a branded version of the basic MSCS store that we examined earlier in the chapter (there are actually a few differences that we'll see in a moment). It is important, however, to understand how the three elements of the page are divided, because this structure is maintained throughout the entire site.

From a technical point of view, as we'll see later on in the book, this corresponds to creating a standard header and footer and then including them in every page using server-side includes:

```
<!--#INCLUDE FILE="i_header.asp"-->

        Body section goes here

<!--#INCLUDE FILE="i_footer.asp"-->
```

The file `i_header.asp` contains not only the common elements that are part of the header, but also all the HTML code that is needed to initialize the page, such as the `<TITLE>` and `<HEAD>` tags, any style sheet declaration, common ASP functions, and so on.

Knowing More About Clocktower

Clicking on the About icon in the home page's header (or any other page's, for that matter), we'll be directed to the page in the following screenshot. As you can see, this page maintains the consistent look and feel of the home page, as we predicted in the previous paragraph, and offers a *substantially* shortened description of what the store does.

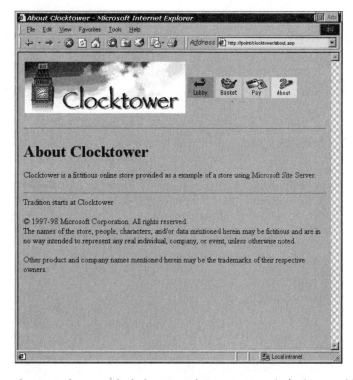

In a real-life store (we'll see how the other samples are a little better at demonstrating this), this would an important part of the site, albeit not one essential to the purchasing of goods itself. In fact, the Internet being such an anonymous medium, it's difficult for a user to really trust a store that doesn't provide a lot of information regarding itself—what the policies are, what kind of services the site provides, and who the people behind it are. If you look at many online stores, *especially* the most popular ones, they do offer a lot of information aimed at making the customer more confident that buying from the site is a safe and good proposition.

Browsing Through the Store

If we click on any of the departments shown on the home page, we are taken to the department page shown in the adjacent screenshot. The layout is, once more, very simple and straightforward: all the products that belong to the department that we selected are displayed in a simple list that includes their name and manufacturer.

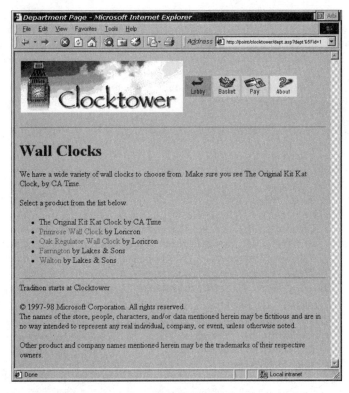

In a real-life store, you would probably include some more data, and possibly provide a direct link to the shopping basket page, so that those users who already know the product they want to buy are not forced into the annoying process of having to go through the product page to do so.

Speaking of the product page, there is one for you to see in this screenshot. This time, because the nature of the products is realistic, you can get a better idea of what the page does. As you can see, the focal elements of the page are a picture of the object (very important in an online store, where the user can't examine the object closely) and a description of it.

Browsing a little through the site, you will notice that all the product pages look the same (and are actually generated by the same ASP script). This is, obviously, a consequence of the fact that all the products are stored in a database, and therefore the pages are displayed using a pre-determined template filled in with the appropriate information. To avoid making your store too "flat" (but without compromising its consistency), it's a good idea to think of ways through which you can customize each page, like, for example, using a slightly different template depending on the department that the product belongs to.

Basket and Ordering Process

The basket page is exactly the same as the one we saw before, although the design is different for obvious reasons. When we are satisfied with its contents, we can proceed to the purchase process. The first step asks us to provide a shipping and a billing address. In this case, the Microsoft Wallet is not even mentioned, and the format is slightly different from the one that we saw in the basic store. There is no specific reason why you should decide to use this method rather than the other, so I suppose that the reason why Clocktower works this way is that whoever designed it wanted to provide a viable alternative to the standard procedure.

It's probably worth noticing that this approach doesn't necessarily simplify the process. As a matter of fact, the customer will still have to go through two different pages to complete the purchase, so no time is saved and, if anything, the user might end up being a little confused about why there are two screens. At the same time, though, the fact that the user is given the opportunity of specifying just one address and then use it both as the shipping and billing destination (by selecting the Same as Shipping Address checkbox) can speed up things and provide a more pleasant experience.

The next page in the sequence provides a summary of the order (which is now possible, since we know where the merchandise is going and we can calculate shipping and taxes appropriately) and requests some credit card data. If all the information entered is correct, we'll end up to the page shown in the following screenshot, which advises us that our order was successful and that we'll have to write down a 26-character long number if we want to keep a record of our purchase.

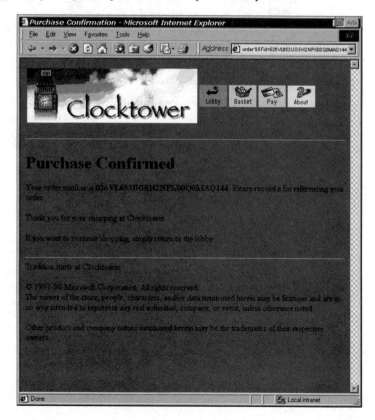

If you make any mistakes along the way, Clocktower will promptly notify you with an error page and advise you on how you can fix the problem. It's interesting to notice that the page's background color changes from green to your default window background color (light blue in my case). It's difficult to tell whether this is just a coincidence or something intentional, but it might be a good idea to attract the user's attention.

Volcano Coffee

The second sample store that we'll examine is called Volcano Coffee (VC) and is a fictitious online site that sells, as the name suggests, coffee and the related paraphernalia. VC is the one store that offers a good balance between its credibility—which makes it good enough to adapt easily to a real-life situation—and its simplicity, which allows us as developers to examine it easily from a technical point of view.

VC is also very important because the MSCS team has improved its functionality significantly and used it for performance tests after the release of SSCE3. A new version of VC, called VCTurbo, was released to the public toward the end of 1998, and is available from the Site Server site at `http://www.microsoft.com/commerce`. It includes several enhancements, most of which are aimed at improving the efficiency of the store as a whole and of the purchase process in particular.

To access the copy of VC that resides on your server, go to the following URL:

http://*your_host*/vc30

where, as usual, *your_host* is the name or IP address of your computer. It is worth noting that the name of the virtual directory where the site is stored is called vc30 because Site Server, Enterprise Edition 2.0 contained a previous version of the store. If you have the older Microsoft software, comparing the way VC works in it with the new one is an interesting exercise that will help you understand the differences between the two versions of Site Server.

Volcano Coffee's Main Page

Upon entering the store, the first thing that you will probably notice is that this store's design has much more personality than Clocktower's. Another interesting feature of the main page is that it only works as a gateway to the store, and offers no functionality by itself. The reason for this is that, contrary to the previous examples, VC does not allow its customers to browse the store anonymously.

As a result, you can only enter the store if you are registered customer. Therefore, the first thing that we must do as soon as we open the home page is to either login or register as a new user. The validity of this approach to online shopping has been the focus of a lot of discussion. Some people, including myself, believe that doing so can be compared to asking people entering a retail mall for their ID—although of course it would be impossible to accomplish anything like that in a practical way, whereas there isn't really any technical problem in doing it online.

However, there are some advantages in asking people who they are from the very beginning. Most notably, the customer enjoys a higher degree of security—the data that he or she communicates to the store is persisted by means of a login procedure and not using a cookie—while the online store owner is able to collect more information right away and use it to provide a better shopping experience. In addition, the store's contents can be customized according to the user's geographical location, for example, or according to other similar parameters.

Ultimately, I think that you should let your customer decide whether they want to shop anonymously or not, explaining to them advantages and disadvantages of both approaches, and noting that, should they decide to make a purchase, they will eventually have to reveal their identities anyway.

The registration procedure, shown in the next screenshot, asks only a few questions of the user; as you can see, these are completely unrelated to the billing data—the rationale being that it's always a good idea not make such data available unless significant security measures are in place (and they aren't here). Returning users can instead use the login page, which only asks for a username—the e-mail address is used here—and password.

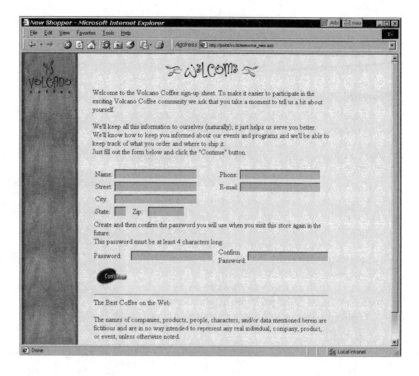

The "Other" Home Page

Once a user has logged in to the site, he or she will be shown the page in the next screenshot, which can be considered the *real* home page of the store. VC takes a different approach to displaying the catalogue of products that offers a more ordered approach to purchasing but adds one more step in the process.

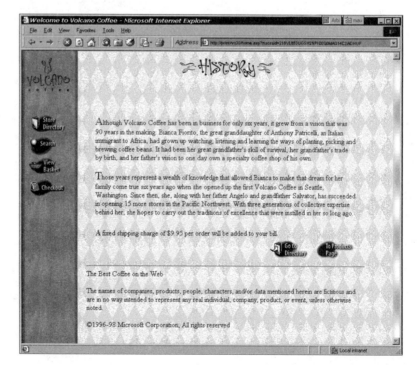

As you can notice, this time the home page does not include any product or category directly. The left side of the screen is reserved for the common navigational elements, the Store Directory replacing the Lobby, and its body provides some generic information about the store in addition to a link to the Store Directory and another one to the Products Page.

Browsing the Store

The Store Directory is fundamentally the same as the Lobby home page in Clocktower: it offers a list of the departments available from which the user can then view a list of products. The only substantial difference, in this case, is in the fact that the departments are organized in a multi-level hierarchy in which only the lowest level categories have products in them.

The Products Page, on the other hand, is basically an expanded version of the Store Directory in which the list of departments also contains the products. From there, it's possible to navigate directly to the Products Page. It's good to keep in mind that this kind of listing works only because VC contains a very limited number of products. If you are planning to go online with *thousands* of items, this approach won't work for you.

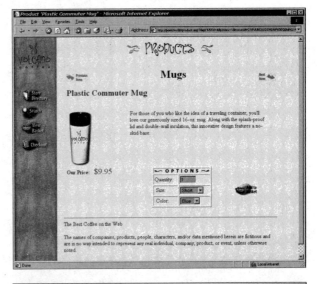

Contrary to the stores that we have examined so far, VC sells a range of products that includes very different items, such as coffee and shirts. Therefore, there is the need to present the products in a different way, and provide support for the fact that certain attributes have to be specified for some of them. If the user wants to purchase a coffee mug (as in the preceding screenshot), for example, he or she will have to specify a size and a color; these specifications, however, do not necessarily apply to a pack of coffee (see the next screenshot). In addition, the store has to be able to handle the fact that some of these attributes might modify the merchandise's price or catalogue number.

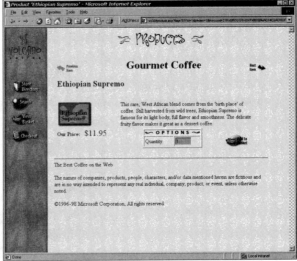

Search Functionality

Product search in VC is, as was the case in other samples that we have seen so far, not one of this store's strong points. In fact, the only option that the user has is to have the store perform a keyword search based on some text that he or she inserts in the text box provided.

The solution that has been used in this case consists, obviously, of a simple SQL query in which the user's input is turned into a parameter for a `like` search:

```
Select * from products where name like '%:1%'
```

If you actually attempt to browse through the store for a while, you'll find that this approach works quite well, although you will easily run up against its limitations if you're not really sure about what you're looking for. But then again, the number of products is very limited, and we can hardly argue that people would be looking for anything but coffee.

Buying from Volcano Coffee

VC's purchase process is similar to the one that we have seen in the basic store that we examined at the beginning of the chapter. Thanks to the fact that we were forced to login at the beginning, the store is automatically able to fill most of the required fields for us, and that's a pleasant surprise, especially if we are returning customers.

Once the process is complete, the usual confirmation page is returned to the user. This time, however, the order number is a link that redirects the customer to a tracking page where he or she can, at any time, review the purchase made. Although this page is not particularly useful as it is (sure, people can be forgetful, but then how are they going to remember that long order number?), it can be expanded to provide additional information. For example, if the store were integrated with a line-of-business system, the inventory status of the items ordered, together with the status of the actual shipment, could be displayed, giving the user a sense of what's happening to the products he or she bought. If you are lucky enough to interface with a courier who provides you with waybill numbers that you can verify online, you could even provide a link to the courier's web site and let users track the status of their shipments.

Volcano Coffe's Store Manager

VC's Store Manager interface differs in only two ways from the basic one that we saw earlier in this chapter. First of all, it provides a means to examine the database of shoppers who have visited or purchased from the site. This interface can be used as a powerful customer support tool, although a higher number of users than ten would probably require some improvement, such as a search function.

The presence of a banner ad is what probably caught your attention first, though. Granted, it's kind of absurd to have advertisement in the Manager of a site, which is only supposed to be visited by authorized users who won't really have much propensity for clicking on it, but let's not forget that this is, after all, a sample site. The ad's real goal is that of showing yet another part of Site Server 3 functionality, called **Buy Now**.

Buy Now makes it possible to create banner ads from which the user can purchase merchandise without leaving the site he or she is currently in. In fact, clicking on the ad brings up a new window (as we can see in the next screenshot) from which it's possible to purchase the merchandise directly in four steps (product selection, shipping, billing and purchase confirmation). Once the process is complete, the pop-up window is closed and the user is once again in the original web site.

There are a few interesting advantages to using Buy Now. First, the user is directed to the purchase process right away rather than having to go through the entire site. This provides a much more targeted advertising approach. Second, the originating site will not lose a customer, which might get the Buy Now store's owner a better deal on online advertising. At the same time, the Buy Now store's owner will have acquired the customer anyway, and will be able to invite him to the store through other methods (i.e. a special offer notice delivered by e-mail).

The Microsoft Press Sample Store

For all of you out there who think that Amazon deserves a lesson, here's a chance to get a jumpstart on your world domination pet projects. The Microsoft Press sample store is a fictitious site that sells books published from Microsoft Press. The real MSPress web site doesn't have an online store, but fulfills orders through a third-party.

To access this sample, use the following URL:

http://*your_host*/mspress30

MSPress presents a number of unique challenges. For one thing, it offers more than 100 different products. Even though all of them belong to a homogeneous category (books)—and therefore don't present the problem of having to handle products of different kinds—their number alone makes most of the search and display techniques seen so far unusable.

With so many products on the table, in fact, it's difficult to simply offer a one-page listing—most users won't be able to find anything by just browsing in it. Also, technical books are seldom searched for by keywords in the title (can you name more than three classics—with the exception of *this* one, of course—in the computer books category?), but rather by topic or by author.

Looking For a Book?

As you can see from the next screenshot, there are a few ways to browse the store. View By Subject corresponds to receiving a list of the departments into which the products are divided, and then starting the drill down from there. This approach is already quite difficult for the user to follow because there are many categories in the store. View by Author provides an alphabetical list of all the authors featured in the site; this approach is well organized, and it would be easy to find a book knowing its author—if that was the way that most people search for books. However, if you're so unlucky that the author you're looking for has a name that starts with the letter Y, you will have to scroll down quite a bit before you'll be able to find the titles you're interested in.

View By Title offers an improved approach to displaying a long list of products. The listing is divided into pages that contain only a limited number of products. It's still somehow difficult to find a title, especially if it's toward the end of the list (which is sorted alphabetically), but at least the user won't have to wait long for the page to load.

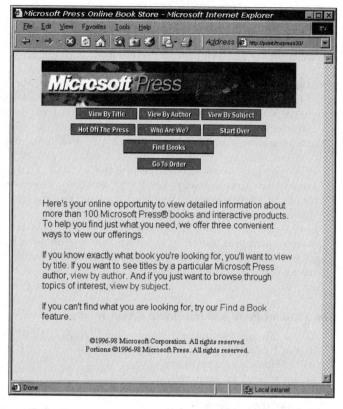

The Hot Off The Press section provides an interesting approach to displaying newly released books. As you can see, the page offers only a few selected titles and displays them together with a picture and a one-line description. The result is quite enjoyable for the user, who might as well make a purchase decision right there. If you take a look at the hot_off_the_press.asp file, which is used to generate this screen, you will notice that the entire page is completely dynamic and responds in real-time to changes in the book database. The list of books is obtained by executing a simple query against the product table:

```
<% cmdTemp.CommandText = "select sku, isbn, title, subtitle, date_published,
list_price from mspress30_product where date_published > {ts '"& new_date &"'}
order by date_published" %>
```

The search functionality offered by MSPress is much more evolved than the one offered by the stores that we have examined so far. This time, there is much more than a simple text box in which the user can type in one or more keywords, and a complete range of options are provided. The whole operation still results in the execution of a SQL query, and a simple one to say the truth, but the user has much more control over how the products are searched for.

Data Caching

Having a dynamic web site is definitely an advantage these days—you can better organize your data and write pages that respond in real-time to any changes to the database. The downside of this approach is in the fact that, if your data doesn't change very often, your pages will continuously hit the database essentially for no really good reason.

A possible solution to this problem could be to create a recordset as part of the store initialization in the `global.asa` file and keep it in the `Application` intrinsic object, which is available to any page in the store. However, using a recordset is not necessarily a good idea, because they are still linked to the database and force a connection to remain open to your SQL Server.

MSPress solves this problem, caused by the nature of the View By Author page, by creating a variable of type **Dictionary** that holds all the data that needs to be displayed and saving it in the Application object. We'll take a better look at the Dictionary component later on, but for the moment you can consider it similar to the `Scripting.Dictionary` object that comes with IIS; as a matter of fact, it can be used to store an arbitrary amount of data in a structured format.

When the page needs to be displayed, the `author_list.asp` file retrieves the data from the Dictionary object instead of hitting the database. The performance of the store increases significantly thanks to this relatively simple improvement, and the only inconvenience that it causes is in the fact that if we update either the author or product database the changes will not be reflected in the page until we force the site's IIS application to reload. This can be done manually as part of normal IIS management procedures, or by closing and opening the store, or even automatically (for example in response to the editing of an existing product or insertion of a new one) by editing the `global.asa` file and simply adding an empty line (This forces the current `Application` to end and triggers the `application_onstart` event handler, reinitializing the program).

The Product Page and Historical Cross-Selling

Either through one of the product lists or by making a search, you will eventually end up in the product page, shown in this screenshot. MSPress offers a more streamlined design than its predecessors in this chapter, and the information presented is more complete and better organized (not to mention more realistic!).

What really should be noted about this page, however, is the last part—the one that begins with the sentence "Other people who have bought this book have also purchased the following titles". This section makes use of Site Server's historical cross-selling functionality and, as you can see, the result is pretty interesting.

Naturally, the information that is loaded as part of the installation procedure for the sample store is completely fictitious, but in a real store it would actually represent the habits of real people and there is a good chance that it would entice other people to buy other books based on the preferences of others who already purchased goods from the store.

The Purchase Process

MSPress' purchase process is very similar to the one offered by VC, and in fact the store asks new users to register while giving returning customers a chance to login to the site to expedite the procedure. Since VC does not provide any order tracking feature to its users, login is only required at this stage and is used exclusively to make the purchase process faster.

You will also notice that the historical cross-selling functionality included in the product pages is also offered in the basket page, with the intent of providing the customer with one more chance to buy additional titles "on impulse".

MSPress' Store Manager

Let's take a quick look at the store management functions provided by MSPress (see the next screenshot). As you can see, we are already familiar with most of the concepts that are presented here. Authors and subjects replace the departments that we have seen so far in the other stores, and simply represent two different ways of organizing the store.

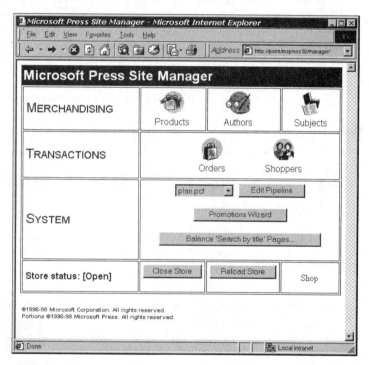

The only section that we should examine a little more in detail is the one that is accessible by clicking on the **Balance 'Search by title' Pages** button. In order to grasp what its goal is, we have to examine the page that lets us view all the products stored in the database and understand how it works.

If you take a look at the `title_list.asp` file, you will see that it makes reference to a table called `mspress30_title_index`. Each record in that table represents the bounds of a chunk of data in the product database, which in turn corresponds to the content of an individual page that is shown to the user in the storefront.

Whenever a user requests to see part of the product listing, the script determines what chunk should be delivered to him or her and extracts the appropriate records from the product database:

```
if IsNull(start_index) then
   query = "select sku, title from mspress30_product where title <= '" &
           Replace(end_index, "'", "''") & "' order by title"
   start_index = ""
elseif IsNull(end_index) then
   query = "select sku, title from mspress30_product where '" &
           Replace(start_index, "'", "''") & "' <= title order by title"
   end_index = ""
else
   query = "select sku, title from mspress30_product where '" &
           Replace(start_index, "'", "''") & "' <= title and title <= '" &
           Replace(end_index, "'", "''") & "' order by title"
end if
```

The result of this operation is that the script only extracts from the database those records that it effectively needs to display, and therefore reduces both the amount of data that has to be transferred from the database server and the computation time that is required to extract it.

Obviously, the records in the index table should be calibrated so that each chunk of data contains approximately the same number of entries, which is exactly what the **Balance 'Search by title' Pages** section does. This operation should be repeated periodically, because the addition, removal or editing of any of the titles in the product database will cause the pages to become uneven.

Trey Research: Not Your Average Store

The last sample store that we'll be looking at is called Trey Research (TR). Contrary to the other samples that we've examined so far, TR doesn't sell any physical goods, but it deals in digital information, in particular trade reports. You can access it by typing in the following URL:

http://*your_host*:5293/tr

The number 5293, which is separated from the hostname by a colon, indicates that the web browser should try to access the site not through the normal TCP/IP port dedicated to HTTP connections, but rather through port number 5293.

> It is important that you use the http:// prefix when typing the URL into your browser, because otherwise the browser will not know what protocol to use when accessing the site, and you will most likely receive an error of some sort.

The reason why we have to go to a different port number in order to get access to TR is that the store interfaces with the Personalization and Membership functionality of SSCE3 and, in order to have its own Membership Directory, it is required to reside on an instance of IIS of its own. As a matter of fact, if you open your Microsoft Management Console and take a look at the IIS configuration, you will notice the presence of a server instance called **Site Server Commerce Membership Samples Web Site** that contains the virtual folder tr. Obviously, this also means that, unless you have P&M installed on your server, you will not be able to view TR.

The Home Page and Login Procedures

Trey Research's home page (visible in the next screenshot) only contains some summary information about the site. Any of the links offered bring us to a login screen that will ask us to either enter our username and password or to register as a new user. The information collected as part of the registration procedure, and the profile that is consequently created, are stored in the Membership Directory, against which they are checked afterwards. As you can from the following snippet of code, extracted from the file verifpwd.asp, this is a very simple process:

```
set x = Server.CreateObject("Membership.verifusr.1")
strUrl = Request("URL")
strUsername = Request("Username")
strPassword = Request("Password")

On Error Resume Next
    y = x.VerifyCredentials(strUsername, strPassword, strUrl)
```

After the VerifyCredentials method of the Membership.verifusr.1 object is executed, an error indicates either that the user data is invalid or that the user doesn't have permission to view the page he or she is requesting.

You can take a look at the users that have registered with your instance of TR by going to the administration part of Site Server, which you will find at the following URL:

http://*your_host*/siteserver/admin

Click on **Membership Directory Manager**, then on **Users**, and finally on **Select Server**. From the resulting page, you should choose **Commerce Membership Server** and then enter the following login data:

Username:	tradmin
Password:	password

This will take you again to the main administration page, from which you can select Users and then User Management. The resulting page contains a list of all the users similar to the one shown in the next screenshot. As you can see, you can view and edit a user's properties, add a new user or delete an existing one and assign different users to the available groups. In this case, all users are by default members of the tr group, which gives them access to the entire site, while those customers who have purchased one or more case studies from the store are given time-limited access to the studies group, and so on for the other products sold.

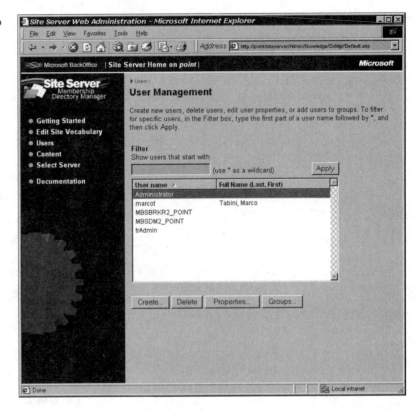

Navigating the Store

TR's store navigation is somewhat similar to the others that we have seen so far. The user is asked to choose one or more document categories, access to which can be purchased in different ways (i.e. one month, three months, and so forth). The options chosen by the user are added to the basket and can be purchased in the traditional way. In addition, TR also lets each user purchase access to the information without specifying a payment option. In that case, a record is entered into a database table that can be used later to produce invoices and bill the customer.

In a real online store, you will probably want to implement this payment system in a different way, as it effectively corresponds to giving credit to your customers, something that you should be very careful about. You could, for example, apply some rule designed to limit any potential fraudulent use of the store, such as allowing billing as an option only to returning customers or to accounts that are specially marked with an attribute by you (and *not* by the users themselves!).

It's also interesting to notice that, because TR doesn't actually send its customer anything, it doesn't ask for a shipping address as part of the purchase process. However, as we shall see in the next few chapters, the system is actually calculating the shipping costs for the purchase—and is setting them to zero—because shipping is a required part of the Order Processing Pipeline.

Trey Research's Management Pages

TR takes full advantage of the possibilities offered by P&M, and uses it for regulating access to the store's manager pages as well. To find out how, let's try to open the Manager's home page, which is located at the following URL:

http://*your_host*:5293/tr/manager

If our browser is IE, we'll be greeted by the Membership Authentication dialogue box (see the next screenshot), which will ask us to enter our login username and password (the combination tradmin/password works well here, too). Clear Text authentication is also supported from non-IE browsers.

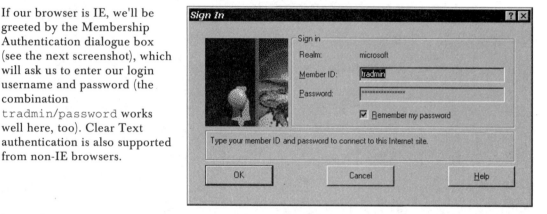

This Manager's home page is not really too different from the others that we have seen so far. As you can see, the store is based on the concept of an article, the basic piece of information to which the user receives access. Articles are grouped in categories, which in turn are organized by provider. Finally, the terms according to which the user is granted the permission to view the articles are expressed as individual products in the database. For example, product 01 represents the right to access the category *case studies* for the duration of one month.

Since the whole site interfaces with P&M, it's interesting to see how the Shoppers and Subscriptions lists are generated. In fact, you will notice that all the lists are generated by the same script, which is a combination of three files:

Include/list.asp	This is the main include file for generating a list. It takes care of creating the necessary data sources and opening a connection to the database/Membership Directory. list.asp also handles the division of the list into manageable chunks (or pages).
Include/list_column.asp	This file generates the header of the list, that is, a list of all the columns that will be printed as part of the page.
Include/list_row.asp	Finally, list_row.asp is used to generate the individual rows that are part of the list.

If you look at the last two files, you will find out that in reality they are simply long case statements designed to handle every possible scenario in the proper way. This ensures that the body of the list generation can be reused each time and that they can be modified by only changing one single file.

The file `list.asp`, as we said, does most of the work. The only problem that it faces is that, while just about all the queries use standard database access, those that have to do with the users and their subscriptions have to go through the P&M interface, which works through an OLE DB provider which is not ODBC-compatible. The script takes care of this problem by using a different initialization method depending on the value of the variable `mem_ds` (which obviously stands for *data source* and *membership*):

```
if not mem_ds then
   Set list = Server.CreateObject("ADODB.Recordset")
   On Error Resume Next
   list.Open cmdTemp, , adOpenKeyset, adLockReadOnly
   If Err.Number <> 0 Then
     Set errorFields = Server.CreateObject("Commerce.Dictionary")
     errorFields("Error") = "<B> Database Error: </B> " + Err.Description
     Response.Clear %>
     <!--#INCLUDE FILE="error.asp" -->
   <% Response.End
   End If
else
   QueryString = SearchDn + ";" + LdapQuery + Fields
   QueryString = QueryString + ";SubTree"
   Set MyConnection = Server.CreateObject("ADODB.Connection")
   MyConnection.Provider = "ADsDSOObject"
   MyConnection.Open "ADs Provider", "",""
   On Error Resume Next
   Set list = MyConnection.Execute(QueryString)

   If Err.Number <> 0 Then
     Set errorFields = Server.CreateObject("Commerce.Dictionary")
     errorFields("Error") = "<B> Internal Error: </B> " + Err.Description
     Response.Clear %>
     <!--#INCLUDE FILE="error.asp" -->
   <% Response.End
   End If

end if
```

As you can see, if the value of `mem_ds` is True, the script proceeds to setting up an OLE DB connection for interfacing with P&M. Otherwise, a normal ODBC connection is created.

Architecture of a Business-to-Business Store

In the previous chapter, we took a quick look at how a business-to-business store differs from a normal retail site open to the public-at-large. It's now time to analyze in more detail the typical structure of such a site and understand how it works. To do so, we'll examine the Microsoft Market (MSMarket) sample that comes with MSCS. MSMarket is a fictitious version of a real Intranet site that Microsoft employees worldwide use to purchase office supplies of any kind, such as books and software.

How Does a Business-to-Business Site Work?

As we mentioned earlier, business-to-business electronic commerce has two faces: corporate procurement and supplier-chain integration. The former is used by online stores that are aimed at providing services to an audience composed primarily by employees of a company, in a scenario where the company itself is paying for their purchases. The latter, on the other hand, is used mainly to exchange documents between two systems (one of which can even be a human, as we'll see later on in the chapter).

MSMarket incorporates both these concepts, in that it is an online store that can only be accessed by authorized users who do not directly pay for their purchases and provides a set of document exchange rules for accomplishing various tasks, such as authorizing orders that go beyond the individual's purchase limit or delivering a purchase order directly to a supplier.

Site Structure

Let's start by looking at how the corporate process works. First of all, you should keep in mind that, in a typical scenario, the store is not selling anything directly to its customers, but it's rather acting as a middle tier between the company's employees and its suppliers. This means that, generally speaking, the store must be well aware of the requisition procedure that must be followed for each supplier, as well as what the buying power of each employee is—that is, how much money he or she can spend before authorization from his or her supervisor becomes necessary in order to complete the purchase.

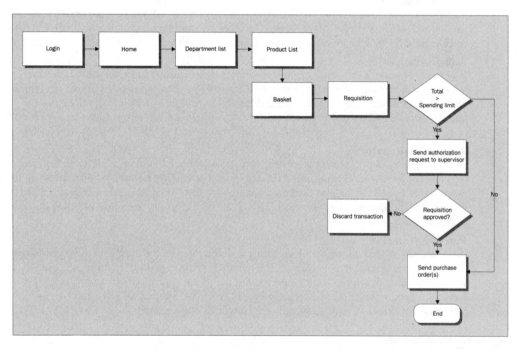

As you can see from the diagram, the purchase process for a business-to-business online store is remarkably similar to its retail counterpart, with the exception that, under normal circumstances, users are not allowed to register themselves with the site but must be inserted in the customer database through some alternative method. This happens because, since the customers will be buying on behalf of the company, they should be added to the list of authorized users from the company's own internal employee database. This will also allow whoever is in charge of doing so to set purchase limits for each individual. MSMarket *does* allow users to register, but only because that is a more practical approach for demonstrating how the store works.

As we'll be going through the store, you will probably notice that MSMarket is much more functional than any other store seen before. In particular, no cross-selling or up-selling is being used—the reason being that the customers who visit this store already know what they are going to buy (and certainly, the company doesn't want to promote more purchases than are strictly necessary!).

The result is a slimmer site, in terms of convenience and speed, that works very well in an Intranet scenario. However, there is also the possibility that a business-to-business store might be configured as an *Extranet* application; this would be the case, for example, if each supplier were to provide its own dedicated store for the company's employees. Most considerations, such as the procurement paradigm and purchase limits, would still apply, but this time the store would be run by somebody who actually has an interest in enticing customers to buy more—the supplier. In this scenario, you would probably want to take advantage of cross-selling and up-selling functionality even though you're not selling your products to the whole world.

The real differences between business-to-business and business-to-consumer come into play once the customer clicks on the Purchase button: the order request goes through a process that is quite unlike anything we've seen before. Let's discuss each of the steps briefly:

> **Purchase authorization**
> As soon as a purchase is submitted by a customer, its total is calculated and verified against the user's purchase limit. If the total is below the latter, the purchase is automatically sent to the last stage, otherwise an authorization request is sent to the user's supervisor.

> **Authorization request**
> Whenever an order's total goes beyond the customer's spending limit, the store sends an authorization request to his or her immediate supervisor. This can happen in one of several ways, and can, for example, be initiated with an e-mail that contains, together with the customer's name and the order's detail, a link to an URL where the supervisor can either authorize or reject the order.

> **Authorization approval**
> At this stage, the supervisor somehow sends a response back to the store either authorizing or rejecting the purchase. Once again, there are several possibilities as to how this can be done; for example, an e-mail can be sent back to the store with the words "accept" or "reject" in a specific spot, or the approval can be submitted through an HTTP post to the store with the appropriate parameters.

> **Purchase request submission**
> If a supervisor rejects an order, the customer is notified (e.g. via e-mail) and the order is generally discarded without further possibility of intervention. If the supervisor authorizes it instead, the store proceeds with sending a purchase request out to the appropriate supplier. As we'll see later on in the chapter, this process is technically similar to the one that we just described for authorizing a purchase, and varies from distributor to distributor.

Setting Up the Site

Before being able to use the MSMarket sample properly, we will have to make some adjustments to its setup. In particular, because the site is largely based on e-mail exchanges, we should make sure that the store knows what SMTP server to use when sending messages out to its users.

To do so, we'll have to enter the store's management site at the following URL:

    http://*your_host*/market/manager

This will take us to the Manager's home page, from which we can click on Configure Email Processes to access the configuration menu. Once here, clicking on Configuration (maildomain) will let us specify the default domain for all the e-mail messages that our site sends to its users, while selecting Configuration (smtphost) will let us type in the hostname of our SMTP mailserver. Finally, you will also have to enter a return e-mail account to be used by the store when sending e-mail; you can do so by clicking on Configuration (siteaccount).

Once you type in a valid mail domain and SMTP server hostname, be very careful when you create new users for testing purposes within the site. In fact, the store *will* send out e-mail messages to these accounts and, if they correspond to real people, you run the risk of flooding their mailboxes! As a general rule, you should use your own e-mail account for all the aliases that are requested by the store; this will also let you monitor how the site works more easily.

Navigating the Store

Now that our settings are done, we can proceed with exploring MSMarket and the way it works. The first step on entering the store is either logging in or registering as a new user. Once again, keep in mind that this happens only because this is a sample store—in real-life there wouldn't be a way to register with the site from the front-end. This time, the registration process asks questions that better fit the business model that is currently being used: not a ship-to address anymore, but rather a room and building number or name.

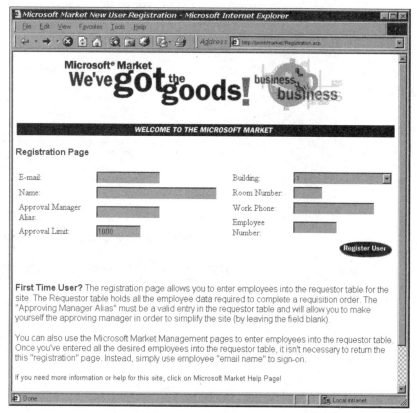

It's interesting to notice that the store is not asking us what department we work for—in many large companies each department has its own budget and keeps track of its expenses separately. As we'll see in a moment, this is done later in the purchase process, when we are asked a cost center code and an account number.

Once we have registered or logged in, we can access the *real* home page, shown in the next screenshot. As you can see, the page's body only contains generic information about the site and the features it provides. What really interests us, though, is the left-side bar, which contains links to the three main areas of the site (international areas are also available, and are treated as different stores altogether). Each of these areas represents a basic category of items, whose products can belong to one or more suppliers.

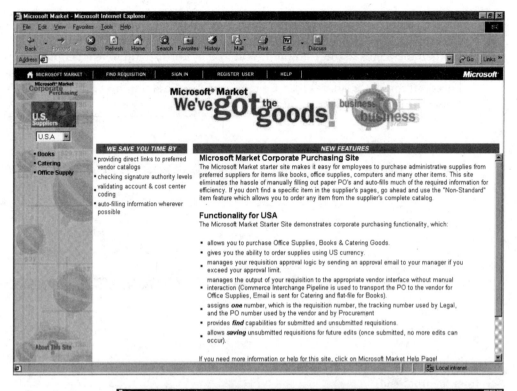

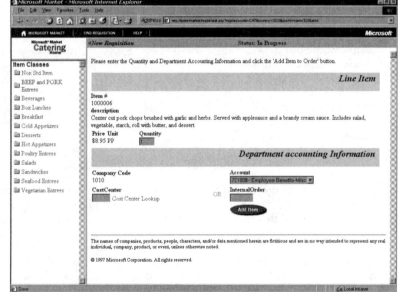

Finding products is a straightforward process, very similar to the one that we have seen so far for the other stores. As soon as we want to add something to the basket, however, some new information appears to be in the product page. As you can see from the adjacent screenshot, the store is asking us to choose an account to which the purchase will be charged, and a cost center, which will be responsible for accounting the order. For frequently purchased items, there is also the possibility of specifying an *Internal Order* code.

Once all the items that we want to purchase are added to our basket, we can proceed with the order fulfillment process. The store asks us for some information regarding the purchase that we are about to make, such as when the merchandise is needed by, or (in the case of catering, for example) when our business or lunch will take place and how many people will be participating.

Continuing with the purchase process causes the store to save our purchase request and, if the order's total exceeds our limit, send an e-mail to our supervisor for approval.

The Approval Process

In our example, it looks like I ordered more food for my event than I can account for. Therefore, my supervisor will receive an e-mail inviting him to review my requisition and either authorize or reject it. In this case, I set myself up as my own supervisor—so that I could better understand what was going on—and I did indeed receive an e-mail from the store, similar to this one:

From: Microsoft Store
To: Marco Tabini
Subject: Requisition # 10005

A requisition is awaiting your approval. To view the details of the requisition click on the link.
http://point:80/market/approveorder.asp?requisitionid=10005&reqclasscode=CAT

Clicking on the link provided by the e-mail brings up the page shown in the next screenshot, which asks me to verify the contents of the order and either approve or reject it.

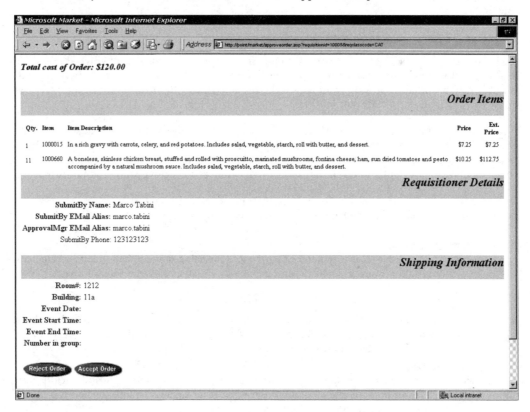

Clicking on Reject Order causes the requisition to be discarded and the following e-mail message sent back to the requisitioner (myself again):

> From: Microsoft Store
> To: Marco Tabini
> Subject: Requisition # 10005
>
> The requisition has been rejected

If I, on the other hand, decide that my own purchase is worth its money, clicking on Accept Order will initiate the transmission of the necessary purchase orders to the various suppliers (there is only one in this case). In this case, no message will be sent out to the requisitioner.

Could It Have Been Better?

It's a good idea to stop for a moment and reflect on what we have seen so far. The MSMarket sample certainly succeeds at streamlining the requisition and approval process, however there is still room for some improvement. First of all, since the supervisor is going to receive an e-mail message anyway, why not make the most out of it?

For starters, it would have been a good idea if a complete detail of the requisition were included in the message; this would have allowed the supervisor to understand what the requisition was about and how urgent it was without having to start his or her browser and go to the store pages. In addition, the process of authorizing the requisition could have been further improved by providing two different links, one to be used by the supervisor when accepting a requisition and another for rejecting it.

How Do Requisitions Work?

We have seen an example of document exchange in the approval process, in which there was the need to generate and transfer documents between the store and the supervisor. A more typical example can be found to pick up right where the process shown in the diagram in the earlier section on the Site Structure of MSMarket left off.

In fact, once a purchase has been definitively approved, the store must proceed to somehow open a communication channel with each supplier's line-of-business system and send purchase orders to it. Ideally, the system should also be able to receive information back from the suppliers—so that it would be able, for example, to track the status of an order or to receive shipment confirmations.

There are three fundamental stages in the submission process, although their exact nature depends on the medium that is being chosen for the transmission of data:

> ➢ **Data preparation**
> As part of the first step, the data must be prepared for being sent out. This includes calculating or generating all the appropriate fields, and making sure that all the necessary information is available.

> ➢ **Data mapping**
> Data will then have to be formatted in such a way that the recipient can understand it. This step varies widely depending on the submission medium that is being used, and can consist of generating a flat text file, or creating an e-mail message, and so on.

> ➢ **Data submission**
> Finally, data is sent over to the recipient using the appropriate method. This can include just about anything, from a printout of a purchase order to more advanced methods, such as EDI (which we'll discuss below), e-mail or other Internet protocols.

At the other end of the submission, a line-of-business system must receive the data and perform the same steps in reverse order. This will allow it to "take apart" the document, map the data it contains to the system's internal storage banks and check its validity.

As you have probably noticed, much of the success of this operation depends on the ability of sender and recipient to agree on a common format for the document and on a medium that is available to both systems. There is, in fact, a standard for the exchange of business-to-business transactions; its name is Electronic Data Interchange (EDI).

EDI is an open-ended standard, in that it only defines rules according to which the data must be formatted and sent to the recipient. There are two sub-standards of EDI: one called X12, maintained by the American National Standard Institute (ANSI) and used mostly in North America; the other called UN/EDIFACT (which stands for Electronic Data Interchange for Administration, Commerce and Transport), managed by the United Nations and primarily used outside North America.

EDI, born before the Internet became a widely available communication medium, has been designed to be sent across a number of different media (primarily telex and other private networks). As a result, it uses an extremely narrow character set (in fact, a subset of the ISO 7-bit set), which becomes even narrower if the medium chosen is telex (unable to transmit letters!).

The core of an EDI communication is called **interchange**, and represents the exchange between two parties of one or more **messages**. Messages, in turn, can be grouped in **functional groups** and can be composed of one or more **data segments**.

Even though (or perhaps, because) it's a generic standard, EDI is very complex and costly to implement, both from a development point of view and from a maintenance standpoint. In fact, mostly for legacy issues, companies that wish to implement it must generally resort to using private (and expensive) networks for the exchange of data. As a result, while many (albeit not all) larger companies are EDI-compliant, almost all the smaller fish are not and resort to more primitive interchange methods (most of the wholesale retail documentation is *still* done by hand).

How does Site Server support EDI? Well, it doesn't—not directly, at least. MSCS includes a complete interchange system that focuses on the Commerce Interchange Pipeline (CIP), which, similar to the Order Processing Pipeline, offers an ordered approach to exchanging documents between two partners. The CIP doesn't favor any exchange protocol in particular, but rather provides a common framework for any format, *including* EDI.

The good news, therefore, is that if you want to develop a store able to communicate with an EDI-compliant system, you'll be able to do so. The bad news is that EDI remains a rather obscure topic for the uninitiated, and you will most likely have to take advantage of the services offered by a third-party consultant that specializes in traditional interchanges.

If, on the other hand, you are looking at *creating* a new interchange system, you'll be happy to know that the CIP is not only fully contained, but also designed to work across the Internet—representing a powerful, and yet significantly less expensive, alternative to EDI. As a matter of fact, once you have established your own document guidelines (i.e. the format for a purchase order, a response, and so on) you will be able to exchange information via e-mail or even HTTP posts.

Remember to Close the Loops

The important thing to remember when designing a business-to-business system is remembering that you should provide a notification system through which the recipient of a message can acknowledge its arrival to the sender. This is particularly important if the correct delivery of the message is vital to the successful completion of a transaction (i.e. if your store sends a purchase order that never arrives, then the order will never be completed!).

It's also a good idea to take full advantage of the concept of interchange and implement a two-way communication system. EDI, for example, provides support not only for messages that go from the store to the line-of-business system (therefore from the requisitioner to the supplier), but that also travel in the opposite direction. This becomes useful, for example, when you want to inform your customers that the merchandise they have ordered has been shipped; in this case, your supplier will send you a notification message, which you can use to set the appropriate fields in your order database.

MSMarket's Store Manager Interface

What does the management interface of a business-to-business store look like? As you can see from the following screenshot, it's a little different from that of a normal retail store. In particular, you will notice that, although many concepts are the same, the terms used are unlike anything we have seen so far.

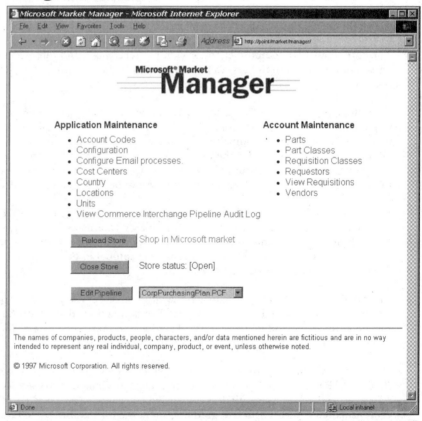

The set of functions on the left side are designed to provide a means to configure several aspects of the store, such as all the e-mail settings, the various locations where employees can be found (including conversion rates for charging customers from foreign countries in their own currency), and the details of the accounts and cost centers that can be used by the users. Each cost center can be assigned to one or more accounts, indicating who can be held accountable for each transaction.

On the right side of the screen, on the other hand, we have access to information about the products that are sold by the store, its customers and a list of requisitions that have been made so far. Products—or **Parts**—are organized in **Part Classes**, which in turn are grouped in **Requisition Classes**, which represent the highest-level departments. Requisition classes are linked to account numbers, so that the right account is used to pay for specific products (i.e. the Office Stationery account is used to buy office supplies, but not catering).

It's important to understand that, unlike any other store that we have seen so far, MSMarket is designed to work without any human interaction. Users could be entered automatically from the company's employee database, while the store could be retrofitted to interface (through an interchange) with the company's own accounting system in order to provide complete feedback on the requisitions that are made. Finally, even the product database can be automatically updated from each supplier's line-of-business system—using another interchange, of course!

Creating a New Store

Now that we understand how an online store works—and we have a better idea of what SSCE has to offer—it's time to take a look at what MSCS has to offer in terms of store creation. Let's start with seeing how the administration model for a Commerce Server host works.

Administration Tools

As in the other parts of SSCE (and the rest of Microsoft's Internet products), MSCS can be administered either online or through the MMC; however, in this case, the web-based management tools are significantly more powerful than their MMC counterparts, to the point where the latter end up opening a browser window if certain tasks have to be carried out. Naturally, online administration has the further advantage of being easily expandable with a little ASP programming.

The next screenshot shows MMC with MSCS's snap-in open to show a list of the stores available on my own server. As you can see, the Microsoft Press sample is selected, and the two options that are available are starting to shop from the store or accessing its management interface. Both actions simply redirect the user to the store's own interface on the Web.

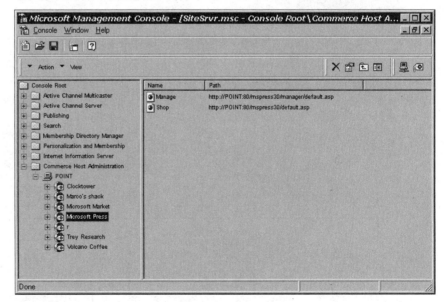

Right clicking on a store and selecting Properties brings up a dialogue box that displays several pieces of information regarding the store's configuration and allows the user to modify them. As we'll see in the next chapter, this data is actually stored in a file inside the store's virtual folder and can be accessed programmatically from ASP. Since it's possible to add an arbitrary number of custom properties to this file, but it is *not* possible to change the snap-in's interface, we have already hit a functionality limit for the MMC administration tools that doesn't apply to their online counterparts.

The online tools can be accessed through this URL:

http://*your_host*/siteserver/admin/commerce/default.asp

Clicking on Server Administration causes the main administration screen—shown in the next screenshot—to be displayed. As you can see, this brings up a list of all the available stores (in a Java applet!), their status and their locations. The number of options available is quite impressive: each store can be opened or closed, shopped in, managed and reloaded. In addition, it's possible create a new store (something that we'll set out to do below), delete an existing one or edit its properties.

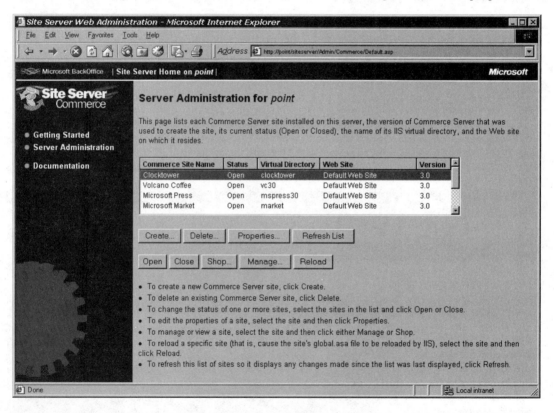

We have already seen the first few options as part of the management interface of each individual store, while the Properties screen presented here offers functionality that is new to us. As part of the configuration of a store, we can specify settings such as the store's base URL for in-clear and secure (HTTPS) transactions, the connection strings that should be used to open the store's database, and so on. It's interesting to notice that any changes we make to the URL configuration of the store (in-clear and secure base URLs, as well as whether HTTPS should be used at all on the site) are immediately reflected on the entire store, including all of its internal links.

Creating a Store Foundation

From the administration tools, it is also possible to start the process that will eventually lead to the creation of a new store. For the MMC snap-in, all you need to do is right-click on a server and then select Create New→Online Store Foundation..., while in the online tool you just have to click on the Create... button.

In both cases, you'll end up in the first step of the **Site Foundation Wizard** (SFW), the first of two online step-by-step store creation tools. The goal of the SFW is to create the building block (called **Store Foundation**) of an online store on which it will be possible to actually build the site.

Wizards have become a widely used tool, mainly because of their ability to break down a problem into smaller, more manageable issues that can be solved by asking a series of questions of the user. Since creating a store is, indeed, a complex process that involves a number of decisions, the use of a wizard simplifies matters through its step-by-step approach.

It's important to remember that, because the SFW is an online tool based on `Session` objects, you will have to proceed through it at a certain speed in order to prevent your session from expiring; this usually happens after twenty minutes of inactivity. If you attempt to continue through the steps of an instance of the wizard after the session has expired, you will be redirected to the administration tool's home page and you'll lose all the information entered up to that point.

Step 1: Selecting a Web Server

The first task in the SFW, shown in the adjacent screenshot, consists of selecting an instance of IIS on which the store will be installed. All you have to do is select one from the list that is provided by the wizard and proceed. By default, the store will be installed in a virtual folder in the IIS server that you select—this is the only way for MSCS to be aware of the store's existence; in addition, the store itself has been designed to work in this configuration.

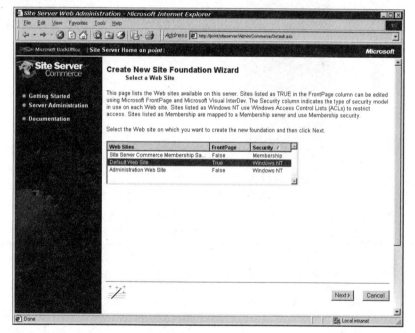

Making a Store Work Inside the Root Folder

If you want your store to be launched in the root folder of a website, the quickest way to do so is to just write a simple script that redirects the user to the site's virtual directory and store it in the site's root as `default.asp`. For example, this code can be used to redirect users to MSMarket when they enter the server's main site:

```
<%
      Response.Redirect ("market")
%>
```

Step 2: Giving Your Store a Name

The next step in the SFW (following screenshot) consists of assigning a name to our store foundation. To be accurate, there are two names that have to be assigned: the **Short Name** and the **Display Name**.

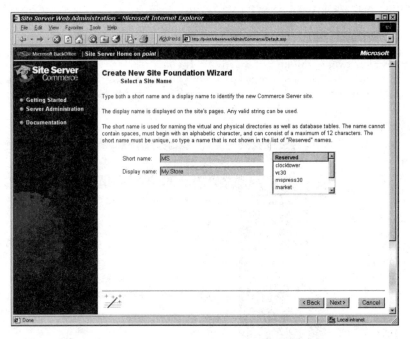

While the Display Name is used, as the name suggests, only for display purposes, and therefore doesn't have to be unique across the system, the Short Name represents the individual instance of MSCS within the computer on which the store foundation is going to be created. As such, it will be used for a variety of purposes: the virtual folder in which the store will reside will be named after it, all the database tables used by the store will have it as a prefix, and so on. The short name is essential because it makes is possible for more than one store to reside in the same IIS instance and for their database tables to be stored inside the same database.

There is a 12-character limit for the Short Name, but you'll usually want to impose a shorter 3-character boundary for most practical uses. In particular, this will ensure that you will not have any trouble in creating database structures with meaningful names later on (as all objects in SQL Server are limited to a maximum of 20 characters, without spaces, for names). In order to allow you to save the data for more than one store in the same database, MSCS will prefix all the tables that belong to one of its instances with its Short Name (i.e. `MT_Product`).

592

To help you choose a name that is not already in use, the wizard provides a list of Short Names that have already been used. Unfortunately, the Java applet that displays the Reserved Names list—and the list itself sometimes—seems to be very fragile and will occasionally refuse to work. When that happens, you will have four options. First, try to guess a name that hasn't been used already. Second, you can try to refresh the page. If that doesn't work, try the "three-finger salute" (*Ctrl + Alt + Delete*, also known as system reboot). Finally—and, believe me, you can actually get to this—when everything else fails, you can always try to reinstall SSCE3.

Step 3: Specifying a Physical Location

At this point, the wizard needs to know where we want the store files to be physically located. By default, the system recommends the creation of a new folder where the root directory of the IIS instance used by the store resides. As you can see from the screenshot following, the default directory is named after the Short Name that we decided in the previous step.

> Once you have created the store foundation, you can change its physical location at will. However, you will also have to change the IIS settings accordingly, and also modify the store properties either through the MMC or the online administration tool.

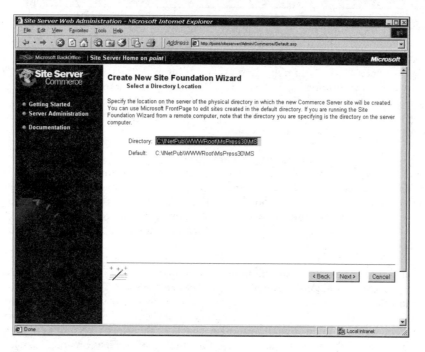

Step 4: Choosing a Data Source

As we have mentioned many times since the beginning of this section of the book, a database is at the core of an online store. The fourth step of the SFW (shown in the next screenshot) lets us choose the data source that should be used by our future store when connecting to *its* database. We are also asked to specify a username and a password for accessing it—the username is required even if the database is not protected (as it is often the case with an Access file).

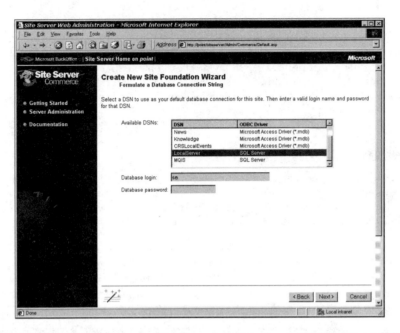

Even though we won't be looking at the database structure of a store created by MSCS until later on, let's think briefly about what criteria you should use to choose a database system for your store. Microsoft Access is an inexpensive solution, but unfortunately it does not work well in a production environment—especially if you are expecting to have a lot of traffic through your store. You could, in principle, use it in your prototypes, and avoid the hassles of having to set up an enterprise-level system like SQL (not to mention having to *buy* another copy of the software). Sadly, the dialect of SQL used by Access differs enough from the one spoken by SQL Server to cause a lot of headaches when you move to a live production environment.

As a result, you should be leaning towards an enterprise-level database system. MSCS supports both Oracle and SQL Server 6.5, so the system that you will choose depends very much on what you are currently using; however, if you're just starting up and need to buy database software anyway, I recommend going with SQL Server, if not for anything else, just for the fact that you can be reasonably sure that future versions of MSCS will support it. In addition, the present version (at the time of writing) of the Site Server installation program does not support creating a Membership directory on Oracle.

You should also think carefully about the login information that you use for the store database. In my example here I chose to use sa, the system administrator alias for SQL Server. This is a reasonable decision when developing a store, because it gives us more freedom and lets us concentrate on the real problems rather than on why we can't execute a certain query. In a production environment, however, this corresponds to an invitation to being hacked; therefore I recommend that you change the login data to that of an account that only has the amount of permissions that is strictly necessary to the correct functioning of the store. You'll probably want to ease the restrictions for the management interface, which *should* use a different account to access the database.

Steps 5, 6 and 7: Selecting an Administration Account

The next three steps are dedicated to letting us choose an NT account that will be used to access the store's management interface. It's worth noting, at this point, that by default there is no integration between MSCS and P&M; as a result, any authentication needs are left in the hands of NT Security.

As you can see from the three screenshots that follow, the only reason why there are three steps for accomplishing this relatively simple task is that the SFW has to progressively discover where the login information should be taken from. To all you Internet Explorer 5.0 users out there, this must look like a serious lack of functionality—just keep in mind that SSCE was published way *before* IE5!

Once again, you should use particular caution when you choose the admin account login. For a prototype, using Administrator makes it possible to avoid any permission problems—as using sa did before—but you will have to settle for something different when you go live with your store, especially if you need to turn on basic-text authentication in order to support non-Microsoft browsers, which will cause passwords to be sent in clear text to the server. A good solution in this case is to manually create a group and grant it access to the management interface's scripts. You can then add individual users to the group (maybe with certain additional safety features, like the need to change their password every two weeks) and deny them access to everything else.

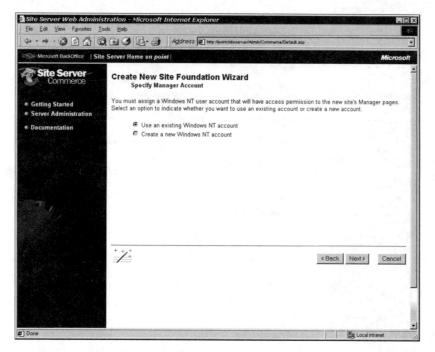

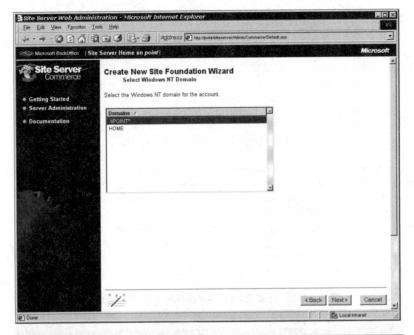

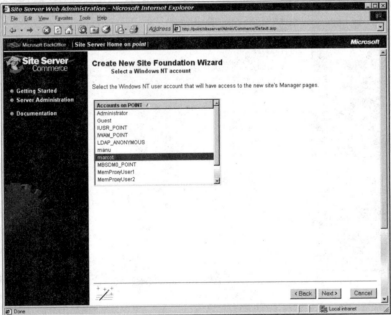

Steps 8 and 9: Creating the Store Foundation

Finally, the last two steps of the SFW take care of actually creating the store foundation. As you can see from the following screenshots, the wizard first asks us for permission to proceed with the creation process, then, when this is complete, provides us with a final page that also contains a link to the store's management pages.

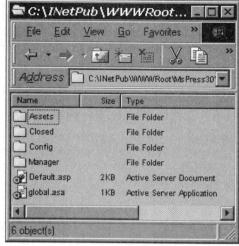

What Has Been Done?

If you try to follow that link, you will find out that the management interface for the newly created store foundation does not actually contain any information, but just a link to the **Site Builder Wizard**, which we'll discuss in the next section.

If you look at the directory structure that has been created by the wizard, shown in this screenshot, you will notice that there are only a handful of files, aimed at providing just the basic functionality needed to display a simple "under construction" page. The Manager folder, too, only contains a bunch of files—very different from what we have seen so far.

What did the SFW really do, then? The answer is in understanding what a store foundation really is—the building block for creating a store. It includes all the structures that are needed by MSCS to be aware that the store exists and to manage its fundamental aspects (i.e. opening/closing, changing the base URLs, and so on), and a basic set of scripts that is intended to offer a possible structure for the store.

This is all that there is to it. As you can see, a store foundation is extremely simple, and at the same time is a powerful starting point for your store, because it provides you with a well thought out structure and many of the global parameters that you will need (which you'll find in the `global.asa` file). Even though you could use it to start your own project from scratch, you will find that using the Site Builder Wizard makes things a lot easier and significantly cuts down development time (and bugs).

The Site Builder Wizard

Once a store foundation has been created, we can run the Site Builder Wizard (SBW). Its goal is to create a store that is as close as possible to the finished product that the developer is looking for, so that he or she will only have to tweak its functionality and will be able to concentrate on implementing advanced features.

Contrary to what happens for the SFW, the SBW can only be launched from within a store's management interface. In the case of a newly created store foundation, a link to it will just about be the extent of the functionality provided by the Store Manager. From a pre-existing store, a Site Builder Wizard button is usually provided as part of the Manager's home page.

> Be very careful about launching the SBW from within the management interface of an existing store. Any modifications that you have made to your site will be lost as a result of the wizard's execution.

What the Site Builder Wizard Does

The functionality provided by the SBW does not just include creating a basic store that you can modify. In fact, you can modify a number of settings, which control the end result:

> ➤ **Product attributes**
> If your store only sells one type of product, like books, for example, you only need a database structure that supports a fixed set of attributes. If the store sells a variety of types of merchandise, however, the fixed-attributes approach doesn't work anymore: the field "number of pages" doesn't work well with a t-shirt, for example. Therefore, the site must be able to handle a number of "dynamic attributes" able to adapt to the nature of each class of products.

> ➤ **Site Structure**
> Another important setting is how products in the store are organized into departments. MSCS offers the possibility of having a single- or multi-level structure. The latter makes it possible to organize the products further into sub-departments.

> ➤ **Payment methods**
> The basic store created by the SBW offers the possibility of automatically validating (but not charging) a number of types of credit cards. All that we have to do is to select the ones that our store should accept, and the wizard will do the rest!

> ➤ **Order tracking**
> Giving your users the possibility of tracking the status of their orders is an important feature for an online store. However, security concerns might make it necessary to avoid supporting it.

> ➤ **Shipping, handling and taxes**
> While handling, when present, is usually an easy matter to manage, dealing with shipping and taxes tends to get close to a nightmare. In the case of shipping charges, the problem is usually trying to offer the best possible deal to our customers, while taxes, being the offspring of political minds, often present the unique challenge of not making any sense. MSCS, luckily, provides a number of possible ways to calculate all these fees that can be configured from within the SBW.

The First Few Steps

The initial steps after starting up
the SBW ask us some questions
that are relatively easy to answer.
Step 1 advises us that running
the wizard on a pre-existing store
might delete its contents,

while Step 2 (next screenshot)
asks us whether we want to
create a custom store or copy
one of the existing samples.

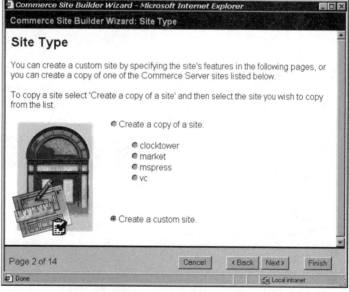

Even though starting from a sample store might look like a good idea, I advise against doing so unless
you are pretty much content with the way the sample works and looks. In fact, these sites have been
created with a very specific purpose in mind, and will not adapt very well to any other business
model that you have in mind. A custom site (which is what our initial basic store was) provides a
much cleaner and unbiased "canvas" that you can change pretty much the way you want. A possible
exception to all this is MSMarket, partly because it offers a kind of functionality that cannot be
generated by the SBW, and partly because it is generic enough to work in a variety of scenarios.

Step 3, shown in the opposite screenshot, asks us to enter some contact information for the store. This data will be available by clicking on the **About** icon in the resulting store. As we said earlier, you will probably need to rewrite and expand this section later on anyway to give your customers more confidence in the store. If this is the case, you don't need to concern yourself too much with what you type in here.

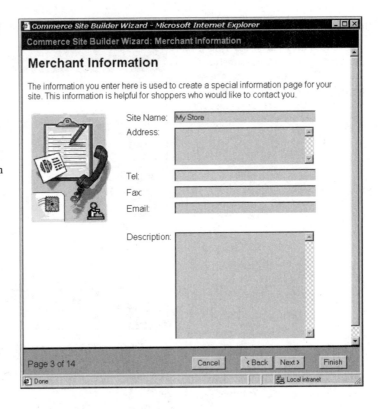

Selecting a Locale

The next step consists of selecting a locale for the store. This will affect the way data is displayed—numbers, currency and date values in particular—but *not* the language in which the store will be generated, which will always be English.

As you can see from the next screenshot, you can only choose one locale for your store. This means that, if you want to provide localized content for your customers, you will have to somehow develop a system to do so. MSCS provides a whole set of functions that take advantage of NT's own locale-formatting API; since the whole store will use those functions, all you will have to do is change the locale identifier to one used in the user's country of origin.

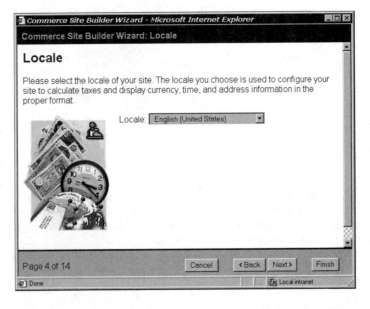

This could be done, for example, in response to a selection made by the customers themselves before entering the site. If your site requires registration, or if it integrates with P&M, the choice might become a permanent part of each user's profile, thus saving him or her the hassle of having to select it every time he or she enters the store.

Choosing a Site Style

The next screenshot shows the SBW's fifth step, which allows us to make a number of design decisions regarding how the store will look. You probably don't need to worry too much about the **Button Style** setting, since most of the time your design team will end up changing the way the site looks anyway.

Choosing the page layout (Navigation Bar), the font and the background color, however, can save a lot of customization work in the development phase. I tend to think that a combination of a vertical navigation bar, white background and the use of Verdana as the main font represent a good starting point that won't force your design team into having to do too many changes. The problem with Verdana, of course, is that it is only supported by version 4 browsers and higher (it comes as part of the installation for IE4); if it is not available on the client's machine however, it usually degrades gracefully to the computer's default proportional font (Times New Roman on PCs).

Supporting Promotions

The next step lets us specify whether we want our store to support and implement cross-selling promotions, price promotions or both. There is no support for historical cross-selling, which must be added manually to the store's functionality; we'll see how to do that in the next chapter.

Support for promotions can also be inserted into an existing store by executing the **Promotions Wizard**, available as part of the normal management functions, which essentially replicates the functionality of this step of the SBW. Remember that, if you decide to run the Promotion Wizard after the store has been created, it will overwrite any changes that you have made to a number of pages, including the product information page.

Features

The seventh step, shown in the screenshot opposite, can be used to set a number of parameters that affect the store's structure. Registration lets us decide whether we want the users to be forced to register in order to use the site. By default, no registration is required– therefore the users are allowed to browse the store anonymously, and the information they enter during the purchase process is not persisted by the store for future visits. It's also possible to ask users to register before they are allowed to enter the site, or when they make a purchase. As the former method presents a significant problem, namely the fact that the users are forced to give away their identity even if they only want to browse around, I recommend that you take the second method into consideration, especially if you are planning to integrate your site with P&M or if you are going to let your customers track their orders.

Department type lets us choose how our store's departments are organized. For a simple store, with only a few products, choosing single-level departments is probably a better idea, while larger stores might need multi-level categorization to avoid having too many products in each department.

Finally, enabling Product Searching will cause the SBW to generate a simple keyword search page in the resulting store. Even though the search functionality provided by MSCS by default is very basic, it's a good starting point that you can use to add more functions.

Product Attributes

The next two steps let us specify how product attributes should be handled by our store. First of all, we should decide whether we need to support static or dynamic attributes. As we saw before, our choice here will depend on what kind of merchandise we'll be selling.

If the choice is static attributes, then step 9 (shown in the next screenshot) will give us the choice of selecting from a list of pre-defined attributes or entering our own. In either case, the attributes that we enter will become part of the product database in the final store. If you have a good idea of exactly what attributes you will be needing, you should take full advantage of the functionality offered by the SBW, which will also add the required input boxes and validation functionality needed to handle the attributes in the store's management interface.

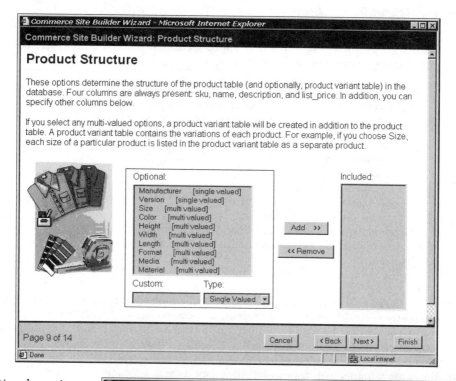

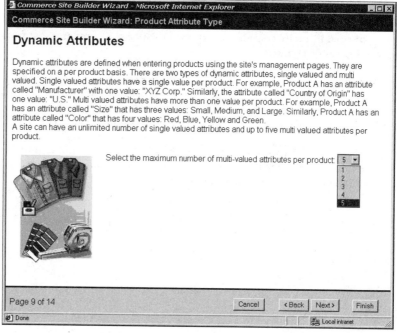

Selecting dynamic attributes will instead cause the system to simply ask you what the maximum number of attributes that you want to use is going to be, as you can see from this screenshot. You will be able to define the attributes from within the Store Manager after the site has been created.

603

Shipping and Handling

Step 10 lets us define the handling and shipping policies for our store. As you will see, the SBW only allows us to specify a per-order fee, which is an approach seldom used by online merchants, who in general prefer to charge a per-item fee instead.

No matter what your shipping needs are, I recommend that you set up the shipping methods that you are going to use anyway, even if they will work on a different basis than per-order fees, because the SBW will take care of setting up all the infrastructure needed to handle them from within the site's pages.

Taxes

Even though your tax needs will vary according to your location (or locations), you will most probably charge some kind of tax fee to your customers. In the US, you can generally get away by charging the sales tax for the state your company is physically located in; in Canada, on the other hand, you will have to charge the Goods and Services Tax, imposed by the federal government, and one or more provincial sales taxes, depending on whether you have offices in any given province. In Europe, each government charges its own Value Added Tax (VAT), although this will probably change thanks to the economic union that is currently under way.

MSCS does provide several tax handling methods, one for each country, that in my opinion serve their purpose pretty well. However, the documentation that comes with SSCE clearly states that this tax functionality should only be used for testing purposes and that a professional consulting firm, or a dedicated tax software package should be used. Personally, I have no problem with getting help from a tax consultant—even in the simplest case, you *will* want to make sure that you are collecting the right tax. If you are not, then you may be forced to pay taxes that you didn't collect, or may risk overcharging your customers and not being competitive. A dedicated tax package, however, sells for several thousand dollars (there are only a handful that integrate seamlessly with MSCS), and should only be used in really complex situations in which the company that runs the store has locations in several states or countries.

In any case, step 11 will let you choose one or more tax rates, depending on the locale information that you selected at the beginning. The next screenshot shows the configuration screen for the United States. Because you can only specify one locale, however, the SBW will assume that the site you just created is only qualified for selling merchandise in the locale's country.

As such, your store will refuse any order coming from any other country (it won't even display a list of possible countries for the ship-to address). In fact, you will have to manually change the configuration of the store to modify this behavior.

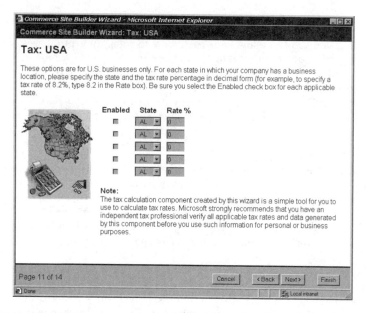

Payment Methods

The next step can be used to select what purchase methods our store should accept. The following screenshot shows that MSCS supports VISA, MasterCard, American Express and Discover. However, as we said before, the store will only check for the validity of the credit card number that the user types in. It will then be up to us to determine whether we can or cannot process the transaction and actually charge the customer's account. Since each credit card type requires the creation of a separate merchant account, you should know what credit card types you are going to accept *before* running the SBW–this will ensure that you won't have to change this information, which is referenced in several places, after the store has been created.

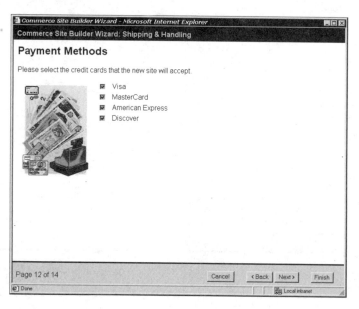

Order Tracking

If you have decided that you want to allow your customers to track their purchases, you should select the Retain order history and receipt information checkbox in step 13. As we mentioned earlier, you should be aware of the potential security concerns that arise from allowing order tracking–in particular the possibility that a user be able to see somebody else's orders. However, if you combine this kind of functionality with customer login (and let customers register as part of the purchase process rather than for being able to access the store), you shouldn't have any problem.

Running the Wizard

After order tracking options have been set, the SBW advises us that it is ready to generate our sample store for us. At this point, you might want to review your settings, but, unfortunately, the only way to do that is by browsing back page by page. In general, if you started out the wizard with clear ideas, you shouldn't encounter any difficulty. In any case, the wizard will take care of persisting the information that you just entered; therefore, you will also be able to rerun it if you find something wrong with your store after you have created it (but *before* you start working on it!).

Contrary to what happens with the SFW, this time you'll actually be able to see what goes on as the SBW builds your store one file at a time. The actual process will vary depending on what options you chose, but it will look somewhat similar to that in the next screenshot. A successful completion of the wizard's execution (something you can't always count on, sadly) will cause your store to be generated and ready to accept transactions (or to be modified, as will probably be the case).

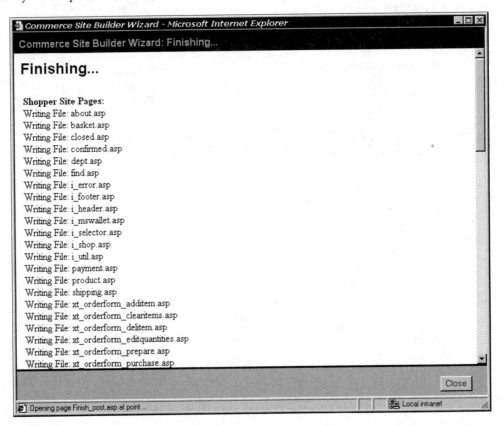

Summary

By now you should have a clear idea of what business-to-consumer and business-to-business stores look like, how they work, and what their structure is. We have also examined in detail the administration and store creation tools provided by MSCS. In all, this should give you enough understanding to be able to design your own store knowing how much work will be needed to expand the basic functionality provided by MSCS.

At this point, it would be worth your while to look around as much as possible to find out what other stores do and how they work. Hopefully, this will give you even more ideas as to what *you* could do with yours. As we go on with this section of the book, you will discover that there is much more to MSCS than meets the eye–in particular, all the functionality that is not directly deployed by the basic store that can be created with the SBW.

16

MSCS Objects Within a Store

In the previous chapter, we examined closely how an electronic commerce store works from a user's point of view – both for the storefront and for the Store Manager, However we haven't yet had a chance to look at any of the code to try to understand how MSCS makes developing an online store easier. That's what we will be doing in this chapter and the next: we'll start from a newly created store and dissect its inner workings, including its database structures. As we move through the technical structure of the store, we'll look in detail at the objects provided by MSCS, taking each one in context.

One of the things that you will undoubtedly notice is that not all of the MSCS functionality is used in a basic store. Most notably, there will be no support for the Commerce Interchange Pipeline, and you will not see any administration objects anywhere. While it's understandable that a store wouldn't normally need to use any of MSCS' administrative functions, you might find it quite odd the CIP is nowhere to be seen. While there is no official explanation for why this happens, it's probably reasonable to think that each implementation of the CIP would be so unique that providing a standard pipeline would prove to be very difficult.

Throughout the chapter, we will look at the various elements of a store that has been created using the Site Builder Wizard (SBW). We'll start from the database structure, then move on to the storefront and the management site. Here's a quick breakdown of what we'll discuss:

> **The database**
> First we'll examine the database tables that the SBW generates as part of the store creation process. We'll also talk about *data marshalling*, a particular system that MSCS uses to save its data in certain database fields.

> **Storage components**
> Next we'll take a close look at the storage components that are provided by Site Server, including the `OrderForm` component and basic building blocks such as the `Dictionary` object.

> **The storefront**
> Following on from data storage, we'll look at how the public portion of the store is structured and how it works from a technical point of view. We will examine the files that make up the storefront and see how they fit together.

> ➤ **Scripts central to the store**
> There are a number of files that are included in all the pages in the store, one of the most important of which is global.asa. We'll walk through these files, examining the built-in MSCS user interface components that are created here.

> ➤ **Store Navigation**
> Finally in this chapter we'll finish off with a look at the files that handle navigation around the sample store.

A Few Notes About My Store

The store that we will be examining in this chapter is called *Marco's Shack*, resides in a virtual directory of my web site called MT, and has been created by specifying the following settings in the SBW:

> ➤ Support for price and cross-selling promotions

> ➤ No user registration is required

> ➤ Simple (single-level) departments are used

> ➤ Product keyword search is enabled

> ➤ Static product attributes are used

> ➤ Shipping costs are $10.00 for "overnight" delivery and $8.00 for "2nd day" delivery

> ➤ No handling fees

> ➤ The store only ships to the United States. Sales taxes are added to orders coming from California

> ➤ Only VISA and MasterCard are accepted

> ➤ Order history is retained for all users

By using the same settings, you can easily recreate the same conditions on your own store. This will help you follow this example more closely.

The MSCS Object Model

The whole interface to the functionality provided by Site Server is in fact implemented through COM. For MSCS in particular, it's fair to say that the entire *product* is based either on ASP or COM components.

The objects shipped as part of MSCS offer a wide array of functionality, ranging from text formatting to operations as complex as managing the entire purchase process. In general, it is possible to divide the components into four categories:

> ➤ **Administration components**
> These components can be used to read or alter the configuration of the store (and its site). Some of them also offer a number of functions that are not related to e-commerce in particular, but can be useful during the development of an e-commerce site.

> ➤ **Storage components**
> These components are used to store data in several ways, such as in a database table or in a file.

> ➤ **User Interface components**
> These components are used to validate the user's input, or to alter the data while preparing it for output, for example to adapt it for a particular locale.

> **Pipeline components**
> These components are used to manage all the pipeline-related operations, such as handling the purchase process.

We'll be looking at the MSCS objects in the last three of these categories over the next few chapters. For information on the administration components please refer to Appendix C, where you can also find a brief summary of using COM components in ASP.

In the course of this chapter, we'll examine those MSCS objects that we find in a basic store: the storage components and the user interface components. For each component, we will take a look at what its intended use is, and how it is created. In the following chapters we'll go on to look at pipeline components.

Note that we'll only be looking at those components that belong to version 3.0 of MSCS. The object set also includes several legacy components inherited from version 2.0, but, because it makes no sense to use them if you are developing a version 3.0 store, we will not go through them.

If you are interested in the legacy Commerce Server Objects that ship with MSCS, check out the documentation at `http://your_host/siteserver/docs/default_com.htm` *– look under Commerce Server Component Reference.*

Also note that if you have problems with some of the MSCS components, such as an "Invalid class string" error, it may be possible that your Commerce installation didn't complete successfully. This particular error means that the DLL in which the component is implemented wasn't properly registered during the installation process. Re-installation is normally the best cure; however, if this isn't an option the knowledge base is probably the next best place to start resolving the problem.

The Directory Structure

In the previous chapter, during our discussion about the Site Foundation Wizard (SFW), we took a look at how the directory structure of a newly created store foundation was organized. After the store generation phase, the SBW adds several files throughout the site, but maintains the directory tree, shown below, essentially intact.

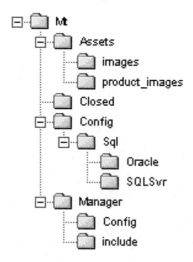

There are five main folders in our site. The root folder contains all the storefront pages and support scripts. The Assets subdirectory is used for storing "support" data that is required by the store's pages, such as images and downloads. In principle, this distinction between Mt and Assets has two main goals. First of all, it helps to organize the files, resulting in a more ordered structure that is easier to read. Second, assuming that all the pages that are in the main folder are scripts, it also makes it possible to separate executable data from data that requires read access, meaning that you can – at least in theory – remove read access from the main folder. This would make your site a little more secure, by preventing malicious users from exploiting any possible security holes that allow a browser to download the contents of a script rather than executing it (like the famous $$DATA bug).

All the configuration files used by the store, such as the Site Dictionary and any pipeline configuration, are stored in the Config folder. In our case, this directory also contains a copy of the SQL scripts that can be used to recreate the database used by the site, both in their Microsoft SQL Server- and Oracle SQL Server-specific version. The Closed folder, on the other hand, contains the files that are accessed by the site when the store is "closed". A completely different set of scripts is executed in that case, in order to let you work on the files that are normally used by the store in its "open" state, which are located in the root folder.

Finally, the Manager folder contains all the scripts that are required by the store management pages. It's interesting to note that, while the root folder is an IIS application, and therefore has its own global.asa file, accessing the Store Manager does not launch a separate application. Therefore, both the Manager and the storefront share the same set of application-level functions that are loaded when the first user accesses the site. Also, the Manager has its own Config folder, which contains the configuration files that it requires. It stores its include files in the Include directory.

The Database

The database that is created by the SBW when it generates a new store has, in most cases, a quite simple structure. While it's true that our store was not produced using the most complicated combination of settings possible, this rule is usually valid even if you elect to use, say, dynamic attributes or multi-level departments.

The following figure shows a simple entity-relationship (ER) diagram of the database tables used by the store. As mentioned in the previous chapter, all of them are named by prefixing their name with the Short Name of the store, mt_ in this example. The dbo prefix indicates a standard database object.

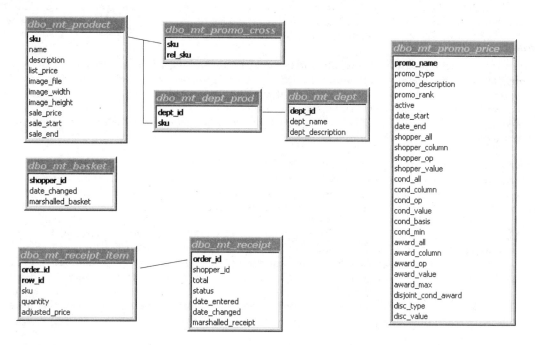

Product Data

Information about the products is stored in three tables: mt_product, which holds the actual products, mt_dept, which contains the various departments in the store, and mt_dept_prod, which is used to join the first two tables. This configuration makes it possible to assign a product to an arbitrary number of departments.

As we'll see later on, the store's logic extracts the list of products in a department by executing a query on mt_dept_prod. Therefore, in order for a product to be visible, it must be assigned to at least one department (that is, it must appear at least once in mt_dept_prod). In addition, the two fields dept_id and sku in mt_dept_prod form a primary key, which means that a particular combination of the two can only appear once, thus preventing a product from being assigned twice to the same department.

Basket and Receipt Information

The mt_basket table, which holds information about the baskets of all the users that have been using the store, is surprisingly simple, considering the fact that it must hold the considerable amount of information that is usually stored in the Orderform.

This happens for a very simple reason: since it's impossible to properly predict the number or nature of the fields that will be stored in the Orderform, the system needs to take advantage of a different storage method in order to hold them all. A very simplistic solution could consist of creating a table that contains many fields and uses them as needed. However, that wouldn't help much because each field could be of a different type, and the system would be rather inefficient overall. In addition, the number of available fields could always prove to be too small, thus causing problems along the way.

Data Marshalling

The solution adopted by MSCS is called **data marshalling**, and it's a concept borrowed from distributed computing. In a distributed environment, two processes can share certain data by "marshalling" it, that is by manipulating it so that is can be accessible to either process. Marshalling is required for reasons such as memory protection, and the fact that the data can represent special objects (such as instances of COM components) that must be reconstructed when they reach their destination.

As a matter of fact, the term "marshalling" is a little improper in the context of MSCS, since the data is not really passed on to another process, but is simply saved for future use. A more appropriate concept is that of "persistency", through which a data element, such as a variable or even a COM object, is represented in a form from which it can be reconstructed later on.

While variables are saved by simply storing their values, COM objects save themselves by "describing" their state (that is, the value of their internal properties), and are later reconstructed by creating a new instance of the COM component and instructing it to restore its state based on the data that was previously saved. The information is persisted in a storage medium that provides a continuous "stream" of data that can be accessed either sequentially or randomly. In order to be capable of being persisted, a COM object must implement a particular set of interfaces that have been designed to provide standard methods to load and save the object's state.

In practical terms, the data stream can be represented by just about any storage medium, including a memory block, a disk file or, as in our case, a database field. In fact, both the marshalled_basket field in mt_basket and marshalled_receipt in mt_receipt are fields of type Binary that contain the marshalled version of an Orderform.

Data Compression

While mt_basket holds dynamic data about a given shopper, and is therefore subject to change at any moment, mt_receipt and mt_receipt_item contain information about orders that have been completed and accepted by the system. It should be noted that mt_receipt_item contains somewhat redundant information, since the marshalled_receipt field of its counterpart already contains all the available order information.

Unfortunately, as much as this looks like a design flaw of the database, it uncovers instead a significant drawback of the fact that, as part of the marshalling process, the data is also compressed, thus resulting in a continuous string of apparently meaningless values:

DS4A8S46D5WW1G5HKJ4I5T62D1VS6

It's practically impossible to find any particular value in a table made of data like this using a simple SQL query. The only way to find, for example, an order placed by a specific shopper, is to un-marshal every single record and then search the resulting Orderform for the desired value. Because marshalling (at least in this version of MSCS) is a very slow operation, even attempting this would prove extremely inconvenient. Therefore, there is a need to store a few "key" values in clear text inside dedicated database fields, which can then be manipulated using normal SQL functions. Thus, mt_receipt_item contains a record for each item that was stored in a particular receipt.

Promotions

Information about the promotions offered by the store is located in the `mt_promo_price` and `mt_promo_cross` tables. The former contains all the parameters that are required by the `DBOrderPromo` pipeline component (we'll look at this component in detail in the next chapter), while the latter is simply used to express an affinity between two products in the product database. As we'll see later on, when the store will need to extract cross-selling information for an item, it will essentially output the results of a simple query performed against this table.

Storage Components

MSCS provides a number of built-in components whose goal is to handle the storage of data in a variety of situations. As you can imagine, the functionality provided by these combined is closely intertwined, as the same data needs to be managed in different ways during the execution of a store; in fact, the database is used as a permanent storage medium for information regarding the customers, while the filesystem contains storewide data. Furthermore, both these sets of data need to be made available to the scripts that run inside the store in a convenient and practical format.

Thus, storage components can be divided in two categories, as illustrated by the following figure:

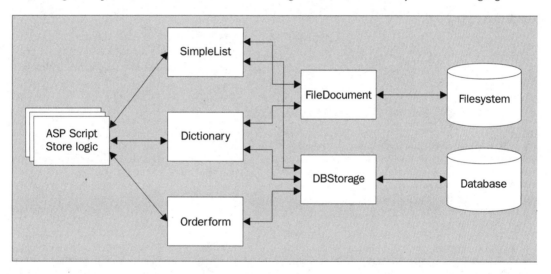

The first category contains those objects that can be used interactively by a script to save and retrieve values: the `SimpleList` object, the `Dictionary` object and the `Orderform` object. The contents of these objects can then be saved permanently to a database or the filesystem, using one of the components belonging to the second category: the `FileDocument` component or the `DBStorage` component.

We'll now go through and look at each of these components in more detail. We'll be discussing them in the following order: `SimpleList`, `Dictionary`, `FileDocument`, `OrderForm`, `DBStorage`.

The SimpleList Component

As the name suggests, SimpleList is an array of Variants that supports enumeration. This means that we can add values to it, and then either retrieve a specific value using a numeric index or iterate through all the values, one at a time.

This object is one of the basic building blocks of a commerce store. As we continue to examine the inner workings of a SBW-created site, you'll see this object many times. Before we see how to use SimpleList however, let's look briefly at its properties and methods.

The Add Method

The Add method can be used to add a new value to a SimpleList object:

```
SimpleList.Add (Value)
```

Where Value is the value or object to be added to the SimpleList object.

Keep in mind that, because SimpleList is, fundamentally, an array of Variants, you can add any kind of data to it, including objects. However, an error occurs if you try to add a duplicate item.

The Delete Method

You'll agree with me that it doesn't really take psychic powers to guess what this method does. You can use it to delete any value from the SimpleList object. However you'll need to know the index number of the item you want to delete in the SimpleList array (note that the array index is zero-based).

```
SimpleList.Delete (iIndex)
```

You'll get an error if the value of iIndex is greater than the number of objects stored in the object minus one.

The Count Property

You can use this property to know how many items are included in the SimpleList object:

```
SimpleList.Count
```

Count returns an integer value corresponding to the number of objects in the SimpleList object.

Using SimpleList

SimpleList is used through a two-step process. First you load all your values into it – the following example loads some strings into a SimpleList object. Next you will want to access them either individually or through enumeration. The following example uses both of these methods to print out the stored strings:

```
<%@ Language=VBScript %>
<HTML>
<HEAD>
<META NAME="GENERATOR" Content="Microsoft Visual Studio 6.0">
</HEAD>
<BODY>

<%
```

```
' Create the SimpleList object

Set slSimpleList = Server.CreateObject("Commerce.SimpleList")

' Load some string values into it

slSimpleList.Add "Unable to print entire file. Your monitor is too short."
slSimpleList.Add "Hard disk full. Feed less."
slSimpleList.Add _
    "Do you want to abort? Click on 'Yes' if you do, otherwise click on 'No'."
slSimpleList.Add "Windows detected. Open curtains for more light?"

' Now, print out the number of items in the SimpleList

Response.Write _
    "The SimpleList object contains " & slSimpleList.Count & " objects.<P>"

' Print one random value

iRndValue = int (rnd * slSimpleList.Count)
Response.Write _
    "Value number " & iRndValue & " is: " & slSimpleList (iRndValue) & "<BR>"

' Finally enumerate through and print out all values

Response.Write "<P><B>Printing all values:</B><BR>"

For Each Value in slSimpleList
    Response.Write Value & "<BR>"
Next
%>

</BODY>
</HTML>
```

The Dictionary Component

The Dictionary and SimpleList components together represent the second half of the basic foundations of most of the storage requirements of MSCS. Therefore, we will analyze it in great detail throughout the book – this is essential in order to understand how an MSCS store works under-the-hood.

A Dictionary object fundamentally behaves like a collection of value/name pairs. Those of you who are familiar with ASP development might have heard of a component called Scripting.Dictionary. Similar to the MSCS Dictionary object, Scripting.Dictionary is a name/value collection that can be used to store an arbitrary number of items.

However, a key difference between Scripting.Dictionary and Commerce.Dictionary is in the fact that the MSCS component can be used in combination with other MSCS storage components, to save the information it contains to either a database or a structured storage file. And, because the values it accepts are Variants, you can basically use it to save anything, including objects.

Another very interesting aspect of Commerce.Dictionary objects—in terms of convenience—is that whenever a name/value pair is added to them, its *name* part becomes a property of the object itself. The following example illustrates this:

```
<%
   Set dDictionary = Server.CreateObject ("Commerce.Dictionary")

   dDictionary.MyName = "MyValue"
%>
```

As you can see, whenever we want to reference a name/value pair, all we have to do is add the name part after the dot, which is really more convenient (and easier to read, if you will) than having to use an explicit method or brackets.

Preventing Values From Being Saved — The Prefix Property

When storing a Dictionary object to either a database or a file (we will see how to do so later on in this chapter), you might want to prevent some name/value pairs from being saved. This can be accomplished using the Prefix property:

```
Public Property Dictionary.Prefix
```

Prefix is used to specify a string prefix that prevents a specific name/value pair from being saved when it is found as the beginning of its name part. For example, the pipeline components in MSCS use the _cc_ prefix to prevent credit card information (such as the _cc_number pair) from being stored to a database.

The Count Property

In a similar way to the SimpleList component, Dictionary allows us to retrieve the number of name/value pairs stored in it by using the Count property:

```
Public Property Dictionary.Count
```

Count returns an integer value that corresponds to the number of name/value pairs that are in the Dictionary object.

The Value Method

As we have seen before, a Dictionary object exposes its name/value pairs as properties that can be accessed directly by putting the name part of the pair right after the Dictionary. expression.

However, there are instances in which this approach doesn't work; for example, if the name of the pair that you want to retrieve has to be built dynamically at runtime. In this case, you will want to use the Value property:

```
Public Property Dictionary.Value (sName)
```

Keep in mind that Value is the default property for the Dictionary component, and therefore it doesn't have to be explicitly called to access a name/value pair stored in a Dictionary. Thus:

```
dDictionary.Value ("MyName")
```

is the same as:

```
dDictionary ("MyName")
```

Iterating Through a Dictionary Object's Collection

Because the `Dictionary` component behaves like a collection, we can iterate through its contents one at a time using the VBScript `For Each...Next` construct. However, because just about anything can be stored in a `Dictionary` object, we must be very cautious in how we treat the data that we get during each cycle.

In particular, we must provide the right code to handle the case in which the value part of a name/value pair is an object. In this case, we must use the `Set` keyword if we are assigning the value to another variable, or create a special case if what we're doing is dumping the `Dictionary` object to the client browser.

MSCS Implementations of Dictionary and SimpleList

As we mentioned earlier, `Dictionary` and `SimpleList` are two building blocks of MSCS – they are used pervasively throughout a store's front end and back end interfaces.

In particular, MSCS takes advantage of the fact that (almost) anything can be stored inside a `Dictionary` object, including `SimpleList` objects and other `Dictionary` objects. We saw an example of this when we were looking at the Site Dictionary, which contains another `Dictionary` object under the name of `ConnectionStringsMap`.

Other implementations of the `Dictionary` object within MSCS include `QueryMap` and `PipeContext`. We'll be looking at both of these over the next few chapters.

The FileDocument Component

If you look at the Commerce Administration objects in Appendix C, you will see that the `AdminSite` object has two methods, `ReadDefaultProperties` and `WriteDefaultProperties`, which can be used to load the Site Dictionary from a file or store it to the same file.

Clearly, being able to do the same with *any* `Dictionary` object would be a definite advantage – you could store a number of data elements for various uses, such as configuration information, and so on. Luckily, MSCS provides the `FileDocument` component to read or write to disk any object that can be persisted.

Now, let's recap what persisting an object means. When you create an object and store information in it, it can be persisted if it is autonomously able to save and retrieve that information in a structured format. Thus, for example, when you load name/value pairs in a `Dictionary` object, it is possible for another object to "persist" them – retrieve them from the `Dictionary` and store them somewhere else. When the data is then loaded back into another instance of `Dictionary`, you can expect that object to behave exactly like its predecessor.

Persisting Objects

There are two methods that you need to use to persist objects. They are `WriteToFile` and `ReadFromFile`:

```
FileDocument.WriteToFile (sFileName, sEntryName, oObject)
FileDocument.ReadFromFile (sFileName, sEntryName)
```

Where:

> ➤ sFileName is the fully qualified path of the file you are writing the object to or reading the object from

> ➤ sEntryName is the name of the entry corresponding to the position within the file where the object is stored

> ➤ oObject is the object to be persisted

Each structured file is composed of one or more objects, each one of which can be given a name as long as 31 characters. When you write an object to a file, that file doesn't necessarily need to exist – WriteToFile will create it for you, or it will add the data in your object that can be persisted to an existing file.

The Scope of Persisted Objects

Because ReadFromFile re-creates the objects that have been persisted, they can only have page scope. This means that they are intended to exist only within the page, and are usually treated as apartment-threaded objects. As we mentioned before however, apartment-threaded objects do not do well in an environment in which multiple calls to them might be made at the same time.

This is the case with Session-wide and Application-wide objects that are intended to be used throughout a user session or an ASP application respectively. These objects can only be created using the <OBJECT> tag in the global.asa file, and therefore ReadFromFile cannot be used to persist them.

The special COM interfaces that enable objects to retrieve their data only allow them to do so as part of the creation process. Therefore, the ReadFromFile method cannot be used when retrieving data that should be stored in an object that already exists (as would be the case with trying to load an application-wide object, which must be created *prior* to any use). The only feasible method would be to manually load each value into the existing object, but this means it would be very difficult to create a persistence method that would be able to handle all objects. We would need a custom method for every possible object – a real stretch even for the MSCS team!

Application-wide objects however, if properly implemented, are extremely efficient. Therefore FileDocument *does* provide a method that makes it possible to persist an object that already exists. It's called ReadDictionaryFromFile and – you guessed it – only works with Dictionary objects.

```
FileDocument.ReadDictionaryFromFile (sFileName, sEntryName, dDictionary)
```

Where (as with the ReadFromFile method):

> ➤ sFileName is the fully qualified path of the file the persisted object must be read from

> ➤ sEntryName is the name of the entry corresponding to the position within the file where the object is stored

> ➤ dDictionary is the Dictionary object the data has to be read into

As we just mentioned, ReadDictionaryFromFile cannot rely on the traditional persistence mechanism, and therefore actively loads each name/value pair into the Dictionary object. This also means that because ReadDictionaryFromFile does not create the object itself, if any other data is already loaded in the object, it will remain there.

Using the FileDocument Component

The following example illustrates the use of `FileDocument`. First, we will load the Site Dictionary from disk, then we'll change the store's `DisplayName` property and finally store it back to disk. We are not using `ReadDictionaryFromFile` here – we'll see how it works in Chapter 17, when we examine the `global.asa` file of the MSCS storefront. Let me remind you that the Site Dictionary is stored in the `/config/site.csc` file in any MSCS site, under the `IISProperties` entry.

```
<%@ Language=VBScript %>
<%
  ' Create the FileDocument object

  Set fdFileDocument = Server.CreateObject ("Commerce.FileDocument")

  ' Load the Site Dictionary
  ' It is located in the /config/site.csc file

  Set dDictionary = fdFileDocument.ReadFromFile (Server.MapPath _
        ("/clocktower/config") & "\site.csc", "IISProperties")

  ' Change the store's display name--again!

  dDictionary ("DisplayName") = "The alternative Clocktower!"

  ' Now, save it to disk

  fdFileDocument.WriteToFile Server.MapPath ("/clocktower/config") _
                        & "\site.csc", "IISProperties", dDictionary
%>
```

Once again, you can test out the result of this script by looking at Clocktower's Store Manager. (Remember that, in order for the changes to take effect, you will need to reload the site. We'll see why this is necessary in Chapter 17).

The OrderForm Component

Let's now examine a very specialized storage component. The `OrderForm` can be used to store order-related information in an ordinate manner. The `OrderForm` is loaded from the database at the beginning of each script that needs to use it, and then saved back into the database at the end of the script.

At its core, an `OrderForm` object corresponds to a specific implementation of the `Dictionary` object containing a set of name/value pairs, some of which are other `Dictionary` or `SimpleList` objects. The following table lists these name/value pairs:

Name	Value
Items	A `SimpleList` of `Dictionary` objects, one for each item that is part of the order
Shopper_ID	The unique identifier for the shopper
ship_to_name	The name portion of the ship-to address

Table Continued on Following Page

621

Name	Value
ship_to_street	The street portion of the ship-to address. Includes street number and apartment number
ship_to_city	City portion of the ship-to address
ship_to_state	The state (or province) portion of the ship-to address
ship_to_zip	The ZIP or Postal Code portion of the ship-to address
ship_to_country	The 3-letter ISO country code portion of the ship-to address
ship_to_phone	Phone portion of the ship-to address
bill_to_name	The name portion of the bill-to address
bill_to_street	Street portion of the bill-to address. Includes the street and any apartment numbers
bill_to_city	City portion of the bill-to address
bill_to_state	State (or province) portion of the bill-to address
bill_to_zip	ZIP or Postal Code portion of the bill-to address
bill_to_country	3-letter ISO country code portion of the bill-to address
bill_to_phone	Phone number portion of the bill-to address
_Basket_Errors	A SimpleList object containing a set of strings, corresponding to all errors that have occurred during the basket preparation phase of the purchase process
_Purchase_Errors	A SimpleList object containing a set of strings, corresponding to all errors that have happened during the purchase process
_cc_name	The name that appears on the credit card to be used to pay for the order
_cc_type	The type of the credit card to be used to pay for the order
_cc_number	The number of the credit card to be used to pay for the order
_cc_expmonth	The credit card expiration date's month portion
_cc_expyear	The credit card expiration date's year portion
order_id	The unique identifier that has been assigned to the order. Becomes available only if the order has been successfully processed
_total_total	The total cost for the whole order. Includes shipping, handling and taxes

Name	Value
_oadjust_subtotal	The cost of all the items in the OrderForm as calculated after the global order adjustments
Shipping_method	The code of the shipping method that should be used to ship the order. Used to calculate the shipping costs
_shipping_total	The total shipping cost included in the order total
_tax_total	The total amount of tax calculated for the order
_handling_total	The total handling cost included in the order total
_tax_included	The amount of tax included in the order total
_verify_with	A Dictionary object that contains the fields that must be checked when verifying that the contents of an order have not been altered during the order process. Used by the Page component (see below)
_payment_auth_code	The authorization code for the payment. Returned by financial institution whenever a transaction is completed

As you can see, there are quite a few values stored here. While some of them will only make sense in the next chapter, after we talk about the Order Processing Pipeline, let's take a closer look at certain interesting ones.

The Items SimpleList

This collection is used to store relevant information about each item in the user's shopping basket. Each of the SimpleList's members is a Dictionary object that typically contains the following information:

Name	Description
SKU	The SKU number for this item
Quantity	Number of items in the basket
Name	Name of the item
list_price	The price of the object when it was added to the basket
_product_name	Name of the product as it appears in the product database
_product_dept_id	Department number of the product as it appears in the database
_product_image_file	Pointer to the image file for the product, as it appears in the database
_product_image_height	Height of the image file for the product, as it appears in the database

Table Continued on Following Page

Name	Description
_product_manufacturer	Manufacturer as it appears in the database
_product_image_width	Width of the image file for the product as it appears in the database
_product_list_price	Price of the item as listed in the product database
_product_sku	SKU of the product as listed in the database
_product_description	Description of the product as it appears in the database
_n_unadjusted	Number of items available to the user (without any adjustments). This value is initially set to the same value as Quantity and then used when calculating the number of available items . (inventory check)
_oadjust_adjustedprice	The total price for all the items of this product after having been adjusted taking into consideration the order as a whole (for example, applying special cross-selling discounts, and so on)
_iadjust_regularprice	The normal price of the item. Normally set to the value of list_price
_iadjust_currentprice	The price of all the items of this product after having been modified keeping into consideration the single item (for example, after having applied quantity discounts)
placed_price	The final price that has been calculated for the single item, keeping into account only the single product.
_oadjust_discount	The discount that was applied to this product when the order was considered as a whole
_tax_total	The total tax calculated for the item
_tax_included	The tax actually included in the final calculation of the order's total

Pairs whose name part is preceded by a _product_ prefix are extracted directly from the database by certain pipeline components.

The Shopper ID

Each shopper who visits the site is assigned a unique identifier that is then used by MSCS for various tracking purposes, including associating basket records and orders with individual shoppers.

The Shopper ID is actually a Global Unique Identifier (GUID) – a number that is guaranteed to be unique within the particular machine running the site. Of course, to create a number that is globally unique, one needs a lot of digits – 128 bits to be accurate – meaning that the Shopper ID is very long.

A GUID was chosen because it is an easy way to encompass all possible database technologies, even those that don't support, for example, automatic numbering. If you know that you will be using a specific type of database server, you can choose to create a different numbering system (you can also use triggers for the purpose).

Ship-To and Bill-To Addresses

The addresses stored in the `OrderForm` component are broken down into their main elements. If you are doing business on the Internet, you will probably lament the absence of an e-mail address. I usually add that under the names of `ship_to_email` and `bill_to_email` (remember, the `OrderForm` is fundamentally a `Dictionary` object, so anything can be added to it).

Notably, the state and ZIP portions of the address look like they are specific to the United States. The truth of the matter is that because these are all `Variants` they can be set to anything, and therefore will work with anything you want. Whenever you create a store and set it to a specific locale in the Store Builder Wizard, however, MSCS might create alternative entries in the `OrderForm`. In the specific example of Canadian stores, the values `ship_to_postalcode` and `ship_to_province` are added – although this is more for aesthetic than practical reasons.

Also, note that the country portion of both addresses is stored using the 3-letter ISO country code. This is an internationally-recognized system that assigns a 3 letter code to each country. Thus, for example, The United States have been assigned the code **USA**, while Canada is **CAN**, and Italy is **ITA**. (These are also the same codes that you will see in the Olympic Games broadcasts besides each athlete's name).

Basket and Purchase Errors

As we have seen while visiting the storefront, there are two moments during the purchase process when we can get errors (or simple communications) from MSCS. One is while looking at the shipping page, and the other is after clicking on **Purchase** in the payment screen. These two moments correspond to two different parts of the purchase process from a technical point of view, and they generate two different sets of error messages, which are stored in the `_Basket_Errors` and `_Purchase_Errors SimpleList` objects.

The Order ID

Whenever an order has been successfully completed and has to be stored, a unique order ID (or order number) is generated by MSCS. This is the very long string that we see in the confirmation screen – and that the user is supposed to write down for future reference! The same string is used when storing the order to a database as its primary key.

Similar to the Shopper ID, the order ID is generated from a GUID. Because it's so long, and difficult for the user to remember, we'll be looking at how to get rid of it in the following chapters.

You have probably noticed that there are several values, both in the `OrderForm` itself and in the `Items` collection, that begin with an underscore ("_"). MSCS sets the `Prefix` value accordingly so that those values are not saved when the `OrderForm` is saved to the database for temporary storage.

Most of these values, however, are of significant importance when the order has been completed. Therefore, MSCS resets the `Prefix` property to an empty string so that when the order is completed and saved to its final storage medium, all the values contained in it are saved.

Adding Your Own Values to the OrderForm

Keep in mind that at the core of the `OrderForm` there is a `Dictionary` object. This means that you can add your own values to it, being very careful with the way you name them (remember, those starting with an underscore are *not* saved to the database). MSCS will not only let you use as many pairs as you want, but will also save them to the order database for you!

In fact, just because of this, the OrderForm becomes an interesting alternative to using sessions. As you know, a major drawback of sessions is that they don't work in a server farm. The OrderForm object, however, is persisted in a database, which is generally accessible to all the servers in the farm. Its consistent use, therefore, will make your stores more scaleable.

Adding Products to the OrderForm

The whole goal of the game in an online e-commerce site – at least if you want to make money out of it – is to get your customer to buy something. Clearly, however, they can't really do so if either knowingly or not you don't let them add products to their baskets.

You could in principle add a product to the basket by simply creating a new Dictionary object and its appropriate entries in the Items dictionary of the OrderForm component. However, the Orderform provides a method that does the trick for you, the AddItem method:

```
OrderForm.AddItem (sSKU, iQuantity, iPrice)
```

Where:

>   sSKU is the SKU of the product that has to be added to the OrderForm

>   iQuantity is the number of items to be added to the order

>   iPrice is the list price for the individual item, expressed in cents, or hundredths of the default currency for the store

AddItem will add the product to the Items collection and set the appropriate pairs. In addition, it will return the Dictionary that was created as its result.

Clearing the OrderForm

There are two methods to clear the contents of an OrderForm object. The first one, ClearItems, cleans up the Items dictionary (corresponding to emptying one's basket – while ClearOrderForm deletes all the values in the object.

The DBStorage Component

As we discussed earlier, one of the key concepts of COM (and DCOM) is *data marshalling*, which takes places whenever certain data must be passed across between two objects that have been created under special conditions. Data marshalling is, fundamentally, a way of packing the data on one end so that it can be successfully transmitted across a medium (or persisted on a storage system and then retrieved) and "unpacked" at its destination.

MSCS uses data marshalling to store the contents of a Dictionary object either in a file or in a database. The marshalled contents of an OrderForm object, for example, will look similar to this:

AJD4DS8W651SA1DS2S6J6F8NV9P

As you can imagine, having this data in a database table causes a few inconveniences, especially the fact that it's impossible to search for any of the OrderForm's contents. Furthermore, packing and unpacking the data takes time, and can adversely affect the performance of your site.

It is obvious, therefore, that a special component is needed to read and write data in that format. Such functionality is provided by DBStorage, which can marshal Dictionary, SimpleList and OrderForm objects directly to a database table. If you remember, the marshalled_basket column in the store_order table is a text-type field, which limits the amount of data that can be saved through DBStorage to about 2 GB for a Microsoft SQL 6.5 database. This is normally enough!

Initializing a DBStorage Component

Before being able to use a DBStorage component, you will need to initialize it. This will make sure that it is connected to a database and that it knows what data to look for and where. The InitStorage method takes care of this for us:

```
DBStorage.InitStorage (sConnectionString, sTable, sKey, sProgID, sMarshalColumn, _
                       sDateChanged)
```

Where:

> ➤ sConnectionString is the connection string that should be used to connect to the database

> ➤ sTable is the name of the table that contains the marshalled information

> ➤ sKey is the name of the table that contains the key used to identify the column

> ➤ sProgID is the name of the object that has been serialized in the table (i.e. Commerce.Dictionary or Commerce.OrderForm)

> ➤ sMarshalColumn is the name of the column that contains the marshalled information. If this parameter is not specified, then DBStorage only maps existing fields to entries in the OrderForm or in the Dictionary that is passed to it. The marshalled value would not be stored.

> ➤ SDateChanged is the name of a date-/time-type column that should be set whenever a row in the database is changed

By default, a DBStorage object will try to map the individual fields inside a record to the entries of the same name in the Dictionary or OrderForm object that is associated with it (or created by it, when a reading operation is performed). If you specify a value for the sMarshalColumn parameter, then all the information in the Dictionary or OrderForm object will be marshalled to the column by that name.

The sKey parameter, on the other hand, is used to specify a field that should be searched upon when looking for a specific record. This field does not necessarily have to contain unique values. Finally, sProgID is used to tell DBStorage which component has been (or should be) serialized in the table. The valid values are Commerce.Dictionary and Commerce.OrderForm.

Reading From The Database

Reading data from the database into an object is a relatively easy operation. If the data you are looking for can be accessed using through the default value for sKey that you specified when calling InitStorage, and if you know that key to be unique, then you can use the GetData method:

```
DBStorage.GetData (oReserved, Key)
```

627

Where:

> ➤ oReserved is included for compatibility with previous versions of MSCS, and should be Null
>
> ➤ Key is the value for the default key that identifies the object being searched for in the database

If, by any chance, the object were to find more than one record, then GetData would return Null (unfortunately, the same happens if GetData is unsuccessful in finding any records). If we are indeed looking at this possibility, we should consider using LookupMultipleData:

```
DBStorage.LookupMultipleData (oReserved, sColumns, Values)
```

Where:

> ➤ oReserved is included for compatibility with older versions of MSCS and should be Null
>
> ➤ sColumns is an array containing the names of the columns that should be used as keys
>
> ➤ Values is an array containing the values that should be searched for

As you can see, this method is significantly more complex than GetData. The sColumns and Values arrays must have the same upper and lower bounds (they must, therefore, have the same size). They are used by LookupMultipleData to create a select statement that looks like:

```
Select * from sTable where sColumns (1) = Values (1) and sColumns (2) = Values
(2)...
```

Of course, this is the simplified version, but the idea here is that LookupMultipleData will try to match every member of the sColumns array with the corresponding entry in the Values array to build a search query. If the lower and upper bounds of the two arrays do not correspond, or if no records are found, then LookupMultipleData returns Null; otherwise, the method returns a SimpleList object containing an OrderForm or a number of Dictionary objects.

Finally, DBStorage offers one more function, which encapsulates characteristics of both GetData and LookupMultipleData:

```
DBStorage.LookupData (oReserved, sColumn, Value)
```

Where:

> ➤ oReserved, again, should be Null and is included for compatibility with older versions of MSCS
>
> ➤ sColumn is the name of the column to be used as a key
>
> ➤ Values is the value that should be searched for

Similar to GetData, LookupData is able to return only one row at a time. It lets us specify an alternative column to be used when searching for that row, however contrary to what happens with LookupMultipleData, only one column can be searched upon.

Writing to the Database

When writing an object to the database, you could be either creating a new record, or updating an existing one. In either case, DBStorage has the right method for you!

If you are storing a Dictionary or OrderForm object in the database for the first time, you should use the InsertData method:

```
DBStorage.InsertData (oReserved, Data)
```

Where:

> ➤ oReserved, as we've seen, should be Null and is included for compatibility with older versions of MSCS

> ➤ Data is the object that should be saved. It must be the same as that specified in the sProgID parameter of InitStorage

Keep in mind that InsertData automatically maps certain values to the corresponding fields in the database – this should include the values that you intend to use as keys.

If you need to update a record that already exists, you would typically read the object from the database first, make modifications to it, and then call the CommitData method:

```
DBStorage.CommitData (oReserved, Data)
```

Where oReserved and Data are the same as for the InsertData method.

Deleting Data from the Database

You can delete data from a DBStorage database table in one of two ways. If your goal is to simply empty the contents of the marshalled object, without actually eliminating the database record where it sits, then you should use DeleteData:

```
DBStorage.DeleteData (oReserved, Data)
```

Where:

> ➤ oReserved should be Null, and is included for compatibility with older versions of MSCS.

> ➤ Data is the object to be deleted. Again, it must be the same as that specified in the sProgID parameter of InitStorage.

DeleteData will look for the correct record in the database, then load the corresponding object into memory. The pairs in this object that have corresponding pairs in the object passed as the value of the Data parameter are subsequently deleted, and finally the object is written back to the database.

This method is useful when deleting a whole record is not convenient; for example, when a user purchases something, his or her basket should be *emptied*, and not *deleted* – thus simply removing the product information from the Items collection is a more efficient solution.

For those cases in which you *really* want to get rid of a whole record, however, there is the `DeleteDataKey` method, which gets rid of an entire row by specifying a value to search for in the key column for the object:

```
DBStorage.DeleteDataKey (oReserved, Value)
```

Where:

> ➤ `oReserved` should be Null, and is included for compatibility with older versions of MSCS
>
> ➤ `Value` is the value in the key column for the object that identifies the row to be deleted

Mapping Values Between a DBStorage-Compatible Object and the Database

If you want to store certain properties from the `OrderForm` (or `Dictionary` object) into the database under a different name, you will need to use the `Mapping` property. This is because `DBStorage` by default only maps fields that have the same name on both ends of the rope. The `Mapping` property is set as follows:

```
Public Property DBStorage.Mapping (sObjectField)
```

Where `sObjectField` is the name part of the name/value pair to be mapped, in the object passed to `DBStorage`.

All you have to do is assign the name of the field in the database table that has to be mapped to `Mapping`, specifying which name/value pair you want to map to it as the value of the `sObjectField` parameter. For example, the following line of code tells a `DBStorage` component that the field `ShipToName` in the database table should be mapped to the `ship_to_name` in an `OrderForm` object:

```
dbsDBStorage.Mapping ("ship_to_name") = "ShipToName"
```

Should You Use DBStorage?

In the previous chapter, we have mentioned how data marshalling is an expensive operation in terms of computational burden. At the same time, if all the data is marshalled to the database, performing searches on that database becomes a nightmare – you have to load each record, decode it and check for the value or the values you are looking for manually until you find what you are looking for. Even if you let `DBStorage` do the job for you, this procedure won't change much.

Thus, if you need to concentrate on developing a fast site using MSCS, you will end up having to discard the `DBStorage` component. This is not just a quirk of my oversized ego talking here – the MSCS team itself has declared the `DBStorage` an outlaw in their white paper on improving the performance of MSCS sites, which also explains how to get rid of it.

You can find the white paper on improving MSCS's performance at
`http://www.microsoft.com/commerce.`

The Storefront

The execution flow of the storefront, shown in the following diagram, is quite complex, even though the root folder of the store contains just twenty-five files. This is simply a consequence of the fact that the entire site was designed with the idea of reusing as much code as possible, thus providing a set of common functionality that could be shared among different files.

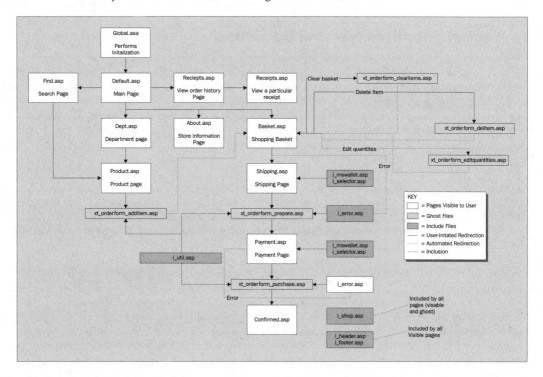

The files whose names begin with an `i_` prefix provide generic functionality, and are included in other files in the store, as shown by the arrows. These include `global.asa`, which is executed upon initialization of the IIS application in which the store resides, and several include files, whose roles range from helping to maintain a consistent look throughout all the pages of the site, to providing a wide array of universal functions.

You will also note the presence of a certain number of "ghost" files, whose names begin with the `xt_` prefix. These are called when particular operations have to be performed in response to the user's input, but no output is normally required. Therefore, all they do is perform whatever task they were designed for and simply redirect the browser to the appropriate page, as shown by the arrows on the diagram above. An exception to this behavior happens when these scripts encounter an error; in that case, they *will* output something to the user, indicating the problem and suggesting a possible way to fix it.

The remaining pages shown on the diagram are those that will be visible to the user. Redirection from these pages is initiated by the user clicking a button, again as shown by the appropriate arrows.

Next in this chapter we'll look at those files whose functionality is taken advantage of by most – or all – of the pages in the site. The most important of these is `global.asa`, where a number of MSCS object instances are created.

Global.asa

The initialization script in `global.asa` is called only once, when the first user attempts to access the store and causes its IIS application to be initialized. No code in the file is intended to be executed at the session level, since – as we mentioned earlier in the book – MSCS stores are designed to work without using the `Session` object and, by default, they turn off support for it inside the IIS metabase.

The Problem With Sessions, and a Solution

While the `Session` object is undoubtedly very useful in a website, it has a few significant drawbacks, in particular the fact that (a) it is based entirely on cookies and (b) its scope is limited to a single server. This means that, if the user's browser does not support cookies, or if the user has turned them off, then sessions won't work. Similarly, you will not be able to implement your site in a web server farm in which access is strictly random. In fact, any time a new page is requested, the browser can end up on any of the web servers in the farm, which might not be the same one that had been accessed previously, and therefore might not be aware of the session that was created on the other machine.

MSCS is able to provide a consistent data storage medium by using an `Orderform` object – available to any script in the site – that is loaded from the `mt_basket` table every time a script starts, and then saved back to the database when the script ends. While this may seem quite heavy in terms of performance, it provides a simple solution to the scope problem, since the database will normally be available to all the machines in a server farm.

What about cookies? Well, MSCS *does* use them to persist the Shopper ID across different connections, which is in turn used to extract the correct record from `mt_basket`. However, it also provides a system that makes it possible to pass this value across two pages by using the URL query string. While this approach allows the store to serve practically any browser, independent of its configuration, it also has one major drawback in that it cannot be used across different sessions. This means that if the user leaves the site and then comes back, his or her browser will not include the Shopper ID in the URL anymore and, as a result, the store will not be able to persist his or her basket.

Global.asa Internals

Generally speaking, `global.asa` takes care of creating several support objects that are later used by most of the scripts in the store. You will notice that all these objects are created using the `<OBJECT>` tag, rather than through a direct call the `Server.CreateObject` method. This makes them a part of the context of any script in the store, which means that they can be accessed directly using their name. We're now going to take a tour of the objects created in `global.asa`. The MSCS objects we'll be looking at, together with their properties and methods, are:

 - ➢ The `StandardSManager` object
 - ➢ The `MSCSDataFunctions` object
 - ➢ The `MSCSQueryMap` object
 - ➢ The `MSCSMessageManager` object
 - ➢ The `Page` object

Before we start with the first of these, note that the Site Dictionary for the store is loaded in the `MSCSSite` object by the `ReadSiteDict` function, which uses an instance of the `Commerce.FileDocument` object to read the dictionary directly from the `.CSC` file in the `/config` folder.

> **The `vRoot` parameter, created at the beginning of the application initialization function, contains the virtual folder of the store. If you ever change your store's location, you will need to update this variable accordingly. Similarly, using the root directory value from the Site Dictionary consistently within your scripts will ensure that you will not need extensive changes in case of such a move.**

The StandardSManager Object

If you remember, a little while ago when we were discussing the `OrderForm` object, we encountered a very important parameter called the Shopper ID. This parameter is used to identify a customer during his or her visit or in subsequent visits, and particular care must be taken in making sure that it is absolutely unique – within your store.

MSCS stores can handle Shopper IDs through the `StandardSManager` component, which takes care of generating, storing and retrieving those pieces of information. The storage and retrieval can be done using one (or both) of two methods: through a cookie and through the URL request parameters.

You are probably already familiar with cookies. A cookie is a small piece of information that is sent to the browser. The browser retains it for a period that varies from the duration of the user session to an indefinite amount of time, and returns it upon request (as long as the requesting server belongs to an authorized domain).

As you can see, cookies are pretty safe but, due to a mix of misleading media coverage and several bugs that have afflicted the major browsers, they are not very popular among the general public. Many people, concerned with the safety of their information – and not knowing any better – turn off their browser's support for cookies, making a user retention system based only on these useless.

As for the URL query string parameters, you have certainly seen – and used – those in the past. Let's for example consider the following URL:

```
http://your_host/default.asp?shopperid=REW2410IJ2120IJAFDI244J
```

Clearly, this URL opens the page `default.asp` on the HTTP server at the address `store.wrox.com`. This leaves us with the portion after the question mark, which is a *parameter* that we can retrieve using the `Request` intrinsic object. This works fine, even if the user's browser has been instructed to refuse cookies. However, it will be impossible to remember who our shoppers are when they return to the site, because their Shopper IDs will be lost (usually, the entrance point to the site is some easy-to-remember address, such as `www.wrox.com`). Naturally, you won't have this problem if you require your customers to login in order to shop at your site.

Initializing StandardSManager Objects

In order to save system resources, you will want to make the `StandardSManager` object that you will use in your own store an application-wide object (MSCS does this for us when we create a store). In addition, other MSCS components will expect to find a `StandardSManager` object in the `Application` object, under the `MSCSShopperManager` key – which makes for a *compelling* reason to create the object in the `global.asa` file of your store.

In order to initialize the object, you must call the `InitManager` method, which takes care of telling the object what store it's working for and what method should be used to store (and retrieve) the Shopper IDs:

```
StandardSManager.InitManager (sStoreName, sMode)
```

Where:

> ➢ `sStoreName` is the short name of the store (this can be retrieved from the Site Dictionary)
>
> ➢ `sMode` instructs the object as to how Shopper IDs should be stored and retrieved, and can take one of the following values:

Name	Description
cookie	The Shopper IDs are written to and read from the cookies.
url	The Shopper IDs are written to and read from the URL query string
cookieurl	The Shopper IDs are written both to the URL query string and to the browser's cookies. When reading, the object attempts first to retrieve the Shopper ID from the cookies, then, if unsuccessful, from the URL query string
urlcookie	The Shopper IDs are written both to the URL query string and to the browser's cookies. When reading, the object attempts first to retrieve the Shopper ID from the URL query string, then, if unsuccessful, from the browser's cookies

Creating, Reading and Writing Shopper IDs

To create a Shopper ID, you can use this method:

```
StandardSManager.CreateShopperID()
```

`CreateShopperID` returns a string that can be used to identify the current user in a unique manner. Keep in mind that you should not attempt to retrieve the Shopper ID on your own – MSCS already provides all the functions you need.

Although `StandardSManager` provides a set of functions that you can use to read and store Shopper IDs, you should use the functions provided by the `Page` component, which we will see in the next section.

Inside `global.asa`, a storewide instance of `StandardSManager` is created by the
`InitShopperManager` function, which, as you can see below, simply initializes the object by
specifying that cookies should be the primary tracking method:

```
Function InitShopperManager
    Call MSCSShopperManager.InitManager(vRoot, "cookieurl")
    Set InitShopperManager = MSCSShopperManager
End Function
```

Handling Data Conversions

Next, `global.asa` creates an instance of the `Commerce.DataFunctions` object, which is stored
in the `MSCSDataFunctions` variable. The goal of `DataFunctions` is to solve two classic problems
that Internet developers – and in particular e-commerce site developers – face continually. First is the
need to localize currency values, numbers, dates and so on to a specific locale. Second is the necessity
of validating user input (or values that end up in the database, for example) to make sure it falls
within certain ranges.

The first problem in particular deserves considerable attention. Windows NT – being, after all an
internationally recognized operating system – does support formatting rules for several locales,
including 13 different versions of the Arabic language and 6 of the English language, among others.
The problem is that the operating system allows you to only set one locale at a time, and all the
formatting functions provided by Windows use that locale by default. The only way to change it is to
actually write a DLL that encapsulates all the relevant operating system functionality – luckily, the
MSCS team has done it for us!

Choosing the Right Locale

According to the latest version of the MSDN library in my possession (the one distributed with Visual
Studio 6.0), Windows supports a total of 107 locales. It is important to understand that a locale is not
only tied to a specific language, but also to the conventions that people from a specific country or
ethnic group share. For example, when considering the difference between Canada and the UK,
although the languages are slightly different, what really matters to us is, for example, the fact that
Canadians use dollars as their currency, whereas people from the UK use pounds sterling.

To instruct a `DataFunctions` object to work with a specific locale, you can set the `Locale`
property:

```
Public Property DataFunctions.Locale
```

For example, the following chunk of code creates a `DataFunctions` object and then uses the
`i_locales.asp` file to set its locale to the identifier for Italy:

```
<!--#Include file="i_locales.asp"-->

<%
    Set dfDataFunctions = Server.CreateObject ("Commerce.DataFunctions")
    dfDataFunctions.Locale = lItalianStandard
%>
```

Converting Values

DataFunctions provides a set of methods for converting a string to a specific data type. In general, all these methods follow the same principle: they return a value of the specified type if they are able to convert the string, otherwise they return Null. We can divide the conversion methods into two groups, dates and numbers.

The date and time methods convert a string that either contains a date, or a time, or a combination of the two to a Date or DateTime variant. The three methods are:

```
DataFunctions.ConvertDateString (sDate, iLocale)
DataFunctions.ConvertTimeString (sTime, iLocale)
DataFunctions.ConvertDateTimeString (sDateTime, iLocale)
```

Where:

> ➢ sDate is a string containing a valid date expression for the locale used

> ➢ sTime is a string containing a valid time expression for the locale used

> ➢ sDateTime is a string containing a valid date and time expression for the locale used

> ➢ iLocale is the locale to be used. If this parameter is not specified, then the method uses the default locale specified for the object

All these conversion functions should work fine – with a couple of exceptions. When converting values that are formatted according to the locales for Latvia and Bulgaria, it might be possible that the conversion methods return Null even if the formatting is correct. In that case, you will have to remove the final portion of the date string that is used as a "postfix" to the date itself.

The other group of conversion functions that can be used is dedicated to converting numbers. The three methods in this category can convert integers, floating-point numbers and currency values:

```
DataFunctions.ConvertInteger (sInteger, iLocale)
DataFunctions.ConvertFloat (sFloat, iLocale)
DataFunctions.ConvertMoneyStringToNumber (sMoney, iLocale)
```

Where:

> ➢ sInteger is a string containing a valid integer for the locale used

> ➢ sFloat is a string containing a valid floating-point number expression for the locale used

> ➢ sMoney is a string containing a valid currency-value expression for the locale used

> ➢ iLocale is the locale to be used. If this parameter is not specified, then the method uses the default locale specified for the object

Formatting Values

While the conversion methods can be used to validate or convert the user's input to a common format, formatting methods perform the opposite operation and can be used to convert values from common format to their string representation for a specific locale.

Once again, we can divide them into two groups—date functions and number/currency functions. The date formatting methods act on `Date` and `DateTime` values and return strings:

```
DataFunctions.Date (dDate, iLocale)
DataFunctions.Time (tTime, iLocale)
DataFunctions.DateTime (dDateTime, iLocale)
```

Where:

- ➤ dDate is a valid `Date` expression
- ➤ tTime is a valid `Time` expression
- ➤ dDateTime is a valid `DateTime` expression
- ➤ iLocale is the locale to be used. If this parameter is not specified, then the method uses the default locale specified for the object

On the other hand, the number/money functions act on integers, floating-point numbers and currency values:

```
DataFunctions.Number (iNumber, iLocale)
DataFunctions.Float (fNumber, iLocale)
DataFunctions.Money (mNumber, iLocale
```

Where:

- ➤ iNumber is a valid `Integer` or `Long` expression
- ➤ fNumber is a valid `Float` expression
- ➤ mNumber is a valid `Currency` expression
- ➤ iLocale is the locale to be used. If this parameter is not specified, then the method uses the default locale specified for the object

Keep in mind that both the currency conversion and formatting methods do not use the standard OLE type for currency values that is used by Visual Basic, but rather the one that is used by MSCS to store currency values in the database. As a result, all the values are in hundredths of the currency for the selected locale. This means cents for the dollar.

The Naked String

Don't you hate it when you ask for a credit card number and the user types in something like:

```
    "      4000 13071535     4079       "
```

I'm sure that you, too, think that these people don't deserve to buy from your store — but, hey, it'd be bad if you were losing that money, right? Luckily for us, `DataFunctions` provides the `CleanString` method that helps us a little bit in solving this problem:

```
DataFunctions.CleanString (sString, iMinLength, iMaxLength, bStripWhiteSpaces, _
                          bStripReturn, iCase, iLocale)
```

Where:

> - sString is the string that has to be "cleaned"
> - iMinLength is the minimum length of the string
> - iMaxLength is the maximum length of the string
> - bStripWhiteSpaces is True if CleanString should remove all the whitespace characters in the string
> - bStripReturn is True if CleanString should remove all the CR+LF pairs – which are inserted when you press the *Return* key – from the string
> - iCase controls how the case of the string is modified. If its value is 0, then no modification is made; if it is 1, then the entire string is converted to uppercase; if it is 2, then the entire string is converted to lowercase
> - iLocale is the locale to be used. If this parameter is not specified, then the method uses the default locale specified for the object

CleanString returns the value of sString modified according to the instructions given.

Validation Methods

To conclude our exploration of planet DataFunctions, let's take a look at its validation methods. These can be used to make sure that the user input falls within certain acceptable ranges. You will usually use them in combination with the conversion methods – first, you convert the strings to a recognizable value, then you check for its accuracy.

There are three validation functions offered by DataFunctions – one for Integer values, one for Floating Point values and one for Date or DateTime values. Keep in mind that, once converted, a currency value also becomes an integer. Here are the three functions:

```
DataFunctions.ValidateNumber (iNumber, MinimumValue, MaximumValue)
DataFunctions.ValidateFloat (fNumber, MinimumValue, MaximumValue)
DataFunctions.ValidateDateTime (dtDateTime, MinimumValue, MaximumValue)
```

Where:

> - iNumber is a valid Integer expression
> - fNumber is a valid Float expression
> - dtDateTime is a valid DateTime expression
> - MinimumValue is the minimum valid value for the expression
> - MaximumValue is the maximum valid value for the expression

All these functions return True if the value passed falls within the specified range, otherwise they return False.

A Central Repository For Queries...

The `InitQueryMap` function is used in `global.asa` to create `MSCSQueryMap`, a `Dictionary` object that contains all the SQL queries used by the store. It's a good idea to add your own queries to this list from within `global.asa`. This will make global updates (such as changes in the names of the tables) centralized and very easy to perform, as opposed of having to scan all the scripts looking for query strings.

Each query in the map is represented by a `Dictionary` of its own, which means the `MSCSQueryMap` is in fact a `Dictionary` object containing other `Dictionary` objects. Name/Value pairs can be added in the normal way. The Name part of the pair, normally a description of the SQL command, is set as a property of the `Dictionary` object, with an SQL command as its value.

...And One For Messages!

Finally, `MSCSMessageManager` is a globally available instance of `Commerce.MessageManager` that contains all the error messages that are generated in the store's pipelines. As is the case with `MSCSDataFunctions`, the Message Manager is initialized with a specific locale – even though it can support more than one.

Using MessageManager

Before you can use a `MessageManager` object, you need to specify what language or languages it will use. This is done through the `AddLanguage` method:

```
MessageManager.AddLanguage (sLanguageName, iLocale)
```

Where:

> `sLanguageName` is an arbitrarily selected string that contains a unique identifier for the language ("Canada", "USA", "Italian", and so on)

> `iLocale` is the locale identifier for the language

You will need a call to `AddLanguage` for every language that you want the system to use. The locale identifier is a number picked from the list that we saw earlier on in the chapter while we talking about the `DataFunctions` component.

Even though you will only need the value of `sLanguageName` to identify a particular language for your calls to `MessageManager`, the `iLocale` parameter is just as important – you can use it, for example, to know what locale you should be using in your calls to `DataFunctions` for the language that is being used to print out messages. Quite convenient, isn't it?

You can also instruct the `MessageManager` object to use a default language. This will make it easier for you to write code, as you won't have to specify a language every time you will be asking for a message. To specify a default language, use the `DefaultLanguage` property:

```
Public Property MessageManager.DefaultLanguage
```

All you have to do is assign a string to it, corresponding to the identifiers for the language you want to use by default. Remember that the identifiers are compared using a case-sensitive algorithm, thus "usa" is different from "Usa" or "USA".

Retrieving Information

There are two pieces of information that you can retrieve from a `MessageManager`: a message and a locale identifier. As we mentioned earlier, you would typically need the latter for your localized calls to a `DataFunctions` object. You can get it by calling `GetLocale`:

```
MessageManager.GetLocale (sLanguageName)
```

Where `sLanguageName` is an optional parameter, specifying the string corresponding to the language for which `MessageManager` should return the local identifier. You can feed this method's output directly to any method of a `DataFunctions` object.

As for the messages, you will have to add them before you can retrieve them! This is done through the `AddMessage` method:

```
MessageManager.AddMessage (sMessageName, sMessage, sLanguageName)
```

Where:

- ➢ `sMessageName` is a string that will be associated
- ➢ `sMessage` is the message itself
- ➢ `sLanguageName` is the language identifier string for the chosen language. If you don't specify this value, `MessageManager` will use the default language specified for the object

As you may have already noticed, the `MessageManager` behaves like a collection object that only accepts string Name/Value pairs. You can use the `GetMessage` method to retrieve a specific message:

```
MessageManager.GetMessage (sMessageName, sLanguageName)
```

Where:

- ➢ `sMessageName` is a string to be matched
- ➢ `sLanguageName` is the language identifier string for the chosen language. If you don't specify this value, `MessageManager` will use the default language specified for the object.

`GetMessage` returns a string that corresponds to the name specified in `sMessageName`.

Messages Used By MSCS

We mentioned above that `MessageManager` messages are most often used during the order process to report errors to the user. MSCS defines a few of these messages by default. Here's a list of them:

Message Name	Message type
pur_badplacedprice	The price of an item in the basket does not correspond to the price in the database
pur_badhandling	The handling cost for the order cannot be computed
pur_badpayment	The payment authorization code has not been set
pur_badshipping	The shipping cost for the order cannot be computed
pur_badsku	The SKU of an item does not correspond to an existing product in the database
pur_badtax	The tax for the order cannot be computed
pur_badverify	The data in the Orderform has been modified and the user must review the order before being able to continue
pur_noitems	There are no items in the order
pur_out_of_stock	At least one of the items in the order is out of stock

I'm sure that most of these values explain themselves. Perhaps the only one you will want to know about is pur_badverify, which happens when the data included in the order changes during the purchase process in a way that might affect the nature of the order itself. This includes, for example, a change in the price of one of the items (for good or, especially, for bad), and so on. Always keep in mind that, once they have entered their credit card number, your customers will expect to pay exactly what they last saw on their screen. Therefore, you must notify them *before* you charge their credit cards, or you'll receive some really upset e-mails!

The Page Component

Finally, the last object created in global.asa is an instance of Commerce.Page. This ubiquitous component handles several HTTP- and HTML-related functions, and is widely used throughout the entire store, as we'll see later on in the chapter.

Handling Shopper IDs

Page offers two functions that can be used to read and write Shopper ID respectively. GetShopperID retrieves a Shopper ID according to the rules established when initializing the site's StandardSManager object:

```
Page.GetShopperID()
```

Similarly, the PutShopperID stores a Shopper ID created by StandardSManager:

```
Page.PutShopperID (sShopperID)
```

Where sShopperID is the Shopper ID that must be stored.

The `Page` component stores and retrieves information either to the browser's cookies, or into the URL query string, or in both. The name of the parameter or cookie in which these are stored is specified by a variable stored in the `Application` intrinsic ASP object under the name `MSCSIDURLKey`. By default, MSCS sets this value to `"mscssiteid"`.

In order to be able to read and write Shopper IDs, a `Page` object needs to be able to locate the `StandardSManager` object for a particular store. As we mentioned before, the latter must be stored in the `Application` object under the name `MSCSShopperManager`.

Creating HTML Form Elements

Forms are the most used interactive elements of HTML. They allow the server to collect information from the user in an easy and intuitive fashion. However, writing forms is rated among the least interesting parts of HTML development (at least by me!)

Although it can't do miracles, the `Page` object can facilitate the creation of checkboxes, radio buttons and drop-down lists. Let's consider checkboxes and radio buttons first. When declaring a checkbox, you will write some code similar to the following:

```
<INPUT TYPE=checkbox NAME="Check1" VALUE="Yes">
```

Obviously, this line of code will only cause the browser to draw a checkbox that is always unchecked. Often, however, you will want to write a checkbox that is checked or unchecked depending on the value of a particular value; in that case, this could be your code:

```
<INPUT TYPE=checkbox NAME="Check1" VALUE="Yes" <% If Check1 = True _
                     Then %>checked<% End If %>>
```

Try writing that ten times, and you will appreciate the practicality of the `Page.Check` method:

```
Page.Check (bValue)
```

Where `Bvalue` is a Boolean value which is `True` if the checkbox should be checked, and otherwise `False`.

`Check` returns the string value `"CHECKED"` if the Boolean condition expressed by `bValue` is True. Here is an example:

```
<% set pPage = Server.CreateObject ("Commerce.Page") %>

<INPUT TYPE=checkbox NAME="Check1" VALUE="Yes" _
       <% = pPage.Check (Check1 = True) %>>
```

Similarly, creating drop-down listboxes can be a painful experience, especially if you want to select the default value. For example, consider this piece of code:

```
<SELECT NAME="Select1">
  <OPTION VALUE="Option 1" <% if Option = "Option 1" then %>SELECTED _
        <% end if %>>Option 1
  <OPTION VALUE="Option 2" <% if Option = "Option 2" then %>SELECTED _
        <% end if %>>Option 2
  <OPTION VALUE="Option 3" <% if Option = "Option 3" then %>SELECTED _
        <% end if %>>Option 3
  <OPTION VALUE="Option 4" <% if Option = "Option 4" then %>SELECTED _
        <% end if %>>Option 4
  <OPTION VALUE="Option 5" <% if Option = "Option 5" then %>SELECTED _
        <% end if %>>Option 5
</SELECT>
```

As you can imagine, it takes a while to write this code, and the result is not elegant at all. Luckily, the `Page.Option` method can be used to take care of the part that determines whether a particular option should be selected:

```
Page.Option (Value1, Value2)
```

Where:

> `Value1` can be any value

> `Value2` can be any value of the same type as `Value1`

This method returns the string `"SELECTED"` if `Value1` equals `Value2`. Going back to our piece of code, it would now look like this:

```
<SELECT NAME="Select1">
  <OPTION VALUE="Option 1" <% = Page.Option (Option, "Option 1") %>>Option 1
  <OPTION VALUE="Option 2" <% = Page.Option (Option, "Option 2") %>>Option 2
  <OPTION VALUE="Option 3" <% = Page.Option (Option, "Option 3") %>>Option 3
  <OPTION VALUE="Option 4" <% = Page.Option (Option, "Option 4") %>>Option 4
  <OPTION VALUE="Option 5" <% = Page.Option (Option, "Option 5") %>>Option 5
</SELECT>
```

Retrieving Information from the URL Query String

Because you will be using forms to collect information from the user, you will also have to retrieve the values stored inside the forms' elements from the query string or from the HTTP parameters. As you probably know, the `Request` ASP intrinsic object provides a few methods that can be used for this purpose. They have the disadvantage, however, of not being able to provide authentication. The `Page` component provides several methods that can be used to retrieve, and at the same time validate, information from the query string or HTTP parameters.

There are a total of eight `Request` methods in the `Page` component. The choice of which one to use depends largely on the final data type of the value you wish to retrieve from the URL query string or HTTP parameters. The methods are:

```
Page.RequestDate (sParameterName, DefaultValue, dLowDate, dHighDate, iLocale)

Page.RequestDateTime (sParameterName, DefaultValue, dtLowDateTime, _
                                                dtHighDateTime, iLocale)

Page.RequestDefault (sParameterName, DefaultValue)

Page.RequestFloat (sParameterName, DefaultValue, fLowValue, fHighValue, iLocale)

Page.RequestMoneyAsNumber (sParameterName, DefaultValue, iLowValue, _
                                                iHighValue, iLocale)

Page.RequestNumber (sParameterName, DefaultValue, iLowValue, iHighValue, iLocale)

Page.RequestString (sParameterName, DefaultValue, iMinLength, iMaxLength, _
                          bStripWhiteSpaces, bStripReturn, iCase, iLocale)

Page.RequestTime (sParameterName, DefaultValue, tLowValue, tHighValue, iLocale)
```

Where for all methods:

> ➢ `sParameterName` is the name of the URL query string parameter or HTTP parameter to be retrieved. The method will look for the parameter first in the URL query string, and then in the HTTP parameters.

> ➢ `DefaultValue` is a valid expression of the appropriate type (date, time etc) to be used as the default value if the parameter specified does not exist or if it contains no value. If no value is specified for `DefaultValue` and the parameter doesn't exist or contains no value, then `RequestDate` returns Null.

> ➢ The third- and fourth-placed `LowValue` and `HighValue` parameters are valid expressions of the appropriate type, representing lower and upper limits for the validation check.

> ➢ `iLocale` is a locale identifier. If no value is specified the validation method will use the default locale specified for the store's `DataFunctions` object.

The `RequestString` method has some additional parameters:

> ➢ `iMinLength` is the minimum length of the string
> ➢ `iMaxLength` is the maximum length of the string
> ➢ `bStripWhiteSpaces` is `True` if white spaces should be eliminated (stripped) from the string, and otherwise `False`.
> ➢ `bStripReturn` is `True` if return characters should be eliminated from the string, and otherwise `False`.
> ➢ `iCase` is 1 if the string should be converted to uppercase, and 2 if it should be converted to lowercase. 0 means no modifications are made to the case of the string

All these methods return Null if the values retrieved by them do not satisfy the conditions expressed by their lower and upper limits. I am sure that almost all the methods are self-explanatory, perhaps with the exception of `RequestDefault`, which corresponds to the simple call to the `Request` object to retrieve a string value without any validation.

Keep in mind that all these functions rely on the fact that a `DataFunctions` object has been created in the store's `global.asa` and stored in the `Application` object under the name `MSCSDataFunctions`. MSCS does this by default when a new store is created, and you should maintain this convention in your own customized stores if you intend to use the `Page` component.

Creating URLs

Putting together a URL can be a tricky task – parameters have to be taken into consideration, the correct protocol has to be used, and so forth. The `Page` component provides several methods that come to our help.

First of all, let's see how we can affect the way that URLs are composed. Most often, we will want to establish whether we want to really use a secure channel, which requires the `https://` prefix, while we are testing our stores. In fact, to be able to use secure communications, we have to obtain a security certificate from a certificate authority, which requires time and money, and is usually just about the last thing we do before going live.

At the same time, we cannot ignore the fact that if we hard-coded the normal `http://` prefix everywhere, we might forget to change some of its occurrences when we later go live, with the risk of leaving pages that contain sensitive information unprotected. The solution to this problem is to use a global function – stored in a file included by all the pages of our store – that encapsulates the functionality of the `SURLPrefix` property or of the `SURL` method. These two methods are called as follows:

```
Public Property Page.SURLPrefix

Page.SURL (sFileName, Parameters…)
```

Where:

> `sFileName` is the name of the file that the URL should point to

> `Parameters` is a set of Name/Value pairs that should be appended as parameters to the URL query string

The results of `SURLPrefix` and `SURL` vary depending on the value of the `DisableHTTPS` value stored in the Site Dictionary. If that is 1, then the prefix used to create the URL will be a simple `http://`, otherwise the `Page` component will assume that the communication should be secure and the `https://` prefix should be used.

While `SURLPrefix` only returns the secure host name for the server where the site is on (i.e. `https://www.wrox.com`), the `SURL` method makes it possible to compose entire URLs very easily. This is done by specifying a set of Name/Value pairs after the name of the file that the URL should point to. For example, consider this call made within the Clocktower store on a computer called Hamilton:

```
pPage.SURL ("default.asp", "par1", "1", "par2", "2", "par3", "3")
```

It will cause the following output to be returned (assuming that the `DisableHTTPS` value is 0):

```
https://Hamilton/default.asp?par1=1&par2=2&par3=3
```

If the `StandardSManager` object for the store has been set to store the Shopper ID into the URL, `SURL` (and all the other URL building functions of the `Page` component) will automatically append the Shopper ID to the URL:

```
https://Hamilton/default.asp?mscsshopperid=D3T2APFZFJIEO23D9D2P3&
                                    par1=1&par2=2&par3=3
```

If you need to create a plain URL, which will not be affected by the value of the `DisableHTTPS` parameter, you can use the `URLPrefix` and `URL` functions – the same considerations above apply to them as well.

It is also possible to create only parts of a URL; this can be useful in those situations where the `URL` and `SURL` methods cannot be used. To create the part of a query string that contains all the parameters, for example, you can use the `URLArgs` method:

```
Page.URLArgs (Parameters…)
```

Where `Parameters` is a set of name/value pairs that should be appended as parameters to the URL query string.

The parameter list is built in the same way as for the `URL` and `SURL` methods, only this time the Shopper ID is never attached to the generated string. For example:

```
pPage.URLArgs ("par1", "1", "par2", "2", "par3", "3")
```

Always returns:

```
par1=1&par2=2&par3=3
```

regardless of how the `StandardSManager` object for the site has been set. If you are interested in retrieving the Shopper ID as well, you can use the `URLShopperArgs` method, which has exactly the same syntax as `URLArgs`. Assuming that the `StandardSManager` object for the site has been set to store the Shopper ID in the URL query string, a call similar to the `URLShopperArgs` call above, will return the following:

```
mscsshopperid=D3T2APFZFJIEO23D9D2P3&par1=1&par2=2&par3=3
```

Finally, it might also be useful to retrieve the name of the virtual directory where the site's files are stored – this is essential if we want to build URLs that point to our own store! The `VirtualDirectory` property comes to our help:

```
Public Property Page.VirtualDirectory
```

As you might have imagined, `VirtualDirectory` returns the name of the virtual directory where the site is stored (e.g. clocktower).

What You See is What You Pay For?

As we have mentioned more than once throughout the book, in the following chapter we will be talking about the Order Processing Pipeline. Because its use pervades Site Server so deeply, however, we are often forced to reference it even if we haven't talked about it yet.

Even the `Page` object ties in with it, by providing a set of functions that can be used to make sure that certain information stored in an `Orderform` does not change between, for example, the payment page and the confirmation page.

You will probably be asking yourselves, how can the user change values in the basket without knowing it? Well, to quote a certain character from Star Trek, "You think in such three-dimensional terms!" Don't forget that while the user is visiting the store using a browser, he or she could get to the payment page and, before making a purchase, open another browser and maybe add something to his or her basket, thus modifying the grand total of the order.

If the user clicks on the purchase button in the first browser, he or she will be under the impression that the old grand total will be charged to his or her credit card – a very wrong impression, because the total has now changed. As you can imagine, this can cause significant problems, and it is both for the user's protection and for yours that the `Page` component provides a simple mechanism for verifying that the information in the `Orderform` has not changed between any two pages.

The mechanism works by storing certain values taken from the `Orderform` while the first page (e.g. `payment.asp`) is being created. The values are output in a set of `HIDDEN` HTML form tags and passed along to the second page through a `GET` or `POST` action. The second page picks them up and compares them against the new values in the processed `Orderform`. If any change is detected, the Order Processing Pipeline generates an error, and the store responds by returning to the first page and prompting the user to review his or her basket.

The `HIDDEN` tags are generated by the `VerifyWith` method:

```
Page.VerifyWith (Orderform, Arguments…)
```

Where:

> `Orderform` is the `Orderform` object from where values need to be extracted
> `Arguments` is a list of strings that contains the names of all the pairs that have to be extracted from the `Orderform` object

Typically, the values that you will want to check against are the grand total of the order (for obvious reasons) and a value from the shipping address that will make it possible to determine if the shipping costs might have changed, or if the current shipping method is available at all to the recipient of the order. In general, this means either the ship-to ZIP code or the ship-to state (or country). For example this line of ASP code:

```
ThePage.VerifyWith (MSCSOrderForm, "ship_to_zip", "_total_total")
```

Will produce the following output:

```
<INPUT TYPE="HIDDEN" NAME="ship_to_zip" VALUE="90211">
<INPUT TYPE="HIDDEN" NAME="_total_total" VALUE="10320">
```

Which means that the total value of the order is $103.20 and the ZIP code of the order's recipient is 90211.

`VerifyWith` can only be used with `Integer`, `Floating Point` and `String` variants. It will not work if you try to use it with `Date` values or objects, even if the latter support property bags.

When you get to the second page, where you want to check that your information has indeed not been changed, you will have to move the information back into the `Orderform`. This is done through the `ProcessVerifyWith` method of the `Page` component:

```
Page.ProcessVerifyWith (Orderform)
```

Where `Orderform` is the `Orderform` object to which values need to be written.

`ProcessVerifyWith` proceeds to write all the values into the `_verify_with` `Dictionary` object inside the pipeline (which, because its names starts with an underscore character, will not be saved by the `DBStorage` component). These values are subsequently verified against the values in the `Orderform` during pipeline processing. We'll take a look at how that happens in the following chapter.

Encoding Functions

You are all probably familiar with the encoding functions that are provided by ASP, like `Server.URLEncode`. The `Page` component offers similar functions that perform a little better than their ASP counterparts.

The `HTMLEncode` method, for example, can be used to convert plain strings into HTML code. This is useful, especially when the string contains "dangerous" characters, such as quotation marks, that can be misinterpreted by an HTML renderer. This method is called as follows:

```
Page.HTMLEncode (sString)
```

Where `sString` is a string value that contains the text to be converted.

The only difference between the `Page.HTMLEncode` method and the ASP-intrinsic `Server.HTMLEncode` method is in the fact that the former returns an empty string if `String` is NULL, whereas the latter simply fails. It's not like we can't live without the method provided by MSCS, but it saves a lot of error handling!

To encode strings into text that can be used as part of a URL (generally in query parameters), we can use the `Page.URLEncode` method, which converts characters that are difficult to digest for a web server into healthier escape sequences:

```
Page.URLEncode (String)
```

Where again `sString` is a string value containing the text to be converted.

Similar to `HTMLEncode`, `URLEncode` acts exactly as its ASP counterpart; the only difference, once again, is in the way the two methods handle NULL values.

Other Attributes Provided by the Page Component

Before we bid our farewell to the `Page` component, we should take a quick look at another two of its properties that can be of interest:

➤ The `SiteRoot` property, as its name suggests, contains the name of the root folder where your store is located.

➤ The `Context` property contains the ASP context for the current page. The context contains interface pointers to all the intrinsic ASP objects, such as `Request`, `Server` and `Response`, and is something that you wouldn't use under normal circumstances. Some MSCS components, however (most notably, the ever-present pipelines) need to have a pointer to it in order to work properly.

The Store Include Files

Now that we have concluded our discussion of the objects created in `global.asa`, and how they can be used, we'll move on to discuss three of the include files in our sample store: `i_shop.asp`, `i_header.asp` and `i_footer.asp`. Of these the most important is `i_shop.asp`.

i_shop.asp

All the scripts in the store, regardless of whether they output something or not, include this file, which provides a number of functions that are generically needed by all the other files.

At the beginning of its execution, `i_shop.asp` defines some constants that are required when dealing with ADO. These turn out to be very convenient, as they save you the hassle of having to either re-define them yourself, or use their corresponding values, which makes the code harder to read.

Next, the script verifies that the store is indeed open. If it isn't, then the browser is redirected to the appropriate page, which is defined in the Site Dictionary as `CloseRedirectURL`:

```
REM -- If store is not open then redirect to closed URL
If MSCSSite.Status <> "Open" Then
  Response.Redirect(MSCSSite.CloseRedirectURL)
End If
```

Hunting for the Shopper

Once it is sure that the store is open, the script continues by attempting to retrieve the user's Shopper ID, which is then used to retrieve the correct record out of `mt_basket`:

```
REM -- mscs = Created on the page; MSCS = created in global.asa
Set mscsPage = Server.CreateObject("Commerce.Page")

REM -- Manually create Shopper ID
mscsShopperID = mscsPage.GetShopperId

REM - Handle shopper
If IsNull(mscsShopperID) then
    mscsShopperID = mscsShopperManager.CreateShopperID()
    mscsPage.PutShopperID(mscsShopperID)
    Call Response.Redirect(pageURL("default.asp"))
End If
```

As you can see from this snippet of code, the Shopper ID is retrieved from an instance of the `Commerce.Page` object created on the spot. The last part of the code, however, should capture your attention, as it can be potentially dangerous. What it does is pretty clear: if the `Page` object is unable to retrieve a Shopper ID, then it creates a new one and then uses the `PutShopperID` method to return it to the user. Finally, it redirects the browser to the main page (`default.asp`), causing the store to start from scratch.

The problem here is that, if you have selected cookies as the method for storing the Shopper ID and the browser does not support or refuses them, the latter will attempt to load `default.asp`, which, however, includes `i_shop.asp`. This, in turn, will still be unable to retrieve and store the Shopper ID properly, and will redirect the browser to `default.asp` once again, entering an infinite loop that will make your site inaccessible to the user.

Why is this happening? After all, in `global.asa`, the Shopper Manager was initialized to support *both* cookies and URLs, therefore we should expect to see the Shopper ID in the URL the second time that the page is loaded. Well, there are two distinct problems here. First of all, as you may remember from earlier, the `Page` object needs to know how the URL query string parameter that contains the Shopper ID should be called. This is stored in the `Application` object, under the `MSCSSIDURLKey` key. `global.asa` is the perfect place to set it, right after initializing all the objects:

```
Application("MSCSSIDURLKey") = "mscssid"
```

Doing this is not sufficient, however, and you will notice no apparent change in the way the site behaves. To understand the problem, in this case, you need to take a closer look at last line of code of the snippet above, the one that redirects the browser:

```
Call Response.Redirect(pageURL("default.asp"))
```

The script obviously expects the `pageURL` function to append the correct Shopper ID to the name of the script to which the browser is being redirected. This function is defined at the end of the script:

```
Function pageURL(pageName)
    pageURL = rootURL & pageName & "?" & emptyArgs
End Function
```

`pageURL` makes use of two variables, `rootURL`, which is supposed to contain the root URL of the site, and `emptyArgs`, which will probably contain the Shopper ID. In fact, these two variables are declared right at the end of the script:

```
siteRoot   = mscsPage.SiteRoot()
emptyArgs  = mscsPage.URLShopperArgs()
```

While the function is available at the time that the Shopper ID is examined and the redirection occurs, however, the declaration of these variables is scoped together with the script's main code and therefore *has not been executed* yet when the `pageURL` is called by our snippet! Therefore, `pageURL` will never be able to attach the Shopper ID to the URL.

In order to make the script work properly, we'll have to change the code snippet to declare the proper variables before redirecting the browser:

```
If IsNull(mscsShopperID) Then
    mscsShopperID = mscsShopperManager.CreateShopperID()
    mscsPage.PutShopperID(mscsShopperID)

  siteRoot    = mscsPage.SiteRoot()
  emptyArgs   = mscsPage.URLShopperArgs()

    Call Response.Redirect(pageURL("default.asp"))
End If
```

Lifesaving Functions

Let's now take a look at the functions that are declared towards the end of the script. We have already encountered and discussed pageURL, which can be used to create a URL that contains all the additional parameters that are required by MSCS. Similarly, pageSURL creates a secure URL that behaves the same way. It's interesting to notice that pageSURL outputs an HTTPS address only if the SURLPrefix name/value pair stored in the Site Dictionary is itself secure. baseURL and baseSURL, on the other hand, can be used to create URLs that do not need to include the additional parameters required by MSCS, or when you need to specify those parameters yourself. They can be used to build URLs that must not be used as active links, such as those that point to image.

Using these four functions consistently throughout your store brings at least two significant advantages. First, your store will automatically and consistently adapt to your needs to switch between secure and non-secure URLs, depending on whether you are in a development or production environment. In addition, you will be able to change the entire store's base address without having to change it throughout the individual pages.

Database à la Carte

The last few lines of code in i_shop.asp are used to create a database connection and ADO Command object that can be used by the page that includes the file. This is quite convenient, since you will not have to rewrite the code to do so in every individual page. On the other hand, it might bring a little overhead if you don't actually need to use the database in all your pages.

i_header.asp and i_footer.asp

These two files are intended to help make the pages in the site consistent. Neither of them includes any code that needs reviewing, although it's worth pointing out that the header, which also prints out the navigation elements that are common to all visible pages, has two minor inconveniences.

First of all, the script is unable to determine what page the user is currently viewing. Therefore, when the browser is displaying, for example, the main page, the Lobby link will still be active, which can prove confusing to the user. It would be better if the script were able to understand that the browser is already on a specific page and act consequently by removing the corresponding link and, maybe, showing a different (i.e. dimmed or grayed) icon.

In addition, when linking to the basket page, the script uses the pageSURL function, which will produce a secure link in a production environment. This is probably unnecessary, since the basket itself doesn't contain any information that can be deemed strictly confidential. An SSL connection, on the other hand, can be significantly slower than a normal one, and prove inconvenient to the user.

Store Navigation

The store navigation files (shown in the following figure) are not very complicated, since their function is essentially that of producing lists of departments or products.

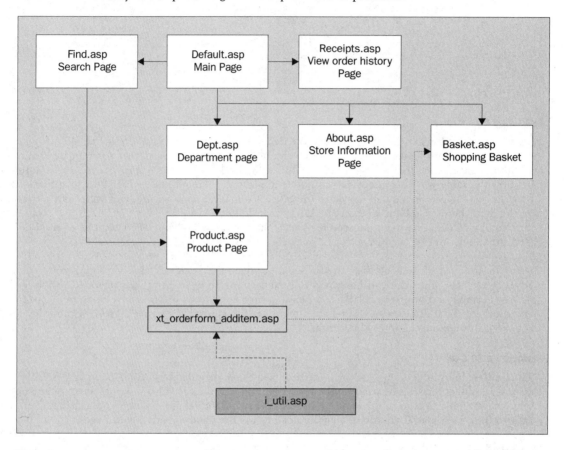

With the exception of about.asp, which is essentially a static page, and xt_orderform_additem, which is a ghost script, these scripts all follow the same basic execution flow: first, a particular query is executed with the appropriate parameters, and then its results are displayed, unless an error of some sort occurs, in which case the scripts are careful to output courteous messages such as "The department you requested is currently unavailable", and so on.

Executing Parametric Queries

By looking at the way database queries are written in global.asa, you might have noticed that most of them contain one or more parameters (usually indicated by :1, :2, and so on) that become known only at execution time. Curiously enough, while ADO knows how to deal with these parameters directly by using a particular syntax, the scripts in the store simply use the VBScript function Replace to replace the placeholder with the parameter's actual value. Here's an example, taken from dept.asp:

```
        cmdTemp.CommandText = _
   Replace(MSCSQueryMap.products_by_dept.SQLCommand,":1",dept_id)
        Set rsProducts = Server.CreateObject("ADODB.Recordset")
        rsProducts.Open cmdTemp, , adOpenStatic, adLockReadOnly
```

Adding Items to the Basket

`xt_orderform_additem.asp` is the first script where we see a reference to the `Orderform`. Up to this point, in fact, there was no need to access it, since all the information that we needed could be taken directly from the database. In this case, however, the user has expressed the will to add an item to his or her basket; therefore, we need to access the `OrderForm` in order to perform this task.

This script is organized in a slightly odd way: the actual functionality is stored in a function (`OrderFormAddItem`), which is called by the script as part of its execution. This is a common format for all the purchase-related pages, and is intended to help you organize things better.

Loading and Saving the Orderform

`xt_orderform.additem.asp` also includes `i_util.asp`, which we haven't encountered yet. This file contains several functions which can be used to manipulate the `Orderform` for load and save operations, and provide the necessary infrastructure to load and execute pipelines.

In our case, only three functions from `i_util.asp` are called. `UtilGetOrderFormStorage` is used to create and intialize an instance of `Commerce.DBStorage` that is used to access the `Orderform` information:

```
   Function UtilGetOrderFormStorage()
        Set orderFormStorage = Server.CreateObject("Commerce.DBStorage")
        Call orderFormStorage.InitStorage(MSCSSite.DefaultConnectionString, _
            "mt_basket", "shopper_id", "Commerce.OrderForm", "marshalled_basket", _
            "date_changed")

        Set UtilGetOrderFormStorage = orderFormStorage
   End Function
```

The script calls this function right away, and passes its return value on to `OrderFormAddItem`, which, in turn, calls `UtilGetOrderForm` to load the basket data into an `OrderForm` object. `UtilGetOrderForm` works by forcing the instance of `Commerce.DBStorage` to load the basket information; if the latter is not available, then the function simply creates a new instance of `Commerce.OrderForm` and returns that.

It's important to notice that the function also returns a flag that indicates whether the `OrderForm` object was loaded or created. This is later used by the `UtilPutOrderForm` function, which is used to store the basket information back into the database. The value of the flag is used to determine whether the database should be simply updated or a new record should be inserted into it.

Inserting an Item in the Orderform

Items are added to the basket using the `AddItem` function of the `OrderForm` object. Since not all the parameters required by this function are available to the script, it extracts them from the database. The method used for carrying out this task is somewhat in contradiction with the rest of the site: in fact, the query that is run against the database (`product_info`) uses question marks to identify parameters that must be substituted at runtime, instead of "named" placeholders like the ones that we have seen so far.

While there isn't anything particularly wrong with doing this (the script runs with no problems), it's worth noting that this isn't a good approach in general. If you were to use this system for all the queries in your store, you would have to be very careful about maintaining the order in which your parameters appear in your scripts, since moving them around will most probably cause the wrong data to appear in the wrong place, with catastrophic results.

Summary

The goal of this chapter was to give you an idea of how the various components of MSCS work together in a store. Although the fact that the storefront is so tightly integrated—revolving around an impressive number of include files and ghost scripts – might be a little scary initially, its structure is not really that complicated in the end. Throughout the chapter, we've also had a chance to discuss potential problems that can be really difficult to catch, and looked at a few tips on what to change when you need to extend your store's functionality.

Now however, we can't move much further on with our discussion of the technical structure of a store without discussing pipelines. Over the next couple of chapters we'll take an in-depth look at pipeline components and stages, and finally examine how they too are used inside the starter store.

17

Pipelines — Stages and Components

Henry Ford, the well-known carmaker who brought the automobile to the masses, didn't invent the concept of a pipeline, but he certainly knew how to use it. His Model T represented a revolution in the way cars were produced and marketed, and it eventually changed these vehicles from a status symbol into a commodity that almost everybody could afford.

The great advantage of the system he used was that of building a car in a specific sequence, optimized so that each step would be preceded and followed by exactly the number of steps needed to get to that point and to complete the car respectively. No time was wasted going backwards because a worker had forgotten a part, and each operation was performed by specialized personnel.

The answer to the question that you are probably asking yourselves by now is that no, a chapter from another book didn't get mixed up with this tome by mistake, and I have not gone crazy (no more than the usual, at least). And, to the purists of computer science, who are frowning at the fact that I am comparing cars to computers, all I have to say is: you're lucky. I could have talked about McDonald's.

This chapter talks about the pipeline technology in Site Server. As we have mentioned before, pipelines offer an ordered approach to the operation of processing an order and of exchanging documents. As such, they are a very important element of both a business-to-consumer and a business-to-business online store.

The chapter is divided into the following sections:

> **Why pipelines?**
> This section will tackle the topic of pipelines in detail, explaining how they work, how they are used in the stores, and why pipeline technology was used in the first place.

> **The Order Processing Pipeline**
> Next, we'll talk about the Order Processing Pipeline (OPP). We'll examine its structure and the way it is used; we'll also take a look at the built-in components that MSCS has to offer.

> **The Commerce Interchange Pipeline**
> As we've mentioned in previous chapters, the Commerce Interchange Pipeline (CIP) is used by a business-to-business store as a data interchange center, but fundamentally it maintains the same basic structure and functioning principles – at least from a technical point of view – as the OPP. Once again, we'll examine the standard set of components that are provided with MSCS.

> **Small is beautiful: Micropipes**
> Micropipes are a particular kind of pipelines that can contain only one component. As we shall see in this section, they can be used to execute a single pipeline component without having to go through all the overheads of executing a standard pipeline.

In the following chapter we'll go on to see how we use the pipelines we've discussed.

Why Pipelines?

Until now, I have been pretty vague as to what a pipeline really is. As a matter of fact, I have limited its description to something similar to "a systematic approach to order processing".

The truth is, the concept of pipelines in MSCS is in no way different from its corresponding concept in the traditional industry of, for example, car making. The reason why a car is built in a pipeline is that the process works well only if a set of steps are taken in a specific order: you can't install the window glass until the body has been painted, or wire the lights before they have been screwed in!

Before Henry Ford came on board, the concept of a pipeline was very different from what it is today: the car stayed in one place, while the workers moved. This meant, for example, that workers had to take all their instruments with them and move from car to car. Ford, who was always looking for a way to make his model T cheaper to produce, and therefore to sell, perceived that the need to continuously move around was a waste of time.

In a bid to improve the process, he made the cars move and his employees stand still at their workstations. As a result, cars were built faster and the correct chain of events was always respected, because the car had to physically move through all the right steps before getting to a particular point.

The pipelines used by MSCS are simply a sequence of steps sorted in a particular order that can be used to complete a process, such as preparing or interpreting a document, or processing an order. To ensure that the data is being processed properly a certain number of checkpoints are built into the pipeline that verify the integrity of certain values and raise errors if they have been compromised.

What is a Pipeline ?

As we shall see later on in the chapter, there are two basic types of pipelines, and although they are intended for very different uses, they share the very same structure, to the point that instances of them are executed using the same group of MSCS objects.

A pipeline is, fundamentally, a collection of COM objects implementing specific interfaces that are executed in a given order (we'll talk more about them in the following chapter). The components are further grouped in **stages**; each stage represents a logical "macro-step" of the pipeline process and usually includes the functionality necessary to validate that what is supposed to happen during its execution has effectively taken place.

The Concept of Pipeline Components

To make a clearer example, let's go back to the concept of car creation. One of its stages might be "seat installation", which, as you can imagine, is dedicated to the correct installation and mounting of the three seats of the vehicle. An important concept to keep in mind here is that the stage logic doesn't have to make sure that the car is in the right condition for the seats to be installed. That's merely a consequence of the fact that all the stages are pre-arranged in a logical order, and that each stage provides its own error-checking functionality at the end of its execution. Therefore, it is reasonable for the "seat installation" stage to assume that whatever steps are necessary for the installation process to successfully take place have already been taken, or the car would have been diverted off the pipeline.

At the same time, it's a good idea to assume that "seat installation" is probably too big a task to be executed in one step. Therefore, it can be broken down into simpler operations, such as "install seat frame", "request seats from inventory", and so on. Each of the individual tasks, which correspond to MSCS's concept of components, has the power to halt the pipeline's execution if an error of some sort is generated or detected.

MSCS Pipelines

As you can imagine, the very same concepts apply to an MSCS pipeline. The main difference is that, while the individual components are responsible for raising errors that are directly connected to their operations, the pipeline container itself acts as a "guardian" that traps any runtime errors unexpectedly caused by the components. As we shall see later on, a component does not raise errors in the pipeline through the usual COM circuit, but rather by notifying the container that an error condition has occurred. This makes it easier for the system to distinguish between errors that are merely accidental and those that are recognized by the component.

In order to function properly, a pipeline needs two important elements: a **context** and a **dictionary**. The former is something that you are probably very familiar with, since it exists also in a normal ASP script (among the other things). The context is simply the collection of data that is intrinsic to the pipeline. In ASP, this includes the `Application`, `Server`, `Response` and `Request` objects, but in a pipeline it can include just about anything, including strings, numerals and other objects.

The dictionary, on the other hand, contains the data that must be computed by the pipeline as it executes. In the case of a purchase, this can include shipping and billing addresses, order information, and so on. For a document interchange, it could include headers or destination addresses. It's important to point out that the term "dictionary" is not used by accident: the data has to be passed within a `Dictionary` object, or some other object that can be manipulated the same way (e.g. the `OrderForm` object).

Handling Alternative Options

One of the biggest issues in a factory pipeline is how optional configurations are handled. In fact, even though it sounds almost like a contradiction, many cars these days are made-to-order. This is simply a consequence of the fact that so many optional items can be installed upon the customer's request, that at least small changes in the way the car is built are required, and therefore a different construction process is needed. Naturally, handling all these custom processes in an efficient way is inherently difficult, as one has to create a number of possible "branches" in the pipeline process in order to manage the possible different outfits.

MSCS's pipelines are not immune from this problem. In fact, the way an order is processed, for example, might differ depending on where it has to be shipped to; or you might be required to use a different component to handle a particular currency when charging customers' credit cards.

Unfortunately, MSCS does not support branching in its pipelines; this means that all the components are executed, unless an error is encountered at some point, in which case the execution simply stops. To ensure that it is possible to provide at least a basic degree of flexibility, MSCS requires that all its components only insert new values in the dictionary, and do not modify existing ones. For example, if Component A determines that the product should be shipped using a specific courier, then it can modify the value of, say, CourierID in the dictionary *only if* the value is NULL. Otherwise, the component should assume that some other component before it has already made a decision and ignore the whole thing.

This "non-interference" rule usually makes it possible to sort the components in a particular order so that a branching scenario can be simulated through a process similar to the one used by the case statement in a programming language. If the components are placed in the correct order, once one of them has found the correct conditions for its execution and fills out certain parameters, the others will not be able to overwrite them – and will not affect the pipeline's execution any longer.

As you can understand, this is a difficult paradigm to follow, because it is sometimes necessary to alter values in the pipeline in order to perform certain operations. At the same time, Microsoft has not enforced this procedure through a certification process, with the result that not many of the MSCS components available from third parties respect it. As we'll see later on, Micropipes can be used to create a pipeline that supports branching, but only with significant performance hits.

How Are Pipelines Used?

In principle, the use of pipelines varies, depending on whether you are running a business-to-consumer or business-to-business store. In the first case, you would probably limit your use of pipelines to processing orders, through the **Order Processing Pipeline**, while in the second case you would use the **Commerce Interchange Pipeline** for exchanging documents with your parties. Clearly, you could just as well use both in your own store, for example if you're running a business-to-consumer store that also communicates with its suppliers and couriers in real-time.

We can answer this question better by looking in detail at first the Order Processing Pipeline and then the Commerce Interchange Pipeline.

The Order Processing Pipeline

As we just mentioned, you will mainly use the OPP for handling the purchase process. Clearly, this does not only include the final task of verifying the entire order and accepting it, but also the operation of creating and maintaining a user basket that displays the actual price (including all discounts) of each item, calculating an order's final price without processing it, and so on.

As a result, there are three pre-defined templates for the OPP. Each of them is designed to handle a particular portion of the purchase process, and for many aspects their roles are complementary, so that you would normally need to use all of them in a business-to-consumer store.

> **Product**
> This type of pipeline is used to generate the information that is displayed in the product detail page of a store. It ensures that the data shown is the most up-to-date and accurate, as it applies all the possible discounts and modifiers to an item's base price stored in the database.

> **Plan**
> The plan pipeline is used to calculate all the information regarding an order without processing it. This makes it possible, among other things, to calculate the true order cost, including shipping and tax fees, and show it to the user *before* he or she makes the final decision on whether to actually complete the purchase.

> *Note that the full name of this pipeline is the Retailing Plan pipeline. However, in the MSCS literature (and also inside the code) it is simply referred to as the Plan pipeline. The only place where its full name is used is inside the pipeline editor.*

> **Purchase**
> Finally, the purchase pipeline is used to complete an order that has already gone through a plan pipeline and is ready to be processed.

In an OPP, the `Dictionary` object is always represented by an instance of the `OrderForm` object that holds all the data necessary to the completion of an order. In the case of the Product pipeline, the `OrderForm` object doesn't necessarily have to hold the entire order, but only the product for which you want to determine information.

The Product pipeline

This kind of OPP is not complex. As we mentioned above, its goal is to generate information to display in the product information page. As such, its structure is extremely simple, as you can see in the following figure:

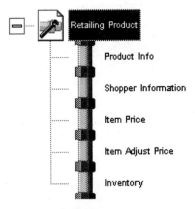

The Product pipeline only contains five stages:

Product Info	This stage can be used to retrieve all the information regarding the items in the `OrderForm` object from the database. Typically, at least a component here is supposed to go through the `Items` collection of the `OrderForm` object and copy the information in the database into each item's dictionary. This is because the system will perform a check at the end of the stage, to make sure that all the information required for each item is available.
	Additional components in this stage can also perform other operations, such as iterating through the list of items and applying special pricing, or pre-calculating certain shipping values – such as weight – in preparation for final computations, and so on.
Shopper Information	The Shopper Information stage can be used to set information regarding the user on behalf of whom the system is retrieving the information. This can be useful, for example, to establish whether the user has a membership in the store's reward program, or other similar tasks. It's interesting to note that this stage is completely optional, as no checking of any kind is done on the data when the execution completes.
Item Price	The goal of this stage is to determine the most current price for each item in the `OrderForm` object. Once the value has been calculated, it has to be stored in the `_iadjust_regularprice` Name/Value pair of each item's dictionary. At the end of the stage, the pipeline makes sure that a value `_iadjust_regularprice` has been set for each item.
Item Adjust Price	This stage is used to determine the actual current price for each item in the `OrderForm` object *including* any discounts. At the end of the stage, the pipeline verifies that a value for the `_iadjust_currentprice` pair is stored in the dictionary for each item.

Inventory	Finally, this stage is used to determine the availability of each item and set the appropriate value (_inventory_backorder) in its dictionary. No checks are done here.

As you can see, at the end of its execution the Product pipeline has simply gone through a list of all the items stored in the OrderForm object and determined an up-to-date price. Using this pipeline is a good idea if your goal is to display to each user how much they will actually be paying for a product while they're looking at it. Otherwise, they would normally have to wait until they get to the shopping basket in order to get the final product price.

The Plan pipeline

If you take a look at the following figure, you will notice that the Product pipeline is really a subset of the Plan pipeline, which is used to determine the complete cost of an order, including shipping and tax fees (when possible).

The Plan pipeline is used at least in two different points of an online store: the shopping basket, for which it calculates the order detail and subtotal, and the payment page, for which it calculates the total amount of the order.

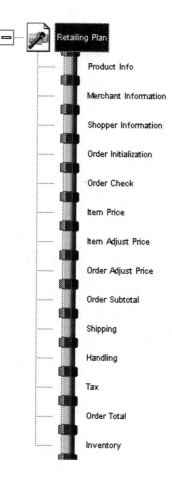

The Plan pipeline is also used after the **Purchase** button is pressed on the payment page to re-calculate the order total and make sure that nothing has changed between when the total was last shown to the user and when he or she actually authorized the purchase. If a difference is found (using the `ProcessVerifyWith` method of the Page component that we saw in the last chapter), then the pipeline will raise an error and cause the system to return to the payment page and authorize the purchase again.

The Plan pipeline is significantly more complex than the Product pipeline, and as such it includes several more stages. Here they are:

Merchant Information	This stage can be used to set information about the merchant for which the purchase is being made. It is completely optional, and can become useful, for example, when you are dealing with more than one merchant sharing the same pipeline. No checking is done at the end of the stage.
Order Initialization	This stage initializes the order information, verifying that the correct quantity for each item (stored in `item.Quantity`) has been set. At the end of this stage the built-in checking system performs several clean-up operations, such as assigning an order ID (unless one has already been assigned), creating the `_oadjust_adjustedprice` entry for each item (which contains the price of each `Item` in the `OrderForm` adjusted for the quantity of items purchased), and deleting several Name/Value pairs that are to be reset during the execution of the pipeline.
Order Check	The Order Check stage verifies that the order can be processed. By default, at the end of the stage the checking logic generates an error if the `OrderForm` object contains no items. The goal of any component in this stage should be to either provide further methods of determining the validity of the order (based on the information available at that point) or to recover from a situation in which the order cannot be processed.
Order Adjust Price	The goal of components in this stage is to determine the final correct price for each item and store it into the `_oadjust_adjustedprice` Name/Value pair in its dictionary. This includes, for example, calculating any order-wide promotions, and so on. At the end of the stage, the pipeline makes sure that the proper Name/Value pairs have been set in the `OrderForm` object.
Order subtotal	The subtotal of the order is calculated here. Typically, this value will be computed by summing together all the `_oadjust_adjustedprice` values and storing the resulting amount in the `OrderForm._oadjust_subtotal` Name/Value pair. The subtotal stored here does not include shipping, handling and taxes, which are calculated later on. The reason why this happens is that those fees are often computed based on the order subtotal, and therefore can only be determined after this stage is complete. In addition, the order subtotal is displayed in the basket, at which point the shipping and tax fees cannot be calculated yet, because the ship-to address is unknown. At the end of this stage's execution the pipeline verifies that a value for `_oadjust_adjustedprice` has been written to the `OrderForm`.

Shipping	Clearly, the shipping stage is used to determine shipping costs for the order. These are, in turn, to be stored in the _shipping_total Name/Value pair of the OrderForm object. At the end of the stage, the pipeline makes sure that this value has been set.
Handling	Similarly, this stage takes care of any handling charge that must be added to the order, which should be stored in the _handling_total Name/Value pair. Once again, the pipeline will verify that the value has been set in the OrderForm.
Tax	The final stage before calculating the order's total cost consists of determining the tax fees. Although the pipeline's logic only checks that the components in the Tax stage have calculated order-wide fees, it's usually a good idea to keep a per-item value as well. This is especially true if you are going to use the records from your online store directly for accounting purposes and you plan to sell tax-free items. In that case, you must be able to determine how much tax was paid and on what items. The components in this stage are expected to set at least two values, _tax_total and _tax_included, respectively used to determine what is the total amount of tax that has to be applied to the order and the amount already included in the order cost.
Order total	This stage takes care of computing the total cost of the order. This is done by summing the order subtotal, shipping, handling and tax fees. In addition, the end-of-stage logic implements the ProcessVerifyWith algorithm (described in the previous chapter) which determines whether certain information should be shown again to the user because a price has changed somewhere along the pipeline's execution. The total should be stored in the orderform._total_total Name/Value pair, which is checked at the end of the stage.

The Purchase pipeline

The goal of the Purchase pipeline is to take an OrderForm object, already processed by the Plan pipeline, and complete the purchase include therein. As such, its structure is extremely simple:

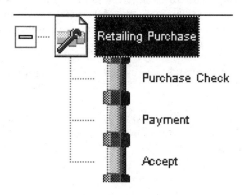

The Purchase pipeline contains only three stages:

Purchase check	This stage can be used to verify that an `OrderForm` is ready for the purchase process. This might include making sure that it has indeed gone through the Plan process (i.e. that the order total has been set, and so forth), and that all the required payment information is present. No checks are performed at the end of the stage.
Payment	The payment stage is where the actual order is processed in the most traditional sense: its goal is to either accept or refuse the order by verifying the customer's ability to pay for it. Any component in this stage should therefore be performing payment-related tasks, such as verifying a user's account status, connecting to a processor and charging a credit card, and so on. At the end of the stage, the pipeline verifies that the `_payment_auth_code` Name/Value pair is set in the `OrderForm`. This indicates that the purchase was successful.
Accept	This final stage takes care of the post-purchase activities, such as updating the inventory, storing the order, sending a confirmation e-mail to the customer, and so on. This stage is entirely optional, and it does not provide any end-of-execution logic.

Business-to-business stores and the OPP

Even if you run a business-to-business store, you will still need at least part of the functionality provided by the OPP. As a matter of fact, as we have seen while examining the MSMarket sample, the purchase process is not that different from the one of a business-to-consumer store, although the payment and order submission methods are probably going to be different.

There are two types of business-to-business OPPs: **Corporate Purchase Plan** and **Corporate Purchase Submit**. As you can imagine, they can be compared to the Plan and Purchase pipelines respectively. You can still use the Product pipeline in your business-to-business store, as it does not contain any stages that can be tied either to business-to-consumer or business-to-business electronic commerce.

The Corporate Purchase Plan Pipeline

The Corporate Purchase Plan pipeline is exactly the same as the Plan pipeline, although some of the names change because we are now talking about requisitions and buyers rather than orders and shoppers. Keep in mind that, even though we are dealing with a business-to-business scenario, the order data is still kept in an `OrderForm` object.

The following figure shows the Plan and Corporate Purchase Plan pipelines side by side, so that you can compare the stages.

> *Note that the Plan pipeline is referred to in the diagram as the Retailing Plan pipeline. As we mentioned earlier on, inside the pipeline editor the Plan pipeline's full name of Retailing Plan is used.*

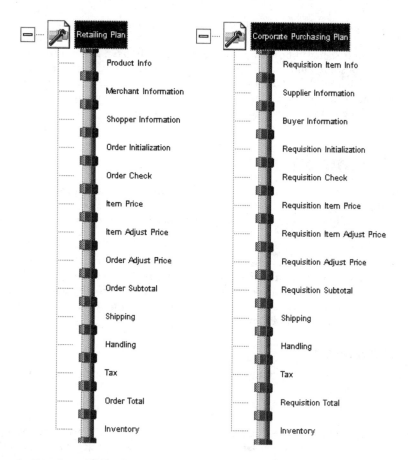

The Corporate Purchase Submit Pipeline

As you can see, the Corporate Purchase Submit pipeline only contains two stages—even fewer than the Purchase pipeline! Their goal is to simply make sure that the requisition is valid (which also includes verifying the buyer's capability of authorizing it) and to submit it to the supplier.

The Purchase Order Validate stage is intended to verify that the order can indeed be completed. This stage is really a combination of the Purchase Check and Payment stages of the Purchase pipeline that we saw a few paragraphs back, as it is also intended to verify that the party who is making the requisition has the authority to complete it. Actions that can be taken in this stage include determining the buyer's purchase limit and sending confirmation requests to a supervisor if that limit is surpassed.

The Purchase Order Submit stage, on the other hand, is a new step: it relays the order to the supplier. Naturally there are many ways of doing this, including fax, e-mail, and manual transfer. In a purely business-to-business scenario however, you will most likely have a direct link to your supplier through an interchange of some kind, such as EDI, or even a system entirely based on the Commerce Interchange Pipeline, which we'll see later on. In this case, a special pipeline component makes it possible for you to transfer the contents of the `OrderForm` to another pipeline (normally a CIP) and launch its execution, which in turn causes an interchange to take place.

Built-in OPP components

I certainly hope that what we have seen so far has helped convince you that pipelines are an excellent platform for executing certain business processes. A platform, however, is only as good as its applications, and as it usually takes time to be adopted by third-party vendors, a certain number of built-in modules must be offered with it.

Pipelines are no exception. They are certainly extensible, as we shall see in the following chapter; however MSCS also comes with a number (and quite a high one, for that matter) of components that are already built in. In this section, we'll take a look at each one of them, divided up according to which stage they belong to. As we will see, some components are ubiquitous, in that they can be used in more than one stage, or even in all of them.

Elements of a Component

From the point of view of an OPP developer, each component is characterized by five elements (in addition to the stage it belongs to):

> **Name**
> This is obviously the name of the COM object that contains the component. Since in a pipeline each component can also be given a label, the Name should be considered more properly the *type* of the component.

> **Properties**
> A component's properties represent the data that can be used to determine its behavior. This could include, for example, the name of a table, or the location of a file, and so on. Each component has its own set of properties – or even no properties at all.

> **Values Read**
> This is a list of values that are read from the `OrderForm` object by the component. It's important to understand that this list is generally provided only as a reference point, as a component doesn't have to implement it to function correctly. However, knowing what information a component accesses can be useful when trying to determine what's wrong with a pipeline (and, believe me, that'll happen often enough!).

> **Values Written**
> Similarly, this is a list of the values that the component writes to the pipeline object. Once again, it's only intended as a reference, and a component need not implement it to work properly.

> ➤ **Context Values Read**
>   This is a list of the Name/Value pairs that are accessed by a component from the pipeline's context. What was said for the other lists also applies to this one, and its role becomes important when you're adding a third-party component to your pipelines, because it might require the context to contain some specific values that are not included in it by default. It's important to note that a component is not supposed to *write* anything in the context (although this is possible, as the context is passed as a Dictionary object), because the latter is discarded and re-created every time that a pipeline is executed.

We'll start our tour of the OPP components offered by MSCS with a component that is not tied to any specific stage, and is also one of the most versatile: the Scriptor component. However, it's important to understand that, even though other components have been designed to work in one or more specific stages, you can also use them anywhere else in the pipeline, as long as the appropriate conditions exist (e.g. that all the Name/Value pairs that they need to function properly have already been set, and so on).

After the Scriptor component, we'll look at each stage in turn, and discuss the built-in OPP components available for that stage.

The Scriptor Component

The Scriptor component can be used to run scripts written with any language that is compatible with the Windows Scripting Host interface. This includes not only VBScript and JavaScript (or JScript), but also other installable languages such as PerlScript.

A neat consequence of the fact that Scriptor is WSH-compatible is the fact that it can interface to COM very easily, and therefore it allows us to take advantage of our usual arsenal of components and objects. Furthermore, there are two more advantages if you decide to use VBScript for your scripts. First, you'll most likely be very familiar with it already, since your ASP scripts work exactly the same way. Second, you'll be able to port your scripts into a Visual Basic component almost without rewriting any code, as we shall see in the following chapter.

Let's start by taking a better look at the component:

Name	Scriptor	
Properties	Scripting Engine	Specifies the scripting engine that will be used to interpret and execute the script. By default, the possible choices include the VBScript, JScript and XML engines, but you will only be able to use the first two, since XML is not a scripting language.
	Source	Determines whether the script is stored internally, as one of the component's properties, or externally in a file.
	Filename	If the source is external, this property contains the path to the file that holds the script text.
	Config	Can be used to set a number of parameters that can be used by the script. This is useful in those cases where you write a generic script that needs configuration settings.
Values Read	Any	
Values Written	Any	
Context Values Read	Any	

When you specify Internal as the source of the script, the script becomes part of the component's properties and is stored together with them. This means that, when your store loads the pipeline (more on this later on), it will also load the script at the same time. If you choose External, on the other hand, the script will be stored in a separate file and it will have to be loaded separately, causing a potential slowdown, since Windows will have to open another file, read from it, and close it. On the other hand, there are instances in which you might want to store the script in an external file because of other practical reasons, particularly if you are in the development phase and there is the necessity of changing the scripts very often.

The MSCSExecute Method

In order to work inside a Scriptor component, a script must include the MSCSExecute method defined below:

```
Function MSCSExecute (Config, Dictionary, Context, Flags)
```

Where:

Config	Is a Dictionary object that contains the configuration data for the component
Dictionary	Is the dictionary that contains the data to be manipulated by the component (e.g. an OrderForm object)
Context	Is a Dictionary object that contains the component's context
Flags	Is a reserved value

Let's look at the first three of these parameters in more detail.

The Config Parameter

The `Dictionary` object specified in `Config` contains a number of parameters, in addition to those that are specified as part of the component's properties. They are:

`Script_type`	Determines whether the script is internal or external. In the first case, it contains the string value `INTERNAL`; otherwise, it contains the string value `EXTERNAL`
`Script_text`	Contains the script's entire text.
`Script_name`	Contains the label that was given to the script within the pipeline.
`Engine_prog_id`	The name of the WSH engine that is being used to execute this script.

From a practical point of view, I have found that it is very unlikely that a script will be using any of these values, with the exception of those that are defined in the component's property box. As a matter of fact, in the long run even these are seldom used, because the scripts are usually written as self-contained entities, that either have all the data they need built-in, or take it from the `OrderForm` object.

The Dictionary Parameter

The `Dictionary` parameter is a `Dictionary` object that contains the data that must be read, manipulated and written by the component. In an OPP, this corresponds to the `OrderForm` object, from which you can read and write any information regarding the order that is being processed.

You should keep in mind a few rules-of-thumb when writing scripts (or pipeline components in general):

➢ As we already mentioned, under normal conditions you should never overwrite a value that is already in the pipeline, and you should instead assume that another component before yours has already determined the correct value for that. Naturally, there are a number of exceptions to this, depending, for example, on how your pipeline components are ordered, and on what values you are dealing with. You can check to see whether a component has been already written (or exists) in the `OrderForm` by using the `IsNull` VBScript function.

➢ It is not a good idea to trap an error using the `On Error Resume Next` statement unless you are completely sure that your script will be able to handle it. WSH and the pipeline-handling objects of MSCS provide default handling for any run-time errors and will notify the store's ASP script automatically, whereas if you fail to trap an error, but the VBScript engine has been instructed to ignore it, your pipelines will appear to work correctly and your headaches will multiply tenfold (at least). If you want to write any error-handling code, do it in your ASP scripts.

➢ Microsoft Transaction Server (MTS) contexts are not available to `Scriptor` scripts. As a result, you will not be able to create a script that is able to commit or rollback a transaction, although the script itself might run within a transaction context if the pipeline is being run using a transaction-friendly MSCS object. We'll discuss the interaction of pipelines with MTS later on in the chapter.

Context

The `Context` parameter is simply a `Dictionary` object that contains the set of values and objects that the script can use to perform certain operations. The context is created by the store as part of the loading and execution of the pipeline (we'll look more into that in the next chapter), and it can contain just about anything, starting from ASP-intrinsic objects (such as `Server` or `Request`), ADO recordsets, string and numeral values, and so on.

I should point out that, although the `Scriptor` component *does* offer a wide variety of possibilities (as a matter of fact, almost just as many as ASP!) it shouldn't be used where complex scripts are needed because of performance reasons. In those cases, `Scriptor` should only be your starting point, and you should be considering porting the component to Visual Basic (a very simple operation, as we'll see later on) or to Visual C++ if need be.

Concluding the MSCSExecute Method

The `MSCSExecute` method returns a numeral value that determines whether its execution was successful or not. A value of 1 means complete success, while a value of 2 corresponds to a status of warning: the script's execution was not successful, but the pipeline can continue running. A value of 3, finally, corresponds to total failure: not only was the script's execution unsuccessful, but the errors encountered were so grave that the entire pipeline should stop running.

Unlike a run-time error, returning a value of 2 or 3 as the result of `MSCSExecute`'s execution does not raise an error that is directly trappable from within an ASP script using the usual method. As a rule, in fact, pipeline components are required to store a description of any error they raise in two dictionaries that are part of the `OrderForm` object: `_Basket_errors` and `_Purchase_errors`. In principle, all the required error checking, once the pipeline has been executed, can be limited to simply making sure that those two `Dictionary` objects do not contain any entry (`Count = 0`).

The `_Basket_errors` collection should be used to indicate errors that are to be trapped by the basket or shipping page. It should therefore be used by components in the Plan pipeline, while the components in the Purchase pipeline should use the `_Purchase_errors` `Dictionary` object.

The MSCSOpen and MSCSClose Methods

In addition to `MSCSExecute`, a `Scriptor` script can also implement two additional methods, `MSCSOpen` and `MSCSClose`:

```
Sub MSCSOpen (Config)
Sub MSCSClose ()
```

Where:

Config	Is a `Dictionary` object that contains the configuration data for the component

`MSCSOpen` is executed before `MSCSExecute`, thus giving the script a chance to perform any initialization routine before the script is actually run. Correspondingly, `MSCSClose` runs after `MSCSExecute`, giving you a chance to perform any necessary cleanup operations before the script's execution ends.

It's important to understand that, although these three methods are defined and recognized by `Scriptor`, the script itself is fully functional, which means that you can define your own functions and subroutines, as long as they are called from within one of the three pre-defined methods (you cannot force a `Scriptor` component to call anything else directly). Thus, while the minimum script contains at least the `MSCSExecute` method, a particular case can include as many functions, variables and subroutines as you want.

> When you create a `Scriptor` component, the pipeline editors (which we'll see later on) will also create the prototypes of `MSCSExecute`, `MSCSOpen` and `MSCSClose` for you. While you are forced to use `MSCSExecute`, you might elect not to implement either `MSCSOpen` or `MSCSClose`, or both. In that case, it's a good idea to delete their declaration. This will prevent WSH from employing valuable CPU cycles trying to execute empty methods.

The Product Info Stage

As we mentioned earlier, the Product Info stage is used to load information about individual products in the order into the `OrderForm` object. As such, the only built-in component that supports this stage, the `QueryProdInfoADO` component, revolves entirely around the interaction between each item and the product database. The `QueryProdInfoADO` component can in fact be used to run a SQL query against each item in the `OrderForm`.

Here are the details of the component:

Name	QueryProdInfoADO	
Properties	Connection String	Specifies the ODBC/OLE-DB connection string to be used when connecting to the database. If no value is given, then the default connection string is extracted from the pipeline's context.
	Query	Specifies the text of the SQL query that has to be executed. Alternatively, specifies the name of the query within the store's Query Manager.
	Parameter list	Contains a space-separated list of all the Name/Value pairs that will be passed to the query.
Values Read	None	
Values Written	(Optional) OrderForm.Item._product_*	
	(Optional) OrderForm.Item._delete	
Context Values Read	(Optional) DefaultConnectionString	
	(Optional) ConnectionStringMap	
	(Optional) QueryMap	

As you can see, this component requires that a certain number of Name/Value pairs be stored in the pipeline's context in order to function properly. In fact, DefaultConnectionString, which contains the store's default ODBC/OLE-DB connection string, and ConnectionStringMap which contains an optional list of all the connection maps that the store can use, are employed by the component to extract a connection string when none is given as part of its properties.

In the property box, when an asterisk (*) is in the list of values read or written, it means "all the values in that subkey". For example:

(Optional) OrderForm.Item._product_*

means that all the values in the OrderForm.Item._product key will be accessed by the component. Also, the (Optional) prefix indicates that the component might—or might not—use any of the values in the list.

The QueryMap Object

If the Query property only contains one word – indicating that it should be considered as a pointer within the Dictionary object rather than a SQL query – QueryProdInfoADO uses the QueryMap object. Naturally, there is the possibility that you might come up with a one-word SQL query: if you're calling a stored procedure. In that case, all you have to do is use the SQL keyword EXEC to make the SQL call two words long!

The QueryMap object is used as a generic repository for all the queries used by the store. It is a Dictionary object commonly created in the global.asa file of a store (we'll see more about that in the next chapter). There is a good reason for keeping all the queries in one place: if you change something in your database, you will not have to scan your entire site to find all the places where you need to change your queries!

It's interesting to notice that the QueryMap object does not contain straight strings, but rather a collection of Dictionary objects, which, in turn, are supposed to have a Name/Value pair called SQLCommand that contains the query's actual text. The reason for this is probably to offer the possibility of adding more data for each individual query, although I have never seen it actually used, even in the sample stores provided with MSCS.

Handling SQL Queries

Regardless of whether the query is specified as a property or as part of the QueryMap Dictionary object, it is possible to store any number of parameters in it by specifying them in the Parameter List property. At the time of execution, the component will read the query, and then attempt to replace any question mark characters in it with the parameters specified in the Parameter List, one at a time. For example, if the following query is specified:

```
Select * from product where sku = '?' and name like '%?%'
```

You could use the following as the text for the parameters:

```
Item.SKU Item.Name
```

As you can see, the individual items extracted in succession by QueryProdInfoADO are given the name Item. You can also retrieve data from the OrderForm by specifying an entry without the Item. prefix.

As a result of its execution, this component stores any column from the first row of the query's result set into the item's own Dictionary within the OrderForm, using the prefix _product_. Thus, if your query returns a column called Price, after the execution of QueryProdInfoADO each item in the OrderForm object will contain the entry _product_Price. It's interesting to notice that, since the parameters set by QueryProdInfoADO start with an underscore character (_), they are not saved to disk or database by the OrderForm, as they are recalculated very often. When the OrderForm is saved in the receipt storage, however, these values *are* saved as well.

If, during its execution, QueryProdInfoADO is unable to find a product (e.g. the query that you specified returns an empty recordset when run using that product's SKU), it sets the Name/Value pair Item.Delete to 1. This can be useful to determine if a product in the user's basket is no longer available, in which case you can advise the customer accordingly.

The Shopper Information Stage

This stage only contains one component, which is called DefaultShopperInfo. Its only task is to load shopper data from the Shopper Dictionary object in the pipeline's context:

Name	DefaultShopperInfo
Properties	None
Values Read	None
Values Written	(Optional) OrderForm._shopper_*
Context Values Read	Shopper

If the Shopper dictionary doesn't contain any data, or if it doesn't exist, DefaultShopperInfo doesn't perform any operation. Keep in mind that, because a store doesn't necessarily need to maintain shopper information (and this is indeed very difficult to do, unless you request that your users register in order to make a purchase or enter the site), the use of DefaultShopperInfo and the Shopper Information stage is entirely optional.

The Order Initialization Stage

There isn't any built-in component that you can configure for this stage. The Plan pipeline does automatically implement an instance of the RequiredOrderInit component, but you wouldn't normally deal with this component as it is part of the end-of-stage logic and is not visible under normal conditions. RequiredOrderInit performs a number of cleanup procedures, including the following:

> If OrderForm.order_id is Null, then it creates a new unique order ID. (Remember, order IDs are GUIDs rendered in base 36, which makes it possible to use all the twenty-six letters of the alphabet, and therefore use fewer digits to express the number).

➢ For each item in the `Items'` `SimpleList` object, it sets the Name/Value pair `_n_unadjusted` (which expresses the number of items of any product shipped to the user before any adjustments) to the value stored in `item.Quantity`, while `_oadjust_adjustedprice` is set to zero.

➢ It sets the following values in the orderform to Null:
```
_total_total
_oadjust_subtotal
_shipping_total
_tax_total
_handling_total
_tax_included
_payment_auth_code
```

The last action ensures that the data in the `OrderForm` is reset whenever the pipeline is run, so that each component does not mistakenly assume that it had already been set.

The Order Check Stage

What we said for the Order Initialization stage applies to the Order Check stage as well. In this case, the end-of-stage logic is provided by `RequiredOrderCheck`, which simply takes care of verifying that the `OrderForm` contains at least one item. If it doesn't, the component adds the relevant error message to the `_Purchase_errors` collection.

The Item Price Stage

The goal of the components in this stage, as we mentioned earlier, is to ensure that the `Item._iadjust_regularprice` Name/Value pair for each item in the `OrderForm` is set. The `_iadjust_` prefix tells us that the price in this pair is calculated taking into account the properties of the individual item rather than the entire order.

The only component available for this stage is `DefaultItemPrice`, which copies the value of `Item._product_list_price` into `Item._iadjust_regularprice`. As you have probably noticed, `Item._product_list_price` would normally be extracted from the database by the `QueryProdInfoADO` component (incidentally, the standard MSCS product table contains a field called `list_price`!). Unless you provide your own price extraction system, you should use `DefaultItemPrice` in all your stores. Always keep in mind that the `_iadjust_regularprice` value simply represents the normal cost of the product, *before* any modifiers have been applied. Therefore, you do not normally need to perform any calculation in this stage, as all the special offers and promotions are calculated later on.

The Item Adjust Price Stage

This stage takes care of adjusting the price of each item in the `OrderForm` so that it accurately reflects any special offers or sale conditions that might be applicable. The resulting adjusted price must be saved in the `Item._iadjust_currentprice` Name/Value pair, which is checked by the end-of-stage logic.

There are two components that are offered by this stage, `SaleAdjust` and `ItemPromo`.

The SaleAdjust Component

`SaleAdjust` is the simpler of the two Item Adjust Price components. It takes care of determining whether a product is on sale and changes its adjusted price accordingly.

Name	SaleAdjust
Properties	None
Values Read	(Optional) Item._product_sale_start
	(Optional) Item._product_sale_end
	Item._product_sale_price
Values Written	Item._iadjust_currentprice
Context Values Read	None

`SaleAdjust` works by comparing the current date and time with the period between `Item._product_sale_start` and `Item._product_sale_end` and, if it falls in between the two dates, will copy the value of `Item._product_sale_price` to `Item._iadjust_currentprice`.

As you may have noticed, the sale Name/Value pairs are in the format that we would expect from the execution of `QueryProductInfoADO`, which means that there should be three fields in your product database called `sale_start`, `sale_end` and `sale_price`.

> **Note that because under normal conditions the dates in the database will be registered as of midnight for the days specified, the day stored in `sale_end` will not be included in the sale period. This means that, if you want to create a sale that lasts until April 15, you will have to specify April 16 as its last day.**

The ItemPromo Component

The other component that can be applied to the Item Adjust Price stage is called `ItemPromo`, and is a somewhat more complex version of `SaleAdjust`, with the difference that it doesn't take the information it needs from the database.

Name	ItemPromo	
Properties	Start Date	Specifies the first date on which the special offer becomes available
	End Date	Specifies the last date on which the special offer is still available
	Condition Order Key	The Name/Value pair on which the condition for the special to be available is checked
	Condition Operator	The logical operator that has to be used to determine whether the condition is true
	Condition Value	The right-hand value of the condition
	Discount Type	The type of discount (percent or dollar amount)
	Discount Value	The amount of the discount (must be an integer).
Values Read	Item._iadjust_regularprice	
	Item._iadjust_currentprice	
Values Written	Item._iadjust_currentprice	
Context Values Read	None	

Before even starting to consider its properties, `ItemPromo` verifies that the `Item._iadjust_currentprice` Name/Value pair has not already been set by another component. Then, it proceeds to verify that the conditions for the special offer are met. The component really checks for *two* conditions to be true.

The first condition is that the current date and time must fall between `Start Date` and `End Date`. These can be specified using any common date format (e.g.: 11/02/1999). The same caveat that we mentioned above, that dates are considered as of midnight, is also valid here.

The second condition is the following:

```
If Item.[Condition Order Key] [Condition Operator] [Condition Value] then apply
discount
```

As you can see, therefore, the Name/Value pair specified in the `Condition Order Key` property is always taken from the individual item's dictionary and compared to the value specified in `Condition Value` using the `Condition Operator`. For example, if we wanted to apply the discount to the product whose SKU is "123" then we'd set the component up as follows:

```
Condition Order Key:  SKU
Condition Operator:   = or ==
Condition Value:      123
```

It is important to understand that the comparison is case-sensitive, so a `Condition Value` of "ABC" is different from "abc". Also, the condition operator = is equivalent to ==, and <> is equivalent to != (as a matter of fact, those among you familiar with both Visual Basic and C – or VBScript and JavaScript – will have recognized that these operators are simply different ways of expressing the same concept in the two languages respectively).

The discount that `ItemPromo` applies can either be a percentage off the product's price, or a fixed money amount. There are two important rules to keep in mind:

> ➢ The discount can only be expressed as an integer value. For dollar amounts, it is specified in hundredths of the currency unit (thus $1 corresponds to a discount of 100). For percentage values, it is expressed in integer points, and cannot be greater than 100.

> ➢ The discount will be applied to the total price of the items, and not to their individual price. This means for example, that a $3 discount will be equally applied to an item that costs $6, whether you buy only one product (which will cost $3 after the discount) or ten (which will cost $57).

The Order Adjust Stage

While the components in the Item Adjust Price stage affect the items in the `OrderForm` individually, those in the Order Adjust stage calculate changes to their prices based on rules that involve the entire order. This includes, for example, the special offers that we saw in Chapter 15, which can be used to specify offers such as "buy x and get y at z% off", and so on.

The price resulting from the calculations–whatever they might be–must be stored in `Item._oadjust_adjustedprice`, which is checked by the end-of-stage logic. This stage is the last occasion in which the price of the items should be changed, and its results will be used by the next stages as final.

The DBOrderPromoADO Component

The only built-in component that MSCS offers for this stage is `DBOrderPromoADO`.

Name	DBOrderPromoADO	
Properties	Connection String	Specifies the ODBC/OLE-DB connection string to be used when connecting to the database. If no value is given, then the default connection string is extracted from the pipeline's context.
	Query	Specifies the text of the SQL query that has to be executed. Alternatively, specifies the name of the query within the store's Query Manager
Values Read	Item._iadjust_adjustedprice	
	(Optional) item._product_*	
	(Optional) _shopper_*	
	Item._n_unadjusted	
	Item.Quantity	

Table Continued on Following Page

Name	DBOrderPromoADO
Values Written	Item._oadjust_adjustedprice
	Item._n_unadjusted
Context Values Read	(Optional) DefaultConnectionString
	(Optional) ConnectionStringMap
	(Optional) QueryMap

DBOrderPromoADO works by applying the promotion information extracted from a database table. A connection to the database is created using either the ODBC/OLE-DB connection string specified in the Connection String property, or the default connection strings stored in the context if this is left empty. The data is generated by executing the SQL command stored in the Query property, which can also be a pointer to the store's QueryMap, (similar to what we saw when we looked at the QueryProdInfoADO component).

The amount of data that the component expects the query to return is quite massive—which shouldn't come as a surprise considering the amount of conditions that must be verified—but it's not very complex to understand:

Cond_column	The individual item's Name/Value pair that must be used as part of the condition that triggers the promotion
Cond_op	The logical operator to be used as part of the condition that triggers the promotion (expressed as a string, such as = or <>)
Cond_value	The value to be used as the right-side operator of the condition that triggers the promotion
Cond_all	An optional integer value that, if set to 1, instructs the component to override the condition that triggers the promotion. If it's equal to 0 (or any other value), the condition will be checked.
Award_column	The individual item's Name/Value pair the must be used as part of the condition that determines whether a promotion can be applied to the item.
Award_op	The logical operator to be used as part of the condition that determines whether a promotion can be applied to a specific item
Award_value	The value to be used as the right-side operator of the condition that determines whether a promotion can be applied to a specific item
Award_all	An optional integer value that, if set to 1, instructs the component to override the condition that determines whether a promotion can be applied to a specific item and force it to apply the promotion to all the items instead. If set to 0 (or any other value), the condition is verified instead.
Shopper_column	The OrderForm object's shopper data Name/Value pair that must be used as part of the condition that determines whether a promotion can be triggered by the customer who is currently making the purchase. The pair will be looked for in the OrderForm._shopper_* list.
Shopper_op	The logical operator to be used as part of the condition that determines whether a promotion can be triggered by the customer who is currently making the purchase.

Shopper_value	The value to be used as the right-side operator of the condition that determines whether a promotion can be triggered by the customer who is currently making the purchase.
Shopper_all	An optional integer value that, if set to 1, instructs the component to ignore the condition that determines whether a promotion can be triggered by the customer who is currently making a purchase.
Cond_basis	The type of check that will be made to verify whether an item meets the minimum requirements to trigger a promotion. A value of P means a price check, while a value of Q means a quantity check
Cond_min	The value that represents the minimum requirements for an item to trigger a promotion. Can be expressed either as a price (in cents, only integer numbers allowed) or a quantity.
Award_max	The maximum number of products that can be affected by the promotion
Disjoint_cond_award	A numeric value that, if set to 1, indicates that the promotion can be *disjointed*, that is, applied to the same item that triggers it.
Disc_type	The type of discount that is applied if the promotion is triggered and an item meets the minimum requirements for it. Can be either "%", for a percentage, or "$" for a dollar amount.
Disc_value	The discount that is applied if the promotion is triggered and an item meets the minimum requirements for it. Can either be a dollar amount expressed in cents (only integer numbers are allowed) or a percentage.
Date_start	The first day of the period during which the promotion is valid
Date_end	The day after the last day during which the promotion is valid

You should be already familiar with most of the concepts that these fields express – if you need to refresh your memory, you just need to take a look at what we said earlier about the SaleAdjust component.

DBOrderPromoADO Component Functionality

Before going any further into the details of the component's configuration, let's examine what this component does. Its ultimate goal is to decide whether a particular promotion (taken from the result set extracted by the query) should be applied to any product in the OrderForm. To do so, it takes into consideration the following conditions:

➤ Was the promotion intended to be triggered by this product?

➤ Was the promotion intended to be triggered when this specific user was making a purchase?

➤ Are any of the products affected by the promotion?

➤ Are they in the OrderForm?

➤ Do they satisfy a minimum requirement of price or quantity?

➤ Can the product affected by the promotions also be the one that triggered it?

681

If the promotion is triggered, then a discount is applied to all the items in the OrderForm that satisfy the other conditions. Optionally, the component can be instructed also to verify whether the current date and time fall within a specific period of time during which the promotion is valid.

As you may have noticed, there is no mention of any ranking for deciding the order in which the promotions are applied. In fact, DBOrderPromoADO doesn't know anything about ranking–it simply stops at the first record in the query's result set that triggers a promotion. In a standard MSCS store, the ranking value is used to sort the various promotions and feed them to the pipeline component, which then applies them in that specific order.

To make this clearer, here is a pseudo-code version of what DBOrderPromoADO does.

Keep in mind that this just an "artist's rendition" of what the component does. As an approximation, it loosely fits all my personal experiences with the component, but it doesn't necessarily represent an accurate reading of what the component's algorithm–which is and remains the property of Microsoft–actually does.

```
' First, set _n_unadjusted to the quantity of each Product
' We'll use this value later on to make sure that each item is only used once for
' a promotion

For Each BasketItem in OrderForm.Items
   BasketItem._n_unadjusted = BasketItem.Quantity
   BasketItem._oadjust_adjustedprice = 0
Next

' Cycle through all the items in the basket

For each BasketItem in OrderForm.Items

  ' Cycle through all the promotions

  For Each Promotion

    ' Check whether this promotion is applicable to the current customer

    If (OrderForm.[Shopper_column] [Shopper_op] [Shopper_value]) or  _
                    (Shopper_all is not Null and [Shopper_all]) then
      Goto next item
    end if

    ' Check whether promotion can be triggered by this item

    If (BasketItem.[Cond_column] [Cond_op] [Cond_value]) or  _
                      ([Cond_all] is not Null and [Cond_all]) then

      ' Check that the minimum conditions for triggering the promotion are met

      If [Cond_basis] = "P" then
        ConditionValue = BasketItem._iadjust_currentprice * BasketItem.Quantity
      Else
        ConditionValue = BasketItem.Quantity
      End if

      If ConditionValue >= [Cond_min] then

        ' Calculate how many times over the minimum conditions are satisfied
        ' The maximum award will be multiplied by the same amount
```

```
            AwardMultiplier = ConditionValue div Cond_min

         ' Iterate through all the Items again -- check whether
         ' promotion is applicable

        For Each ApplyItem in OrderForm.Items

           ' First, check if award condition is satisfied

           If (ApplyItem._product_[Award_column] [Award_op] [Award_value]) or _
                        ([Award_all] is not null and [Award_all]) then

              '. Condition satisfied -- now apply the maximum discount possible
              ' considering the number of items still unaffected

              If [Disc_type] = "%" then
                 DiscountedPrice = ApplyItem._iadjust_currentprice / _
                                 100 * (100 - [Disc_value])
              else
                 DiscountedPrice = ApplyItem._iadjust_currentprice - [Disc_value]
              End if

              ApplyItem._oadjust_adjustedprice = _
              ApplyItem._oadjust_adjustedprice + max _
              (ApplyItem._n_unadjusted, [Award_max] * AwardMultiplier) * _
                 DiscountedPrice

              ' Because each item can only be affected only once, now decrease the
              ' number of items unaffected for this product by the number of items
              ' that were affected by this promotion

              ApplyItem._n_unadjusted = ApplyItem._n_unadjusted - max _
              (ApplyItem._n_unadjusted, [Award_max] * AwardMultiplier)
           End if

        Next

         ' Promotion has been triggered -- now exit this loop
         ' And move on to the next Item

        Exit For

      End if

    Next

  Next

  ' Before exiting, add the cost of all the unaffected items to
  ' _oadjust_adjustedprice

  For Each BasketItem in OrderForm.Items
     BasketItem._oadjust_adjustedprice = BasketItem._oadjust_adjustedprice + _
              BasketItem._iadjust_currentprice * BasketItem._n_unadjusted
  Next
```

As you can see, this algorithm is pretty complex. First of all, it's important to understand one specific rule: each item in the basket can be considered part of a promotion only once. I realize that the term "item" is a little confusing—in this case it means an individual unit of a product in the OrderForm.

So, for example, if you add three books to your basket, the "book" is your product, and each of the three units you have added is an item. The number of items for each product that have not been affected by a promotion yet is stored in `Item._n_unadjusted`, initially set to the same value as `Item.Quantity` (because no item has been affected yet).

During its execution, the component progressively reduces the value of `Item._n_unadjusted` as the individual items are affected by each promotion. It's interesting to notice that, while the minimum requirements must be met in order for a promotion to be triggered, if these are exceeded by an integer number of times greater than one, the amount specified in `Award_max` is multiplied accordingly.

For example, let's consider a case in which you have a promotion that offers a fifty percent discount on 1 pair of pants if you buy three shirts. If you add three shirts and one pair of pants to your basket, you will get 50% off the pants. If you add another pair of pants, however, you will not get any discount on those, because your order only meets the minimum requirements to get discount on one item only. The only way to get a fifty percent discount on the second pair of pants is to add three more shirts to your basket.

Finally, you should keep in mind that the complexity of the algorithm above can take its toll on your server's performance, especially if you implement a large number of special offers in your store and the user is making a large purchase. In the best possible scenario, in which the first promotion in the query's result set is triggered by all products, the algorithm will make a number of iterations at least equal to the number of items in the `OrderForm` squared. In the worst case, the one in which the last promotion extracted by the query is triggered by all products, that number will increase significantly, because for each iteration through the products in the `OrderForm`, the system will be forced to iterate through the promotions as well. On average, the number of iterations (i) that the algorithm will do, can be expressed by this simple formula:

$$i = a \cdot \left(\sum_{b \lor P(k)=1}^{k=1} \left(a \cdot P(k) \right) \right) + \sum_{a}^{1} k$$

Where a is the number of items in the `OrderForm`, b is the number of promotions returned by the query, and $P(k)$ is the probability that the promotion number k is triggered by a particular item.

The Order Subtotal Stage

The goal of the components in this stage is to calculate the order's subtotal and store it in the `OrderForm._oadjust_subtotal` Name/Value pair. The only built-in component provided by MSCS for this stage is `DefaultOrderSubTotal`, which simply calculates the sum of all the `Item._oadjust_adjustedprice` values.

You won't normally need to add any other component here, unless you need to calculate the order subtotal in a particular way (e.g there has to be a minimum spending).

The Shipping Stage

As you can imagine, the task of the components that reside in this stage is to calculate any shipping costs that are associated with the order. The resulting amount should be stored in the `OrderForm._shipping_total` Name/Value pair, which is checked by the end-of-stage logic.

MSCS comes with several built-in components that have been designed to run in the Shipping stage. The simplest one is called `DefaultShipping`, and simply stores the value 0 in the shipping total pair. Clearly, you would use this component only if you are not going to apply any shipping charges to your orders.

The remaining components can be used to calculate shipping costs based on a fixed per-order amount, a per-item fee or a fee schedule stored in a database. In all cases, the determination of the shipping costs is based, at least in part, on the value of the `OrderForm.shipping_method` Name/Value pair, which contains the shipping method selected by the customer for the delivery of his or her order (e.g. regular mail, express courier, and so on). In a typical MSCS starter store, this value is selected in the Shipping page, and is usually equal to a string similar to `"shipping_method_n"`, where n is the number of the entry in the Shipping Method select box. However, you can assign any value you want to the pair, as long as it is consistent through the store *and* the pipeline.

The FixedShipping Component

The first component that we'll take a look at is called `FixedShipping`. As you can imagine, it can be used to associate a fixed shipping cost to the order, based on a specific shipping method:

Name	FixedShipping	
Properties	`Apply when`	Specifies the condition which must be satisfied by `OrderForm.shipping_method` in order for the component to apply the specified shipping cost to the order. If it is set to `Always`, then the shipping fee is applied regardless of whether the shipping method has been set. If it contains `Has any value`, then the shipping fee is applied as long as the shipping method pair contains some value (is not null). If it set to `Equal to Method`, then the fee is applied only if the shipping method pair contains a string that is exactly the same as the value of the `Method` property.
	`Method`	Contains the string to which the shipping method pair must be compared in order for the discount to apply. The comparison is case-sensitive.
	`Cost`	The cost of the shipping fee, in hundreds of the main currency (thus, the value $1 is stored as 100). Only integer values are allowed.
Values Read	`shipping_method`	
Value Written	`_shipping_total`	
Context Values Read	None	

There isn't much to say about this component, except for the fact that you can't have more than one instance of it in the same pipeline with the Apply When property set to Always. If you do, only the first one will be executed and will therefore write the appropriate shipping values in the pipeline, while the others will be ignored because they cannot overwrite previous data. Similarly, you should not put an instance of FixedShipping with the Apply When property set to Always before any other component, because this will also then not be executed.

The LinearShipping Component

A slightly more complex shipping computation system is provided by the LinearShipping component, that can be used to calculate the fees based on the multiplication of a fixed rate by one or more values in the OrderForm:

Name	LinearShipping		
Properties	Apply when	Specifies the condition which must be satisfied by OrderForm.shipping_method in order for the component to apply the specified shipping cost to the order. Same details as for the FixedShipping component, above.	
	Method	Contains the string to which the shipping method pair must be compared in order for the discount to apply. The comparison is case-sensitive.	
	Basis Item Key	Expresses the key in the OrderForm that is used as a multiplier for calculating the rate. Can be one of the following:	
		Order.[fieldname]	A specific Name/Value pair (fieldname) from the OrderForm (i.e.: Order._oadjust_subtotal).
		Sum.[fieldname]	The sum of individual values taken from each item in the OrderForm. For example, specifying Sum.Quantity is equal to ordering the sum of the Quantity values for all the items. Thus, if you have 3 shirts and 2 ties in your basket, Sum.Quantity for your OrderForm is equal to 5.
		Sumq.[fieldname]	Represents the sum of individual values taken from each item in the OrderForm multiplied by the value of the Quantity Name/Value pair for each item.
		Count	The total number of **unique** products in the OrderForm (ignoring the quantities).
	Rate	The basic rate that has to be multiplied by the result of the Basis Item Key.	

Name	LinearShipping
Values Read	(Optional) *
	(Optional) Item.*
	Shipping_method
Values Written	_shipping_total
Context Values Read	None

The meaning of the Basis Item Key can be a little confusing, but all you really have to do in order to understand it better is try to examine the framework in which the component needs to run. When calculating a shipping fee you fundamentally have three scenarios to keep in mind:

> **Per-product cost**
> The rate is applied to the order based on the amount of unique products purchased, or some other order-wide parameter. This is covered either by the *Count* or the *Order.fieldname* methods.

> **Per-item cost**
> The rate is multiplied by the number of items, or a similar value. This is covered by the *Sum.fieldname* method.

> **Per-linear quantity cost** (e.g. weight)
> The multiplier is calculated based on the amount of items times the linear quantity cost for each of them. For example, specifying Sumq.Weight, assuming that your OrderForm contains an Item.Weight Name/Value pair for each product, will cause the rate to be multiplied by the quantity for each item times its weight:

$$ShippingCost = \sum_{Count\ (Items)}^{i=1} Items\ (i).Quantity \ \cdot Items\ (i).Weight$$

The TableShippingADO Component

The third and last component that can be applied to this stage is `TableShippingADO`, which can be used to retrieve the shipping cost for the order based on the information stored in a database.

Name	TableShippingADO		
Properties	Apply when		Specifies the condition which must be satisfied by `OrderForm.shipping_method` in order for the component to apply the specified shipping cost to the order. The details are the same as for the `FixedShipping` component.
	Method		Contains the string to which the shipping method pair must be compared in order for the discount to apply. The comparison is case-sensitive.
	Connection String		The connection string that must be used to connect to the database. If no string is specified, the component looks in the pipeline context for default values.
	Query		The query that has to be executed in order to retrieve the database information. Can be either a straight SQL statement or a pointer to a `Query` object.
	Parameters		Contains a space-separated list of all the parameters that are required by the query in order to return the correct result set. Each parameter can be one of the following:
		Order. [fieldname]	A specific Name/Value pair (fieldname) from the `OrderForm` (e.g. `Order._oadjust_subtotal`).
		Sum. [fieldname]	The sum of individual values taken from each item in the `OrderForm`. For example, specifying `Sum.Quantity` equals to ordering the sum of the Quantity values for all the items. Thus, if you have 3 shirts and 2 ties in your basket, `Sum.Quantity` for your `OrderForm` is equal to 5.
		Sumq. [fieldname]	Represents the sum of individual values taken from each item in the `OrderForm` multiplied by the value of the `Quantity` Name/Value pair for each item.
		Count	The total number of unique products in the `OrderForm` (ignoring the quantities).
	Column		The name of the column in the query's result set that contains the shipping rate.
Values Read	(Optional)	*	
	(Optional)	Item.*	
	(Optional)	Shipping_method	

Name	TableShippingADO
Values Written	_shipping_total
Context Values Read	(Optional) DefaultConnectionString
	(Optional) ConnectionStringMap
	(Optional) QueryMap

Once executed, the component starts by verifying that it is compatible with the shipping method currently selected in the OrderForm, using the same system that we have already illustrated. Next, it prepares the query for execution. This is done in a way similar to the one used for the QueryProdInfoADO component: the query text initially contains a series of question marks, which are progressively replaced by the values specified in the Parameters property. When the query is ready, the component executes it and then stores the value of the field expressed by the Column property in the OrderForm.Shipping_Total Name/Value pair.

Keep in mind that only the first row of the query's result set is considered by TableShippingADO, and the value of the rate column is stored in the database as it is, without being modified in any way. Therefore, you should create your database table so that it returns the correct amount given all the possible parameters (quantity, weight, and so on). Also, the component does not allow you to calculate the shipping costs for each individual item, but only of the order as a whole.

One final note: although you can react to different shipping methods by adding an instance of TableShippingADO to the pipeline for each possible value of the Shipping_method pair, you can also incorporate this functionality in your query. In that case, all you will need to do is the following:

> Start by modifying your database table so that it can calculate the right amount for each shipping method

> Change the query so that it passes the shipping method along as a parameter

> Add Order.Shipping_method to the Parameters property

> Set the ApplyWhen property to Has any value.

Keep in mind that you should not set the Apply When property to Always, because you will most likely need the shipping method pair to have a valid value in order to make a correct computation of the shipping costs.

The Handling Stage

Components in this stage take care of calculating "handling" fees. These are usually connected to operations such as packing of the products, gift wrapping, and so on. The built-in components that are provided as part of the Handling stage perform exactly the same functions as the ones in the Shipping stage, to the point that they are based on the OrderForm.Shipping_method Name/Value pair and have very similar names. However, they store their result in the OrderForm.Handling_total Name/Value pair instead.

There are four components provided for this stage:

> The `DefaultHandling` component—similar to `DefaultShipping`—limits itself to storing a value of 0 in the handling total pair. As such, you will normally use it only when your store does not charge any handling fee.

> `FixedHandling` performs exactly as `FixedShipping`, and has the same properties. You will want to use it when you charge a fixed, per-order handling fee.

> `LinearHandling`, which provides the same functionality as `LinearShipping`, is used instead when the shipping fee is based on values such as weight or quantities.

> `TableHandlingADO`, finally, calculates handling costs based on the contents of a database table, exactly in the same way as `TableShippingADO`.

The Tax Stage

The Tax stage is used—as its name vaguely suggests—to calculate any tax charges for your items. The end-of-stage logic only checks that a value has been stored in the `OrderForm._tax_total` and `OrderForm._tax_included` Name/Value pairs, indicating the total amount of tax charged for the order, and the amount of tax that is included in the total cost of the order. Normally, the cost of the order (order subtotal) does not contain any tax amounts, so you will leave `OrderForm._tax_included` set to 0.

Contrary to what happens for shipping and handling charges, the tax fees are calculated on a per-item basis, because different items might be subject to different tax rate, or none at all. As such, it's also a good idea to store some tax information for each item, so that it will be easier later on to determine how much tax was exactly applied where.

MSCS includes several built-in components for this stage, each one designed to provide support for a particular tax model. However, you should always keep in mind that taxes are a very difficult subject to tackle (after all, they are conceived by politicians), and therefore the built-in components might not be able to adequately cover your particular situation. Since miscalculations in how you apply taxes can result in heavy losses (not to mention trouble with the government) it might be a good idea to get in touch with a tax consultant before you decide whether to use the built-in components or a third-party plug-in (there are several that provide a much more complete and up-to-date computation system).

The Default Tax Component

The simplest tax component that MSCS provides...doesn't actually calculate any taxes! It's called DefaultTax and, similar to all the other "Default" components that we have seen so far, limits itself to setting both `OrderForm._tax_total` and `OrderForm._tax_included` to zero. As before, you will want to use this component only if you decide that your store charges no taxes (this is not such an uncommon occurrence in electronic commerce, since most of the individual governments have not caught up with the fact that most of the online sales will take place outside the local area where your business resides).

The SimpleUSTax Component

If you wish to charge sales tax in the United States, you can use the `SimpleUSTax` component. As you may know, sales tax in the US is charged by the individual states, and usually applies only to those sales that fall within a state where the company that runs your store has a physical location.

Name	SimpleUSTax	
Properties	Apply when	Specifies the condition under which the value of the `OrderForm.ship_to_country` Name/Value pair triggers the component's execution. Can be set to `Always`, in which case the component is always executed, `Has any value`, which causes the component to be executed as long as the ship-to country pair has a value (is not null), or `Equal to country`, in which case the value of the pair is compared to the string stored in the `Country` property.
	Country	Contains the string to which the ship-to country pair must be compared if the `Apply When` property is set to `Equal to country`. The comparison is case-sensitive; by default, MSCS stores 3-letter ISO country codes in that pair (USA for the US).
	State Rate List	A space-delimited list of state codes and their sales tax rates. Each entry in the list consists of the two-letter state code and the percent value of the rate, separated by a colon (e.g. California, 5.4% tax = CA:5.4)
Values Read	Ship_to_state	
	Item._oadjust_adjustedprice	
	Ship_to_country	
Values Written	Item._tax_total	
	Item._tax_included	
	_tax_total	
	_tax_included	
Context Values Read	None	

Before starting the tax calculation, this component checks whether the right conditions have been met. This is decided using a method similar to the one used for the shipping and handling components. You might be wondering why you need to tell the component what country it should apply the tax to (nothing prevents you from entering anything different from USA), since it has been designed to work specifically for the United States. The reason for this is that the component conforms to a tax model that *happens* to be the one used in the States, but that could also be used somewhere else. This will become more evident later on, when we talk about the VAT tax component, which works with the tax methods used in Europe.

The SimpleCanadaTax Component

For Canadian stores, you might want to use the `SimpleCanadaTax` component, which supports the tax system used in Canada. As you may know, Canadians usually have to pay two sales taxes: the Goods and Services Tax (GST) and the Provincial Sales Tax (PST). Unfortunately, this is not always true, as in some regions the two taxes are incorporated in what is called the Harmonized Sales Tax (or HST). `SimpleCanadaTax` can handle both GST and PST, but not HST (at least not as such, as we'll see in a moment):

Name	SimpleCanadaTax	
Properties	Apply when	Specifies the condition under which the value of the `OrderForm.ship_to_country` Name/Value pair triggers the component's execution. Can be set to `Always`, in which case the component is always executed, `Has any value`, which causes the component to be executed as long as the ship-to country pair has a value (is not null), or `Equal to country`, in which case the value of the pair is compared to the string stored in the `Country` property.
	Country	Contains the string to which the ship-to country pair must be compared if the `Apply When` property is set to `Equal to country`. The comparison is case-sensitive; by default, MSCS stores 3-letter ISO country codes in that pair (CAN for Canada).
	GST Item Key	The Name/Value pair that contains the GST rate for a certain item.
	PST Item Key	The Name/Value pair that contains the PST rate for a certain item.
	Province List	A space-delimited list of two- or three-letter province codes to which the rates apply.
Values Read	Item._oadjust_adjustedprice	
	Ship_to_state	
	Ship_to_country	
	(Optional) Item.GSTKey	
	(Optional) Item.PSTKey	
Values Written	Item._tax_total	
	Item._tax_included	
	_tax_total	
	_tax_included	
	_tax_total_gst	
	_tax_total_pst	
Context Values Read	None	

You may be wondering why the GST and PST are not specified as global parameters, but rather as two Name/Value pairs within each item's dictionary. The reason for this is that Canadians do not pay the same tax rate on every project. There are cases in which only GST is applicable, others–much less frequent–in which the PST is the only tax paid, and cases in which no tax is paid at all (for example food). As such, it's not possible to apply the same tax rate to all the products.

The component gives us the possibility of specifying what the tax rate is for each product. This can be easily done if you add two fields (one for the GST and one for the PST) to your product database and store them in each item's dictionary, for example using the QueryProdInfoADO component. Keep in mind that you do not necessarily need to add two fields with the actual GST and PST rates for each product in the product table–this would pose a problem if the tax rates change. Instead, you can store the rates in separate tables and only provide "links" to them in the product table, then using the query that you pass on to QueryProdInfoADO to extract the correct rates.

The problem with the HST is obviously that the component simply doesn't support it. Even though you might be able to work around the issue by using a combination of GST and PST (which is exactly what the HST is), you will still have to provide the necessary logic to recognize the tax as HST and display it as such (which is mandatory).

The SimpleJapanTax Component

Japanese stores can use the functionality provided by the SimpleJapanTax to apply taxes for that country. This component is the only one that keeps track of the _tax_included Name/Value pair, indicating that the price of some items might already be inclusive of any applicable tax fee. When this happens, the component does not recalculate the tax for those items, storing the amount of tax already included in the price in the appropriate Name/Value pair.

Name	SimpleJapanTax	
Properties	Apply when	Specifies the condition under which the value of the OrderForm.ship_to_country Name/Value pair triggers the component's execution. Details are the same as for the previous tax component.
	Country	Contains the string to which the ship-to country pair must be compared if the Apply When property is set to Equal to country. The comparison is case-sensitive; by default, MSCS stores 3-letter ISO country codes in that pair (JPN for Japan).
	Include Item Key	The Name/Value pair that contains the amount of tax already included in the price for a certain item.
	Rate Item Key	The Name/Value pair that contains the tax rate for a certain item.
Values Read	Item._oadjust_adjustedprice	
	Ship_to_country	
	(Optional) Item.IncludeItemKey	
	(Optional) Item.RateItemKey	

Table Continued on Following Page

Name	SimpleJapanTax
Values Written	Item._tax_total
	Item._tax_included
	_tax_total
	_tax_included
Context Values Read	None

`SimpleJapanTax` works similarly to the Canadian component, in that the included tax and tax rates are extracted on a per-item basis. In this case, however, it is going to be difficult to use the same trick that we used before for the data retrieval, because the amount of tax included in each item will be entirely dependent on the item itself. In addition, you will have to adjust the amount of tax included for each product times the number of items that the customer is buying.

The SimpleVATTax Component

European stores, finally, can compute their sales tax using the `SimpleVATTax` component:

Name	SimpleVATTax	
Properties	Apply when	Specifies the condition under which the value of the `OrderForm.ship_to_country`. Details are the same as for the other tax components..
	Country	Contains the string to which the ship-to country pair must be compared if the `Apply When` property is set to `Equal to country`.
	Rate Item Key	The Name/Value pair that contains the tax rate for each individual item in the `OrderForm`.
Values Read	Item._oadjust_adjustedprice	
	(Optional) Item.RateItemKey	
Values Written	Item._tax_total	
	Item._tax_included	
	Item._tax_vat_item	
	_tax_total	
	_tax_included	
Context Values Read	None	

This component, too, works in the same way as the last two. The particular problem here is that, following the birth of the European Union, European retailers in some member states do not charge VAT only to the customers from their own country, but to all residents of the EU. As such, you can't really use the `Apply when` property to force the application of taxes on just one country, because, if you do, you will have to insert more than one copy of the component in the pipeline for doing, essentially, the same thing. A possible workaround is to "change" the meaning of the `OrderForm.Ship_to_country` Name/Value pair so that it contains a common value (i.e. "EUR") if the ship-to country is in the EU. You could do this, for example, using a small `Scriptor` component at the beginning of the Tax stage, and another one at the end to restore the original ship-to country in the `OrderForm`.

One final note about tax components: if you decide to write your own components for this stage, try to keep in mind that sometimes you must apply tax fees not only to the products, but also to the shipping and handling fees, for example. The built-in components do not do this by default, so you will have to provide the functionality yourselves (a quick `Scriptor` component will help you out in this case as well).

The Order Total Stage

After the tax stage, it's time to calculate the total cost of the order. This should be stored in the `OrderForm._total_total`. MSCS offers only one component for this stage, called `DefaultTotal`, which simply calculates the sum of the order-wide values calculated to this point (subtotal, shipping, handling and taxes).

The Inventory Stage

The Inventory stage can be used to update the inventory status of all the items in the `OrderForm` before the order is sent to the Purchase pipeline. Doing so will ensure that the user will know which products are available immediately and which ones are in backorder. Unfortunately, in order to be able to give a reasonable estimate of the product availability, you will also have to have a direct link to your line-of-business system, which, as we already mentioned, is not always a viable possibility.

Also, most online stores have settled on the standard approach of not charging their customers for backordered items until (or if) these items become available. As you may imagine, having the Inventory stage at the end of the Plan pipeline is not really compatible with this approach, and therefore you will have to be a little creative in how you handle availability-related issues. A possible solution would be to use some Inventory-stage component early in the pipeline, for example in the Product Info stage. This is certainly possible (don't forget that the stage affinity of a component is simply indicative, but not mandatory), although not particularly elegant. As an alternative, you might consider re-organizing the pipeline's stages—thus creating your own pipeline (we'll see how to do that later on in this chapter).

The LocalInventory Component

The `LocalInventory` component can be used to determine whether one or more items in the pipeline are out of stock. The `LocalInventory` component works by comparing the quantity for each item to the `Item._product_local_inventory` Name/Value pair, which can for example be loaded by the `QueryProdInfoADO` component that we saw earlier. If the quantity requested for each item is more than what is available, then the component stores the difference in the `Item._inventory_backorder` pair and, optionally, stops the execution of the pipeline so that the user can be notified of the fact that some items are in backorder.

Name	LocalInventory	
Properties	Disallow backorder	Specifies whether the component should stop the pipeline's execution if one or more items are in backorder
Values Read	Item._product_local_inventory	
	Item.Quantity	
	Item.SKU	
Values Written	Item._inventory_backorder	
Context Values Read	None	

An important characteristic of LocalInventory is the fact that it works by SKU, and not by item. This means that, if the same item appears twice in an OrderForm, the component will sum the two quantities and compare *those* to the product availability. A different approach is offered however by the FlagInventory component.

The FlagInventory Component

This component limits the inventory availability control to the individual item.

Name	FlagInventory	
Properties	Disallow backorder	Specifies whether the component should stop the pipeline's execution if one or more items are in backorder
Values Read	Item._product_in_stock	
	Item.Quantity	
Values Written	Item._inventory_backorder	
Context Values Read	None	

In this case, the inventory availability should be stored in the Item._product_in_stock Name/Value pair, which could as usual be retrieved by the QueryProdInfoADO component in the Product Info stage.

The third and final component that has affinity with the Inventory stage is called ReduceLocalInventory, and is used to update the inventory information in the product database once an order is completed. As such, that component should not be part of the Plan pipeline, but should rather be included in the Accept stage of the Purchase. We'll talk about it there.

The Purchase Check Stage

Let's move now on to the Purchase pipeline. Its first stage is Purchase Check, which, as we mentioned earlier, can be used to determine whether all the information in the OrderForm is correct and therefore payment can be applied. It's important to understand that this stage should *not* be used to process a payment, as its goal is exactly to make sure that everything else is ready before proceeding to the Payment stage.

The ValidateCCNumber Component

MSCS provides only one component that has affinity with this stage, and one that you will probably use very often! Its name is `ValidateCCNumber`, and it is used to verify that a credit card number is valid.

Name	ValidateCCNumber	
Properties	Apply When	Specifies the condition under which the value of `Order._payment_method` is verified to determine whether the component should run. It can be set to `Always`, in which case no check is done, Has any value, in which case the component runs as long as the pair is set to any value (is not null), or `Equal to method`, in which case the pair's value must be equal to the string stored in the `Method` property
	Method	A string that must be compared against the value of the `Order._payment_method` Name/Value pair. The comparison is case-sensitive.
Values Read	`_cc_number`	
	`_cc_expmonth`	
	`_cc_expyear`	
	`cc_type`	
Values Written	(Optional) `_Purchase_Errors`	
Context Values Read	None	

The component verifies that (a) the expiration date stored in the `OrderForm` is set in either the current or a future date, and that the credit card number is set to a number that satisfies the algorithm that we described in chapter 15. If one of these two checks fail, `ValidateCCNumber` interrupts the pipeline's execution and stores an error in the `OrderForm._Purchase_Errors SimpleList` object.

The Payment Stage

During the payment stage, components in the pipeline should take care of verifying that the payment information submitted by the customer is satisfactory for completing the order. Typically, this corresponds to connecting to a credit card processor and charging the customer's credit card for the appropriate amount. However, other payment methods, such as online micro-payment systems, might be used as well.

MSCS doesn't offer any particular component for this stage, its nature being so generic that you will have to integrate your own solution with the pipeline. Many third-party ISVs who develop credit card processing software, however, are beginning to offer Site Server 3 plug-ins for their products.

The end-of-stage logic here checks for the existence of the `OrderForm._payment_auth_code` Name/Value pair. If you do not need to insert any third-party component in the stage, for example because you charge credit cards manually, you can use the built-in `DefaultPayment` component, which stores the code "FAITH" in the Name/Value pair.

697

The Accept Stage

The final stage of the OPP handles all the activities that have to take place after an order has been approved by the store. This includes inventory updates, receipt storage, or even business-to-business transactions with your suppliers. Given the wide variety of tasks that can be accomplished in this stage, it's no surprise that MSCS includes a number of built-in components that have affinity with it.

One thing that we have already discussed is the inventory update. In the paragraph dedicated to the Inventory stage, I mentioned the existence of the `ReduceLocalInventory` component, which can be used to update the inventory count in the product database for each item in the `OrderForm`. Unfortunately, that component has a small—but important—problem: it doesn't support transactions, while the Purchase pipeline should always be run in a transaction-friendly environment. This is because the operations that it carries out often affect database data (not to mention "wallet" data when you charge a credit card!) and should therefore be reversible.

The same functionality offered by `ReduceLocalInventory` can however be replicated using a component which both supports transactions and is of a more generic use, and is called `SQLItemADO`.

The SQLItemADO Component

Name	SQLItemADO	
Properties	Connection String	The connection string that must be used to connect to the database. If no string is specified, the component looks in the pipeline context for default values.
	Query	The SQL query that the component is supposed to executed for each item in the `OrderForm`. Can either be a straight SQL statement or a pointer to the store's `QueryMap` object.
	Parameter List	A space-delimited list of parameters that have to be passed as part of the query.
Values Read	(Optional)	*
	(Optional)	Item.*
Values Written	None	
Context Values Read	(Optional)	DefaultConnectionString
	(Optional)	ConnectionStringMap
	(Optional)	QueryMap

`SQLItemADO` works by scrolling through the entire list of items in the `OrderForm` and executing the same query for each one of them. As in other components before this one, the SQL query can contain a number of parameters, marked by question marks in the statement. As usual, the prefix `Order.` instructs the component to retrieve a parameter's value from the `OrderForm`, while the prefix `Item.` indicates that the value should be taken from the individual item. `SQLItemADO` also recognizes two special parameters: `count` represents the number of products (individual SKUs) in the `OrderForm`, while `index` corresponds to the index, within the `OrderForm`'s `Items` collection, of the item being used by the component.

In order to update the inventory count for all the items in the OrderForm, thus imitating the behavior of the ReduceLocalInventory component, you can use a query similar to the following:

```
UPDATE prod_table SET inventory_field = inventory_field - ? WHERE sku_field = ?
```

And pass this parameter list:

```
Item.Quantity Item.SKU
```

This setup will force the component to go through the list of products in the OrderForm and effectively reduce the inventory count for each one of them by the amount set in the Item.Quantity Name/Value pair.

The SQLOrderADO Component

The SQLOrderADO component offers a functionality similar to the one provided by SQLItemADO, with the exception that the SQL query is executed only once, and its scope is the entire OrderForm:

Name	SQLOrderADO	
Properties	Connection String	The connection string that must be used to connect to the database. If no string is specified, the component looks in the pipeline context for default values.
	Query	The SQL query that the component is supposed to execute for each item in the OrderForm. Can either be a straight SQL statement or a pointer to the store's QueryMap object.
	Parameter List	A space-delimited list of parameters that have to be passed as part of the query.
	Use Child Object	Specifies whether the order information should be taken from the pipeline's main dictionary or from an object that resides within it.
	Child Object Name	The name of the Name/Value pair within the pipeline's main dictionary that holds the object from which the order information should be taken. Used in conjunction with the Use Child Object property.
Values Read	(Optional) *	
Values Written	None	
Context Values Read	(Optional) DefaultConnectionString	
	(Optional) ConnectionStringMap	
	(Optional) QueryMap	

As you can see, the only difference betweeen the two components is the concept of a "child object". If you were to specify one, SQLOrderADO would try to extract the order information from an object that resides within the pipeline's main dictionary. Now, in an OPP, the main dictionary is the OrderForm itself, and it would make very little sense to have another OrderForm object within the main OrderForm object! As such, you will probably never use this feature. However, this component can also be used in a CIP, as we'll see later on, in which the order information is not part of the main dictionary, but rather of an OrderForm object that is stored in one of its Name/Value pairs.

SQLOrderADO supports the same types of parameters used by SQLItemADO, with the following exceptions:

> The Item. prefix is not recognized

> The Sum.[pair] expression causes the component to calculate the sum of all the [pair] Name/Value pairs for each individual Item in the OrderForm.

> The same effect is obtained by using the Sumq.[pair] expression, with the difference that the sum is also multiplied by the Item.Quantity value for each item.

The MakePO Component

Another interesting inhabitant of the Accept stage is called MakePO. Its goal is to transfer the information stored in the pipeline into text format (for example, to generate a Purchase Order) using a user-specified template.

Name	MakePO	
Properties	Template Filename	The complete filename and path of the file that contains the template. Can also be set using the **Browse** button.
	Script Language for the template	The WSH language that should be used to interpret the code in the template. By default, can either be VBScript or JavaScript
	Output Property Name	The Name of the Name/Value pair where the template's output will be stored.
	Use Child Object	Specifies whether the order information should be taken from the pipeline's main dictionary or from an object that resides within it.
	Child Object Name	The name of the Name/Value pair within the pipeline's main dictionary that holds the object from which the order information should be taken. Used in conjunction with the Use Child Object property.
Values Read	(Optional) *	
	(Optional) Item.*	
Values Written	(Output Property Name)	

Name	MakePO
Context Values Read	(Optional) DefaultConnectionString
	(Optional) ConnectionStringMap
	(Optional) QueryMap

The template used by MakePO is in most respects similar to an ASP file, in that it can contain both text and scripting code. The two main differences will be that you probably will not need to use HTML in your templates, but plain text instead, and that scripts will be delimited by the symbols <%% and %%> (rather than the usual <% and %>).

In addition, the component will make the OrderForm object (either the main dictionary or the child object) an integral part of the template's scripting context, under the name Items. The OrderForm's individual Name/Value pair will also be part of the *default* scripting context, which means that you will be able to address them directly without any need for a prefix. So, for example, Items.Ship_to_country will be the same as Ship_to_country.

Unfortunately, this arrangement comes with one big string attached. In fact, you are probably used to including local variables in your ASP scripts without declaring them– assuming, of course, that you use VBScript. This is generally considered a bad habit by professional developers but, let's face it, there is nothing really wrong with it in a scripting environment (especially considering that the environment itself doesn't really care). The problem is that this is a difficult habit to lose, and it can be damaging if you use it in a template, because any variable that is not declared belongs by definition to the default context. In the case of MakePO, though, the default context is the OrderForm! This means that, if you do not declare *all* your variables using VBScript's Dim statement, you will be adding new Name/Value pairs to it.

A Purchase Order Template

As an example of what can be done with this component, let's take a look at this simple template, which creates a simple Purchase Order (PO) containing all the items in the OrderForm and their quantities.

```
<%%
  ' Make PO sample
  ' Creates a simple PO with bill-to and ship-to information
  ' and a list of all the SKUs in a table

  ' Function FormatString
  ' Formats a string with a fixed number of preceding spaces
  ' We use it to format the columns with a fixed width (will only
  ' work if you use a fixed-type font)

  Function FormatString (sString, iLength)
    If Len (sString) > iLength - 1 Then
      sString = Left (sString, iLength - 1)
    Else
      FormatString = String (iLength - Len (sString), " ") & sString
    End If
  End Function

  ' The following pre-defined array tells the script
  ' what values to extract from the item dictionary
```

Continued on Following Page

```
    Dim sItemPairs
    sItemPairs = Array ("_product_sku", "_product_name", "Quantity")

    ' The following pre-defined array tells the script
    ' how big the column for each value should be

    Dim iItemPairColumns
    iItemPairColumns = Array (10, 20, 5)

    ' The following pre-defined array contains the column
    ' headers for the table

    Dim sItemColumnHeaders
    sItemColumnHeaders = Array ("SKU", "Name", "Qty.")
%%>

Marco's Used Shoes Shack
1 Nowhere St.
Elsewhere, MD 14232
USA

Phone:  ++1-416-555-7789
Fax:  ++1-416-555-7788


  P U R C H A S E    O R D E R


  Order ID:  <%% = order_id %%>

  Ship To:  <%% = Ship_to_name %%>
       <%% = Ship_to_address %%>
       <%% = Ship_to_city %%>, <%% = Ship_to_state %%> <%% = Ship_to_zip %%>
       <%% = Ship_to_country %%>



  Bill To:  <%% = Bill_to_name %%>
       <%% = Bill_to_address %%>
       <%% = Bill_to_city %%>, <%% = Bill_to_state %%> <%% = Bill_to_zip %%>
       <%% = Bill_to_country %%>

<%%
  ' Print the column headers

  dim iCounter
  dim sSeparator

  For iCounter = 0 to UBound (sItemColumnHeaders - 1)
    %%><%% = FormatString (sItemColumnHeaders (iCounter), iItemPairColumns _
                          (iCounter)) & " " %%><%%
    sSeparator = sSeparator & String (iItemPairColumns (iCounter), "-") & " "
  Next
%%>
<%% = sSeparator %%>
<%%
  dim Item
```

```
    For each Item in Items.Items
       For iCounter = 0 to UBound (sItemColumnHeaders - 1)
          %%><%% = FormatString (Item.Value (sItemPairs (iCounter)), _
                                 iItemPairColumns (iCounter)) & " " %%>
  <%%
     Next
   Next
%%>

   Shipping Costs:    <%% = _shipping_total %%>
   Handling Costs:    <%% = _handling_total %%>
   Taxes:       <%% = _tax_total %%>

    T O T A L    <%% = _total_total %%>
```

You have probably noticed that I have not used any of the usual ASP intrinsic objects, such as `Server` and `Response`. This is because they are not available inside the template. As such, the only way to output text is by using the implicit printing command `(=)`, which sometimes forces you to use strange syntax. If your script is correct, its results will be stored in the `OrderForm`, using the Name/Value pair specified in the `Output Property Name` property.

It's reasonable to expect that, stored in the `OrderForm`, the PO will not really do you any good. In most cases, you will want to somehow get it to the outside. This can be done by combining two different components, `POToFile` and `ExecuteProcess`.

The POToFile component

The `POToFile` component takes care of saving a PO to a text file:

Name	POToFile	
Properties	Source Field Name	The Name/Value pair that contains the PO's text
	Destination	The name of the file that will receive the PO. Can be either a specific file (File Name), a file whose pathname is specified in a Name/Value pair in the `OrderForm` (File named in field) or a temporary file, which is created by the component and whose name is subsequently stored in the specified Name/Value pair (Temporary File, name saved in field).
	Append to file instead of overwriting file	Specifies whether the PO text should be appended to an existing file or if the file should be deleted altogether.
Values Read	(Optional) SourceFieldName	
Values Written	None	
Context Values Read	None	

Once the PO has been saved to a file, it can be fed to an external program, for example, for sending it over a phone line or to an EDI partner. The ExecuteProcess component can be used to run such a program.

The ExecuteProcess Component

Name	ExecuteProcess	
Properties	Path name of the executable	The complete path name of the program that has to be executed. (The anonymous user that IIS impersonates must have execute permission on the file)
	Arguments to the executable	The command-line parameters to the executable. One of the parameters can be the placeholder %1, which will be substituted with the value of the Name/Value pair specified in the Field Name of substitutable parameter property
	Field Name of substitutable parameter	Specified the Name/Value pair whose value must be substituted for the placeholder in the Arguments to the executable property.
Values Read	(Optional) SubstitutableParameter	
Values Written	None	
Context Values Read	None	

This component works by running the executable specified in the properties. Optionally, it is possible to specify a series of command-line parameters that are passed to the program, including one parameter that is taken from the OrderForm.

The SaveReceipt Component

Another important task that can be carried out in the Accept stage is saving the order information to the database. This can also be done in the ASP script once the pipeline has terminated its execution, and in fact the MSCS basic stores act in this way. However, the SaveReceipt component can also be used to store the data in the database.

Name	SaveReceipt	
Properties	No save key prefix	Specifies a prefix used to identify data in the OrderForm, which should not be saved to the database.
Values Read	(Optional) *	
	(Optional) Item.*	
Values Written	None	
Context Values Read	ReceiptStorage	

SaveReceipt works by using the properly initialized DBStorage object, which should be present in the pipeline's context in the ReceiptStorage Name/Value pair, to save all the data in the OrderForm to a database. Those Name/Value pairs whose name begins with the string specified in the No save key prefix are not saved. For example, specifying _cc_ causes all the credit-card related data not to be saved.

The PipeToPipeTransfer Component

Finally, if you are using Site Server to manage business-to-business communications with your suppliers, you will have to transfer a successful purchase to a CIP in order to send a purchase request over to the appropriate partner. You can certainly do so in your ASP scripts by first executing the OPP, then transferring the data over to a Dictionary object and using that to run the CIP, but it might be easier to use the built-in PipeToPipeTransfer component, which takes care of loading an existing CIP, transferring the OrderForm data over to it, and executing it.

Name	PipeToPipeTransfer	
Properties	Calling pipeline object	Specifies whether the OrderForm data should be taken from the calling pipeline or from a Name/Value pair thereof.
	Receiving pipeline object	Specifies whether the OrderForm data should be passed as the root of the receiving pipeline, or as a child thereof. Also, specifies whether the receiving pipeline is a Dictionary (for the CIP) or an OrderForm (for the OPP).
	Pipeline configuration filename	The pathname of the file that contains the configuration for the receiving pipeline.
	Pipeline type	The type of pipeline object that should be used to create the receiving pipeline.
Values Read	(Optional) *	
	(Optional) Item.*	
Values Written	None	
Context Values Read	(Optional) DefaultConnectionString	
	(Optional) ConnectionStringMap	
	(Optional) QueryMap	

As you can see, the component works by creating a new pipeline object (we'll discuss the MSCS pipeline objects in detail later on in this chapter), loading its configuration from the specified file, and then copying the contents of the originating pipeline into it. The newly created pipeline is then executed, and any errors reported to the originating pipeline, which continues its execution normally.

The Commerce Interchange Pipeline

After talking so much about it, we have finally come to the point where we can talk about the CIP in detail. As mentioned more than once above, its goal is to provide an ordered approach to the exchange of documents between two parties. It's important to understand that, even though the CIP provides the necessary support for both sending and receiving business documents, you do not need to have a Site Server site on both ends of an interchange in order to use it, as long as your interchange partner has the ability to understand the messages you send, and send you messages you can understand.

As a matter of fact, in most cases you will not be dealing with Site Server sites, as most of your suppliers and partners will probably still use legacy systems, such as IBM AS/400 minicomputers. Naturally, not all your interchange partners will be able to support all the advanced features offered by the CIP, so you will have to be careful about how the documents are exchanged.

Since the CIP is all about sending and receiving documents, there are only two types of pipeline to deal with here:

> **Transmit**
> The Transmit pipeline is used to – you guessed it – process a set of data into a form that is suitable for transmission to a partner, and then perform all the necessary steps for sending it.

> **Receive**
> When you're on the other end of the partnership, you can use the Receive pipeline to accept an interchange, verify its integrity, process any requests for receipts, and map it back into a form that can be used by your Site Server application.

In a CIP, the pipeline's dictionary is represented by a `Dictionary` object – not an `OrderForm` as in the case of the OPP.

Sending Documents

It's probably a good idea to spend a moment investigating a little more the meaning of the word "document" in this specific context. Generally speaking, two businesses usually "talk" to each other by exchanging one or more sets of data whose format has been pre-determined, so that one end can understand what the other sends. These are the documents that we talk about when we discuss the CIP; they can be as familiar as Purchase Order, shipping manifests and receipts, or developed specifically for a particular purpose.

The Transmit pipeline

As you can see from the following figure, the transmit pipeline has a very simple structure—six stages in total—but it's very different from the OPP:

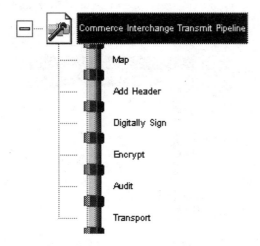

Map	The first stage in the pipeline takes care of converting the data in the `Dictionary` into a format that is suitable for transmission.
Add Header	This stage's task is to wrap a header around the dictionary data so that the receiving end knows what kind of information it is.
Digitally Sign	One of the advanced features of the CIP is the ability to digitally sign an outgoing exchange, using a digital certificate. A digital signature (which does *not* encrypt the data) can be used to verify that the data has not been changed along path that takes it from the sender to the receiver.
Encrypt	The Encrypt stage can be used to encrypt the interchange so that, even if it is intercepted before it reaches its intended recipient, unauthorized parties cannot have access to it.
Audit	Components in this stage are used to write data to a database every time that the pipeline runs. This audit information can be used to verify whether a certain transaction took place, when, and so on.
Transport	The final stage of the Transmit pipeline is used to effectively send the interchange to its intended recipient. There are many ways of doing this, although MSCS only provides components for the most commonly used Internet protocols.

As you can see, the procedure here is really to turn the contents of a `Dictionary` object (or some other object that exposes the same functionality, such as an `OrderForm`) into some form that is suitable for the transmission system used in the Transport stage. By default, all the stages work by progressively building the interchange in a Name/Value pair of the pipeline's main dictionary called `working_data`, however you can choose to use some other pair if you need to.

The Receive pipeline

The Receive pipeline pretty much follows the reverse process of the Transmit pipeline that we just saw, with a couple of exceptions. Its goal, as a matter of fact, is to "deconstruct" an interchange received by the system and turn it into a form that can be used by your application, which—as we shall see in a moment—*doesn't* necessarily need to be an ASP site.

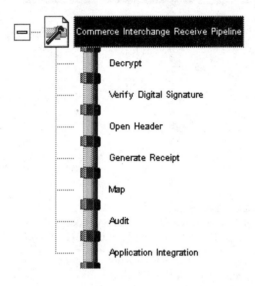

A Receive pipeline is made up of the following stages:

Decrypt	The first step in the pipeline makes it possible to decrypt an interchange (assuming that it has been encrypted in the first place). Keep in mind that you *must* know in advance whether the interchange is encrypted, and you cannot rely on a flag in the header, because the header itself will have been encrypted with the rest of the data!
Verify Digital Signature	Next, the interchange's digital signature (again, if present) is verified.
Open Header	In this stage, the interchange's header is opened, examined and removed from the interchange. This makes it possible to recognize several parameters that might have been transmitted by the sender.
Generate Receipt	If a receipt has been requested by the sender, the components in this stage can be used to generate and send it, generally using yet another pipeline.
Map	This stage is used to map the data in the interchange to an MSCS object (such as a `Dictionary` or an `OrderForm`).
Audit	Audit information is once again handled by this stage, which can be used to store a log of all the pipeline's activity into a database (or a log file, if you prefer).

Table Continued on Following Page

Application Integration	The final stage in the Receive pipeline can be used to transform the data received as part of the interchange into a form that is suitable for the uses of the application that executed the pipeline. In many cases, you will not use this stage unless you want, for example, to store the interchange data in a database, or if you indeed need to transform the data for the use of another application.

It's interesting to note the presence of the last stage, in which the data in the interchange can be transformed for use by another application. Although we will not explore this possibility in detail, it indicates that the pipeline technology can be used by many different programs, and is not limited to electronic commerce and ASP sites.

Built-in CIP Components

Let's now take a look at the built-in components that MSCS provides for use in the CIP. As we'll see, these are far fewer than those offered for the OPP, but several OPP components can be recycled for use in the CIP–we'll mention them as we will go through the various stages.

The Map Stage (Transmit pipeline)

As mentioned above, the Map stage is used in the Transmit pipeline to render the data to be sent in a format suitable for the transmission medium that is going to be used. In many cases, the best format is some sort of organized text, for example a comma-delimited string, or even XML.

MSCS provides two built-in components for this stage. One is MakePO, which we have already seen in the Accept stage of the OPP. Since it can be used to render the OrderForm data in text format, you can also use it to create the body of the interchange, if you need to.

> **Keep in mind that, when dealing with a CIP, the OrderForm is normally placed as a child object inside the pipeline's main dictionary, and not in the main dictionary itself!**

The other component that we are going to examine for this stage is called MapToXML.

The MapToXML Component

The MapToXML component can be used to map an entire dictionary into XML format. The main difference between MapToXML and MakePO is that the former automatically maps an entire object, whereas the latter relies on your scripts to do so. In addition, MapToXML is able to persist entire COM objects that are stored inside the dictionary, as long as they support the appropriate COM persistence functionality.

Name	MapToXML	
Properties	Object source key	Specifies the name of the Name/Value pair where the source dictionary is located. The component determines the object type of the dictionary automatically.
	Results XML key	The name of the Name/Value pair that will contain the component's XML output
	Preferred data format	The format that should be used to render the dictionary in XML. If XML Tags is selected, then the object is rendered using a series of text-only XML tags, whereas selecting Encoded Binary will cause the component to simply encapsulate the object's binary representation within simple XML tags.
Values Read	ObjectSourceKey	
Values Written	ResultsXMLKey	
Context Values Read	None	

In most cases, you will want to make sure you're using the XML Tags format, which renders the entire object using exclusively text – this would be a solution if you were planning to send data through e-mail or HTTP posts. In addition, you should keep in mind that only persistable COM objects – those that support either the standard IPersistStreamInit COM interface, or the Site Server-defined IPersistXML interface – will be rendered by the component. Non-persistable objects will simply be ignored.

Finally, it's important to understand that, if you render an object in XML expecting to be able to rebuild the object entirely at the other end of the interchange, you should make sure that all the components you are persisting are also installed on the recipient's computer.

The Add Header Stage

The Add Header stage is used to encapsulate the data that has to be sent over so that the recipient will be able to identify the kind of data it's receiving, where it's coming from, and so on. MSCS offers two components for this stage: AddHeader and EncodeMIME.

The AddHeader Component

AddHeader can be used to add a custom header that encapsulates the following information:

➤ Unique transaction ID (generated by the component)
➤ Receipt request
➤ Date and time the request was sent
➤ Type of the document
➤ Source of the document
➤ Destination of the document

The header generated is appended to the data as a series of XML tags, and can only be decoded if at the other end of the interchange there is a Receive pipeline properly set up.

Name	AddHeader	
Properties	Input field	Specifies the location of the interchange data within the pipeline's main dictionary. This will usually be the output of `MapToXML`.
	Output field	The name of the Name/Value pair that will contain the component's output. Will normally be the same as `Input field`, but it can be different if required.
Values Read	InputField	
	Receipt_requested	
	Document_type	
	Document_source	
	Document_destination	
	Txid	
Values Written	Txid	
	OutputField	
Context Values Read	None	

The EncodeMIME Component

If you are planning to send your data via e-mail or HTTP, you might want to encode it using the `EncodeMIME` component, which turns your interchange data into the Internet-standard MIME format.

Name	EncodeMIME	
Properties	Content Type	Specifies the content type of the MIME-encoded data. The three values allowed by the component (`UN/EDIFACT`, `ANSI X12` and `EDI-Consent`) correspond to three well-known EDI systems in use throughout the world.
	Content encoding	Specifies the method through which the data itself should be encoded. Can be `Quoted Printable`, which allows only for the use of the standard ASCII character set in the data, or `Base64`, which encodes extended characters and binary values as well.

Table Continued on Following Page

711

Name	EncodeMIME	
Properties	`Read from field`	Specifies the location of the interchange data within the pipeline's main dictionary.
	`Write to field`	The name of the Name/Value pair that will contain the component's output. Will normally be the same as `Read from field`, but it can be different if required.
Values Read	`ReadFromField`	
Values Written	`WriteToField`	
Context Values Read	None	

The MIME encoding system is a standard used by many Internet applications, such as web browsers and e-mail clients, to exchange data over the network. MIME makes it possible to easily recognize the type of data being transmitted—and therefore invoke the appropriate handler—and properly encodes the information so that it can be sent safely through common Internet systems.

> *The need for data encoding is not due to limitations in how the Internet works, as many seem to think, but rather is due to how these protocols were originally designed. In fact, most protocols were designed for terminals that only knew the standard 7-bit ANSI ASCII. As a consequence, for compatibility reasons, it's impossible to send extended ASCII codes (which are 8 bits long) or common binary data through many e-mail systems. Therefore, the information must be encoded with some system that turns 8-bit long bytes into 7-bit long strings, such as Base64.*

The Digitally Sign Stage

Digital signatures are an interesting method of calculating a checksum of a set of data and expressing it in such a way that it cannot be tampered with. They can therefore be used to check whether data has been modified since it was initially signed. This is an important step, especially if you decide to transmit your interchanges over a public network such as the Internet—just think of the damage that a hacker could do!

There are two pipeline components for this stage: `DigitalSig` and `EncodeSMIME`.

The DigitalSig Component

`DigitalSig` can be used to calculate the digital signature of an interchange and then store it as part of the data that has to be sent over. The digital signature can be calculated using any of the algorithms available on your computer, and either appended to the data as an XML tag or encoded together with the rest of the interchange using the Public Key Crypto System (PKCS).

Name	DigitalSig	
Properties	Signature [and message] in xxx format	Specifies how the interchange and the signature should be formatted. It's possible to store both of them in XML format (Signature and Message in XML format) or in the PKCS format (Signature and Message in PKCS7 format). Optionally, it is also possible decide to leave the interchange as-is and simply store the signature in the PKCS format (Signature only in PKCS7 format).
	Input field	Specifies the location of the interchange data within the pipeline's main dictionary.
	Signed output field	The name of the Name/Value pair that will contain the component's output. Will normally be the same as Input field, but it can be different if required.
	Hash algorithm	Specifies the algorithm used to calculate the digital signature. The actual list of algorithms available depends on the algorithms that are installed on your computer and their strength.
	Hash Algorithm ID Field	The field where the component will store the ID of the algorithm used to calculate the digital signature.
	Signer Certificate	The digital certificate that should be used to sign the data. Using a digital certificate will enable the recipient not only to verify that the data's integrity has not been corrupted, but also who the sender really is.
Values Read	InputField	
Values Written	SignedOutputField	
	HashAlgorithmIDField	
Context Values Read	None	

This component takes advantage of the Microsoft Crypto-API to perform all the necessary signature and formatting functions. The Crypto-API is a standard component of many newer Microsoft applications, such as IIS4, IE4 and higher, and so on. Its most interesting feature is the fact that it only provides a generic encryption, decryption and digital signature interface layer, while the actual functionality is provided by an arbitrary number of plug-ins. Depending on what plug-ins you have installed on your server, you will be able to use different algorithms to encrypt and sign your data.

> In order to use an encryption or signing algorithm, it must be installed both on the originating and destination server. If the algorithm is only installed on the originating server, the destination server will not be able to verify the interchange's digital signature or, even worse, to decrypt the interchange in the first place!

The EncodeSMIME Component

The EncodeSMIME component can be used to encrypt and digitally sign the interchange using the Internet-standard SMIME format.

It should be pointed out that SMIME was not yet a standard when Site Server was released into the market. As such, this component supports a draft of the standard that is not compatible with its final version.

Name	EncodeSMIME	
Properties	Operation	Specifies what kind of action should be carried out by the component; Plain text forces the component to leave the interchange as it is (no operation), Sign instructs the component to digitally sign the interchange, Encrypt causes the interchange to be encrypted. Sign and encrypt causes the interchange to be both signed and encrypted.
	Character set	Specifies the character set to be used in the output. The character set chosen must be installed in the system in order for the component to work properly.
	Signature Certificate	The digital certificate which will be used to digitally sign the interchange.
	Encryption Certificate	The digital certificate used to encrypt the interchange.
	Signature Algorithm	Specifies what algorithm to use to digitally sign the interchange. The actual list changes, depending on the algorithms that you have installed on your server.
	Encryption Algorithm	Specifies the algorithm used to encrypt the exchange. As for the Signature Algorithm property, the list will only display those algorithms that you have installed on your server.
	Read from field	Specifies the location of the interchange data within the pipeline's main dictionary.
	Write to field	The name of the Name/Value pair that will contain the component's output. Will normally be the same as Read from field, but it can be different if required.
Values Read	ReadFromField	

Name	EncodeSMIME
Values Written	WriteToField
Context Values Read	None

As you can see, the functionality of this component does not strictly apply solely to the Digitally Sign stage – it is also relevant to the Encrypt stage. Keep in mind that, while you will use your own digital certificate to sign the interchange – thus signaling that you are its originator – you will need to use the recipient's certificate to encrypt it. If you don't, the recipient will not be able to decrypt the message!

As before, if you decide to use this component, you should make sure that the algorithms you choose are installed and properly selected on both ends of the interchange.

The Encrypt Stage

There are two components built-in for the Encrypt stage. One is EncodeSMIME, which we've just seen. The other is EncryptPKCS.

The EncryptPKCS Component

The EncryptPKCS component can be used to encrypt the interchange using one of the algorithms supported by the Microsoft Crypto-API.

Name	EncryptPKCS	
Properties	Plain text field	Specifies the location of the interchange data within the pipeline's main dictionary.
	Encrypted text field	The name of the Name/Value pair that will contain the component's output. Will normally be the same as Plain text field, but it can be different if required.
	Encryption Algorithm	Specifies the algorithm to be used when encrypting the exchange.
	Receiver certificate	Specifies the digital certificate that should be used to encrypt the exchange.
Values Read	ReadFromField	
Values Written	WriteToField	
Context Values Read	None	

If you are thinking that there is a little redundancy in the functionality provided by the encryption and signing components that we have seen so far, you're right—and you're not. As a matter of fact, EncodeSMIME alone performs almost the same tasks as DigitalSig and EncryptPKCS together, with one important exception: it also formats the data according to the SMIME specifications. Now, this is fine if you are going to send the data through the Internet and your interchange partner is able to handle SMIME. Many legacy systems, however, might be able to handle public-key encryption, but not SMIME, which is a relatively new standard. As such, you will want to use EncodeSMIME when sending data through the Internet to another CIP, while DigitalSig and EncryptPKCS should be used in all the other cases.

The Audit Stage (Transmit pipeline)

This stage takes care of saving certain information from the dictionary into a database, so that a permanent trace of the pipeline's execution is left behind. The audit data can become useful, for example, to keep track of what transmissions have been received by your partners. All you have to do is audit the transmission, request a receipt, audit the receipt and cross-relate the database information to verify that an interchange has been received correctly.

The only component provided by MSCS for this stage is called – as the imaginative among you might have already guessed – Audit.

The Audit Component

The Audit component writes an arbitrary number of Name/Value pairs to a user-specified database.

Name	Audit	
Properties	Connection String	Specifies the connection string to be used when connecting to the database. If no string is specified, the default connection string is taken from the pipeline's context.
	Table	The name of the table that will receive audit information.
	Add a field/Fields to record	Specifies a list of Name/Value pairs that will be saved in the database table.
Values Read	(Optional) *	
	Txid	
Values Written	None	
Context Values Read	(Optional) DefaultConnectionString	
	(Optional) ConnectionStringMap	

In order for Audit to work properly, you will need to make sure that the table contains the appropriate number of fields, and that those fields are named exactly as the Name/Value pairs they will be mapped to. Keep in mind that the component will automatically map the two Name/Value pairs Txid and utc_datetime, which indicate the transaction ID created by the AddHeader component and the Universal Coordinated Time at which Audit was run.

The Transport Stage

The last stage of the Transmit pipeline takes care of sending an interchange through the appropriate medium. As mentioned above, MSCS only provides built-in components for the most used Internet protocols, such as SMTP, HTTP and DCOM transmissions. If you are going to be dealing with more "traditional" partners, however, you will most likely need to write your own components for communicating with them, because they won't be accessible through the Internet but through some other network, such as DataPAC or EDI.

The SendSMTP Component

The `SendSMTP` component sends interchanges using the Simple Mail Transport Protocol, which is used to transmit Internet e-mail:

Name	SendSMTP	
Properties	From	Specifies the identity of the message's sender.
	SMTP Host	Specifies the IP of the SMTP server that will be used to send the message.
	To	The Name/Value pair in the dictionary that contains the e-mail address(es) of the message's recipient(s).
	CC	The Name/Value pair in the dictionary that contains the e-mail address(es) of the carbon-copy message recipients
	Subject	The Name/Value pair that contains the message's subject
	Character set for subject	The character set to be used for encoding the message body.
	Message Body	The Name/Value pair that contains the message body (will generally be the interchange itself)
	Message Body contains	Specifies the format of the message body. If MIME header and body or Text body are selected, then the component will not perform any further processing, while selecting Binary body causes the component to encode the message using Base64.
Values Read	To	
	CC	
	Subject	
	MessageBody	
Value Written	None	
Context Values Read	None	

It's interesting to notice that you can send the e-mail to multiple recipients by separating them using a semicolon. In addition, keep in mind that the use of this component is not limited to the CIP–and to this specific stage. In fact, you can use it in the OPP to send a purchase confirmation (for example, by using the MakePO component to create a receipt), or in the CIP to request supervisorial authorization if an order exceeds the customer's purchase limit.

The real problem with using e-mail to send your interchange is that, in most cases, you will not be able to automatically trigger the execution of a Receive pipeline if your partner also runs an MSCS site. In fact, the only way to do so is by using a mail server that supports scripting and that will let you execute a process whenever a new message arrives, such as Microsoft Exchange.

The SendHTTP Component

A better solution is offered by the SendHTTP component, which can be used to transmit your interchanges using the HTTP protocol, which is normally used by your browser and web servers. In this case, the HTTP POST action will cause the recipient's web server to launch a script, and the automatic execution of a pipeline becomes thus possible.

Name	SendHTTP	
Properties	URL	Specifies the URL that has to be invoked at the recipient's end.
	Field to be posted	The Name/Value pair to be posted as part of the component's operation (normally the pair that contains the interchange).
	As type	Specifies how the data should be posted to the server.
	Store response in field	The Name/Value pair (optional) in which the component will store the remote server's response.
	From Type	Specifies the format in which the response will be transmitted by the remote server.
Values Read	FieldToBePosted	
Values Written	(Optional) StoreResponseInField	
Context Values Read	None	

You should make sure to examine the response that the remote server sent back from the remote server, because the component will report connection problems (e.g. server not found, unable to connect, and so on), but not HTTP failures.

The SendDCOM Component

Finally, the "high-high-tech" way to send your interchanges to another MSCS host is by using the SendDCOM built-in component. This will cause an instance of the ReceiveDCOM2.dll (which is also built-into Site Server) to be created at the recipient's end. ReceiveDCOM2.dll is able to create an instance of a pipeline object, load a pipeline and execute it with the interchange transmitted by the sender.

Name	SendDCOM	
Properties	Machine name	The name of the receiving machine (can be either a UNC name or an Internet IP).
	From field	The Name/Value pair that contains the interchange.
	To field	The Name/Value pair in which the interchange will be stored in the remote pipeline's main dictionary
	PCF File Name	The name of the remote file that contains the Receive pipeline to be run by ReceiveDCOM2.dll
	Transacted pipe	Specifies whether the remote pipeline should be executed in a transaction-friendly environment.
Values Read	FromField	
Values Written	None	
Context Values Read	None	

The Decrypt Stage

It's now time to move on to the Receive pipeline. As you have already seen before, its first stage takes care of decrypting the interchange data (assuming, naturally, that it has been encrypted in the first place). The components in this stage correspond somewhat to similar components in the Transmit pipeline, with the exception, of course, that they perform the opposite tasks.

The DecryptPKCS Component

DecryptPKCS can be used to decrypt an interchange that had been encrypted using the EncryptPKCS component.

Name	DecryptPKCS	
Properties	Encrypted text field	Specifies the location of the interchange data within the pipeline's main dictionary.
	Plain text field	The name of the Name/Value pair that will contain the component's output. Will normally be the same Encrypted text field, but it can be different if required.
	Text output	Specifies whether the interchange data should be saved in text rather than binary format. Your choice should depend on whether you had text data to start with.
	Write certificate used for decryption to field	Specifies the name of the Name/Value pair used to store the name of the digital certificate used to decrypt the interchange.
Values Read	EncryptedTextField	
Values Written	PlainTextField	
	WriteCertificateUsedForDecryptionToField	
Context Values Read	None	

The component is able to automatically determine what digital certificate should be used to decrypt the interchange, as long as that certificate is indeed installed on your computer. If the required certificate is not available, the component will raise an error and cause the pipeline to fail.

The DecodeSMIME Component

If the Transmit pipeline was instructed to use the EncodeSMIME component to encrypt and/or digitally sign the interchange, you can use the DecodeSMIME component in your Receive pipeline in order to decrypt the interchange and verify its digital signature.

Name	DecodeSMIME	
Properties	Read from field	Specifies the location of the interchange data within the pipeline's main dictionary.
	Write to field	The name of the Name/Value pair that will contain the component's output. Will normally be the same as Encrypted text field, but it can be different if required.
	Write signature certificate to field	Specifies the name of the Name/Value pair used to store the name of the certificate used to digitally sign the interchange.
	Write crypt certificate to field	Specifies the name of the Name/Value pair used to store the name of the digital certificate used to decrypt the interchange.
Values Read	ReadFromField	
Values Written	WriteToField	
	WriteSignatureCertificateToField	
	WriteCryptCertificateToField	
	Signature_result	
Context Values Read	None	

This component decodes the contents of the interchange, assuming they have been encoded using the SMIME protocol, and verifies that the digital signature (if present) is valid, storing the verification results in the signature_result Name/Value pair of the main dictionary. If the interchange has been encrypted, it also decrypts it. Once again, you must have the decryption digital certificate installed on your machine in order for the decryption process to work properly. You do not need to have the signature certificate installed, however.

The Verify Digital Signature Stage

The DecodeSMIME component can also belong to the next stage in the pipeline, which is dedicated to the verification of the interchange's digital signature. This also happened in the Transmit pipeline with the EncodeSMIME component, mainly because of the fact that SMIME's functionality spans both stages.

The VerifyDigitalSig Component

If the sender of the interchange opted *not* to use SMIME to encode the data, but relied on DigitalSig to sign it, you can use the VerifyDigitalSig component to verify the validity of the signature.

Name	VerifyDigitalSig	
Properties	Verify signature and Message in… format	Specifies the format of the digital signature. Depends on what was selected in the Transmit pipeline for the DigitalSig component
	Message field	The Name/Value pair that will contain the interchange
	Signature	If Verify Signature Only in PKCS7 Format was selected, specifies the Name/Value pair that contains the digital signature data.
	Verified Message field	The output field for the component. If both the signature and the message are verified, the component writes the original interchange (without the signature) into this field.
	Text/Binary output	Specifies whether the verified interchange should be written as binary or text data.
	Write certificate used to verify signature to field	Specifies the Name/Value pair where the component will write the name of the certificate used to verify the signature.
Values Read	MessageField	
	(Optional) Signature	
Values Written	VerifiedMessageField	
	WriteCertificateUsedToVerifySignatureToField	
Context Values Read	None	

The Open Header Stage

This stage takes care of "unwrapping" the interchange and stripping it of its header (assuming it has one). MSCS provides a built-in component, called OpenHeader for this stage.

The OpenHeader Component

This component takes care of mapping the contents of a header created by the `AddHeader` component that can be run in the Add Header stage of a Transmit pipeline.

Name	OpenHeader	
Properties	Input field	Specifies the location of the interchange data within the pipeline's main dictionary.
	Output field	The name of the Name/Value pair that will contain the component's output. Will normally be the same as the `Input field` property, but it can be different if required.
Values Read	InputField	
Values Written	OutputField	
	Txid	
	(Optional) msg_digest	
	(Optional) return_receipt_requested	
	(Optional) document_type	
	(Optional) document_source	
	(Optional) document_destination	
	Send_datetime	
Context Values Read	None	

You are probably already familiar with most of these fields, since we have examined them as part of the `AddHeader` component description. Perhaps the one you have not seen yet is `msg_digest`, which simply represents a "digest" of the interchange—a sort of a "recap" of the message that was sent across by the originator that can be used as the body of a receipt, as we shall see in the next paragraph. The originator also sends across the algorithm with which the digest must be computed by the component.

The DecodeMIME Component

Alternatively, if the originator used `EncodeMIME` to add a header to the interchange, you can use the corresponding `DecodeMIME` component in the Receive pipeline to unwrap the interchange and store your data (still to be mapped) in the `Dictionary` object.

Name	DecodeMIME	
Properties	Read from field	Specifies the location of the interchange data within the pipeline's main dictionary.
	Write to field	The name of the Name/Value pair that will contain the component's output. Will normally be the same as Read from field, but it can be different if you need so.
Values Read	ReadFromField	
Values Written	WriteToField	
Context Values Read	None	

The Generate Receipt Stage

If the originator of your interchange has requested that a receipt be sent back to it when the recipient processes the message, you will want to include any component that takes care of doing so here. It's interesting to notice that a "receipt" is nothing more than another interchange, and as such will have its own Transmit pipeline and–if another MSCS site is at the other end–its own Receive pipeline as well.

In the standard MSCS environment, the system will expect a request for a receipt to be stored in the return_receipt_requested Name/Value pair, while the receipt itself will be stored in the receive_msg_digest pair.

The GenerateReceipt Component

The only built-in component provided for this stage is GenerateReceipt, which can be used to launch a Transmit pipeline for sending a receipt back to the originator.

Name	GenerateReceipt	
Properties	Send Receipt PCF Filepath	The path name of the configuration file for the Transmit pipeline to be used for sending the receipt over to the interchange's originator
Values Read	Receipt_requested	
	Txid	
	Receive_msg_digest	
	Receive_digest_algorithm	
	(Optional) Document_type	
	Receive_datetime	
	(Optional) Document_source	
	(Optional) Document_destination	
Values Written	None	
Context Values Read	None	

GenerateReceipt works by creating a new pipeline object, loading the configuration file specified in the Send Receipt PCF Filepath property, and then copying all the values it reads from the originating pipeline into the new pipeline's main dictionary.

> **Transmit pipelines for return receipts should never include a request for another receipt in their interchange. If they do, you can end up into a loop in which receipts are endlessly exchanged between the two interchange partners. A good way to protect yourselves from this problem is to ignore return receipt requests in your Receive pipelines for receipts.**

The Map Stage (Receive pipeline)

Components in this stage are dedicated to mapping the contents of the interchange – which, by now, should have been decrypted, digitally verified, and stripped of any header – back into the MSCS object that originated them (or in the appropriate MSCS object if the originator was not using Site Server). The only built-in component provided by MSCS is complementary to the MapToXML component that can be inserted in the Map stage of a Transmit pipeline.

The MapFromXML Component

As you can image, `MapFromXML` is used to turn the contents of an XML interchange into a copy of the MSCS object that was originally used to create it.

Name	MapFromXML	
Properties	XML Source key	Specifies the Name/Value pair that contains the XML-mapped interchange, decrypted and stripped of any header or encoding.
	Result Object Key	The name of the Name/Value pair that will contain the component's output.
Values Read	XMLSourceKey	
Values Written	ResultObjectKey	
Context Values Read	None	

It's important to remember that if the MSCS object that was originally mapped to XML contains any objects, these will only be presented in `MapFromXML`'s output if the COM components of which they are instances are installed on the receiving server.

The Audit Stage (Receive pipeline)

As in the Transmit pipeline, the Audit stage can be used to write a log of the transactions that take place inside a Receive pipeline, normally to a database or to a file.

The `Audit` component that we saw in the corresponding stage of the Transmit pipeline can be used here as well to save certain elements of the exchange to a database table. If your Receive pipeline has been designed to handle receipts, however, you might want to use the `AuditReceipt` component to update your log information with regards to a specific transaction.

The AuditReceipt Component

Name	AuditReceipt	
Properties	Input field	Specifies the Name/Value pair that contains the receipt information received by the pipeline.
	Connection String	The connection string to be used to connect to the database. If nothing is specified, the component attempts to retrieve the default connection string from the pipeline's context.
	Table	Specifies the name of the table where the component should write the receipt information.
Values Read	InputField.receive_datetime	
	InputField.txid	
	InputField.receive_msg_digest	
	InputField.receive_digest_algorithm	
	InputField.document_type	
Values Written	None	
Context Values Read	(Optional) DefaultConnectionString	
	(Optional) ConnectionStringMap	

To better understand the basis on which this component works, you should keep in mind that, in a Receive pipeline created to handle receipts, the receipt data *is* the interchange itself. Therefore after all the operations of decryption, header management and mapping, you will end up with a dictionary containing the data which is read by AuditReceipt.

The component works by opening a connection to the database and mapping the Name/Value pairs from the receipt data into the fields of the database table that have the corresponding name (which *must* have the same name as the pairs). The txid field is used as a primary key. AuditReceipt attempts first to create a new record in the database; if that operation fails because of a primary key violation, the component proceeds to update any existing record instead.

The following figure shows the whole process of exchanging a complete interchange.

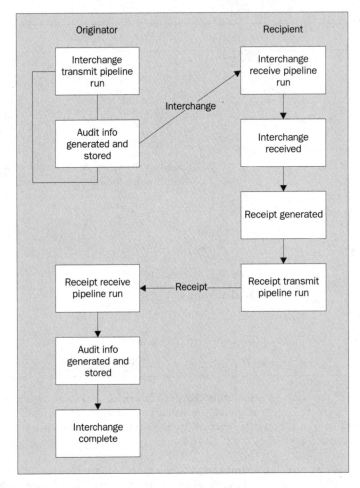

As you can see, a record in the audit database is created at first when the Transmit pipeline is called, and is *updated* when receipt information is received by the originator—thus making sure that the transmission was entirely successful.

In an interactive environment, you may elect to use a timeout mechanism to determine whether a transmission is successful: if a receipt is not sent back within a certain timeframe, the originator assumes that the recipient did not receive the interchange and sends it again. Naturally, in this case, you will have to make sure that the interchange is marked as a duplicate, so that if the recipient has indeed received the original interchange, but the receipt never made it back to the originator, no duplicates are created by mistake.

Unfortunately, you cannot use timers in ASP applications, and therefore you will have to get a little creative in how you decide to handle this issue. A simple solution is to create a WSH script that simply verifies what transactions are still open and proceeds to re-send the interchanges that have not been acknowledged after the prescribed amount of time. You can schedule the execution of this script by using the Windows NT Scheduling System (or similar software).

The Application Integration Stage

The final stage in the pipeline, as we mentioned above, is used to transform the data extracted from the interchange so that it can be used in your own application. In most cases, if you are running an ASP application, you will not need to use this stage at all, since the end result of the pipeline will be a dictionary that you can already use in your scripts.

Let's not forget, however, that pipelines are a totally COM-based affair and, as such, you might think of running them from within another type of application, like a Visual Basic or Visual C++ executable. If you consider how much easier pipelines make it to exchange information in an ordered manner, this is not such an unreasonable possibility. In this case, you may want to transform the dictionary data into a form more suitable for your programs in this stage—you could, for example, turn the information into a file (i.e. comma delimited), or store it into a database.

Because the scope of this stage is so generic, MSCS does not provide any built-in component that has affinity with it.

Small is Beautiful: Micropipes

Finally in this chapter we're going to take a quick look at micropipes. Once you've worked with pipelines for long enough, you begin to wonder (a) why there are no branching capabilities in the pipeline technology and (b) how nice it would be to execute a pipeline component without needing to load and execute an entire pipeline.

While there is no immediate solution to the first problem, you can work around the second by creating a custom pipeline that only contains one stage and one component, but that leaves you with a system that wastes a lot of system resources, since the pipeline configuration will have to be loaded every time, and the overhead of running an entire pipeline versus just a component will become apparent.

MSCS, however, includes a component, called `MicroPipe`, which can be used to execute a single pipeline component. `MicroPipe` offers functionality similar to that provided by the pipeline objects we'll see in the next chapter, including activity logging, but doesn't support transactions in any way.

Using the Micropipe Component

To use a `Micropipe` we first need to create and set the component that we want the `Micropipe` to execute. We do this in three steps.

First we create a `Micropipe` instance with a call to `Server.CreateObject`.

```
Set mPipe = Server.CreateObject ("Commerce.MicroPipe")
```

Next we want to create the component instance that our `Micropipe` will execute. In this example we're going to execute a `FlagInventory` component.

```
Set obj = Server.CreateObject ("Commerce.FlagInventory.1")
```

We would then pass the component, `obj`, to the micropipe's `SetComponent` method:

```
mPipe.SetComponent (obj)
```

> *You can find out what the correct Program ID for the built-in components are by looking at their properties in the Win32 editor. For example, the FlagInventory component is registered as* `Commerce.FlagInventory.1`.

Executing the Component

The `MicroPipe` component provides an `Execute` method that is in all aspects the same as the one offered by the other pipeline objects:

```
MicroPipe.Execute (MainDictionary, Context, Reserved)
```

Where:

> ➤ `MainDictionary` is the pipeline's main dictionary
> ➤ `Context` is the pipeline's context
> ➤ `Reserved` is a reserved long value which must be zero.

As for the other pipeline objects, the execution of a `MicroPipe` will return a long integer value of 1 for success, 2 for a recoverable error and 3 for an unrecoverable failure.

You can also set the component to log its activities, using the `SetLogFile` method:

```
MicroPipe.SetLogFile (sFilename)
```

Where `sFilename` is the complete path of the log file.

> **If you wish to run more than one component in the same page using `MicroPipe`, you can do so by reusing the same `Micropipe` instance over and over again—you don't need to create a new one every time.**

Using MicroPipes to Simulate Branching in a Pipeline

If you have an absolute need for having branching capabilities in a pipeline, you can use the `MicroPipe` component to do so, even though the result will neither be easy to maintain, nor provide good performance.

This technique consists fundamentally in writing a script (I recommend an include file, which will be easier to maintain) in which the execution of a pipeline is broken down into its components, which in turn are executed one by one using a single instance of `MicroPipe`. Clearly, between the execution of a component and the next one, you can insert whatever branching you like, since you're essentially running ASP code inside a web page.

Setting the Component's Properties

The problem here is, of course, that since you are not loading a configuration file for your pipeline, you cannot set the component's properties before you load it as you have done so far. As a matter of fact, if the components you are going to need have been developed in a certain way, you will be able to access their functionality anyway.

Components that are compatible with ASP development (and every component should be, because otherwise it wouldn't be possible to set their properties from within the web-based editor) should expose two methods, called `GetConfigData` and `SetConfigData`. The former returns the configuration parameters for the component in a `Dictionary` object, while the latter accepts changes to the configuration parameters from a `Dictionary` object that is passed to it:

```
Component.GetConfigData
```
or
```
Component.SetConfigData (ConfigData)
```

Where `ConfigData` is a dictionary object that contains the configuration parameters to be set.

Your problem now is that you do not know how each component's parameters are stored in the configuration dictionary, since the individual properties will be saved in Name/Value pairs whose names do not appear anywhere in this book or in MSCS's documentation. As a matter of fact, there *is* an easy way to find out what the properties for a given component are–all you have to do is call its `GetConfigData` method and dump the contents of the `Dictionary` object that you receive in return. For example, the following script extracts all the properties exposed by the `TableShippingADO` component:

```
<%
   Set objDump = Server.CreateObject ("Commerce.TableShippingADO")

   Set ConfigDictionary = objDump.GetConfigData

   Response.Write "Property count: " & ConfigDictionary.Count & "<BR>"

   For Each PropertyPair in ConfigDictionary
      Response.Write PropertyPair & "<BR>"
   Next
%>
```

Naturally, all you have to do in order to extract the properties of another component is change the class ID in the call to `Server.CreateObject` that appears in the first line of the listing.

Summary

In this chapter we began by establishing what exactly a pipeline is. We looked at how a pipeline is made up of stages, and how components within each stage carry out the tasks necessary for execution of the pipeline.

We've then looked in detail at the two Commerce pipelines, the Order Processing Pipeline and the Commerce Interchange Pipeline. For each of these we walked through the different pipelines that make up the OPP and the CIP, and then looked in detail at each different stage and examined the built-in components for that stage available with MSCS. We also saw the non-stage-specific `Scriptor` component.

By now you should have a good understanding of all the elements involved in a pipeline and how you would be able to use them. But how exactly do you use them? This is the question we'll go on to answer in the next chapter.

18

Using Pipelines

Until this moment, we have been talking about pipelines in a rather abstract manner. As a matter of fact, you probably know everything about them, with the exception of how to run them—a not so small detail in real-world applications! In this chapter, therefore, we'll talk about how pipelines are used from within an MSCS application.

The chapter is divided into the following sections:

> **Managing pipelines**
> In this section, we'll take a look at the two pipeline editing technologies that come with MSCS, and see how we can use them to create new pipelines or modify existing ones.

> **Creating supporting objects**
> Here we'll delve into the details of how pipelines can be executed from within your own scripts, using the objects and methods provided by MSCS. We'll also take a look at caching pipelines.

> **Pipeline log files**
> In this section we'll look at how to view pipeline log files, and how to make sense of them.

> **Using pipelines in a typical store**
> Finally in this chapter we'll look at where pipelines fit in to the typical technical structure of a store, using the example store we set up in chapter 17. We'll see which components are called from which ASP pages, and how they map into a typical purchase process.

Managing Pipelines

The following figure illustrates the process that has to be followed in order to successfully create and execute a pipeline object. The first step consists of creating what I call the *support objects*, that is the set of data that is required for the pipeline to work properly. Next, a **pipeline object** will have to be created; this acts as a container in which the pipeline is loaded and executed.

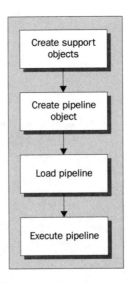

Once a pipeline object is available, the pipeline itself is loaded from a file–either on the hard drive or on the network–called a **pipeline configuration file**, usually with the extension .PCF. Finally, the pipeline is executed and its results are passed back to the ASP script. Optionally, it's also possible to cache a configuration file so that, when a pipeline is executed more than once in the same application, it doesn't have to be reloaded every time. Before we can get into how pipelines are run, however, we'll have to talk extensively about how they can be created and modified.

Pipeline Editors

MSCS provides two different editors for creating and managing pipelines. One is Win32-based, and can only be run from a machine on which (a) the pipeline configuration file is reachable and (b) all the required components are installed. The other is entirely web-based, and can be run from just about anywhere the MSCS server is reachable through the network.

In choosing one editor or the other, you should mainly keep into consideration their convenience versus their capabilities. In general, the Win32-based editor provides a wider array of functionality, including the possibility of creating your own pipeline templates, in which the names and order of the stages are not necessarily those pre-determined by the MSCS standard pipelines. On the other hand, the web-based editor gives you the convenience of being able to edit your pipelines from just about anywhere: all you need is a web browser and the appropriate credentials to access your store's management pages.

The Web-Based Editor

We'll start from the web-based editor, which you will most likely use a lot when you do not have direct access to your server, or if you do not have Site Server installed on your local computer. The following figure shows the editor's main screen for a Plan pipeline, which is reached by clicking on the Edit Pipeline button of the Store Manager's main page. As you can see, Microsoft takes the metaphor of a pipeline pretty seriously!

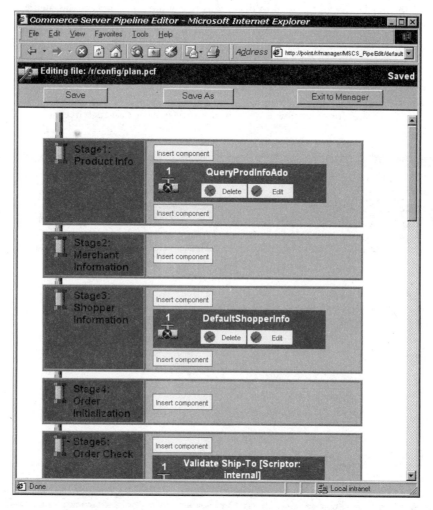

The editor is very easy to use. The section at the top, which is enclosed in a frame so that it remains visible even as you scroll down the pipeline, is used to perform activities such as saving the pipeline with the same or a different filename, or going back to the Store Manager's main page. It's interesting to notice that the Save and Save As buttons do not cause the browser to navigate back to the Manager's main page, so you will have to click on Exit to Manager *after* you have saved your pipelines anyway. If you forget to save, a message will notify you that continuing to the main page will cause all the changes that you have made to be lost. You can verify whether your pipeline's changes have already been saved by looking at the upper right corner of the screen, which will read Not Saved in a bright red if you have not yet saved your edited configuration file.

By default, the editor is only able to load and display the pipeline files that belong to a specific store. Even if you decide to use the Save As function, you will still only be able to save the files within your store's virtual folder. This is not a limitation, but rather an obvious security measure. In fact, since this editor can be executed without having physical access to the server, it's reasonable to expect that the person using it might only have access to his or her own store's virtual root, and should not be allowed to reach any other file in the system. For example, this would apply particularly to an ISP re-selling Site Server functionality on its servers. Allowing somebody to save their configuration files anywhere on the hard drive might lead to disastrous consequences (such as the owner of one store overwriting somebody else's pipelines!).

Editing and Deleting a Component

You can edit a component that is already in the pipeline by clicking on its Edit link (each component is represented with an icon of what looks like a hydraulic valve, within the green box of a stage). Doing so will take you to a page lets you specify the properties of the component that you have selected. This screenshot for example shows the property page for an instance of the QueryProdInfoADO.

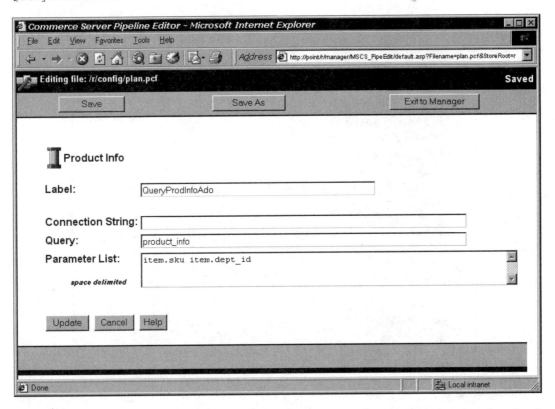

As you can see, you can also specify a *label* for the component, that will be displayed in the editor's main screen. The value of the label field bears no importance in how the pipeline or the components are executed, but it can be used to make the role of each component in the pipeline easier to understand.

To delete a component, go to the editor's main screen and click on the Delete link that appears beside the component. The editor will not ask you for a confirmation before deleting the component, and there is no undo functionality, so make sure that you're certain you want to delete it!

Inserting a New Component

To insert a new component, click on any Insert Component box. As you may have noticed from the previous screenshots, the link appears twice for each stage. This lets you decide whether you want your component to be added at the beginning or at the end of a stage.

Clicking on the Insert Component link takes you to another page that lists all the components that show affinity with your stage. You can also select the component that you want to add from a list of all the components that are available on the server.

> **Although you can add any component to any stage regardless of the affinity rules, you should be careful in adding a component to a stage it doesn't show affinity for. In many cases, the component might require that certain values be set in the pipeline's main dictionary, and those values might only be set in or before the component for which it shows affinity.**

Once you've added a component, you can elect to move it around in the stage by using the small arrows that are on its right side in the editor's main page.

How Does The Editor Work?

The editor is simply an ASP application that has been designed to handle configuration files through an undocumented MSCS object called `Commerce.PipeManager`, which is also used at the end of the Store Builder Wizard to create the pipeline configuration files for a store, and has the ability of loading and manipulating configuration files.

When a store is first created, MSCS adds a virtual folder to it called `MSCS_PipeEdit`, which points to the following location:

`MSCSRoot\SiteServer\Admin\Commerce\PipeLine Configuration`

where `MSCSRoot` is the installation directory of your copy of Site Server, Commerce Edition. This folder contains the pipeline editor's source files. Oddly enough, they show little consistency in the way the code is written, mainly because part of the ASP scripts are written in JScript, while the rest are in VBScript.

The Win32-Based Editor

Working with the Win32 pipeline editor is a somewhat speedier process, and the functionality that it provides is in many ways superior to that offered by the web-based editor, although the latter is obviously more convenient. Naturally, you do not necessarily need to be on the server in order to edit a pipeline configuration file, but you will have to have all the pipeline components installed on your workstation in order for the program to work properly outside a server environment.

If you are using a machine on which Site Server is installed, you may run the editor by selecting Programs|Microsoft Site Server|Commerce|Pipeline Editor from the Start menu. This will load the editor – you should then see the following interface:

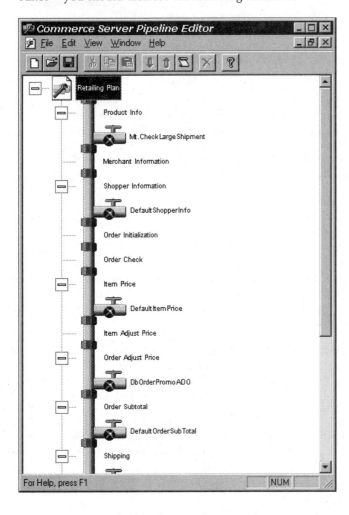

As you can see, the basic look of the editor is not that different from that of its web-based counterpart, with exception of the Win32 common elements (i.e.: menus, buttons, and so on) that you obviously couldn't have in your browser window. The first big difference that you will notice, however, is in the fact that this editor does not load any pipeline configuration file by default – in fact, you have the choice of creating a new pipeline from scratch.

Editing or Deleting a Component

To edit a component that already sits in the pipeline, all you have to do is double click on it. The editor will display a dialog box with a several tabbed panels. Their actual number varies, depending on how many property pages each component has, but in general you will see any combination of the following:

> **Property pages**
> Each property page (components rarely have more than one) contains the configurable properties for the component. The title of the tab for this panel is decided by the component's developer, and therefore varies considerably from component to component. This is the property page for an instance of the Scriptor component:

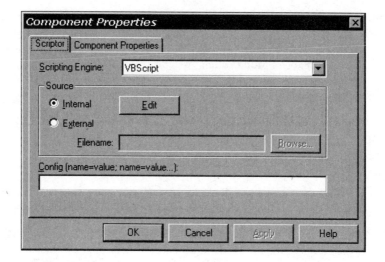

> **Component properties**
> This panel, not to be confused with the property pages, is always present for all components, and provides basic information about them. This includes the label, the COM Class ID, the COM Program ID and a description. Both the label and the description can be modified to better explain what a component does and how it has been configured.

> **Values Read/Written**
> This optional panel contains a list of all the values that the component reads and writes to the main dictionary, and reads from the pipeline's context.

Deleting a component is a very easy operation: just select it by clicking on it with your mouse, then either select Delete from the Edit menu, or press the *DEL* key on your keyboard. Contrary to what happens with the web-based editor, the Win32 editor will ask you for a confirmation before proceeding, but will not provide any undo functionality once you've taken your decision.

Inserting a New Component

To insert a new component in your pipeline, you can right click on either an existing component or on a stage. In the first case, the resulting popup menu will give you the possibility of adding a component before or after the existing one, while in the second case you will be simply adding a component to the beginning of the stage you selected.

In both cases, the editor will display a dialog box that will list all the components available for the stage you are currently in. As before, you can also select your component from a list of all the components available on the server. Naturally, the same caveats apply!

Since the Win32 editor does not run in the safety of your browser, it is more prone to hanging and crashing than its web counterpart. Save your configuration files often to minimize the risk of losing important work if the editor crashes or stops working.

The Expert Mode

Wouldn't it be nice if you could create your own pipelines? As we have mentioned more than once in this chapter, such a possibility exists, and it is only available when you use the Win32 editor in *Expert Mode*, also known as Enhanced Mode. When the editor is running in this mode it is possible to add, move and delete entire stages, as well as deciding what the end-of-stage logic does. As you can imagine, the possibilities are almost limitless, so let's get started!

In order to run the pipeline editor in Expert Mode, you need to start it from the command line. To do so, click on Run from the Start menu, then type in the following:

```
"SiteServer Root\bin\pipeeditor.exe" /e
```

where `SiteServer Root` is the installation folder of your copy of Site Server (for example, in my case, its value would be `C:\Microsoft Site Server`). Make sure that you include the quotation marks in your command line.

At first glance, the editor in Expert Mode looks exactly the same as it does normally. As soon as you either create a new pipeline or open an existing one, however, differences become obvious, as you can see from the following figure:

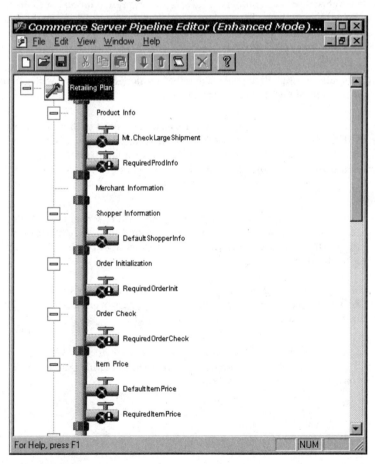

The first difference that you will probably notice when opening an existing Plan pipeline is the presence of certain components that were not there before. They all start with Required... and are designed to handle the end-of-stage logic.

If you try to delete one of those components, the editor doesn't complain and will actually let you take the components out. After all, that's what the Expert Mode is all about: giving you more freedom in choosing what goes in and out of a pipeline. If you now try to access the properties for any component, and select the Component Properties tab, you will notice the presence of an apparently innocuous checkbox that reads Required. If you select that box, the component will be marked as required, and the editor will simply not show it in the pipeline when run in normal mode.

Modifying Stages

Another very interesting feature of Expert Mode is the ability to treat stages as you do components: you can move them around, add new ones, or delete existing ones. To move a stage from its current position, right-click on it and select either Move Up or Move Down. To insert a new stage, click on an existing stage and select Insert Stage, then Before or After, if available. To delete an existing stage, simply select it and press the DEL key on your keyboard. It's that simple.

When you add stages, you will notice by right clicking on them that you can change their label and add a comment. In addition, the editor generates (and lets you change) a GUID for the stage, which will be used to determine what components have affinity to it (we'll talk more about how components are assigned to stages later on in this chapter). Finally, you can specify the minimum execution mode in which a stage will run (as specified by the pipeline objects that we'll examine shortly), as well as the maximum error level that a stage will be able to tolerate. If the error level returned by any of the components at any point in the stage goes beyond that level, the pipeline execution will stop immediately. The possible levels are those that we examined briefly when we were talking about the Scriptor component.

You will notice that a few properties are available also for the pipeline as a whole by right clicking on it and selecting Properties (the pipeline is identified by the first icon that appears in the editing window). As you can see, along with the usual label and description fields, there is a drop-down list that reads Transaction Compatibility, which can be used to determine whether the pipeline requires a transacted environment, is transaction-neutral or requires that it be run in an environment that does not require transaction. We'll talk more about pipelines and transactions in the next section.

Creating a New Pipeline

If you're on to something really new and you want to create your own pipeline from scratch, the editor provides you with an empty template that you can use. To create a new pipeline based on it, simply select Empty.pcf from the dialog box that the editor displays when you click on File/New. Speaking of which, wouldn't it be nice if you could create your own pipeline template and then make it available through the File|New mechanism? To do so, all you need to do is copy the configuration file that contains your template to the following location:

```
SiteServer Root\Bin\Templates
```

Where, as usual, SiteServer Root is the installation folder for your copy of Site Server, Commerce Edition.

It's worth noting that Expert Mode deserves its name. Shuffling stages around requires a certain amount of planning, and can lead to disastrous consequences for the stability of your pipeline (and of your psyche, as well). Before starting to play with Expert Mode, you should make a backup of every pipeline that you intend to modify.

Creating the Supporting Objects

As we've seen, each pipeline requires two supporting objects in order to run properly:

> **The context**
> The context is usually a `Dictionary` object that is initialized to contain a number of "environment" objects required by the pipeline at execution time. This includes ASP intrinsic objects, connection strings, query strings, and so on.

> **The main dictionary**
> The main dictionary is either an `OrderForm` object (for OPP pipelines) or a `Dictionary` object (for CIP pipelines), and contains the data that the pipeline is supposed to manipulate.

Clearly, both the context and the main dictionary must be created before the pipeline can execute. Generally speaking, you can elect to create the context only once, for example in the `Application_OnStart` method of the `global.asa` file, and then store it in the `Application` object. However the main dictionary will probably vary every time a pipeline is executed.

Creating the Context Object

As we just said, the context object is a `Dictionary` object, and it should contain whatever values the components in your pipeline require to run. By default, a basic MSCS store creates a dictionary that contains the following Name/Value pairs:

`MessageManager`	An instance of Commerce.MessageManager that is generally created in the store's `global.asa` file, which contains all the possible error messages for the pipeline's components.
`DataFunctions`	An instance of Commerce.DataFunctions, usually created and initialized in the store's `global.asa` file.
`QueryMap`	An instance of `Commerce.Dictionary`, usually created and initialized in `global.asa`, which contains a list of all the SQL queries used by the store.
`ConnectionStringMap`	A Dictionary object that contains a list of the connection strings available to the store
`SiteName`	The display name of the store
`DefaultConnectionString`	The default connection string to be used by the store
`Language`	The default language/locale used by the store (must be defined in the MessageManager object)

You can obviously add whatever objects or other values you like to the context dictionary, including the ASP intrinsic objects (which are not by default available to the pipeline components). For example, if you need to read the user's cookies from within the pipeline, you can add the `Request` object to the context as follows:

```
Set objContext = Server.CreateObject ("Commerce.Dictionary")
Set objContext.Request = Request
```

Creating the Main Dictionary

For OPP pipelines, the creation of the main dictionary is a process that most of the time spans the entire site. In fact, the `OrderForm` is used from when the user first enters the store until when he or she either leaves or makes a purchase to hold all of his or her personal information and basket contents.

For a CIP, the main dictionary is usually created right before the pipeline's execution, and loaded with whatever values are needed. A CIP can also be created by a component within another pipeline—as is the case with `PipeToPipeTransfer` and `GenerateReceipt`.

Pipeline Objects

Pipelines are executed by using specialized objects provided by MSCS. There is no difference between the way an OPP and a CIP are executed, except, naturally, the fact that in one case the main dictionary is a Dictionary object, while in the other, it is an `OrderForm` object. As such, the procedure for loading and executing a CIP and OPP is exactly the same.

The reason MSCS provides two different objects for loading and executing a pipeline is one of convenience. Since the introduction of the Microsoft Transaction Server, many Microsoft products have been developed to be fully transaction-friendly, and Site Server is no exception—the pipeline is an excellent candidate for the benefits that transactions bring along. As we'll see in the next chapter, however, pipelines are used pervasively throughout the MSCS store, and their role is almost never to perform tasks which would make more sense as part of a transaction. The only time when you will really need transactions is when a customer purchases something (and, in fact, the Purchase pipeline is automatically marked as "transaction required"). For all the other instances, using transactions would only add a useless overhead and therefore limit the capacity of your site.

The MtsPipeline Object

The `MtsPipeline` object is used to load and execute pipelines that do not require transactions. The first operation that you must take care of is that of actually loading the pipeline from its configuration file.

The LoadPipe Method

Calling the `LoadPipe` method will load a pipeline from the configuration file you specify:

```
MtsPipeline.LoadPipe (sPath)
```

Where `sPath` is the complete pathname of the pipeline configuration file.

This method will attempt to retrieve and load the pipeline configuration file that you specify, therefore you can expect a runtime error if the file cannot be found or is not accessible (for example because of permission problems). However, you can also expect problems if the pipeline file you are trying to load has been marked for transacted execution (more about that later)—in that case, since MtsPipeline does not support transactions in any way, you will not be able to execute the pipeline. The default extension for a pipeline configuration file is .PCF.

The Execute Method

Assuming that everything went fine with your call to LoadPipe, you can attempt to execute the pipeline using the Execute method:

```
MtsPipeline.Execute (lMode, MainDictionary, PipeContext, lReserved)
```

Where:

> lMode is the mode in which the pipeline must be executed (1 under normal conditions).

> MainDictionary is the pipeline's main dictionary

> PipeContext is the pipeline's context

> lReserved is a reserved value, which must be zero.

The lMode parameter is implemented mainly for legacy reasons. You should never use a value of zero, which will prevent *any* component from running.

> *In Site Server 2, only one pipeline per store could be used, and therefore it was necessary to differentiate between Plan and Purchase pipeline by stuffing all the components in a single pipeline and marking them with an "execution mode". The pipeline was then executed with a specific mode, which prevented certain components from running.*

All the built-in pipelines provided by MSCS that we have seen so far are designed to run when lMode has a value equal to or greater than one. Naturally, you can design your own pipelines to run only in specific modes, as we'll see later on in the chapter, but in doing so you will force the pipeline objects to load the entire pipeline configuration file every time even though you might be needing only a handful of components. This will increase your overhead significantly, and will make your store perform worse than if you had simply used more than one pipeline file in the first place.

Execute returns a value of type Long that expresses the level of success of the pipeline's execution, similar to the one that is set by using the Scriptor component that we saw in the previous chapter.

> A value of 1 corresponds to a successful execution, meaning that all the components were run without any problem.

> A value of 2 means that a "recoverable" error occurred and, while the pipeline's execution was not entirely successful, it might have continued until the end.

> A value of 3 corresponds to an unrecoverable failure, and means that the pipeline's execution was not successful.

In general, you should consider the pipeline's execution unsuccessful unless you receive a return value of 1.

The SetLogFile Method

Make no mistake about it: pipelines are a pesky critter at times. Their biggest problem–the one that will sometimes keep you stuck for hours–is that they are extremely difficult to debug, because you cannot even see the code for most of the components (`Scriptor` being an obvious exception). Luckily (or *unluckily*, if you're the it's-never-enough-for-me type), pipeline objects are able to write all the actions that components perform on the pipeline's main dictionary to a log file. Clearly, this is not something that you would want the objects to do every time (log files tend to be *very* large with time), and therefore you must turn on this behavior by calling the `SetLogFile` method:

```
MtsPipeline.SetLogFile (Path)
```

Where `Path` is the pathname of the log file.

It's important to make sure that the file chosen can be accessed for writing by the pipeline component–this includes the fact the appropriate permissions are set and that the file is not read-only. Pipeline log files can be quite complex to understand–but only because they usually contain a lot of data and are not very easy to read. We'll take a look at them right after we have talked a bit about how transacted pipelines are run.

> Always remember to turn off pipeline activity logging when you go to a production environment. If you don't, your store's performance will suffer, and your hard drive will rapidly run out of space (log files can be *really* big!).

The MtsTxPipeline Object

This MSCS object can be used to run pipelines that require a transaction-enabled environment. `MtsTxPipeline` supports exactly the same set of methods provided by `MtsPipeline`, with no difference whatsoever in their parameters or return values. However, there are a number of differences that you should take into account when using either component.

As mentioned above, pipelines that require transactions can only be run using `MtsTxPipeline`. Likewise, if you mark a pipeline as requiring a non-transacted environment, you will not be able to run it unless you use `MtsPipeline`.

`MtsTxPipeline` can use the transaction context of your ASP script, if you create one. If you do not, the object will automatically create one and run the pipeline within it. Because of the stateless nature of web serving, you cannot create an instance of `MtsTxPipeline` in one script (for example, in `global.asa`) and then use it in another. This is something that, in theory, you could do with `MtsPipeline`, although it's not recommended. You will need to create a new instance of the object every time you need to use it.

When you create a transacted pipeline, always remember to use components that support transactions. In particular, you should make sure that all the components that access a database do so through transaction-aware ODBC-compliant COM objects, such as ADO. The same recommendation is valid if you decide to develop your own pipeline components, a topic that we will tackle later on in this chapter.

Caching Pipelines

As you can imagine, the action of loading a pipeline from disk every time that it is run can waste a lot of valuable system resources. Luckily, MSCS provides us with the Commerce.ConfigurationCacheHelper component, which can be used to cache a pipeline configuration file once it's been loaded from disk.

In order to use this component, you must first create an instance of either MtsPipeline or MtsTxPipeline, which you will use to load the configuration file that you want to cache.

The SaveToCache Method

Once the file has been loaded, you can save it into an instance of ConfigurationCacheHelper by calling its SaveToCache method:

```
ConfigurationCacheHelper.SaveToCache (Pipeline)
```

Where Pipeline is an instance of MtsPipeline or MtsTxPipeline that contains the pipeline configuration file to be cached.

SaveToCache will return a unique token that you can use to retrieve your pipeline. It's important to understand that the component will not save the pipeline object, but only its configuration. As such, you can use the cached configuration files anywhere in your store, and you should save the unique token in a location that is accessible by all the scripts (i.e.: the Application object).

The LoadFromCache Method

To use cached configuration files you need to call the LoadFromCache method instead of loading the pipeline configuration file from disk as you would normally do.

```
ConfigurationCacheHelper.LoadFromCache (Pipeline, CacheToken)
```

Where:

> ➢ CacheToken is the unique token returned by SaveToCache when the configuration file was saved to the cache.

> ➢ Pipeline is an instance of MtsPipeline or MtsTxPipeline that will receive the configuration file from the cache.

Once you've called LoadFromCache, your pipeline object is ready to go, without the need to continuously access the server's hard drive to load the configuration files.

The DeleteFromCache Method

Should you require to delete one or more configuration files from the cache, you can do so by calling the DeleteFromCache method:

```
ConfigurationCacheHelper.DeleteFromCache (Pipeline, CacheToken)
```

Where, again:
> ➢ CacheToken is the unique token returned by SaveToCache when the configuration file was saved to the cache.

> ➢ Pipeline is an instance of MtsPipeline or MtsTxPipeline that will receive the configuration file from the cache.

In general, you will initialize an instance of this component in your store's `global.asa` file, so that the configuration files commonly used will be available to all the pages in your site. If you do so, you should remember to delete the cache entries when your application ends, so that you will be able to reclaim all the memory used by them.

Interpreting Pipeline Logfiles

So you've got a pipeline problem? When one of your components isn't working—or is not properly configured, as happens in many cases—the best way to solve the problem consists of looking at the log file that the pipeline objects generate. Always remember that you *have* to turn logging on every time you execute a pipeline, because the objects do not provide this behavior by default. At the same rate, as we mentioned earlier, you should always remember to turn logging off as soon as you stop needing it.

Choosing a Location for the Log File

The first thing that you should do once you decide that you need pipeline logging is establish a good location for your log files. Debugging a pipeline is an excruciating process under normal circumstances, so you shouldn't try to make it even more difficult by placing your logs in a location that is difficult to reach. Best of all, if you are modifying the site remotely, you should make sure that the files will be easy to retrieve from where you are.

In general, your log files should be placed in a place that is easy enough to reach, and at the same time easy to clean up as well. (Thus, the server's root folder (C:\) does not qualify for our good spot contest. The same goes for the \Winnt directory!) Depending on what kind of access you have to the hard drive, I recommend that you create a folder one level below the root and use that exclusively for logging. That way, you can easily wipe out old log files by simply getting rid of everything that lives in that folder.

Examining the Log File

Unfortunately for us, MSCS does not come with a log file viewer, which means that you'll have to load and examine the logs in a normal editor. I find that Notepad does a really good job from this point of view, at least if you're using the Windows NT version (the one that comes with Windows 9x has the terrible problem of being limited to only reading up to 64kb of data). The following screenshot shows a log of the execution of a Purchase pipeline, loaded in Notepad.

You can also use other programs to import the log files. Excel seems to work a lot better than any other, as long as you import the file as a tab-delimited database. However, the spreadsheet program tends to confuse numbers and strings (for example, credit card numbers are taken as numbers, with terrible consequences) and I find the whole process of having to import the file every time a bit annoying (you will too, after the third time that you have to look at a log in a ten-minutes timespan).

Once you get past their mass, however, log files are relatively easy to understand. As you can see by looking at one, they start with an entry that records when the pipeline object was first executed:

```
Sink started at 1999/04/26 18:23:56.0857
```

Next, an entry is used to record that the pipeline was executed:

```
PIPELINE:++ 1999/04/26 18:23:56.0857 Pipeline Execution starts (lMode==0x1,
lFlags==0x0)   7 components in the list (MTS is enabled)
```

This line tells us that the mode specified in the Execute method of the originating pipeline object was 1 (lMode in the log), that there are seven components in the pipeline, and that the originating object was an instance of MtsTxPipeline, since MTS is enabled. You have probably noticed that the line begins with the text PIPELINE:++, which indicates the beginning of a task. Similarly, the end of a task is indicated by the text PIPELINE:--. In fact, going forward in the log, we notice the following:

```
PIPELINE:++ component[0x0] about to be called ProgID: Commerce.Scriptor.1
RootObject: ReadValue _Purchase_Errors VT_DISPATCH PV=[0x33bc60] VT_EMPTY __empty__
RootObject: ReadValue bill_to_name VT_BSTR Marco VT_EMPTY __empty__
RootObject: ReadValue bill_to_street VT_BSTR 100 Nowhere Rd. VT_EMPTY __empty__
RootObject: ReadValue bill_to_city VT_BSTR Toronto VT_EMPTY __empty__
RootObject: ReadValue bill_to_state VT_BSTR ON VT_EMPTY __empty__
RootObject: WriteValue _payment_auth_code VT_NULL _null_ VT_BSTR FAITH
RootObject: ReadValue bill_to_zip VT_BSTR M4H1L3 VT_EMPTY __empty__
RootObject: ReadValue bill_to_country VT_BSTR USA VT_EMPTY __empty__
PIPELINE:-- component [0x0] returned hr: 0x0 in 60 milliseconds
```

As you can see, this set of entries corresponds to an entire task, that is, the execution of component number 0 in the pipeline, which is an instance of Scriptor. The entries within the task correspond to individual accesses of the object to the main dictionary. They all begin with RootObject: and can express either read or write operations. Read operations include the following information:

Read Operation	Description
Action type	Always `ReadValue`, indicating that this entry corresponds to a read operation.
Source Name/Value pair	The name of the Name/Value pair that was read from the main dictionary.
Source pair's type	The type of data that was read from the main dictionary. Contains one of the possible subtypes of a COM Variant variable.
Value read	The value that was actually read from the main dictionary.
Destination Name/Value pair type	The Variant sub-type of the variable passed to the main dictionary by the component to receive the value.
Destination Name/Value pair value	The contents of the destination Name/Value pair *before* the main dictionary copied the new value into it.

For write operations, the following information is logged:

Write Operation	Description
Action type	Always `WriteValue`, indicating that this is a write operation.
Destination Name/Value pair	The name of the Name/Value pair whose value is being changed.
Original type	The Variant sub-type of the Destination Name/Value pair *before* the change.
Original Value	The value of the Destination Name/Value pair *before* the change.
New type	The Variant sub-type of the Destination Name/Value pair *after* the change.
New value	The value of the Destination Name/Value pair *after* the change.

At the end of the pipeline, you will find two lines similar to the following:

```
PIPELINE:-- 1999/04/26 18:23:58.0940 Pipeline Execution completed returning hr:
0x0      i: 0x7     hrLoop: 0x0 *plErrorLevel: 1 (MTS committed)
Sink stopped at 1999/04/26 18:23:58.0940
```

They indicate that the pipeline has ended its execution (the pipeline itself is considered one task, and therefore has an opening and closing entry, just like the individual components). In particular, you want to take a look at the last few words of the first line, which indicate the error level at the end of the pipeline (1 in this case) and, if you're running an instance of `MtsTxPipeline`, what happened to the transaction in which the pipeline was running (in this case, it was committed).

What to Look For in a Pipeline Log

When you have a problem the first thing you should be looking for is where the pipeline stopped. If it stopped in response to an error raised by a component, take a look at the values read and written by it. In most cases, the log will be able to tell you what was wrong. For example, if a pipeline stopped its execution because a component wasn't expecting a value to be Null, take a look at what the last value read by it was, and act accordingly.

If your pipeline didn't stop in response to a runtime error, then you are probably trying to look at how one or more Name/Value pairs were modified during the pipeline's execution. If your log file is very cluttered, it might be worth going through it and deleting all the read or write entries that do not have anything to do with the pairs you're interested in. This way, you'll end up with a list of all the changes that your pair went through during the pipeline's execution.

Pipelines Within a Store

Finally in this chapter we're going to see how pipelines are used inside an example store. In chapter 16, we started looking at the technical structure of a starter store. The one aspect of the site that we couldn't get too much into detail about was the purchase process, which makes heavy use of pipelines. Now that we have a better handle on them, it's a good time to go back to *Marco's Shack* for more shopping fun!

First of all let's look again at the diagram from Chapter 16. which shows the files that were created by the Site Builder Wizard to make up our basic store, as well as their functions, and how they interact:

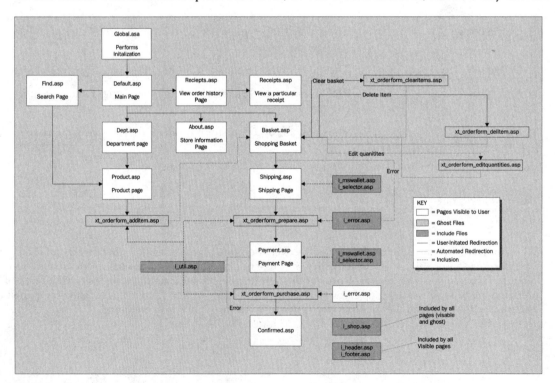

In Chapter 16 we went through the files that make up the storefront, such as I_shop.asp. Here we'll cover the remaining files that make up the actual purchase process. The first page in which the pipeline is used—which also happens to be where we finished two chapters ago — is the basket, so that's where we'll start. After this we'll follow the execution flow onwards from shipping.asp, and conclude with a quick look at the receipt pages.

The Basket

Basket.asp is arguably one of the most complex scripts in the whole store. Its goal is not only to display the basket's contents, but also to calculate their correct price, as well as the order subtotal.

The script starts by setting its own expiration date ten years in the past:

```
<% Response.ExpiresAbsolute=DateAdd("yyy", -10, Date) %>
```

While this may seem a little weird, it's goal is simply to make sure that no browser or proxy server will ever cache this page, since its contents may change at any time.

The next step consists of updating the information that is stored in the OrderForm. This is done by calling the UtilRunPlan function from i_util.asp, which, in turn, ends up executing the store's Plan pipeline. UtilRunPlan works by executing a number of steps required to create the appropriate environment before it proceed to run the pipeline. The diagram below shows its operation flow:

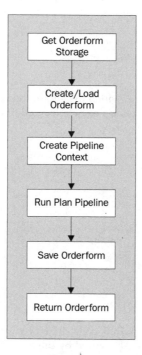

As you can see, the function begins by retrieving the OrderForm data, using the UtilGetOrderFormStorage and UtilGetOrderForm functions that we have already seen before. Next, it retrieves the pipeline's context by calling UtilGetPipeContext, which works by instantiating a new Dictionary object and storing the appropriate data in it:

```
function UtilGetPipeContext()
    Set pipeContext = Server.CreateObject("Commerce.Dictionary")
    Set pipeContext("MessageManager")         = MSCSMessageManager
    Set pipeContext("DataFunctions")          = MSCSDataFunctions
    Set pipeContext("QueryMap")               = MSCSQueryMap
    Set pipeContext("ConnectionStringMap")    = MSCSSite.ConnectionStringMap
    pipeContext("SiteName")                   = displayName
    pipeContext("DefaultConnectionString")    = MSCSSite.DefaultConnectionString
    pipeContext("Language")                   = "USA"

    Set UtilGetPipeContext = pipeContext
end function
```

If your own pipeline needs additional values stored in the context, this is the place where you would add them to it. You can even add data that is taken from ASP's own context, such as `Server` or `Request`:

```
function UtilGetPipeContext()
    Set pipeContext = Server.CreateObject("Commerce.Dictionary")
    Set pipeContext("MessageManager")         = MSCSMessageManager
    Set pipeContext("DataFunctions")          = MSCSDataFunctions
    Set pipeContext("QueryMap")               = MSCSQueryMap
    Set pipeContext("ConnectionStringMap")    = MSCSSite.ConnectionStringMap
    pipeContext("SiteName")                   = displayName
    pipeContext("DefaultConnectionString")    = MSCSSite.DefaultConnectionString
    pipeContext("Language")                   = "USA"

    Set pipeContext ("Server") = Server
    Set pipeContext ("Request") = Request

    Set UtilGetPipeContext = pipeContext
end function
```

Finally, the function calls `UtilRunPipe`, which essentially takes care of creating an instance of `Commerce.MtsPipeline` (thus the pipeline to be executed doesn't require transactions), loading the pipeline's configuration file, and executing it:

```
function UtilRunPipe(file, orderForm, pipeContext)
    Set pipeline = Server.CreateObject("Commerce.MtsPipeline")

    Call pipeline.LoadPipe(Request.ServerVariables("APPL_PHYSICAL_PATH") & _
                    "config\" & file)

    REM Call pipeline.SetLogFile(Request.ServerVariables("APPL_PHYSICAL_PATH") & _
                        "config\pipeline.log")

    errorLevel = pipeline.Execute(1, orderForm, pipeContext, 0)

    UtilRunPipe = errorLevel
end function
```

As you can see, the configuration file's path is constructed by mapping the store's `config` directory and adding the filename. The filename is provided by the caller and, in this case, is `plan.pcf`. The function also contains a commented line that can be used to instruct the pipeline object to log its activity to your choice of text file. You can uncomment this line if you need to debug your store; just remember to comment it back once you're done, or you will end up with a huge log file.

After the pipeline has been executed, UtilRunPlan simply saves the OrderForm back to the database using a method similar to what we saw earlier and returns the data to the basket's script.

The Plan Pipeline

The accompanying figure shows the structure of the store's Plan pipeline. For the most part, it is organized along fairly simple lines; however, I'd like to point your attention to a few interesting things. First, you will notice how the **QueryProdInfoAdo** component is used at the beginning of the pipeline to load information about each item in the OrderForm. If you look at its configuration, you will notice that it uses an empty connection string, forcing the component to use the store's default string, and that it references the product_info query, which is defined in our Global.asa as follows:

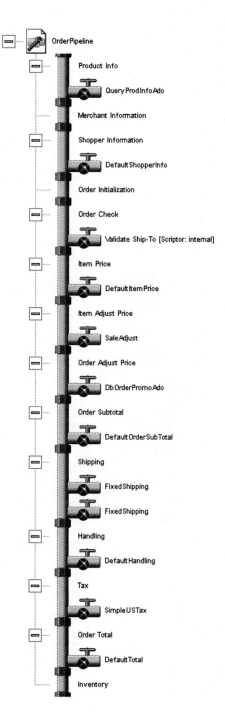

```
SELECT
  pf.sku,
  pf.name,
  pf.list_price,
  pf.sale_price,
  pf.sale_start,
  pf.sale_end,
  dept.dept_id
FROM
  mt_product pf,
mt_dept_prod deptprod,
  mt_dept dept
WHERE
  pf.sku = ?
and
  pf.sku = deptprod.sku
and
  dept.dept_id = deptprod.dept_id
and
  dept.dept_id = ?
```

As you can see, the query has two parameters, which are substituted with the two values specified in the <u>Parameter List</u> text box of the configuration screen (`item.sku` and `item.dept_id` respectively).

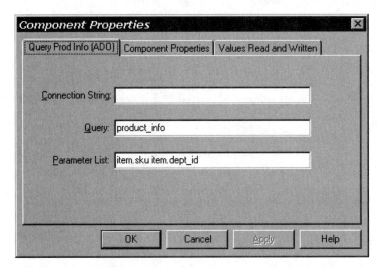

Another aspect of the pipeline that is worth examining is the `Validate Ship-To` script, whose goal is to determine whether the shipping address is valid or not. Most of the script is quite easy to follow. However, if you're planning to sell outside the country specific to the locale you selected when creating the store using the SBW, you should remember this line of code:

```
If orderForm.ship_to_country <> "USA" then 'call
errors.Add(msg_mgr.GetMessage("val_shipcountrymustbe")) : result = 2
```

This if-then statement forces the ship-to country to be the United States. As we'll see in the next section, the shipping page forces this value onto the user (the page doesn't even show a list of countries to choose from).

> **For a ship-to country other than the USA you need to modify this code in basket.asp.**

The store will not work even if you decide to make it possible to specify the country manually, unless you remove (or modify appropriately) this line of code.

Keep in mind that the basket itself doesn't really care about this section of code. As a matter of fact, when you get to the basket, the pipeline will most likely fail at this point, since you have not specified any ship-to information yet. However, you will notice that the Validate Ship-To script uses the _Purchase_Errors collection to store its error messages, and therefore the basket will simply ignore it.

Basket Execution

Once the Plan pipeline has been executed, the script determines whether the basket is empty (that is, the number of items in the OrderForm is zero), and whether any errors occurred, in which case they are shown to the user.

The basket itself is built by creating a table and iterating through each item in the OrderForm, printing out its SKU (displayed as Label), its name, the per-item price, an editable quantity, and the total. In addition, a Delete Item link is printed at the end of each line.

It's interesting to notice that items are kept track of according to their ordinal position inside the OrderForm. For example, here's how the Delete Item link is formed:

```
<A HREF="<%= baseSURL("xt_orderform_delitem.asp") &
mscsPage.URLShopperArgs("index", iLineItem) %>">
```

As you can see, this creates a link that calls xt_orderform_delitem.asp with a parameter that equals the position of the product in the Items collection, essentially telling it to "delete item number *x*". While this works well in most cases, it can lead to certain problems.

> **Users can experience some unexpected results due to this method of tracking OrderForm items by ordinal position.**

For example, let's assume that the user reaches the basket page, then opens a new browser window and ends up on the same page. This is not an unreasonable scenario, since it's common to use more than one browser window for convenience reasons. Whatever is now done on the first basket page inevitably puts the other one out of sync. In fact, if the user deletes an item from the first page, the second will still list it as available. What's worse, if the user attempts to delete it from the second basket, he or she might end up deleting something else!

A possible solution to this problem could be to use the SKU instead. However, you will also have to change the xt_orderform_additem.asp script so that it will be able to recognize whether a particular product has already been added to the basket and change its quantity instead of adding it again if that's the case. This will prevent double entries from showing up in the basket, which, in turn, will avoid annoying problems when manipulating its contents.

Manipulating the Basket

There are three actions that can be taken from the basket page whose goal is to somehow change the its contents: remove an item, change the quantity of one or more items and wipe out the entire order altogether. In the first case, xt_orderform_delitem.asp simply loads the OrderForm, deletes the items whose number is specified by the index URL parameter and stores the OrderForm back into the database.

The item quantities are changed all at the same time in the xt_orderform_editquantities.asp script, which simply iterates through the Items collection updating the Quantity field with the contents of the URL parameters that are passed by the basket page. The actual form that generates these parameters is composed of the individual quantity edit boxes that are shown in basket.asp.

Finally, when the user clicks on **Empty Basket**, the browser loads the xt_orderform_clearitems.asp script, which simply loads the OrderForm, calls its ClearItems method and saves it back to the database.

Generally speaking, all the ghost scripts that are used to manipulate the basket's contents contain minimal error checking, and they do not include any code to create the OrderForm if it doesn't already exist. Clearly, this happens because—at least in theory—a user should never end up running out of them outside a controlled environment, in which (a) the OrderForm exists (and, in most cases, must not be empty), and (b) the parameters passed are pre-checked by the basket page.

The Purchase Process

We can trace the purchase process within our sample store through a set of files from shipping.asp to receipt.asp. The following diagram shows the files we'll be examining in the last section of this chapter – they are a subset of the full collection of scripts that make up our store.

For the sake of simplicity this diagram shows only the links relevant to the discussion here; to remind yourself of how the purchase process files fit into the overall process flow please refer back to the diagram at the beginning of this section, Pipelines Within a Store.

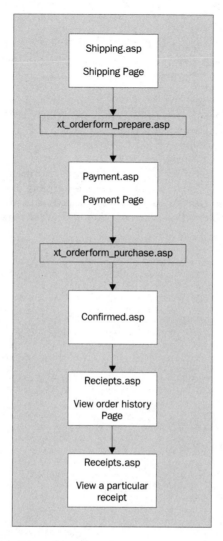

We'll go through and look at each of these scripts in turn, to see how the pipeline theory we've discussed is used within the store.

The purchase process begins when the user clicks on the Purchase button on the basket page, which causes the browser to navigate to shipping.asp.

Shipping.asp

This script contains support for showing both the Wallet and traditional HTML forms. Most of the decisions from this point of view are made by the `I_MSWallet.asp` include file, which, in turn, includes `I_selector.asp`.

These two files work by using the `MSWC.BrowserType` component to determine whether the browser is capable of displaying the Wallet. In case of doubt (which, as we have mentioned in the previous chapter, can also be caused by an obsolete `browscap.ini` file), or if the URL parameter `use_form` is 1, HTML forms are used.

Keep in mind that, while the functions in `I_selector.asp` perform most of the decision making process, the actual inclusion of the Wallet is done inside the shipping page by verifying that the browser is able to support it (`I_selector.asp` stores a value of True inside the `fMSWltUplevelBrowser` variable in that case) and then passing the appropriate HTML code along to the browser:

```
    <% if fMSWltUplevelBrowser then %>
' code omitted
        <TD VALIGN="TOP">Ship-To Address:</TD>

        <TD VALIGN="TOP" ALIGN="CENTER">
        <% if fMSWltActiveXBrowser then %>
            <OBJECT
                ID="addrSelector"
                CLASSID="<% = MSWltIEAddrSelectorClassid() %>"
                CODEBASE="<% = MSWltIECodebase() %>"
                HEIGHT="123"
                WIDTH="154"
            >
            </OBJECT>
        <% elseif fMSWltLiveConnectBrowser then %>
            <EMBED
                NAME="addrSelector"
TYPE="application/x-msaddr"
                PLUGINSPAGE="<%= MSWltNavDwnldURL("plginst.htm") %>"
                VERSION="<%= strMSWltDwnldVer %>"
                HEIGHT="123"
                WIDTH="154"
            >
        <% end if %>
```

The `fMSWltActiveXBrowser` variable is used to determine whether the browser at hand is able to contain ActiveX objects. If it isn't, the script assumes that it must be a Netscape product and act consequently. In the `<BODY>` tag of the page, you will notice a cryptic line of code:

```
<BODY
    BGCOLOR="#FFFFFF"
    TEXT=    "#000000"
    LINK=    "#FF0000"
    VLINK=   "#FF0000"
    ALINK=   "#FF0000"
    <% if fMSWltUplevelBrowser and CBool(nOrderItems > 0) then
        %>onLoad="<% = MSWltLoadDone(strDownlevelURL) %>"<%
    end if %>
>
```

As you can see, if the browser is able to display the Wallet, and if the `OrderForm` is not empty, the `MSWltLoadDone` function is called once the page has finished loading. This function, located in `I_selector.asp`, provides specific code for Netscape browser, which are unable to automatically download and install plug-ins the way Internet Explorer does. Therefore, if the user is running a version of Navigator that supports plug-ins and the Wallet is not installed, this script outputs an elegant box, complete with Load button, that instructs the user to load and install it.

`I_MSWallet.asp` also includes two important settings that you can override and change for your own purposes. The first one is a piece of commented code that can be used to instruct the browser to load the Wallet's installation files from a location different than the standard one (which is usually on the Microsoft.com website). You will need to use if your store resides on a local Intranet that doesn't have direct access to the Internet:

```
     REM -- For intranets not connected to the internet, override default
     REM    download location here.  For example:
     '  If LCase(CStr(Request("HTTP_UA_CPU"))) <> "alpha" Then
     '      strMSWltIEDwnldLoc  = "/" & siteRoot &
"/manager/MSCS_Images/controls/MSWallet.cab"
     '  Else
     '      strMSWltIEDwnldLoc  = "/" & siteRoot &
"/manager/MSCS_Images/controls/MSWltAlp.cab"
     '  End If
     '  strMSWltNavDwnldLoc = "/" & siteRoot & "/manager/MSCS_Images/controls"
```

In this case, if you uncomment the text, it will by default assume that the Wallet's files are stored in your `/manager/MSCS_Images/controls/MSWallet.cab`. `MSCS_Images` is a virtual folder that the SBW creates when it generates the store, and points to the `SiteServer\Admin\Commerce\Images` folder of your Site Server installation. It contains several downloadable files that are required by the administrative wizards used by MSCS, such as the SBW, the promotions wizard, and so on.

The other setting that might come in handy is used to determine what payment methods are accepted by the store:

```
    REM -- Set wallet control accept credit card types. strMSWltAcceptedTypes =
    "visa:clear;mastercard:clear;"
```

The Missing Country

If you take a look at the HTML-only form, you will notice that there isn't an input box for the ship-to country. In fact, the country is hard-coded on the page:

```
    <INPUT TYPE="HIDDEN" NAME="ship_to_country" VALUE="USA">
```

As a result, you will have to remove this tag and add something different if you want your store to support foreign countries.

Xt_orderform_prepare.asp

This ghost script's goal is essentially of storing into the `OrderForm` the data that the user inputs in the shipping page. Therefore, it works by loading the `OrderForm`, retrieving each individual parameter using the various `Request` methods of the `Page` component and then stores the purchase information back into the database.

Errors are handled by the I_error.asp generic include file, which simply dumps the contents of a Dictionary object (that can either be one the error collections that can be found inside the OrderForm after executing the pipeline or a collection created by the calling script) to the browser and invites the user to click on the back button to correct the problem.

Payment.asp

The payment page starts by running the Plan pipeline once more, this time with the shipping information in the OrderForm. Contrary to what happened in the basket, the errors here are looked for in both the _Purchase_Errors and _Basket_Errors collections, since the entire pipeline should now be able to run without any problem.

For the rest, the page behaves similarly to shipping.asp, and it either displays the payment interface of the Wallet or the corresponding HTML forms. It's interesting to note that, while the address interface of the Wallet is consistent and can therefore be successfully replaced by a pre-defined HTML form, the same cannot be said of its payment counterpart. You will have to make sure that your store supports the same payment methods both with and without the Wallet, or you may risk losing customers–for example because their browser doesn't support the Wallet and therefore they can't use the payment method they want.

What we said about the ship-to country being hard-coded in the shipping page is valid for the payment page as well. In fact, about halfway down the script, we find the following HTML tag:

```
<INPUT TYPE="HIDDEN" NAME="bill_to_country" VALUE="USA">
```

> **Once again, if you are planning to let customers from places other than the United States buy from your store, you will have to change this code.**

Xt_orderform_purchase.asp

This is where the final act of the purchase process takes place. In fact, this script takes care of incorporating the values entered in the payment page into the OrderForm and of executing the Purchase pipeline at the same time.

As before in xt_orderform_prepare.asp, the data is entered by the OrderForm OrderformPurchaseArgs function in the OrderForm by reading each parameter using one of the Request methods provided by the Page object. This, in turn, is called by OrderFormPurchase, which, in the meantime, has loaded a copy of the purchase information in an OrderForm object.

If no errors are encountered while retrieving the HTTP parameters, the function then saves the OrderForm back to the database (the pipeline might raise a runtime error, which would otherwise cause all the data to be lost). The Plan pipeline is then run one last time, with the intent of (a) making sure that nothing has changed since the last time it was executed, and that (b) the OrderForm data is still all valid. You will notice that, this time, the script uses a different approach than before:

```
             REM Set the verify with flags onto the OrderForm
             call mscsPage.ProcessVerifyWith(mscsOrderForm)

             REM Create the basic pipe context
             set mscsPipeContext = UtilGetPipeContext()

             REM Run the plan
             errorLevel = UtilRunPipe("plan.pcf", mscsOrderForm, mscsPipeContext)
```

There are at least two reasons why the UtilRunPlan function is not used here. First of all, the OrderForm data has already been loaded; second, the script performs a call to the ProcessVerifyWith method of the Page component, which causes the pipeline to look for differences between the new calculations and the data that was previously viewed by the user. If they don't match, then the user is asked to review the data before approving the purchase again.

If no errors are returned by the Plan pipeline, the script proceeds to execute the Purchase pipeline to complete the order:

```
        if mscsOrderForm.[_Basket_Errors].Count = 0 and
  mscsOrderForm.[_Purchase_Errors].Count = 0 and errorLevel = 1 then

             REM Create the receipt storage
             Set mscsReceiptStorage = UtilGetReceiptStorage()

             REM Add the receipt storage into the pipe context...the Save Receipt
  component uses it
             Set mscsPipeContext.ReceiptStorage = MSCSReceiptStorage

             REM Run the transacted pipe
             errorLevel = UtilRunTxPipe("purchase.pcf", mscsOrderForm, mscsPipeContext)
        end if
```

This time, the pipeline is run using the UtilRunTxPipe function, which is located inside I_util.asp and is essentially identical to UtilRunPipe, with the exception that it runs the pipeline in a transacted environment:

```
function UtilRunTxPipe(file, orderForm, pipeContext)
    Set pipeline = Server.CreateObject("Commerce.MtsTxPipeline")

    Call pipeline.LoadPipe(Request.ServerVariables("APPL_PHYSICAL_PATH") &
"config\" & file)

    REM Call pipeline.SetLogFile(Request.ServerVariables("APPL_PHYSICAL_PATH") &
"config\txpipeline.log")

    errorLevel = pipeline.Execute(1, orderForm, pipeContext, 0)

    UtilRunTxPipe = errorLevel
end function
```

> You will need to uncomment the call to SetLogFile in this function as well if you want to log the Purchase pipeline's activity.

The Purchase Pipeline

The following figure shows the structure of the purchase pipeline. As you can see, it's simpler than the Plan pipeline, and the function of all the scripts is pretty straightforward. The one thing that you might want to note is that the `Validate CC Info` script contains a few lines of code that output an error if the credit card is not of a type that is accepted by the store. If you plan to add more credit card types, you will need to modify this script as well.

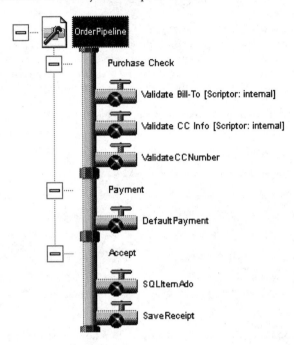

Finally, it's worth noting that, in the accept stage, an instance of `SQLItemADO` is used to store information about the individual products that are part of the order inside the `mt_receipt_item` table. The `SaveReceipt` component, on the other hand, is used to insert the appropriate record, together with a copy of the marshalled basket, into the `mt_receipt` table. It's interesting to note that the properties of `SaveReceipt` are programmed so that the component will not save the credit card information as part of the marshalled basket:

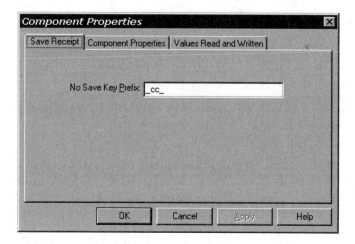

If you are processing your credit card online—or if you need to keep them on file—you should change this setting by using an empty string in the **No Save Key Prefix** text box.

`SaveReceipt` requires that an instance of `Commerce.DBStorage` be saved inside the `OrderForm`. This is done in `xt_orderform_purchase.asp` by calling the `UtilGetReceiptStorage` function, which is identical to `UtilGetOrderformStorage`, with the exception that it instructs its instance of DBStorage to access the `mt_receipt` table.

Confirmed.asp

The confirmation page is extremely simple, as it limits its functionality to returning the order_id string to the user, and providing a link to `receipt.asp`, which can be used to review his or her order.

Order Viewing

The only two pages of the storefront that we haven't yet had a chance to examine are `receipts.asp` and `receipt.asp`. The former can be used to produce a history of the orders placed by a particular customer, while the latter will provide more detail about a specific order, given its identifier.

Receipts.asp

This script works by executing a query against the `mt_receipts` table, looking for all the records whose primary key corresponds to the shopper ID of the user. It's important to understand that this page will only work properly if you are using cookies to store the shopper ID, or if you require your customers to login—if you aren't, the shopper ID will be only temporary and it will be changed the next time the user logs in.

Receipt.asp

Finally, this script works similarly to the basket, with the only exception that the `OrderForm` is loaded from the `mt_receipts` table, rather than from `mt_basket`. You will also notice that the page includes some more additional information, such as the ship-to and bill-to address. No credit card information is specified—since the pipeline is programmed not to save it—so you will have to manually add it in yourselves if you need to.

Summary

Well, this is the end of our discussion of what pipelines are and how you can use them in your sites. As you have probably noticed, the basic concept behind this technology is not very complicated—its goal is essentially that of providing a properly ordered environment for operations to be carried out. At the same time, however, its implementation, as well as the sheer number of components available, make it somewhat more difficult to master well.

The only solution to this problem is to practice a lot with different scenarios, trying to understand how different pipeline configurations can help you translate your business needs into working solutions. If you're planning to work with Site Server in the future, you can rest assured that it will time well spent. There is little doubt that pipelines are what truly distinguishes Site Server from other ecommerce systems, and it's probably fair to say that they are here to stay.

19

Extending Your Pipelines

In the previous chapter, we had a chance to take an in-depth look at what pipelines are and how they work. As such they can be considered a very exciting technology, however, they wouldn't be nearly as interesting if it wasn't possible to extend them so that they can provide more functionality.

As a matter of fact, we have already discovered that this can be done by using the `Scriptor` component to execute ASP-like scripts that can act directly on the pipeline's contents and interact with the outside world through COM. The biggest limitation of this approach, however, is that `Scriptor`'s performance can become a problem in large implementations, and that its possibilities are still restricted to what a scripting language can do.

During the course of this chapter, we will examine how pipelines can be extended by writing custom components in either Microsoft Visual Basic or Microsoft Visual C++. We'll also focus on how pipeline components work internally and how they interact with the pipeline data and execution objects:

> **Understanding pipeline components**
> First of all, we'll take a look at how a pipeline component is structured, and how it works internally. As we'll see, a component is essentially a COM object that supports at least one interface – `IPipelineComponent`. Additional interfaces can be implemented in order to provide specific capabilities, such as persistence and property pages.

> **Writing pipeline components in Visual Basic**
> Visual Basic is the simplest environment in which you can write a pipeline component, since it supports COM natively and is very easy to program. On the flip side, Visual Basic's performance might not be sufficient for large-scale applications that are meant to serve a high-traffic client base.

> **Writing pipeline components in Visual C++**
> Finally, we'll tackle the development of pipeline components in Visual C++. As you may imagine, components written in VC++ are more difficult to implement – mainly because the language itself is more complex (and complete) than VB – but the Site Server SDK includes some tools that make it much easier. Using VC++, you will be able to go beyond the limits of the Visual Basic language and the performance of your components will be greatly enhanced.

Understanding Pipeline Components

As we have mentioned more than once, pipeline components essentially belong to a special class of COM objects that are compatible with the pipeline technology by implementing a particular set of interfaces. Pipeline components are also peculiar in that they must be registered following a particular procedure, or the pipeline editing tools will not be able to recognize them.

Pipeline Interfaces

Let's take a brief tour of the COM interfaces that must be implemented in a pipeline component. As you can see from the list below, there is only one interface that is required (meaning that the component will not work unless it implements it), while the others are optional and server a number of different purposes.

Interface Name	Required	Description
IPipelineComponent	Yes	The main pipeline interface. Provides the means for the pipeline objects to control the component for execution.
IPipelineComponentAdmin	No	Provides ASP-based property management capabilities.
IPipelineComponentDescription	No	Used to provide a description of the values that the component reads and writes.
IPersistStreamInit	No	Used to save and/or load a component from a storage medium.
ISpecifyPropertyPages	No	Used to communicate to the Win32-based editor what property page(s) are implemented by the component.

Even though only IPipelineComponent is a required interface, a "serious" component will most likely implement IPipelineComponentAdmin and IPipelineComponentDescription, which will provide support for the web-based editor, and for the list of values read and written that appears in the Win32-based editor.

If your component requires property pages, you will also need to implement ISpecifyPropertyPage, which will make the Win32 editor aware of them. However, a special procedure will have to be followed to let the web editor know about these property pages, as we'll see later on in the chapter.

IPipelineComponent

The main interface that a pipeline component must implement provides two methods, one of which you are already very well familiar with, since we illustrated it when we were discussing the Scriptor component.

`EnableDesign` is used to "prepare" the component for execution in one of two modes: design mode, which corresponds to the editing phase, and execution mode, which corresponds to the production phase. In principle, during the editing phase the component should be more tolerant of possible errors, while in execution mode it should report all the errors properly. The truth is, no component is ever executed in design mode – at least as far as I've been able to see – and the only errors that you normally report during the editing phase are those related to the validity of the properties that the user enters.

```
HRESULT IPipelineComponent::EnableDesign(BOOL fEnable /* in */);
```

```
Sub IPipelineComponent_EnableDesign(ByVal fEnable As Long)
```

Where:

> ➤ `fEnable` specifies whether the component should be executed in design mode (TRUE or <> 0) or in execution mode (FALSE or 0)

The implementation of `EnableDesign` is completely optional. In my personal experience with pipeline components, I have never found the need to use it.

One method that you just have to use is `Execute`, which we met earlier when we were talking about `Scriptor`. `Execute` is called whenever the pipeline component is run from within a pipeline object.

```
HRESULT IPipelineComponent::Execute(IDispatch* pDispOrder   /* in */,
                                    IDispatch* pDispContext /* in */,
                                    long lFlags             /* in */,
                                    long* pErrorLevel /* out, retval */);
```

```
Function IPipelineComponent_Execute(ByVal pDispOrder As Object, _
                                    ByVal pDispContext As Object, _
                                    ByVal lFlags As Long) As Long
```

Where:

> ➤ `pDispOrder` is the pipeline's main dictionary
> ➤ `pDispContext` is the pipeline's context
> ➤ `lFlags` is a reserved value. Should always be zero
> ➤ `pErrorLevel` is a pointer to the return value for the function

In the case of Visual C++ implementations, the `HRESULT` function return value must be complemented by setting `*pErrorLevel` to the appropriate return code for the component's execution, while Visual Basic implementations will simply use this as the return value for their function. The possible values for this variable are those that we have already seen earlier for the pipeline objects, although a fourth one is also defined for "catastrophic failure" errors:

1	Success: the pipeline execution was successful.
2	Warning: a non-fatal error was raised. The pipeline component may elect to continue the pipeline's execution. In an MSCS store, the Plan pipeline is designed to withstand this error level, while the Purchase pipeline terminates with an error. The error level withstood by a pipeline can be set in its properties when the Win32 editor is running in Expert Mode.
3	Failure: an error was raised. The pipeline execution should terminate immediately.
4	Fatal error: a fatal (catastrophic) error was raised. The pipeline execution should terminate immediately.

As a rule, level 2 errors are raised when the problems can be fixed by the user's interaction (e.g. re-entering a credit card number, and so on), while level 3 errors represent user-independent issues, such as communication failures and inability to connect to a database. Level 4 is never used.

IPipelineComponentAdmin

This interface is used to provide a means for ASP pages to access a component's properties directly. You will most likely implement this interface if you expect your component to be usable for MicroPipe operations. In order for the properties to be passed along, you must include them in an instance of Dictionary.

IPipelineComponentAdmin provides two methods, one for loading and the other for saving the properties. GetConfigData is used to return the configuration parameters:

```
HRESULT IPipelineComponentAdmin::GetConfigData(IDispatch** ppDict /* out */);
```

```
Function IPipelineComponentAdmin_GetConfigData() As Object
```

Where:

> IDispatch is the return value of the function's C++ implementation

Even when your component's properties are not set, you should always return a complete Dictionary object when GetConfigData is called. This will let whoever uses your component find out what the correct names for the properties are, just like we did while looking at the MicroPipe component.

Properties are saved using the SetConfigData method, to which the caller passes a Dictionary object that contains all the appropriate Name/Value pairs:

```
HRESULT IPipelineComponentAdmin::SetConfigData(IDispatch* pDict /* in */);
```

```
Sub IPipelineComponentAdmin_SetConfigData(ByVal pDict As Object)
```

Where:

> pDict is the Dictionary object that contains the Name/Value pairs of the properties to be set

Your implementation of `SetConfigData` should be flexible enough to recognize the scenario in which the caller has only set a few of the properties: in that case, only those properties that have been set in the `Dictionary` should be changed.

IPipelineComponentDescription

The `IPipelineComponentDescription` interface is implemented to pass a list of the values that are accessed by a component to the Win32 editor, which in turn, displays them in the Properties dialog box for that component. Each method in this interface returns a COM `Variant` variable that contains a `SAFEARRAY` of `Variant`s, which, in turn, are initialized with wide-character string values.

> **It's important to understand that, because they are entirely COM-based, pipeline components should store and retrieve all string values in wide-character (Unicode) format.**

The list of values read from the pipeline's main dictionary is returned by the `ValuesRead` method:

```
HRESULT IPipelineComponentDescription::ValuesRead(
    VARIANT* pVarRead /* out */);
```

```
Function IPipelineComponentDescription_ValuesRead() As Variant
```

Where:

> ➤ pVarRead is the return value of the function

Similarly, `ValuesWritten` and `ContextValuesRead` are used to report the Name/Value pairs that a component writes to the main dictionary and reads from the context respectively.

```
HRESULT IPipelineComponentDescription::ValuesWritten(
    VARIANT* pVarRead /* out */);
HRESULT IPipelineComponentDescription::ContextValuesRead(
    VARIANT* pVarRead /* out */);
```

```
Function IPipelineComponentDescription_ValuesWritten() As Variant
Function IPipelineComponentDescription_ContextValuesRead() As Variant
```

Where:

> ➤ pVarRead is the return value of the function

IPersistStreamInit

This is a standard COM interface that is used to save and load data to and from a streaming storage medium, such as a file or a database field. A pipeline component needs to support it in order for the editor to load and save its configuration. Obviously, if the component does not expose any properties, it doesn't need to implement this interface. Also, you should keep in mind that Visual Basic implements this interface through the property bag mechanism. As such, if you're writing your components in VB, you don't need to worry about `IPersistStreamInit`.

The `InitNew` method is called whenever a new instance of the component is created from scratch, rather than loaded from a storage medium:

```
HRESULT IPersistStreamInit::InitNew(void);
```

Although you normally don't have to do much in this method, you must implement it, and you can use it to initialize the properties that your component exposes if necessary. When a component is instead loaded from a storage medium, the pipeline editor (or pipeline object) will call the `Load` method:

```
HRESULT IPersistStreamInit::Load(IStream* pStm /* in */);
```

Where:

> `pStm` is an instance of `IStream` from which the component properties are to be read

Reading from an instance of `IStream`, as we'll see later on, is not a very complex operation. All you have to do is use the `Read` method defined below:

```
HRESULT IStream::Read(void*   pv        /* out */,
                      ULONG   cb        /* out */,
                      ULONG*  pcbRead   /* in */);
```

Where:

> `pv` is a pointer to a buffer that will receive the information read
> `cb` is the number of bytes to read
> `pcbRead` is the number of bytes actually read

As for any streaming operation, you will have to save your data in a way such that it will be possible to retrieve it easily from the stream. For example, if you decide to save a string, you must do so by making sure that the `Load` method will know how long the string is before reading the data from the stream. In general, you should use the built-in COM `Variant` variables available to an ATL VC++ project when developing your components, since they interface with `IPersistStreamInit` directly.

When it comes to saving a component's property to a stream, a particular sequence of events takes place. First of all, the editor will call the `IsDirty` method to establish whether the component has been saved since the last time it was changed.

```
HRESULT IPersistStreamInit::IsDirty(void);
```

`IsDirty` should return `S_OK` if the component's properties have been modified, and `S_FALSE` if they haven't. It's a good idea to always return `S_OK`, so that there will never be the possibility that certain information will not be saved.

If `IsDirty` indicates that the component's data should be saved, the editor calls the `GetSizeMax` method to determine how much space on the stream is required to save the information:

```
HRESULT IPersistStreamInit::GetSizeMax(ULARGE_INTEGER* pcbSize /* out */);
```

Where:

> `pcbSize` is a pointer to a 64-bit integer variable that receives the number of bytes required to save the object.

`GetSizeMax` should always return the upper bound of the possible space required to save the object, even though the actual requirements might end up being lower. This is because the stream that you might receive for saving the data could be limited in size to the amount returned by the method.

Finally, the data is saved to the stream by the `Save` method:

```
HRESULT IPersistStreamInit::Save(IStream* pStm        /* in */,
                                 BOOL     fClearDirty /* in */);
```

Where:

> `fClearDirty` is a flag that indicates whether the dirty flag should be cleared.

> `pStm` is an instance of `IStream` to which the component properties are to be written.

Before you run to your e-mail programs and send flames to the author, let me explain that the "dirty" flag is simply an indication of whether the component has been modified or not since the last time it was saved. I assure you that it is my intention to keep this book (or at least my part of it) in the G rating!

Similar to what happened for the `Load` method, the `IStream` interface provides us with the appropriate method for writing data to it:

```
HRESULT IStream::Write(void const* pv         /* out */,
                       ULONG       cb         /* out */,
                       ULONG*      pcbWritten /* in */);
```

Where:

> `pv` is a pointer to the buffer that holds the data to be written

> `cb` is the number of bytes to write

> `pcbWritten` is the number of bytes actually written to the stream

ISpecifyPropertyPages

The last interface that we will examine is used to report all the property pages that a component supports. Like `IPersistStreamInit`, `ISpecifyPropertyPages` is a standard COM interface that is normally used by all components (VB components implement it automatically).

The only method that this interface requires is supposed to return a counter array containing the GUIDs of all the property pages that the component supports (keep in mind that a property page is simply another COM component):

```
HRESULT ISpecifyPropertyPages::GetPages(CAUUID* pPages /* out */);
```

Where:

> ➤ pPages is a variable of type CAUUID that contains the required structures to return an array of GUIDs.

The CAUUID structure is defined as follows:

```
typedef struct tagCAUUID
{
    ULONG       cElems;
    GUID FAR* pElems;
} CAUUID;
```

where cElems is an unsigned long variable that contains the number of elements in the array, and pElems is a pointer to the buffer that holds the array, which must be allocated using the CoTaskMemAlloc function.

Writing Pipeline Components in Visual Basic

There's no doubt that Visual Basic is the ideal environment for developing COM objects, since it's largely based on the Component Object Model to start with. As such, VB is an optimal platform for writing pipeline components, since it's much easier to manage in the development phase.

However, VB has also several limitations if you compare it to Visual C++, in particular the fact that it doesn't support the Free-Threaded threading model, which is the ideal model for pipeline components. Thus, in general, you will probably want to use VB for prototyping purposes – just because it's faster to write components with it – while VC++ should be your choice for production-grade code.

Before You Start

I should probably point out that you can't use just any version of a Visual Basic component for developing a pipeline component. In fact, the pipeline objects require every component to be based either on the Apartment or Free-threading model, and neither of them is supported by any version of VB prior to 5.0 SP1.

Therefore, you will need to either have installed Service Pack 1 for Visual Basic 5.0 (available for free from the Microsoft web site) or Visual Basic 6.0 and higher (also available from Microsoft, but not for free, I'm afraid). This will enable you to create Apartment-threaded COM objects, and write pipeline components that will actually work.

Preparing the Project

In order to create a new pipeline component, you must first create a project of type ActiveX DLL or ActiveX Control. Next, you will need to create the actual component, which should either be a User Control or a Class Module. This choice depends largely on whether you expect to need one or more property pages, in which case you will need a Control, or not, in which case either type will work for you.

In addition, you should check your project's properties to make sure that your component is being created using the Apartment-threading model.

Implementing the Basic Component Functionality

In order to make the component work, you will need, at a minimum, to implement the IPipelineComponent interface. In order to do so, you need to reference the Pipeline 1.0 Type Library from the Project/References dialog box. If that library doesn't appear in your list, you can also include it by adding a reference to the \bin\pipeline.dll file in your Site Server installation folder.

Once you have added a reference to the pipeline library, you can instruct VB that you intend to implement the IPipelineComponent interface in your component:

```
Implements IPipelineComponent
```

If you look at your editing window, you will notice that the Object list now contains the IPipelineComponent interface, which, in turn, provides you with the Execute and EnableDesign methods.

```
Private Sub IPipelineComponent_EnableDesign(ByVal fEnable As Long)

End Sub

Private Function IPipelineComponent_Execute(ByVal pdispOrder As Object, _
                                            ByVal pdispContext As Object, _
                                            ByVal lFlags As Long) As Long

End Function
```

When the Execute method is called, you can access both the context and the main dictionary directly from the component as you would do from an ASP script – that's the beauty of a language so well integrated with COM!

Let's suppose, for example, that we want to write a component to handle a special promotion conceived by our marketing department that provides orders whose item count falls between two boundaries. We'll store – for the moment – those boundaries in two private variables, called lLowerBound and lUpperBound, and the special shipping price in lShippingPrice. As you can see from the code below, we'll just go through all the items in the Orderform using a simple For...Next loop:

```
Option Explicit

Implements IPipelineComponent

Private lLowerBound As Long
Private lUpperBound As Long
Private lShippingPrice As Long

Private Sub IPipelineComponent_EnableDesign(ByVal fEnable As Long)

End Sub

'========================
' Execute method of IPipelineComponent
'
' Called when the pipeline component is executed
'========================

Private Function IPipelineComponent_Execute(ByVal pdispOrder As Object, _
                                   ByVal pdispContext As Object, _
                                   ByVal lFlags As Long) As Long

    Dim lTotalQuantity As Long
    Dim Item

    ' Only run if the shipping costs have not been set yet

    If Not IsNull(pdispOrder.[_shipping_total]) Then Exit Function

    lTotalQuantity = 0

    ' Calculate total number of items in the Orderform

    For Each Item In pdispOrder.Items
        lTotalQuantity = lTotalQuantity + Item.Quantity
    Next

    ' If total number of items within boundaries, apply special pricing

    If (lTotalQuantity > lLowerBound) And (lTotalQuantity < lUpperBound) Then
        pdispOrder.[_shipping_total] = lShippingPrice
    End If

    ' Return success value

    IPipelineComponent_Execute = 1

End Function
```

Reporting the Values Read and Written by the Component

In order to report the values read and written by our component, we'll need to implement the
IPipelineComponentDescription interface. To do so, however, you will need to have the Site
Server SDK, which comes with SSCE, installed on your computer. This will allow you to add a
reference to the pipecomplib.tlb object library, which is located in the lib_386 folder of the
SDK's main installation folder.

Adding the following line to our component's source:

```
Implements IPipelineComponentDescription
```

Will let us add the code to support the interface's three methods. In our case, we are not reading any value from the context, but we are certainly reading and writing to the main dictionary:

Values Read	Item.Quantity
	_shipping_total
Values Written	(Optional) _shipping_total

As such, we'll have to return the appropriate Variant arrays to the editor:

```
'=======================
' IPipelineComponentDescription implementation
' Used to report the values read and written by the component
'=======================

Private Function IPipelineComponentDescription_ContextValuesRead() As Variant
    Dim ReturnValue(0) As Variant

    ReturnValue(0) = "[None]"

    IPipelineComponentDescription_ContextValuesRead = ReturnValue
End Function

Private Function IPipelineComponentDescription_ValuesRead() As Variant
    Dim ReturnValue(1) As Variant

    ReturnValue(0) = "Item.Quantity"
    ReturnValue(1) = "_shipping_total"

    IPipelineComponentDescription_ValuesRead = ReturnValue
End Function

Private Function IPipelineComponentDescription_ValuesWritten() As Variant
    Dim ReturnValue(0) As Variant

    ReturnValue(0) = "[Optional] _shipping_total"

    IPipelineComponentDescription_ValuesWritten = ReturnValue
End Function
```

Adding and Supporting Properties

It's pretty much obvious that our component uses three properties: the lower and upper boundaries, and the special shipping price. As such, we can start by implementing them using standard VB code:

```
'=======================
' Component properties, implemented using standard VB functionality
'=======================

Public Property Get LowerBound() As Variant
    LowerBound = lLowerBound
End Property
```

```
Public Property Let LowerBound(Value As Variant)
    lLowerBound = CLng(Value)
End Property

Public Property Get UpperBound() As Variant
    UpperBound = lUpperBound
End Property

Public Property Let UpperBound(Value As Variant)
    lUpperBound = CLng(Value)
End Property

Public Property Get ShippingPrice() As Variant
    ShippingPrice = lShippingPrice
End Property

Public Property Let ShippingPrice(Value As Variant)
    lShippingPrice = CLng(Value)
End Property
```

Now, all we need to do is create a property page for the component and add the appropriate control and check logic to it. We can do that by selecting **Add Property Page...** from the **Project** menu. In general, I prefer to use the VB Property Page Wizard, which takes care automatically of creating a property page for me. Whatever your choice, you will end up with something similar to what is shown in the following screenshot; make sure that your property page appears in the property page list for your components (accessible by selecting **Property Pages** from the component's properties).

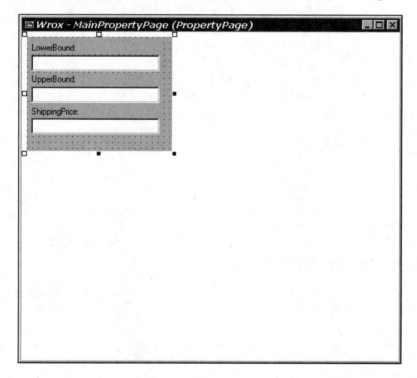

It's a good idea to have your property pages perform at least some basic checks on the validity of the selection that the user makes for the property values. In my case, I've added to my property page the code needed to make sure that all the values entered are valid positive integer numbers, and that the lower boundary is less than or equal to the upper boundary. In the following code, I've left the wizard generated sections un-highlighted.

```
Private Sub txtShippingPrice_Change()
    Changed = True
End Sub

Private Sub txtShippingPrice_Validate(Cancel As Boolean)
    On Error Resume Next

    If CLng(txtShippingPrice.Text) < 0 Then
        Cancel = True
    End If

    ' if an error is detected the text entered cannot be converted to a long
    ' integer

    If Err.Number <> 0 Then
        Cancel = True
    End If
End Sub

Private Sub txtUpperBound_Change()
    Changed = True
End Sub

Private Sub txtUpperBound_Validate(Cancel As Boolean)
    On Error Resume Next

    If CLng(txtUpperBound.Text) < 0 Then
        Cancel = True
    End If

    ' if an error is detected the text entered cannot be converted to a long
    ' integer

    If Err.Number <> 0 Then
        Cancel = True
    End If
End Sub

Private Sub txtLowerBound_Change()
    Changed = True
End Sub

Private Sub txtLowerBound_Validate(Cancel As Boolean)
    On Error Resume Next

    If CLng(txtLowerBound.Text) < 0 Then
        Cancel = True
    End If

    ' if an error is detected the text entered cannot be converted to a long
    ' integer

    If Err.Number <> 0 Then
        Cancel = True
    End If
End Sub
```

```
Private Sub PropertyPage_ApplyChanges()
    SelectedControls(0).ShippingPrice = txtShippingPrice.Text
    SelectedControls(0).UpperBound = txtUpperBound.Text
    SelectedControls(0).LowerBound = txtLowerBound.Text
End Sub

Private Sub PropertyPage_SelectionChanged()
    txtShippingPrice.Text = SelectedControls(0).ShippingPrice
    txtUpperBound.Text = SelectedControls(0).UpperBound
    txtLowerBound.Text = SelectedControls(0).LowerBound
End Sub
```

Since our component already exposes all of its properties directly, there is very little point in implementing the `IPipelineComponentAdmin` interface, but we'll do it anyway – just for the fun of it. In this case, we already have added a reference to the appropriate type library when we implemented `IPipelineComponentDescription`, and therefore we should be able to implement this interface right away. In fact, adding the following line:

```
Implements IPipelineComponentAdmin
```

Lets us insert the `GetConfigData` and `SetConfigData` members into our code. However, we're still unable to create the instance of the `Dictionary` object that we will need in order to return the properties to our callers. To make our component "Dictionary-aware", we can include a reference to the **Commerce – MSCSCore Type Library** that should be available on our computer. Note that the MSCS objects are available as part of the `MSCSCoreLib` group: for example, a Dictionary object is identified as `MSCSCoreLib.CDictionary`. Next, we are finally able to add the implementations of the `IPipelineComponentAdmin` interface:

```
' =======================
' GetConfigData/SetConfigData
'
' Implemented from IPipelineComponentAdmin
' =======================

Private Function IPipelineComponentAdmin_GetConfigData() As Object

    Dim dConfigData As MSCSCoreLib.CDictionary

    ' Create a dictionary object

    Set dConfigData = New MSCSCoreLib.CDictionary

    ' Fill it with the configuration data

    dConfigData.LowerBound = lLowerBound
    dConfigData.UpperBound = lUpperBound
    dConfigData.ShippingPrice = lShippingPrice

    Set IPipelineComponentAdmin_GetConfigData = dConfigData

End Function

Private Sub IPipelineComponentAdmin_SetConfigData(ByVal pDict As Object)

    ' Save values passed into properties
```

```
        lLowerBound = CLng(pDict.LowerBound)
        lUpperBound = CLng(pDict.UpperBound)
        lShippingPrice = CLng(pDict.ShippingPrice)

    End Sub
```

The only thing missing, at this point, is support for loading and saving the component's properties from a storage medium. Visual Basic provides all the functionality required through the `ReadProperties` and `WriteProperties` methods:

```
'=======================
' Persistency functions
'=======================

Private Sub UserControl_ReadProperties(PropBag As PropertyBag)
    lUpperBound = PropBag.ReadProperty("UBound", 0)
    lLowerBound = PropBag.ReadProperty("LBound", 0)
    lShippingPrice = PropBag.ReadProperty("ShippingPrice", 0)
End Sub

Private Sub UserControl_WriteProperties(PropBag As PropertyBag)
    PropBag.WriteProperty "UBound", lUpperBound, 0
    PropBag.WriteProperty "LBound", lLowerBound, 0
    PropBag.WriteProperty "ShippingPrice", lShippingPrice, 0
End Sub
```

Making the Component Visible

If you now go to the Win32 editor (we'll talk more about the web editor later on in the chapter), you'll notice that the component we just created...doesn't appear anywhere! Not to worry, though: this is happening only because we haven't properly registered it.

In fact, in order for the editor to know that a COM component is really a pipeline object, a few extra entries must be done in its Registry key. The same must be done in order to declare the affinity of a component with one or more particular stages. Let's start by opening the Registry Editor and look for the component; assuming that you called it `Wrox.ShippingSpecial`, just like I did, you'll find it under **HKEY_CLASSES_ROOT/Wrox.ShippingSpecial**. Within that key, you will find a sub-key called **CLSID**, whose default value contains the Class ID for the component. If you copy that into the clipboard and then use it to make a search starting from the **HKEY_CLASSES_ROOT/CLSID** key, you will find the component's main registry entries.

One of the sub-keys in the component's main entry is called **Implemented Categories**, and contains several other sub-keys that reference a number of Class IDs. This sub-key is used to express what kind of component is described in the Registry, and that's where the editor looks to see whether a COM object is indeed a pipeline component.

In order to be marked as such, a pipeline component needs to implement the following category:

```
{CF7536D0-43C5-11D0-B85D-00C04FD7A0FA}
```

Then, it also needs to specify the stages that it shows affinity for. MSCS provides a different category for each possible stage, plus a special category for those components that work in any stage. They are all listed in the `Include\Microsoft Site Server\Commerce\Pipe_Stages.h` C++ include file. In our case, we will add the implemented category for the Shipping stage, which is:

{D82C349A-43C5-11D0-B85D-00C04FD7A0FA}

Once the appropriate GUIDs have been added to our component's Implemented Category list, we'll finally see it appear in the Win32-based editor. The editor will also show our property page and the values read and written by our component!

Using the Component in the Web-Based Editor

If you now try to add the component to a pipeline using the web-based editor, you will notice that it is unable to display a property page for it. That's because web editing works in a slightly different way than Win32 editing: you'll have to provide ASP-based property pages!

The editor will automatically recognize your property pages, as long as their names follow the following convention:

> ➢ The main property page must be called with the name of the component, taking care that any dots are turned into underscores. For example, the property page for Wrox.ShippingSpecial should be called Wrox_ShippingSpecial.asp.

> ➢ The "post" page, used to validate and save the values of the properties should be called with the same name as the main page, with the _Post suffix appended to it (i.e. Wrox_ShippingSpecial_Post.asp).

Both pages should be stored in the following folder:

SiteServer Root\SiteServer\Admin\Commerce\Pipeline Configuration

In addition, the main page should include two files provided by MSCS, which create the header and footer for the actual page displayed by the web browser, including all the structures required to access the component and post the newly entered values. The header include file is called pe_3rd_party_edit_header.asp, while the footer is called pe_3rd_party_edit_footer.asp. The header handles the component to be configured automatically, and makes it available in the ComponentConfig variable, so that all you have to do in the main page is add the proper HTML controls to display the properties and let the user change them. For example, here's a simple property page for our shipping control:

```
<%@ Language=VBScript %>

<!--#include file = "pe_3rd_party_edit_header.asp"-->

Lower boundary:
<INPUT TYPE="TEXT" NAME="LBound" Value="<% = ComponentConfig.LowerBound %>">
<BR>

Upper boundary:
<INPUT TYPE="TEXT" NAME="UBound" Value="<% = ComponentConfig.UpperBound %>">
<BR>

Shipping cost:
<INPUT TYPE="TEXT" NAME="SCost" Value="<% = ComponentConfig.ShippingPrice %>">
<BR>

<!--#include file = "pe_3rd_party_edit_footer.asp"-->
```

If you add this file to the editor's folder with the name `Wrox_ShippingSpecial.asp`, you will notice that the editor will not complain anymore, and the property page will finally become visible, although you will not be able to save the information you type in yet. To do so, you'll need to write the post script `Wrox_ShippingSpecial_Post.asp`, which must include the `pe_3rd_party_post_header.asp` file at its beginning:

```
<%@ Language=VBScript %>

<!--#include file = "pe_3rd_party_post_header.asp"-->

<%
    ComponentConfig.LowerBound = Request ("LBound")
    ComponentConfig.UpperBound = Request ("UBound")
    ComponentConfig.ShippingPrice = Request ("SCost")
%>

<!--#include file = "pe_3rd_party_post_footer.asp"-->
```

As you have certainly noted, in this case we have used the properties that the component exposes directly – exactly like our VB property page does – but we could have just as well used the configuration dictionary that we exposed as part of our implementation of `IPipelineComponentAdmin`.

Writing Pipeline Components in Visual C++

The task of developing a pipeline component in Visual C++ is certainly not an easy one, although it's fair to say that the tools provided by MSCS *do* help the programmer a lot. The real challenge, unfortunately, is in the language itself, which is necessarily more complex than Visual Basic, even though the results you can achieve are far better in terms of stability and performance.

As a result, I strongly recommend that you at least consider using VB for your development needs, unless there is a very good reason to do otherwise. When a component starts behaving erratically, you'll want to be able to fix it as quickly as possible, and not waste precious time digging into some C++ snafu. Now that you're warned...

Getting Started

The first time I tried to write a pipeline component in VC++, I ended my day a desperate man. Sure, the documentation explained a lot (although, I must say, there are a few mistakes here and there), but dealing with all the problems of managing a COM component *plus* taking care of all the little idiosyncrasies of working with MSCS objects was a little too much for my little brain.

Then, one day, I decided that for once I'd actually take a look at what the whole package had to offer and found out that MSCS comes with a built-in ATL wizard that has been designed specifically for creating pipeline components. After a few minutes of head-banging on the wall, I installed it and...voilà! A whole new world opened before my eyes, a world in which developing a pipeline component didn't take an IQ of 150!

The ATL wizard is the first thing that you have to install if you want to use VC++ for writing your components. It's located in the `SiteServer\Commerce\SDK\Commerce\Samples\ATLWizard` subfolder in your SSCE installation's main directory. All you really need to do is the following:

1. **Register the wizard's DLL**. This is located in the i386 directory and is called `CommerceDLG.dll`. You can register it by selecting Run from the Start menu, then typing in the following:

    RegSvr32.exe *SiteServer*
    Root\SiteServer\Commerce\SDK\Commerce\Samples\ATLWizard\i386\CommerceDlg.dll

    Where *SiteServer Root* is, as usual, the location where you installed SSCE. The COM server registration utility should pop up a dialog box similar to the one shown in the next screenshot, indicating that the `dll` was properly registered.

2. **Copy the template files to the VC++ folder**. Doing this will enable the wizard to use certain files as templates for the component's creation. You'll find the templates in the Template folder in the wizard's directory. If you are running Visual C++ 5.0, you must copy them to the `C:\Program Files\DevStudio\SharedIDE\Template\ATL` folder, assuming that `C:\Program Files\DevStudio` is where you installed Visual Studio. If you're using VC++ 6.0, you should copy these files to the `C:\Program Files\Microsoft Visual Studio\Common\MSDev98\Template\ATL` directory, assuming, once again, that `C:\Program Files\Microsoft Visual Studio` is where you installed Visual Studio 98 in the first place.

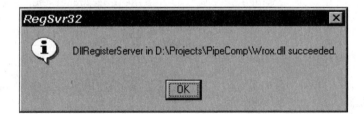

Unfortunately, this will only work well if you run VC++ 5.0. If you're using version 6, moving the files to the right location will not suffice. In fact, you will have to download a file from Microsoft's technical support site, which is available by looking at the following Knowledge Base article:

    http://support.microsoft.com/support/kb/articles/q214/8/32.asp

Once you have downloaded and unzipped the file, all you have to do is follow the instructions that come with it and you're ready to go!

Creating the Component

In order to create a new pipeline component, you must first of all create a new project of type ATL COM AppWizard. In my case, I named it Wrox and chose it to be a DLL that does not support either MFC or MTS.

Once the project is ready, you can create a pipeline component by selecting **New ATL Object** from the **I**nsert menu, then double-clicking on the **Commerce Component** icon. This will cause the Pipeline Component ATL Wizard to pop up and ask you a few questions, such as the component's name (I chose `VCShippingSpecial`) and, if you click on the **C**ommerce Component tab, what additional MSCS interfaces you want the component to support. Our component will support all three available interfaces, so check those boxes!

The good thing here is that the wizard does almost all the work for you – to the point that you will only need to worry about actually implementing the component and its methods, rather than writing the code to declare its interface. You will notice that our newly created component already exposes all the methods required to implement `IPipelineComponent`, `IPipelineComponentDescription`, `ISpecifyPropertyPages` and `IPersistStreamInit`, although it doesn't (yet) support `IPipelineComponentAdmin`.

> To get access to some of the header files that the wizard generated component requires, you need to add the `<SDK Install Directory>\include` directory to the paths that Visual Studio searches through. This can be done from the **Tools | Options** menu.

Accessing MSCS Objects

While accessing MSCS objects in VB was a relatively easy task – thanks, once again, to the language's built-in integration with COM – this time it's going to be a little more difficult, because VC++ won't know anything about them, nor does it provide easy-to-use functionality to handle `Variant`s and Unicode strings.

Luckily, however, MSCS does that for us and, as part of the global methods of our project, it provides a wide variety of functions that can be used for many purposes, as we are about to see.

Dictionary Manipulation

An instance of `IDictionary` can be extracted from an `IDispatch` pointer by calling `GetDictFromDispatch`:

```
GetDictFromDispatch (IDispatch* pdisp, IDictionary** ppdict);
```

Where:

- ➤ `pdisp` is the instance of `IDispatch` from which the `Dictionary` object must be extracted
- ➤ `ppdict` is a pointer to the `IDictionary` pointer that will receive the instance of `IDictionary`.

Once you've got an instance of IDictionary, you can use one of the GetDictValue functions to retrieve a value from it:

```
HRESULT GetDictValue(IDictionary* pdict,
                     LPCWSTR       name,
                     BSTR*         pvalue);

HRESULT GetDictValue(IDictionary* pdict,
                     LPCWSTR       name,
                     VARIANT*      pvalue);

HRESULT GetDictValue(IDictionary* pdict,
                     LPCWSTR       name,
                     int*          pvalue);
```

Where:

> ➢ pdict is the instance of IDictionary from which the value must be extracted
> ➢ name is the name of the Name/Value pair that holds the value to be extracted. Must be a Unicode string
> ➢ pvalue is a pointer to the variable that will receive the value extracted. The actual type depends on what version of the method is called.

Similarly, you can store value in a Name/Value pair of a Dictionary object by using the PutDictValue method:

```
HRESULT PutDictValue(IDictionary* pdict,
                     LPCWSTR       name,
                     LPCWSTR       value);

HRESULT PutDictValue(IDictionary* pdict,
                     LPCWSTR       name,
                     VARIANT&      value);

HRESULT PutDictValue(IDictionary* pdict,
                     LPCWSTR       name,
                     int           value);
```

Where:

> ➢ pdict is the instance of IDictionary to which the Name/Value pair must be written
> ➢ name is the name of the Name/Value pair that must be stored
> ➢ value is the value that must be stored. Its actual type depends on the version of the function that is being called.

You can also loop through the contents of a Dictionary object by using three functions that are used to extract the enumeration interface from it:

```
HRESULT InitKeyEnumInDict(IDictionary*    pdict,
                          IEnumVARIANT**  ppenum);
```

Where:

> - pdict is the instance of IDictionary that must be enumerated
> - ppenum is a pointer to the IEnumVARIANT pointer that will receive the enumeration interface. IEnumVARIANT is a standard COM interface used for enumeration

```
HRESULT GetNextKeyInDict(IEnumVARIANT* penum,
                         BSTR*         pbstrkey);
```

Where:

> - penum is the enumeration interface of the Dictionary object from which the next available key should be extracted
> - pbstrkey is a pointer to the BSTR variable that will receive the name of the next Name/Value pair in the Dictionary

```
HRESULT DeInitKeyEnumInDict(IEnumVARIANT** ppenum);
```

Where:

> - ppenum is the enumeration interface that has to be released

As you may have imagined, in order to use the enumeration functions we must first of all obtain an enumeration interface by calling InitKeyEnumInDict, then we can start looping through the object's Name/Value pairs using GetNextKeyInDict. This function only changes the value of the pbstrkey parameter if the retrieval operation is successful, therefore we can determine whether we are at the end of the list by initializing the parameter to NULL before calling the function. Once we're done with the enumeration, we must release the enumeration object by calling the DeInitKeyEnumInDict function.

Here's an example that goes through the entire main dictionary:

```
IDictionary*   dict;
IEnumVARIANT*  penum;
BSTR           pname;

// We'll assume that the dictionary is already
// loaded

// Get an enumeration interface for the dictionary

InitKeyEnumInDict(&dict, &penum);

// Now, start looping through the dictionary
// until GetNextKeyInDict stops changing the value
// or pname

do
{
    pname = NULL;
    GetNextKeyInDict(penum, &pname);
```

```
      // Use the pair here
  }
  while(pname);

  // Release the enumeration object

  DeInitKeyEnumInDict(&penum);
```

It's important to understand that `GetNextKeyInDict` does not return the actual values of the
Name/Value pairs in the `Dictionary` object, but rather their name part. Therefore, you will still
have to use either a `GetDictValue` or `PutDictValue` function in order to access the pairs.

Naturally, you can also extract a `SimpleList` object from within a `Dictionary`. There are two
global functions for doing so; `GetListFromDict` is a generic function that can be used to extract a
`SimpleList` if the name of the Name/Value pair that holds it inside the `Dictionary` object is
known:

```
HRESULT GetListFromDict(IDictionary*   pdict,
                        LPCWSTR        wszName,
                        ISimpleList**  pplist);
```

Where:

> ➤   pdict is the `Dictionary` object from which the `SimpleList` should be retrieved

> ➤   wszName is the name of the Name/Value pair that holds the `SimpleList` object

> ➤   pplist is a pointer to the `ISimpleList` pointer that will receive the `SimpleList` object

The second function provides us with a shortcut for retrieving the `Items` collection of an
`Orderform` object:

```
HRESULT GetListItems(IDictionary*   pdict,
                     ISimpleList**  pplistItems);
```

Where:

> ➤   pdict is the `Orderform` object from which the `Items` collection should be retrieved

> ➤   pplistItems is a pointer to the `ISimpleList` pointer that will receive the `Items` collection

SimpleList Manipulation

The manipulation of a `SimpleList` object begins with obtaining an instance of it. This can be done,
as we have just seen, by extracting it from a `Dictionary` object, but the global functions also
provide a method for extracting it directly from an instance of `IDispatch`:

```
HRESULT GetSimpleListFromDispatch(IDispatch*     pdisp,
                                  ISimpleList**  pplist);
```

Where:

- ➤ pdisp is the instance of IDispatch from which the SimpleList object will be instantiated
- ➤ pplist is a pointer to the ISimpleList pointer that will receive the SimpleList object

Next, you can determine how many items are in the list by calling the GetNumItems function:

```
HRESULT GetNumItems(ISimpleList* plistItems,
                    long*        pcItems);
```

Where:

- ➤ lSimpleList is the SimpleList object whose item count must be retrieved
- ➤ pcItems is a pointer to the Long-typed variable that will receive the item count

Extracting items from a SimpleList is a relatively easy operation using its get_Item method, which corresponds to using the Item property in VBScript. However, since the only SimpleList that you will normally use in a pipeline component is the Items collection of the Orderform object, you might find it convenient to use the GetNthItem function to retrieve a Dictionary object (corresponding to an individual product in the Orderform) from it:

```
HRESULT GetNthItem(ISimpleList*  plistItems,
                   long          lItem,
                   IDictionary** ppdictItem);
```

Where:

- ➤ plistItems is the SimpleList object whose item must be retrieved
- ➤ lItem is the number of the Item that should be retrieved
- ➤ ppdictItem is a pointer to the IDictionary pointer that will receive the item

No global functions are provided for adding an item to a SimpleList (with the exception of certain "special" SimpleList objects, whose global functions are discussed in the General Purpose section). However, you can call its put_Item method, which corresponds to using the Item property in VBScript, to store any Variant variable in it.

To delete an item, you can call the DeleteNthItem function:

```
HRESULT DeleteNthItem(ISimpleList* plist,
                      int*         lItem,);
```

Where:

- ➤ plist is the SimpleList object whose item must be deleted
- ➤ litem is the number of the item that has to be deleted

General Purpose Functions

The global functions also include several general-purpose functions that can be used to carry out various tasks. For example, GenUniqueID is used to generate a unique ID based on a GUID plus an optional four-byte random value:

```
HRESULT GenUniqueID(unsigned short* buf,
                    BOOL*           fAddRandom,);
```

Where:

> ➤ buf is the buffer that will receive the unique ID

> ➤ fAddRandom specifies whether an optional 4-byte long random value should be appended to the GUID generated by the function

The unique ID is returned in base 32, which is the same used by MSCS for shopper and order IDs, and will be returned as an array of Unicode characters (which means that the buffer passed on to the function must be at least 64 bytes long).

At time, you will need to extract text messages from the store's MessageManager object (which is located in the context dictionary). The GetMsgFromMsgMan function will help you in this:

```
HRESULT GetMsgFromMsgMan(IDispatch* pdispMsgMan,
                         LPCWSTR*   wszErrMsgName,
                         BSTR*      pbstrMessage);
```

Where:

> ➤ pdispMsgMan is the instance of IDispatch that points to the MessageManager object

> ➤ wszErrMsgName is the name of the error message that has to be extracted

> ➤ pbstrMessage is a pointer to the BSTR variable that will receive the error.

If you need to report an error into an Orderform, however, you should usually extract the message from the pipeline's context, and then store it into either _Purchase_Errors or _Basket_Errors. Or, you can use the AddErrToList global function, which will do all the work for you!

```
HRESULT AddErrToList(IDictionary* pdictOrder,
                     LPCWSTR      wszErrListName,
                     IDispatch*   pdispContext,
                     LPCWSTR      wszErrMsgName);
```

Where:

> ➤ pdictOrder is the Orderform object where the error will be stored

> ➤ wszErrListName is the name of the error list to use

> ➤ pdispContext is the pipeline's context, still in its IDispatch form, from whose MessageManager object the error message will extracted

> ➤ wszErrMsgName is the name of the error message that should be extracted

The next two functions let us extract typed values from a `Variant` variable:

```
HRESULT GetNumValueOfVariant(VARIANT* pvar,
                             int*      pvalue);
```

Where:

> ➤ `pvar` is a pointer to the `Variant` variable whose integer value must be extracted
> ➤ `pvalue` is a pointer to the integer variable that will receive the value

```
HRESULT GetStringValueOfVariant(VARIANT* pvar,
                                BSTR*     pvalue);
```

Where:

> ➤ `pvar` is a pointer to the `Variant` variable whose string value should be extracted
> ➤ `pvalue` is a pointer to the string variable that will receive the value

Registry Access

As we've had a chance to find out while developing our Visual Basic component, the registry plays an important role in making a pipeline component work correctly. The problem with the VB component is that it won't be easy to deploy, since you will have to somehow force the user to add one or more registry keys manually. You could, naturally, write a registry script or even an installation program to do so, but it would still be less practical than taking advantage of the fact that a COM `dll` must be able to register itself and, therefore, contains code to do so.

In VB, you do not have access to this code – and, even if you did, you wouldn't have the appropriate functions to use the registry handy. In VC++, however, the `UpdateRegistry` method of each component is promptly available to the developer. By default, they call the standard methods that register your object's main features, such as the `ClassID`, the threading model, and so on. However, nothing prevents you from adding your own code to them, and the pipeline component template provides three very helpful functions for doing so.

`RegisterCATID` can be used to add an entry to the **Implemented Category** key, and thus to mark a pipeline component as such, as well as specifying what stages it has affinity with:

```
HRESULT RegisterCATID(const CLSID& clsid,
                      IID          newCATID);
```

Where:

> ➤ `clsid` is the Class ID of the component
> ➤ `pvalue` is the ID of the category that has to be added

The file `Pipe_Stages.h`, which we encountered while discussing the creation of a component in VB, can be included directly in our project, so that we will be able to use the symbols that have been defined by the MSCS team for us, rather than having to deal with GUIDs directly. For example, to register a pipeline component as such, we can use the symbol `CATID_MSCSPIPELINE_COMPONENT`, and so on.

You have probably noticed how the name displayed by the pipeline editor for the built-in components is not the same as the one that is stored as the component's main name in the Registry. For example, `DefaultShipping` is really called `Commerce.DefaultShipping`. Although the same doesn't happen with the components we create, this is not simply a consequence of the fact the editor already "knows" about the built-in components. In fact, the editor is looking at what is known as the "short display name" of the object, which VB sets normally to the Program ID of the object itself. The global function `RegisterName` lets us do specify our own choice of name from within the component registration method:

```
HRESULT RegisterName(const CLSID& clsid,
                     LPCWSTR      wszName);
```

Where:

> `clsid` is the Class ID of the component
> `wszName` is the short display name for the component

If you are using your components within a transaction-enabled pipeline, you should specify what threading models they support by creating the **ThreadingModel** entry in the **InProcServer32** subkey. As you may know, the possible threading models are the following:

Model	Value of ThreadingModel
Single	None (the entry should not be made)
Apartment	Apartment
Free	Free
Both	Both

The `RegisterThreadingModel` global function can be used to create the threading model entry from the component's registration methods:

```
HRESULT RegisterThreadingModel(const CLSID& clsid,
                               LPCWSTR      wszThreadingModel);
```

Where:

> `clsid` is the Class ID of the component
> `wszThreadingModel` is the string to store in the `ThreadingModel` entry

Return Values

As you may have noticed, all the functions that we have seen so far return a value of type `HRESULT`. This is because often the functions they call do the same, and it's certainly more convenient to maintain this convention up to the highest level. The values returned by the functions can vary, although they are all documented in the MSDN library; in general, if a function succeeds, it returns `S_OK`, while any other value corresponds to some error condition. In particular, a return value equal to `E_INVALIDARG` means that at least one of the parameters you passed to the function is invalid. Common instances include passing a wrong type (i.e., an `IDispatch` pointer where `IDictionary` was needed, and so on).

Providing Basic Component Functionality

Similarly to what happened for the VB component, the VC++ component is run by calling the `Execute` method that it inherits from `IPipelineComponent`. We will attempt to port the functionality of the VB component into VC++ (this might also be interesting if you want to run some performance comparisons between the two versions), so we'll start by defining the three global variables that we need as part of the public declarations of the component's class, `CVCShippingSpecial`. We'll do this in the `VCShippingSpecial.h` include file:

```
...

public:

    long lLowerBound = 0;
    long lUpperBound = 0;
    long lShippingPrice = 0;

...
```

Next, we'll write the implementation of `Execute` so that it calculates the number of items in the `Orderform` and, if appropriate, applies the correct discount. The following code shows the changes to be made to `VCShippingSpecial.cpp`:

```
STDMETHODIMP CVCShippingSpecial::Execute(IDispatch*  pdispOrder,
                                         IDispatch*  pdispContext,
                                         LONG        lFlags,
                                         LONG*       plErrorLevel)
{
    VARIANT         varDummy;
    IDictionary*    lpdictOrderform = NULL;

    ISimpleList*    lpItems = NULL;
    IDictionary*    lpItem = NULL;
    long            lItemCount;
    long            lProductCount;
    long            i;
    int             lItemQty;

    *plErrorLevel = OPPERRORLEV_SUCCESS;    // Let's be optimistic here!

    // First, let's get an IDictionary pointer to the Orderform

    if (GetDictFromDispatch(pdispOrder, &lpdictOrderform) != S_OK)
        goto labelError;

    // Next, check whether the shipping cost has already been set

    if (GetDictValue(lpdictOrderform, L"_shipping_total", &varDummy) != S_OK)
        goto labelError;

    if (!((varDummy.vt == VT_NULL) || (varDummy.vt == VT_EMPTY)))
        return S_OK;

    // Now, let's find out how many items are in the order

    lItemCount = 0;

    if (GetListItems(lpdictOrderform, &lpItems) != S_OK)
```

```
        goto labelError;

    if (GetNumItems(lpItems, &lProductCount) != S_OK)
        goto labelError;

    for (i = 0; i < lProductCount; i++)
    {
            if (GetNthItem(lpItems, i, &lpItem) != S_OK)
                goto labelError;

            if (GetDictValue(lpItem, L"Quantity", &lItemQty) != S_OK)
                goto labelError;

            lItemCount += lItemQty;

            lpItem->Release();
            lpItem = NULL;
    }

    lpItems->Release();
    lpItems = NULL;

    // Apply the discount, if appropriate

    if ((lItemCount > lLowerBound) && (lItemCount > lUpperBound))
        PutDictValue(lpdictOrderform, L"_shipping_total", (int)
                    (lShippingPrice));

    // Exit (successful)

    lpdictOrderform->Release();
    lpdictOrderform = NULL;

    return S_OK;

    // Exit (unsuccessful)

labelError:

    if (lpItem)
    {
        lpItem->Release();
        lpItem = NULL;
    }

    if (lpItems)
    {
        lpItems->Release();
        lpItems = NULL;
    }

    if (lpdictOrderform)
    {
        lpdictOrderform->Release();
        lpdictOrderform = NULL;
    }

    // Return failure code

    *plErrorLevel = OPPERRORLEV_FAIL;

    return S_OK;
}
```

As you can see, the code is a little more complex than before. In particular, there are a number of checks that we must continuously perform in order to make sure that any call to global functions and methods of the various interfaces that we use are successful. In our case, we limit ourselves to returning a failure error code, although we could do exactly the same thing that VB does: raise a runtime error through normal COM mechanisms. Considering the errors that we were trying to trap, we couldn't use the error `SimpleList` objects within the `Orderform`.

The following `#include` must also be added to the top of `VCShippingSpecial.cpp`:

```
#include "mspu_guids.h"
```

This header file is required to use the pipeline interfaces.

Reporting The Values Read

If we take a look at our project, we will notice that the ATL wizard has already created all the methods we need to implement the `IPipelineComponentDescription` interface; as such, all we need to do is add the code!

C++ arrays are not good enough for us here, since COM uses `SAFEARRAY` objects to store arrays, which we will have to use to pass along the values read and written by our component. Luckily, the template already contains most of the code needed to implement them. Therefore, making the changes needed to return the values that the component uses is a breeze:

```
//
// IPipelineComponentDescription Methods
//

STDMETHODIMP CVCShippingSpecial::ContextValuesRead(VARIANT *pVarRead)
{
    // allocate the safearray of VARIANTs

    SAFEARRAY* psa = SafeArrayCreateVector(VT_VARIANT, 0, 0);

    // set up the return value to point to the safearray

    V_VT(pVarRead) = VT_ARRAY | VT_VARIANT;
    V_ARRAY(pVarRead) = psa;

    return S_OK;
}

STDMETHODIMP CVCShippingSpecial::ValuesRead(VARIANT *pVarRead)
{
    VARIANT      varElement;
    long         i;

    // allocate the safearray of VARIANTs

    SAFEARRAY*   psa = SafeArrayCreateVector(VT_VARIANT, 0, 2);

    // Populate the safearray variants

    i = 0;
```

```
                varElement.bstrVal = SysAllocString (L"Item.Quantity");
                varElement.vt = VT_BSTR;

                SafeArrayPutElement (psa, &i, &varElement);

                i = 1;

                varElement.bstrVal = SysAllocString (L"_shipping_total");
                varElement.vt = VT_BSTR;

                SafeArrayPutElement (psa, &i, &varElement);

                // set up the return value to point to the safearray

                V_VT(pVarRead) = VT_ARRAY | VT_VARIANT;
                V_ARRAY(pVarRead) = psa;

            return S_OK;
        }

        STDMETHODIMP CVCShippingSpecial::ValuesWritten(VARIANT *pVarWritten)
        {
                // allocate the safearray of VARIANTs

                SAFEARRAY* psa = SafeArrayCreateVector(VT_VARIANT, 0, 1);

                // Populate the safearray variants

                VARIANT* pvarT = (VARIANT*)psa->pvData;
                V_BSTR(pvarT) = SysAllocString(L"[Optional] _shipping_total");
                V_VT(pvarT) = VT_BSTR;

                // set up the return value to point to the safearray

                V_VT(pVarWritten) = VT_ARRAY | VT_VARIANT;
                V_ARRAY(pVarWritten) = psa;
                return S_OK;
        }
```

These few lines of codes demonstrate three possible approaches to creating the SAFEARRAY objects that we need in order to return the values accessed by our component. The first method, ContextValuesRead returns an empty array. This is a slightly different approach from what we did in VB (where we passed an array that contained the string [None]). In VC++, we can pass an empty array, and the editor automatically recognizes it.

The second approach uses the SafeArrayPutElement method to add the strings to the SAFEARRAY object. As you can imagine, code like this works well only if you access only a few values (which is usually the case). For larger arrays, you might want to implement a loop that reads the values from a constant standard array defined globally.

The third approach, which is the one provided by the template, works well if you've only got one value to return. In this case, the pvData member of the SAFEARRAY structure can be used directly as the pointer to the only element of the array.

Adding and Supporting Properties

As before, our first step in adding properties to our component is to expose them through normal COM mechanisms. To do so, all we have to do is right-click on IVCShippingSpecial in the project explorer and add three properties: LowerBound, UpperBound and ShippingCost. Next, we'll have to write their implementation in VCShippingSpecial.cpp, which, as you can see below, is not complex at all:

```
STDMETHODIMP CVCShippingSpecial::get_LowerBound(VARIANT *pVal)
{
    pVal->lVal = lLowerBound;
    pVal->vt = VT_I4;

    return S_OK;
}

STDMETHODIMP CVCShippingSpecial::put_LowerBound(VARIANT newVal)
{
    HRESULT hr;

    // Attempt to convert variant to long integer

    hr = VariantChangeType (&newVal, &newVal, 0, VT_I4);

    if (hr == S_OK)
        lLowerBound = newVal.lVal;

    return hr;
}

STDMETHODIMP CVCShippingSpecial::get_UpperBound(VARIANT *pVal)
{
    pVal->lVal = lUpperBound;
    pVal->vt = VT_I4;

    return S_OK;
}

STDMETHODIMP CVCShippingSpecial::put_UpperBound(VARIANT newVal)
{
    HRESULT hr;

    // Attempt to convert variant to long integer

    hr = VariantChangeType (&newVal, &newVal, 0, VT_I4);

    if (hr == S_OK)
        lUpperBound = newVal.lVal;

    return hr;
}

STDMETHODIMP CVCShippingSpecial::get_ShippingCost(VARIANT *pVal)
{
    pVal->lVal = lShippingPrice;
    pVal->vt = VT_I4;

    return S_OK;
}
```

```
STDMETHODIMP CVCShippingSpecial::put_ShippingCost(VARIANT newVal)
{
    HRESULT hr;

    // Attempt to convert variant to long integer

    hr = VariantChangeType (&newVal, &newVal, 0, VT_I4);

    if (hr == S_OK)
        lShippingPrice = newVal.lVal;

    return hr;
}
```

All three properties are exposed as Variants, because that's the native language used by VBScript (in fact, VBScript is only able to create Variants, and the only way to pass variables of a specific type is to typecast them). Obviously, this means that we'll have to handle all the conversion from VARIANT to long integer within the code, but even that is quite easy to do, thanks to the built-in VARIANT-manipulation function VariantChangeType.

Next, we'll have to create and implement a property page. To do so, we'll use another ATL wizard. We'll start by selecting New ATL Object... from the Insert menu, then clicking on Controls and, finally, double-clicking on Property Page. I've called my property page VCSSProp, and left all the other settings as they were. In your implementation, you might want to change the title of the property page from "Title" to something more significant, though!

Add the following controls to the property page:

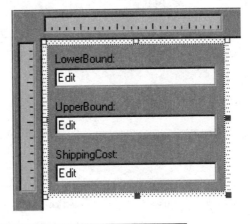

Control	Value	ID
Edit box		IDC_LBOUND
Edit box		IDC_UBOUND
Edit box		IDC_SCOST
Static text	LowerBound:	
Static text	UpperBound:	
Static text	ShippingCost:	

Next we'll add a method called `Activate`, which will be called when the property page is first displayed. We'll use it to load and convert the property values from our component. Add the following `public` method declaration to `VCSSProp.h`:

```
STDMETHOD(Activate)(HWND hWndParent, LPCRECT pRect, BOOL fModal);
```

and the following implementation to `VCSSProp.cpp`:

```
STDMETHODIMP CVCSSProp::Activate(HWND hWndParent, LPCRECT pRect, BOOL fModal)
{
    VARIANT     varPropValue;

    IPropertyPageImpl<CVCSSProp>::Activate(hWndParent, pRect, fModal);

    // First, retrieve a pointer to the component

    CComQIPtr<IVCShippingSpecial,
            &IID_IVCShippingSpecial>pVCShippingSpecial(m_ppUnk[0]);

    // Next, retrieve all the properties and set the text boxes appropriately

    // ...Retrieve value

    pVCShippingSpecial->get_LowerBound(&varPropValue);

    // ...Convert to string

    VariantChangeType(&varPropValue, &varPropValue, 0, VT_BSTR);

    // ...Store in text box

    SetDlgItemText(IDC_LBOUND, varPropValue.bstrVal);

    // Now for the others

    pVCShippingSpecial->get_UpperBound(&varPropValue);
    VariantChangeType(&varPropValue, &varPropValue, 0, VT_BSTR);
    SetDlgItemText(IDC_UBOUND, varPropValue.bstrVal);

    pVCShippingSpecial->get_ShippingCost(&varPropValue);
    VariantChangeType(&varPropValue, &varPropValue, 0, VT_BSTR);
    SetDlgItemText(IDC_SCOST, varPropValue.bstrVal);

    SetDirty(FALSE);

    return S_OK;
}
```

As you can see, we have to juggle a little bit with the fact that the properties are exposed as `Variant`s, but, as you can see below, they come pretty handy when we're going to respond to a request to apply the changes that the user has made to them in the `Apply` method.

Remove the wizard generated definition of the `Apply` method from `VCSSProp.h` and replace it with the simple `public` declaration:

```
STDMETHOD(Apply)(void);
```

Next, add the following implementation to `VCSSProp.cpp`:

```
STDMETHODIMP CVCSSProp::Apply(void)
{
    VARIANT     varLBound;
    VARIANT     varUBound;
    VARIANT     varSPrice;
    CComBSTR    combstrTextboxValue;

    // Obtain a pointer to our pipeline object
    // We'll only have one object at a time, so we'll directly get the first
    // IUnknown interface

    CComQIPtr<IVCShippingSpecial,
             &IID_IVCShippingSpecial>pVCShippingSpecial(m_ppUnk[0]);

    // Get the lower boundary, check it for validity

    GetDlgItemText (IDC_LBOUND, combstrTextboxValue.m_str);

    varLBound.vt = VT_BSTR;
    varLBound.bstrVal = SysAllocString (combstrTextboxValue);

    if (VariantChangeType (&varLBound, &varLBound, 0, VT_I4) != S_OK)
    {
        MessageBox (L"Lower bound must be a valid integer number",
                    L"ERROR", MB_OK | MB_ICONEXCLAMATION);
        return E_UNEXPECTED;
    }

    if (varLBound.lVal < 0)
    {
        MessageBox (L"Lower bound must be greater then zero",
                    L"ERROR", MB_OK | MB_ICONEXCLAMATION);
        return E_UNEXPECTED;
    }

    // Now, get the upper boundary, check it for validity

    GetDlgItemText (IDC_UBOUND, combstrTextboxValue.m_str);

    varUBound.vt = VT_BSTR;
    varUBound.bstrVal = SysAllocString (combstrTextboxValue);

    if (VariantChangeType (&varUBound, &varUBound, 0, VT_I4) != S_OK)
    {
        MessageBox (L"Upper bound must be a valid integer number",
                    L"ERROR", MB_OK | MB_ICONEXCLAMATION);
        return E_UNEXPECTED;
    }

    if (varUBound.lVal < 0)
    {
        MessageBox (L"Upper bound must be greater then zero",
                    L"ERROR", MB_OK | MB_ICONEXCLAMATION);
        return E_UNEXPECTED;
    }

    // Finally, it's the shipping cost's turn

    GetDlgItemText (IDC_SCOST, combstrTextboxValue.m_str);
```

```
        varSPrice.vt = VT_BSTR;
        varSPrice.bstrVal = SysAllocString (combstrTextboxValue);

        if (VariantChangeType (&varSPrice, &varSPrice, 0, VT_I4) != S_OK)
        {
            MessageBox (L"Shipping cost must be a valid integer number",
                        L"ERROR", MB_OK | MB_ICONEXCLAMATION);
            return E_UNEXPECTED;
        }

        if (varSPrice.lVal < 0)
        {
            MessageBox (L"Shipping must be greater then zero",
                        L"ERROR", MB_OK | MB_ICONEXCLAMATION);
        return E_UNEXPECTED;
        }

        // If all values OK, then save them to our component

        pVCShippingSpecial->put_LowerBound(varLBound);
        pVCShippingSpecial->put_UpperBound(varUBound);
        pVCShippingSpecial->put_ShippingCost(varSPrice);

        SetDirty (FALSE);
        return S_OK;
    }
```

In this code, we take full advantage of the `VariantChangeType` function to check whether the user has inserted a valid integer value. `Variant`s also come in handy to manage all the text values that come from the input boxes, which are in wide-character format. Finally, you should be very careful (both in the `Activate` and `Apply` methods) to properly set the "dirty" flag so that the caller (that is, the editor) knows that the any changes to the edit boxes have been properly taken care of.

The task is not yet complete, though. In fact, we're still missing a real-time response to the changes in our input boxes. We'll make it so that the **Apply** button in the editor's properties dialog box is initially grayed, and will become active as soon as one of the properties is changed. In order to do this, we should set the "dirty" flag to `TRUE` whenever we detect a change in our input boxes; we can do so by handling the `OnChange` event for all three of them.

To add these event handlers, right click on the `CVCSSProp` class in the **ClassView** window and select **Add Windows Message Handler**. Select each of `IDC_LBOUND`, `IDC_UBOUND` and `IDC_SCOST` in turn, adding handlers for the `EN_CHANGE` event for them. This will add `COMMAND_HANDLER` entries to the `MSG_MAP` in `VCSSProp.h`, along with handler functions for these events. We'll move the implementation of these functions into the `.cpp` file, so modify the declarations in the header to read:

```
    STDMETHOD(Apply)(void);
    STDMETHOD(Activate) (HWND hWndParent, LPCRECT pRect, BOOL fModal);
    LRESULT OnChangeLbound(WORD wNotifyCode, WORD wID, HWND hWndCtl, BOOL&
                        bHandled);
    LRESULT OnChangeScost(WORD wNotifyCode, WORD wID, HWND hWndCtl, BOOL&
                        bHandled);
    LRESULT OnChangeUbound(WORD wNotifyCode, WORD wID, HWND hWndCtl, BOOL&
                        bHandled);
```

Add the following implementations of these functions to `VCSSProp.cpp`:

```
LRESULT CVCSSProp::OnChangeLbound(WORD wNotifyCode, WORD wID, HWND hWndCtl,
                                  BOOL& bHandled)
{
   if (wNotifyCode == EN_CHANGE)
      SetDirty (TRUE);
   return 0;
}

LRESULT CVCSSProp::OnChangeScost(WORD wNotifyCode, WORD wID, HWND hWndCtl,
                                 BOOL& bHandled)
{
   if (wNotifyCode == EN_CHANGE)
      SetDirty (TRUE);
   return 0;
}

LRESULT CVCSSProp::OnChangeUbound(WORD wNotifyCode, WORD wID, HWND hWndCtl,
                                  BOOL& bHandled)
{
   if (wNotifyCode == EN_CHANGE)
      SetDirty (TRUE);
   return 0;
}
```

> **When trying to compile the component after adding the property page, the linker might complain about being unable to find the _main entry point. This is caused by the fact that some of your functions now require the CRT library, which, by default, is excluded by an ATL project in order to save space. To eliminate this problem, just go to the project properties and remove the pre-processor directive called _ATL_MIN_CRT.**

We're still missing support for access to the properties through the configuration dictionary. Since our project does not yet support the `IPipelineComponentAdmin` interface, we'll have to implement it ourselves. In most cases, we can implement interfaces by right-clicking on our class (`CVCShippingSpecial` in this case) in the project explorer view and selecting **Implement Interface**. In order for VC++ to recognize this particular interface, we'd have to point it to the right type library, located in the `\lib\_386\PipeCompLib.tlb` of the SDK directory, by clicking on the **Add typelib** button. However, in this case Visual Studio defines several objects in its standard inclusions which would give us compilation errors were we to implement the interface in this way. Instead, we can include the following GUID definition at the top of `VCShippingSpecial.h`:

```
extern "C" const GUID __declspec(selectany) LIBID_PipeCompLib =
   {0xf4100721,0x498b,0x11d1,{0xa7,0x28,0x00,0xc0,0x4f,0xd7,0xa1,0x05}};
```

Once the pipeline is implemented, the system will add the `GetConfigData` and `SetConfigData` members to our component, which we will implement with this simple code – similar, at least conceptually, to the one we wrote for the VB version of the component:

```
STDMETHODIMP CVCShippingSpecial::GetConfigData(IDispatch** ppDict)
{
    IDictionary* dictCData;

    if (ppDict == NULL)
        return E_POINTER;

    if (CoCreateInstance(CLSID_CDictionary, NULL, CLSCTX_INPROC_SERVER,
                        IID_IDictionary, (void **) (&dictCData)) != S_OK)
        return E_UNEXPECTED;

    PutDictValue (dictCData, L"LowerBound", lLowerBound);
    PutDictValue (dictCData, L"UpperBound", lUpperBound);
    PutDictValue (dictCData, L"ShippingPrice", lShippingPrice);

    dictCData->QueryInterface (IID_IDispatch, (void **) ppDict);

    dictCData->Release();

    return S_OK;
}

STDMETHODIMP CVCShippingSpecial::SetConfigData (IDispatch * pDict)
{
    IDictionary *dictCData;

    GetDictFromDispatch (pDict, &dictCData);

    GetDictValue (dictCData, L"LowerBound", (int *) &lLowerBound);
    GetDictValue (dictCData, L"UpperBound", (int *) &lUpperBound);
    GetDictValue (dictCData, L"ShippingPrice", (int *) &lShippingPrice);

    dictCData->Release();

    return E_NOTIMPL;
}
```

We also need to modify the `GetPages` method such that it specifies the right Property Page, make the changes as follows (making sure you remove the /* and */ statements so that the body of this method is not commented out):

```
STDMETHODIMP CVCShippingSpecial::GetPages(CAUUID *pPages)
{
    if (NULL == pPages)
        return E_INVALIDARG;

    pPages->cElems = 1;
    pPages->pElems = (GUID*)CoTaskMemAlloc(1*sizeof(GUID));
    if(!pPages->pElems)
    {
        pPages->cElems = 0;
        return E_OUTOFMEMORY;
    }
    memcpy(pPages->pElems, &CLSID_VCSSProp, sizeof(GUID));

    return S_OK;
}
```

Finally, we can implement the `IPersistStreamInit` methods, so that our component can be saved to and loaded from a disk by the editor. The trick here is to load and save the data to the stream in the correct order:

```
STDMETHODIMP CVCShippingSpecial::Load(IStream *pStm)
{
    HRESULT hRes = S_OK;

    pStm->Read (&lLowerBound, sizeof (long), NULL);
    pStm->Read (&lUpperBound, sizeof (long), NULL);
    pStm->Read (&lShippingPrice, sizeof (long), NULL);

    return hRes;
}

STDMETHODIMP CVCShippingSpecial::Save(IStream *pStm, BOOL fClearDiry)
{
    HRESULT hRes = S_OK;

    pStm->Write (&lLowerBound, sizeof (long), NULL);
    pStm->Write (&lUpperBound, sizeof (long), NULL);
    pStm->Write (&lShippingPrice, sizeof (long), NULL);

    return hRes;
}

STDMETHODIMP CVCShippingSpecial::GetSizeMax(ULARGE_INTEGER *pcbSize)
{
    // Modify size to be the size of your data
    pcbSize->LowPart  = sizeof (long) * 3;
    pcbSize->HighPart = 0;
    return S_OK;
}

STDMETHODIMP CVCShippingSpecial::InitNew(void)
{
    // Add any component initialization

    lLowerBound = 0;
    lUpperBound = 0;
    lShippingPrice = 0;

    return S_OK;
}
```

You will have probably noticed that I have also implemented the `InitNew` method, which we didn't take into account in the VB version of the component. This is because VB automatically initializes all long integer variables to zero, while VC++ doesn't do the same. Therefore, we'll have to force zero values on our properties manually.

The implementation of `GetSizeMax` is also included here – as mentioned earlier, it's necessary to implement it in order for the `IStream` object to be sized properly.

Making the Component Visible

Thanks to the global functions generated by the ATL wizard, creating the appropriate Registry entries to make the component visible in the editor is extremely easy. We'll even change the "short display name" to something more pleasant to the eye, while we will not worry about specifying a threading model because our component is not transaction-friendly. As discussed above, the right place to do all this is the `UpdateRegistry` method, which we'll modify as follows:

```
static HRESULT WINAPI UpdateRegistry(BOOL bRegister)
{
    HRESULT hr = _Module.UpdateRegistryClass(GetObjectCLSID(),
                    _T("Wrox.VCShippingSpecial.1"),
                    _T("Wrox.VCShippingSpecial"),
                    IDS_PROJNAME, THREADFLAGS_BOTH, bRegister);

    wchar_t wsName[50] = L"Wrox Shipping Special";

    if (SUCCEEDED(hr))
    {
        // TODO: Add stage affinities here
        hr = RegisterCATID(GetObjectCLSID(), CATID_MSCSPIPELINE_COMPONENT);
        hr = RegisterCATID(GetObjectCLSID(), CATID_MSCSPIPELINE_SHIPPING);
        hr = RegisterName (GetObjectCLSID(), &wsName[0]);
    }
    return hr;
};
```

If we now try to add the component using the Win32 editor, it will show the short name – which is much easier to understand than the Program ID!

Summary

This chapter concludes our discussion on pipelines; you should now have a complete picture of this technology, and you should be able to expand it to suit any of your needs. Even though I have already mentioned this earlier in the chapter, I reiterate the fact that, whenever possible, you should use a two-phase approach to writing new components.

Visual Basic offers you an environment in which you can focus on what your components do, rather than on whether the language itself will behave the way you think, which is what happens with Visual C++. As such, it is a good idea to use it when you're developing your pipeline extension. If your store has a lot of traffic, however, the component will prove to be a bottleneck because it won't perform nearly as well as a free-threaded VC++ component. Thanks to the supporting tools provided by the Site Server SDK, developing a component using VC++ is not nearly as difficult as it would be if you were starting from scratch.

20
Using the Ad Server

When television was in its infancy (that is, when people stared at a TV screen in awe, rather than looking at it with disgust), video advertisement was far from being the perfected art it is today. Ad agencies were not yet born, and commercials limited themselves to associating an image with the sounds that everybody was used to hearing as coming from a radio box.

Sixty years later, television advertisement is a thriving business – a business that, in most countries, truly drives any effort in the television industry. Standards have been defined, techniques have been developed, and professional tools have been created.

Online advertisement is going through a similar phased growth. Clearly, the Internet has a significant advantage over other traditional media: interactivity. While everybody receives the same television signal (at least for the same channels), each person who browses the Web establishes a bi-directional line of communication with the sites he or she visits.

Therefore, the ads on a web site should be tailored to the individual user's needs, very much like content should be. SSCE comes with a very powerful tool, called **Ad Server**, that lets you do exactly this at a fraction of the cost of other similar systems on the market.

What This Chapter Covers

As we shall see in due course, there are two important aspects of using the Ad Server: being able to actually employ its services for scheduling the delivery of ads on a web site, and programming a web site so that it can display ads. This may seems a highly convoluted way of thinking, but the truth is that, in order for effective ad serving to take place, your site must be properly equipped.

This chapter is divided into three sections:

> **Introducing the Ad Server**
> In this section, we'll go through the functionality that the Ad Server provides, analyzing how it can fit into a web site and how it integrates with the other Site Server technologies.

> **Running and configuring the Ad Server**
> This part of the chapter will focus on the way the Ad Server is configured and run from an administrative point of view. Thus, we won't get into any code at this point, but we'll see how ad delivery works and how it is used.

> **Using the Ad Server in your site**
> Finally, we'll examine how a site is prepared in order to serve ads properly; this includes not only writing the script that actually calls the Ad Server components, but also supporting ad targeting and exposure limits.

Introducing the Ad Server

While the ultimate goal of the Ad Server is, obviously, to deliver ads to a client on the web, this is a much more complex task than it might seem at first. There are, in fact, many different aspects of ad delivery that must be taken into consideration, such as whether a particular set of ads is being delivered in the appropriate timeframe, or whether the user is able to view the ad in the format in which the server sent it.

The Ad Server in the Big Picture

The Ad Server (or AS) is a standalone product that can be used without requiring any other Site Server technology. This doesn't mean, however, that it can't be integrated with the other products in the package; in particular, you can use Personalization and Membership to target the ads that it delivers according to the user's own preferences. Similarly, you could use Commerce Server for billing purposes, and so on.

Installation

The AS is part of the Commerce Edition of Site Server, and is located in the second CD of the set. You will be able to install it during the Site Server setup. Naturally, if you haven't installed it the first time, you can always go back and install it again.

An easy way to check whether the Ad Server is installed properly is to try and open the following URL in your web browser:

```
http://your_host/admanager/default.asp
```

If you get an HTTP error, then you should go back to your Site Server setup program and make sure that all the software has been properly installed. Otherwise, you can proceed to displaying ads in your site!

A Little Terminology

It's a good idea to start by setting forth a few terms that we will use throughout the chapter. This is particularly true if you consider that online advertisement is beginning to form as an industry of its own and, as such, is developing its own terminology.

Banner and Button Ads

The most common form of online advertisement is the **banner ad**. This term is commonly used to identify a portion of a web page (such as a small horizontal strip) that is dedicated to a commercial advertisement. In its most common form, the banner ad is an image, generally stored as a GIF, displayed at the top or at the bottom of the page. More recently, banner ads have been created in different forms, such as HTML, DHTML and Java, that allow for a higher degree of interactivity with the user.

The industry has settled on a standard format for banner ads of 468x60 pixels. These dimensions allow for the banner to be displayed in any screen resolution without going out of the browser's window.

Another commonly used format for ads is the **button**, which is essentially a smaller version of an image banner. Buttons are often used to provide a less expensive form of advertising, as they occupy less space – and, therefore, are less evident – than a full-size banner. No standard size has been defined for button ads.

In general, it's a good idea to think of ads as a special kind of content. From that point of view, most of the considerations that we have made about the need to personalize their delivery are still valid. As we shall see later on, in fact, the Ad Server does provide the means for us to determine how the ads are shown on the site according, for example, to a certain user's profile.

Click-Through Rate and Redirect URLs

The goal of an online ad is – as you know – to convince the user to click on it. The number of times an ad has been clicked on divided by the number of impressions that it received is called its **click-through rate**, and is usually expressed as a percentage value:

$$ClickthroughRate = \frac{CLICKS}{IMPRESSIONS} \times 100$$

For example, a click-through rate of 0.2% means that 2 visitors out of 1,000 clicked on the ad.

In an environment where the ads are delivered on a non-targeted basis, you can expect the click-through rate to be rather low: a value of anywhere between 2% and 5% is generally considered to belong to a successful campaign. Targeted deliveries often show a higher rate, mainly because of the fact that they are displayed in front of people who are more likely to be interested in them. Campaigns are sometimes paid for on a 'per-click' basis.

Many ad agencies, and several ad servers, use a redirection page in order to maintain statistical data about the click-through rate of their ads. This redirection page, sometimes referred to as a **redirect URL**, does nothing other than update a log file or database table (or call a method of the Ad Server that does so) and redirect the browser to the appropriate destination URL for the ad.

Ad Deliveries

The delivery of online advertisements (also known as **ad impression**) is usually paid for by the thousand. Thus, a Price-per-mil (PPM) is established between the seller and the buyer, and the seller commits to the delivery of the number of impressions agreed upon in accordance with a specific schedule. The latter not only establishes a start and end date for the delivery, but also during what days and hours the delivery should take place.

One or more delivery schedules for an individual customer can be grouped into a **campaign**. Often, the number of impressions to be delivered is established for the entire campaign rather than for the individual ad. The buyer can also request that a specific ad not be shown to any user for more than a certain number of times during a single session. This number is called the **exposure limit**.

Ad Targeting

If you visited a major search engine recently, you will have probably noticed that the ads that are displayed in the results pages – those displayed after you make a search – often seem to be related to the search terms that you have specified. Naturally, this doesn't happen by mistake, but is the result of a technique called **ad targeting**. As we'll see later on, there are several types of targeting methods, but in general they are all used to determine how ads are chosen based on the user's behavior or profile.

What the Ad Server Can Do

All in all, the Ad Server is a pretty flexible platform, as it can handle most of the scenarios and techniques that we have just reviewed. Its only problem is that almost all the functionality is provided by one single COM object; this does result in an extremely high performance, but not as much flexibility as one would probably like to have.

Delivery Formats

One of the aspects of the AS that I like most is the fact that it is not tied to any specific ad format. As a matter of fact, the technology on which the Ad Server works can be considered to be somewhat similar to a content delivery system, to the point that interfacing it with the membership technology of SSCE can be an interesting exercise that will probably yield excellent returns.

Thus, you can deliver any kind of ad you wish, as long as your browser will somehow be able to display it. If you intend to use the Ad Server as-is, you will find that anything you intend to deliver has an "upper-technology limit" of client-side scripting; i.e. the most complex content you can serve up contains at most some script code to be run on the client. In fact, since you will be using ASP to retrieve the ad itself, you will not be able to deliver server-side scripting with it.

However, at least in theory, it would be possible to write a server-side component that could be fed an ASP script, whose output would be the ad itself. Even better, you could use a micropipe running a `Scriptor` instance to do the job.

The AS comes with the most commonly used ad formats (i.e. banner ad, HTML banner ad, button, and so on) built-in and ready to use. However, the situation is pretty flexible from this point of view – you can specify just about any custom format.

Customers, Campaigns and Delivery Schedules

The fundamental unit recognized by the AS is the **campaign item**. This represents the schedule for a particular ad, intended as the set of rules that decide when the item is displayed to a particular user.

The AS is able to deliver ads based on a target number of impressions over a certain period of time, during certain hours of the day and during specific days of the week. In addition, it's possible to determine whether an item has been paid for, in which case it will receive a higher priority in the display hierarchy, or is a "house" ad, in which case it is used as a "filler" when no other ads can be displayed to the user.

It is also possible to associate each ad delivery location (i.e. the spot on a page where a banner should be displayed) with an arbitrary number of keywords that characterize it in a meaningful way. For example, these keywords may include a description of the user's profile, the nature of the page, and so on.

Upon delivery, the AS compares the delivery location's keywords with a set of rules, which are created by associating a particular keyword with one of three actions:

> **Required**
> Required keywords must be present when the delivery mechanism is executed in order for an item to be displayed.

> **Exclude**
> Exclude keywords make the ad visible only when they are not part of the delivery location's keyword lists.

> **Target**
> Target keywords are used to express an affinity between the ad and the keyword–a concept similar to the Required action but not as strict. Target-keyworded ads are preferably displayed when the keyword is present, even though its presence is not necessary.

One or more items can be grouped in a campaign, for which default start and end dates can be set. The ad delivery of the items in a campaign can be scheduled by impressions, or by clicks.

Finally, campaigns are arranged in **customer** groups, which represent the highest-level entities that the AS recognizes. Customers have no functional role, but contain information that is useful to identify and contact advertisers.

It's important to understand that, while the AS has been designed to schedule the delivery of the ads so that the established goals can be met, it can by no means guarantee that this will actually happen. You should keep in mind, in fact, that there are many factors that determine whether a schedule will be successfully completed, including, for example, whether enough users access the ads in the timeframe set.

Reporting

The AS has the capability of providing real-time reporting on the ad impression and click-through activity for any given item. The results are calculated by tallying the log data that is collected at time of delivery and of click-through at regular intervals. The information generated by the real-time reporting functions, accessible via a web browser, is limited in accuracy and detail, but can certainly be used to give a much-needed 'at-a-glance' overview of how your ads are doing.

Very accurate reports can be created using the Analysis tools that ship with SSCE. The sampling data, in this case, is collected directly from the log that the AS creates in a file or database table.

Running and Configuring the Ad Server

Let's now move on to a more practical approach to understanding how the AS works and is operated. First of all, it's important to understand that its scope is machine-wide. This means that all the customers, campaign and items that you will use for all the sites on a computer will be shared. While in theory this could cause ads meant to be displayed on one site to be shown on a different one, keep in mind that you can correct this problem through accurate targeting.

The "control center" of the AS is the **Ad Manager**, a web application that can be accessed at the following URL:

```
http://your_host/admanager
```

where, as usual, `your_host` is the name or IP of your computer. As you can see from the screenshot that follows, the main page of the Ad Manager is quite unimpressive, but gives us access to its four main sections:

> **Customers**
> Through this section, it is possible to access all the customers, campaigns and items

> **Performance**
> Real-time performance statistics can be accessed through this section

> **Ad Sizes**
> As mentioned above, the AS gives the site owner the capacity to customize the sizes for the ads that will be available through his or her system

> **Refresh**
> While real-time performance statistics are automatically re-calculated on a pre-determined schedule, it's possible to force a recalculation at any time by entering this section

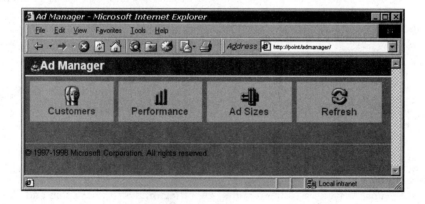

The Customers Section

Clicking on the Customers icon or link from the Ad Manager's main page takes us to the screen shown in the next screenshot, which shows us a list of all the customers currently on our server, together with some fundamental data about them. (In my case, it shows a few sample customers that the SSCE setup program installs automatically.)

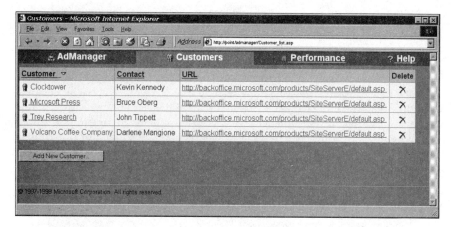

Adding a New Customer

Clicking on the Add New Customer... button brings up the page shown in the screenshot that follows, which prompts us for several pieces of information about the customer that we want to add. These are all pretty self-explanatory, and therefore there is no need to cover them in detail. The only thing that is probably worth mentioning is that the Customer Type field is there only for your personal reference, and it doesn't have any importance from a functional point of view.

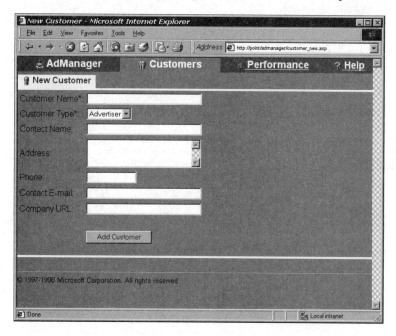

Viewing, Editing and Deleting an Existing Customer

It's possible to view the complete set of information that the AS keeps about an individual customer by clicking on the name from the Customers list. You can edit the information in the same screen. The right side of the screen also displays a list of the campaigns that belong to the customer, which we'll see in a few moments.

To delete a customer, you can click on the Delete icon that appears beside it. The AS will ask you whether you are sure or not – which will save you when you impulsively click on the icon after a tough call from your clients!

Creating and Managing Campaigns

The creation of a new campaign must be done from within a customer entry by clicking on the Add New Campaign... button. Doing so will bring up a page similar to the one shown in the next screenshot. As you can see, the Ad Manager will ask us for a name to give to our campaign, as well as default start and end dates, which will be used when creating a new item for the campaign.

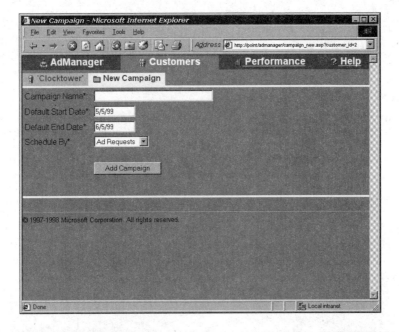

> The default start and end dates for a campaign have no bearing on the way the ads are actually displayed. They are only used to determine what start and end dates an item will be assigned by default during the creation process. You can modify the start and end dates for an item at any time.

The measurement of ad delivery goals for a particular campaign can be based either on the number of impressions – called **Ad Requests** by the AS – or on the number of click-throughs that the ads receive. This setting, which is selected through the Scheduled By list box is global to all the items that belong to a certain campaign and cannot be changed once the campaign has been created.

To edit a campaign, you can click on its name from the customer entry it belongs to. This will cause a page like the one in the next screenshot to be shown. As you can see, similarly to what happened for the customer entries, the left side of the page contains the editable elements of the campaign, while the right side contains a list of the items that belong to it. It's very important to remember that, if you decide to edit any of the fields for a particular campaign, you *must* click on the Update Properties button in order for the changes to take effect. If you go on to editing or adding new campaign items, the changes you made to the campaign properties will not be recorded by the system.

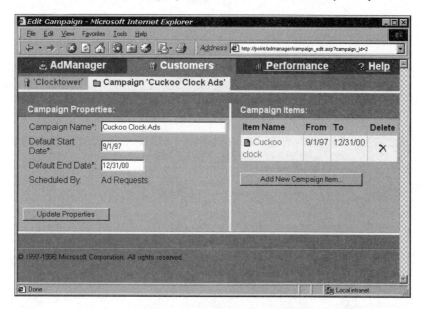

Deleting a campaign is equally easy – all you have to do is click on the Delete icon that appears right beside it in the campaign list for a given customer. The deletion operation is hierarchical – meaning that if you delete a campaign you will also delete all the items that belong to it.

Creating and Managing Campaign items

The creation and management of campaign items is probably the trickiest part of using the AS (at least from an administrator's point of view) and, as we are about to see, it's not complicated at all.

In order to add a new item, you will need to click on the Add New Campaign Item... button, which will bring the first step of a simple wizard. The page asks us to select what type of item we want to create:

Item Type	Description
IMG	The simplest of banners: a clickable image
TEXT	A text-only ad
HTML	An ad that can contain any HTML or DHTML code, including client-side scripts

Table Continued on Following Page

817

Item Type	Description
NOCLICKING	An image that cannot be clicked upon
BUYNOW	A Buy-Now ad (described in the earlier chapters about MSCS)
NETSHOW	A NetShow streaming video that can be clicked upon
ENLIVEN	An ad that takes advantage of a new technology called Enliven (you can find more information about it at `http://www.enliven.com`)

The wizard needs to know the type of ad to be displayed in order to display the correct information in the next page, shown in the next screenshot, that asks us for some additional information about the item. In my case, I have chosen to create an item of type IMG, but the scenario doesn't change particularly if you chose a different type.

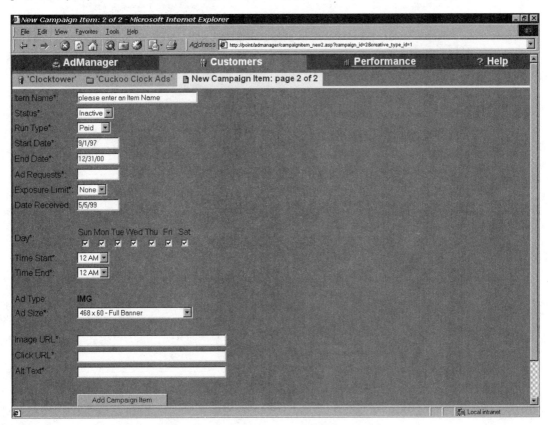

Here's a quick rundown of what these fields mean:

Name	Description
Item Name	The name of the item (used for display purposes during reporting and editing functions).
Status	Determines whether the item is actively being displayed to customers or not.
Run Type	Determines whether the ad is paid for, in which case it enjoys a higher priority in the display sequence, or whether it's a "house fill", in which case it is used to "fill in" the empty spots when all the paid ads have already been displayed.
Start Date	The date on which the ad delivery should start.
End Date	The date on which the ad delivery should end.
Ad Requests	The number of ad impressions that should be considered as being the goal for the ad delivery over the period of time that goes from the Start Date to the End Date. *Note:* If you chose Clicks as the Schedule By value for your campaign, then this field will be replaced by the number of clicks.
Exposure Limit	The maximum number of times that an ad can be displayed to a specific user during a session.
Date Received	The date on which the ad was received for insertion. This field has no functional role, but can be used for your own purposes.
Day	The day(s) of the week during which the ad can be displayed.
Time Start	The hour of the day starting from which the ad can be displayed. This setting is global to the entire week, that is, it applies to all the active days.
Time End	Determines when the ad delivery must stop during the day. Similar to the previous one, this setting is global to the entire week.
Ad Type	The type of the ad being entered (determined by the first step of the wizard, and cannot be changed)
Ad Size	The size of the ad. This list is compiled from the customizable list of sizes that the user can specify (see below).
Image URL	The URL of the image that must be displayed
Click URL	The URL where the user should be taken to when the ad is clicked upon. Not to be confused with the redirection page.
Alt Text	The text that should be displayed instead of the image in graphics-incapable browsers.

Ad Targeting

Once you have added your campaign item, you will have to enter its targets, assuming you need any. Because every ad starts out without any targets, you might want to always create your items as inactive, then create the targets, and finally make them active. If you don't follow this procedure, there is a risk that a newly created item will enter into the delivery schedule without being properly set.

As we have already mentioned, there are three types of targets, corresponding to requirement, exclusion and affinity. When a delivery decision has to be made by the AS engine, all the targets that have been defined for an item are ANDed together, and compared to the environment in which the delivery has to be made. Let's suppose, for example, that the following keywords are passed to the AS as part of the environmental conditions:

```
Male
MidForties
Canada
```

If the following targets were defined for an item:

```
Require      Canada
Target       Male
Exclude      MidForties
```

Then the ad wouldn't be delivered, because the MidForties keyword is indeed defined. The following ad, on the other hand, might or might not be delivered:

```
Require      Canada
Target       MidForties
```

It's important to understand that the fact that, while an ad that does not meet target conditions is *certainly* not displayed, one that does is simply added to a "pool" of displayable items, from which a final decision is made based on several other factors, such as performance and scheduling.

You can only add and delete targets (no edits are allowed). To add a new target, just enter its value, then select its type and click on the Add New Target button. To delete a target, simply click on the Delete icon beside it.

> Keep in mind that the changes you make to an ad do not become automatically effective, but are applied at the next scheduled refresh. If you cannot wait until then, you can force a refresh of the system (see below).

The Performance Section

The real-time performance information that the Ad Server displays becomes very useful when you need to have an immediate impression of how a particular ad or campaign is doing. In my experience, it's been a great lifesaver, since you get to make a phone call to your clients *before* the delivery quota isn't met, and not afterwards.

The one thing I particularly like about the performance page, shown in the next screenshot, is that it's complete and yet it's very easy to understand. As you can see, for each ad the page shows the start and end dates, the number of impressions or clicks scheduled for delivery, the quantity actually delivered and the click-through rate for the ad. In addition, a colored bar is used to visually represent the performance of an item: red means severe under-performance, while green means that the item is either on schedule or even over delivered.

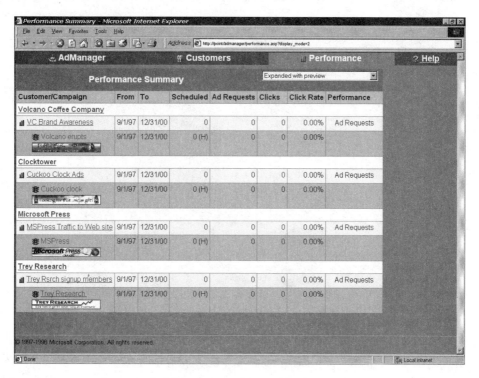

A list box at the top-right corner of the page can be used to determine how the performance data is displayed:

List Box Option	Description
Collapsed	Only a per-campaign report is generated. In order to access the performance data for the items of a particular campaign the user must access a separate page.
Expanded	Each campaign is expanded into its individual items, for which a report is generated as well.
Expanded with preview	Same as above, but also displays a "preview" of the ad.
Expanded with date range	Same as Expanded, but the data is generated from samples taken between the specified start and end dates.
Expanded with preview and date range	Same as Expanded with preview, but the data is generated from samples taken between the specified start and end dates.

Defining Ad Sizes

Clicking on the Ad Sizes link from the Ad Manager's main page lets us define the dimensions of the ads that we are displaying. As you can see from the following screenshot, the list of default sizes that are created when the Ad Server is installed is very comprehensive, in that it includes most of the dimensions commonly used throughout the industry.

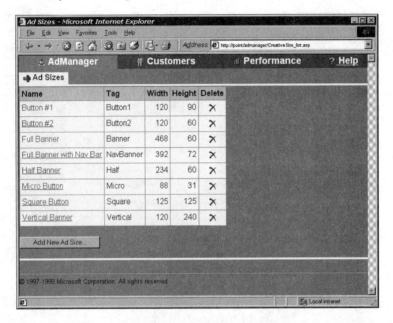

Adding a new ad size is an extremely straightforward operation: all you need to do is click on the Add New Ad Size... button and fill in the blanks. While most of the fields requested here are self-explanatory, you are probably wondering what the Tag field is used for.

The answer to your question is quite simple: when a delivery request is made, the requester can also specify what type of ad should be displayed as part of the environment keywords (more about that later on).

Editing and Deleting Ad Sizes

You can edit an ad size by clicking on it. Keep in mind that whatever changes you make will directly affect all the items that use that ad size, so you should be very careful. The same considerations go into deleting an ad size, although the Ad Manager won't let you delete one if one or more items use it.

Refreshing the Ad Server

No, this is not about drinks. What we are talking about is refreshing the ad schedule and, at the same time, the ad performance data of the Ad Server. The AS generally performs this operation automatically at regular intervals, but occasionally you might find yourself in a situation that requires you to refresh the schedule manually. You may want to do this, for example, if you have made a change to one of your ads – perhaps because it wasn't working properly – and you need it to become effective right away, rather than at the next scheduled refresh.

By clicking on the Refresh link from the Ad Manager's main page, you will be shown a list of all the AS-enabled applications that currently reside on your server. In order to refresh the delivery schedule for one of them, all you need to do is click on the Refresh icon beside it.

Using the Ad Server in Your Site

We are finally heading into what is certainly the last section of this chapter, but undoubtedly not the least interesting: how to change your site so that it can use the functionality provided by the AS.

Step 1: Setting up Global.asa

The entire functionality of the AS is provided by one single instance of the Commerce.AdServer component, which works by loading the entire delivery schedule into memory (for performance reasons) and can then be used to make delivery decisions. The fact that the entire schedule is loaded in memory forces us to create a single instance of the component that can be made available to every script in the site. It also explains why the schedule and performance data is only refreshed every once in a while.

Generally speaking, you will want to modify your global.asa file so that its Application_OnStart method is used to create an instance of Commerce.AdServer:

```
Set ASInstance = Server.CreateObject ("Commerce.AdServer")
Set Application ("AS") = ASInstance
```

Next, we will specify what ODBC connection string should be used by the component when connecting to the database that contains schedule information. It's a good idea to retrieve this value from the Site Dictionary – assuming that you are running an MSCS store – or from some external file, so that, if by accident somebody gains access to your copy of global.asa, he or she will not be able to get a login for your database server as well:

```
AsInstance.ConnectionString = MSCSSite.DefaultConnectionString
AsInstance.TimeOut = 30
```

The second line of code tells the AS component that, if it is unable to connect to the database, it should attempt to reconnect after thirty seconds.

In order for the ad delivery to work properly, we will also have to define a redirection URL that the Ad Server will use as a click-through counter for our ads:

```
AsInstance.RedirectURL = "http://myserver/redirect/click.asp"
```

The redirection script – which, once again, should *not* be confused with the Click URL that is defined in the Ad Manager – should take care of recording a banner click and then redirect the user to its ultimate destination (see the following screenshot). A click event can be logged by using the RecordEvent method of the AS component:

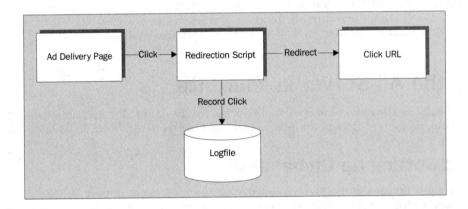

Syntax:

```
Sub AdServer.RecordEvent (Response, ciid, evt)
```

Response   The intrinsic ASP Response object, used to log events to the IIS log
             (which is later processed by the Analysis components of SSCE for
             reporting purposes).

ciid   The unique ID of the item for which the event has to be recorded.
             Generated and passed by the AS.

evt   The type of event that should be recorded. Should always be equal to
             "CLIK"

By default, a redirection request from the AS will be formulated as follows:

```
http://redirect_url?ciid=ciid&url=url
```

where *ciid* is the unique ID of the campaign ID being clicked on, and *url* is the URL to which the
script should redirect. For example, here's a simple redirect script that records a click event and uses
the Response.Redirect method to redirect the browser to the appropriate URL:

```
<%
  Application ("AS").RecordEvent (Application, Request ("ciid"), "CLICK")
  Response.Redirect (Request ("URL"))
%>
```

Finally, we should enter a name for our site in the instance of the AS, which will use it to identify our
IIS application in the Ad Manager:

```
ASInstance.Application = "My Application"
```

In addition to these settings, we can also decide how often the component will refresh its schedule and update the performance data:

```
AsInstance.RefreshInterval = 120          ' in seconds
```

> Keep in mind that short refresh times can reduce the performance of your system, as the AS component will be forced to reload all the information more often.

Another interesting setting that you might want to be aware of is `PenalizeUnmatchedTargets`, which can be used to tweak the way the AS engine determines what ads should be displayed. When this property is set to `True`, the fitness of a particular ad is determined not only according to the number of targets that it has in common with the environment, but also on those that it does not have in common. For example, if item A has the following targets:

```
Target       Male
Target       Mid40s
Target       HasChildren
Target       IsMarried
```

It might be less likely to be displayed when the environment contains both Male and Mid40s than another item that only has the following target:

```
Target       Male
```

This is because, while item A has more hits than item B, it also has more misses (since the last two targets are not hit at all), and therefore receives a penalty. If `PenalizeUnmatchedTargets` is set to `False`, which is also its default value, then item A is chosen over item B because it contains more matches.

You can set `PenalizeUnmatchedTargets` to the appropriate value in `global.asa`:

```
PenalizeUnmatchedTargets = True
```

Enabling Design Mode

When running in its production mode, the AS component does not produce any error, even if one occurs. Instead, it delivers what is called the "default" ad, which can be specified as follows:

```
ASInstance.DefaultAD = "<default ad html>"
```

The default ad will be displayed when the component is unable to display any other item for any reason, including the database server not being available. As such, the default ad must be specified as the actual HTML code that will be used to display the item, rather than the name of an item in the ad schedule.

During the development phase of your site, however, you might want to turn off this behavior, so that the errors raised by the component will be printed out to the page rather than hidden by the default ad. You can do so by adding this line of code:

```
ASInstance.DesignMode = True
```

> You should remember to remove this line of code when you go into production with your site. When design mode is enabled, the default ad is never displayed. In both cases, the errors are always logged to the NT Event Log.

Step 2: Delivering the Ad

Before being able to deliver an ad on our pages, we must create a list of targets, and then create and maintain a session-wide "impression history". These will let us target our ads and support the exposure limit functionality respectively.

Creating a List of Targets

When making a delivery request to the AS component, we will be passing along a list of targets stored in an array of strings. Each string in the array will define an individual target, such as `Under40`, or `Male`. The AS itself defines three reserved targets that begin with the `Ad.` prefix:

`Ad.Size.Name`	Specifies that only items of a particular size should be displayed. *Name* should correspond to one of the sizes defined in the Ad Manager.

`Ad.TargetFrame._top`
`Ad.TargetFrame._self`
`Ad.TargetFrame._parent`
`Ad.TargetFrame.Name`
	Specifies in which frame the Click URL should be displayed. You can use this target to make the Click URL load in a different window, for example.

`Ad.Border.Size`	Specifies how big the border around the ad should be. It can be any integer value greater than or equal to zero.

It's obviously possible to combine one or more **Ad.Size** targets so that only certain types of banners are displayed. Here's an example of a target list:

```
TargetList = Array ("Ad.Size.Banner", "Ad.TargetFrame._new", "Mid40s", "Female")
```

Creating an Impression History

The impression history is very simply a string that the AS component automatically updates at every delivery attempt. The problem, however, is storing that list so that it is preserved between one page and the next.

If you are not running an MSCS store, then you might want to use the `Session` object to do so, even though you should be aware of its limitations, including the fact that it won't be available if the user's browser does not support or refuses cookies.

If your site is an MSCS store, on the other hand, you will not be able to use the Session object. However, you will be able to use the Orderform object that holds the shopping cart information for your customers to store the impression history. In fact, the Orderform behaves in a very similar way to the Session object, since you can add any kind of information to it. For example:

```
<!--#Include File="i_util.asp"-->

<%
' Load the Orderform
' Note: you should only do this if you are in a page
' that doesn't already automatically load the Orderform
' as a result of its execution

Set mscsOrderFormStorage = UtilGetOrderFormStorage()
Set mscsOrderForm = UtilGetOrderForm(mscsOrderFormStorage, created)

' Get the impression history

sImpressionHistory = mscsOrderForm.sImpressionHistory

If IsNull (sImpressionHistory) Then

' Create new

sImpressionHistory = ""

End If

' Deliver the Ad here.

mscsOrderForm.sImpressionHistory = sImpressionHistory

' Save the Orderform
' Note: you should only do this if you are in a page that
' doesn't already do it automatically.

Call UtilPutOrderForm(orderFormStorage, mscsOrderForm, created)
%>
```

The only thing that you will have to be extremely careful about will be cleaning it up whenever the user returns to the store, since the Orderform object will be preserved in its entirety in the database between sessions.

Delivering the Ads

Finally, we come to the moment of truth, in which we officially request an ad from the AS component. The syntax for doing so is quite simple: all you have to do is call its GetAd method:

Syntax:

```
Function AdServer.GetAd (Response, TagList, HistoryString)
```

`Response`	The intrinsic ASP `Response` object (used for login and reporting operations)
`TagList`	An array that contains the list of targets
`HistoryString`	A string, entirely handled by the component, that contains the impression history for this session

`GetAd` returns a string that contains the actual text for the ad that should be displayed (if design mode is enabled and an error occurred, then the return value will be the text of the error). Unless you need to process it any further, you can output the returned value directly using a `Response.Write` command.

Here's a quick example that creates a target list, retrieves the user history from the `Session` object and uses them to deliver an ad:

```
<%
  Set As = Application ("AS")

  TargetList = ("Ad.Size.Banner", "Ad.TargetFrame._new", "Mid40s",
                "Female")
  HistoryString = Session ("HistoryString")

  If IsNull (HistoryString) Then
    HistoryString = ""
  End If

  Response.Write As.GetAd (Response, TargetList, HistoryString)
%>
```

Summary

In this chapter, we have examined the Ad Server in detail. As you have seen, it's a rather simple product, very easy to use and yet flexible. Its simplicity, however, is its real power, as it provides an extremely high level of customizability with relatively little effort.

As you experiment more with it, you will begin missing two functional elements: the ability to include server-side scripts inside the ads and the possibility of delivering ads from a server that does not have the AS installed. The first problem can be solved, as we mentioned briefly at the beginning of the chapter, by using the `Scriptor` component within a Micropipe. You will still have to cope with the fact that both the text and the script must be stored together in the ad but separated when fed to the `Scriptor` component.

As for the second problem, Microsoft has released a very interesting whitepaper that explains some, albeit not all, of the techniques that can be used to deliver ads on non-AS sites. You will find it at `http://www.microsoft.com/commerce`.

21

The Microsoft Wallet

Many online stores seem to have been designed with the intent of doing just about anything to prevent a shopper from buying something. If you consider your time valuable, buying as many things as possible on the Internet is fast and convenient. The only annoying thing is having to enter your personal information again every time you go through a purchase process. Credit card numbers tend to become particularly pesky. I, for one, would gladly avoid the physical exercise of having to take my card out of the wallet (and the wallet out of my pocket) if I only could.

Microsoft has tried to solve this problem by providing a client-side storage system that could be accessible to any web site and secure for the shopper to use. This system is called the Microsoft Wallet and was originally shipped with Site Server Enterprise Edition 2.0. When Internet Explorer 4.0 came out, the Wallet was an integral part of the product, and it is still available in Internet Explorer 5.

We've already come across the Wallet in some of the preceding chapters, as we've looked at the structure of an online store. This short chapter should draw together the aspects of the Wallet we've discussed, and give you an understanding of the whole picture. We'll start by looking at what the Wallet is and how it works. Then we'll discuss how it can be included in your own stores.

> ➤ What is the Microsoft Wallet?
>   This section briefly explains some fundamental facts about the Wallet, from its basic working principle to how it is installed by a browser, as well as how it works from a user's point of view.

> ➤ Using the Wallet in your store.
>   We'll see what you need to do in order to use the Wallet in your own store. We'll also take a look at the Browscap.ini file and how it can affect the Wallet's functionality.

What is the Wallet?

The rationale behind the Wallet is that users need a common storage system that they can use to save their personal information, and that can be accessed by any web site, with the user's permission, to retrieve it. This eliminates the need to remember and type repetitive information.

Until Internet Explorer 5.0 came out, there was no way for individual sites to create anything that would have been able to play a similar role without exchanging personal information about their customers, a practice that cannot be considered good business for privacy reasons. IE5 helps to solve this problem by providing the AutoComplete feature, which however requires different stores to use the same name for the various fields needed for the user's personal information.

It was clear that a more definitive answer to this problem would have to work locally from the user's machine, rather than on each server. Thus was born the Wallet, which stores sensitive data locally and then releases it to a web site after requesting the user's permission.

Security and privacy are important concerns, and the Wallet addresses them by encrypting the information that it needs to save to the hard drive and then protecting the information with a password, that is needed whenever the data must be accessed, even for editing. Any extension to the Wallet must be digitally signed with a valid certificate for it to be installed on the user's computer.

Accessing the Wallet

A user will typically access the Wallet in two phases, the first one to create a dataset that contains his or her own personal information and the second one to release the information to a web site. It's worth noting that these two phases can happen at the same time. While the user is visiting a web site, he or she can enter his or her personal data and, at the same time, release it to a site.

Browser Support

The Wallet provides its functionality to a web site through a browser plug-in. Currently (in Version 3.0), the plug-in supports both Internet Explorer 3.0 and higher, and Netscape Navigator 3.0 and higher. Thus, if a customer doesn't use one of these browsers, he or she will not be able to use the Wallet.

Installation

Internet Explorer browsers are at an advantage here. In fact, if the plug-in is not already installed on the client machine, the browser will automatically start to download it and will then proceed through the installation process with minimal user intervention.

With Navigator browsers, however, the user has to manually download and install the plug-in before they can use the Wallet. This operation sometimes requires the user to close the browser window and then launch it again. Since the user often won't find out that the Wallet isn't installed on his or her machine until he or she gets to the web pages that require it, this can become quite annoying.

In both cases, when the Wallet isn't installed on the client machine, downloading it can be quite a painful experience, especially for users who have slow connections. Therefore, it could be a good idea to use the Wallet as a second choice and to use standard HTML forms by default. That way, users who have the Wallet and want to take advantage of it will be able to do so, while those who don't will not have any major problems.

Address and Payment Interfaces

The Wallet works through two different interfaces, one dedicated to storing addresses and the other to storing payment information. The address interface is integrated with the system's Address Book (which is also shared by several other Microsoft applications, such as Office and Internet Explorer) and is the same for any address that it stores.

The payment interface, however, can be extended to support an arbitrary number of payment systems (i.e.: private label credit card, CyberCash, and so on) and therefore presents a slightly different interface depending on the method that the user chooses. It's interesting to note that the Wallet is able to automatically install additional payment methods by downloading them from a web site. In addition, a web site can specify what payment methods it supports, and the Wallet will consequently make the unsupported methods unavailable to the user. By default, the Wallet comes with support for the most common credit cards (VISA, American Express, MasterCard, Novus and Discover).

Both the address and payment interfaces provide support for multiple data instances, which do not need to belong to the same user. Each instance is protected by a password and can only be released by a user who knows that password. Thus, the Wallet makes it possible to safely share the same computer among several people.

Using the Wallet

In recent versions of IE, the Wallet can be accessed directly through the browser's interface, by selecting Internet Options from the Tools menu. In the resulting dialogue box, you can click on the Contents tab to gain access, among other things, to the Wallet's configuration interface.

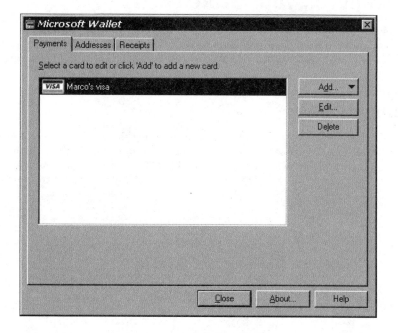

From here it's possible to access, add, edit and delete any of the payment and user information instances that the Wallet has stored. You can even access a list of "receipts" that have been delivered to the Wallet by MSCS stores. Microsoft has probably added this functionality, which wasn't available before Version 3.0, because the order IDs generated by MSCS are so long and difficult to remember.

In Chapter 15, we saw how the Wallet is used inside a typical MSCS store. It's important to understand, however, that a password is required in order to release an instance of payment information.

Using the Wallet in your Store

There are two separate problems that you will face if you decide to use the Wallet in your store. As we will see later, MSCS provides most of the functionality that you need, but you will still need to fully understand how to make the best of it and provide an enjoyable shopping experience to your users.

Browser Compatibility

Before you decide to use the Wallet, you will need to be sure that the user's browser will be able to display it. Since only IE and Navigator Version 3.0 will be able to install the plug-in, any other browser should be automatically directed to the standard HTML forms. To find out which browser is running at the other end of the wire, you will need to use the MSWC.BrowserType object that ships with IIS.

```
Set objBrowser = Server.CreateObject ("MSWC.BrowserType")

If (objBrowser.ActiveXControls) and (objBrowser.MajorVer >= 3) then
     ' IE 3.0 +
     ' You may also want to determine what CPU is running at the other end,
     ' so that you will point the user to the right files if he or she
     ' needs to install the Wallet

     If (UCase (CStr (Request ("HTTP_UA_CPU"))) = "ALPHA" then
          ' ALPHA CPU
     Else
          ' x86 CPU
     End If
Else
     If (objBrowser.Browser = "Netscape") and (objBrowser.MajorVer >= 3) then
          ' Navigator 3.0 +
End if
```

The problem with this system is that MSWC.BrowserType returns its values by comparing the agent information that is passed along by the browser with the contents of the browscap.ini file, which is normally found in the \winnt\system32\inetsvr folder.

Since the information changes not only between different browsers, but also between different versions of the same product, the contents of browscap.ini tend to become obsolete quite rapidly, so your site can be tricked into thinking that a browser doesn't support the Wallet just because its agent information is too new for your browscap.ini file. This is quite a common problem and can only be solved by keeping your files current. Microsoft used to maintain a periodically updated version of the ini file, but has now turned its control over to CyScape (http://www.cyscape.com), a third-party company that also produces additional browser detection products.

Displaying the Address Selector

The address selection interface, also known as Address Selector, is displayed by adding the appropriate tag into your HTML pages. For example, if you're targeting an Microsoft browser running on an 80x86 platform, you will use something similar to the following.

```
<OBJECT
     ID="Selector"
     CLASSID="clsid:87D3CB63-BA2E-11cf-B9D6-00A0C9083362"
     CODEBASE="mswallet.cab"
     HEIGHT="123"
     WIDTH="154"
>
</OBJECT>
```

A corresponding <EMBED> tag can be used for Navigator, although you will also have to provide some functionality that will degrade the page gracefully if the plug-in isn't installed.

The Wallet by itself, however, will not send out any information through an HTTP connection, but will store it into a set of input parameters that are in your HTML page. The plug-in is advised of these parameters, which will typically be hidden <INPUT> tags in an HTML form, by the MSWltPrepareForm function, which is available by default to all MSCS stores.

Displaying the Payment Selector

The techniques that apply to the address selector are also valid for the payment interface, called the Payment Selector. The main difference here is that you will also have to inform the selector of what payment methods your site supports. This is done by passing a string formatted following the appropriate syntax when the plug-in is created.

```
<OBJECT
     ID="paySelector"
     CLASSID="<% = MSWltIEPaySelectorClassid() %>"
     CODEBASE="<%= MSWltIECodebase() %>"
     HEIGHT="123"
     WIDTH="154">
     <PARAM NAME="AcceptedTypes" VALUE="visa:clear;mastercard:clear;">
</OBJECT>
```

As you can see, the string is composed of a series of tokens separated by a semicolon. Each token, in turn, contains two parameters, separated by a colon. The first parameter expresses the name of a payment method (VISA, MasterCard, and so on), while the second specifies the transmission method that should be used. The Wallet, by default, supports both clear text (unencrypted) transmission and SET transmissions.

Since your store will not probably be ready for SET yet, you will have to settle for clear text transmission. Keep in mind, however, that your payment pages should be protected using SSL, which provides the necessary security layer.

Summary

As you have seen, while there are a few things that you should be aware of if you intend to use Microsoft Wallet, proper planning and a little maintenance can provide a secure and enjoyable shopping environment for your customers.

Historical Cross-Selling and the Predictor Component

At the beginning of the section of this book dedicated to MSCS, we briefly introduced the concept of historical cross selling. As we mentioned, this technique works by comparing a user's behavior on the site to historical information that was collected from previous customers in the past, attempting to predict what he or she will be more interested in based on what his or her predecessors have done.

Historical cross selling is a widely used technique in online sites these days. Often, it's used to show the user who is looking at a particular product what else other people who bought that product also purchased. This works very well, especially with merchandise in which the choice of a particular item has a high probability of indicating a preference for a specific category of products. For example, in a bookstore that sells technical books, there's a good chance that all the people who bought a copy of *Professional Site Server* will be interested in Microsoft technology and will therefore buy other related books. Thus, if we were to look at the Pro Site Server page, the site would tell us that other users have bought titles that will probably be of interest to us as well.

On the other hand, if you go to an online grocery store and purchase a carton of eggs, it's difficult for the site to tell whether you want to bake a pie or play a nasty practical joke on your neighborhood (not that you would ever do that, of course). In scenarios similar to this one, the store cannot make a reasonably correct prediction based simply on the product that you are looking at, but has to extend its calculations to include the contents of your basket and, possibly your own purchase history.

The goal of this short chapter is to examine the historical prediction capabilities included in MSCS, which are provided by the Predictor component. The chapter is divided into three parts:

> **The prediction process**
> First of all, we'll take a look at how the prediction process can help you in your store and how it works from a conceptual point of view. As we'll find out in this section, it's not nearly as simple as it looks.

> **Using Predictor**
> Next, we'll introduce the Predictor component and see how it can be used in your stores. We'll also discuss how to best program it so that it doesn't take up too many resources while still providing optimal prediction capabilities.

> **Other uses of the prediction engine**
> Finally, we'll take a look at how Predictor can be used for more than simply offering historical cross-selling capabilities. In particular, we'll quickly review how it can be used to provide simple implicit personalization.

The Prediction Process

The first time one looks at an online store making historical predictions, the natural reaction is to think that it must be quite easy to reproduce this behavior. Then, once the development team starts to put a prototype together, the problems start to come out and things tend to get very complex.

This isn't a Crystal Ball

The basic issue with the prediction process is that it's very simple to handle *if* the conditions on which it is based are simple to start with. However, when the conditions are very simple, predictions tend to be inaccurate – to the point that, unless they are based on a sufficiently large amount of data, you may run the risk of driving away customers who can't understand why you're offering them merchandise that – in their opinion – is completely unrelated to what they're interested in.

Let's take an example, just to make things a little clearer. Suppose you're running a bookstore that sells technical books and somebody buys a copy of a book on Site Server and a copy of a book on IBM DB/2. If you were to base your prediction only on this fact, it would be very easy to recommend the DB/2 book to another person who bought the Site Server tome.

On the other hand – and your personal experience would probably suggest that this is the case in our scenario – the one historical piece of information that you have might be a statistical fluke and not represent the actual preferences of the majority of people who will buy Site Server books (or DB/2 books, for that matter) from you. What's worse, in this case you have actually revealed what another customer had purchased from your store, information that should be usually considered confidential.

To make a correct prediction, you will in fact need to first collect a quantity of statistical information large enough to provide a sample that will represent your entire customer base reasonably well. At this point, the prediction process becomes increasingly complex, because you will have to take into consideration many different pieces of information in order to make a correct calculation and offer the right merchandise to your users. In addition, simply collecting a lot of data does not automatically get rid of the spurious entries that we just saw above, which you must be able to recognize and ignore. Finally, you might not only have to consider the category your merchandise belongs to, but also other factors, such as price, availability, shipping costs, and so on, that have influenced purchases in the past and are likely to influence the customer at hand now.

It Wasn't Just an Apple!

A typical problem in many experimental fields of science, like physics or astronomy, is trying to extrapolate a general law based on a finite number of observations. For example, it's very difficult to determine the Earth's trajectory around the sun by sampling the position of each celestial body with respect to the other once (or twice, or even three or four times!) All you can expect by doing so is, at the very best, a wild guess. This is not to say that it's impossible, of course: if, going back to our previous example, a person buys a book on Site Server and one on ASP programming, and you make a prediction based on that, it's probably a good one. On the other hand, the chances of that happening in real life are slim (or non-existent, if you keep Murphy's law in consideration).

Clearly, the only way to determine the general law that regulates Earth's path around the sun, is to measure their relative positions often, and then try to figure out how the whole thing works. While this can be an easy task if you plot all your measurements on a piece of paper and try to make a guess "by eye", it's a task much more difficult to accomplish mathematically, which is your only chance of success in our field, since a computer can neither "see" nor "guess".

Although we won't go into any mathematics, it's not difficult to imagine how things which are already quite complicated when you're drawing a two-dimensional line on a piece of paper, can get *a lot* more complex if you start considering other possible dimensions. The Earth revolves around the sun so that its center always lies on a specific plane. However, it also has the unfortunate habit of moving along a third dimension, which you will have to consider if we are to accurately predict not only the distance of our planet from our star, but also the angle at which they will be facing each other.

In a real life store, it's difficult to have things in two dimensions; each aspect of a product or purchase that you consider as part of a prediction will represent a different dimension, and will complicate the calculations even further. In addition, let's not forget that statistical errors do still happen. We need the prediction engine to be able to recognize and purge them from its calculations; unless we want a single person among a million who has purchased that DB/2 book make our store think that all Site Server users also like to play with IBM's database system.

The Predictor Component

Luckily for all of us, MSCS includes a very useful component, called `Commerce.Predictor`, that can perform complex historical cross-selling predictions and that, incidentally, is also very easy to use.

How It Works

Predictor, whose algorithm by the way came straight from Microsoft's research laboratories, works by analyzing a set of information that contains a collection of purchases made through a given store. The results of this analysis are compiled in a look-up system, which is then consulted at run time so that the information about the individual customer can be used to infer the correct prediction.

This approach, as opposed to doing everything on-demand, is necessary because the calculations required to analyze the data are so complex that they would represent a serious performance problem if they were performed in real-time. Clearly, there is a major drawback in the fact that you will periodically have to refresh the results of the initial analysis, or your data will eventually become obsolete. We'll get to all this later on.

Getting Started

In order to be able to use Predictor, you will first have to retrofit your store so that it collects the information required by the component to perform its analysis operations. This should be stored in its own database table, which, in turn, should contain one entry for each product that was purchased by all your shoppers.

> *Since the data collection onus is on you, you can also decide to filter the purchases that you feed Predictor. However, you should only decide to do so very carefully and with good reasons. In this chapter, we'll assume that no filtering is done.*

The following fields are required by the component:

> ➢ SKU of the product sold
>
> ➢ Quantity of the product sold
>
> ➢ Unique ID of the shopper

You will notice that there is no chronological information in the data required by Predictor, although it might be useful for you to add the date on which a purchase was made, so that you can delete obsolete entries later on. For example, we can add the following table to the MT store:

```
Create table mt_predictor
(
   ShopperID varchar (32),
   SKU varchar (100),
   Quantity int,
   DateEntered datetime default GetTime(),
)
```

Collecting Historical Data

Next, we'll have to change the store so that it records the appropriate information in `mt_predictor` whenever a new purchase is made. There are essentially two ways of doing this: in the pipeline, or in `xt_orderform_purchase.asp`, right after the Purchase pipeline has been run.

In the first case, the best option is to use the `SQLItemADO` component to execute a query similar to the following:

```
Insert into mt_predictor values (?, ?, ?)
```

Note that we do not insert any value into the `DateEntered` field, since the database server will automatically fill in a value for it. However, it's important that you specify this field as the last of the table when you create it, or you'll have to use a different syntax for the insertion query.

Setting up our instance of SQLItemAdo, which goes in the Purchase pipeline after the Payment stage, is easy enough. First of all, we'll have to add the query to the store's Querymap object, which, as you may remember from Chapter 16, is defined in global.asa. Next, you will specify the name you gave the query in the Query property of the item, while you can probably leave the Connection String parameter empty – thus forcing the component to use the store's default connection specifications. Finally, you can set the list of data that has to be inserted in the query where the question marks are, in the exact same order in which you want them to appear in the SQL command:

```
Orderform.ShopperID SKU Quantity
```

Modifying xt_orderform_purchase.asp

If you decide that you do not want to record the purchase information during the pipeline's execution, you can insert some ASP code inside xt_orderform_purchase.asp that performs the same operations. One way of doing this is by executing a straight SQL query, as in this example:

```
For Each Product in Orderform.Items
   sQuery = "insert into mt_predictor values ('" & _
      Orderform.ShopperID & "', '" & _
      Product.SKU & "', " & _
      Product.Quantity & ")"
   MSCS.Execute sQuery
Next
```

Keep in mind, however, that you would at least need some basic kind of error checking functionality in this routine, which can complicate things a little bit.

Another possibility, assuming that you decided not to use the pipeline because you wanted to have more control over what orders you add to mt_predictor, could be to use a Micropipe component instead and still run an instance of SQLItemAdo. This will save the requirement of doing all the error checking yourselves and give you all the flexibility you need.

> Because Predictor works with a statistical model, you will need to collect a certain amount of data before you can start making predictions. It's a good idea to experiment with a sample page until you get reasonable results before going live with the prediction engine.

Initializing Predictor

It's now time to add the Predictor component to our store. The first step consists of modifying global.asa so that it initializes our instance of the component. As we have mentioned above, we must do this in global.asa because at initialization time Predictor will perform an analysis of the historical data collected so far, which may take some time.

An instance of Predictor is initialized by calling its InitPredictor method:

```
Predictor.InitPredictor (sDSN,
                         sTable,
                         sUserColumn,
                         sSKUColumn,
                         sQuantityColumn,
                         iMaxMemory)
```

Where:

- ➢ sDSN is the name of the datasource to be used when accessing the table
- ➢ sTable is the name of the table that contains the historical data
- ➢ sUserColumn is the name of the column that contains the unique user ID
- ➢ sSKUColumn is the name of the column that contains the SKU of the product purchased
- ➢ sQuantityColumn is the name of the column that contains the quantity of items purchased
- ➢ iMaxMemory is the maximum amount of memory (in kB) that the object can allocate for its internal structures.

Although the purpose of most of the columns is straightforward, you should pay particular attention to the value given to iMaxMemory. If this parameter is too small, Predictor will only store the analysis results that are "richer" in information – i.e. that contain more products and can therefore cover more situations. The documentation that comes with MSCS recommends a minimum value of 1,000, corresponding to about 1MB of storage space. Unless you have strict memory requirement, a value of 4,000 should be enough to satisfy all your needs.

In order to add prediction functionality to our store, we can add the following lines of code into the Application_OnInit event handler of global.asa:

```
Set Predictor = Server.CreateObject ("Commerce.Predictor")

Predictor.InitPredictor (MSCSSite.DefaultConnectionString,
                         "mt_predictor",
                         "ShopperID",
                         "SKU",
                         "Quantity",
                         4000)

Set Application ("Predictor") = Predictor
```

It's important to understand that this will cause the instance of Predictor to be created and initialized only once the first user enters the site after you have modified `global.asa,` or stopped and then restarted IIS or the IIS application where your store resides. This, of course, means that that first user will have to wait for Predictor to complete all its analysis before being able to access and browse the site. Since this can be a rather unpleasant experience for a customer, it's a good idea that you access the main page – to any other page, if you prefer – of your store yourself and wait for the prediction engine to load whenever you do something that will cause the IIS application, in which the store resides to reload.

Making Predictions

It's now time to modify the store so that it can actually make predictions and show them to its customers. This is done by calling the `GetPredictions` method:

```
Predictor.GetPredictions   (slItems,
                            iMaxPredictions,
                            fPopularItemFilter,
                            iRequiredMatches)
```

Where:

- > `slItems` is a `SimpleList` object that contains the items currently in the user's basket
- > `iMaxPredictions` is the maximum number of predictions that should be returned by the method
- > `fPopularItemFilter` is a `Floating Point` number, between 0 and 1, that expresses the possibility that "popular" items could be filtered (that is, removed) out of the list of prediction. 0 means that no filtering will be done, while 1 means that all popular items will be filtered out.
- > `iRequiredMatches` is the minimum number of historical baskets that a prediction must be matched against in order to be considered credible and returned by `GetPredictions`.

There are two parameters here that require a little more explanation. The first one is `fPopularItemFilter`, which is used by the object to improve the effectiveness of the prediction by removing all the items that seem to be particularly "popular" in association with what the user has in his or her basket.

For example, if your store sells computer hardware and somebody builds his or her own system, you may not want to remind him or her that other customers have bought keyboards with their computers, and instead use the prediction for less obvious items. At the same time, it's also true that sometimes customers tend to forget the most obvious things – one typical example being purchasing batteries with electronic products – and it might therefore be useful to allow popular items to be included in your predictions.

In general, I recommend that you experiment a little with `fPopularItemFilter` before settling on a specific value, since finding the best setting depends on examining how your store works and what your customer's feedback on the quality of your predictions is.

Another important parameter to `GetPredictions` is `iRequiredMatches`, which expresses the number of historical baskets against which the prediction engine needs to match the current user's shopping cart against in order to consider a prediction statistically credible. The concept here is very similar to what we were discussing a little earlier in the chapter: it's very difficult to make an accurate prediction if you can only examining a little data.

Thus, if a user's basket contains a combination of items that has occurred only a few times before, Predictor might run the risk of coming up with a list of predictions that do not accurately reflect a valid statistical sample of your customer base. In general, the documentation that comes with Site Server recommends that you use a value between 4 and 6 for iRequiredMatches, which will give you a reasonable degree of accuracy without requiring an incredibly high amount of data collection.

GetPredictions returns a SimpleList object that contains a Dictionary object for each prediction made by the engine. Each Dictionary object contains the following name/value pairs:

>   SKU: the SKU of the product for this prediction.

>   Weight: The number of items that, according to the prediction, the user is likely to buy.

>   MatchSupport: the "level of confidence" (or estimated accuracy) of the prediction. Set to the same value for all the predictions made.

Maintaining Your Prediction Engine

As mentioned earlier in the chapter, there is a certain amount of maintenance that your prediction engine will require. First of all, you will need to periodically re-initialize your instance of Predictor, which in turn will cause the object to perform a new analysis of the data stored in the historical basket table.

While there are a number of methods for doing this, the simplest by far is by adding a new page to the Store Manager, which calls the InitPredictor method of your instance of Predictor stored in the Application object. Make sure that the store is closed before you do this, or your customers may encounter errors while the analysis is under way.

Another maintenance tip that you might want to take into consideration is the fact that the historical data table will need to be periodically cleaned of obsolete entries. If you do not do this, the initial analysis will take longer every time you perform it, and the obsolete data can prove to be spurious because it contains information that is no longer representative of reality. For example, if a new version of Windows is out, people will progressively be less and less interested in the old one, but your historical table might still "confuse" the Predictor engine because the old basket that contain the previous version of Windows will still create matches during the prediction process and cause wrong results to be displayed.

Other Uses of the Prediction Engine

With a little stretch of our imagination, it's possible to conceive other tasks that can be performed by the Predictor component. The first step in doing so is trying to abstract the concepts that we have seen so far, so that all the references we have made about historical cross-selling will be out of the picture.

Looking back at the table where we collect the historical basket data, it's possible to see how the Shopper ID is simply a way to group the data in a logical way, while the SKU is a way to identify the individual units of data. The Quantity field, on the other hand, has a slightly more complex meaning. In fact, this is actually the importance that any given entry has with the respect to the other data. The prediction engine partly uses this value to determine whether information of unusual nature should be considered spurious or not.

Predictor & Site Personalization

With the abstracted data in our hands, we can now move on to exploring how Predictor can be used to provide personalization services rather than historical cross-selling. First of all, for clarity's sake, we'll follow a simple example: we'll suppose that our store offers articles divided into three main categories:

> ➢ News
>
> ➢ Press releases
>
> ➢ Reviews

Our goal will be to offer links to particular articles in the site based on what other users have chosen in the past, with the intent of driving traffic to the highest possible level by personalizing the site's behavior to the individual visitor.

Part 1 — Collecting historical information

Similar to what was happening for the basket information, we would need to somehow collect data about the habits of our users, in order to build enough historical information for the prediction engine to base its analysis on. We'll do that by mapping the following information on to the information categories we were collecting in the previous shopping basket example:

Baskets	Articles
Shopper ID	Session ID
SKU	Article ID
Quantity	# of times visited

As you can see, we are assuming that we will be tracking the users with some sort of session-keeping system, such as the `Session` object in IIS or even the shopper ID in MSCS when cookies are turned off. Clearly, you could be tracking users rather than sessions, but that is not always the case in sites that only sell articles, so we'll not make it a requirement.

The data collection process will also have to change from the one we used earlier. In fact, we will have to collect information throughout the entire site – as opposed to only once every time a purchase is successfully completed. In particular, the site should be able to create a new record (or update an existing one) every time an article is read. We can do this easily if our article delivery system is purely dynamic (e.g.: all the information about each article, including its body, is taken from the database), in which case we'll most likely have only a few centralized pages handling all the workflow.

Part 2—Delivering Predictions

In order for our store to be able to deliver predictions based on the current user's data, we would have to also keep track of his or her own personal profile for this session. This corresponds to maintaining the user's basket in a store.

Probably, the easiest way to perform this operation is to simply create a `SimpleList` object, in which we store a `Dictionary` object for each unique page visited by the user. This would represent an `Orderform` object. Remember that Predictor will go looking for the name/value pairs that are normally found in the basket, so you will have to save the article information using the same conventions, that is, by storing the article ID under the name `SKU` and the number of visits as `Quantity`. Naturally, you will also have to do a similar conversion when recovering the information from the list of predictions.

Summary

The good thing about the Predictor component is that it is much more powerful that one would expect at first sight. As we saw at the beginning of the chapter, providing historical cross-selling functionality is not an easy task but it can yield a high return in improving the commercial performance of your site and the overall shopping experience for your customers.

At the same time, it's important that you proceed carefully in implementing the prediction engine in your own store, because it will not work well unless the store is appropriately equipped and the historical information is properly maintained.

23

Case Study — Outlining a Business-to-Business Solution

This case study outlines an application of Site Server technology to a real world business situation. It emphasizes the following aspects:

> ➢ Understanding of the market strategy behind the Site Server product
> ➢ Focuses on specific Site Server features that create business value
> ➢ Presents a guide for scoping and planning your own project
> ➢ Provides real world metrics to use in performance and project management

Let's waste no time in delving into the first of these.

Creating a Path Towards Electronic Commerce

Finding success in an Internet-based electronic commerce (or e-commerce) project is difficult. If the end goal of your project is to achieve some positive business result, then the risks associated with Internet e-commerce projects are great. The problem with e-commerce projects is that the entire concept seems to be a moving target. It was only a couple of years ago that people frequently understood e-commerce as meaning Electronic Data Interchange, or EDI. Now e-commerce still applies to EDI, but it also means a whole lot more. Today you might think that e-commerce means buying and selling over the Internet, a.k.a. The CyberStore. But even this concept is rapidly expanding in scope to include new initiatives in telephony, artificial intelligence, and a tremendous series of innovations.

From a business perspective, many people view e-commerce as the vehicle for implementing tremendous business process change and implementation of Total Quality Management. It is a vehicle for establishing new and different customer relationships. As such, e-commerce has become the banner for the march to the 21st century. Even if you believe all this grand rhetoric, the point to make here is that understanding the need for e-commerce is not the same as understanding the path toward e-commerce. Even those that feel e-commerce is a good idea are lost when it comes to understanding how to proceed in a market full of complex commerce enabling products. Achieving a positive business result, whether it is cost saving, or profit, or market presence, depends on understanding not only the technology, but factors such as legal issues, product promotion, process scalability, availability, customer service, partner alliances, and so on.

One of the great advantages of Site Server is that it provides the infrastructure to provide a path and framework to move one toward e-commerce. Of course, having Site Server as a project infrastructure doesn't guarantee a successful project any more than having the right wood and bricks will win you architectural awards for a building. But Site Server is a great start!

As you venture forward on your own project you need to picture yourself as an adventurer/explorer of cyberspace. Maybe it is overly simplistic and immature to see oneself hacking a path through the jungle of cyberspace. But there are plenty of ways to get in trouble... and it takes a multi-talented team to survive. Maybe your problems will be as simple as severely underestimating the number of visitors to your site and having a million visitors arrive on your first day. Perhaps you would consider this the best kind of problem. But Internet-based projects present technology problems far in excess of the planning issues of only a few years ago. Server sizing, database sizing, LDAP configuration, security hacking, you name it; it's a zoo of problems.

And there are plenty of challenges beyond technology.... I can remember vividly one experience where I was trying to help the client figure out if their cyberstore deserved it's own loading and docking space at their distribution warehouse. There are lots of issues to consider.

A case approach to learning helps to unveil some of the not so obvious factors that contribute toward a project. You can make a pretty good case, (no pun intended), that e-commerce projects are more risky than traditional computer projects. Final project business results can appear to depend on the whims of fashion and culture, not so much on technology. Here's a list of but a few of the key factors to consider:

- ➢ Reliability of technology
- ➢ Project budget
- ➢ Executive sponsorship

- ➢ Company organization
- ➢ Ability to innovate
- ➢ Security/knowledge sharing
- ➢ End user involvement
- ➢ Internet bandwidth
- ➢ Database creation
- ➢ Team building

I suppose the lesson here is that this case approach is not so much a cookbook as a reference on nutrition. An e-commerce project is more of a lifestyle than a meal. The project will never end. There is always a next phase.

This case study will help the technical reader apply the features available in Site Server and relate to business concepts to drive home the idea of establishing a firm foundation for e-commerce. The foundation is part technology and two parts cyber-enterprising or total quality management. At the end of the case study there's some additional discussion that explores the non-technology issues that contribute toward project success.

Case Content

In considering a case study for Site Server I wanted to find something that spoke to the abilities of the product, beyond what might be considered the basics of commerce, the cyber store. To that end, this chapter presents a case for a manufacturing supplier communication application. While the case centers on the textile industry, specifically on a company called BroadCloth, the concepts fit companies in chemicals, insurance, financial services, and many others. In all industries the theme is the same, how to coordinate an alliance of suppliers into a cohesive network that provides a synergy of value additions to a product. The key business pattern or process in the case is a situation where a product is sent out to a supplier who makes changes to the product and then returns or forwards the product on to the next link in the chain.

As a preface to whet your appetite, within this case study you will have everything necessary to create your own Java and XML based Supplier Chain Management system. Forget all those $300,000 fancy EDI solutions. It isn't bending the truth too much to say that you have a complete EDI solution in this case. However, I should say from the onset that I am not an expert in the fields of manufacturing, supplier chain management, or logistics. I can also say that I do not think this lack of experience is important in terms of the immediate value a company can produce from Microsoft Site Server. However, I think there are people who will read this case and will recognize that we might have missed some of the traditional tenets of manufacturing control.

I like the idea that our project team didn't know any better, so we invented something simple that works. All right, yes, we acknowledge that the Site Server brand of supplier chain management is not on par with the features you would purchase in a multi-year implementation of an Enterprise Resource Planning system. On the other hand, did the companies that implemented this situation save a lot of money? Yes they did! Did they pay for the solution within a matter of months? You bet!

I was first called to consult with the company concerned based on the invitation of a major systems integrator that had plenty of LAN experience but was weak in the Internet Services venue. The case actually started a couple of years ago, prior to the introduction of Site Server. After gaining some experience with Web page forms the client could easily appreciate the somewhat subtle advantages of Microsoft IIS and Site Server. The various features and nuances of Site Server are best appreciated by those teams that have already had some experience with internet based e-commerce.

Case Format

The case is presented in the outline of a project scope and extends into a functional specification. In defining a project scope the goal of the document is as follows:

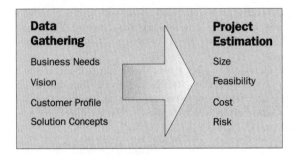

As you start your own project you will want to try to firmly establish the scope of the project. More than a few times I have been invited to meet with clients where the middle managers in attendance at the meeting are almost hysterical because the CEO has demanded that they pursue a crash course toward e-commerce.

As a Microsoft endorsement, the Microsoft Consulting Services division offers a series of training courses on a software engineering discipline called the Microsoft Solutions Framework (MSF). The MSF is a series of concepts, tools and best practices that create a foundation for building and deploying projects. If for no other reason, it provides a great mechanism for getting a project team to communicate using a common set of project management processes and terminology.

In keeping with the Microsoft MSF, the idea of a project scope is to:

> Define the development team's role in the Information System project
> Bound the Information System project by clearly defining the business processes with which a system will interact
> Provide the opportunity for development personnel to gain experience with the organization, its stakeholders, the needs that must be fulfilled, and the operating environment
> Protect the client, BroadCloth, and the development team from unrealistic expectations in project delivery.

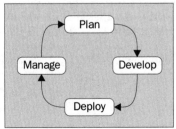

This project Scope document constitutes the first milestone in a development process that includes four major milestones:

> ➤ · Plan
> ➤ · Develop
> ➤ · Deploy
> ➤ · Manage

Let's now look at the first stage of the data gathering process.

Business Needs

One of the first steps in your project will be to gather the people who will have a vested interest in the project's success and try to move the project from business need definition to project specification. We begin this case by carefully laying down the business justification for the technology implementation. In performing this exercise, we will show how the features of Site Server relate to common business needs.

The Client

BroadCloth is not the real name of the target case company. However, even if I presented the real name of the company chances are fair that you had never heard of them. They are but one cog in the US industrial machine that is comprised of thousands of companies providing goods and services in a business-to-business network. They are a big cog; their annual gross income is more than a billion US dollars and chances are pretty good that if you live in the US, you own one of BroadCloth's products. Sure, your pants, dress, or shirt may have a designer label but in reality, the item was manufactured by the BroadCloth Company.

The Need

The critical business need behind the BroadCloth Company Inc. Supplier Coordination System (SCS) project is a need to enhance the communication between BroadCloth Company Inc. and its suppliers. Improved communications will result in better and more timely information, high quality operations, and a reduction in the time required to produce products.

Key Facts

BroadCloth is a textile manufacturing company that has about thirty primary suppliers with a total of about 1,000 users who would participate in a supplier communications solution. Most of the users of the system work for the suppliers and are not employees of BroadCloth. The application is very much one where knowledge is shared across enterprises.

The BroadCloth supplier chain is global in nature. Although it is nothing to joke about, the suppliers of BroadCloth's products are located in the economically disadvantaged developing countries and are known by the politically incorrect expression, "sweatshops". Low cost labor is the name of the game in textiles. A very important factor in this case is the concept that BroadCloth wants to use the Internet as a communication vehicle to Third World countries. Previous to this new project, communication with suppliers was conducted through a variety of intermediaries who used phones and fax equipment. The average telecom phone expenses exceed $30,000 US dollars a month. To bring that budgetary amount home, the cost of a fax to a plant in Madagascar, when the project was initiated, was more than $30 a minute. I'm sure a lot of you are comparing the phone rate amounts just presented with your own knowledge of rates and thinking about the feasibility and risks associated with trying to get Internet service to the "Third World" developing countries. I was very skeptical of the proposition when I first heard the vision for the project. Keep in mind that a phone call to a country like Madagascar has no comparison with an international call between more developed areas such as the US and Europe.

But phone charges are not the real money pit. In the main, BroadCloth's problems lie in its production cycle. It takes more than 75 days, more or less, to take a work batch from fabric to finished product. As BroadCloth is a production broker for textile products their basic business is as follows:

> Buy fabric
> Ship fabric
> Produce product
> Ship to client

BroadCloth can save many thousands of dollars by improving the quality of finished products and the cycle time required to produce them. As many experts in manufacturing will tell you, one of the key factors to successful manufacturing is found in inventory control.

Business Needs

The executives of BroadCloth instantly see great advantages in the Internet telecommunications revolution. BroadCloth is the epitome of a global company. They do business in dozens of countries. What makes this case interesting is the fact that BroadCloth is not only international but also doing business with less developed countries, not the typical industrial power nations.

As we proceeded toward project scope discovery we tried to answer a few basic questions:

> What business problems can be solved through the Internet?
> What is the target audience for the project?
> How will other parts of the company want to participate?
> What project tasks need to be accomplished?
> What resources and skills will be necessary?
> Is there the technical expertise to build and maintain a Web site?
> How much time should BroadCloth be expected to devote to maintaining a site?
> How will success of the site be measured?

Need Discovery

As the project moved forward a list was developed for basic business requirements. You will notice that these requirements are quite vague enough to fit almost any commerce project. In addition, many of you might jump to the conclusion that e-mail might be an adequate solution to the problem. Perhaps you are right. As we proceed here we will try to dig deep into requirements from a high level and proceed to greater understanding.

BroadCloth industries must establish a communication system that:

> ➢ Can be operated on a cost efficient basis
> ➢ Is available all the time (24 x 7 x 365)
> ➢ Provides for a structured framework for exchanging data
> ➢ Offers a cross platform open way for a suppliers to communicate easily
> ➢ Provides adequate security
> ➢ Offers an effective investment and growth potential for long term use
> ➢ Minimizes support expense

Issues With the Current System

In project discovery sessions the basic root causes of business needs were uncovered. Obviously you may take issue with validity of these concepts and you would be justified in doing so. It is beyond the scope of this case presentation to provide all the details that were collected by the project team.

> ➢ World economics suggest getting the most profitable deals in manufacturing, meaning that you move production to areas were the labor is inexpensive. The name of the game here is an economic tradeoff between labor and transportation logistics.

> ➢ Supplier relations are changing at an increasing rate, owing to global competitive economics. Suppliers are becoming more independent. BroadCloth Company has no control other than business leverage over suppliers. This means that corporations have less opportunity to control all vertical segments of production. It used to be that General Motors Corporation or Ford would grow the sheep that provided the wool that went into the fabric for the auto seats, etc. The auto industry is now a conglomeration of many firms working together.

> ➢ English is becoming more accepted as a world language (i.e. less translation required)

> ➢ Personal Computer Technology is becoming less expensive than phone communications. Phone and fax communications are not decreasing in price fast enough. Industrialized nations are experiencing rate drops faster than developing countries. Meanwhile, Internet access is becoming more globally available at a better rate.

> ➢ Data received from suppliers is not timely.

> ➢ Data received from suppliers is often not complete.

A listing of key manufacturing facts includes:

> ➢ When is raw material received?
> ➢ How does material received compare to material shipped?
> ➢ When is a batch work order started?

> ➢ When order is finished?
>
> ➢ When will an order ship?
>
> ➢ How will an order ship?
>
> ➢ When will the order arrive in the States?
>
> ➢ What sizes and styles are included in the order?
>
> ➢ Data is not structured and must be transcribed

Having made these issues explicit it becomes easier to home in on the requirements for the new web based application.

The Vision

The client executives and the project team worked to create a vision statement for the project. The vision statement provided a bridge between requirements gathering and solution formation. It may seem like a trivial exercise but it is interesting to see how many times a project team is drawn back to the vision statement while in the midst of arguing the virtues of one possible solution versus another.

The vision for the SCS is to create a system that will improve connectivity to suppliers world wide. In implementing a solution via the Internet, BroadCloth is pioneering a cost effective solution that will provide open but secure access to the exchange of critical manufacturing data. The clarity, currency and quality of the data will be enhanced by using structured electronic forms that will aid in providing the correct information required. Both BroadCloth and their suppliers will benefit from timely, quality data.

Measuring Success and Business Objectives

Vision statements are great but the ultimate success of the SCS project will be measured against whether or not BroadCloth's operational objectives are achieved. Will BroadCloth achieve a positive business result? In order to measure this concept of success, BroadCloth's objectives were quantified with best estimates. The project team wrote down a list of quantifiable and intangible benefits for the project and then tried to match each business objective back to a specific business need.[1]

Project Justification Factors

It is interesting to see how difficult it is for businesses to quantify their business results. Let's look at some of the quantifiable benefits first:

Tangible business benefit project justification factors

> ➢ Communications reduction in expense
>
> ➢ Quality of data as measured by opinions in Operations and Supplier Resources
>
> ➢ Inventory Reduction Value
>
> ➢ Value of data on fabric receipts
>
> ➢ Value of data on work in progress

---

[1] For those of you who are consultants, or future consultants, it might be important to note that the consulting team didn't sign a contract to achieve business results, they were more focused or limited to the technology implementation. On the other hand, and more recently, there have been instances where large consulting enterprises have created contracts where they actually share in the business results with the client.

- ➢ Value of data on outbound finished goods
- ➢ Elimination of data entry operations

Along with the factors that could be quantified, the project team identified the factors that might be intangible but nonetheless important for project success. In today's stock market, a company's stock valuation might rise several percent merely by them announcing that they are thinking about an Internet project.

Intangible business benefit additional considerations

- ➢ Business partner relations
- ➢ Customer service
- ➢ Overall quality
- ➢ Establishing a competitive position on the Internet
- ➢ Maximizing the price of the client's stock

Table for Business Objectives

The above considerations were then honed down to a core set of objectives, and the means by which these objectives would be met:

Business Need	Objective	Means
Timely quality data	Quality objective of 95% on time and complete, 75 day production cycle	E-mail and Web-based forms that structure: Fabric Receipts, Fabric Cuts in Sizes, and Outbound Finished Goods
Inexpensive communication mechanism	Reduce communication expenses that currently exceed $30,000 per month	Use Internet for inexpensive global communications.
To establish an Internet infrastructure model	Validate Internet application model by subjective opinion	Establish easy to use application with a report generator to convert raw data into useful information

Finally, the project team tried to make a statement that narrowed the project down to a technological basis for defining success. This might seem strange, but if you are a Java developer or a database guru, you might appreciate that you are not being held responsible for raising your company's revenue by 25%. After all, you would want to be paid like the CEO if you had those objectives in your performance plan.

The SCS project will be technically successful if it:

> Establishes an infrastructure via the Internet for conducting business with suppliers.

> Creates a Web site that allows for the exchange of information on Fabric:
> 1) Receiving
> 2) Cut sizes
> 3) Work-in-progress summary and/or
> 4) Outbound finished goods, (assumed to be the same data in different states of being).

> Implements a report generation facility to create information on the data that is received via the Web.

Stakeholder Profiles

Given that everyone agreed on the business needs for the project, the next step was to agree on what the roles were of the people who would make or break the project in terms of success. These roles are called Stakeholders in the terminology of the Microsoft Solutions Framework, (refer to the case introduction). The Stakeholders are the people that have a vested interest in the project's success.

Stakeholder	Project Goals and Priorities	Constraints	Tolerance for Risk
Suppliers	Compliance with BroadCloth policies	Low overhead environments	Unknown
Operations Department	Overall efficient production responsibility	Limited power over suppliers,	Unknown
Supplier Resources Department	Quality supplier outsourcing	Communication facilities	Unknown
Management Information Systems (MIS)	Efficient data operations	MIS distributed to divisions	Moderate
Controller	Inventory Control	OUT OF SCOPE	Unknown
Customers	Overall service and results	OUT OF SCOPE	Low

At this point you will probably wonder, as I first did, about the suppliers and their participation in the project. Why should they participate? Would they have the right equipment? Would they like the usability of the application? All of these are of course valid questions. In the first phase of this engagement, the project team had very little opportunity to work with the most important stakeholders of the project, the suppliers. You should make every effort to establish solid communications with all your project stakeholders. You need to understand their needs. You should be able to articulate what I call their "performance plans". That is to say, how and why do they get compensated in their jobs? While lack of supplier communication access has not been a problem on this project, I can admit that I participated in another project, a salesforce automation system, where the "marketing" department felt they could speak for and represent the needs of the company's salesforce. That was a tremendous mistake! The speed with which the salesforce killed the project was amazing.

Notice that the Controller and the Customer were excluded from the project. Some clarification is in order here. In this situation, the idea of the customer meant the ultimate customer for the goods and services of BroadCloth (i.e. the consumers of the products). Therefore, they were really not involved in the scope of the project since it involved internally focused product manufacturing.

It is less clear as to why the Controller would be excluded. The project team decided to exclude the company's controller from this project not because the role was not a Stakeholder, but moreover, the project team was worried about the Controller's influence on the project. The project was envisioned as a communication system. The team felt that the Controller could quickly turn the project into an overall inventory management system, and the scope of the endeavor would rapidly grow out of control.

I guess the end message here is that there is a degree of risk mitigation and politics that seems to creep into every project. It is something you need to be artful of detecting and controlling for maximizing positive results.

Solution Analysis

In crafting an overall analysis for a solution there are two domains of concern:

> Creating the right technology solution – The Solution Design
> And implementing the project as a consulting engagement – The Solution Implementation

Let's now look at the first of these.

The Solution Design

The idea underlying arriving at a Solution Design is to distill the business requirements and translate them into computer system specifications. We will start with a high level review of the business applications and technology resources that were used to design the systems for the application. Then we will look at the system architecture in more depth and address performance and operational issues.

Business Applications

In what might be an over simplification, the BroadCloth manufacturing process was distilled into the following four major phases of production.

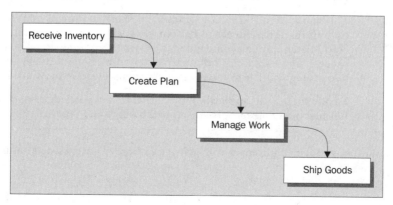

The manufacturing process is presented at a high level, but in actual practice there are many sub-steps to each major phase of production. The "Receiving Inventory" phase, for example, includes the tasks associated with handling import and customs activities and then reconciling what was received to what was shipped. In "Creating a Plan", the manufacturing plan for a batch, the supplier must arrive at a plan for efficiently cutting fabric into the best assortment of shapes and sizes. You may think that all this could have been dictated by BroadCloth prior to the arrival of the goods, but the reality is that the cloth can easily become damaged due to theft, water, or just plain old dirt. Therefore, the final analysis for a manufacturing plan is best done at the supplier's factory.

Having previously documented the business issues and then identified the stakeholders in a new solution, BroadCloth created some business objectives and then brainstormed on possible application solutions to address their needs. In the end, BroadCloth distilled the business requirements of the SCS into five key applications.

1. Raw Material Analysis	This application concerns the acknowledgment and analysis of raw materials (cloth or garment components) that have arrived on site. In this application, the supplier needs to communicate what was received back to BroadCloth. Inventory is frequently damaged or missing on shipment.
2. Shipping Reconciliation	This application provides correlation of shipping to receiving. It seems very similar to the first one and indeed we could have called the applications Receiving Goods 1a and 1b. However, the Shipping Reconciliation application is more focused on serving internal BroadCloth departments and their needs to control inventory and manufacturing plans. If a shipment of fabric goes to India, the actual number of shirts, their styles, and their sizes may not be decided until the material actually arrives at the supplier's factory. BroadCloth departments, from Operations, all the way to Sales, need to be able to predict product futures.
3. Batch Design	This application provides quality education and references for the supplier. It is like a handbook for the production requirements of goods to be assembled. The ultimate vision is vaguely like a Computer Aided Design, or CAD, system for garments. Batch design involves the supplier planning for a production run of a manufacturing batch. The supplier has some latitude on creating a proposal for what can be produced from the goods as received. However, BroadCloth also dictates such product quality characteristics as the style and quantity of stitching, seams, etc.
4. Production Control	This application is similar to traditional Work in Process or Production lot tracking. There needs to be some way to monitor a Work in Process (WIP) batch through some number of steps within the manufacturing process. Once a batch work order is started it moves through an assembly line of steps similar to the manufacturing involved in most products.
5. Final Shipping	Finally there is an application that provides acknowledgment that the finished materials have been shipped by date and mode.

Each of these applications provides a domain with a scope or border for crafting a solution. We will discuss these applications later on as we investigate the application architecture.

Technology Resources

Next we look at the technology available for crafting a solution. This review will present the solution at a high level, relating the technology to business needs.

From the onset of the project, the client product manager for this project suggested that an Internet based solution was the target for the technology. In considering solutions, the project team could have considered various groupware technologies, including Microsoft Exchange, Lotus Notes, etc. As we mentioned previously, one possible, and acceptable solution to the business needs may be plain old e-mail.

And e-mail is a great solution! Having electronically entered documents was a big advance over the methods that were in place for transcribing faxes. As the project started there must have been at least a dozen data entry operators that were transcribing faxes into electronic form. How much did those people cost? Probably more than the cost of Site Server in terms of a single month of salaries and administrative overhead. However, eventually the problem you discover with e-mail is that it is too unstructured to easily get data into database managers (this was prior to the introduction of XML).

The project team decided that in order to accomplish a solution for BroadCloth, a system would need to be designed so that BroadCloth suppliers could connect to the Internet through a browser program that would act as a gateway for exchanging manufacturing information. The idea of the browser program was intended to mean both the traditional concept of a Web browser, but also a mechanism to send e-mail.

While we are here, I might mention that controlling the scope of a new project and it's integration into legacy business infrastructure, or future business vision is very important. There was some consideration given to a future need for the SCS to include connectivity to the an IBM AS/400 application as well as the expansion of new forms of information and graphics that are exchanged via the SCS browser program. The project team decided to table these considerations for future phases of the project, meaning that they were out of the scope of the first phase of the project, but that they also somewhat drove the team to emphasize the use of Web site pages and forms in lieu of e-mail based solutions.

Hierarchy of communication perfection

In contemplating a solution the project team eventually considered that there is a hierarchy of technology that needs to be acknowledged in integrating a value chain of suppliers. Some suppliers have very rudimentary connections to the Internet with basic equipment. The price of connecting to the Internet varies tremendously from country to country. Other suppliers enjoy ample bandwidth and use the latest in Intel and Microsoft technology. Therefore a system needs to be developed that will recognize a profile of supplier capabilities and then communicate with the supplier with the most efficient method to enhance the operations between the two companies.

The following is a list of the preferred methods of doing business with BroadCloth.

Preferred Technology Mechanisms (in order):

- ➢ Secure XML Transactions
- ➢ Traditional EDI transactions
- ➢ Web pages and Forms

> ➢ Transfer Microsoft Office documents
>
> ➢ E-mail
>
> ➢ Fax
>
> ➢ Phone
>
> ➢ Tin Cans and String (postal isn't even an option, submit your own joke here...)

In reality there is not a good profile of the average supplier. We need to reinforce the idea that suppliers come in many sizes and capabilities and are spread over the globe. The relationships between suppliers change daily. There is an entire BroadCloth department that is devoted to resourcing suppliers. Some suppliers are large businesses in their own rights, having many factories, others are one shop operations.

At the onset of the project, BroadCloth actually had a "traditional" Premenose EDI system and was using it to communicate with some suppliers. Other suppliers just barely had phone service. Furthermore, it was envisioned that supplier technology is a moving target. Currently, (1999) the rate of growth in Brazil is incredible. Other countries have changed little in the last two years. When the SCS project was started a Personal Computer still cost about $1,500 to $2,500. Now you can obtain one in the US for a few hundred dollars, (and some are even free, via Internet promotions). Developing a one-size-fits-all solution to this problem is very difficult. Therein lies one of the advantages of Site Server – flexibility to cope with change.

Site Server Potential

From the onset the design team began discussing the technology needs of implementing a solution. While there are distinct differences in jargon, the design team felt that business-to-business commerce technology should be similar to consumer to business technology but perhaps more robust. To say this another way, there are a lot of great products being developed to create what we call cyberstores. In the architectural concept of the cyberstore there is a structure to a Web site that offers a product database, shopping basket, product selection, financial transactions, and so forth. The project team felt that there was a lot of good code being offered in cyberstores that could be adapted to the needs of communicating between two businesses. In other words, they came to the conclusion that a cyberstore-like commerce system could be adapted to the needs of manufacturing communication and control. The team liked the idea of Microsoft Site Server Commerce Server and its adaptability to manufacturing.

Technology Need	Microsoft Product Features
Authentication and security	Personalization and Membership, NT based ACLs, Certificate Server
Publishing configuration management	Publishing Content Management and Deployment
Personalization to suppliers	Personalization and Membership and Active Server Pages
News distribution	E-mail and Channels

Technology Need	Microsoft Product Features
Searching	Index Server and Search Server
Scalability	NT, BackOffice, IIS
Internationalization	Commerce Server
Flexibility to cope with change	Commerce Server

Basically Site Server provides a new form of groupware, or collaboration software for distributed teamwork.

Derived Systems

As a result of comparing business requirements to technology the project team began to organize the SCS project into the following basic systems. Each system addresses one or more business requirements. This organization of systems, or really sub-systems, allows a way to compartmentalize, not only the computer organization of the project, but also the business organization of the project. Each of these systems is discussed further as we present the Target Systems Architecture.

> **SCS Communications WebGate**
> Provides the basic interface between the supplier and BroadCloth. Must be able to accommodate wide cross-platform variance. This system provides a logical concept for the gateway that all suppliers would use to access the facilities of BroadCloth. The WebGate encompasses both Web and e-mail services. In the cyberstore analogy, the WebGate is equivalent with the principle store.

> **SCS Management and Maintenance Facility**
> Provides an interface to the SCS for BroadCloth departments. Allows BroadCloth personnel access to the total SCS application. In the cyberstore analogy, the Management and Maintenance Facility, or MMF, is similar to the Microsoft Commerce Server Store Manager.

> **SCS Information Query Facility**
> Provides an OLAP-like capability for data that is derived from the SCS. As the data collected by the SCS WebGate and MMF increases in volume, there is a need to provide decision support services. These services should be handled by a separate system that would not disturb production operations.

> **SCS Support Service**
> An ongoing support and development maintenance service to provide operations support for the total SCS application. Includes the setup and rollout of the application to new suppliers. As suppliers come and go, frequently on a monthly basis, there needs to be some process for getting new suppliers on board with the BroadCloth applications, as well as addressing the changes to new applications that become available to current suppliers.

> **SCS Network Infrastructure Engineering**
> Provides network engineering and network support for the application. Interfaces to ISPs as required. Finally there needs to be an organization and system that deals with the intricacies that are inherent to the Internet. Issues included here are: Routers and Domain Name Services, Security, Supplier Connection, etc.

In the five major systems of SCS, most of the code involved in the application is involved in the first two systems, the WebGate and the Management and Maintenance Facility. The SCS Information Query Facility is pretty much a developing OLAP application using canned software from the Statistical Analysis System, or SAS (http://www.sas.com). The final two systems, the Support Service and Network Infrastructure Engineering address the project needs of rollout and providing continuous administrative services for a project where most of the users are not employees of BroadCloth. As another way to view these sub-systems, the creation of the sub-systems is done to provide an organization for different departments of BroadCloth. Support and Engineering are really more similar to departmental services than applications, but all the applications involve Web sites and the creation of Web pages, so perhaps we are making too much of a differentiation in the details. However, as you proceed with your own project you might look out for issues that involve integrating many departments of your company into your project. Internet projects often have a wide span of influence on the various departments of a company.

Mapping Technology to Requirements

Early on in the design stage of the project there was an activity to map the application needs to technology. The resultant spreadsheet is a tool to ensure that the technology features meet business requirements. You can elaborate this simple chart by adding various weightings for business requirements or product features and develop a more elaborate ranking mechanism for a variety of product candidates that meet a certain business need. What follows is a good initial example.

SCS Applications	Telecom Phone/Fax	E-mail	Office	SiteServer Personalization P&M	Search	Publishing ContMgt	ContDepl	Knowledge Manager KM	Push Channels	Commerce Server CIP	Certificate Server CertServ
Raw Material Analysis	5	2	2	3	4	1		3	5	2	5
Shipping Reconciliation	5	2	2	3						1	5
Batch Design	5	2		3	1	1		2		3	5
Production Control	5	5		3	1				5	1	5
Final Shipping	5	5		3						1	5

1 = Major Importance
5 = Minor Importance

Legacy Technical Architecture

Prior to delving into the solution, there are some considerations involved in understanding the current IT infrastructure and how it fits the Site Server solution. First of all, the Site Server solution doesn't really replace a legacy system per se. Prior to venturing into SCS, the client had registered a domain name and had set up some Web site operations. Getting some minor experience on the Internet helped the BroadCloth staff appreciate some of the features of Site Server and IIS 4.0. By that we mean the ideas associated with ASP establishing session state, having IIS configure sites to run in their own processes, etc. BroadCloth has both an IBM S/390 class machine as well as an AS/400. The AS/400 runs manufacturing process control, inventory, order processing, shipping and accounting. BroadCloth is working toward getting data into and out of the AS/400 but at the time of the project initiation it was not considered a high priority for the scope of the project. BroadCloth had some experience with Premenose, an EDI package for the AS/400 so they understood the elements of EDI. EDI in its traditional forms, from vendors such as Sterling and Premenose was considered a more expensive solution than what could be obtained with Internet technology.

More importantly for the purpose of this project, BroadCloth was already using Microsoft Office and Microsoft Mail, but not Exchange.

Target Systems Architecture

Up to this point we have taken the time to walk through the business needs for BroadCloth. The idea behind this exercise is to illustrate that the needs of BroadCloth are no different to the needs of hundreds, if not thousands of businesses in dozens of industries. Basically the idea of creating a virtual distributed manufacturing team entails the sharing of timely quality knowledge. Now we will look more carefully at how this is accomplished and look specifically at the technology involved in the Microsoft Commerce Interchange Pipeline.

As a brief reminder, the manufacturing process for BroadCloth and suppliers consists of the following:

> ➤ Transport and receive fabric inventory at the supplier.
> ➤ Create a manufacturing plan for handling the received inventory.
> ➤ Begin creating products and manage the work in process.
> ➤ Ship finished goods to the back to BroadCloth or the final destination.

Different semantics but the concepts are the same

It is worth noting that the terminology may seem different but the concepts associated with implementing a supplier management system are the same as in operating a cyberstore. During the engagement we spent a considerable amount of time exploring this theory and eventually came to some conclusions that you could adjust many business processes to fit the Site Server model.

Manufacturing Glossary	
Business-to-Consumer	**Textile Mfg**
Customer/Shopper	Supplier
Shopping Basket	Bill of Materials
Add to Basket	Add to Inventory
Empty Basket	Clear Batch
Purchase	Authorize
Checkout	Complete Requisition

It may be a mental stretch to see how Site Server might fit the needs of your industry. For BroadCloth, the alternatives to this idea were to simply gain the benefits of using the Internet to exchange documents via e-mail. Or, on the more expensive side of the range of ideas, BroadCloth could have put in a more custom-tailored and proprietary solution for EDI and supplier chain management. A key concept in viewing the problem domain is to view the features of Site Server as utilities for implementing Distributed Teamwork. A more passé term is called Groupware and the family of software has more recently been known as Collaboration products.

Let's walk through a sample case for a manufacturing batch and then see how the features of Site Server fit the business processes.

Supplier Coordination Flow of Information

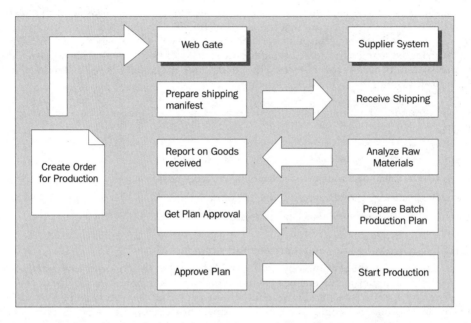

The project team originally decided to delimit tasks and activities of the manufacturing process on the events associated with communicating with suppliers. Therefore the first step in the process is focused on the need to request that a supplier create a batch work order of goods. However, as a preface to the supplier manufacturing process, there are other activities that are involved the use of Site Server. Prior to creating an order there are processes such as the selection and purchase of raw materials, and in this case we mean fabric. It is basically out of scope to worry about how fashion dictates whether purple bath towels or silk shirts will be in fashion next year. But the point is that the entire SCS process starts when there is a need to create a manufacturing work order for a batch of goods or products and we are excluding the initial processes involved with recruiting suppliers or finding the raw materials that are used to create products.

Basically, an order is a manufacturing request to a supplier. However, it is more like the creation of a proposal than a request. Within the proposal there needs to be information on the nature of the fabric used in manufacturing, however, there is also much more that needs to be included. Many of us don't consider the number of details that go into a product as common as a shirt. For example:

- ➤ What style of shirt will be required?
- ➤ What sizes?
- ➤ What gender?
- ➤ How many buttons?
- ➤ What kind of main seam?
- ➤ Is the main seam double lined?

➢ How will the buttons be stitched?

➢ How many stitches go into the seam?

➢ What kind of stitches are used?

Multiple BroadCloth departments specify the requirements for a production batch. BroadCloth departments use the Intranet based SCS Management and Maintenance Facility to create batch requisitions, but at this point the Site Server technology of Content Management and Knowledge Manager are providing some utility. Site Server Publishing offers a content publishing process that enables multiple content authors to submit and tag content via a drag-and-drop Web interface, and site editors to approve and edit content. Initially it was decided that the deployment of content from intranet-based servers to the SCS was unnecessary and so was phased for the future. Basically this means that Content Deployment isn't being used, but it could certainly fit the problem.

Since the application at this point is more focused on stakeholders who are working within BroadCloth and who are also using Microsoft Windows and Office software (as opposed to a supplier workstation environment that is more indeterminate and could be Windows, Unix, Linux, Mac, etc.), the use of COM objects at the client workstation level is encouraged.

Membership and Personalization plays an important role in guiding the business process, even though the participants of the process at this point are internal employees and staff of BroadCloth. The end result of all this activity is really to create a folder of information that will be used in production. There are probably a lot of ways to achieve this end result. BroadCloth could have used Lotus Notes, Microsoft Exchange or other forms of groupware. However, Site Server sets the stage for the application because the Internet first offers inexpensive connectivity, and then Site Server offers a set of utilities that offer a browser based drag-and-drop environment that is very easy to use.

Eventually we get to the point where we are ready to officially begin the manufacturing process. A manufacturing request and shipping manifest is created. The process starts when BroadCloth manufacturing operations department uses the SCS Management and Maintenance Facility, (think of it like the Site Server Commerce Server Store Manager), to create an order for a production batch. The order is entered in via a Web page, and as we will see shortly, it is delivered to a supplier via an XML formatted SMTP e-mail.

Of course, we keep in mind that there will be situations where the operations department continues to make expensive phone calls to some far-flung third world factory, but the big vision is to automate the process and establish Internet-based transactions.

Raw Material Analysis

The request for a manufacturing work order, …think of it as a service, is delivered to a supplier via e-mail. Later we'll look at this process in more detail because it is interesting in that it involves the Microsoft Commerce Server Interchange Pipeline (CIP) performing XML generation. The XML based e-mail containing an order can be deciphered with a wide variety of programs and we have provided an example that is specifically provided to show that the job is non-Microsoft, and platform agnostic, (using Java). From a systems perspective the Management and Maintenance Facility (MMF) creates the order but from the supplier's perspective, all collaboration with BroadCloth is handled through the public interfaces of the SCS WebGate.

Perhaps a bit of explanation is in order here. The Commerce Interchange Pipeline, CIP, is a Microsoft Commerce Server pipeline. As you read earlier in the book the idea of a pipeline is a concept where you can create a transaction and pass data, or in this case, a manufacturing object through a series of COM objects that, in the case of the CIP, prepare an order for transfer. The CIP is a data format-independent and transport-independent mechanism allowing for support of native Web formats and transports such as HTTP and SMTP.

It is easier to think of the WebGate as using the Commerce Interchange Pipeline to ratify initial project confirmations, although this may be confusing and isn't quite technically correct. The reader should focus on the idea of a Commerce Server store that has been adapted to manufacturing. The Commerce Server store has both a front, public store, and a back, private store manager.

The receipt of the e-mail is only a beginning. After the supplier receives their initial order, they can follow up on many details via the SCS WebGate. Standard Forms usage is available in instances where the supplier can't conform to the requirements of the CIP, and most of them do not. In plainer language this means that it would be great if both the supplier and BroadCloth were both using Microsoft Site Server. However this is not the case. The hardware/software environment at the supplier end has a great deal of variance. However each supplier and a profile of their information technology is represented in Personalization and Membership. This provides the supplier with a personalized work order based on the supplier's available technology and profile of manufacturing capabilities. In the end, a work order requisition may be sent via fax, e-mail, traditional EDI, or CIP-XML. However, CIP-XML is preferred.

The supplier performs an analysis on what raw materials are received and how the materials received will match to the initial batch work order. The supplier's interaction with the SCS is tailored via Personalization and Membership. The original idea was that the supplier would learn about a project and its requirements by visiting a Web site and visiting their own sub-site of a sort, dedicated to a specific work order. In reality, many suppliers like to download the Microsoft Word documents that are supplied at the site. There is less browsing than expected, and more downloading.

WebGate Sample Site Organization for an Order

You can see from the profile provided above that the supplier has the option of getting BroadCloth news, contact information, or can tailor a personal profile (again leading back to Site Server Membership). Most of the supplier's time is spent on the project workbench. The workbench will be the primary mechanism for the supplier, and correspondingly BroadCloth, to manage work.

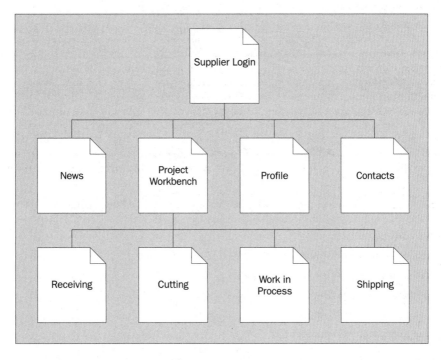

For the most part, the supplier enters information via standard forms. Using forms to capture data provides for greater data validation than might be offered via unstructured e-mails. There is an option for the supplier to report back to BroadCloth using the CIP but this would only fit suppliers that have installed Site Server and at this point the activity is mostly related to beta testing of the concept. I should also mention that the supplier may move office documents back to BroadCloth using e-mail or Content Management upload capability or FTP of Microsoft Office documents. FTP is very popular, but once again, the quality of the data suffers when data can't be conveniently captured in fields, meaning that an ASP web form sending direct to SQL Server is much preferred over receiving some document with data in Microsoft Word.

The pages of the SCS Webgate site are similar to the former paper documents that were familiar to the suppliers.

- An inventory of materials received
- A plan for cutting fabric, sizes and styles
- A project plan on manufacturing schedules

Shipping Reconciliation

Data returned from the supplier is available for analysis via the SCS Management and Maintenance Facility, MMF, in the same sense that a merchant would look at customers, orders, and products in the Microsoft Commerce Server Store Manager. Shipping Reconciliation is an intranet-based portion of the Supplier Communication System. Approvals are required for deviations from the original plan for a work order, based on raw materials received at the supplier. Missing and damaged raw goods reconciliation is an important factor in the overall profitability of a work order and for the most part the activity of shipping reconciliation involves the BroadCloth internal staff and not suppliers. The technology involved concerns Content Management as well as Commerce Server CIP. A general ability to perform OLAP-type analysis on SQL-based data is considered critical and so the project team decided to develop a separate system to service this need. (As we discuss further in the hardware architecture section, it is important to isolate potentially complex queries from production operations).

The following sub-processes are involved in performing Shipping Reconciliation:

> ➤ Forecasting
>
> ➤ In Transit Inventory Analysis
>
> ➤ Work In Process "What If" Analysis
>
> ➤ Receiving and Auditing
>
> ➤ Supplier Contacts Directory
>
> ➤ Support Contacts Directory

While we are here and discussing an intranet application it is a good time to mention that the SCS Management and Maintenance portion of the overall application allows for a central place to manage workflow-like issues such as tracking approvals, entering in new suppliers, publishing news, and providing (uploading) information relating to support.

Work Order Batch Design

Perhaps the greatest payback from the SCS can be found in having a handy online repository for obtaining the right manufacturing specifications to create an efficient plan for manufacturing a batch work order. Based upon initial estimates and approvals, a batch design is created for the number of units of product to be manufactured. In clothing there are issues in finding the optimum production quantity of sizes within styles. Plans for production are created based on the CAD[2]-like materials provided by BroadCloth. While the vision of the system is CAD-like, the actual implementation is more like providing a great variety of graphics and images on manufacturing processes. The supplier actually doesn't have access to any interactive design software, as you would usually find in CAD. Perhaps there is a future for some sort of Java applet. Batch design plans encompass details such as the style and configuration of stitches to implement on the various seams of a garment or product. Search and Knowledge Manager are the key technologies, backed by P&M and Content Management.

---

[2] CAD or Computer Aided Design is a vision that in this situation really means the exchange of CAD-like drawings, rather than the interactive design of drawings via some actual CAD system.

Searching may be key during the design phase of the work order. Some information may be specific to a certain batch, but other information may be related to BroadCloth in general or the industry in general, and thereby lend itself to the Site Server Search features. The feature of having Search look beyond the scope of Web page HTML and venture into Microsoft Office documents is greatly appreciated. While we are talking about Microsoft Office, the feature of allowing users to FTP download documents, including Microsoft documents is very popular. One problem with FTP however is that it is hampered by firewalls. In these situations, which are actually quite few in number, Content Management and the Site Server Posting Acceptor are showing promise.

Production Control

Previously we discussed a hierarchy of technology in establishing communications with suppliers. As in all the other aspects of the SCS, BroadCloth is trying to be flexible to accommodate a variety of methods in communication, while also stressing the benefits of Site Server and specifically, the Commerce Interchange Pipeline. During the Work in Process, Production Control aspect of the SCS we perform the actual management of manufacturing. Fabric goes through various states of cutting, sewing, and assembling into final products. Each supplier must maintain records of production and transmit those records to BroadCloth. As much as I hate to say it, there are still suppliers who are using faxes. However, there are also a preferred group that are uploading or e-mailing documents. We have a group of suppliers that has begun the task of implementing the sort of leading edge work processes that will probably be more common as Microsoft rolls out their new XML-based BizTalk strategy in the next version of Site Server. In the Production Control process, suppliers receive project plans and accounting on each batch work order. One supplier may need to coordinate production at several factories, usually within a 'local' area, but still hundreds of miles distant from each other.

Searching may be important depending on various production situations. XML provides a great method for providing more categorization over data content. It allows for the easy transfer and more meaningful searching of content.

Final Shipping

Final shipping involves the reporting of finished goods inventory and the brokerage of return transportation, either back to BroadCloth or drop shipped directly to a final client. Searching may be useful for various issues involved in transport and import/export issues.

In rounding out a review of the business process and Site Server solution it may be beneficial to return to the key issues in developing a solution.

Technological Issue	Site Server Solution
Authorization	Both individuals within BroadCloth and various suppliers must be authorized to provide and access information. The SCS application is small enough to allow for NT ACL based authentication versus the alternative security available in Site Server called Membership authentication.

Table Continued on Following Page

Technological Issue	Site Server Solution
Profiling the Supplier Company, the Plant and the user	Site Server Membership allows BroadCloth set up a profile of key supplier groups and apply member personalization to tailor the SCS WebGate to situations involving specific work orders.
Exchanging production data	Content Management has been valuable in offering a structured method for uploading documents, first by the various departments that contribute to the creation of a work order, and later by suppliers who choose to exchange design plans and design batch modification requests via uploading documents.
Tracking and Auditing Communications exchanges	The Commerce Server Commerce Interchange Pipe, CIP offers an auditing facility that has been very useful, if hampered only by the time that has been required to get both BroadCloth and suppliers to use more advanced transaction processes, (meaning more advanced than e-mail, and such).
Support for Internet technology in developing countries	The acceptance of Internet technology in developing nations has been surprising. Access to the Internet is relatively much more expensive there than what we take for granted in industrialized nations, and yet the availability of communications is pretty good and getting better every day. Even such exotic new solutions as Iridium Satellite communications, while seeming expensive to the consumer, can easily be justified by a factory operating in a developing country.
Providing help in the manufacturing process	Having ready access to manufacturing guides is, all by itself, a great factor in reducing the time required to produce work orders. The further deployment of that information in CAD-like images as well as Microsoft Office documents has greatly enhanced the quality of production.

Commerce Interchange Pipeline

In the original vision for the SCS system, the solution was to improve the efficiency of the communications between suppliers and BroadCloth and thereby improve the speed and quality of the production cycle. A primary means for achieving that vision is Site Server Commerce Edition. Most people would think that the Commerce Server is used to build cyberstores. Well, yes it does that, but there's more. A key feature of Commerce Server is the idea of a pipeline. Basically the pipeline provides a transaction-like environment for executing a series of COM objects. In reference to business-to-business type communications there is a specific model for a pipeline called the Commerce Interchange Pipeline (CIP). The CIP allows businesses to communicate with each other by offering a mechanism for transmitting and receiving communications, via pipelined COM objects.

A pipeline has multiple steps. You can use the Win32-based Pipeline editor to configure COM objects to position them at each position on the pipe, called a **stage**.

The basic idea behind the pipeline is to set up a transaction where each stage in the pipe is executed serially and data is passed from stage to stage. While Microsoft Transaction Server, MTS, is not a pipeline requirement, the concept of the pipeline is perfect for MTS.

Transmit and Receive Pipelines

The Commerce Interchange Pipe has both Transmit and Receive pipelines. In the BroadCloth case they mostly use a transmit pipeline as you will see in a following example. However, in a business-to-business transaction situation, the preferred BroadCloth situation, you would have two servers running Commerce Interchange Pipelines, one at each end of the transaction. Of course what this means is that both the BroadCloth and the supplier had licenses to Site Server. Perhaps now the problem is much more in focus. Thus far it has been enough of a challenge to get suppliers connected to the Internet but there is at least one situation where a large supplier has agreed to implement Site Server. Still though, the idea behind the pipelines will continue to grow and it is a good foundation for the future. Site Server is not a terribly expensive solution in comparison to other EDI applications.

In the following graphic we see how each stage of a pipeline would serve the needs of BroadCloth and a supplier who were both using Commerce Interchange Pipelines.

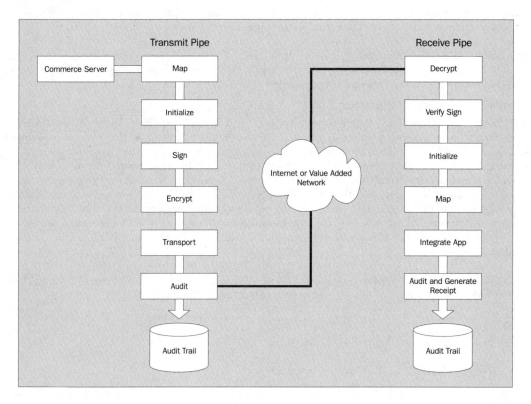

System Architecture

I'm sure it will be no surprise that the general architecture for the SCS system is Microsoft BackOffice and Site Server. The core of the system is Internet Information Server IIS 4.0, and the Site Server products, but also SQL Server and Active Server Pages (ASP). While ASP creates dynamic site content, Java COM objects have been created to encapsulate key business logic processes and enhance site performance. (We will show how to do this in a moment.) SQL Server 6.5 is used as a database manager.

General System Schematic for SCS

Conceptually the design is considered a three-tier client/server system. To make that a little clearer, we mean that the supplier's browser is the first layer of the architecture, the User Interface tier. The IIS Web server and Site Server comprise the second layer, the Business Logic tier, where most of the business logic is kept. The final layer, the Data Services tier, is found in several SQL Server data servers that provide production data, OLAP analytical data, and Membership LDAP data. The data servers keep a nice encapsulation of the data content separate from the business logic[3]. The SCS Information Query Facility (IQF) OLAP application could really be positioned on the same tier as the WebGate, from a business logic perspective. In the following diagram it has been presented on the opposite side of the database to symbolize that it is more of an intranet and non-production application, away from the browser or e-mail based users at the suppliers.

---

[3] There are always a number of business rules that get implemented in client side validation routines, or Database stored procedures so the pure notion of business rules being resident only in a middle tier is never quite perfect in reality.

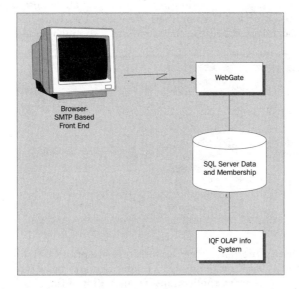

Perhaps a more simplistic vision is shared in the following.

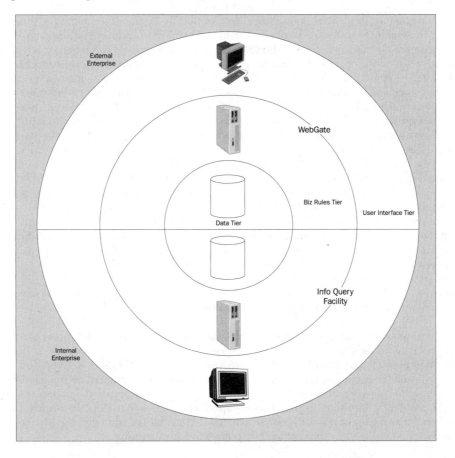

Following are the major processes involved in the SCS and their allocation to processors. Microsoft now offers a Site Server Resource Kit, (free on their Web site). I wish we had obtained access to that kit much sooner than it was released because the kit contains so much good performance information.

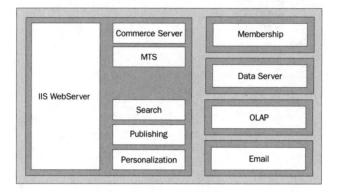

I think the benefits of a three-tier client/server architecture are pretty well known so I won't extol the virtues of the concept here, at least not too much. I might mention that a three-tier conceptual architecture seems perfect for Internet applications because a lot of the applications are new and dynamically changing so that it is great to encapsulate business logic so that it can be easily changed.

In terms of performance guidelines, as a general rule of thumb, let me drive home the message that you should try to isolate SQL Server performance from your Web server operations. In the first graphic we presented on the system, the Membership, Data Server and OLAP Server are all SQL Server intensive processor operations. As a bit of a war story, one of my first cyberstores involved Site Server 2.0. The client was cash poor and we were anxious to pursue the engagement so we tried to build all the store and database into a dual Pentium Pro 200 complex. What a mistake! There was plenty of horsepower but the system was constrained by a single SCSI drive and was always starved for finding faster disk access. I guess that was my first lesson: that it pays to study up a little on SQL Server and its installation configuration. Microsoft now has a pretty good SQL Server planning document available via their web (http://www.microsoft.com/sql/). In case you are new to Site Server, you should know that SQL Server skills are a make or break factor for success. At least from my experience, even simple ASP development involves extensive ADO calls to SQL Server (Yes, I realize that there is Microsoft Access as well). It is almost impossible to impart much SQL Server planning knowledge in the space of this case, but I'll bet a lot of readers would be surprised to learn that a slower processor with a lot of memory and a lot of SCSI disk access can easily outperform the speedier Pentiums, and even the Alphas. Once again, the secret to SQL Server architecture success, as if there was one easy answer, is found in making sure you have SCSI controllers, or something similar, that will allow for asynchronous disk access.

So basically, you want to make sure that the Web server portion of your system is not adversely affected by the potential for SQL Server to perform long queries.

The production manufacturing data is kept on the Database Server. The OLAP server is a replicated server that gets data off production and isolates the complex queries that are sometimes, no, make that all too often produced by the Market Research and Operations Research departments. It wouldn't be unusual for some guy in Operations Research to want to understand the average spacing between the buttons on every shirt produced for the last five years. In more than a few instances we have found a problem where some researchers will perform queries that will take twenty or thirty minutes to complete. The problem with this is that ADO connections and even the Microsoft Internet Explorer browser have timeouts that are usually not set to wait that long.

The Membership Server is an LDAP server but at its heart, it is basically SQL Server. As perhaps a gross over-generalization, you should treat it with the same respect if not more than you would provide your Microsoft NT domain controller. In the couple of engagements that I have witnessed the Membership server has either been used very little or almost too much for my sense of risk. The LDAP Membership Server is relatively new technology and it would be well to heed the advice to tread cautiously as you integrate it into your application designs. Therein lies part of the reason for putting it into its own processor complex.

A separate e-mail server was 'grandfathered' into the system complex because it predated the Site Server project. I might also mention that the e-mail server is one of the key components of the solution that was not Microsoft technology and came from SeattleLabs.

Even though we have gone to all this trouble of providing separate machines for the various servers I think that overall, the BroadCloth case doesn't make a very good example for performance planning in Site Server. The total user population is only about a thousand users and even though they are located around the globe, meaning that the system needs to be available 24X7, the users are not really hammering away on the system all day and all night. Nonetheless, even with a solution of this scale it pays to over-engineer the system to cope with expansion.

Server Architecture

For those of you who are hardware groupies, the hardware configuration at BroadCloth uses Compaq Proliant servers, featuring Pentium Pro 200s, mostly in dual processor motherboards, and possibly upgraded to higher processor complexes by press time. Disk systems are SCSI and disk space seems almost limitless. RAID configurations have been a combination of RAID 5 and combos of RAID 1 and RAID 0, often called RAID 10. Following is a table describing the hardware schema bill of materials.

Server	Qty	Services
Web Server	1	IIS 4.0 Microsoft Transaction Server (MTS) 2.0 Commerce Pipeline Objects Commerce Server Search Publishing
Data Server	1	SQL Server
Membership Server	1	SQL Server Site Server Membership Directory Authentication Service
OLAP	1	SQL Server MTS 2.0 Site Server Usage Analyst
E-mail and Staging Server	1	IIS 4.0 Site Server Publishing

Client Systems

A discussion of the system architecture would not be complete without at least a small glimpse of the expectations for supplier hardware. Basically, there are none, but I say that as a bit of humor. One of the major risk items in this project involved the compliance and participation of the suppliers. BroadCloth is really in no position to have a strong influence over the IT plans of its suppliers.

Here are the founding assumptions for the supplier's browser software:

> 1. Must support forms

> 2. Must support a grid component or Java applet like a grid

> 3. Does *not* need to perform any validation of calculations at the client

> 4. Does *not* need to implement any encryption method such as Netscape SSL

> 5. Cryptography is not a requirement

> 6. Does *not* need to support any audio or video

> 7. Graphics usage will be kept minimal

Obviously a client meeting the minimum of the specifications here is not your dream supplier. Still though, when you are having expensive phone conversations and transcribing faxes, the idea of having any supplier with any browser seems like a big step forward.

I'm sure a lot of people would also question what seems like a total absence of security requirements such as SSL. In defense of that position I can say that SSL is actively used in the project today, but there is a difference between the minimum requirements and the preferred execution environment. BroadCloth would not reject a potential supplier due to the fact that their browser or e-mail could not support a secure mechanism such as SSL.

A Pipeline Example

We have talked a little about the Microsoft Commerce Interchange Pipeline without really explaining enough how it is useful for BroadCloth's business-to-business communication needs. Hopefully you will have inferred from all the above discussion that the central problem involves improving BroadCloth's capacity to communicate rapidly and effectively with its suppliers.

As we previously mentioned, the CIP is designed to offer great connectivity between two organizations that both have Site Server installed. However, Site Server to Site Server connectivity is not a requirement for using the product. In the BroadCloth case, the company wanted to communicate with suppliers who were unlikely to even have Microsoft Windows, much less BackOffice or Site Server. Since data in XML format is basically just a structured text document, and can be transmitted via HTTP, enabling the transactions to be accomplished in XML format is thus key to surmounting the problems of BroadCloth's capacity to interoperate with suppliers who do not have Site Server technology at their end. Comparatively simple client-side mechanisms can be used for the suppliers to receive, display the data in acceptable ways, and send responses back to the BroadCloth SCS.

There's one more problem or challenge, depending on your point of view. In the Microsoft vision the kind of data that is passed along a pipeline is known as a business object. A business object is a data container for something like a shopping basket order, a purchase invoice, a billing record, or in the case of BroadCloth, a manufacturing work order. Beyond that conceptual introduction, a business object is represented as one of the following:

> ➢ An ADO recordset

> ➢ OLEDB rowset

> ➢ Commerce Server Dictionary object

> ➢ Commerce Server SimpleList object

> ➢ Commerce Server OrderForm object

To make a long story short, this is an impressive list of objects but they all share a common technological heritage, they are Microsoft technology. That is to say, if you receive one of these objects, you pretty well need to have a Microsoft-based platform to take advantage of the object[4]. BroadCloth wanted to use the best part of the CIP architecture but also pass more generic business objects to suppliers. Therefore they developed their own pipeline component to handle the mapping of a manufacturing work order to an XML format. Microsoft offers a pipeline object to map to XML, but once again, it will only map an ADO recordset, Commerce Server Dictionary object, SimpleList, etc.

In the following example we want to show that implementing a combination of ASP and COM objects via J++ Java is a great solution to BroadCloth's main problem of communicating with less equipped suppliers in terms of both effort and performance. What follows is a step-by-step guide for creating your own CIP objects to perform XML mapping. This example will provide you with a basis for your own EDI system. I think that you will see from this example that developing COM components for Site Server is easy. In this example we will set up a sample Web site, using Microsoft Commerce Server. We will then develop our own Java based COM component that does XML mapping. Finally we will show how the CIP is called from an ASP page and then e-mails a work order to a supplier.

ASP Kickoff: Setting Up Your Web Site.

First we will need to set up a Commerce Server Web site to serve as a test bed for our example. In doing this you will get a look at how to set up a `global.asa` file as well as the ASP code that is used to set up the execution of a pipeline.

The installation is crucial in most Site Server projects. For the project that we are about to walk through I used the following setup:

> ➢ Commerce Server

> ➢ Commerce Server Service Pack 2

> ➢ Commerce Server SDK, (via custom install of Commerce Server)

> ➢ Visual J++ version 6.0 October '98 release

You might also need the Java SDK2, as this was on my machine at the time I was working, but I suspect that everything that it contains is also in the version 6.0 '98 release of Visual J++.

---

[4] Technically speaking you could debate about the feasibility of working with Microsoft business objects on non-Microsoft Windows platforms and argue that there are alternatives that let you extend the Microsoft world to other platforms; ChiliSoft offers ASP on Unix, etc.

881

By now I'm sure you are familiar with the Site Server concept of integrating Site Server functions with Active Server Pages. If you want to create this example for your own use, then I suggest you begin the process by using the Commerce Server Store Builder Wizard to create a store similar to the Microsoft Market sample. If you choose this route, then you will have a great example of Site Server programming to study, as well has having the example from this book. Moreover, the reason why I make that recommendation is due to the fact that the Site Server wizard configures your site within IIS and within the Commerce Server administrative programs.

Using the wizard is not a requirement. Basically the ASP portion of the example involves setting up a Web site and copying over four resources:

> `global asa` provides site initialization and session setup.

> `testorder.asp` is the ASPpage that kicks off the CIP pipeline.

> `bctransmit.pcf` is a pipeline configuration

> `site.csc` is a Commerce Server configuration setup

Of these four resources, the site.csc file is pretty much untouched since it was created as part of the setup for a Microsoft Market sample. The other resources are significantly altered and must be substituted for the resources you create when you set up your site in Commerce Server, or Visual Studio. You will need to place both the pipeline configuration and the site configuration files in a subdirectory for your site called "Config". This will be created automatically if you configure your site using the Commerce Server wizard.

As you perform your site setup you may look at the `global.asa` and notice that a database is not required in this example. Therefore we don't need to get into the details of customizing ODBC connection objects and such. I guess the point here is that the `global.asa` has been greatly simplified from the file you would probably set up for your own project but we have still created a good code construction to set up a variety of pipelines which could then be called from various pages within your site.

Here's a listing of the global.asa code:

```
<SCRIPT LANGUAGE=VBScript RUNAT=Server>
Option Explicit
REM ##########################################################
REM
REM    GLOBAL.ASA
REM    Microsoft bcSCS
REM    Microsoft Commerce Server v3.00
REM ##########################################################

    Sub Session_OnStart
     ' Sub Application_OnStart  'After testing you can
     ' make this procedure part of the Application and not the Session.
    Dim SiteName
    SiteName = "bcSCS"

    REM -- Read Site Dictionary
    Dim FD, MSCSSite
    Set FD = Server.CreateObject("Commerce.FileDocument")
    Set MSCSSite = Server.CreateObject("Commerce.Dictionary")
    Dim configdir
```

```
        configdir = "/" & SiteName & "/config/"
        Call FD.ReadDictionaryFromFile( Server.MapPath(configdir & _
                                "site.csc"), "IISProperties", MSCSSite)

        Dim  pipemap,bctransmit
        Set pipemap = server.createobject("commerce.dictionary")
        bctransmit =  Server.MapPath(configdir & "BCtransmit.pcf")
        pipemap("BCTRANSMIT") = bctransmit

        REM Set up the Application instrinsic object
    ' Application.Lock  'Don't perform locking until the application
    ' is developed.
        Set session("MSCSSite") = MSCSSite
        session("HTMLEncodedName") = Server.HTMLEncode(MSCSSite.DisplayName)
        session("SiteName") = SiteName
        set session("pipemap") = pipemap
        ' Application.Unlock
    End Sub

</SCRIPT>
```

Prior to execution of the example, there are two Webmaster related administration details that will need to be performed at the server:

➢ You will need to bring up your Commerce Server pipeline editor and make sure your `bctransmit.pcf` pipeline is properly installed and customized for your installation

➢ You will need to enable Session management for your site at the IIS MMC console.

Let's delay a discussion of the first task until I show you how to create your own COM component. However, now is a good time to make sure your session state is enabled. If you use the Commerce Server to setup your Microsoft Market store then the ability to have sessions is not enabled.

Those of you who are familiar with the history of Active Server Pages or follow the development of the product in newsgroups know that there is a pretty active debate on the value of maintaining sessions. The background to all this involves the fact that Internet activity, the interaction of a user with a Web site is "stateless". Basically the server has a difficult time keeping track of who's who when users visit a site. The solution to managing state is to create a tracking mechanism. Various methods are used and most of them involve the exchange of cookies with the users. The problem with all this is the idea that maintaining state, i.e. sessions for a large body of interactive users has a penalty in terms of memory usage and in general site performance.

You will need to consider this in the architecture of your own site. When designing your own site, you can construct a scope to your variables that detail the length of time they may be active. Options are:

- *"page" – the time a page is active within your site.*

- *"session" – the time a visitor interacts with your site.*

- *"application" – the time that your site is resident and active within the scope of IIS.*

883

In most of the examples that you can create using the Commerce Server wizard the variables for a site are set up with application level scope. The problem with doing this during development is the fact that it is difficult to abandon an application without rebooting your server. The problem involves the fact that COM objects are executed and instructed to stay resident and in general that makes them pretty resilient to being shut down. This is ideally what you want in production, but it is a different story when you are trying to debug a COM object. Therefore, we have set up our example so that it has session state and not application state.

Enabling session state is easy. You need to find your example site in the Internet Information Server part of your Microsoft Management Console. You will then need to look at the properties for your site and find the Configuration button for your application settings. The button may be on a Virtual Directory tab or a Directory tab, depending on how you've configured your site within IIS. Eventually you will find you way to the App Options tab where there is a check box that enables session state. The box is usually enabled if you created your site without the use of the Commerce Server Store Builder Wizard.

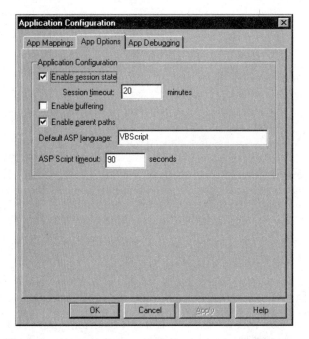

At this point you've configured your site and you could run the example, except for the fact that we have not created the star player of the example, your COM XML mapping object.

Further on is the ASP code, `testorder.asp`, that kicks off the pipeline example. If you are new to ASP coding, then this example provides you with a pretty good template to use in setting up your ASP pages. The code will actually write a lot of comments to the user's screen to trace the activity of creating the pipe. Only recently, within the last year or so has Microsoft come out with a good debugging tool to use for ASP pages, and previously you had to pretty much write comments to the screen to trace the execution of your program. Old habits are difficult to get rid of.

I tried to make the code as self-documenting as possible. In setting up a pipeline for execution there is a series of activities that you must set up.

> ➤ Is your order ready for transmittal?
> ➤ Have you created the business object that serves as the container to hand to the pipe?
> ➤ Will you handle error conditions appropriately?

In a moment, after we present the code, we will show you the output of a transaction and you will see the steps that were involved in setting up a pipeline.

When you run this example, the page will set up a manufacturing work order and then call a Commerce Interchange Transmit pipeline. The pipeline, which is composed of COM objects, will take responsibility for preparing your order for transmittal, mapping the order to XML, and then actually sending the order out via e-mail, SMTP. Here's the `testorder.asp` code:

```
<%@ LANGUAGE="VBSCRIPT" %>
<%
'-----------------------------------------------------------------
' Name: testOrder.asp
'
' Purpose: This pages will test the CIP pipe.

'-----------------------------------------------------------------


Option Explicit
Response.Expires = 0
Response.Buffer = True



'-----------------------------------------------------------------
' Include Files
'-----------------------------------------------------------------

%>
<!--no include files -->
<%

'-----------------------------------------------------------------
' Global Variables
'-----------------------------------------------------------------

Const PAGE_NAME = "Pipeline Test Page"

Dim ProdMfgOrder

'-----------------------------------------------------------------
' Main
'-----------------------------------------------------------------
Main

'-----------------------------------------------------------------
' Function: Main
'
' Purpose: Entry point for the page.
'-----------------------------------------------------------------
Sub Main
%>
```

```
<!DOCTYPE HTML PUBLIC "-//IETF//DTD HTML//EN">
<HTML>
<HEAD>
    <TITLE><%= PAGE_NAME %></TITLE>
</HEAD>

<BODY BGCOLOR="#FFFFFF">
<%

debug "This is a sample page to kick off a "
debug "Commerce Interchange Pipeline pipe. "

debug "First we create a transport dictionary."
    Dim TransportDictionary
    Set TransportDictionary = server.createobject("commerce.dictionary")

debug "Now the Pipeline Transport is set."

debug "Then we set up an order."
debug "The loadOrder procedure will load some data."
    Set TransportDictionary = loadOrder(TransportDictionary)

'Look down to see the dummy data load

debug "Next we set up error control processing for the pipe."
    Dim ErrNumber, ErrText, iError
    ErrNumber = Err.Number
    ErrText = Err.description

debug "Now we actually create the Pipeline: BCappSamp "

    TransportDictionary.working_data = null
    TransportDictionary.suppliername = "sjedens@netsail.net"
    TransportDictionary.mfgsubject = "a test of the pipe"
    TransportDictionary.test = "test body of letter"

    Dim mscsMtsTxPipeline
    set mscsMtsTxPipeline = server.createobject("commerce.MtsPipeline")

debug "OK... looks like we have a go for liftoff: The Pipeline is set"

    Dim MSCSSite
    Dim pipemap

    Set MSCSSite = session("MSCSSite")  'Application("MSCSSite")
    Set pipemap = session("pipemap")  'application("pipemap")
    call mscsMtsTxPipeline.loadpipe(pipemap("BCTRANSMIT"))

debug "Final setup proceeds by settting the MTS Context and error control."
    Dim ierrorlevel,context
    set Context = server.createobject("commerce.dictionary")
    Context.DefaultConnectionString = MSCSSite.DefaultConnectionString
    Context.SiteName = MSCSSite.DisplayName
    set Context.CIP_receiveerrors = Server.CreateObject("Commerce.SimpleList")
    set Context.CIP_receiveDBerrors = Server.CreateObject("Commerce.Dictionary")

debug "Here we go on executing the CIP pipe!"
    on error resume next
    ierrorlevel = mscsMtsTxPipeline.execute(1, TransportDictionary, Context, 0)
```

```
          REM -- Errors are logged to the W3SVC error logs.In order for the specified
          REM -- string to be recorded in the log file,
          REM -- select the URI Query option of the Extended Logging Properties
          REM -- sheet for the site.

    debug "<br><br> We are now done with the pipe execution. <br>"

          ErrNumber = Err.Number
          REM -- store the errors if any, and display if no errors raised by
          REM -- other pipeline components.
          ErrText = Err.description

    'debug " error: " & ErrNumber & " errtxt= " & ErrText
    'debug " ierrorlevel error level = " & ierrorlevel

          on error goto 0

          for each iError in Context.CIP_receiveDBerrors
              Response.AppendToLog(Context.CIP_receiveDBerrors(iError))
          next

          for iError = 0 to Context.CIP_receiveerrors.Count - 1
              Response.AppendToLog(Context.CIP_receiveerrors(iError))
          next

          if (0 = Context.CIP_receiveDBerrors.count) and (0 = _
             Context.CIP_receiveerrors.count) and (0 <> ErrNumber)
            then
                Response.AppendToLog("#:" & ErrNumber & "," & ErrText)
          end if

          if (1 < iErrorlevel) then
              Response.AppendToLog(E_PIPELINE_ERRORLEVEL)
          end if

          If ErrNumber <> 0 Then
             Response.End
          Else
             Response.Write "<br> Your manufacturing order has been sent."
          end if
%>
</BODY>
</HTML>

<%
End Sub
Response.End

'-------------------------------------------------------------------
' Client-Side Functions
'-------------------------------------------------------------------
%>
<SCRIPT LANGUAGE="JavaScript">

function template()
{
// Empty template
}
```

```
    </SCRIPT>

    <%
    '----------------------------------------------------------------
    ' Server-Side Functions
    '----------------------------------------------------------------
    %>

    <SCRIPT LANGUAGE="VBScript" RUNAT="Server">


    Function loadOrder(TransportDictionary)
        TransportDictionary.batchorderid = "1008"
        TransportDictionary.batchsize = "2"
        TransportDictionary.batchname = "Test1"
        TransportDictionary.batchvalue = 10000
        TransportDictionary.batchtax = 100

        Set loadOrder = TransportDictionary
    End Function

    Sub debug(String)
        Dim prtTime
        prtTime = Time
        Response.Write "<br> " & prtTime & ":     " & String
        Response.Flush
    End Sub

    </SCRIPT>

    <%
    '----------------------------------------------------------------
    ' End of Page
    '----------------------------------------------------------------
    %>
```

In our example, a server side procedure called `loadOrder` will prepare a dummy order for transmittal. In the actual case the ASP page instantiates a Java-built COM object that then does the necessary database calls and other marshalling necessary to prepare an order for transmittal. The goal of the activity is to make sure that all the right data, in the right format is presented and ready for transmission.

Here is the output you will receive when you finally run your ASP page. It is not very glamorous but serves its purpose.

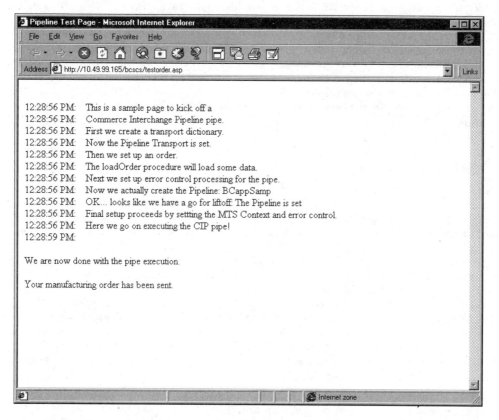

This page is actually a review of the steps that are processed on the page. As you run the page on a slow server, or Internet connection, the steps to set up the pipe will be written serially and appear on the page one after another. In the example presented you can see that the page took about three seconds to execute. The setup of the pipeline took about a second and the execution of the pipeline took two seconds. If you don't have ready access to the Internet then you will receive an SMTP pipeline error message telling you about it at the last step. In our example, a work order was prepared and sent via e-mail thereby presenting a final conclusion message at the bottom of the page.

We are getting a little ahead of our plan here because we have not yet created our pipeline component.

Building a Pipeline Component in J++

Let's now build a Java based COM object. As I said previously there is a slight issue with the Commerce Server Interchange Pipe in the respect that it expects to handle and transmit Microsoft Business Objects such as Commerce Server Dictionaries. In the BroadCloth case, there was no assurance of what technology would be found once an order arrived at a supplier's location. The answer to this dilemma is to construct a more flexible pipeline component that can handle a wider variety of data formats.

The idea of encoding the data in XML is pretty incidental to the application *per se*. BroadCloth could probably have prepared a work order in comma-delimited text and it would have the same value. XML really is a good fit for situations where there is less communication between the partners of a transaction and the receiving party, in this case the supplier, isn't sure about the format of the data. In this case, BroadCloth can be very specific in telling the supplier about the format of the data. Of course, XML is a hot technology, the wave of the future, and it makes sense to go with that technology for a wide variety of reasons beyond its technology merits. Additionally, XML is a good fit for situations where the platform technology between the partners in communication is indeterminate, as is the case with the SCS. (If you need a good introduction to XML try *XML Applications* from Wrox Press (ISBN 1861001525).)

Java COM Programming

Prior to jumping into development I should offer the disclaimer that I assume the reader has some familiarity with the way object classes are crafted in either C++ or Java. As you try your hand at working with this example, you will be interested in the Commerce Server Software Development Kit, or SDK. The SDK provided the foundation for this example. In the kit there is an example called MinMaxShip. What Microsoft provides is an example of a pipeline COM object, as it is constructed in C++, Java, and Visual Basic. You will want to compare the code between the three mechanisms for creating objects. The C++ environment provides the richest but most complicated method of component development. On the other hand, Visual Basic is a nice environment for development but Visual Basic has traditionally suffered from being somewhat backward in its apartment threading model. Threading has improved but there are still limitations in crafting Visual Basic COM objects that integrate well with Microsoft Transaction Server. Therefore, Java offers a great middle ground for object development. The object-oriented world of Java allows you to create objects that are generally cleaner and less complicated the C++ but have a great deal of the same functionality and none of the limits associated with Visual Basic.

> *A more recent consideration in choosing a language might be the future support that Microsoft offers for Java, but this was not an issue when BroadCloth originally considered which development environment to use in creating the SCS application.*

Site Server and COM go hand in hand. As you begin serious development of components you will want to reference several of the good books that have been developed exclusively for COM. Wrox offers an excellent reference, *Professional DCOM Programming* by Dr. Richard Grimes (ISBN 186100060X).

In this example we are creating a COM object that is designed to integrate into the CIP. However, if you want to create just any old, "Hello World" type COM object it is incredibly simple using J++. (The following assumes you have Microsoft's IIS or Personal Web Server on your machine.) Here are the steps:

1. Open J++ and go to the File | New Project option. In the dialog box that appears open the Visual J++ Projects folder in the browse window on the left and click on the Components folder. Select the COM DLL icon, type in a name for your project in the Name edit field (I used "JavaCom"), and then click on the Open button. You will then see a couple of dialog boxes about Microsoft Java extensions (click OK on these) before a new project is created. If you have the VJ++ Project Explorer open you will see the new project appear in the window. Otherwise, to open the Project Explorer go to the View menu and select it.

2. In the Project Explorer window, click on the plus sign to the left of your project's name to reveal a .java file (usually labeled Class1.java). Put some code in your main class that says "Hello World!" My class code looks like this:

```
public class Class1
{
    public String message = "Hello World!";
}
```

Then, on the main menu, select Build | Build. VJ++ will then compile the code, create the COM DLL, *and* register the component on your machine.

3. Create an ASP that calls your new COM component using the Server.CreateObject command in an ASP. Here's the code I used:

```
<%@ LANGUAGE="VBSCRIPT" %>
<%
Dim out
set out = Server.CreateObject("JavaCom.Class1")
Response.write out.hello
%>
```

If you then save this ASP in a directory on your Web server and view the page with your browser (I created a directory called Test under the Wwwroot directory of my Personal Web Server and called the page "comtest.asp", so I would access the page in my browser as http://localhost/test/comtest.asp) you should then see the message "Hello World!" displayed.

Using the J++ COM creation capacity makes it all very straightforward, but there are a couple of points to watch out for if you are going to try this out now.

The point of doing this is to recognize that you can create all manner of COM objects that are then called from your ASP pages. The performance of your site will improve dramatically if you use these compiled COM objects as a replacement for long ASP scripts and procedures.

Following is the main code for our COM object. Without providing a big tutorial on Java, what we are doing here is to provide Java code that implements a series of **interfaces** that are required to implement a pipeline COM object. The idea behind Java interfaces is pretty simple. The original author of the interface was making a suggestion that went something like: if you create your program and use my ideas on interfacing in your program, then we will have programs that will all link together.

Of course that is a pretty simplistic overview of Java interfaces. From this example you can see that the Java world and the COM world are pretty similar in the respect that they are both trying to present the developer community with some standard ways of creating code that can be shared and reusable.

As you create your own pipeline component it will basically import some interfaces and then use the interfaces to build your application. Let's look at this in slightly more detail. Here's the line of code that instructs the compiler to import the interfaces:

```
import pipecomplib.*;
```

This is an import statement in Java that will bring a library of interfaces into your program. "Where is this code?" you may wonder.

If you installed the Commerce Server SDK on your machine then you should be able to find a file called `pipecomplib.tlb`. One quick way to ensure that the relevant pipecomplib interface classes are imported by the compiler as the COM DLL for your code is generated, is to import the `pipecomplib.tlb` type library file into your project prior to compilation. To do this, right-click on the name of your project in the Project Explorer window of VJ++, and from the drop-down menu that appears select **Properties**. A dialog box for the project's settings will then appear. In the COM Classes tab, select **Use existing Type Library** and then click on **Select....** Another dialog box will appear with a long list of the COM templates already installed on your machine. Click on the **Browse...** button on the right-hand side and then navigate to where the `pipecomplib.tlb` file is stored in your file system. Select it then click on **Open**. In the COM Templates dialog click on **OK**. You might then see a couple of dialog boxes appear, one warning you about Microsoft Extensions and the other containing a legal disclaimer. Click on **OK** for both, then click **OK** in the project's Properties dialog too. If you then look at the Project Explorer window you should see that a new folder has appeared containing lots of pipeline related `.java` interface class files.

Now let's take a look at a Java Class statement. In creating a class called `XMLOut1` we are telling Java that we are going to use certain interfaces that are defined in the `pipecomplib` library package.

```
// ------------------------------------------------------------
/** XMLOut1: implements Commerce Interchange Pipeline component to map
 *  manufacturing order into XML
 */
public class XMLOut1 implements
    IPipelineComponentAdmin,
    ISpecifyPipelineComponentUI,
    IPipelineComponent,
    IPipelineComponentDescription,
    IPersistDictionary
//  this class statement is not complete.
```

Here we are implementing the interfaces that are necessary to create a pipeline component. In keeping with the model provided by the MinMaxShip example in the Site Server Commerce SDK, we have provided two custom variables that you will see can be set from the Commerce Server Pipeline editor. The variables are used to set an excise tax rate and to set a floor limit for a minimum excise tax. Such taxes are pertinent in the import/export business of shipping inventory to suppliers. In providing these variables, you will get a chance to see how you can create your own custom parameters and use the user interface of the Pipeline Editor to control your application. You also get a chance to see how VB-style dictionaries are handled within the world of Java.

There are actually three classes involved in this application. The class `XMLOut1` is the main class for coordinating the activities of two other classes. `XMLOut1UI` addresses the needs of a user interface for the pipeline COM object. `XMLMapper` is a class that actually does the mapping of an order to XML. We will talk about the `XMLMapper` in more detail later, but the `XMLOut1UI` user interface is provided in the code archive that goes along with the book that can be downloaded from `http://www.wrox.com`.

Here is the code for the XMLOut1 class:

```java
/**
 *  XMLOut1.java
 */

package XMLMapper;

import java.io.*;
import com.ms.com.*;
import mscscore.*;
import pipecomplib.*;

// -------------------------------------------------------------------
/** XMLOut1: implements Commerce Interchange Pipeline component to map
 *  manufacturing order into XML
 */
public class XMLOut1 implements
    IPipelineComponentAdmin,
    ISpecifyPipelineComponentUI,
    IPipelineComponent,
    IPipelineComponentDescription,
    IPersistDictionary
{
    private int minTax = 100;
    private float exciseTaxRate = 0.0f;
    private boolean isDirty;

// -------------------------------------------------------------------
    /** IPipelineComponentAdmin
     */
    public void SetConfigData(Object dict)
    {
        Variant v = new Variant();
        v = ((IDictionary)dict).getValue("exciseTaxRate");
        this.exciseTaxRate = v.getFloat();
        v = ((IDictionary)dict).getValue("minimumTax");
        this.minTax = v.getInt();
    }

    /* Set up values that are custom properties of the component. */
    public Object GetConfigData()
    {
        IDictionary dict = (IDictionary)new CDictionary();
        Variant v = new Variant();
        v.putInt(minTax);
        dict.setValue("minimumTax", v);
        v.putFloat(exciseTaxRate);
        dict.setValue("exciseTaxRate", v);
        return dict;
    }-------------------------------------------------------------
    /** ISpecifyPipelineComponentUI
     */
    public String GetPipelineComponentUIProgID()
    {
        return "Commerce.XMLOut1UI";
    }


// -------------------------------------------------------------------
    /** IPipelineComponent
     *
     */
```

```java
    public int Execute(Object order, Object context, int flags)
    {


        Variant vBatchvalue = new Variant();
        Variant vBatchtax = new Variant();
        vBatchvalue = ((IDictionary)order).getValue("batchvalue");
        int iBatchValue = vBatchvalue.toInt();

        // handle taxes
        int tax = (int)((float)iBatchValue * this.exciseTaxRate);
        if (tax < this.minTax)
        {
            tax = this.minTax;
        }
        vBatchtax.putInt(tax);
        ((IDictionary)order).setValue("batchtax",vBatchtax);

        XMLMapper mapper = new XMLMapper();
        String sWorkingData = mapper.mapXML(order);

        sWorkingData = "Manufacturing Order from BroadCloth Company\n" +
                "Contact SCScontrol@broadcloth.com with questions.\n\n" +
                sWorkingData;

        Variant vXMLdata = new Variant();
        vXMLdata.putString(sWorkingData);

        ((IDictionary)order).setValue("working_data",vXMLdata);
        return 1;
    }

    public void EnableDesign(int flag)
    {
        // Empty implementation
    }

// -----------------------------------------------------------------
    /** IPipelineComponentDescription
     *Note: following functions assume that you have
     *installed Microsoft Java SDK 2.0
     */
    public Variant ContextValuesRead()
    {
        Variant[] varray = new Variant[0];
        Variant vRet = new Variant();
        vRet.putVariantArray(varray);
        return vRet;
    }

    public Variant ValuesRead()
    {
        Variant[] varray = new Variant[1];
        varray[0] = new Variant();
        varray[0].putString("working_data");
        Variant vRet = new Variant();
        vRet.putVariantArray(varray);
        return vRet;
    }
```

```
   public Variant ValuesWritten()
   {
      Variant[] varray = new Variant[1];
      varray[0] = new Variant();
      varray[0].putString("working_data");
      Variant vRet = new Variant();
      vRet.putVariantArray(varray);
      return vRet;
   }

// -------------------------------------------------------------------
   /**
    *  IPersistDictionary
    */
   public String GetProgID()
   {
      return "Commerce.XMLOut1";
   }

   public void InitNew()
   {
      isDirty = false;
   }

   public void Load(Object dict)
   {
      minTax = ((IDictionary)dict).getValue("minimumTax").getInt();
      exciseTaxRate  = ((IDictionary)dict).getValue("exciseTaxRate").getFloat();

      isDirty = false;
   }

   public int IsDirty()
   {
      return 0;
   }

   public void Save(Object dict, int fResetDirty)
   {
      isDirty = isDirty && (fResetDirty != 0);
      Variant v = new Variant();
      v.putInt(minTax);
      ((IDictionary)dict).setValue("minimumTax", v);
      v.putFloat(exciseTaxRate);
      ((IDictionary)dict).setValue("exciseTaxRate", v);
   }

   public void setValues(int minTax, float exciseTaxRate)
   {
      this.minTax = minTax;
      this.exciseTaxRate = exciseTaxRate;
   }

// method for testing class code before implementation----------------
/*    public static void main(String [] argv)
      {
         // dummy
      }
*/
}  // End of class
```

Almost all the code is dedicated to what I call "data housekeeping". That is to say, the code associated with making sure that we are implementing all the interfaces and getting data into and out of persistent data stores. All the real action, the true business value and logic for the application takes place in the `Execute()` method. So where's the XML mapping you might wonder? Look inside the `Execute()` method and you'll find the following code:

```
XMLMapper mapper = new XMLMapper();
String sWorkingData = mapper.mapXML(order);
```

In these two lines of code we instantiate a new object from the class `XMLMapper`. We then call the object and feed it the order that we received as a Transport Dictionary in the CIP.

Following is the `XMLMapper` code. In the actual case for the company for which BroadCloth is a pseudonym the code is considerably more complicated but the point here is to provide some code that performs the process of wrapping the data in XML markup. The XML generation code here merely wraps the relevant tags around the data values obtained from the pipeline's `Dictionary` object in the process of building up the `sWorking_Data` string. The string is then returned to the `Execute()` method of `XMLOut1.java`.

```
package XMLMapper;

import com.ms.com.*;
import mscscore.*;

// -----------------------------------------------------------------
/** XMLMapper:  Core logic for providing XML mapping here.
 */
public class XMLMapper
{

// -----------------------------------------------------------------
/** mapXML:
 * Create a dummy manufacturing order for a demo.
 */

    protected String mapXML(Object order)
    {
    // Core component logic goes here.

        Variant vBatchOrderId = new Variant();
        Variant vBatchsize = new Variant();
        Variant vBatchname = new Variant();
        Variant vBatchvalue = new Variant();
        Variant vBatchtax = new Variant();

        vBatchOrderId = ((IDictionary)order).getValue("batchorderid");
        vBatchsize = ((IDictionary)order).getValue("batchsize");
        vBatchname = ((IDictionary)order).getValue("batchname");
        vBatchvalue = ((IDictionary)order).getValue("batchvalue");
        vBatchtax = ((IDictionary)order).getValue("batchtax");

        String sWorking_Data = "<BatchOrder>\n" +
            "<BatchOrderID>" + vBatchOrderId.toString() +
            "</BatchOrderID>\n" +
            "<BatchSize>" + vBatchsize.toString()  + "</BatchSize>\n" +
            "<BatchName>" + vBatchname.toString() + "</BatchName>\n" +
```

```
              "<BatchValue>" + vBatchvalue.toString()  + "</BatchValue>\n" +
              "<BatchTax>" + vBatchtax.toString() + "</BatchTax>\n" +
              "</BatchOrder>\n";

          return sWorking_Data;
      }

      XMLMapper()
      {
          // main constrctor
      }
  }
```

That's pretty much it for the coding. You compile these classes in J++ and you are almost home. Be sure and note the location of the output from your complication. I suggest you make sure that your new classes are compiled into your `Java\Classes`, or `Java\TrustLib` directories. In doing this you will avoid situations where your system won't be able to find your code. The `Java\Classes` and `Java\TrustLib` directories are included in the Classpath setup when you install J++. If you are experienced with Java you have no doubt established your own system for keeping track of your class code.

COM Registration

There's one final task that is necessary prior to taking a run at our example. You must register your new COM component in your server. Following are the steps to registering your COM program. These steps are also included in a `readme` file in the code archives for the book.

First, make sure your system path parameters include:

➢ `\Program Files\DevStudio\vj\bin` – (for midl and javaTLB)

➢ `\Microsoft Site Server\Site Server\Commerce\SDK\Commerce\lib\x86` –
(for the dlls that are needed as typelibs)

➢ `\Program Files\DevStudio\SharedIDE\bin` – (for jvc)

A lot of this is done when you install Site Server and J++. However, that would assume that you are doing development on your Site Server server, which you probably will not want to do. I have a development workstation and I needed to look at the path statements on the production Web server and then make some adjustments to the path parameters as defined on my workstation. In most cases, I pointed to disk shares to find the right resources that were installed and resident on the production server.

We are almost there. You need to register your COM objects. A good way to do this is run the regsvr32 utility that comes with NT. Note down the file path of your COM DLL (we're assuming here that you compiled the project with the name XMLOut1) and then type in at the **Start | Run** command prompt:

```
  regsvr32 C:\<yourpath>\XMLOut1.dll
```

You should then see a small dialog box that reports that the registration of the DLL succeeded.

At this point you can search in the HKEY_CLASSES_ROOT of your registry (type regedit at the Windows command prompt to bring up the registry editor) and find your COM object right next to what are probably hundreds of other COM objects that have been registered through numerous Microsoft program product installations.

There's one more step. If you have ever worked with the Commerce Server pipeline editor you may have noticed that when you try to insert a component into the pipe you are presented with a choice. Do you want the components that are right for this specific pipe stage or do you want to see everything? You probably don't want to add a shipper selector component to the tax stage of your cyberstore. On the other hand, there may be cases where a certain component, say a customer name validation routine, might fit many stages. In the final step of COM registration you can set the implemented categories or stages in which a component may be useful. In our case, we have identified two situations:

> The XMLMapper component can be listed with all the other pipe components

> The XMLMapper needs to be listed along with the other components for the Map stage of the CIP Transmit pipeline.

If you look at the entry in the registry for your component you should see a folder called Implemented Categories. We need to put some new category entries in here to make our component visible to the Site Server pipeline editing tools. At this point you will want to go back to your Windows Explorer and look in the folders of your installation of the Site Server SDK 1.1 (available free from http://www.microsoft.com/siteserver/commerce/default.htm). If you go into the include folder of the SDK you should be able to find a file called pipe_stages.h. If you then open up this file with a text editor you will see a list of the registry entries for the categories of various Commerce Server pipeline stages and components. In our case we want to register our component as both a generic pipeline component, and we want to give it affinity with the Map stage of the Transmit pipeline. The key entry we want to set our component as a generic pipeline component is the long hexadecimal number at the top of this entry in pipe_stages.h:

```
//  cf7536d0-43c5-11d0-b85d-00c04fd7a0fa
DEFINE_GUID( CATID_MSCSPIPELINE_COMPONENT,
  0xcf7536d0,0x43c5,0x11d0,0xb8,0x5d,0x00,0xc0,0x4f,0xd7,0xa0,0xfa);
```

In the entry for your component in the registry editor, right click on the Implemented Categories folder and select New... then Key. Copy and paste the hexadecimal code above into the name for the new key (not forgetting to put curly brackets at either end of the number):

{CF7536D0-43C5-11D0-B85D-00C04FD7A0FA}

To give the component affinity with the Map stage of the pipeline, repeat the process with this entry from pipe_stages.h (this one comes with brackets provided):

```
// {d3a71c30-ffc7-11d0-b885-00c04fd7a0f9}
DEFINE_GUID( CATID_MSCSPIPELINE_MAP,
  0xd3a71c30,0xffc7,0x11d0,0xb8,0x85,0x00,0xc0,0x4f,0xd7,0xa0,0xf9 );
```

If you now open up a Transmit pipeline in the pipeline editor you should be able to see your component in the list of available components for the Map stage when you attempt to insert a component into the stage.

Plumbing the Pipe

I could not resist using a plumber analogy to reference the activity that you will pursue in customizing your pipeline. In order to do this you have the option of using an HTML or a WIN32-based pipeline editor. While the two are similar, the Win32 editor is better looking and offers more functions than the HTML based editor. We will use the Win32 editor here. You can find the editor under the other programs associated with Commerce Server.

In the following illustration we have created a CIP Transmit pipe and have placed two components into the pipeline. The first component is the XMLMapper Java object we just completed. The other component is an SMTP e-mail component to send the BroadCloth work order to a supplier. For simplicity in this example I have excluded loading the components to encrypt, digitally certify, audit, etc.

The XML Mapper (Custom Component)

In the screenshot that follows we can see our XMLMapper component inserted into the Map stage of the Transmit pipeline.

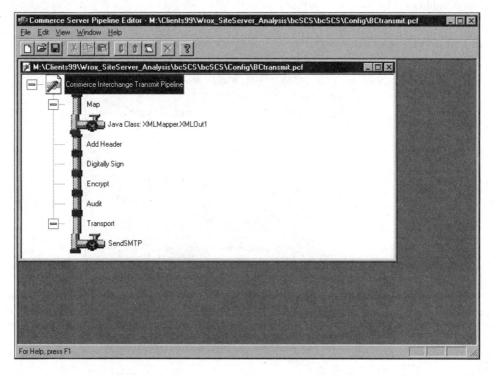

Including components on the pipeline is quite straightforward. Customizing the individual components is more complicated. In the following graphic we have displayed the basic properties of the XMLMapper component.

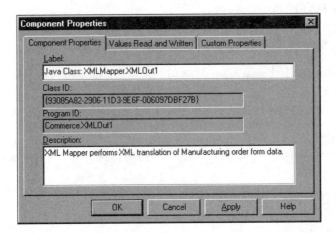

Part of the value of the Commerce Server pipeline is the organization that it provides in helping you set up a transaction. In the following example we can open a window to view a list of the variables read and written by our component. From within the pipeline editor you can also save out a list of all the values used by your pipe.

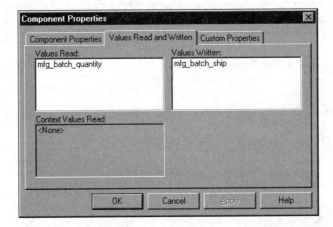

Finally we are presented with the option of modifying the custom properties we designed into our object. The Java code involved in presenting this window was contained in the XMLOut1UI class.

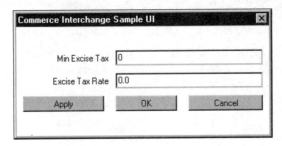

SMTP Mailer

In order to use the SMTP mail component you will need to install Internet Explorer 4.01 or greater on the IIS Server with Site Server Commerce to enable the SMTP functionality. You will also need a convenient e-mail server.

As we look at the SMTP mailer Microsoft COM object, we are offered similar options for configuring our component. Most of the configuration action takes place on the window shown in the screenshot that follows. The example is pretty straightforward. However, in the lower portion of the screen there are several text boxes where you fill in variable names that you load into your Transport `Dictionary` business object. The names are not significant. You could make up anything. If you return to our `testorder.asp` page you can find the following code that loaded data to the manufacturing work order. The concept is like addressing an envelope.

```
TransportDictionary.suppliername = "sjedens@netsail.net "
TransportDictionary.mfgsubject = "a test of the pipe"
TransportDictionary.test = "test body of letter"
```

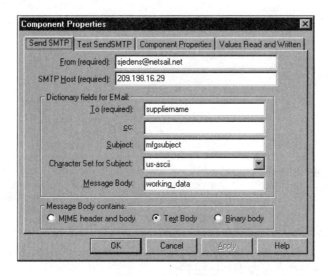

> Don't forget to substitute your own e-mail address in the `suppliername` field of the `Dictionary` object in `testorder.asp` before you test out the custom pipeline.

Now you are ready to test. As a final cautionary measure, it is useful to close your pipeline editor and then reopen the same pipeline you just configured. Sometimes you will notice that a specific component has been badly configured. To continue the overly cute analogy of the pipe, your broken component will have a "broken" pipe as an indication of your error. You can then click on the broken component and receive a diagnosis of the error.

Unfortunately, one popular error in creating your own pipeline components is to create a class formatting error within your Java code. You can do this easily by trying to typecast a `Variant` object into the superclass named `Object`. You will not receive an error during compile but your pipes will break as surely as if you'd drilled holes in them. When and if this happens, you only need to fix the error in the Java code and reload your pipe.

So let's assume you are in a condition to fire it up at this point. You simply bring up your browser and type in the URL of your test web. In my case it is `http://10.49.99.131/bcSCS/testorder.asp`. As we had previously shown, the Web page lists the steps in completing the pipeline. Your project will not want to present the same user interface, although you may want to try the exercise during debugging.

In any event, if you are successful you will have a special e-mail waiting for you the next time you open your mail.

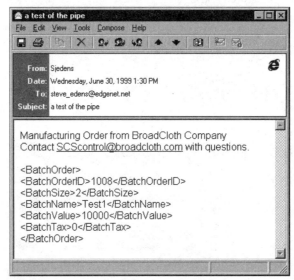

The content of this e-mail message is the XML. Of course the real work order is considerably longer and more complicated. The XML code may confuse the average person but most people in program development can easily get the idea that XML is marking up meta-information about data content.

Building a Client XML Program

As we said previously, the suppliers may not have Microsoft technology so XML was chosen as an EDI like vehicle for communicating manufacturing data. How do the users receive the data?

Glad you asked. One of the benefits of XML is that it not only represents a standard but it represents a very popular standard. There are lots of free programs rapidly being developed and offered via the Internet. In the BroadCloth case, BroadCloth doesn't have much leverage over suppliers. BroadCloth can't dictate what software each supplier should use. However, the beauty of XML is that it can be implemented on many platforms.

Here is a Java program that the users can run to turn the manufacturing data into information. The user can run this application from the command line of any platform that supports a Java Virtual Machine. The program will take an e-mail document saved as a file and then parse out the XML content from within the document. This can be used as part of a platform-independent application for receiving and viewing the content at the client end. (I won't discuss the details of the viewing application here. I'll leave its design and construction as an exercise for the reader to pursue.)

The original code on which this is based was published by Todd Sundsted in an article called "*XML and Java Tackle Enterprise Application Integration*" at Javaworld.com (http://www.javaworld.com/javaworld/jw-06-1999/jw-06-howto.html). However, I have made a number of changes to suit the BroadCloth manufacturing order XML. The code involves an XML parser from IBM. Microsoft offers an XML parser but it is currently represented as a COM object, which thereby restricts its usage to platforms that support COM. In addition, the example uses a set of Java classes called the Simple API for XML or SAX. This is another independently developed set of classes that are offered as freeware. The URLs for the base free Java code packages are included in comments, within the code below. In order to keep this example short I have not included the standard Java I/O classes that would be used to perform disk I/O. The primary purpose of this example is really to indicate that extracting the data from the XML message for use in client side application is not that complicated. The messages generated by the SAX parser as it checks the structure of the XML are used to trigger string handling processes for lifting the values out. These processes would be coded into the clientSCS class at the points within startElement() and endElement() currently containing comments.

```
package SCSgate;

import org.xml.sax.Parser;
import org.xml.sax.Locator;
import org.xml.sax.DocumentHandler;
import org.xml.sax.ErrorHandler;
import org.xml.sax.HandlerBase;
import org.xml.sax.AttributeList;
import org.xml.sax.SAXException;
import org.xml.sax.SAXParseException;
import org.xml.sax.helpers.ParserFactory;

/** clientSCS: Sample program to parse XML based manufacturing order.
 * Simple API for XML (SAX):
 * http://www.megginson.com/SAX/index.html
 * IBM's XML parser and IBM's useful XML parser toolkit:
 * http://www.alphaworks.ibm.com/tech/xml4j
 */
public class clientSCS
{

// --------------------------------------------------------------------
/**
 * Load the IBM parser.
 */
private static final String _stringParserClass =
                    "com.ibm.xml.parsers.ValidatingSAXParser";

/**
 * The main class here does not provide implementation for obtaining
 *an XML document from it's persistent form,
 *(I.e. no disk reading code here.)
 */

public static void main(String [] rgstring)
{
    try
    {
    // Create the parser.
```

```
Parser parser = ParserFactory.makeParser(_stringParserClass);
HandlerBase handlerbase = new HandlerBase()


public void startElement(String stringTagName,
                         AttributeList attributelist)
{
   if (stringTagName.equals("BatchOrder"))
   {
      /* Provide processing for the variable here. */
   }
   else if (stringTagName.equals("BatchOrderId"))
   {
      /* Provide processing for the variable here. */
   }
   else if (stringTagName.equals("BatchSize"))
   {
      /* Provide processing for the variable here. */
   }
   else if (stringTagName.equals("BatchName"))
   {
      /* Provide processing for the variable here. */
   }
   else if (stringTagName.equals("BatchValue"))
   {
      /* Provide processing for the variable here. */
   }
   else if (stringTagName.equals("BatchTax"))
   {
      /* Provide processing for the variable here. */
   }
} // end of startElement

public void endElement (String stringTagName)
{
   if (stringTagName.equals("BatchOrder"))
   {
     /* handle the XML end tag. */
   }
   else if (stringTagName.equals("BatchOrderId"))
   {
      /* handle the XML end tag. */
   }
   else if (stringTagName.equals("BatchSize"))
   {
      /* handle the XML end tag. */
   }
   else if (stringTagName.equals("BatchName"))
   {
      /* handle the XML end tag. */
   }
   else if (stringTagName.equals("BatchValue"))
   {
      /* handle the XML end tag. */
   }
   else if (stringTagName.equals("BatchTax"))
   {
      /* handle the XML end tag. */
   }
} // end of endElement
```

```
        public void characters(char [] rgc, int nStart, int nLength)
        {
          // handle character data
        }

        public void error(SAXParseException saxparseexception)
                   throws SAXException
        {
          throw saxparseexception;
        }

          parser.setDocumentHandler((DocumentHandler)handlerbase);
          parser.setErrorHandler((ErrorHandler)handlerbase);

          for (int i = 0; i < rgstring.length; i++)
          {
              parser.parse(rgstring[i]);
          }

    }
    catch (Exception exception)
    {
        exception.printStackTrace();
    }
  }
}
```

Note that the data extraction methods `startElement` and `endElement` are specific to the data in this case study, containing element names like `BatchOrder` and `BatchTax`. Clearly it would not be difficult to change the names in the `stringTagName.equals()` methods to match those of your own XML formatted data structures, or you could even add in extra "`else if (stringTagName.equals("TagName"))`" statements to deal with extra tags nesting within your XML structures.

Now let's look at one last cause for concern in dealing with large-scale Site Server projects.

Site Server Project Management

I believe I could write a BroadCloth project management handbook that is at least as long as the case we have just presented. Microsoft has recently published some excellent planning documents in their Commerce Server Resource Kit as well as on their SiteBuilder MSDN Web site. All these resources are free.

Site Server offers an excellent foundation for a wide variety of Internet-based enterprise ventures. The BroadCloth case is but the tip of the iceberg in relation to the potential for Site Server. If I had to come up with one critical success factor that can make or break the value of Microsoft Site Server to an organization I would have to say it is teamwork. There is something about Internet projects that seems to place new stresses on a lot of companies. It might be fair to argue that SiteServer really brings these new stresses into focus. A successful Site Server implementation will probably require at least three basic skills. I think of them as personality types. They are: Managerial/Leadership, Marketing, and Technical. Of course you can probably think of a great many more roles but I feel comfortable slotting people into one of these three categories. Not only will these three primary roles need to work as a team, but their integration and cooperation with all the departments of a company is usually an important factor to the final success of a project. Rather than trying to suggest various methods to create effective teams I will leave it to the reader to find a path toward teamwork that works within the culture of their company or project.

Perhaps more to the point, I have offered a sample organization for a Site Server team. It is much larger than the original three roles, but still organized into columns that correspond to Marketing, Management, and Technical.

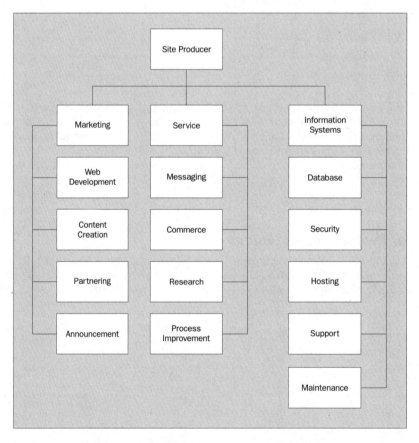

I have also outlined the scope of the various roles in this table. (The main managerial roles for the project are in bold.):

Site Producer	**The overall project manager for a Site Server site production.**
Marketing	**The manager for the marketing aspects of a site production.**
Web Development	Includes the graphic arts and HTML, non- programming aspects of site page creation.
Content Creation	A writer
Partnering	Responsible for alliances in what logos or advertising a site presents, as well as the partnering with other businesses, through a site production.
Announcement	The publicity for a site.
Service	**The overall business manager or sponsor for a site production.**
Messaging	The activity involved with insuring that the right company messages are being conveyed through a site production.
Commerce	Drives a company's business to electronic commerce.
Research	Provides industry research so that a site production is strategic to a company's long-term goals.
Process Improvement	Implements quality and process re-engineering via a site production.
Information Systems	**The manager for the technology end of a production.**
Database	The DBA as well as other development staff doing the coding.
Security	The security guy who knows the art of hacking and cracking.
Hosting	Responsible for making sure that a site is hosted in the right place.
Support	Provides customer service.
Maintenance	Provides operational control of a site and coordinates maintenance.

Obviously, depending on the size of the project and the number of employees available and their skills, some of these specialized roles may have to be blended together in an individual. Nonetheless all the roles are definitely present in any professional Site Server project, and the above table provides a good guide for ensuring that you have all the angles covered for any given project.

Summary

Hopefully, with this case study I have managed to convey to you not only the global scale and complexity of applications that can be readily achieved with Site Server, but also some insight into adapting the mechanisms within Site Server to suit custom implementations. We have walked through the process of translating the business aims of a major company into application specifics, as well as examining the implementation details of a crucial aspect of the use of Site Server technologies to provide a key part of the solution to BroadCloth's global communication needs.

Connecting to Data

In a perfect environment, all of your Oracle/DB2/Mainframe and SQL data would be accessible and easily manipulated from any location through a common interface like a Web browser. Sounds like a good idea, right? Well, as technologies change and improve, we are not far off having that capability. With the right tools and platform, we can start to take advantage of both your legacy data and the power to display the results over the World Wide Web.

Now that the Internet and Web technologies and their universal standards are pervasive in commerce, many companies are exploring the possibilities of linking their existing data with the power and functionality of the Web. In reality, however, roughly eighty percent of all data throughout the world still resides on an assortment of non-Microsoft databases such as IBM Mainframes, AS/400s and Oracle databases spread throughout the world in a range of environments. Compared to these data storage systems, Microsoft SQL Server is still in its infancy.

Many of you may be curious as to why Microsoft Site Server would play such a vital role with legacy data. Well, much of the power of the Web is realized through connecting different databases via Web applications. This allows people to view and manipulate the data via a universal platform. As Microsoft technologies continue to mature and integrate into different markets, accessing and integrating with legacy databases is crucial to their success.

As a platform for managing Web sites, Microsoft Site Server is commonly used to manage content and SQL Server databases. But it is also important that companies that use Site Server can access the legacy data that plays such an important role in the their businesses. For most companies e-commerce Web sites are merely an extension of their existing business processes into a wider context. Companies will want to leverage the power and functionality of Site Server to manage their site, and any transactions made over the Web with their customers, yet still use their legacy databases without having to make significant modifications thus taking maximum advantage of their existing assets whilst extending the business' potential market for their products or services.

Companies simply have too much time and money invested in their legacy systems to let all of their work slip away. In most companies' mindset, they still want to leverage the best of both worlds.... their legacy systems and the power of the World Wide Web, specifically Microsoft Site Server and Active Server Pages.

So legacy data is here to stay, and as you may have guessed, Microsoft is planning on being there to help with every step of the Web site development process. This includes a series of development tools and platforms that will allow you to access and manipulate either relational or non-relational databases.

Universal Data Access is Microsoft's covering term for enabling access to any type of data, in any type of environment. It consists in providing an assortment of ways to tap into relational and non-relational databases using a series of programming interfaces that will allow you to take advantage of your existing data sources. Microsoft's notion of Universal Data Access relies on the technologies of OLE DB, ADO (ActiveX Data Objects) and ODBC (Open Database Connectivity). Coupled with Microsoft's COM technology, connecting to any type of database in any location across the enterprise is now a valuable and viable option.

The best part about the new developments that Microsoft have provided in their Universal Data Access suite is that as long as you have the necessary tools, you can access and manipulate different data sources as if they were all on a common platform and interface. By allowing you to readily access different forms of data in different environments, you now have the power to take advantage of your existing infrastructure, and make the most of your legacy data in any form imaginable.

This appendix presents a survey of some of the options that are available to Site Server users for connecting to some of the most popular non-Microsoft systems in use today. Computer technology, especially in terms of Microsoft Windows and the Internet, is changing rapidly, and by empowering the way developers can connect Web-enabled applications to various data systems, Microsoft stays at the forefront of the development world. Keeping up with these changes and maintaining a connection to data storage systems that are either too expensive, complicated, or critical to change or port to another environment is exactly what this chapter is about.

The Beginning of Legacy Systems

In the early days of data processing, programmers soon found the need to store the data that they needed to use repeatedly. Saving this information, or making it persistent, allowed these early programmers to retain data for reuse as they ran different processes. This simple need soon gave rise to the development of modern day databases as we know them today.

There have been many definitions of a database over the years. For our purposes we should formally define that here:

A database is an organized group of data collected for a central purpose. The organization of this data allows it to be stored, and formatted in a manner that allows for consistent access.

Although a lot of people may argue with this definition as not being complete enough, it gives us a simple base upon which to build. We've all seen examples of information that can be stored in a database, such as address, telephone, or customer information. We often think of databases in terms of business data, but a database can store other types of information that would not normally be thought of as storable in a database: scientific, personal, or military data, for example.

Also, a database may contain different types of data. When we think of data stored in a database we think in terms of numbers or text-based data that can be organized or catalogued. However, databases commonly contain other types of data such as images, video, audio or binary file formats.

This is an important concept to grasp with new technologies and databases such as Oracle8i and its concept of an "Internet File System." This database can hold on to a variety of objects such as HTML pages, video, spreadsheets and a multitude of different documents.

Databases are often used within a department or smaller unit of an organization or enterprise. However, modern databases are often brought together from different parts of an organization to form one large database, often called a data warehouse. With the advent of Internet technology, databases and data warehouses now frequently serve as back ends for Web browser front ends.

Although a database can be used to store and retrieve data, not all databases are created equal. Back in the old days, most of the data was stored in data sources such as AS/400s and IBM Mainframes. As time has gone by, technological developments have resulted in a number of different database systems designed to run on different operating systems. It is not unusual now for companies to have several types of databases in different environments that all store important data, but until recently they didn't have a way to access that data easily in a standard fashion. With the advent of the Web, and with Universal Data Access, the situation has changed.

Often we hear the term legacy database or legacy system without really understanding what the term means. A legacy system or database is really any system that has been in existence for more than a couple of years or that exists on a system other than the one that we currently use or are changing to. Often the person or people that created the system are no longer available to work on or assist with converting the system. As a result there is probably no one in the company that really understands the structure or design of the system. This is where the beauty of UDA comes into play. By using the tools of Universal Data Access, you don't have to worry about where your data is located, or who still knows your legacy database. Of course you're still going to need to know some basics of the legacy database, but UDA (specifically ADO) works at a level where most of the hard work is done for you.

Legacy databases that are present on mainframe systems can present a special problem when trying to integrate them with your Web system. These databases can be based on hierarchical or network database models instead of the current relational or object oriented models. The time and effort needed to understand or convert these systems can sometimes far outweigh the benefits of conversion or access. Usually, the investment required to start a rewrite of a database to provide Web integration wouldn't be cost effective. This is one of the issues that you're going to have to take into consideration before deciding to tackle a large project that requires access to legacy data. Database conversions and rewrites are what we're trying to prevent by using UDA with Microsoft Site Server, thus easing the process of developing Web applications whilst avoiding large-scale conversion of legacy data sources.

Legacy Data Access Options

As Web sites become more sophisticated and dynamic, their ability to access and manipulate data must also become more sophisticated. Businesses today are looking to move more of their information to a Web based platform and more of their applications to a client/server environment. Included in this is all of the legacy data that companies have been amassing for decades. This legacy data may include company reports, sales information or employee records.

Legacy data and applications may take many forms, so there are diverse challenges when trying to connect to this data. Not only are there the challenges of the types and formats of the data itself, and of the data management systems in place, but also the challenge presented by the fact that the data systems might be on a different operating system.

Businesses are beginning to understand that using the Web as a universal interface, all of the information that a company wishes to make available can be made available, to whoever needs it, no matter where in the world they may be located. This enterprise approach to employing Web technology to best advantage however can be difficult to achieve. Mission-critical data can be stored in a variety of forms such as host-based file systems and relational databases on IBM mainframes or AS/400 computers. In the past, trying to deliver any sizeable amount of data to a widely dispersed group of users was both very expensive and problematic. Developing a custom application to deliver or translate data between proprietary hardware or software systems was essentially the only available option.

In this appendix we will look at several available options for connecting your Web site to, and communicating with, legacy data and applications including:

> Connecting to and communicating with Oracle databases

> Using Microsoft SNA Server 4.0 and Microsoft COM Transaction Integrator to access IBM host data and applications

> Replicating data from legacy system to Microsoft's SQL Server

> Migrating Web applications to Microsoft Internet Information Server

Let's look a little more closely at the architecture of integrating legacy data sources with Web applications.

Enterprise Web Applications

The main interest in opening your legacy data sources to Web access is the ability to reach a wider audience through a common interface. Never before has such a universal medium come into place, with an unprecedented effect on the nature of international commerce. In theory, as long as a person has a Web browser on their desktop, they have an unlimited gateway to a wealth of information. We all know that the Web is a great tool for checking your stock quotes and finding out what is going on in the world, but companies are beginning to utilize this power and functionality for their business needs.

Basically, instead of implementing expensive and complicated client/server applications, the entire burden of development is being placed on the middle-tier and backend systems by having the Web act as the client interface. However, if the middle tier can provide services that avoid the problems involved with matching the standard user interface provided by the browser to a variety of data systems, then all that is left to do is to provide the necessary business logic functions in the middle tier. Microsoft's UDA suite provides these data access services, easing the development of Web applications over existing business systems.

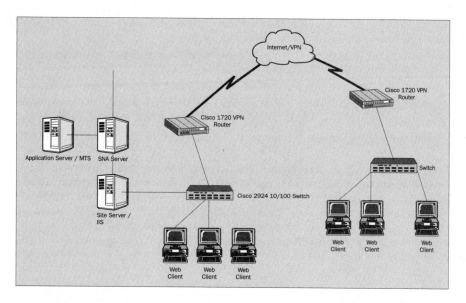

Universal Data Access

As we've said already, UDA is based on the premise of accessing any type of data stored in a wide variety of different environments. The key to understanding Universal Data Access is to become familiar with the three key namespaces within UDA that the platform is based upon: ADO, OLE DB and ODBC. While many of you are probably familiar with Open Database Connectivity (ODBC) and its interoperability with data sources such as Oracle and SQL Server, you might not be very familiar with OLE DB and ADO.

With ODBC, you have a standard programming interface, but with ADO and OLE DB you have additional functionality. OLE Database and ActiveX Data Objects are where the real power exists for connecting to legacy data sources. By combining these two technologies, you can open up a brave new world of database connectivity.

The most promising technology is the ActiveX Data Objects. ADO is the easy to use medium that works at a high-level of data access while dependent on an OLE DB provider to access different types of legacy databases. OLE DB provides the data access and services to almost any type of database you can imagine including Oracle, DB2, Microsoft Exchange and AS/400s.

Before we look at ADO and OLE DB in more detail though, let's just take a quick look at ODBC.

ODBC

ODBC or Open Database Connectivity is probably the most popular method available to access a variety of traditional relational data sources. Created in the late 1980s, ODBC was designed to provide a uniform interface for client access to relational databases. The ODBC interface actually provided for the following:

> A library of function calls that allow the client program to execute SQL statements against the database

> A specific SQL syntax that client applications use to query the data

> A standard set of error codes and messages to deliver to the client program

ODBC is made up of a number of components that work together to provide maximum flexibility in dealing with relational database systems. The main parts are:

> **The Client Application:** This can be Visual Basic, Visual C++, or any customized Web application that is retrieving or updating the information in the relational database.

> **Driver Manager and ODBC:** The driver manager is a Microsoft DLL that provides entry points for the individual drivers. ODBC drivers are created to access specific relational database systems.

> **Data Source:** The data source is the actual database that contains the required data.

Up until now, ODBC has been the common thread to developing and sharing data through compliant databases such as Microsoft SQL Server and Oracle. ODBC works at a level that allows you to talk to the database via ODBC instead of knowing the native syntax of the SQL*Net. ODBC gives you more flexibility and exposure to more developers by being able to work with ODBC instead of native SQL*Net. It has been thought that using the native syntax would offer better performance, but ODBC offers similar or even superior performance with SQL*Net for accessing the data. To talk to either database, all that is required is the necessary driver that was supplied by the software vendor.

While ODBC was a great technological leap forward at the time it was released it did lack the capacity to connect to non-relational data sources. However, it wasn't long before Microsoft released a new technology to do this, OLE DB.

OLE DB

OLE DB is Microsoft's answer to allow developers to connect to a variety of relational and non-relational data sources. But what is the difference between the two types of data source? A relational database is a collection of data organized in a set of structured tables and where data can be accessed or reassembled in many different ways without having to reorganize the database tables. Non-relational databases consist of non-structured data such as a Microsoft Exchange, Microsoft Office documents or even e-mail messages.

OLE DB put the power in the hands of the developers by giving them access to almost any type of data source available. OLE DB works by using the using the provider-consumer model to allow connectivity to relational and non-relational databases. Combined with ADO, data access is simplified by only having to work with the data at a high-level. Whereas you manipulate the data with ADO, OLE DB works at the level that accesses and then ensures that the data provided is structured so you don't have to. Typically the consumer application is coded to ADO and with OLE DB providing the data access.

For non-Microsoft types of relational and non-relational databases, you can use third-party drivers and tools with OLE DB to provide access.

While much of the buzz in today's computing world is about OLE DB, the reason OLE DB came into being was to expand on ODBC. This expansion or increase in functionality for data access is accomplished in a couple of ways, but perhaps the most significant is that OLE DB is based on Microsoft's Component Object Model (COM) technology.

Thus OLE DB actually provides us with a lower-level interface for accessing data sources. Programmers who use C++ or J++ can access OLE DB directly to manipulate their data sources. However, Visual Basic and Web programmers using scripting languages still need to go through additional interfaces, such as ADO, for access to OLE DB.

As we mentioned above, OLE DB can be thought of in terms of two different kinds of applications, consumers and producers.

> ➤ **OLE DB Consumer:** An OLE DB consumer is an application that uses the OLE DB interface.

> ➤ **OLE DB Provider:** An OLE DB provider is an OLE DB interface that actually communicates with the data source.

Below is an example of how the OLE DB provider works with an Oracle database. We're calling the "Provider" with the name "MSDAORA" in our code and having the OLE DB connection take care of the work.

```
Set DataConn = Server.CreateObject ("ADODB.Connection")
DataConn.Provider = "MSDAORA"
DataConn.Open = "DSN=Commerce";UID=Oracle;PWD=oracle"
```

No doubt you are now wondering whether connecting to legacy data sources can really be as simple as installing and using OLE DB with three lines of code. And you'd be right if you thought that it couldn't quite be...

Site Server and non-SQL Server Data Sources

There are many pros and cons to actually trying to integrate the Site Server-Universal Data Access combination and other Microsoft relational databases together with databases such as Oracle or DB2. The benefits to using Site Server to manage your Web data and applications are pretty obvious. If you can take advantage of the powerful Web management tools that are available today along with your legacy databases of yesteryear, you can save yourself a lot of time and money in re-engineering costs. However, the cons of trying to integrate two completely different technologies and platforms also exist. With two different technologies, you are likely to need two sets of developers, two systems people and more to manage such a large project.

Connecting to legacy databases is not as easy or as powerful as connecting to your average SQL Server as you might expect. When you invest in a Site Server and SQL Server solution, you are getting a complete solution that is supposed to work together and increase functionality. Much of the functionality for operating with SQL Server was already in place with Internet Information Server (IIS) when Microsoft began developing the tools for Site Server.

Although this level of proprietary integration brings dividends if you make use of the complete package, things are not so straightforward if you don't: for example, the lack of the ability to use Site Server Personalization and Membership without additional coding with other databases besides Microsoft SQL Server. There are certain stored procedures that are written specifically for SQL Server, and which won't work under any other databases such as Oracle. If you plan to implement Personalization and Membership on your Web site, you should think twice about using a non-SQL data source on the back end. By using Site Server to manage other technologies, you run the risk of losing sight of the basic purpose of the Site Server/IIS/NT suite – "out of the box" power and ease of use.

This practice is also evident with the development tools that Microsoft provides. I'm not trying to discourage your connection to legacy databases, I just want to highlight that it is not as easy as Microsoft's marketing department might convey, and that it should be thoroughly contemplated before moving to implementation.

Let's now take a look at the developer tools Microsoft provide to help with data source integration.

Microsoft Data Access 2.1 SDK

In order to take advantage of many of the useful tools that are available to the average Web developer, you need to get your hands wet, and play with the technology. With the concept of Universal Data Access, Microsoft has released a series of tools that will allow you to test and work with legacy databases, found in the Data Access 2.1 SDK. This tool kit is the prime source for learning to take advantage of the Microsoft data access technologies. You'll find a huge assortment of tools and code samples that will help you with any questions that might arise when accessing legacy data. Besides the variety of code examples, the documentation also includes a series of projects that will assist you as you work.

Below is an example of the Microsoft OLE DB Interface TEST (ITEST) tool that can help practice your COM objects and make you better versed at the OLE DB programming model. Although for most purposes ADO will provide the interface you need, it can still be useful to know something about the OLE DB COM interfaces.

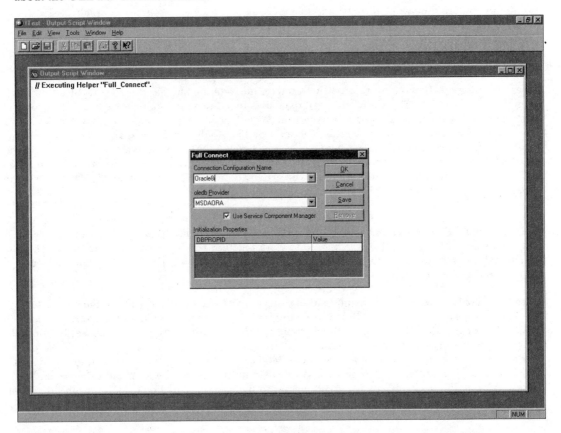

You can find these tools and other available downloads at Microsoft's Universal Data Access Download page: http://www.microsoft.com/Data/download.htm

Visual InterDev and Legacy Databases

Another popular tool you can use with an assortment of databases is Visual InterDev 6 (also available as part of the Visual Studio suite). It has a variety of customized tools that allow you to access and manipulate your data through a series of wizards and the Data View option. The Data View interface allows you to "see" your data in a common window in Visual Interdev so you won't have to constantly be moving back and forward between data and code as you build your application.

To begin a data project with Visual InterDev 6, you can just open up a new database project and specify which data source you would like to connect to. You can either use a pre-configured DSN or create one 'on the fly' to establish a data connection. Once you specify your data connection, and make the connection, you can access the data with much of the functionality you would have with the database's own management system.

Creating a System DSN

In order for your application and the database to communicate, you're going to need a DSN to connect to the data source in your application. A Data Source Name is simply a pointer to the database that is specified to allow access to the data. This is essentially the first step in the process of getting your application to a point where you can start manipulating the data in your database.

You'll notice the importance of the System DSN when you start coding and opening up a connection to your data source. You can define an ODBC data source name using the ODBC Data Source Administrator in the Control Panel. A data source is a connection definition to a specific database. The data source contains several pieces of information that are important for accessing data from the database. You can open the **ODBC Data Source Administrator** by clicking on the **ODBC 32** icon in the control panel.

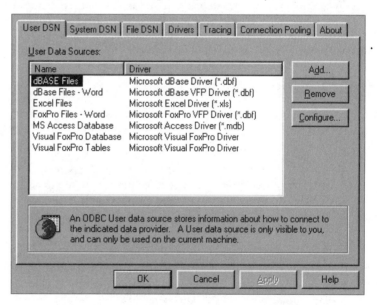

A System DSN is probably one of the most common data sources that you will create for use with Web applications. Clicking on the System DSN tab will bring you to the screen for setting up a system data source name. Click the Add button to add a new system DSN to your Data Source Administrator.

This will bring up the
Create New Data Source
dialog box from which
you can view a list of
ODBC drivers that are
installed on your system.
Highlight an item in the
list and click on Finish.
This will launch an ODBC
Driver Setup dialog from
which you can configure
the particular data source.

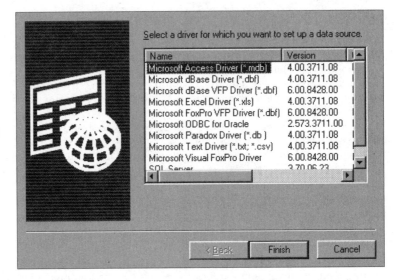

Driver configurations are dependent on the data source that they are connecting to. Creating a data source name to an Oracle data source is a little different from connecting to an Access data source. The information required by the setup screen could be unique to the data source that you are accessing.

Connecting to Oracle

Most of you have probably encountered an Oracle database in your travels. Oracle is a great tool for data warehousing because of its speed and reliability with extremely large amounts of data. This is evident in such large sites as Yahoo! and Amazon.com.

Whereas you don't have to be an Oracle DBA to work with an Oracle database, a little knowledge will go a long way in preparing you to connect your site to an Oracle backend. We'll go over some Oracle basics to begin with, and what makes Oracle different from SQL Server.

Oracle Relational Database Management System, or RDBMS, has been around storing large amounts of data for thousands of companies, for many years before SQL Server came on the scene. Designed to allow simultaneous access to a large amount of stored information, and to allow access by many simultaneous users, the Oracle RDBMS is supported on over 80 different operating system environments, ranging from IBM mainframes, DEC VAX minicomputers, UNIX-based minicomputers, Windows NT and several proprietary hardware-operating system platforms.

With such a large installation base, it's obvious that many companies want to take advantage of their existing commitment to Oracle. To heighten its strength within the Internet community, the latest version of the Oracle software is Oracle 8i, which highlights the Internet File System or IFS. The Internet File System allows you to users store Web pages, graphic files, and other traditional documents directly within an Oracle database. Depending on the security, you can search the database through a standard Web browser. You can even view relational data independently from the client you're using to access the database.

Connecting to an Oracle Data Source

There is no particular rule about whether to use ODBC or OLE DB to connect to an Oracle Server, although you will get better performance if you can connect to your data though the OLE DB provider, as this does not go through an intermediary ODBC layer.

When you connect to an Oracle database through ODBC you have two methods that you can follow, as with any ODBC connection. The first is to use a DSN that is registered on your machine. The second is to use the connection string directly in your code.

To establish your connection to the Oracle database, you'll need a validated SQL*Net connection string. SQL* Net Easy Configuration is a tool that allows you to create an alias that you can reference in an ODBC DSN to connect to your Oracle Server. It is added to your install group by the Oracle installer.

Creating an Oracle Data Source

When setting up a DSN for your Oracle connection, you have the option of using the latest Microsoft Oracle driver or the Oracle Driver that is installed when on your workstation. Once you specify your driver, you are then prompted for an Oracle server. This is where you type in your instance name. If you are using your local instance in Personal Oracle you can use "2:". If you are using an older Microsoft driver, a third-party driver or an Oracle driver, you may be prompted for a connection string.

Installing the Oracle Client

Before we can connect to an Oracle server we need to install the Oracle Client software on our machine. The Oracle Client installation will install all the components we need to access an Oracle server. Some of the tools that we will need to interact with an Oracle database include:

> **SQL*Plus:** This is the primary interface for access to an Oracle system.
> **Net*8:** This component includes the client-side networking components and administrative tools.

We won't go through the Oracle Client install process here – following the install wizard from the Oracle CD is straightforward.

Making the Oracle Connection

Having installed Oracle Client, we need to supply a valid SQL*Net connection string in order to connect to an Oracle database using ODBC. We can setup an alias using the SQL Net Easy Configuration. This utility will allow us to create a connection alias to our Oracle database that we can reference in the ODBC setup.

SQL Net Easy Configuration is a simple-to-use wizard-type utility that guides you though the process of creating a database alias for an Oracle database. Bring up the Wizard by clicking on Start | Programs | Oracle on Windows NT | SQL Net Easy Config.

The first screen allows you to define the option that you wish to configure. Click **Add New Service** and type in your database alias in the **New Service Name** box.

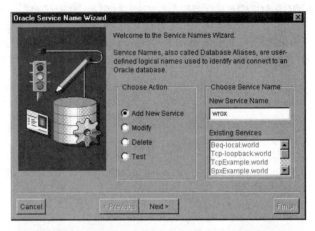

Next you can select the networking protocol that you need to connect to the Oracle database. The most common option for Oracle will be TCP/IP, but if you are working locally for development, you can use the IPC connector.

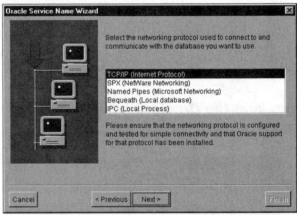

Click **Next** to bring up the configuration options for the TCP/IP protocol option. This screen will prompt you for the host name of the computer that houses your Oracle database. If you are connecting to an Oracle database, you will need to make sure that port 1521 is available. This is especially important if your enterprise Web application connects to users behind a firewall. Your system administrator can create a plug for port 1521 that will allow for the client to talk to the Oracle Server.

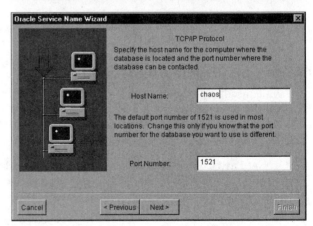

Finally you will be prompted for the System Identifier of the Oracle database instance that you wish to connect to. The default instance name is usually ORCL.

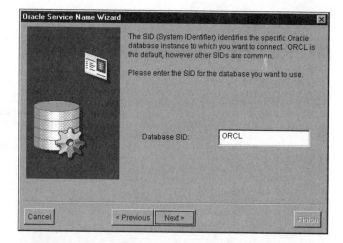

If all is well at this point you can test the connection to your database server. For testing services, Oracle has created a user Scott with the password of "tiger." You can test that you have a valid connection with this password and user ID.

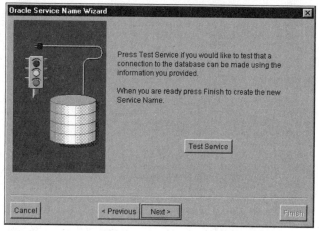

Creating an Oracle ODBC Data Source

Finally we can create a data source connection for use by our system. To create a system DSN open the 32-Bit ODBC control from the control panel, or click Start | Programs | Oracle for Windows NT | 32-Bit ODBC Administrator.

> Click the System DSN tab to add a system DSN, and then click on Add.

> Select the Microsoft ODBC for Oracle driver to display the dialog box as shown opposite.

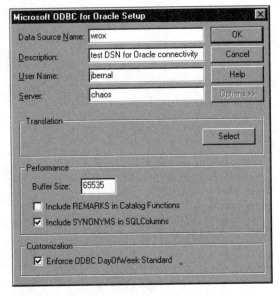

Fill in the required information to and then click OK to complete the installation. Here is a description of the information that you will require to complete the installation.

> Data Source Name: Enter a name for the DSN that you wish to create.
> Description: Enter a description of the Oracle Server that you are connecting to.
> User Name: Enter a user name to access the Oracle database identified by the connection string or alias.
> Server: Enter the SQL*Net Easy Configuration alias that you created earlier.

Connecting to Legacy Systems

With an estimated eighty-percent of all data in the world residing on IBM Mainframe computers, there is a good chance that somewhere along your career you'll be asked to be part of a development process that needs to access and manipulate the data. Connection to this type of system can be approached using System Network Architecture (SNA), a networking architecture developed by IBM in the early 70s.

SNA is actually a series of models and protocols that allowed IBM the ability to inter-operate various systems that were available at the time. It is important to realize that the SNA architecture was developed over time or in stages as new problems or challenges were encountered. In the early 80s IBM introduced Advanced Program-to-Program Communication (APPC) and Advanced Program-to-Program Networking (APPN) to answer one of the challenges concerning distributed processing and communications.

SNA uses a layered approach to describe the many protocols and communications that take place under the architecture. It is important to realize that SNA is not an open architecture environment. SNA defines a complete network environment and the protocols and models that make up that network.

Using Microsoft's SNA Server

OK, you've learned a little bit about SNA, so what does that have to do with us? To answer that in some detail we will take a look at Microsoft's SNA Server 4.0. SNA Server 4.0 runs on Windows NT Server 4.0 and can communicate on an SNA network to provide access to a wide variety of legacy data and applications. Because you cannot connect directly to an IBM mainframe directly from a Windows computer, you need a system that can form the translation. This is where an IBM Mainframe can still add a lot of value to your Windows network. This way you can take advantage of the power and functionality of your Mainframe for your Windows network. Here is a diagram of how a Microsoft SNA Server integrates with an IBM Mainframe computer.

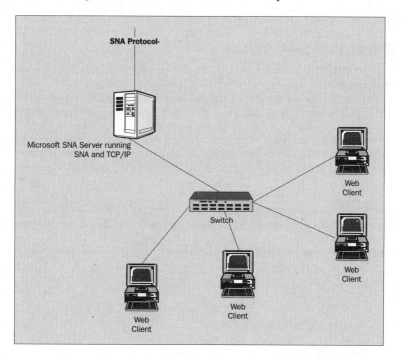

The SNA Server works by encapsulating the SNA protocol into TCP/IP and communicating with the hosts through their web browsers. The capabilities of Microsoft's SNA Server can be summarized as follows:

> **Provides access to host terminal applications, allows printer emulation, or file access to shared folders:** SNA Server supports several terminal emulation modes, which allow access to mainframe or AS/400 systems. This configuration allows access to host applications, shared folders, and supports PC-based printer emulation.

> **Access to relational and non-relational host databases:** SNA server provides a wide variety of ODBC drivers and OLE DB interfaces that allow connection to both relational databases and non-relational data sources in IBM and AS/400 systems.

925

> ➤ **Replicating of host data to Microsoft's SQL Server:** The Host Data Replicator is a new tool developed to allow the replication of data in IBM's DB2 databases with Microsoft's SQL Server.

> ➤ **Transaction Integration on host systems using Microsoft's COM Transaction Integrator (COM TI):** COM TI is a SNA Server component that allows developing applications that operate with IBM host transaction services and applications.

Using Microsoft's SNA Server 4.0 computers running Windows NT Server 4.0 can communicate on an SNA network. SNA Server can translate information coming from Windows NT to the LU 6.2 protocol commands. This is a very powerful solution for connecting your Windows NT applications to legacy systems including both legacy applications and databases.

Most importantly for us, SNA Server 4.0 also has a Solutions Development Kit that will provide much of what you'll need to connect your Web application to an SNA Server. You can find more information on the SNA Server SDK on Microsoft's site at

```
http://msdn.microsoft.com/library/sdkdoc/sna/legal_9hda.htm
```

Installing Microsoft's SNA Server

While we won't cover every detail about the installation and configuration of SNA Server, it is important that we understand some of the options that are available to use within the system. However, complete understanding of SNA networks and inter-operability of heterogeneous systems is a complex and time consuming task that may take the advice of experiences professionals.

Microsoft's SNA Server is a member of the BackOffice family and runs under Windows NT 4.0. As a BackOffice product, it is designed to integrate well with other members of the BackOffice family, and still provides a powerful set of tools for connecting Windows NT networks to mainframe environments.

Because ordinary clients cannot speak with IBM Mainframes directly without special hardware or software, Microsoft SNA Server acts as a "go-between" between the Mainframe and the client.

Hardware and Software Requirements for SNA Server

Since SNA Server is a member of the BackOffice family, most of the requirements you are already familiar with. However, here is a short list of the minimum requirements you will need for installing the system.

> ➤ Pentium or higher CPU (Alpha AXP).

> ➤ Windows NT Server 4.0 with Service Pack 3.

> ➤ 32 MB of RAM with 64 or more recommended.

> ➤ 50 to 100-MB available hard disk space.

> ➤ Communication interface for communicating with the network that you are trying to access. Remote Access Services, Token Ring interface, TCP/IP services, etc.

> ➤ IE 4.0 or later. Microsoft Data Access Components required for most of the ODBC or OLE DB connections.

> ➤ For interface with IIS components such as IIS and MTS, the Windows NT Option pack is required.

Running through the SNA Server setup program is straightforward. We'll look at just a few of the screens in detail, starting with the fourth screen, **SNA Server Components and Services**.

SNA Server Components and Services

This section contains the main components of SNA Server. Items found here will be components to attain host connectivity, printing services, file sharing, terminal access and security:

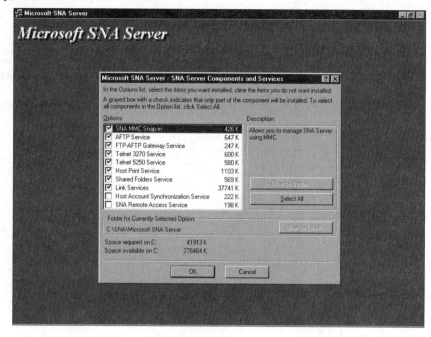

The components you can see on the screen shot are as follows:

> **SNA MMC Snap-in:** This is a MMC snap-in allowing you to manage SNA Server and integration components.

> **AFTP Service:** AFTP is an FTP service that uses the APPC protocol instead of TCP/IP. This protocol is often used to transfer files between host systems running SNA.

> **FTP-AFTP Gateway Service:** This is an SNA Server component that allows FTP clients to access AFTP services on host systems. The component acts as a translator between the FTP and AFTP systems.

> **Telnet 3270 Service:** This service supports TN32XX series client emulation for terminal and printer access over TCP/IP.

> **Telnet 5250 Service:** This service supports TN5250 client emulation for terminal emulation.

> **Host Print Service:** This service provides printer emulation services via LU protocols to IBM host and AS/400 system.

> **Shared Folders Service:** This is a file access that allows access to files from Windows NT.

> **Link Services:** Link Services support SNA communication adapters.

> **Host Account Synchronization Service:** Synchronizes password changes between Windows NT and host systems.

> **SNA Remote Access Service:** Remote Access Services allow Windows NT RAS users to communicate over SNA.

When you've selected those components you require, click OK to move on to the Applications and Development Tools screen.

Applications and Development Tools

This section contains components for developers who are looking to develop applications that integrate with a host system.

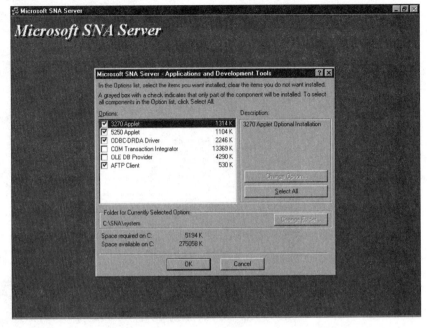

Here, the options are as follows:

> ➤ 3270 Applet and 5250 Applet: These applets provide access to these services as discussed in the previous section.

> ➤ ODBC-DRDA Driver: A customer ODBC driver that provides access to relational data files on host systems using the Distributed Resource Data Access (DRDA) server.

> ➤ COM Transaction Integrator: Development tools and components for integrating MVS, CICS, and IMS programs with Microsoft Transaction Server.

> ➤ OLE DB Provider: This component provides record level access to non-relational data stored on AS/400 and VSAM files.

> ➤ AFTP Client: Client software for transferring files using AFTP.

The next screen is Host Connectivity SDK. This section contains sample code and SNA system documentation for application developers. To get you moving in the right direction, it's a good idea to install this SDK and examine the code examples.

Next you will be prompted to decide which type of server that you wish to install. If this is the first installation of SNA Server than you must choose a Primary configuration server. Installing any other type of server as a first installation will cause setup to fail.

After being asked what protocols you want SNA to work with, setup then prompts you for a SNA Server sub domain. A single Windows NT domain can contain several SNA Server sub domains, however in most cases the setup program will prompt you with the name of the current Windows NT domain that the server exists within. For administration purposes it is probably better to install separate SNA servers on the same sub domain.

Finally, SNA Server services require a service account from which to run. The **Server Domain Account Information** dialog box will prompt you for this account information. Setup will create a new account if the information contained in this dialog box does not exist. If you have additional SNA Servers on the same sub domain, they may be configured to use the same services account.

Connecting to VSAM and AS/400 Files

In the beginning of this chapter we talked about ODBC vs. OLE DB and how OLE DB was developed to expand on the popularity of ODBC. In addition we mentioned that OLE DB was designed to allow client applications or consumers to gain access to information that is not stored in a relational system. SNA Server provides an OLE DB driver (Provider) for AS/400 and VSAM (Virtual Sequential Access Method) to allow you access to some of the most common non-relational storage systems in use today.

The OLE DB provider supports all file types for AS/400 and most of the data types available in VSAM. This makes it a powerful tool in gaining access to indexed and sequential files at both a file and record locking level. The provider is designed to support the following AS/400 file types and VSAM data set file types:

> Keyed and non-keyed physical files
> Logical Files with external descriptions
> Basic Sequential Access Method (BSAM) data sets
> Queued Sequential Access Method (QSAM) data sets
> Entry-Sequenced Data Sets (ESDS)
> Key-Sequenced Data Sets (KSDS)
> Fixed Length Relative Record Data Sets (RRDS)
> Variable Length Relative Record Data Sets
> Partitioned Data Set (PDS) and Partitioned Data Set Extended (PDSE)

Installing and Configuring the OLE DB Provider for AS/400 and VSAM

The OLE DB provider for AS/400 and VSAM is designed to run under SNA Server 4.0 either as a server-based deployment or a client-based deployment. Since the OLE DB provider is designed to work under SNA Server for Windows, many of the requirements of the provider are the same as for SNA Server or SNA Server client:

> Windows NT Server 4.0 with Service Pack 3
> SNA Server 4.0 or Client for SNA Server 4.0

There is also a Windows 95 SNA Server client that is designed to run under Windows 95

The OLE DB Provider is also designed to work in conjunction with Distributed Data Management (DDM) server systems:

> Data Facility Storage Management Systems (DFSMS) for MVS
> OS/400 Version 2

If you download and install SNA Server 4.0 Service Pack 1, you can work with the SNA OLE/DB Provider.

Using Replication to Gain Access to Legacy Data

Replication is the process of making data available at one location, also available at another location. This replication process can be conducted by copying or moving data between servers so that the same data can be made available at several different locations. Replicating data in Microsoft's SQL Server can take many forms, including:

> **Transactional-based replication:** In transactional replication the data is modified at the host or Publishers site and then replicated to all subscribers of the data. With the release of SQL Server 7.0, it is now possible to use transactional replication in a bi-directional manner. Bi-directional replication does not have to be used however, since in many cases replication is best used in a one-way scenario.

> **Snapshot replication:** Snapshot replication takes a picture of the data at a given point in time. This is the simplest type of replication to use and essentially makes a copy of the data for use at another site.

> **Merge replication:** Merge replication allows users to make a copy of the database for use at another location and then merge or replicate any changes to the data with the original data source at a later time.

> **Immediate Updating Subscribers replication:** Immediate update is another form of SQL Server 7.0 update replication in which changes are replicated on an ongoing basis

Rather than creating processes to interact with the data on legacy systems, we can sometimes simply create a process to replicate the data we require to a platform and format that we can work with. One of the tools that Microsoft has created to assist with this process is called the Host Data Replicator.

Using the Host Data Replicator

The Host Data Replicator (HDR) is a SQL Server application that provides access to DB2 Databases. DB2 is a database management system provided by IBM and is a very popular database that allows for mainframe connectivity. HDR uses the ODBC driver for DB2 to create the interface to SQL Server.

The Host Data Replicator copies pre-defined data from DB2 tables to SQL Server tables. The HDR can also perform this replication process at scheduled intervals as required. This process can be made bi-directional so that updates to the SQL Server data can be pushed back to the DB2 system as well. To ensure high-availability, the HDR maintains localized copies of the enterprise data that is controlled through the SQL Server end.

Because the Host Data Replicator uses ODBC for communication between database systems, it provides for a very flexible environment where data can be replicated. HDR is most useful where data does not need to be replicated or updated in real time, or where the user simply needs a snapshot of the data at regular intervals. The HDR can process and replicate up to one gigabyte an hour for mid-range computers and up to five gigabytes for Mainframe class systems. Any NT-based application, which can access an ODBC data source including IIS and SNA Server, can take advantage of the HDR to access available data. Here is a listing of the system requirements that you'll need to implement the Host Data Replicator.

System requirements for the Host Data Replicator are:

- ➢ Single/multiprocessor system with Intel Pentium, Pentium PRO, or Alpha AXPTM
- ➢ 64 MB of memory (includes SQL Server memory requirements)
- ➢ 10 MB of available hard-disk space
- ➢ Microsoft Windows NT Server v3.51 or later
- ➢ Microsoft SNA Server 3.0 or later
- ➢ Microsoft SQL Server 6.5 or later

If you need this type of functionality, you'll have to purchase this product as an add-on to your existing system. The software license for this tool is presently $1795 and is available from most Microsoft software resellers. Even if you don't want to use the Host Data Replicator explicitly, you may still have reason to connect to an existing DB2 database that may exist on a host system. For this you can use the ODBC driver for DB2.

The ODBC Driver for DB2

The ODBC for DB2 driver is an optional component that can be installed with SNA Server. This component converts SQL requests from client applications to Distributed Relational Database Architecture (DRDA) Protocol commands that can be transmitted through SNA to a DB2 system.

Migrating Web Applications

Windows NT really hasn't been around that long compared to UNIX. But it is starting to make a name for itself, and organizations are starting to see benefits in switching platforms from older legacy systems to NT-based development environments. The addition of IIS and Active Server Pages has turned Windows NT into a powerful Web server that is capable of handling just about any Web application requirement.

Older Web applications that have any type of dynamic content are usually built around the Common Gateway Interface or CGI specification. CGI scripts are compiled applications or code that is run in an interpreted environment to perform some action on the fly and generate Web content as needed. Both Perl and C are common languages used for writing these powerful CGI scripts.

Switching your existing Web applications to run on NT can be performed by setting up your existing Web pages and then recompiling the CGI scripts that support those existing pages on your new platform. Internet Information Server fully supports the CGI specification and will run your existing site with little modification. However, you may find that CGI performance is considerably reduced under Windows NT, due to the fact that a new process is spawned for each CGI request – not a problem in a Unix environment, but slower under Windows NT which is designed to use threads.

Transaction Processing

Transaction processing is a technology that has been around for some time and is currently starting to enjoy some popularity under Windows NT, thanks to the creation of the Microsoft's Transaction Server. Transaction processing itself can be a confusing process to understand in light of the level of knowledge that you need to have before you can understand the principles of transaction processing itself.

A transaction is a multi-part update process in which the update is committed or completed only if all the parts of the transaction are completed successfully. An online transaction is an update process that is initiated and carried out over a data network. In most cases transaction processing is the process of communicating with databases.

This communication can be one or a series of steps that combine to create a single transaction. A transaction server is designed to perform these transactions and allow for the possibility that a transaction may not be performed completely. In the case of an error or problem, the transaction must be rolled back and returned to the state that it was before the transaction was started. Often we use the term **ACID** to describe transaction processing.

> **Atomic:** The term atomic is used to describe a single element or abstract idea. In this case we can think of the steps that we perform for a specific transaction are combined into a single atomic unit. This is used to ensure that the entire process be complete before the changes are committed to the database.

> **Consistent:** Each transaction must be consistently executed step by step. This requirement goes hand in hand with the requirement for isolation. This ensures that each transaction is the same as every other transaction and anomalies do not occur.

> **Isolated:** Transactions need to be isolated from one another, in order to protect the data involved.

> **Durable:** Once a transaction is complete it needs to be saved in a way that will make it durable. Any transaction that occurs and completes must be made durable even in the event of a system failure.

These **ACID** properties are kind of a guarantee that transactions will function properly and data will remain true and consistent. Without these requirements, transaction processing would not be possible.

Recent developments in the use of the Internet for exchanging information and the growth in the development of distributed technology has spawned new life into transaction processing for use on the Web. These new technologies have increased the ability to interact with databases, which require a transaction manager to ensure that the updates and changes are preformed smoothly.

In addition there are currently many existing transaction systems on existing legacy networks that provide important processing on a daily basis. Organizations often feel they are stuck in an existing environment because of the need to continue updating existing applications with new modifications or functionality. This can often not be the best solution in terms of cost and development time required updating what may be outdated solutions.

The COM Transaction Integrator

Now that you know a little bit about transaction processing, let's take a look at how that technology will allow us to access legacy processes. We actually have a couple of choices. First we can rewrite all of our legacy transaction processing systems to run in MTS or another transaction monitor; or we can use Microsoft's COM Transaction Integrator (COM TI) to migrate our processes at a little slower pace, which allow current systems to utilize the resources they already have.

We can use COM TI to extend existing transaction management processes to include new processes written for MTS. By migrating parts of the existing transaction processing we can begin to extend our existing legacy applications to a client/server front-end.

As we all know the Web is quickly becoming the front-end interface of choice. However as we continue to grow and move into the future we are still held in check by the existence of legacy systems that can't be changed or updated due to cost or complexity. COM TI is a technology that bridges that gap and allows us to integrate our client/server systems with legacy host transactions. This can allow us to take full advantage of both worlds and ensure that we still meeting the needs of your organization. Below is a listing of different processing systems for Mainframes.

> **Information Management System:** Information Management System (IMS) is a mainframe-based transaction manager. IMS is a message-based system that interacts with it's own database. IMS receives messages from clients in its message queue. It then launches transaction applications to perform the requested operation and returns the results to the client.

> **Customer Information Control System:** Customer Information Control System (CICS) is a Transaction Processing monitor and manager which provides online transaction processing services. CICS doesn't contain a built - in database, instead using DB2 to contain the information for managing the transaction requests and results.

The following list summarizes how COM TI gains access to CICS application and integrated data returned from CICS TPs with Internet Information Server through Active X Data Objects (ADO) and MTS:

> Gains access to CICS Transaction Processes.
COM TI directly supports any TP that executes in CICS or IMS. Because COM TI can access CICS programs, developers can issue application calls to legacy environment by using CICS to gain access to any program under its control. This includes DB2 databases, VSAM files, or IMS databases.

> Redirects method calls.
COM TI is a generic proxy for the mainframe. IT intercepts method calls from the client application and redirects those calls to TPs running on the mainframe. For example, when an Internet browser sends data that ASP interprets as requiring COM TI, IIS forwards the data to COM TI.

> Reformats method calls.
When COM TI intercepts the method call, it converts and formats the method's parameters from Automation data types into IBM System 390 mainframe data types.

> Handles return values.
COM TI handles the return of all output parameters and values from the mainframe and converts and reformats them for IIS as needed.

> COM TI runs under Windows NT, not on the SNA host.
Its processing takes place on a computer running Windows NT Server, and does not require any new executable code to be installed on the mainframe, or on the desktop computer that is running the Internet browser. COM TI communicates through SNA Server and uses standard communication protocols (for example, LU 6.2 provided by Microsoft SNA Server version 4.0) to communicate between the computer running Windows NT Server and the mainframe TP.

Using COM TI

COM TI functions as an on-line Transaction Processing Proxy service that processes host transaction programs through COM objects. COM TI works by intercepting calls to COM components in transaction server and passing the data to host transaction programs. COM IT then receives the results from the host transaction and returns it to the COM component for use by the calling application.

In this sense you are extending the functionality of legacy host applications for use by COM components within Microsoft Transaction server. This provides an excellent upgrade or migration path to eventually replacing original legacy transaction processes with full-featured client/server applications.

We can install COM TI when we do the initial install of SNA Server or later as we add components to our SNA Server installation. COM TI consists of the following components:

> **Administration Component:** The administration component collects information about the user's SNA environment.

> **Run-time Component:** The run-time component intercepts the method calls to the mainframe and uses the COM TI-created component library to perform the actual conversion and formatting of the method parameters. In addition, the run-time component interacts with SNA Server and builds LU 6.2 packets, which are sent to the mainframe.

> **Development Components:** Development Components include the component builder, a GUI used to create component libraries from the mainframe COBOL programs. You can find out more about this product by visiting the SNA Server Home Page (http://www.microsoft.com/sna).

Summary

Hopefully you have an idea of some of the options available for accessing non-Microsoft systems and legacy data. Over the course of this appendix we have discussed a number of issues in trying to access some of the more common forms of host systems that are available. As we have mentioned time and time again, in many cases it is often the best solution to leave legacy solutions in place and build client/server systems around what you already have. Not only can this be more cost effective, for many legacy systems it is a cost savings with the same functionality that you originally desired in your NT applications.

Anytime you try and mix different technologies, such as legacy data and the entire Microsoft Web Tools you can run into a multitude of problems. These technologies were never meant for interoperability in the beginning, and you might run into some difficulties down the road.

In a perfect environment, all of your relational and non-relational databases would interact without another thought, but unfortunately, that is not the case. However, the times are changing for the better and we are getting closer to a standard development platform that will empower both the developer and the end-user that can access data anywhere in any location.

Navigation in the MMC

When we first discussed the Microsoft Management Console in Chapter 5, we mentioned that there were different ways of navigating around it. This appendix provides a quick reference for mouse navigation and keyboard shortcuts within the MMC.

Using the Mouse

You move through the MMC console tree by expanding and collapsing branches with the plus sign (+) and minus sign (-) keys, or by clicking and double-clicking with the mouse.

Click	Selects an item.
Double-click	Displays or hides items contained by the selected item. Displays properties for or opens an item.
Right-click	Displays the Action shortcut menu for the selected item.

Keyboard Shortcuts

CTRL+O	Opens a saved console.
CTRL+N	Opens a new console.
CTRL+S	Saves the open console.
CTRL+M	Adds or removes a snap-in.

Table Continued on Following Page

CTRL+W	Opens a new window.
ALT+SPACEBAR	Displays the MMC window menu.
ALT+F4	Closes the active console.
CTRL+P	Prints the current page or active pane.
ALT+ MINUS SIGN	Displays the window menu for the active console window.
SHIFT+F10	Displays the Action shortcut menu for the selected item.
ALT+A	Displays the Action menu for the active console window.
ALT+V	Displays the View menu for the active console window.
F1	Opens the Help topic, if any, for the selected item.
F5	Refreshes the content of all console windows.
CTRL+F10	Maximizes the active console window.
CTRL+F5	Restores the active console window.
ENTER	Displays the properties dialog box for or opens the selected item.
F2	Renames selected item.
CTRL+F4	Closes the active console window. When a console has only one console window, this closes the console.
TAB or F6	Moves forward between panes in the active console window.
SHIFT+TAB or SHIFT+F6	Moves backward between panes.
CTRL+TAB or CTRL+F6	Moves forward between console windows.
CTRL+SHIFT+TAB or CTRL+SHIFT+F6	Moves backward between console windows.
+ on numeric keypad	Expands the selected item.
- on numeric keypad	Collapses the selected item.
* on numeric keypad	Expands the entire console tree below the root item in the active console window.
UP arrow	Moves the selection up one item in a pane.
DOWN arrow	Moves the selection down one item in a pane.
PAGE UP	Moves the selection to the top item visible in a pane.
PAGE DOWN	Moves the selection to the bottom item visible in a pane.

HOME	Moves the selection to the first item in a pane.
END	Moves the selection to the last item in a pane.
RIGHT arrow	Expands the selected item. If the selected item doesn't contain hidden items, behaves like the DOWN arrow.
LEFT arrow	Collapses the selected item. If the selected item doesn't contain exposed items, behaves like the UP arrow.

More on MSCS Objects

As we saw in Chapter 16, *MSCS Objects within a Store*, the MSCS object model provides a number of different components with a wide range of functionality. However, how do we actually use these components in our scripts? This appendix starts by providing a general summary of the basics of using components in ASP pages.

Also in Chapter 16, we looked at the MSCS data storage and user interface components, and discussed their place in the typical ASP pages that make up an online store. In addition, you may remember we mentioned that MSCS includes a number of components that can be used for management and maintenance tasks. In this appendix we'll talk about these remaining components and their properties and methods.

Using the MSCS Components

In order to be able to understand how MSCS components work, we must first make sure that we know how to use them in our ASP scripts.

Once upon a time, languages used to be based on the concepts of *structured programming*. These are focused on the idea that the language, and therefore the developer, should focus on the procedures that have to be carried in out in order for an operation (the program) to be completed. That was the time when Fortran, C, Pascal, Basic and COBOL ruled the world of computer programming (some say that COBOL still does, but we'll just ignore them and go on).

Almost twenty years ago, however, a gentlemen by the name of Alan Kay wrote a language that he called *SmallTalk*, which was based on the concept of Object-Oriented Programming (OOP). Contrary to any other language until then, it focused on the *data* that had to be manipulated in order for the program to be completed. If you consider a multiplication, for example, structured programming focuses on the operations that have to be made so that the result can be calculated, while OOP focuses on the two numbers that have to be multiplied and decides what to do based on their nature. This means that OOP languages can be more flexible than their traditional counterparts, because they make it easier to write code that adapts to the data being used.

COM takes full advantage of the basic concepts of OOP – in particular the possibility of reusing objects and providing a uniform interface that can be used across several languages – and represents one of Microsoft's most actively used technologies. A COM component is, fundamentally an object composed of any number (including zero) of data members, known as **properties**, and procedural members, known as **methods.**

ASP and COM

COM objects are not only available, but even intrinsic to ASP. In fact, objects such as `Server`, `Application` or `Response` are COM components made available to any ASP script that is executed.

With a few exceptions, an instance of a COM component (which we'll call an *object*) must be created and assigned to an object variable before the component's functionality can be used in an ASP script. This is done using the `Server.CreateObject` method:

```
Server.CreateObject (ObjectStringID)
```

`ObjectStringID` is a string that identifies a particular component. Each component is given a unique string that can be used to identify it. This string is made of three parts:

```
Class.Name.Version
```

Where:

> ➤ *Class* is the name of the group of objects to which the component belongs. For example, all the Commerce components belong to the class `Commerce`.

> ➤ *Name* is the name of the component itself, such as `Page`.

> ➤ *Version* can be used to refer to a specific version of the component, e.g. `1`.

The *Version* portion of the string can be omitted; in this case, the default version of the object, generally the most recent one, will be created.

Once an object has been created, its members can be accessed by appending a dot (.) to the variable's name, followed by the members name:

```
Set MyObject = Server.CreateObject ("My.Object")

' Executes a procedure

MyObject.Proc Value1, Value2

  ' Executes a function

a = MyObject.Funct (Value1)


  ' Reads a property

Response.Write MyObject.Property1
```

Now we've covered the necessary basics for using MSCS components, the rest of this appendix will discuss the last category of MSCS objects.

MSCS Administration Objects

There are three administration components supplied with MSCS. With these we can access IIS to modify its configuration, change the store's setup, open and close the store and so on. One other component is used to access text or binary files in a way similar to the `Scripting.FileSystemObject` used with scripting on the server but with a simpler and more powerful interface.

The starter store, which we examined in the main commerce chapters, does not use any of these components in its storefront, although some of them are used in the Store Manager. Normally, you will not need to use any of them, unless you need complete control over your store from an administrative point of view.

In the remainder of this appendix, we will examine the administration components that come with SSCE:

> `AdminFile`
> This component is used to access a file on the server's hard drive or through a network connection and to read its contents either in text or in binary format. Although its uses are similar to those of the standard object, `Scripting.FileSystemObject`, it provides a one-step approach to file access and some much needed additional functionality.

> `AdminWebServer`
> This component is allows your script to access the IIS metabase, a repository of all the settings of your web server. Through it, you can also read the MSCS properties of your store, which are normally visible through the MMC or administration website.

> `AdminSite`
> `AdminSite` is used to directly manage an instance of MSCS. It can create store foundations, delete existing stores, and so on.

The AdminFile Component

If you have used ASP to output a binary file, such as an image, you will know that it isn't easy. The `Scripting.FileSystemObject` that can be used with ASP has a limitation in the fact that it can only read text files, which are handled internally using the Unicode standard (2 bytes for each characters) and can't be used to output binary data. Most people, those who don't have MSCS at least, end up writing their own components to handle this kind of data.

Luckily, MSCS comes with the `Commerce.AdminFile` component, that can be used to read information from a server-side binary or text file. `AdminFile` has only two methods, `ReadFromBinaryFile` and `ReadFromFile`.

The ReadFromBinaryFile Method

This function is used to read the contents of a binary file. The whole file is read into an array of bytes that can be outputted directly using the `Response.BinaryWrite` function:

```
AdminFile.ReadFromBinaryFile (sFilename)
```

Where `sFilename` is the complete pathname of the file.

As we have seen, this function can be useful if you want to examine or alter the contents of a binary file, or if you want to output them to the user's browser. In the latter case, you will have to do a little more than just using the `Response.Write` command. The following example loads and outputs a GIF.

```
<%
' Turn on error checking
On Error Resume Next

' Declare some vars
Dim afAdminFileObject
Dim bFile

' Create AdminFiles object
Set afAdminFileObject = Server.CreateObject ("Commerce.AdminFile")

' Load file into memory
bFile = afAdminFileObject.ReadFromBinaryFile ("C:\myfile.gif")

' Now, tell the browser that it will be receiving a GIF
Response.ContentType = "image/gif"

' Finally, output the file
Response.BinaryWrite (bFile)

' Handle errors
If Err.Number <> 0 Then
     Response.ContentType = "text/html"
%>
     <HTML><HEAD><TITLE>Error!</TITLE></HEAD>
     <BODY><B>Unable to load image file!</B></BODY>
     </HTML>
<%
End If
%>
```

You must use the `ContentType` member of the `Response` object to let the browser know that it is about to receive an image and not plain text or HTML, which it expects by default. Using `BinaryWrite` ensures that all eight bits that make a byte are sent to the client; in ASCII, or text, mode. The system will only transmit the lowest seven bits of the byte with disastrous consequences in our case.

The `ReadFromBinaryFile` method can be useful in a number of ways, such as when your e-commerce site is selling digital goods. You must perform some kind of authentication to make sure that the user who is attempting to download a file is authorized to do so, so you cannot just give the users direct access to the file via a URL such as `http://your_host/downloads/file.zip`. This would either give all the users indiscriminate access to the file or create a security nightmare if you tried to manage the access list dynamically. Instead, you could write a simple ASP script, similar to the example above but with some authentication checking functionality, that would only output the file if the user is authorized to download it.

The ReadFromFile Method

This function is very similar to ReadFromBinaryFile, although it returns the contents of a file as a text string. Therefore, it cannot be used to read binary files, and its functionality is somehow redundant, since the same effect can be obtained by using the Scripting.FileSystemObject component that ships with ASP.

```
AdminFile.ReadFromFile (sFilename)
```

Where sFilename is the complete pathname of the file.

It's obvious, however, that it is much easier to use ReadFromFile (with just one call), than to create an instance of FileSystemObject, than open a text file, read the file's contents and then close the file. The functionality provided by ReadFromFile is used by the Trey Research sample store when delivering online content.

The AdminWebServer Component

While AdminFile is more of a "server-side access" component, Commerce.AdminWebServer can be used to access a few specific parameters relating to the configuration of Internet Information Server. Although IIS already provides a set of ASP components that can be used to fully administer a web server, AdminWebServer has been designed with an eye to the specific needs of MSCS.

> For more information about the IIS configuration objects, visit MSDN online at http://msdn.microsoft.com.

AdminWebServer has three methods, GetWebSites, GetWebSiteProperties and GetCommerceSites.

The GetWebSites Method

The GetWebSites method can be used to enumerate all the instances of IIS (web sites) that are available on the server. It has no parameters.

```
AdminWebServer.GetWebSites()
```

The result of a call to GetWebSites is an array of numbers that contains an entry for each instance of IIS installed on the computer. These numbers can be used as parameters to several functions, such as GetWebSiteProperties and other methods belonging to the AdminSite component, as we shall see a little further on.

> The default web site's instance number is 1.

To retrieve the dimension and lower bound of the array, you can use VBScript's Lbound and Ubound functions as in the following example.

```
<%
    ' Dim some variables
    Dim awsAdminObject
    Dim nIISInstances
    Dim i

    ' Create instance of AdminWebServer
    Set awsAdminObject = Server.CreateObject ("Commerce.AdminWebServer")

    ' Retrieve array of IIS instances
    nIISInstances = awsAdminObject.GetWebSites

    ' Output instances
    For i = LBound (nIISInstances) to UBound (nIISInstances)
        Response.Write nIISInstances (i) & "<br>"
    Next

    ' Destroy objects

    Set awsAdminObject = Nothing
%>
```

The GetWebSiteProperties Method

The GetWebSiteProperties method is used to retrieve several of the properties of an IIS instance when its number is known:

```
AdminWebServer.GetWebSiteProperties (iInstance)
```

Where iInstance is the number of the IIS instance whose properties have to be retrieved.

The result of GetWebSiteProperties is a Dictionary object. As with all Dictionary objects you can access its members by name:

```
Set dProperties = AdminWebServer.GetWebSiteProperties (1)

' This prints the virtual root's path of the IIS instance
Response.Write dProperties ("VrPath")
```

If you try to call the GetWebSiteProperties method from a web site with anonymous access, you will get the following message.

Commerce.AdminWebServer.1 error '80070005'

Access is denied.

This happens because, if you are logged in as the IIS anonymous user (by default called IIS_USR*MachineName*, where *MachineName* is your server's NetBIOS name), you do not have access to the configuration parameters for IIS. If you think about it, this is an obvious security feature, but it tends to take you by surprise when you are trying to make your script work. If you really want to use GetWebSiteProperties, you should do it from a web site or virtual directory where you can login as a member of the administrative group for IIS.

The GetCommerceSites Method

As we have seen, the creation of a new e-commerce site only requires a reserved virtual directory on a specific instance of IIS. Thus, each IIS web site can contain any number of MSCS stores. The `GetCommerceSites` method provides a way to enumerate all the MSCS stores that are installed in a specific instance of IIS.

```
AdminWebServer.GetCommerceSites (iInstance)
```

Where `iInstance` is the number of the IIS instance for which the installed MSCS stores must be retrieved.

The value of `iInstance` can be retrieved using `GetWebSites`. The `GetCommerceSites` method is similar to that function and returns an array that contains all the MSCS sites installed on the IIS instance specified.

The AdminSite Component

While `AdminFile` is more of a "server-side access" component, `Commerce.AdminSite` can be used to access the configuration of an MSCS site. Because it can be used for a variety of purposes, including creating and deleting e-commerce sites, it is a powerful tool, particularly if you want to develop your own site creation tools. For example, if you are an ISP reselling MSCS-based hosting to your clients, then you will not want to give them access to all the functionality provided by the administration system that is provided by MSCS, although you can develop a simpler set of functions whose scope is limited to what you want the clients to be able to do.

Using the AdminSite Component

There are three uses for the `AdminSite` component. You can use it to create a new IIS site or MSCS store, with the `Create` method. You can delete a site using the `Delete` method, and finally you can also use it to access an existing site and to access or modify its properties.

This third use requires that you initialize an instance of `AdminSite`, with the `Initialize` or `InitializeFromMDPath` methods. You can then edit the properties of the site that it represents in a three-step process. You use the `ReadDefaultProperties` or `ReadManagerProperties` methods to read the site's properties. You can then modify them by accessing their values through the `Dictionary` object and save your changes using `WriteDefaultProperties` or `WriteManagerProperties`.

Let's look at all of these methods in a bit more detail.

The Create Method

In Chapter15, we saw that we need to use either the MMC or the online administration tool to create a new store foundation. However, you can also create a new store programmatically through the `Create` method of the `AdminSite` component.

```
AdminSite.Create (iServerInstance, sVirtualDirectory, sPhysicalPath,
              bIsApplication, bIsCommerceSite)
```

Where:

> ➤   iServerInstance is the number of the IIS instance for which the installed MSCS stores must be retrieved.

> ➤   sVirtualDirectory is the name of the virtual directory where you want the site installed. Also the short name of the store.

> ➤   sPhysicalPath is the physical path where you want the store to be created.

> ➤   bIsApplication is True if an IIS application should be created, and otherwise False.

> ➤   bIsCommerceSite is True if the directory support for an MSCS store should be created and if the site should be marked for administration through MSCS. False otherwise.

In general, you wouldn't need to use this function in your own scripts unless you are writing your own version of the Store Foundation Wizard.

The value of iServerInstance can be retrieved using the GetWebSites method of the AdminWebSite component. You can also specify 1 for the default website. The value of bIsApplication should be True when you want to use ASP within the site you are creating, and this *definitely* includes MSCS stores!

It is important to understand that Create does *not* perform the same functions as the Store Builder wizard, but it rather provides the basic tool for creating a store foundation that will have to be populated appropriately. If you set bIsCommerceSite to True, Create will create the /Config folder and its subfolders.

The Initialize Method

As mentioned above, we need to initialize an instance of AdminSite before we can use it to retrieve a store's configuration parameters. This will cause the object to connect to a particular instance of IIS so that we can access its properties. We have a choice of two methods to initialize our AdminSite instance. The InitializefromMDPath method allows us to use a Metabase path (we'll look at this next). The Initialize method below on the other hand requires an IIS instance number.

```
AdminSite.Initialize (iInstance, sVirtualDirectory)
```

Where:

> ➤   iInstance is the number of the IIS instance to be referenced by the object.

> ➤   sVirtualDirectory is the virtual directory (store) to be referenced by the object.

Initialize is, typically, the first call that should be made when using the AdminSite component. You should always make sure that you have administrative privileges when accessing a site's properties. (We discussed how to do this while we were looking at the AdminWebSite component.) Otherwise, you will be denied access to the IIS information Metabase.

The InitializeFromMDPath Method

You can also initialize an instance of `AdminSite` with the `InitializeFromMDPath` method, which uses a Metabase path to create a reference to a site that can then be used by the functions of `AdminSite`.

A Metabase path for an IIS site has the following format.

*/machine/*W3SVC*/instance/*virtual*folder*

where *machine* is the server's NetBIOS name, *instance* is the IIS site's instance number and *folder* is the virtual directory where the MSCS store is.

```
AdminSite.InitializeFromMDPath (sMetabasePath)
```

Where `sMetabasePath` is the IIS Metabase path to be used for referencing an MSCS site.

The obvious advantage of `InitializeFromMDPath` when compared to `Initialize` is that you are able to specify the machine where you want to read the information. However, you can only access MSCS sites that are at the virtual directory level (as opposed to a sub-directory).

> **You can use the value `"LM"` to indicate that the server you want to connect to is your local machine.**

The Delete Method

Once you have initialized an instance of `AdminSite` with a reference to a specific web site, you can use the `Delete` method to remove the web site from the IIS metabase. This method has no parameters:

```
AdminSite.Delete()
```

Always remember that `Delete` only removes the IIS metabase entries (the information that is stored inside the IIS's own registry) – it doesn't delete the site's files and folders.

The ReadDefaultProperties Method

When you have initialized an instance of `AdminSite` to reference the site of your choice, you will want to access its properties. This can be done using the `ReadDefaultProperties` method. This method has no parameters.

```
AdminSite.ReadDefaultProperties()
```

`ReadDefaultProperties` returns a `Commerce.Dictionary` object. This dictionary is a particular collection of data, known as the **Site Dictionary**, which contains relevant information about an MSCS site. This information is stored in and retrieved from the `/config/site.csc` file (using a method of the `FileDocument` component that we saw in Chapter 16).

The Site Dictionary contains a number of name/value pairs that can be used to change several settings of the store.

CloseRedirectURL	The URL where the user is redirected when the store is closed.
ConnectionStringMap	A Dictionary object that contains all the ADO/ODBC connection strings available to the site.
DefaultConnectionString	The default connection string used by the site.
DisableHTTPS	0 if the pages that are marked as secure on the site should be called using the https:// URL prefix. 1 if those pages should be called using a standard http:// prefix. Extremely useful for testing purposes. See the Page object in Chapter 16 for more information.
DisplayName	The long name of the store, which is displayed prominently in several locations, including the Store Manager.
NonsecureHostName	The name of the host that should be used when building non-secure URLs. (See the Page component and the PageURL and PageSURL methods below).
SecureHostName	The name of the host that should be used when building secure URLs.
Status	The current status of the store. Can assume the values, "Open", "Closed" and "Invalid".

The WriteDefaultProperties Method

This method saves changes to the configuration data stored in the Site Dictionary back to the site.csc file.

```
AdminSite.WriteDefaultProperties(dSiteDictionary)
```

Where dSiteDictionary is a variable that contains the Site Dictionary for the site to which the instance of AdminSite points.

Using ReadDefaultProperties and WriteDefaultProperties

ReadDefaultProperties and WriteDefaultProperties are an easy combination of functions to use. All you have to do is to create an AdminSite object, reference it to an existing MSCS site or create a new one, and call ReadDefaultProperties to retrieve the Site Dictionary. When you have made your changes, you simply write the dictionary back to the site.csc file using WriteDefaultProperties.

In this example, a store's Site Dictionary is loaded and its contents dumped to the output of a file. The store's Display Name is then changed, and the Site Dictionary is saved back to disk using `WriteDefaultProperties`.

```
<%@ Language=VBScript %>
<HTML>
<HEAD>
<META NAME="GENERATOR" Content="Microsoft Visual Studio 6.0">
</HEAD>
<BODY>

<%
    ' Create and intialize an instance of AdminSite

    set asAdminSite = Server.CreateObject ("Commerce.AdminSite")
    asAdminSite.Initialize 1, "ClockTower"

    ' Load the site dictionary

    set dSiteDictionary = asAdminSite.ReadDefaultProperties

    ' Dump all the properties

    For Each Property in dSiteDictionary
            If Not IsObject (dSiteDictionary (Property)) Then
                    Response.Write Property & " = " & dSiteDictionary (Property) & _
                    "<br>"
            Else
%>
                    <table>
                        <tr>
                            <td>
                             <% = Property %> =
                            </td>
                            <td>
<%
                                    For Each SubProperty in dSiteDictionary (Property)
                                            Response.Write (SubProperty) & "<br>"
                                    Next
%>
                            </td>
                        </tr>
                    </table>
<%
            End If
    Next

    ' Change the display name of the store

    dSiteDictionary ("DisplayName") = "The New ClockTower!"

    ' Save the modified Site Dictionary

    asAdminSite.WriteDefaultProperties (dSiteDictionary)

    ' Unreference all objects

    set dSiteDictionary = Nothing
    set asAdminSite = Nothing
%>

</BODY>
</HTML>
```

The For Each ... Next loop dumps all the properties that are included in the Dictionary object. As you can see, there is a condition before printing out the value of the property that checks whether the property itself is an object. As we have seen, the Dictionary object can also contain other objects and we cannot print out these objects directly, because this would generate a VBScript error.

Here, we are just assuming that if we find an object, then it is going to be a collection of some kind, and therefore we attempt to iterate through its properties. It is important to understand that we are making this assumption because we know that normally the only object that we'll find is a ConnectionStringMap, and *that* is a Dictionary object. This assumption might not always be correct, however, and therefore we must be very careful as to how we handle Dictionary objects.

Once you have run the this script you can go to the Clocktower Store Manager (assuming that Clocktower is installed in the /ClockTower virtual directory of the default IIS site) to see that it has indeed altered the Display Name for the store:

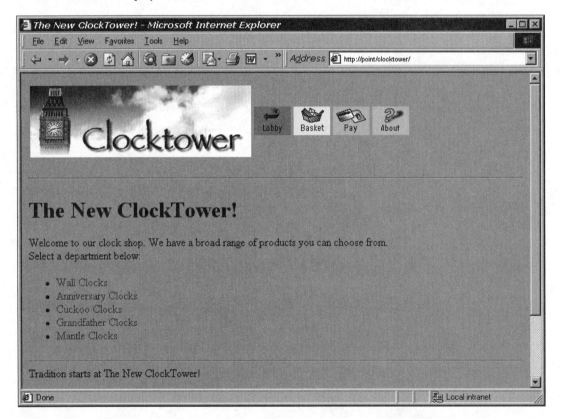

The ReadManagerProperties and WriteManagerProperties Methods

Similarly to the Site Dictionary, which is stored in the storefront, the manager has its own configuration file, which is stored in the /manager/config/site.csc file. This configuration file only contains the DefaultConnectionString and ConnectionStringMap properties. It can be accessed by using the ReadManagerProperties and WriteManagerProperties methods. The ReadManagerProperties method has no parameters:

```
AdminSite.ReadManagerProperties()
```

Like `ReadDefaultProperties`, the `ReadManagerProperties` method returns a `Dictionary` object that contains all the configuration parameters. You can make changes to this `Dictionary` object, and store the changes with the `WriteManagerProperties` method:

```
AdminSite.WriteManagerProperties (dDictionary)
```

Where `dDictionary` is the `Dictionary` object containing all the parameters to be stored in the configuration file.

The Status Property

The `Status` property is used to open and close an MSCS store and to find out whether it is open through an instance of the `AdminSite` component. It has no parameters.

```
Public Property AdminSite.Status
```

The `Status` property accepts and returns Boolean values, indicating whether the store referenced by the `AdminSite` object is open (`True`) or closed (`False`). Assigning a value to this property causes the store to be opened or closed, and the value of the status parameter in the Site Dictionary to be set accordingly.

Keep in mind that whenever you change the value of `Status`, MSCS has to change a few files in your store. If you don't have enough permissions to access those files (or if the files are marked as read-only), you might not be able to open or close a store.

The Version Property

As we have mentioned, probably more than once, MSCS is also able to handle stores that have been created using Version 2.0 of the software. Although we do not explore that possibility in this book, it *is* a possibility, so being able to distinguish between stores created using Versions 2 and 3 may be useful. This can be done through the `Version` property. It has no parameters.

```
Public Property AdminSite.Version
```

The `Version` property returns the integer value, 2, if the store referenced by the `AdminSite` object has been created using the previous version of MSCS. It returns 3 otherwise.

The Directory Property

This property can be used to determine the physical path where the currently selected MSCS site is stored. You can use this value, for example, in a function that automatically generates links to files in the store. This property has no parameters.

```
Public Property AdminSite.Directory
```

The return value here is a string that contains the fully qualified path to the folder where the site is stored. Because IIS supports UNC paths, this may involve non-local paths (in the `\\machine\folder\` format).

953

The IsValidName Method

At times, you might want to know whether a certain store really exists in an instance of IIS. This can be done using the `IsValidName` method.

```
AdminSite.IsValidName (sSiteName, iInstance)
```

Where:

> ➤ `sSiteName` is the short name (or virtual directory name) of the MSCS store whose existence has to be verified.

> ➤ `iInstance` is the numeric instance of IIS where the MSCS site is expected to be found.

`IsValidName` returns a Boolean value – `True` if the parameters passed match an existing store and `False` otherwise.

Summary

As you have seen, MSCS offers functionality that would otherwise be very time-consuming. In the next chapter, we will take a look at the pipeline technology, how it works and how we can use it inside our stores. When we'll have acquired that knowledge, we'll be ready to examine the structure of an online store from a code perspective.

D

ADSI for the Membership Directory

Site Server as a product provides a number of interfaces and wizards through which to administer and configure your site. It is possible to set up and use a Site Server site without having to delve into the code behind the scenes, in fact the strength of Site Server is that you don't have to code your own web solution from scratch. However, as we have seen throughout this book, there are a number of occasions when you will want to directly manage the code behind the scenes.

One of the situations in which you'll most commonly want to write your own code is managing the Membership Directory. While you can manage and view objects in the Membership Directory through the Membership Directory Manager, in the MMC, this can be a time-consuming process. The Membership Directory Manager is oriented around individual tasks – adding one member is simple, but if you want to add a thousand members you will probably want to write a script to do this for you. To accessing the Membership Directory through code you need to use Active Directory Service Interfaces or ADSI.

There are upwards of fifty Active Directory Service Interfaces. Only five of these however are supported by the Membership Directory, and therefore relevant to Site Server. This appendix provides definitions for these five interfaces. All the properties and methods listed are those supported by the ADSI LDAP provider, as this is the provider through which we access the Membership Directory.

You can find full documentation for ADSI on the Microsoft web site, in the MSDN online library at http://msdn.microsoft.com/library/. Select and expand Platform SDK | Networking Services | Active Directory | Active Directory Service Interfaces.

Active Directory Service Interfaces

ADSI is built on the COM object model. All the properties and methods of an object that can be accessed using ADSI are implemented by one of a number of underlying COM interfaces.

The Membership Directory supports the following ADSI interfaces:

> IADs

> IADsContainer

> IADsClass

> IADsProperty

> IADsOpenDSObject

The first two of these can be described as general-purpose interfaces. As in any directory structure, objects in the Membership Directory are either container objects or leaf objects. All objects support the IADs interface, which allows you to manage the object's properties and retrieve the object's parent and schema objects. ADSI container objects also support the IADsContainer interface, which allows enumeration, creation and deletion of objects in a container.

The next two interfaces, IADsClass and IADsProperty, are schema management interfaces. They provide methods to manage classes and attributes, such as defining the range of values for an attribute.

Finally the IADsOpenDSObject interface is used to bind securely to the Membership Directory.

The following interface definitions are for ADSI 2.5.

> **Note that there are some compatibility issues with MDAC 2.1, ADSI 2.0 and ADSI 2.5.**

There are some known problems with Site Server if Microsoft Data Access Components (MDAC) 2.1 and ADSI 2.0 are both installed on the same machine as Site Server. MDAC 2.1 is installed automatically as part of the SQL Server 7.0 install, and Site Server uses ADSI 2.0, so if you install SQL Server 7.0 and Site Server on the same machine you will experience some problems.

You can resolve this issue by upgrading to ADSI 2.5 – you can download it from
http://www.microsoft.com/Windows/server/Technical/directory/adsilinks.asp

However be aware that with ADSI 2.5 you may also need to work around a problem with creating new Membership Servers. You can find full details in the following article from the Microsoft Knowledge Base:

http://support.microsoft.com/support/kb/articles/Q216/7/09.asp

The General Purpose Interfaces

IADs – All ADSI objects require this interface.

Method	Description
Name	Gets the relative name of the object, returned as a String.
AdsPath	Gets the ADsPath of the object.
Class	Gets the schema class of this object, returned as a String.
GUID	Gets a unique identifier for this member. Returned as a String.
Parent	Gets the ADsPath of the object's parent.
Schema	Gets the ADsPath of the object that represents this object's schema class in the schema.

The methods listed above can all be described as property methods, in that they return a specific property for the object. They are all used in the same manner: first we need bind to the Membership Directory, and then use the bound object to call the method. In the code snippet below we create an instance of the AUO and then retrieve the `Parent` property for that member object:

```
Set objAUO = Server.CreateObject("Membership.UserObjects.1")
Response.Write objAUO.Parent
```

In addition to these property methods, IADs also supports the following six methods:

Method	Parameters	Description
GetInfo	None	Reloads the object cache with all the property values.
SetInfo	None	Commits property values from cache to the directory service.
Get	Property_Name (String)	Retrieves the value of the named property. Property value is returned as a variant.
Put	Property_Name (String) Property_Value (Variant)	Sets the named property to the value specified.
GetEx	Property_Name (String)	Retrieves value(s) for a single or multi-valued named property.

Table Continued on Following Page

Method	Parameters	Description
PutEx	Control_Code (Long) Property_Name (String) Property_Value (Variant)	Modifies a named single or multi-valued property, depending on the value of Control_Code: 1 removes the property from the class instance 2 sets the property to the specified value 3 appends the specified value to the (multi-valued) property
GetExInfo	Property_Array (Variant) Reserved_Parameter (Long)	Reloads the object cache with the values for the properties in the specified array of Strings (as opposed to GetInfo, which reloads the object cache with the values of ALL properties). The second parameter is reserved and must be 0.

IADsContainer – All container objects in the Membership Directory implement this interface.

Method	Description
Filter	Gets / Sets the filter on an object class. The filter describes which object classes will be returned during an enumeration.
Hints	Indicates which properties should be loaded.
GetObject	Returns the IADs interface of the item in the container that is identified by the object's name and class.
Create	Creates an object of the class specified, with the name specified. Note that the object is not created in the directory service until a SetInfo is called on the new object.
Delete	Deletes the object specified.
CopyHere	Creates a new object in this container identical to the specified object. Objects may not copy across namespaces.
MoveHere	Moves an object to this container. Same as copy except the source is removed.

Note: GetInfo/SetInfo affects the properties of the container object, not the properties of objects in the container.

The Schema Management Interfaces

IADsClass – defines a class of objects that can be created in the namespace.

Method	Description
CLSID	Gets/Sets a class ID.
OID	Gets/Sets the Object ID defining their class.
Abstract	Gets/Sets VARIANT_BOOL indicating whether this class is abstract (can only be used as a parent class).
Auxiliary	Gets/Sets VARIANT_BOOL indicating if this class is auxiliary (a source of extra properties for another class).
MandatoryProperties	Gets/Sets an array of Strings listing the properties that must be set for this class.
OptionalProperties	Gets/Sets an array of Strings listing the additional properties that may be set for this class.
NamingProperties	Gets/Sets an array of Strings listing the properties that provide for the Relative Distinguished Name (such as o, ou and cn in the Membership Directory).
PrimaryInterface	Gets/Sets the Interface ID for objects of this class.
DerivedFrom	Gets an array of String names of the immediate parent classes of this class.
AuxDerivedFrom	Gets an array of String names of the auxiliary classes contributing to this class (see Auxiliary above).
PossibleSuperiors	Gets/Sets an array of String names of classes that can contain an instance of this class.
Containment	Gets the object types that can be contained within this container.
Container	Gets a Boolean value that indicates whether this is a container.
HelpFileName	Gets/Sets the name of the Help File containing further information about objects of this class.
HelpFileContext	Gets/Sets a context ID within the Help File specified in HelpFileName, above. The context ID can be used to locate information on this class within the Help File.

IADsProperty – describes class properties.

Method	Description
OID	Gets/Sets the object identifier for this property.
Syntax	Relative path of the schema syntax object.
MaxRange	Gets/Sets the upper limit of values assigned to this property.
MinRange	Gets/Sets the lower limit of values assigned to this property.
Multivalued	Gets/Sets a Boolean value specifying whether or not this is a property that supports multiple values.

The IADsOpenDSObject Interface

The IADsOpenDSObject interface allows you to specify security credentials when binding to an object, as the OpenDSObject method requires a username and password.

Method	Description
OpenDSObject	Binds to an object. Requires four parameters: the ADsPath to the object, the username to provide the security context, the password for the username, and a parameter specifying the type of bind.

The fourth parameter for this method, specifying the type of bind to be performed, is an enum value, ADS_AUTHENTICATION_ENUM. This enum can have one of the values listed below. You can use an integer value for this parameter, but it is better practice to define and use one of the following constants:

Constant	Value
ADS_SECURE_AUTHENTICATION	0x1
ADS_USE_ENCRYPTION	0x2
ADS_USE_SSL	0x2
ADS_READONLY_SERVER	0x4
ADS_PROMPT_CREDENTIALS	0x8
ADS_NO_AUTHENTICATION	0x10
ADS_FAST_BIND	0x20
ADS_USE_SIGNING	0x40
ADS_USE_SEALING	0x80

Further Site Server Objects

This appendix presents a quick reference to the objects provided with the Content, Search and P&M areas of Site Server 3.0. (For those Commerce components not discussed in the book, please refer to Appendix C). We won't be listing the syntax for every method and property, as this is available in the Site Server documentation; instead this appendix will show the range of objects available for development with Site Server, and for each one, describe how it can be used.

Content Deployment

The content deployment objects provide a set of functionality to programmatically manage replication of files across directories or servers. The following diagram provides an overview of the content deployment objects:

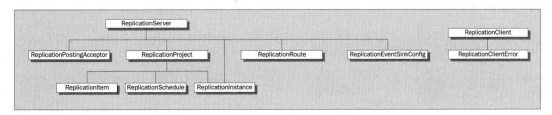

The ProgId for creating instances of content deployment objects takes the form CrsApi.ObjectName. The ReplicationServer and ReplicationClient objects are created with the CreateObject() method:

```
dim objReplicationServer
set objReplicationServer = CreateObject("CrsApi.ReplicationServer")
```

The remaining content deployment objects can then be created from either of these objects, as shown on the object model diagram.

The content deployment objects and documentation can be found in the Site Server SDK.

A content deployment project (a `ReplicationProject` object) has information about what files are to be replicated (`ReplicationItem` objects) and when any automatic replication is scheduled (`ReplicationSchedule` objects). Replication can take place over a specified route of servers (managed through `ReplicationRoute` objects), and specific parameters can then be set on destination servers with the `ReplicationPostingAcceptor` object. All objects are listed in the table below.

Object	Description
ReplicationServer	The `ReplicationServer` object enables you to manage aspects of the Content Deployment service. Through this object you can (among other things) add, delete, list etc aspects such as event sinks, routes, projects (however adding a project has to be done through the `ReplicationProject` object). You can also stop and start the Content Deployment server, check the access permissions of the current user, or get/set/list the parameters of the content deployment service.
ReplicationRoute	The `ReplicationRoute` object's main function is to manage destinations for the route, although it also allows you to view and set the base directory where the route is stored.
ReplicationProject	The `ReplicationProject` object enables you to manage projects; for instance open an existing project or create a new one (both with the `OpenProject` method), apply or rollback a replication transaction, and grant or remove a user's access to the project.
ReplicationSchedule	The `ReplicationSchedule` object has a number of properties that specify when the schedule is to run, and methods to either commit changes to the schedule or remove the schedule from the project.
ReplicationInstance	The `ReplicationInstance` object provides information about a replication, such as the number of files and bytes sent and received. It also enables you to cancel a current replication.

Object	Description
ReplicationItem	The ReplicationItem object represents a file or directory to be replicated, and enables you to read file attributes such as file type, size and time of last modification.
ReplicationPostingAcceptor	The ReplicationPostingAcceptor object has a number of read/write parameters specifying posting details, such as the source and destination URLs and the maximum number of concurrent transactions.
ReplicationEventSinkConfig	This object enables you to administer an event sink, for example specifying the event to listen for.
ReplicationClient	The ReplicationClient object allows you to run a replication of individual files, without the Content Deployment server.
ReplicationClientError	Any errors produced by the ReplicationClient object can be retrieved through its GetExtendedErrorInfo method, returning an array of ReplicationClientError objects, which can be queried for extra information about the error.

Search

To program with Site Server Search you can use the objects supplied with the Site Server SDK and Site Server Search.

The following two objects are included with Site Server Search:

Object	Description
Query	The Query object has a number of properties that specify aspects of a search query, such as the catalogs to be searched and how the results are to be sorted. The search query itself is specified in the object's Query property. To create this object use MSSearch.Query. (Note that you will get an error if you try and create the Query object under an application that does not have session state enabled).
Utility	The Utility object supplies five methods to handle displaying the results of a search query, such as truncating strings at the next whitespace character. To create this object use MSSearch.Util.

For more information on these objects see the Site Server documentation.

The Search objects in the SDK provide a set of functionality to programmatically manage building catalogs of indexed content. The following diagram provides an overview of the Search objects:

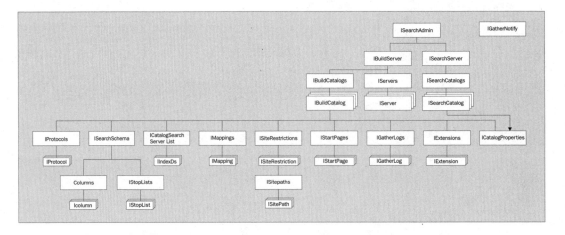

Object	Description
IBuildCatalogs/ IBuildCatalog	IBuildCatalogs maintains a collection of IBuildCatalog objects. IBuildCatalog has properties to specify a catalog definition and methods to implement catalog builds or propagation.
IBuildServer	IBuildServer manages settings for the server running the catalog build, such as the account to use when crawling sites and the amount of resources to allocate.
ICatalogProperties	ICatalogProperties specifies the properties of a catalog, such as its size (in MB) and when it was built.
ICatalogSearch ServerList	ICatalogSearchServerList is associated with an IBuildCatalog object, and maintains a collection of search servers to which that catalog will be propagated.
IColumns/IColumn	IColumns maintains a collection of IColumn objects. IColumn describes which columns will be indexed or retrieved.
IExtensions/IExtension	IExtensions maintains a collection of IExtension objects, which have a single property specifying a file type extension for Search to crawl or avoid.
IGatherLogs/IGatherLog	IGatherLogs maintains a collection of IGatherLog objects, which each represent a log containing crawl details from a catalog build.
IGatherNotify	IGatherNotify is used when a catalog has a project type of Notification, to notify Search when a document in the catalog has changed (so a build can be performed to update the catalog). It is created using CreateObject("GatherSvc.GatherNotify").
IIndexDs	IIndexDs represents a host to which a catalog will be propagated. A collection of IIndexDs objects is maintained by ICatalogSearchServerList.
IMappings/IMapping	IMappings maintains a collection of IMapping objects, which specify a mapping of the physical location of a file (where it is crawled) on to a display location (such as a URL).
IProtocols/IProtocol	IProtocols maintains a collection of IProtocol objects, whose properties specify a handler for a protocol and whether that protocol should be included in a search.
ISearchAdmin	This object represents Search on a particular host, and provides properties to retrieve the name of the host, and the IBuildServer and ISearchServer objects for that host. It is created using Server.CreateObject("Search.SearchAdmin").

Table Continued on Following Page

Object	Description
ISearchCatalogs/ ISearchCatalog	ISearchCatalog maintains a collection of ISearchCatalog objects, each of which represents a catalog for Search to search.
ISearchSchema	ISearchSchema specifies what properties of a document Search will retrieve or index, based on the IColumns object specified through its Columns property. The Stoplists property also allows you to specify words for Search to ignore.
ISearchServer	This object provides properties to define where the catalogs should be located, which should be the default catalog, and the level of resources to be devoted to searching. Through this object you can also access the list of available catalogs and thus their properties.
IServers/IServer	IServers maintains a collection of IServer objects, which through their hitInterval property, specify the rate at which Search requests documents from the site (in seconds).
ISitePaths/ISitePath	ISitePaths maintains a collection of ISitePath objects, which specify a path within a site and whether it (and any sub-directories) should be crawled.
ISiteRestrictions/ ISiteRestriction	ISiteRestriction maintains a collection of ISiteRestriction objects, each of whose properties specify the name of a site, whether that site is to be crawled, and if so, what type of authentication and what user account to use.
IStartPages/IStartPage	IStartPages maintains a collection of IStartPage objects, which define a page (in their URL properties) for Search to start crawling a site. There are also properties to specify the extent of the search on that site, in terms of hops and links to follow.
IStopLists/IStopList	IStopLists maintains a collection of IStopList objects, which specify a file (in their Filename properties) containing a list of words to ignore in a catalog build.

For more information on these objects see the Site Server SDK documentation.

Personalization and Membership

In addition to managing the Membership Directory through ADSI, as we saw in Appendix D, the Personalization and Membership section of the Site Server SDK provides a number of objects to programmatically administer the Personalization and Membership system. We can divide these into two groups:

> ➤ Membership objects
> ➤ Administrative objects

The following tables deal with each of these groups in turn.

Membership Objects

The most important P&M object is the AUO (we looked in detail at the AUO in Chapter 10). The AUO is used with sites that are using Membership authentication, to handle user properties from the various ADs providers for Site Server. It is most commonly used to handle members stored in the Membership Directory.

The AUO actually provides three interfaces; IADs and IADsContainer that we saw in the previous appendix, and IUserObjects, described below. To create an instance of the AUO, you create a UserObjects instance:

```
Set objAUO = Server.CreateObject("Membership.UserObjects")
```

We've specified the ASP Server.CreateObject method to create objects in an ASP page, so that the object is initialized with the correct context. You might not want this for an instance of the AUO if, for example, you want to initialize it with the context of a user other than then user running the page, for some specific Membership Directory task. In this case you can create the instance with a simple CreateObject call.

All Membership objects are listed in the following table.

Object	Description
UserObjects	Create with Server.CreateObject("Membership.UserObjects"). Used to manage information about individual users, eg setting the user name, or binding to an ADSI object as a particular user. Also exposes the IADs and IADsContainer interfaces.
SchemaObjects	Create with Server.CreateObject("Membership.SchemaObjects"). Allows you to bind to the ADSI objects defining the user schemas.
AuoConfig	Provides AUO configuration information, stored on the Membership Server. Used by UserObjects to put together an AUO instance. Create an instance of this object using the COM ObjCreator object, as described below for the Administrative objects. The progid for this object is MemAdmin.AuoConfig.
VerifUsr	Manages Membership Server-related cookies and certificates, including methods for issuing cookies and verifying credentials. Create with Server.CreateObject("Membership.VerifUsr")
GuidGen	Create with Server.CreateObject("Membership.GuidGen"). Used to generate a GUID for an object.

The Administrative Objects

All these objects can be created with a simple `CreateObject()` call. However this will only give you read access to the objects, for all the objects listed below except the `LdapCfg` object. For this reason you should create all the Administrative objects (except `LdapCfg`) with the COM object `ObjCreator` as shown:

```
Set objCreator = CreateObject("ObjCreator.ObjCreator ")
Set objBrokServers = ObjCreator.CreateObjAuth("MemAdmin.BrokServers")
```

The following table lists the Administrative objects for P&M:

Object	Description
BrokServers	Create an instance of this object with `MemAdmin.BrokServers`. Manages the Membership Authentication service, such as mapping to a website, and setting the authentication type. Also handles creating and deleting or stopping and starting servers, and testing a user's permissions.
BrokConfig	Create an instance of this object with `MemAdmin.BrokConfig`. Gets and changes configuration of a particular Membership Authentication service – properties include specifying whether to map NT groups to Membership groups.
LdapCfg	Create an instance of this object with `MemAdmin.LDAPConfig`. Manages and configures LDAP Server instance, including properties specifying the backend database for the LDAP server.
TMAdmin	Create an instance of this object with `MemAdmin.TMAdmin`. Manages and configures Direct Mail server instances.
SetupStore	Create an instance of this object with `MemAdmin.DSConfig`. Manages backend databases (SQL Server or Access) for an LDAP server. Provides methods for functions such as creating the table structure in a database which is necessary for an LDAP directory.

Site Server Counters

In Chapter 4 we discussed how to use Performance Monitor to read performance counters, for purposes such as logging and issuing alerts. The Site Server installation includes a large number of Site Server-specific performance counters. These counters can be used to measure the activity levels of a variety of Site Server services.

This appendix lists all the Site Server performance counters, and provides a description for each one of what it can be used to monitor. The Site Server counters can be divided into the following categories:

- ➤ Authentication Service counters
- ➤ Content Deployment counters
- ➤ Search Gatherer counters
- ➤ Search Gatherer project counters
- ➤ Search Indexer counters
- ➤ LDAP Service counters
- ➤ Message Builder service counters
- ➤ Search counters
- ➤ Search Catalog counters

We'll list the counters for each category in turn.

Site Server Authentication Service Counters

Counter	Description
Logon Operation Successes	Number of successful logon operations.
Logon Operation Failures	Number of failed logon operations.
Logon Operation Successes	Number of successful logon operations per second.
Logon Operation Failures	Number of failed logon operations per second.
Clear Text/Basic Auth Successes	Number of successful Clear Text/Basic Authentication logon operations.
Clear Text/Basic Auth Failures	Number of failed Clear Text/Basic Authentication logon operations.
DPA Auth Successes	Number of successful DPA Authentication logon operations.
DPA Auth Failures	Number of failed DPA Authentication logon operations.
HTML Forms Auth Successes	Number of successful HTML Forms Authentication logon operations.
HTML Forms Auth Failures	Number of failed HTML Forms Authentication logon operations.
Automatic Cookie Auth Successes	Number of successful Automatic Cookie Authentication logon operations.
Automatic Cookie Auth Failures	Number of failed Automatic Cookie Authentication logon operations.
Membership Directory Connections Succeeded	Number of times a password has been accepted and the Authentication Service has established a connection to the Membership Directory.
Membership Directory Connections Failed	Number of connection attempts the Authentication Service has made to the Membership Directory where the password is not accepted, or the connection is dropped before a password is provided. It may indicate there is no problem with the connectivity between the Authentication Service and the Membership Directory.
Membership Directory Connections Dropped	Number of times the Authentication Service connection to the Membership Directory has dropped for any reason.
Requests Served from Cache	Number of Membership Authentication requests that have been served from the cache of the Authentication Service.
Requests Sent to the Membership Directory	Number of authentication requests that resulted in a request being sent to the Membership Directory.
Connections Attempted by Denied Users	Number of connections attempted by denied users.

Counter	Description
Clear Text/Basic Auth Success	Number of successful Clear Text/Basic Authentication logon operations per second.
Clear Text/Basic Auth Failures Per Second	Total number of failed Clear Text/Basic Authentication logon operations.
Certificate Auth Successes	Number of Client Certificate Authentication successes per second.
Certificate Auth Failures	Number of Client Certificate Authentication failures per second.
Certificate Auth Successes	Number of successful Client Certificate Authentication logon operations.
Certificate Auth Failures	Number of failed Client Certificate Autentication logon operations.
HTML Forms Auth Successes	Number of successful HTML Forms Authentication logon operations per second.
HTML Forms Auth Failures	Number of failed HTML Forms Authentication logon operations per second.
DPA Auth Successes	Number of successful DPA logon operations per second.
DPA Auth Failures	Number of failed DPA logon operations per second.
Automatic Cookie Auth Successes	Number of successful Automatic Cookie Authentication logon operations per second.
Automatic Cookie Failures	Number of failed Automatic Cookie Authentication logon operations per second.
Membership Directory Status	The current status of the connection with the Membership Directory. 1 if the Authentication Service is connected to the Membership Directory. 2 if the Authentication Service is not connected to the Membership Directory.

Site Server Content Deployment Counters

Counter	Description
Active Threads Total	The total number of currently active threads.
API Calls Total	The total number of API calls since the service started.
API Calls/sec	The number of API calls per second.
Bytes Received Total	The total number of bytes received.
Bytes Received/sec	The rate that bytes are received.
Bytes Sent Total	The total number of bytes sent.
Bytes Sent/sec	The rate that bytes are sent.

Table Continued on Following Page

Counter	Description
Bytes Total	The combination of bytes sent and bytes received.
Bytes Total/sec	The rate that bytes are sent and received.
Connections Current	The current number of incoming and outgoing socket connections.
Connections Total	The total number of incoming and outgoing socket connections which have been established since the service started.
Current Replications Total	The total number of replications currently running.
Directory Change Notifications	The number of directory change notifications since the service started.
Directory Change Notifications/sec	The number of directory change notifications per second.
Events Logged Total	The total number of events logged.
Events Logged/sec	The rate that events are logged.
Files Deleted Total	The total number of files deleted.
Files Deleted/sec	The rate that files are deleted.
Files Received Total	The total number of files received.
Files Received/sec	The rate that files are received.
Files Sent Total	The total number of files sent.
Files Sent/sec	The rate that files are sent.
Maximum Concurrent Replications	The maximum number of concurrently running replications that occurred.
MD5 Hash Calculations Total	The total number of MD5 Hash calculations.
MD5 Hash Calculations/sec	The rate that MD5 Hash calculations are made.
Privileged API Calls Total	The total number of privileged API calls since the service started.
Privileged API Calls/sec	The number of privileged API calls per second.
Retransmits	The number of retransmits since the service started.
Retransmits/sec	The number of retransmits per second.
Threads Total	The total number of threads.
Transactions Applies Total	The total number of replication transaction applications.
Transaction Applies/sec	The current Rate of replication transaction applications.
Transmits Total	The total number of transmit operations.
Transmits/sec	The rate at which transmit operations are being performed.

Site Server Search Gatherer Counters

Counter	Description
Notification Sources	Currently connected external notification sources.
Notifications Received	The total number of notifications received from all notification sources.
Notifications Rate	The rate of external notifications received per second.
Admin Clients	The number of currently connected administrative clients.
Heartbeats	The total number of heartbeats counted since startup. A heartbeat occurs once every 10 seconds while the service is running. If the service is not running there will be no heartbeat and the number of ticks will not be incremented.
Heartbeats Rate	Displays one heartbeat every 10 seconds.
Filtering Threads	The total number of filtering threads in the system.
Idle Threads	The number of threads waiting for documents.
Document Entries	The number of document entries currently in memory.
Performance Level	Indicates the amount of system resources that the Gatherer service is allowed to use.
Active Queue Length	The number of documents waiting for robot threads. If this number is not 0, all threads should be filtering.
Filter Processes	The number of filtering processes in the system.
Filter Processes Max	The maximum number of filtering processes that have existed in the system since startup.
Filter Process Created	The total number of times a filter process was created or restarted.
Delayed Documents	The number of documents delayed due to site hit frequency rules.
Server Objects	The number of servers recently accessed by the system.
Server Objects Created	The number of times a new server object had to be created.
Filter Objects	The number of filter objects in the system. Each filter object corresponds to a URL currently being filtered.
Documents Filtered	The number of times a filter object was created. Corresponds to the total number of documents filtered in the system since startup.
Documents Filtered Rate	The number of documents filtered per second.
Accessing Robots.Txt File	The number of current requests for robots.txt. Robots.txt is requested by the system implicitly, for every host, through HTTP.
Robots.Txt Requests	The total number of requests for robots.txt.

Table Continued on Following Page

Counter	Description
Timeouts	The total number of timeouts detected by the system since startup.
Servers Currently Unavailable	A server becomes unavailable when a number of requests to that server time out.
Servers Unavailable	A server becomes unavailable when a number of requests to that server time out.
Threads Accessing Network	The number of threads waiting for a response from the filter process.
Threads In Plug-ins	The number of threads waiting for plug-ins to complete an operation.
Documents Successfully Filtered	The number of documents successfully filtered.
Documents Successfully Filtered Rate	The number of successfully filtered documents per second.

Site Server Search Gatherer Project Counters

Counter	Description
Document Additions	The number of add notifications.
Document Add Rate	The number of document additions per second.
Document Deletes	The number of delete notifications.
Document Delete Rate	The number of document deletions per second.
Document Modifies	The number of modify notifications.
Document Modifies Rate	The number of modify notifications per second.
Waiting Documents	The number of documents waiting to be processed.
Documents In Progress	The number of documents in progress.
Documents On Hold	The number of documents on hold because a document with the same URL is currently in process.
Delayed Documents	The number of documents delayed due to site hit frequency rules.
URLs in History	The number of files (URLs) in the history list.
Processed Documents	The number of documents processed since the history has been reset.
Processed Documents Rate	The number of documents processed per second.
Status Success	The number of successfully filtered documents.

Counter	Description
Success Rate	The number of successfully filtered documents per second.
Status Error	The number of filtered documents which returned an error.
Error Rate	The number of filtered documents which returned an error per second.
HTTP Errors	The number of HTTP errors received.
HTTP Errors Rate	The number of HTTP errors received per second
File Errors	The number of file protocol errors received while getting documents.
File Errors Rate	The number of file protocol errors received per second.
Accessed HTTP	The number of documents accessed via HTTP.
Accessed HTTP Rate	The number of documents accessed via HTTP per second.
Accessed Files	The number of documents accessed via file system.
Accessed File Rate	The number of documents accessed via file system per second.
Filtered HTML	The number of HTML documents filtered.
Filtered HTML Rate	The number of HTML documents filtered per second.
Filtered Office	The number of office documents filtered.
Filtered Office Rate	The number of office documents filtered per second.
Filtered Text	The number of text documents filtered.
Filtered Text Rate	The number of text documents filtered per second.
Crawl In Progress Flag	The Crawl in Progress flag indicates if a crawl is currently in progress.
Gatherer Paused Flag	The Gatherer Paused flag indicates if the Gatherer has been paused.
Recovery In Progress Flag	The Recovery in Progress flag indicates if recovery is currently in progress.
Not Modified	The number of documents which were not filtered because no modification was detected since the last crawl.
Iterating History In Progress Flag	The Iterating History in Progress flag indicates if the Gatherer is currently iterating over the URL history.
Current Crawl is Incremental	This indicates if the current crawl is an incremental crawl.
Filtering Documents	The number of documents currently being filtered.
Started Documents	The number of documents initiated into the Gatherer service. This includes the number of documents on hold, in the active queue, and currently filtered.

Table Continued on Following Page

981

Counter	Description
Notifications On Hold	The number of external notifications on hold until the notification crawl is completed.
Retries	The total number of times a document access has been retried.
Retries Rate	The number of retries per second.

Site Server Search Indexer Counters

Counter	Description
Wordlists	The total number of wordlists.
Persistent Indexes	The number of persistent indexes.
Index Size (MB)	The current size of index data in megabytes.
Files To Be Filtered	The number of files waiting to be filtered and added to the catalog.
Unique Keys	The number of unique words and properties in the catalog.
Merge Progress	The percentage of merge complete for the current merge.
Documents Filtered	The number of documents filtered since the catalog was mounted.
Number of documents	The number of documents in the catalog.
Documents In Progress	The number of documents for which data is being added.
Active Documents	The number of documents currently active in Content Index.
Build In Progress	An index build is in progress.
Number Of Propagations	The number of propagations in progress.

Site Server LDAP Service Counters

Counter	Description
Bytes Sent	Total number of bytes sent.
Bytes Sent	Rate that bytes are being sent (number of bytes sent per second).
Bytes Received	Total number of bytes received.
Bytes Received	Rate that bytes are being received (number of bytes received per second).
Authentication Failure	Total number of authentication failure messages received.
Connection Attempted	Total number of attempted connections.
Connection Total	Total number of successfully completed connections.

Counter	Description
Connection Current	Number of current connections.
Connection Max	Maximum number of connections handled simultaneously.
Total Request Handled	Total number of requests handled by the LDAP Service.
Request Handled	Number of requests handled per second by the LDAP Service per second.
Pending LDAP Request	Number of LDAP requests pending.
Static Add	Total number of adds to the static records of the Membership Directory database.
Static Add per sec	Number of adds per second to the static store of the Membership Directory database per second.
Static Delete	Total number of deletes to the static store of the Membership Directory database.
Static Delete	Number of deletes per second to the static store of the Membership Directory database per second.
Static Modify	Total number of modifies to the static store of the Membership Directory database.
Static Modify	Number of modifies per second to the static store of the Membership Directory database per second.
Static Modify Distinguished Name	Total number of modifies to distinguished names in the static store of the Membership Directory database.
Static Modify DN	Number of modifies per second to the static store of the Membership Directory database per second.
Static Search	Total number of search operations to the static store of the Membership Directory database.
Static Search	Number of search operations per second to the static store of the Membership Directory database per second.
Static Compare	Total number of compare operations to the static store of the Membership Directory database.
Static Compare	Number of compare operations per second to the static store of the Membership Directory database per second.
Static Extended Request	Total number of extended requests to the static store of the Membership Directory database.
Static Extended	Number of extended requests per second to the static store of the Membership Directory database per second.
Dynamic Add	Total number of adds to the dynamic store of the Membership Directory database.

Table Continued on Following Page

Counter	Description
Dynamic Add	Number of adds per second to the dynamic store of the Membership Directory database per second.
Dynamic Delete	Total number of deletes to the dynamic store of the Membership Directory database.
Dynamic Delete	Number of deletes per second to the dynamic store of the Membership Directory database per second.
Dynamic Modify	Total number of modifies to the dynamic store of the Membership Directory database.
Dynamic Modify	Number of modifies per second to the dynamic store of the Membership Directory database per second.
Dynamic Modify DN	Total number of modifies to distinguished names in the dynamic store of the Membership Directory database.
Dynamic Modify DN	Number of modifies to distinguished names per second to the dynamic store of the Membership Directory database per second.
Dynamic Search	Total number of search operations to the dynamic store of the Membership Directory database.
Dynamic Search	Number of search operations per second to the dynamic store of this Membership Directory database per second.
Dynamic Compare	Total number of compare operations to the dynamic store of this Membership Directory database.
Dynamic Compare	Number of compare operations per second to the dynamic store of this Membership Directory database per second.
Dynamic Extended Request	Total number of adds to the dynamic store of the Membership Directory database.
Dynamic Extended	Number of deletes per second to the dynamic store of the Membership Directory database per second.
Dynamic Object Timeout	Number of timeouts to the dynamic store of the Membership Directory database.
Current Dynamic Object	Number of current objects in the dynamic store of the Membership Directory database.
Current Dynamic Attributes	Number of attributes currently in the dynamic store of the Membership Directory database.
Current Dynamic Value	Number of values currently in the dynamic store of the Membership Directory database.
TTL	Time-to-live thread state in the dynamic store of the Membership Database.
ULP Resolve	Total number of ULP (User Locator Protocol) resolves to the Membership Directory database.

Counter	Description
ULP Resolve	Number of ULP resolves per second to the Membership Directory database per second.
ULP Directory	Total number of ULP Directory operations to the Membership Directory database.
ULP Directory	Number of ULP Directory operations per second to the Membership Directory database per second.
ULP Add User	Total number of ULP add user operations to the dynamic store of the Membership Directory database.
ULP Del User	Total number of ULP delete user operations to the Membership Directory database.
ULP Add App	Total number of ULP add application operations to the Membership Directory database.
ULP Del App	Total number of ULP delete application operations to the Membership Directory database.
Repl Server	Total number of replication servers connected to the Membership Directory database.
Active Repl Server	Number of active replication servers connected to the Membership Directory database
Replication Add In	Total number of add operations replicated to the Membership Directory database.
Replication Add In	Number of add operations per second replicated to the Membership Directory database per second.
Replication Del In	Total number of delete operations replicated to the Membership Directory database.
Replication Del In	Number of delete operations per second replicated to the Membership Directory database per second.
Replication Modify In	Total number of modifies replicated to the Membership Directory database.
Replication Modify In	Number of modify operations per second replicated to the Membership Directory database per second.
Replication Modify DN In	Total number of modify distinguished name (DN) operations replicated to the Membership Directory database.
Replication Modify DN In	Number of modify DN operations per second replicated to the Membership Directory database per second.
Replication Total In Op	Total number of operations replicated to the Membership Directory database.
Replication Total In Op	Number of operations per second replicated to the Membership Directory database per second.

Table Continued on Following Page

985

Counter	Description
Replication Add Out	Total number of adds replicated to other databases.
Replication Add Out	Number of adds per second replicated to other databases per second.
Replication Del Out	Total number of deletes replicated to other databases.
Replication Del Out	Number of deletes per second replicated to other databases per second.
Replication Modify Out	Total number of modify operations replicated to other databases.
Replication Modify Out	Number of modify operations replicated to other databases per second.
Replication Modify DN Out	Total number of modify DN operations replicated to other databases.
Replication Modify DN Out	Number of modify DN operations replicated to other databases per second.
Replication Total Out Op	Total number of operations replicated out.
Replication Total Out Op	Number of operations replicated out per second.
Replication Conflict	Total number of replication conflicts.
Replication Commit	Total number of replication operations committed.
Replication Reject	Total number of replication operations rejected.
Replication Error	Total number of replication errors.
Replication Queue Size	Total size of the replication queue.

Site Server Message Builder Service Counters

Counter	Description
Messages Sent/sec	Number of messages sent per second.
Total Messages Sent	Total number of messages sent since the last restart.
Errors/sec	Number of errors generated per second.
Total Errors	Total number of errors generated since the last restart.
Flow Control Rate	Current flow control rate in number of messages per second.
Idle Worker Threads	Number of worker threads waiting for the I/O or new mailings.
Messages Processed/sec	Number of messages processed per second.
Total Messages Processed	Total number of messages processed since the last restart.

Site Server Search Counters

Counter	Description
Current Connections	The number of currently established connections between the Search service and all clients.
Maximum Connections	The maximum number of instantaneous connections to this service over the lifetime of the service.
Connection Managers	The number of connection manager objects in the service. Typically, the initial value is four and can be increased as additional connections are made to the service.
Active Connections	The number of connections that are currently processing a request on behalf of a client or are queued for processing.
% Active Connections	The percentage of active connections currently processing requests or queuing requests for processing on behalf of a client.
Bytes Received	The number of bytes received by the Search service from the query interface.
Bytes Received Rate	The number of bytes received by the Search service from the query interface per second.
Bytes Sent	The number of bytes sent by the Search service to the query interface.
Bytes Sent Rate	The number of bytes sent by the Search service to the query interface per second.
Heartbeats	The total number of heartbeats counted since startup. A heartbeat occurs once every second while the service is running. If the service is not running there will be no heartbeat and the number of ticks will not be incremented.
Heartbeats Rate	The number of heartbeat ticks per second. Under normal operation, the search service generates one heartbeat per second. If the service is not running there will be no heartbeat and the number of ticks will not be incremented.

Site Server Search Catalog Counters

Counter	Description
Threads	The total number of threads in the thread pool.
Active Threads	Number of threads that are currently processing queries.
% Active Threads	Percentage of threads in that are currently processing queries.

Table Continued on Following Page

Counter	Description
Maximum Response Time	The maximum response time for a single query over the lifetime of the catalog. The response time is the number of milliseconds the service spends on a single query, measured from when the Search server first receives the query until the last result has been returned.
Average Response Time	The average response time of all queries answered over the last second. The response time is the number of milliseconds the service spends on a single query, measured from when the Search server first receives the query until the last result has been returned.
Queue Length	The number of queries waiting for thread resources.
Cumulative Queue Duration	The total number of milliseconds that all queries have spent in the queue over the lifetime of the service.
Maximum Queue Duration	The maximum number of milliseconds that a single query has spent in the queue.
Average Queue Duration	The average number of milliseconds that all queries have spent in the queue in the previous minute.
Queries	Cumulative number of queries posted to the catalog.
Queries Rate	The number of queries posted to the catalog per second.
Failed Queries	The number of queries that have failed.
Failed Queries Rate	The number of failed queries per second.
Results	The cumulative number of results returned to clients.
Results Rate	The number of results returned to the client per second.
Successful Queries	The number of queries that produce successful searches.
Successful Queries Rate	The number of queries per second that produce successful searches.
Persistent Catalogs	The number of persistent catalogs.
Catalog Size (MB)	Size of catalog data in megabytes.
Unique Keys	Number of unique words and properties in the catalog.
Number Of Documents	The total number of documents in the catalog.

ADSI and LDAP Codes

There are a number of ADSI error codes and LDAP event messages that you may encounter when developing with Site Server. This appendix provides a quick reference for some of the most common codes for first ADSI and then LDAP.

ADSI Error Codes

To always have a complete and up-to-date listing of error codes you'll need to make sure you have the latest Platform SDK (available to download from the Microsoft web site). You'll find the ADSI and Win32 error code definitions in the `adserr.h` and `winerror.h` header files respectively. You can also find documentation on these error codes on the Microsoft web site, at:

`http://msdn.microsoft.com/library/sdkdoc/adsi/ds2_error_0t9v.htm`

Hex Error Code Constant Name Description	Notes
0x80005000 E_ADS_BAD_PATHNAME An invalid Active Directory pathname was passed	The Active Directory Path, i.e. `LDAP://Wrox/o=Wrox`, is invalid. Check the ADsPath value passed to ensure it points to a valid directory service.
0x80005001 E_ADS_INVALID_DOMAIN_OBJECT An unknown Active Directory domain object was requested	Not applicable to the Site Server Membership Directory.

Hex Error Code Constant Name Description	Notes
0x80005002 E_ADS_INVALID_USER_OBJECT An unknown Active Directory user object was requested	The user object requested is invalid. Check the list of available user objects that the directory supports.
0x80005003 E_ADS_INVALID_COMPUTER_OBJECT An unknown Active Directory computer object was requested	Not applicable to the Site Server Membership Directory.
0x80005004 E_ADS_UNKNOWN_OBJECT An unknown Active Directory object was requested	The Active Directory object requested does not exist. Please check the validity and type of the object and try again.
0x80005005 E_ADS_PROPERTY_NOT_SET The specified Active Directory property was not set	The ADSI property was not set and will not be updated in the directory.
0x80005006 E_ADS_PROPERTY_NOT_SUPPORTED The specified Active Directory property is not supported	The ADSI property you are attempting to use is not supported.
0x80005007 E_ADS_PROPERTY_INVALID The specified Active Directory property is invalid	The ADSI property is invalid. This will usually occur in a Membership Directory when a request is made for a user property and that property does not exist.

Hex Error Code Constant Name Description	Notes
0x80005008 E_ADS_BAD_PARAMETER One or more input parameters are invalid	The parameter value passed for the property is invalid. Check the property type of the object and pass the correctly typed value for this property.
0x80005009 E_ADS_OBJECT_UNBOUND The specified Active Directory object is not bound to a remote resource	The Active Directory object is not bound to a remote object. To use the object, it must first be bound to an ADs object – such as the ou=members container in the Membership Directory.
0x8000500A E_ADS_PROPERTY_NOT_MODIFIED The specified Active Directory object has not been modified	The ADs property has not been modified.
0x8000500B E_ADS_PROPERTY_MODIFIED The specified Active Directory object has been modified	The ADs property has been modified.
0x8000500C E_ADS_CANT_CONVERT_DATATYPE The Active Directory datatype cannot be converted to/from a native DS datatype	Check the data types supported by the directory provider. Next make sure the object type passed matches the acceptable object types for the provider.
0x8000500D E_ADS_PROPERTY_NOT_FOUND The Active Directory property cannot be found in the cache.	Either the property does not exist, or the cache needs to be refreshed. To refresh the cache, call GetInfo from the object whose properties need to be refreshed.
0x8000500E E_ADS_OBJECT_EXISTS The Active Directory object exists.	The Active Directory object attempting to be created already exists – use a different naming value for the new object.

Hex Error Code Constant Name Description	Notes
0x8000500F E_ADS_SCHEMA_VIOLATION The attempted action violates the DS schema rules.	The schema of the directory does not support this action.
0x80005010 E_ADS_COLUMN_NOT_SET The specified column in the Active Directory was not set.	The column for the search was not set, therefore the search cannot continue.
0x00005011 S_ADS_ERRORSOCCURRED One or more errors occurred	An unknown error has occurred.
0x00005012 S_ADS_NOMORE_ROWS No more rows to be obtained by the search result.	Occurs if a request is made past the number of available rows.
0x00005013 S_ADS_NOMORE_COLUMNS No more columns to be obtained for the current row.	Occurs if a request is made past the number of available columns.
0x80005014 E_ADS_INVALID_FILTER The search filter specified is invalid	The search filter specified for the search is invalid. Please examine the syntax of the query – additionally, check the allowed types set by the, Membership Server.

LDAP Event messages

The LDAP server writes event messages to the event log of the Windows NT 4.0 machine it runs on. There are three different categories of errors: **error**, **warning**, and **informational**, decreasing in severity in that order.

Severity: Error

Event Number Constant Definition; Action (if applicable)	Explanation
396 LDAP_EVENT_TIMEBOMB The evaluation period for this product has expired and could no longer be started.	Uninstall this beta version and purchase the retail version of Site Server 3.0
400 LDAP_EVENT_CANNOT_INITIALIZE_SECURITY Site Server LDAP Service cannot initialize its security. **Action**: Check Windows NT configuration and reboot the server.	Check the broker account and the account used to run the LDAP service on the computer. Either the broker or the account running the service does not have the proper permissions configured.
401 LDAP_EVENT_CANNOT_INITIALIZE_WINSOCK Site Server LDAP Service cannot initialize the socket library. **Action**: Check the TCP/IP configuration.	LDAP uses TCP/IP to communicate across the network. TCP/IP must be installed and properly configured to use LDAP.
402 LDAP_EVENT_MAX_CONNECTION_REACHED Site Server LDAP Service rejected the connection attempt because there are too many users connected.	The maximum number of users that can be connected to the system has been reached. Use the P&M snap-in to configure support for more connections or add another service.

Hex Error Code Constant Name Description	Notes
404 LDAP_EVENT_CANNOT_LOCATE_LDAP Site Server LDAP Service cannot open the LDAP/TCP service. The data area, shown below, contains the return error code.	The LDAP service is unavailable due to problems with the TCP/IP configurations. Check the machine settings.
405 LDAP_EVENT_CANNOT_CREATE_CONNECTION_SOCKET Site Server LDAP Service cannot create the main connection socket. The data area, shown below, contains the return error code.	The LDAP service is unavailable due to problems with the TCP/IP configurations. Check the machine settings.
406 LDAP_EVENT_CANNOT_CREATE_CONNECTION_THREAD Site Server LDAP Service cannot create the main connection thread. The data area, shown below, contains the return error code.	The LDAP service is unavailable due to problems with the TCP/IP configurations. Check the machine settings.
407 LDAP_EVENT_CANNOT_CREATE_CLIENT_CONN Virtual Server %1: Site Server LDAP Service cannot create a client connection object for user at host %2. The connection to this user is terminated. The data area, shown below, contains the return error code.	A connection was refused on virtual server number %1 (Membership Server #) for the user at %2 (IP address).
408 LDAP_EVENT_SYSTEM_CALL_FAILED A call to a system service failed unexpectedly. The data area, shown below, contains the return error code.	System error.
409 LDAP_EVENT_CLIENT_TIMEOUT User %1 at host %2 timed out after %3 seconds of inactivity.	The threshold for the user session (named) at host (IP address) has timed out – default set for 10 minutes.

Hex Error Code Constant Name Description	Notes
417 LDAP_EVENT_CANNOT_OPEN_SVC_REGKEY Site Server LDAP Service cannot open the LDAP registry key %1.	Ensure that the registry key is available and that the ACEs on this key allow for the account running the LDAP service to gain access.
418 LDAP_EVENT_CANNOT_READ_SVC_REGKEY Site Server LDAP Service cannot read registry key %1.	Ensure that the registry key is available and that the ACEs on this key allow for the account running the LDAP service to gain access.
481 LDAP_EVENT_CANNOT_INITIALIZE_OBJECT Site Server LDAP Service cannot initialize the following object: %1.	Check the security requirements of the object and ensure that the LDAP service account has the proper permissions for this object.
1003 LDAP_EVENT_GLOBAL_ERROR Error %1 Solution	Dependent upon returned error code.
2133 LDAP_BOOT_ERROR The server has detected a previous instance and will not boot until the old instance goes away. **Action**: After waiting some time, try to start the service. The data is the error code. Error description is % 1.	Apparently another instance of the LDAP service attempting to be started is already running. Check the LDAP instance configurations through the PMAdmin.vbs utility for duplicate instance.

Hex Error Code Constant Name Description	Notes
2500 LDAP_DSCORE_INIT_ERROR The server failed to start due to an initialization error. **Action**: Verify the configuration. Error description is % 1.	See the returned error code.
2501 LDAP_DSCORE_RUNTIME_ERROR The server failed due to a runtime error. Error description is % 1.	See the returned error code.
2503 LDAP_SECURITY_BAD_SD The Security Descriptor data was not valid. %1	The security descriptor for the object is corrupt. Use the commerce security objects to check the security descriptor for problems.
2600 LDAP_REPL_INIT_ERROR Dynamic replication for the Site Server LDAP Service failed due to an initialization error. **Action**: Verify the configuration. Error description is % 1.	Dynamic data replication failed. Ensure that all RPC services are accessible for the machine needing to communicate – additionally, check firewall settings if on separate segments.
2601 LDAP_REPL_RUNTIME_ERROR Dynamic replication for the Site Server LDAP Service failed due to a runtime error. Error description is % 1.	See the returned error code.
2700 LDAP_EVENT_GENERIC_LDAP_ERROR General error for the Site Server LDAP Service: %1 (where %1 is name of the error).	See the returned error code

Hex Error Code Constant Name Description	Notes
2701 LDAP_EVENT_CANT_MONITOR_IPBLIST There was a problem monitoring the IP blacklist file for changes.	The IP blacklist text file is either corrupt or missing.
2703 LDAP_EVENT_ERROR_UPDATING_IPBLIST There was a problem monitoring the IP blacklist file for changes.	The IP blacklist text file is either corrupt or missing.
2708 LDAP_EVENT_KEKEY_INVALID The Key Encryption Key needs to be updated for the instance number %1	The key encryption key for a Membership Server Instance has been changed, and needs to be changed in other Membership Server Instances. Use the kekey.exe utility found in the \bin\P&M directory.
2711 LDAP_EVENT_KEKEY_UPDATE_FAILED The Key Encryption Key has failed to be updated for Site Server LDAP Service instance number %1	Make sure the LDAP service is stopped before attempting to change the key.
2712 LDAP_EVENT_KEKEY_UPDATE_DS_FAILED The Encrypted Password Encryption Key failed to be updated for the database for Site Server LDAP Service instance number %1	Check the value of the PE – the PE in the database should never be changed.

Severity: Warning

Event Number Constant Definition; Action (if applicable)	Notes
397 LDAP_EVENT_SSL_FAILED Site Server LDAP Service could not establish Secure Sockets Layer (SSL) channel. **Action:** Verify that a proper certificate is installed correctly. The data area, shown below, contains the return error code.	See the data returned for specific error information. Ensure that port 636 is used for SSL communications.
398 LDAP_EVENT_OUT_OF_MEMORY Cannot allocate %1 because there is not enough memory available.	Install more memory.
399 LDAP_EVENT_OUT_OF_POOL Cannot allocate %1 because the pre-allocated limit has been reached	Check the number of accounts used to access the database providing the services for the Membership Directory – more open accounts may need to be added.
482 LDAP_EVENT_COMMAND_TOO_BIG The Site Server LDAP Service command that was requested is too big for this server to process.	Trim the LDAP service command into smaller segments.
485 LDAP_EVENT_NT_CALL_FAILED A system call (%1) failed unexpectedly. The data area, shown below, contains the return error code.	The system call to the specified NT item, event, or service failed.
2603 LDAP_REPL_RUNTIME_LOG Dynamic replication warning for Site Server LDAP Service %1.	The specified LDAP service is having problems replicating the dynamic data. Check the data being replicated for any unnecessary information.

Hex Error Code Constant Name Description	Notes
2502 LDAP_DSCORE_RUNTIME_LOG Site Server LDAP Service directory server %1.	Internal error.
2704 LDAP_EVENT_SHORTTERM_IPBLACKLISTED Rejected connection attempt from IP address %1. Address is on short-term blacklist.	The ip address requesting LDAP service has been rejected since it is on the short-term ip blacklist – either remove the ip address from the blacklist or ignore.
2706 LDAP_EVENT_SHORTTERM_ACCT_BLACKLISTED Rejected binding attempt to account %1. Account is on short-term blacklist.	The account requesting LDAP service has been rejected since it is on the short-term blacklist – either remove the account from the blacklist or ignore.
2707 LDAP_EVENT_BLACKLISTING_INITIALIZE_ERROR %1 blacklisting failed to initialize. This feature will be turned off for the current session.	No blacklist files found – blacklist disabled.

Severity: Informational

Event Number Constant	Notes
483 LDAP_EVENT_SET_MAX_SIZE_ACCEPTED	Virtual Server %1: The maximum accepted message size is set to %2.
484 LDAP_EVENT_SET_MAX_SIZE_BEFORE_CLOSE	Virtual Server %1: The maximum message size accepted before the socket is forced closed is set to %2.
530 LDAP_EVENT_SERVICE_STARTED	Site Server LDAP Service has been started.
531 LDAP_EVENT_SERVICE_STOPPED	Site Server LDAP Service has been stopped.
532 LDAP_EVENT_SERVICE_INSTANCE_STARTED	Site Server LDAP Service instance %1 has been started.
533 LDAP_EVENT_SERVICE_INSTANCE_STOPPED	Site Server LDAP Service instance %1 has been stopped.
534 LDAP_EVENT_SERVICE_INSTANCE_PAUSED	Site Server LDAP Service instance %1 has been paused.
535 LDAP_EVENT_SERVICE_INSTANCE_UNPAUSED	Site Server LDAP Service instance %1 has been un-paused.
536 LDAP_EVENT_SERVICE_INSTANCE_CREATED	Site Server LDAP Service instance %1 has been created.
537 LDAP_EVENT_SERVICE_INSTANCE_DELETED	Site Server LDAP Service instance %1 has been deleted.
538 LDAP_EVENT_SSL_NEGOTIATION_FAILED	Site Server LDAP Service failed to negotiate Secure Sockets Layer (SSL) connection.
539 LDAP_EVENT_CONNECTION_TIMED_OUT	The connection timed out.
2602 LDAP_REPL_RUNTIME_INFO	Dynamic replication information for the Site Server LDAP Service: %1.

Event Number Constant	Notes
2699 LDAP_EVENT_LONGTERM_BLACKLIST_DISABLED	The %1 file could not be found. Permanent blacklisting for the instance is disabled.
2702 LDAP_EVENT_CAN_MONITOR_IPBLIST	The problem with monitoring the IP blacklist file has been resolved. Will resume monitoring the file for changes.
2705 LDAP_EVENT_LONGTERM_IPBLACKLISTED	Rejected connection attempt from IP address %1. Address is on permanent blacklist.
2709 LDAP_EVENT_KEKEY_UPDATED	The Key Encryption Key has been successfully updated for the Site Server LDAP Service instance number %1
2710 LDAP_EVENT_KEKEY_UPDATED_DS	The Key Encryption Key has been successfully updated for the database for Site Server LDAP Service instance number %1

Useful Resources

General

Microsoft Site Server Documentation – ideally make sure you have the main Site Server documentation, the Commerce Edition documentation and the SDK documentation.

Websites

General

http://msdn.microsoft.com/default.asp
http://www.microsoft.com/support/
http://www.microsoft.com/data
http://www.15seconds.com

Microsoft's Site Server Web Site

http://www.microsoft.com/siteserver

Site Server Software Development Kit

http://www.microsoft.com/siteserver/commerce/30/downloads/sdk.asp

Site Server 3.0 Commerce Edition Resource Kit

http://www.microsoft.com/siteserver/commerce/30/downloads/reskit.asp

Site Server Resource Web Sites

http://www.siteserver.com
http://www.siteserverresources.com
http://www.15seconds.com/focus/Site Server.htm
http://www.siteserver101.com/

Active Server Pages Web Site
`http://www.activeserverpages.com`

Security Information Web Site
`http://www.microsoft.com/security`

Scripting Web Site
`http://msdn.microsoft.com/scripting/default.htm`

Newsgroups and Communities

Microsoft's Site Server newsgroups
`microsoft.public.siteserver.general`
`microsoft.public.siteserver.per-mbr`
`microsoft.public.siteserver.commerce`

15 Seconds Site Server List
`http://www.15seconds.com/listserv.htm`

The Mulberry XSL List
`http://www.mulberrytech.com/xsl/xsl-list/index.html`

Imperial College XML List
`http://www.ch.ic.ac.uk/hypermail/`

Microsoft Online Site Server Seminars
`http://www.microsoft.com/seminar/98/ve/siteserver/portal.htm`

Books

Site Server 3.0 Personalization and Membership. Robert Howard – Wrox Press 1998. ISBN 1-861001-94-0.
`http://www.wrox.com/Store/Details.asp?Code=1940`

SQL Server 7 The Complete Reference. Gayle Coffman – Osborne/McGraw Hill 1999. ISBN 0-078824-94-x

Microsoft SQL Server 7.0 DBA Survival Guide. Mark Spenik *et al.*, – Sams Publishing 1999. ISBN 0-672312-26-3

Professional Active Server Pages. Francis et al. – Wrox Press 1998. ISBN 1-861001-26-6

Implementing LDAP. Mark Wilcox - Wrox Press 1999. ISBN 1-861002-21-1

ASDI ASP. Steven Hahn -Wrox Press 1998. ISBN 1-861001-69-X

MSDN Articles

"Getting the Most Out of Site Server Knowledge Manager" by Drew DeBruyne
`http://msdn.microsoft.com/workshop/server/nextgen/kmpaper.asp`

"Microsoft Site Server 3.0 Membership Directory Configuration and Tuning Guidelines" by John Ostlund and Alex Weinert
`http://msdn.microsoft.com/library/techart/msdn_memdirct.htm`

"Creating a Search Catalog for Your Site with Site Server 3.0" by Dina Berry
`http://msdn.microsoft.com/workshop/server/nextgen/searchcatalog.asp`

Content Management

Microsoft white paper: "Site Server Multiple Approval Process for Publishing"
`http://www.microsoft.com/siteserver/site/30/whitepapers/MultipleApproval.htm`

Search

Microsoft white paper: "Implementing Search in the Enterprise"
`http://www.microsoft.com/siteserver/site/30/gen/searchwp.htm`

Microsoft white paper: "Creating a Search Catalog with Site Server 3.0"
`http://www.microsoft.com/siteserver/site/30/whitepapers/SearchCat.htm`

Knowledge Manager

MSDN Article: "Getting the Most Out of Site Server Knowledge Manager"
`http://msdn.microsoft.com/workshop/server/nextgen/kmpaper.asp`

Support and Errata

One of the most irritating things about any programming book is when you find that bit of code you've just spent an hour typing simply doesn't work. You check it a hundred times to see if you've set it up correctly and then you notice the spelling mistake in the variable name on the book page. Of course, you can blame the authors for not taking enough care and testing the code, the editors for not doing their job properly, or the proofreaders for not being eagle-eyed enough, but this doesn't get around the fact that mistakes do happen.

We try hard to ensure no mistakes sneak out into the real world, but we can't promise that this book is 100% error free. What we can do is offer the next best thing by providing you with immediate support and feedback from experts who have worked on the book and try to ensure that future editions eliminate these gremlins. The following section will take you step by step through the process of posting errata to our web site to get that help. The sections that follow, therefore, are:

➢ Wrox Developers Membership

➢ Finding a list of existing errata on the web site

➢ Adding your own errata to the existing list

➢ What happens to your errata once you've posted it (why doesn't it appear immediately)?

There is also a section covering how to e-mail a question for technical support. This comprises:

➢ What your e-mail should include

➢ What happens to your e-mail once it has been received by us

So that you only need view information relevant to yourself, we ask that you register as a Wrox Developer Member. This is a quick and easy process, that will save you time in the long-run. If you are already a member, just update your membership to include this book.

Wrox Developer's Membership

To get your FREE Wrox Developer's Membership click on Membership in the navigation bar of our home site – http://www.wrox.com. This is shown in the following screenshot:

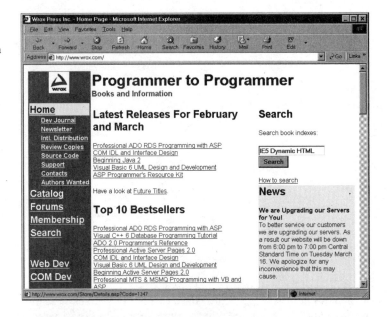

Then, on the next screen (not shown), click on New User. This will display a form. Fill in the details on the form and submit the details using the Send Form button at the bottom. Before you can say 'The best read books come in Wrox Red' you will get the following screen:

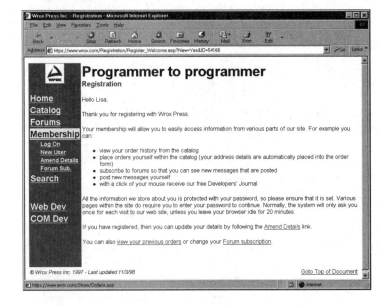

Finding an Errata on the Web Site

Before you send in a query, you might be able to save time by finding the answer to your problem on our web site – http://www.wrox.com.

Each book we publish has its own page and its own errata sheet. You can get to any book's page by clicking on Support from the left hand side navigation bar.

From this page you can locate any book's errata page on our site. Select your book from the pop-up menu and click on it.

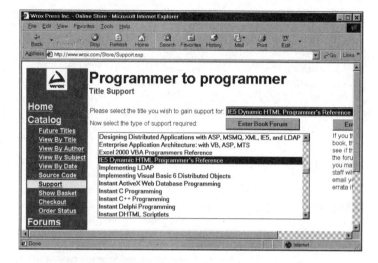

Then click on Enter Book Errata. This will take you to the errata page for the book. Select the criteria by which you want to view the errata, and click the Apply criteria... button. This will provide you with links to specific errata. For an initial search, you are advised to view the errata by page numbers. If you have looked for an error previously, then you may wish to limit your search using dates. We update these pages daily to ensure that you have the latest information on bugs and errors.

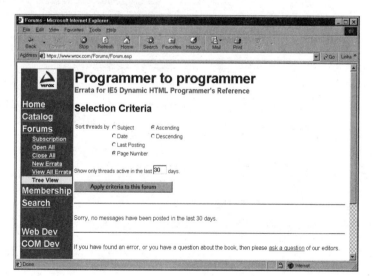

Adding an Errata to the Sheet Yourself

It's always possible that you may find your error is not listed, in which case you can enter details of the fault yourself. It might be anything from a spelling mistake to a faulty piece of code in the book. Sometimes you'll find useful hints that aren't really errors on the listing. By entering errata you may save another reader hours of frustration, and of course, you will be helping us provide even higher quality information. We're very grateful for this sort of advice and feedback. You can enter errata using the 'ask a question of our editors' link at the bottom of the errata page. Click on this link and you will get a form on which to post your message.

Fill in the subject box, and then type your message in the space provided on the form. Once you have done this, click on the Post Now button at the bottom of the page. The message will be forwarded to our editors. They'll then test your submission and check that the error exists, and that the suggestions you make are valid. Then your submission, together with a solution, is posted on the site for public consumption. Obviously this stage of the process can take a day or two, but we will endeavor to get a fix up sooner than that.

E-mail Support

If you wish to directly query a problem in the book with an expert who knows the book in detail then e-mail support@wrox.com, with the title of the book and the last four numbers of the ISBN in the subject field of the e-mail. A typical email should include the following things:

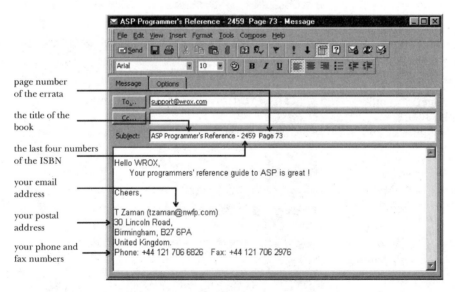

We won't send you junk mail. We need the details to save your time and ours. If we need to replace a disk or CD we'll be able to get it to you straight away. When you send an e-mail it will go through the following chain of support:

Customer Support

Your message is delivered to one of our customer support staff who are the first people to read it. They have files on most frequently asked questions and will answer anything general immediately. They answer general questions about the book and the web site.

Editorial

Deeper queries are forwarded to the technical editor responsible for that book. They have experience with the programming language or particular product and are able to answer detailed technical questions on the subject. Once an issue has been resolved, the editor can post the errata to the web site.

The Authors

Finally, in the unlikely event that the editor can't answer your problem, s/he will forward the request to the author. We try to protect the author from any distractions from writing. However, we are quite happy to forward specific requests to them. All Wrox authors help with the support on their books. They'll mail the customer and the editor with their response, and again all readers should benefit.

What We Can't Answer

Obviously with an ever growing range of books and an ever-changing technology base, there is an increasing volume of data requiring support. While we endeavor to answer all questions about the book, we can't answer bugs in your own programs that you've adapted from our code. So, while you might have loved the help desk systems in our Active Server Pages book, don't expect too much sympathy if you cripple your company with a live adaptation you customized from Chapter 12. But do tell us if you're especially pleased with the routine you developed with our help.

How to Tell Us Exactly What You Think

We understand that errors can destroy the enjoyment of a book and can cause many wasted and frustrated hours, so we seek to minimize the distress that they can cause.

You might just wish to tell us how much you liked or loathed the book in question. Or you might have ideas about how this whole process could be improved. In which case you should e-mail feedback@wrox.com. You'll always find a sympathetic ear, no matter what the problem is. Above all you should remember that we do care about what you have to say and we will do our utmost to act upon it.

Index

N

Name
Create New Direct
Mailing wizard
mail packages, creating, 452
Order Processing
Pipeline, components, 668
**name the membership
directory and create
account screen**
New Membership Server
Wizard, 276
Named Pipes
SQL Server, 69
namespace partitions
Membership Directory, 33
naming conventions
Site Server, 38
navigation
online store, 652
parametric queries,
executing, 652
shopping basket, adding
items, 653
net command
command line, 120
services, starting, 120
services, stopping, 120
Netscape Navigator
authentication, problems
with
NT Authentication, 296
Wallet, 832
network bandwidth
Search, 190
**Network Infrastructure
Engineering**
BroadCloth Company,
case study, 865
Network Libraries
Multi-Protocol Network
Library, 69
Named Pipes, 69
SQL Server, 68
TCP\IP Sockets, 69
default library, 71
New Attribute Wizard
group attributes
*Membership Directory
Citix Consultants Inc, case
study, 471*

**New Catalog Definition
Wizard**
Search
*Citix Consultants Inc, case
study, 502*
New Group Wizard
access level groups
*Membership Directory
Citix Consultants Inc, case
study, 471*
**New Membership Server
Wizard**
complete the
configuration screen, 281
create local LDAP service
screen, 279
Membership
Authentication, 270
Membership Directory,
moving, 179
Membership Server,
creating, 270
Message Builder
configuration screen, 280
name the membership
directory and create
account screen, 276
screens, 271
select authentication
mode screen, 275
select configuration mode
screen, 272
select configuration
options screen, 273
select the database type
screen, 277
select the membership
directory screen, 274
splash screen, 272
SQL Server, 270
type SQL database
information screen, 278
New Object Wizard
distribution list, creating,
455
site vocabulary
*Citix Consultants Inc, case
study, 476*
New Project Wizard
deployment projects,
creating, 181
staging server content, 181

New User Wizard
Membership Directory
*Citix Consultants Inc, case
study, 470*
member attributes, 475
Notification type Catalog
Search, 202
NT
installation
*paging file size, increasing,
74*
Site Server, installation, 73
NT Accounts
Membership Directory,
282
NT Authentication
Allow Anonymous Access
IIS, authentication, 291
Basic Authentication
IIS, authentication, 293
compared to Membership
Authentication, 269
configuring
IIS, authentication, 290
IIS security, 53
IIS, authentication, 289
*Allow Anonymous Access,
291*
Basic Authentication, 293
*methods, combinations of,
296*
*Netscape Navigator, problems
with, 296*
NT Challenge/Response, 295
*trusted domain
authentication, 296*
membership, 267
Membership Directory,
275
logon anonymously, 286
logon using, 287
methods, combinations of
IIS, authentication, 296
Netscape Navigator,
problems with
IIS, authentication, 296
NT Challenge/Response
IIS, authentication, 295
NT security features, 267
trusted domain
authentication
IIS, authentication, 296
NT Challenge/Response
NT Authentication
IIS, authentication, 295

Index

wrox

PROGRAMMER TO PROGRAMMER™

Wrox writes books for you. Any suggestions, or ideas about how you want
information given in your ideal book will be studied by our team.
Your comments are always valued at Wrox.

Free phone in USA 800-USE-WROX
Fax (312) 397 8990

UK Tel. (0121) 687 4100   Fax (0121) 687 4101

Professional Site Server 3.0 - Registration Card

Name _____

Address _____

_____

_____

_____

City_____ State/Region _____

Country_____ Postcode/Zip _____

E-mail _____

Occupation _____

How did you hear about this book? _____

☐ Book review (name) _____

☐ Advertisement (name) _____

☐ Recommendation _____

☐ Catalog _____

☐ Other _____

Where did you buy this book? _____

☐ Bookstore (name)_____ City _____

☐ Computer Store (name)_____

☐ Mail Order _____

☐ Other _____

What influenced you in the
purchase of this book?

☐ Cover Design

☐ Contents

☐ Other (please specify) _____

How did you rate the overall
contents of this book?

☐ Excellent   ☐ Good

☐ Average   ☐ Poor

What did you find most useful about this book? _____

_____

What did you find least useful about this book? _____

Please add any additional comments. _____

_____

What other subjects will you buy a computer
book on soon? _____

What is the best computer book you have used this year?

_____

*Note: This information will only be used to keep you updated
about new Wrox Press titles and will not be used for any other
purpose or passed to any other third party.*

2696   **Check here if you DO NOT want to receive support for this book** ☐   2696

wrox
PROGRAMMER TO PROGRAMMER™

NB. If you post the bounce back card below in the UK, please send it to:

Wrox Press Ltd., Arden House, 1102 Warwick Road,
Acocks Green, Birmingham B27 6BH. UK.

Computer Book Publishers